# VALUES
# AMERICANS
# LIVE BY

THE GREAT
CONTEMPORARY
ISSUES

# VALUES
# AMERICANS
# LIVE BY

𝕿𝖍𝖊 𝕹𝖊𝖜 𝖄𝖔𝖗𝖐 𝕿𝖎𝖒𝖊𝖘

ARNO PRESS

NEW YORK/1974

**GARRY WILLS**

Advisory Editor

Copyright © 1974 by The New York Times Company.
Library of Congress Cataloging in Publication Data.
Main entry under title:
Values Americans live by.
    (The Great contemporary issues)
    "A Hudson group book."
    Collection of Articles appearing in the New York times.
    Bibliography: p.
1. United States—Social conditions—Addresses, essays, lectures. 2. Social values—Addresses, essays, lectures. I. Wills, Garry, 1934-      II. New York times.
III. Series.
HN57.V34      301.2′1′9073      73-16036
ISBN 0-405-04166-7
Manufactured in the United States of America by Arno Press, Inc.

The editors express special thanks to The Associated Press, United Press International, and Reuters for permission to include in this series of books a number of dispatches originally distributed by those news services.

A HUDSON GROUP BOOK

Edited by Joanne Soderman

# Contents

# Publisher's Note About the Series

It would take even an accomplished speed-reader, moving at full throttle, some three and a half solid hours a day to work his way through all the news THE NEW YORK TIMES prints. The sad irony, of course, is that even such indefatigable devotion to life's carnival would scarcely assure a decent understanding of what it was really all about. For even the most dutiful reader might easily overlook an occasional long-range trend of importance, or perhaps some of the fragile, elusive relationships between events that sometimes turn out to be more significant than the events themselves.

This is why "The Great Contemporary Issues" was created—to help make sense out of some of the major forces and counterforces at large in today's world. The philosophical conviction behind the series is a simple one: that the past not only can illuminate the present but must. ("Continuity with the past," declared Oliver Wendell Holmes, "is a necessity, not a duty.") Each book in the series, therefore has as its subject some central issue of our time that needs to be viewed in the context of its antecedents if it is to be fully understood. By showing, through a substantial selection of contemporary accounts from THE NEW YORK TIMES, the evolution of a subject and its significance, each book in the series offers a perspective that is available in no other way. For while most books on contemporary affairs specialize, for excellent reasons, in predigested facts and neatly drawn conclusions, the books in this series allow the reader to draw his own conclusions on the basis of the facts as they appeared at virtually the moment of their occurrence. This is not to argue that there is no place for events recollected in tranquility; it is simply to say that when fresh, raw truths are allowed to speak for themselves, some quite distinct values often emerge.

For this reason, most of the articles in "The Great Contemporary Issues" are reprinted in their entirety, even in those cases where portions are not central to a given book's theme. Editing has been done only rarely, and in all such cases it is clearly indicated. (Such an excision occasionally occurs, for example, in the case of a Presidential State of the Union Message, where only brief portions are germane to a particular volume, and in the case of some names, where for legal reasons or reasons of taste it is preferable not to republish specific identifications.) Similarly, typographical errors, where they occur, have been allowed to stand as originally printed.

"The Great Contemporary Issues" inevitably encompasses a substantial amount of history. In order to explore their subjects fully, some of the books go back a century or more. Yet their fundamental theme is not the past but the present. In this series the past is of significance insofar as it suggests how we got where we are today. These books, therefore, do not always treat a subject in a purely chronological way. Rather, their material is arranged to point up trends and interrelationships that the editors believe are more illuminating than a chronological listing would be.

"The Great Contemporary Issues" series will ultimately constitute an encyclopedic library of today's major issues. Long before editorial work on the first volume had even begun, some fifty specific titles had already been either scheduled for definite publication or listed as candidates. Since then, events have prompted the inclusion of a number of additional titles, and the editors are, moreover, alert not only for new issues as they emerge but also for issues whose development may call for the publication of sequel volumes. We will, of course, also welcome readers' suggestions for future topics.

# Introduction

# Values Americans Live By

Mark Twain knew what to do with the new century, in its glow of baby self-fascination. He counted the lynchings. They were running about a hundred a year at the time—and Americans were singing "You Can't Keep a Good Man Down." Out on the Chautauqua circuit, William Travers Jerome was defending the trusts: "This is commerce, this is competition—it is war and strife. I do not say that this is moral. It is immoral. But do not tell me that if the men at the crossroads had more power they would not use it to their own advantage, or that they would use it any better than Rockefeller uses it." To the winner, the spoils; and to everyone, the advantage of an excellence tested in fires of competition.

Americans have to ask each other what their values are. Only the pollster really knows. What the market is to products, and election to our politics, the survey is to morals. Kinsey would shock people in the forties, but only by asking blunter questions. The rules of the game were set up long ago. When Herbert Spencer came to America, New York's society threw a great dinner for him at Delmonico's. William Graham Sumner was there, and Oliver Wendell Holmes. The first toast was "To Sociology," and the toastmaster praised the man who taught us to worship whatever prevails on the market: "It matters little whether such a system as this is called scientific or not. It is practical, and redounds to the good of mankind." It may not be moral, but it works. Besides, morality is what people do—as politics is who they vote for. Kinsey could ask, "Who are you to tell people what morals are? You do not even know. I know, because I asked. Morality is what men will admit to." As Rockefeller admitted to acquisitiveness.

This was not an argument for amorality, but for the true morality. The lazy and indolent do not prevail; only the industrious, striving up. As the toastmaster said to Spencer: "Whatever may be said of your system of philosophy, however it may be compared by scientific men to other and different systems, we must all agree that it is practical, serious, and benevolent; that it treats evil, not as eternal, but as evanescent, and that it aims to bring man to that condition of life where he shall find perfect happiness and contentment."

Energetic contentment marked the time, piety and the quicker punch. Teddy Roosevelt was being strenuous, while prohibition made headway in the states. In 1906 Roosevelt won the Nobel Peace Prize, and the nation started singing "Anchors Aweigh." The next year he sent off the Great White Fleet, and the year's song was "You Splash Me and I'll Splash You." Judge Kenesaw Mountain Landis fined Standard Oil $29,240,000 and everyone was getting cleaner every day. In a victory for the Sunday schools and universities, men elected Woodrow Wilson in 1912; the big hit was "Sweetheart of Sigma Chi."

It was time for America to discover the world, by saving it. Wilson did not hedge on the matter: "America has the infinite privilege of fulfilling her destiny and saving the world." Only by following up the War with the League could Americans "make good their redemption of the world." Well, we needed *some* excuse to see Paris. The first pose was of an innocence bailing out sophistication. But there was envy behind our enlightening impulse. America wanted a little of that sophistication too, if there was any to spare. The Golden Horseshoe crowd had already bought artists the way Carnegie bought libraries. America had purchased the world's greatest musicians, made itself opera's consumer capital of the world. Conductors like Toscanini, Muck, Koussevitsky, and Rachmaninoff were brought here—but Muck was kicked out when he hesitated to lavish his skill on exculpatory Star Spangled Banners before each performance. He could not lower himself to inform Americans there is a difference between a Swiss and a German. Well, artists didn't have to get huffy on us, just when we were saving them (and paying their salaries). Better stick with the English; they make the fanciest butlers anyway.

The talkies did a lot for British accents—and dragged cinematic drama out of the Victorian and into the Edwardian age. Griffith, with all his technical innovations, was filming Dickens novels. Words jumped us up to drawing room comedy, with suave continental types, the men all nasal and dinner-jacketed, the women slinky and looking sedated. Luckily, honest farmers and milkmaids somehow found their way into the drawing room and redeemed it. One has to remember that these films were being produced by Jewish immigrants impressed with the virtues that made native robber barons rise to the level of English aristocracy. Aristocrats would dance and drawl all through the Depression, people getting sappier as they got sadder. Culture meant Europe—even the comedy of Chaplin, Keaton, and Stan Laurel came from the British music hall. When jazz went "respectable," it had to be under the baton of Paul Whiteman in his tie and tails.

In 1932, F.D.R. took us back to the Spencer dinner with William Graham Sumner's phrase, "the Forgotten Man." Disney was producing hit songs to go with his cartoons: "Who's Afraid of the Big Bad Wolf?" America decided you can't keep a good nation down—and, next year, went on another lynching spree. The Democrats now had the Klan *and* a "Brains Trust." Professors were in the White House, and artists in the WPA. There was a thirties vogue for things Oriental—Mr. Moto and the Green Hornet's Kato would have to change nationalities when the war came, but Terry's pirates were on the right side. Still, America was acquiring its own style in adversity. It was a golden time for Tin Pan Alley, Broadway musicals, the detective story, movies, and the novel. English butlers were out of work. Roosevelt had given us a *native* patrician manner.

War came, and more righteousness. Americans needing each other had grown almost lovable in the thirties, despite internal conflict. Now they smugly united in killing Huns and Japs. There was an instant deliberate coarsening of national life. Songs and the movies went mindlessly off to war, with "Lucky Strike Green." Zealots whipped us out of our misgivings, and the virtue of doubt was not indulged. Archibald MacLeish said, "The real battlefield of this war is the field of American opinion"—i.e., we must turn the war into a crusade, to wage it viciously enough. Rex Stout preached at length on the theme, "We shall hate, or we

shall fail." Evil always sends recruiting sergeants into the pulpit. So we locked up the Nisei, urged total war toward unconditional surrender, and worked our way up to Hiroshima by way of Dresden and Tokyo. Only the colossal evil of the kilns, revealed in the course of the war and afterward, retroactively excused our own first eagerness to hate. What surprises is not that war degrades, but that we took our degradation for ennoblement.

We got ennobled on the cheap. We waged the huge campaigns and unleashed force without parallel—yet our shores were not touched, and our losses were, in proportion to total population, among the lowest in the world. Our economy, still sludgy with effects of the Depression, finally soared free. Blacks moved and found jobs; women got out of the home; the young went off early, with good hope, to war or to work—and returned to improved chances for schooling on the GI Bill. The war gave America power, pride, wealth, and self-righteousness. There was nothing we couldn't do—which made some people wonder if there was nothing we wouldn't do. After all, we had dropped the bomb.

We spent over twenty years chafing because we could not drop it again. Frustrated crusaders get all itchy under their armor. And now it was harder to keep back doubt. A laving tide of piety came washing in on us, a stream of forgiveness. Eisenhower was its spokesman, more because it was saleable, and he was a great salesman, than from any compulsion toward the pew. In 1957, *McCall's* coined the term "togetherness," and the bestseller lists of the fifties were cluttered with Salvation: *The Big Fisherman, A Man Called Peter, The Robe, The Silver Chalice, The Seven Storey Mountain, Life is Worth Living, Witness, The Greatest Faith Ever Known, The Power of Positive Thinking.* Dale Evans sang the hymns, and it was happy time: "Love and Marriage," "Cherry Pink and Apple Blossom White," "April Love." Teen-agers were excruciatingly clean in their beach party bikinis, with their trochee names (Tammy, Gidget, Debbie, Cindy). Female Fashion had moved a long way from the platinum blonde (Harlow and Lombard) through the stages of blonde virginity in the forties (June Allyson and Doris Day), the fifties (Grace Kelly and Doris Day), the sixties (Eva Marie Saint and Doris Day). The trochee girls had monosyllabic last names: Sandra Dee, Tuesday Weld, Sally Fields—all led by their den mother, Doris Day. Under all the sugar there was a percolating espresso of Beatnik doubt and Rock sensuality. But Kennedy distracted us from that, for a while.

America had marked time under the General. Now we had to be shaped up *and* shipped out: Cubans back to their own island, to get clobbered; kids to Africa in the Peace Corps, to suffer mosquitos and doubt; Green Berets god-knows-where, to show Dulles was all wrong about massive retaliation; and Jackie to Paris, as a boost for the fashion trade—all this at the blink and beck of that computered intelligence David Halberstam finally described as a kind of Brains Swindle. Fluted and trumpeted back up to our World War II sense of glamorous danger, we marched into waisthigh Reality's mud, and foundered there.

The nation, needing punishment, elected Richard Nixon. Since moral heroics had failed us, we turned to the moral dwarfs, expiating Vietnam with Watergate. If Asians rebuked us for wrecking their country, we could at least say, look what we did to our own.

**Garry Wills**

THE GREAT
CONTEMPORARY
ISSUES

# VALUES
# AMERICANS
# LIVE BY

# Industrial America

*Ford's Model T*

# PHILOSOPHY AT DINNER

## HERBERT SPENCER'S GENTLE REPROOF TO AMERICA.

A BANQUET GIVEN TO THE ENGLISH PHILOSOPHER—THE GUEST'S REMARKS ON AMERICAN DEVOTION TO WORK—ADDRESSES BY MR. EVARTS, PROF. MARSH, MR. BEECHER, PROF. SUMNER, AND OTHERS.

It is seldom that Delmonico's banquet hall is filled with a gathering of scholars and gentlemen so distinguished as that which assembled there last evening to participate in a farewell complimentary dinner to Herbert Spencer, the famous English philosopher, who is to sail for home to-morrow afternoon. The dinner was tendered by a committee of citizens consisting of E. R. Leland, Prof. John S. Newberry, W. W. Appleton, Prof. Henry Draper, F. F. Marbury, and W. J. Youmans, and 200 gentlemen sat at the table with the guest. In deference to the simple tastes of Mr. Spencer, who has a natural repugnance to any great display, no attempt at decorating the large hall was made, and the tables presented the usual *pièces montées*, no special designs being prepared for the occasion. At the raised table set apart for the more distinguished guests, the Hon. William M. Evarts, who presided at the dinner, occupied the centre seat. On his right sat Herbert Spencer, Prof. W. G. Sumner, Prof. John Fisk, of Yale; Gen. Benjamin F. Bristow, Henry Ward Beecher, Prof. E. L. Youmans, and E. R. Leland. To his left were Carl Schurz, Prof. O. C. Marsh, of Yale; Sir Richard Temple, and Mr. Edward Lot, of England, and the Hon. Abram S. Hewitt. Among the more prominent of the gentlemen at the five long tables on the floor were Congressman Perry Belmont, L. Bradford Prince, Hamilton Cole, Albert Bierstadt, Algernon S. Sullivan, Chauncey M. Depew, Dr. G. M. Weeks, R. H. Manning, Dr. W. A. Hammond, Dr. Spitzka, F. J. de Peyster, Prof. V. Botta, the Rev. Lyman Abbott, Prof. J. S. Newberry, Salem H. Wales, John Bigelow, J. Spencer Turner, Charles A. Coombs, the Rev. Mr. Morgan, Charles A. Dana, Prof. Henry Draper, John P. Townsend, Brayton Ives, Simon Sterne, S. H. Scudder, Dr. A. Alexander, Erastus Winans, Cyrus W. Field, David Dudley Field, Horace White, H. C. Van Voorst, W. W. Appleton, E. D. Appleton, Parke Godwin, and S. B. Eaton.

It was 9:30 o'clock before the elaborate *menu* prepared by Delmonico had been fully discussed and cigars were lighted. Then William M. Evarts rapped for order, and the busy hum of conversation ceased at once. Mr. Evarts made a very short eulogistic speech in regard to Mr. Spencer. "We are met to-night," he said, "to express the feelings of Americans toward the distinguished man who sits by my side. No banquet hall, no city even, can hold all his friends and admirers, and we are here in a representative capacity to speak for them all. In primitive times they had a custom when men were desirous of possessing themselves of the learning, the wisdom, the philosophy, or the great traits of any person of eating him up as soon as he was dead. It is a little hard on the natural instincts that we should take up the subject of evolution at this end of the dinner, [laughter,] but you can see how, by a multiplication of causes and effects, we have gradually progressed, until out of this barbarous custom we have come to a dinner of a dozen courses and wines of almost as many different varieties." Turning to Mr. Spencer, who sat with his eyes cast modestly down, Mr. Evarts said: "Mr. Spencer, we are glad to greet you here! [Applause.] We are glad to see you here and to have you see us. We are glad to see you, for we recognize in the breadth of your knowledge a greater comprehension of philosophical truth than has been shown to this generation by any other living man. We acknowledge your labors in the search for truth as surpassing those of any other man. [Applause.] You have already treated us to a little lesson in the science of vivisection, [laughter,] and we are now expecting that the world will be instructed concerning our many merits and our few faults when you get to the other side of the water. Whatever may be said of your system of philosophy, however it may be compared by scientific men to other and different systems, we must all agree that it is practical, serious, and benevolent; that it treats evil, not as eternal, but as evanescent, and that it aims to bring man to that condition of life where he shall find perfect happiness and contentment. It matters little whether such a system as this is called scientific or not. It is practical, and redounds to the good of mankind." Turning to the company again at this point, Mr. Evarts said: "Gentlemen, fill your glasses and drink to th health of our guest, Herbert Spencer."

### MR. SPENCER'S SECOND CRITICISM.

The toast was drank standing and in silence, and Mr. Spencer then arose to respond. He was greeted with a loud outburst of applause, and his benevolent and thoughtful-looking face flushed as he stood bowing in recognition of this demonstration. He spoke in a low but perfectly distinct tone as soon as silence had been restored, and his speech, which occupied some 20 minutes, was listened to with profound attention. Mr. Spencer said:

MR. PRESIDENT AND GENTLEMEN: Along with your kindness there comes to me a great unkindness from fate; for, now that, above all times in my life, I need full command of what powers of speech I possess, disturbed health so threatens to interfere with them that I fear I shall very inadequately express myself. Any failure in my response you must please ascribe, in part at least, to a greatly disordered nervous system. Regarding you as representing Americans at large, I feel that the occasion is one on which arrears of thanks are due. I ought to begin with the time, some two-and-twenty years ago, when my highly-valued friend, Prof. Youmans, making efforts to diffuse my books here, interested on their behalf the Messrs. Appleton, who have ever treated me so honorably and so handsomely, and I ought to detail from that time onward the various marks and acts of sympathy by which I have been encouraged in a struggle which was for many years disheartening. But, intimating thus briefly my general indebtedness to my numerous friends, most of them unknown, on this side of the Atlantic, I must name more especially the many attentions and proffered hospitalities met with during my late tour, as well as, lastly and chiefly, this marked expression of the sympathies and good wishes which many of you have traveled so far to give at great cost of that time which is so precious to the Americans. I believe I may truly say that the better health which you have so cordially wished me will be in a measure furthered by the wish, since all pleasurable emotion is conducive to health, and, as you will fully believe, the remembrance of this event will ever continue to be a source of pleasurable emotion, exceeded by few, if any, of my remembrances.

And now that I have thanked you, sincerely though too briefly, I am going to find fault with you. Already, in some remarks drawn from me respecting American affairs and American character, I have passed criticisms, which have been accepted far more good-naturedly than I could reasonably have expected; and it seems strange that I should now again propose to transgress. However, the fault I have to comment upon is one which most will scarcely regard as a fault. It seems to me that in one respect Americans have diverged too widely from savages. I do not mean to say that they are in general unduly civilized. Throughout large parts of the population, even in long-settled regions, there is no excess of those virtues needed for the maintenance of social harmony. Especially out in the West, men's dealings do not yet betray too much of the "sweetness and light" which we are told distinguish the cultured man from the barbarian. Nevertheless, there is a sense in which my assertion is true. You know that the primitive man lacks power of application. Spurred by hunger, by danger, by revenge, he can exert himself energetically for a time; but his energy is spasmodic. Monotonous daily toil is impossible to him. It is otherwise with the more developed man. The stern discipline of social life has gradually increased the aptitude for persistent industry; until, among us, and still more among you, work has become with many a passion. This contrast of nature has another aspect. The savage thinks only of present satisfaction, and leaves future satisfactions uncared for. Contrariwise, the American, eagerly pursuing a future good, almost ignores what good the passing day offers him; and, when the future good is gained, he neglects that while striving for some still remoter good.

What I have seen and heard during my stay among you, has forced on me the belief that this slow change from habitual inertness to persistent activity, has reached an extreme from which there must begin a counterchange—a reaction. Everywhere I have been struck with the number of faces which told in strong lines of the burdens that had to be borne. I have been struck, too, with the large proportion of gray-haired men; and inquiries have brought out the fact that with you the hair commonly begins to turn some 10 years earlier than with us. Moreover, in every circle I have met men who had themselves suffered from nervous collapse due to stress of business, or named friends who had either killed themselves by overwork, or had been permanently incapacitated, or had wasted long periods in endeavors to recover health. I do but echo the opinion of all observant persons I have spoken to, that immense injury is being done by this high-pressure life—the physique is being undermined. That subtle thinker and poet whom you have lately had to mourn, Emerson, says, in his essay on the gentleman, that the first requisite is that he shall be a good animal. The requisite is a general one—it extends to the man, to the father, to the citizen. We hear a great deal about "the vile body;" and many are encouraged by the phrase to transgress the laws of health. But nature quietly suppresses those who treat thus disrespectfully one of her highest products, and leaves the world to be peopled by the descendants of those who are not so foolish.

Beyond these immediate mischiefs there are remoter mischiefs. Exclusive devotion to work has the result that amusements cease to please; and, when relaxation becomes imperative, life becomes dreary from lack of its sole interest—the interest in business. The remark current in England that, when the American travels, his aim is to do the greatest amount of sight-seeing in the shortest time, I find current here also; it is recognized that the satisfaction of getting on devours nearly all other satisfactions. When recently at Niagara, which gave us a whole week's pleasure, I learned from the landlord of the hotel that most Americans come one day and go away the next. Old Froissart, who said of the English of his day that "they take their pleasures sadly after their fashion," would doubtless, if he lived now, say of the Americans that they take their pleasures hurriedly after their fashion. In large measure with us, and still more with you, there is not that abandonment to the moment which is requisite for full enjoyment; and this abandonment is prevented by the ever-present sense of multitudinous responsibilities. So that, beyond the serious physical mischief caused by overwork, there is the further mischief that it destroys what value there would otherwise be in the leisure part of life.

Nor do the evils end here. There is the injury to posterity. Damaged constitutions reappear in children, and entail on them far more of ill than great fortunes yield them of good. When life has been duly rationalized by science, it will be seen that among a man's duties care of the body is imperative, not only out of regard for personal welfare, but also out of regard for descendants. His constitution will be considered as an entailed estate, which he ought to pass on uninjured, if not improved, to those who follow; and it will be held that millions bequeathed by him will not compensate for feeble health and decreased ability to enjoy life. Once more, there is the injury to fellow-citizens, taking the shape of undue disregard of competitors. I hear that a great trader among you deliberately endeavored to crush out every one whose business competed with his own; and manifestly the man who, making himself a slave to accumulation, absorbs an inordinate share of the trade or profession he is engaged in, makes life harder for all others engaged in it, and excludes from it many who might otherwise gain competencies. Thus, besides the egotistic motive, there are two altruistic motives which should deter from this excess in work.

The truth is, there needs a revised ideal of life. Look back through the past, or look abroad through the present, and we find that the ideal of life is variable and depends on social conditions. Every one knows that to be a successful warrior was the highest aim among all ancient peoples of note, as it is still among many barbarous peoples. When we remember that in the Norseman's heaven the time was to be passed in daily battles, with magical healing of wounds, we see how deeply rooted may become the conception that fighting is man's proper business, and that industry is fit only for slaves and people of low degree. That is to say, when the chronic struggles of races necessitate perpetual wars, there is evolved an ideal of life adapted to the requirements. We have changed all that in modern civilized societies, especially in England, and still more in America. With the decline of militant activity, and the growth of industrial activity, the occupations once disgraceful have become honorable. The duty to work has taken the place of the duty to fight; and in the one case, as in the other, the ideal of life has become so well established that scarcely any dream of questioning it. Practically business has been substituted for war as the purpose of existence.

Is this modern ideal to survive throughout the future? I think not. While all other things undergo continuous change, it is impossible that ideals should remain fixed. The ancient ideal was appropriate to the ages of conquest by man over man, and spread of the strongest races. The modern ideal is appropriate to ages in which conquest of the earth and subjection of the powers of nature to human use is the predominant need. But hereafter, when both these ends have in the main been achieved, the ideal formed will probably differ considerably from the present one. May we not foresee the nature of the difference? I think we may. Some 20 years ago, a good friend of mine and a good friend of yours, too, though you never saw him, John Stuart Mill delivered at St. Andrews an inaugural address on the occasion of his appointment to the Lord Rectorship. It contained much to be admired, as did all he wrote. There ran through it, however, the tacit assumption that life is for learning and working. I felt at the time that I should have liked to take up the opposite thesis. I should have liked to contend that life is not for learning, nor is life for working, but learning and working are for life. The primary use of knowledge is for such guidance of conduct under all circumstances as shall make living complete. All other uses of knowledge are secondary. It scarcely needs saying that the primary use of work is that of supplying the materials and aids to living completely, and that any other uses of work are secondary. But in men's conceptions the secondary has in great measure usurped the place of the primary. The apostle of culture as it is commonly conceived, Mr. Matthew Arnold, makes little or no reference to the fact that the first use of knowledge is the right ordering of all actions; and Mr. Carlyle, who is a good exponent of current ideas about work, insists on its virtues for quite other reasons than that it achieves sustentation. We may trace everywhere in human affairs a tendency to transform the means into the end. All see that the miser does this when, making the accumulation of money his sole satisfaction, he forgets that money is of value to purchase satisfactions. But it is less commonly seen that the like is true of the work by which the money is accumulated—that industry, too, bodily or mental, is but a means, and that it is as irrational to pursue it to the exclusion of that complete living it subserves, as it is for the miser to accumulate money and make no use of it. Hereafter, when this age of active material progress has yielded mankind its benefits, there will, I think, come a better adjustment of labor and enjoyment. Among reasons for thinking this, there is the reason that the process of evolution throughout the organic world at large, brings an increasing surplus of energies that are not absorbed in fulfilling material needs, and points to a still larger surplus for humanity of the future. And there are other reasons, which I must pass over. In brief, I may say that we have had somewhat too much of "the gospel of work." It is time to preach the Gospel of relaxation.

This is a very unconventional after-dinner speech. Especially it will be thought strange that in returning thanks I should deliver something very much like a homily. But I have thought I could not better convey my thanks than by the expression of a sympathy which issues in a fear. If, as I gather, this intemperance in work affects more especially the Anglo-American part of the population—if there results an undermining of the physique not only in adults, but also in the young, who, as I learn from your daily journals, are also being injured by overwork—if the ultimate consequence should be a dwindling away of those among you who are the inheritors of free institutions and best adapted to them, then there will come a further difficulty in the working out of the great future which lies before the American Nation. To my anxiety on this account, you must please ascribe the unusual character of my remarks. And now I must bid you farewell. When I sail by the Germanic on Saturday I shall bear with me pleasant remembrances of my intercourse with many Americans, joined with regrets that my state of health has prevented me from seeing a larger number.

## THE OTHER SPEECHES.

When the prolonged applause which followed Mr. Spencer's remarks had ceased, Mr. Evarts read a letter of regrets from Oliver Wendell Holmes, dated Boston, Nov. 6. The "autocrat of the breakfast table" said that it would have been a great pleasure to have testified by his presence that he "shared the feelings of respect and admiration of which this occasion is a passing manifestation." "Mr. Spencer," he wrote, "has come nearer to the realization of Bacon's claim of all knowledge as his province than any philosopher of his time. It is a life's work to expand a single specialty as it must be studied to-day. * * * The man who takes the survey of the entire order of things as his specialty must needs have a long stride and a clear outlook. He must have a well measured and largely extended base line of ascertained fact to begin with, and command the views which expand themselves from all the heights of the various sciences. The facts of development furnished Mr. Spencer with his base line. From the summit of one branch of knowledge after another, he has brought its phenomena into relations with the base line and with each other. * * * All is development, and the standing illustration of it was laid before the world by the bird of Chanticleer, when she proclaimed to the virgin creation that she was a mother. * * * May Herbert Spencer live to place the cap-stone on that pyramid of achievements which is already one of the wonders of the intellectual world."

The Rev. Heber Newton, of this City, wrote from Garden City, as follows: "I am sure that all the best representatives of the clerical vocation, however they may differ from Mr. Spencer, entertain the profoundest respect for his abilities and character, and the sincerest gratitude for the single-minded service he has rendered the cause of truth." The Hon. Hugh McCulloch sent a letter of regrets from Holly Hills, Md., in which he said: "Mr. Spencer is eminently a teacher in whom there is no guile, and thousands of those who differ radically with him in his religious views, and who cannot quite follow him in some of his philosophical teachings, greatly honor him for his independence and uprightness."

The first regular toast of the evening was "The Science of Sociology," which was responded to by Prof. William G. Sumner, of Yale College. The speaker said that he regarded with the deepest respect the science of sociology, and he fully appreciated its value and importance. It is a fact that is generally overlooked that the great advancements that have been made in science and the arts during the past 100 years have reached out until they produced the most important of social results. These advancements are producing new hopes and new faiths in the various classes of the population. The new ideas that are constantly arising are of such importance that they require to be criticised carefully and intelligently in order to separate the good from the bad. Old traditions are inadequate to accompany and explain the new social problems that are being produced in the advancements in science and the arts. In the present day our discussions far surpass our deliberations, and our deliberations surpass our information. Sociology is discussed in all places and by all classes of people, but the crude method of most of these discussions is such as to confuse people. What is needed is intelligent classification, in order that the guiding lines of the study of sociology may be properly established. Herbert Spencer is looked upon as being the man who has opened the way to a well-defined oa of sociology. It is in the doman of evolution that a solution of the all-importtant social problems is to be found, and in that domain Mr. Spencer stands pre-eminent. The speaker expressed the hope that the honored guest would be spared to the world for many years to come in order that he might complete his work. Cordial applause followed the expression of this wish.

"The Doctrine of Evolution" was the theme of interesting remarks by Prof. Marsh, of Yale College. He traced the history of the philosophy of evolution, the first scientific theory of which was advanced by Lamarck in the beginning of the present century. Cuvier opposed the new idea with all his authority, and evolution was pronounced to be without foundation. This triumph of Cuvier delayed the progress of evolution for half a century. "In the first decade of the present half century," said Prof. Marsh, "Darwin, Wallace, Huxley, and our honored guest, were all at the same time working at one problem, each in his own way, and their united efforts have firmly established the truth of organic evolution. Our guest to-night did not stop to solve the difficulties of organic evolution, but with that profound philosophic insight which has made him read and honored by all intelligent men, he made the grand generalization that the law of organic progress is the law of all progress. The evolution of life and of the physical world are now supplemented by the evolution of philosophy, of history, of society, and of all else pertaining to human life, until we may say that evolution is the law of all progress, if not the key to all mysteries. The battle has been fought and won. A few stragglers on each side may still keep up a scattered fire, but the contest is over and the victors have moved on to other fields. The doctrine of evolution has brought light out of darkness, and marks the path of future progress. What the law of gravitation is to astronomy, the law of evolution is now to natural science. It is no longer a theory, but a demonstrated truth, accepted by naturalists throughout the world. The most encouraging feature in natural science, indeed in all science to-day, is the spirit in which the work is carred on. No authority is recognized which forbids the investigation of any question, however profound; and, with that confidence which success justly brings, no question within the domain of science is now believed to be insoluble. Not even the grand poblems now before us—the antiquity of the human race, the origin of man, or even the origin of life itself."

The Hon. Carl Schurz spoke to the sentiment, "The Province of Science Tends to International Harmony." He elicited uproarious applause by announcing at the outset that Herbert Spencer appeared more like an American than an Englishman. Mr. Schurz agreed with Mr. Spencer in the idea that "the results of the attempts to protect men from the results of their own follies peoples the world with fools." The speaker, however, said that he would displace the word "fools" in the quotation by "dyspeptic philosophers," and as he believed that too much mental exertion after a hearty meal was injurious to health he proposed to be careful and not become a "dyspeptic philosopher." He said that while serving in the Army during the late rebellion he happened to get hold of a copy of Herbert Spencer's "Social Statics," and he had frequent opportunities of studying that work during the long nights of camp life. After reading the book through, he became convinced that it was the duty of the Federal soldiers to hammer Mr. Spencer's ideas on "social statics" into the heads of the slaveholders. Mr. Schurz said that he greeted Herbert Spencer as one of the builders up of science, as the great apostle of evolution, as the representative of the democratic tendency and of that great development of thought which had burst the bonds of the closet; as the hero of thought who had vindicated the divine right of science as against the intolerant authority of tradition.

Chairman Evarts announced that the next regular toast was, "Evolution and Religion; that which Perfects Humanity cannot Destroy Religion." He said that it would be necessary to have such a sentiment responded to by a duet, [laughter] and he should first call upon Prof. John Fiske, of Harvard College, and afterward the Rev. Henry Ward Beecher. [Applause.] Prof. Fiske said that he regarded evolution and religion as being important factors of a true understanding of science. He thought that Herbert Spencer's services to religious thought had been no less signal than his services to science and philosophy.

The Rev. Henry Ward Beecher made a characteristic and witty speech. He said that Herbert Spencer had done immense harm, for there were very few ministers who had not been put to a peck of trouble by trying to reconcile Herbert Spencer's advanced ideas with their old-fashioned doctrines. As for himself, Mr. Beecher said that he found it hard to reconcile Herbert Spencer with St. Augustine. He could not get along with Spencer and Calvin both. [Great laughter.] But whatever might be said about Mr. Spencer's intrinsic utterances of advanced thought, there was no getting around the fact that Mr. Spencer had come into the world of thought, and he had come to stay. Whether people liked it or not, Mr. Spencer's theory of evolution was going to revolutionize theology entirely, It was going to open new ways to theologians. It was going to bridge over some of the muddy streams which the theologians had hitherto had to wade, and it was going to cast light on many dark points of biblical literature. Some men had maintained that religion was the art of putting people on an anvil and hammering them into perfect manhood. Such a theory did not clash with Mr. Spencer's theory of the power and effect of thought and knowledge. The object of religion was not to insure men against fire in another world. The true disciples of religion were not in the insurance business. [Laughter.] With reference to the theory of evolution, Mr. Beecher said that it was a hypothesis that men of the present day were but the prolongation of a lower animal life; and were he to judge by some men that he knew he would be inclined to believe in the absolute truth of this theory. [Laughter.] "I had just as lief have descended from a monkey," said he, "if I have descended far enough." Mr. Beecher believed that from the earliest period of the world's history people had undergone steady but erratic changes for the better. There were evidences of an inevitable plan of developement which could not be truthfully characterized by the assertion that "all these changes are due to the interposition of Providence." There was nothing more in the quarrel between science and religion, said the speaker, than there was in a quarrel between man and wife. In both cases it might be regarded simply as "an adjustment of differences." [Laughier and applause.] Mr. Beecher said that to believe in the theory of gradual development did not make necessary a man's disbelieving any of the teachings of the Scriptures. All that was true and good in the Bible might easily be adjusted to the facts developed by the careful researches of the students of science. Man was certainly a progressive animal, and just so far as true science opened the way for him to see, just so far would his moral status improve. "Our physical being is in constant conflict with our moral being," exclaimed the speaker. "We are constantly in our moral natures resolving to do things which our physical natures refuse to do, but the physical as well as the moral natures are improving from year to year, which carries out the theory of progressive development." Mr. Beecher paid a warm and eloquent personal tribute to Mr. Spencer, whose works, he said, had been meat and drink to him for 20 years. He felt under deep personal obligations to Mr. Spencer for giving him ideas and suggestions which had enabled him to see many things in a clearer and better light, and had, he thought, brought him nearer to the Divine presence. Mr. Beecher's remarks were cheered at their conclusion, most of the gentlemen rising to their feet and waving handkerchiefs and napkins.

Mr. Evarts then requested the gentlemen once more to drink to "the health, long life, and prosperity of their guest." After the glasses had been emptied Mr. Spencer said: "I am too much overcome by the good wishes expressed this evening to say more than Thank you!" The formalities being declared closed, the assemblage quickly dissolved.

## ARE CITIES TO RULE THE COUNTRY?

There has been a good deal of discussion in recent years as to the capacity of the people of large cities to govern themselves, especially under the principles of representative government which have been established in this country, but the figures of each successive census suggest with increasing clearness the possibility of a time not very far off when cities may hold the ruling power of State and Nation. Out of that suggestion arise questions even more serious than that of local self-government for cities. One hundred years ago only about 3⅓ per cent. of the population of this country was massed in cities, and at that time the city of New-York had little more than 33,000 inhabitants. Fifty years ago the proportion of city population to the whole had risen to 8½ per cent., and New-York contained 312,852 people. The rate of increase in the ratio of urban population in the last half century has been still greater, and the new census will show that more than one-fourth of the people of the country live in cities. The proportion is considerably higher than this in some of the older States, and, though the census tables showing the actual result of the last enumeration are not yet at hand, there is no doubt that in this State more than one-third of the population is massed together in incorporated municipalities. The causes of this movement in the distribution of population will doubtless continue to operate, and the time is not far distant when a majority of the people will dwell in cities, and those cities will exercise a controlling power in all affairs of government.

The causes of this transfer of the preponderance of numbers and of power from rural to urban communities are not difficult to find. It is the result of the general development of industrial appliances and of the means of interchange for the products of labor. The application of machinery to agricultural processes and the immense increase of the scale upon which farming operations are carried on have diminished the relative number of people necessarily employed in strictly rural labor. A far greater effect has been produced by the enormous development of manufacturing industries through the application of machinery. This has brought population together at central points, and, while it has done away with a great variety of widely distributed hand labor, it has so vastly increased the number and variety of the products into which raw materials are wrought that a much larger proportion of the people are employed in manufacturing than before. Not only the invention and application of machinery but the massing of capital by incorporation has promoted this imposing movement of labor from the soil to the workshop and the factory. Accompanying this industrial movement has been the rapid development of means of conveyance and communication by railroads, which has done away with necessity for the nearness of population to the sources of supply. A city may draw its supply of food and materials from a distance of a thousand miles with almost as much certainty, celerity, and cheapness as it could obtain them from the country about it, if that were capable of producing them, and its people are no longer dependent upon their immediate environment. With the expansion of mechanical industries and the growth of facilities of communication has come an enormous development of trade and of agencies employed in the operations of exchange, employing multitudes of people.

In short, it is the evolution through which production and trade have been going for two generations that has built up cities and concentrated population, and the movement has been going on all over the civilized world. There is no reason for supposing that it will not continue until the people who are scattered in rural communities and engaged in occupations necessarily carried on in such communities will be in the minority. Heretofore the State has created and practically controlled City Governments, and it has been judicially held that municipal government is a subordinate branch of State government and subject to any change which the Legislature may ordain. The city of New-York is to-day dependent for such measure of self-government as it may exercise and for the privilege of supplying its most important civic needs upon the Legislature at Albany, in which a large majority of the members represent rural communities. In an important sense it is ruled by the scattered population of the country districts, which has no conception of its requirements. Country legislators have even prevented the cities from having their due share of representation in the law-making body upon which they so largely depend. But the time will come when cities must control the Legislature and make the government of the State. Though they may still be nominally the creatures of the State, they will secure local self-government by their power to control the agency which now controls them, and the position of dependence may be changed from the cities to the rural towns.

When the preponderance of population is in cities of constantly-increasing size they will not only control Legislatures and make and unmake State Governments, but they will have the controlling voice in the Congress of the Nation and determine the character and policy of the National Administration. Thus the tendency of population to congregate in cities, the industrial and commercial development which draws the forces of the country more and more into employments that mass the people together in great urban communities, with their manifold and complex activities and interests, will ultimately put a new phase upon problems of government.

December 15, 1890

## CHRISTIANITY AND EDUCATION.

THE TIMES printed on Wednesday an interesting letter in which Mr. JOHN JAY collated the judicial decisions which maintain that Christianity is the law of the land. The letter was written in answer to an editorial remark in these columns upon the use of that proposition by the Methodist Conference. It was used by that body to enforce the demand that religious instruction should be given in the public schools. For that purpose the declaration seemed too vague to be relevant or valuable.

There are cases no doubt for which the doctrine is specific enough for judicial purposes. Mr. JAY cites one of them in which a man was indicted for reviling the Scriptures, and it was held that he could rightly be convicted and punished even though there were no statute directed expressly at his offense. That decision could perhaps be rested as strongly upon other grounds. Whoever wantonly offends the religious sensibilities of his neighbors is guilty of a violation of public decency for which all right-minded persons must censure him and desire to see him punished, even though they do not themselves share the sensibilities he outrages. There are very few Americans, no matter what their religious belief or want of it may be, who are not shocked by ribald references to the doctrines of Christianity. It is quite intelligible, and it is no infringement at all of the principle of religious liberty that, for the purpose of punishing such offenses, Christianity should be held to be part of the law of the land.

But this is not the question. The question is whether Christianity shall be taught in the public schools, and, if so, what Christianity and how much. Toward the answer to this question the assertion that Christianity is part of the law of the land takes us a very little way. In England, from which our courts have borrowed the expression, it has a definite meaning. It means Christianity as formulated by the Established Church of the country, even including the denunciation in the articles of the "vain talk" of "certain Anabaptists." Where the Church and the State are one, the doctrine taught in the State schools is the doctrine of the Church. But how does it help us in considering whether the common schools shall give religious instruction to be told that Christianity is part of the law of the land? No law book lays down what the Christian doctrines are in which courts have a judicial belief, or what doctrines are essential and what unessential. The Judges who have delivered the doctrine have been compelled to generalize it. One of the most impressive statements of it, that quoted by Mr. JAY from DANIEL WEBSTER, is also one of the vaguest—"Christianity, Christianity independent of sects and parties, general, tolerant Christianity, is the law of the land."

This is doubtless impressive, but it scarcely affords the material for a curriculum of religious instruction in the secular schools. Where is "Christianity independent of sects and parties" to be found? Suppose we admit that general, tolerant Christianity should be taught in the common schools, though no other part of the law of the land is so taught, where is unsectarian Christianity to be found? Is there any Christian authority which is not also a sectarian authority? The Methodist pastor and the Catholic priest might admit each other to be Christians, though each of them would probably have so many qualifications to make that the Christianity of the other would appear to be as unimportant as it was general. Each of them, at any rate, professes and calls himself a Chris-

tian, and each would have as good a right as the other to say how much Christianity and what Christianity the common schools should teach. Everybody knows that they would not in the least agree about it, even though they professed to make it as "general" as possible. The Roman Catholic would insist that "the simple reading of the Scripture without note or comment," which seems to be the ultimatum of the evangelical Protestants, was either too much or too little, and certainly was not a proper teaching of general Christianity. We can imagine the horror, on the other hand, with which the Methodist would recoil from any scheme of religious instruction that the Roman Catholics would propound. As there is, practically speaking, no unsectarian Christianity, the only resource would be to invite all the Christian sects to unite in preparing a suitable course of religious instruction, and this it is certain that they could not agree upon. Yet their rights as citizens are precisely the same. Anglican Christianity is part of the law of England, but no American court has yet decided that either Protestantism or Catholicism is part of the law of this country, any more than any court has denied that both Protestantism and Catholicism are entitled to be consid-

ered forms of Christianity. Yet no religious instruction can be given in the schools upon which Catholics and Protestants will agree, although all Catholics and a limited number of Protestants agree that some religious instruction should be given. If the majority of the voters could be brought to this opinion, the division of the school fund which the Roman Catholics desire would be the natural solution of the difficulty. We believe, and we believe that a majority of the voters believe, that this would be a grievous public calamity. The only way to avert it is to hold that the instruction of the common schools should be exclusively secular, and that anybody who insists upon the necessity or desirableness of adding religious instruction to it shall be at liberty to add it in his own way and at his own cost, but not in the common schools nor at the cost of the taxpayers. A man whose money is taken from him by the State to administer religious instruction which he disapproves is certainly not in the enjoyment of the religious liberty guaranteed to him by the Constitution. To quote, in justification of this abstraction, that Christianity is part of the law of the land is idle, meaningless, and exasperating.

April 20, 1890

### NO MORE MIXED CLASSES.
The Board of Control of the Art Students' League decided last night that Mr. St. Gaudens's mixed class in drawing from the nude should not be resumed this term. The class consisted of three men and nine young women. Objection was made to their drawing together from a nude figure, and one girl left the school on this account.

This stirred up quite a controversy in the league over the subject, and the work of the class was stopped. The vote last night upon a motion to resume the class was 6 to 6, a majority being necessary to carry the measure.

### TRANSMITTED MUSIC.
Miss Lillian Russell will sing into a long-distance telephone to-morrow night for the edification of Mr. Thomas A. Edison and a party of his friends in Washington. A transmitter has been rigged up in Miss Russell's dressing room at the Casino especially for the occasion. Mr. Edison has also arranged with Miss Russell to visit her residence next week and bottle up the singer's voice in the cylinder of a phonograph for preservation and reference.

May 10, 1890

### SUNDAY AMUSEMENTS.
The arrest of two baseball teams at Rochester for playing a public game on Sunday is a fact of some importance in the history of the Sunday question. In the West, where the traditionally American rigor of the observance of Sunday is very much relaxed, professional games have been common for some years. A majority, however, of the people who attend such games on week days in the Eastern States would feel a certain shamefacedness about attending them on Sunday. Even if there were no legal interference, the playing of professional games on Sunday would bring the association that countenanced it into a disrepute for which the attendance upon these games would not compensate.

There is no doubt that the more respectable and orderly part of the community is

much opposed to public amusements on Sunday which are merely amusements. Many persons who are heartily in favor of the opening on Sunday of libraries and museums and picture galleries, and who have no scruples about attending concerts of good music on that day, would object to Sunday baseball. The distinction is, perhaps, rather fine, but it is none the less real. The whole Sunday question is, indeed, one of sentiment rather than of reason. The distinction in this case is that attendance upon libraries and museums and concerts is not merely an amusement. It is also instructive, and has or may have a positive educational value. Going to see a game of baseball, on the other hand, is an amusement pure and simple, and cannot be construed into anything else. Moreover, the game or any ath-

letic entertainments given out of doors is not merely public, but attracts an assemblage necessarily more or less noisy and even tumultuous. It is undoubtedly a disturbance to the quiet of the neighborhood in which it is given, and hinders the people who hold the puritanical view of Sunday from observing the day in their own way. As a matter of public policy and public decency there is no good reason why the Sunday laws should be relaxed in favor of baseball.

A much more important question has arisen touching the observance of Sunday in connection with the World's Fair at Chicago. Last Sunday a public meeting was held in that city to protest against the opening of the fair on Sunday and to request the Legislature to make sure that it be closed on that day. The people of Chicago are not very strict Sabbatarians, and it is not likely that such a meeting would have been called if there had not been an intention on the part of some of the promoters of the fair to keep it open on Sunday. Undoubtedly a World's Fair is a means of instruction as well as amusement. According to the distinction we have noted it is so for one of the entertainments that are permissible without reducing Sunday to the level of a secular day or interfering with it as a day of rest. All Americans, whether or not they attach any value to the religious sanctions by which the day is preserved, are in favor of preserving it as a day of rest. A World's Fair, however, is so large an "institution," and requires so large a force of attendants and exhibitors, that to keep it open on Sunday is to keep going a very extensive business. Each exhibitor may be described as a shop-keeper, and the number of exhibits is the number of shops that are kept open. The reason adduced for keeping them open would be the number of persons employed

during the week who are shut up to the alternatives of seeing the exhibition on Sunday or of not seeing it at all. In New-York, with the Saturday half holiday, of which the observance is extending every year, this consideration would lose most of its force. It is to be assumed that the business men of Chicago will arrive at some such arrangement as will allow everybody in their employ to visit the exhibition on a week day if the exhibition be closed on Sunday.

If the decision is left to the managers of the exhibition it will doubtless depend upon their judgment as to the more profitable course to pursue. It seems to us not doubtful that the success of the exhibition will be promoted by closing it on Sunday. The remonstrants in Chicago appealed with much force to the example of the Centennial. That the Centennial was successful without a Sunday opening of course does not of itself prove that it would not have been successful with a Sunday opening,

but we are inclined to believe that its success would have been less marked. In Chicago the case is stronger, because the Columbian Exposition will be much more exclusively American than the Centennial Exposition. The selection of Chicago and the enactment, even in a highly modified form, of the McKinley bill will effectually deter European exhibitors, who would not be deterred in the least by the opening of the exhibition on Sunday. There are many American exhibitors who would be deterred by that fact, which also would have a considerable effect upon the attendance. To announce that the exhibition would be open on Sundays would be to draw down upon it in advance the denunciation of the pulpits of all denominations. To array all the Churches against an enterprise of this character would be about as unwise a step as could be taken, and there is no reason to expect that the managers of the Chicago fair will commit so great a blunder.

July 22, 1890

---

### VAGRANTS AND BEGGARS.

The movement against vagrancy and street beggary that was begun yesterday has not been set on foot until after it was obviously and urgently needed. The object, of course, is to make it certain that nobody who is able to support himself shall be supported by public and promiscuous charity because he is unwilling to work. On the other hand, it is to make it more certain than it now is that nobody who is actually unable to support himself shall be left destitute. In order to bring about these two results and to insure that the charity of the charitable shall be utilized and not wasted, it has been necessary to secure co-operation between several municipal departments. The police must arrest casual beggars; the Police Magistrate must hold them; the Charity Organization Society must investigate the cases of mendicancy, and, finally, the Commissioner of Correction must convince the sturdy beggars that mendicancy is not so easy or pleasant a way of getting a living as honest labor.

There is no doubt that the practice of promiscuous alms-giving is responsible for the institution of an order of sturdy, or, as they are called in the ancient English statutes, of "valiant" beggars. Nobody is to be praised, on the contrary everybody deserves censure, who adopts this easy method of salving his own conscience with respect to appeals made upon him for aid. It is no doubt easier to give a poor devil something than to make investigation concerning him. But whoever adopts this easy method helps to encourage the adoption of beggary as an easy trade. It is within the experience

of most people that appeals made in the name of hunger are apt to be made in the real behalf of thirst, and that a gift that can be used only for the purpose for which it is asked is apt to be rejected. Those provident persons who in past seasons have provided themselves with meal tickets redeemable at an agency of charity to be given in lieu of money have found that their offerings were either rejected outright by the more impudent beggars, or quickly thrown away by the more modest, as not meeting their requirements.

One of the saddest results of such an experience is that it induces the charitably disposed to generalize too rashly, and tends to harden their hearts against what may be really deserving applications. The best method of sifting the worthy from the unworthy that has yet been discovered, in respect to able-bodied applicants, is to offer them food in exchange for work. Wherever this choice has been presented, it has been found to have a marvelous effect in reducing the number of unfortunate poor men who are looking for work, but in the meanwhile require gifts of money. It is a very simple test, and it is not very creditable to this municipality that it should not have been as extensively and systematically applied here as it has been in other places. The application of it is part of the scheme that went into operation yesterday. Of course, the mere weeding out of the undeserving is only a preliminary to a proper organization of charity. But is is a necessary preliminary, and it is gratifying that it should have been at last seriously taken up by the authorities.

February 2, 1897

---

## ECKELS ON "INDIVIDUALISM."

### Ex-Controller Makes a Defense of Trusts and Says Talent Is Rewarded.

*Special to The New York Times.*

CHICAGO, Feb. 5.—James H. Eckels, ex-Controller of the Currency, spoke in the University of Chicago to-day on "Individualism." He made a defense of trusts in general and during his remarks said:

"Many men seem to think there is no room for individuals in modern commercial life, but in my opinion at no time in our history has there been so much opportunity for individual effort and action as at present. Combinations of capital in business are looked upon with distrust, but I am free to confess that I see nothing at all harmful, detrimental, or dangerous in combinations, provided the combination is properly made and under an honorable management."

Mr. Eckels spoke on railroads as an example of beneficial corporations or trusts, and said:

"Railroad corporations give better service, cheaper rates, and better accommodation, and no railroad organization has been formed for the purpose of fleecing a community. In railroad combinations and all others, the individual that displays talent for business will rapidly advance, and never has there been such opportunity of such remuneration for talent."

February 6, 1901

# TALK ABOUT TRUSTS MOSTLY BOSH---JEROME

## Nothing Touched by Them That Is Not Improved, He Says.

## GOOD WORD FOR WALL STREET

### Tells Kansans They Hurt Themselves When They Strike at the Country's Financial Interests.

*Special to The New York Times.*

OTTAWA. Kan., July 7.—One of the points of the Ottawa Chautauqua always has been that if possible its speakers shall advocate reform of some sort. The programme was arranged this year with especial reference to just that principle, the officers of the assembly selecting Gov. La Follette of Wisconsin, Thomas W. Lawson of Boston, and William Travers Jerome of New York. Mr. Jerome, who spoke to-day, said in part:

" You of the West have kept and do keep a vital interest in everything, and for that I admire you. You are fitted with good minds out here, and you look at the world with healthy eyes and rare minds. You lack the cynicism of the East, but you should not forget how differently we live. In the West you make mistakes, sometimes, of course, a bad bond for a State Treasurer is taken, or you have a bad failure, but you pick up courage and go ahead into the field of commerce and make another start. Those things are experiments with you.

" In the East, with its dense population, we cannot try those experiments. We must be conservative. You think of us as effete Easterns, crushed beneath the iron heel of Pierpont Morgans, Russell Sages, and such, and we think of you as downtrodden, Populist-ridden Kansans. You think of Wall Street and you groan.

" My dear people, Wall Street has legitimate functions. Who is building your railroads, digging your wells, financing your great undertakings, if not Wall Street? When you strike a blow at financial interests of the country you hurt yourselves. This may not please you, but I did not come all the way out here to say something to please you.

" All this talk about trusts is mostly nonsense. I tell you, and I hold no brief from the trusts, that no man has been in a position to know more of the iniquities of trusts than I have, and yet I declare that nothing in this country has been touched by a trust that has not grown and improved. Despicable a man as is John D. Rockefeller, you have only to look at your own country crossroads to find men, in a smaller way, doing exactly as he has done.

" This is business, and business is war. This is commerce, this is competition—it is war and strife. I do not say that this is moral. It is immoral. But don't tell me that if the men at the crossroads had more power they would not use it to their own advantage, or that they would use it any better than Rockefeller uses it."

## GROPING OUR WAY.

Mr. JAMES J. HILL has been talking to a representative of our neighbor The Herald in that discursive and enlightening way that is characteristic of his newspaper interviews, which always show that he has done a great deal of thinking himself and are apt to stimulate thinking in others. This time Mr. HILL is in a somewhat critical mood. He finds that " there are too many hampering influences on commerce from Governmental and individual quarters," and he thinks that " there are too many quack political theories which clash with sound business." We are working, eighty millions of us, to develop the natural resources of the country, but from a trade and business point of view " we are making a poor job of it." " The country is richer far than England or Germany," says Mr. HILL, " and yet the fruits of trading are exceedingly small compared with what they ought to be." We are swapping jackknives with each other when we ought to be selling immense volumes of commodities to foreigners. And all the time we are hampered because " individual effort is restrained by political theorists and demagogue leaders," but " five or ten years hence this country will deplore the present policy of political interference locally and nationally."

The National customs and policies with which Mr. HILL thus frankly expresses his impatience are the fruit of our youth and inexperience. We are at present groping our way amid a multitude of unsolved problems. One of these problems is that of " political interference " with private business. It was inevitable that this problem should confront us, and we are trying to solve it. In the last fifteen years, and notably in the last ten years, some very powerful corporations have been created. The tendency has been toward building up big corporations by putting small ones together. Some of these corporations were outrageously greedy and rapacious; they destroyed their competitors, they preyed upon the people, they made the cost of living higher. In self-defense the people enacted protective statutes. Here is where the demagogues have notoriously " come in." Any man who assailed the corporations and Trusts and advocated the putting of restraints upon them, whether he was a ranting demagogue or a friend of the people prompted by sincere convictions, was sure of a wide hearing. One consequence is that we have put upon the statute books, State and Nation, enactments intended to curb the capitalists and the corporations. Another consequence is that in enacting and applying some of these statutes we have made a frightful mess of it. But by experience we get wisdom. After a long period of contests between the people and the combinations, a struggle that will certainly last for years, we shall be able to draw with wisdom and precision the safe line that defines the rights of the people and the privileges of the corporations.

It is perfectly true, as Mr. HILL says, that " what is needed the country over is a great awakening, a sort of revival in its business methods, in domestic and foreign trade." We want to rid ourselves of the " hampering influences." But here again we are groping our way, and although there is light enough to show the true path there are those among us who make it their business to see that the people's eyes are bandaged all the time. Germany exports twice, and England three times, our annual volume of exported manufactures. Why? Because we stubbornly stick to the jackknife swapping policy. Instead of sending their agents everywhere to drum up foreign trade and find markets the world over, our great manufacturers and captains of industry have preferred to look to Government bounty for profits. Mr. CARNEGIE's steel works, which were the basis of the great United States Steel Corporation, made $41,000,000 of profits in one year. So long as our tariff laws enabled Mr. CARNEGIE to charge American consumers prices that would yield him that enormous gain, why should he trouble himself about " abroad "? When an American manufacturer finds his business languishing he packs his carpetbag for Washington, not for Europe. Mr. HILL says that American ships cost more to build and operate than foreign ships. Instead of finding a natural trade remedy for that condition our shipbuilders and shipowners draw up subsidy bills which they beseech Congress to pass. The immense fortunes that have been built up by our protective tariff and the influence that comes with them are freely used to perpetuate the high tariff policy, until tariff reformers have abandoned pretty much all hope. Even our resolute President, who in a moment of haste and inadvertence recently declared that the Panama Canal was to be considered outside of the scope of the Dingley tariff, was promptly persuaded to reconsider his decision.

The business awakening of which Mr. HILL speaks is long overdue. We ought not to export agricultural products— that is the business of raw countries. We ought not to be buyers of foreign Government bonds bearing low rates of interest—if we were wide awake our own trade and industries would offer more profitable investments to capitalists. Our foreign trade ought to be double its present volume, it would be doubled if we had not for so many years been groping in darkness. Of course we have done great things, we have accomplished big results. But compared with what we might have done, with what we shall do when we have come to a full sense of our opportunities, our achievement thus far is, as Mr. HILL says, a poor job. One of these days there may be a sudden awakening.

July 18, 1905

## MOB BURNS NEGRO AT STAKE.

### Immense Crowd Sees Lynching on Texas Town's Court House Square.

SULPHUR SPRINGS, Texas, Aug. 11.— Tom Williams, a negro charged with attacking the fourteen-year-old daughter of a widow near here early this morning, was caught and burned at the stake in the Sulphur Springs Court House Square to-day.

The town was alarmed about an hour after the attack, and a posse of armed horsemen immediately started in pursuit of the assailant. When captured, the negro was chained to a stake on the Court House Square and burned before an immense crowd of excited citizens. Little resistance was made to the mob by the officers.

August 12, 1905

# Who Shall Own America? A Study of the Corporation Problem

JUDGE PETER S. GROSSCUP of the United States Circuit Court of Appeals in Chicago, whose decisions in trust cases have brought him to the front as an authority on corporate problems, has propounded a new plan for controlling corporations so that they may benefit the many instead of the few. Judge Grosscup's plan is to bring all corporations under Federal instead of State control and to so order their issues of securities that financial juggling of these will be impossible.

The scheme is set forth in an article in the current issue of the American Illustrated Magazine, and has already elicited a host of comments and criticisms favorable, in whole or in part, from other eminent students of the problem of regulating the corporations. Ex-President Grover Cleveland has written to the publishers of the magazine that while he does not agree with some of Judge Grosscup's far-reaching conclusions, he regards the most of what the Judge says as "sound common sense clothed in such a way as readily to be understood," and as a "very valuable contribution to the efforts now being made to solve the troublesome problems which affect our body politic."

President Lucius Tuttle of the Boston and Maine Railway does not agree at all with the Judge's conclusions or his plan. Prof. John Bates Clark, who holds the Chair of Political Economy in Columbia University, thinks that one may dissent as to details, while earnestly supporting the Judge's main contention. John Bassett Moore, ex-Assistant Secretary of State, declares Judge Grosscup's proposals not in themselves extravagant nor the ends sought to be attained by them undesirable. Congressman J. Sloat Fassett approves the proposals. Congressman Esch of Wisconsin has grave doubts as to whether the end desired can be brought about solely through legislative means.

### State Socialism No Remedy.

Judge Grosscup's article is entitled "Who Shall Own America?" He calls it a problem and a solution. The first conclusion he reaches is that unless something is done about it speedily America will be owned by the corporations, although the very basis of the Republic has been the ownership of the property of the country by individual citizens. He instances the policy under which the land was parceled out among individual owners in proof of this.

Then the Judge propounds his plan for controlling the corporations, keeping them in the proper path in the future and letting in the many—the hosts of individuals of small means—to share their profits. "Peopleizing" the corporations, he calls it. He says he would "have no mad remedies—dealing with the institutions of the new domain as an endangered people would deal with a mad dog."

"It is one thing to destroy," says Judge Grosscup, "another to reconstruct. What we want in the solution of the problem before us is not some supposed retribution; what we want is reform—some practical, workable reform."

For that reason he would avoid State Socialism. Respecting municipal owner-ship of public utilities, could the movement be confined to that field, he has nothing to say. But he fears that after State Socialism has widened out to include the railroads, the telegraphs, and telephones, the programme would be extended to the coal and ore mines. And in the end the whole institution of private property would be endangered. Therefore the Judge reaches these conclusions:

### The Real Way Out.

First, he says, the beginning of the way out is National incorporation. The sole way in which the work of reorganization can go on is under the eye of the master instead of five and forty masters.

Mr. Bryan, Commissioner Garfield, and possibly Mr. Roosevelt favor what is called Federal license. The object of Federal license is to bit and curb the present corporation, to the end that it travel not ungoverned in the matter of prices. I am for National incorporation as against Federal license, not because the two are nearly alike, as some people suppose, but because in the end to be attained they are wholly unlike—National incorporation being the only method that will directly and effectively go to the root of the disease, the peopleization of the ownership of the new domain. I would have the corporation of the future deal fairly with the people in the matter of prices. But I set above that, as the supreme object to be attained, this other thing: That the people of the country be brought back into the ownership of the property of the country. And to attain this, the Nation must have its hand, not simply in the guidance of existing corporations, but in the construction of the new corporation.

### Two Classes of Securities Enough.

Second, the new corporation must be constructed on lines of simplicity.

There never has been need, from any sound financial or economic point of view, for the labyrinthian constructions that seem the order of the day—securities so overlying each other, and often so involved, that no one not an expert buying a security can locate his claim. Two classes of securities ought in every case to be sufficient—the security that represents actual cash paid in, or its equivalent in property, and the security that may be issued from time to time as the value of the property actually increases, and to cover such increased value. The corporation that cannot be financially launched upon lines thus plainly put before the eye ought not to be launched at all, for here, as elsewhere, mystery means not something essential to success, but something open to uses other than the corporation's success.

Simplicity in the issue of securities such as I have pointed out would not interfere with any legitimate financial need of the corporation. The corporation could still borrow money at stated rates of interest, issuing bonds secured by mortgage upon the properties. But such bonds would be a part of the security that represented actual cash paid in, or its equivalent in property, and for all time, and through all change and consolidation, such bonds, together with the stock securities originally represented by cash or property equivalent, would be the fundamental securities, on which interest or dividends must be paid before the second class of securities could share in the earnings—these secondary securities representing the increment of value, the increase in earning power, the good-will of the property, as distinguished from the cash investment constituting the fundamental security.

### Labor Must Share Ownership.

Third, provision should be made to interest labor in ownership. The securities issued on account of increased value should be issued only as the increase is shown, not by prediction or expectation, but by such experience as proves the fact, and provision should be made that such securities may be divided equitably between the capital invested and the labor put in, and expedients be adopted to encourage corporations formed on that basis.

Fourth, the corporation being trustee for its owners, the Government must be given opportunity to exercise a constant watch that the trust is executed. Under supervision, something like the watch the Government holds over the National banks—seeing to it that financial conditions are always correctly reported, that no capability of the corporation is diverted to private gain, and that transgressions meet with swift punishment—personal schemes would be reduced to a minimum. And, what is more, corporate activity would be lifted to a higher plane of personal and moral responsibility. Under such supervision, too, public utility corporations, deriving their existence from the United States, could be made to obey those laws that look to the giving of equal opportunity to all, because they could be punished by the Government for any form of discrimination or favoritism, not simply by a fine, but by possession taken by the Government as the Government now takes possession of recusant National banks, and such possession continued until the corporation was brought to obey the law.

### Federal Stock Exchange Needed.

Fifth, provision should be made for a Government exchange, or a private exchange under Government supervision, through which the securities of National corporations could be bought and sold. In this way would be drawn a distinctly visible line between the securities of National corporations and securities in corporations that refuse to nationalize—a line that would soon be understood as the boundary between corporations that were willing to be faithful trustees of the owners, faithful at the same time to their duties to the people and corporations that had inner and ulterior designs. My own opinion is that this distinct differentiation of the National from the hybrid corporation would in time lead every incorporation engaged in inter-State commerce voluntarily to incorporate under the National law. A just plan of organization and supervision being offered, the people would not long permit the bank and insurance accumulations to be absorbed in corporations that refused the plan.

Having thus stated his plan, Judge Grosscup gives his reasons for believing it capable of fulfillment. He says:

That the vast new domain of property withheld from the ownership of the people by the corporate lawlessness of the past can, without disorder, be restored to the people, requires some faith. That it will be restored by setting those things right that heretofore have been allowed to go wrong requires faith that things once set

right and kept right will work themselves out right—that a righteous cause, righteously begun and righteously maintained, draws aid from a power that, though not fully compassed by our vision, enters mightily into shaping the destinies of mankind.

### Don't Tear Down; Build Up.

I have that faith. Whether the world knows it or not, that faith is the faith of the world. More than anything else it has moved the world. And the immediate work that lies before those who believe with me in the regeneration of the corporation is to reach the faith that underlies American character—to set in vibration the moral fibre in our character, that once set in vibration will not rest until the work of regeneration has been begun, and once begun, has been accomplished.

The great fact of to-day is the domain of private property under corporate ownership. Widely and individually owned, in accordance with the instincts of a republican people, this new domain would be the pride of the Republic. Narrowly owned, under processes which kept going are bound to narrow its ownership still more, this new domain is the peril of the Republic. The prevailing temper of the day is to tear it down. But the real problem is, not how to tear it down, nor how to hamper this new great domain, but how to honorably reclaim it from present conditions that, like the great landed domain distributed by our fathers among the people, this new domain may come likewise into the proprietorship individually of the people. In the end some organization will give to this work the momentum of a political movement. The practical question is, When will some party set out upon this movement? With the cloud that already hangs over the horizon, seamed and streaked with flashes of a people's impatience, that when becomes a question full of significance.

### Comments on the Plan.

The comments on Judge Grosscup's scheme, which have already reached The American Magazine publishers, cover a wide range. This is Mr. Cleveland's:

"I have been exceedingly interested in the perusal of Judge Grosscup's article, and, although I do not quite agree with some of his far-reaching conclusions, I regard the most of what he says in the article as sound common sense, clothed in such a way as to be readily understood by any reader who will give the subject with which he deals careful attention. On the whole, I regard it as a very valuable contribution to the efforts now being made to solve the troublesome problems which afflict our body politic."

Congressman John J. Esch of Wisconsin has written:

"I agree with Judge Grosscup in the proposition that the concentration of ownership of corporate wealth as against the peopleization thereof is a wrong tendency, and yet is perhaps the most characteristic tendency of our times. It will take a tremendous force to equalize corporate ownership with landed ownership. I have grave doubts as to whether such a consummation can be brought about solely through legislative means. A National incorporation act with attendant Federal supervision, control, and inspection, might do much hereafter, but how could it change materially the present ownership of corporate wealth?

"The Illinois Central for some years has been permitting its employes to secure stock, and has thus interested them in the road as part owners. I understand that the United States Steel Company has

done likewise, and there may be many other small corporations which have thus appreciated the great fact, called attention to by Judge Grosscup, that labor should have some participation in the profits which it creates. Good and desirable as this tendency is, would Judge Grosscup's plan hasten or enlarge it?"

### Doubts of Prof. John B. Clark.

Prof. John Bates Clark of Columbia says of the Federal charter for corporations that the plan is so excellent that no objection resting on tradition or prejudice and no political opposition ought to weigh against it. As to the other remedies he says:

"One may dissent as to details while earnestly supporting the main contention. I should say that the article conveys the impression that the consolidation effected by a trust insures a larger economy than it actually does, and that it conveys the further impression that the owning by laboring men of stock in the companies which employ them is likely to come about earlier than it is, and that it is more unequivocally desirable.

"An ultimate remedy for some large ills it should certainly be, but as things are and will probably long continue to be, a body of workers can afford to buy stock in their employing corporation only when they have a positive assurance that they can sell it at pleasure and at a rate that will insure them against loss. They must at all events retain their right to bring pressure on the corporation to raise their wages."

### J. Bassett Moore Commends It.

John Bassett Moore, former Assistant Secretary of State, calls Judge Grosscup's proposals not in themselves extravagant nor the ends sought to be obtained undeniable. If National incorporation be limited to companies engaged in inter-State commerce, he says, it represents a tendency which is not unnatural and may fairly be regarded as inevitable.

"As between National incorporation and Federal license there would appear to be little room for hesitation. Even if the remedy of National incorporation were deemed inadmissible, the license plan would still be undesirable, because of its intrinsic defects. Of all the measures of National intervention that have been suggested it seems to be the most unadvised and impracticable. The granting and revocation of licenses would involve on the part of the officials by whom it was done the exercise of a power altogether inordinate and full of mischievous possibilities.

"But the exaction of licenses in respect of our own corporations would be only the beginning of the trouble. If our own corporations were thus taken in hand, there would spring up a demand for the imposition of like conditions on the right of the foreign corporations to do business, and the weapon invented by ourselves would be equally available to foreign Governments for the purpose of restraining the activities and covertly counteracting the competition and enterprise of our own great companies."

### Would It Work? Asks Fassett.

Congressman J. Sloat Fassett fears that Judge Grosscup has hardly shown how the great mass of the real owners of the real money of the country are to be brought into that ownership and control of the new domain of corporate wealth.

"Wipe out by Federal control," he says, "all of the manifest, and many of the latent, abuses attendant now upon the launching and conducting of corporate enterprises and render humanly perfect the methods of proper public regulation and control, and still the question of ownership and control are untouched, are they not? Whether the perfected and simple and honest securities of the perfected and simple and uniform corporations are floated by underwriters or private promoters or established exchanges, or a new Federal exchange, the affairs of every corporation must still be conducted by a limited set of agents or Trustees or Directors. The door of opportunity to buy, and through purchase to enter into ownership, is not open one whit wider.

"This does not seem to suggest any new departures in the actual machinery of administration of corporations. The evils he has pointed out are very real, very prevalent, and very threatening, but are not the basic errors moral rather than mechanical? Will the perfection of the instrument eliminate dangers of its improper use?"

### Railroad President Against It.

President Lucius Tuttle of the Boston and Maine Railroad is very doubtful about the value of any of the measures Judge Grosscup suggests. He has written to the publishers:

"His beginning of 'the way out' is National incorporation. What convincing evidence does he present of the probable success of his plan? He uses in its support practically the only form of National incorporation that we now have—the National bank—and suggests that under supervision something like the watch the Government holds over the National banks in the formation and control of National corporations, 'a peopleization' of their ownerships is likely to result.

"Is it not true that this very watch and supervision of the Government over National banks, with the attendant risks and the responsibilities of their stockholders, is rapidly 'depeopleizing' this very corporate domain? Is it not well known that many of the smaller National banks are liquidating and passing into the hands of larger National banks, and is it not also known that centralization of their ownerships has already so far progressed that they are now in many sections largely controlled by savings banks, insurance and trust companies, and other fiduciary institutions, so that it has become more or less difficult to find the necessary number of suitable persons willing to accept the responsibilities and perform the duties of stockholders and Directors in them? Is it not also true that there appears to be an uncontrollable tendency on the part of possessors of small sums of money to relieve themselves of personal care in the investment thereof, by depositing these small sums in various fiduciary institutions whose officers are willing to assume the responsibility of their investments and who will, in a way, guarantee periodical payments of interest or dividends thereon?

### It Might Not "Peopleize."

"Have we, therefore, taking the National bank as the criterion, any real evidence that National incorporation and control of corporate interests is likely to produce a 'peopleization' of the corporate domain such as most thinkers will undoubtedly agree with Judge Grosscup is desirable?"

Judge Grosscup himself is said to be very pleased with the rapid progress of this warm discussion of his plan.

# ROOSEVELT FOR TAX ON WEALTH

## Would Prevent Inheritance of Great Fortunes.

## FAVORS A FEDERAL LAW

## Congress Leaders Talk of a New Political Issue

## PRESIDENT ON MUCKRAKES

## Condemns Indiscriminate Assaults on Public Men— Cornerstone of House Office Building Laid.

### TAX FORTUNES— ROOSEVELT

#### From the President's Speech.

*As a matter of personal conviction, and without pretending to discuss the details or formulate the system, I feel that we shall ultimately have to consider the adoption of some such scheme as that of a progressive tax on all fortunes, beyond a certain amount, either given in life or devised or bequeathed upon death to any individual—a tax so framed as to put it out of the power of the owner of one of these enormous fortunes to hand on more than a certain amount to any one individual; the tax, of course, to be imposed by the National and not the State Government. Such taxation should, of course, be aimed merely at the inheritance or transmission in their entirety of those fortunes swollen beyond all healthy limits.*

*Special to The New York Times.*

WASHINGTON, April 14.—President Roosevelt's speech at the laying of the corner stone of the new office building of the House of Representatives this afternoon is the sensation of Washington.

It was not the muck rake feature of the address that attracted attention. It was his new scheme for the progressive taxation of fortunes.

The notice that had been given as to what he was to say about the magazine critics had excited no little curiosity, and the big crowd that heard him to-day gave him the closest attention while he was speaking to that text. But his declaration in favor of a progressive inheritance tax on large fortunes, which shall be practically confiscatory after a certain to be determined upon size is attained, immediately overwhelmed the muck rake feature, and when the crowd was dispersing the only part of the President's remarks that excited any comment was this new proposition.

It took Mr. Roosevelt half an hour to get through with what he had to say about the muck rake sort of criticism and critics. But little more than a minute sufficed to declare this new proposition.

Yet as the throng left the stands and moved away this was the only subject mentioned. Senators and Representatives questioned one another about it, and those who do not belong to the legislative circle showed themselves equally interested.

One question, often asked, was, "Is it the keynote of the next Presidential campaign?" And often it was answered by the assertion, "It is."

### THE PRESIDENT'S SPEECH.

Mr. Roosevelt said:
"Over a century ago Washington laid the cornerstone of the Capitol in what was then little more than a tract of wooded wilderness here beside the Potomac. We now find it necessary to provide by great additional buildings for the business of the Government. This growth in the need for the housing of the Government is but a proof and example of the way in which the Nation has grown and the sphere of action of the National Government has grown. We now administer the affairs of a Nation in which the extraordinary growth of population has been outstripped by the growth of wealth and the growth in complex interests. The material problems that face us to-day are not such as they were in Washington's time, but the underlying facts of human nature are the same now as they were then. Under altered external form we war with the same tendencies toward evil that were evident in Washington's time, and are helped by the same tendencies for good. It is about some of these that I wish to say a word to-day.

**Man with the Muck-Rake.** "In Bunyan's 'Pilgrim's Progress' you may recall the description of the Man with the Muck-rake, the man who could look no way but downward, with the muck-rake in his hand; who was offered a celestial crown for his muck-rake, but who would neither look up nor regard the crown he was offered, but continued to rake to himself the filth of the floor.

"In 'Pilgrim's Progress' the Man with the Muck-rake is set forth as the example of him whose vision is fixed on carnal instead of on spiritual things. Yet he also typifies the man who in this life consistently refuses to see aught that is lofty, and fixes his eyes with solemn intentness only on that which is vile and debasing.

"Now, it is very necessary that we should not flinch from seeing what is vile and debasing. There is filth on the floor, and it must be scraped up with the muckrake, and there are times and places where this service is the most needed of all the services that can be performed. But the man who never does anything else, who never thinks or speaks or writes save of his feats with the muckrake, speedily becomes, not a help to society, not an incitement to good, but one of the most potent forces for evil.

"There are, in the body politic, economic and social, many and grave evils, and there is urgent necessity for the sternest war upon them. There should be relentless exposure of and attack upon every evil man, whether politician or business man, every evil practice, whether in politics, in business, or in social life. I hail as a benefactor every writer or speaker, every man who, on the platform, or in book, magazine, or newspaper, with merciless severity makes such attack, provided always that he in his turn remembers that the attack is of use only if it is absolutely truthful.

"The liar is no whit better than the thief, and if his mendacity takes the form of slander, he may be worse than most thieves. It puts a premium upon knavery untruthfully to attack an honest man, or even with hysterical exaggeration to assail a bad man with untruth. An epidemic of indiscriminate assault upon character does not good, but very great harm. The soul of every scoundrel is gladdened whenever an honest man is assailed, or even when a scoundrel is untruthfully assailed.

### Easy to Twist President's Words.

"Now, it is easy to twist out of shape what I have just said, easy to affect to misunderstand it, and, if it is slurred over in repetition, not difficult really to misunderstand it. Some persons are sincerely incapable of understanding that to denounce mud slinging does not mean the indorsement of whitewashing, and both the interested individuals who need whitewashing and those others who practice mud slinging, like to encourage such confusion of ideas.

"One of the chief counts against those who make indiscriminate assault upon men in business or men in public life is that they invite a reaction which is sure to tell powerfully in favor of the unscrupulous scoundrel who really ought to be attacked, who ought to be exposed, who ought, if possible, to be put in the penitentiary. If Aristides is praised overmuch as just, people get tired of hearing it, and overcensure of the unjust finally and from similar reasons results in their favor.

"Any excess is almost sure to invite a reaction, and, unfortunately, the reaction, instead of taking the form of punishment of those guilty of the excess, is very apt to take the form either of punishment of the unoffending or of giving immunity, and even strength, to offenders. The effort to make financial or political profit out of the destruction of character can only result in public calamity. Gross and reckless assaults on character, whether on the stump or in newspaper, magazine, or book, create a morbid and vicious public sentiment, and at the same time act as a profound deterrent to able men of normal sensitiveness and tend to prevent them from entering the public service at any price.

"As an instance in point, I may mention that one serious difficulty encountered in getting the right type of men to dig the Panama Canal is the certainty that they will be exposed, both without, and, I am sorry to say, sometimes within, Congress, to utterly reckless assaults on their character and capacity.

### Sane War on Corruptionists.

"At the risk of repetition, let me say again that my plea is, not for immunity to, but for the most unsparing exposure of, the politician who betrays his trust, of the big business man who makes or spends his fortune in illegitimate or corrupt ways. There should

be a resolute effort to hunt every such man out of the position he has disgraced. Expose the crime, and hunt down the criminal; but remember that even in the case of crime, if it is attacked in sensational, lurid, and untruthful fashion, the attack may do more damage to the public mind than the crime itself. It is because I feel that there should be no rest in the endless war against the forces of evil that I ask that the war be conducted with sanity as well as with resolution.

"The men with the muck-rakes are often indispensable to the well-being of society; but only if they know when to stop raking the muck, and to look upward to the celestial crown above them, to the crown of worthy endeavor. There are beautiful things above and round about them; and if they gradually grow to feel that the whole world is nothing but muck, their power of usefulness is gone. If the whole picture is painted black there remains no hue whereby to single out the rascals for distinction from their fellows. Such painting finally induces a kind of moral color-blindness; and people affected by it come to the conclusion that no man is really black, and no man really white, but they are all gray. In other words, they neither believe in the truth of the attack, nor in the honesty of the man who is attacked; they grow as suspicious of the accusation as of the offense; it becomes well-nigh hopeless to stir them either to wrath against wrongdoing or to enthusiasm for what is right; and such a mental attitude in the public gives hope to every knave, and is the despair of honest men.

"To assail the great and admitted evils of our political and industrial life with such crude and sweeping generalizations as to include decent men in the general condemnation means the searing of the public conscience. There results a general attitude either of cynical belief in and indifference to public corruption, or else of a distrustful inability to discriminate between the good and the bad. Either attitude is fraught with untold damage to the country as a whole. The fool who has not sense to discriminate between what is good and what is bad is well-nigh as dangerous as the man who does discriminate and yet chooses the bad.

"There is nothing more distressing to every good patriot, to every good American, than the hard, scoffing spirit which treats the allegation of dishonesty in a public man as a cause for laughter. Such laughter is worse than the crackling of thorns under a pot, for it denotes not merely the vacant mind, but the heart in which high emotions have been choked before they could grow to fruition.

### Lofty Work Being Done

"There is any amount of good in the world, and there never was a time when loftier and more disinterested work for the betterment of mankind was being done than now. The forces that tend for evil are great and terrible, but the forces of truth and love and courage and honesty and generosity and sympathy are also stronger than ever before. It is a foolish and timid, no less than a wicked, thing to blink the fact that the forces of evil are strong, but it is even worse to fail to take into account the strength of the forces that tell for good. Hysterical sensationalism is the very poorest weapon wherewith to fight for lasting righteousness. The men who with stern sobriety and truth assail the many evils of our time, whether in the public press or in magazines, or in books, are the leaders and allies of all engaged in the work for social and political betterment. But if

they give good reason for distrust of what they say, if they chill the ardor of those who demand truth as a primary virtue, they thereby betray the good cause, and play into the hands of the very men against whom they are nominally at war.

"In his 'Ecclesiastical Polity' that fine old Elizabethan divine, Bishop Hooker, wrote:

He that goeth about to persuade a multitude that they are not so well governed as they ought to be, shall never want attentive and favorable hearers; because they know the manifold defects whereunto every kind of regimen is subject, but the secret lets and difficulties, which in public proceedings are innumerable and inevitable, they have not ordinarily the judgment to consider.

"This truth should be kept constantly in mind by every free people desiring to preserve the sanity and poise indispensable to the permanent success of self-government. Yet, on the other hand, it is vital not to permit this spirit of sanity and self-command to degenerate into mere mental stagnation. Bad though a state of hysterical excitement is, and evil though the results are which come from the violent oscillations such excitement invariably produces, yet a sodden acquiescence in evil is even worse.

"At this moment we are passing through a period of great unrest—social, political, and industrial unrest. It is of the utmost importance for our future that this should prove to be not the unrest of mere rebelliousness against life, of mere dissatisfaction with the inevitable inequality of conditions, but the unrest of a resolute and eager ambition to secure the betterment of the individual and the Nation. So far as this movement of agitation throughout the country takes the form of a fierce discontent with evil, of a determination to punish the authors of evil, whether in industry or politics, the feeling is to be heartily welcomed as a sign of healthy life.

"If, on the other hand, it turns into a mere crusade of appetite against appetite, of a contest between the brutal greed of the 'have-nots' and the brutal greed of the 'haves,' then it has no significance for good, but only for evil. If it seeks to establish a line of cleavage, not along the line which divides good men from bad, but along that other line, running at right angles thereto, which divides those who are well off from those who are less well off, then it will be fraught with immeasurable harm to the body politic.

### Crimes of Capital and Labor.

"We can no more and no less afford to condone evil in the man of capital than evil in the man of no capital. The wealthy man who exults because there is a failure of justice in the effort to bring some trust magnate to an account for his misdeeds is as bad as, and no worse than, the so-called labor leader who clamorously strives to excite a foul class feeling on behalf of some other labor leader who is implicated in murder. One attitude is as bad as the other, and no worse; in each case the accused is entitled to exact justice, and in neither case is there need of action by others which can be construed into an expression of sympathy for crime.

"It is a prime necessity that if the present unrest is to result in permanent good the emotion shall be translated into action, and that the action shall be marked by honesty, sanity, and self-restraint. There is mighty little good in a mere spasm of reform. The reform that counts is that which comes through steady, continuous growth; violent emotionalism leads to exhaustion.

"It is important to this people to grapple with the problems connected with the amassing of enormous fortunes, and the use of those fortunes, both corporate and individual, in business. We should discriminate in the sharpest way between fortunes well-won and fortunes ill-won; between those gained as an incident to performing great services to the community as a whole, and those gained in evil fashion by keeping just within the limits of mere law-honesty. Of course no amount of charity in spending such fortunes in any way compensates for misconduct in making them.

**Progressive Tax on Great Fortunes.** "As a matter of personal conviction, and without pretending to discuss the details or formulate the system, I feel that we shall ultimately have to consider the adoption of some such scheme as that of a progressive tax on all fortunes, beyond a certain amount, either given in life or devised or bequeathed upon death to any individual—a tax so framed as to put it out of the power of the owner of one of these enormous fortunes to hand on more than a certain amount to any one individual; the tax, of course, to be imposed by the National and not the State Government. Such taxation should, of course, be aimed merely at the inheritance or transmission in their entirety of those fortunes swollen beyond all healthy limits.

**Rate Bill a First Step.** "Again the National Government must in some form exercise supervision over corporations engaged in inter-State business—and all large corporations are engaged in inter-State business—whether by license or otherwise, so as to permit us to deal with the far-reaching evils of overcapitalization. This year we are making a beginning in the direction of serious effort to settle some of these economic problems by the railway rate legislation. Such legislation, if so framed, as I am sure it will be, as to secure definite and tangible results, will amount to something of itself; and it will amount to a great deal more in so far as it is taken as a first step in the direction of a policy of superintendence and control over corporate wealth engaged in inter-State commerce, this superintendence and control not to be exercised in a spirit of malevolence toward the men who have created the wealth, but with the firm purpose to do justice to them and to see that they in turn do justice to the public at large.

"The first requisite in the public servants who are to deal in this shape with corporations, whether as legislators or as executives, is honesty. This honesty can be no respecter of persons. There can be no such thing as unilateral honesty. The danger is not really from corrupt corporations; it springs from the corruption itself, whether exercised for or against corporations.

"The Eighth Commandment reads, 'Thou shalt not steal.' It does not read, 'Thou shalt not steal from the rich man.' It does not read, 'Thou shalt not steal from the poor man.' It reads simply and plainly, 'Thou shalt not steal.' No good whatever will come from that warped and mock morality which denounces the misdeeds of men of wealth and forgets the misdeeds practiced at their expense;

which denounces bribery, but blinds itself to blackmail; which foams with rage if a corporation secures favors by improper methods, and merely leers with hideous mirth if the corporation is itself wronged.

"The only public servant who can be trusted honestly to protect the rights of the public against the misdeed of a corporation is that public man who will just as surely protect the corporation itself from wrongful aggression. If a public man is willing to yield to popular clamor and do wrong to the men of wealth or to rich corporations, it may be set down as certain that if the opportunity comes he will secretly and furtively do wrong to the public in the interest of a corporation.

"But, in addition to honesty, we need sanity. No honesty will make a public man useful if that man is timid or foolish, if he is a hot-headed zealot or an impracticable visionary. As we strive for reform we find that it is not at all merely the case of a long uphill pull. On the contrary, there is almost as much of breakneck work as of collar work; to depend only on traces means that there will soon be a runaway and an upset.

"The men of wealth who to-day are trying to prevent the regulation and control of their business in the interest of the public by the proper Government authorities will not succeed, in my judgment, in checking the progress of the movement. But if they did succeed they would find that they had sown the wind and would surely reap the whirlwind, for they would ultimately provoke the violent excesses which accompany a reform coming by convulsion instead of by steady and natural growth.

**Opponents of Real Reform.** "On the other hand, the wild preachers of unrest and discontent, the wild agitators against the entire existing order, the men who act crookedly, whether because of sinister design or from mere puzzle-headedness, the men who preach destruction without proposing any substitute for what they intend to destroy, or who propose a substitute which would be far worse than the existing evils—all these men are the most dangerous opponents of real reform. If they get their way they will lead the people into a deeper pit than any into which they could fall under the present system. If they fail to get their way they will still do incalculable harm by provoking the kind of reaction, which in its revolt against the senseless evil of their teaching would enthrone more securely than ever the very evils which their misguided followers believe they are attacking.

"More important than aught else is the development of the broadest sympathy of man for man. The welfare of the wage-worker, the welfare of the tiller of the soil, upon these depend the welfare of the entire country; their good is not to be sought in pulling down others; but their good must be the prime object of all our statesmanship.

"Materially we must strive to secure a broader economic opportunity for all men, so that each shall have a better chance to show the stuff of which he is made. Spiritually and ethically we must strive to bring about clean living and right thinking. We appreciate that the things of the body are important; but we appreciate also that the things of the soul are immeasurably more important. The foundation stone of National life is, and ever must be, the high individual character of the average citizen."

## SETS SENATORS TO LAUGHING.

Mr. Roosevelt was evidently in high good humor throughout the delivery of the speech. The Senators occupied a stand together adjoining the cornerstone. The Representatives were in another stand further removed from the Speaker's platform. Occasionally the President turned to them while he uttered a few words, but more than nine-tenths of the speech was fired straight into the ranks of the Senators who sat directly in front of and beneath him.

In the very beginning, when he referred to some of the things that make for evil in the public life of to-day, Mr. Roosevelt swung his arm, with a wide sweeping gesture over the heads of the Senators and cried out: "It is about these things that I wish to speak." The Senators saw the joke and roared, and Mr. Roosevelt joined heartily in the laughter.

On several other occasions, when his references to the Senate or to bills pending there now brought forth responsive laughter from the Senators, the President could not keep the smile from his face, and when he spoke of his hope for the Rate bill there was a shout in which he joined heartily.

A programme embodying speeches by Speaker Cannon and Col. Hepburn and ex-Representative Richardson, the members of the Building Commission of the new office buildings, had been prepared. But the Masonic ceremony of laying the cornerstone consumed so much time that when it was finished Speaker Cannon bounded up on the speakers' platform, and without reference to the three addresses scheduled for delivery before the President's, introduced "the man who needs no introduction, Theodore Roosevelt."

Wherever two Senators or Representatives got together this evening the thing they talked about was the proposition of the President for the control of large fortunes through a graduated inheritance tax. Senators were particularly interested in the subject, and were already studying the exact language.

There was little hesitation in expressing opinions, although the Senators were, as a rule, inclined to be more guarded in their acceptance of Mr. Roosevelt's scheme than were the members of the House. As a rule, Republican Representatives were outspoken in favor of the proposition, but it was a Republican—Mr. Gardner of New Jersey—who expressed the most vigorous opinion against it.

Several Democrats hailed the expression of the President as a declaration of Democratic doctrine, and Senator Clay of Georgia, whom the President said on his Southern tour last Fall that he always consulted when he wanted advice, was quite prepared to claim the President as a convert to his own party.

### Licenses for Corporations.

In the general excitement over the President's inheritance tax scheme a highly significant part of his speech passed almost unnoticed. It was his declaration in favor of supervising corporations "whether by license or otherwise." This is the scheme which Commissioner Garfield proposed in his annual report, and it is an open secret that Mr. Garfield inserted the recommendation after a conference with the President.

Mr. Roosevelt did not force the issue, realizing that he had his hands full with the Railroad Rate bill. Congress will pass a rate measure at this session, and the plan which the President next takes up will be Federal franchises or licenses for corporations engaged in inter-State business. He will probably begin the fight at the second session of the Fifty-ninth Congress next December, but it is doubtful if it can be forced through at a short session. Next Winter's work on the subject will be educational, and the real work probably cannot be accomplished before the meeting of the Sixtieth Congress.

The inheritance tax part of the Roosevelt programme, it is understood, will not be pushed until the Federal license fight has been won or at least begun.

April 15, 1906

## DIDN'T MEAN ME—STEFFENS.

**Magazine Writer Disagrees with Muck-Rake Speech in One Particular Only.**

*Special to The New York Times.*

CLEVELAND, April 16.—Commenting upon President Roosevelt's "muck-rake" speech, Lincoln Steffens says in an article in an evening newspaper:

"If it is understood, the President's muck-rake speech will do good, but it was misunderstood when it was first delivered. That was at the speaker's dinner to the Gridiron Club in Washington, and the men who heard it then—statesmen, railroad men, bankers, and correspondents—all seemed to think that the President had hit at the magazine writer.

"And they rejoiced. Some of them laughed at me, saying the President had taken a fall out of me. But when I asked him about it the next morning he said he didn't mean me. And he told me some of those he did mean.

"I disagree with the President only on one fundamental point. He wants us to go on 'hunting' bad men; and he shows that he means individuals. The longer I live the more I feel that the individual is not so much to blame—not even the worst individuals, not even the 'best' citizens—as the system of corruption which has grown up about us, and which rewards an honest man with a mere living and a crook with all the magnificence of our magnificent modern life."

April 17, 1906

## BRYAN ON ROCKEFELLER:

**Thinks He Should Be Isolated by Refusals to Take His Money.**

INDIANAPOLIS, Oct. 23.—William J. Bryan, during his second day's tour through Indiana, delivered a speech at Wabash in which he referred to John D. Rockefeller.

Until recently, he said, the Churches had been willing to accept money without asking questions about it, but one of the demonations had been stirred to its very depths by a controversy as to whether it should accept money from Mr. Rockefeller.

"I believe," he continued, "that if the Churches and charitable societies would stand up and say to Mr. Rockefeller, 'Keep your money; you stole it from the public; we will not accept it,' they would come near to making him feel how lonesome a man can be in this world who has nothing but money, and no conscience back of it."

October 24, 1906

# CONANT OPPOSES REGULATING TRUSTS

**Commissioner of Corporations Is for Competition, Not Paternalism.**

## AGAINST TRADE COMMISSION

**Says It Would Mean Abandonment of Competition—Admits Necessity of Railroad Regulation.**

WASHINGTON, Feb. 21.—Luther Conant, Jr., Commissioner of Corporations, to-day came out in opposition to the much-discussed proposition for toleration of monopolies under Governmental regulation and urged the continuation of the policy which permits competition among the industries of the United States.

In his annual report to Secretary Nagel, made public to-day, the Commissioner says that recent decisions under the Sherman Anti-Trust act have demonstrated that the statute is effective to reach consolidations which so cross the border line of monopolistic control as to be detrimental to the public interest.

"It is remarkable," he adds, "that after years of effort to maintain the vital principle of the Sherman Anti-Trust act the first real success in this direction, so far as industrial combinations are concerned, should be accompanied by a rather widespread demand for the practical abandonment of that principle and the substitution therefore of regulated monopoly. It should not escape notice that among the foremost advocates of such regulated monopoly are the representatives of some of the most powerful consolidations of the time."

The creation of a proposed trade commission with powers of regulation over private corporations similar to those exercised by the Inter-State Commerce Commission would mean, the Commissioner says, "the substitution of a marked degree of paternalism for that freedom of individual action under which, despite admittedly flagrant abuses, the country has attained an almost unparalleled prosperity." Says Mr. Conant:

"Up to the present time the idea of a trade commission has been in the main associated with regulation rather than with maintenance of competition. Indeed, any proposal for a trade commission with substantially the same jurisdiction over private business corporations as is now given to the Inter-State Commerce Commission over common carriers, is in large measure a proposition for the abandonment of competition and for the acceptance of concentration and combination on the ground that regulation will sufficiently protect the public welfare.

"For there can be no doubt that the old idea that unrestricted competition among railroad companies is desirable has been largely abandoned. Instead, public

opinion has recognized that, to a considerable extent at least, such enterprises do not permit of free competition, although even here it is noteworthy that where competition has been virtually destroyed, as in the case of certain New England railroads, the results have proved exceedingly unsatisfactory from the public standpoint. However, it may be conceded that, so far as railroad and certain other quasi-public corporations are concerned, the public has definitely accepted the principle that competition must largely be subordinated to regulation. But to assume that the same principle should be adopted in dealing with the private corporations of the country is a radical departure.

"Undoubtedly there are industries outside the field of railroad transportation and other public service enterprises where the competitive principle is not entirely applicable, but these instances present exceptional problems to be dealt with on their individual merits.

"One fact seems obvious: The opportunity for regulating monopoly cannot be lost by attempts to maintain the competitive principle. If, on the other hand, the experiment first be tried of regulating monopoly, there is grave danger that competition may be destroyed to an extent which would make its restoration exceedingly difficult. Certainly it seems the part of wisdom, just as the competitive principle has been sustained and vitalized by the highest court of the land, to continue its application under new conditions, instead of hastily abandoning it for an experiment involving obvious difficulties and grave dangers."

Discussing the Bureau of Corporation's recent recommendation that the Federal Government should retain the ownership of the remnant of timber land now owned by it, and increase its holdings by such lands as may be recovered through forfeiture suits, the Commissioner explains: "The bureau did not advocate Government ownership of timber in general, but simply the retention in public ownership of certain timber until the time of actual use. This recommendation, instead of being a indorsement of the principle of Government ownership in general, should have a contrary effect by preventing conditions for which Federal control and Federal ownership are now so often sought as a panacea."

While the act creating the Bureau of Corporations expressly provided for investigations of insurance corporations, Mr. Conant announced that inquiries of that character had been abandoned, owing to doubtful jurisdiction, as the United States Supreme Court had repeatedly held that insurance was not commerce.

Substantial results have followed in the wake of the bureau's campaign of publicity, the primary purpose of its existance, says the Commissioner. The rebate and dissolution suits against the Standard Oil Company and the suit against the United States Steel Corporation were, he says, to a very large extent predicated upon facts published by the bureau, while certain of the bureau's information was used in the Government's litigation against the Tobacco Trust. In addition, he adds, many corporations have corrected faults pointed out by the bureau, and in other instances the country has received information for the basis of a constructive policy in dealing with economic problems. Mr. Conant urged that corporations be required to submit regularly and automatically to the Bureau of Corporations elementary data relating to their organization, capitalization, business, and profits, especially the larger Inter-State concerns.

These investigations by the bureau are still pending:

International Harvester Company, final reports on the tobacco and steel industries, and further reports on water transportation, lumber, and State taxation of corporations.

The cost of some of the important investigations by the bureau, exclusive of administrative expenses, as shown by the report, was:

Lumber, $323,802; oil, $143,588; iron and steel, $106,131; tobacco, $119,385; water transportation, $106,834, and harvester, $90,167.

## PRESIDENT McKINLEY'S COFFIN.

### It Was Made in Oneida, N. Y., and Is of Special Design.

*Special to The New York Times.*

BUFFALO, Sept. 14.

> WILLIAM McKINLEY.
>
> Born January 29th, 1843.
>
> Died September 14th, 1901.

The foregoing is the inscription on the coffin that will contain the remains of the martyred President. It was furnished by the National Casket Company of Oneida and is elaborate in design. It is made of solid crotched Santo Domingo mahogany. It measures 6 feet 3 inches in length, is 22 inches wide, and 20 inches deep inside. It is entirely hand carved, with mahogany extension bar handles. On top of the casket are two carved panels of swell design. Instead of a metallic name plate the deceased President's name and the date of his birth and death are carved inside of a scroll.

Inside of the mahogany shell is a metallic case lined with copper plate, and which has a full-length bevel-edged glass on top. When the body is placed in the case the case will be hermetically sealed. This metallic case is lined with cream grosgrain silk of the heaviest texture, shirred at the top and caught up with imported silk thread and trimmed at top with milliner's fold. Inside of the case are also a silk mattress and pillow of the same material.

The coffin was ordered by a committee selected from the President's Cabinet advisers. It was designed by John Maxwell, manager of the National Casket Company, assisted by Superintendent James A. Anderson, both of this city.

The company will also ship a plain black broadcloth-covered coffin of hard wood to Buffalo, to be used providing Mrs. McKinley does not desire the elaborate one already prepared.

September 15, 1901

## EXECUTION OF CZOLGOSZ.

### Request to State Department to be Represented—26 Witnesses to be Admitted—1,000 Applications.

ALBANY, N. Y., Oct. 14.—Superintendent Cornelius V. Collins will send a request to Secretary of State Hay to designate an official representative of the Government to be present at the execution of Leon F. Czolgosz, the murderer of President McKinley. There will be but twenty-six witnesses in the chamber of death when the sentence of the law is executed.

Warden Mead of Auburn Prison has sent to Superintendent Collins the requests he has received for permission to attend the execution—over 1,000 in all. The Superintendent will decide who the witnesses will be.

It was stated at the State Department of prisons to-day that statements to the effect that Czolgosz is in a continuous state of collapse and that he breaks down and weeps every time anything is said to him concerning the execution are false. Superintendent Collins had a talk with the condemned man some days ago, and at that time Czolgosz said he knew that he had to die.

He expressed no fear as to the execution, but said that he would not care to go outside of the prison, for he believed that the people would kill him. Since his confinement at Auburn Prison several thousand letters have been received for him at the prison, as well as a large number of express packages containing flowers and fruit.

Neither the letters nor the flowers nor the fruit have ever reached the condemned man. The flowers and fruit, it is learned, have been sent by Christian societies, as have a number of letters intended to console him in his last moments. Other letters have come from cranks, who have written about the species of torture to which they would put him if they had in control the execution of justice.

It is stated, however, that it would be a matter of surprise if the names of senders of fruit and flowers were made public. The State Prison Department has pursued a uniform policy in regard to Czolgosz. An effort has been made to prevent the murderer from gaining any notoriety while awaiting death and to secure for him as perfect an isolation from the world as possible.

October 15, 1901

## MARK TWAIN'S FAREWELL ?

It is reported that Dr. CLEMENS, after the variegated and admirable speech recently made by him on receiving his latest degree, announced that it was his last appearance as a speaker in public.

We must all hope that it is only the first of a long series of last appearances. Probably there is no genius now known to the English-speaking world who can impart such vitality to a pleasantry of ripe age as can Mark Twain. Let us trust that he is illustrating this happy facility in the present instance and that his announcement is but an incident in the continuous exercise of his unique and precious function in this generation. We have many humorists of more or less distinction in " occasional " talk. There are some who have aspired to association, and even to rivalry with him. Some of them have approached him on a few of the many sides he has turned to a delighted public. No one has attained his rank. No one is so familiar and so uniformly surprising. Of no one can we be so sure that he will be funny and so utterly at a loss to predict what form or direction his fun will take. It would be a great pity if at future entertainments his " turn " should be missing.

Every one will read with pleasure the accounts of Dr. CLEMENS's material prosperity, and hope that they are far short of the fact. He has proved his possession of that rarest claim to fortune—the capacity to face deprivation and hard work for the satisfaction of his own conscience and his emancipation from even indirect responsibility for losses incurred through him. His title is very clear to the best that can possibly come to him. And, of course, he is entitled to repose if he wishes it. But it is hard to connect his retirement from the public stage with the notion of repose. He has borne his part with such ease and apparent spontaneity, it has seemed so much more natural for him to talk in his own way than to keep silent, that one can imagine his self-repression only as an act of self-denial. It would certainly be unkindness to the public for whom he has so long been indulgent. We prefer to regard his announced intention as a practical joke, which, like most practical jokes, has in it an element of cruelty.

June 7, 1902

# NATIONAL EDUCATORS MEET IN BOSTON

## President Eliot on "The New Definition of Cultivated Man."

### He Outlines the Essentials of Culture in This Age—Several Thousand Teachers Listen to His Address.

BOSTON, July 6.—The forty-second annual convention of the National Education Association was formally opened in this city to-day, with two sessions of the National Council, a meeting of the Department of Indian Education, and finally the general session, practically a mass meeting in the largest hall in the city, at which fully a fifth of the whole of the host of 16,000 teachers from all parts of the country who have come to attend the convention were present. The general session which was held in Mechanics' Hall was naturally the feature of the day, and the two addresses, one by President Eliot of Harvard University, and also President of the General Association, and the other by Andrew F. West, Dean of the Graduate School of Princeton University, were listened to with great attention.

President Eliot's topic was "The New Definition of the Cultivated Man." In the course of his address he said:

"The ideal of general cultivation has been one of the standards in education. I propose to use the term cultivated man in only its good sense in Emerson's sense. Emerson taught that the acquisition of some form of manual skill and the practice of some form of manual labor were essential elements of culture, and this idea has more and more become accepted in the systematic education of youth.

"The idea of some sort of bodily excellence was, to be sure, not absent in the old conception of the cultivated man. The gentleman could ride well, dance gracefully, and fence with skill, but the modern conception of bodily skill as an element in cultivation is more comprehensive, and includes that habitual contact with the external world which Emerson deemed essential to real culture. We proceed to examine four elements of culture:

"Character. The moral sense of the modern world makes character a more important element than it used to be in the ideal of a cultivated man. Now, character is formed, at Goethe said, in the 'stream of the world,' not in stillness or isolation, but in quick moving tides of the busy world, the world of nature and the world of mankind. To the old idea of culture some knowledge of history was indispensable.

"Language. A cultivated man should express himself by tongue or pen with some accuracy and elegance; therefore linguistic training has had great importance in the idea of cultivation.

"The store of knowledge. The next great element in cultivation to which I ask your attention is acquaintance with some parts of the store of knowledge which humanity in its progress from barbarism has acquired and laid up. This is the prodigious store of recorded, rationalized, and systematized discoveries, experiences, and ideas—the store which we teachers try to pass on to the rising generation.

"Imagination. The only other element in cultivation which time will permit me to treat is the training of the constructive imagination. The imagination is the greatest of human powers, no matter in what field it works—in art or literature, in mechanical invention, in science, government, commerce, or religion, and the training of the imagination is, therefore, far the most important part of education.

"Zola, in 'La Bête Humaine,' contrives that ten persons, all connected with the railroad from Paris to Havre, shall be either murderers or murdered, or both, within eighteen months; and he adds two railroad slaughters criminally procured. The conditions of time and place are ingeniously imagined, and no detail is omitted which can heighten the effect of this homicidal fiction.

"Contrast this kind of constructive imagination with the kind which conceived the great wells sunk in the solid rock below Niagara that contain the turbines that drive the dynamos, that generate the electric force that turns thousands of wheels and lights thousands of lamps over hundreds of square miles of adjoining territory; or with the kind which conceives the sending of human thoughts across 3,000 miles of stormy sea instantaneously on nothing more substantial than ethereal waves. There is going to be room in the hearts of twentieth century men for a high admiration of these kinds of imagination, as well as for that of the poet, artist, or dramatist.

"Let us as teachers accept no single element or variety of culture as the one essential; let us remember that the best fruits of real culture are an open mind, broad sympathies and respect for all the diverse achievements of the human intellect at whatever stage of development they may be to-day—the stage of fresh discovery, or bold exploration, or complete conquest. The moral elements of the new education are so strong that the new forms of culture are likely to prove themselves quite as productive of morality, high-mindedness, and idealism as the old."

Prof. West's topic was "The Present Peril of Liberal Education."

July 7, 1903

# NATIONAL STRENGTH IS THANKSGIVING DAY TEXT

## Roosevelt's Proclamation Deals with the Mission of the Country.

## PROSPERITY ALSO A THEME

### "Reward Has Waited Upon Honest Effort," Says the President—Appeal to Maintain High Average of Citizenship.

WASHINGTON, Nov. 1.—The President to-day issued the Thanksgiving Day proclamation, setting aside Thursday, Nov. 24, "to be observed as a day of festival and thanksgiving by all the people of the United States, at home and abroad." The proclamation follows:

"It has pleased Almighty God to bring the American people in safety and honor through another year, and, in accordance with the long unbroken custom handed down to us by our forefathers, the time has come when a special day shall be set apart in which to thank Him who holds all nations in the hollow of His hand for the mercies thus vouchsafed to us.

"During the century and a quarter of our National life, we, as a people, have been blessed beyond all others, and for this we owe humble and heartfelt thanks to the Author of all blessings. The year that has closed has been one of peace within our own borders as well as between us and all other nations. The harvests have been abundant, and those who work, whether with hand or brain, are prospering greatly. Reward has waited upon honest effort. We have been enabled to do our duty to ourselves and to others.

"Never has there been a time when religious and charitable effort has been more evident. Much has been given to us and much will be expected from us. We speak of what has been done by this Nation in no spirit of boastfulness or vainglory, but with full and reverent realization that our strength is as nothing unless we are helped from above. Hitherto we have been given the heart and the strength to do the tasks allotted to us as they severally arose. We are thankful for all that has been done for us in the past, and we pray that in the future we may be strengthened in the unending struggle to do our duty fearlessly and honestly, with charity and good will, with respect for ourselves and love toward our fellow-men.

"In this great Republic, the effort to combine National strength with personal freedom is being tried on a scale more gigantic than ever before in the world's history. Our success will mean much, not only for ourselves, but for the future of all mankind, and every man or woman in our land should feel the grave responsibility resting upon him or her, for in the last analysis this success must depend upon the high average of our individual citizenship, upon the way in which each of us does his duty by himself and his neighbor.

"Now, therefore, I, Theodore Roosevelt, President of the United States, do hereby appoint and set apart Thursday, the 24th of this November, to be observed as a day of festival and thanksgiving by all the people of the United States, at home or abroad, and do recommend that on that day they cease from their ordinary occupations and gather in their several places of worship or in their homes, devoutly to give thanks unto Almighty God for the benefits he has conferred upon us as individuals and as a Nation, and to beseech Him that in the future His divine favor may be continued to us.

"In witness whereof I have hereunto set my hand and caused the seal of the United States to be affixed.

"Done at the City of Washington this 1st day of November, in the year of our Lord one thousand nine hundred and four, and of the independence of the United States the one hundred and twenty-ninth.

"THEODORE ROOSEVELT.

"By the President.

"JOHN HAY,
"Secretary of State."

November 2, 1904

# COMSTOCK TAKES HAND IN PHYSICAL CULTURE SHOW

## Has Promoters Arrested for Putting Up Posters.

### SHOWMAN SAYS HE'LL FIGHT

#### How Can Any One Show How Physical Culture Has Improved the Body if the Body Is Clothed?

When the "Mammoth Physical Exhibition" opens next Monday at Madison Square Garden for a week's run there is likely to be trouble between its management and Anthony Comstock's Society for the Suppression of Vice. Mr. Comstock is already so horrified at the bare, printed posters advertising the exhibition that yesterday afternoon he had Bernarr MacFadden, who backs the exhibition, and Benjamin F. Provandie, the young man who is attending to the posters, arrested and taken to the Tenderloin Police Station, charged with having in their possession obscene pictures. Five hundred pounds of the posters were confiscated.

Late last night Thomas J. Bimberger, one of Comstock's agents, arrested Gomer Reese of 102 West Ninety-eighth Street, on the same charge. The warrant was issued by Justice Wyatt. Reese is the manager of the show. He was locked up in the Mercer Street Station.

The first two were arrested at 29 East Nineteenth Street, the office of The Physical Culture Magazine, of which MacFadden is editor. MacFadden gave his address as Physical Culture City, N. J. He wore sandals and a broad-brimmed hat, and other clothes as well. The prisoners were arrested on warrants obtained by John J. Deering of the Vice Society. They were bailed out with a $1,000 bill, put up by counsel for Mr. MacFadden. This is the first cash bail accepted by Capt. Dooley since Magistrate Moss lectured one of his Sergeants on oppression.

The posters which Mr. Comstock considers objectionable are said to be photographs of contestants who took part in last year's exhibition at Madison Square Garden. One of them shows the women prize winners, ten or twelve young women in white union suits with sashes around their waists standing or reclining in various positions. Another poster shows a man wearing a pair of sandals and a leopard's skin as a breech-cloth.

Most of the posters printed for the exhibition already have been put up. Mr. MacFadden thinks the S. S. V. will have a time tearing them all down.

"The purpose of this exhibition, which now has become annual," said MacFadden yesterday afternoon, "is to show how the spread of physical culture has improved the human body. Manifestly that cannot be done if the exhibitors are covered with clothing.

"There will be various athletic contests. The men contestants will be nude from the waist up; the women will wear white tights or union suits with sashes around their waists. To impress upon the audience the good of physical culture the men and women will pose before a black curtain and under a light.

"All this was done last year, and nobody became indignant. Women in tights are seen in every circus; men nude from the waist up or even nude altogether with the exception of a breech cloth are seen at all sorts of athletic exhibitions.

"Comstock's intentions are good, no doubt, but he is going too far. I shall fight this case through every court in the land before I'll let it drop. If he beats me in — t to-morrow I'll modify the posters a — le for the benefit of the coming show. If I beat him the same old posters will go up. The exhibition itself will come off on schedule time, and in the way we intended.

"More than 100 men and 35 young women will take part in the exhibition, and it is too late now to either call it off or change the rules governing it.

"The posing of the contestants we consider one of the most beneficial parts of the exhibition. Contestants are coming from all parts of the country."

October 6, 1905

---

# SPEND NEARLY $30,000 A YEAR EACH ON AUTOS

## J. J. Astor Has 20 Cars and C. K. G. Billings 13.

### THE COST TO A POOR MAN

#### For a Small Runabout $600 or More, and for a Tonneau Car $3,300 a Year.

"Why is it so many second-hand machines are on the market?" asked a young automobilist.

"Simple enough," was the reply. "It's because a lot of people have enough money to buy better and faster machines, while others have discovered that they haven't sufficient money to own one. The reasonable price of good machines, particularly of the little two-passenger runabouts that you can buy for from $600 to $750, has led many young fellows with comfortable incomes to join the ranks of automobile owners.

"But the cost of a motor car doesn't really begin until you get it. When a man buys a horse he usually figures on the expense of keeping the animal at a livery stable or at his suburban home. With the automobile, however, hundreds of purchasers go it blind and learn by experience that an automobile has as voracious an appetite as any horse. A simple runabout that is kept busy the greater part of the year will cost about as much as a man pays for his six or seven room flat."

### Autos Cost Billings $30,000 a Year.

What a man can pay for the use and maintenance of an automobile is regulated entirely by his own resources. C. K. G. Billings, for instance, who disposed of all his fast horses last week except Lou Dillon, Major Delmar, and Hontas Crook, and is now devoting his attention and money to automobiles, pays nearly $30,000 a year for his private garage and to keep his thirteen cars in good running condition. Col. John Jacob Astor probably pays as much, if not more, for the care of his twenty machines in his private garage on his Rhinebeck estate. The man who keeps a number of automobiles is by no means a rarity. In fact, a stable of automobiles is coming to be recognized as the proper thing for the man of wealth, just as his private yacht, his box at the Opera, and his town and country houses.

But all men do not possess a superabundance of money, and yet most of them would like to own automobiles. How cheaply, then, can a machine be kept? The cheapest car that a man can buy is of course one of the little open runabouts. He can easily run from forty to 50 miles with it in an afternoon, while its mechanical construction is so simple that his wife can learn to manage it. A car of this sort costs from $650 to $1,000, the maximum price including a canopy top and better upholstering.

If the owner lives in an apartment he must arrange to have the car stored for him. In the automobile district of the city, from about Thirty-eighth to Sixty-fifth Street, adjoining Broadway, he will find several garages that will store his car, keep it washed, polished, and in good condition for $15 a month. His gasoline bill will be in proportion to the distance he travels.

Assuming that the owner will use his car mainly on Saturdays and Sundays, with perhaps a few hours on the other days, he will consume from fifteen to twenty gallons of gasoline a week. With his runabout equipped with a single cylinder, four gallons of gasoline ought to carry him 100 miles and one gallon of lubricating oil will last him 400 miles. The best lubricating oil costs $1 a gallon. A gallon of oil will be needed every week, while for 400 miles, sixteen gallons of gasoline will be required. Purchasing this at retail, the cost will be 20 cents a gallon. This means a weekly outlay of $3.20. With $1 for oil, his weekly cost for fuel alone is $4.20, or about $17 a month. This, added to his storage charge, will bring his monthly bill up to $32.

But the expense does not end here. There will be repairs. How much will depend entirely upon the owner's care in driving, and his knowledge of his car's mechanical construction. Then, too, good luck must be reckoned with to some extent.

### $37 a Month a Low Estimate.

Notwithstanding the utmost care, a tire may suddenly go to pieces, and if one has to pay from $30 to $40 for a new tire very often it will make a big difference in his automobile bill. At the lowest possible estimate tire troubles and general repairs will cost $5 a month. This will make the bill $37 a month, which is a very reasonable estimate.

"If the owner of a runabout gets through the year on that average he will be one of the fortunate ones," said the manager of a garage. "His actual expense is likely to be nearer $50 a month."

The next step in automobile development is the ownership of a tonneau body touring car of from twenty-five to forty horse power and with two or four cylinder motors. This car will require more fuel and more attention, while its greater weight and more complicated machinery will increase the breakdowns and tire troubles. The garage will charge $25 a month to store this car. This includes washing and polishing, everything, in fact, except actual repairs. The charge for repairs made in the garage is 75 cents an hour, and there are few repairs that can be made that will cost less than $5. At a conservative basis, the monthly repair bill will be $30. More than twice the quantity of gasoline and oil that is necessary for the small one-cylinder car will be needed. About forty gallons of gasoline a week will not be excessive when the car is used nearly every day in pleasant weather, and about two gallons of oil. This will mean $10 a week for fuel, or $40 a month.

While the owner of a car of this size will probably drive it himself, he will also require a chauffeur. The chauffeur is needed, not so much to drive the car, for any one can learn to do that in a short time, but to keep it in good order and know what to do if anything happens while on the road. Every chauffeur should be a capable mechanician, and what he will save an owner in preventing breakdowns may often amount to more than his month's salary.

### Hire a Good Chauffeur.

"Get a good chauffeur or none at all," is the advice of a veteran in garage management. "The good man is worth his price, while the cheap man is worth nothing. To give you an example: A customer of mine employed a man for $12 a month to run his car, and started on a tour through New England. The next day I got a telephone call from him near Stamford asking me to send up a car and tow him home. I sent a car, and when we began to look for the trouble, what do you think we found? A little soft mud had gone through the radiator and clogged up some of the pipes. One of the workmen got it out with a hairpin in fifteen minutes. We couldn't tell the owner that, so we had to keep the machine all night and send him a bill for $5. We also coached the chauffeur and perhaps he will know better next time. However, it cost the owner $75 to be towed to the city, plus $5 for repairs, and besides the loss of time and extra hotel bills."

A good chauffeur gets $25 a week, but a capable man who has had experience with several makes of machines finds no difficulty in finding a place paying from $100 to $150 a month. The demand for first-class chauffeurs is greater than the supply. One of the schools in this city that instructs new men and does not give a chauffeur a certificate until he has passed a rigid examination has a place waiting for every man who finishes the course.

The chauffeur also receives his board and clothes. His overalls and his leather suit, cap, goggles and gloves must be supplied. Where no arrangements are made to board and lodge the chauffeur at the owner's home, it is customary to allow him $10 a week, and he finds his own lodgings.

This is a conservative estimate of the monthly cost of a high-class touring car:

| | |
|---|---|
| Storage | $25 |
| Gasoline and oil | 40 |
| Repairs of all kinds | 30 |
| Chauffeur | 125 |
| Board, lodging, and clothing of chauffeur | 55 |
| Total | $275 |

This is $3,300 a year, and many owners who are not rated as men of wealth pay a great deal more. By far the largest item for repairs will be for tires. The larger and heavier the car the more severe will be the wear and tear upon the tires. Here again the most expensive is the best. For the big touring cars the best tires, including the inner tube, will cost from $50 to $90 each, while for the same size of imported tires, that the owners of the best foreign cars use, the price will be $105. It is therefore to the interest of every owner to get along with as few tires as possible.

Besides the tires there are a number of things about the car that will need constant repairing. A good chain which costs about $20 will usually last a year. New spark plugs will be needed frequently. They cost $3 apiece. A new igniter costs $15. The clutch leathers and clutch bars must be renewed every three or four months. To do this it is necessary to take the clutch out, and on some cars the entire transmission has to be removed. This will take the better part of two days, so that added to the cost of $4 or $5 for a new clutch leather, the owner will have a bill of $15 for twenty hours work.

C. K. G. Billings undoubtedly pays more than any other automobile owner in this city for the care and running of his automobiles. But the bills of Harry Payne Whitney, Judge Gary, Charles M. Schwab, Temple Bowdoin, I. E. Emerson, and many others are by no means small.

### Has Thirteen Cars.

Mr. Billings has thirteen cars, and their estimated cost is $100,000. All but two are of foreign make. The American cars are a Woods electric runabout and a home-made electric car built by his head chauffeur for the use of Mr. Billings's son. It is one of the most compact little cars ever built outside of a regular factory, and can reel off fifteen miles an hour with ease. For touring purposes Mr. Billings has the choice of two richly upholstered cars, one a twenty-five horse power C. G. V. and the other a forty horse power machine of the same make. This car cost $11,000, but his thirty-five horse power Panhard with limousine body cost $15,000, and is one of the finest automobiles in the city. It will accommodate seven passengers. He also has a sixteen horse power Panhard with limousine body and a forty horse power Mercedes of the same style. In landaulet bodies there are five cars, two being C. G. V. machines of

eighteen and twenty-five horse power each, a fourteen horse power Renault, a 20-30 Renault, and a Gallia electric. In addition, there is an eighteen horse power Mors open touring car and a French electric brougham, for use in wet weather and in the evening.

Mr. Billings has two stables in East Seventy-fifth Street, for which he pays $150 a month each. He has his own workshop and the electric plant for charging the electric cars. The cost of his shop and electric plant is about $1,000 a month. His monthly bill for lighting will amount to $50. Mr. Billings pays his head chauffeur $225 a month, and he has three other chauffeurs who receive $150 each. He has two washers at $50 a month, one being on duty in the day and the other at night.

His tire repair bill is probably close to $400 a month. As he buys his gasoline by the barrel, he gets it at the wholesale rate of 12 cents a gallon. He will probably use close to ten barrels a month, and three barrels of lubricating oil, which at barrel rates will cost about 40 cents a gallon. His monthly bill for new parts will be about $100. His chauffeurs live in the garage, and his bill for cleaning, living expenses, and clothing will perhaps be $200 a month. At this estimate Mr. Billings will pay for the care of his thirteen automobiles close to $2,000 a month. At 3½ per cent., the interest on $100,000, the estimated cost of the cars, will be $3,500, making an annual outlay of $27,500.

### Some Other Owners.

Harry Payne Whitney has four cars, which he keeps at a garage near Broadway. He gives his cars plenty of use, and his monthly expense, exclusive of chauffeurs, is about $800. He has three chauffeurs, the head man getting $200 a month and the others $150. One of Mr. Whitney's cars is a theatre coach. All of his cars are foreign vehicles, one being a German Mercedes and the others French machines.

Judge Gary, the steel man, has three automobiles, which are stored with the Whitney cars. One is a 60-horse-power Mercedes, which cost $15,000. The second is a 20-horse-power Mercedes, with landaulet body, and the third is a Columbia electric brougham for city and night use. He has two chauffeurs, who receive $175 and $125 respectively. His monthly bills for storage, repairs, and new parts is about $400.

Temple Bowdoin of the J. Pierpont Morgan banking house has four foreign cars and two chauffeurs. I. E. Emerson owns five cars, a 40-horse-power Bollee with canopy top, a 15-horse-power Mors, a 20-horse-power Clement hansom, a 24-horse-power Mors, with limousine body, and a 20-horse-power Mercedes. Mr. Emerson employs a single chauffeur, who receives $225 a month. His bill is not so large as where several cars are kept in frequent use. About $300 a month will pay his repairs and storage bills.

# CARNEGIE ASSAULTS THE SPELLING BOOK

## To Pay the Cost of Reforming English Orthography.

## CAMPAIGN ABOUT TO BEGIN

### Board Named, with Headquarters Here—Local Societies Throughout the Country.

Announcement was made yesterday that an organization, including prominent men of affairs as well as men of letters, has been formed to urge the simplification of English spelling. This new body is called the Simplified Spelling Board. It will appeal to all who for educational or practical reasons wish to make English spelling easier to learn. Andrew Carnegie has undertaken to bear the expense of the organization. Mr. Carnegie has long been convinced that English might be made the world language of the future, and thus one of the influences leading to universal peace; and he believes that the chief obstacle to its speedy adoption is to be found in its contradictory and difficult spelling.

The Simplified Spelling Board contains some thirty members, living in various parts of the Union. Some of them are authors of wide reputation; some are professed scholars connected with leading universities; some are editors of the foremost American dictionaries; some are men distinguished in public life, and some are men of affairs, prominent in civil life.

The membership is not yet complete, but it now includes Chancellor Andrews of the University of Nebraska, Justice Brewer of the United States Supreme Court, President Butler of Columbia University, O. C. Blackmer of Chicago, Andrew Carnegie, Mark Twain, Dr. Melvil Dewey, Dr. Isaac K. Funk, editor and publisher of The Standard Dictionary; Lyman J. Gage, ex-Secretary of the Treasury; Richard Watson Gilder, editor of The Century Magazine; Dr. William T. Harris, United States Commissioner of Education and editor of Webster's International Dictionary; Prof. George Hempl of the University of Michigan, Col. Thomas Wentworth Higginson, Henry Holt, Prof. William James of Harvard, President Jordan of Leland Stanford University, Prof. Thomas R. Lounsbury of Yale, Prof. Francis A. March of Lafayette, Prof. Brander Matthews of Columbia, Dr. Benjamin E. Smith, editor, and Dr. Charles P. G. Scott, etymological editor, of The Century Dictionary; President H. H. Seedley of the Iowa State Normal School, Cedar Falls; Col. Charles E. Sprague, President of the Union Dime Savings Institution; Prof. Calvin Thomas of Columbia, Dr. William Hayes Ward, editor of The Independent, and President Woodward of the Carnegie Institution of Washington.

The establishment of the Simplified Spelling Board is the result of an effort made within the last year to obtain the use, by men of position, of certain simplified spellings, adopted some years ago by the National Educational Association and now used by several important publications. The response to this request was cordial. Hundreds of signatures were received, pledging the writers to use these simpler forms in their personal correspondence. The members of the Simplified Spelling Board believe that the time is now ripe for a forward movement.

They do not intend to urge any violent alteration in the appearance of familiar words. They will not advance and extreme theories. They will not expect to accomplish their task in a day or in a year. They wish, in brief, to expedite that process of simplification which has been going on in English, in spite of the opposition of conservatives, ever since the invention of printing, notably in the omission of silent and useless letters.

The immediate activities of the Simplified Spelling Board will be directed by an Executive Committee chosen from the members residing in New York. An office will be opened in New York to serve as headquarters for the work, and from this office the campaign of education will be conducted by a competent staff. Local societies will be organized wherever a group of willing workers can be gathered together. Comprehensive plans are being mapped out, which will take years for their full accomplishment.

---

# MOB BURNS TWO NEGROES.

### First Hangs Them to Goddess of Liberty in Springfield, Mo.

*Special to The New York Times.*

SPRINGFIELD, Mo., April 14.—A mob of several hundred persons broke into the county jail here to-night, dragged out two negroes charged with attacking a white girl named Mabel Edwards last night, hanged them to the Goddess of Liberty in the Public Square, and burned them to death in the presence of more than 3,000 persons, who cheered the performance.

There were six men concerned in the assault on a white girl last night, but only two suspects were arrested, the other four escaping to the country.

To-day there was no intimation of what was to happen to-night, but a great mob gathered from all over the city in front of the jail and rushed the doors.

The Sheriff did not or could not resist, and the guards were soon overpowered.

While the mob was picking out its victims a crowd of 3,000 gathered in the square. Some of these got fuel, ropes, and oil, and when the negroes were brought out they were tied to the electric light poles and burned.

The crowd witnessing their agonies cheered and jeered. The mob is now searching for the four men who escaped.

Last night, while Miss Edwards and a young man named Cooper were riding in a buggy, they were stopped by two negroes, who beat Cooper into unconsciousness before attacking Miss Edwards. Two negroes, Duncan and Copeland, were arrested on suspicion, but there was no evidence against them.

One thousand men gathered at the city jail to-night, and, on learning that the negroes were not there, hastened to the county jail, where the prisoners were confined.

Instead of attacking the jail at first, the mob stormed the residence of the Sheriff, breaking down doors, smashing windows, destroying the furniture in the lower part of the house, and rendering the Sheriff's wife unconscious from fright. Then the mob obtained the key to the jail and gained entrance therto. The mob had no difficulty in finding the cells of Duncan and Copeland.

When the committee which entered the jail came out with the two negroes the mob began to clamor for summary execution, shouting "Hang them!" "Burn them!" The negroes were taken to the public square and hanged to a statue of the Goddess of Liberty and a fire was kindled under them, in which they were roasted, 3,000 persons watching their agony.

March 12, 1906

April 15, 1906

18

# JOHNSON WINS IN 15 ROUNDS; JEFFRIES WEAK

## "I Couldn't Come Back," Says Former Champion, Helpless After Third Knockdown.

## POOR FIGHT, SAYS SULLIVAN

## White Man Outclassed by His Opponent from the First Tap of the Gong.

## CROWD'S SYMPATHY AROUSED

## Yells to Referee to Save Jeffries from a Knockout and His Seconds Jump Into the Ring.

## JOHNSON'S SHARE, $70,600

## While Jeffries Takes $50,400 from the Purse—The Moving-Picture Rights Bring Them More Thousands.

### By JOHN L. SULLIVAN.

*Special to The New York Times.*

RENO, Nev., July 4.—The fight of the century is over and a black man is the undisputed champion of the world.

It was a poor fight as fights go, this less than fifteen-round affair betweeen James J. Jeffries and Jack Johnson. Scarcely ever has there been a championship contest that was so one-sided.

All of Jeffries's much-vaunted condition and the prodigious preparations that he went through availed him nothing. He wasn't in it from the first bell tap to the last, and as he fell bleeding, bruised, and weakened in the twenty-seventh second of the third minute of the fifteenth round no sorrier sight has ever gone to make pugilistic history. He was practically knocked out twice in this round.

Johnson's deadly left beat upon his unprotected head and neck, and he went down for the count just before the second minute had gone in the fifteenth round. As Johnson felled him the first time he was conscious, but weakened. He tactfully waited for the timekeeper's call of nine before he rose. When he did John-

son caught him flush on the jaw again, and he fell almost in the same spot, but further out, and as he leaned against the lower rope his great bulk crashed through outside the ring.

His seconds and several newspaper men hauled him into the ring again, and he staggered weakly over to the other side. Johnson slowly followed him, measured his distance carefully, and as Jeff's head always hangs forward, struck him hard in the face, and again that terrible left hand caught him, sending him reeling around to a stooping posture.

Johnson pushed his right hand hard as Jeffries wheeled around, and quick as a flash whipped his left over again, and Jeff went down for the last time. His seconds had given it up.

They didn't wait for the ten seconds to be counted, but jumped into the ring after their man. Billy Delaney, Johnson's chief second, always watchful for the technicalities, yelled his claim for the fight for his man on the breach of the rules by Jeff's handlers. Tex Rickard, in the meantime, was trying to make himself heard, and he was saying that the fight was Johnson's.

### Result Left the Crowd Dazed.

By this time the crowd was realizing that Johnson had won out, but there was very little cheering. Jeff had been such a decided favorite they could hardly believe that he was beaten and that there wouldn't still be a chance for him to reclaim his lost laurels. The crowd was not even willing to leave the arena, and as poor old Jeff sat in his corner being sprayed with water and other resuscitating liquids he was pitied from all sides.

The negro had few friends, but there was no real demonstration against him. They could not help but admire Johnson, because he is the type of prize fighter that is regarded highly by sportsmen. He played fairly at all times and fought fairly. He gave in wherever there was a contention and he demanded his rights only up to their limit, but never beyond them.

### Had Picked Johnson to Win.

I have never witnessed a fight where I was in such a peculiar position. I all along refused to announce my choice as to the winner. I refused on Jeff's account, because he was sensitive and I wanted to be with him some time during his training. I refused on Johnson's account, because of my well-known antipathy to his race, and I didn't want him to think that I was favoring him from any other motive than a purely sporting one. He might have got this impression, although since I know him better, in the last few weeks, I am rather inclined to believe that he hasn't many of the petty meannesses of human character.

You will deduce from the foregoing that I really had picked Johnson as the winner. My personal friends all know it, and even Jeffries accused me of it one day, but I denied it in this way. I said:

"Jeff, I have picked the winner, but I haven't done it publicly. A few personal friends know who I think will win, and I am not going to tell you before the fight. I don't want you to get any wrong impression."

However, the fact remains that three weeks ago I picked Johnson to win. It seems almost too much to say, but I did say inside of fifteen rounds. It's all over now, and it does not matter who I picked to win to either Jeff or Johnson, but the main theory I based my decision on was the old one that put me out of the game. Jeff could not come back. Jeffries was a mere shell of his former self. All the months of weight reducing, involving great feats of exercise, had come to naught.

The experts who figured that a man

must receive his reward for such long, conscientious, muscle-wearing and nerve-racking work, figured that he must get it even providentially.

It seemed only just to human nature that Jeffries must win, even in the face of all the features resting on the other side of the argument. For it is true, and probably would only be denied by Johnson himself, that the big colored champion did not train conscientiously. As subsequent events proved he didn't have to train more than he did, but nevertheless he took a chance, and, by his manner and deportment, seemed perfectly willing to stand the consequences, whatever they were. The result was success for him in its fullest meaning.

Johnson got scarcely a hard knock during the whole encounter, and was never bothered by Jeffries's actions one little bit. He came out of the fray without a mark, if one except the cut lip he got in the third round, which proved to be only the opening of the old cut that George Cotten gave him the other day when Gov. Dickerson was out at his training quarters.

Never before has there been a fight for the championship of the world with so many peculiar ends to it, because never before has a black man been a real contender for the championship. Johnson, of course, was the credited champion even before to-day's fight by virtue of his defeat of Tommy Burns, but just the same the rank and file of sporting people never gave him the full measure of his title. Jeffries has always been the bugaboo of Johnson's championship career, and it seemed to many that if only the big boilermaker would go back into the fighting game and get himself into condition he could obliterate this so-called blot on the pugilistic map.

Jeffries was persuaded against his will, and he went to work with a willingness and determination that brought about wonderful results, but that couldn't bring back outraged old nature.

### Johnson Never in Doubt.

Probably never before was a championship so easily won as Johnson's victory to-day. He never showed the slightest concern during the fifteen rounds and from the fourth round on his confidence was the most glaring thing I ever saw in any fighter. He was the one person in the world at that moment who knew that Jeffries's best blow was packed away in his last fight and on the road and by the running brooks from which he lured the fish during his preliminary training for his fight.

He was a perfect picnic for the big negro, who seemed to be enjoying himself rather than fighting for 60 per cent. of a $101,000 purse. It could not have been all assumed, either, as his remarks during the contest to me, while I sat below and near him at the ringside, showed that he had honestly a good opinion of himself.

Once in the interval between the fifth and sixth rounds he leaned over and said: "John, I thought this fellow could hit."

I said: "I never said so, but I believe he could have six years ago."

Johnson continued with conversation when he should have been paying attention to the advice his seconds were giving him, and said: "Yes; five or six years ago ain't now, though."

By that time the bell had rung and he was up and at it again.

My, what a crafty, powerful, cunning left hand he has. He leads with it, of course, but he does most of his work in close, and some of his blows look as though he were trying to lead with his right while his left is traveling to its goal.

He is one of the craftiest, cunningest boxers that ever stepped into the ring, and poor old Jeffries could not get set or anywhere near him for an effective punch. As a matter of fact, he didn't have any. They both fought closely all during the fifteen rounds. It was just the sort of a fight that Jeffries wanted. There was no running around and ducking like Corbett did with me in New Orleans. Jeffries didn't miss so many blows, because he hardly started any. Johnson was on top of him all the time, and he scarcely attempted a blow that didn't land. There wasn't a full swing during the whole fifteen rounds, something unusual in this latter-day fighting.

The only thing that wasn't actual fighting to-day was the many clinches that occurred, and here, instead of Jeff getting in the fatal work, it was Johnson. None of the plans that all of the experts and critics have been talking about for the last six months materialized. Jeffries's fearful rushes were not there. The awful wallops that he was going to land on Johnson's body, where were they? Johnson didn't receive a blow during the whole encounter that would have hurt a 16-year-old boy. From the time Jeff got his right eye closed in the sixth round it was all over as far as I was concerned. I felt then that if Jeffries had all this power behind that had been claimed for him, he would get mad and he would at least take a desperate chance. Probably he had some such idea in mind himself, for he did step in viciously in the next round, but a gloved fist always stopped his onward way.

When I saw Johnson throw Jeffries away from him in one of the many clinches in the eighth or ninth round I was still further convinced that the negro was the winner.

This had been one of his favorite stunts during his training, and he was expected to at least attempt it here. He didn't get gay at all with Jeffries in the beginning, and it was always the white man who clinched, but Johnson was very careful, and he backed away and took no chances, and was good-natured with it all.

### Probably the Last Big Fight Here.

There were those in the throng to-day who will probably say it was the greatest fight the world ever saw, but that is because it was the most peculiar fight crowd the world ever saw, for half of them never saw a fight before. It was the greatest fight this class ever saw, but, as a matter of fact, it was about the poorest fight that has ever been fought for the championship. It will probably be the last big fight in this country, notwithstanding the crowd's enthusiastic reception of Billy Muldoon's sentimental speech. "Let us give three cheers for the great, broad-minded State of Nevada and its great, broad-minded Governor," because it will be hard to work up the fervor that has existed all through the arrangements for this fight.

It will go down in history as the greatest fight that ever took place in some respects, and from a purely sporting point of view the very worst.

Nevertheless, the best man won, and I was one of the first to congratulate him, and also one of the first to extend my heartfelt sympathy to the beaten man.

JOHN L. SULLIVAN.

# OLYMPIC PRIZES LOST; THORPE NO AMATEUR

## Carlisle School Indian Admits He Once Played Professional Baseball in the South.

## DIDN'T REALIZE HIS DECEIT

### Our Committee Must Return Decathlon Cup and Pentathlon Trophy, Reducing Our Points from 85 to 80.

James Thorpe, a Sac and Fox Indian student of the Carlisle Indian School, confessed to the Amateur Athletic Union officials yesterday that he had played professional baseball in 1900 and 1910, thereby automatically disqualifying himself for any amateur competition since the Summer of 1909.

Thorpe's deception and subsequent confession deals amateur sport in America the hardest blow it has ever had to take, and disarranges the scheme of amateur athletics the world over. We must now return to the Swedish Olympic Committee the Pentathlon trophy awarded by the King of Sweden and the Decathlon Cup presented by the Czar, both of which were won by Thorpe in the guise of an amateur, for reward to the foreigners who were second to him. Our total points in the Olympic games are thus reduced from 85 to 80, and Sweden's rise from 27 to 33. Our internal athletic readjustments will be almost as important.

The letter which Thorpe sent to James E. Sullivan, Chairman of the Amateur Athletic Union Registration Committee, was in response to a request by Mr. Sullivan that he answer certain charges made by one Charles Clancy in Worcester, Mass., last week. Here is the letter:

### Thorpe's Confession.

Carlisle, Penn., Jan. 26, 1913.
James E. Sullivan, New York, N. Y.:
Dear Sir—When the interview with Mr. Clancy stating that I had played baseball on the Winston-Salem team was shown me, I told Mr. Warner that it was not true, and, in fact, I did not play on that team. But so much has been said in the papers since then that I went to the school authorities this morning and told them just what there was in the stories.

I played baseball at Rocky Mount and at Fayetteville, N. C., in the Summer of 1909 and 1910 under my own name. On the same teams I played with were several college men from the North who were earning money by ballplaying during their vacations and who were regarded as amateurs at home. I did not play for the money there was in it because my property brings me in enough money to live on, but because I liked to play ball. I was not very wise to the ways of the world and did not realize that this was wrong and it would make me a professional in track sports, although I learned from the other players that it would be better for me not to let any one know that I was playing, and for that reason I never told any one at the school about it until to-day.

In the Fall of 1911 I applied for readmission to this school and came back to continue my studies and take part in the school sports and, of course, I wanted to get on the Olympic team and take the trip to Stockholm. I had Mr. Warner send in my application for registering in the A. A. U. after I had answered the questions and signed it, and I received my card allowing me to compete in the Winter meets and other track sports. I never realized until now

what a big mistake I made by keeping it a secret about my ballplaying, and I am sorry I did so. I hope I will be partly excused by the fact that I was simply an Indian schoolboy and did not know all about such things. In fact, I did not know that I was doing wrong because I was doing what I knew several other college men had done except that they did not use their own names.

I have always liked sport and only played or run races for the fun of the thing, and never to earn money. I have received offers amounting to thousands of dollars since my victories last Summer, but I have turned them all down because I did not care to make money from my athletic skill. I am very sorry, Mr. Sullivan, to have it all spoiled in this way, and I hope the Amateur Athletic Union and the people will not be too hard in judging me.

Yours truly,
(Signed) JAMES THORPE.
### World's Greatest Athlete.

Thorpe, by the performances he made in the Pentathlon and Decathlon events at the Olympic games in Stockholm last July, when he competed in the United States team, as well as through his efforts in winning the all-around championship of America last year, clearly established his right to be considered the greatest athlete in the world. In fact, he was so described by King Gustave V. of Sweden at the prize giving in connection with the Olympic sports.

The admitted breaking of the amateur laws by the Indian has upset the whole athletic machinery of two continents. His confession makes it obligatory upon his part to return to the American Olympic Committee for transmission abroad to the Swedish Olympic Committee the Pentathlon trophy awarded by the King of Sweden, and the Decathlon Cup presented by the Emperor of Russia.

His last athletic victory was the all-around championship of America, won at Celtic Park Sept. 2, 1911, when he amassed the wonderful total of 7,476½ points for the ten events, which included 100-yard dash, 16-pound shot, running high jump, 880-yard walk, 16-pound hammer, pole vault, 120-yard high hurdle, 56-pound weight, running broad jump, and one-mile run. His versatility is immediately apparent when it is realized that during this series he jumped 6 feet 1½ inches high; put the shot 44 feet 3¼ inches, and broad jumped in the next to the last event 23 feet 3 inches.

At Stockholm, where he won the Pentathlon with four firsts of a possible five, the runner-up was F. R. Bie of Norway, to whom the trophy will now go. With the readjustment of the places which will be made necessary by Thorpe's confession, J. J. Donohue of California will get second place.

In the Decathlon, the ten-event series, Thorpe was first with 8,412 points figured on the American percentage system, while three Swedes, H. Wieslander, G. Lomberg, and G. Holmer tallied 7,724, 7,413, and 7,347, respectively; therefore Wieslander will get the trophy presented by the Emperor of Russia.

In the other events contested by Thorpe during the Olympic games he was fourth in the running high jump with 6 feet 1 inch and seventh in the running broad jump with 22 feet 7¼ inches.

### Our Olympic Total Lowered.

The grand total of the American points scored in the games is decreased from 85 to 80, while Sweden's tally will be increased from 27 to 33, by which advance it will be able to claim second place in the purely athletic series over Finland, which scored 29, and which country is in no way benefited by the establishing of Thorpe's guilt.

Looking still further backward, it is recalled that Thorpe, among his other features of athletic supremacy, has been conceded to be one of America's most wonderful football players, having been chosen almost unreservedly by the pickers of all-America teams as one of the premier half backs of this country during the years of 1911 and 1912. In these seasons, respectively, Thorpe has figured in thirteen and twelve games.

By his confession Thorpe makes easy the work of the Amateur Athletic Union officials in the matter of eliminating his name from the record books and all championship lists. A canvass of the members of the American Olympic Committee yesterday revealed that there was not one who did not feel the stigma he had put upon American amateurism, but each had a certain measure of satisfaction in the acknowledged point that Thorpe had not sinned against the laws in their immediate connection with the Amateur Athletic Union or any of its allied bodies.

As Thorpe was, however, immediately under the supervision of the Amateur Athletic Union by virtue of his having been a registered amateur and because of his having been chosen by the American Olympic Team Selection Committee for competition abroad last year, it became incumbent upon members of that committee—Gustavus T. Kirby, President of the Amateur Athletic Union and Vice President of the American Olympic Committee; James E. Sullivan, Chairman of the Registration Committee and Secretary of the Amateur Athletic Union and American Olympic Committee, and Bartow S. Weeks, Chairman of the Legislation Committee of the Amateur Athletic Union and Vice President of the American Olympic Committee—to make a statement. They issued the following:

### Statement by Olympic Committee.

The Team Selection Committee of the American Olympic Committee selected James Thorpe as one of the members of the American Olympic team, and did so without the least suspicion as to there having ever been any act of professionalism on Thorpe's part.

For the last several years Thorpe has been a member of the Carlisle Indian School, which is conducted by the Government of the United States at Carlisle, Penn., through the Indian Department of the Department of the Interior. Glenn Warner, formerly of Cornell, a man whose reputation is of the highest and whose accuracy of statement has never been doubted, has been in charge of the athletic activities of the institution. During the period of Mr Thorpe's membership at Carlisle he competed on its football, baseball, and track and field teams, and represented it in intercollegiate and other contests, all of which were open only to amateurs, as neither Carlisle nor any of the institutions with which it competes has other than amateur teams. Thorpe's standing as an amateur had never been questioned, nor was any protest ever made against him nor any statement ever made as to his even having practiced with professionals, let alone having played with or as one of them.

The widest possible publicity was given to the team selected by the American Olympic Committee, and it seems strange that men having knowledge of Mr. Thorpe's professional conduct did not at such time for the honor of their country come forward and place in the hands of the American Olympic such information as they had. No such information was given, nor was a suggestion even made as to Thorpe being other than the amateur which he was supposed to be. This country is of such tremendous territorial expanse and the athletes taking part therein are so numerous that it is sometimes extremely difficult to ascertain the history of an athlete's past. In the selection of the American team the committee endeavored to use every possible precaution, and where there was the slightest doubt as to a man's amateur standing his entry was not considered.

Thorpe's act of professionalism was in a sport over which the Amateur Athletic Union has no direct control. It was as a member of a baseball team in a minor league and in games which were not reported in the important papers of the country. That he played under his own name would give no direct notice to any one concerned, as there are many of his name. The reason why he himself did not give notice of his acts is explained by him on the ground of ignorance. In some justification of this position, it should be noted that Mr. Thorpe is an Indian of limited experience and education in the ways of other than his own people.

The American Olympic Committee and the Amateur Athletic Union feel that, while Mr. Thorpe is deserving of the severest condemnation for concealing the fact that he had professionalized himself by receiving money for playing baseball, they also feel that those who knew of his professional acts are deserving of still greater censure for their silence.

The American Olympic Committee and the Amateur Athletic Union tender to the Swedish Olympic Committee and through the International Olympic Committee to the nations of the world their apology for having entered Mr. Thorpe and having permitted him to compete at the Olympic games of 1912.

The Amateur Athletic Union regrets that it permitted Mr. Thorpe to compete in amateur contests during the last several years, and will do everything in its power to secure the return of prizes and the readjustment of points won by him, and will immediately eliminate his records from the books.

### Regret of Carlisle School.

The foregoing statement followed an interview between Glenn S. Warner, Athletic Director of the Carlisle Indian School, and James E. Sullivan, in the latter's office. Mr. Sullivan immediately placed two communications which had been presented to him by Warner before the attention of Gustavus T. Kirby and Bartow S. Weeks, with the above result.

One of the letters which Warner brought with him from Carlisle was the confession of Thorpe; the other came from M. Friedman, Superintendent of the Carlisle Indian School, attesting the ignorance in regard to the matter on the part of the authorities at the Indian School. Mr. Friedman's letter follows:

U. S. Indian School, Carlisle, Penn.,
Jan. 26, 1913.

James E. Sullivan, Secretary Amateur Athletic Union, New York City:

My Dear Sir: Immediately on hearing of the newspaper charges made against James Thorpe, a Sac and Fox Indian student of this school, to the effect that he played professional baseball previous to the Olympic Games last July, the school authorities instituted a thorough investigation. I have just learned that Thorpe acknowledges having played with a Southern professional baseball team.

It is with profound regret that this information is conveyed to you, and I hasten to assure your committee that the Faculty of the school and the athletic director, Mr. Glenn Warner, were without any knowledge of this fact until to-day.

As this invalidates Thorpe's amateur standing at the time of the games in Stockholm, the trophies which are held here are subject to your disposition. Please inform me of your desires in the matter. It is a most unpleasant affair, and has brought gloom on the entire institution. Very respectfully,
M. FRIEDMAN, Superintendent.

### Thorpe's Case Discussed.

Even those who are least impressed with either the importance or the value of competitive athletics can understand that there is a decidedly serious side to the discovery of the fact that the young Indian, THORPE, had once played baseball for money and therefore was a professional among amateurs when he made his magnificent records at Stockholm. By doing so he revealed a personal conscelessness which neither his origin nor the brevity of his education goes far to mitigate. His own disgrace, however, though lamentable enough, is a trivial matter in comparison with the humiliation which he has brought upon his country—with the derision and denunciation which all Americans will long have to bear from the foreign critics who are sure to make the most of the chance given them for saying that with us sport is a business and that we lack the instinct of fair play.

This we must bear with what patience we can, and get what consolation—and mercy—there is to be derived from full confession and prompt reparation. THORPE himself is now doing his best in these directions—that much at least may be said for him—and the officials of the Amateur Athletic Union have taken precisely the right action in the matter. They are concealing nothing, and their instant action in canceling THORPE's records and in returning his prizes to their rightful owners, while of course only their plain and obvious duty, yet has been taken with a readiness and completeness that will or ought to have some effect in setting us right in the eyes of the world.

Bad as the case is, it might have been worse. Surely it is something that the disclosure of the offense committed and the punishment of the offender have been not less "American" than was the violation of the athletic decencies. Really unpardonable are only the men who knew before THORPE went to Stockholm, while he was there, and after he returned, that he was not eligible for amateur honors and yet kept silent while he took them. Their guilt is greater even than that of the young Indian, and the work of the Amateur Athletic Union will not be done until every one of these utterly despicable wretches has suffered the heaviest penalties, official and others, which honest sportsmen can inflict. Such folly as theirs is simply intolerable.

January 28, 1913

January 29, 1913

## SOUTHERN CHILD WORKERS

### Are They, or Are They Not, Ground in the Mills?

Dawley—Thomas Robinson Dawley, Jr., to be exact—has written a book, and a very startling book it is. It is called "The Child That Toileth Not," and is intended to correct some of the many misapprehensions in the public mind as to the actual conditions of the children employed in the Southern cotton mills who have been much exploited by those engaged in the work of making such conditions easier. The book is announced as "the story of a Government investigation hitherto suppressed," and is particularly interesting for this reason, and for the additional reason that it is packed with a great deal of information obtained by the writer, who was employed as one of the field agents of the Government in the prosecution of his work. Cutting out the argument, the disclosures made by Mr. Dawley are sufficiently exciting to justify Congressional inquiry. If the facts be as they are stated by Mr. Dawley—and there is much corroborative detail to sustain the truth of what he says—there has been much misrepresentation, for what reason it is not necessary here to inquire, and, as the subject has already been discussed in Congress, it would be in the interest of both cotton mill workers and employers if Congress should provide for the appointment of a special commission of its own members to sift the matter to the bottom without regard to the previous findings of any of the professional experts or bureaucratic agencies who have hitherto made investigations and apparently with the object of proving their case. The method adopted by Mr. John D. Rockefeller, Jr., in the investigations of the "social problem" is the method that should be followed in this and all other like matters—an entire absence of preconceived opinion or theory based upon undemonstrated facts; the open mind being regarded by him and his associates as a condition precedent to sound judgment and effective remedial measures. There is no question that there is a social problem; there is equally little doubt that there have been hard conditions—unsanitary surroundings, long hours, small wages and squalid living in some of the mill communities; but it does not stand to reason that the cotton mill owners and managers have formed a trust for the oppression of their people.

It wouldn't pay. The statement is ventured that a thorough investigation made, by a Congressional committee, organized to find the facts, not to prove a case, might show that the average condition of the cotton mill workers in the South is better than the average condition of the workers on the farms, in the mines and in other of the productive industries; that the cotton mill workers, as a rule, are living in far better circumstances than before they went into the mills, and that instead of being the objects of professional commiseration as a class they are to be felicitated upon their happier estate.

\* \*

Mr. Beveridge, in January, 1907, made a speech in the United States Senate pleading for a Federal child labor law. Congress passed a joint resolution directing the Secretary of Commerce and Labor to investigate and report upon the industrial, social, moral, educational and physical condition of woman and child workers in the United States. Appropriations amounting to $300,000 were made to cover the expense of the investigation. The Commissioner of Labor was charged with the inquiry. A number of field agents were appointed under the authority of the Civil Service Commission to prosecute the work. Mr. Dawley was one of these agents. He was assigned to the Southern field to study the conditions in the Carolinas, Tennessee, Georgia and Alabama, and particularly in the rural districts, from which the main supply of labor employed in these mills is drawn. He found much to distress him in the poverty of the people, in their surroundings, but nowhere did he find among the managers of the mills any lack of sympathy for the people employed by them, or any disposition to fatten upon the necessities of the poor. Generally he found a disposition to improve the condition of the workers. He did not find that young children were employed generally in the mills or anywhere that they were regarded as desirable. He found not only that the men and women from the mountain districts were densely ignorant, but that they had been almost invariably improved by their change of residence and occupation; that the industrious among them were successful, that the idle and vicious were in no worse plight, but were really in better condition in the mills than they had been on the mountain farms, where they had always lived a hopeless life; that the "poor whites" from the mountain districts were brought into closer touch with

schools and churches and other agencies of civilization; in a word, that the movement from the mountains to the mills had been of very distinct advantage, generally speaking, and specifically in a number of well authenticated cases, to the mill workers and their families.

\* \*

Mr. Dawley seems to have made his studies with great care and in the right spirit. He has illustrated his text with abundant illustrations from actual photographs, showing the shanties of the mill workers before they left their mountains, scenes in the mills and in the mill villages, the school houses and playgrounds and churches built for their benefit, and pictures of the mill workers "before and after taking." He does not spare criticism of the pitiful conditions he found in some communities and in certain mills; but he does not withhold praise from the places and the men who have been planning intelligently, in their own interest as well as in the interest of their people, to improve the condition of this great manufacturing industry.

\* \*

But Mr. Dawley has a grievance. He claims that he "was literally thrown out by the Bureau of Labor" because his findings did not suit the case as made up by the Commissioner of Labor, acting in concert with the Child Labor committees and allied organizations, and that his report, in the making of which he spent two years of unremitting labor, was suppressed. This statement is made by Mr. Dawley:

> While thousands of dollars were squandered by the Federal Bureau of Labor, in its investigation of woman and child labor, to prove that the manufacturers are rascals; that they lie with respect to the ages of the children employed; that they hide them away when investigators are sent to report upon them; and that they employ them because they get their labor cheaper than they get the same labor from adults; and, finally, that they compel them to work when they should be in school, and underfeed and underpay their employes generally—not a word of the revelations showing the misrepresentations of the agitators, reformers and other interests of the kind was allowed to go before the public in the report.

\* \*

It does not matter particularly about Mr. Dawley; but in view of the vast importance of the cotton manufacturing industry in the South and the alleged misrepresentations in a Government report of conditions obtaining in the Southern mills, Congress should direct an investigation on its own account and by its own members, "let the chips fall where they will."

J.C.H.

January 31, 191

---

# CHILD LABOR LAW HAS AIDED SCHOOLS

### Prof. John Dewey of Columbia Says Much More Should Be Done for Young Workers.

### PLEA FOR DULL CHILDREN

#### They Most of All Need Vocational Training — Praise Henry Street Settlement.

That the new Child Labor law of the State of New York has increased the demand for schools and for courses of study better adapted to the needs of boys and girls about to enter industrial pursuits, is the assertion of Prof. John Dewey, of Columbia University, in an introduction to the Directory of the Trades and Occupations taught at the day and evening schools in Greater New York.

This directory is published by the Committee for Vocational Scholarships of the Henry Street Settlement at 265 Henry Street, and was compiled by Mrs. Mortimer J. Fox. Among those who are interested in the movement to enable boys and girls to secure employment for which they best are fitted are Mrs. Max Morgenthau, Jr., Miss Elsie Borg, Mrs. William Ehrlich, Miss Margaret Brown, Miss Harriet West Knight, Miss Alice Lewisohn, Miss Irene Lewisohn, Mrs. Wesley C. Mitchell and Miss Lillian D. Wald.

According to Dr. Dewey, the educational problem faced by the city of New York, as by every other great industrial centre, is whether the community as a whole shall care for the education of the children or whether the education of the largest number shall be left to the unregulated conditions of factory life.

"Child labor laws have, upon the whole, approached the question from the negative side," Dr. Dewey writes. "They have kept the children out of industrial pursuits until they have reached a certain age, and have presumably secured a certain amount of schooling. The problem will not be adequately dealt with on its positive and constructive side until the community furnishes to the large number of boys and girls, who are about to become wage-earners, educational facilities that equip them intellectually and morally for their callings in life; and until continuation schools, in some form or other, are provided for at least all children between fourteen and sixteen, who are engaged in factory work.

"The new child labor law of the State of New York, while more stringent as a preventive measure than the older law (since it requires the boys and girls to have attained the Grade of 6B or the age of 16 years), actually increases the demand for more schools and courses of study better adapted to the needs of those going into industrial pursuits. Naturally, it is the duller children who, not reaching the 6B Grade, have to remain in school till they are 16 years old. To a large extent these children, backward in book studies, are just the ones to whom instructions that use the hands and the motor energies would appeal. Meantime, they are kept out of industry,

and yet are not adequately prepared for any useful activity in life.

"The public is indebted to the Henry Street Settlement, which maintains a system of scholarships for the benefit of those boys and girls who might otherwise leave school and go to work at 14. The purpose of the scholarships is to give as many children as possible two years of further education and vocational training during that period which has been called the "two wasted years." The giving of scholarships to the comparatively few children fortunate enough to secure this protection and the supervision of their education keeps the committee in close touch with the educational agencies throughout the city.

"While we must rejoice that the showing is as good as it is, and that such excellent work is done by these schools, nevertheless we must confess that the showing is a meagre and inadequate one. When one considers the thousands and thousands of children destined to wage-earning pursuits, the obvious conclusion from the exhibit found in this directory is that neither by public activity nor by voluntary agencies has the City of New York as yet made more than a bare beginning. The directory should thus serve a double purpose, in that it gives information—otherwise very difficult to procure—regarding existing facilities, and in that it makes evident the immense work that remains to be done."

The Scholarship Committee of the Henry Street Settlement offers its second directory of the educational resources of the city to teachers and settlement workers, parents and children because it often becomes the duty of both teacher and settlement worker to advise boys and girls about to leave school as to their future occupation. The committee hopes that the directory may render the choice less difficult and insure a vocation more appropriate to the capacity of the various boys and girls who apply to it for aid.

Conferences on vocational guidance and training, held during the past two years in Boston and New York, demonstrate that interest in this problem is growing. Meanwhile, opportunities for vocational education have not increased proportionally either to this interest or to the school population. In 1909 there were 27,152 children graduated from the elementary schools, and in 1913 there were 41,151. To meet this increase of 50 per cent., three new public trade schools have been established, and eight schools conducted by private organizations, four of which are special schools for the blind and the crippled, the other four, electrical, corporation and Children's Aid Society schools. Since the first directory was published in 1909 two schools have been discontinued.

December 21, 1913

# CHILD LABOR LAW UPSET BY COURT

## Action of Congress Declared Unconstitutional by 5 to 4 on Final Test.

## HELD TO EXCEED POWERS

### Holmes Reads Dissenting Opinion— Move for New Law or Constitutional Amendment.

*Special to The New York Times.*

WASHINGTON, June 3. — On the ground that Congress, in passing the child labor law, unwarrantably invaded the rights of the States to control their own commerce, the Supreme Court today declared the law unconstitutional.

The decision was concurred in by five of the nine members of the court, Chief Justice White, and Justices Day, Van Devanter, Pitney, and McReynolds. Justice Holmes read a dissenting opinion, concurred in by Justices Brandeis, Clarke, and McKenna.

The court's action caused the utmost surprise. It was received with much regret by those who worked for nearly fifteen years in Congress for the passage of the law, which prohibited the shipment in interstate commerce of the products of child labor.

"The controlling question for decision is," said Justice Day, who handed down the prevailing opinion, "is it within the authority of Congress in regulating commerce among the States to prohibit the transportation in interstate commerce of manufactured goods, the product of a factory in which, within thirty days prior to their removal therefrom, children under the age of 14 have been employed or permitted to work, or children between the ages of 14 and 16 have been employed or permitted to work more than eight hours in any day, or more than six days in any week, or after the hour of 7 o'clock P. M. or before the hour of 6 o'clock A. M.?"

### Called Purely Local Question.

This question the majority opinion answered as follows:

"To sustain this statute would not be in our judgment a recognition of the lawful exertion of Congressional authority over interstate commerce, but would sanction an invasion by the Federal power for the control of a matter purely local in its character, and over which no authority has been delegated to Congress in conferring the power to regulate commerce among the States."

Justice Day said:

"All will admit that there should be limitations upon the right to employ children in mines and factories. That such employment is generally deemed to require regulation is shown by the fact that every State in the Union has a law limiting the right thus to employ children.

"We have neither authority nor disposition to question the motives of Congress in enacting this legislation. The purposes intended must be attained consistently with constitutional limitations, and not by an invasion of the powers of the States. This court has no more important function than that which involves upon it the obligation to preserve inviolate the constitutional limitations upon the exercise of authority, Federal and State, to the end that each may continue to discharge, harmoniously with the other, the duties intrusted to it by the Constitution.

### Boundaries of Trade Freedom.

"In our view, the necessary effect of this act is, by means of a prohibition against the movement in interstate commerce of ordinary commercial commodities, to regulate the hours of labor of children in factories and mines within the States, a purely State authority. Thus the act in a twofold sense is repugnant to the Constitution. It not only transcends the authority delegated to Congress over commerce, but also exerts a power as to a purely local matter to which the Federal authority does not extend.

"The far-reaching result of upholding the act cannot be more plainly indicated than by pointing out that if Congress can thus regulate matters intrusted to local authority by prohibition of the movement of commodities in interstate commerce all freedom of commerce will be at an end, and the power of the States over local matters may be eliminated, and thus our system of Government be practically destroyed."

Justice Day pointed out that the mak-

ing of goods or the mining of coal were not in themselves commerce, even though the goods or the coal were afterward to be shipped in interstate commerce. He cited this in support of his argument that the law in effect aims "to standardize the ages at which children may be employed in mining and manufacturing."

"If the mere manufacture or mining were part of interstate commerce," Justice Day said, "all manufacture intended for interstate shipment would be brought under Federal control to the practical exclusion of the authority of the States, a result certainly not contemplated by the framers of the Constitution when they vested in Congress the authority to regulate commerce among the States."

### Dissenting Opinion by Holmes.

In the dissenting opinion, Justice Holmes stated that Congress in his judgment was clearly within its rights, as defined by the Constitution, in enacting the law, even if it constituted interference with the individual rights of States to regulate commerce.

"The national welfare," said Justice Holmes, "is higher than the rights of any State or States, and Congress was clearly justified in using all its efforts along that line."

Justice Holmes expressed surprise that this question of the right of Congress to invade State rights of commercial control should have entered into the decision. He pointed out that in the oleomargarine case, various cases under the Sherman anti-trust law, and under the Pure Food and Drug act, as well as under the Mann act, the Supreme Court had decided that in the broad general interest of the nation, Congress had a right to trample upon the individual rights of States.

The suit decided today was brought by Roland H. Dagenhart in behalf of his children, Roland, Jr., Reuben, and John, who were employed in the mill of the Fidelity Manufacturing Company at Charlotte, N. C. Mr. Dagenhart sought an injunction to prevent the concern from discharging his children.

The Federal Court for the Western District of North Carolina decided that Mr. Dagenhart's contention that the law was unconstitutional was well founded. The Government at once appealed, and today's decision is the result.

Representative Keating of Colorado and Senator Kenyon of Iowa, ardent supporters of the child labor law, stated today they would immediately begin a campaign for a new law, or for an amendment to the Constitution, which would permit Congress to enact such a law. Mr. Keating suggested that the situation might be met by taxing the products of factories employing children.

A meeting will be held in Washington soon to plan a new campaign for a child labor law that will meet the Supreme Court's objections.

June 4, 1918

# SAYS ALIEN LABOR IS A DANGER TO US

## Chief of Bureau in Immigration Department Urges Regulation of the Number.

## LITERACY TEST CONDEMNED

### Congressman Nye and ex-Congressman Bennet Speak Against It at Republican Club Luncheon.

W. W. Husband, Chief of the Bureau of Investigation in the United States Bureau of Immigration, told the members of the Republican Club, at their weekly luncheon yesterday, that the proper adjustment of the immigrant labor supply to the demand for such labor and the welfare of the American workingman was the chief immigration problem of the day. Mr. Husband took a leading part in the discussion, during which the question was considered from a dozen angles. Congressman Frank Mellen Nye of Minnesota was alone in opposing restrictive legislation. The other speakers were Congressman Benjamin K. Focht of Pennsylvania, ex-Congressman William S. Bennet of New York, who was a member of the commission which made a three years' study of the problem, and Edward Kellog Baird, who presided. Mr. Bennet said that as a result of his investigations he was satisfied that the number of immigrants should be restricted, but he joined with Congressman Nye in attacking the proposed "illiteracy test," which he characterized as ridiculous and impossible of enforcement. Immigration Commissioner William Williams attended the luncheon, but did not make an address.

In opening the discussion Mr. Baird said that there was a popular impression among the uninformed that America was the dumping ground for the scum of Europe. The exact reverse was true, he said, and it was in the main the most desirable class which sought our shores.

Mr. Husband referred to the attitude taken by Dr. Eliot, President Emeritus of Harvard College, against the admission of unmarried men. Senator Dillingham, sponsor for the Senate Immigration bill, he said, had taken the same attitude. On an average, said Mr. Husband, about three-fourths of the new immigrants were males. In 1900, he said, the census showed that there were 117 males of foreign birth in the country for every 100 females, and in 1910 the ratio had increased to 129 to 100. The tendency of the men was not to bring families here, he said.

The immigrants who have come to the country in recent years, said Mr. Husband, have been largely city dwellers. Very few of them entered agricultural pursuits, and 65 per cent. had gone to New York, Pennsylvania, Massachusetts, New Jersey, and Connecticut. Naturally the effect on wages was one of the important problems. Nearly three-fourths of all those who reported occupations on their arrival were unskilled laborers, and it was a fact, said the speaker, that they had nearly monopolized the unskilled labor facilities in many industries, and the so-called semi-skilled occupations as well.

Skilled labor, said Mr. Husband, thrived on what unskilled labor produced and the tendency of immigration had been to force the demand for skilled labor without furnishing a corresponding increase in that labor. Mechanical devices which could be operated by immigrants who could be obtained for $1.50 a day, a wage which seemed princely to them, he added, were steadily pulling to a lower economic level the occupations that but yesterday yielded an American income to an American family.

"Of course, an embargo on inventive genius is not conceivable," said Mr. Husband in conclusion, "and improved and new machinery will continue to usurp the field of skilled artisanship, but while the introduction of improved machinery cannot be regulated, the influx of alien laborers can be controlled."

Congressman Nye aimed most of his shafts at the proposed literacy test and said that foreigners should not be excluded because they had not been able to obtain the advantages abroad which this country could give them. He said that the poor of the country were its safeguard and charged that it was the educated and clever men who made fortunes overnight by gambling on the Stock Exchange or selling fake mining stock and undermined the moral strength of the country.

"The educational system of the country is top heavy. It has no moral basis on which to found citizenship," said Mr. Nye. "Our great educational system is not one that emphasizes righteousness. It is the college graduate or high school graduate who goes out not to add strength to this republic, but to weaken it. If a radical law to restrict immigration is necessary, then there is something wrong with our civilization. All over the land there is a demand for labor; the farmer needs it, the mines need it, the factories need it."

The literacy test clause of the Dillingham bill was defended by Congressman Focht.

He said he was a protectionist on the tariff and he believed in the protection of the American workingman who stood to-day on the free list.

Mr. Bennet closed the discussion devoting most of his time to an attack on the literacy test. Whoever prepared the clause in the Dillingham bill, he said, apparently knew nothing of conditions at Ellis Island.

February 2, 1913

## SUNDAY DANCE STIRS CAPITAL

### Much Comment In Washington Over German Attache's Entertainment.

*Special to The New York Times.*

WASHINGTON, Feb. 18.—Washington society is split over the fact that A. C. Horstmann, Third Secretary of the German Embassy, gave a dance to-night at Rauscher's. This is not the first time dances have been given here on Sunday, as a member of the Austro-Hungarian Embassy staff three years ago did the same thing. But that was done very quietly; few except those in attendance knew about it, and little talk was aroused.

Mr. Horstmann's dance, however, is causing much comment. He preceded it with a dinner party, at which young people were guests, and other dinner parties, whose guests later went to the dance, made the whole thing public. Mr. and Mrs. Joseph Leiter and Mr. and Mrs. Perry Belmont were among the hosts at dinners preceding the dance.

The dance was a small affair, but invitations were sent out widely enough to elicit several declinations. Washington society almost invariably rehearses dramatic productions on Sunday, but in every such production there are some who skip the Sunday meetings. It is from these that the declinations came.

February 19, 1912

# PRESIDENT VETOES IMMIGRATION BILL

## Asserts Literacy Test Constitutes a Change in Nation's Policy Which Is Not Justified.

## ALSO MIGHT CAUSE TROUBLE

### Would Be Unwise to Pass Judgment on Laws of Foreign Nations— House Will Try to Override Veto.

*Special to The New York Times.*

WASHINGTON, Jan. 29. — President Wilson, as was expected, vetoed the Immigration bill today. In the statement of his reasons for refusing for the second time in his Administration to give his approval to the measure, the President stated that the provision incorporated in the bill to admit illiterates who may come to the United States seeking a refuge from religious persecution involved the responsibility on the part of United States immigration officials to pass on the laws and practices of foreign Governments, and this he regarded as an invidious function for any administrative officer of this Government to perform.

Singularly this feature of the bill was inserted to meet the objections raised by President Wilson in his first veto of the bill. The President's veto message follows:

"I very much regret to return this bill without my signature.

"In most of the provisions of the bill I should be very glad to concur, but I cannot rid myself of the conviction that the literacy test constitutes a radical change in the policy of the nation which is not justified in principle. It is not a test of character, of quality, or of personal fitness, but would operate in most cases merely as a penalty for lack of opportunity in the country from which the alien seeking admission came. The opportunity to gain an education is in many cases one of the chief opportunities sought by the immigrant in coming to the United States, and our experience in the past has not been that the illiterate immigrant is as such an undesirable immigrant. Tests of quality and of purpose cannot be objected to on principle, but tests of opportunity surely may be.

"Moreover, even if this test might be equitably insisted on, one of the exceptions proposed to its application involves a provision which might lead to very delicate and hazardous diplomatic situations.

"The bill exempts from the operation of the literacy test 'all aliens who shall prove to the satisfaction of the proper immigration officer or to the Secretary of Labor that they are seeking admission to the United States to avoid religious persecution in the country of their last permanent residence, whether such persecution be evidenced by overt acts or by laws or Governmental regulations that discriminate against the alien or the race to which he belongs because of his religious faith.'

"Such a provision, so applied and administered, would oblige the officer concerned in effect to pass judgment upon the laws and practices of a foreign Government, and declare that they did or did not constitute religious persecutions. This would, to say the least, be a most invidious function for any administrative officer of this Government to perform, and it is not only possible, but probable, that very serious questions of international justice and comity would arise between this Government and the Government or Governments thus officially condemned, should its exercise be adopted.

"I dare say that these consequences were not in the mind of the proponents of this provision, but the provision separately and in itself renders it unwise for me to give my assent to this legislation in its present form."

Representative Burnett, Chairman of the House Committee on Immigration, announced in the House late today that he would move to reconsider and pass the measure over the President's veto on Thursday. By unanimous consent it was agreed the veto message shall remain on the Speaker's table until that time.

The House vote on the motion to override the veto undoubtedly will be close, Mr. Burnett expressed confidence today that the required two-thirds majority will be obtained, but both sides are now engaged in telegraphing for absentees, and a half dozen votes may decide the issue. The House lacked four votes when it attempted to override a similar veto two years ago. When President Taft vetoed a similar measure the Senate succeeded in overriding him by more than a two-thirds majority, but the House fell short by about a dozen votes. The bill which the President vetoed today passed the House last March by a vote of 306 to 87, and the Senate in December by 64 to 7.

Representatives Burnett and Sabath, the latter representing the opponents of the Immigration bill, agreed today that the roll call on reconsideration shall be preceded by a debate of an hour and a half.

January 30, 1917

# Gen. Rosalie Jones and Her Suffrage Hikers In Washington.

## ARMY ENDS ITS HIKE; GEN. JONES SCORES

---

**Will Have Nothing More to Do with Message to Wilson, Despite Request.**

---

**CROWDS BLOCK THE PARADE**

---

**No Demonstration on the Part of the Antis—Thirteen Walked Entire Distance.**

---

*Special to The New York Times.*

WASHINGTON, Feb. 28.—General Rosalie Jones, leader of the suffragist hikers, made a laconic entry in her diary tonight. It was: "And so marching they came to Washington." In the diary General Jones has chronicled faithfully the happenings on the long hike. The Army of the Hudson reached here shortly after noon, and its reception must have filled the heart of General Jones with pride. From the boundary line of the District of Columbia, from which point mounted policemen escorted them, all the way to the headquarters of the local organization in F Street, near Fifteenth Street Northwest, the weary hikers, the war correspondents, and camp followers marched through a lane of interested spectators.

At some points the crowd was enthusiastic, but for the most part it was merely attracted by curiosity. There were occasions when the crowd pushed so closely against the hikers that Gen. Jones had to halt the line and wait until the mounted policemen had opened the lane again. At the suffrage headquarters the street was blocked. When Gen. Jones stood in an automobile to speak a cheer went up that made the Treasury building windows rattle.

It was the weather of a Summer day when the Army of the Hudson marched down the Bladensburg road into the District of Columbia. The hikers entered the city by way of the old toll gate at Fifteenth Street Northeast and Maryland Avenue. Gen. Jones, with her pilgrim's cloak draped about her and her staff in her hand led the way. She walked some paces ahead of the army. At her side walked Milton Wend. Behind Gen. Jones came Col. Ida Craft and walking with her Mrs. George Wend. To the left was Dr E. S Stevens of Philadelphia, carrying a large American flag. Behind came the others of the army in informal formation. War correspondents marched as they desired Bringing up the rear were Miss Elizabeth Freeman, driving Lausanne, the noted Newark bargain horse, and Miss Marguerite Geist, driving Jerry the donkey.

As the army reached the beginning of Maryland Avenue the hikers caught sight for the first time of the dome of the Capitol.

Gen. Jones called a halt, and for a few moments the army gazed upon the dome glistening in the sunlight.

"We are here," said Gen Jones, turning to her companions and pointing ahead with her staff.

The army cheered and again took up the hike. For a time it seemed as if there would be no welcome for the hikers. The original plan was to enter the city by way of Rhode Island Avenue. The automobile containing the delegation headed by Miss Alice Paul and the escort of women on horseback went to Rhode Island Avenue and waited some time before they learned that the army was coming in another direction.

"We will enter the city by our own way," was the comment of Gen. Jones, who halted the army for a little time to await the arrival of the welcoming delegation. In more orderly formation after a little she ordered the advance. The hikers had been marching only a short time when Mrs. Margaret Hopkins Morrell and Mrs. Lucy Reid came up on horseback. Both wore white corduroy riding habits and large white plumed hats with the rims caught up on one side. They at once took the lead in the parade. Then came the automobile, in which were Miss Alice Paul, Miss Margaret Foley of

Boston, and Mrs. Lawrence Lewis of Philadelphia. Miss Paul welcomed Gen. Jones and her army. She explained how the escort had gone in the wrong direction to meet the hikers. Mrs. Richard Pope Burleson, Mrs. Russell MacLennan, and Mrs. Frank Baker, joining the welcoming party, fell into line with the escort.

"Three cheers for Rosalie Jones" shouted a crowd of men as the head of the parade turned into North Capitol Street. The cheers were given with a will. Then there were cheers for Col. Craft. The marchers swung into Pennsylvania Avenue, and there Gen. Jones halted her command and ordered the hikers, who had made the entire journey, to form a line across the street. There were thirteen in that first line, and every one had walked every step of the distance. At one end of the line was Dr. Stevens with the flag. At the other end Milton Wend with the bugle. Behind the first line came the women who marched most of the way. Then came a line of women who had walked only a fraction of the distance, and the escort which had joined at different places. Behind came Miss Freeman in the yellow wagon, and behind her Miss Geist in her donkey cart. In the rear was the baggage automobile with Alphonse Major at the wheel.

The formal parade was led by a squad of mounted policemen. Next came the automobile carrying the women of the Washington headquarters of the National Suffrage Association. Then came women on horseback. At the request of Gen. Jones the war correspondents acted as her personal escort. There was no band. It was hard marching at times because of the crowds along the way. Once a woman pushed forward, dodged a policeman and succeeded in reaching the hikers. She presented a bunch of violets to one of the hikers. "I believe you have done a great work for the cause," she said. "Others may talk and work at home, but you have taken the gospel into the country."

A man held a little girl up so that she might see the marchers. Gen. Jones walked to the side of the street and kissed the child. The crowd cheered. "Good for you," it shouted. At Ninth Street the spectators pressed so closely that the line had to halt while the policemen fought to open up the way. The worst confusion occurred when the hikers turned at Fifteenth Street to march to F Street and the local headquarters. There was no demonstration on the part of the anti-suffragists. A number of young men in an automobile decorated with the colors of the antis, according to the pilgrim's twice attempted to block the line of march, but that was all.

At the suffrage headquarters the police had trouble in opening up a way. It was a friendly crowd, and when Gen. Jones arose to speak she was cheered heartily. She told the crowd how glad she was to get to Washington.

"We have come through," she said, "and we thank you for this welcome."

As Gen. Jones spoke she glanced often toward the scout car, in which sat Mrs Oliver Livingston Jones, her mother. Mrs. Jones is a pronounced anti-suffragist, and she has more than once expressed her opinion of the hiking activities of her daughter. Evidently, however, she enjoyed her daughter's triumph and smiled at her as she spoke. Inside the headquarters the hikers rested for half an hour and then went to a restaurant for luncheon.

Gen. Jones's day of triumph really began when a telegram was received from the National Woman's Suffrage Association in New York telling her that the hikers could accompany the Congressional committee and the officers of the association when the message is presented to President Wilson. Gen. Jones was quite upset by the action of the association, which had intrusted the message to her to deliver and had, near the journey's end, intercepted her and taken the message away. In the telegram the officers of the association expressed regret that there had been a misunderstanding, and invited the hikers to go along and help them deliver the message. This telegram did not soothe the feelings of Gen. Jones. The hikers will not assist in the delivery of the message.

"I am through," said Gen. Jones. "I was asked to give up the message that I had received in New York to deliver to President Wilson. I did so. It is now out of my hands, and so far as I am concerned that ends the matter."

Shortly after her arrival here Gen. Jones was visited by a delegation of students from the Maryland Agricultural College. The college authorities deny the reports that some of the students made insulting remarks to the hikers as they passed the college grounds. The students say that the remarks were made by outsiders.

The hikers now await the suffrage demonstration on March 3. The anti-suffragists held a meeting to-day in the Belasco Theatre.

March 1, 1913

# "ART" IN THE ARMORY

## Resembles the Ancient Brush-marks of Prehistoric Man.

*To the Editor of The New York Times:*

A painter and student of matters of art—please note the distinction—would like the privilege of your columns to say: Do not be disturbed—you have not gone crazy, and art, the dainty goddess, still is. I address you as having visited the exhibition now at the Sixty-ninth Regiment Armory.

Savages and children practice this art sincerely, and get over it as fast as they can. In the new Encyclopaedia Britannica (see Painting) there is a picture of the extinct European bison, done 50,000 years ago. It is the oldest painting known. It is identically the art of the armory, only it is real and not an imitation.

Observe that brush marks may do two things; they may depict solids imaginatively extant behind the canvas—which implies a knowledge of the forms of the solids; and they may please by their inherent beauty, which implies the enjoyment of abstract order—taste. And the whole history of painting is a series of compromises between these two different ends. Abstract order, pattern, or, if I use a popular barbarism, decoration, exists for its own beauty only; whereas depiction is for representing objects of assorted interests. For 2,000 years European painting has been increasing the emphasis upon depiction, which means a growth away from design and taste, and toward representation and knowledge. The antique sculpture merely helped the people of the Renaissance to forget that painting had another field. Thereby came into existence a pictorial art having exactly the motive of the "living picture." And in 600 more years after Cimabue this art arrives at—Carolus Duran.

In all academic art the object of the painter is the rotundity of a nude figure, exactly as in sculpture, so that painting, as an art having powers denied to sculpture, ceases to exist. Yet this pseudo painting has been enthroned in Europe for centuries—not, however, because of its beauty, but because of its ability to present objects having other interests, as those of religion, war, personal vanity, &c. Esthetically, this art wearies us by the contradiction between its theory of an illusion of depth and its inability to give the illusion because the eye is compelled to remain at focus on the picture plane. It is inherently imperfect, and, in a way, the better it is the worse it is. This is painting as it is understood in the Ecole des Beaux Arts, the Royal Academy, and the like. Its logical and ultimate result is Bouguereau and Alma Tadema. And yet Turner, Corot, Rousseau, Whistler, Courbet, Maret, Inness, Tryon, Twachtman, and Wyant have gone quite other ways and have given us better work.

But the conflict between depiction and decoration is fundamental, and the ground between them that they have truly in common is very small. In early Italian painting the pattern, while not the sole concern, was yet always clear. And in his group of Primavera girls Botticelli achieves the most perfect balance ever effected between depiction and decoration, between knowledge and taste. With more knowledge and less taste you get Ingres; with more taste and less knowledge you get Koriusai.

Now as to those louder armory pictures—disregarding cubism, &c.—one has no difficulty in seeing that they consist of a jumble of lines and patches, and that they are very ugly. The formula for their production is to compel a painter to use only 2 per cent. of either his knowledge or his taste. With greater knowledge, they would be more like natural things—with greater taste, more like beautiful patterns. Having the least possible quantity of either, they neither interest nor please, they are neither words nor music. As to color—it does not exist; its place is taken by mere pigment. As a whole, they are to art what "pi" is to literature.

Brains and taste, labor and skill, love and patience, are back of all art. Omit these and you get—these other things.

The art of the future will carry the art of the past not backward, but forward. Pictorial painting, practiced as art and not as illustration, far from being exhausted has been but touched. The esthetic masters of light have been few—masters of color, still fewer. And the world awaits an art that shall give in the flat perfectly all that the flat can perfectly give of the spirit of Ingres and the spirit of Koriusai. Why not?

BOLTON BROWN.
New York, Feb. 27, 1913.

March 1, 1913

## 50,000 VISIT ART SHOW.

**Armory Exhibit a Big Success, Press Dinner Guests Are Told.**

Art and noise met last night when the Press Committee of the International Exhibition of Modern Art entertained at Healy's, Sixty-sixth Street and Columbus Avenue, their "friends and enemies of the press." Though art was present, the affair had little of the Latin quarter air, and Bohemian trimmings were absent. The chief contributor to the noise was D. Putnam Brinley, the artist.

The affair was a beefsteak dinner in the log cabin room. In the intervals of passing about the beef young women, also artists, sang and danced. When they were not dancing Mr. Brinley, who is nearly seven feet tall, danced.

The climax came in a high-kicking contest, which was won by Mr. Brinley. Frederick James Gregg, Chairman of the Press Committee, was Chairman. Mr. Gregg insisted upon reading a short address he had prepared to deliver at the opening of the exhibition, but had no chance to "put it across."

John Quinn, who is a lawyer and not an artist, spoke upon the success of the present show, which, he said, was one of the most important international exhibitions of contemporary art that had been held in any country in the last quarter of a century.

"In the nineteen days that it has been open," he said, "nearly 50,000 persons have visited the exhibition in the Sixty-ninth Regiment Armory. There have been sold over 160 works of art, and the association has entered into a contract with the Chicago Art Institute, by which a major part of the works exhibited here will be exhibited in Chicago.

"Its success in attendance and sales demonstrates that the American people as an art-loving people are second only to France. Even as to the Cubists, our association has shown true courage. I will not here attempt an explanation of the Cubists or of Cubist art. I might, however, compare the Cubists to the members of eugenic societies in England and other countries. The Cubists are trying to improve the breed of painters, as the eugenists are apparently trying to improve the breed of men. Some of the intermediate types may not be perfect or examples of wondrous beauty, but they are alive and vital, and we may say for them that 'they don't know where they're going, but they know they're on the way,' which is not only true of the Cubists, but of all art that is living and vital and progressive."

March 9, 1913

# CONCEDE BIGGER TAX ON LARGE INCOMES

**High as 7% Above $1,000,000 by Leaders' Plan, but Radicals Demand 10%.**

**NEW BLOW AT SPECULATION**

**Cummins Introduces Amendment Taxing Future Sales 10 Per Cent. —Would End Short Selling.**

*Special to The New York Times.*

WASHINGTON, Sept. 1.—In an effort to satisfy the radical element of the Democratic Party, the majority membership of the Senate Finance Committee has decided upon sweeping increases in the surtax levied by the tariff bill on large incomes. These increases, which carry the levy on that part of incomes in excess of $1,000,000 a year up to seven per cent., is still regarded as too low by many extremists, and a fight, it is expected, will be made in caucus to-morrow afternoon to have the rates graded up to ten per cent. While there is some talk among radical Democrats of vitiating the caucus rule so far as income tax is concerned if the rate be not increased, it is expected that the party ranks will not be broken materially.

As now proposed, the surtax, in addition to the normal one per cent. levy, will be four per cent. on incomes between $100,000 and $250,000. On incomes between $250,000 and $500,000 the rate will be five per cent.; between $500,000 and $1,000,000 it will be six per cent. The seven per cent. rate will apply to all incomes above $1,000,000.

It is estimated that there are 550 persons in this country with incomes between $250,000 and $500,000; 350 with incomes between $500,000 and $1,000,000, and more than 100 with incomes above $1,000,000.

**Tax on Cotton Futures.**

Considerable difference of opinion within and without the Democratic ranks developed to-day in the Senate's debate over the provision in the Tariff bill imposing a tax of one-tenth of a cent a pound on undelivered future cotton sales. Senator E. D. Smith of South Carolina, long prominent in the fight of the Farmers' Alliance to raise the price of cotton, attacked the measure as likely to prove a heavy burden on the producer. Other Southern Democrats were of the same opinion, though Mr. Clarke of Arkansas, President pro tempore of the Senate, spoke warmly in support of the tax, of which he was the originator. Mr. Clarke bitterly assailed the New York Cotton Exchange as wholly vicious, declared it ought to be destroyed, and quoted various authorities as saying that the Exchange supplied the legitimate trade no additional facilities for handling the cotton crop.

Senator Cummins of Iowa, a radical Republican, seemed to agree with Mr. Clarke as to the general principle involved, but he thought the Clarke provision did not go far enough. He offered a substitute amendment taxing contracts of sale in all commodities 10 per cent. in cases where the seller was not the actual owner of the commodity.

The Democratic supporters of the Clarke provision have contended that the tax would not entirely destroy future sales, but would merely eliminate the more wildly speculative of them and at the same time raise revenue. Mr. Cummins admitted that his idea was to put an end to all undelivered future transactions.

"The railroad stocks attempted to be sold in 1912 on the New York Stock Exchange," said Mr. Cummins, "represented three-fourths or more of all the railroad stocks in the United States. Ninety-five per cent. of these sales were fictitious. Not 10 per cent. changed hands. Yet three-fourths of the entire amount of railway stock were sold on the New York Exchange alone, not taking into account the Exchanges of Boston, Philadelphia, Chicago, and other great cities of the country."

**Would Prevent Short Selling.**

"Short sales constitute the greatest menace to industrial stability and financial strength now presented to the American people. Some time we must take up the problem of suppressing these gigantic gambling transactions, and this is the time to do it. We ought to employ the taxing power to put an end to the evil. If the tax is imposed next year, there will be but a tithe of the gambling that has been flaunted in the face of the American people. It will not interfere with honest and legitimate business methods, and the market places of the country will be made more secure. The Stock Exchanges are not now places for the actual transfer of commodities. They are places where unscrupulous men balance their wits."

Mr. Cummins cited figures showing that the sales of stocks of various railroads and industrial corporations on the New York Stock Exchange in 1912 exceeded in many cases the entire amount of the stocks in existence. In the case of the Lehigh Valley, the listed stock of which aggregates $60,571,000, the sales were $175,625,000, said Mr. Cummins. Instead of stabilizing the price of stocks, Mr. Cummins said, the price ranged from 155⅞ to 185¾ as a result of speculative manipulation. In the case of the American Beet Sugar Company, the total stock of which is $15,000,000, said the Senator, the sales were $108,-612,400, more than seven times the entire amount of the stock outstanding.

"The Atchison, Topeka & Santa Fé had $168,430,000 of stock listed on the Exchange," he said. "At the end of the year its stockholders had changed but little, yet 129,000,000 shares had been 'traded in.'

"The stock of the St. Paul Road was listed at $116,348,000, yet the trades amounted to $149,277,000, and the price ranged from 99⅜ to 117⅝ a share. There was no reason for this fluctuation; there was but little change in ownership," declared Senator Cummins.

"The Reading road's capital stock amounted to $42,480,000," he continued, "yet the trades were twenty-five times that, or over $1,114,000,000. Stock Exchange brokers pretended to sell nearly three times the entire capital stock of the Lehigh Valley Road, and passed back and forth $119,000,000 of Great Northern stock, when there was but little change of ownership."

**Smith Urges His Own Bill.**

In his speech, Senator Smith of South Carolina declared that under the Clarke amendment the cotton producers would indirectly pay the tax. He argued in support of his own bill, making it mandatory for every contract for cotton to specify the grade to be delivered, declaring that under present contracts, with twenty-seven different grades of cotton, the purchaser never knew what sort of cotton he would get. He declared that if the contract provided for the delivery of a specified grade of cotton no man would dare go short on the Cotton Exchange.

"The Senators seem inclined to help the bulls in their fight with the bears," said Senator Clarke.

"I am in favor of putting an end to the miserable iniquity in New York," rejoined Senator Smith, "but in putting it out of business I do not want to hurt the producers of cotton."

Senator Ransdell of Louisiana objected to the designation of the New Orleans Cotton Exchange as a "parasite" of the New York Exchange. He declared that the New Orleans rules and regulations were entirely different, that the dominating groups were different, and that the New Orleans Exchange had an actual commercial settlement by an Exchange committee.

Senator Clarke said he referred to the New Orleans Exchange as a "parasite" only with the idea that it could not itself control or dominate the cotton market.

"Our business there is just as fairly conducted as it can be," declared Senator Ransdell, "and we have no connection with New York. New Orleans is strictly a spot cotton market. The Government grades of cotton were immediately adopted by the New Orleans Exchange; they haven't yet been adopted by New York."

Senator Clarke said he believed the proposed tax on cotton futures would in the end break up the trading in futures. For a time, he said, it would bring in a substantial revenue for the Government, but in time the future trading would greatly decrease.

September 2, 1913

# ROOT WANTS TO TAX SMALL INCOMES, TOO

## Burden Should Not All Be Placed on Industrial States and Big Fortunes.

## "HIS PEOPLE" SUFFER MOST

### Senator Lewis Attacks New Yorker in Reply, Asking If All His People "Nest in Wall Street."

*Special to The New York Times.*

WASHINGTON, Sept. 2.—In a speech to-day, during the consideration of the Tariff bill in the Senate, Senator Elihu Root of New York protested against the Democratic proposition to levy a heavy tax on large incomes and exempt persons of small incomes. He was in favor of the principle of the income tax, he said, but in his opinion, the exemption now fixed at $3,000 in the pending Tariff bill should be reduced to $1,000.

Mr. Root's argument was that the great industrial States should not have the burden of the tax so shifted that they would have to bear the greater part of it, while the lesser States, with populations mainly in receipt of small incomes, would have very little of this burden to bear. He pointed out that through the voluntary consent of the larger States, when the Union was formed, the smaller States of the Union were given equal representation with the larger in the Senate, and this consent had been given because the larger States trusted to the sense of fairness of the other States not to misuse the power thus conferred. As an example to sustain his contention, Mr. Root said that Nevada, with a total population of 84,000, had as much voice in the Senate as New York with its 10,000,000 population.

"I am in favor of an income tax," he said, "and I believe in the principle of it. I think it fair, and I voted for the income tax amendment to the Constitution, and urged it upon my people. I have no fault to find with an income tax or a graded tax, but if you impose too great a tax upon the industrial States you will, to that extent, diminish their taxable resources for State or other local purposes.

### New York's Great Taxes.

"Last year the State of New York imposed direct taxes amounting to $234,000,000, a far greater amount than you expect to raise in the whole country from this excise. We tax inheritances and franchises. Last year we raised $13,000,000 from inheritance taxes and $10,000,000 from franchises. In levying your taxes you should not treat the taxable resources of our State less fairly than you treat the resources of other States.

"The pending bill will diminish the taxable resources of New York more than the old income tax law. If you go on making the rate on the incomes of the wealthy higher and higher, simply to take it away from them, you will diminish the resources of the State proportionately, and you are enabled to do this because New York has placed herself voluntarily in your power and relinquished her constitutional rights, trusting to your sense of fairness as between States."

Senator James Hamilton Lewis of Illinois undertook to reply to Senator Root, and spoke of Mr. Root's reference to "My people." He asked if the Senator from New York considered his own people "only the brood of gentlemen who nest about Wall Street."

Mr. Lewis mentioned Wall Street, the Waldorf-Astoria, Bar Harbor, and Palm Beach as boundary points within which Mr. Root's "people" were congregated. Mr. Lewis said Senator Root had advocated in the Roosevelt Administration that the Federal Government should step in to conduct the affairs of States that had not been able to conduct them properly for themselves. The high income tax, he said, was an application of this idea to New York, which had failed to collect taxes from the wealthy classes.

"I did not say that," replied Mr. Root sadly. "I never have said it and I never shall say it. I am humiliated that the Senator has not read my speech to which he refers," and then Mr. Root smiled and continued to smile during the rest of Senator Lewis's remarks.

### Senator Gallinger Assails Bill.

During the tariff discussion Senator Gallinger of New Hampshire replied to the recent speech by his Democratic colleague, Senator Hollis, who declared New England was not discriminated against in the Tariff bill, and hotly assailed the textile manufacturers for recent labor troubles.

"New England believes in a protective tariff," declared Senator Gallinger, "and no man who supports the bill now under consideration, or defends men like Ettor, Haywood and others of their ilk, represents in any way her views." He also assailed the Democratic bill as a whole.

Senator Hollis replied that his presence in the Senate was proof that the people of New Hampshire had rejected high protection.

Senator Thompson, Democrat, declared he proposed to support the bill in every particular and that his only difference with other Democrats on free sugar had been as to the time the schedule should become effective. He referred to charges that President Wilson was influencing Senators in favor of the bill by Federal patronage.

"No patronage has ever been withheld or given by the President because of the position of any Congressman upon any public question," said he.

Democratic Senators in a caucus which began to-night will endeavor to settle all differences over the income tax, cotton future tax, and other questions.

Chairman Simmons of the Finance Committee expects to confer with President Wilson upon the latter's return from Cornish about some of the disputed features before the caucus finally decides. Mr. Simmons looks for a vote on the bill the latter part of next week.

---

## THE INCOME TAX.

The estimate that 425,000 persons must pay the income tax does not exempt the rest of the population from informing themselves regarding the details of this most popular tax. The presumption is against the citizen claiming exemption. Those contending that the law does not apply to them must make that fact clear to the officials whose duty is to maintain the contrary. The ordeal which corporations have undergone under the application of the excise tax now confronts multitudes who have never kept books, or who have kept them only in their minds, and now are confronted with the necessity of keeping them in a manner satisfactory to the law under penalty of fine and imprisonment.

The law contemplates that every taxpayer shall receive a tax bill, but the failure to get one does not exempt the taxpayer. At his own risk he must report himself, and must make his statement subject to criticism. The taxpayer must make return of his gross income, and the Government will make the deductions. The law requires the presentation by the Government of a blank return to be filled, and the Treasury will prepare regulations for itself which also will serve for the guidance of those perplexed by the numberless cases of actual or supposed doubt in the application of the law. The Government asks only for the facts. The computations and the assessment it makes for itself, leaving the taxpayer who is caught the same option that the eel has about being skinned.

Doubtless many will slip through the meshes of the law, but those hoping or planning to do so must remember that the Government has better sources of information than the State officials who have levied the personal property tax. Their means of information were directories which disclosed the residents upon fashionable streets, rosters of expensive clubs, jury lists, and pure guesses. The income tax law is a more serious matter for tax dodgers. Wages paid must be borne by those who pay them. Taxes payable on large classes of income "deducted at the source" will simply be taken from corporations on their own account, and on account of those receiving income through them, such as interest on bonds. The provision in this case illustrates the manner in which the law throws the presumption against the exemption. The tax payable in respect of accrued interest is deducted irrespective of the exemption, and in the first instance is collected even though the owner of the bond and recipient of the interest is exempt. In order to secure the return of such collection the individual taxpayer must make affidavit. Dividends are deductible by the individual who reports them in his gross income, but not otherwise.

It must be admitted that the tax is more burdensome in its manner than in its amount. Those who must pay the largest amount—6 per cent. upon the excess above $500,000—will feel it least in both respects. Necessarily without regard to the law they must have books kept for them. The mere payment of whatever amount means no such sacrifice to them as the smaller amounts mean to the larger number of small payers, who must do the work themselves, and pinch themselves into the bargain, even though the tax is only moderate at the bottom of the scale. One per cent. upon the excess above $3,000 for bachelors, or $4,000 for married couples living together, is little for those whose income is $5,000, or even $10,000. If the option were to pay the amount of the tax and escape the nuisance many would rejoice. But there is no such option. The only means of escape is the receipt of an income provably below $3,000, and that means that the ordeal must be undergone probably by more persons just below the exemption than by those above it.

It would be repetitious to give here the language of the law, or the exposition of it by its author in yesterday's TIMES. The taxpayer must read the law for himself, and must read it aright at his peril. Next New Year's is the day upon which his duty begins. Between then and March, 1914, first he must make his return in respect to his income from March 1 to the end of 1913, the period to be calculated as five-sixths of a year. After this year the return will be for the full year. He will receive notification of the tax due under his return on June 1, and must pay within the month. If the taxpayer neglects to make return the Collector may make one for him at any time within three years. If the tax is not paid there will be added to the tax due 5 per cent., and 1 per cent. monthly. The penalty for refusal to make return is a fine from $20 to $1,000. The making of a false return is a misdemeanor, punishable by a fine of $2,000, or a year's imprisonment, or both. Those making returns for others as the law requires are held personally liable under the law. It is an alluring prospect, especially when it is considered that each State for itself may make similar requirements, as some have already done, and others are likely to do, so great is the popularity of the law with those who do not pay it, and have the power to impose it upon others.

## EDISON SEES MISS KELLER.

### Inventor Thinks He Can Give Her Actual Sound Perceptions.

A meeting, which had been much desired by both for many years, was arranged between Helen Keller and Thomas A. Edison at the Edison home in Llewellyn Park last Sunday afternoon, just before Miss Keller and her teacher, Mrs. Macy, started West, to continue a lecture tour. Miss Keller was much interested in all that Mr. Edison told her of recent experiments and inventions.

"Tell me more about your wonderful inventions," she said over and over again.

Mr. Edison showed deep interest in Miss Keller's keenness and delicacy of touch perception. After testing it in various ways he declared his confidence that he could translate sound waves into electrical vibrations, which would give Helen Keller actual sound perceptions.

Miss Keller and Mrs. Macy will spend a day with Mr. Edison in his laboratories on their return from the West, for the purpose of assisting in experiments to this end.

December 16, 1913

## 'THE BIRTH OF A NATION.'

### Film Version of Dixon's "The Clansman" Presented at the Liberty.

"The Birth of a Nation," an elaborate new motion picture taken on an ambitious scale, was presented for the first time last evening at the Liberty Theatre. With the addition of much preliminary historical matter, it is a film version of some of the melodramatic and inflammatory material contained in "The Clansman," by Thomas Dixon.

A great deal might be said concerning the spirit revealed in Mr. Dixon's review of the unhappy chapter of Reconstruction and concerning the sorry service rendered by its plucking at old wounds. But of the film as a film, it may be reported simply that it is an impressive new illustration of the scope of the motion picture camera.

An extraordinarily large number of people enter into this historical pageant, and some of the scenes are most effective. The civil war battle pictures, taken in panorama, represent enormous effort and achieve a striking degree of success. One interesting scene stages a reproduction of the auditorium of Ford's Theatre in Washington, and shows on the screen the murder of Lincoln. In terms of purely pictorial value the best work is done in those stretches of the film that follow the night riding of the men of the Ku-Klux Klan, who look like a company of avenging spectral crusaders sweeping along the moonlit roads.

The "Birth of a Nation," which was prepared for the screen under the direction of D. W. Griffith, takes a full evening for its unfolding and marks the advent of the two dollar movie. That is the price set for the more advantageous seats in the rear of the Liberty's auditorium.

It was at this same theatre that the stage version of "The Clansman" had a brief run a little more than nine years ago, as Mr. Dixon himself recalled in his curtain speech last evening in the interval between the two acts. Mr. Dixon also observed that he would have allowed none but the son of a Confederate soldier to direct the film version of "The Clansman."

March 4, 1915

## EGG NEGRO SCENES IN LIBERTY FILM PLAY

### Police Quell Disturbers at "Birth of a Nation," and Arrest Indignant Southerner.

A mixed crowd of white men and negroes who had obtained seats in the front row of the gallery started a demonstration against the film play, "The Birth of a Nation," at the Liberty Theatre at 10:30 o'clock last night.

Policemen, ushers and private detectives who had been stationed at convenient intervals in anticipation of a demonstration swarmed down upon the noise makers and seized two of the leaders. As they did so two eggs splattered over the screen, blotting out portions of a picture showing a white Southern girl in the act of leaping off a cliff to escape from a negro pursuer.

A white man, who gave the name of Howard Schaeffle, was hurried from the theatre after private detectives had asserted it was he who threw the eggs. He cried out, " Rotten, rotten," as the detectives pushed him down the stairs toward the street. He was taken to the West Thirty-seventh Street station on a charge of disorderly conduct.

A negro who walked with a slight limp followed the white man out with the help of detectives. He protested loudly that " that play's a libel on a race. It's got to be stopped."

A negro arose some minutes after the main party had left.

" On the anniversary of Lincoln's assassination," he shouted. " it is inappropriate to present a play that libels 10,000 loyal American negroes. I think President Lincoln wouldn't like this play." The negro, who said his name was Cleveland G. Allen and that he was the head of a colored news agency, was ushered to the street.

At the West Thirty-seventh Street Station Schaeffle was searched and a paper bag containing three eggs was found in his overcoat pocket.

" I was taking the eggs home for breakfast," he said, " and I stopped in to see this play. I am a Southerner and a libertarian, and I believe in the education and the uplifting of the negro. It made my blood boil to see the play and I threw the eggs at the screen. The play will have to be removed from the boards."

Schaeffle said he was born in Maryland. A negro lawyer, escorted by a delegation of negroes who had not been in the theatre, appeared at the station to take charge of Schaeffle's case.

The management of the theatre pointed out this scene as a refutation of the charge that the play was meant to libel the negroes, or show them in an especially bad light. The management insisted that most of the applause during the progress of the play was for scenes showing negroes performing heroic acts.

April 15, 1915

# FIVE DOLLAR MOVIES PROPHESIED

## D. W. Griffith Says They Are Sure to Come with the Remarkable Advance in Film Productions.

By Richard Barry.

DAVID GRIFFITH is today the biggest figure in the moving-picture world. As the creator who is stalking ahead of the procession and lifting it literally by its own boot straps, he is now a marked man throughout filmdom. He has done more subtle things, more delicate things, and more gigantic things on the screen than any other man.

However, it was not in his capacity as a showman only that I approached Mr. Griffith. While he is a producer without a rival and a generalissimo of mimic forces whose work has never been equaled, it was as a thinker pondering the new problems of filmland, a triumphant Columbus of the screen, that he talked with me for THE SUNDAY TIMES recently.

"It is foolish to think that the moving picture has reached its climax of development," said he. " We have the moving-picture theatre as well built and as well run as any other theatre; we have the moving-picture show that brings $2 a seat; we have the foremost actors and the foremost writers of the world working for us. So people are prone to think we have gone the limit and there is nothing more to be done. But I tell you that moving pictures are still only in their swaddling clothes."

"Would you mind predicting something about the maturity of this promising infant?" I suggested.

He smiled that courteous, humorous, knowing smile of the Southerner, (his father was a Kentucky Colonel, brevetted Brigadier General of Volunteers by the Confederate States of America.) He said that he had been obliged to predict so much for motion pictures while talking of their possibilities to capitalists that he would welcome the chance to go into the prophecy business, where it costs nothing to make good.

"But," he added seriously, " I am not a dreamer in the sense that I see fantastic things unlikely of realization. I haven't dreamed an impossible thing in seven years—since I started in pictures. That is the beauty of this work. It makes dreams come true.

"My first prediction is that a moving picture will be made within three or four years for which the entrance money will be $5 and $6 a seat. It is easy to predict that."

"But will the public pay $5 a seat merely to see a picture?"

"They are already doing it—to ticket speculators. When I first proposed asking $2 a seat for my new film not a single man in the theatrical business could be found to say I was making a sound business move. Regular theatres on all sides were cutting prices, not advancing them, and 50 cents a seat had always heretofore been considered a record price for the best films.

"The public is quick to see values. If they are willing to pay 5 cents to see a picture that costs $500 to produce and 50 cents to see a picture that costs $50,000 to produce, they are willing to pay $2 to see one that costs half a million to produce.

"And when we can put on a picture that will cost $2,000,000 to produce the public will be willing to pay $5 a seat for it."

"Two million dollars!" I exclaimed. "Where are you going to get the money and how are you going to spend it?"

"If you had asked me a year ago where we could get the money I would have believed it would be impossible," replied Mr. Griffith, "for up to that time an investment of $50,000 was considered utterly daring for a picture; but the days of little things in the pictures are gone by forever. When I started in the business only seven years ago a producer who spent $500 on a picture was considered very extravagant. Not today. We spend that much on a single scene that runs less than a minute, and then often throw it away because it doesn't fit, or is not just right.

"The experimental work on a big picture costs thousands of dollars. The trying out of new effects to see if they will reproduce is a costly process, and when one has the inventive faculty and is anxious to produce new things he is likely to bankrupt his promoters."

The mellow smile came back to the Griffith countenance. "However," he added, "that is the only known way to get the big, new effects."

"What will happen to the regular theatre when its prices are being cut while yours are advancing?"

"The regular theatre," he continued, "will, of course, always exist, but not, I believe, as now. The pictures will utterly eliminate from the regular theatre all the spectacular features of production. Plays will never again appeal to the public for their scenery, or their numbers of actors and supernumeraries. Pictures have replaced all that.

"The only plays that the public will care to see in the regular theatre wi be the intimate, quiet plays that can b staged in one or two settings within four walls, and in which the setting is unimportant, while the drama will be largely subjective. Objective drama, the so-called melodrama, will be entirely absorbed in the pictures.

Photo by Bangs.

**D. W. Griffith.**

"The audiences for these old-fashioned theatres will be drawn from old-fashioned people who remember the days of old and how plays were produced by Belasco and Frohman when 'I was a boy.' The new generation will be wedded to the movies. You won't be able to satisfy them with anything else."

"What of the written and spoken word that is so vital to true drama? Do you intend to kill that, too?"

"On the contrary, we intend to vitalize it. The bane of the drama is verbosity, but we can't produce any picture without some words. In one of my pictures we throw on the screen over 7,000 words, in which there are at least four pages from Woodrow Wilson's history of the United States. That is more words than are used in the average short story.

"We are coming to pay more and more attention to the words we use on the screen. The art of writing for the pictures is developing almost as rapidly as the art of acting for them. And the great rewards to be gained there by a

writer will be a powerful incentive for him to learn to tell his story more crisply, more tellingly, more alluringly, than he ever could, even in the best spoken drama."

"But this will mean a great revolution in our methods of thought?"

"Of course," answered the multiparous Griffith, "the human race will think more rapidly, more intelligently, more comprehensively than it ever did. It will see everything—positively everything.

"That, I believe, is the chief reason that the American public is so hungry for motion pictures and so loyal to a good one when it comes along. They have the good old American faculty of wanting to be 'shown' things. We don't 'talk' about things happening, or describe how a thing looks; we actually show it—vividly, completely, convincingly. It is the ever-present, realistic, actual now that 'gets' the great American public, and nothing ever devised by the mind of man can show it like moving pictures."

At this point the director, who counts that day lost whose low descending sun finds no new idea hatched, produced an illumination for the future right out of his egg, (we were at breakfast.)

"The time will come, and in less than ten years," he went on, "when the children in the public schools will be taught practically everything by moving pictures. Certainly they will never be obliged to read history again.

"Imagine a public library of the near future, for instance. There will be long rows of boxes or pillars, properly classified and indexed, of course. At each box a push button and before each box a seat. Suppose you wish to 'read up' on a certain episode in Napoleon's life. Instead of consulting all the authorities, wading laboriously through a host of books, and ending bewildered, without a clear idea of exactly what did happen and confused at every point by conflicting opinions about what did happen, you will merely seat yourself at a properly adjusted window, in a scientifically prepared room, press the button, and actually see what happened.

"There will be no opinions expressed. You will merely be present at the making of history. All the work of writing, revising, collating, and reproducing will have been carefully attended to by a corps of recognized experts, and you will have received a vivid and complete expression.

"Everything except the three R's, the arts, and possibly the mental sciences can be taught in this way—physiology, chemistry, biology, botany, physics, and history in all its branches."

Seven years ago this man who talks thus glibly of "revolutions" was an actor out of work, and a director without a prospect. He was walking along Broadway as are thousands of others today.

While now his annual salary is reputed to be $100,000, Griffith at that time was so hard up that he clutched desperately at the chance to earn fifteen a week as extra man in "pictures." His play, "A Fool and a Girl," had been produced out of town by James K. Hackett and had run one consecutive week. He had been an actor in California and once had received as much as $27 a week.

Yet he was just turned thirty, in perfect health, with an excellent education. He walked to the office of a little motion-picture concern, the Kalem Company, and asked its manager, Frank Marion, for a job as extra man. Usually in those days actors changed their names before dropping so low; not Griffith.

He also kept his nerve. Griffith said o Marion: "I believe motion pictures might be dignified and put on a par with the spoken drama. In my opinion you've got to change your whole style of acting. At present it's only horseplay and not true to life. Moreover, you don't use the right kind of stories and your photography is rotten."

"I'm afraid I can't use you," said Marion, "you seem to be a bit visionary."

The next place Griffith applied was at the office of the Biograph Company, up in the Bronx. He kept his opinions to himself and he got a job at $15 a week. What happened after that is a vital part of the history of moving pictures.

To say that Griffith almost single-handed revolutionized the moving-picture business is only to repeat what many of its students and historians have said before. He introduced naturalistic acting and he began, in a small way, the development of handling crowds that has led to the half-million-dollar picture with 18,000 people and 1,500 horses.

As soon as he had induced the Biograph people to let him direct a picture in his own way his advancement was rapid. Within four years his annual salary with the Biograph was said to be $50,000. The Mutual bought him away only at the published price of $100,000 a year and a percentage of the profits.

Many of the big stars of the pictures, from Mary Pickford to Blanche Sweet, were "discovered" by Griffith, and a large number of the best directors have learned their trade under him.

For seven years he has been leading the motion-picture procession. If he makes one-quarter the "discoveries," "improvements," and "revolutions" in the business in the next seven years that he has in the past seven, then the prophecies of today may be less absurd than was his comment to the manager who first refused him because he was "visionary."

## GROWTH OF THE MOVIES.

What of the movies? There has been a great deal of controversy about them lately from various points of view, artistic, moral, and commercial. A theatre manager has said that they will destroy the drama within ten years. Others have proclaimed that they blunt the artistic sense and retard aesthetic development, and there is a more reasonable complaint that some of the picture shows deal with violence and crime and have a debasing moral tendency. This last complaint, however, is restricted to a kind which is least likely to endure. We do not believe that the newly created movie public has an inherent liking for this kind. As for the complaint on behalf of the theatre, or, to speak more accurately, the drama, it has been made as ineffectually against the motor car and the game of golf. That in the drama which is fit to endure will not be injured by the competition of picture shows. They are not essentially dramatic. The element of suspense, of course, is not absent in a well-contrived movie, but you cannot interpret SOPHOCLES or SHAKESPEARE with the camera, and, after all, we doubt if the real stars of the movies are the actors of the dramatic stage who have been temporarily enticed into them by huge cash payments for their services and the use of their advertised names. The genuine movie actor seems to have been born to that particular calling. It is a new form of art, and let us admit freely that it is art as often as the stage play of this era is art.

But the movie needs no defense. While we are by no means sure that a large proportion of the millions who find so much of their entertainment in the movies and so much of their instruction, too—for the educational side of the pictures is not to be ignored—would go to the theatre if there were no movies, it is true that large numbers of people of good mental equipment derive real enjoyment from the clear, varied, and fascinating succession of pictures on the screen. The tendency to depict the ways of criminals and the perpetration of crimes of violence will pass away. It is characteristic of a habit of the hour, and it has been persisted in, probably, because of the pride the movie makers take in their knowledge that they can do such things so well. It is tolerably certain that the purely spectacular stage play has a strong and effective rival in the more lifelike and beautiful moving picture. That should be a wholesome influence in dramatic reform. What we look for in the drama is acting, not pictures. When the art of color photography is so far advanced that the movies may present scenes of life in all the colors of life the manufactured crime spectacle will not long survive.

March 28, 1915

October 31, 1915

# Text of the President's Address

## Gentlemen of the Congress:

I have called the Congress into extraordinary session because there are serious, very serious, choices of policy to be made, and made immediately, which it was neither right nor constitutionally permissible that I should assume the responsibility of making.

On the 3d of February last I officially laid before you the extraordinary announcement of the Imperial German Government that on and after the first day of February it was its purpose to put aside all restraints of law or of humanity and use its submarines to sink every vessel that sought to approach either the ports of Great Britain and Ireland or the western coasts of Europe or any of the ports controlled by the enemies of Germany within the Mediterranean. That had seemed to be the object of the German submarine warfare earlier in the war, but since April of last year the Imperial Government had somewhat restrained the commanders of its undersea craft, in conformity with its promise, then given to us, that passenger boats should not be sunk and that due warning would be given to all other vessels which its submarines might seek to destroy, when no resistance was offered or escape attempted, and care taken that their crews were given at least a fair chance to save their lives in their open boats. The precautions taken were meagre and haphazard enough, as was proved in distressing instance after instance in the progress of the cruel and unmanly business, but a certain degree of restraint was observed.

The new policy has swept every restriction aside. Vessels of every kind, whatever their flag, their character, their cargo, their destination, their errand, have been ruthlessly sent to the bottom without warning and without thought of help or mercy for those on board, the vessels of friendly neutrals along with those of belligerents. Even hospital ships and ships carrying relief to the sorely bereaved and stricken people of Belgium, though the latter were provided with safe conduct through the proscribed areas by the German Government itself and were distinguished by unmistakable marks of identity, have been sunk with the same reckless lack of compassion or of principle.

I was for a little while unable to believe that such things would in fact be done by any Government that had hitherto subscribed to humane practices of civilized nations. International law had its origin in the attempt to set up some law which would be respected and observed upon the seas, where no nation has right of dominion and where lay the free highways of the world. By painful stage after stage has that law been built up, with meagre enough results, indeed, after all was accomplished that could be accomplished, but always with a clear view, at least, of what the heart and conscience of mankind demanded.

This minimum of right the German Government has swept aside, under the plea of retaliation and necessity and because it had no weapons which it could use at sea except these, which it is impossible to employ, as it is employing them, without throwing to the wind all scruples of humanity or of respect for the understandings that were supposed to underlie the intercourse of the world.

I am not now thinking of the loss of property involved, immense and serious as that is, but only of the wanton and wholesale destruction of the lives of noncombatants, men, women, and children, engaged in pursuits which have always, even in the darkest periods of modern history, been deemed innocent and legitimate. Property can be paid for; the lives of peaceful and innocent people cannot be. The present German submarine warfare against commerce is a warfare against mankind.

It is a war against all nations. American ships have been sunk, American lives taken, in ways which it has stirred us very deeply to learn of, but the ships and people of other neutral and friendly nations have been sunk and overwhelmed in the waters in the same way. There has been no discrimination.

The challenge is to all mankind. Each nation must decide for itself how it will meet it. The choice we make for ourselves must be made with a moderation of counsel and a temperateness of judgment befitting our character and our motives as a nation. We must put excited feeling away. Our motive will not be revenge or the victorious assertion of the physical might of the nation, but only the vindication of right, of human right, of which we are only a single champion.

When I addressed the Congress on the 26th of February last I thought that it would suffice to assert our neutral rights with arms, our right to use the seas against unlawful interference, our right to keep our people safe against unlawful violence. But armed neutrality, it now appears, is impracticable. Because submarines are in effect outlaws, when used as the German submarines have been used against merchant shipping, it is impossible to defend ships against their attacks as the law of nations has assumed that merchantmen would defend themselves against privateers or cruisers, visible craft giving chase upon the open sea. It is common prudence in such circumstances, grim necessity indeed, to endeavor to destroy them before they have shown their own intention. They must be dealt with upon sight, if dealt with at all.

The German Government denies the right of neutrals to use arms at all within the areas of the sea which it has proscribed, even in the defense of rights which no modern publicist has ever before questioned their right to defend. The intimation is conveyed that the armed guards which we have placed on our merchant ships will be treated as beyond the pale of law and subject to be dealt with as pirates would be. Armed neutrality is ineffectual enough at best; in such circumstances and in the face of such pretensions it is worse than ineffectual; it is likely only to produce what it was meant to prevent; it is practically certain to draw us into the war without either the rights or the effectiveness of belligerents. There is one choice we cannot make, we are incapable of making; we will not choose the path of submission and suffer the most sacred rights of our nation and our people to be ignored or violated. The wrongs against which we now array ourselves are no common wrongs; they cut to the very roots of human life.

With a profound sense of the solemn and even tragical character of the step I am taking and of the grave responsibilities which it involves, but in unhesitating obedience to what I deem my constitutional duty, I advise that the Congress declare the recent course of the Imperial German Government to be in fact nothing less than war against the Government and people of the United States; that it formally accept the status of belligerent which has thus been thrust upon it; and that it take immediate steps not only to put the country in a more thorough state of defense, but also to exert all its power and employ all its resources to bring the Government of the German Empire to terms and end the war.

What this will involve is clear. It will involve the utmost practicable co-operation in counsel and action with the Governments now at war with Germany, and, as incident to that, the extension to those Governments of the most liberal financial credits, in order that our resources may so far as possible be added to theirs.

It will involve the organization and mobilization of all the material resources of the country to supply the materials of war and serve the incidental needs of the nation in the most abundant and yet the most economical and efficient way possible.

It will involve the immediate full equipment of the navy in all respects, but particularly in supplying it with the best means of dealing with the enemy's submarines.

It will involve the immediate addition to the armed forces of the United States, already provided for by law in case of war, of at least 500,000 men, who should, in my opinion, be chosen upon the principle of universal liability to service, and also the authorization of subsequent additional increments of equal force so soon as they may be needed and can be handled in training.

It will involve also, of course, the granting of adequate credits to the Government, sustained, I hope, so far as they can equitably be sustained by the present generation, by well conceived taxation.

I say sustained so far as may be equitable by taxation, because it seems to me that it would be most unwise to base the credits, which will now be necessary, entirely on money borrowed. It is our duty, I most respectfully urge, to protect our people, so far as we may, against the very serious hardships and evils which would be likely to arise out of the inflation which would be produced by vast loans.

In carrying out the measures by which these things are to be accomplished we should keep constantly in mind the wisdom of interfering as little as possible in our own preparation and in the equipment of our own military forces with the duty—for it will be a very practical duty—of supplying the nations already at war with Germany with the materials which they can obtain only from us or by our assistance. They are in the field and we should help them in every way to be effective there.

I shall take the liberty of suggesting, through the several executive departments of the Government, for the consideration of your committees, measures for the accomplishment of the several objects I have mentioned. I hope that it will be your pleasure to deal with them as having been framed after very careful thought by the branch of the Government upon whom the responsibility of conducting the war and safeguarding the nation will most directly fall.

While we do these things, these deeply momentous things, let us be very clear, and make very clear to all the world, what our motives and our objects are. My own thought has not been driven from its habitual and normal course by the unhappy events of the last two months, and I do not believe that the thought of the nation had been altered or clouded by them. I have exactly the same things in mind now that I had in mind when I addressed the Senate on the 22d of January last; the same that I had in mind when I addressed the Congress on the 3d of February and on the 26th of February. Our object now, as then, is to vindicate the principles of peace and justice in the life of the world as against selfish and autocratic power, and to set up among the really free and self-governed peoples of the world such a concert of purpose and of action as will henceforth insure the observance of those principles.

Neutrality is no longer feasible or desirable where the peace of the world is involved and the freedom of its peoples, and the menace to that peace and freedom lies in the existence of autocratic Governments, backed by organized force which is controlled wholly by their will, not by the will of their people. We have seen the last of neutrality in such circumstances. We are at the beginning of an age in which it will be insisted that the same standards of conduct and of responsibility for wrong done shall be observed among nations and their Governments that are observed among the individual citizens of civilized States.

We have no quarrel with the German people. We have no feeling toward them but one of sympathy and friendship. It was not upon their impulse that their Government acted in entering this war. It was not with their previous knowledge or approval. It was a war determined upon as wars used to be determined upon in the old, unhappy days, when peoples were nowhere consulted by their rulers and wars were provoked and waged in the interest of dynasties or of little groups of ambitious men who were accustomed to use their fellow men as pawns and tools.

Self-governed nations do not fill their neighbor States with spies or set the course of intrigue to bring about some critical posture of affairs which will give them an opportunity to strike and make conquest. Such designs can be successfully worked out only under cover and where no one has the right to ask questions. Cunningly contrived plans of deception or aggression, carried, it may be, from generation to generation, can be worked out and kept from the light only within the privacy of courts or behind the carefully guarded confidences of a narrow and privileged class. They are happily impossible where public opinion commands and insists upon full information concerning all the nation's affairs.

A steadfast concert for peace can never be maintained except by a partnership of democratic nations. No autocratic Government could be trusted to keep faith within it or observe its covenants. It must be a league of honor, a partnership of opinion. Intrigue would eat its vitals away; the plottings of inner circles who could plan what they would and render account to no one would be a corruption seated at its very heart. Only free peoples can hold their purpose and their honor steady to a common end and prefer the interests of mankind to any narrow interest of their own.

Does not every American feel that assurance has been added to our hope for the future peace of the world by the wonderful and heartening things that have been happening within the last few weeks in Russia? Russia was known by those who knew her best to have been always in fact democratic at heart in all the vital habits of her thought, in all the intimate relationships of her people that spoke their natural instinct, their habitual attitude toward life. The autocracy that crowned the summit of her political structure, long as it had stood and terrible as was the reality of its power, was not in fact Russian in origin, character, or purpose; and now it has been shaken off and the great, generous Russian people have been added, in all their naïve majesty and might, to the forces that are fighting for freedom in the world, for justice, and for peace. Here is a fit partner for a League of Honor.

One of the things that has served to convince us that the Prussian autocracy was not and could never be our friend is that from the very outset of the present war it has filled our unsuspecting communities, and even our offices of government, with spies and set criminal intrigues everywhere afoot against our national unity of counsel, our peace within and without, our industries and our commerce. Indeed, it is now evident that its spies were here even before the war began; and it is unhappily not a matter of conjecture, but a fact proved in our courts of justice, that the intrigues which have more than once come perilously near to disturbing the peace and dislocating the industries of the country, have been carried on at the instigation, with the support, and even under the personal direction of official agents of the Imperial Government, accredited to the Government of the United States.

Even in checking these things and trying to extirpate them we have sought to put the most generous interpretation possible upon them because we knew that their source lay, not in any hostile feeling or purpose of the German people toward us, (who were, no doubt, as ignorant of them as we ourselves were,) but only in the selfish designs of a Government that did what it pleased and told its people nothing. But they have played their part in serving to convince us at last that that Government entertains no real friendship for us, and means to act against our peace and security at its convenience. That it means to stir up enemies against us at our very doors the intercepted note to the German Minister at Mexico City is eloquent evidence.

We are accepting this challenge of hostile purpose because we know that in such a Government, following such methods, we can never have a friend; and that in the presence of its organized power, always lying in wait to accomplish we know not what purpose, can be no assured security for the democratic Governments of the world.. We are now about to accept the gauge of battle with this natural foe to liberty and shall, if necessary, spend the whole force of the nation to check and nullify its pretensions and its power. We are glad, now that we see the facts with no veil of false pretense about them, to fight thus for the ultimate peace of the world and for the liberation of its peoples, the German peoples included; for the rights of nations, great and small, and the privilege of men everywhere to choose their way of life and of obedience.

The world must be made safe for democracy. Its peace must be planted upon the tested foundations of political liberty. We have no selfish ends to serve. We desire no conquest, no dominion. We seek no indemnities for ourselves, no material compensation for the sacrifices we shall freely make. We are but one of the champions of the rights of mankind. We shall be satisfied when those rights have been made as secure as the faith and the freedom of nations can make them.

Just because we fight without rancor and without selfish object, seeking nothing for ourselves but what we shall wish to share with all free peoples, we shall, I feel confident, conduct our operations as belligerents without passion and ourselves observe with proud punctilio the principles of right and of fair play we profess to be fighting for.

I have said nothing of the Governments allied with the Imperial Government of Germany because they have not made war upon us or challenged us to defend our right and our honor. The Austro-Hungarian Government has, indeed, avowed its unqualified indorsement and acceptance of the reckless and lawless submarine warfare, adopted now without disguise by the Imperial German Government, and it has therefore not been possible for this Government to receive Count Tarnowski, the Ambassador recently accredited to this Government by the Imperial and Royal Government of Austria-Hungary; but that Government has not actually engaged in warfare against citizens of the United States on the seas, and I take the liberty, for the present at least, of postponing a discussion of our relations with the authorities at Vienna. We enter this war only where we are clearly forced into it because there are no other means of defending our right.

It will be all the easier for us to conduct ourselves as belligerents in a high spirit of right and fairness because we act without animus, not with enmity toward a people or with the desire to bring any injury or disadvantage upon them, but only in armed opposition to an irresponsible Government which has thrown aside all considerations of humanity and of right and is running amuck.

We are, let me say again, the sincere friends of the German people, and shall desire nothing so much as the early re-establishment of intimate relations of mutual advantage between us, however hard it may be for them for the time being to believe that this is spoken from our hearts. We have borne with their present Government through all these bitter months because of that friendship, exercising a patience and forbearance which would otherwise have been impossible

We shall happily still have an opportunity to prove that friendship in our daily attitude and actions toward the millions of men and women of German birth and native sympathy who live among us and share our life, and we shall be proud to prove it toward all who are in fact loyal to their neighbors and to the Government in the hour of test. They are most of them as true and loyal Americans as if they had never known any other fealty or allegiance. They will be prompt to stand with us in rebuking and restraining the few who may be of a different mind and purpose. If there should be disloyalty, it will be dealt with with a firm hand of stern repression; but, if it lifts its head at all, it will lift it only here and there and without countenance except from a lawless and malignant few.

It is a distressing and oppressive duty, gentlemen of the Congress, which I have performed in thus addressing you. There are, it may be, many months of fiery trial and sacrifice ahead of us. It is a fearful thing to lead this great, peaceful people into war, into the most terrible and disastrous of all wars, civilization itself seeming to be in the balance.

But the right is more precious than peace, and we shall fight for the things which we have always carried nearest our hearts—for democracy, for the right of those who submit to authority to have a voice in their own Governments, for the rights and liberties of small nations, for a universal dominion of right by such a concert of free peoples as shall bring peace and safety to all nations and make the world itself at last free.

To such a task we can dedicate our lives and our fortunes, everything that we are and everything that we have, with the pride of those who know that the day has come when America is privileged to spend her blood and her might for the principles that gave her birth and happiness and the peace which she has treasured.

God helping her, she can do no other.

# PLOTTERS HERE AGAINST DRAFT UNDER WATCH

## Federal Authorities Discover the Trail of Anarchist Agitators Against Conscription.

## EMMA GOLDMAN IS ACTIVE

## 15,000 Letters Sent Assailing "Patriotic Claptrap" Meant to "Prussianize America."

## GREGORY ORDERS ACTION

### Instructs Attorneys and Marshals to Seize and Prosecute Offenders.

The activities of various organizations and individuals in New York City opposed to the enforcement of the Selective Draft act are under investigation by the Federal and local authorities, and any move to interfere with the enforcement of the law before, on or after next Tuesday will be dealt with promptly, according to statements made last night.

Press dispatches yesterday continued to show that the anti-draft propaganda was nation-wide in extent. Injunction proceedings against the draft registration law were begun in Kansas City on the ground that it violated the State Constitution. From Chicago it was reported that an anti-conscription conspiracy had been found in the Central West, and a legal fight against the Conscription act was renewed in California.

One of the organizations in this city which is actively at work to nullify the selective draft act, whose members say that they are working "within the law," is called the No-Conscription League, at the head of which are various persons more or less well known in anarchistic and I. W. W. circles. The office of the league is at 20 East 125th Street, where it was said yesterday that Emma Goldman, Leonard Abbott, and others with similar beliefs were prominent in its management.

Another organization opposed to the draft, it is asserted, represents thousands of college students in all parts of the country, a great many of whom, it is declared, will resist conscription and will refuse to register on Tuesday. The Anti-Militarist League is another organization, which, it was said at the 125th Street headquarters last night, was in sympathy with the movement, the participants in which, it was said, were "men who will be shot before they will shoot."

It was said at the No-Conscription League offices that within the past few days at least 100,000 copies of a pamphlet entitled "No Conscription," had been mailed to all parts of the country. This pamphlet urges those to whom it is sent to resist conscription and to organize protest meetings.

### "Patriotic Claptrap."

A letter urging anti-war agitation, it was said, also had been mailed to more than 15,000 persons. Both the pamphlet and the letter display a picture of a workingman standing before a cannon tearing in pieces a paper on which is printed the word "Conscription." The letter, of which 15,000 copies have been mailed, reads in part as follows:

We are sure that you are interested in the anti-war agitation. You cannot fail to realize that the patriotic claptrap which is now propagated on such a huge scale by the press, the pulpit, and the authorities only represents a desperate effort to blind the people to the real issues confronting them. The main issue now is the Prussianizing of America.

Already America has demonstrated its autocratic tendencies in passing the conscription bill without making even the slightest proviso for conscientious objectors to human slaughter. There are thousands of men who will not under any circumstances allow themselves to be conscripted. First, they consider all wars a fight between thieves who are too cowardly to do their own fighting, hence force the masses to do the cruel thing for them. Secondly, they will not be conscripted because they refuse to be coerced into taking human life at the behest of their masters. Something must be done to sustain these men to whom the ideal of liberty and human solidarity is not a mere phrase, but a vital, living fact.

With that in view, we have organized the No-Conscription League. Its first public activity took place on Friday evening, May 18—a mass meeting attended by 8,000 men and women who pledged their decision not to register or to be conscripted into killing. It was an inspiring demonstration and so tremendous in its scope that all the dailies were stirred from their usual attitude of silence.

More than any other Government, perhaps, the Washington authorities are very sensitive to publicity and criticism, especially on the part of those who can reach large sections of the people both here and abroad. The American Government cannot afford to have the world know that, while it pretends to be interested in democracy and to fight against Prussianism in Germany, it is at the same time Prussianizing America. We, therefore, feel that the agitation of the league, energetically started in New York and undoubtedly spreading over the whole country, will create sufficient sentiment to morally compel the authorities to recognize conscientious objectors.

### Emma Goldman Prophesies.

When asked if the No-Conscription League was in a position to estimate the number of men in this city between the ages of 21 and 31 years, who would refuse to register on Tuesday Emma Goldman said yesterday that she could state that the number would certainly be more than 5,000 and probably as high as 10,000.

"Are you advising men of the ages affected by the draft act not to register?" she was asked.

"No, we are not doing that. What we are doing is to make the issue plain to them and then leave it to them to act on their own initiative. But we will stand behind all who refuse to register and will see to it that they get all legal protection and that their rights in this matter are maintained."

Commissioner of Elections Edward F. Boyle, who is in charge of the registration in New York City, said yesterday that every precaution had been taken to see to it that the registration of the 600,000 New Yorkers affected by the selective draft law should not be interfered with.

"Despite a lot of talk on the part of irresponsible persons and others," Commissioner Boyle said, "I do not anticipate any trouble next Tuesday. But if there is any it will be promptly and efficiently disposed of by the police."

### Federal Authorities Prepared.

It was announced at the Federal Building yesterday that the Grand Jury for the Southern District of New York would convene on Monday prepared to take up any violations of the President's selective draft proclamation.

"We are not going to tolerate any monkey business in this district," said Assistant United States District Attorney John C. Knox, "and will be ready to handle any and all troublemakers who try to interfere with the proper carrying into effect of the law. Any man or woman who tries to dissuade any man from registering will find accommodations in jail."

Chief Magistrate William McAdoo sent a letter yesterday to the City Magistrates and employes of the Magistrates' Courts requesting that the courts be kept open all day on Tuesday.

"In view of the great interests at stake," wrote the Chief Magistrate, "both to New York City and the nation on registration day, June 5, I beg to suggest to each of the presiding Magistrates in the District Courts on that day that the same be kept open, with a reasonable recess, from 8 A. M. to 6 P. M."

Maurice Cohen, 22 years old, a salesman, of 822 Eastern Parkway, Brooklyn, was arrested on a subway train yesterday afternoon by Benjamin W. MacLaren, a traveling salesman, of 130 Fifth Avenue. Roselle, N. J., after he had given MacLaren a circular announcing a mass meeting called "A Conference of Peace Terms," to be held in Madison Square Garden tomorrow night. He was arraigned in the Men's Night Court last night on a charge of disorderly conduct. Magistrate Simms imposed a penalty of $25 fine or ten days in the City Prison.

The formal charge against Cohen was disorderly conduct for annoying Mr. MacLaren by explaining to him that the mass meeting announced in the circular was a meeting against conscription. MacLaren testified that he took Cohen to task for distributing the circulars and that two men attacked him.

### PATRIOTS' DAY.

The outlook for Registration Day is encouraging. The Government expects a prompt and loyal response to its summons. Care will be taken in all parts of the country to guard against possible interference with the registration by weak-minded pacifists and crafty agents of the enemy. In this city the precautions will be thorough. About 600,000 registrations are expected here, and there are more than 2,000 registering stations. Of the 600,000 not more than 30,000 will be drafted in the national army within a year or more. There will probably be fewer than 15,000 of them in the first increment. It is well for every man to remember that positive proof of his exemption from military service does not render him exempt from registration. All men born between June 6, 1886, and June 5, 1896, inclusive, must register, whether they are citizens or aliens.

The spirit of this day was aptly expressed yesterday by FRANKLIN K. LANE, Secretary of the Interior, in a speech delivered at Washington. As an appeal to the reason of the comparatively few who have not yet comprehended the call of the nation to arms, Secretary LANE answered again that question so often asked, so often satisfactorily answered, Why are we at war? "Ours," he said, "is a war "of self-defense. * * * We could "not keep out. * * * It is a war "to save America, to preserve self-"respect, to justify our right to live "as we have lived, not as some one "else wishes us to live. In the name "of Freedom we challenge with ships "and men, money, and an undaunted "spirit that word 'Verboten' which "Germany has written upon the sea "and land."

For self-defense, to save America, to preserve our national self-respect, 10,000,000 Americans will register their names today, prepared to respond hereafter to any call for service the nation may make. They have already volunteered. The whole nation has volunteered. "Feudalism," says Mr. LANE, "is making its last stand against democracy." We are resolved to overthrow feudalism for all time.

May 30, 1917

June 5, 1917

## DEMOCRACY LIMITED.

At first one might suppose that the militant suffragists have suffered a sad relapse from immutable principle in the interest of momentary expediency. Having failed to annoy the President into forcing the passage of the Federal woman suffrage amendment, they now appeal to the people; those ladies who suffered for their convictions in Oceoquan jail are to tour the country on a train known to the profane as the Prison Special, to the elect as the Democracy Limited, " to make it clear to the people that " the Administration is responsible for " the fact that American women are " forced to endure imprisonment in " their effort to secure the passage of " the amendment."

Of course, the women endured imprisonment—if that verb may be applied to an action which savored much of passionate desire for a not too onerous martyrdom—because they tried to make the President too uncomfortable to work at a time when the nation was at war. At this assault at once upon the majesty and the welfare of the United States public sentiment rose to the President's relief, and it can hardly be doubted that the militants lost more than they gained. But their new method does not mean the abandonment of terrorism; it is only a change in objective. The militants will go from State to State stirring up trouble for recalcitrant Senators; eventually they may be able to bulldoze enough of them to pass the amendment.

It is quite in the new theory of government which has lately been demonstrated with such distinction by the Anti-Saloon League. The Democracy Limited goes forth to do its work on a limited democracy, a democracy modified by terrorism. State rights have lately been abridged in order to make the North conform to the standards necessary in the South, and the militant suffragists, observing the triumph of the militant prohibitionists, can hardly be blamed for seeing some hope that a still further abridgment may be effected to make the South follow the lead of the North. The secret of the State has been divulged—that the nation can be dominated by well-paid flying squadrons of agitators. Nobody is likely to forget this

fact for some years to come, for everybody will use the method. It is announced that in the cultural centre of Syracuse University there has been born the organization which will conduct the crusade for the anti-tobacco amendment to the Constitution. The W. C. T. U. is actively behind it, the Y. M. C. A., though it has taken down the "No Smoking" signs, is furnishing co-operation by its propaganda on the dire effects of nicotine, which ought to make considerable impression on the returning soldiers. Under the circumstances, the passage of the woman suffrage amendment, the anti-tobacco amendment, or any other amendment is only a question of the persistence, the affluence, and the implacability of its supporters.

January 28, 1919

# FOR ACTION ON RACE RIOT PERIL

## Radical Propaganda Among Negroes Growing, and Increase of Mob Violence Set Out in Senate Brief for Federal Inquiry

EVEN though recurring race riots have made the public aware that the negro problem has entered upon a new and dangerous phase, only those in touch with the inner forces that are playing in ignorance, prejudice, and passion, realize how great this menace is. Bloodshed on a scale amounting to local insurrection at least will be threatened in more than one section where large white and black populations face each other unless some program of conciliation is adopted to forestall influences that are now working to drive a wedge of bitterness and hatred between the two races.

So far this problem, in some respects the most grave now facing the country, has been allowed to drift. The States have done nothing. The Federal Government has done nothing. The only move made at Washington is the introduction by Senator Charles Curtis of Kansas of a resolution calling for the appointment of a subcommittee of the Senate Committee on Judiciary to investigate recent riots and lynchings and to report what remedies should be employed to prevent their recurrence. Senator Curtis said in Washington the other day that information in his possession made it clear that there should be no delay in grappling the problem and that he would press for action. A brief containing new information as to the extent of race clashes which he will lay before the committee accompanies this article. It shows that since the beginning of the year there have been since Jan. 1, 1919, thirty-eight race riots and clashes in cities and other communities in various parts of the country. Senator Curtis is uncertain whether Congress has the authority to pass a law against riots and lynchings; this may be a question for action by the States, but he is certain that, after an investigation has laid bare the

causes of the growing antagonism between white and black, recommendations can be made that will show the urgent need of a policy of organized conciliation, backed by the better elements in each race, in every community wherever whites and blacks confront each other in considerable numbers.

#### The War's Responsibility.

Out of the war has come a new negro problem—that, observers agree, is the first fact to be recognized in taking up the question. Before the war negro leaders, still under the influence of Booker Washington, were in the main for a policy of conciliation. For all the scattered injustice and oppression that the negro still suffered the majority of the negro leaders still held in clear prospective the great benefits granted the negro race in this country, the fact that their freedom had been won by the sacrifice of an immense number of white men's lives, that in no other country in the world where a large colored population lived in contact with the white race did the principle of the laws confer equal recognition to the black man. In a word, there was still active among the negro leaders a sense of appreciation tracing back to the civil war period. Whenever friction threatened, leaders of this type, believing that by forbearance and thrift on the part of the black man a fair and harmonious adjustment of the two races would be attained, steadily argued conciliatory methods. Some of these leaders remain, but they are growing fewer. The assertion is made in explanation that these moderate leaders have been without the support of white leaders. Under heavy attack of radicals and militants, charged with being at heart the betrayers of the negro race, they have been unable, according to this attempted elucidation of the situation, to point to any organized co-operation on the part of the whites to see, for example, that police officers

and courts dealt justly with the negro, to remove unjust treatment of the negro wherever found. The other side proclaims that there is no evidence that the great majority of the white men in this country, who as the result of a civil war had bestowed on the black man opportunities far in advance of those he had in any other part of the white man's world, were still the friend of the negro. They ask proof that forbearance, not militancy, is the course to follow.

#### Reds Inflaming Blacks.

Every week the militant leaders gain more headway. They may be divided into general classes. One consists of radicals and revolutionaries. They are spreading Bolshevist propaganda. It is reported that they are winning many recruits among the colored race. When the ignorance that exists among negroes in many sections of the country is taken into consideration the danger of inflaming them by revolutionary doctrine may be apprehended. It is held that there is no element in this country so susceptible to organized propaganda of this kind as the less informed class of negroes. The other class of militant leaders confine their agitation to a fight against all forms of color discrimination. They are for a program of uncompromising protest, " to fight and to continue to fight for citizenship rights and full democratic privileges." The former leadership of Booker Washington is derided. A negro paper of wide circulation said in a recent editorial: " * * * the late Booker T. Washington was selected by a group of Southern and Northern philanthropists and business men who sympathized with them to teach the negro to know his place. * * * Under the Frederick Douglass propaganda we gained freedom and citizenship. Under the Booker Washington propaganda we lost our citizenship in the Southland and saw the spread of mob violence all over the country. The

thing to do is to get back to the teachings of Frederick Douglass, * * * "

W. E. B. Du Bois, a foremost leader in this class of militants, says in the leading editorial in the current issue of his magazine, The Crisis:

" We have cast off on the voyage which will lead to freedom or to death. For three centuries we have suffered and cowered. No race ever gave passive submission to evil longer, more piteous trial. Today we raise the terrible weapon of self-defense. When the murderer comes, he shall no longer strike us in the back. When the armed lynchers gather, we too must gather armed. When the mob moves, we propose to meet it with bricks and clubs and guns."

There is no doubt that owing to recent experiences many negroes have provided themselves with arms, and that unless Governmental efforts, based on some carefully considered policy, are made to stop the riots and race clashes and to remove their causes, that outbreaks of far greater extent than any of those that have yet occurred may take place. The one approach to a betterment of conditions is asserted to be through those negro leaders who are opposed to militant methods, but it is pointed out, while they preach co-operation, they insist also that the only solution is " full justice, manhood rights and full opportunities for the negro American."

#### Industrial Clashes.

New industrial contacts between white and negro workers aggravate the problem. Three weeks before the riot last week in Omaha investigators from Washington reported that a clash was imminent owing to ill-feeling between white and black workers in the stockyards. It is estimated that during the war period 500,000 negro workers migrated from the South to the North. In whatever Northern city they have settled in numbers there is the menace of racial clash, and consequently the immediate need of some agency of conciliation, in which both whites and negroes shall be represented, as a medium for clearing those misunderstandings that spring from rampant prejudice. An illustration of changes in Northern industrial centres is provided by the case of Detroit. In 1914 there were probably not 1,000 negroes in that city. At present it is estimated there are between 12,000 and 15,000 engaged in the automobile industry there. In the steel plants of Pittsburgh the number of negro workers has increased 100 per cent in some of the plants. In New York City many negro girls are now at work in the cheaper branches of the garment trade. This is one of the many industries in the North in which they have won or are seeking to win a place.

On this phase of the problem, Dr. George E. Haynes, a leading negro educator, and now Director of Negro Economics of the Department of Labor, recommends:

"To be concrete, the first step in this direction seems to be for local and national officials to call into conference and counsel the liberal-minded citizens of both races and with them to map out some plan to guarantee greater protection, justice, and opportunity to negroes that will gain the support of law-abiding citizens of both races. Co-operative local committees on matters involving race relations, both under private and governmental auspices, especially during the war, have demonstrated that far-reaching practical results can be secured by such efforts."

The brief on which the projected investigation of the race problem by the Senate Committee on Judiciary will be based follows, the more detailed information being summarized at several points. It is headed: "Why Congress Should Investigate Race Riots and Lynchings," and is divided into five heads:

### I. The Facts—1919.

A. Race riots:

Washington, D. C.: "Nation's Capital at Mercy of the Mob"—headline on Page 1 of Washington Post Tuesday, July 22, 1919. Rioting in the main streets of national capital was unchecked during four nights from Saturday, July 19, until Wednesday, July 23. Six persons were killed outright, 50 severely wounded, and a hundred or more less seriously wounded.

Chicago, Ill.: At least 36 persons were killed outright, by official report, in race rioting which lasted from Sunday, July 27, to Friday, Aug. 1. According to unofficial reports, the number killed was much larger. Houses were wrecked and burned, mobs roamed the streets, and it was necessary to put seven regiments of State militia under arms.

Knoxville, Tenn.: On Aug. 30 a mob of white persons stormed the Knox County Jail, firing on officers of the law, liberating 16 white prisoners, of whom several were convicted murderers; looting the house of the Sheriff, stealing stocks of confiscated whisky. The mob then wrecked and looted shops and invaded the colored district. At least seven persons were killed and twenty or more injured.

Longview, Texas: Four or more men were killed outright in a riot on the night of July 10, when a mob of white men invaded the negro residence district, shooting and burning houses.

Norfolk, Va.: Receptions of the home-coming negro troops had to be suspended because of riots July 21, in which six persons were shot, necessitating the calling out of the marines and sailors to assist the police.

Philadelphia, Penn.: A riot call was sent to all West Philadelphia stations July 7; eight arrests were made and one man was taken to a hospital in consequence of a race riot at a carnival.

Charleston, S. C.: One or more men were killed and scores were shot or beaten in a race riot led by United States sailors May 10; city placed under martial law.

Bisbee, Ariz.: Clashes occurred on July 3 between local police and members of the 10th United States Cavalry, (colored.) Five persons were shot.

There were in addition race clashes in the following cities:

Tuscaloosa, Ala., July 9.
Hobson City, Ala., July 26.
New London, Conn., June 13.
Sylvester, Ga., May 10; one reported killed.
Putnam County, Ga., May 29.
Mullen, Ga., April 15; seven reported killed.
Blakely, Ga., Feb. 8; four reported killed.
Dublin, Ga., July 6; two reported killed.
Ocmulgee, Ga., Aug. 29; one reported killed.
Bloomington, Ill., July 31.
New Orleans, La., July 23.
Annapolis, Md., June 27.
Baltimore, Md., July 11.
Monticello, Miss., May 31.
Macon, Miss., June 27.
Hattiesburg, Miss., Aug. 4.
New York City, N. Y., Aug. 21.
Syracuse, N. Y., July 31.
Coatesville, Penn., July 8.
Philadelphia, Penn., July 31.
Scranton, Penn., July 5.
Darby, Penn., July 23.
Newberry, S. C., July 28.
Bedford County, Tenn., Jan. 22.
Memphis, Tenn.; one killed.
Memphis, Tenn., June 13.
Port Arthur, Texas, July 15.
Texarkana, Texas, Aug. 6.
Morgan County, W. Va., April 10.

B. Lynchings:

Forty-three negroes, four white men lynched from Jan. 1 to Sept. 14.

Eight negroes burned at the stake, one of the burnings extensively announced beforehand in newspapers of Louisiana and Mississippi. Copies of these papers are filed as exhibits with the brief. Of the number sixteen were hanged. Others were shot. One was cut to pieces.

#### 1889-1918.

Two thousand four hundred and seventy-two colored men, 50 colored women, 691 white men and 11 white women lynched. Less than 24 per cent. of these lynchings were ascribed to be on account of attacks on women.

#### 1918.

Five negro women, 58 negro men and 4 white men lynched. No member of any mob was convicted. In only two cases were trials held.

### II. The Failure of the States.

The States have proven themselves unable or unwilling to stop lynchings, as the figures show. Even attempts to prosecute are so rare as to be exceptional. Before the burning at the stake of John Hartfield, at Ellisville, Miss., June 26, 1919, Governor Bilbo of Mississippi said:

"I am utterly powerless. The State has no troops, and if the civil authorities at Ellisville are helpless, the State's are equally so. Furthermore, excitement is at such a high pitch throughout South Mississippi that any armed attempt to interfere with the mob would doubtless result in the death of hundreds of persons. The negro has confessed, says he is ready to die, and nobody can keep the inevitable from happening."

The Houston Post, Texas, in a widely quoted editorial, said:

"The Post believes * * * that the half-century old lynching problem is about to pass from the jurisdiction of State authority into the domain of Federal action. Surely, in the light of half a century of lynchings, in which the victims have been numbered by the thousands, the failure of the States must be confessed."

### III. A National Problem.

Lynching and mob violence have become a national problem. President Wilson was aroused by the danger of mob violence to make a statement July 26, 1918, in which he called the subject one which "vitally affects the honor of the nation, and the very character and integrity of our institutions. * * * I say plainly that every American who takes part in the action of a mob or gives any sort of countenance to it is no true son of this great democracy, but is its betrayer, and does more to discredit her by that single disloyalty to her standards of law and right than the words of her statesmen or sacrifices of her heroic soldiers in the trenches can do to make a suffering people believe in her, their savior."

The extension of lynching to Northern States with white men as victims shows it is idle to suppose murder can be confined to one section of the country or to one race.

#### IV. Consequences of Lynching.

1. Race riots: Persistence of unpunished lynchings of negroes fosters lawlessness among white men imbued with the mob spirit, and creates a spirit of bitterness among negroes. In such a state of public mind a trivial incident can precipitate a riot.

2. Industrial: Property values and productivity are lessened and business is disturbed in districts from which people are forced to migrate to escape mob violence.

3. Psychological: Brutalization of men, women, and children who take part in and witness hangings, burnings at stake, and the horrors of lynchings. Dr. A. A. Brill, neurologist, assistant Professor of Psychiatry at the Post Graduate Medical School, says:

"The torture which is an accompaniment of modern lynchings shows that it is an act of perversion only found in those suffering from extreme forms of sexual perversion." Of course, not all lynchings are conducted in that way, but it is not uncommon to read accounts telling that the victim was tortured with hot irons, that his eyes were burned out, and that other monstrous cruelties were inflicted upon him. Such bestiality can be recognized only as a form of perversion. Lynching is a distinct menace to the community. It allows primitive brutality to assert itself and thus destroys the strongest fabric of civilization. Any one taking part in or witnessing a lynching cannot remain a civilized person."

4. Political: The position of the United States before the world is impaired by its failure to accord protection and trial by law to its own citizens within its own borders.

### V. The Danger.

1. Disregard of law and legal process will inevitably lead to more and more frequent clashes and bloody encounters between white men and negroes and a condition of potential race war in many cities of the United States.

2. Unchecked mob violence creates hatred and intolerance, making impossible free and dispassionate discussion not only of race problems, but questions on which races and sections differ.

## 82 LYNCHED IN 1919.

### Tuskegee Statistics Show an Increase of 18 Over 1918.

TUSKEGEE, Ala., Dec. 31.—Eighty-two persons were lynched in the United States during the year, an increase of eighteen over 1918, the Department of Records and Research of Tuskegee University announced tonight through its annual report. Seventy-five of those who met death at the hands of mobs were negroes, and seven were whites. One negro woman was included in the list.

Seventy-seven of the lynchings were in the South and five in the North and West.

# HUNDREDS OF REDS ON SOVIET 'ARK' SAIL SOON FOR RUSSIA

**United States Transport Will Start Within Ten Days with Load of Anarchists.**

## GOLDMAN GOES WITH THEM

**Withdraws Her Appeal, Saying She Prefers Jail or Deportation to Ellis Island.**

## RED OFFICIAL MET BULLITT

"Secretary" of Soviet Here Saw Him in State Department Before Bullitt Went to Lenin.

A United States transport will leave this port within ten days for Russia carrying several hundred Russian Reds held for deportation. Emma Goldman and Alexander Berkman will be among them. Emma Goldman, whose appeal against deportation is before the United States Supreme Court, withdrew her appeal yesterday on hearing from her lawyer that the "Soviet Ark" would start within less than two weeks with most of the leaders of the Russian Red movement in this country.

While Harry Weinberger, the lawyer for Emma Goldman and Berkman, was carrying the news of the "Red transport" from Commissioner General of Immigration Anthony J. Caminetti at Washington to the Ellis Island Soviet, the Secretary of the Soviet "Embassy" here was testifying that he had had frequent conferences with William C. Bullitt before that young diplomat made his visit to Soviet Russia on behalf of President Wilson.

Testimony also was introduced, although denied by Ludwig C. A. K. Martens, the Soviet representative, to show that the Soviet Bureau had aided the formation of the Communist Party in this country and had sought to aid that revolutionary organization in establishing relations with the Bolshevist Government.

### Goldman Withdraws Appeal

Mr. Weinberger sent notice last night to the office of the Attorney General at Washington, saying that Emma Goldman wished to withdraw her appeal. According to Mr. Weinberger, he was informed by Mr. Caminetti and an official of the Department of Labor that the Government had decided to send the transport within ten days, but he could not learn to what port it was to go. Mr. Weinberger said that he thought Kronstadt was its destination, thus landing them in Soviet territory, by an agreement with the Soviet Government. He said that he was not sure of this, and added that he had been informed that the question of finding a port and making the delivery of the Reds to Soviet territory was being handled by the State Department. The plan urged by Congressman Isaac Siegel of New York has been that of sending a ship loaded with all Russians held for deportation to Libau to be forwarded by the Letts, at the request of this Government, to Soviet territory.

There are ninety Russian anarchists held on Ellis Island for deportation and several hundred others held for deportation in other parts of the country, some of whom are now on their way to this port.

The United States Supreme Court held that Berkman had no ground for his appeal from the order of deportation, but postponed decision in the case of Emma Goldman, because of her plea that she had been illegally deprived of her citizenship and could not properly be sent away as an alien.

### Prefers Jail to Ellis Island.

In his letter to the Attorney General, however, Mr. Weinberger said:

"Miss Goldman instructs me to inform you that she desires to withdraw her application for writ of error, or appeal, stay and release on bail. This is especially her decision, for if the Supreme Court of the United States should allow the appeal, but refuse bail pending argument on or decision of the appeal, jail or deportation would be preferable to continued custody on Ellis Island without proper opportunity for exercise, and where the censor of the Department of Justice comes only once or twice a week to examine and allow mail to pass back and forth and visitors are only seen through a wire screen."

He gave as a further reason for withdrawing the appeal that Miss Goldman was unwilling to put her friends to the expense involved in an appeal. Although the original order of deportation was made in her case several months ago, Miss Goldman made a statement through her lawyer deploring the shortness of the time allowed to her to wind up her affairs in this country.

"I did not expect," she said, "that I would be given time to arrange my affairs, as the sudden calling for my deportation shows the hysteria of the Government officials, which has communicated itself to the courts, and to print the tremendous record of books and exhibits in the case which the Government introduced would drain my friends who have so nobly stood by me and would be of little avail, in my opinion, as I have no faith in the courts.

"Having lived thirty-four years in this country, and having many business and personal affairs to arrange, yet I do not get time to settle any of them. I expect while in Soviet Russia to shortly read of American-born citizens being deported from America to the Island of Guam or some other colonial possession of America, despite the Constitution, which guarantees free speech and a free press."

### Red Secretary Met Bullitt.

Santeri Nuorteva, the Secretary of the Soviet "Embassy," admitted to the Lusk committee that he had had several conferences with William C. Bullitt with regard to Russian affairs. He also admitted having had some correspondence with Bullitt after Bullitt returned from his semi-official mission to Russia with Lincoln Steffens and others, complaining that President Wilson had neglected him, Lloyd George had deceived him, and Secretary Lansing had, in a private and confidential correspondence, condemned the League of Nations.

"Are you acquainted with William C. Bullitt?" asked Deputy Attorney General Samuel A. Berger.

"Yes. I met him in March, 1918, in the State Department at Washington."

"Have you had any correspondence with him since that time?"

"Yes. I have been in correspondence with him in the same manner that I have been in correspondence with many people. I have put him on our mailing list. There may have been some personal correspondence."

"Did you have any correspondence with him before he started on his trip to Russia?"

"I had several conferences with him in the Spring of 1918, but I did not see him immediately before he went to Russia. He was in Paris before he went to Russia."

"Are you personally acquainted with Lincoln Steffens?"

"Yes, I met him twice or thrice."

Mr. Nuorteva said that the Soviet Bureau had received through its secret messengers a letter containing an account of the arrival of the Bullitt Mission, and its negotiations with the Lenin Government which led to the proposals for peace between Soviet Russia and the Allies, which were carried by Bullitt to Paris.

### Lenin Recognized Bullitt.

Chairman Martin asked the witness if the letters from Russia showed that the Lenin Government had accepted the Bullitt Mission as an official body from the United States Government. Secretary Nuorteva replied that it had so accepted them.

"Have you any knowledge of who suggested the names of those who served on the Bullitt Mission?" asked Mr. Berger.

"No, sir, I have no inside information on that."

Mr. Berger was asked later what the object of this question was, and he replied that he sought to confirm through the witness information which he had received from other sources as to the origin of the Bullitt-Steffens visit to Soviet Russia.

Nathan Chabrow was the emissary of the Communist Party of this country to Soviet Russia, who was aided by the Soviet Bureau here, according to John Chabrow, his brother, who appeared before the Lusk Committee yesterday. Chabrow said that his brother failed to get through to Russia and was stranded in Stockholm without funds. After hearing of his brother's predicament, he said that he went to Martens in August of this year, and that Martens promised to send cablegrams to Soviet representatives which would smooth the way for his brother.

A letter was introduced from Nathan Chabrow, thanking his brother, saying that he had received $100 from the Communist Party here and other money and was getting along fine. He also acknowledged receipt of copies of the Revolutionary Age and the platform of the Mexican Communist Party. He said that the Mexican Communist Party was formed in Mexico City, and that its literature was handled in this city at the Communist headquarters at 43 West Twenty-ninth Street.

Martens, the Soviet representative, testified that he knew nothing about this matter, and had not helped Chabrow in any manner.

### Denies Attacking Government.

Nuorteva made denials in answer to questions intended to discover whether he had made speeches in Ohio or Pennsylvania during the steel strike. He admitted that in addresses he had attacked the capitalists of Finland and Russia, but he denied that in this country he had made any attacks on the United States Government. He said that the letters of instruction which they had received from Russia directed them to use their utmost efforts to procure the lifting of the blockade and the resumption of trade relations, but said the Lenin Government also instructed the Soviet Bureau to refrain absolutely from taking part in radical movements in this country or interfering in American affairs. He admitted that he had done his utmost to make people believe that the present Russian Government was a good Government and ought to be recognized.

Nuorteva declined to answer questions relating to the whereabouts of the correspondence with Russia or the names of messengers carrying it, contending that his "diplomatic position" protected him in such a stand. He was asked if he and Martens had not recently been discussing their action of some weeks ago in sending this correspondence out of the jurisdiction. He replied:

"No, sir, your dictaphone must have worked wrong."

Archibald E. Stevenson and Mr. Berger, the lawyers for the committee, were instructed to go ahead with proceedings for contempt against Martens, Nuorteva and Dr. Michael Mislig, all of whom have declined to give information to the committee. Mr. Berger said that they would probably go to the Supreme Court on Monday to ask for the punishment of these men for contempt. It was admitted, however, that Martens and Nuorteva, because of their claim of diplomatic immunity, might be able to carry the appeal in the contempt proceedings as far as the United States Supreme Court, possibly prolonging the contempt proceedings beyond the life of the legislative committee. The committee adjourned to meet next Thursday morning at the City Hall.

# J. P. MORGAN'S LIFE ONE OF TRIUMPHS

## Born to Wealth, Yet Made His Own Career and Became Master of Finance.

## HELPED IN '95 BOND ISSUE

## Climax of His Fame When He Stopped the Panic of 1907—His Family Life.

J. Pierpont Morgan had been the leading figure in American finance for almost as many years as the present generation could remember and had often been described as the biggest single factor in the banking business of the entire world. Combination, concentration, and development were his aims and the story of his life is indissolubly intertwined with the periods of expansion in this country in the world of railroads, industrial organization, and banking power.

The pinnacle of his power was reached in the panic of 1907 when he was more than 70 years old, and to some extent had withdrawn from participation in active affairs. By general consent he was put at the head of the forces that were gathered together to save the country from financial disaster, and men like John D. Rockefeller and E. H. Harriman, to say nothing of Presidents of banks and trust companies, put themselves and their resources at his disposal. Secretary of the Treasury Cortelyou, coming to New York to deposit Government funds where they would most aid in holding up the tottering financial structure, recognized his leadership and acted on his advice in every particular.

Unlike many of the men of great wealth in this country, Mr. Morgan, who was born in Hartford on April 17, 1837, in pursuing the career that led to this preeminence, did not have the incentive of poverty to spur him on in the early stages of his career. He was not born poor. On the contrary, he was heir to a fortune estimated at from $5,000,000 to $10,000,000. It was one of the notable fortunes of the country in the fifties, and when John Pierpont Morgan went into business here in the early sixties there was open to him a career entirely honorable and very comfortable, that would have carried him to an inconsequential old age and an unhistoric grave. He did not choose this career, but rather chose to work as few men have worked in the last half century.

The decade from 1880 to 1890 was characterized by most extensive and most destructive competition between the various railroad systems of the country, and it was during this period that J. P. Morgan had occasion to develop publicly the policy regarding railroad affairs that he stood for ever after. It found its concrete expression in the famous West Shore deal in 1885, which ended a period of warfare between the New York Central and the West Shore Railroad almost without parallel for its severity, even in those days of rate-cutting and kindred devices.

The West Shore was the only route connecting the cities of New York, Albany, and Buffalo that was not controlled by the New York Central, and the Vanderbilts undertook, straightway upon its opening in the early 80's, to crush it. By 1885 things had reached the point where the only question at issue was as to which road would go into a receiver's hands in the end, and it was at this point that J. P. Morgan stepped in. It was not an easy task, for the Vanderbilts of that day were fighters, and concessions from them were out of the question. Mr. Morgan's proposal—the only one to which he could gain their assent—was that he should acquire the West Shore in the interest of the New York Central without compensation for himself, and it was on Dec. 5, 1885, that the West Shore Railroad Company was incorporated to succeed the New York, West Shore & Buffalo Railroad Company, and leased to the Central for 475 years, with a renewal option, at a rental of the interest on its $50,000,000 of bonds.

The entire capital stock of $10,000,000 was taken by the Central. Mr. Vanderbilt was so pleased that he gave his banker a silver service which cost $300,000, and then had the dies broken, so that it never could be replaced.

But Mr. Morgan's activities in the suppression of destructive competition were by no means confined to the railroads in which he had a direct banking interest. The records of railroading from 1884 to 1889 are replete with "gentlemen's agreements" between the Presidents of roads all over the country, and in these negotiations Mr. Morgan played always a prominent part.

### Reconstructing Northern Pacific.

Meantime the Northern Pacific Railroad Company had passed into a receiver's hands. The success of the reorganization in which the Morgan syndicate furnished the $45,000,000 cash necessary to put the road on its feet temporarily, is a matter of record. The story is told in the appreciation of the common stock from the time when it sold at less than the assessment of $15 a share that was placed upon it in the reorganzation to the time when it sold under normal conditions at upward of $200 a share, and all virtually within ten years.

Quite true, the administrative success of the railroad was the achievement of James J. Hill rather than of J. P. Morgan, but it must also be considered that Mr. Hill entered the Northern Pacific at Mr. Morgan's invitation, buying some $30,000,000 of the stock for himself and his friends at $18 a share.

Some men would have found their hands reasonably full in conducting the Northern Pacific reorganization, with its $80,000,000 of new common stock, its $75,000,000 of new preferred, its $130,000,000 of prior lien 4 per cent. bonds, and its $60,000,000 of general lien 3 per cents. But not so with J. P. Morgan, for the Philadelphia & Reading had been coming at recurrent stages of its illness back to the Hospital for Crippled Railroads until eventually it was decided that it must submit to a major operation if its life was to be spared at all. This was performed, and a corporation with $28,000,000 first preferred stock, $42,000,000 second preferred stock, $70,000.00 common stock, and a bonded indebtedness of $105,000,000, was turned out with some $20,000,000 ready cash to live on until its recovery should be complete.

So it would be possible to go on even at greater length with this series of reorganizations, which included minor railroads apparently innumerable. But in this maze of adjustments of securities and security values there was one undertaking of J. P. Morgan & Co., as the New York end of the Morgan-Drexel combination long before had become known, that made for itself a permanent place in the financial history of the country. That was the so-called Cleveland bond issue of 1895.

### To the Treasury's Relief.

For causes growing out of the depression of 1893, the situation of the National Treasury at the opening of 1895 was worse, according to competent authority, than at any time since the resumption of gold payments in 1879. Throughout the month of January there were heavy withdrawals of gold from the Treasury both for domestic purposes and for shipment, the exports of one week being $11,000,000. President Cleveland sought from Congress legislation to relieve the condition, but without effect, although on Jan. 28, when one of his messages was sent in, the free gold in the Treasury was less than $45,000,000.

Then came the contract with the Morgan-Belmont syndicate to supply to the Government $65,117,500 in gold in return for $62,317,500 thirty-three year 3 per cent. bonds. The syndicate undertook to import the gold, where necessary, to pay for the bonds, and had its payments to the Government in progress by Feb. 15. Almost instantly there was a change for the better in conditions, and by March the syndicate, in complete control of the foreign exchange situation, had stopped the gold exports entirely. By June the syndicate had completed, in advance of the time set, payment for the foreign half of the loan, and before the close of that month the free gold in the Treasury had reached the $107,000,000 mark.

Again, in the following year, when the nomination of William J. Bryan for the Presidency had alarmed the country, Mr. Morgan took the initiative in a somewhat similar undertaking. It was in July, when the outflow of gold became so rapid as to alarm the most conservative financiers, that Mr. Morgan called a meeting of bankers and leading dealers in exchange and formed a syndicate within an hour which undertook to furnish practically an unlimited supply of bills of exchange.

The formation of the syndicate restored confidence almost instantly, and while the members of the syndicate as individuals furnished about a million dollars of such bills, no general syndicate operation was necessary. This was in effect a forerunner of the famous "Faith Cure" pool of December, 1902, when J. P. Morgan, James Stillman, and George F. Baker got together a group of banks to furnish some $40,000,000 loanable funds in the face of a tight-money scare, but didn't have to render any aid in the actual event, as the announcement served automatically to restore normal conditions.

The year 1899 marked an epoch in American finance in which J. P. Morgan had a pretty large part, for then it was that he negotiated the first foreign loan of any size ever placed in this country. This was to take up and refund the entire national debt of Mexico, and the amount of the loan was $110,000,000. It was followed the next year by an American participation of $25,000,000 in the British war loan, which was handled on this side of the water by J. P. Morgan in connection with Baring, Magoun & Co.

### The Chief and His Cabinet.

So at the opening of the new century Mr. Morgan was easily the largest financial figure on this side of the water, if not in the world. He had gathered around his a notable group of men—Francis Lynde Stetson, his personal counsel and "Attorney General"; Charles Steele, lawyer and financier; Samuel Spencer, President of the Southern Railroad; George F. Baker, President of the First National Bank, with which Morgan had more intimate relations than with any other institution, and George F. Baer, President of the Reading Railroad and head of the great anthracite coal interests that that road represents; Robert Bacon, afterward Assistant Secretary of State.

So far as the affairs of the Northern Pacific Railroad were concerned, James J. Hill would have to be considered as within this group, although his personal railroad interests in the Great Northern made him a factor of importance in the railroad world quite aside from his connection with the road that Morgan reorganized. And woven in all through the Directorates of all the roads that had come under Morgan influence during the reorganization period was the fibre of varied financial interests, for this was the corporate carrying out of the community of interest idea that J. P. Morgan himself had entertained on behalf of the railroads of the country from the time in the eighties when he used to try to settle rate-cutting disputes by getting up "gentlemen's agreements" among the Presidents.

Big things began to happen with the opening of 1901, and the biggest figure in the doing of them was J. P. Morgan. In January it was announced that he had bought the Jersey Central Railroad and turned it over, with its valuable coal properties, to the Reading. Soon after came word that the Pennsylvania Coal Company, the Hillside Coal Company, and others had been bought and turned over to the Erie, two acquisitions which brought the control of the anthracite traffic practically within the Morgan sphere of influence. Then went forth into the Street rumors that a consolidation of Northern Pacific, Great Northern, and the St. Paul Roads was imminent, but these were forgotten when, in the latter part of the month, came news that Andrew Carnegie was going to start a steel plant at Conneaut, Ohio, to manufacture "merchant pipe" in competition with Mr. Morgan's Federal Steel Company and John W. Gates's American Steel and Wire Company.

### Launching of the Steel Corporation

Here was a denial of the very principle, in the case of the most important industrial enterprise in the country, which Mr. Morgan had been working for in the railroad field for twenty years, and if one must needs wonder how he found the time to give the matter attention, it is easy enough to conceive the motive that led to the formation. That great institution, with its original capitalization of $1,154,000,000, was launched in February to take over the Carnegie Steel Company, the Federal Steel, the American Steel and Wire, the American Tin Plate, the American Steel Hoop, the American Sheet Steel, and various smaller steel companies. By March 20, when the time expired for depositing the stocks of the subsidiary corporations, the smallest percentage so deposited was 92 and the largest 99. On April 1, to which time an extension was granted for the deposit, an average of 96½ per cent. of all the subsidiary securities had been deposited under the plan.

The Steel Corporation had achieved the greatest success in its flotation that had ever been known, and, despite an increase in its capitalization in the Summer of 1901 and the strike of the steel workers in that Summer, by May of the following year there was a profit of $10,000,000 to be distributed to the members of the original syndicate, who stood ready in the beginning to put up $200,000,000 if called upon. The amount actually advanced had been $25,000,000.

This United States Steel enterprise was perhaps as notable an example of J. P. Morgan's persistent optimism as anything in his whole life. It was capitalized on the expectation that the conditions of the most prosperous year in the history of the country up to that time would continue indefinitely. When the depression of 1903 came along, and the Steel stocks dropped off until the preferred, with its 7 per cent. dividend, was selling under 50, and the common, dividendless, was down to 8¾, a banker went to Mr. Morgan to ask him what he thought about it.

"I am not concerned with the stock market conditions of the Steel stocks," was the gruff reply, "but I can tell you that the possibilities of the steel business are just as great as they ever were."

This is a fair statement of the principle that J. P. Morgan applied to all enterprises having to do primarily with the potential energy of this country.

### The Northern Pacific Episode.

In the meantime, Mr. Morgan's attempt to secure the control of the St. Paul in behalf of the Northern Pacific and Great Northern had come to nothing, but Mr. Hill had managed to buy for the two roads a controlling interest in the Chicago, Burlington & Quincy. With all these tremendous affairs apparently settled, Mr. Morgan went to Europe, and was still there when, in May, Edward H. Harriman, deciding that the Burlington deal was too great a matter to be left out of, tried to buy control of the Northern Pacific in the open market, and precipitated the panic of May 9, but it may be supposed that the master mind of the Morgan firm was the one that dictated the settlement of contracts which the shorts on the Stock Exchange had made in the wild days preceding, to the end that deliveries were allowed at $150 a share of the stock which had sold up to $1,000 a share in the height of the panic itself.

The eventual settlement of the matter from a railroad point of view—until the United States Government broke it up through the Northern Securities litigation—was one that was the flower of the community-of-interest idea. In connection with the Northern Securities Company, the $400,000,000 holding corporation formed in November of 1901, to hold the stocks of the Northern Pacific and Great Northern, it was arranged that the troublesome Harriman holdings in the Northern Pacific should be retired through exchange for the securities of the holding company, while the Harriman interests should have a representation in the Burlington Road, which was deemed the factor in the situation of the greatest importance to them.

### Active Also in England.

An interesting illustration of the prestige attaching to the Morgan name in this period came in April of 1902, when John W. Gates succeeded in getting the control of the Louisville & Nashville Road away from August Belmont. The corner developed by the contest for control had the shorts in somewhat the same predicament as were the shorts on that famous May day of 1901. By agreement between Mr. Gates and the Belmont interests the entire situation was placed in the hands of J. P. Morgan & Co., to the end that the Louisville & Nashville was turned over to the Atlantic Coast Line not many months later.

The reputation attained on this side of the water was now duplicated abroad. Every time Mr. Morgan crossed the water, whether in search of health or of rare objects of art, the European press was filled with stories that he was buying everything in sight. So the Leyland Line purchase in 1901 was supposed to herald a combination of the shipping interests of the world even more extensive than developed a year later, when the International Mercantile Marine Company was organized.

It has been said that a bright Irishman, the head of a great shipbuilding firm which had one of the constituent companies deeply in its debt, talked Mr. Morgan into the purchase of that particular company, and eventually suggested the idea of general consolidation.

### Mr. Morgan in the 1907 Panic.

When the first rumblings of the storm that was to break in the furious panic of October, 1907, began to be heard, Mr. Morgan was regarded by many as already out of active life. He was 70 years old and for several years had spent most of his time when in this country at his home and library uptown, while J. P. Morgan, Jr., and the other partners in the firm carried on its current business.

"Morgan is out of it" was a somewhat common view in Wall Street. "He is old and tired and his reputation has suffered from his flotation of United States Steel and International Mercantile Marine. Even if he were able to take the lead, confidence in his judgment has been shaken. We must look elsewhere for leadership."

How erroneous these ideas were it took but a few weeks to show, but at the moment Mr. Morgan's own attitude toward financial affairs fitted in with them. While nearly all the captains of finance in Wall Street were lying awake nights in the Spring of 1907, wondering how much longer they could stand the strain, Mr. Morgan was in Europe paying fabulous prices for works of art. In the very week that the late Henry H. Rogers was forced to make his great loan to carry his Virginian Railway project through the panic Mr. Morgan was in Italy spending his money lavishly collecting treasures for his library.

Mr. Morgan had put his house in order long before the storm broke. He had had his bitter experiences several years before in the Northern Pacific panic, and he told his partners then that never again must the house of Morgan run into stormy weather with its coffers drained of gold. It was the "silent panic," two years later—the "undigested securities" panic—that hurt the prestige of Mr. Morgan, not only in America, but in Europe. He and his imitators had manufactured hundreds of millions more of new securities than the country could absorb.

When the stampede to convert great masses of these securities into cash caused a panic in Wall Street, international bankers predicted that Mr. Morgan would never regain his financial prestige. At that time it was the Rockefeller-Rogers-Harriman contingent that was in possession of great cash resources and in the slump that came in Steel shares this group was accused of putting the knife into Morgan. He is said to have dug deep into his personal securities and to have taken millions of his best investment stocks to Boston in order to obtain funds to use in staying this decline.

Since that, however, the marvelous industrial growth of the country had given Mr. Morgan an opportunity to repair his fences. During the three years he waited, apparently idle, while rival captains of finance went ahead with great speculative projects involving the collapse of credit in 1907. Throughout the speculative furor of 1906 he went ahead quietly, emptying his strong boxes of securities of uncertain value and strengthening his credit in the banking capitals of the world.

At the beginning of 1907 business had continued extremely active. There was a recrudescence of hostility toward the railroads, and reports were in circulation that President Roosevelt had adopted the radical ideas of Senator La Follette. The Inter-State Commerce Commission began its investigation which resulted in many disclosures as to the operations of E. H. Harriman. At the same time new purchases of interests in other roads by the Union Pacific increased the public feeling against Harriman. There was uneasiness, too, about the possibility of the withdrawal of Government deposits from the banks when Leslie M. Shaw should retire as Secretary of the Treasury on March 4.

In the meantime, Heinze, Morse, and Thomas were building up the house of cards in the control of banks that was to play a conspicuous part in the panic a few months later. Augustus F. Heinze got control of the Mercantile National Bank in January, and the Trust Company of America, afterward a storm centre, absorbed the Colonial Trust. An early sign of the impending crash was the failure of a $12,000,000 bond issue by the Erie Railroad, about three-fourths of it being left in the hands of the underwriting syndicate.

**Cause of the Panic.**

Harriman's Alton deal, by which that road was loaded up with a big bond issue to the great personal profit of Harriman and his associates, was disclosed in February, and in March came the first signs of panic in the stock market. This was another "silent panic" and world-wide financial disturbance followed a phenomenal break on the New York Stock Exchange. The break was due chiefly to the impairment of public confidence in the value and stability of railroad securities, helped along by tight money, caused by some withdrawals of Government funds, and uncertainty as to the probable course of the new Secretary of the Treasury, George B. Cortelyou. The decline continued until, on March 14, there was a terrific collapse which carried prices to lower levels than in the Northern Pacific corner in 1901.

The immediate cause of the crash on March 14 was the failure of efforts made by Mr. Morgan to obtain from President Roosevelt some sign that he would stay his hand in his attacks on the railroads. Mr. Morgan went to the White House on March 11 and suggested that Mr. Roosevelt confer with Presidents Mellen of the New Haven, Hughitt of the Northwestern, Newman of the New York Central, and McCrea of the Pennsylvania. The public took it for granted that such a conference was to be held, and the slump in the market was halted for a few days.

Two days later Mr. Morgan sailed for Europe, and on the next day it became known that his sugestion to President Roosevelt was entirely informal, and that none of the railroad Presidents he had named had had anything to do with it. No basis had been laid for a conference, and none was called by President Roosevelt. Several railroad Presidents called at the White House later as individuals, but nothing was forthcoming from the President that would tend to reassure the holders of railroad securities.

The market on March 15, however, took a better turn on rumors that a fund of $25,000,000 had been made up for purposes of market support. It never became definitely known whether Mr. Morgan had taken steps of this kind before he sailed or not, and if the fund had been raised it was never used. It was known as the "faith cure fund" from the market effect of its rumored existence. In the week following there was a sharp recovery in stocks, but the month was not to end without another crash, which left it supine and inert until the final blow in October. No sooner had the faith cure had its full effect than fears in London over the fortnightly setlement on March 27 disclosed serious weakness there. The result was an outpour of stocks here on Monday, March 25, in which prices crumbled as they had on March 14. There were no failures, however, at that time, and the anxious money kings breathed a little more freely.

A substantial recovery followed, and the money stringency vanished. Trouble continued brewing outside of the Stock Exchange, however. More two-cent-fare laws were passed by various State Legislatures, and any expectation that President Roosevelt would modify his position was rudely shattered by his famous controversy with Harriman, in which he classified him as an undesireable citizen, and said one of his statements should be characterized by "an uglier and shorter word."

**Helps City Bond Issue.**

Several bond issues that were brought out failed and had to be taken over by underwriting syndicates, and in June a city bond issue also failed. It was Mr. Morgan who came to the relief of the city's finances after his return from Europe. An issue of $40,000,000 at 4½ per cent. was decided on, upon his assurances that it would be a success. When the offering was made in September it was announced that Mr. Morgan had formed a syndicate which had agreed to take at least half the issue at par, and the result was that it was oversubscribed many times.

The immediate cause of the October panic was the collapse of F. Augustus Heinze's pool in United Copper shares, following a slump in the copper market in September and the early days of October. Otto H. Heinze & Co., who had undertaken to corner the stock, said that one of its members had sold out the others, and there were intimations that the member referred to was Charles W. Morse.

Since his return from Europe Mr. Morgan had been quietly studying the situation, from which he held rather markedly aloof. He sat at his desk nearly every day and listened to reports, but said nothing. He was still studying the situation when the panic came.

Again he showed a disposition to keep out of the coming turmoil, in which he was, however, to be the central figure. The National Bank of Commerce, one of the chief Morgan banks, gave notice that after Oct. 22 it would no longer clear for the Knickerbocker Trust Company. On the night of Oct. 21 the leading bankers held a conference with Mr. Morgan at his house, and it was reported that he had refused to extend any aid to the trust companies that were on the ragged edge.

The next day the Knickerbocker Trust closed, after paying out $8,000,000 to depositors. That night there was another conference over the affairs of the Trust Company of America, and on the next morning a run on that institution started.

The panic was on in earnest, and Secretary of the Treasury Cortelyou was sent to New York by President Roosevelt to help afford relief to the banking situation. On the night of Oct. 23 Mr. Morgan and other bankers met Secretary Cortelyou at the Manhattan Hotel, and the Secretary agreed to add $25,000,000 to the Government's deposits.

**Mr. Morgan Takes Command.**

Again the situation pointed to Mr. Morgan as the only possible leader. The banks were associated together in the Clearing House, and the Clearing House Committee had already been hard at work on the situation, but the trust companies, among which were the greatest danger points, were not members of the Clearing House. They had no association among themselves, and when a meeting of their Presidents was called in Mr. Morgan's office, several of them had never met before, and had to be introduced to one another. A little coherence was brought into their relations by the formation of a committee of five Presidents to represent them at conferences.

None of these agencies, however, could handle the relief to be extended by the Treasury Department. The Government funds could be deposited only in National banks, to begin with. Then Mr. Cortelyou explained that he could not give relief to individual banks but must deal with the situation as a whole. There was more or less jealousy among the National banks, and there was no direct way by which the tottering trust companies could be benefited by Government deposits in National banks. One man who could superintend the whole field was needed, and, of course, Mr. Morgan was the man.

When he entered his office the next morning his power was absolute. He was the arbiter between the banks, the trust companies and the National Treasury. His was the power to say who should and who should not borrow money. Stock speculation was brought to an end by his fiat. In the days that followed John D. Rockefeller came to him with an offer of $10,000,000 in bonds to be used in securing Government deposits for the afflicted banks. His office was crowded continuously with men like E. H. Gary, head of the Steel Corporation, with $75,000,000 in cash; James Stillman, representing the untold millions of Standard Oil money, and lesser lights. Even Harriman, his enemy, it is said, gave him temporary support.

Mr. Morgan may have taken a grim satisfaction in this turning of the tables, since the days of the silent panic in which he had been compelled to carry the load of United States Steel and other combinations almost out of his own resources while the "Standard Oil crowd" and Harriman smiled at his difficulties. Now it was Morgan who had the liquid assets and was directing the distribution of the Government millions.

On that first day, with Mr. Morgan fully in the saddle, the Hamilton Bank, a Thomas institution, and the Twelfth Ward Bank closed. The run on the Trust Company of America went on, with hundreds in line. The streets in the financial district were filled with frenzied throngs. All that day Mr. Morgan sat at his desk, listening to reports, which he received with short, gruff comments. Across the street, at the Sub-Treasury, Secretary Cortelyou distributed his Government money as Mr. Morgan decided and as the legal securities were brought to him. George W. Perkins, then the most active of Mr. Morgan's partners, dashed back and forth from Morgan to Cortelyou. At the Clearing House the council of bankers worked out the details of the distribution which were submitted to Mr. Morgan for his assent and to Mr. Cortelyou for execution. Bankers hurried into Mr. Morgan's office to get their instructions as to the further distribution of the money they received among the banks and trust companies that needed it most.

**$25,000,000 to Help Brokers.**

On the next day, Oct. 24, a run started in the Lincoln Trust Company, and behind this and the Trust Company of America Mr. Morgan determined to make his stand. This was the big day of the panic, for, as securities were thrown into the vortex of the Stock Exchange by frightened investors and by banking institutions that must perforce liquidate their holdings to meet the demands of the money-hungry lines before their doors, call money on the Exchange soared to incredible heights, touching 125 per cent. Finally no money was to be had at any price, and early in the afternoon R. H. Thomas, President of the Exchange, went to President Stillman of the National City Bank, usually a large lender on call, and told him that $25,000,000 was needed to prevent many failures or the closing of the Exchange. What followed was graphically told by Mr. Thomas before the Pujo Committee.

"Mr. Stillman," he said, "replied 'Go right over and tell Mr. Morgan about it. I will telephone him you are coming.' I went to the office of J. P. Morgan & Co. The place was filled with an excited crowd. After a time Mr. Morgan came out from his private office and Mr. Perkins joined us. 'I'm going to let you have $25,000,000,' Mr. Morgan said to me. 'Go over to the Exchange and announce it.' I said there was one suggestion I would like to make. 'What is it?' asked Mr. Morgan. 'If you will divide the money up among several,' I said, 'it will have a better effect.' 'That's a good suggestion,' said Mr. Morgan, 'Perkins, divide that up into lots.'

"I went back to the Exchange and one of the officials said to the loan crowd who were swarming about the post, 'Wait a minute; Mr. Thomas will make a statement.' I said to them: 'I haven't any money, but relief is coming. You can depend on that.' I didn't say how much was coming. The crowd greeted the statement with cheers. The money came in about a minute and a half—certainly less than five minutes. It appeared in different parts of the crowd. I couldn't tell who had it. The rate dropped and I left."

Stilling the Stock Exchange panic was one of the hardest things Mr. Morgan had to do, although he did it in a few minutes. Secretary Cortelyou had said specifically that he could do nothing for the Stock Exchange. The banks that had been receiving the Government deposits the day before and since had been called on by Mr. Morgan to transfer part of the money to the threatened trust companies and were hoarding the rest to conserve their own reserves.

As soon as Mr. Stillman telephoned, Mr. Morgan called a conference of bank Presidents in his office, and it gathered in a few minutes. While President Thomas waited the $25,000,000 pool was made up. The money was pledged but was not all used before call money rates became normal.

On the next day some of the smaller banks, including several in Brooklyn, closed, while the run on the two trust companies kept up. Another money pool—this time of $10,000,000—was made up in Morgan's office, the banks having still continued to receive Government deposits. Savings banks decided to require sixty days' notice of withdrawal of deposits. From the first Mr. Morgan had fought against the issue of Clearing House loan certificates as a partial suspension of cash payments, but on Oct. 26 this became necessary, and the resulting release of funds gave additional help to the threatened institutions. The Government deposits went on, and by the end of the week amounted to $82,000,000.

Conferences were held at Mr. Morgan's house on Sunday, Nov. 3, and at the Waldorf, some of them lasting till 5 in the morning. There had been no cessation of the runs on the Lincoln Trust and the Trust Company of America despite the millions they had paid out. They had been found solvent by the Clearing House Committee, and at these conferences it was decided that they should have the support of the trust companies as a whole.

The second day following was Election Day and afforded another breathing spell. Final plans were made on that day and the next for saving the two trust companies. These involved the taking over of the stock of the Tennessee Coal and Iron Company by the United States Steel Corporation. Oakleigh Thorne, President of the Trust Company of America, was one of the syndicate which had pooled the controlling stock of the Tennessee Company. Moore & Schley were heavily involved in this syndicate and in other industrial stocks.

Tennessee Coal and Iron stock was being thrown out as collateral by the banks, and it was felt that the failure of the brokerage firm was imminent and would bring down many others, including several banks and trust companies. The substitution of Steel Corporation bonds as collateral would save Moore & Schley and prevent the catastrophe.

Judge Gary and H. C. Frick were called to Mr. Morgan's house and were asked if the Steel Corporation would take the property. They said that they would do so if they were satisfied that it would not mean the prosecution of the Steel Trust under the Sherman law. Mr. Morgan told them they had better go to Washington and see President Roosevelt at once, and they went by special train, arriving at the White House on Monday. On President Roosevelt's assurance that he saw no reason to interfere, the deal was consummated, and the officers of the Steel Corporation sat up all night signing bonds to exchange for the T. C. & I. stock.

Whatever question may have been raised since as to this transaction, all of those concerned either as buyers or sellers, have said that it was the one thing that could have prevented an enormous extension of the panic. That the panic immediately ended is a matter of history. To relieve further the monetary stringency the Government issued bonds to permit an increase in the issue of National bank notes, and Mr. Morgan, through his Paris branch, arranged for the shipment of gold from France, which still further eased the situation.

### After the Panic.

In the aftermath of the panic—particularly the drawing together of financial institutions into the so-called "Money Trust" and the elimination of the weaker vessels—Mr. Morgan naturally played an important part. In these combinations the compulsory sale of bank and other stocks by the big life insurance companies was a considerable element. The Equitable Trust Company absorbed the Bowling Green Trust Company, and the Mutual Life sold part of its holdings in the United States Mortgage and Trust Company. In December, 1909, Mr. Morgan bought a majority of the stock of the Equitable Life Assurance Society, continuing the voting trust established by Thomas F. Ryan. A little later he bought the controlling interest in the Guaranty Trust Company from the Mutual Life and the Harriman estate, and in January, 1910, it was consolidated with the Morton Trust and the Fifth Avenue Trust.

The troubles that followed the closing of the Carnegie Trust Company on Jan. 7, 1911, brought Mr. Morgan forward again for a brief time in the rôle he had played in the panic. The next day, which was Sunday, saw conferences in his library and elsewhere to prevent an extension of the trouble to the Madison Trust Company and the Twelfth and Nineteenth Ward Banks. It was arranged after midnight that the Madison Trust should be absorbed by the Equitable Trust, and Mr. Morgan agreed to advance money enough to the two banks to see them through.

A little later the Equitable and Mutual Life sold large blocks of stock of the National Bank of Commerce, and Presidents Hine of the First National and Wiggin of the Chase National, both Morgan institutions, entered the board. With them went President Vanderlip of the National City Bank. The Bankers' Trust Company took over the Mercantile Trust through the purchase by parties identified with it of the stock holdings of the Equitable Life controlled by Mr. Morgan.

In September, 1911, there was another conference at Mr. Morgan's house. This time it was due to rumors that the Steel Corporation was to be prosecuted as a trust, and that it would voluntarily dissolve. The outcome was a statement signed by Mr. Morgan and Judge Gary defending the Steel Corporation, saying it was not organized to restrain trade, had always scrupulously observed the law, and would not voluntarily dissolve. A sharp rise in the shares followed, but a month later the suit was filed, and Mr. Morgan was named among the defendants.

Shortly after the panic Mr. Morgan again came to the assistance of the city, when he organized a syndicate that bid for an entire issue of $30,000,000 bonds, with the result that it was oversubscribed. In April, 1908, he prevented a receivership for the Erie Railroad by underwriting $5,000,000 of new notes without commission.

In the last few years Mr. Morgan had continued to spend much of his time in Europe. He was a witness before the Pujo Committee on Dec. 18 and 19, 1912, and it was then noticed for the first time that he was failing physically. The first day, after his trip from New York, he was plainly nervous and tired, but on the following day he withstood a long examination at the hands of Samuel Untermyer and stood his ground in defense of the financial system in which he believed.

### MR. MORGAN'S FAMILY LIFE.

#### He Was Twice Married—Succeeded by His Son, J. P. Morgan, Jr.

J. P. Morgan was married twice. His first wife was Amelia Sturges, daughter of Jonathan and Mary Cady Sturges of Manhattan. They were married in 1861. Her death occurred in 1862. In 1865 he married Frances Louise Tracy, who survives him, daughter of Charles Tracy, one of the leading attorneys here in the seventies. Their children, all of whom are living, are Louisa, wife of Herbert L. Satterlee; J. Pierpont Morgan, Jr.; Juliet, wife of William P. Hamilton, and Miss Anne Tracy Morgan.

Eleven grandchildren survive—Mabel Morgan Satterlee and Eleanor Morgan Satterlee, daughters of Mr. and Mrs. Herbert L. Satterlee; two sons and two daughters of Mr. and Mrs. J. Pierpont

# Mr. Morgan's Widow and Children.

MISS ANNE MORGAN

J. P. MORGAN JR

Morgan, Jr., Junius Spencer, Jane Norton, Frances Tracy, and Henry Sturges Morgan; two daughters and three sons of Mr. and Mrs. William P. Hamilton, Helen Morgan, Pierpont Morgan, Laurens Morgan, Alexander, and Elizabeth Schuyler Hamilton. There are six nephews and two nieces, four grandnieces, and two grandnephews, the children and grandchildren of Mr. Morgan's sisters, Sarah Spencer Morgan, who married George Hale Morgan; Mary Lyman Morgan, who married Walter Haynes Burns, and Juliet Pierpont Morgan, who married the Rev. John B. Morgan, rector of the American Episcopal Church, Paris, France. Junius Spencer Morgan, J. P. Morgan's only brother, died in 1858, at the age of 12.

The town house of J. P. Morgan, at the corner of Madison Avenue and Thirty-sixth Street, is notable because of the attractive gardens lying between it and that of J. P. Morgan, Jr., at Thirty-seventh Street. Including the Morgan building which houses the Morgan private library and art treasures, this is one of the most attractive groupings of private residences in the heart of the city.

In recent years the younger Morgan has largely taken his father's place in the banking office here, occupying his desk during his long absence abroad and acting for the firm in all of its largest transactions. Like his father, he is a Director in many corporations, including the United States Steel Corporation. He is a big man physically, as was his father, and shows the same aptitude for hard work and the strength to continue at it.

Mrs. Satterlee, Mr. Morgan's eldest daughter, often his companion in his travels here and abroad, went with him to Washington and sat beside him while he testified before the Pujo Committee. She also accompanied him on his last trip. She is the wife of Herbert L. Satterlee, attorney, author, and a former Assistant Secretary of the Navy. In 1910 Mr. Morgan purchased as a gift for Mrs. Satterlee an estate of 117 acres at Great Head, Bar Harbor.

Mrs. Hamilton, Mr. Morgan's third child, is the wife of William Pierson Hamilton, a member of the firm of J. P. Morgan & Co. He testified last October in the Government's suit against the International Harvester Company, concerning the agreements between J. P. Morgan & Co. and the vendors for the deposit on the stock they received in the voting trust.

Miss Anne T. Morgan, the youngest child of Mr. and Mrs. Morgan, has for several years been actively engaged with other prominent women in the effort to improve conditions surrounding workers in industrial lines here and throughout the country. Associated with

MRS. J. P. MORGAN

women of the Civic Federation, Miss Morgan established a restaurant for the workers in the Brooklyn Navy Yard in June, 1909, which sought to provide them with good and moderate-priced food. In addition she has done much charitable work, and has studied strike conditions. Frequently reports have had it that Miss Morgan was to marry. To a friend a month ago, Miss Morgan said: "I have not yet met a man whose wife I'd rather be than the daughter of J. Pierpont Morgan."

### PATRIOT, SAYS MR. TAFT.

Ex-President Taft paid a graceful tribute to the memory of J. Pierpont Morgan last night at the home of his brother, Henry W. Taft, shortly after his arrival from Augusta, Ga.

"I knew Mr. Morgan personally," said Mr. Taft, "but our relations were never intimate. However, he always impressed me as a man of remarkable administrative force and executive ability. He was without doubt the greatest financier that America has ever produced, and certainly was one of the impressive world figures of his time. I regret his death exceedingly.

"Mr. Morgan was a patriotic American and was a genuine patron of art. He performed a patriotic service in bringing to our shores countless valuable paintings and art objects of the Old World, and for this service the American people should be and are deeply appreciative. The City of New York is especially indebted to Mr. Morgan for his generous display of civic spirit in giving to its citizens one of the most important collections of old masters in the United States."

MRS. HERBERT L. SATTERLEE

# CARNEGIE STARTED AS A BOBBIN BOY

## Came to America When He Was 12 Years Old and Left Some $500,000,000.

---

## MADE FORTUNE IN STEEL

---

### Rose to be Dominant Figure in Industrial World and Great Benefactor.

---

Until he was a septuagenarian, Andrew Carnegie believed that he was born in 1837. Then on a return visit to his native town in Scotland he learned that the date 1837 in the church records merely meant that the records were commenced in that year, and he was listed as a living child in the first census. He announced his correction of the date of his birth by clicking the news to his brother telegraphers on a miniature telegraph instrument at his plate at the dinner they were giving in his honor, supposing it to be his seventy-first when it was really his seventy-third birthday.

He was born Nov. 27, 1835, in Dunfermline, a little manufacturing town in Fifeshire, Scotland, at that time noted for its weaving. His father and his ancestors for a long way back had been weavers, and at the time of Andrew's birth the elder Carnegie owned three or four hand looms, one of which he operated himself, and hired extra hands for the others as the trade required. Andrew was to have been a weaver, too, but new inventions were soon to abolish the industry, and William Carnegie, his father, was the last of the weaving line.

"I owe a great deal to my mother," he wrote in 1914. "She was companion, nurse, seamstress, cook, and washerwoman, and never until late in life had a servant in the house. Yet she was a cultivated lady, who taught me most of what I know."

He earned his first penny by reciting Burns's long poem, "Man Was Made to Mourn," without a break. There is a story that in Sunday school, being called upon to recite some Scripture text, he astonished the assembly by giving this: "Look after the pence, and the pounds will take care of themselves."

### Wealth Put at $500,000,000.

Estimates of Mr. Carnegie's wealth made yesterday put it at possibly $500,000,000. When he retired in 1901 he sold his securities of the Carnegie Steel Company to the United States Steel Corporation for $303,450,000 in bonds of that company. He was possessed of large interests in addition to those bonds. When he started in 1901 to endow his great benefactions he made inroads into his capital for several years in gifts to libraries, for peace propaganda, and to other philanthropic causes.

The fortune of $303,450,000 in 5 per cent. bonds, if allowed to increase by the accumulation of interest and reinvestment since 1901 would amount to about a billion dollars today, but his numerous benefactions prevented this. According to financial authorities, however, the ironmaster's ambition to die poor was not realized, and, despite the scale of his philanthropies, it was believed that his fortune was at his death as large as it ever was.

Elihu Root, Jr., son of former United States Senator Root, whose father for years has been Mr. Carnegie's counsel, declined yesterday to discuss Mr. Carnegie's affairs other than to say that he was a citizen of New York City and to admit that his will doubtless would be probated here.

When he was 12 years old the steam looms drove his father, the master weaver, out of business, and, reduced

to poverty, the family emigrated to America. There were four, the parents and two boys, Andrew and Thomas. They settled at Allegheny City, Penn., across the river from Pittsburgh, in 1848. The father and Andrew found work in a cotton factory, the son as bobbin boy. His pay was $1.20 in this, his first job. He was soon promoted, at a slight advance to be engineer's assistant, and he stoked the boilers and ran the engine in the factory cellar for twelve hours a day.

It was at this time, he afterward said, that the inspiration came for his subsequent library benefactions. Colonel Anderson, a gentleman with a library of about 400 books, opened it to the boys every week-end and let them borrow any book they wanted. Carnegie made full use of the opportunity. "Only he who has longed as I did for Saturdays to come," he said, "can understand what Colonel Anderson did for me and the boys of Allegheny. Is it any wonder that I resolved, if ever surplus wealth came to me, I would use it imitating my benefactor?"

### Becomes a Telegraph Messenger.

At 14 he became a telegraph messenger. The Superintendent of the office, James Reid, also a Scot, took a liking to the new boy. Indeed, it was his Scotch accent that warmed Reid's heart toward him, and got him the job. Andrew had not been there a month before he asked Mr. Reid to teach him telegraphy, and spent all his spare time in practice. "My entrance into the telegraph office," said Carnegie, "was a transition from darkness to light—from firing

a small engine in a dark and dirty cellar into a clean office with bright windows and a literary atmosphere, with books, newspapers, pens, and pencils all around me. I was the happiest boy alive."

One day a death message came before the operators arrived. Carnegie took it, and delivered it, and this led to his promotion to be an operator. When the Pennsylvania Railroad put up a telegraph wire of its own he became clerk under Divisional Superintendent Thomas A. Scott, at a salary increased to $35 a month. Mr. Scott got $125 a month, "and," Carnegie said, "I used to wonder what on earth he could do with so much money."

At that time telegraphy was still new. The dots and dashes were not read by sound, but were all impressed on tape, and Carnegie is said to have been the third operator in the United States to read messages by sound alone. He was now Colonel Scott's private secretary. One morning when Colonel Scott was late coming down the trains were getting tangled up in the yards. The young private secretary wrote out such orders as he knew his chief would give and put them on the wires. When Colonel Scott arrived, greatly disturbed over what he supposed, and prepared to plunge into the work of straightening things out, Carnegie told what he had done and said the trains were all under way. Scott said nothing to him, but to the President of the road he reported that he "had a little Scotch devil in his office who would run the whole road if they'd only give him a chance."

### His First Investment.

His father died when Andrew was 16, and as the breadwinner of the family he advised his mother to make

her investment, $600, in ten shares of Adams Express stock. She mortgaged her home to do it, and there was a monthly dividend of 1 per cent. "I can see that first check of $10 dividend money," he said after his retirement. "It was something new to all of us, for none of us had ever received anything but from toil."

This first investment was made on the advice of Scott, who had told him that it would be a good one and had offered to help him if he could not raise enough.

Colonel Scott became General Superintendent of the Pennsylvania in 1858 and Vice President in 1860, taking Carnegie along with him at each rise. In May, 1861, the civil war had broken out and Scott was appointed Assistant Secretary of War in charge of military railroads and telegraphs, and again he took Carnegie with him. Carnegie was now Superintendent of the Western division of the road, and did not want to go to Washington, but Scott insisted.

Mr. Carnegie was placed in charge of the Government telegraph communications. He went to Annapolis and opened communications which the Confederates had interrupted. He started out on the first locomotive which ran from Annapolis to Washington. While passing Elbridge Junction he noticed that the wires had been pegged down by the enemy. He stopped the engine, jumped down beside the wires, and cut them. One of them sprang up and gave him a wound in the cheek, the scar of which remained with him all through life.

He was on the field at Bull Run in charge of the communications, and was the last man on the last train that left for Washington when the rout began.

### Meets Sleeping Car Inventor.

While traveling on his division of the road one day he met a man who said his name was T. T. Woodruff, and that he had invented a sleeping car. Mr. Carnegie was interested, and after seeing a model he became convinced of its advantages. He arranged an interview between Woodruff and Scott, and they formed a small company which resulted in the use on the Pennsylvania of the first sleeping cars ever used in the world. They gave Carnegie an interest, but when his assessment, $217.50, came due, he had not the money; he borrowed it, however, from a banker in Altoona and repaid the loan at the rate of $15 a month. His other assessments were paid from his share of the earnings of the car, and he made a profit on this venture of about $200,000.

Mr. Carnegie's first attempt to invest the fortune he was beginning to make came when he put $40,000 in a company formed for the development of an untried piece of oil land. But oil was not found, he grew discouraged and he finally succeeded in selling out one-third of his holdings for $3,000. Then he went to Europe, and while he was away the company struck oil, and the share remaining to him was worth a quarter of a million.

Two of his fellow workmen, named Piper and Schiffler, had attracted his attention by their work on bridges. He proposed to them to organize a company for building bridges, and the Keystone Bridge Company was formed about 1863. His brother Thomas had become interested in iron works, and Andrew, after consulting with him, organized the Cyclops Iron Mill for the production of structural iron, to be used in railway bridges.

Colonel Scott joined with them, but the project was not successful, and Andrew Carnegie had to turn to Thomas to help him get out of it. He proposed that his brother and Henry Phipps, Thomas's partner, should form a combination that would relieve him of his rolling mill, and a union of interests was brought about in 1865. The result was the Union Iron Mills.

It was just at the right time. The civil war had just ended and the great expansion was beginning. The new concern made great profits, and Carnegie proposed further ventures. It was the era of the building of railroads and the development of the West. Steel rails had become worth $80 to $100 a ton.

### Adopts Bessemer Steel Process.

By this time Andrew Carnegie was recognized as the leader of this Napoleonic combination, which, with every new success, reached out further. On a visit to England in 1868 he discovered the success being obtained there with the Bessemer process, and brought the idea home with him and adopted it in his mills. After he introduced the Bessemer steel process in this country he became principal owner of the Homestead and Edgar Thomson

**ANDREW CARNEGIE**
*Who Died Yesterday at His Home in Lenox, Mass.*

Steel Works and other large plants as head of the firms of Carnegie, Phipps & Co. and Carnegie Brothers & Co.

In 1899 the interests were consolidated in the Carnegie Steel Company, which in 1901 was merged in the United States Steel Corporation, when Mr. Carnegie retired from business.

The only great clash with labor which occurred while Mr. Carnegie was in business was the Homestead strike of 1892. He was in Europe at the time, and came in for much criticism for not returning and for letting the trouble go to a finish without any action by him. He, however, made an explanation long afterward.

"I was coaching through the Scottish Highlands on my holiday," Mr. Carnegie told the Industrial Relations Commission in 1915, "and did not hear of the lamentable riot at Homestead until days after it occurred. I wired at once that I would take the first steamer home, but was requested not to come."

He said that after his return he told the Homestead rollers that his partners had offered liberal terms and he could not have offered more, and that one of the men said: "Oh, Mr. Carnegie, it wasn't a question of dollars. The boys would have let you kick them, and they wouldn't let another man stroke their hair." And he also told the commission a story of his treatment of Burgess McLuckie, one of the Homestead men who disappeared to avoid arrest after the riots. Professor van Dyke of Rutgers College told him that he had met McLuckie working as a laborer in a mine at Sonora, Mexico. Carnegie asked the professor to offer McLuckie any help he might need, and on his return to the West he did so.

He found that McLuckie had obtained a position with the Sonora Railway, driving wells, and was prospering. "You don't know," said the professor, "whose money I was told to help you with." He did not. "Well, it was Mr. Carnegie's." "Then," related Mr. Carnegie, "came the slow, earnest response: 'That was damned white of Andy.' When I heard this I suggested to my friend Van Dyke that it wouldn't be a bad epitaph to grace one's tombstone. If it ever did I hoped there would be no long blank between the d's. Each letter should be put down to give McLuckie's proper expression."

He sold out to the Steel Corporation for $420,000,000, and in his testimony before the Stanley Committee in 1912, referring to this bargain, he exclaimed, "What a fool I was! I have since earned from the inside that we could have received $100,000,000 more from Mr. Morgan if we had placed that value on our property."

## His Peace Propaganda.

Of all his fields of public activity he took most interest, probably, in his peace propaganda. An offshoot of his peace labors was his interest in bringing about arbitration in Central and South America. He aided in the organization of various leagues and commissions to this end. When ex-Secretary of State Elihu Root returned from his tour of South America Mr. Carnegie at once gave Mr. Root's alma mater, Hamilton College, $200,000, in memory of the services of Senator Root in behalf of international peace." In 1907 he sent a peace commission to the Latin-American republics.

"Not so long ago," said Mr. Carnegie in 1907, "a speaker recited in my hearing how he had seen the most powerful naval vessel in the world—the Dreadnought with her 18,000 tons displacement. When my turn came I said that I must regret to dispute the statement. I myself had seen the most powerful naval vessel in the world. She was a tiny yacht-like vessel, painted in beautiful white, with a flag at her masthead and a toy cannon on her deck—for use in firing salutes, mostly.

"Such dainty vessels as these serve to maintain the neutrality of the North American great lakes. The little white yacht was the true dreadnought. The name of the other, the vast, gloomy and terrible engine, should be 'Dread-everything'—dread wounds, dread shot, dread drowning, dread savage, hellish passions; dread miserable, tortured, fruitless death."

If there seemed an inconsistency in his attacks on armament and the making of it, in that he himself had once engaged in the manufacture of armor plate, he had an answer ready. He had engaged in it reluctantly. He declined to bid to President Cleveland for armor manufacture, despite Secretary Whitney's pleadings to him to reconsider. President Harrison and Secretary Tracy had urged him, but he had refused. Then, while he was coaching in Scotland, he received a telegram from Tracy saying: "The President considers it your duty to contract for the armor for your country; the ships now wait for it." Carnegie, according to his story, replied: "That settles it. That command from the President of my country is a command from on high."

## His Famous Utterance.

His famous utterance about "dying disgraced" appeared in an article in the North American Review in 1898, in which he said:

"The day is not far distant when the man who dies leaving behind him millions of available wealth, which were free for him to administer during life, will pass away 'unwept, unhonored, and unsung,' no matter to what use he leaves the dross which he cannot take with him. Of such as these the public verdict will be, 'The man who dies thus rich dies disgraced.'"

When he came back to the United States in 1907 he was the central figure of the dedication of the Carnegie Institute at Pittsburgh, which had cost him $6,000,000. In a remarkable speech he said that he could not bring himself to a realization of what had been done. He felt like Aladdin, when he saw this building and was aware that he had put it up, but he could not bring himself to a consciousness of having done it any more than if he had produced the same effect by rubbing a lamp. He could not feel the ownership of what he had given, and he could not feel that he had given it away.

In "Problems of Today," a book published in 1907, Mr. Carnegie expressed some views on wealth which are unusual in a millionaire. He declared socialism, viewed upon its financial side, to be just, and said, "A heavy progressive tax upon wealth at death of owner is not only desirable, it is strictly just."

And he favored an income tax. Before the passage of the Underwood law he said in a speech at Montrose, Scotland: "Great Britain is ahead of the United States in having a progressive income tax. But do not flatter yourselves, we shall catch up with you very soon." A little later he expressed himself as pleased with the Underwood bill, so far as the income tax feature was concerned.

Mr. Carnegie did not believe in almsgiving. His idea was to help others help themselves, which was why he said, of his gifts of organs to churches, "I now only give one-half the cost, the congregations first provide the other." As for beggars, he was proud of his indifference to them: "I never give a cent to a beggar, nor do I help people of whose record I am ignorant; this at least is one of my really good actions."

# JOHN D. ROCKEFELLER DIES AT 97 IN HIS FLORIDA HOME; FUNERAL TO BE HELD HERE

## SUCCUMBS IN SLEEP

### Suffers Heart Attack Suddenly After Brief Period in Coma

### LEADERS MOURN DEATH

### Nation Shocked at Passing of Oil Man Who Dominated an Industrial Era

### NOTED FOR PHILANTHROPY

### Gifts Totaled $530,000,000— He Turned Most of Billion Fortune Over to Heirs

#### By PAUL CROWELL
Special to THE NEW YORK TIMES.

ORMOND BEACH, Fla., May 23.—John D. Rockefeller Sr., who wanted to live until July 8, 1939, when he would have rounded out a century of life, died at 4:05 A. M. here today at The Casements, his Winter home, a little more than two years and a month from his cherished goal.

Death came suddenly to the founder of the great Standard Oil organization—so suddenly that none of his immediate family was with him at the end. Less than twenty-four hours before the aged philanthropist died in his sleep from sclerotic myocarditis, his son, John D. Rockefeller Jr., had been assured that there was nothing about his father's condition to cause concern.

#### Known as Philanthropist

Once called the world's richest man, Mr. Rockefeller had given more than $530,000,000 to various educational, scientific and religious institutions, thus winning for himself the right to be called the world's greatest philanthropist.

Long since retired from active participation in business, he had given most of his great fortune to his heirs before he died, and close associates expressed doubt today that his estate, which they said was relatively small and very liquid, would amount to as much as $25,-000,000.

Soon after word of Mr. Rockefeller's death reached New York a special car was sent to Florida to bring back his body and plans were made for a simple private funeral on Wednesday from his official residence at Pocantico Hills, where he had planned to celebrate his ninety-eighth birthday next July.

#### Burial to Be in Cleveland

Burial will be Thursday in Lakeview Cemetery, Cleveland, where Mr. Rockefeller got his business start as a $12-a-month clerk. In accordance with his wishes he will be buried beside his wife, Laura Spelman Rockefeller, who died more than twenty years before him.

The funeral services probably will be conducted by the Rev. Dr. Harry Emerson Fosdick, pastor of the Riverside Church, which the oil man endowed. Only members of the family and intimate friends will be permitted to attend.

As the news of the passing of the great industrialist, who will be remembered both as a philanthropist and as America's first billionaire, spread across the country and to Europe, leaders in educational, religious and charitable organizations paid tribute to his memory.

Mr. Rockefeller had lived in and been a part of the industrialization of a continent. In his lifetime he saw automobiles replace horses and carriages, airplanes challenge automobiles and railroad trains as common carriers.

He saw great steel combines grow as his oil empire grew. He was a man when the Civil War was fought and it was not until late in his lifetime that the last frontier was reached.

Behind the closed gates at Pocantico Hills, where John D. Rockefeller Jr. and his family were alone with their grief, and here at The Casements, where faithful employes and servants prepared for the sad journey north, there was mourning. Flags on the estate and on public buildings here flew at half staff.

Dr. H. L. Merryday of Daytona Beach, personal physician to Mr. Rockefeller, said that Mr. Rockefeller, as recently as last Wednesday, had appeared to be in good health. On Thursday and Friday he suffered sinking spells, but apparently rallied. On Saturday his condition had improved. About midnight Saturday Mr. Rockefeller sank into a coma, which continued until his death, four hours later.

Before he lapsed into the coma he whispered to his nurses, "Raise me a little higher." Once during the coma he muttered a few words in tones so low that none at the bedside was able to understand them.

With him when he died were Dr. Merryday, Mrs. Fannie A. Evans, a cousin; John E. Yordi, a nurse and companion who had attended him for many years, and Roy C. Sly, another nurse.

Mr. Rockefeller came to The Casements in October, following an annual custom of many years' standing.

The undertakers, the Baggett, Wetherby & McIntosh Company of Daytona Beach, declined to name the time of departure tomorrow. A study of schedules of the Florida East Coast Railway indicated that it would be late in the afternoon, with arrival in New York scheduled for Tuesday.

Mr. Rockefeller's death came as a shock to the residents of Ormond Beach and Daytona Beach, to whom his spare figure was a familiar sight. Since his arrival here in October he was accustomed to take daily automobile rides along the beach back of his estate, or along the tree-shaded highways of Daytona Beach.

For the last few years Mr. Rockefeller's failing strength has forced him to abandon his golf games on the Ormond Beach links.

As recently as Wednesday he took his usual automobile ride, and even on Friday and Saturday, after rallying from sinking spells, he sat in his wheelchair in the gardens of his estate.

Early this morning, when news of Mr. Rockefeller's death spread through Ormond Beach and Daytona Beach, hundreds of automo-

biles made the trip across the Halifax River to the massive gates of The Casements. They were turned away by guards.

The river highway between the estate and the Halifax, was blocked off along the entire estate frontage and cars were directed to adjacent roads.

The twenty-five employes on the estate were a saddened group. They could be seen through the entrance gates on Granada Avenue talking in muffled tones about the passing of "the mister." Within the low-roofed, rambling structure where Mr. Rockefeller died, members of the household staff could be seen moving slowly from room to room.

During the last two weeks, according to "old timers" who had watched Mr. Rockefeller's comings and goings in the years that he made his Winter and Spring home here, there was no indication that his health was declining. On Monday he paid a visit to Dr. Sidney G. Main of Daytona Beach, his dentist. At that time he appeared to be in his usual health.

Only a few were aware of his absence from the beach on Thursday and succeeding days, or of his failure to take his automobile ride to Daytona Beach. As recently as Wednesday, the Rev. James M. Anderson, a Baptist minister in Daytona, called at The Casements and talked with Mr. Rockefeller, noting that his health seemed to be as usual.

At the Union Baptist Church in Ormond, where Mr. Rockefeller was a frequent attendant up to three years ago, the bell in the steeple was tolled to mark his passing.

James Davis, the Negro sexton of the church, to whom Mr. Rockefeller had given many a shiny silver dime during the twenty-three years he had been coming to Ormond Beach, pointed out the pew in which the late oil man used to sit.

"He was a fine, gentle soul and a real Christian," the sexton said.

He pointed to the hymnal board near the pulpit. It bore the announcement that the first psalm of the day would be the Twenty-third.

"It was his favorite psalm," Mr. Davis said. "Even though I walk in the valley of the shadow of death I shall fear no evil."

## Rockefeller Was Author Of Inspirational Poem

ORMOND BEACH, Fla., May 23 (*P*).—John D. Rockefeller Sr., who loved poetry and had a passionate desire to see others succeed in life, once wrote a poem of five lines describing his life.

As far as is known, it was the only poetry from his pen. He had it printed on cards and distributed many copies. It read:

I was early taught to work as well as play;
My life has been one long, happy holiday—
Full of work, and full of play—
I dropped the worry on the way—
And God was good to me every day.

# DR. BELL, INVENTOR OF TELEPHONE, DIES

## Sudden End, Due to Anemia, Comes in Seventy-Sixth Year at His Nova Scotia Home.

### NOTABLES PAY HIM TRIBUTE

### Lived to See Speech Reproduced Across the World—Pioneered in Aeronautics.

SYDNEY, N. S., Aug. 2.—Dr. Alexander Graham Bell, inventor of the telephone, died at 2 o'clock this morning at Beinn Breagh, his estate near Baddeck.

Although the inventor, who was in his seventy-sixth year, had been in failing health for several months, he had not been confined to bed, and the end was unexpected. Late yesterday afternoon, however, his condition, brought about by progressive anemia, became serious, and Dr. Ker of Washington, a cousin of Mrs. Bell, a house guest and a Sydney physician, attended him.

With Mr. Bell when he died were Mrs. Bell, a daughter, Mrs. Marion Hubbard Fairchild, and her husband, David G. Fairchild of Washington. The inventor leaves another daughter, Mrs. Elise M. Grosvenor, wife of Gilbert Grosvenor of Washington, who now is with her husband in Brazil.

At Sunset on Friday, on the crest of Beinn Breach Mountain, the body of Dr. Bell will be buried at a spot chosen by the inventor himself. The grave of the venerable scientist, the immensity of whose life work was attested by scores of Telegrams which came today to the Bell estate from the world's prominent figures, is at a point overlooking the town of Baddeck, Cape Breton. The sweeping vista from the mountain top, so admired by Dr. Bell, stretches far over the Bras d'Or Lakes. Sunset, chosen as the moment when the body will be committed to the sturdy hills, gilds the waters of the lakes until they are really what their name means—"the lakes of the arm of gold."

Dr. Bell asked to be buried in the countryside where he had spent the major portion of the last thirty-five years of his life. The inventor came to Cape Breton forty years ago, and five years later purchased the Beinn Breagh estate. His last experiments, dealing with flying boats, were made on Bras d'Or Lake.

American specialists who were rushing to the bedside of Dr. Bell were today returning to the United States. They were told of his death while aboard fast trains, bound for Baddeck, and, being too late, turned back.

*Special to The New York Times.*

WASHINGTON, Aug. 2.—Because of his long residence in Washington, his scientific position and his wide circle of friends, news of the death of Dr. Alexander Graham Bell shocked many in the national capital.

Officials of the National Geographic Society, of which Dr. Bell was a founder and a trustee, received advices that Dr. Bell had "passed away peacefully" from his son-in-law, David S. Fairchild of the United States Department of Agriculture.

On learning of his death President Harding sent this telegram to Mrs. Bell:

"The announcement of your eminent husband's death comes as a great shock to me. In common with all of his countrymen, I have learned to revere him as one of the great benefactors of the race and among the foremost Americans of all generations. He will be mourned

and honored by human kind everywhere as one who served it greatly, untiringly and usefully."

President Thayer of the American Telephone and Telegraph Company ordered the Bell system throughout the country to half-mast flags on its buildings. Mr. Thayer sent this telegram to Mrs. Bell:

"In behalf of all the men and women of the telephone system which bears his name, we extend our deepest sympathy and express grief in the passing of Dr. Bell. History will record the inestimable value of his services to mankind, but we who are carrying on the telephone art founded on his great discovery are peculiarly appreciative of his genius."

Dr. Bell's Washington home at 1,131 Connecticut Avenue is closed. A cousin, Charles J. Bell, President of the American Security and Trust Company and a civic leader, lives here.

News of Dr. Bell's death was cabled by the National Geographic Society to Dr. and Mrs. Gilbert Grosvenor, who are on their way to Rio de Janeiro, Brazil, where Dr. Grosvenor, who is President of the National Geographic Society, was to attend the Congress of Americanists as a delegate from the United States to that scientific gathering.

WEST ORANGE, N. J., Aug. 2.—Thomas A. Edison today paid the following tribute to his fellow-inventor, Alexander Graham Bell:

"I am sorry to learn of the death of Alexander Graham Bell, the inventor of the first telephone. I have always regarded him very highly, especially for his extreme modesty."

MIAMI, Fla., Aug. 2.—Dr. Alexander Graham Bell, who spent last Winter at the home of his son-in-law, Dr. David Fairchild, at Cocoanut Grove, near here, devoted much of his time to an attempt to develop a process to distill salt water in the event of disaster at sea, an invention which he declared would be of great benefit to the human race. He had not completed his experiments when he left for the North.

*Special to The New York Times.*

HARRISBURG, Pa., Aug. 2.—The death of Alexander Graham Bell recalls the litigation that extended over a period of eight years to determine whether Bell or Daniel Drawbaugh, noted inventor of Eberlys Mills, Cumberland County, was the original inventor of the telephone. Mr. Drawbaugh died eight years ago.

The first suit was brought by the American Bell Telephone Company against the Peoples Telephone Company, which had purchased Drawbaugh's invention. Through a number of courts the case was taken on appeal until a decision finally was rendered in favor of the Bell Company by the United States Supreme Court on March 19, 1888.

Drawbaugh, who was called the "Edison of the Cumberland Valley" and who invented many labor-saving devices, never took out a patent on his "talking machine," although he is known to have conceived the idea of creating it before 1875, the earliest date Bell is known to have started similar experiments.

Bell's patents were taken out in 1876 and 1877, and he claimed that his first work on the telephone was done on June 10, 1875. The final decision in Bell's favor was rendered by a divided court, Chief Justice Waite casting the deciding vote when the six Justices were evenly divided in their opinion.

Although a subsequent suit was brought in 1890 to invoke Bell's patents and to determine whether Drawbaugh or Bell was the inventor of the telephone, this suit was dragged out by counsel for Drawbaugh until the Bell patents had expired and there was no further reason to prosecute the action.

*Special to The New York Times.*

SCHENECTADY, N. Y., Aug. 2.—In paying tribute to Dr. Alexander Graham Bell, E. W. Rice Jr., honorary Chairman of the Board of Directors of the General Electric Company, said today:

"The news of Dr. Bell's death will come as a great shock to all those who ever had the rare pleasure of his acquaintance. His cheerful greeting and the stimulus of his great intellectual activity will be sorely missed. It seems too bad that such a personality cannot live forever in this world. However, of no man can it be more truly said that his deeds will live after him. He will, of course, be acknowledged as one of the world's greatest benefactors. His contribution to the telephone has made possible the achievements of modern business.

"His invention was not due to his knowledge of electricity. While Bell

**DR. ALEXANDER GRAHAM BELL,**
Inventor of the Telephone, Who Died Yesterday.

had a limited knowledge of electricity at that time, his profound knowledge of the nature of sound waves which accompany human speech and of the mechanics of its transmission and reproduction led him to his great discovery."

OTTAWA, Ont., Aug. 2.—Premier Mackenzie King tonight sent the following message to the widow of Dr. Alexander Graham Bell:

" My colleagues in the Government join with me in expressing to you our sense of the world's loss in the death of your distinguished husband. It will ever be a source of pride to our country that the great invention, with which his name is immortally associated, is a part of its history. On behalf of the citizens of Canada, may I extend to you

an expression of our combined gratitude and sympathy."

Alexander Graham Bell lived to see the telephonic instrument over which he talked a distance of twenty feet in 1876 used, with improvements, for the transmission of speech across the continent, and more than that, for the transmission of speech across the Atlantic and from Washington to Honolulu without wires. The little instrument he patented less than fifty years ago, scorned then as a joke, was when he died the basis for 12,000,000 telephones used in every civilized country in the world. The Bell basic patent, the famed No. 174,465, which he received on his twenty-ninth birthday and which has been sustained in a historic court fight, has been called the most valuable patent ever issued.

Although the inventor of many con-

trivances which he regarded with as much tenderness and to which he attached as much importance as the telephone, a business world which he confessed he was often unable to understand made it assured that he would go down in history as the man who made the telephone. He was an inventor of the gramophone, and for nearly twenty years was engaged in aeronautics. Associated with Glenn H. Curtiss and others whose names are now known wherever airplanes fly, he pinned his faith in the efficacy for aviation of the tetrahedral cell, which never achieved the success he saw for it in aviation, but as a by-product of his study he established an important new principle in architecture.

Up to the time of his death Dr. Bell took the deepest interest in aviation. Upon his return from a tour of the European countries in 1909 he reported that the continental nations were far ahead of America in aviation and urged that steps be taken to keep apace of them. He predicted in 1916 that the great war would be won in the air. It was always a theory of his that flying machines could make ever so much more speed at great heights, in rarefied atmosphere, and he often said that the transatlantic flight would be some time made in one day, a prediction which he lived to see fulfilled.

### A Teacher of Deaf Mutes.

The inventor of the telephone was born in Edinburgh, on March 3, 1847. Means of communication had been a hobby in the Bell family long before Alexander was born. His grandfather was the inventor of a device for overcoming stammering and his father perfected a system of visible speech for deaf mutes. When Alexander was about 15 years old he made an artificial skull of guttapercha and India rubber that would pronounce weird tones when blown into by a hand bellows. At the age of 16 he became, like his father, a teacher of elocution and instructor of deaf mutes.

When young Bell was 22 years old he was threatened with tuberculosis, which had caused the death of his two brothers, and the Bell family migrated to Brantford, Canada.

Soon after he came to America, at a meeting with Sir Charles Wheatstone, the English inventor, Bell got the ambition to perfect a musical or multiple telegraph. His father, in an address in Boston one day not long after, mentioned his son's success in teaching deaf mutes, which led the Boston Board of Education to offer the younger Bell $500 to introduce his system in the newly opened school for deaf mutes there. He was then 24 years old, and quickly gained prominence for his teaching methods. He was soon named a professor in Boston University.

But teaching interfered with his inventing and he gave up all but two of his pupils. One of these was Mabel Hubbard of a wealthy family. She had lost her speech and hearing when a baby and Bell took the most acute interest in enabling her to hear. She later became Mrs. Bell.

### Works Three Years on Telephone.

Bell spent the following three years working, mostly at night, in a cellar in Salem, Mass. Gardiner G. Hubbard, his future father-in-law, and Thomas Sanders helped him financially while he worked on his theory that speech could be reproduced by means of an electrically charged wire. His first success came while he was testing his instruments in new quarters in Boston. Thomas A. Watson, Bell's assistant, had struck a clock spring at one end of a wire and Bell heard the sound in another room. For forty weeks he worked on his instruments, and on March 10, 1876, Watson, who was working in another room, was startled to hear Bell's voice say:

" Mr. Watson, come here. I want you."

On his twenty-ninth birthday Bell received his patent. At the Centennial in Philadelphia he gave the first public demonstration of his instrument. He had not intended to go to the exposition. He was poor and had planned to take up his teaching again. In June he went to the railroad station one day to see Miss Hubbard off for Philadelphia. She had believed he was going with her. As he put her on the train and it moved off without him, she burst into tears. Seeing this, Bell rushed ahead and caught the train, without baggage or ticket.

An exhibition on a Sunday afternoon was promised to him. When the hour arrived it was hot, and the judges were tired. It looked as if there would be no demonstration for Bell, when Dom Pedro, the Emperor of Brazil, appeared, and shook Mr. Bell by the hand. He had heard some of the young man's lectures. Bell made ready for the demonstration. A wire had been strung along the room. Bell took the transmitter, and Dom Pedro placed the receiver to his ear.

" My God, it talks! " he exclaimed.

Then Lord Kelvin took the receiver. " It does speak," he said. " It is the most wonderful thing I have seen in America."

The judges then took turns listening, and the demonstration lasted until 10 o'clock that night. The instrument was the centre of interest for scientists the rest of the exposition.

The commercial development of the telephone dated from that day in Philadelphia.

### His Other Inventions.

While Alexander Graham Bell will be best remembered as the inventor of the telephone, a claim he sustained through many legal contests, he also became noted for other inventions. With Sumner Tainter he invented the gramophone. He invented a new method of lithography, a photophone, and an induction balance. He invented the telephone probe, which was used to locate the bullet that killed President Garfield. He spent fifteen years and more than $200,000 in testing his tetrahedral kite, which he believed would be the basis for aviation.

The inventor was the recipient of many honors in this country and abroad. The French Government conferred on him the decoration of the Legion of Honor, the French Academy bestowed on him the Volta prize of 50,000f., the Society of Arts in London in 1902 gave him the Albert medal, and the University of Wurzburg, Bavaria, gave him a Ph. D. Dr. Bell regarded the summit of his career as reached when in January of 1915 he and his old associate, Mr. Watson, talked to one another over the telephone from San Francisco to New York. It was nearly two years later that by a combination of telephonic and wireless telegraphy instruments the engineers of the American Telephone and Telegraph Company sent speech across the Atlantic.

In 1915 Dr. Bell said that he looked forward to the day when men would communicate their thoughts by wire without the spoken word.

" The possibilities of further achievement by the use of electricity are inconceivable," he said. " Men can do nearly everything else by electricity already, and I can imagine them with coils of wire about their heads coming together for communication of thought by induction."

In April of 1916 he declared that land and sea power would become secondary to air power. He expressed then the opinion that the airplane would be more valuable as a fighting machine than the Zeppelin and urged that the United States build a strong aerial fleet.

The inventor's last few years were spent in energetic efforts to materialize new dreams and in seeing wider and wider applications of his greatest one. In December, 1920, he was in London when that city talked by wireless with Geneva. That same year he perfected a device for cooling houses. Always he kept working at something, more often than not a something far afield from his earlier interests.

The telephone, in fact, had palled on him. There had piled up 3,000 patents atop his original basic one, and meantime he had put in some of his hardest years trying to develop flying. It was on his seventy-fifth birthday that he disclosed that he would not have a telephone in his own study, and that there was no telephone in the Cocoanut Grove home of his daughter-in-law, Mrs. Fairchild, in the Miami suburb where he was spending the Winter working toward fresh inventions.

Dr. Bell went abroad the last time two years ago, making a farewell visit to his native Edinburgh, and returning to say that he had found himself a stranger in a strange land, and that he was glad to get back to America, where he had lived most of his life.

Throughout his life Dr. Bell maintained his interest in deaf mutes. He founded the American Association to Promote Teaching of Speech to the Deaf and contributed $250,000 to its support. He was a member of many of the leading American societies of learning.

# WORLD MADE OVER BY EDISON'S MAGIC

**He Did More Than Any One Man to Put Luxuries Into the Lives of the Masses.**

---

**CREATED MILLIONS OF JOBS**

---

**Electric Light, the Phonograph, Motion Pictures and Radio Improvements Among Gifts.**

---

**LAMP ENDED "DARK AGES"**

---

He Held the Miracle of Menlo Park, Produced on a Gusty Night 50 Years Ago, His Greatest Work.

---

### By BRUCE RAE.

Thomas Alva Edison made the world a better place in which to live and brought comparative luxury into the life of the workingman. No one in the long roll of those who have benefited humanity has done more to make existence easy and comfortable. Through his invention of electric light he gave the world a new brilliance; when the cylinder of his first phonograph recorded sound he put the great music of the ages within reach of every one; when he invented the motion picture it was a gift to mankind of a new theatre, a new form of amusement. His inventions gave work as well as light and recreation to millions.

His inventive genius brooded over a world which at nightfall was engulfed in darkness, pierced only by the feeble beams of kerosene lamps, by gas lights or, in some of the larger cities, by the uncertainties of the old-time arc lights. To Edison, with the dream of the incandescent lamp in his mind, it seemed that people still lived in the Dark Ages. But his ferreting fingers groped in the darkness until they evoked the glow that told him the incandescent lamp was a success, and that light for all had been achieved. That significant moment occurred more than fifty years ago—on Oct. 21, 1879.

### The Miracle of Menlo Park.

A blustering wind beat gustily on the unpainted boards of a small laboratory in Menlo Park, N. J. A tall, lean figure stooped over a shaky table, his steel-blue eyes filled with the impassioned light of discovery. Beside him was a thin, nervous assistant. The dull golden glow of kerosene lamps, puffing off an oily odor, cast grotesque shadows on the walls, as every chance gust of air blown the lamp chimneys twisted the erratic flame.

Straining weary eyes in the dim and uneven light, the assistant fluttered the pages of a notebook—jottings on a miracle about to be performed. The corners of the laboratory were deep in shadow and the outside world was a waste of darkness, shot by occasional rifts of light. A few miles away was New York, with gas light in some of its homes, but table lamps still a household necessity. The hoofbeats of its leisurely traffic passed along streets brightened only by the pale yellow pools of light that circled the wide-spaced lamp posts. On Broadway the fabled midnight supper of the Victorian era was served under crystal chandeliers and gas globes; there was no spotlight in the theatres and the footlights were feeble gestures at illumination.

The two men in the laboratory were looking from a dim present into a dazzling future, from darkness to Broadway's brightest display. Gravely Francis Jehl told Mr. Edison that the lamp on the table had a good vacuum. An organ pump in a corner was started to force the air from the lamp. A minute or two went by in breathless silence. Then the inventor tested the vacuum. It was right, and he told Jehl to seal the lamp. The great moment was at hand. They moved to the dynamo and started it. Light sprang from the lamp like a newly created world to the watching men. Edison put on more power. He thought the makeshift filament would burst. Instead it grew bright. More power and more light. At last it broke. But the incandescent lamp had been invented.

### Tribute of a World Aglow.

Fifty years later the fruition of that night's work was dramatized in the golden anniversary of the electric light. Broadway, Piccadilly, the Champs Elysées, Unter den Linden flashed in golden brilliance. Cape Town, Rio de Janeiro, Peiping, Bangkok, Melbourne, Moscow—cities the world over, blazed an unconscious tribute, and at Dearborn, Mich., Edison feebly re-lived that memorable night in the history of scientific progress. In a reconstructed Menlo Park, with President Hoover and Henry Ford looking on, he and his faithful aide re-enacted the discovery of a half a century before, but with a different climax. The original scene at Menlo Park had been faithfully reproduced and every light extinguished, except the oil burners in the laboratory itself. At the second that the filament burned and Mr. Edison turned with a smile to the President, the dim yellow flame of the oil lamps leaped to a golden spray of amperes as a Ford foreman pulled a master switch. Dearborn leaped from the darkness, and powerful lights turned the night into noontime. Buildings emerged in twinkling frames, and airplanes, with their wings and fuselage outlined in electric lights, dipped and circled as the inventor, now grown feeble and silver-haired, returned to the dining hall to hear the President hail him as the benefactor of all mankind. He counted this the best of his gifts to humanity.

### The Magic Release of Music.

Then, in 1877, Edison invented the cylinder phonograph, a crude affair which was not perfected until 1890, and which was still undergoing refinement when the World War broke out in 1914. The average parlor music up to that time was provided by the harmonium, or the piano on which some musical maid practiced her scales or laboriously picked out tunes like "Hearts and Flowers." There was a monotony and a tameness to the household melody, even in the cities, and the fiddle held undisputed sway in rural districts. Then came the phonograph—at first a novelty, then a luxury and, finally, a commonplace. It brought the great arias of opera into the tenements. Caruso's voice soared for flat-faced Tibetans in the hill villages near Darjeeling. Traders saw to it that the spear-carrying natives of Central Africa had a chance to hear crack orchestras from Broadway and Piccadilly grind out jazz, with a faintly reminiscent note. And, fifty years from now, the voice of Caruso and all his contemporaries will be heard by those not yet born.

Edison had a hand even in the perfection of the radio, that invention which has given his phonograph a back seat in the march of progress. In 1876 he perfected the carbon telephone transmitter, which, in turn, helped in the evolution of the microphone. To complete his contribution to radio, it should be pointed out that in 1883, while studying the flow of current, he evolved what is known as the Edison Effect. This, in principle, is the basis for the De Forest radio lamp or tube.

### Stilled Images Brought to Life.

He first produced a motion picture camera in 1887, but it was not until 1891 that he perfected it. Curiously enough, this historic machine did not interest him to any great extent. He failed utterly to envision Hollywood and the huge industry that his genius made possible. To Edison a succession of flashes thrown on a screen so rapidly that they made a continuous picture had possibilities only as peep shows in penny arcades. When some one suggested that the pictures be shown in theatres he demurred, on the ground that to do so would interfere with the arcades. He did harbor the idea, however, that the pictures might be synchronized with the phonograph. This he never worked out, because of the failure of his early attempt to link conversation to moving pictures.

Thus he permitted others to carry on his pioneering in this fertile field, but it is because of his early discoveries that America leads the world in screen effects, and that the penny arcade, with its shooting gallery and knockout fight films, has yielded to the cathedrals of the screen. Also, because of Edison, it is possible for the natives of Kamchatka to sit impassively, row upon row, and see how the high school champion diving team of Rural Centre, Ill., put on a water carnival and raised money to pay the church mortgage. And vice versa, for the students of Rural Centre to see what the well-controlled native of Bengal does when a hungry tiger charges him. Edison did more than light the lamp at Menlo Park.

**THOMAS ALVA EDISON,**
From the Painting by Ellis M. Silvette.

# HENRY FORD IS DEAD AT 83 IN DEARBORN

## PIONEER IN AUTOS

### Leader in Production Founded Vast Empire in Motors in 1903

### HE HAD RETIRED IN 1945

### Began Company With Capital of $28,000 Invested by His Friends and Neighbors

By The Associated Press.

DETROIT, April 7—Henry Ford, noted automotive pioneer, died at 11:40 tonight at the age of 83. He had retired a little more than a year and a half ago from active direction of the great industrial empire he founded in 1903.

When he retired Mr. Ford was in excellent health, but turned over the management of the vast empire to his grandson, Henry Ford 2d, because, he said, he wanted to devote more time to personal interests.

Death came to the famed industrialist at his estate in Fairlane, in suburban Dearborn, not far from where he was born in 1863. At the Ford Company news bureau offices it was said that the exact cause of death would not be known until Henry Ford 2d, his grandson, could reach the family home, perhaps within an hour.

Mr. Ford was reported to have been in excellent health when he returned only a week ago from his annual winter visit to the Ford estate in Georgia.

### Kept Interest in Research

The automobile industry leader dropped completely out of the management of the far-flung Ford Company when he resigned as president late in 1945. He had been able to spend some time each week at the Ford engineering laboratory, where he maintained a private office and workshop, but was rarely seen about the administration building, where affairs of the big company were directed.

There were many reports that the elder Ford had given up his leadership of the Ford interests at the insistence of other members of his family, particularly the widow of his only son, the late Edsel B. Ford. Although never confirmed officially, reports had it that she was dissatisfied with the course of company affairs.

He leaves a widow, the former Clara Bryant, whom he married in 1887, and two grandsons, Henry 2d and Benson.

### Father of Mass Production

Henry Ford was the founder of modern American industrial mass production methods, built on the assembly line and the belt conveyor system, which no less an authority than Marshal Josef Stalin testified were the indispensable foundation for an Allied military victory in the Second World War.

Mr. Ford had many other distinctions. As the founder and unchallenged master of an industrial empire with assets of more than a billion dollars, he was one of the richest men in the world. He was the apostle of an economic philosophy of high wages and short hours that had immense repercussions on American thinking. He was a patron of American folkways and in later years acquired a reputation as a shrewd, kindly sage. But these were all relatively minor compared with the revolutionary importance of his contribution to modern productive processes.

His career was one of the most astonishing in industrial history. Nearing the age of 40 he was looked upon as a failure by his acquaintances — as a day-dreaming mechanic who preferred to tinker with odd machines than to work steadily at a responsible job. Yet within a dozen years he was internationally famous, and his Model T automobile was effecting changes in the American way of life of profound importance.

He lived to see the Ford Motor Company, which he founded with an initial investment of $28,000 put up by a few friends and neighbors who had faith in him, produce more than 29,000,000 automobiles before the war forced the conversion of its gigantic production facilities to weapons of war. Then he directed its production of more than 8,000 four-motored Liberator bombers, as well as tanks, tank destroyers, jeeps and amphibious jeeps, transport gliders, trucks, engines and much other equipment.

Struck a cruel blow shortly before his eightieth birthday by the death of his only son, Edsel Ford, on May 26, 1943, Mr. Ford unfalteringly returned to the presidency of the Ford Motor Company, which he had yielded to his son twenty-four years previously. He remained at its helm as it reached the peak of its gigantic war production, directing the war-expanded force of 190,000 workers.

Mr. Ford was born on July 30, 1863, on a farm near Dearborn, nine miles west of Detroit. He was the eldest of six children. His mother died when he was 12 years of age. He went to school until he was 15. Throughout his schooldays he worked on the farm after school hours and during vacations.

His mechanical bent first showed itself in an intense interest in the mechanism of watches. When he was 13 he took a watch apart and put it together again so that it would work. He had to do this work secretly at night, after he had finished his chores on the farm, because his father wanted to discourage his mechanical ambitions. His tools were home-made and were limited to a screwdriver and a pair of tweezers, fashioned respectively from a knitting needle and an old watch spring.

In 1879, at the age of 16, he took the step that foreshadowed his remarkable career. He ran away from home. Walking all the way to Detroit, almost penniless, he went to work as an apprentice in a machine shop. He did this in order to learn all he could of the making of machinery. He received $2.50 a week for ten hours a day, six days a week—a far cry from the wages paid in the Ford factories today. As he had to pay $3.50 a week for board and lodging, he took another job, working from 7 to 11 o'clock every night for a jeweler, for $2 more a week.

### Built a Steam Tractor

Returning to his father's farm to live, he spent his spare time for several years endeavoring to evolve a practical farm tractor of relatively small size and cost. He succeeded in building a steam tractor with a one-cylinder engine, but was unable to devise a boiler light enough to make the tractor practicable. For several years he confined himself to cutting the timber on forty acres his father had given him; operating a sawmill and repairing farm machinery for his neighbors.

Convinced that the steam engine was unsuited to light vehicles, he turned to the internal combustion engine, which he had read about in English scientific periodicals, as a means of locomotion for the "horseless carriage" of which he and other automobile inventors had dreamed. For several years he spent most of his spare time reading about and experimenting with the gasoline engine.

In 1890 he got a job as engineer and machinist with the Detroit Edison Company at $45 a month, and moved to Detroit. He set up a workshop in his backyard and continued his experiments after hours. He completed his first "gasoline buggy" in 1892. It had a two-cylinder engine, which developed about four horsepower, and he drove it 1,000 miles. The first, and for a long time the only automobile in Detroit, it was too heavy to suit Mr. Ford, who sold it in 1896 for $200, to get funds to experiment on a lighter car. Later, when he became successful, he repurchased his first car for $100 as a memento of his early days.

#### Named Chief Engineer

Meanwhile, he had become chief engineer of the electric company at $125 a month, but his superiors had no more use for his gas engine experiments than had his father. They offered to make him general superintendent of the company, but only on condition that he give up gasoline and devote himself entirely to electricity. He had the courage of his convictions, and he quit his job at the age of 36, on Aug. 15, 1899—a most important date, in view of later developments, in the automotive industry.

Mr. Ford had no money, but he persuaded a group of men to organize the Detroit Automobile Company to manufacture his car. The company made and sold a few cars on his original model, but after two years Mr. Ford broke with his associates over a fundamental question of policy. He already had envisioned the mass production of cars which could be sold in large quantities at small profits, while his backers were convinced that the automobile was a luxury, to be produced in small quantities at large profits per unit.

### RENTED ONE-STORY SHED

#### Built Car for Barney Oldfield Which Won All Its Races

Renting a one-story brick shed in Detroit, Mr. Ford spent the year 1902 experimenting with two-cylinder and four-cylinder motors. By that time the public had become interested in the speed possibilities of the automobile, which was no longer regarded as a freak. To capitalize on this interest, he built two racing cars, the "999" and the "Arrow," each with a four-cylinder engine developing eighty horsepower. The "999," with the celebrated Barney Oldfield at its wheel, won every race in which it was entered.

The resulting publicity helped Mr. Ford to organize the Ford Motor Company, which was capitalized at $100,000, although actually only $28,000 in stock was subscribed. From the beginning Mr. Ford held majority control of this company. In 1919 he and his son, Edsel, became its sole owners, when they bought out the minority stockholders for $70,000,000.

In 1903 the Ford Motor Company sold 1,708 two-cylinder, eight horsepower automobiles. Its operations were soon threatened, however, by a suit for patent infringement brought against it by the Licensed Association of Automobile Manufacturers, who held the rights to a patent obtained by George B. Selden of Rochester, N. Y., in 1895, covering the combination of a gasoline engine and a road locomotive. After protracted litigation, Mr. Ford won the suit when the Supreme Court held that the Selden patent was invalid.

From the beginning of his industrial career, Mr. Ford had in mind the mass production of a car which he could produce and sell at large quantity and low cost, but he was balked for several years by the lack of a steel sufficiently light and strong for his purpose. By chance one day, picking up the pieces of a French racing car that had been wrecked at Palm Beach, he discovered vanadium steel, which had not been manufactured in the United States up to that time.

With this material he began the new era of mass production. He concentrated on a single type of chassis, the celebrated Model T, and specified that "any customer can have a car painted any color he wants, so long as it is black." On Oct. 1, 1908, he began the production of Model T, which sold for $850. The next year he sold 10,600 cars of this model. Cheap and reliable, the car had a tremendous success. In seven years he built and sold 1,000,000 Fords; by 1925 he was producing them at the rate of almost 2,000,000 a year.

He established two cardinal economic policies during this tremendous expansion: the continued cutting of the cost of the product as improved methods of production made it possible, and the payment of higher wages to his employes. By 1926 the cost of the Model T had been cut to $310, although it was vastly superior to the 1908 model. In January, 1914, he established a minimum pay rate of $5 a day for an eight-hour day, thereby creating a national sensation. Up to that time the average wage throughout his works had been $2.40 for a nine-hour day.

## DEVISED CONVEYOR LINE

### Each Workman Performed One Specialized Operation

These policies were made feasible by the revolutionary organization of production devised by Mr. Ford. Under the old factory system, a single workman constructed an entire spring, using several dif-

ferent tools and performing many different operations in the process. Mr. Ford substituted an arrangement under which each worker performed a single specialized operation, which was simplified to the utmost by scientific study.

To make a single leaf of a spring, for instance, eleven workmen stood in line, each using a single tool. A moving conveyor belt carried the steel from which the leaf was made along the line, at waist-high level. The workers never had to stoop or move to get anything, and the speed at which they worked was controlled by the speed of the conveyor rather than the desires of the workmen.

Every part of the automobile had its own conveyor line, carefully integrated to bring the various parts to completion in the proper ratio. In later years Mr. Ford found it wasteful to assemble the cars at the great River Rouge plant in Dearborn, Mich., which instead was limited to the manufacture of parts. These were shipped to assembly plants scattered throughout the United States and in many foreign countries.

### Bought Own Mines and Forests

In order to reduce costs and eliminate intermediate profits on raw materials and transportation, Mr. Ford purchased his own coal mines, iron mines and forests, his own railways and his own lake and ocean steamships, all of which he operated on the Ford system of high wages, high production and low cost. Ownership of these collateral industries enabled Mr. Ford to keep down waste in men, time and material.

At the River Rouge plant, for example, iron from the furnace goes directly into the foundries and is poured without reheating. The slag from the furnace is used in a cement plant and all the steel scrap is converted by a combination of electric furnaces and a large rolling mill. In the Ford sawmills the parts are sawed directly from the logs, instead of converting the logs into lumber first. All the wood-working is done at the forest mill, the waste goes to a wood-distillation plant, and there is no waste in shipment.

The phenomenal success of the new system of production made Mr. Ford not only fabulously rich, but internationally famous, within a comparatively few years. His own very positive and often unusual opinions added to his renown. In the winter of 1915-16 he was convinced by a group of pacifists, of whom Rozika Schwimmer was the best known, that the warring nations in Europe were ready for peace and that a dramatic gesture would be enough to end the war.

### Chartered Peace Liners

Mr. Ford chartered an ocean liner, the Oskar II, with the avowed purpose of "getting the boys out of the trenches by Christmas," and sailed from New York on Dec. 4, 1915, with a curiously assorted group of companions. The mission was ridiculed and

failed to achieve anything. Mr. Ford himself left the party at Christiania, now Oslo, and returned home.

"We learn more from our failures than from our successes," was his comment.

When the United States declared war on Germany in April, 1917, Mr. Ford placed the industrial facilities of his plants at the disposal of the Government, although he had previously refused orders from belligerent countries. During the war he produced large quantities of automobiles, trucks, ambulances, Liberty airplane motors, munitions, whippet tanks and Eagle submarine chasers.

President Wilson persuaded Mr. Ford to become a candidate for United States Senator in 1918, although the manufacturer had never before displayed any particular interest in party politics. Going before the voters in the primaries on both the Democratic and Republican tickets, he received the Democratic nomination, but was defeated in the election by Truman H. Newberry, Republican, whose majority was reduced from 7,567 to 4,000 in a Senate recount. Previously Michigan had normally returned a Republican majority of 100,000, so that the closeness of the 1918 election showed Mr. Ford's personal popularity with the voters.

Mr. Ford retired as active head of the Ford Motor Company in 1918, at the age of 55, turning over the presidency to his son, Edsel, and announcing his intention of devoting himself thereafter to the development of his farm tractor, the Fordson, and to the publication of his weekly journal, The Dearborn Independent.

### Sued Chicago Tribune

In 1919 Mr. Ford sued The Chicago Tribune for $1,000,000 on the ground of libel, because of an editorial which was headed "Ford is an Anarchist," and which accused him of having been pro-German during the war. The jury awarded him a verdict of 6 cents, but only after counsel for the defense had subjected him to a pitiless cross-examination which revealed him to be almost without knowledge of subjects outside his own field.

His activities as publisher of The Dearborn Independent involved him in another highly publicized libel suit. The weekly published a series of articles, which were widely criticized as anti-Semitic. Aaron Sapiro, a Chicago lawyer, brought suit for $1,000,000 on the ground that his reputation as an organizer of farmers' cooperative marketing organizations had been damaged by articles which charged that a Jewish conspiracy was seeking to win control of American agriculture.

On the witness stand Mr. Ford disclaimed animosity toward the Jews. It was brought out that, although a column in the paper was labeled as his, he did not write it nor did he read the publication. The editor wrote articles expounding Mr. Ford's economic and social ideas after consulting with him. Mr. Ford settled the suit without disclosing the terms of settlement and discontinued the paper. He

appeased his critics by making a public apology, in which he explained he had discovered the articles were doing harm by the prejudice they created.

## WEATHERED 1921 CRISIS

### Refused Assistance of Bankers And Proved Resourcefulness

The 1921 business depression brought the Ford Motor Company its most severe financial crisis, and served to demonstrate both Mr. Ford's antipathy to bankers, and his resourcefulness. When it became acute the company had obligations of $58,000,000 due between Jan. 1 and April 18, and only $20,000,000 with which to meet them.

Investment bankers were convinced that he would have to go to them "hat in hand," and an officer of one large New York bank journeyed to Detroit to offer Mr. Ford a large loan on the condition that a representative of the bankers be appointed treasurer of the Ford Motor Company with full control over its finances. Mr. Ford silently handed him his hat.

He loaded up Ford dealers throughout the country with all the cars they could possibly handle and compelled them to pay cash, thereby adding nearly $25,000,000 to the funds in hand. Then, by purchasing a railroad of his own, the Detroit, Toledo & Ironton, and by other economies, he cut one-third from the time his raw materials and finished products were in transit. Thereby he was able to decrease by one-third the inventory of goods he needed on hand for uninterrupted production, and to release $28,000,000 from capital funds to ready cash.

### Raised More than Needed

In addition he realized nearly $8,000,000 from the sale of Liberty bonds, nearly $4,000,000 from the sale of by-products and $3,000,000 in collections from Ford agents in foreign countries.

On April 1, consequently, he had more than $87,000,000 in cash, or $27,000,000 more than he needed to wipe out all the indebtedness. Furthermore, by rigid economies of labor and materials hitherto thought impossible, he cut the overhead cost on each car from $146 to $93.

The crisis over, Mr. Ford severed all connections with the banks, except as a depositor. In fact, he became a competitor of the banks, frequently loaning several millions on call in the New York money market. He made a practice of carrying tremendous amounts on deposit in banks throughout the United States and in other countries. Bankers reported that he invariably drove a hard bargain in placing these funds. He often exacted a special rate of interest when his balance was to be above a certain amount for a certain time.

During the calm and increasingly prosperous years of the middle Nineteen Twenties Mr. Ford's business continued to grow, but more and more of his energies were devoted to his outside interests. He attempted in vain to interest the younger generation in old-fashioned dances and fiddlers. In 1923 he purchased the Wayside Inn at South Sudbury, Mass., which had been the subject of Longfellow's "Tales of a Wayside Inn," and restored it.

Mr. Ford startled the country late in 1926 by announcing the permanent adoption of the five-day week for his factories, after trying it out for some time. He declared that the five-day week would open the way to greater prosperity than that which the country then enjoyed and which he attributed to the eight-hour day and high wages, because they gave people time and money to consume the goods they produced. Without the five-day week, he said, the country would not be able to absorb the results of mass production and remain prosperous.

## DEVELOPED MODEL A

### Met Chevrolet Competition by Turning Out New Car

Late that same year Mr. Ford met his greatest industrial crisis. In 1924 the Ford company had manufactured about two-thirds of all the automobiles produced in this country, but by 1926 the Chevrolet car, manufactured by the General Motors Corporation, had become a serious competitor. Its production mounted from 25,-000 in January, 1926, to 77,000 in November, while Ford sales dropped.

Mr. Ford closed his plants late in 1926 while he experimented with a six-cylinder engine. He finally abandoned the Model T the next year, substituting the Model A, which became almost as well known. To produce the new model Mr. Ford had to make over almost his entire system of production, retooling his plants and retraining his workers, a feat of industrial renovation which many experts had contended would prove impossible.

The new model proved popular with the buying public, and the Ford Motor Company continued to expand. In 1928 Mr. Ford organized the British Ford Company, and subsequently began operations in other European countries. In Germany the German Ford Company was organized with the German dye trust as one of its principal stockholders.

### Aided Soviet Industrialization

Mr. Ford had long regarded Soviet Russia as a potential market of great importance. By agreeing to aid in the construction of an automobile factory at Nizhni-Novgorod, and by providing technological assistance in the development of the automobile industry in the Soviet Union, Mr. Ford sold $30,-000,000 worth of products to Russia, and, incidentally, gave added impetus to the industrialization of that country, which was to prove of such importance in later years.

When the stock market collapse of October, 1929, precipitated the great depression, Mr. Ford was one of the business and industrial leaders who were summoned to the White House by President Hoover. Unlike some industrialists who favored deflation of wages, Mr. Ford argued that the maintenance of purchasing power was of paramount importance.

Although the Ford Motor Company lost as much as $68,000,000 in a single depression year, Mr. Ford maintained his wage policy until the autumn of 1932, when it announced a readjustment from "the highest executive down to the ordinary laborer," including a new minimum wage scale of $4 a day, $1 less than that which he had put into effect eighteen years before. As the depression waned, however, he reverted to his high-wage policy and in 1935 established a minimum of $6 a day.

Mr. Ford was a central figure in the banking crisis which led to the closing of the Detroit banks in February, 1933, which in turn precipitated the chain of events that resulted in the national bank holiday when President Roosevelt was inaugurated the next month. When the collapse came the Ford Motor Company had about $32,500,000 on deposit in various banks of the Guardian Detroit Union group, and Edsel Ford personally and the Ford Motor Company had made loans of about $12,000,000 in cash and securities to try to stave off the closing.

How much the Ford interests lost because of the closing was never publicly revealed, but Edsel Ford subsequently helped to organize and capitalize a new national bank, the Manufacturers National Bank of Detroit, which took over most of the assets and obligations of the Guardian National group. Meanwhile the General Motors Company, Mr. Ford's closest business rival, aided by the Reconstruction Finance Corporation, opened another new bank, the National Bank of Detroit.

### Early Foe of New Deal

Mr. Ford, who had supported Herbert Hoover for re-election in 1932, was regarded as one of the leading foes of the New Deal in the early days of President Roosevelt's Administration, and he refused to sign the automobile code of the National Recovery Administration, which stipulated that employes had a right to organize. In 1936 he supported Gov. Alf M. Landon, stating that the election would "determine if labor and industry in this country can continue under a system of free enterprise."

Despite Mr. Roosevelt's triumphant re-election with the strong support of the Committee for Industrial Organization, then headed by John L. Lewis, Mr. Ford remained outspokenly antagonistic to unions. In an interview on Feb. 19, 1937, he advised all workers to "stay out of unions." At the same time he declared that no group of strikers would ever take over a Ford plant.

The United Automobile Workers, a CIO union, began a vigorous drive to organize the workers in the Ford plants. The opening blow was a sit-down strike in the Ford plant at Kansas City, ended only by the promise of officials there to treat with the union, a step the Ford company had never taken before. Other sporadic strikes occurred in Ford plants in other sections of the country.

Mr. Ford fought back with the argument that his policy of high wages and short hours was satisfactory to the bulk of the workers in his plants. He charged that a group of international financiers had gained control of the unions and were utilizing their power to exploit labor and management alike.

## HIS TROUBLE WITH UNION

### UAW Won 70% Votes After NLRB Ordered Election

On May 26, 1937, a group of UAW organizers, including Richard T. Frankensteen and Walter Reuther, were distributing organizing literature outside the gate of the Ford plant at River Rouge, when they were set upon and badly beaten. The union charged that the beatings were administered by Ford company police. The Ford Motor Company denied this.

After lengthy hearings the National Labor Relations Board found the Ford Motor Company guilty of unfair labor practices. The Ford company fought the issue through the courts to the United States Supreme Court, which, in effect, upheld the finding by refusing to review it. In April, 1941, the UAW called a strike in the Ford plants and the NLRB held an election under the Wagner Act to determine the collective bargaining spokesman for the employes.

When the votes were counted in June, 1941, the UAW was found to have won about 70 per cent of them. With characteristic vigor, Mr. Ford, long looked upon as perhaps the strongest foe of unionism, did a complete about face. He signed a contract with the union which gave them virtually everything for which they had asked, including a union shop and a dues check-off system.

In the early days of the second World War, Mr. Ford opposed our entry into it and, true to his pacifist convictions, refused to manufacture airplane motors for Great Britain. He compelled the cancellation of a contract made by his son, Edsel, calling for the production of 6,000 Rolls-Royce engines for Great Britain, and 3,000 of the same type for the United States. To support his contention that the United States was in no danger Mr. Ford, in May, 1940, stated that if it should become necessary the Ford Motor Company could "under our own supervision, and without meddling by Government agencies, swing into the production of a thousand airplanes of standard design a day." As the pressure for re-armament became greater, Mr. Ford was compelled by public opinion to agree to build planes for the United States.

The net result was the celebrated

Willow Run plant for the construction of four-motored bombers. At its construction it was the largest single manufacturing establishment in the world, occupying a building 3,200 feet long and 1,280 feet wide, with 2,547,000 feet of floor space. In addition there were hangars with another 1,200,-000 feet of floor space, and an adjacent air field larger than La Guardia Field in this city.

## PRODUCED 8,000 B-24'S

### Plant at Willow Run Turned Out One Bomber an Hour

Ground was broken for the plant on April 18, 1941, and the first of the thirty-ton B-24-E bombers came off its assembly line a little more than a year later, in May, 1942. For a time the plant was under severe criticism on the ground that it was not producing at the rate that had been anticipated, but this was eventually stilled when the gigantic factory began turning out bombers at the rate of one an hour, twenty-four hours a day.

By the spring of 1945, when the War Department announced that the production of Liberator bombers would be discontinued, Willow Run had produced more than 8,000 of them. In May, 1945, a spokesman for the company revealed that it had no plans for the post-war utilization of the gigantic factory, and that it planned to turn it back to the Defense Plant Corporation, the Government agency which had put up the $100,000,-000 it cost.

When Mr. Ford resumed the active management of the company, after the unexpected death of his son, Edsel, he began a series of changes in its high officials. In March, 1944, Charles E. Sorenson, who had been considered for years as its greatest production expert, announced his retirement from the company. Not long after that Mr. Ford's personal secretary, Ernest G. Liebold, was dismissed, after having been one of the company's top executives for many years.

The Ford Company asked for and obtained the release of Henry Ford 2d, son of Edsel Ford, from the Navy, in which he had served for two and a half years and had risen to the rank of lieutenant, on the ground that he was needed in the executive end of the business. Mr. Ford let it be known that he was grooming his grandson and namesake, then 26 years old, for the eventual leadership of the business.

From time to time Mr. Ford gave interviews in which he emphasized his favorite beliefs: the folly of war, the need for world federation, the decentralization of industry, the advantages of hard work, utilitarian education, abstemiousness and simple pleasures. He was opposed to the use of tobacco and liquor, and he hated idling.

In a characteristic interview in September, 1944, he made known his adherence to his old doctrine of high wages for his employes. Declaring his intention of raising the wages of his workers as soon as the Government would allow him to do so, Mr. Ford said:

"As long as I live I want to pay the highest wages in the automobile industry. If the men in our plants will give a full day's work for a full day's pay, there is no reason why we can't always do it. Every man should make enough money to own a home, a piece of land and a car."

Mr. Ford was an ardent collector of Americana. In 1928 he established, and endowed with $5,000,000, a museum at Dearborn to commemorate the inventions of his old friend, Thomas A. Edison. The Menlo Park Laboratory, in which Mr. Edison perfected the electric light, was completely restored in the museum.

Mr. Ford also built Greenfield Village, a reproduction of the community in which Mrs. Ford, who was Clara Bryant before their marriage in 1887, was born. There he brought the original log cabin in which McGuffey, author of the celebrated reader, was born; the court house in which Abraham Lincoln first practiced law, and the home of Stephen Foster's parents, as well as momentos of his own youth.

One of his lifelong interests was in the training of youths to earn a livelihood, and he established various vocational schools for the purpose. He also made it a policy to employ a fixed proportion of blind persons and other handicapped individuals in his plants, and took a keen interest in the rehabilitation of wounded war veterans. At its convention in September, 1944, the American Legion awarded to him its Distinguished Service Medal for his efforts in behalf of disabled veterans of both world wars.

# World Leaders in Tribute

In the capitals of the world yesterday, as in the humble homes of the country, the passing of Henry Ford was sincerely mourned. British newspapers carried the story of Mr. Ford's death with streamer headlines, pointing out that the English Ford Company now employs many thousands in a huge plant outside London.

In Amsterdam, the Netherlands, the flag above the big plant of the Netherlands Ford Company was flown at half staff. In Rio de Janeiro, Brazil, all evening papers carried Mr. Ford's picture, calling him "world benefactor."

Among the tributes were:

### President Sends Message

President TRUMAN—In a message to Mr. Ford's widow and family: In the sorrow which has come with such sudden and unexpected force I offer to you and to all who mourn with you this assurance of deepest sympathy.

ALFRED P. SLOAN Jr., Chairman of the Board of General Motors—The impact of Henry Ford's inventive and productive genius on the well-being of America is incalculable. He typified the best in American enterprise. He pioneered mass production, which has become the keystone of American economy. He contributed directly and by example to our high living standards. The nation's debt to him is large and enduring.

C. E. WILSON, President of General Motors—His life and example will continue to be an inspiration to the youth of America. His perseverance in overcoming heavy odds at a time when things he worked at were considered impractical provides an outstanding example of what can be done in America.

ORVILLE WRIGHT, airplane pioneer—He did more to promote the welfare of the American people, and particularly the working class, than any man who ever lived in this country. The present great wealth of this country has come indirectly from Mr. Ford through his development of mass production.

MRS. THOMAS A. EDISON, widow of the inventor—We have lost a friend and one near and dear to all of us.

CHARLES EDISON, former Governor of New Jersey, son of the inventor—I am grieved and shocked. My father was devoted to him and admired him enormously. His contributions to civilization have been beyond measure. He was my friend and no one ever had a better one.

### Called Industrial Genius

THOMAS E. DEWEY, Governor of New York State—Our nation has suffered the loss of one of the great men of our times. His industrial genius contributed mightily to the development of our country. His philanthropic activities did much to bring our people educational, social and cultural gifts.

Senator ARTHUR H. VANDENBERG of Michigan—His death ends one of the greatest and most thrilling careers in the life of his country. It is the vivid epitome of what a man can do for himself and his fellow-men under our system of American freedom through his own irresistible genius and courage. He not only rose from humble obscurity to fame and fortune but founded a new national economy of mass production which blessed his hundreds of thousands of employes with high wages and his millions of customers with low prices.

Representative GEORGE A. DONDERO of Michigan—A great man, who brought transportation within the reach of the average man. An ordinary American, he was willing to work, and through his work and concentration of effort he rose to the top.

B. E. HUTCHINSON, vice president of the Chrysler Corporation—He conceived and dramatized to his country and the world the possibility of the mass production of material goods for the benefit of all people. A great vision faithfully adhered to.

GEORGE ROMNEY, general manager of the Automobile Manufacturers Association—The greatness of the American automotive industry is largely the result of others applying his methods and ideals.

GEORGE MASON, president of the Automobile Manufacturers Association — One of the greatest creative forces of our time. He joined Edison, Pasteur and other

immortals. His Model T car has become a symbol of an era.

### Praise from Britain

Sir MILES THOMAS, Vice Chairman of the Nuffield Organization, One of Britain's Largest Automobile Companies—Everyone who uses a motor car ought to pay tribute to his pioneer work, because it was he who first put motoring within the reach of the ordinary man. He was a mechanic with a profound sympathy for metals. Many of the engineering principles of his Model T car have stood the test of time.

HARVEY S. FIRESTONE, President of the Firestone Tire and Rubber Company—It was a great privilege to have known him, and I feel a deep sense of personal loss in his passing. Few men in history have made so profound a contribution to the advancement of civilization and the welfare of mankind. Through his genius, personal transportation has brought a higher standard of living to millions. He exemplified the virtues of hard work, vision and service which made this country great, and sought to preserve these virtues through his philanthopy so that the human, simple, pioneering spirit of America might be perpetuated.

Count GIANCARIO CAMARINI, Vice President of the Fiat Automobile Company of Rome, Italy—His death made a very deep impression on the executives of my company, which is a little Ford of Italy. It was especially shocking as it occurred only eighteen months after that of Giovanni Agnelli, founder of Fiat, who was closely attached to Mr. Ford.

WILLIAM S. KNUDSEN, chairman of the board of the Hupp Motor Car Corporation—A great teacher, and a great inspiration to all of us in American industry. He will be forever remembered for the things he has done and the beautiful example of his personal life.

PAUL H. GRIFFITH, National Commander, American Legion—His spirit will ever remain an inspiration for those who admired him.

EDDIE RICKENBACKER, president, Eastern Airlines—Deeply regret the untimely passing of my good friend, Mr. Ford, and hasten offer my condolences and deepest sympathy to you and other members of the family.

JOSEPHUS DANIELS, former Secretary of the Navy—I wish he could have lived to see the world peace that was near his heart.

# NATION GOES DRY UNDER WARTIME ACT; SOME WILL SELL BEER AND LIGHT WINES, BUT PALMER REFUSES TO GIVE IMMUNITY

## BEER SELLERS RISK PENALTY

### "Pendency of Litigation No Protection Against Prosecution."

### SEEKS EARLY COURT RULING

### Meanwhile Attorney General's Department Stands Ready to Act on Complaints.

### 'DRYS' INTRODUCE NEW BILL

### Seek Legislation for Prohibition Between End of Demobilization and Jan. 16, 1920.

*Special to The New York Times.*

WASHINGTON, June 30.—With the strong arm of the Federal Government prepared to enforce it, the wartime prohibition law of Nov. 21, 1918, went into effect at midnight tonight.

The Department of Justice will have exclusive jurisdiction over the enforcement of the act. The Bureau of Internal Revenue of the Treasury Department will not be responsible for enforcement, but, all internal revenue officers have been instructed by Internal Revenue Commissioner Roper to co-operate with the Department of Justice.

* * * * *

While he does not specifically say so in his announcement, the Attorney General, pending decision by the courts whether 2¾ per cent. beer is intoxicating, is understood to have decided to permit Federal District Attorneys to prosecute in cases where complaint has has been made that the law has been violated through the sale or manufacture of beer containing more than 1½ per cent. of alcohol. It is understood that it is not the intention of the Attorney General at this time to make any drive of his own against violation of the law through sale of beer containing from one-half of 1 per cent. to 2¾ per cent. of alcohol, but where complaint is made, or where warrants and prosecution are sought for sale or manufacture of beer containing more than one-half of 1 per cent. of alcohol, the legal machinery of the Department of Justice, in its many ramifications throughout the country will be made available for prosecution.

The Attorney General's statement did not say distinctly that prosecutions would be made for sale of beer containing more than one-half of 1 per cent. of alcohol, but it was pointed out by a high official at the Department that it also does not say distinctly that there will not be prosecutions and arrests for such sales. But the clear inference was permitted to be drawn at the Department of Justice that when complaint is made that sale of beer containing more than one-half of 1 per cent. of alcohol has violated the law, that the Department will act.

### Will Not Initiate Prosecutions.

The position of the Attorney General is understood to be that he does not of his own volition, pending decision of the courts respecting beer containing less than 2¾ per cent. of alcohol, care to pile up a lot of the 2¾ per cent. cases, but that he cannot interfere with prosecutions where complaint has been made, arrests effected, or prosecutions sought for sale of beer containing more than one-half of one per cent. of alcohol. After the courts have made their rulings in the cases now pending in the 2¾ per cent. cases, the Attorney General will be guided by their decision.

Meanwhile it is understood the initiation of arrests in cases involving making and sale of beer containing more than one-half of 1 per cent. for beer will be left to those who care to make complaints, and in all such cases, it is understood, the Department of Justice will act. It was asserted tonight that since there is no doubt that complaints will be filed by prohibition leaders, Anti-Saloon organizations, and others who are opposed to the sale of one-half of 1 per cent. beer, there can be no doubt that there will be prosecutions in such cases instituted by agents of the Department of Justice on such complaints.

In his statement the Attorney General appeals for the co-operation of local authorities, State and municipal, and says that warrants for offenders will be issued by District Attorneys on evidence furnished by agents of the Bureau of Investigation of the Department of Justice, agents of the Internal Revenue Department, local officers, and "others," and that all such warrants will be served promptly by United States marshals and their deputies. The use of the word "others" is important. It means that action will be taken on the basis of evidence submitted by private individuals and by the Anti-Saloon League and other prohibition organizations.

How long the law will remain in effect is problematical, but there were developments today indicating that—unless held unconstitutional by the courts—war-time prohibition will be continued in effect until national prohibition goes in effect on Jan. 16, 1920, and that the country will never again be wet.

President Wilson has indicated that he will exercise his power to lift the ban and wipe out war-time prohibition when the demobilization of the army has terminated. The most favorable opinion is that the army will not be demobilized inside of six or seven weeks, and some believe it will take ninety days to bring about a reduction of the army to a point where the President would feel justified in issuing his proclamation of demobilization.

### "Drys" Press Their Advantage.

Were this the only obstacle in the path of lifting the ban on war-time prohibition those who are opposed to the country's going dry might hope for a return to normal conditions somewhere between Aug. 15 and Sept. 1. But the prohibition elements are now on fighting edge and prepared to press their present advantage to the limit, and do not propose to have any breathing spell granted the "wets" between now and the going into effect of national prohibition, if they can possibly prevent it. Anticipating that when the army is demobilized the President will keep his promise to lift the ban on war-time prohibition, the "drys" are planning to urge legislation to keep the country dry between the termination of demobilization and the going into effect next January of national prohibition.

A step in this direction was taken today by Representative Charles H. Randall, Prohibition member from Los Angeles, who introduced a bill in the House "to keep the country from going on a whiskey-drinking basis" in the period from demobilization until the effective date of constitutional prohibition. The Randall bill would prohibit the removal of distilled spirits from bond for beverage purposes, and prevent the shipping in interstate or foreign commerce of all distilled malt, vinous, and other intoxicating liquors.

The wets, who appear to be in a hopeless minority in the present Congress, are planning to do away with wartime prohibition as quickly as possible. Representative Igoe of St. Louis, a member of the House Judiciary Committee, announces that he will seek to have the Volstead Prohibition Enforcement bill amended so as to give the President power immediately to lift the wartime prohibition ban.

Anti-saloon leaders are well organized and intend to make a very active campaign against violators with a view to furnishing evidence to agents of the Department of Justice.

### Promises Prosecutions at Once.

"The saloons in 90 per cent. of the cities will close at midnight, never to open again," said Representative Randall, father of wartime prohibition, today. "The owners of 10 per cent. will face the Federal courts within forty-eight hours after they defy the law. The dry forces are thoroughly organized to assist in the prompt enforcement of wartime prohibition, believing that effective enforcement is highly important at the beginning of nation-wide prohibition."

The bill which Mr. Randall introduced today for the purpose, among other things, he said, of keeping the country from "going on a whiskey-drinking orgy between the termination of demobilization and the going into effect of national prohibition, follows:

"That from and after the approval of this act no distilled spirits held in bond shall be removed therefrom for beverage purposes. The Commissioner of Internal Revenue is hereby authorized and directed to prescribe rules and regulations, subject to the approval of the Secretary of the Treasury, in regard to the removal of distilled spirits held in bond, for other than beverage purposes.

"After the approval of this act no distilled, malt, vinous, or other intoxicating liquor shall be imported into or exported from the United States, nor shall any such liquor be transported by common carrier or by any person in any manner from one State, Territory or district, to another State, Territory or district of the United States. Any person who shall violate this act or any rule or regulation made thereunder, shall be punished by a fine not exceeding $5,000, or by imprisonment for not more than two years, or both."

# PROHIBITION TO BLAME

## Psychologist Places Crime Wave, Immorality Wave and Gluttony Wave at Its Door

THE crime wave, the murder wave, the immorality wave, the gluttony wave, the return in triumph of absinthe after years in exile, the new fad of drinking eau de cologne as a routine beverage, the smut on the stage and in windows of novelty and tobacco shops, the drunkenness of people who used to be temperate, the carnivals of intoxication at many public dinners where men used to behave, the drinking in homes where liquor was previously unknown, the growing taste of once nice people for unexpurgated Oriental-plus dancing—these are a few of the outward symptoms of a profound national moral breakdown due largely to prohibition, as its effects are seen by Dr. A. A. Brill, the psychologist and specialist in nervous and mental diseases.

Dr. Brill asserts that more alcohol is being consumed than ever before, that people are drinking who never used to drink, that moderate drinkers have become heavy ones, that the former consumers of beer and light wines are drinking whisky, brandy, gin, raw alcohol and other concentrated spirits.

One of his patients, he said, makes a pure alcoholic beverage out of tomatoes. An engineer friend of his makes his own whisky in his kitchen. Others of his friends and patients make their own gin. Among his patients are several confirmed eau-de-cologne sots. They resorted to it originally during brief panicky periods when spirits were hard to obtain, and grew quickly to like it, so that they now consume it by preference.

The only man not getting his share of liquor, according to Dr. Brill, is the working man. When he does get his share, it is usually in the form of a terrific dose of some fluid only a few degrees milder than knock-out drops.

The men who have taken to crime in the last few years, according to Dr. Brill, are defectives who would be in the main harmless, except to themselves, if they were allowed to drink under different conditions. Prohibition, he says, makes desperate criminals of them in two ways—in some cases the absence of liquor gives free rein to the half-insane tendencies which formerly evaporated in alcoholic dreams and vaporings; in some cases, drugs or the poisonous, maddening intoxicants of a prohibition era inflame the morbid imaginations and send them forth to kill and rob.

#### Moral Injuries.

One of the deep-seated moral injuries wrought on the nation by prohibition, according to Dr. Brill, is the fact that hundreds of thousands of men and women, who formerly would never have dreamed of violating any law, consciously violate the dry laws in patronizing bootleggers and make a national jest of the subject. Hardly a jury ever sits in judgment on a criminal, he said, without several of the jurors knowing that they themselves have been violating the law with regularity. The whole proceeding, he said, gives a nation a bad conscience. The man of integrity who is the backbone of the country has lost something of the former consciousness of rectitude which made him the highest type of citizen.

"Our so-called nice people or best people," he said, "are now breaking the law all the time. I have gone to public dinners where there formerly was a little decent drinking, but no one intoxicated. Now word is whispered around in advance that every one is to bring something with him. There is heavy drinking, and the affair ends in a disgraceful scene.

"Cocktails and hard liquors are served to guests now in private homes, where this custom did not formerly prevail. It has become now the universal practice. The guests expect it. The hosts would feel that they were not as good as their neighbors if they did not serve plenty of liquor. I have seen Judges and well-known men drinking openly in public places. The conversation is often a discussion of the merits of this bootlegger as against that one. Now, all this is degrading and demoralizing. It cannot just pass off without any effect. It is having a far-reaching bad effect."

Dr. Brill said that there were on every hand signs of an increase of gluttony since prohibition.

"Overeating kills more than overdrinking," he said. "That is not questioned by anybody who has had any medical experience. The consumption of pastry and candy as a substitute for alcohol has increased enormously. Candy eating is much more harmful than moderate drinking, and it does not give the benefit as an emotional outlet that comes from moderate drinking."

Dr. Brill said that he had always regarded the saloon as a pernicious institution peculiar to America, and that he regarded its destruction as one of the compensations of prohibition.

"But instead of controlling something that would be a benefit to the community and that offers a good outlet psychologically," he said, "we have in absolute prohibition taken a course which puts a premium upon crime.

"Before prohibition came there were only a comparatively few people who gave us a problem. Those habitual drunkards were all defective persons. When you take alcohol from them, they are an ever-greater menace to society. The worst they used to do was to become drunk, get sick and go to a hospital or a prison. But when alcohol is taken from them they always resort to something else which is much worse to society. A defective will always remain a defective. He will never be able to adjust himself to society, and will always do something contra-social. It is just a question of what he will do.

"But prohibition has done great harm to the normal people who used to drink moderately. It has never been shown in any scientific way that this moderate drinking decreased their efficiency. On the contrary, the moderate drinkers have belonged to the higher type of people in the best civilization—as against the non-drinking Turks, Chinese and Africans.

"The average normal individual has never been a problem to the community as a result of indulging in alcoholic beverages, until now that the legal right to do so has been taken away from him.

"Wherever there has been a prohibition of anything, it means that there has been a strong abuse. Now, prohibition started in small provincial communities, where the people were below the standards of cosmopolitan education. In other words, it took hold in places where there were lynchings, camp meetings and heavy drunkenness, even among people of high type. These were not communities in which people had recreations of the better sort or artistic, esthetic and intellectual pleasures. Prohibition started in narrow spheres, where everything primitive still prevailed."

The abuse of alcohol, while excessive in such communities, has been shown by experience to be a lesser evil than prohibition, according to Dr. Brill. Immorality, he said, had been promoted, as well as crimes of violence.

"There is no question at all that all primitive impulses are enhanced as a result of prohibition. When people cannot get an outlet through alcohol, which was a very concentrated good outlet for the average normal persons, they have to get it in something else. The extreme forms of dancing which have made their appearance, the inability of reform organizations to control any longer the publishers of indecent pictures, the degradation of some of the theatrical productions, are partly due to the stimulation which prohibition has given to primitive impulses. These evils are also able to manifest themselves because the disgust of the public with reform and restrictive legislation is such that they will have no more of it.

"And all this has been brought about with the object of protecting from alcohol the smallest minority, the type of defectives who furnished the habitual drunkards. They cannot be protected. They are killing themselves off now as fast, or perhaps faster, than ever. It is important for the human race that this stock should not be preserved. Misguided sympathy has for years actually protected the unfit to the great detriment of the normal person. As far as prohibition saved them, it would have injured society. But the unbalanced, inferior types are bound to fall in one way or another. Prohibition is possibly hastening their end, but in increasing their addiction to crimes of violence has unfortunately caused the death of many good citizens and a great loss to society.

"Last, but not least, prohibition is destroying the fabric of our society by forcing the highest type of law-abiding people to violate the law. They are not going to give up a life-long habit in which they see no harm because a reformer wants them to do it."

# CINCINNATI AND DETROIT: EXPERIMENTERS WITH LABOR

## Two Cities Adopt Contrasting Methods in Meeting Cost of Living, and Americanization— Question—What the Middle West Thinks of Prohibition, About the Peace Treaty It Thinks Little

By CHARLES A. SELDEN.

NOT only has our wartime effort to see the world as a whole vanished, but we are split into many experiment stations to deal with national questions, and so are only locally considering local fragments of them.

This is not intended as a summary of the labor situation, perhaps the greatest of those problems, but as a condensation of facts and impressions acquired in Ohio, Indiana, and Michigan, at the outset of a journey intended to cover the United States and to determine what the people are thinking, what they are earning, whether they are discontented, and how they are living at the end of this first year since the armistice.

Cincinnati and Detroit illustrate strikingly the divergence in our methods of meeting the labor question. In Cincinnati, which is not a strong union labor town, there is an increasing opinion among some of the employers that now it would be the part of wisdom for manufacturers to accept and support the conservative element in labor as organized by craft rather than risk conflict later on with the radical labor element, organized, not by craft, but by industry and approaching "the one big union" as its ultimate goal. In other words, there are former ultra conservatives among bankers and manufacturers in Cincinnati and the industrial region which it dominates who would support Samuel Gompers in his present struggle against the radicals who are trying to get control of the American Federation of Labor, and who have been able so far to compel Federation endorsement of the coal strike and the granting of Federation charters to the police of Boston and other cities.

But there is no such tendency noticeable in the open-shop City of Detroit, where Gompers is still as cordially detested and as vigorously fought by the Employers' Association as he is by such radical labor organizations as the Auto Workers' Union.

There is another difference between Cincinnati and Detroit which seems paradoxical in view of the one already indicated. Cincinnati attributes its industrial peacefulness of the moment, its freedom from race riots and labor disturbances, accompanied by violence, largely to the fact that it has kept intact and very much alive and in fighting trim its volunteer armed Home Guard, which came into existence at the beginning of the war. On the other hand, Detroit has a Mayor and Police Commissioner who have succeeded in keeping order by giving, or in spite of giving, wide scope to the activities of the radicals and by allowing "free speech" to the extent of letting Emma Goldman and others like her address public meetings in support of political amnesty.

This article is based on talks with statesmen who admit they don't know what is going to happen next and with politicians who do not hesitate to predict exactly what will happen in 1920; on talks with decent, level-headed, farseeing employers for whom the word "welfare" is something more than a technical term recently added to the vocabulary of workshop management; on talks with a few employers who are farseeing in the other direction. They can look backward twenty-five years and revel in the view, but they can't or won't look ahead twenty-five minutes. There are just a few such left. They seem to enjoy talking about the use of machine guns and the quantity production of corpses in American streets as a necessary preliminary to the orderly peaceful quantity production of any other commodity.

Also it is based on talks with laborers and labor leaders who are level-headed and farseeing, who can't be bought or fooled by the free use of a pair of dumbbells or a set of dominoes or with a two-cent cup of coffee in the noon hour, but who, nevertheless, look upon employers as fellow-beings whom they have no desire to eliminate. It's true, of course, that many of these have ideas wisely or unwisely differing from those that for a long time have prevailed, but they have no wish for the adoption of those ideas by any methods other than are provided by the law of the land.

Further, it is based on talks with workers or misleaders of workers who are as red as they are painted. But these, too, are few. In proportion to the whole number of workers the number of Red radicals, the advocates of violence, is probably no greater than the number of machine gun advocates, or what Bishop Williams of Michigan calls the Red reactionaries, is to the whole number of employers. The trouble is that each class of Reds can, in hectic moments of danger, swing many individuals of their respective groups to their color.

### Free Speech and Suppression.

People of this or that city or State are far more interested in what their returned soldiers are doing as members of their local branch of the American Legion than in what those soldiers did in France as members of the great American Expeditionary Force.

Different counsels seem to guide the American Legion in different places. In Cincinnati I was referred to a small hall in Vine Street as the real danger spot of the city, the headquarters of the Reds of all sorts. The hall was empty, but in a combination kitchen and office opening from it was Lotta Burke, a white-haired woman, with a paper sweeping cap on her head, dividing her attention between writing a speech and stirring something on the range to prevent its burning. I do not know whether it was hell broth, or which was hotter, the speech or the stuff in the kettle. The woman was much like Mother Jones, who used to go to Hoboken and Paterson a generation ago to stir up the silk workers. Lotta Burke contented herself with saying that almost everything was wrong, and for further particulars referred me to a heap of Communist Labor newspapers on the kitchen table.

That evening the American Legion of Cincinnati raided this Vine Street hole. Nobody was there. The raiders took away as a trophy a big American flag, which had hung over the stage of the hall, and threw the newspapers and propaganda leaflets into the street, where they burned them. But in the course of the dancing about the bonfire the Legionaries cheered the Cincinnati police, the same police who went on strike in September for more pay and recognition of their union, which they had organized under charter of the American Federation. The Home Guard, already mentioned, took the place of the policemen in September, and there was no violence nor increase of crime nor decrease in number of arrests. After a strike of several days all the policemen were allowed to return to their jobs. But the principle involved was exactly the same as in the Boston police' strike, where the men were not taken back, on the ground that they had been deserters from official public duty. When Calvin Coolidge was re-elected Governor of Massachusetts by an unprecedented majority on this very Boston police issue there was no city in the country which rejoiced more over this New England rebuke to disorder and desertion of public duty than the City of Cincinnati, which had restored its own police deserters to duty and pay without any hesitation.

Several nights after this bonfire in Pine Street and the cheering of the former Cincinnati police deserters by the Cincinnati members of the American Legion I was sitting in the Detective Bureau of Police Headquarters at Detroit talking with Detective Clarke, who had charge of that city's police work to keep the Reds in control. It was the night before Emma Goldman was to speak in Auto Workers' Hall at Detroit. William D. Haywood, by the way, was scheduled to speak in the same place a week later. Clarke's telephone bell rang and I heard his end of the conversation. He said: "Yes, it is true, Goldman is going to speak tomorrow night and Haywood a week from tomorrow night. They will have permission of the police and will be allowed to speak without molestation if they do not violate the Michigan Syndicalism act. We will have to protect them against disorder."

### What's the American Way?

After hanging up the receiver the detective told me that he had been talking to a representative of the American Legion.

"I hope nothing happens," added Clarke, "for it would be very embarrassing. I am a member of the Police Department and have become convinced that the policy of Dr. Inches, the head of the department, to allow anybody to say anything that is not in violation of the law is the best policy for the situation in Detroit. But I am also a member of the American Legion."

When asked what he would do in case Goldman did not violate the Michigan law, but the Legionaries did try to break up the meeting, the detective replied: "Well, I'm an American above everything else, and I'd try to think quickly what, under the circumstances at the moment, would be the most American thing to do."

Good answer! Clarke was in the Army Intelligence Service of the General Staff during the war.

The embarrassing situation did not arrive. Members of the Legion decided to abide by the ruling of the police, and, much to the surprise of the police, Emma Goldman did not violate the Michigan law. They had supposed that she would do so deliberately to get herself tangled up in a State court, hoping thereby to delay the Federal deportation proceedings pending against her. She did tell the meeting that she would fight deportation to the last stage by taking her case to the Supreme Court of the United States. A newspaper headline, with nothing in the story under it but that reference to the Supreme Court, said, "Goldman Defies the Government." Emma probably does defy the Government about five days a week, but she didn't happen to on this occasion when she declared for a hearing before its highest court.

The attitude of the newspapers of Detroit generally on labor matters is more or less peculiar to their city. It is their avowed policy, which has the indorsement of the Employers' Association and the Board of Commerce, not to print news of strikes and labor activities unless there is violence or something else sensational involved. This fact is held as a grievance against the papers on the part of the workers, who number about 325,000 of the city's million inhabitants and who consider that their affairs are news regardless of their merits or demerits. It is worth remarking, by the way, that the bitter resentment of manufacturers and business men of Detroit against Mayor Couzens and Dr. Inches, because of their theories as to what constitutes the safest way of handling radicals, is dying out to a great extent. Mr. Culver, the secretary and authorized spokesman of the Employers' Association, said to me, "Perhaps Dr. Inches has got the right idea. He seems to be able to apply his free-speech theory and at the same time save the city from violence or public violation of the law." The Cincinnati raid in Vine Street and the Emma Goldman meeting in Detroit serve to show how differently these two big manufacturing cities meet the Red question.

#### Safety First in Detroit.

Detroit, having gone more than 80,000 beyond the million mark in her number of inhabitants, doesn't want to run any unnecessary risks of losing her present lead in population over her chief rival, the City of Cleveland, on the opposite shore of Lake Erie. So the Michigan city is enjoying a series of picturesque safety-first campaigns to save her citizens from being run down by her 80,000 automobiles. At every spot in the city where a person has been killed in the last year, there is a sort of memorial, black bordered poster stuck on a lamp post to record the tragedy and warn the populace. But the most picturesque things in the enterprise are the round pulpits erected in the centres of the liveliest circles seven feet above the street surface, from which policemen preach all day sermons of safety by pantomime and semaphore to the dodging crowds afoot and the whirring crowds awheel circling around them on the pavement below. It is an effective method except for such newly arrived pedestrians as become so fascinated by watching the police preachers that they stand stock still in front of a car, and so get a direct, forcible, personal exhortation from the man in the pulpit with a sort of responsive chant from the chauffeurs. The lofty safety pulpits of Detroit are a good text, indeed, on which to hang a discussion of the Mid-West situation, for these policemen, just a little above the wild whirlpools of traffic coming into the circle from and going out in seven directions, seemed remarkably symbolic of the sane leaders of employers and employes in these three highly industrial and industrious States who are trying to save their part of the world from disastrous collision by convincing the reactionaries that they must go fast enough and the radicals that they must not go too fast.

**To go back to the beginning, there is so much that's right with the country that there's probably enough** of it to justify all the reasonable optimism there is. But it doesn't make so much noise as the wrong. For example, the people of Detroit who make the small individual bank deposits have in the city's savings institutions at the present time $186,000,000, as against $150,000,000 a year ago. But for facts like that you must dig a little. There's no trouble in finding a mass meeting in that same city called to protest against the cost of living.

Among the major subjects which naturally might be supposed to hold the intense interest of the people now are the not yet adopted treaties of peace with Germany and Austria, the Presidential election of 1920, prohibition, and the labor situation, with its allied problem of the cost of living. But the supposition is hardly justified by facts with reference to the treaties, the League of Nations, or the approaching national political campaign. Prohibition is rapidly losing ground as a live topic and being more and more widely accepted as a fact accomplished. The live questions, and they are getting more alive every day, are those concerning work and wages and profits, with the conflicting proposals for solution, selfish or disinterested, from many sources. About these things you may say, with literal accuracy, everybody is thinking and talking. However, a summary of somewhat negative results in trying to learn opinion on the other matters is of some interest.

#### Vague Knowledge of Treaties.

If the League of Nations is recalled to a citizen of the Middle West, he or she generally expresses the desire that it become a reality because he or she has heard or read that the League is the only tangible plan in sight to minimize the chances of war. But there's no such thing as popular, widespread familiarity with the provisions of the League or with the arguments which have been offered for and against it. Perhaps the number of people in any community who could discuss it intelligently would about equal the number of those who could discuss the Constitution intelligently. But probably many more people know of the prohibition amendment to the Constitution than about Article X. of the covenant of the League of Nations.

Interest in the pending treaties, beyond that portion of them establishing the League, is much more on the wane and a thousand times more vague than that in the League itself. Soldiers are home, demobilized, and back at their civilian jobs, and there are no more casualty lists. With those facts assured, there is no popular concern whatever on the question whether or not we are technically still at war with Germany; unless, perhaps, the answer to that question is a factor in deciding whether there may be a wet interval between wartime emergency prohibition and permanent constitutional prohibition. People remember seeing a great deal in the newspapers about the Paris Peace Conference nearly a year ago, but details of that event have slipped about as far back in public memory in the Middle West as have other great conferences which ended previous wars.

At the present moment, for example, popular interest in the coal mines in the United States leaves no room for discussion of the coal output from the Sarre Basin and from Westphalia. That is a case of contrasting two extremes, but the same suggestion holds good through the whole triple range of interests—those that are international, those that are national, and those that are local or provincial.

**Even in 1917, when America was under stress of the emotion of going into the war, Hoover said it was difficult to produce a sufficient degree of internationał mindedness to meet the requirements of the world emergency. With the ending of that emotionalization of war the painful effort to be international minded has dwindled almost to a negligible quantity under pressure of domestic anxieties and difficulties. Spiritually we are once more split into local communities. National and widespread as the coal strike may be, the popular interest in it within any given locality is primarily and naturally based on the immediate local effect of it, on the size of the reserve coal pile in that particular region. At least, that is the evidence of Ohio, Indiana, and Michigan.**

I'd like to say a little concerning what the people in these three States are thinking or saying about next year's Presidential election.

In Ohio they are saying the most, which is not much, and that is because Ohio has two Senators each of whom would like to be President and perhaps hopes that he can be: Harding, Republican, and Pomerene, Democrat. The best that Ohio Republican politicians seem to expect for Harding is that the convention situation might narrow down to him as the result of deadlock between two bigger men. Not for a moment does anybody in Ohio believe now that Harding would be a first-crack candidate. They fear that he belongs to a period which seems to have passed for good, that Harding would have been more in the picture in the palmy Senate days of the Aldrich and Platt régime, and even then would have been in the background. Harding does not antagonize anybody.

When Colonel Procter of Cincinnati, who is a member of the Republican Advisory Committee, declared himself for General Leonard Wood, and followed it up next day by assuring the public that he had spoken only as an individual and in no sense as the representative of the committee, the incident caused hardly a ripple. One comment on it by a banker and friend of Procter was that the Colonel was evidently hoping to play Hanna to Wood's McKinley. Democrats don't go beyond the point of mentioning Pomerene as a remote possibility, because they have not now sufficient confidence in the result of the election itself next November to be eager about what the nominating convention may do in June.

The only thing in Indiana that saves the general run of people in the State from 100 per cent. indifference as to next year's politics is the fact that some of them hope the Republican nomination will fall to Governor Goodrich. In Michigan a group of friends of General Wood and believers in him have formally declared their preference, but Michigan as a whole is not yet thinking anything about Presidential conventions or election. It's too early, and there are too many other things to think about.

#### Prohibition Making Its Case.

Now for prohibition: In Cincinnati, the President of a trust company said to me: "I have changed my mind just 50 per cent. on prohibition. I voted against it, and at that time I was against it on every count. I considered it unfair, an attack on personal liberty, and I thought also that it would do little good for the community as a whole and much harm. I still think it unfair and will tell you why. I have in my cellar a five-year supply of drinks. My chauffeur has not got a drop. That is discrimination. But, on the other hand, I have changed my mind as to the effect of prohibition on the community. We formerly had as a daily average 800 prisoners in our workhouse. Now we have seventy-five. The town is more orderly than ever before. My manufacturing friends tell me that Monday morning absenteeism of workmen because of Saturday and Sunday drinking has practically disappeared. Savings bank deposits have greatly increased. So I am still against prohibition on the score of fair play to everybody, but very much in favor of it as a practical good for this community. Financially, it has not hurt us, for most of the brewers saw it coming long before it came and took steps accordingly."

I did not see the banker's chauffeur, but talked to various workingmen without cellars in Cincinnati, and found a desire for beer, but not any conviction that the country was going to the devil without beer.

In Indianapolis the workhouse is empty and useless to the county. A man who had voted against prohibition (an editor this man was), said: "Thank God, we have not had whisky as a factor in this period of labor upheaval."

In Cleveland the total number of prisoners on the police correction farm during the four months of June, July, August and September of 1918, in the wet régime, was 2,053. In the corresponding four months of this year under the dry law the total was 685. Of course, there are violations and blind tigers in all towns, but they are not open or flagrant. The stranger cannot buy a drink. In the course of a fortnight's cruising about these three States I did not see a case of intoxication. I ate at clubs, hotels, restaurants with men who never had been total abstainers, but on no occasion did anybody attempt to produce a drink. What was more significant nobody mentioned a drink or thought to apologize for its lack, because the lack had ceased to be a novelty.

In Cleveland there had been more blind tigers than anywhere else in

**AMERICA'S PROBLEM, as Symbolized by the "Detroit Traffic Cop" Who Stands on a Raised Pulpit-Like Platform.**

*These policemen just a little above the wild whirlpools of traffic * * * seemed remarkably symbolic of the sane leaders * * * who are trying to save their part of the world from disastrous collision by convincing the reactionaries that they must go fast enough and the radicals that they must not go too fast."*

his part of the country until a sensational tragedy caused them to be closed. A police Lieutenant and two patrolmen, off duty and not in uniform, went to one of these places, where the Lieutenant got drunk. A civilian friend came along with an automobile and invited the three policemen for a ride. It was a joy ride that ended with the Lieutenant's shooting and killing his friend, who owned the car.

**Detroit's Dryness.**

In Detroit, where no Sunday law is enforced, where there is professional Sunday baseball and where all the regular theatres, as well as the motion picture shows, give Sunday performances, there is nevertheless a general observance, so far as my observation goes, and a somewhat resigned acceptance, of prohibition. Both employers and employes take issue with Samuel Gompers's charge that prohibition is the cause of all the labor unrest in Detroit. Michigan went dry on May 1, 1918. In the twelve months prior to that there had been in Detroit 10,299 arrests for felonies, 43,858 for misdemeanors, and 11,279 for drunkenness. In the first year of prohibition, beginning May 1, 1918, the corresponding Detroit figures were 6,318 arrests for felonies, 22,963 arrests for misdemeanors and 4,032 arrests for drunkenness.

Although these are police record figures, they are given to me by the Employers' Association representative, who seemed to think that they were among the best things he had to show concerning Detroit. He produced a clipping containing Gompers's charge, and said the head of the American Federation was as far from right on prohibition in Michigan as on other matters. He also said that Detroit manufacturing concerns were having fewer accidents and no Monday morning absentees. On this one subject the employers and William A. Logan, head of the Auto Workers' Union, are in accord. As to the lack of saloons, Logan said: "We are getting used to it and we have better meetings of the union, because the men talk better and think better. They also pay their union dues much more promptly and regularly than ever before."

There was no beverage-making distillery in Detroit before prohibition. The twenty-two breweries there had an annual output of only a million barrels and employed only 2,000 men. Fifteen of the twenty-two are making nonalcoholic drinks. Seven are closed. Detroit had 4,000 bartenders, most of whom have gone into factories.

**Mid-West Americanization.**

As to Americanism: There is more uniformity among the cities in their methods of promoting Americanism than in any other activity, and there is no dangerously acute or sharply defined foreign problem with reference to any one nationality or race. Cincinnati and Indianapolis, with their large negro populations, had nothing of the race rioting which upset Chicago and Washington last Summer, and have no fear of such a thing. The nearest approach to serious trouble in Indianapolis was the result of speeches made there by a negro who had been in Europe as a Government representative, to report on the condition of America's negro troops. This man told the colored people of Indiana that with our allies, the French and the English, there was no color line and no race question, that in Paris and London he had seen the best of white women on the streets and in the restaurants with black men. That mis-

leading sort of information caused some bitter resentment among the negroes of Indiana, but their own leaders undid the mischief which had been started by the jackass from Europe before anything serious came of it.

Save for her 20 per cent. of Germans, Cincinnati is very much an American stock city and she has no German problem left except in the continued social ostracism of the few wealthy Germans who were disloyal. The effort to keep up their ostracism in a business way is not so well sustained. During the war there was a fight in the Cincinnati Board of Education over the question of barring the teaching of German from the lower schools. A German member of the board voted not to bar it, but the chief advocate of continuing the study of German in these schools was an American with no German blood in him. Several weeks ago both of these men were candidates for re-election to the School Board. The German was defeated and the American who had made the hardest fight for the German language teaching was re-elected.

Both Detroit and Cleveland have

about 75 per cent. foreign-born and first generation foreign population. But no one nationality stands out in either place as particularly troublesome or particularly helpful. Cleveland had a German language newspaper which was so disloyal in the war that the Government had to take control of it, but it has been restored to its former management and is not now offending. Cleveland has a Hungarian newspaper with a circulation throughout the State of about 100,000. It is described as a publication that stands for nothing but good, wholesome Americanism. There is a wide difference of opinion everywhere as to immigration and its restriction, but the American who damns an immigrant merely because he is an immigrant is hard to find.

**Secretary Lane on Americans.**

In a publication of the Detroit Americanization Committee there appeared recently something on the foreigner by Franklin K. Lane, Secretary of the Interior. Perhaps it has been printed elsewhere, but it is worth referring to whenever the subject of Americanization is under discussion. And it indicates the spirit in which the committees in these three near-West States are going about their work of helping the immigrants to become American. It was printed under the title, "Each Brought His Gift," and was as follows:

"America is a land of but one people, gathered from many countries. Some came for love of money and some for love of freedom. Whatever the lure that brought us, each has his gift. Irish lad and Scot, Englishman and Dutch, Italian, Greek and French, Spaniard, Slav, Teuton, Norse, negro—all have come bearing gifts and have laid them on the altar of America.

"All brought their music—dirge and dance and wassail song, proud march and religious chant. All brought music and their instruments for the making of music, those many children of the harp and lute.

"All brought their poetry, winged tales of man's many passions, folksong and psalm, ballads of heroes and tunes of the sea, lilting scraps caught from sky and field, or mighty dramas that tell of primal struggles of the profoundest meaning. All brought poetry.

"All brought art, fancies of the mind, woven in wood or wool, silk, stone or metal—rugs and baskets, gates of fine design and modeled gardens, houses and walls, pillars, roofs, windows, statues and painting—all brought their art and handcraft.

"Then, too, each brought some homely thing, some touch of the familiar home field or forest, kitchen or dress—a favorite tree or fruit, an accustomed flower, a style in cookery or in costume—each brought some homelike, familiar thing.

"And all brought hands with which to work.

"And all brought minds that could conceive.

"And all brought hearts filled with hope—stout hearts to drive live minds; live minds to direct willing hands.

"These were the gifts they brought.

"Hatred of old-time neighbors, national prejudices and ambitions, traditional fears, set standards of living, graceless intolerances, class rights and the demand of class—these were barred at the gates.

"At the altar of America we have sworn ourselves to a single loyalty. We have bound ourselves to sacrifice and struggle, to plan and to work for this one land. We have given that we may gain, we have surrendered that we may have victory. We have taken an oath that the world shall have a chance to know how much of good may be gathered from all countries and how solid in its strength, how wise, how fertile in its yield, how lasting and sure is the life of a people who are one, but have come bearing gifts from many countries."

**The Community Unit.**

Cincinnati is still trying the community unit experiment, which has been described in newspapers. It is intended by its advocates for national use. Just now it is meeting with opposition in Cincinnati from the City Administration and from others who were its well-wishers and supporters at the start. It has been denied participation in the community chest for the financial aid of welfare organizations. The objections to it are that it costs too much to be practical, that it creates a Government within a Government, and that its administrators are Socialists and using it for Socialist propaganda. That last charge is not true. There is one thing the community unit organization can do, and that is to get exact information concerning the needs of a given locality. That, apparently, is one of the things Ohio needs; for the estimates of the State experts as to the number of feeble-minded citizens who should have public care range from 7,000 to 15,000.

**Labor in Cincinnati.**

There is a tendency in Cincinnati and Cleveland and Indianapolis on the part of business men to ask if they had better not co-operate with conservative organized labor rather than run the risk of being confronted with something more radical later on. This is by no means unanimous. In Procter & Gamble, for example, there is no thought of any such thing with reference to their soap factory. This concern is solving the labor problem in its own way in its own open shops, and apparently to the complete satisfaction of all its employes. Three of these employes, elected by their fellow-workmen, were recently taken into the Directorate of the company. A national labor leader of the American Federation told me that if all concerns were like Procter & Gamble there would be little need of trade unions.

But there seems to be an absence of bitterness in Cincinnati between labor and capital. One illustration of it is in the relationship between Fred Geier, head of the Cincinnati Milling Company, which is one of the big open-shop concerns of Ohio, and James Wilson, national head of the Pattern Makers' Union. These two men are absolutely opposed to each other on the question of union and nonunion labor. Neither will yield an inch to the other on that question, but they are most friendly personal associates in public welfare enterprises growing out of the war in which they are both enlisted. Each is good-humoredly confident that the other will eventually yield on the main question. One open-shop advocate remarked that if all union men were like Jim Wilson he'd accept the union, thus returning the compliment paid to Procter & Gamble.

There is a bitterness in Detroit. Outside of the stove-making industry and some minor trades, the American Federation of Labor has no control in the Michigan city. The Auto Workers' Union, which claims only 18,000 members in the whole country, has only 7,000 in Detroit, where there are more than 300,000 factory workers, two-thirds of whom are in the automobile industry. But, nevertheless, the Auto Workers' Union is feared or at least hated by the Employers' Association and the press. They accuse the union of being an I. W. W. organization in disguise. As evidence the employers cite the fact that the Auto Workers' Union allows Emma Goldman and those like her to use its hall and declare that their labor newspaper is inflammatory.

Logan, the head of the union, who is a Socialist, declares that neither he nor the organization has any affiliation with the I. W. W. or any other radical group. He is opposed to Gompers and the American Federation system of organization by craft, because the Auto Workers are organized on the basis of the entire industry in which they are employed, and a strike in one department of a concern means a simultaneous strike automatically in all the departments of that concern.

The Ford shops are difficult for the Auto Workers' Union or any other union to get a foothold in. Union men explain that by saying that the Ford employe is so stupefied by the monotony of his routine essential to the Ford method of quantity production that he can't listen to or understand argument at the end of his eight-hour day. A manufacturer in Cincinnati told me a story to go with that. It was about a mechanic who came to Cincinnati from Detroit in search of a job. He had been employed in the Ford plant. When asked why he left there he replied: "Well, I worked for Ford six months and had to quit or go nutty. I couldn't stand handling bolt No. 86 another hour."

I understood better what that story meant after spending half a day in the Ford plant watching 55,000 employes turn out automobiles at the rate of 3,500 a day and seeing each man standing in the long line of fellow-workmen doing his one bit over and over again for eight hours, as the engine or the body or the cushion, or whatever other part of the car it might be, passed slowly in front of him on a mechanical conveyor.

**High Pay in Detroit.**

But bitter or not, monotonous or not, Detroit, the biggest of the Middle Western cities next to Chicago, is surely prosperous. It is so rich that you feel it as you walk on the streets. You feel that if Detroit were drinking anything it would be champagne. It is no mere joke that in the city of cars the workmen, too, have their cars. In front of Bricklayers' Hall twenty Ford cars were parked at one time. They belonged to the bricklayers. Artisans by the thousand own their cars. In the automobile factories piece work wages run from $1 to $1.50 an hour; on day work they run from 55 to 75 cents. Steam hammer operators get $20 a day; metal finishers $15. Washwomen get $4 for an eight-hour day, with two meals and carfare both ways. Inexperienced home servants get $15 a week as a minimum, with board and lodging.

But there is discontent. A dollar an hour man who has had those wages for a year said that he had been able to save only $100 in twelve months after supporting a family of three adults and two children. He did not think he was getting a fair deal.

The value of Detroit's manufactured output in 1914 was $569,519,227. This year it is $1,400,000,000. The cost of material is estimated at over half a billion and the pay roll of employes at another half billion in round numbers. Yes, Detroit is so rich and growing so fast that it is funny in spots. It has the atmosphere of a bonanza town. In one store window was a quantity of rock showing indications of gold ore as an advertisement for gold mining stock guaranteed to pay 150 per cent. In a broker's window near by was an offer to buy Liberty bonds accompanied by latest quotations. In the same window was a sign which read: "We advise you to keep your Liberty bonds, but if you must sell our facilities are at your disposal."

In a labor quarter of the city near the House of the Masses a shoe store window was filled with drummers' samples. None of these shoes was new, but the lowest price was $5.9[illegible] a pair. Most of them were more than $7.

In the shops de luxe, of which Detroit has many, the rush of trade is not waiting for Christmas. In a "popular price" restaurant running thirty feet or more back from the sidewalk, but so narrow that only one row of customers could sit down at a time, every place was taken and a row of people were standing behind the eaters waiting for their places at the counter. The sign in front of the restaurant said "Klean Kitchen." I asked the joyous proprietor how he accounted for it. "Don't know," he said. "Perhaps it's because they like the way I spell clean and perhaps its because Detroit is putting Cleveland off the map, for size and money. But the cash register rings now as constantly as the electric buzzer used to buzz over the door to attract people's attention to the place." In restaurants with prices that are popular with those who do not care how much they spend, there is a tendency on the part of some of the male clientele to be a trifle overmanicured and a trifle too sleek as to the hair.

At the theatre one evening in Detroit a young man in evening clothes sat down in the orchestra chair next to mine. "Here we are again," he exclaimed. "This afternoon I sold you a newspaper and now we are seeing a show together." He explained that he sold 5,000 papers a day, and had the most profitable street stand in Detroit. He regretted that he could not make his money in Detroit and live in New York, where he would find more theatres.

# Latest Works of Fiction

MAIN STREET. By Sinclair Lewis. Harcourt, Brace & Howe.

IT is the portrait of a town—typical, one of thousands of common little American towns scattered all over the country, each with its own markings, its idiosyncrasies, of course, but alike in essentials, alike as the average small town person, who is found quite as usually in the cities and the country as in the village or the towns, the common person, the common people, of whom there are so many. Nothing is so self-satisfied as this type, be it human or aggregate human. As one of them expresses it, " After all, Gopher Prairie standards are as reasonable to Gopher Prairie as Lake Shore Drive standards are to Chicago. And there's more Gopher Prairies than Chicagoes, or Londons. * * *" There you have it. Gopher Prairie may be small in itself, but it can point with pride, and certainly will do so, to myriads like itself.

A remarkable book is this latest by Sinclair Lewis. A novel, yes, but so unusual as not to fall easily into a class. There is practically no plot, yet the book is absorbing. It is so much like life itself, so extraordinarily real. These people are actual folk, and there was never better dialogue written than their revealing talk. The book might have been cut without harm, possibly, for there is an infinite amount of detail, yet this very detail has its power, exerts its magic. The latter half is the more forcefully, clearly written, moves more soundly. In fact, one cannot shake off the impression that this book was begun long ago, when Mr. Lewis was but recently out of college, laid aside, and taken up lately, to be rewritten and reconstructed and finished. There is the sharp reaction of youth to so much of it, a personal note in the hatred Carol has for the people, the ways, the thoughts and the place of Gopher Prairie, a reaction and a note that savor of the agony, undimmed by intervening years, of a sensitive young creature coming from the free outlook and tolerant sympathies of a broader environment into such a prison atmosphere as that of this small Minnesota town. This impression that the book is partly by a college boy and partly by a man with many contacts with life and the world will not down; there are some poorly written pages, some jejune bits that add to it. Yet one would not wish to eliminate this youthful stand in the book. It belongs there.

As we have said, the book is a portrait of a town. It is also an amazing study of the girl Carol, the foil and critic of that town.

Carol is an alien. She comes of New England parentage, of a home that had its tone and color, and reached back to rich things that were lost. She had had a college training of a sort, some experience of Chicago, and she had been a librarian in St. Paul. She had known hopes and visions, a desire to transform the dull and the ugly into charm and beauty, but she had fallen into the routine of work, and the dream to go forth and to improve had faded. Then the man comes, a man she drifts into liking, into the belief of loving, the doctor of Gopher Prairie, " some live burg," as he and his townsmates never tire of saying.

Will Kendicott is his name, and soon it becomes Carol's name. She marries and she goes with her husband to the burg he loves and admires. From that moment she and Gopher Prairie are at grips.

First it is the hopeless ugliness of Main Street that strikes at her, then the deadliness of the social life of the creators of this street, the leading citizens of the town. There is genius in Mr. Lewis's description of the party given in honor of the homecoming of the bride and groom. The awful stiffness of human beings to whom the joys of social intercourse are not alone unknown but distrusted, whose sole notion of entertainment consists in the performance of stunts. " Let's have some stunts, folks," cries the host to the circle that has sat silent and watchful, or rattling personalities, or surreptitiously watching Carol. And they shriek assent. Upon which the few who can do stunts take their turn doing them. There is Dave—" Say, Dave, give us that stunt about the Norwegian catching a hen," and there is Ella Stowbody, spinster, with her recitation, " That Old Sweetheart of Mine." And there were four other stunts. They concluded the social part of the evening. What is more, they appeared at each and every party of the leading set of Gopher Prairie, and when they had been done the party sank back into coma until the coming of the refreshments, practically identical at each house. About then the party began to be natural. That is, the men got together and talked of their shops and their hunting, the women herded and discussed their servants and their children and their sicknesses.

And Carol, brave with youth's unreadiness, foolish with that youth, not any too expert herself, starts to make Gopher Prairie beautiful and amusing, to give it some notion of the world outside its own limits, to bring in art and literature and landscape gardening.

And in the end she is allowed to plant a few geraniums in a vacant lot. But a great deal comes in between.

In the first place, she finds that the town doesn't want to be reformed; that the people in it resent the fact that she has seen and done more than they; that they are critical and sneering:

> She had tripped into a meadow to teach the lambs a pretty educational dance, and found that the lambs were wolves. There was no way out between their pressing gray shoulders. She was surrounded by fangs and sneering eyes.

And for a while Carol is terror-stricken. She cannot walk the streets without the feel of those eyes on her; she cannot talk naturally to any one, thinking of the gossip and the criticism that is being poured upon her; she dreads to go to the stores, where the merchants grin superciliously over her requests for something they don't keep—in Gopher Prairie it is a virtue not to keep things you haven't kept before.

But this does not last. Once again she decides that she will do what in her lies to prod the town:

> What if they were wolves instead of lambs? They'd eat her all the sooner if she was meek to them. Fight or be eaten. It was easier to change the town completely than to conciliate it! She could not take their point of view; it was a negative thing, an intellectual squalor, a swamp of prejudices and fears. She would have to make them take hers * * * the tiniest change in their distrust of beauty would be the beginning of the end: a seed to sprout and some day with thickening roots to crack their wall of mediocrity.

She begins by trying to make Will like poetry. He is very nice about it. Listens sheltered behind his cigar, says " yes, great stuff, shoot," and asserts that he likes poetry—" James Whitcomb Riley and some of Longfellow." But it won't do, and when he tells her, after she has read Kipling with a great deal of emphasis, that she can " elocute just about as good as Ella Stowbody," she bangs the book down and they go to the movies.

Yet she has recovered from her terror and her slump, and she finds that some of the people do like her. There is the pariah of the village, the Red Swede, the handy man of the town, who senses her difference from the villagers and who talks

to her one day, laughs at the prejudices and the narrowness of the place, makes fun of its big men, gives the girl a realization that freedom does exist, after all. And here and there some one is kind, smiling, affectionate. She bucks up. She joins the Thanatopsis Club, which is engaged in culture, she stops being either scared or patronizing, and she dreams of tearing down the blank horror that does service for a City Hall and of seeing in its place a Georgian structure of warm brick and white stone, &c.

Of course, it won't do. No individual could conquer a town like Gopher Prairie. No alien can bring sweetness and light where it is not wanted or missed. Carol is a silly girl. She does not know as much as she thinks she does, she misses doing what good she might because she cannot see the good there is. But she is sensitive, proud and keen. She is alive, and she moves in a different strata from the townspeople of the prairie town. She has no business there, and yet she is caught there, by the fact of her marriage, by the later fact of her child. She gives up, she sinks almost to coma—and then, for a while she is awakened, yanked back to the feeling of her own individual existence and reality by falling rather feebly in love with the tailor, the one man who has some vision, some despair to match her own.

It doesn't last. But it leads to a wonderful interview between wife and husband, a few pages that are as good as anything can be. There are more such pages in this book than in any other book we have read this year, perhaps in several years, written by an American.

In a way Carol is beaten. But she isn't lost. She runs away, goes to Washington and war work, and finally comes back. Gopher Prairie is the same. Insufferably conceited, insufferably ugly, mediocre, common, drab, though it has made money out of the war. And it has no more use for Carol than it ever had. But she retains her vision and her hope, and she has two children to fight for. And it is they who will win. She points out her small daughter to Will, saying:

> Do you see that object on the pillow? Do you know what that is? It's a bomb to blow up smugness. If you Tories were wise you wouldn't arrest anarchists; you'd arrest all these children while they're asleep in their cribs. Think what that baby will see and meddle in before she dies in the year 2000!

But Gopher Prairie sits tight, ignoring its dangerous babies.

# Getting at the Truth About an Average American Town

## A Study Which Gives Statistical Support to the Derogatory Lewises and Menckens

MIDDLETOWN. A Study in Contemporary American Culture. By Robert S. Lynd and Helen Merrell Lynd. 550 pp. New York: Harcourt, Brace & Co. $5.

### By R. L. DUFFUS

THE American town and small city have had to take some hard knocks in recent years, mostly from ungrateful natives who had escaped from them to Chicago, New York or the south of France. But these exposures have generally taken the form of fiction, and it was always possible to say that their authors had grievances. This particular charge cannot be brought against the authors of this book, who are scientific and sociological almost to a fault. They have looked at their sample American community with the cool eyes of anthropologists studying the habits of an alien species. They have collected case reports and their pages are larded with percentages and statistics. They had, consciously, at least, no axe to grind. According to Professor Clark Wissler, who writes a brief introduction, "no one had ever subjected an American community to such a scrutiny." Those who cling to their childhood illusions about their native land will wish that the Lynds had scrutinized the Patagonians instead. For the portrait of Middletown is not flattering. Not only does it make the reader wonder whether all that has happened since 1890 has been progress. It even arouses some doubt in his mind as to whether the present inhabitants of America have attained greater happiness per capita than did the Indians who preceded them. Of course this may be merely the result of viewing an objective piece of work in a subjective way. Even Athens under Pericles or Rome under the Antonines might have shown up badly under the statistical method. It may not be so much Middletown as the fundamental conditions of human life that are at fault. The American reader is shocked because, despite Sinclair

Lewis, Theodore Dreiser, H. L. Mencken and others, he is invincibly optimistic.

Middletown comes into the picture as a town which has made great physical progress. In 1885 it was "an agricultural county seat of some 6,000 persons"; now it is an industrial city which in 1920 had a population of more than 35,000. Its wealth has greatly increased. Its inhabitants have more things in their houses, better clothes on their backs and more means of amusement, and its health is decidedly better. But it gets less fun out of its job, its home life has pretty well gone to

tive returning to the familiar scenes notes a dismaying change. "These people are all afraid of something," he writes. People are hemmed in by their social and economic affiliations. As the authors put it:

Confronted by the difficulty of choosing among subtle group loyalties the Middletown citizen, particularly of the business class in this world of credit, tends to do with his ideas what he does with his breakfast food or his collars or his politics—he increasingly accepts a blanket pattern solution. He does not try to scratch the "good-fellow" ticket but votes it straight. To be "civic" and to "serve" is put over "Magic Middletown," the church, the party,

of Commerce naturally gets behind the "Buy in Middletown" campaign, but it does not hesitate to let contracts for its new building go to a builder using materials bought out of town. Competition is still the gospel of the city's business classes. A church which is raising a building fund refuses to lend its kitchen to another smaller church of the same denomination which is giving a benefit for its own building fund. The smoke nuisance is allowed to continue because prominent men own stock in the electric light company which is largely responsible for it. A movement to abolish grade

From the Jacket Design for "Middletown."

or Rome under the Antonines might have shown up badly under the statistical method. It may not be so much Middletown as the fundamental conditions of human life that are at fault. The American reader is shocked because, despite Sinclair

pot, it is inefficiently and often corruptly governed, and its ideas and habits are almost as regimented as those of a South Sea Islander under the taboo system. The individualism with which we endow the older generations is disappearing. A na-

a get-together dinner, a financial campaign, one's friends; it is to be a "booster, not a knocker"; to accept without question the symbols.

This group loyalty is more fatal to ideas than to action. The Chamber

crossings is killed because a group of manufacturers discover that elevated tracks would cause them inconvenience in loading their cars. But all of upper-crust Middletown was sure in 1924 how it felt about Mr. La Follette and what it would do to any civic traitors caught voting for him. Even in small details it imposes a kind of pattern. There was talk when one well-to-do family moved a little way out of town and built its house back from the road and partially hidden by a grove of trees. In social and business life the man who conceals his thoughts, or possibly who has no thoughts, gets along best—assuming that we mean by thoughts a questioning of accepted beliefs. Of course, there are mavericks who indulge in private a fondness for speculative books, for the arts, even for producing literature. But they do not boast about these tastes unless—and this is a large exception in Middletown—they make money by them. Money making and money spending are current measures of quality in Middletown. A citizen explains that this is partly because they are such easy tests.

Now for some details. Forty-three out of every hundred Middletowners are gainfully employed. A healthy adult male who does not work loses caste, no matter what his income. One out of five of the paid workers is a woman. For the manual workers the job has become less interesting since 1890, the respect for skill less, the hope of promotion less, the dread of unemployment at least as great. Organized labor is not so strong as it used to be. On the

other hand, the standard of living, measured by appliances used in the home and means of diversion, has gone up. The single-family residence houses 86 per cent. of the population. Practically all of them are wired for electricity, though some of them have as yet no plumbing. People seem to marry younger than they did. They also get divorced oftener—six times as often as in 1890. Families seldom get together—an ironic contrast with the large number of "get-together" organizations. Young people astound and worry their elders, as they do elsewhere. Social life in the high school is so complicated and expensive as to be a severe burden. The proportion of high school and college students to population is, however, rapidly increasing. Defeated ambition in the parents often expresses itself in educational ambitions for the children. Yet teachers are not looked up to—nor are clergymen, not as they were a generation ago.

There is a good deal of reading of books, magazines and newspapers though the first category seems to be largely left to the women. The men are not strong for literature,

music or the arts. The automobile has, of course, revolutionized ways of finding recreation. A boy without a car is entirely out of the social swim. Most cars are bought on credit. Sometimes a family mortgages its home rather than be without one. There is some sense in this, for Middletown judges people as much by their cars as by their homes. The occasional performances in the "Opera House" a generation ago have been succeeded by nine motion-picture houses open ten hours a day every day in the year, and every one goes at least once a week. The social system is rigid and based largely on estimated income. Cards and dancing are the principal social diversions, with dancing becoming less important after the age of 30. The churches do not have the hold they used to, except among certain sections of the working class, and the younger generation is liberal in its practices as well as in its views. The authors think the religious impulse is perhaps more widely diffused than it was, showing itself in some helpful civic enterprises. Gov-

ernment, including the administration of justice, is cumbersome and no longer enlists the best talents. Voting is falling off. In health and in caring for the unfit there have been real gains, though local newspapers still unblushingly run many columns of quack patent medicine advertisements.

The impression with which the reader is left is that of a curiously contradictory community—united in supporting the meaningless gymnastics of the high school basketball team, clubbed together in numberless organizations for mutual advantage, yet rarely seeing or seeking true community good. Above all, Middletown seems to possess no sense of a community civilization. It is sophisticated in the mechanism of living and pitifully naive in almost everything having to do with the purposes of living. Our authors do not tell us this in so many words. They are too unbiased and too scientific to do so. But the portrait of a community, representative of millions of our population, barely groping for a national culture still to be born, jumps out of their careful paragraphs. The only comfort is the possibility that Middletown is not altogether representative, after all.

*January 20, 1929*

## WITH COLLEGE MEN

THIS SIDE OF PARADISE. By F. Scott Fitzgerald. New York: Charles Scribner's Sons. $1.75.

THE glorious spirit of abounding youth glows throughout this fascinating tale. Amory, the "romantic egotist," is essentially American, and as we follow him through his career at Princeton, with its riotous gayety, its superficial vices, and its punctilious sense of honor which will tolerate nothing less than the standard set up by itself, we know that he is doing just what hundreds of thousands of other young men are doing in colleges all over the country. As a picture of

the daily existence of what we call loosely "college men," this book is as nearly perfect as such a work could be. The philosophy of Amory, which finds expression in ponderous observations, lightened occasionally by verse that one thinks could have been evolved only in the cloistered atmosphere of his age-old alma mater, is that of any other youth in his teens in whom intellectual ambition is ever seeking an outlet. Amory's love affairs, too, are racy of the soil, while the girls, whose ideas of the modern development of their sex seem to embrace a rather frequent use of the word "Damn," and of being kissed by young men whom they have no thought of marrying,

quite obviously belong to Amory's world. Through it all there is the spirit of innocence in so far as actual wrongdoing is implied, and one cannot but feel that the sexes are well matched according to the author's presentment. Amory Blaine has a well-to-do father and a mother who lives the somewhat idle, luxurious life of a matron who has never known the pinch of even economy, much less of poverty, and the boy is the creature of his environment. One knows always that he will be safe at the end. So he is, for he does his bit in the war, finds afterward that his money has all gone and goes to work writing advertisements for an agency. Also, he has his supreme love

affair, with Rosalind Connage, which is broken off because the nervous temperaments of both would not permit happiness. At least, so the girl thinks. So Amory goes on the biggest spree noted in the book—a spree which is colorfully described as taking in everything in the alcoholic line from the Knickerbocker "Old King Cole" bar to an out-of-the-way drinking den where Amory is "beaten up" artistically and thoroughly. The whole story is disconnected, more or less, but loses none of its charm on that account. It could have been written only by an artist who knows how to balance his values, plus a delightful literary style.

*May 9, 1920*

# EIGHT WHITE SOX PLAYERS ARE INDICTED ON CHARGE OF FIXING 1919 WORLD SERIES; CICOTTE GOT $10,000 AND JACKSON $5,000

## COMISKEY SUSPENDS THEM

### Promises to Run Them Out of Baseball if Found Guilty

### TWO OF PLAYERS CONFESS

### Cicotte and Jackson Tell of Their Work in Throwing Games to Cincinnati.

### BOTH ARE HELD IN CUSTODY

### Prosecutor Says More Players Will Be Indicted and Gamblers Brought to Task.

*Special to The New York Times.*

CHICAGO, Sept. 28.—Seven star players of the Chicago White Sox and one former player were indicted late this afternoon, charged with complicity in a conspiracy with gamblers to "fix" the 1919 world's series. The indictments were based on evidence obtained for the Cook County Grand Jury by Charles A. Comiskey, owner of the White Sox, and after confessions by two of the players told how the world's championship was thrown to Cincinnati and how they had received money or were "double-crossed" by the gamblers.

The eight players indicted are:

EDDIE CICOTTE, star pitcher.

"SHOELESS JOE" JACKSON, left fielder and heavy hitter.

OSCAR "HAP" FELSCH, centre fielder.

CHARLES "SWEDE" RISBERG, shortstop.

GEORGE "BUCK" WEAVER, third baseman.

ARNOLD GANDIL, former first baseman.

CLAUDE WILLIAMS, pitcher.

FRED McMULLIN, utility player.

The specific charge against the eight players is "conspiracy to commit an illegal act," which is punishable by five years' imprisonment or a fine up to $10,000, but this charge may be changed when the full indictments are drawn by the Grand Jury.

No sooner had the news of the indictments become public than Comiskey suspended the seven players, wrecking the team he had given years to build up and almost certainly forfeiting his

chances to beat out Cleveland for the American League pennant.

**Would Run Them Out of Baseball.**

His letter notifying the players of their suspension follows:

Chicago, Sept. 26.

To Charles Risberg, Fred McMullin, Joe Jackson, Oscar Felsch, George Weaver, C. P. Williams and Eddie Cicotte:

You and each of you are hereby notified of your indefinite suspension as a member of the Chicago American League Baseball Club.

Your suspension is brought about by information which has just come to me directly involving you and each of you in the baseball scandal resulting from the world's series of 1919.

If you are innocent of any wrongdoing you and each of you will be reinstated; if you are guilty you will be retired from organized baseball for the rest of your lives if I can accomplish it.

Until there is a finality to this investigation it is due to the public that I take this action, even though it costs Chicago the pennant.

CHICAGO AMERICAN BASEBALL CLUB.

By CHARLES A. COMISKEY.

Officials of the Grand Jury lifted the curtain on the proceedings and declared that Cicotte and Jackson made open confessions, Cicotte admitting receiving $10,000 and throwing two games, and Jackson admitting receiving $5,000 of $20,000 promised him by the gamblers and telling of his efforts to defeat his own team.

**Cicotte Breaks Down and Weeps.**

Cicotte's confession came after he and Alfred S. Austrian, counsel for the White Sox management, had conferred with Judge Charles A. McDonald in the latter's chambers.

Toward the end of this conference they were joined by Assistant State Attorney Hartley Replogle. A few moments later he and Cicotte proceeded to the Grand Jury room.

There the great baseball pitcher broke down and wept.

"My God! think of my children," he cried. Cicotte has two small children.

"I never did anything I regretted so much in my life," he continued. "I would give anything in the world if I could undo my acts in the last world's series. I've played a crooked game and I have lost, and I am here to tell the whole truth.

"I've lived a thousand years in the last year."

Describing how two games were thrown to Cincinnati, Cicotte, according to court officials, said:

"In the first game at Cincinnati I was knocked out of the box. I wasn't putting a thing on the ball. You could have read the trade mark on it when I lobbed the ball up to the plate.

"In the fourth game, played at Chicago, which I also lost, I deliberately intercepted a throw from the outfield to the plate which might have cut off a run. I muffed the ball on purpose.

"At another time in the same game I purposely made a wild throw. All the runs scored against me were due to my own deliberate errors. I did not try to win."

Cicotte, it was learned late tonight, confessed first to Comiskey. He went to the latter's office early in the morning.

"I don't know what you'll think of me," he said, "but I got to tell you how

I double-crossed you. Mr. Comiskey, I did double-cross you. I'm a crook, and I got $10,000 for being a crook."

"Don't tell it to me," replied Comiskey, "tell it to the Judge."

Cicotte told it to the Judge in tears and shame, slowly, haltingly, hanging his head, now and then pausing to wipe his streaming eyes.

"Risberg and Gandil and McMullin were at me for a week before the world's series started," he said. "They wanted me to go crooked. I didn't know—I needed the money. I had the wife and the kids. The wife and kids don't know this. I don't know what they'll think.

**Says He Needed It to Pay Mortgage.**

"I bought a farm. There was a $4,000 mortgage on it. There isn't any mortgage on it now. I paid it off with the crooked money.

"The eight of us [the eight under indictment] got together in my room three or four days before the games started. Gandil was the master of ceremonies. We talked about throwing the series. Decided we could get away with it. We agreed to do it.

"I was thinking of the wife and kids and how I needed the money. I told them I had to have the cash in advance. I didn't want any checks. I didn't want any promise, as I wanted the money in bills. I wanted it before I pitched a ball.

"We all talked quite a while about it, I and the seven others. Yes, all of us decided to do our best to throw the games to Cincinnati.

"When Gandil and McMullin took us all, one by one, away from the others, and we talked 'turkey,' they asked me my price. I told them $10,000. And I told them that $10,000 was to be paid in advance.

"'Cash in advance,' I said. 'Cash in advance, and nothing else.'

"It was Gandil I was talking to. He wanted to give me some money at the time, the rest after the games were played and lost. But it didn't go, with me.

"'I said cash,' I reminded him. 'Cash in advance, and not C. O. D. If you can't trust me, I can't trust you. Pay or I play ball.'

"Well, the arguments went on for days—the arguments for 'some now and some later.' But I stood pat. I wanted the $10,000 and got it.

"And how I wish that I didn't.

"The day before I went to Cincinnati I put it up to them squarely for the last time, that there would be nothing doing unless I had the money.

"That night I found the money under my pillow. There was $10,000. I counted it. I don't know who put it there, but it was there. It was my price. I had sold out 'Commy'; I had sold out the other boys; sold them for $10,000 to pay off a mortgage on a farm, and for the wife and kids.

"If I had reasoned what that meant to me, the taking of that dirty crooked money—the hours of mental torture, the days and nights of living with an unclean mind; the weeks and months of going along with six of the seven crooked players and holding a guilty secret, and of going along with the boys who had stayed straight and clean and honest—boys who had nothing to

trouble them—say, it was hell.

"I got the $10,000 cash in advance, that's all."

**Jackson Only "Tapped" Ball.**

Cicotte after his testimony was taken from the courtroom by a back door, and shortly afterward Austrian appeared with Joe Jackson. There was another conference in the chambers of Judge McDonald and a meeting with Assistant State Attorney Replogle, and then Jackson ran the gantlet of newspaper cameramen to the Grand Jury room.

Jackson hung his head and covered his face with his hands. Replogle tried to keep the cameramen away. They refused and there was a volley of flashes. Jackson cursed newspapermen, gamblers and baseball and fled to the security of the jury room.

His story, it was learned, was a confirmation of Cicotte's. It was the story of a slow "feeling out" of the cupidity of players by Gandil, McMullin and Risberg.

Joe Jackson, in his confession, said he went into the deal through the influence of Gandil and Risberg. He was promised $20,000 and got $5,000, which was handed to him in Cincinnati by "Lefty" Williams. When he threatened to say about it, Williams, Gandil and Risberg said, "You poor simp, go ahead and squawk. Where do you get off if you do? We'll all say you're a liar, and every honest baseball player in the world will say you're a liar. You're out of luck. Some of the boys were promised a lot more than you, and got a lot less."

"And that's why I went down and told Judge McDonald and told the Grand Jury what I knew about the frame-up," said Jackson tonight. "And I'm giving you a tip. A lot of these sporting writers who have been roasting me have been talking about the third game of the World's Series being square. Let me tell you something. The eight of us did our best to kick it and little Dick Kerr won the game by his pitching. And because he won it these gamblers double-crossed us for double-crossing them.

"They've hung it on me. They ruined me when I went to the shipyards. But I don't care what happens now. I guess I'm through with baseball. I wasn't wise enough, like Chick, to beat them to it. But some of them will sweat before the show is over.

"Who gave me the money? Lefty Williams slipped it to me the night before I left for Cincinnati and told me I'd get the other $15,000 after I delivered the goods. I took Lefty's word for it. Now Risberg threatens to bump me off if I squak. That's why I had all the bailiffs with me when I left the Grand Jury room this afternoon.

"I'm not under arrest yet and I've got the idea that after what I told them old Joe Jackson isn't going to jail. But I'm not going to get far from my protectors until this blows over. Swede is a hard guy."

Jackson testified, according to the officials, that throughout the series he either struck out or hit easy balls when hits would mean runs.

Jackson also testified, it is said, that Claude Williams received $10,000.

**Jackson Comes Out Smiling.**

Jackson was before the Grand Jury nearly two hours, and he came out walking erect and smiling.

"I got a big load off my chest," he told a friend who accosted him. "I'm feeling better."

"Don't ask Joe any questions," Replogle cautioned the newspaper men. "He's gone through beautifully and we don't want him bothered."

Joe intimated he was "willing to tell the world now, if they'll let me."

The crowd outside the Criminal Court buildings cheered and jeered as he rode off in the custody of bailiffs.

Cicotte is also in the custody of officers from the State Attorney's office.

"We are taking no chances on anything," was the only explanation Mr. Replogle offered of this.

Mrs. Henrietta Kelley, owner of an apartment house on Grand Boulevard with whom many of the players and their families lived, gave testimony in the morning, which Mr. Replogle declared was extremely important.

Mrs. Kelley herself denied that she had given any important evidence.

President Heydler of the National League also was a witness. No hint of the nature of his testimony could be obtained from the prosecutors. Mr. Replogle dismissed questioners with his stock statement, "it is of great importance."

Mr. Austrian, attorney for the White Sox, said:

"Mr. Comiskey and myself, as his counsel, have been working on this for a year. We have spent a great deal of Mr. Comiskey's money to ferret it out. It is because of our investigation the lid has been blown off this scandal."

"Mr. Heydler is also testifying," he said: "Mr. McGraw will appear also—of their own volition, of course."

The significance of Heydler's testimony appeared when it was announced that two National League players would be summoned by the Grand Jury, Olsen, shortstop, of Brooklyn, and Rawlings, second baseman, of Philadelphia. Each is said to have won $2,000 on the first two games of the 1919 world's series.

The announcement of the calling of these players was followed by the intimation from the State Attorney's office that the investigation would soon reach far beyond Bill Maharg, former pugilist, Bill Burns, a retired ball player, now interested in the oil industry of Texas, and Abe Attell who so far have been named in the investigation as connected with the gamblers' end.

The Grand Jury recessed for the day with the conclusion of Jackson's testimony, but there was promise of more fireworks tomorrow.

"It'll be hotter, and there'll be more of it," Mr. Replogle promised. He declined to say whether immunity had been promised Jackson and Cicotte or whether it would be promised any others.

Two witnesses, Dr. Raymond B. Prettyman, a friend of Buck Weaver and John J. McGraw, manager of the New York Giants, who appeared to testify today, were told they could not be heard until tomorrow.

Claude "Lefty" Williams, the man who handed Joe Jackson $5,000, will be the central figure in the baseball investigation tomorrow.

Williams will be asked who handed him the money. He also may be asked as to his career in the Coast League, and he he may be asked as to his knowledge of a scandal regarding fixed games after Salt Lake City entered the league.

Williams was questioned tonight as to his part in the conspiracy, but was non-committal.

**Comiskey Commends Court.**

Mr. Comiskey tonight made the following statement:

"The consideration which the Grand Jury gave to this case should be greatly appreciated by the general public. Charles A. McDonald, Chief Justice, and the foreman of the Grand Jury, Harry Brigham, and his associates, who so diligently strived to save and make America's great game the clean sport which it is, are to be commended in no uncertain terms by all sport followers, in spite of what happened today.

"Thank God it did happen. Forty-four years of baseball endeavor have convinced me more than ever that it is a wonderful game and a game worth keeping clean.

"I would rather close my ball park than send nine men on the field with one of them holding a dishonest thought toward clean baseball—the game which John McGraw and I went around the world with to show to the people on the other side.

"We are far from through yet. We have the nucleus of another championship team with the remainder of the old world's championship team."

He named the veterans, Eddie and John Collins, Ray Schalk, Urban Faber, Dick Kerr, Eddie Murphy, Nemo Leibold and Amos Strunk and declared that, with the addition of Hodge, Falk, Jordan and McClellan, "I guess we can go along and win the championship yet."

Buck Weaver, when seen just after receiving notice of his suspension, declared he never received any of the money said to have been distributed and denied all knowledge of the deal to throw games in the world's series. He said his own record, in the series of 1919, in which he batted .333 and made only four errors out of thirty chances, ought to exonerate him.

"Any man who bats .333 is bound to make trouble for the other team in a ball game," he said. "The best team cannot win a world's championship without getting the breaks."

September 29, 1920

# WHITE SOX PLAYERS ARE ALL ACQUITTED BY CHICAGO JURY

## Two Others, Indicted With Them, Are Also Declared Not Guilty.

## WILD SCENES IN THE COURT

## Cheers Greet Verdict and Jurors Lift tne Freed Players to Their Shoulders.

## JUDGE FRIEND IS PLEASED

### Defense Lawyer Calls It Vindication of Most Maltreated Players—State Attorneys Silent.

CHICAGO, Aug. 2. (Associated Press).—The seven former Chicago White Sox baseball players and two others on trial for alleged conspiracy to defraud the public through throwing of the 1919 world series games were found not guilty by a jury tonight.

The jury took only one ballot.

The verdict was reached after two hours and forty-seven minutes of deliberation, but was not returned until forty minutes later, Judge Hugo M. Friend being out of court when the decision was reached.

Announcement of the verdict was greeted by cheers from the several hundred persons who remained in court for the final decision, with shouts of "Hooray for the clean Sox!"

Judge Friend congratulated the jury, saying he thought it a just verdict.

Eddie Cicotte was the first of the defendants to reach the jurors. He grabbed William Barrett by both hands, shouting his thanks.

Joe Jackson, Claude Williams and the others were close behind, and the jurors lifted them on to their shoulders, while flashlight photographs were taken.

Bailiffs vainly pounded for order and, finally noticing Judge Friend's smiles, joined in the whistling and cheering.

Hats sailed high in the air, papers were thrown around and the courtroom was the scene of the wildest confusion in any recent Cook County criminal case.

As the jurors filed out of the room they were slapped on the back, and the spectators shouted congratulatory words.

**They Had Paced the Floor.**

The defendants, on hearing the nine verdicts solemnly read by the Court Clerk, gave vent to their feelings in varied manners. Throughout the hours the jury deliberated the men on trial had paced up and down at times, gathered in little groups quietly to discuss the case or remained secluded.

When the three loud knocks on the jury room door were heard, indicating a verdict, every one jumped for the courtroom; but the excitement was momentary, it being some time before Judge Friend could be reached.

Buck Weaver and "Swede" Risberg were the most excited over the verdict, grabbing each other by the arms and shouting. Felsch and Williams merely smiled, while Joe Jackson took the decision very quietly. Gandil shook hands with a few friends and slipped from the courtroom.

"I'll give a sailor's farewell to Ban Johnson," said Gandil. "Good-bye, good luck and to —— with you."

"I knew I'd be cleared," said Weaver, "and I'm glad the public stood by me until the trial was over."

Williams termed the verdict a "true one," saying he was proud to have "come through clean."

Cicotte and Risberg rushed to telegraph offices to notify their wives.

David Zelcer will return to his home in Des Moines immediately and Carl Zork plans to leave for St. Louis tomorrow.

Henry Berger, defense counsel, termed the verdict a "complete vindication of the most mistreated ball players in history."

The State's attorneys were silent.

The case was placed in the hands of the jury at 7:52 o'clock in a special session of the court tonight, after Judge Hugo Friend had instructed the jury as to the numerous legal points involved.

**Arguments Concluded in Afternoon.**

The closing arguments were concluded this afternoon when George Gorman, Assistant State's Attorney in charge of the prosecution, in a brief closing address informed the jury that in his opinion the State had presented such a conclusive case that a long address was unnecessary.

Judge Friend in his instructions, which he spent most of the afternoon in preparing, told the jury that the State must prove that it was the intent of the Chicago White Sox players and others charged with conspiracy, through the throwing of the 1919 world series to defraud the public and others and not merely to throw baseball games.

Those indicted by the Grand Jury as a result of the baseball scandal were:

"Eddie" Cicotte, former star pitcher of the White Sox.

Claude Williams, former White Sox pitcher.

Arnold ("Chick") Gandil, former first baseman.

Charles (Swede) Risberg, former shortstop.

George ("Buck") Weaver, former third baseman.

Joe Jackson, former outfielder.

Oscar ("Happy") Felsch, former outfielder.

Abe Attell, former pugilist and alleged gambler.

Hal Chase, former baseball player.

William ("Bill") Burns, former player and alleged go-between.

Rachael Brown, alleged New York gambler.

John J. ("Sport") Sullivan, alleged Boston gambler.

David Zelcer, Des Moines (Iowa) advertising man and alleged gambler.

Louis Levi and Ben Levi, brothers, of Kokomo, Ind.

Carl Zork of St. Louis.

When the trial began, it was discovered that only seven of the indicted ball players were apprehended and ready for trial. They were Cicotte, Williams, Gandil, Weaver, Risberg, Felsch and Jackson. Only four of the alleged gamblers, the Levi brothers, Zork and Zelcer, were apprehended and ready for trial. After the State had finished its case, the prosecution voluntarily dismissed the charges against the Levi brothers, as no evidence was submitted to incriminate them.

The defense, led by Attorney Henry A. Berger, then moved to dismiss the cases against Zork, Weaver and Felsch. Judge Friend indicated that he would not allow a verdict to stand against these men, but the State insisted upon going to the jury with them.

**Twelve Counts in Indictments.**

The indictments upon which the defendants were tried contained twelve counts, but the State moved to dismiss three after presenting its evidence. The remaining counts charged the following offenses:

Statutory conspiracy to obtain divers sums of money from divers persons by means and use of the confidence game.

Statutory conspiracy to obtain divers sums of money from divers persons by false pretenses and to cheat and defraud the same.

Common law conspiracy to injure the business and reputation of the American League Baseball Club.

Statutory conspiracy to obtain from the public generally and any individual whom the defendants might meet divers sums of money by means and use of the confidence game.

Statutory conspiracy to obtain from the public generally and any individual whom the defendants might meet divers sums of money by false pretenses.

Statutory conspiracy to obtain from the public generally divers sums of money by false pretense and to cheat and defraud the same.

Statutory conspiracy to obtain from the public generally divers sums of money by means of the confidence game.

Common law conspiracy to cheat and defraud the American League Baseball Club of large sums of money by causing and inducing the players improperly and erroneously and not in accordance with their skill and ability to execute plays required of them.

Burns in his story asserted that Cicotte and Gandil were the originators of the scheme to throw the series for $100,000. According to Burns, Abe Attell, who was supposed to be the lieutenant of Rothstein, double-crossed the players and gave them only $10,000 of the promised $100,000.

During the entire trial the defendants' attorneys contended continuously that Ban Johnson, President of the American League, had instigated the prosecution because of a feud between himself and Charles A. Comiskey, owner of the White Sox.

During the trial it became known that the original confessions said to have been made by Cicotte, Williams and Jackson, along with the immunity waivers which they had signed, had been stolen from the State's Attorney's office. It was charged that Eastern gamblers had made up a pot of $10,000 to obtain these documents.

**Rumors Led to Investigation.**

Even while the 1919 world's series was in progress there were persistent reports in sporting circles that the White Sox were "throwing" games to Cincinnati. After Cincinnati won these reports were whispered all through that Winter, and continued during the 1920 baseball season.

It was not until September, however, that the scandal was given publicity. President Comiskey of the White Sox and other baseball officials had hired detectives to investigate the alleged "fixing," but with no definite results. Then in September, 1920, a rumor got about that a game between the Cubs and Philadelphia had been fixed for Philadelphia to win. This led to a thorough inquiry into the gambling end of baseball, and eventually uncovered the 1919 world's series scandal.

When the news first was published William Maharg of Philadelphia, a former pugilist, volunteered a confession. He said he and William (Bill) Burns, the former White Sox pitcher, had acted as go-between for the White Sox players and the alleged gamblers who sought to fix the series. His story named the players who were later indicted.

Maharg's story was followed by alleged confessions by Eddie Cicotte, Claude Williams and Joe Jackson. They later repudiated the confessions, however, and demanded trials.

True bills against the players named by Maharg were voted by the Grand Jury last September, but these indictments finally were quashed by Judge Dever. The players and gamblers named were reindicted and were brought to trial last month. Two weeks were consumed in getting a jury.

Abe Attell, former featherweight pugilistic champion, and Hal Chase, former White Sox player, who were named as "fixers," beat extradition proceedings in New York and California, respectively. Fred McMullen, White Sox utility man in the 1919 series, gave bond on the first indictment, but never was apprehended on the second.

Ben Franklin of St. Louis, alleged to have been implicated in the gamblers' end of the plot, was too ill to be brought here for trial. Rachel Brown of New York and John J. (Sport) Sullivan of Boston, alleged gamblers, said to have been implicated, were never arrested.

Arnold Rothstein of New York was mentioned repeatedly in connection with the case. He denied all knowledge of the alleged "fixing," however, and declared the gamblers probably used his name to win the confidence of the players.

August 3, 1921

### PURIFIED BASEBALL.

The Chicago Sox are once more whiter than snow. A jury has said that they are not guilty, so that settles that. If hair-splitting moralists are still in doubt as to the exact nature of the offense of which the defendants have been acquitted, that must be ascribed to the wide scope of the arguments of their own lawyers. Counsel for the defense held that the players were not under contract for the world's series—presumably they took part in the games only as a favor to COMISKEY—and that there was nothing in their contracts obliging them to try to win games anyway. The Court instructed the jury, according to Chicago dispatches, that it had to determine "whether the defendants in-"tended to defraud the public and "others and not merely to throw ball "games." To the lay mind this sounds very much like asking whether the defendant intended to murder his victim or merely to cut his head off, but the law is a mystery not open to the speculations of the profane.

If the innocence of the players is established, in all this labyrinth of subtleties it is rather hard to find out just what the jury decided they didn't do. Against some of them, certainly, there was little evidence; some of the others had confessed, but without prejudicing their case in the minds of the jury. Everybody will be pleased with what the counsel for the defense called "a complete vindication of the "most mistreated ballplayers in his-"tory"; but nearly everybody will be still better pleased with the prompt and decisive action of Judge LANDIS in barring the "vindicated" athletes from organized baseball. In such a situation the old National Commission would probably have exhausted its energies in twiddling its thumbs and finally come to the conclusion that it couldn't go back of the verdict of the jury. But the new High Commissioner is not much troubled by that respect for quibbles and technicalities which is the Western idea of justice. He goes straight to the essential rights and wrongs in the good old Oriental manner—the manner of HAROUN-AL-RASCHID.

August 4, 1921

# PALMER UPHOLDS RED REPRESSION

## Replies to Federal Attorney Kane, Who Opposed Raids on Radicals.

## ACCEPTS HIS RESIGNATION

## Attorney General Shows Communists Planned Overthrow of Government by Force.

## QUOTES THEIR MANIFESTO

### Cites Their Alliance with Moscow Internationale for Armed Rule by Proletariat Here.

*Special to The New York Times.*

WASHINGTON, Jan. 23.—Attorney General Palmer tonight issued a statement in justification of the recent raids on the Communists and the general attitude of the Department of Justice toward radicals and their organizations. The statement was in the form of a letter to Francis Fisher Kane, attorney for the Eastern District of Pennsylvania, who on Jan. 12 sent his resignation to President Wilson and apprised the Attorney General of his action, and in both letters gave as the reason for his resignation his lack of sympathy with the attitude of the Attorney General and the Department of Justice toward the radical elements.

Mr. Kane, just before the series of nation-wide raids on the Communists, had protested against the plan in a letter to the Attorney General, who had replied that the protest was too late. In his letter of resignation Mr. Kane not only condemned the raids and the general policy of the Attorney General toward radicals, but expressed his opposition to the pending Sterling-Graham sedition bill as a measure whose enforcement he would not care to aid.

The Attorney General, having received Mr. Kane's letter from the White House, accepts the resignation in his reply, in which he states the reasons underlying his acts relating to the Communist parties and other radical organizations. His chief reasons are the affiliation of the Communist parties with the Third Internationale, which declared at Moscow for the establishment of the rule of the proletariat and the overthrow of the State by force of arms, and the fact, as stated in their manifesto issued in the United States, "that the aim of the Communists of America is for the destruction of the Government."

The Attorney General also calls Mr. Kane's attention to the fact "that the organizations of Communists in the United States are pledged to destroy the great and loyal labor organization of America, namely the American Federation of Labor."

The Attorney General began his reply to Mr. Kane by saying:

"I have carefully read your views upon this matter, and in view of the frankness with which you have stated the same I feel impelled to reply at some length, in order that you may have a full understanding as to the reason in mind for the necessity for the recent actions of this department against the radical, anarchistic elements in the United States."

He then related how dissension in the ranks of the Socialist Party early in 1919 caused the formation last September of the Communist Party of America and the Communist Labor Party.

"These two organizations," the letter continued, "are identical in aim and tactics, the cause for their separate existence being due to the desire of certain individuals connected with the so-called Left Wing elements of the Socialist Party to be leaders. For the sake of convenience I shall refer to members of the Communist Party of America and the Communist Labor Party as 'Communists.'

"Immediately upon the formation of the Communist parties a program and manifesto were adopted by these parties, based upon the manifesto of the Third Internationale, adopted March 6 at Moscow. The Assembly at Moscow, as you know, was international in scope, and represented the gathering together of communists from all sections of the world, and at the meeting plans were laid to spread the doctrines of communism throughout the world. As specifically stated in the manifesto of the Third Internationale and its program, the accomplishment of its aims was not to be reached by merely the conquest of the political power of the so-called bourgeois State, but was to be reached by the destruction of the 'State.'

"Again in the manifesto is found the statement that it will be necessary 'to disarm the bourgeois and to arm the laborers and to form a communist army as the protector of the rule of the proletariat and the inviolability of the social structure. Further in the same manifesto we find enunciated the principle that in order to accomplish the aims of the proletariat it will be necessary to annihilate the enemies' apparatus of government, namely, its police, jailers, Judges, priests, Government officials, and others. One particular important statement contained in the manifesto, under the heading 'The Way to Victory,' is the following:

"'The revolutionary era compels the proletariat to make use of the means of battle which will concentrate its entire energy, namely, mass action, with its logical resultant direct conflict with the governmental machinery in open combat. All other methods, such as revolutionary use of bourgeois parliamentarism, will be of only secondary significance.'

"It is not necessary for me further to point out the ideas that permeated the minds of the persons attending the conference at Moscow to indicate that their sole and ultimate aim was to accomplish not only the conquest but the destruction of the idea of the 'State,' as understood by loyal American citizens. This destruction was not to be accomplished by parliamentary action, for it is specifically stated that it is to be by armed conflict with governmental authority.

"It is this manifesto which was adopted by the Communist parties in the United States as their program of action, and on the membership card of the Communist Party of America there is printed the fact that the organization is affiliated with the Third Internationale. However, the mere statement of affiliation was not the principal reason for the stand taken by this department against the Communist parties in this country. Not satisfied with the statement of affiliation with the Third Internationale at Moscow, the Communist parties in this country adopted in addition separate and distinct programs of action.

"In the program of the communists in the United States we find such statements as the following:

"'Communism rejects the conception of the State; it rejects the idea of class reconstruction and the parliamentary conquest of capitalism. The Communist Party alone is capable of mobilizing the proletariat for the revolutionary mass action to conquer the power of the State.'

#### Quotes Communist Manifesto.

After referring to the communists as being the chief instruments in causing the labor unrest of the last several months as part of the plan to overthrow the Government, the Attorney General again quotes from the manifesto:

"'The objective is the conquest by the proletariat of the power of the State. Communism does not propose to capture the bourgeois parliament of any State, but to conquer and destroy it.'

"We thus find stated in very clear and plain language the fact that the aim of the communists of America is for the destruction of the Government. This shows clearly," he continues, "that the organizations of communists in this country aim, not at the change of the Government of the United States by parliamentary or political methods, but in the overthrow and the destruction of the same by mass and direct action by force and violence.

"Another point of particular significance which I feel I should call to your attention is the fact that the organization of communists in the United States are pledged to destroy the great and loyal labor organization of America, namely, the American Federation of Labor, which, according to the Communist Party of America, is considered to be reactionary and a bulwark of capitalism. Another particularly significant pledge of the communists of America is to carry on agitation of the negro workers of America."

"Certainly such an organization as the Communist Party of America and also the Communist Labor Party," says Mr. Palmer, "cannot be construed to fall within the same category as the Socialist Party of America, which latter organization is pledged to the accomplishment of changes of the Government by lawful and rightful means.

"The immigration laws of the United States provide that any person who is a member of an organization which advocates the overthrow of the Government of the United States by force and violence shall be deported. There is no discretion placed in the hands of the officers administering this law which permits them to discriminate between active and non-active members, but it has been the policy of this department and the Department of Labor, which has rendered hearty co-operation in these matters, to take into custody only such persons as have been actively identified with pernicious organizations of the nature of the Communist parties and who are cognizant of the purposes of these organizations.

#### Defends Scope of Arrests.

The Attorney General quotes the pledge which those joining the Communist Party must sign, by which the member declares his adherence to the principles and tactics of the party and the Communist internationale and agrees to submit to the discipline of the party as stated in its constitution and pledges himself to engage actively in this work, as fixing the member's responsibility.

Merely to have arrested individuals would have been as useless as to endeavor to curb a great epidemic by isolating a single case, Mr. Palmer says. It was necessary to apprehend simultaneously all persons who were active members of the organizations so that their records would not be destroyed.

Regarding Mr. Kane's criticism of deportation proceedings, Mr. Palmer says careful study has failed to reveal a single instance where injustice had been done to an alien. "In every step of the proceedings the alien is accorded a full and fair opportunity to show cause why he should not be deported," explained the Attorney General. "It is incumbent upon the Government to prove that the man is an alien and to prove that he falls within the provisions of the law. After the decision of the Secretary of Labor has been reached, and if it is unfavorable to the alien, the attorney for the alien may, if he so desires and if he feels that he has not been accorded a proper and sufficient hearing, sue out a writ of habeas corpus, and the court will then inquire as to whether or not the rights of the alien have been fully safeguarded."

Unfortunate predicaments in which the families of the arrested aliens may find themselves must be faced by every Judge when dealing with a violator of the law, the Attorney General adds.

#### Opposes Sterling-Graham Bill.

"I have failed to find any large number of cases of families actually in want," says the letter. "In the few cases reported wherein families have actually been in need they have been cared for by charitable organizations.

"You seem to be laboring under a misapprehension as to my attitude with respect to proposed sedition legislation. I told a committee of the Senate last Summer that I did not favor an extension of the Espionage act beyond the war period, and in a report that I made to the Senate on Nov. 14 last I said:

"'I have felt that it was limited to the acts and utterances which tended to weaken the waging of actual hostilities.'

"I did ask, however, legislation which would make it possible for us to deal with citizens who seek the overthrow of the Government by force or violence, and in November I submitted to the Senate a draft of a proposed bill defining sedition and providing for punishment therefor and defining the promotion of sedition and providing for a penalty. This bill is one to which no loyal American can take exception. It makes it a crime for any person, with intent to injure or destroy the Government or its agencies, to commit or attempt or threaten to commit an act of force or violence against public property or public officials. It does not to the slightest extent abridge or interfere with the guarantee of free speech and the right of assembly.

"The Senate subsequently prepared and reported a bill known as the Sterling bill and the Judiciary Committee of the House reported a bill known as the Graham bill, both of which are very much more drastic and far reaching than the legislation which I proposed and, neither of which I have at any time approved. I had no part in their preparation and have no responsibility for either of them.

"I believe that the greatest safety of the country lies in the free expression of ideas. I am willing that any man should advocate the most radical reforms as long as he proposes to accomplish them by the methods devised by the people for accomplishing all change in our Government; but when he steps over the line and threatens to use physical force to accomplish such results, he goes beyond the bounds of the guaranty of free speech.

"Every man who comes to our shores from a foreign country ought to understand that his revolution has been fought and won when he sets foot on American soil. While there may be such a thing as a right of revolution, there is no room for revolution in a people's government, founded upon the Democratic principles of our Republic. The Government should encourage free political thinking and political action, but it certainly has the right for its own preservation, to discourage and prevent the use of force and violence to accomplish that which ought to be accomplished, if at all, by parliamentary or political methods."

So long as the deportation statute is the law, says the Attorney General in closing his letter, "it must be enforced. No person has been arrested who does not come within the provisions of that law. Your suggestions seems to be that we should disregard the law and refuse to enforce it. Of course, I cannot subscribe to any such doctrine, and I should not want any man to be associated with the Department of Justice who does not believe in the law.

"In view of your misunderstanding of the real facts in connection with the matters herein discussed, and of your apparent misconception of the duties of the Department of Justice in the enforcement of the laws as written, I am bound to say that your resignation seems to me to be quite the proper step for you to take."

In a later and separate statement, following a discussion of his views in the House, the Attorney General reiterated the foregoing views on the Sterling-Graham bill.

# IMMIGRATION BILL PASSED BY HOUSE

## Measure in Substantially Same Form as Vetoed by Wilson Wins Without Rollcall.

## STUBBORN FIGHT FOR IRISH

### Mondell Says Amendments, Which Are Defeated, Would Admit "William the Damned."

*Special to The New York Times.*

WASHINGTON, April 22.—Without material amendment and without a rollcall the House today passed the bill to limit immigration of aliens into the United States. The measure, which limits immigration from May 10, 1921, until June 30, 1922—fourteen months less ten days—to 3 per cent. of the number of foreign-born persons of such nationality in the United States as determined by the census of 1910, is in substantially the same form as vetoed by President Wilson in the last session of Congress.

Despite strenuous efforts to destroy the real purpose of the bill that of prohibiting immigration of undesirables from countries where Bolshevism thrives, the House stubbornly rejected many amendments intended to weaken the bill. The efforts of Irish sympathizers, led by Representative Sabath of Illinois and Representative W. Bourke Cockran of New York, to have political refugees exempted failed. A motion to amend the bill to permit Lord Mayor O'Callaghan of Cork to remain here was also rejected.

The House debated for more than an hour the political refugee amendment which was denounced as a move to break the backbone of the bill. After the House had rejected more than a dozen motions to exempt political refugees, Representative Frank W. Mondell, Republican floor leader, attacked the moves and quickly brought the debate to an end and forced a vote on the bill.

"Under Mr. Sabath's amendment," said Mr. Mondell, "not only could William the Damned come here, but Charles, late Emperor of Austria, and all the kings and princes who have been spurned and spewed out by the people of Europe could come.

"Every Russian opposed to the régime of Lenin and Trotzky would gain admission to our shores under it, and tomorrow, when, let us hope, the pendulum shall swing and these murderers and thieves fall from their present seats of power, Lenin and Trotzky and all the foul hordes that follow them could come in and we could not close the doors against them, even though they were avowed anarchists. That is what this amendment would do.

"Of course, we are all for America first, but the only way we can prove that is not by words, but by votes. That is what we are called upon to do now. He that careth not for his own household is worse than an infidel, and what shall it profit America if she shall afford an asylum to all the world and lose her own soul."

Two unimportant amendments were accepted today. One, offered by Representative Fish of New York, gave preference to the alien relatives of ex-service men. Representative Cooper of Wisconsin succeeded in having his amendment adopted which exempted from the provisions of the bill aliens under 18 years of age who are children of citizens of the United States.

The 3 per cent. immigration based on the 1910 census would permit in one year the following immigration from the various countries of Europe:

| Northwestern Europe. | | | |
|---|---|---|---|
| Belgium | 1,482 | Sweden | 19,956 |
| Denmark | 5,440 | Switzerland | 3,745 |
| France | 3,523 | United King. | 77,206 |
| Germany | 75,040 | | |
| Netherlands | 3,624 | Total N. W. | |
| Norway | 12,116 | Europe | 202,212 |

| Outside Northwestern Europe. | | | |
|---|---|---|---|
| Austria | 50,117 | Turk in Europa | 957 |
| Bulgaria | 345 | Turkey in Asia | 1,792 |
| Serbia | 139 | | |
| Greece | 3,088 | Tot. outside N. | |
| Montenegro | 161 | N.W. Europe. | 153,249 |
| Italy | 40,294 | Total N. W. | |
| Portugal | 1,781 | Europe | 202,212 |
| Rumania | 1,918 | | |
| Spain | 663 | Grand total | 355,461 |
| Russia | 51,974 | | |

The measure as passed now goes to the Senate, where early action will be recommended.

# NO MELTING POT, SAYS ELIOT

### Races Here Retain Characteristics, Harvard Educator Tells Students.

BOSTON, May 5.—Students from thirty-seven counties, undergraduates at colleges in or near this city, heard President (Emeritus) Charles W. Eliot of Harvard University tonight picture a future federation of the world.

The educator asserted that the figure of the melting pot as applied to the United States was in error, and that there had been no such thing in this country as assimilation or amalgamation. Each of the races that had settled here, he said, had retained characteristics, while giving to the whole the strength of all.

The address was made at a dinner given by the Chamber of Commerce for the foreign students at institutions in Greater Boston. Four hundred young men, including the Crown Prince of Siam, were present.

"We have in the United States no such thing as a melting pot, no such thing as assimilation of all these races as a common stock," Dr. Eliot told the students. "There never has been; there never will be.

"That is the spectacle offered by all these nationalities, living together here, sometimes in large groups, sometimes scattered. Each race has held aloof from the others; they do not mix, they do not intermarry, or, at least, they have done so only to a degree so slight that it would take thousands upon thousands of years to affect the country.

"Those who have eyes may see here an example for the whole world: many races living apart, but together; though different, in harmony, and more and more acquiring the common ideals of liberty and law. Let that be your picture of the world hereafter: The nations living side by side, just like the States of our Union. It will be a federation of states, uneven in size, but a united people composed of different racial elements in great variety.

"The separate merits, virtues and gifts of each will be as they have been here, preserved, not extinguished by intercourse or commerce, but instead strengthened to the good of the whole. That is the case in our country; so must it be in the federation of the world."

# WHAT EUROPE THINKS OF US

### *Our Materialism in Pursuit of Ideals Generally Mistaken for Precisely the Opposite*

#### By ESTHER EVERETT LAPE

BUT you see, my dear, America in these matters is about where we were in 1868."

"These matters" were industrial relations and the degree of political expression achieved my minorities. The speaker was the host at a London luncheon table, patiently endeavoring to put his bewildered wife au courant with American politics.

Most London luncheon table talk seems to begin with Ramsay MacDonald, under whose charm, if not power, the empire seems to have fallen. "He looked more the duke than any one else there." This enthusiastic approval of the Labor Prime Minister's appearance at court the night before came not from an American but from, so to speak, an old hand at the presentations. Nature's nobleman. Quite a pretty little political idyl which England had decided to enjoy.

From Labor in England you will admit that luncheon tables travel easily to Labor in America and American politics and, indeed, America at large: Why did Labor and the Left generally and all that come so little into the speculations on the national conventions? Fashions in dealing with Lefts has changed all over the European world, but you'd never know it to look at America. Did the American Left, assuming we had one, never get into the Government? Oh, we had one Socialist in Congress! But how amusing. And we had the Farm Bloc. And we had some Socialists in the New York State Legislature —but hadn't they been retired as unconstitutional or something like that? And the Irreconcilables — oh, they were not Left at all! What then were they irreconcilable to? Just irreconcilable in the abstract? Ah yes, that did happen.

But our hostess, a gentle soul with the vaguest possible notions of American life outside the sheltered circles of the few American cities she had known, simply could not understand: Here was England with a minority actually in power. Here was France gone to the Left, for a spell at least. Here was Germany— well, it was hard to say just how the Right and Left weighed against each other there at present, because so many of the old Right and Left had rather got bunched together in the Centre, but they had the leftest kind of Left in those sixty-two men and women in the Reichstag—that is, such of them as weren't in jail. To say nothing, of course, of Russia. The guests had heard that over in America we didn't talk much about Russia except as a horrible example. England, now, considered it quite respectable to "speak to" Russia, though, to be sure, the Anglo-Russian conference then in session wasn't going forward so very fast. Really, America was confusing.

Yes, of course, they realized the different conditions produced by our two-party system. But even so, wouldn't it be better if America recognized frankly how many forces go into the making of the political life of a great nation? Wouldn't it be healthier if even within our two-party system we worked out some scheme for defining minorities better? If you never defined them, never forced them to issues and a vote, how did you ever know just how powerful or how weak they were? Whether you wanted the minorities to thrive or whether you wanted them squelched, wasn't it better, in either case, to have them defined, with a clear path to the tribune? Weren't we "blinking things a bit?"

"But you see, my dear, America in these matters is about where we were in 1868."

Not a bit of color of comment in our host's voice; no air of making a charge; just a calm supplying of a fact left out of the reckoning up to this point. If only he had been a bit mean and cynical about it; if only he had had the air of making a mot. But it had merely been stated with British calm by a clear and genial observer who has lived with us and is affectionately known in America.

1868! Reactionary America! To be charged with the faults of youth and a generous audacity, that we have always been able to endure with equanimity. But it is one thing to be called a gay young dog; another to be spoken of forbearingly as not young but belated, a bit blind here and a bit deaf there. To hear ourselves, the liberal, the uninhibited, the free, polished off as politically confused, reactionary, with a tinge of distinctly middle-aged, nay, even Victorian, hypocrisy—well, that is baptism by immersion into what they think

"Materialism in the pursuit of ideals"—the Wright Brothers.

of us. I came up for air and waited for the next.

It came a few days later in Paris. I had been taken to see one of the Ministers of the present Government—no, by this time it is the one before the present! We were talking about America and France and the peace of the world.

"Ah, yes," he said, "I have seen that a number of Americans have come to talk glibly of 'militaristic France.' " He was silent a moment, a shadow on his face. "Can you not tell America for France," he said at last, slowly, "that to us here and now it is America who seems 'militaristic,' very far from preoccupied, shall I say, with the vision of peace which she held up to France and all the world in 1919? It is America who seems regardless of the shadows of war still so far from dispelled, so little conscious of Europe's longing for peace."

A fine string of adjectives I was collecting across the Continent of Europe. "Militaristic" America, "Reactionary" America, not exactly intolerant of its protestant minorities, but awkwardly incapable of fitting them in.

Not only in this but in many other respects, I think, Europe rather generally finds us lacking in political savoir vivre. Naturally, countries in which changes of Cabinets, sharp fluctuations in currency, new elections, and even revolutions, may follow each other within the space of a few months get to regarding political life as a free-for-all, and political crises as the order of the day, not to be taken too seriously. They find us naive in our intensity about our very moderate political problems, while what we regard as the iron hand of our two-party system represses, they think, the free play of thought and action they consider essential to representative democratic government. They find us deficient in ability to take heavy political events with well-mannered lightness. We could never, for instance, carry off a conference with Russia (especially with our defined habit of ominousness toward Russia) as England does. All England did not give the effect of believing that civilization was hanging in the balance. She simply waited with a kind of disinterested calm for the Russians to show their hand about how far they would go toward assuming debts in order to get credits! Meanwhile in the revue halls good performers reproduced faithfully the manner of speech of the non-English-speaking Russian delegates and the audiences rocked with laughter.

And it isn't our great national memorial, prohibition, that intrigues the foreigner nearly so much as our momentous attitude toward having got it. True it is that all travelers returned from America to their native heath write endless columns on prohibition. But that is because we make it impossible for them to do otherwise. We steer them up to prohibition and insist that they contemplate it. We give them no choice. Yesterday, in Berlin, I tried to get my taxi driver to take me directly to a certain part of Berlin where my objective was people. But in spite of repeated directions in very fair academic German he insisted upon driving me around the other way in order that I might contemplate certain Denkmäler I already knew and never want to see again. Prohibition is our greatest American Denkmäl. We insist that travelers to our shores shall not take it lightly. They come to share our intensity. Probably if our visitors had found American hosts accepting prohibition more as a matter of course, not say a fait accompli, they would not be discussing it so copiously in their "impressions of America."

I think the British capacity for assimilating political crises more calmly is due to the firmest belief that British institutions are permanent and finished and unassailable, and that political crises of whatever nature are therefore unimportant. Perhaps they would say, if they analyzed us, that the reason we feel ourselves less independent of history is that our fun-

damentals, our institutions, are constantly showing themselves more subject to the influences of wind and tide than theirs are. There is a good deal of real and ill-concealed British distrust of at least some of our institutions. The Church, for instance. Only a few weeks ago an Englishman told me he never could, so to speak, get the hang of the Church in America—it seemed such an individual thing there, hardly an institution at all. "I'm a churchman myself, but in America the Church seems to me—well, rather like a small bowler hat. More like a rudimentary growth or excrescence than a fundamental limb. Not even a proper sized hat." Something detached, incongruous, even a little ludicrous, perhaps, in the way it failed to fit into this man's conception of a perfect civilization. This Englishman, it should be said, is of the type who has made only brief professorial trips to America on that "exchange" basis which is obviously better than no exchange at all, but which often results in curiously literal application of fleeting generalizations.

Our courts we take so largely from England, with so fundamental an adoption of the Anglo-Saxon common law, that we should expect the British to regard American courts as good old home brew. Yet the true Briton views with alarm what he regards as an undue flexibility in American courts. While I was in England lately, former Lord Justice Darling introduced a bill which proposed enlarging the legal interpretation of insanity as determining criminal responsibility. He suggested that all juries be instructed to decide whether the criminal at the moment of his crime was in such a state of mental disease as to be incapable of resisting the impulse to commit it. But the bill "didn't take" at all in England, in spite of its distinguished source. It struck the press and Lord Justice Darling's colleagues and the British mind generally as an attempt to blur the sacred Anglo-Saxon method of determining right and wrong, by introducing complexities. Once given up the sharp old Anglo-Saxon black and white—

conception of right and wrong, and where are you? In dismissing with horror the proposal in Lord Justice Darling's bill, more than one editorial that I saw claimed that it tended in an American direction: "We do not want Thaw cases in the British law courts or expert witnesses testifying to the reality or otherwise of brainstorms, or juries too confused by medical jargon to give a clear and sensible verdict."

So far as the editorial objections to Lord Justice Darling's proposal were founded on a belief that "only rich men would have the means to pursue this type of justice," a large part of American opinion would support them. But one cannot help suspecting that British opinion balks even more at any idea which in its operation would take away one jot or one tittle of the ancient and absolute prestige of the good old jury. Lombroso began knocking at that door a long time ago with his suggestion that how the Lord endowed or failed to endow a human soul

should have something to do with the character of the human justice meted out to it. Many groups in America have been intrigued by this aspiration toward a finer justice than a jury is capable of. The hardest point on earth for our English friends to get is that idealism and aspiration may and sometimes must take the course of modifying landmarks.

I daresay the reason why things like Leagues of Nations find existence so rocky is simply the host of hoary and grotesque popular misconceptions people simply have to maintain about countries and peoples they don't know. Did it ever occur to you to imagine how the average Britisher who has never been to see us pictures New York? I got the photograph clearly several weeks ago. "Come with me," as the valedictorians say, to the top of a bus going out Hampton Courtway on a beautiful afternoon. In front of me sat a woman and her husband taking a long ride in order to get a glimpse of the horsechestnuts scheduled to be in full blossom in Bushey Park. The bus passed a building being demolished. The woman lamented it with a repetition which her husband endured with phenomenal patience. I heard its shrill culmination: "Some people would be perfectly willing to have all the old landmarks taken away and let the world get just like New York." I could see it, her New York. Years of an ancient tradition of a raw America would make it quite impossible for her to believe even that the evening dusk comes graciously over Madison Square or that the spirit of all the ages broods over the vast city seen from Brooklyn Bridge at nightfall.

I should have been happy to present her—had it been possible—with another mind picture of New York, for I was charmed with the pilgrimage she and her husband were making to see the horsechestnuts, meanwhile planning another to the bluebells at Kew. We Americans view with some amusement the conscious and somewhat solemn enjoyment Londoners show in their rare good weather. But I think they really are capable of a more frank and simple pleasure in sun and flowers and birds than we are. Of course, we haven't any nightingales. If we had, I wonder if we should have thought of broadcasting their song. The news of a week while I was in London was the broadcasting of the song of the nightingales from Sussex woods. A lady playing a harp in her garden had noticed that when she played the nightingales sang. Which gave the radio people the means of capturing its song for all England.

If I was enlightened by an average Englishwoman's traditional conception of New York, I was more so by a much more-than-average Frenchman's traditional conception of New York women. It was at the Comédie Française. The woman described in the cast of characters as a New Yorker, upon her entrance struck such a curiously inharmonious and overemphatic note in an otherwise almost perfect presentation, that I hastily looked up the text. There she was described by the author, with rare simplicity, as an American "avec aucune aristocratie, mais avec la hauteur des dames de New York." One dame de. New York looked agape at her national representative, heavily accented, unspeakably raucous, big and blond and noisily giggly, a very raw article among those presented as of the demi-monde of other countries. So much for our "hauteur." I am sure les hommes de New York wouldn't have had any trouble in classifying this specimen!

Hoariest and mossiest of foreign conceptions is the jealously preserved belief that, if Americans are faster workers, they are, by the same token, infinitely more superficial and sloppy workers, daring all things and finishing few. I had some contacts with a certain English committee. Almost every one of them, at some point in the negotiations, fixed me with his eye and told me I must remember "an *Englishman* will never undertake anything unless he can do it *thoroughly*." Business of accenting. A splendid alibi, this sentiment, for work. I humbly allowed America in my person to be classified with the hasty and superficial workers. Yet I left England musing on the amount of laziness that might travel under a much more respectable name, and wondering if I should ever dare to suggest that there is a world of ancient error in the assumption that slowness and thoroughness are one and the same.

Or in the assumption that because America is often practical she is therefore "materialistic." The oldest saw of all. Sooner or later every American millionaire works out some method of spending his money for an idea. It is the great American tendency. Yet over here we still figure as the "Dollarmenschen" as I saw us yesterday displayed in a Berlin bookshop—the epithet being spread out over a Ford car constructed out of an American flag. And last night, in a very distinguished English review, I read a critique of a book of President Coolidge's which the reviewer chose to regard as the epitome of the American spirit because, to him, it showed our traditional "curious idealism in the pursuit of material objects." He and most foreign analysts of the American spirit miss the point entirely: our characteristic is not a "curious idealism in the pursuit of material objects"; it is a curious materialism in the pursuit of ideals.

It strikes the observer sometimes that a very little genuine international interpreting would make such an immense difference. Really, we shall have to work out a better means of accomplishing it. Take the

Olympic games, obviously a magnificent opportunity for international contact—if there are not too many preconceived misunderstandings. The French soul, or the French taste, or the French something was sorely tried by the noisiness of our folk at the games. The barbarity of our organized cheering struck them as an assault. The French failed completely to get the point that our noisiness didn't in the least mean preoccupation with victory, hadn't a thing in the world to do with the insolence of the conqueror, but is just a little habit we have of being stirringly articulate in sport, whether victorious or vanquished. But the breach at one point reached almost diplomatic proportions.

When you think of the material out of which the rank and file of the foreign population gets its idea of us, small wonder it is that distorted pictures result. Try collecting on any given day the grist of American news in the foreign press. Rushing, when I landed in Europe, for all available newspapers, like the true newspaper hound that I am, in order to get word of all that had been doing after a week at sea with only a meagre wireless bulletin each day, I found: a story of money taken by airplane from one Missouri town to another in order to avoid a run on a bank; a story of fourteen miners entombed in Colorado; of a member of the House found guilty of possessing an illegal permit for liquor; of the chasing of bootleggers by the police in New York and the killing of two innocent bystanders in the consequent shooting. That was the grist—save for one long, slow, deadly dull column on the American political situation, the "news" in it so old that it might have come over in a rowboat. And so barren withal. A tale of stark outlines only, with no philosophy either behind or ahead, with the strange remoteness that colors a tale told by an uninterested writer to uninterested readers.

There is another source of information on America: At present in the foreign press there is a tremendous run of "impressions of America" by returned journalists, novelists and what not. A naïve collection. Would that American editors would pay for such. It has been many a long year since the American editor printed the casual meanderings of the very casual tripper abroad. I have before me one week's collection comprising three articles on America by three distinguished travelers returned to their

several countries: One begins with a picture of Americans characteristically consuming ice cream soda and large pieces of layer cake in drug stores at 11 in the morning (poor observation—the 11 o'clock ice cream soda fiend is male and rarely takes cake). Another—by nothing less than a Lord–philosophizes as usual on how many of us are Babbitts, whither we are tending with respect to the negro whose "dark invasion" of certain sections of our cities is unfailingly regarded as a sign of progressive black domination. This reporter, or I should say his lordship, answers the burning question as to whether our artisans go to and from work in "motors." They do—he has seen the motors parked. The third article is the simplest of all. It appeared a few days ago in a Berlin paper under the signature of a man who habitually discusses subtleties at home. But from America he sent to his paper a long story describing Fifth Avenue and Park Avenue—i. e., telling the most obvious facts about them—and with the Deutsch completeness distinguishing between the two.

At this rate it will take a long time to convey America to Europe. But there are hopeful signs: A London bookseller told me that he is selling now in England ten books on America to the one he sold some years ago. "Account for it? Oh, I don't know. More Englishmen emigrating to America, of course, and wanting to read of conditions there. But I think, too, it's the result of the war, in a way. People saw America come over and build a four-track railway in no time and put up all kinds of buildings with speed and dispatch and power. And they want to know more about the people that did these things and how they do it. That's all."

It isn't quite all. There are other infiltrations. Later years have seen, for instance, a new kind of pilgrim to Europe not known in Henry James's day. It is the American economic student, investigator or social worker, gone abroad to study and compare methods, &c. The very new international interest in America has penetrated the many American movements for "uplift" and they are sending representatives abroad on intellectual and research missions of all kinds. In numbers! Right now we are keeping the English, especially, busy showing zealous Americans this and that and expounding their "methods" to us. They complain bitterly but they love it.

# Scott Fitzgerald Looks Into Middle Age

*THE GREAT GATSBY. By F. Scott Fitzgerald. New York: Charles Scribner's Sons. $2.*

OF the many new writers that sprang into notice with the advent of the post-war period, Scott Fitzgerald has remained the steadiest performer and the most entertaining. Short stories, novels and a play have followed with consistent regularity since he became the philosopher of the flapper with "This Side of Paradise." With shrewd observation and humor he reflected the Jazz Age. Now he has said farewell to his flappers—perhaps because they have grown up—and is writing of the older sisters that have married. But marriage has not changed their world, only the locale of their parties. To use a phrase of Burton Rascoe's—his hurt romantics are still seeking that other side of paradise. And it might almost be said that "The Great Gatsby" is the last stage of illusion in this absurd chase. For middle age is certainly creeping up on Mr. Fitzgerald's flappers.

In all great arid spots nature provides an oasis. So when the Atlantic seaboard was hermetically sealed by law, nature provided an outlet, or inlet rather, in Long Island. A place of innate natural charm, it became lush and luxurious under the stress of this excessive attention, a seat of festive activities. It expresses one phase of the great grotesque spectacle of our American scene. It is humor, irony, ribaldry, pathos and loveliness. Out of this grotesque fusion of incongruities has slowly become conscious a new humor—a strictly American product. It is not sensibility, as witness the writings of Don Marquis, Robert Benchley and Ring Lardner. It is the spirit of "Processional" and Donald

F. Scott Fitzgerald.
*Author of "The Great Gatsby." New York: Charles Scribner's Sons.*

Douglas's "The Grand Inquisitor"; a conflict of spirituality caught fast in the web of our commercial life. Both boisterous and tragic, it animates this new novel by Mr. Fitzgerald with whimsical magic and simple pathos that is realized with economy and restraint.

The story of Jay Gatsby of West Egg is told by Nick Carraway, who is one of the legion from the Middle West who have moved on to New York to win from its restless indifference—well, the aspiration that arises in the Middle West—and finds in Long Island a fascinating but dangerous playground. In the method of telling, "The Great Gatsby" is reminiscent of Henry James's "Turn of the Screw." You will recall that the evil of that mysterious tale which so endangered the two children was never exactly stated beyond a suggested generalization. Gatsby's fortune, business, even his connection with underworld figures, remain vague generalizations. He is wealthy, powerful, a man who knows how to get things done. He has no friends, only business associates, and the throngs who come to his Saturday night parties. Of his uncompromising love — his love for Daisy Buchanan—his effort to recapture the past romance—we are explicitly informed. This patient romantic hopefulness against existing conditions, symbolizes Gatsby. And like the "Turn of the Screw," "The Great Gatsby" is more a long short story than a novel.

Nick Carraway had known Tom Buchanan at New Haven. Daisy, his wife, was a distant cousin. When he came East Nick was asked to call at their place at East Egg. The post-war reactions were at their height—every one was restless—every one was looking for a substitute for the excitement of the war years. Buchanan had acquired another woman. Daisy was bored, broken in spirit and neglected. Gatsby, his parties and his mysterious wealth were the gossip of the hour. At the Buchanans Nick met Jordan Baker; through them both Daisy again meets Gatsby, to whom she had been engaged before she married Buchanan. The inevitable consequence that follows, in which violence takes its toll, is almost incidental, for in the overtones—and this is a book of potent overtones—the decay of souls is more tragic. With sensitive insight and keen psychological observation, Fitzgerald discloses in these people a meanness of spirit, carelessness and absence of loyalties. He cannot hate them, for they are dumb in their insensate selfishness, and only to be pitied. The philosopher of the flapper has escaped the mordant, but he has turned grave. A curious book, a mystical, glamourous story of today. It takes a deeper cut at life than hitherto has been essayed by Mr. Fitzgerald. He writes well—he always has—for he writes naturally, and his sense of form is becoming perfected.

EDWIN CLARK.

# Mr. Barton Makes a "Success Story" of the Life of Christ

## "Stripped of All Dogma," He Says, "This Is the Grandest Achievement Story of All."

*THE MAN NOBODY KNOWS: A Discovery of Jesus. By Bruce Barton. 220 pp. Indianapolis: The Bobbs-Merrill Company. $2.50.*

ONE of the high priests of modern advertising has written a book about Jesus Christ. It is a book different from any other that has been written about Him. Mr. Barton's interpretation is certain to shock many readers, though it is reverent; it will convince many, though others will find it often dropping into absurdity. But it will interest everybody.

"The Man Nobody Knows" was written out of sincere conviction. That much is evident from the first page to the last. It is the product of a revolt that began, Mr. Barton tells us, in Sunday school. As a boy he could not see why his teacher repeatedly told him that he must love Jesus. He was not attracted by the frail figure, the sad face that looked down on him from the wall. He liked the pictures of Daniel and David and Moses, but this Jesus was "the lamb of God," He was "meek and lowly," he was "a man of sorrows" and went around telling people not to do things. As he grew up he began to wonder about Jesus.

He said to himself: "Only strong, magnetic men inspire great enthusiasm and build great organizations. Yet Jesus built the greatest organization of all. It is extraordinary."

He decided to go back to the original sources, to free his mind from old conceptions and to see what the Gospels said. And Mr. Barton "was amazed."

A physical weakling! Where did they get that idea? Jesus pushed a plane and swung an adze; He was a successful carpenter. He slept outdoors and spent His days walking around His favorite lake. His muscles were so strong that when He drove the money-changers out nobody dared oppose Him!

A kill-joy! He was the most popular dinner guest in Jerusalem. The criticism which proper people made was that He spent too much time with publicans and sinners and enjoyed society too much. They called Him a "wine-bibber and a gluttonous man."

A failure! He picked up twelve men from the bottom ranks of business and forged them into an organization that conquered the world.

From those three paragraphs you can catch the outlines of the picture Mr. Barton builds up. It is a picture which when finished portrays Jesus not so completely as it does those manly characteristics enshrined in the creed of American salesmanship. It is a picture in which the go-getter, the worshiper of "personality" and of the "human dynamo," the mixer, the man who can "sell himself" and who can "put his message across" will take comfort. Says Mr. Barton: "Stripped of all dogma this is the grandest achievement story of all!"

It is, of course, entirely reasonable to suppose that Jesus was of a different physical type than the religious painters have habitually pictured Him. The very conditions of His life give support to that belief. He must have done hard manual labor in His youth, for, as Mr. Barton points out, a carpenter's work was more exacting then than now; and during the years of His ministry His life was of the sort to keep Him in robust physical condition.

Nor does one need any more evidence than the Gospels provide to see that Jesus enjoyed the company of men. He was no recluse like John the Baptist. Mr. Barton is sure that He laughed, and probably He did.

So far, well enough. But Mr. Barton is not content to emphasize the healthy humanity of Jesus. He must defend Him from the charge of being a failure, and one wonders why the author feels the necessity of that. But spiritual triumph, apparently, is not enough; there is a "success story" here in terms which the twentieth century can understand. Jesus was a born executive, unerring in His perception of how to pick His subordinates and how to get the most out of them; a born organizer; the founder of modern advertising, who knew how to make the front page every day.

In filling out that side of his picture Mr. Barton, without at all meaning to, belittles the meaning and purpose of his subject's work. Possessed by this Rotarian vision of his, he swings the Gospels forcibly into line with the commandments of the business world. What did Jesus mean, he asks, when He said: "And whosoever shall compel thee to go a mile, go with him twain?" Why, this is the very gospel of achievement; this is admonition for the clock-watchers; Jesus is telling us to work after hours. Had Mr. Barton so soon forgotten that this was part of the Sermon on the Mount, that the sentence he quotes was immediately preceded by these:

But I say unto you, That ye resist not evil; but whosoever shall smite thee on thy right cheek, turn to him the other also.

And if any man sue thee at the law and take away thy coat, let him have thy cloak also.

And all three of these admonitions led up to the counsel that followed:

But I say unto you, Love your enemies, bless them that curse you, do good to them that hate you and pray for them which despitefully use you and persecute you.

There was the incident of the stilling of the tempest. As the story is told in the Gospels, Jesus was awakened by the frightened disciples, who feared their boat would sink.

And He saith unto them, Why are ye fearful, O ye of little faith? Then He arose and rebuked the waves and the sea, and there was a great calm.

Faith may be all very well, but the picture of an unflurried executive, with "2 o'clock in the morning courage," issuing "a few quiet orders" so that "presently the menaced boat swung around into the smoother waters of safety" is better suited to Mr. Barton's purpose. Even his emphasis on the physical characteristics of Jesus becomes distorted when he makes Pilate, "his cheeks fatty with self-indulgence" and with "the colorless look of indoor living," exclaim in admiration when he brought Jesus out before His accusers, "Behold the man!" Those were Pilate's words, but in their context they are perfunctory, a mere identification.

The reasons why Mr. Barton recommends to the attention of sales managers every one of Jesus' conversations, "every contact between His mind and others," are fairly obvious. Jesus knew how to secure attention, how to work concisely and simply toward His point, how to drive it home by repetition. He knew the value of homely illustration, the worth of a story. But it is a bit hard to reconcile Mr. Barton's belief that He was consciously an advertiser in the modern sense, "the greatest of His time," with Jesus' own repeated instructions to those whom He healed to "let no man know of this."

Mr. Barton's book, it may be added, is itself a model of crisp advertising English.

Bruce Barton.

© *Pirie MacDonald.*

May 10, 1925

## BRYAN CALLS SCIENTISTS DISHONEST SCOUNDRELS

### Declares They Are 'Burrowing in the Ground' and Stealing Away Children's Faith.

*Special to The New York Times.*

PHILADELPHIA, May 13.—William J. Bryan, in an address at Westchester today, accused the scientists of America of being "dishonest scoundrels" afraid to tell their beliefs—burrowing in the ground and stealing away the faith of your children."

"But we've got 'em now where they've got to come up and fight," added Mr. Bryan. "In Tennessee there is a law they can't teach that man is descended from any lower form of life. Now that law deliberately has been violated. The Fundamentalists are so interested in the case that I said I'd be one of their counsel if the law department of the State of Tennessee doesn't object.

"This is a matter for the nation. It is one of the greatest questions ever raised—the question of the right of the people who created and support the schools to control them. If not they, then who?"

Mr. Bryan's address was delivered at the third annual interdenominational conference on fundamentals held by the Sure Foundation Reformed Episcopalians, Lutherans and Goshen Baptists of Westchester.

"The Fundamentalists," said Mr. Bryan, "are trying to establish the doctrine that the taxpayer has a right to say what shall be taught—the taxpayers and not the scientists.

"There are only 11,000 members of the American Association for the Advancement of Science," Mr. Bryan went on. "I don't believe one in ten thousand should dictate to the rest of us. Can a handful of scientists rob your children of religion and turn them out atheists? We'll find 109,000,000 Americans on the other side. For the first time in my life I'm on the side of the majority."

# BRYAN IN DAYTON, CALLS SCOPES TRIAL DUEL TO THE DEATH

### If Evolution Wins, He Declares, Christianity Goes, for Both Cannot Survive.

## SEES THE BIBLE AT STAKE

### Trying to Destroy It, He Asserts, on Evidence That Would Not Convict a Habitual Criminal.

## CROWD CHEERS HIS ARRIVAL

### Malone and Hays of Defense Counsel Leave Here Today, Expecting Colby to Join Them Later.

*Special to The New York Times.*

DAYTON, Tenn., July 7.—William Jennings Bryan arrived in Dayton today to direct the prosecution of John Thomas Scopes for teaching evolution and ten minutes after he landed in this little town he was walking down the main street in his shirt sleeves, with helmet protecting his bald head from the Summer sun.

Incidentally, Mr. Bryan confessed today that the inheritance of acquired characteristics had played some part in his own life, for he inherited his baldness and his handwriting from his father. Once upon a time the elder Bryan signed his firm name "Bryan & Kegge" to a letter and when the reply came back it was addressed to "Barrell & Keg," which the ardent advocate of grape juice related with many chuckles. As Mr. Bryan carefully made corrections in copies of a speech which he made tonight he laughed at his penmanship and said he would give the copies out to the impatient reporters on the theory of "the survival of the fittest."

Altogether, Mr. Bryan was in good humor. He had been met at the station by about 300 people, 50 of whom were reporters and photographers, had been paraded up the main street in an automobile, had shaken hands with all those on the side of the prosecution and some interested in the defense, had had a long talk with the lawyers with whom he will be associated, had been interviewed, had an ice cream soda in the drug store, and made a speech at a dinner in his honor. It was Bryan day, for there was no other distinguished visitor in town. He even looked at the court house where he will declaim against evolution, sitting far back from the road behind a green lawn and trees, and pronounced it good.

### Cheered on His Arrival.

When he stepped from the train which had brought him on the last stage of his long journey from Miami there was a cheer from the assembled townsfolk and three local clergymen. He met F. R. Rogers, at whose bungalow he will stay while in Dayton; Sue and Herb Hicks, J. G. and Ben McKenzie and Wallace Haggard, all of whom will be associated with Mr. Bryan and E. T. Stewart of the Attorney General's office in the case against Scopes. Dr. John R. Neal, tired and covered with dust, with a two days' growth of beard, after his long night journey over the mountains from Cookeville, where he tried to get a Federal injunction against the State prosecution, also stepped up and gripped the Commoner's hand.

The pith helmet was the most conspicuous thing in the automobile procession that wound its way up the street to the Rogers home, with the exception of a large truck bearing a model of a Florida house, which edged its way into the line three cars behind Mr. Bryan. Big signs on its sides shrieked the good news about Tampa, which is on the other side of the peninsula from Mr. Bryan's favorite spot, Miami, where real estate is also a marketable commodity. He noticed it and smiled with the look of one who could afford to be magnanimous.

When he reached the Rogers home he stood on the steps, surveyed the crowd of photographers and townspeople before him, and exclaimed with satisfaction:

"This is the day I have been waiting for."

After his conference with the Hicks brothers and the visit to the drug store Mr. Bryan strolled through the streets, his shirt-sleeved figure and pith helmet, the cynosure of all of Dayton, which gathered in store windows, against fences and under trees to watch their champion go by. He smiled and waved merry greeting.

### He Declares the Bible Is on Trial.

There was a very real earnestness in Mr. Bryan's voice as he sat in the Hicks law office later correcting his speech. He looked with determination over his glasses, and, pencil in hand, pronounced against the stupidities of scientists.

"Why, these men would destroy the Bible on evidence that would not convict a habitual criminal of a misdemeanor," he said. "They found a tooth in a sand pit in Nebraska with no other bones about it, and from that one tooth decided that it was the remains of the missing link. They have queer ideas about age, too. They find a fossil and when they are asked how old it is they say they can't tell without knowing what rock it was in, and when they are asked how old the rock is they say they can't tell unless they know how old the fossil is."

"How about radio-activity?" asked a man who has been sitting up nights with books on evolution. But Mr. Bryan bent over his work and did no reply. The age of the earth has been estimated by a study of radio-activity.

Mr. Bryan's speech before the Dayton Progressive Club tonight made it very plain that the Fundamentalists are planning to get just as much out of the publicity of the Scopes trial as are the evolutionists.

"The contest between evolution and Christianity is a duel to the death," he said dramatically. "It has been in the past a death struggle in the darkness. From this time on it will be a death grapple in the light. If evolution wins in Dayton Christianity goes—not suddenly, of course, but gradually—for the two cannot stand together. They are as antagonistic as light and darkness, as good and evil."

### Says the Truth Must Triumph.

"Heretofore evolution has been like the pestilence that walketh in darkness. Hereafter it will be the destruction that wasteth at noonday."

His words were a paraphrase of Goethe's remarks, who, on hearing of the debate between Frederic Cuvier and Geoffrey de Saint Hilaire on evolution, exclaimed:

"It is out in the open now. They will not be able to keep it in conference rooms from this time on.

"The atheists, agnostics and all other opponents of Christianity understand the character of the struggle," continued Mr. Bryan, "hence this interest in this case. From this time forth the Christians will understand the character of the struggle also. In an open fight the truth will finally triumph.

"Believing that revealed religion offers mankind the truth, the only abiding religious truth, Christians will fight evolution as their only great foe. If they are wrong they will of course be defeated, and in their defeat will be compelled to abandon the Bible as the word of God.

"If the information furnished at the trial and brought out afterward because of the trial shows evolution to be unproven and therefore unworthy of acceptance, science will have to fall back upon demonstrated truth which has no terrors for Christianity. Christianity is not afraid of any truth, it only opposes hypotheses put forth in the name of science but unsupported by facts."

Mr. Bryan came to the support of Dayton, and said that it was very fitting that this trial should be held in a small town, for Bethlehem and Nazareth were both small towns. This peaceful community forms a fitting environment, he said, for uncovering the attack which has been made for a generation on revealed religion.

The drug store, "where it all started," was the spot to and from which George W. Rappelyea, termed "general manager" of the Scopes defense, moved most of the day. The little tables, particularly the one with the inscription under glass that tells of the origin of the case, were filled all day with girls eating ice cream and newspapermen trying to cool off, and both the prosecution and the defense were represented there at intervals. Dr. John R. Neal, chief counsel for Scopes, was sitting at one of these tables when Rappelyea came in with a batch of telegrams and greatly excited. He had good news about his witnesses, but what it was Dr. Neal did not want to reveal at this time.

There is no doubt, however, that the defense will be able to bring to the stand some scientists of real standing, and clergymen of liberal tendencies and of wide repute.

There has been some misunderstanding, Dr. Neal said, of the reasons for the attempt to obtain a Federal injunction. There was little hope that the trial of Scopes would be stopped, and the defense did not wish it stopped. But they did want to pave the way for a suit which might later, no matter what happens at this trial, be taken to the United States Supreme Court. That was the reason for bringing the taxpayers' action to demand that the State does not interfere with freedom of teaching in Tennessee.

"In the Oregon case it was pointed out in the Supreme Court decision that the right of the Legislature to regulate the curriculum was not in question," said Dr. Neal. "That point has never been raised in the Federal courts, but Justice McReynolds did say that the Legislature has no right to attempt to conventionalize the mind of a child against the wishes of its parents. That is a very wonderful statement. This taxpayers' action we have brought is to protest against the limitation by the State of the curriculum.

Judge Neal said that the action at Cookeville was merely for the purpose of the record, and that at any time he will be able to make a similar motion before three Judges, one of whom must be a Circuit Judge, which will insure the issue being brought before the United States Supreme Court. But that action has nothing to do with the case against Scopes, who, incidentally, was not in Dayton today to see his famous prosecutor, Mr. Bryan, arrive.

# LINDBERGH DOES IT! 1,000 MILES THROUGH CHEERING FRENCH

## COULD HAVE GONE 500 MILES FARTHER

### Gasoline for at Least That Much More— Flew at Times From 10 Feet to 10,000 Feet Above Water

### ATE ONLY ONE AND A HALF OF HIS FIVE SANDWICHES

### Fell Asleep at Times but Quickly Awoke—Glimpses of His Adventure in Brief Interview at the Embassy.

---

### LINDBERGH'S OWN STORY TOMORROW.

*Captain Charles A. Lindbergh was too exhausted after his arrival in Paris late last night to do more than indicate, as told below, his experiences during his flight. After he awakes today, he will narrate the full story of his remarkable exploit for readers of Monday's New York Times.*

---

#### By CARLYLE MACDONALD.
Copyright, 1927, by The New York Times Company.
Special Cable to The New York Times.

PARIS, Sunday, May 22.—Captain Lindbergh was discovered at the American Embassy at 2:30 o'clock this morning. Attired in a pair of Ambassador Herrick's pajamas, he sat on the edge of a bed and talked of his flight. At the last moment Ambassador Herrick had canceled the plans of the reception committee and, by unanimous consent, took the flier to the embassy in the Place d'Iena.

A staff of American doctors who had arrived at Le Bourget Field early to minister to an "exhausted" aviator found instead a bright-eyed, smiling youth who refused to be examined.

"Oh, don't bother; I am all right," he said.

"I'd like to have a bath and a glass of milk. I would feel better," Lindbergh replied when the Ambassador asked him what he would like to have.

A bath was drawn immediately and in less than five minutes the youth had disrobed in one of the embassy guest rooms, taken his bath and was out again drinking a bottle of milk and eating a roll.

#### "No Use Worrying," He Tells Envoy.

"There is no use worrying about me, Mr. Ambassador," Lindbergh insisted when Mr. Herrick and members of the embassy staff wanted him to be examined by doctors and then go to bed immediately.

It was apparent that the young man was too full of his experiences to want sleep and he sat on the bed and chatted with the Ambassador, his son and daughter-in-law.

By this time a corps of frantic newspaper men who had been madly chasing the airman, following one false scent after another, had finally tracked him to the embassy. In a body they descended upon the Ambassador, who received them in the salon and informed them that he had just left Lindbergh with strict instructions to go to sleep.

As Mr. Herrick was talking with the reporters his son-in-law came downstairs and said that Lindbergh had rung and announced that he did not care to go to sleep just yet and that he would be glad to see the newspaper men for a few minutes. A cheer went up from the group who dashed by Mr. Herrick and rushed upstairs.

#### Expected Trouble Over Newfoundland.

In the blue and gold room, with a soft light glowing, sat the conqueror of the Atlantic. He immediately stood up and held out his hands to greet his callers. THE NEW YORK TIMES correspondent being first to greet him.

"Sit down, please," urged every one with one voice, but Lindbergh only smiled again his famous boyish smile and said:

"It's almost as easy to stand up as it is to sit down".

Questions were fired at him from all sides about his trip across the ocean, but Lindbergh seemed to dismiss them all with brief, nonchalant answers.

"I expected trouble over Newfoundland because I had been warned that the situation there was unfavorable. But I got over that hazard with no trouble whatsoever."

#### Sleet and Snow for 1,000 Miles.

"However, it wasn't easy going. I had sleet and snow for over 1,000 miles. Sometimes it was too high to fly over and sometimes too low to fly under, so I just had to go through it as best I could.

"I flew as low as 10 feet in some places and as high as 10,000 in others. I passed no ships in the daytime, but at night I saw the lights of several ships, the night being bright and clear."

Everyone then wanted to know if the flier had been sleepy on the voyage.

"I didn't really get what you might call downright sleepy," he said, "but I think I sort of nodded several times. In fact, I could have flown half that distance again. I had enough fuel

# TO PARIS IN 33½ HOURS; SNOW AND SLEET; CARRY HIM OFF FIELD

left to go 1,000 miles, I think—certainly 500—although I had no time to examine my fuel tanks, the crowds were so terrific.

"If it wasn't for the soldiers and two French aviators I think I might have been injured by wild enthusiasts in the throng. Anyway, I paid no attention to economy of fuel during the voyage."

### Saw Flares Forty Miles From Le Bourget.

Ambassador Herrick then asked the young aviator if he had any difficulty finding his way once he reached Europe.

"Well, you know this is my first trip to Europe, and I just had to take a chance," was his reply.

He added, with another of his smiles, that he liked what he had seen of Paris and he wanted to stay as long as he could.

The American youth said that never once during the trip had he doubted his eventual success, and when he was over Cherbourg, or what he thought was Cherbourg, he knew he would make it.

"About forty miles away from Paris," he continued, "I began to see the old trench flares they were sending up at Le Bourget. I knew then I had made it, and as I approached the field with all its lights it was a simple matter to circle once and then pick a spot sufficiently far away from the crowd to land O. K.

"I landed perfectly. Then the crowd descended on me, and it was all over but the handshaking."

Lindbergh refused to take seriously the problem of flying the Atlantic, when he was asked how he had performed the almost unbelievable feat.

"You know, flying a good airplane doesn't require near as much attention as a motor car," he explained.

### Ate Sandwich and a Half on the Way.

"I had four sandwiches when I left New York," he said. "I only ate one and a half during the whole trip and drank a little water. I don't suppose I had time to eat any more, because you know it surprised me how short a distance it is to Europe."

By this time the interview had lasted for seven or eight minutes and Mr. Herrick insisted that it would involve too much strain on the flier to submit him to further questioning. Every one then withdrew, and with a cheery "good night" and a final handshake with the Ambassador, Lindbergh hopped into bed like a schoolboy after a hard day's play, and before this correspondent left the embassy word came downstairs that Lindbergh was sound asleep.

### Herrick Cables Lindbergh's Mother.

Immediately after this Mr. Herrick sent the following cable to Linbergh's mother in Detroit:

"Warmest congratulations. Your incomparable son has honored me by becoming my guest. He is in fine condition and sleeping sweetly under Uncle Sam's roof.

"MYRON HERRICK."

Lindbergh brought no baggage, so a hasty wardrobe was assembled for him at the embassy from the personal effects of Ambassador Herrick and his son, Parmely.

The young flier, however, did bring three letters, the only excess baggage he carried. Two were from Theodore Roosevelt for Ambassador Herrick and his son, and the third was addressed to the Ambassador and was from Charles Lawrence of the Wright firm that built the motor for the Spirit of St. Louis.

May 22, 1927

## A TRIBUTE TO CHARACTER.

There has been no complete and satisfactory explanation of the enthusiasm and acclaim for Captain LINDBERGH, which have run through the nation like an infection and which will have overpowering manifestations in these first days after his return home. One element in it all is clear. If the youthful aviator won unstinted admiration by his daring, he conquered every mind and heart by his demeanor. It would have been so easy for him to spoil his wonderful feat by braggadocio, by stupid talk, by disregard of the finer courtesies. But young LINDBERGH was guarded through every peril of that kind, partly no doubt by his skilled and friendly advisers, but mainly by his own instinctive sense of the right and delicate, tactful and manly thing to do.

It is not too much to say that most Americans watched him during those first days of his in Europe with a kind of trembling anxiety. They feared some slip, some awkwardness, some boorishness. But soon they began to see that this young man had perfect taste as well as perfect poise. And it is really to the high qualities of character which he has displayed that the tribute of his countrymen is paid. These things come not by accident or even by training. They are inborn. The mother has almost outshone the son in the quiet dignity with which she has accepted her new honors. As for Captain LINDBERGH himself, he recalls the definition of true eloquence given by STERNE when he said that it was a " mingling of simplicity and majesty." It is the blending of unaffected modesty with courage, of clear seeing and straight thinking with an incommunicable sense of personal high-mindedness that has captured the applause of all the world for CHARLES LINDBERGH.

June 11, 1927

## TOPICS OF THE TIMES.

**Lindbergh a Plain American.** In expressing to the Swedish colony in Paris his regret that he could not visit the "land of his ancestors" Captain LINDBERGH genially reminded his hearers that Sweden was the home of only some of them, inasmuch as he also had French, Irish and Manx blood in him.

In other words, LINDBERGH is what we have all instinctively recognized and loved in him—a plain American. He is proud of his European ancestry and wants to see the place where his father was born in Sweden. But, like the many other millions of Americans who have the blood of various European races in their veins, he has no special partiality for any one group here or abroad.

The failure to realize that for many millions of our people there can be no such leanings is the great weakness of those professionally organized foreign groups in this country which seek to exploit the hyphen. LINDBERGH's Swedish name has been used by several European groups in this country to taunt the native American element with his foreign origin. This attitude is deplorable primarily because it shows that such foreign groups are incapable of realizing that a man's ancestry has no bearing on his Americanism so long as he has truly absorbed the spirit of America. This LINDBERGH has done infinitely better than those who seek to capitalize his glory in order to further the selfish interests of hyphenated groups.

June 6, 1927

### Lindbergh's "Unslicked" Hair.

*To the Editor of The New York Times:*

What a relief to see once more a young man with hair unslicked! Every picture of Charles Lindbergh brings pleasure. The young men of today are too shiny-looking to be real, just like highly varnished furniture that scratches easily and shows poor wood underneath. And when these young men smooth their hair back, and, as sometimes is the case, have receding chins and slightly prominent teeth, they look like water rats!                                   A MOTHER,
New York, June 6, 1927.

June 8, 1927

## LINDBERGH FLIGHT HAILED IN PULPITS

### Flier's Skill, Courage, Modesty, Clean Life Furnish Themes for Many Sermons.

### SEEN AS SYMBOL OF FAITH

#### Adelphi and Brooklyn Polytechnic Graduates Hear Dr. Baldwin and Dr. Simons Praise Him.

Colonel Charles A. Lindbergh's epochal flight from New York to Paris, his courage, his skill, his clean life, his modesty, his simplicity, furnished the theme for many sermons in New York churches, including two baccalaureate sermons before the graduating classes of Adelphi College and the Polytechnic Institute, Brooklyn. He was extolled as a model and inspiration for youth, as a symbol of faith and religion, as a bond between nations replacing world strife with international brotherhood, as an example of perfect sportsmanship, as "a hero and a Christian gentleman," and as a messenger of peace. In one sermon, also, he was warned to accept all the fruits of his feat as quickly as possible, lest he suffer the common fate of heroes and be forgotten by the public. Several preachers also eulogized Clarence D. Chamberlin and Charles A. Levin, who flew from New York to Germany, as well as Colonel Lindbergh.

#### Lays Success to Ideals.

It was not luck but ideas and ideals that enabled Colonel Lindbergh to complete his flight successfully, said the Rev. Dr. Fritz W. Baldwin in his baccalaureate sermon to the graduating class of Adelphi College yesterday morning in the Clinton Avenue Congregational Church, Clinton and Lafayette Avenues, Brooklyn. He told them that "success, human affection and Christ-like service to others" were "the springs of human living."

The senior class, in academic robes, were led down the main aisle by the members of the Faculty, the minister of the church and the members of the junior class—also in cap and gown—who served as guard of honor to the outgoing class.

Dr. Baldwin stressed to the graduating girls the necessity of dreams in a well-rounded and successful life. "The world is tingling today over the exploits of two youths who dreamed, over the exploits of Lind-

bergh and Chamberlin," said Dr. Baldwin, "and the world is agog with dreams of what the future may hold for it."

It is not luck, "pull" or good-fortune that leads the successful man on, according to Dr. Baldwin, but the ability to dream, the formation of ideas and the crystallization of ideals.

"The dream of personal success has its place as well as any other dream," Dr. Baldwin went on to say. "In the past the church has been so prone to disapprove of personal ambition, and it has had reason for its disapproval, but I tell you that the acquiring of wealth, power and knowledge in the proper manner is to be commended! The successful individual is a necessity to the successful commonwealth. You are in a country where every chance is given you to succeed; you have the equipment to succeed. Your motto should be 'Give me new worlds to conquer!' You should strive ever upward and onward."

#### Calls Organization the Secret.

Organization was the secret of Colonel Lindbergh's success, and accounts for the difference between persons and between characters, the Rev. Dr. Minot Simons said yesterday in his baccalaureate sermon to the graduating class of the Polytechnic Institute, Brooklyn, in the Unitarian Church of the Saviour, Pierrepont Street and Monroe Place. The service was the first event of Commencement Week at the institute. Ninety-five seniors were present in academic dress.

"Lindy, who has just come home, has astounded us because he has been so well organized. His accomplishment wasn't the most difficult thing that the human race has ever done; but it was done by a great man—a charming fellow," Dr. Simons declared.

Recalling the exposure of the Tweed Ring by THE NEW YORK TIMES, he continued:

"That was a great deed. An emissary of the Tweed forces offered the editor of THE NEW YORK TIMES five million dollars. When he refused the offer, the editor replied, 'I suppose the devil will never make a higher bid for my soul.' This man was able to act nobly because he had disciplined himself and organized his life."

Speaking directly to the members of the graduating class, Dr. Simons said, "You have reached this event in your life because you have applied the principle of organization. No doubt you have anticipated that you may not reach the goal you now vision—that the forces of disintegration may be too great for you." He pointed to parallel between the forces in nature, of attraction and repulsion, and the forces in human nature, of self-control and self-indulgence. Self-control means integration and integration means organization, according to the speaker. Great men do not act without preparation, he told his auditors, they act in accord with their character, which has been built by a lifetime of concentrated effort.

June 13, 1927

# SACCO AND VANZETTI PUT TO DEATH EARLY THIS MORNING

## WALK TO DEATH CALMLY

### Sacco Cries 'Long Live Anarchy'; Vanzetti Insists on His Innocence.

### WARDEN CAN ONLY WHISPER

### Much Affected as the Long-Delayed Execution Is Carried Out.

### MADEIROS FIRST TO DIE

### Machine Guns Bristle, Searchlights Glare During Execution—Crowds Kept Far From Prison.

From a Staff Correspondent of The New York Times.

CHARLESTOWN STATE PRISON, Mass., Tuesday, Aug. 23.—Nicola Sacco and Bartolomeo Vanzetti died in the electric chair early this morning, carrying out the sentence imposed on them for the South Braintree murders of April 15, 1920.

Sacco marched to the death chair at 12:11 and was pronounced lifeless at 12:19.

Vanzetti entered the execution room at 12:20 and was declared dead at 12:26.

To the last they protested their innocence, and the efforts of many who believed them guiltless proved futile, although they fought a legal and extra legal battle unprecedented in the history of American jurisprudence.

With them died Celestino F. Madeiros, the young Portuguese, who won seven respites when he "confessed" that he was present at the time of the South Braintree murder and that Sacco and Vanzetti were not with him. He died for the murder of a bank cashier.

**Defense Works as They Die.**

The six years' legal battle on behalf of the condemned men was still on as they were walking to the chair and after the current had been applied, for a lawyer was on the way by airplane to ask Federal Judge George W. Anderson in Williamstown for a writ of habeas corpus.

The men walked to the chair without company of clergy, Father Michael Murphy, prison chaplain, waited until a minute before twelve and then left the prison.

Sacco cried, "Long live anarchy!" as the prison guards strapped him into the chair and applied the electrodes. He added a plea that his family be cared for.

Vanzetti at the last made a short address, declaring his innocence.

Madeiros walked to the chair in a semi-stupor caused by overeating. He shrugged his shoulders and made no farewell statement.

Warden William Hendry was almost overcome by the execution of the men, especially that of Vanzetti, who shook his hand warmly and thanked him for all his kindnesses.

The Warden was barely able to pronounce above a whisper the solemn formula required by law:

"Under the law I now pronounce you dead, the sentence of the court having been legally carried out."

The words were not heard by the official witnesses.

After Governor Fuller had informed counsel for the two condemned radicals that he could take no action, their attorney, Michael A. Musmanno, made a dash to the prison in an automobile and tried to make another call on Sacco and Vanzetti, but Warden Hendry refused, as the legal witnesses were just about to pass into the execution chamber.

**The Witnesses Gather.**

The witnesses gathered in the Warden's office an hour before midnight. They were instructed as to the part they would take.

W. E. Playfair of The Associated Press was the only reporter permitted to attend the execution, as the State law designated one representative of the press as a witness. The assignment was handed to him six years ago after Sacco and Vanzetti had been convicted in Dedham for the murder of William Parmenter and Alexander Berardelli.

At 11:38 all but the official witnesses were asked to leave the Warden's office. Led by Warden Hendry the official witnesses walked toward the rotunda of the prison. He rapped three times on the inner door. A key grated in the lock. Just then Mr. Musmanno dashed in breathlessly.

"Please, Warden," he said, touching Mr. Hendry on the arm. "A last request."

His voice was faint and broken.

"No, no," the Warden said, sternly, slightly unnerved at the last-minute interruption. Mr. Musmanno turned away, weeping. He had refused to accept as a farewell gift a book from Vanzetti because he felt that the men would be saved.

"I only tried to see them the last time and he refused me," said Musmanno through tears.

**The Executions.**

The witnesses walked through the prison and entered the death house with the Warden. They took their places and then Madeiros was escorted into the chamber. He walked without support, attended by two guards, one at each side. He was strapped in the chair at 12:03 and at 12:09 he was pronounced dead.

He was officially pronounced dead by Dr. George Burgess MacGrath, Medical Examiner of Norfolk County, and Dr. Howard A. Lothrop, Sur-

geon-in-Chief of the Boston City Hospital. Stethoscopes were also applied to Madeiros's chest by Dr. Joseph I. MacLaughlin, the prison physician, and Colonel Frank P. Williams, Surgeon-General of the Massachusetts National Guard. The same procedure was followed in the case of Sacco and Vanzetti.

Sacco, whose cell was next to that of Madeiros, was the next. A guard opened his door. Sacco was ready. His face was pale from his long confinement. Without a word he took his place between the guards. Walking slowly but steadily, he traversed the seventeen steps into the death chamber. He required no support and sat down in the chair. As the guards were finishing their work Sacco cried out in Italian:

"Long live anarchy."

In English he shouted: "Farewell, my wife and child, and all my friends!"

He has two children, Dante, 14, and Inez, 6, but his difficulty in speaking English and the excitement of the occasion were responsible for the slip.

"Good evening, gentlemen," he said, jerkily. Then came his last words: "Farewell, mother."

Warden Hendry waited until Sacco apparently was satisfied that there was no more to say. Then he gave the signal. Sacco was pronounced dead at 12:19:02.

Vanzetti's cell door was opened. He, too, was calm. He shook hands with the two guards and kept step with them. He had four more steps to the death chair than Sacco. On entering the chamber he spoke to the Warden, shaking his hand and saying:

"I want to thank you for everything you have done for me, Warden."

Vanzetti spoke in English. His voice was calm throughout. There was not the slightest tremor or quaver.

Then, addressing the witnesses, he said:

"I wish to tell you that I am innocent, and that I never committed any crime but sometimes some sin."

They were almost the same words he addressed to Judge Webster Thayer in the Dedham courtroom last April when he was sentenced to die during the week of April 10, the sentence having been deferred because the Governor's advisory committee was working in the case.

"I thank you for everything you have done for me," he went on, calmly and slowly. "I am innocent of all crime, not only of this, but all. I am an innocent man."

Then he spoke his last words:

"I wish to forgive some people for what they are now doing to me."

Vanzetti stepped into the chamber at 12:20:30. At 12:26:55 he was declared dead.

**Warden Broke News to Them.**

Before midnight Warden Hendry told reporters how he broke the news to Sacco and Vanzetti.

"I simply told them that it was my painful duty to convey to them the information that they were to die shortly after midnight," he said. "I told them that their lawyers had informed me that they had done all they could and had failed."

Father Michael J. Murphy, Prison Chaplain, again offered the men his services, but they refused his offer of the last rites. Earlier in the day.

the Chaplain visited the men, and on coming from the death house said:

"I offered them the consolation of religion, but all three preferred to die as they had lived—outside the pale. They can call on me at any time before the execution, and I will hear their confessions and give them communion."

Warden Hendry received two telegrams, one addressed to himself, which he did not make public, and another addressed to Sacco. After reading the Sacco telegram, the Warden refused to make known its contents to the prisoner, explaining that he did not know the writer.

The telegram read:

"Take heart, men. It is justice that dies. Sacco and Vanzetti will live in history." It was signed Epstein and sent from New York.

The police, despite their elaborate precautions, had a surprise about an hour before midnight, when it was discovered that some one had penetrated the lines thrown around the prison for blocks and made his way to the very entrance of the Warden's office, where he had passed an envelope to one of the regular guards and strolled off.

The envelope contained a two-page letter, the contents of which the Warden withheld. An investigation was begun at once to learn how the mysterious messenger had gained entrance to the guarded area.

The first of the legal witnesses to arrive at the prison were Dr. Joseph I. McLaughlin, the prison physician, and Dr. Edward A. Lathrop, a surgeon of the Boston City Hospital. They reached the prison at 9:40 P. M.

**Electricians Test Chair.**

Warden Hendry at 9 P. M. made his second visit to the death house. He informed newspaper men on his return to his office that he had found the trio resigned to their fate. Sacco requested him to have his body sent to his home in Italy. The Warden declared that they showed no change regarding their religious viewpoint and entertained the belief that they would go to the chair without spiritual aid.

At 10 P. M. Granville Greenough, chief electrician, and John Mullaney, assistant electrician, made a final test of the electric chair and found it to be in good working order.

**Police Break Up Crowds.**

Superintendent Crowley's men broke up a meeting of nearly 500 Italians in Salem Street, in the North End, as midnight approached. They threatened to hold a demonstration in front of the Bunker Hill Monument, and also threatened to hold a protest meeting before the State House and on the Common.

Mounted policemen charged a crowd of several thousand that gathered just outside the roped-off area surrounding the jail at the hour of execution. Two hundred Sacco and Vanzetti sympathizers had congregated in Thompson Square to join a parade out to Bunker Hill. Policemen afoot were unable to control the excited crowd. The charge of the mounted police drove men, women and children back in a wave. Several persons were crushed. Two women were arrested charged with sauntering and loitering.

More than 1,000 cars were blocked in a traffic jam along Main Street, obstructing the passage of pedestrians and police. The street became a tangled mass of automobiles and other vehicles. There was a terrific din as policemen shouted orders, the iron-shod hoofs of their mounts clattered over pavements and hundreds of automobilists sounded their sirens continuously.

Charlestown prison was armed and garrisoned as if to withstand a siege. Machine guns, gas and tear bombs, not to mention pistols and riot guns, constituted the armament and to man it were 500 patrolmen, detectives and State constables besides the usual prison guard.

They took their posts at 7 o'clock, cutting off Rutherford Avenue and other streets approaching the long, gloomy brick walls of the prison. No one was allowed to pass either on foot or in vehicles unless on official business.

A truck filled with State police jangled and clanged along the cobblestones and into the glare of light about the entrance to the prison. Forty mounted policemen clamped over the Prison Point Bridge. All reported to Captain Goff, then deployed down streets and alleys.

### Barricade Prison Entrance.

The south and west walls of the death house and cell blocks facing on the Boston & Maine Railroad yards were lined with machine guns and searchlights in clusters of three at twenty-yard intervals. The powerful lights flooded the railroad yards in a brilliant glare that accentuated the pitchy blackness of shadows. Across the tracks marine patrol boats could be seen moving slowly up and down the river in the region of the prison. Each of the police vessels was equipped with flares and searchlights that played along the gloomy prison walls.

From the comparative gloom of the cement walk along the siding came the click, click of horses hoofs as mounted patrolmen rode up and down. A prison entrance facing on the railroad yards was heavily barricaded with ladders, doors and other lumber.

At 11 P. M. searchlights installed by the police on the roof of the State House were turned on. Their brilliant rays were kept sweeping up and down the adjacent streets. Twenty policemen armed with riot guns were stationed at intervals between the searchlights. It was the first time in Massachusetts's history that such a scene had been enacted.

Chapman Street, Austin Street, Miller Street, as well as Rutherford Avenue were completely cut off as far as automobile or pedestrian traffic was concerned, but those living in houses in this district, warned by the police not to leave them, leaned out of windows. On other houses occasional sweeps of searchlights revealed entire families, including babies in arms, perched on roof tops.

In Main Street, the street nearest the prison on which traffic was permitted, a throng circulated. At a late hour adherents of Sacco and Vanzetti were not in evidence. Most of the men and women chattered excitedly, but without attempting to make any sort of demonstration. Rather, they were merely curious and interested in the display of martial power. Passengers of elevated trains crowded to windows on the side near the prison. Some who tried to alight were urged not to by the police.

### All Streets Are Cut Off.

All streets leading toward the sprawling collection of steel barred brick and cement buildings were closed off at 8 P. M. and no one could get within blocks of the entrance. Police stood in little knots. Inside the area of restriction was an entire platoon of mounted policemen, their horses stamping restlessly in the yellow glare of street lights. For the first time in the records of the police department, roll call was taken on post instead of in station houses.

Persons living within the restricted area were kept as closely to their houses as during an air raid. When they ventured to their doors they were told to stay inside unless their business was extremely urgent and were warned that they might have difficulty getting back. Gasoline filling stations and small shops were ordered to close and stay closed until tomorrow.

Captain N. J. Goff of the Charlestown Station was in charge of police arrangements at the prison. All Boston police, State Constabulary and special detectives assigned to duty there reported to him for instructions. Despite the elaborate police precautions, windows of the officers' room of the prison, which was given over to newspaper men, were nailed down and blinds drawn as a precaution in case some one should "try to throw something in," according to Captain Goss.

A weird and martial picture was presented when motion picture photographers held aloft flaming calcium torches, lighting up a passing detail of mounted State police with a ghastly flicker and silhouetting their silent figures against the grim gray of the prison walls.

### Last Visit to the Men.

Mrs. Rose Sacco and Miss Luigia Vanzetti called three times at the death house during the day. Their last visit was at 7 o'clock in the evening, when they remained five minutes and departed weeping. Gardiner Jackson and Aldini Felicani of the Defense Committee, who accompanied the women, arranged with Warden Hendry for the transfer of the bodies to the relatives.

Mrs. Consuelo Aruda of New Bedford, sister of Madeiros, was the first of the relations of the condemned men to go to the prison. Madeiros was worried because his mother did not visit him Sunday. His sister told him that his mother had had a breakdown and could not come to Boston. Madeiros was much affected by the news of his mother's condition. The two spoke for an hour in Portuguese and the young woman left in tears with a last message for her mother.

Mrs. Sacco and Miss Vanzetti arrived at the prison for the first time in the day at 11 A. M. Dr. Joseph I. McLaughlin, the prison physician, was in the death house at the time and Vanzetti introduced his sister to him. The two women were downcast. They pressed their faces close to the heavily barred cell doors under the eyes of the guards.

An hour passed and the interview ended with tearful farewells. Fare-

well embraces were not permitted. There were handclasps and faces were pressed to the cell doors. The bars are an inch thick and an inch apart and heavily meshed.

Madeiros at noon seemed quite calm and smoked many cigarettes. Vanzetti worked on a letter to his father. Sacco paced up and down his cell. But when Michael A. Musmanno of defense counsel called on Sacco and Vanzetti at 2:30 P. M. he found them depressed and ready for death. They told him they were convinced that no power on earth would save them. Sacco begged to see his wife again. Vanzetti regretted that his sister had come from Italy to be with him in his last moments of agony. He was sorry that her last memories of him would be clouded with knowledge of the gray prison, the death cell and the electric chair.

At 3:10 P. M. the two women returned to the death house in an automobile driven by Miss Edith Jackson of New Haven. Mrs. Sacco, who has always presented a tearless and composed face to the public, wept for the first time as she approached the gate. Miss Vanzetti's arm supported her as the two passed into the death house for the second time in the day. They greeted the men again through the wire mesh and remained an hour. Sacco spoke of his children and Vanzetti of his old home in Italy. The women remained an hour and they were weeping when they stepped into the automobile.

Joseph F. Linhares, a lawyer, of Somerville, called at the prison on behalf of Madeiros and asked permission to see him. The warden refused, after calling up the State House on the telephone.

### Thompson Calls on Men.

William G. Thompson, former counsel for Sacco and Vanzetti, called on them late in the day. Mr. Thompson had returned from his Summer home at South Tamworth, N. H., at the request of Vanzetti and visited both men at the death house. He spent nearly an hour there. When he left he said that Sacco and Vanzetti had reasserted that they were absolutely innocent of the South Braintree murders. He declared also that there was no truth in the report that he had been offered an opportunity to inspect the files of the Department of Justice and had refused.

The conversation with Vanzetti, said Mr. Thompson, was partly on the man's political and philosophical beliefs. He declined to discuss the report of Governor Fuller or that of the Advisory Committee other than to say that, having read both documents with care, he found nothing in them which altered his opinion "that these two men are innocent and that their trial was in a very real sense unfair."

Mr. Thompson left, and half an hour later Mrs. Sacco and Miss Vanzetti arrived for their third and final visit, to the condemned men. They were in an automobile with Gardner Jackson and Aldini Felicani of the Defense Committee. The men stepped out, while the women waited. Jackson and Felicani asked Warden Hendry for permission to have the women see their unfortunate relatives for the last time. The request was granted. During the final visit, which lasted five minutes, Mr. Jackson and Mr. Felicani arranged for the bodies of the two men to be turned over to Mrs. Sacco and Miss Vanzetti.

---

## POEM BY MISS MILLAY ON SACCO AND VANZETTI

### Written as Her Contribution to the Campaign to Save Them.

Ruth Hale, who has been active in the Sacco-Vanzetti defense campaign, sent to THE TIMES yesterday the following poem by Edna St. Vincent Millay, who, Miss Hale says, wrote it "as her contribution to the registering of the feeling many of us have about the Sacco-Vanzetti execution":

### JUSTICE DENIED IN MASSACHUSETTS.

#### By Edna St. Vincent Millay.

Let us abandon then our gardens and go home
And sit in the sitting room.
Shall the larkspur blossom or the corn grow under this cloud?
Sour to the fruitful seed
Is the cold earth under this cloud.
Fostering quack and weed we have marched upon but cannot conquer;
We have beat the blades of our hoes against the stalks of them.
Let us go home and sit in the sitting room.
Not in our day
Shall the cloud go over and the sun rise as before,
Beneficent upon us
Out of the glittering bay,
And the warm winds be blown inward from the sea,
Moving the blades of corn with a peaceful sound.
Forlorn, forlorn,
Will stand the blue hay-rack by the empty mow;
And the petals drop to the ground,
Leaving the tree unfruited.
The sun that warmed our stooping backs and withered the weed uprooted—
We shall not feel it again.
We shall die in darkness and be buried in the rain.
What from the splendid dead we have inherited—
Furrows sweet to the grain, and the weed subdued—
See now the slug and the mildew plunder.
Evil does overwhelm the larkspur and the corn;
We have seen them go under.
Let us sit here, sit still,
Here in the sitting room until we die;
At the step of Death on the walk, rise and go;
Leaving to our children's children this beautiful doorway,
And this elm,
And a blighted earth to till,
With a broken hoe.

# ROTHSTEIN A POWER IN GAMBLING WORLD

## Forsook Business Career in Youth to Find Excitement in Games of Chance.

## LAID SUCCESS TO BRAINS

### But Denied He Had Ever Taken Part in Dishonest Play—Fortune Put at Millions.

To the man in the street Arnold Rothstein was mostly a legend. He readily admitted that he was—or "had been"—a powerful figure in the gambling world. But nothing dishonest was ever proved against him; he was absolved of charges of participation in "crooked" gambling; and his statement, made with quiet pride, that he won perpetually through sheer mental superiority had to be taken at its face value.

Rothstein did not fit that popular stereotype of the professional gambler—a man with a "poker face." Imbued with great nervous energy, he could sit up most of the night at dice and then appear at his office for a twelve or fifteen hour day of jumbled interviews, telephone conversations, and the skillful juggling of a score of enterprises that were continually in ferment. He was well-mannered and soft of speech, but his associates were chary of trifling with him. He had an overweening confidence in his own brain, and was apt to be impatient with those who "dubbed along."

Once, while he was going to court day after day in connection with the Fuller-McGee bankruptcy proceedings, he served notice upon those who were conducting the hearings that he would come to court "just once more." "I have been here twenty times or more," he said, "and the questions I have been asked have been 1 per cent. relevant. The other 99 per cent. of the questions have been asked by attorneys who are seeking newspaper headlines."

### "Never in Crooked Deal," He Said.

When the world series scandal in 1919 was going full blast and Rothstein's name was coupled with it by Ban Johnson, President of the American League, Rothstein suddenly announced:

"My friends know that I have never been connected with a crooked deal in my life, but I am heartily sick and tired of having my name dragged in on the slightest provocation whenever a scandal comes up."

He declared he was tired of being considered a "social outcast" and asserted that he was disposing of his gambling interests. Henceforward, he said, he was to be a real estate operator. He threatened to sue Ban Johnson. He was cleared in a Chicago court of complicity in the "throwing" of the 1919 world's series. But his statement that he was through with gambling was taken with several grains of salt by those who knew him.

Rothstein began gambling at an early age. He was the son of orthodox Jewish parents and was headed for a safe success in his father's dress goods business. His nervous energy soon overflowed the bounds of commercial fields and he began gambling—always, however, with a cool head and the acumen of a successful speculator. He got his early training from "Honest John" Kelly, an ex-ball player, and Richard Canfield. While Rothstein was never forceful in the Kelly manner, and never a dandy, as was Canfield, he applied Kelly-Canfield business principles to his chance-taking. In other words, he made a study of the law of averages.

He determined always to "play fair," declaring that "all crooks are fools." At 17 he was a veteran at stuss in the old Tenderloin. Dice followed. Then came faro, roulette poker and the races. In 1909 Rothstein played a game of pool in Philadelphia that lasted thirty-two hours. His opponent was Jack Conway, and Rothstein took $4,000 from him. With that game Rothstein claimed the "marathon" pool-playing record.

### Opens Gambling "Business."

A year later found him in business for himself. It was at his gambling establishment in West Forty-sixth Street that Charles G. Gates, son of "Betcher-Million" Gates, lost $40,000 in one night at roulette and faro. The losses were part of Gates's celebration following his return to Broadway after an appendicitis operation.

The murder of Herman Rosenthal, the gambler, dealt a blow to the operation of gaming establishments and forced Rothstein to the expedient of moving his headquarters from one hotel suite to another. Even after his announced retirement from the business of wagering he patronized the "floating crap games" that drifted up and down Broadway.

No sooner had Rothstein's name become a symbol than it was linked to all manner of mysterious double-dealing. He was indicted in 1919 on a charge of felonious assault when three policemen were shot at, and two wounded, from behind a door. The police had descended on what they believed was a crap game at

Rothstein's place in 301 West Fifty-seventh Street. Later Rothstein was dismissed by Judge McIntyre in General Sessions.

At one time August Belmont ruled Rothstein off the race track. Later the gambler was reinstated. He said he had simply gone to Belmont, convinced him that his enormous winnings were the product of superior intelligence, and made the banker admit that Rothstein's moral code was better than that of many business men. "The majority of the human race are dubs and dumbbells," Rothstein asserted. "They have rotten judgment and no brains, and when you have learned how to do things and how to size people up and dope out methods for yourself they jump to the conclusion that you are crooked."

Rothstein added that at 15 he knew his limitations. Since that time, he said, he had never played with a man he was sure he couldn't beat.

### Accused of Income Tax Fraud.

In 1924 Rothstein was accused of "concealment and perjury" in his Federal income tax returns for 1921. The accusation had it that he admitted to $7,257.29 profit, whereas his net gains were said to be in reality $45,940.32. The case never reached a court decision. When he was charged with helping Fuller of the brokerage firm of Fuller & McGee in hiding assets through fake betting losses, Rothstein took the stand to deny he had ever bet very heavily with Fuller.

In his later years Rothstein boasted of friendships with persons listed in the Social Register. His fortune was estimated at anywhere from two to ten million. He made $500,000 on the first Dempsey-Tunney fight. His philosophy, he often said, was summed up in the word "friendship," and he was known for his generosity. Chorus girls, actors, all the types of Broadway, were tided over at one time or another by Rothstein. Not only did he make money in gambling, but he turned considerable sums buying and selling real estate and participating in financial deals. He owned the building in which his real estate office is situated at 45 West Fifty-seventh Street, and also the building across the street from it at 30 West Fifty-seventh. The Fairfield Hotel, 20 West Seventy-second Street, was his property. At one time he was said to have had 1,000 furnished apartments in the city, which he subleased to his own gain.

Since his indictment for felonious assault in 1919 Rothstein had dispensed with carrying arms. Instead, he hired a bodyguard. Abe Attell, one-time featherweight champion, was his bodyguard for a time, but quit when Rothstein placed the "fixing" of the 1919 World's Series at the pugilist's door. Later, when he had been annoyed by threats of kidnapping, Rothstein increased his escort to two. He was not kidnapped.

## IT MIGHT HAVE BEEN MORE BITTER.

Opinions differ about what may be called the psychology of this Presidential election. Mr. HUGHES has seen in it evidences of an unusually "keen interest." Others have thought it rather dull. But this may be because they have missed the high excitement, with an element of public fear in it, which has marked certain remembered contests for the Presidency. That there has been deep concern this year may be argued from the extraordinarily large registration of voters, but there certainly has been no alarm. Fanatics have predicted no subversion of the Government if Governor Smith is elected President, but no man in the full possession of his senses has believed them. Yet with all the good nature and orderly behavior which have characterized the campaign, it has undeniably had one source of much bitterness caused by the injection into it of the religious controversy.

Without going back now to its unpleasing and humiliating aspects it may be said thankfully that it has been spared one thing which would have made it far more angry and repulsive. We refer to the fact that Catholics have exhibited such wonderful restraint under attacks upon their Church. They have kept silent even in the face of notorious misrepresentation and calumny. No priest or Catholic publication of any prominence has noticed the violent challenges of Senator HEFLIN, Bishop CANNON and others. Had the Catholic hierarchy in any way entered the lists against its political assailants, the country would have resounded with clamorous and bitter cries that would have sounded in all ears and filled thoughtful Americans with a sense of public disgrace. Fortunately, that *amari aliquid* was not thrown into our political cup. Comparisons need not be made, but at least it should be said in fairness that those who, under great stress, when reviled, reviled not again, illustrated the more excellent way—the Christian way.

We are aware that this dignified course of the higher Catholic clergy is said to be only one proof more of the conspiracy of Rome. Orders to keep silent were, it is hinted, sent direct from the Vatican to American Catholics. Another evidence, people exclaim, of the dangerous solidarity of the Catholic Church! There is no way of proving or disproving this assertion, but the fact remains that the refusal of Catholics to enter into the religious dispute, thrust into this Presidential election, has been both prudent and salutary. It was the wisest thing to do, and it was also most in accord with the spirit of the Founder of Christianity. It is recorded that under the most severe accusations, He "answered not a word."

# LEADERS DISPEL TELEVISION FEARS

## "Make it a Radio Christmas," Is Slogan of the Industry—Utility of New Sets Not Threatened by Revolutionary Changes

WHILE the slogan in the stock market is "Higher with Hoover," the radio market has adopted "Make this a radio Christmas," and if it comes true the radio industry, too, will go "Higher with Hoover." "What receiving set shall I buy as a Christmas gift, or should I wait another year?" asks the man with the pocketbook.

"Why wait another year?" asks the radio man. "Just think of all the fine radio entertainment you will miss during 1929 if you keep your home and family out of tune with the ether."

"Well, I wonder if the set I buy today will be obsolete within a year. What about television arriving to change the broadcasting system and associated receiving apparatus? And the other day I read where Radio Commissioner Caldwell advised those who now own radio sets of the 1924-5 type to buy new ones so that they could get satisfactory results from broadcasting. He said that sets of such vintage are not hearing 1928 radio but 1925 calibre as far as tone quality is concerned. It made me think. If I buy a set now, will come Radio Commissioner advise me in 1932 to get a new set? If I spend a hundred or more dollars in radio, I expect it to serve me more than three years. If a 1925 set is no better now with the new wave lengths in effect, what will a 1928 set be like in 1932?"

As to television, leaders in the industry remove all apprehension that it will make present-day sets obsolete over night.

### Television Needs Nurturing.

"The latest child of the electrical arts requires careful nurturing if it is to grow into a great public service," asserts David Sarnoff, vice president of the Radio Corporation of America. "In the present stage of public interest it would be easy to cry, 'Television is here'; to broadcast light reflections on the basis of catch who catch can; to provide crude receiving equipment for the will-o'-the-wisps of the air. It would be easy, and it might be profitable, but it would not advance the day when sight is added to sound in an adequate service to the home through the medium of radio communication." Mr. Sarnoff points out that, in the light of progress thus far made, it is clear:

1. That television now, despite the latest engineering and mechanical developments, is still in an experimental stage.

2. That many refinements, improvements and even new engineering solutions are involved in the transmission and reception of light images by radio.

3. That the broad highway in the ether, necessary for the establishment of a television service, requires continued research into the problem of locating suitable wave lengths.

4. That a service comparable to sound broadcasting must be created to justify visual broadcasting on a scale which would encourage the use of television receivers in the home.

"In other words, the great problem of television is not the problem of making a magic box through the peephole of which one may view diminutive reflections of passing men and events," said Mr. Sarnoff. "The fundamental principles of sight transmission and reception are well understood. The greater problems of television are still bound up in the secrets of space.

"Meantime, it must be remembered, with the poets, that art is long and time is fleeting. There is no shortcut in the logical unfolding of an art that promises to extend the range of the eye, as it has extended the range of the ear, to the four corners of the earth."

### Three Years From Now.

How will the Christmas sets this year perform in 1932? It is true that within the past three years vast improvements have been made to give superior tonal quality. The development of power tubes and improved loud-speakers, especially the electro-dynamic unit, has gone a long way to make radio reproduction more real. And on top of this there is the all-electric set now available to Christmas shoppers in a form that no one need fear as far as results are concerned. It is just as easy today to get excellent tonal quality, sharp tuning and long-distance stations with a set that plugs into the lighting socket for its current supply as it is from a battery-operated set.

The rush to buy has already started. Inquiry among dealers attests to the fact, beyond a doubt, that the all-electric set, the dynamic loudspeaker and new sets of tubes will be among the most popular radio gifts this season. So many refinements have been crowded into the past three years that it is doubtful if the next three will witness such radical or rapid advances. Today the all-electric set has arrived. It had not in 1925.

However, radio will not come to a complete halt from 1929 to 1932. It never will, for that matter. The man who hesitates to buy this Christmas will find little things, from year to year that will threaten improvements. But if he waits for each one, he will grow old missing all the joys of broadcasting. The same is true in the automobile field. Each year there are improvements. The man who waits for the final, perfect motor car will have a long wait and he will miss the pleasures of motoring. Today he has better roads and more of them than in 1925. Today in radio the listeners have forty cleared channels in the broadcasting system on which distant stations ride from coast to coast without the interference experienced in 1925. The courageous man despises the future, according to Napoleon, so to enjoy the present and the future, now is the time to equip the home with radio. It is a Christmas joy for the entire family not only in the Yuletide but for years to come.

### Automatic Tuners Available.

This season the Christmas buyer finds automatic tuning among the improvements. All one need do is to press one of nine levers and the favorite station is automatically tuned in. This is a feature of the new Zenith models. The initial adjustment is simple. The station is tuned in as usual. Then a little cap at the end of the lever is unscrewed and the lever pressed downward at which point the cap is tightened. Thereafter, whenever the operator desires to tune in that station, he has only to press down that particular lever.

There are plenty of magnetic cone loudspeakers and electro-dynamic types in the Christmas market place. The latter gives greater depth of volume, which can be regulated from a whisper to sufficient intensity to fill a hall with clear musical tones. In fact, one manufacturer contends that the dynamics "ring as true as the cathedral chimes." The magnetic cones are less expensive than the dynamics. The cones run from $15 to $35 while the dynamics generally cost from $50 to $100; many, however, sell around $60 and $70. The man who buys a loudspeaker should select it by comparison and choose it in accordance with the way it pleases his ear. One may like a cone and another a dynamic. What is ideal for one is not ideal for another. So it is best to pick the loudspeaker that suits your ear and not always the one which a neighbor lauds.

### All-Electric Sets Popular.

The all-electric sets, some equipped with the dynamic units inside the console cabinets and others with magnetic cones, are winning popularity this season. Inquiry among retailers indicates that there is a much greater demand for expensive console sets this year than ever before. It is believed to indicate that the public feels that radio has reached a stage of permanence and they are willing to put more money into it and to make it part of their furniture. Incidentally, radio is now closely allied with furniture and one manufacturer speaks the mind of many when he advertises, "Built for permanence with assurance of permanent satisfaction."

What is a good Christmas gift for the man who already owns a set? There are numerous accessories that he will be happy to see hanging on or placed beneath the Christmas tree. A new set of tubes is always a good thing to have on hand; a new loudspeaker; an automatic voltage regulator to prevent excesses in line voltage from burning out the tubes; an electric phonograph pick-up that electrifies the old phonograph and brings the melodies from the radio loudspeaker instead of the phonograph sound box. There are tables for the radio set and kits for those who like to assemble their own outfits. The boy experimenters will be happy with a short wave set kit; a broadcast receiver kit or the parts for an experimental television machine.

All in all Santa Claus has many fine radio presents in his warehouse in the Northland. He is receiving an abundance of orders and is busy packing his bag. His representatives are holding an advance showing at the radio shops throughout the land. In radio "to hear is to believe."

# Babe Ruth, Baseball's Great Star and Idol of Children, Had a Career Both Dramatic and Bizarre

## WORLD-WIDE FAME WON ON DIAMOND

Even in Lands Where Game Is Unknown, Baseball's Star Player Was Admired

SET HOME RUN MARK IN '27

First a Talented Pitcher, Then Foremost Batter, He Drew Highest Pay of His Time

Probably nowhere in all the imaginative field of fiction could one find a career more dramatic and bizarre than that portrayed in real life by George Herman Ruth. Known the world over, even in foreign lands where baseball is never played, as the Babe, he was the boy who rose from the obscurity of a charitable institution in Baltimore to a position as the leading figure in professional baseball. He was also its greatest drawing-card, its highest salaried performer—at least of his day—and the idol of millions of youngstehs throughout the land.

A creation of the times, he seemed to embody all the qualities that a sport-loving nation demanded of its outstanding hero. For it has always been debatable whether Ruth owed his fame and the vast fortune it made for him more to his ability to smash home runs in greater quantity than any other player in the history of the game or to a strange personality that at all times was intensely real and "regular," which was the one fixed code by which he lived.

He made friends by the thousands and rarely, if ever, lost any of them. Affable, boisterous and good-natured to a fault, he was always as accessible to the newsboy on the corner as to the most dignified personage in worldly affairs. More, he could be very much at ease with both.

He could scarcely recall a name, even of certain intimates with whom he frequently came in contact, but this at no time interfered with the sincerity of his greeting. Indeed, by a singular display of craft, he overcame this slight deficiency with consummate skill. If you looked under 40 it was "Hello, kid, how are you?" And if you appeared above that line of demarcation it was "Hello, doc, how's everything going?"

### How Ruth Aided Small Boy

The story is told of the case of Johnny Sylvester, a youngster whose life doctors had despaired of unless something unusual happened to shock him out of a peculiar malady. The boy's uncle, recalling how fond he always had been of baseball, conceived the idea of sending word to Babe Ruth and asking his aid.

The next day the Babe, armed with bat, glove and half a dozen signed baseballs, made one of his frequent pilgrimages to a hospital. The boy, unexpectedly meeting his idol face to face, was so overjoyed that he was cured—almost miraculously.

A year later an elderly man accosted the Babe in a hotel lobby and, after receiving the customary whole-hearted greeting of "Hello, doc," said:

"Babe, I don't know whether you remember me, but I'm Johnny Sylvester's uncle and I want to tell you the family will never forget what you did for us. Johnny is getting along fine."

"That's great," replied the Babe. "Sure, I remember you. Glad to hear Johnny is doing so well. Bring him around some time."

After a few more words they parted and no sooner had the man removed himself from earshot than the Babe turned to a baseball writer at his elbow and asked:

"Now, who the devil was Johnny Sylvester?"

### Never Lost Carefree Spirit

Nor must this be mistaken for affectation, for there was never a doubt that the Babe at all times was tremendously sincere in his desire to appear on friendly terms with all the world. And though in later years he acquired a certain polish which he lacked utterly in his early career, he never lost his natural self nor his flamboyant, carefree mannerisms, which at all times made him a show apart from the ball field.

Single-handed, he tore the final game of the 1928 world's series in St. Louis to shreds with his mighty bat by hitting three home runs over the right-field pavilion. That night, returning to New York, he went on a boisterous rampage and no one on the train got any sleep, including his employer, the late Colonel Jacob Ruppert.

Such was the blending of qualities that made Babe Ruth a figure unprecedented in American life. A born showman off the field and a marvelous performer on it, he had an amazing flair for doing the spectacular at the most dramatic moment.

Of his early days in Baltimore even Babe himself was, or pretended to be, somewhat vague during his major league baseball career. Thus various versions of his childhood were printed over the years with neither denial nor confirmation from Ruth as to their accuracy.

However, the following account of his boyhood years appeared in a national magazine under Ruth's own "by-line:"

"In the first place I was not an orphan. * * * My mother, whose maiden name was Schanberg, lived until I was 13. My father, George Herman Ruth, lived until my second year in the majors. Few fathers ever looked more like their sons than my pop and I. My mother was mainly Irish, and was called Kate. My father was of German extraction. It is not true that our family name was Erhardt, as has been repeatedly written. Or Ehrhardt, or Gearhardt.

"But I hardly knew my parents. I don't want to make any excuses or place the blame for my shortcomings as a kid completely on persons or places. * * * Yet I probably was a victim of circumstances. I spent most of the first seven years of my life living over my father's saloon at 426 West Camden Street, Baltimore. * * *

"On June 13, 1902, when I was 7 years old my father and mother placed me in St. Mary's Industrial School in Baltimore. It has since been called an orphanage and a reform school. It was, in fact, a training school for orphans, incorrigibles, delinquents, boys whose homes had been broken by divorce, runaways picked up on the streets of Baltimore and children of poor parents who had no other means of providing an education for them.

"I was listed as an incorrigible, and I guess I was. * * * I chewed tobacco when I was 7, not that I enjoyed it especially, but, from my observation around the saloon it seemed the normal thing to do.

In Hollywood, where he was portraying himself in a motion picture dealing with the life of his team-mate, the late Lou Gehrig, played by Gary Cooper (right).                    Associated Press

### Gaps in School Life

"I was released from St. Mary's in July, 1902, but my parents returned me there in November of the same year. My people moved to a new neighborhood just before Christmas, 1902, and I was released to them again. This time I stayed out' until 1904, but then they put me back again and I was not released again until 1908. Shortly after my mother died I was returned to St. Mary's once more by my father. He took me back home in 1911 and returned me in 1912. I stayed in school—learning to be a tailor and shirt-maker—until Feb. 27, 1914. The last item on my 'record' at St. Mary's was a single sentence, written in the flowing hand of one of the teachers. It read:

" 'He is going to join the Balt. Baseball Team.' "

Ruth said he played in the band at St. Mary's and always pointed with pride to this accomplishment, frequently reminding friends that he also was a musician as well as a ball player. Curiously enough, however, no one ever discovered what instrument the Babe played, although he always stoutly denied that it was the bass drum.

But baseball captivated his fancy most and now began a train of circumstances that was to carry this black-haired, raw-boned youngster to fame and a fortune that has been estimated as close to $1,000,000. It also happened that Brother Benedict, one of the instructors at St. Mary's, was a great lover of the national pastime.

Using baseball, therefore, as the most plausible means to a laudable end in keeping the Babe out of mischief as much as possible, the good Brother encouraged the youngster to play as much as he could. The Babe scarcely needed encouragement. Every hour he was allowed to spare from his classrooms found him on the ball field.

He batted left-handed and threw left-handed. He played on his school team, also on a semi-professional team. He also played pretty nearly every position on the field. At the age of 19 he astounded even his sponsor, Brother Benedict, who now saw a real means of livelihood ahead for the young man, though little dreaming at the time to what heights he would soar.

He recommended the Babe to his friend, the late Jack Dunn, then owner of the Baltimore Orioles of the International League, and Ruth received a trial, alternating in the outfield and in the pitcher's box. That was in 1914. The same summer he was sold to the Boston Red Sox for $2,900, and after a brief period of farming out with Providence was recalled to become a regular.

Under the direction of Bill Carrigan, then manager of the Red Sox, Ruth rapidly developed into one of the most talented left-handed pitchers ever in the majors. He had tremendous speed and a baffling cross-fire curve, which greatly impressed Ed Barrow, later to become associated with Colonel Ruppert as general manager of the Yankees, Barrow became the leader of the Red Sox in 1918 and gave much time to Ruth's development.

But even then he also displayed unmistakable talent for batting a ball with tremendous power and with unusual frequency, and Barrow, one of baseball's greatest men of vision, decided to convert Ruth permanently into an outfielder on the theory that a great hitter could be built into a greater attraction than a great pitcher.

It was quite a momentous decision, for in the 1918 world's series against the Cubs Ruth had turned in two masterful performances on the mound for the Red Sox, winning both his games. He had also turned in one victory for the Red Sox against Brooklyn in the world's series of 1916.

But Barrow had also seen Ruth, in 1918, hit eleven home runs, an astonishing number for that era, particularly for a pitcher, and his mind was made up.

The next year—1919—Ruth, pitching only occasionally, now and then helping out at first base, but performing mostly in the outfield, cracked twenty-nine home runs and the baseball world began to buzz as it hadn't since the advent of Ty Cobb and the immortal Christy Mathewson. This total surpassed by four the then accepted major league record for home runs in a season, set by Buck Freeman with the Washington Club in 1899.

But it was the following year—1920—that was to mark the turning point, not only in Babe Ruth's career but in the entire course of organized baseball. Indeed, baseball men are almost in accord in the belief that Babe Ruth, more than any individual, and practically single-handed, rescued the game from what threatened to be one of its darkest periods. Not only rescued it, but diverted it into new channels that in the next decade were to reap an unprecedented golden harvest.

The first sensation came early that winter when Ruth was sold by the late Harry Frazee, then owner of the Red Sox, to the Yankees, owned jointly by the two Colonels, Jacob Ruppert and Tillinghast L'Hommedieu Huston, for a reported price of $125,000. It may even have been more, for in making the purchase the Yankee owners also assumed numerous financial obligations then harassing the Boston owner, and the matter was very involved. But whatever the price, it was a record sum, and New York prepared to welcome its latest hero prospect.

The Babe did not disappoint. The Yankees were then playing their home games at the Polo Grounds, home of the Giants, and before the close of the 1920 season they were already giving their more affluent rivals and landlords a stiff run for the city's baseball patronage.

Ruth surpassed all expectations by crashing out the unheard-of total of fifty-four home runs and crowds which hitherto had lavished their attention on the Giants now jammed the historic Polo Grounds to see the marvelous Bambino hit a homer.

### Crisis in History of Game

But scarcely had the echoes from the thunderous roars that greeted the Ruthian batting feats subsided than another explosion was touched off that rattled the entire structure of baseball down to its sub-cellar. The scandal of the world's series

When he broke into the big leagues in 1914 as a pitcher for the Boston Red Sox.

of 1919 broke into print and through the winter of 1920-21 the "throwing" of that series by certain White Sox players to the Reds was on every tongue.

The baseball owners of both major leagues were in a panic, fearful that the public's confidence in what they had so proudly called America's national pastime had been shaken beyond repair. True, they had induced the late Kenesaw Mountain Landis, a Federal judge, to assume the position of High Commissioner with unlimited powers to safeguard against a repetition of such a calamity, but they feared it was not enough.

With considerable misgivings they saw the 1921 season get under way and then, as the popular song of the day ran, "Along Came Ruth."

Inside of a fortnight the fandom of the nation had forgotten all about the Black Sox, as they had come to be called, as its attention became centered in an even greater demonstration of superlative batting skill by the amazing Babe Ruth. Home runs began to scale off his bat in droves, crowds jammed ball parks in every city in which he appeared and when he closed the season with a total of fifty-nine circuit clouts, surpassing by five his own record of the year before, the baseball world lay at his feet.

In addition to that, the Yankees that year captured the first pennant ever won by New York in the American League, and Ruth was now fairly launched upon the first chapter of the golden harvest. With the help of his towering war club, the Yankees won again in 1922 and repeated in 1923, in addition to winning the world's championship that year.

Also in 1923 came into being the "House That Ruth Built," meaning the great Yankee Stadium with its seating capacity of more than 70,000, which Colonel Ruppert decided to erect the year previous in order to make himself clear and independent of the Giants, whose tenant he had been at the Polo Grounds. The right-field bleachers became "Ruthville." Homers soared into them in great abundance and the exploitation of Babe Ruth, the greatest slugger of all times, was at its height.

### Spent Earnings Freely

But now there crept in a dark episode, decidedly less glamorous, though spectacular enough, and which must be chronicled in order to appreciate more fully the second chapter of the golden harvest. Money was now pouring upon the Babe and was being poured out as speedily. In 1921 he had drawn $20,000 and the following season he signed a five-year contract at $52,000 a season. In addition to this he was collecting royalties on all sorts of ventures.

But money meant nothing to the Babe, except as a convenient means for lavish entertainment. He gambled recklessly, lost and laughed uproariously. The Ruthian waistline began to assume alarming proportions. He still took his baseball seriously enough on the field, but training had become a horrible bore.

Of such phenomenal strength, there seemed to be no limits to his vitality or stamina. It was no trick at all for him to spend an evening roistering with convivial companions right through sun-up and until game time the next afternoon and then pound a home run.

Along in the 1924 season Colonel Ruppert began to fear he had made a mistake in having signed the Babe to that long-term contract at $52,000 per season which ran from 1922 to 1926 inclusive. The Yankees lost the pennant that year and there came ominous rumblings that Miller Huggins, the mite manager who had just piloted the Yankees through three successful pennant years, was not in harmony with the Babe at all.

There even had been trouble back in 1921 when Ruth openly flouted Commissioner Landis by playing on a barnstorming tour that fall after the limit date set by the commissioner. The following spring Landis, in order to demonstrate his authority, suspended Ruth for thirty days from the opening of the season.

But it was not until 1925 that the real crash came and high living proved as exacting in collecting its toll as the high commissioner. Coming north at the end of the training season Ruth collapsed at the railroad station at Asheville, N. C., from a complication of ailments.

He was helped aboard the train, carried off on a stretcher on the team's arrival in New York and spent weeks in a hospital. He did not appear again in a Yankee line-up until June 1.

Nor had all the lesson been yet fully learned. Later in the same campaign Huggins, exasperated beyond all measure at the Babe's wayward way of deporting himself, slapped a $5,000 fine on him for "misconduct off the ball field." It was the highest fine ever imposed on a ball player, and Ruth at first took it as a joke. But Huggins stuck by his guns, received the backing of Colonel Ruppert, who was now the sole owner of the club, and the fine came from the Babe's pay check.

Now the lesson was learned and another startling change came over the Babe. He became, almost overnight, one of Miller Huggins' stanchest supporters. He trained faithfully in 1926, hammered forty-seven homers as against a meager twenty-five in 1925, and started the Yankees on another pennant-winning era. Sixty homers, a new record sailed off his bat in 1927, and Ruth was a greater figure in baseball than ever.

Another pennant followed that year and still another in 1928, on top of which the Yankees swept through two world series triumphs in those two years without the loss of a single game.

## Became Good Business Man

In the Spring of 1929, several months after his first wife, from whom he had been estranged for a number of years, died in a fire in Boston, the Babe married Mrs. Claire Hodgson, formerly an actress, and to her also is given a deal of credit for the complete reformation of the Babe, who in the closing years of his baseball activities trained as faithfully to fulfill what he considered his obligation to his public as it was humanly possible.

Simultaneously with this Ruth suddenly became a shrewd business man with an eye to the future. Giving heed to the advice of Colonel Ruppert and Ed Barrow, the Babe invested his earnings carefully. In 1927 he became the highest salaried player of his time with a three-year contract at $70,-000 a year. In 1930 he signed a two-year contract at $80,000 per season, but in 1932 acceding to economic pressure of the times, accepted a $75,000 stipend for one season.

That proved an excellent investment, for the Yankees won another pennant that year and defeated the Cubs in four straight games, Ruth causing a sensation by indicating to the spectators in Chicago where he meant to hit the ball when he made two home runs in the third game of the series for the championship. The next year saw a further decline in the salary of the star to $52,000, and in 1934 he signed for $35,000.

At the close of his baseball career it was estimated that in his twenty-two years in the major leagues he had earned in salaries $896,000, plus $41,445 as his share of world series receipts. In addition, he was reputed to have made $1,000,000 from endorsements, barnstorming tours, movies and radio appearances.

Coaching students at a school in Saint-Cloud during a visit to France in 1935.

The New York Times

As a consequence, when he retired the Babe was able to live in comfort, maintaining a large apartment on New York's West Side. For, despite his earlier extravagances, he later invested so well he was able to realize a monthly income of $2,500 by the time he had reached 45.

In addition to the great crowds he had drawn steadily to major league parks, he also brought vast sums into the Yankee coffers from spring exhibition tours. In 1929 and 1930 the Yanks booked two tours through Texas and the Middle West on their way north from the training camp in Florida and played to record-smashing crowds that stormed hotel lobbies and blocked traffic in all directions to get a glimpse of baseball's most famous character.

And through all this new homage showered upon him, he steadfastly remained the same Babe, more serious-minded, but as cordial and affable as ever. The youngsters he worshiped possibly as much as they worshiped him. In Waco, Tex., he broke up an exhibition game by inviting some of the kids to come out on the field and roll around on the grass. They poured out of the stands by the thousands, overran the field, swamped the local police and ended the game.

Ruth came to the parting of the ways with the Yankees after the 1934 season. He had always aspired to be a manager, and that Winter he asked Colonel Ruppert, with his accustomed bluntness, to make him leader of the New York team.

Ruppert was satisfied with the results obtained by Joe McCarthy in winning the 1932 world series after coming from the Cubs in 1931 and refused. However, he said that he would not stand in the way of Ruth if the latter could find a place as manager.

The opening came in the spring of 1935, when Judge Emil Fuchs, then president of the Boston National League Club, offered Ruth a contract as a player at $25,000 a year, with a percentage from exhibition games and a percentage of the gain in the earnings of the club, together with a promise of becoming manager the following season. Ruppert gave Ruth his release and he joined the National League team at its training camp in St. Petersburg, Fla., that spring.

Ruth never was a success with the Braves. He was his old self as a batsman and player only in spots and the team sank into the National League cellar. On May 25, 1935, in Pittsburgh he showed the last flash of his former greatness when he batted three home runs in consecutive times at bat at Forbes Field, but a week later, on June 2, after a dispute with Fuchs he asked for and received his release. He had several offers from minor league teams after that, but refused them all.

It was not until June 17, 1938, that his chance came to re-enter the big leagues. Then he was named coach of the Dodgers. Burleigh Grimes, the manager of the team, recommending the move, said "you can't keep a man like

that out of baseball." Although the team was a loser, Ruth entered into the work of upbuilding enthusiastically and was hailed with the usual acclaim around the circuit and in towns where he played in exhibition games.

Although Ruth's continued popularity helped the Dodgers to draw additional fans through their turnstiles, a service for which the club paid him a $15,000 salary, he was not re-engaged as coach at the close of the 1938 season.

It was then that Leo Durocher was appointed manager to succeed Grimes. Ruth, taking his dismissal in good spirit, explained that a new manager necessarily would want to make his own choice for the coaching jobs, and he wished the Dodgers good luck.

The Bambino once again became the retired business man, and as he returned to the role of "baseball's forgotten man," he increased his activities on the links. His name soon became associated with some of golf's leading players, while his scores consistently ran in the low 70's.

### At World's Fair Baseball School

However, he never overlooked lending a hand to his first love wherever baseball offered him some opportunity for showing himself. During 1939 he appeared at the World's Fair baseball school in the role of instructor, took part in the old-timers' game in the baseball centennial celebration at Cooperstown, played a prominent role in the Lou Gehrig appreciation day ceremonies and in the spring of 1940 appeared for a time with a baseball training school at Palatka, Fla.

During 1941, Ruth, principally through the medium of his golfing prowess, stayed in the public eye. During the summer he engaged in a series of matches with his old diamond rival, Cobb, the proceeds going to the British War Relief Fund and the United Service Organizations. Cobb, victor in the first match in Boston, 3 and 2, lost the second match at Fresh Meadow, New York, 1 up on the nineteenth hole, but came back to defeat the Babe in the deciding tilt in Detroit, 3 and 2.

Later in the year Ruth signed a contract to appear in the Samuel Goldwyn motion picture based on the life of his famous team-mate, Lou Gehrig, with the Babe appearing as himself.

The Babe hit the headlines and frightened his friends before 1942 scarcely had begun. On the morning of Jan. 3 he was removed to a hospital in an ambulance, the reason being "an upset nervous condition," partly brought on by an automobile accident in which he was involved.

But three weeks later Ruth was off on a hunting trip in up-State New York and by February was in Hollywood, teaching Gary Cooper (who was to portray Gehrig) how to bat left-handed and signing autographs for screen stars.

On April 9 Ruth went to the Hollywood Hospital suffering from pneumonia and described by his doctor as "a border line case," but two days later the Babe's countless friends and well-wishers were cheered by the same physician's statement: "I believe he is over the hump." Ruth was out of the hospital by April 22 and back on the movie lot to complete his work in the Gehrig film.

During that and succeeding war years Ruth answered any and all demands for his appearance at war bond rallies and charity enterprises. He played in golf tournaments, went bowling and sold bonds. On Aug. 23, 1942, he paired with the late Walter Johnson, another of baseball's immortals, at the Yankee Stadium to aid in a benefit show for two war services.

With Johnson pitching, the Babe came through, as he always had, by hitting a "home run" into the right field seats and "rounding the bases" via a short cut from first to third base. That was his final homer.

### Wrong on War Prophecy

Late in 1943 Ruth proved a bad prophet when he predicted that major league baseball would become a war casualty in 1944, "if not sooner." His prophesying was as wholehearted as his ball playing had been, for he said: "It's a cinch they won't open the ball parks next year."

Although never realizing an ambition to manage a major league club, Ruth became manager for a day in mid-July of 1943, when he piloted a team of all-stars, including such players as Ted Williams and Dom DiMaggio, to a triumph over the Boston Braves as part of a charity field-day program in Boston. A dozen days later he filled the same role in a similar game at Yankee Stadium.

Ruth's activity in aiding war causes increased in 1944 and it was in March of that year that he was the subject of one of the oddest dispatches of the conflict. It came from Cape Gloucester, New Britain, where United States Marines were fighting the Japanese and recounted that when the little men charged the Marine lines their battle cry was:

"To hell with Babe Ruth!"

Babe's rumbling comment to that was:

"I hope every Jap that mentions my name gets shot—and to hell with all Japs anyway!"

The Babe didn't know, or care, that nine years before the Japanese sounded that battle cry a Japanese

publisher had been assassinated by a Japanese fanatic and that Ruth was partly blamed for it. The assassin had said the publisher's crime was in sponsoring the Japanese tour of a group of American ball players, headed by Babe Ruth.

In June of 1944 Ruth went into the hospital once more, this time to have a cartilage removed from his knee. Reports immediately followed that he might try to play ball again as a pinch-hitter.

Early in 1946 Ruth took a trip to Mexico as a guest of the fabulous Pasquel brothers, "raiders" of American organized baseball. This resulted in a rumor that he would become commissioner of the Mexican National League, the Pasquel loop, but as usual nothing came of it.

On his return to New York Ruth disclosed that he had sought the manager's berth with the Newark club, owned by the Yankees, but that "all I got was a good pushing around" by Larry MacPhail. The Babe also praised the Pasquels and at the same time revealed that he had turned down an offer of $20,-000 from the Federal League while getting $600 a season from Baltimore.

"I turned it down because we were told by organized baseball that if we jumped we would be barred for life. But nobody was barred for life and I just got jobbed out of $20,000 without a thank-you from anybody."

There was scarcely room for real bitterness in the expansive and warm Ruthian temperament, but the big fellow undoubtedly did feel at times a resentment against the owners in major league baseball because no place in it ever was found for him. And whatever slight flame of resentment may have lighted in him was frequently fanned by many writers who openly chided the baseball moguls for sidestepping the great Bambino.

Through the unhappy medium of a protracted illness and a serious neck operation that kept him hospitalized from late November 1946, to mid-February, 1947, Ruth came back into the public eye. Recurrent reports that his condition was critical resulted in deluge of messages from sympathetic well-wishers.

There was general rejoicing

among his legions of followers whe he was sufficiently recovered t leave the hospital. That this fee ing was shared in official baseba circles was promptly indicate when Baseball Commissioner A. I (Happy) Chandler paid unprece dented tribute to the Sultan Swat by designating April 27, 194 as "Babe Ruth Day."

All organized baseball joined o this date in honoring the man wh contributed so much to the gam Ruth himself was present at th Yankee Stadium, where a crow of 58,339 turned out for cere monies that were broadcast ove the world and piped into the oth major league ballparks.

Extremely conscious of his det to the "kids of America," to whos loyal support he attributed his su cess, Ruth identified himself wit welfare programs after his di charge from the hospital. He w engaged by the Ford Motor Con pany as a consultant in connectio with its participation in the Ame ican Legion junior baseball pr gram and he was named by Mayo William O'Dwyer of New York permanent honorary chairman the Police Athletic League.

In May, 1947, he established an made the first contribution to th Babe Ruth Foundation, Inc., a organization whose resources we to be devoted to the interests underprivileged youth.

Although the ravages of his il ness left little of his once robu physique, the Babe, now gaunt an bent and his once resonant voic reduced to a rasping whisper, con tinued to astound his physicians b tackling his new job with all h oldtime vigor. Throughout th summer he made innumerable pu lic appearances all over the cou try.

On Sunday, Sept. 28, the fin day of the 1947 championship sea son, he returned to the Yanke Stadium to receive another thun derous ovation. On this day, un der the direction of MacPhail, galaxy of more than forty stars former Yankee and other Amer can League world championshi teams, assembled to engage in a Oldtimers Day.

They included such immortals a Ty Cobb, Tris Speaker, Cy Young George Sisler, Waite Hoyt, Bo Meusel and Chief Bender and wit the Babe looking on from a bo

the grizzled vets played a two inning game. The entire day's re ceipts were turned over to th foundation.

Ruth continued his role as con sultant, making appearances a over the country. He went t Hollywood to help with the filmin of his life story. While there, th Babe was informed that th Yankees were planning to cele brate the twenty-fifth anniversar of the Yankee Stadium. He readil agreed to participate in the cere monies. He accepted the manager ship of the 1923 Yankees, wh were to play an abbreviated exhibi tion game against later-yea Yankees, to be piloted by Barrow.

June 13, 1948, was the date se for "Silver Anniversary Day." I turned out to be a memorable day one that Ruth, despite his physi cal condition, would not hav missed for anything. Despite wretched day—rain, fog, etc.—th Babe donned his old uniform wit the No. 3 on the back. When h was introduced and walked slowl to home plate, a thunderous ova tion from 49,641 men, women and children greeted him.

Many in the gathering wept a Ruth, in a raspy voice, told hov happy he was to have hit the firs homer ever achieved in the Stadi um; how proud he was to have been associated with such fin players and how glad he was to be back with them, even if only for day.

Bob Shawkey, Sad Sam Jones Whitey Witt, Bob Meusel, Waite Hoyt, Carl Mays, Bullet Joe Bush Wally Pipp, Mike McNally, Wally Schang and others from the 192 club that annexed the first world championship by a Yankee aggre gation; Bill Dickey, Lefty Gomez George Selkirk, Red Rolfe and others who came later—all were on hand to pay homage to the Babe.

It was the last time that No. was worn by a Yankee player. For the Babe turned his uniform over to the Hall of Fame, retired for all time. It was sent to the base ball shrine at Cooperstown, N. Y., where it was placed among the Ruth collection there.

Ruth's team scored a 2-0, two inning victory that day and the man to whom a big-league man ager's job was never given man aged a winner in the "House That Ruth Built."

# Full Text of Hoover's Speech Accepting Party's Nomination for the Presidency

You bring, Mr. Chairman, formal notice of my nomination by the Republican Party to the Presidency of the United States. I accept. It is a great honor to be chosen for leadership in that party which has so largely made the history of our country in these last seventy years.

Mr. Chairman, you and your associates have in four days traveled 3,000 miles across the Continent to bring me this notice. I am reminded that in order to notify George Washington of his election, Charles Thompson, Secretary of the Congress, spent seven days on horseback to deliver that important intelligence 230 miles from New York to Mount Vernon.

In another way, too, this occasion illuminates the milestones of progress. By the magic of the radio this nomination was heard by millions of our fellow citizens, not seven days after its occurrence, nor one day, nor even one minute. They were, to all intents and purposes, present in the hall, participants in the proceedings. Today these same millions have heard your voice and now are hearing mine. We stand in their unseen presence. It is fitting, however, that the forms of our national life, hallowed by generations of usage, should be jealously preserved, and for that reason you have come to me, as similar delegations have come to other candidates through the years.

Those invisible millions have already heard from Kansas City the reading of our party principles. They would wish to hear from me not a discourse upon the platform—in which I fully concur—but something of the spirit and ideals with which it is proposed to carry it into administration.

Our problems of the past seven years have been problems of reconstruction; our problems of the future are problems of construction. They are problems of progress. New and gigantic forces have come into our national life. The World War released ideas of government in conflict with our principles. We have grown to financial and physical power which compels us into a new setting among nations. Science has given us new tools and a thousand inventions. Through them have come to each of us wider relationships, more neighbors, more leisure, broader vision, higher ambitions, greater problems. To insure that these tools shall not be used to limit liberty has brought a vast array of questions in government.

The points of contact between the Government and the people are constantly multiplying. Every year wise governmental policies become more vital in ordinary life. As our problems grow so do our temptations grow to venture away from those principles upon which our Republic was founded and upon which it has grown to greatness. Moreover we must direct economic progress in support of moral and spiritual progress.

Our party platform deals mainly with economic problems, but our nation is not an agglomeration of railroads, of ships, of factories, of dynamos, or statistics. It is a nation of homes, a nation of men, of women, of children. Every man has a right to ask of us whether the United States is a better place for him, his wife and his children to live in because the Republican Party has conducted the Government for nearly eight years. Every woman has a right to ask whether her life, her home, her man's job, her hopes, her happiness, will be better assured by the continuance of the Republican Party in power. I propose to discuss the questions before me in that light.

With this occasion we inaugurate the campaign. It shall be an honest campaign; every penny will be publicly accounted for. It shall be a true campaign. We shall use words to convey our meaning, not to hide it.

## Tells of Hard Task Faced 8 Years Ago

The Republican Party came into authority nearly eight years ago. It is necessary to remind ourselves of the critical conditions of that time. We were confronted with an incompleted peace and involved in violent and dangerous disputes both at home and abroad. The Federal Government was spending at the rate of five and one-half billions per year; our national debt stood at the staggering total of twenty-four billions. The foreign debts were unsettled. The country was in a panic from overexpansion due to the war and the continued inflation of credit and currency after the armistice, followed by a precipitant nation-wide deflation which in half a year crashed the prices of commodities by nearly one-half. Agriculture was prostrated; land was unsalable; commerce and industry were stagnated; our foreign trade ebbed away; five millions of unemployed walked the streets. Discontent and agitation against our democracy were rampant. Fear for the future haunted every heart.

No party ever accepted a more difficult task of reconstruction than did the Republican Party in 1921. The record of these seven and one-half years constitutes a period of rare courage in leadership and constructive action. Never has a political party been able to look back upon a similar period with more satisfaction. Never could it look forward with more confidence that its record would be approved by the electorate.

Peace has been made. The healing processes of good-will have extinguished the fires of hate. Year by year in our relations with other nations we have advanced the ideals of law and of peace, in substitution for force. By rigorous economy Federal expenses have been reduced by two billions per annum. The national debt has been reduced by six and a half billions. The foreign debts have been settled in large part and on terms which have regard for our debtors and for our taxpayers. Taxes have been reduced four successive times. These reductions have been made in the particular interest of the smaller taxpayers. For this purpose taxes upon articles of consumption and popular service have been removed. The income tax rolls today show a reduction of 80 per cent. in the total revenue collected on income under $10,000 per year, while they show a reduction of only 25 per cent. in revenues from incomes above that amount. Each successive reduction in taxes has brought a reduction in the cost of living to all our people.

Commerce and industry have revived. Although the agricultural, coal and textile industries still lag in their recovery and still require our solicitude and assistance, yet they have made substantial progress. While other countries engaged in the war are only now regaining their prewar level in foreign trade, our exports, even if we allow for the depreciated dollar, are 58 per cent. greater than before the war. Constructive leadership and cooperation by the Government have released and stimulated the energies of our people. Faith in the future has been restored. Confidence in our form of government has never been greater.

## Finds Opportunity in America Widening

But it is not through the recitation of wise policies in government alone that we demonstrate our progress under Republican guidance. To me the test is the security, comfort and opportunity that has been brought to the average American family. During this less than eight years our population has increased by 8 per cent. Yet our national income has increased by over $30,000,000,000 per year or more than 45 per cent. Our production—and therefore our consumption—of goods has increased by over 25 per cent. It is easily demonstrated that these increases have been widely spread among our whole people. Home ownership has grown. While during this period the number of families has increased by about 2,300,000, we have built more than 3,500,000 new and better homes. In this short time we have equipped nearly 9,000,000 more homes with electricity, and through it drudgery has been lifted from the lives of women. The barriers of time and distance have been swept away and life made freer and larger by the installation of 6,000,000 more telephones, 7,000,000 radio sets, and the service of an additional 14,000,000 automobiles. Our cities are growing magnificent with beautiful buildings, parks and playgrounds. Our countryside has been knit together with splendid roads.

We have doubled the use of electrical power and with it we have taken sweat from the backs of men. The purchasing power of wages has steadily increased. The hours of labor have decreased. The twelve-hour day has been abolished. Great progress has been made in stabilization of commerce and industry. The job of every man has thus been made more secure. Unemployment in the sense of distress is widely disappearing.

Most of all, I like to remember what this progress has meant to America's children. The portal of their opportunity has been ever widening. While our population has grown but 8 per cent. we have increased by 11 per cent. the number of children in our grade schools, by 66 per cent. the number in our high schools, and by 75 per cent. the number in our institutions of higher learning.

## The People Save, but Are Not Selfish

With all our spending we have doubled savings deposits in our banks and building and loan associations. We have nearly doubled our life insurance. Nor have our people been selfish. They have met with a full hand the most sacred obligation of man—charity. The gifts of America to churches, to hospitals and institutions for the care of the afflicted, and to relief from great disasters, have surpassed by hundreds of millions any totals for any similar period in all human record.

One of the oldest and perhaps the noblest of human aspirations has been the abolition of poverty. By poverty I mean the grinding by under-nourishment, cold, and ignorance and fear of old age of those who have the will to work. We in America today are nearer to the final triumph over poverty than ever before in the history of any land. The poorhouse is vanishing from among us. We have not yet reached the goal, but, given a chance to go forward with the policies of the last eight years, and we shall soon, with the help of God, be in sight of the day when poverty will be banished from this nation. There is no guarantee against poverty equal to a job for every man. That is the primary purpose of the economic policies we advocate.

I especially rejoice in the effect of our increased national efficiency upon the improvement of the American home. That is the sanctuary of our loftiest ideals, the source of the spiritual energy of our people. The bettered home surroundings, the expanded schools and playgrounds, and the enlarged leisure which have come with our economic progress have brought to the average family a fuller life, a wider outlook, a stirred imagination, and a lift in aspirations.

Economic advancement is not an end in itself. Successful democracy rests wholly upon the moral and spiritual quality of its people. Our growth in spiritual achievements must keep pace with our growth in physical accomplishments. Material prosperity and moral progress must march together if we would make the United States that commonwealth so grandly conceived by its founders. Our Government, to match the expectations of our people, must have constant regard for those human values that give dignity and nobility to life. Generosity of impulse, cultivation of mind, willingness to sacrifice, spaciousness of spirit—those are the qualities whereby America growing bigger and richer and more powerful, may become America great and noble. A people or Government to which these values are not real, because they are not tangible, is in peril. Size, wealth, and power alone cannot fulfill the promise of America's opportunity.

## Farm Relief Most Urgent Problem

The most urgent economic problem in our nation today is in agriculture. It must be solved if we are to bring prosperity and contentment to one-third of our people directly and to all of our people indirectly. We have pledged ourselves to find a solution.

In my mind most agricultural discussions go wrong because of two false premises. The first is that agriculture is one industry. It is a dozen distinct industries incapable of the same organization. The second false premise is that rehabilitation will be complete when it has reached a point comparable with pre-war. Agriculture was not upon a satisfactory basis before the war. The abandoned farms of the Northeast bear their own testimony. Generally there was but little profit in Mid-West agriculture for many years except that derived from the slow increases in farm-land values. Even of more importance is the great advance in standards of living of all occupations since the war. Some branches of agriculture have greatly recovered, but taken as a whole it is not keeping pace with the onward march in other industries.

There are many causes for failure of agriculture to win its full share of national prosperity. The after-war deflation of prices not only brought great direct losses to the farmer but he was often left indebted in inflated dollars to be paid in deflated dollars. Prices are often demoralized through gluts in our markets during the harvest season. Local taxes have been increased to provide the improved roads and schools. The tariff on some products is proving inadequate to protect him from imports from abroad. The increases in transportation rates since the war have greatly affected the price which he receives for his products. Over 6,000,000 farmers in times of surplus engage in destructive competition with one another in the sale of their product, often depressing prices below those levels that could be maintained.

The whole tendency of our civilization during the last fifty years has been toward an increase in the size of the units of production in order to secure lower costs and a more orderly adjustment of the flow of commodities to the demand. But the organization of agriculture into larger units must not be by enlarged farms. The farmer has shown he can increase the skill of his industry without large operations. He is today producing 20 per cent. more than eight years ago with about the same acreage and personnel. Farming is and must continue to be an individualistic business of small units and independent ownership. The farm is more than a business; it is a state of living. We do not wish it converted into a mass production machine. Therefore, if the farmer's position is to be improved by larger operations it must be done not on the farm but in the field of distribution. Agriculture has partially advanced in this direction through cooperatives and pools. But the traditional cooperative is often not a complete solution.

## Conflicting Opinions Retard Solution

Differences of opinion as to both causes and remedy have retarded the completion of a constructive program of relief. It is our plain duty to search out the common ground on which we may mobilize the sound forces of agricultural reconstruction. Our platform lays a solid basis upon which we can build. It offers an affirmative program.

An adequate tariff is the foundation of farm relief. Our consumers increase faster than our producers. The domestic market must be protected. Foreign products raised under lower standards of living are today competing in our home markets. I would use my office and influence to give the farmer the full benefit of our historic tariff policy.

A large portion of the spread between what the farmer receives for his products and what the ultimate consumer pays is due to increased transportation charges. Increase in railway rates has been one of the penalties of the war. These increases have been added to the cost to the farmer of reaching seaboard and foreign markets and result therefore in reduction of his prices. The farmers of foreign countries have thus been indirectly aided in their competition with the American farmer. Nature has endowed us with a great system of inland waterways. Their modernization will comprise a most substantial contribution to Mid-West farm relief and to the development of twenty of our interior States. This modernization includes not only the great Mississippi system, with its joining of the Great Lakes and of the heart of Mid-West agriculture to the Gulf, but also a shipway from the Great Lakes to the Atlantic. These improvements would mean so large an increment in farmers' prices as to warrant their construction many times over. There is no more vital method of farm relief. But we must not stop here.

An outstanding proposal of the party program is the whole-hearted pledge to undertake the reorganization of the marketing system upon sounder and more economical lines. We have already contributed greatly to this purpose by the acts supporting farm cooperatives, the establishment of intermediate credit banks, the regulation of stockyards, public exchanges and the expansion of the Department of Agriculture. The platform proposes to go much further. It pledges the creation of a Federal Farm Board of representative farmers to be clothed with authority and resources with which not only to still further aid farmers' cooperatives and pools and to assist generally in solution of farm problems but especially to build up with Federal finance, farmer-owned and farmer-controlled stabilization corporations which will protect the farmer from the depressions and demoralization of seasonal gluts and periodical surpluses.

## Rules Out Cost as Objection to Program

Objection has been made that this program, as laid down by the party platform, may require that several hundred millions of dollars of capital be advanced by the Federal Government without obligation upon the individual farmer. With that objection I have little patience. A nation which is spending ninety billions a year can well afford an expenditure of a few hundred millions for a workable program that will give to one-third of its population their fair share of the nation's prosperity.

Nor does this proposal put the Government into business except so far as it is called upon to furnish initial capital with which to build up the farmer to the control of his own destinies.

This program adapts itself to the variable problems of agriculture not only today but which will arise in the future. I do not believe that any single human being or any group of human beings can determine in advance all questions that will arise in so vast and complicated an industry over a term of years. The first step is to create an effective agency directly for these purposes and to give it authority and resources. These are solemn pledges and they will be fulfilled by the Republican Party. It is a definite plan of relief. It needs only the detailed elaboration of legislation and appropriations to put it into force.

During my term as Secretary of Commerce I have steadily endeavored to build up a system of cooperation between the Government and business. Under these cooperative actions all elements interested in the problem of a particular industry, such as manufacturer, distributor, worker, and consumer have been called into council together, not for a single occasion but for continuous work. These efforts have been successful beyond any expectation. They have been accomplished without interference or regulation by the Government. They have secured progress in the industries, remedy for abuses, elimination of waste, reduction of cost in production and distribution, lower prices to the consumer, and more stable employment and profit. While the problem varies with every different commodity and with every-different part of our great country, I should wish to apply the same method to agriculture so that the leaders of every phase of each group can advise and organize on policies and constructive measures. I am convinced that this form of action, as it has done in other industries, can greatly benefit farmer, distributor and consumer.

The working out of agricultural relief constitutes the most important obligation of the next Administration. I stand pledged to these proposals. The object of our policies is to establish for our farmers an income equal to those of other occupations; for the farmer's wife the same comforts in her home as women in other groups; for the farm boys and girls the same opportunities in life as other boys and girls. So far as my own abilities may be of service, I dedicate them to help secure prosperity and contentment in that industry where I and my forefathers were born and nearly all my family still obtain their livelihood.

## Speaks for the Protection Principle

The Republican Party has ever been the exponent of protection to all our people from competition with lower standards of living abroad. We have always fought for tariffs designed to establish this protection from imported goods. We also have enacted restrictions upon immigration for the protection of labor from the inflow of workers faster than we can absorb them without breaking down our wage levels.

The Republican principle of an effective control of imported goods

and of immigration has contributed greatly to the prosperity of our country. There is no selfishness in this defense of our standards of living. Other countries gain nothing if the high standards of America are sunk and if we are prevented from building a civilization which sets the level of hope for the entire world. A general reduction in the tariff would admit a flood of goods from abroad. It would injure every home. It would fill our streets with idle workers. It would destroy the returns to our dairymen, our fruit, flax, and livestock growers, and our other farmers.

No man will say that any immigration or tariff law is perfect. We welcome our new immigrant citizens and their great contribution to our nation; we seek only to protect them equally with those already here. We shall amend the immigration laws to relieve unnecessary hardships upon families. As a member of the commission whose duty it is to determine the quota basis under the national origins law I have found it is impossible to do so accurately and without hardship. The basis now in effect carries out the essential principle of the law and I favor repeal of that part of the act as calling for a new basis of quotas.

We have pledged ourselves to make such revisions in the tariff laws as may be necessary to provide real protection against the shiftings of economic tides in our various industries. I am sure the American people would rather entrust the perfection of the tariff to the consistent friend of the tariff than to our opponents, who have always reduced our tariffs, who voted against our present protection to the worker and the farmer, and whose whole economic theory over generations has been the destruction of the protective principle.

## Stand of American Labor Praised

Having earned my living with my own hands I cannot have other than the greatest sympathy with the aspirations of those who toil. It has been my good fortune during the past twelve years to have received the cooperation of labor in many directions and in promotion of many public purposes.

The trade union movement in our country has maintained two departures from such movements in all other countries. They have been stanch supporters of American individualism and American institutions. They have steadfastly opposed subversive doctrines from abroad. Our freedom from foreign social and economic diseases is in large degree due to this resistance by our own labor. Our trade unions, with few exceptions, have welcomed all basic improvement in industrial methods. This largeness of mind has contributed to the advancing standards of living of the whole of our people. They properly have sought to participate—by additions to wages —in the result of improvements and savings which they have helped to make.

During these past years we have grown greatly in the mutual understanding between employer and employe. We have seen a growing realization by the employer that the highest practicable wage is the road to increased consumption and prosperity and we have seen a growing realization by labor that the maximum use of machines, of effort and of skill is the road to lower production costs and in the end to higher real wages. Under these impulses and the Republican protective system our industrial output has increased as never before and our wages have grown steadily in buying power. Our workers with their average weekly wages can today buy two and often three times more bread and butter than any wage-earner of Europe. At one time we demanded for our workers a "full dinner pail." We have now gone far beyond that conception. Today we demand larger comfort and greater participation in life and leisure.

The Republican platform gives the pledge of the party to the support of labor. It endorses the principle of collective bargaining and freedom in labor negotiations. We stand also pledged to the curtailment of excessive use of the injunction in labor disputes.

The war and the necessary curtailment of expenditure during the reconstruction years have suspended the construction of many needed public works. Moreover, the time has arrived when we must undertake a larger visioned development of our water resources. Every drop which runs to the sea without yielding its full economic service is a waste.

Nearly all of our greater drainages contain within themselves possibilities of cheapened transportation, irrigation, reclamation, domestic water supply, hydro-electric power and frequently the necessities of flood control. But this development of our waters requires more definite national policies in the systematic coordination of those different works upon each drainage area. We have wasted scores of millions by projects undertaken not as a part of a whole, but as the consequence of purely local demands. We cannot develop modernized water transportation by isolated projects. We must develop it as a definite and positive interconnected system of transportation. We must adjust reclamation and irrigation to our needs for more land. Where they lie together we must coordinate transportation with flood control, the development of hydro-electric power and of irrigation, else we shall as in the past commit errors that will take years and millions to remedy. The Congress has authorized and has in process of legislation great programs of public works. In addition to the works in development of water resources, we have in progress large undertakings in public roads and the construction of public buildings.

All these projects will probably require an expenditure of upwards of one billion dollars within the next four years. It comprises the largest engineering construction ever undertaken by any government. It involves three times the expenditure laid out upon the Panama Canal. It is justified by the growth, need and wealth of our country. The organization and administration of this construction is a responsibility of the first order. For it we must secure the utmost economy, honesty, and skill. These works which will provide jobs for an army of men should so far as practicable be adjusted to take up the slack of unemployment elsewhere.

I rejoice in the completion of legislation providing adequate flood control of the Mississippi. It marks not alone the undertaking of a great national task, but it constitutes a contribution to the development of the South. In encouragement of their economic growth lies one of the great national opportunities of the future.

## Repeats Opposition to Dry Law Change

I recently stated my position upon the Eighteenth Amendment which I again repeat:

"I do not favor the repeal of the Eighteenth Amendment. I stand for the efficient enforcement of the laws enacted thereunder. Whoever is chosen President has under his oath the solemn duty to pursue this course.

"Our country has deliberately undertaken a great social and economic experiment, noble in motive and far-reaching in purpose. It must be worked out constructively."

Common sense compels us to realize that grave abuses have occurred—abuses which must be remedied. And organized searching investigation of fact and causes can alone determine the wise method of correcting them. Crime and disobedience of law cannot be permitted to break down the Constitution and laws of the United States.

Modification of the enforcement laws which would permit that which the Constitution forbids is nullification. This the American people will not countenance. Change in the Constitution can and must be brought about only by the straightforward methods provided in the Constitution itself. There are those who do not believe in the purposes of several provisions of the Constitution. No one denies their right to seek to amend it. They are not subject to criticism for asserting that right. But the Republican Party does deny the right of any one to seek to destroy the purposes of the Constitution by indirection.

Whoever is elected President takes an oath not only to faithfully execute the office of the President, but that oath provides still further that he will to the best of his ability preserve, protect and defend the Constitution of the United States. I should be untrue to these great traditions, untrue to my oath of office, were I to declare otherwise.

## Holds Economic System Proved Right

With impressive proof on all sides of magnificent progress no one can rightly deny the fundamental correctness of our economic system. Nothing, however, is perfect but it works for progress. Our pre-eminent advance over nations in the last eight years has been due to distinctively American accomplishments. We do not owe these accomplishments to our vast natural resources. These we have always had. They have not increased. What has changed is our ability to utilize these resources more effectively. It is our human resources that have changed. Man for man and woman for woman we are today more capable whether in the work of farm, factory, or business than ever before. It lies in our magnificent educational system, in the hardworking character of our people, in the capacity for far-sighted leadership in industry, the ingenuity, the daring of the pioneers of new inventions, in the abolition of the saloon, and the wisdom of our national policies.

With the growth and increasing complexity of our economic life the relations of Government and business are multiplying daily. They are yearly more dependent upon each other. Where it is helpful and necessary, this relation should be encouraged. Beyond this it should not go. It is the duty of Government to avoid regulation as long as equal opportunity to all citizens is not invaded and public rights violated. Government should not engage in business in competition with its citizens. Such actions extinguish the enterprise and initiative which has been the glory of America and which has been the root of its pre-eminence among the nations of the earth. On the other hand, it is the duty of business to conduct itself so that Government regulation or Government competition is unnecessary.

Business is practical, but it is founded upon faith—faith among our people in the integrity of business men, and faith that it will receive fair play from the Government. It is the duty of Government to maintain that faith. Our whole business system would break down in a day if there was not a high sense of moral responsibility in our business world. The whole practice and ethics of business has made great strides of improvement in the last quarter of a century, largely due to the effort of business and the professions themselves. One of the most helpful signs of recent years is the stronger growth of associations of workers, farmers, business men and professional men with a desire to cure their own abuses and a purpose to serve public interest. Many problems can be solved through cooperation between Government and these self-governing associations to improve methods and practices. When business cures its own abuses it is true self-government which comprises more than political institutions.

One of the greatest difficulties of business with Government is the multitude of unnecessary contacts with Government bureaus, the uncertainty and inconsistency of Government policies, and the duplication of Governmental activities. A large part of this is due to the scattering of functions and the great confusion of responsibility in our Federal organization. We have, for instance, fourteen different bureaus or agencies engaged in public works and construction, located in nine different departments of the Government. It brings about competition between Government agencies, inadequacy of control, and a total lack of coordinated policies in public works. We have eight different bureaus and agencies charged with conservation of our natural resources, located in five different departments of the Government. These conditions exist in many other directions. Divided responsibility, with the absence of centralized authority, prevents constructive and consistent development of broad National policies.

## Favors Reduction of Federal Agencies

Our Republican Presidents have repeatedly recommended to Congress that it would not only greatly reduce expenses of business in their contacts with Government but that a great reduction could be made in Governmental expenditure and more consistent and continued national policies could be developed if we could secure the grouping of these agencies, devoted to one major purpose, under single responsibility and authority. I have had the good fortune to be able to carry out such reorganization in respect to the Department of Commerce. The results have amply justified its expansion to other departments and I should consider it an obligation to enlist the support of Congress to effect it.

The Government can be of invaluable aid in the promotion of business. The ideal state of business is freedom from those fluctuations from boom to slump which bring on one hand the periods of unemployment and bankruptcy and on the other speculation and waste. Both are destructive to progress and fraught with great hardship to every home. By economy in expenditures, wise taxation and sound fiscal finance it can relieve the burdens upon sound business and promote financial stability. By sound tariff policies it can protect our workmen, our farmers and our manufacturers from lower standards of living abroad. By scientific research it can promote invention and improvement in methods. By economic research and statistical service it can promote the elimination of waste and contribute to stability in production and distribution. By promotion of foreign trade it can expand the markets for our manufacturers and farmers and thereby contribute greatly to stability and employment.

Our people know that the production and distribution of goods on a large scale is not wrong. Many of the most important comforts of our people are only possible by mass production and distribution. Both small and big business have their full place. The test of business is not its size—the test is whether there is honest competition, whether there is freedom from domination, whether there is integrity and usefulness of purpose. As Secretary of Commerce I have been greatly impressed by the fact that the foundation of American business is the independent business man. The department, by encouragement of his associations and by provision of special service, has endeavored to place him in a position of equality in information and skill with larger operations. Alike with our farmers his is the stronghold of American individuality. It is here that our local communities receive their leadership. It is here that we refresh our leadership for larger enterprise. We must maintain his opportunity and his individual service. He and the public must be protected from any domination or from predatory business.

## Moral Responsibility of Government

I have said that the problems before us are more than economic, that in a much greater degree they are moral and spiritual. I hold that there rests upon Government many responsibilities which affect the moral and spiritual welfare of our people. The participation of women in politics means a keener realization of the importance of these questions. It means higher political standards.

One-half of our citizens fail to exercise the responsibilities of the ballot box. I would wish that the women of our country could embrace this problem in citizenship as peculiarly their own. If they could apply their higher sense of service and responsibility, their freshness of enthusiasm, their capacity for organization to this problem, it would become, as it should become, an issue of profound patriotism. The whole plane of poltician life would be lifted, the foundations of democracy made more secure.

In this land, dedicated to tolerance, we still find outbreaks of intolerance. I come of Quaker stock. My ancestors were persecuted for their beliefs. Here they sought and found religious freedom. By blood and conviction I stand for religious tolerance both in act and in spirit. The glory of our American ideals is the right of every man to worship God according to the dictates of his own conscience.

## Assails Indifference to Corruption

In the past years there has been corruption participated in by individual officials and members of both parties in national, State and municipal affairs. Too often this corruption has been viewed with indifference by a great number of our people. It would seem unnecessary to state the elemental requirement that government must inspire confidence not only in its ability but in its integrity. Dishonesty in government, whether national, State or municipal, is a double wrong. It is treason to the State. It is destructive of self-government. Government in the United States rests not only upon the consent of the governed but upon the conscience of the nation. Government weakens the moment that its integrity is even doubted. Moral incompetency by those entrusted with government is a blighting wind upon private integrity. There must be no place for cynicism in the creed of America.

Our Civil Service has proved a great national boon. Appointive office, both North, South, East and West, must be based solely on merit, character, and reputation in the community in which the appointee is to serve; as it is essential for the proper performance of their duties that officials shall enjoy the confidence and respect of the people with whom they serve.

For many years I have been associated with efforts to save life and health for our children. These experiences with millions of children both at home and abroad have left an indelible impression—that the greatness of any nation, its freedom from poverty and crime, its aspirations and ideals are the direct quotient of the care of its children. Racial progress marches upon the feet of healthy and instructed children. There should be no child in America that is not born and does not live under sound conditions of health; that does not have full opportunity of education from the beginning to the end of our institutions; that is not free from injurious labor: that does not have every stimulation to accomplish the fullest of its capacities. Nothing in development of child life will ever replace the solicitude of parents and the surroundings of home, but in many aspects both parents and children are dependent upon the vigilance of government, national, State and local.

I especially value the contribution that the youth of the country can make to the success of our American experiment in democracy. Theirs is the precious gift of enthusiasm, without which no great deeds can be accomplished. A Government that does not constantly seek to live up to the ideals of its young men and women falls short of what the American people have a right to expect and demand from it. To interpret the spirit of the youth into the spirit of our Government, to bring the warmth of their enthusiasm and the flame of their idealism into the affairs of the nation, is to make American government a positive and living force, a factor for greatness and nobility in the life of the nation.

## Pledges Foreign Policy Toward Peace

I think I may say that I have witnessed as much of the horror and suffering of war as any other American. From it I have derived a deep passion for peace. Our foreign policy has one primary object, and that is peace. We have no hates; we wish no further possessions; we harbor no military threats. The unspeakable experiences of the great war, the narrow margins by which civilization survived from its exhaustion, is still vivid in men's minds. There is no nation in the world today that does not earnestly wish for peace—that is not striving for peace.

There are two cooperating factors in the maintenance of peace—the building of good-will by wise and sympathetic handling of international relations, and the adequate preparedness for defense. We must not only be just; we must be respected. The experiences of the war afforded final proof that we cannot isolate ourselves from the world, that the safeguarding of peace cannot be attained by negative action. Our offer of treaties open to the signature of all, renouncing war as an instrument of national policy, proves that we have every desire to cooperate with other nations for peace. But our people have determined that we can give the greatest real help—both in times of tranquillity, and in times of strain—if we maintain our independence from the political exigencies of the Old World. In pursuance of this, our country has refused membership in the League of Nations, but we are glad to cooperate with the League in its endeavors to further scientific, economic and social welfare and to secure limitation of armament.

We believe that the foundation of peace can be strengthened by the creation of methods and agencies by which a multitude of incidents may be transferred from the realm of prejudice and force to arbitration and the determination of right and wrong based upon international law.

We have been and we are particularly desirous of furthering the limitation of armaments. But in the meantime we know that in an armed world there is only one certain guarantee of freedom—and that is preparedness for defense. It is solely to defend ourselves, for the protection of our citizens, that we maintain armament. No clearer evidence of this can exist than the unique fact that we have fewer men in army uniform today than we have in police uniforms, and that we maintain a standing invitation to the world that we are always ready to limit our naval armament in proportion as the other naval nations will do likewise. We earnestly wish that the burdens and dangers of armament upon every home in the world might be lessened. But we must and shall maintain our naval defense and our merchant marine in the strength and efficiency which will yield to us at all times the primary assurance of liberty, that is, of national safety.

## Would Safeguard Equal Opportunity

There is one of the ideals of America upon which I wish at this time to lay especial emphasis. For we should constantly test our economic, social and governmental system by certain ideals which must control them. The founders of our Republic propounded the revolutionary doctrine that all men are created equal and all should have equality before the law. This was the emancipation of the individual. And since these beginnings, slowly, surely and almost imperceptibly, this nation has added a third ideal almost unique to America—the ideal of equal opportunity. This is the safeguard of the individual. The simple life of early days in our Republic found but few limitations upon equal opportunity. By the crowding of our people and the intensity and complexity of their activities it takes today a new importance.

Equality of opportunity is the right of every American—rich or poor, foreign or native-born, irrespective of faith or color. It is the right of every individual to attain that position in life to which his ability and character entitle him. By its maintenance we will alone hold open the door of opportunity to every new generation, to every boy and girl. It tolerates no privileged classes or castes or groups who would hold opportunity as their prerogative. Only from confidence that this right will be upheld can flow that unbounded courage and hope which stimulate each individual man and woman to endeavor and to achievement. The sum of their achievement is the gigantic harvest of national progress.

This ideal of individualism based upon equal opportunity to every citizen is the negation of socialism. It is the negation of anarchy. It is the negation of despotism. It is as if we set a race. We, through free and universal education, provide the training of the runners; we give to them an equal start; we provide in the Government the umpire of fairness in the race. The winner is he who shows the most conscientious training, the greatest ability and the greatest character. Socialism bids all to end the race equally. It holds back the speedy to the pace of the slowest. Anarchy would provide neither training nor umpire. Despotism picks those who should run and those who should win.

Conservative, progressive and liberal thought and action have their only real test in whether they contribute to equal opportunity, whether they hold open the door of opportunity. If they do not they are false in their premise no matter what their name may be.

It was Abraham Lincoln who firmly enunciated this ideal as the equal chance. The Sherman law was enacted in endeavor to hold open the door of equal opportunity in business. The commissions for regulation of public utilities were created to prevent discrimination in service and prevent extortion in rates—and thereby the destruction of equal opportunity. Equality of opportunity is a fundamental principle of our nation. With it we must test all our policies. The success or failure of this principle is the test of our Government.

## Coolidge Hailed as Great President

Mr. Chairman, I regret that time does not permit the compass of many important questions. I hope at a later time to discuss the development of waterways, highways, aviation, irrigable lands, foreign trade and merchant marine, the promotion of education, more effective administration of our criminal laws, the relation of our Government to public utilities and railways, the primary necessity of conservation of natural resources, measures for further economy in government and reduction of taxes —all of which afford problems of the first order.

I would violate my conscience and gratitude, I feel, did I not upon this occasion express appreciation of the great President who leads our party today. President Coolidge has not only given a memorable Administration, he has left an imprint of rectitude and statesmanship upon the history of our country. His has been the burden of reconstruction of our country from the destruction of war. He has dignified economy to a principle of government. He has charted the course of our nation and our party over many years to come. It is not only a duty but it is the part of statesmanship that we adhere to his course.

No man who stands before the mighty forces which ramify American life has the right to promise solutions at his hand alone. All that an honest man can say is that within the extent of his abilities and his authority and in cooperation with the Congress and with leaders of every element in our people, these problems shall be courageously met and solution will be courageously attempted.

Our purpose is to build in this nation a human society, not an economic system. We wish to increase the efficiency and productivity of our country but its final purpose is happier homes. We shall succeed through the faith, the loyalty, the self-sacrifice, the devotion to eternal ideals which live today in every American.

The matters which I have discussed directly and deeply affect the moral and spiritual welfare of our country. No one believes these aspirations and hopes can be realized in a day. Progress or remedy lies often enough at the hand of State and local government. But the awakening of the national conscience and the stimulation of every remedial agency is indeed a function of the national Government. I want to see our Government great both as an instrument and a symbol of the nation's greatness.

The Presidency is more than an administrative office. It must be the symbol of American ideals. The high and the lowly must be seen with the same eyes, met in the same spirit. It must be the instrument by which national conscience is livened and it must under the guidance of the Almighty interpret and follow that conscience.

August 12, 1928

84

# FINANCIAL "SPEAKEASIES" NET "SUCKERS"

### By W. F. WAMSLEY.

WALL STREET'S financial speakeasies, blood brothers to the old fashioned bucket shop but equipped with new schemes and operating from angles calculated to trap the inexperienced and unwary investor, have robbed the American people of more than $5,000,000 in recent months, according to United States Attorney Tuttle, who, in cooperation with the Attorney General's security bureau and the Better Business Bureau, is engaged in a campaign to drive from the fringes of legitimate finances these racketeers who prey on the hopes of the financially ignorant. A powerful weapon is being employed—one that slashes through to the very core of the illegalities. It is the Federal statute providing punishment for conviction on the charge of using the mails in a scheme to defraud.

This law, now brought strongly into play in connection with dealings in illegitimate securities, already has started several of the racketeers on the road to Atlanta and has been the basis for complaints against many stock tipsters, market sheets and shady brokerage houses. But, what is probably still more important, the application of the law and the publicity involved have caused a legion of financial racketeers to fold their tents and silently steal away.

It could hardly be said with assurance that Wall Street at last is free of the racketeer and his paraphernalia, shrewdly camouflaged to entrap the dollars of the prosperous American investor who believes all that he reads. It is not. Nevertheless, a good start has been made, and the racketeer is wary, knowing that the powers that be are aroused and on his trail.

### The Financial Speakeasy.

As in the case of the speakeasy that purveys liquor illegally, the country probably will never be entirely rid of the financial speakeasy. One closed up is likely to open in the next block under another name. So long as markets continue to soar and fortunes are made in them by skillful traders, so long will some men take a chance on garnering fast and illegitimate profits by the distribution of dubious or worthless securities. This has been true since speculation began. It will always be true. There is present, on the fringe of every big market, such as has been the one of this year and last, a certain percentage of unscrupulous individuals chasing what appears to them to be the easy dollar by means of false representations and promises hopeless of fulfillment.

The game waxes and wanes as the legitimate markets wax and wane. It is prosperous and expands when people the country over have money with which to buy securities, and when active and rising markets tempt the speculator on to quick riches. It contracts when markets are dull and listless, when public interest in securities is at low ebb, or when public attention is drawn sharply to the methods of skulduggery, as is being done at present.

As a matter of fact, financial speakeasies are not new. They represent merely the refinement of an age-old game that was going strong when a few brokers gathered under a butternut tree and formed the New York Stock Exchange. The association was made, largely, to protect themselves from the shysters, crooks and racketeers of those days.

Less than twoscore years ago one could walk into any number of bucket shops on Broad Street and "bet with the tape." That is, if X. Y. Z. shares were selling at $100 on the tape, one could "buy" 100 shares (or any number) by putting up ten points, or could "sell" the same number from the last quotation. It was simply a gamble, with no thought in mind of delivery of stock to the buyers. One simply won or lost, as the market fluctuated.

This became a little too raw, and out of the tape game developed the bucket shop, in which the broker made the same bet—that the customer was wrong—but camouflaged it by a purchase of the stock (for the purpose of obtaining a buyer's name) even though it was immediately sold, the house bucketing the order. The term bucket shop originated from the bucket or basket kept by the brokerage offices into which were thrown the incoming orders that were never executed or, if executed on the buying side, immediately sold out.

The bull market of 1919-20 put an end to most of them. They could not pay off the customers whose orders had been bucketed, because, for once, the customers had won their bets that the market would go higher. The bucket shops failed rapidly and with loud reports resembling the touching off of a bunch of firecrackers.

### The Unsuspecting Customer.

Then came the bull markets of 1927, 1928 and 1929 and with them the financial speakeasy, whose merchandise is dressed up in such a pleasing fashion, and its sale urged so skillfully and adroitly, that the unsuspecting customer usually has the pretty—but generally worthless—certificates and the racketeer the money before the buyer realizes what it is all about.

Incidentally, the metamorphosis of the bucket shop into the financial speakeasy eliminated the necessity for ornate and elaborate offices with which to awe the sucker who is being given an uneven break. These show rooms, which used to dot the financial district, paid high rent in advantageous locations and by their very appearance of class and prosperity aided the racketeers' "front." Now they are not needed, because of the absence of personal contact between broker and customer; and consequently the financial speakeasy proprietor spends no foolish money in Persian rugs and mahogany tables and chairs. Two or three rooms, usually hidden away, are enough.

There are three physical requisites for a financial speakeasy. First, a stock to sell; second, a "sucker list" of customers to sell it to; third, means of communication with those customers, mainly by telephone, telegraph and mail. All of them are comparatively easy to procure.

Mining shares, formerly the popular sucker bait, have gone out of fashion. Now it is the oil shares, the public utility issues, aviation stocks, the motors and others of the sort which are in popular favor. So the racketeer hunts out a small company engaged in one of these lines—one that has encountered hard sledding because of competition, because of lack of capital or from other causes—and buys or options as much of the stock as he can acquire. Usually it is for a few cents a share, but sometimes the price runs up to $10 or more a share.

Seldom is there any open market for this stock. It is not listed on any exchange, nor is it dealt in over the counter. The racketeer can arbitrarily fix its selling price at any figure he thinks the traffic will bear.

The "sucker lists" come from a variety of sources, mainly from telephone and city directories, from newspaper articles containing names and addresses and from corporation stockholders' lists. Several firms make a specialty of gathering and selling these names and addresses, their prices ranging from 10 cents per name up to a dollar or so.

### The Tipster Sheet.

The tipster sheet is the newest and most elaborate adjunct of the financial speakeasy and the factor that probably leads most people astray. No less than 100 of them are published daily in the Wall Street district, under one high-sounding name or another. Usually they are well written from the standpoint of the stock market, printed on good paper and mailed free of cost or at a small subscription price to each name on the "sucker list."

They purport, of course, to give advice about the market, to answer questions about particular securities and to give a résumé of corporation and financial news developments such as would be of interest to the ordinary reader of the financial section of a daily newspaper. Tucked away among the legitimate news, however, is always a carefully worded boost for the particular issue being distributed by the financial speakeasy which owns the tipster sheet.

One of the most successful of these, now out of business because the racketeer who owned it faces a long term in Atlanta, on conviction of the charge of using the mails to defraud, had a daily circulation of 200,000, at a charge of $1 per year—a publication which, over and above that income, cost the racketeer $300,000 a year to maintain.

With his stock in hand and his tipsheet circulating, the proprietor of the financial speakeasy is ready to establish his "boiler room." This is merely a room containing a table at which sit the glib-tongued salesmen, known as "dynamiters," who have previously been versed in and rehearsed in their "canvass."

Most of the high-pressure work is done over the telephone, a large part of it long-distance messages at high rates. One racketeer recently paid a $6,000 telephone bill for one month's service. Both telephone and telegraph are used lavishly. Many a financial speakeasy proprietor will be astonished to learn, when he comes up for trial, that complete stenographic records of many of his phone calls have been made and are in the safes of the authorities.

Some of the financial speakeasies concentrate on New York customers, some on both New York customers and those in outlaying cities and towns. But no call is too long if there is a chance to sell a block of phony stock. One recently raided racketeer had his staff of dynamiters divided into sections, a section for each borough of New York. With the telephone book of their borough before them, each was engaged in going assiduously through the entire book, in alphabetical fashion, calling each subscriber and giving whoever answered what the racketeers call "a canvass."

The greatest damage, of course, has been done to the purses of the financially inexperienced, and at the forthcoming trials witnesses, many of whom have lost their life savings, will be brought from all sections of the country, reflecting the widespread activity of the "boiler rooms" and the tremendous distribution of the questionable market letters and tipsheets. Small-town merchants, clergymen, school teachers, farmers and lawyers appear to have been the favorite quarry of the racketeers, as disclosed by the investigation made by officials now engaged in smoking them out. The losses were generally from $1,000 to $5,000 to the individual, but at times they ran into greater sums.

Considerable astute psychology enters into the successful operation of

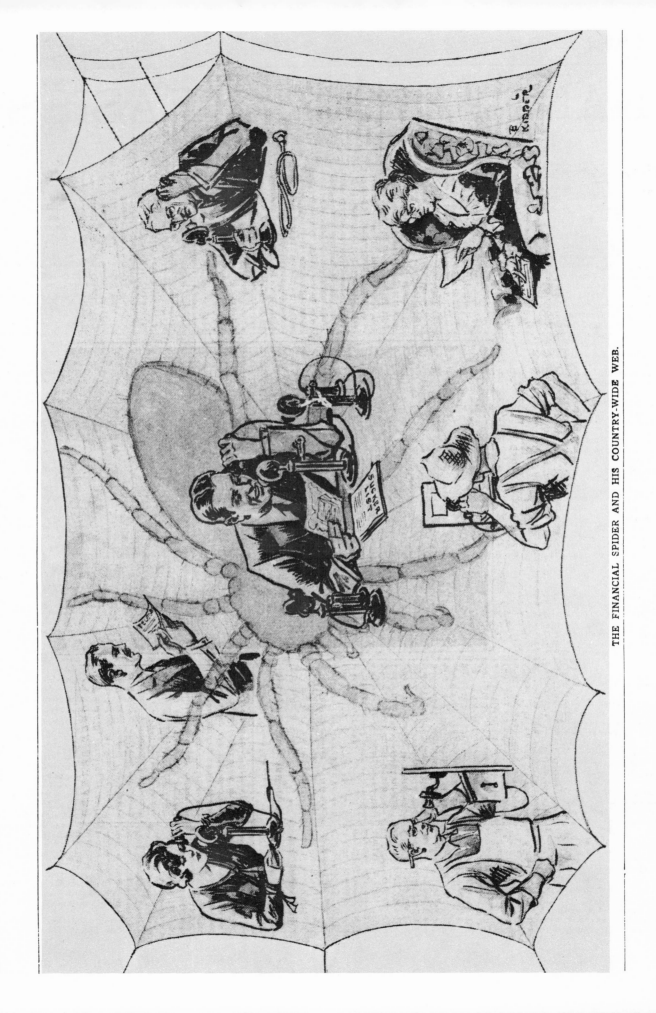

THE FINANCIAL SPIDER AND HIS COUNTRY-WIDE WEB.

a financial speakeasy, the investigators have ascertained. First, there is the fact that markets and finance represent a subject about which there is widespread ignorance; second, the average man who has saved a few thousand dollars believes that he can enhance his fortune by "playing the market"; third, such a novice seeks to be shown the ropes by one who evidently knows all about it, and he readily welcomes advice and does not inquire too closely about its source. There is, too, the fact that the public mind has been inflamed by the wave of speculation which has swept the country in the last two years or so and the frequent stories of tremendous stock market exploits and winnings.

The dynamiter has, naturally, all of these facts in mind and knows well, too, the individual desire for financial independence. The field is a fertile one, ready plowed and awaiting the planting.

Details of the sale of dubious stock are monotonous in their similarity. The telephone bell on the desk of a small-town merchant rings and he is informed that he is being called long distance by New York. When he answers he is told by a pleasant and suave voice that its owner represents the firm of A. B. C. & Co. and that they want to make some money for him. The name of the shares being urged by the financial speakeasy are casually eased into the conversation, and he is told of a coming big rise in the market for this stock, of the corporation's earnings and possibilities.

The canvass is so well rehearsed, so complete and, to the uninitiated, so plausible that many sales are made on the first call. If not, the prospective customer is deluged with telegrams, letters and additional telephone calls, each cunningly designed to break down his sales resistance.

That practically worthless stock certificates have been sold in large quantities throughout the country is demonstrated in the complaints which have deluged the Federal and State officials. Most of them, unfortunately, are from people of modest circumstances, who can ill afford to lose their savings and to whom the success of the glib-tongued dynamiter spells tragedy.

The favorite adjunct of the present form of larceny is the "trade-out." It will be assumed that the prospective speakeasy customer is the owner of a few shares of a standard stock listed on an exchange and actively dealt in. He is urged to send this in, that it may be used as margin to finance the purchase of X. Y. Z. shares. Of course, his shares are sold immediately by the financial speakeasy and he is "put in" to the new stock. Sometimes he is advised that it has moved up a point or so, but that the big move is just ahead and that he should buy more, and on no consideration sell out at this time. Sometimes he is told that his shares have depreciated a few points, and he is advised to buy additional stock to "average" or, again, is switched into something else which the speakeasy is boosting.

In most cases it is not until the customer's determination to sell and secure his cash is final that he realizes he has been in the hands of a "gyp" and has been literally shorn of his fleece. It is seldom that there is a market for any of the stocks boosted by financial speakeasies. A few of the racketeers, alarmed at the investigations under way and seeking a softening of the charges made or to be made against them, have rebought stock sold at the prices paid, but these cases are few and far between. Some have fled with their ill-gotten gains, others have changed individual and firm names and addresses. Former financial speakeasy proprietors in New York are bobbing up in Chicago, St. Louis, Philadelphia and Pittsburgh. Financial speakeasies are as difficult to control and keep in hand as are liquor speakeasies.

### The Crook Who Met His Match.

Now and then cases come to light in which the law is taken into their own hands by irate customers. The story is told in Wall Street of a Denver man who lost $10,000 through the purchase of an illegitimate security sold over the long-distance telephone by high-pressure salesmanship. He came on to New York, tried to get his money back and failed, being unable to get further than the peep-hole at the outside of the financial speakeasy.

Finally, with his dander thoroughly up, the Westerner assembled half a dozen husky New York friends and in force they descended on the speakeasy just before noon on a busy day. The door was quickly broken down with an iron bar; the Denver man and his associates rushed in and started to work, swinging at every jaw in sight. The proprietor was located and got the beating of his life, which did not cease until he had written his check for the full amount of the Denver man's loss. Just as a matter of precaution he was held in his chair until the office boy had returned from the bank with the cash, as instructed. Two of the dynamiting salesmen and the proprietor spent several cheerless days in Broad Street Hospital recovering from their experience.

But all of the school teachers and clergymen and struggling merchants who have trustingly sent their money along to the financial speakeasies, in the hope that the bread thus cast on the speculative waters will return to them as cake, cannot come to New York and engage in hand-to-hand combat with the speakeasy proprietors with any hope of success in getting their money back. Most of the duped ones will never see their earnings again.

What can be done, however, and what is now being done, is authoritative disruption of the cheating business through raids and subsequent prosecutions which may result in stiff penitentiary sentences for the racketeer, who is fearful of but one thing—a term in Atlanta.

It has been the experience of officials of the Better Business Bureau in connection with the sale of worthless or questionable securities that the campaign against the financial speakeasies, if it is to prove effective and lasting, must be a continuous one. Like the liquor speakeasy, the financial speakeasy bobs up in unexpected places with alarming regularity and starts to operate with amazing rapidity and efficiency. Convictions are more difficult to obtain than in the case of the liquor speakeasy, for a raid on the liquor speakeasy usually reveals a bottle or so of liquor. In the case of the financial speakeasy, the campaigners must prove that customers have been defrauded, that the mails have been used in furtherance of the business and that the certificates sold are practically worthless.

### Testimony Hard to Obtain.

Many people who have been thus defrauded hesitate to make a formal complaint. The small-town business man especially does not want his neighbors and business associates to know that he has been duped. It doubtless would prove injurious to his credit and would tend to make him the laughing stock of the town. Usually he cannot spare the time or money to come to New York and testify about the details of his case. There are few men, even wealthy and experienced business men, whose executors do not find a few "cats and dogs" in their estates after their death, mute evidence of the campaign of a racketeer.

But the guns of the 1929 dynamiters are trained on the small game, the men and women with a few thousand dollars, which in the aggregate run into the millions. The guess of the United States Attorney that $5,000,000 has been sopped up from the financially inexperienced by the speakeasies of Wall Street in the last few months is probably as good as any other. No one knows the complete details and all their ramifications or the prices paid by the victims and their losses. Probably, with all facts under consideration, the figure would be much higher.

Officials of the Better Business Bureau, who have for long maintained a securities department for ferreting out securities crimes, say that the aggregate losses to the people of the country through the sale to them of worthless or nearly worthless securities by high-pressure methods will run into a total of billions rather than millions.

The financial speakeasy is probably more dangerous than was the old-fashioned bucketshop. It uses more subtle and far more plausible methods, nicely calculated to attract the dollars of the inexperienced investor. The wariness of the dynamiter does not usually arouse the suspicions of the victims, because of the secrecy usually surrounding stock market transactions.

Two methods may be employed to stamp out the racketeer and put an end to the financial speakeasy. The first is by direct action, such as is now being taken; second, and perhaps the more effective method, the continuous campaign of education carried on by the Better Business Bureaus of the country in cooperation with the legitimate exchanges. Every prospective investor is thus urged to buy no stock of any sort from a stranger, or by telephone solicitation, and to consult with his banker or otherwise obtain informed investment counsel before closing the deal.

August 25, 1929

## 'NEW ERA' THEORY FAILS, BANKERS SAY

Teachings of "Jazz Economists" Reviewed in Light of Stock Markets' Break.

### FACTORS OVERESTIMATED

Buying Power of Investment Trusts and Institutions Less Than Was Expected.

Wall Street's financiers were looking last week upon the wreckage of various economic theories which had been advanced during the bull markets of recent years and which now are held to have been exploded by the sweeping decline in stocks. These theories, which sought to account for high prices of shares and relatively low yields on the ground that the nation was entering a new financial era, were advanced by a group which the bankers have labeled "jazz economists."

Commenting on the collapse of these theories, several bankers said yesterday that the appearance of the "new era" school of economists this year was one of the most significant danger signals to men who had seen panics come and go. Previous to every collapse in security prices in the last half century, they asserted, similar schools of prophets had arisen to account for unreasonably high prices by saying the financial world was entering a "new era."

### Theories of New School.

The basic thesis of the school of 1929 was that stock prices had entered a new holding zone from which major reactions were unlikely. In support of this theory, the economists pointed to the vast buying resources of millions of investors who had entered the market in recent years, and to the huge funds in the hands of insurance companies, investment trusts and other institutions which would be placed in common stocks after any reaction of 10 or 15 points. This group asserted that panics had been made impossible by the creation of the Federal Reserve System, and that major reactions were also unlikely because there was no apparent inflation of commodities. Since the basic industries of the country were expanding their operations steadily, these economists predicted a fairly steady rise for several years at least in the quotations of pivotal issues. The high prices of these issues, and the fact that many stocks were selling at figures from thirty to fifty times their earnings, were defended by the group on the ground taht the prices were merely discounting future earning power.

The optimistic views of these economists were shared by many persons who bought pivotal issues at ascending prices, on the ground that these "blue chip" stocks would have an increased scarcity value within a short time. Buying stocks for appreciation in price, rather than on the basis of yield, was the rule among a large section of the trading and investing public. it is now conceded by Wall Street. These speculative policies were reinforced by the principles of the "new era" economists, who predicted steadily rising values. as a result of the increasing prosperity of the country.

### Flaw in Reasoning Sought.

While Wall Street has not definitely agreed as to what is the weak link in the reasoning of these economists, most financiers there hold that the chief error of the school was its failure to recognize the development of an overbought, over-bulled position in the stock markets. The reserve buying power of investment trusts and small investors upon which the economists counted to check a major reaction was totally inadequate, it is seen now, to stem any general wave of selling caused by anxiety concerning the speculative outlook. Bankers say that investing institutions and the public were so heavily committed in common stocks at high prices last September that a major reaction was inevitable sooner or later, owing to the weak technical position.

One of the keenest disappointments to the new economists was the failure of the investment trusts to bring their resources to bear as stabilizing forces in stopping the decline. Bankers now agree that the importance of the investment trust movement was vastly overemphasized. With a total capital of approximately $3,000,-000,000, more than two-thirds of which was invested in securities, the trusts were a relatively insignificant factor in comparison with the total value of securities listed on the New York Stock Exchange, which amounted to more than $85,000,000,-000 at the beginning of October. Other financial institutions, whose capital also was tied up in securities, were equally powerless to check a tide of liquidation. The reserve buying power which the economists saw was overwhelmed when the public decided to sell $5,000,000,000 or $10,-000,000,000 of securities.

### Trusts Reluctant to Buy.

Not only were the investment trusts powerless to cope with the situation, it is pointed out, but many of them were quite unwilling to buy stocks when the decline gathered headway. Several institutions were reported to have been convinced, even before the crash assumed panic proportions, that the nation was about to enter a transitory period of business recession. This pessimistic view was based on the accumulation of stocks of rubber, sugar, non-ferrous metals and other commodities, and a feeling that manufacturers of automobiles and other products had not gauged their markets correctly. One investment trust executive predicted more than a month ago that corporation earnings for the fourth quarter of the year would show a marked decrease. He said the effect of the impact of reports of smaller earnings upon a stock market geared for increased earnings would be terrific. In line with this theory, many investment trusts were unwilling to buy stocks except at genuine bargain prices, Wall Street now believes. Other trusts were reported to have exhausted their buying power early in the recession and were unable to assist in checking the decline.

The theory of the new school of economists that good industrial stocks would never again sell upon a basis of ten times earnings, and that utility stocks would never be seen on a twenty-times-earnings basis has been thoroughly exploded, financiers say, by a crash which has brought many industrials down to ten times earnings and some utilities to twelve times earnings. Much of the solid buying which has developed in the last week, they add, has been stimulated solely by the high yields which the economists predicted had been banished forever.

November 17, 192

---

# WORST STOCK CRASH STEMMED BY BANKS; 12,894,650-SHARE DAY SWAMPS MARKET; LEADERS CONFER, FIND CONDITIONS SOUND

## LOSSES RECOVERED IN PART

Upward Trend Start° With 200,000-Share Order for Steel.

### TICKERS LAG FOUR HOURS

Thousands of Accounts Wiped Out, With Traders in Dark as to Events on Exchange.

### SALES ON CURB 6,337,415

Prices on Markets in Other Cities Also Slump and Rally —Wheat Values Hard Hit.

The most disastrous decline in the biggest and broadest stock market of history rocked the financial district yesterday. In the very midst of the collapse five of the country's most influential bankers hurried to the office of J. P. Morgan & Co., and after a brief conference gave out word that they believe the foundations of the market to be sound, that the market smash has been caused by technical rather than fundamental considerations, and that many sound stocks are selling too low.

Suddenly the market turned about, on buying orders thrown into the pivotal issues, and before the final quotations were tapped out, four hours and eight minutes after the 3 o'clock bell, most stocks had regained a measurable part of their losses.

### Losses at Close Not Excessive.

The break was one of the widest in the market's history, although the losses at the close were not particularly large, many having been recouped by the afternoon rally.

It carried down with it speculators, big and little, in every part of the country, wiping out thousands of accounts. It is probable that if the stockholders of the country's foremost corporations had not been calmed by the attitude of leading bankers and the subsequent rally, the business of the country would have been seriously affected. Doubtless business will feel the effects of the drastic stock shake-out, and this is expected to hit the luxuries most severely.

It was by far the biggest market day in the country's history. Total sales on the New York Stock Exchange were 12,894,650 shares, as compared with the 8,246,000-share record set on March 26, and on the Curb 6,337,415 shares, as compared with the 3,715,400 record established Monday. A total of 974 separate issues were dealt in on the Exchange, this figure, of course, establishing a new record. Bonds, which were strong, reached a volume of $23,233,000, the biggest day in that market since April 28, 1926, and unlike stocks, the fixed investments were strong, with the exception of the convertible issues, whose fluctuations synchronize with the selling price of the stocks to which they are prior.

**Thousands Sacrifice Holdings.**

The total losses cannot be accurately calculated, because of the large number of markets and the thousands of securities not listed on any exchange. However, they were staggering, running into billions of dollars. Fear struck the big speculators and little ones, big investors and little ones. Thousands of them threw their holdings into the whirling Stock Exchange pit for what they would bring. Losses were tremendous and thousands of prosperous brokerage and bank accounts, sound and healthy a week ago, were completely wrecked in the strange debacle, due to a combination of circumstances, but accelerated into a crash by fear.

The ticker services maintained by the New York Stock Exchange and the New York Curb Exchange proved pitifully inadequate for the task of recording history's biggest market. By 10:30 o'clock the Exchange ticker had fallen 15 minutes behind and that of the Curb Exchange 16 minutes; by 11:30 this was stretched to 48 for the Exchange and 47 for the Curb; at 1 o'clock they were 92 minutes late; by 2 o'clock, 131 minutes late for the Exchange and 116 for the Curb tickers, and by 2:30 the Exchange quotations were 147 minutes late and the Curb tickers 130 minutes behind. The New York Stock Exchange tickers did not complete the task of printing the market until 8½ minutes past 7 o'clock last night, while the Curb tickers finished at 5:54.

**Financial District in Confusion.**

Under these circumstances of late tickers and spreads of 10, 20 and at times 30 points between the tape prices and those on the floor of the Exchange, the entire financial district was thrown into hopeless confusion and excitement. Wild-eyed speculators crowded the brokerage offices, awed by the disaster which had overtaken many of them. They followed the market literally "in the dark," getting but meager reports via the financial news tickers which printed the Exchange floor prices at ten-minute intervals.

Rumors, most of them wild and false, spread throughout the Wall Street district and thence throughout the country. One of the reports was that eleven speculators had committed suicide. A peaceful workman atop a Wall Street building looked down and saw a big crowd watching him, for the rumor had spread that he was going to jump off. Reports that the Chicago and Buffalo Exchanges had closed spread throughout the district, as did rumors that the New York Stock Exchange and the New York Curb Exchange were going to suspend trading. These rumors and reports were all found, on investigation, to be untrue.

**Opening Is Fairly Steady.**

The early market gave no hint of the smash that was to follow. Stocks opened moderately steady, although on a big volume that forecast trouble. Biggest blocks at the opening were 20,000 shares of Kennecott Copper, which opened up 11; 20,000 of General Motors, off fractionally; 15,000 of Sinclair Oil, 15,000 of Standard Brands, 10,000 of United Corporation, 12,000 of United Gas Improvement, 10,000 of Westinghouse, 13,000 of Packard Motors, 10,000 of Alleghany Corporation, and a long list of 5,000-share blocks of a large number of other leading shares. The pressure became more impressive at the end of the first half hour, however, and with all following of the market from the ticker out of the question, the confusion and liquidation increased.

It was not the calm slipping away of stocks as had been the case in many previous markets. By 11 o'clock it had become a wild scramble, with "sell at the market" resounding in every brokerage office in the country and the effect was perhaps the most astonishing crash of open market values that the Street has ever seen. If there was any support in the market at all, it was swept forcibly aside, as leading stocks crashed down and down by 1 point, 2 points, and even 5 and 10 between sales as the violence increased.

**Steel Falls Below 200.**

Margins by the thousands became exhausted and frightened stockholders in all parts of the country seemed to have become terror stricken. Ineffectual attempts to keep Steel above 200 proved unsuccessful, although there was a short, sharp battle around the Steel post because of the general knowledge that if Steel crashed through 200 it would exert a tremendously disquieting effect on the balance of the market. But crash through it did, and before the market was saved from itself the market leader, which had opened at 205½, had smashed its way down to 194½.

The break of stocks which have been in the speculative limelight was followed with breathless interest in all parts of the country. General Electric broke from 319¾ to 302¾, American Telephone & Telegraph from 274¾ to 265, Johns-Manville from 180 to 140, Montgomery Ward from 84 to 50, Auburn Motors from 260 to 190, National Biscuit from 209 to 193½, Atchison from 264½ to 253¼, New York Central from 213⅞ to 197 and practically every other stock on the list in proportion.

Stocks were thrown in, in tremendous volume, for just what they would bring at forced sale. The greatest damage and the lowest prices were reached between 11:15 and 12:15. Soon after that time, leading bankers were observed en route to the offices of J. P. Morgan & Co. With the knowledge that a statement would soon be made from the Morgan offices, the Street guessed that it would relate to market support. There was an immediate turn-about in stocks, and the leaders started their fast climb up the ladder of fluctuations, down which they had so ingloriously tumbled an hour before.

**200,000 Steel Order Placed.**

Steel got the first recognized support. It was 200,000 shares. Then strength spread to all sections of the list and by 2 o'clock the market had turned vigorously and definitely upward, almost as wide, in leading stocks, as had been the decline. Faint hearted stockholders, on the verge of selling out, withdrew their orders; a vast amount of bear covering was started and pivotal issues rebounded in strong fashion.

The rally in United States Steel was started by a 25,000-share buying order placed in the hands of Richard Whitney of Richard Whitney & Co., and a brother of George Whitney, who is a partner in J. P. Morgan & Co. His bid of 205 for 25,000 shares of Steel electrified the group around the Steel post and communicated buying enthusiasm to other parts of the floor. It was assumed that Mr. Whitney, who is frequently spoken of as a "Morgan broker," had received the order from the house of Morgan or interests identified with it. Prior to the bid of 205 the bid had been hovering around 195.

On the upswing, there was just as much confusion about the state of the market as there was on the downswing, if not more, for the volume had increased measurably. At 4 and 5 o'clock the tickers were still printing prices which represented the lowest levels of the day, and it was not until the later prices came on, between 6 and 7 o'clock that an idea could be obtained of the extent and breadth of the recovery. Gains on this rally ran from 5 to 30 points or more, and a few stocks were able to close the day with a gain, although the list was a ragged and irregular one at the close, with many stocks showing very wide losses on the day's trading.

**Wheat Markets Are Affected.**

Such a sweeping smash always has widespread ramifications and because of the importance of this country in the scheme of international finance, reverberations from American markets resound loudly abroad. That was the case yesterday. American commodity markets were lower, also. Wheat broke 12¾ cents in Chicago amid scenes of wildest confusion, but rallied when the stock market shook off its fear and closed 5 to 5⅝ cents lower. In Winnipeg, wheat ended 5⅝ to 6¼ cents weaker. Corn rallied briskly at the close.

Commodity prices declined on the various local exchanges in response to the weakness in the stock markets, with the volume of trading in silk futures setting a high record, with prices down 3 to 4 points at the close. Burlap eased 10 to 14 points, and rubber ended down 10 to 30 points after earlier losses of 40 to 50 points. Raw hide futures were unchanged to 50 points lower. Coffee was 3 points higher to 30 points lower for the A and 40 to 135 points lower for the D contracts. Sugar fell 2 to 4 points, and cocoa, an exception to the general rule, was unchanged to 8 points higher. Cotton futures fell 40 to 50 points on the local market but were 7 to 20 points higher on the close as a result of strong support.

Sterling continued its advance to $4.88 1/16, the effect of the continued transfer of funds from this country to London, as a result of the liquidation of extremely heavy holdings in our stock markets. That this country will lose gold to England now appears certain, and it is expected that France, too, will get some of the exports if an outbound movement develops.

**Tables Show Losses.**

The following table shows the day's market history of leading stocks on the Exchange, with Wednesday's closing prices, yesterday's low, the recovery from the low and the net change for the day:

| | Wednesday's Close. | Yes-t'day's Low. | Re-covery From Low. | Net Ch'ge For Day. |
|---|---|---|---|---|
| Air Reduction | 193½ | 176⅛ | 15⅝ | −3⅝ |
| Allis Chalmers | 56⅝ | 44 | 5 | −6⅝ |
| Am Bank Note | 125 | 113 | 2 | −8 |
| Am Foreign Power | 112 | 88 | 9⅛ | −14½ |
| Am Home Prod | 59¾ | 49¾ | .. | −10 |
| Am International | 65¾ | 53 | 4 | −8¾ |
| Am Rolling Mill | 115½ | 100¾ | 2¾ | −12½ |
| Am Tel & Tel | 272 | 245 | 24 | −3 |
| Am Water Works | 120¼ | 93 | 16¾ | −16½ |
| Anaconda Cop | 102 | 92 | 10 | .. |
| Auburn Motor | 260 | 190 | 45 | −25 |
| Baldwin Loco, new | 35 | 15 | 18 | −2 |
| Bendix Aviation | 51 | 40 | 3 | −8 |
| Bohr Aluminum | 73 | 50 | 15 | −8 |
| Bethlehem Steel | 101¼ | 92½ | 9 | +¼ |
| Burroughs Add Mach. | 84¼ | 59 | 6 | −19¼ |
| Byers (A M) Co | 121¼ | 76 | 35 | −10¼ |
| Can Dry Gin Ale | 80½ | 60 | 9 | −11½ |
| Ches & Ohio | 257½ | 231 | 11 | −15½ |
| Columbia Carbon | 255 | 210 | 21 | −24 |
| Gen Elec | 314 | 283 | 25 | −6 |
| Gen Motors | 57⅜ | 49 | 4½ | −3⅜ |
| Grigsby Grunow | 43⅛ | 30 | 2½ | −10⅜ |
| Inter Business Mach | 231⅜ | 201 | 5 | −25¾ |
| Inter Tel & Tel | 110⅜ | 79 | 27 | −4¾ |
| Johns Manville | 180 | 140 | 30 | −10 |
| Kennecott | 67 | 69 | 6 | +8 |
| Ludium Steel | 70½ | 59 | 12¼ | −7⅜ |
| Montgomery Ward | 83¼ | 50 | 24 | −9¼ |
| Radio Corp | 68½ | 44½ | 13¾ | −10¼ |
| Republic Steel | 105⅜ | 90 | 5 | −10⅜ |
| U S Indus Alcohol | 201¼ | 169 | 7 | −25¼ |
| U S Steel | 204 | 193½ | 12½ | +2 |
| Western Un Tel | 235 | 220 | 23 | +8 |

On the Curb, the day's record of the leading stocks was:

| Stock. | Wed. Close. | Yest. Low. | Recov. from Low. | Net Ch'ge for Day. |
|---|---|---|---|---|
| Allied Pow & Lt | 67⅝ | 40⅛ | +18¾ | −6½ |
| Aluminum Co Amer | 374½ | 300 | ... | −74½ |
| Am & F Pow (war) | 93 | 75¼ | +14¾ | −3 |
| Am Gas & El | 140½ | 130⅛ | +16⅞ | −6½ |
| Am Lt & Trac | 280 | 250 | +10 | −30 |
| Am Superpower | 36⅞ | 25 | +7¾ | −4⅛ |
| Assoc Gas & El | 59 | 50⅜ | +6 | −2⅝ |
| Brazilian Tr Lt | 61 | 52 | +7 | −2 |
| Cent States Elec | 49¾ | 43½ | +4½ | −1¾ |
| Cities Service | 59 | 45 | +6½ | −7½ |
| Comm Edison | 354 | 325 | +1 | −28 |
| Consol Gas Balt | 114⅛ | 108⅛ | +⅞ | −5¼ |
| Crocker Wheeler | 49 | 25 | +⅛ | −23⅞ |
| Deere & Co | 564 | 500 | +29 | −44 |
| Driver Harris | 630 | 585½ | ... | −44½ |
| El Bond & Share | 112½ | 91 | +16½ | −5 |
| Elec Investors | 180 | 141 | +29¾ | −10¼ |
| Elec Pow Asso | 47 | 28¼ | +8⅝ | −10⅛ |
| Do A | 42 | 30 | +1¼ | −10¾ |
| Firestone T & R | 228 | 195 | +10 | −23 |
| Goldman Sachs | 84½ | 65 | +15 | −4½ |
| Gulf Oil Penn | 175⅛ | 158¾ | +5¼ | −11⅛ |
| Humble Oil | 114⅝ | 107⅝ | +½ | −6½ |
| Ill Pipe Line | 302 | 295 | ... | −7 |
| Indian Ter | 35½ | 21 | +10⅞ | −3⅞ |
| Insull Util | 85 | 67¼ | +12⅝ | −5 |
| Lehman Corp | 99½ | 92½ | +5 | −2 |
| Mid West Util | 38 | 29 | +7½ | −1½ |
| Newmount Mining | 198⅛ | 160 | +25 | −13⅛ |
| Nor States P. A | 200 | 188 | +12 | .. |
| Sisto Fin Corp | 53 | 40⅛ | +8⅞ | −4 |
| Southern Corp | 15½ | 10 | +4¼ | −1¼ |
| Standard P & L | 136 | 127 | +3¾ | −5¾ |
| Tampa Elec | 75⅛ | 69⅞ | ... | −5¼ |
| Thermoid Co | 29½ | 24½ | +4¼ | −¾ |
| Tri Cont Allied | 80 | 70 | +10 | ... |
| Tri Cont Corp | 32⅝ | 18 | +11 | −3⅝ |
| Tubize Art Silk | 275 | 223 | +45 | −5 |
| Unit Corp (war) | 25⅛ | 17¼ | +8⅝ | −½ |
| Unit Gas Co | 36½ | 30 | +2 | −4½ |
| Unit L & P. A | 37¼ | 30 | +6⅞ | −⅜ |
| U S Gypsum | 73 | 65⅝ | +2⅞ | −4½ |
| Utility & Ind | 34⅛ | 29 | +2⅞ | −2¼ |
| Utility P & L | 24⅞ | 19⅝ | +5⅝ | +⅛ |
| Utility Equities | 25⅜ | 20 | +⅛ | −5¼ |
| Walgreen Co | 88 | 78⅛ | ... | −9⅞ |
| Walgreen Co (war) | 65 | 52 | ... | −13 |
| Vesta Auto Supply | 58 | 50 | +1 | −7 |

The immediate future of the stock market will interest the world, because of the attitude leading bankers have taken and the possibility that as goes the market for the balance of the year, so will go business. There are many complexities in the situation, and many readjustments to be made, in view of the wide declines which have taken place since Sept. 1. It is usually the case that the development of a record-breaking day, such as yesterday's, marks the culmination of a trend, on either the up or down side, and many persons in Wall Street anticipate a stiffening of prices until stocks regain their equilibrium and the last vestige of hysteria has been wiped out.

# BANKING BUOYS UP STRICKEN STOCKS

## Action of Morgan and Others Something New in History of Buying Pools.

### PLAN CAREFULLY ARRANGED

#### Original Group of Five Houses Had Active Cooperation of Other Large Institutions.

When the financial history of the past exciting week is finally written an unusual chapter will be that devoted to the formation of a coalition of the city's leading bankers to support the stricken stock market.

The phrase "banking support" has been a favorite one with stock market commentors for years, but never before has Wall Street had definite information of the formation of a pool by bankers, the identity of whom is definitely known, to bring to bear upon a demoralized stock market the tremendous strength of their combined buying power.

Bankers have always scoffed at the popular belief that leading financiers agree in times of stress to act in concert. Only a few days before the rout of the stock market on Thursday Charles N. Mitchell, chairman of the National City Bank and a prime mover in the formation of the banking group, asserted that in all his long experience of Wall Street affairs he had yet to learn of any such organized movement as the term "banking support" in generally suppose to connote.

In the past there have been not infrequent instances when bankers have thrown money into the market to avert a panic. But the crisis of last week was not one which could be stemmed by the offer of a few million dollars to be lent on call. It was a crisis which called first of all for some gesture to quiet the hysterical fears of trapped market speculators all over the country.

This was the chief virtue of that dramatic meeting at the offices of J. P. Morgan & Co. The word went out that "they" were coming to the rescue and almost at once fears were quieted. But it had to be proved also that the bankers stood ready to carry through with the heavy purchase of securities. They said nothing about "a pool." They specifically announced that they intended to say nothing about "concerted action."

There was no need to say anything about such a plan. It was enough for Wall Street that floor traders known to have the handling of Stock Exchange business for the bankers involved appeared immediately after the meeting and calmly offered to purchase heavy blocks of pivotal issues.

The next day Wall Street received confirmation from reliable sources of its belief in the existence of a buying pool. It learned further that the original group of five great banks did not stand alone, but had the active support of other large banking institutions of the city and had been joined in its conferences by a representative of a sixth distinguished bank.

Shortly after noon on Thursday, when stock market prices were crashing dizzily, when offers of stock on the floor of the Exchange met no bids at all, or, at best, bids far below the previous quotations, Charles F. Mitchell, chairman of the National City Bank, was seen to enter the offices of the Morgan firm.

The news was flashed out on the tickers and Wall Street held its breath. Mr. Mitchell had once before come to the rescue of the market earlier in the year when a severe squeeze in money had forced the call rate to 20 per cent and threatened to precipitate a panic. At that time, March 26, Mr. Mitchell threw funds into the market and made known the fact that he was prepared to offer additional amounts up to $25,000,000 at the rate of $5,000,000 at 15 per cent and a like amount at each succeeding advance of 1 per cent in the call rate.

When the head of the country's largest bank was seen to enter the offices of the powerful private banking firm, the financial community concluded at once that a rescue party was about to be organized. Succeeding flashes on the news tickers told of the entrance into the Morgan offices of Albert H. Wiggin, chairman of the Chase National Bank, William C. Potter, president of the Guaranty Trust Company, and Seward Prosser, chairman of the Bankers Trust Company. In less than half an hour the meeting was over. The bankers departed and Thomas W. Lamont, partner of the house of Morgan, spoke reassuringly to waiting reporters. On the floor of the Stock Exchange United States Steel common stock rallied from 193½ to 206 and the panic was over.

Next day it was learned that George F. Baker Jr., son of the dean of American banking, had joined the conferences of the banking group to represent the First National Bank. The adherence of this great institution, carrying with it the prestige of George F. Baker, further strengthened the faith of the financial community, and Wall Street settled down to quieter trading, confident that the danger of panic had been averted.

# WICKERSHAM STUDY LAYS RISE IN CRIME TO UNEMPLOYMENT

## This Is Experts' Finding, but Commission Holds All Theory on Causes Disputable.

### ONE MEMBER DISAGREES

#### H. W. Anderson Blames Bad Laws and Urges "Institute of Human Research."

### SING SING RECORDS GIVEN

#### Experts Say These Show Effect of Idleness—Corrupt Police Here Called Crime Factor.

*Special to The New York Times.*

WASHINGTON, Aug. 16.—Asserting that the underlying factors in this era of widespread lawlessness in the United States are too complicated and theoretical to be boiled down to more than a controversial social philosophy, the Wickersham Commission, in its thirteenth report to President Hoover, made public at the White House today, frankly admitted that "we find it impossible comprehensively to discuss the causes of crime or factors in non-observance of law."

The report, entitled "Causes of Crime" and signed by ten of the eleven Wickersham commissioners, declared it would serve "no useful purpose" to put forth theories as to criminology, either generally or in America, on the basis of some one current psychology or social philosophy, with the certainty that it represents only one phase of the thought of the time and "will not long hold ground." "For the same reason," said the report, "it would be quite as useless to develop the potentialities of each of the current theories."

But the commission's report totals about 250,000 words, so far its most lengthy document, and is composed mainly of treatises by recognized students of the subject, including Morris Ploscowe, Sheldon Fellow of Harvard University; Miss Mary Van Kleeck of the Department of Industrial Studies of the Russell Sage Foundation; Clifford R. Shaw, head of the Department of Research Sociology, and Henry D. McKay, associate criminologist of the Institute of Juvenile Research and the Behavior Research Foundation of Chicago.

#### Commission's Comment Brief.

The commission itself used only three paragraphs of the lengthy report to set forth its own views. Those views were summarized by the mere statement of its inability to put its finger on crime causes and the added assertion that "the most that was feasible was to conduct a certain number of studies of limited scope but with possibilities of general application, and bring together, in a critical review, what has been done thus far in the way of theories of criminality."

Throughout the treatises of the experts, such elements as unemployment, political influence on enforcement machinery, defective mentality, bad environment, particularly in the city slums; improper family life, broken homes and complex system of laws received important places in their discussions as to the causes of crime. The Wickersham commission presented these conclusions as strictly those of the experts, however, and did not specifically adopt any of them as its own. The law enforcement body left the whole matter without conclusion.

One of the commissioners, Henry W. Anderson of Virginia, however, refused to join with his fellow-members in making this disposition of the subject. Mr. Anderson expressed the opinion that the commissioners should not refrain from stating their own views on crime causes along with those of the so-called experts; that each had had experience with the subject and had had a chance to review it while sitting on the law enforcement committee.

Judge William S. Kenyon of Iowa likewise did not sign the report, but made no explanation in the document of his reasons.

#### Anderson Cites Lawlessness.

Mr. Anderson said that the American people have created the largest body of laws and the most complex system of government now in existence as a restraint and control of the individual conduct, but that every stage in their development has been characterized by a large and ever increasing degree of lawlessness and crime.

"No candid investigation," he said, "can ignore these facts, or the conclusions which they naturally suggest." The underlying factors in crime could no more be found in a day than could those factors be done away with by the "thoughtless enactment of laws which often serve to increase the evil." The subject demanded "thorough, consistent and scientific study, followed by courageous and constructive social action." To this end he proposed the establishment in the Federal Government of an "institute of human research," to study the broad subject of the relation of the human being to society, with special reference to the crime problem, and to coordinate material

October 27, 1929

on the subject for study and instruction.

Mr. Anderson quoted from a letter of former President Roosevelt to Sir Edward Grey in which Mr. Roosevelt said:

"Nine-tenths of wisdom is in being wise in time; and if a country lets its time for wise action pass, it may bitterly repent when a generation later it strives under disheartening difficulties to do what could have been done so easily if attempted at the right moment."

**Urges "Wisdom in Time."**

"This expression from a statesman of great foresight and of large human sympathies," said Mr. Anderson, "is fully sustained by the records of history which show one nation after another arising to play its short part in the great drama, seeking to expand its influence by power to maintain domestic order by repressive laws, only to crumble in the end as a result of social disease and internal weakness.

"The general and increasing prevalance of crime gives adequate warning that the American people should be 'wise in time' in the deeper causes to which it is due. The economic results will more than justify the expenditure and effort, but the results in social security and human happiness will be far more important in their bearing upon the future of American civilization."

Miss Mary Van Kleeck was loaned to the Wickersham commission by the Russell Sage Foundation to gather and compile certain data on causative factors in crime. Assisted by Dr. Emma A. Winslow and Ira De A. Reid, director of research for the National Urban League, Miss Van Kleeck made a special statistical study of the histories of men in Sing Sing prison, the results of which were embodied in the Wickersham report and the "Relationships Between Employment and Crime Fluctuations as Shown by Massachusetts Statistics." She also included in a separate chapter "Certain Notes on Fluctuations in Employment and Crime in New York State." Mr. Reid made a separate investigation of the special problem of the Negro as related to both work and crime.

**Idleness Held Crime Breeder.**

After a careful checking of the records of 300 of the 1,051 men who entered Sing Sing Prison, largely from Greater New York in the year ended Feb. 28, 1930, Miss Van Kleeck came to the conclusion that the ranks of the unemployed yield more material for criminals than do the ranks of the employed; that the record of unemployment among men committed is larger in hard times and less in good times; that unemployment is a circumstance present mostly in crimes against property, which constitutes 64 per cent of the crimes for which men are serving sentences in Sing Sing.

She suggested that it might be better for New York State to establish a large number of effective employment bureaus "than to build new prisons to which to send men under 30 with a past record of skill in employment and no evidence of intention to break the law."

Miss Van Kleeck cited the case of a 27-year-old man who, born in a Western State came to New York to seek employment. He could not get a job at his trade as a printer because he did not have the necessary money to pay the initial dues in the Typographical Union. He drifted from pillar to post until one day while seeking work on Long Island, he saw a purse protruding from under the arm of a woman passerby. Being actually hungry, the man snatched the purse, containing $11.89, but bungled the theft, was caught and sent to Sing Sing for a sentence of a year and a half to three years for grand larceny.

Of the group of Sing Sing prisoners studied for the report, 52 per cent were out of work at the time of the commission of crime.

**City Populates Sing Sing.**

"Within the counties of the jurisdiction of Sing Sing Prison," Miss Van Kleeck said, "the larger majority of prisoners come from Greater New York, varying from 83.3 per cent to 92.2 per cent in the ten-year period ended June 30, 1929. This means that the crimes of those men have been committed in the great majority of instances in the city.

"They are not, however, committed by non-residents. According to the prison statistics for the year ended June 30, 1929, of the 1,098 admitted in that year only 10 were non-residents of the State; 584 had been in both the locality and the State for five years or more.

"New York City and State appear to be responsible for the careers of the men at Sing Sing and conditions in the community are not favorable to law observance. By the same sign, it seems evident that, in so far as the community can control these conditions and prevent crime, New York has the opportunity to develop a program, for the men in prison have lived in the State and the locality long enough to be influenced by it and have for the most part attended the public schools there."

In separate notes on employment and crime in New York State, Miss Van Kleeck established a close concurrence between crime and business fluctuations, asserting that the record of crime from 1930 "suggests interesting inquiries which would trace changes in social and economic conditions during 100 years in New York State."

**Data on Causes "Inadequate."**

Mr. Ploscowe's part in the lengthy report of causes of crime consisted of a critical examination of literature on the subject. He concluded from his examination that a thoroughgoing investigation of the criminal situation in light of the social, political and economic development of the country has not yet been made. He granted that such an examination would be extremely difficult but said that it is an essential step "so that a program of crime prevention can aim at fundamental causes and not at effects."

Mr. Ploscowe told of various works that had been done in the morphological and psychological elements in criminality, but out of all of it he said he found "only suggestive theories rather than convincing data on the operation of physical deficiencies in the production of criminal behavior."

Neither did he find much of a convincing nature in his studies of the literature on mental factors in the growth of criminals. He attributed this, however, to the infancy of crime psychology and psychiatry. The techniques of psychologists and psychiatrists in dealing with criminal problems are still imperfect, he said.

The writings on social factors, Mr. Ploscowe found to be a bit more convincing.

"It may be stated," he said, "that while the literature on social factors does not provide completely unassailable data, it does point out specific conditions which may well be considered contributory factors in criminality.

"There seems to be no escaping the conclusion that the family is fundamental; it is the State's first bulwark against the formation of antisocial tendencies. At present it seems that in the very places where the family inadequacy is apt to be greatest, instead of offsetting the results, the community makes them worse.

**Many Convicts From Slums.**

"If nothing intervenes between the children and adult demoralizing influences, a point of almost direct contact is provided by the gang, the children's play group. Finally, the evidence as to the failure of institutional treatment points in some cases to a direct subversion of its airms."

Mr. Ploscowe noted that the New York Crime Commission, in a report published in 1928, concluded, from a study of 145 cases in Sing Sing and Elmira prisons, that the offenders from Greater New York came principally from six congested slum sections of the city. The New York commission stated in its report that until more comprehensive statistics prove or disprove his theory, the urban sociologist must be presumed to be correct when he states that isolated slums are the breeding places of crime, or at least of such types of crime as robbery, burglary and theft.

Mr. Ploscowe concluded from his study of available literature on this subject that although the lowest economic strata do furnish an undue proportion of delinquents, their contribution to the delinquent population is not very much greater than might be expected from their proportion in the general population.

Very little "except by way of declamation" had been done up to this time to show the influences on crime of the underlying philosophy of the present social and economic system "and of such manifestations of the present social order as the existence of inequality of fortune, the existence of a leisure class, the constant stimulation of needs."

**Gravity of Situation Stressed.**

"Perhaps it may be found," he said, "that the price the present organization of society must pay for its continued existence is the necessity of dealing with some individuals who will refuse to accept a material status which does not permit them to enjoy all the things they see others enjoying. Finding their justification in the existing social philosophy, in order to satisfy their desire, they may use methods which must be repressed if the present system is to continue."

The literature studied by Mr. Ploscowe left no doubt in his mind about the contribution of political influence to the "gravity" of the American criminal situation.

"The more serious aspects of the breakdown, the link between politics and crime and the consequent influence exerted over the processes of criminal justice by the politicians, the acceptance of protection money by the police, certainly contributed directly to crime," he stated.

Mr. Ploscowe said that many documents attest the practice of New York and Chicago police taking money from criminals and permitting in return the continuation of their anti-social activities. These documents consist of official investigations, statements from students of police conditions and statements of professional criminals themselves.

"In both cities," Mr. Ploscowe said, "the practice of police protection of criminals has a long history. In 1875 a legislative investigation into the causes of the increase of crime in New York stated that 'headquarters detectives are not only in collusion with thieves, but that when certain thieves have tried to reform and lead honest lives they have been instigated and actually compelled into crime.'

**Police Corruption Here Cited.**

"The Lexow investigation of the New York police force made twenty years later found the usual payment of protection of money by gambling and disorderly houses along with similar payment by swindlers, thieves, abortionists and other criminals. Nor do conditions appear to be very much better in New York at present in view of the disclosures of corruption in the police department revealed by the Seabury investigations during the past Winter.

A footnote to this last sentence referred to "the front pages of THE NEW YORK TIMES Feb. 16, 17 and 18 and March 1, 19, 20, 21, 1931. Reference again was made to THE NEW YORK TIMES of Aug. 24, 1930, for substantiation of the statement that "the present New York City investigation of the lower courts has also furnished some striking examples of political subservience, misconduct, and, what is even more important, downright lack of integrity existing in the judiciary."

Mr. Ploscowe concluded from all his studies that they only served to accentuate the need for a more fundamental examination of criminality.

In his study of the Negro phase of crime causes, Mr. Reid came to the conclusion that the part the black citizens of America play in crime is not due to any inherent racial criminality, but more to poverty and the restricted opportunity for employment. He expressed the view that the volume of crimes among Negroes is susceptible to vast improvement by merely changing some of those underlying factors.

The whole second volume of this longest report of the commission, itself comprising 410 pages, was taken up with the study of "social factors in juvenile delinquency" made by Mr. Shaw and Mr. McKay. As they are connected with welfare organizations in Chicago, their study had largely to do with that city.

**Delinquency a Group Behavior.**

They listed the results of their study in twenty-four separate findings, but all to the major purport that the delinquent child is the potential criminal and "a delinquent or criminal act is a part of a dynamic life process and should be considered as such in the treatment of cases."

While the larger part of the Shaw-McKay study dealt with Chicago, investigations were made of the child problem also in Philadelphia, Richmond, Cleveland, Seattle and Denver, for purposes of confirmation of the general conclusion. One of the major purposes of the inquiry was to establish, through a study of these representative cities, the influence of city environment on the problem of juvenile delinquency.

It was found, for instance, that juvenile delinquents in Chicago come largely from areas adjacent to the central business district and industrial areas which are characterized by physical deterioration, decreasing resident population, high rates of dependency and high rates of adult crime.

It was found also that the rate of delinquency among families of immigrant origin decreases as the foreign born groups migrate further from these established delinquency areas. Juvenile delinquency, they found, is largely a matter of group behavior, as only 25 per cent of the cases studied involved delinquent acts committed singly, and the whole problem is a product of natural development, resulting from the "inter-action" between the individual and the successive social situations in which he lives.

# KIDNAPPING STIRS NATION

## WORLD AFFAIRS ASIDE

All Else Faded in Importance Before the Empty Cradle in the Lindbergh Home.

## PROGRESS IN WASHINGTON

Economic Rehabilitation Advanced—Stock Exchange Inquiry Ordered.

**By ARTHUR KROCK.**
Special to The New York Times.

WASHINGTON, March 5.—An empty cradle in a house on Sourland Mountain in New Jersey filled the heart and the mind of America last week. The great nation of more than sixscore millions thought of little else. What were the perversions of humanity which could prompt so cruel a plan as the kidnapping of small Charles A. Lindbergh Jr.? Was the baby being properly cared

for in the custody of unthinkable people like these? Would he be safely restored to his despairing parents?

The Chinese and the Japanese might broaden their bloody shambles at Shanghai. The Assembly of the League of Nations at Geneva might meet or evade the issue in the Far East. The Democrats and the Republicans in Congress might break the truce that never had existed. Tax bills might be drawn and new amendments to the Constitution proposed. But for the bulk of the week no one in America seemed to care, and few in the world. Until the infant, "just learning to toddle," was back in his crib again, the ordinary great concerns of men seemed uninteresting.

This national concentration on the tragedy near Hopewell, N. J., was not the result of hero worship. There was something of Burns's lament of "man's inhumanity to man." It was not that the daughter of Dwight Whitney Morrow and the young man who first and alone flew the Atlantic were presumed to love their baby more than obscure parents love theirs. The stolen child suddenly became a symbol of the home men and women toil and suffer to achieve. And to shatter that home, putting an unfair penalty on courage and fame, seemed to the American people the most despicable of crimes.

March 6, 1932

---

## THE GOVERNOR'S ADDRESS.

### Mr. Roosevelt Is Accused of Ignoring Some Well-Known Facts.

To the Editor of The New York Times:

Governor Roosevelt's charge in his speech delivered last night, that the administration is not doing anything for the farmer or for the small banks and loan companies, exposes him to the danger of being classified with the "shallow thinkers" for whom he expresses his scorn.

Is it possible that so well posted a man as Governor Roosevelt is supposed to be has not heard of the immense loans which have been made by the Farm Board with the express purpose of trying to peg the price of wheat for the benefit of the farmer and the small banks? Has he never heard of the $50,000,000 fund which has been provided for the farmers in order that they may borrow to plant their crops? And has he heard of any loans being made to large banks by the Reconstruction Finance Corporation, whom he accuses of loaning to large banks, who do not need the loans, rather than to small banks which have not been properly managed, which do need the loans and who are getting them?

He speaks of restoring the purchasing power of the farmer, but does not tell us how he would propose to do it. The secret ought to be worth a great deal, and I wonder if he will keep it until he gets in the White House, meanwhile promising every one that he can perform this miracle which the Farm Board has

not been able to bring about with all its hundreds of millions. The Governor just expects us to take his word for it and vote him into the White House, when he will divulge his wonderful secret, which it would not do to reveal at this time, even if a languishing country might benefit immensely from it immediately, as the Republicans might apply his wonderful remedy and then claim all of the credit for it!

If the Governor wishes to escape the accusation of "shallow thinking," he ought to find something nearer the truth to complain about, such as the delay to balance the budget; but that would strike his own party as well as the opposition. But if he were a real leader, he would point out how the English budget was balanced in a fraction of the time that Congress has been trying to balance ours; how they laid aside all political motives and considerations and all parties, except the Labor party; united patriotically to reduce expenses, starting first by a reduction of 10 per cent in all official salaries which our Governor, I believe, does not advocate; and now England has turned the corner, while we are still languishing and waiting for something constructive to come out of Washington!

A real patriot could make such an appeal, and how the politicians who are wasting time playing politics would scurry to their rat-holes!

HOWARD W. STARR.
New York, April 9, 1932.

April 11, 1932

---

# BONUS ARMY INVASION NEW CAPITOL WORRY

Greater Influx Feared as Costigan Asks $75,000 for 525 Camped in the City.

Special to The New York Times.

WASHINGTON, May 30.—While the nation was celebrating Memorial Day, 525 veterans of the World War, 300 from the Pacific Coast and 225 from scattering States, camped here today after arriving yesterday in trucks, prepared, their leader said, to stay here until Congress accedes to their demand for immediate cash payment of their bonus certificates. They were quartered in two vacant buildings in different parts of the city and fed by army rolling kitchens.

"We are going to stay here until the bonus is paid, whether it is next year or 1945," George Kleinholz of Portland, Ore., second in command of the Pacific Coast group, asserted.

"There are only 300 in the Portland group, but 75 per cent of them are property owners and married men who have been without work for the past two years. They don't care what happens to them until the bonus is paid. Don't intimate

that we are holding any power over individual members of Congress. Just take a look at these fellows. If you offer any one a job at $1 a day tomorrow he will take it. There is not a radical in this group."

**Food and Bed Sacks Supplied.**

The Chief of Police, Pelham D. Glassford, a retired Brigadier General, obtained the two rolling kitchens from the War College. Secretary Hurley ordered 2,000 bed sacks delivered to police for the veterans, and General Glassford asked social organizations to contribute two tons of straw to fill them. Until the straw is supplied the veterans will be compelled to sleep on bare floors.

General Glassford has served notice on the unwelcome visitors that when funds for their support are exhausted, and if Congress fails to authorize an appropriation, he will request them to leave within forty-eight hours.

Leaders of Congress are showing anxiety over the predicament caused by the arrival of the bonus demonstrators, whose leaders predicted tonight that they would number at least 25,000 within the next two weeks.

"If they come in here and sit down and have three meals furnished free every day, then God knows what will happen to us," a leader of the House said. "There are more than 8,500,000 persons out of work in the country, most of them with families. If the government can feed these who are here, then we can expect an influx that will startle the entire country."

Walter W. Waters of Oregon, com-

---

# HOOVER ORDERS EVICTION

Blaming Reds, He Asserts Bonus Camps Included Many Criminals.

## QUICK ACTION BY SOLDIERS

Eject Squatters After Police Fall and Then Burn Camps In and Near Capital.

Special to The New York Times.

WASHINGTON, July 28.—Amidst scenes reminiscent of the mopping-up of a town in the World War, Federal troops late today drove the army of bonus seekers from the shanty village near Pennsylvania Avenue in which the veterans had been entrenched for months. Earlier in the day the police had fought and lost

# TROOPS DRIVE 1 KILLED,

a battle there which resulted in the death of one veteran, possibly fatal injuries to a policeman and a long list of other casualties, many of them serious.

Ordered to the scene by President Hoover after the District of Columbia authorities confessed defeat, detachments of infantry, cavalry, machine-gun and tank crews laid down an effective tear-gas barrage which disorganized the bonus-seekers, and then set fire to the shacks and tents left behind by the veterans on the government land near Third and Pennsylvania Avenues, scene of the earlier clash with the police.

**Begin to Clear Anacostia.**

After the disputed area near the Capitol had been cleared, the troops moved late in the evening on Camp Marks, on the Anacostia River, the bonus army's principal encampment. At 10 o'clock this evening infantrymen with drawn bayonets advanced into the camp, driving the crowd before them with tear gas bombs. Then they applied the torch to the shacks in which the veterans lived. Troops shortly afterward halted at the main bonus camp in response to mander of the Portland contingent, predicted additions to the ranks.

"When they find the heart of the nation is willing to house and feed us until we are treated as the government promised, they will—and should—come on here. We mean to stay until the bonus is paid, whether it is next year or 1945."

Representative Patman of Texas, who is trying to force a vote on the bonus on June 13, conferred with Waters and is understood to have told him not to lose faith that the bonus would be paid before the expiration of the present session of Congress.

### Lewis Rebukes Marchers.

In an address delivered at the National Soldiers' Home, Senator Lewis of Illinois declared that by "abandoning the plea for justice and adopting in its place threat and coercion veterans are causing their fellow-countrymen to wonder whether their soldiers served for patriotism or merely for pay."

If the veterans persisted in "terroristic tactics," they would endanger their chances of receiving any favorable treatment whatsoever. The present period of national distress was one which demanded of the veterans service instead of criticism.

Instead, the country was treated to the sight of veterans marching on Washington to threaten Congress that it must grant them favors and money. By "taunt and terror" the veterans counted on intimidating Congress.

"I warn you as your fellow-soldier and friend," he continued, "that you risk the defeat of the relief measures you now have a right to hope for by placing yourselves where the charge can be made that you have come here to terrorize the public servants and force their surrender through weakness or cowardice."

Instead of capitulating, legislators would "lean backward and defy" even the rightful demands of the veterans.

## BONUS MARCHERS ENCAMPED AT WASHINGTON.

Associated Press Photo.

Group of the advocates of immediate payment of the bonus gathered around an army kitchen at the Capitol. A bugler announces that the food is ready. The new Department of Agriculture Building is in the background.

May 31, 1932

# VETERANS FROM CAPITAL; SCORES HURT IN DAY OF STRIFE

what General Perry L. Miles, commanding the soldiers, said was a Presidential order. Theodore G. Joslin, the President's secretary, later denied positively that the President had issued any such order, and word came from the camp that the troops would resume operations within an hour.

At 11:15 P. M. the first troop of cavalry had moved into the disordered camp, now a mass of flames as the bonus-seeking veterans set fire to their own miserable shacks. At midnight practically all the veterans had left the place.

War _ that the soldiers would use tear gas the veterans had arranged to evacuate the 600 women and children earlier.

The normal population of Camp Marks was augmented by more than 2,000 veterans who had been evicted from other camps, bringing the total male population to 7,000.

### Troops Avoid Bloodshed.

Soon after the khaki-clad regulars descended on the various camps along Pennsylvania Avenue this afternoon the bonus seekers were straggling sullenly away from the ominous blue mist of the tear gas, leaderless and apparently demoralized, seeking shelter in other open places scattered afar through the city. A few of them were sore from minor bruises, but on the whole the Federal troops had conducted their offensive without bloodshed. The veteran who was killed in the earlier clash with the police was identified tonight as William Hashka of Chicago.

The day's disturbances were blamed on the radical element among the bonus-seekers. Walter W. Waters, the young veteran from Oregon who led the unsuccessful bonus march to Washington, disclaimed responsibility for his followers' part in resisting the first eviction order of the police. Waters announced tonight that he was "through."

"The men got out of control. There was nothing and there is nothing that I can do to control them," he said.

With the bonus army in the city proper dispersed into straggling and woebegone remnants, the hovels and tents which had been their homes were the scene of another kind of fight tonight—when numerous fire crews were called out to control the flames started by the torches of the victorious army troops. The bonus men will be unable to "dig in" to their old camp sites in the city because the land is now being prepared for the Federal building operations which government authorities have decided should not be delayed any longer.

The clash with the police earlier in the day was short and furious. The advancing police, met by a hail of brickbats, first used their nightsticks and then began to shoot, after one of the bluecoats, George Scott, was felled by a brick that fractured his skull. His condition tonight was serious, and so was that of one of the wounded veterans.

In ordering out the troops to take the situation in hand after the police had failed, President Hoover explained that many of the bonus seekers who had stayed on after Congress had adjourned, were not veterans. The President said that many were "Communists and persons with criminal records."

The necessity of proclaiming martial law was avoided by War Department officials through an order to the army officers to turn over all prisoners to the civil authorities.

The order issued by Secretary of War Hurley to General Douglas MacArthur, chief of staff, which quickly brought the troops from near-by forts and camps in Virginia, read as follows:

"The President has just informed me that the civil government of the District of Columbia has reported to him that it is unable to maintain law and order in the District.

"You will have United States troops proceed immediately to the scene of the disorder. Cooperate fully with the District of Columbia police force, which is now in charge. Surround the affected area and clear it without delay.

"Turn over all prisoners to the civil authorities.

"In your orders, insist that any women and children who may be in the affected area be accorded every consideration and kindness. Use all humanity consistent with the due execution of this order."

Soon afterward the troops, with steel helmets and fixed bayonets, were marching down Pennsylvania Avenue past a throng of citizens, some of whom jeered them and cheered the veterans. Cavalry, tanks, machine gunners, engineers and infantrymen went to work immediately. Meanwhile huge army trucks waited in readiness to carry off those who refused to move. Ambulances were mobilized to care for possible casualties.

On side streets army tanks and machine gunners waited to reduce to rubble and smoking ruin the shanty towns which the veterans had stubbornly refused to vacate, even in the face of a sweeping eviction order that was issued by Attorney General Mitchell after the first fight with the police.

\* \* \* \* \*

July 29, 1932

# Text of the Inaugural Address; President for Vigorous Action

### "This Is Pre-eminently the Time to Speak the Truth," He Says, in Demand That "the Temple of Our Civilization Be Restored to the Ancient Truths."

Special to The New York Times.

WASHINGTON, March 4.—*President Roosevelt's inaugural address, delivered immediately after he took the oath, was as follows:*

President Hoover, Mr. Chief Justice, my friends:

This is a day of national consecration, and I am certain that my fellow-Americans expect that on my induction into the Presidency I will address them with a candor and a decision which the present situation of our nation impels.

This is pre-eminently the time to speak the truth, the whole truth, frankly and boldly. Nor need we shrink from honestly facing conditions in our country today. This great nation will endure as it has endured, will revive and will prosper.

So first of all let me assert my firm belief that the only thing we have to fear is fear itself—nameless, unreasoning, unjustified terror which paralyzes needed efforts to convert retreat into advance.

In every dark hour of our national life a leadership of frankness and vigor has met with that understanding and support of the people themselves which is essential to victory. I am convinced that you will again give that support to leadership in these critical days.

In such a spirit on my part and on yours we face our common difficulties. They concern, thank God, only material things. Values have shrunken to fantastic levels; taxes have risen; our ability to pay has fallen; government of all kinds is faced by serious curtailment of income; the means of exchange are frozen in the currents of trade; the withered leaves of industrial enterprise lie on every side; farmers find no markets for their produce; the savings of many years in thousands of families are gone.

More important, a host of unemployed citizens face the grim problem of existence, and an equally great number toil with little return. Only a foolish optimist can deny the dark realities of the moment.

Yet our distress comes from no failure of substance. We are stricken by no plague of locusts. Compared with the perils which our forefathers conquered because they believed and were not afraid, we have still much to be thankful for. Nature still offers her bounty and human efforts have multiplied it. Plenty is at our doorstep, but a generous use of it languishes in the very sight of the supply.

## Charges "Money Changers" Lack Vision.

Primarily, this is because the rulers of the exchange of mankind's goods have failed through their own stubbornness and their own incompetence, have admitted their failure and abdicated. Practices of the unscrupulous money changers stand indicted in the court of public opinion, rejected by the hearts and minds of men.

True, they have tried, but their efforts have been cast in the pattern of an outworn tradition. Faced by failure of credit, they have proposed only the lending of more money.

Stripped of the lure of profit by which to induce our people to follow their false leadership, they have resorted to exhortations, pleading tearfully for restored confidence. They know only the rules of a generation of self-seekers.

They have no vision, and when there is no vision the people perish.

The money changers have fled from their high seats in the temple of our civilization. We may now restore that temple to the ancient truths.

The measure of the restoration lies in the extent to which we apply social values more noble than mere monetary profit.

Happiness lies not in the mere possession of money; it lies in the joy of achievement, in the thrill of creative effort.

The joy and moral stimulation of work no longer must be forgotten in the mad chase of evanescent profits. These dark days will be worth all they cost us if they teach us that our true destiny is not to be ministered unto but to minister to ourselves and to our fellow-men.

Recognition of the falsity of material wealth as the standard of success goes hand in hand with the abandonment of the false belief that public office and high political position are to be valued only by the standards of pride of place and personal profit; and there must be an end to a conduct in banking and in business which too often has given to a sacred trust the likeness of callous and selfish wrongdoing.

### "Confidence Thrives Only on Honor."

Small wonder that confidence languishes, for it thrives only on honesty, on honor, on the sacredness of obligations, on faithful protection, on unselfish performance. Without them it cannot live.

Restoration calls, however, not for changes in ethics alone. This nation asks for action, and action now.

Our greatest primary task is to put people to work. This is no unsolvable problem if we face it wisely and courageously.

It can be accomplished in part by direct recruiting by the government itself, treating the task as we would treat the emergency of a war, but at the same time, through this employment, accomplishing greatly needed projects to stimulate and reorganize the use of our natural resources.

Hand in hand with this, we must frankly recognize the overbalance of population in our industrial centres and, by engaging on a national scale in a redistribution, endeavor to provide a better use of the land for those best fitted for the land.

The task can be helped by definite efforts to raise the values of agricultural products and with this the power to purchase the output of our cities.

It can be helped by preventing realistically the tragedy of the growing loss, through foreclosure, of our small homes and our farms.

It can be helped by insistence that the Federal, State and local governments act forthwith on the demand that their cost be drastically reduced.

It can be helped by the unifying of relief activities which today are often scattered, uneconomical and unequal. It can be helped by national planning for and supervision of all forms of transportation and of communications and other utilities which have a definitely public character.

There are many ways in which it can be helped, but it can never be helped merely by talking about it. We must act, and act quickly.

Finally, in our progress toward a resumption of work we require two safeguards against a return of the evils of the old order; there must be a strict supervision of all banking and credits and investments; there must be an end to speculation with other people's money, and there must be provision for an adequate but sound currency.

### Must Deal First With Home Emergency.

These are the lines of attack. I shall presently urge upon a new Congress in special session detailed measures for their fulfillment, and I shall seek the immediate assistance of the several States.

Through this program of action we address ourselves to putting our own national house in order and making income balance outgo.

Our international trade relations, though vastly important, are, in point of time and necessity, secondary to the establishment of a sound national economy.

I favor as a practical policy the putting of first things first. I shall spare no effort to restore world trade by international economic readjustment, but the emergency at home cannot wait on that accomplishment.

The basic thought that guides these specific means of national recovery is not narrowly nationalistic.

It is the insistence, as a first consideration, upon the interdependence of the various elements in and parts of the United States—a recognition of the old and permanently important manifestation of the American spirit of the pioneer.

It is the way to recovery. It is the immediate way. It is the strongest assurance that the recovery will endure.

In the field of world policy I would dedicate this nation to the policy of the good neighbor—the neighbor who resolutely respects himself and, because he does so, respects the rights of others—the neighbor who respects his obligations and respects the sanctity of his agreements in and with a world of neighbors.

If I read the temper of our people correctly, we now realize, as we have never realized before, our interdependence on each other; that we cannot merely take, but we must give as well; that if we are to go forward we must move as a trained and loyal army willing to sacrifice for the good of a common discipline, because, without such discipline, no progress is made, no leadership becomes effective.

We are, I know, ready and willing to submit our lives and property to such discipline because it makes possible a leadership which aims at a larger good.

This I propose to offer, pledging that the larger purposes will bind upon us all as a sacred obligation with a unity of duty hitherto evoked only in time of armed strife.

### Action Feasible Under Our Form of Government.

With this pledge taken, I assume unhesitatingly the leadership of this great army of our people, dedicated to a disciplined attack upon our common problems.

Action in this image and to this end is feasible under the form of government which we have inherited from our ancestors.

Our Constitution is so simple and practical that it is possible always to meet extraordinary needs by changes in emphasis and arrangement without loss of essential form.

That is why our constitutional system has proved itself the most superbly enduring political mechanism the modern world has produced. It has met every stress of vast expansion of territory, of foreign wars, of bitter internal strife, of world relations.

It is to be hoped that the normal balance of executive and legislative authority may be wholly adequate to meet the unprecedented task before us. But it may be that an unprecedented demand and need for undelayed action may call for temporary departure from that normal balance of public procedure.

I am prepared under my constitutional duty to recommend the measures that a stricken nation in the midst of a stricken world may require.

These measures, or such other measures as the Congress may build out of its experience and wisdom, I shall seek, within my constitutional authority, to bring to speedy adoption.

But in the event that the Congress shall fail to take one of these two courses, and in the event that the national emergency is still critical, I shall not evade the clear course of duty that will then confront me.

### May Ask Congress for Broad Power.

I shall ask the Congress for the one remaining instrument to meet the crisis—broad executive power to wage a war against the emergency as great as the power that would be given to me if we were in fact invaded by a foreign foe.

For the trust reposed in me I will return the courage and the devotion that befit the time. I can do no less.

We face the arduous days that lie before us in the warm courage of national unity; with the clear consciousness of seeking old and precious moral values; with the clean satisfaction that comes from the stern performance of duty by old and young alike.

We aim at the assurance of a rounded and permanent national life.

We do not distrust the future of essential democracy. The people of the United States have not failed. In their need they have registered a mandate that they want direct, vigorous action.

They have asked for discipline and direction under leadership. They have made me the present instrument of their wishes. In the spirit of the gift I take it.

In this dedication of a nation we humbly ask the blessing of God. May He protect each and every one of us! May He guide me in the days to come!

March 5, 1933

---

# SHOALS BILL HELD SECURITIES PERIL

## W. L. Willkie Says Utility Holdings of $400,000,000 in South Would Be Worthless.

## POWER LINES ARE OFFERED

### Hearing Is Told That the Government Could Not Compete on Fertilizer.

Special to THE NEW YORK TIMES.

WASHINGTON, April 14.—Passage of a Muscle Shoals bill with Federal construction of transmission lines provided would make worthless $400,000,000 of securities of six Southern utilities companies, W. L. Willkie, president of the Commonwealth and Southern Corporation, declared today before the House Military Affairs Committee.

He said that enactment would virtually mean confiscation of property of the companies concerned, stripping them of constitutional rights.

"Every security house in New York," he testified, "has sent word to their customers that passage of the bill would ruin their securities. If the purpose of the measure is to distribute the greatest power to the greatest number at the lowest rate we offer you the means to do it.

"We will absorb the power as fast as we can. If it is necessary we will contract to carry your power and pass the savings on to the ultimate consumer."

Mr. Willkie reiterated the faith of his companies in the President's general development plan for the Tennessee Valley, but declared that it would be "worse than a crime" to destroy the existing companies by depriving them of their market.

"The officials of these companies are trustees and every single dollar of the $400,000,000 outstanding has been approved by a State agency in the State where they were sold," he said.

"Thousands of letters have come to us from disturbed investors and if this bill passes as now written, those securities will be destroyed."

### Opposes Fertilizer Proposal.

Opposition from another source developed during the afternoon session, when Charles J. Brand, executive secretary of the National Fertilizer Association, insisted that fertilizer could not be manufactured at the Muscle Shoals plant as cheaply as by private industry.

Much of his testimony was a repetition of statements he has made before the committee during the last twelve years as to previous Shoals legislation, and at one point he expressed regret that Representative James, former chairman of the committee, had to listen again to this "tiresome" story.

Replying to Representative Goss of Connecticut, Mr. Brand said he knew that the government could not produce fertilizer as cheaply as private concerns, and that he had also been told that electricity could not be produced as cheaply by the government.

"The President wants to," Mr. Goss said.

"I wonder if he does," answered Mr. Brand.

He saw no occasion for putting the government into business, remarking:

"Don't knock out a window to kill a fly."

Replying to Mr. Goss again, he declared that he still held an opinion he expressed last year, that it would not be a bad arrangement to lease the shoals to private industry.

Representative Brown of Kentucky appeared this afternoon to ask that the legislation be amended to provide for development of the Cumberland River. He said that a dam near Jamestown would develop 800,000,000 kilowatt hours, which would care for the needs of the State. It would make the river navigable, he added, and benefit the mountainous section of Kentucky.

### Trend Toward Steam Plants.

"During the last administration the Red Cross fed the hungry Republicans down in our State," he said, "and our Highway Department fed the Democrats. A lot of our people lost money in Insull Utilities investments and we want a chance for cheap power to help our people."

Mrs. Harris T. Baldwin, chairman of the Living Cost Department of the League of Women Voters, told the committee that her organization endorsed the general purposes of the bill, but objected to government manufacture of fertilizer on a large scale.

J. M. Barry, vice president and general manager of the Alabama Power Company, said gross revenue of the company in 1932 was $15,583,840, a decrease of $2,174,603 from 1931, and that his company paid $1,981,661 in taxes in 1932.

Outstanding in securities were $132,680,603, 51 per cent of which were owned by Alabama women. He said steam generating plants cost but $70 per kilowatt to build, whereas hydro-electric plants cost $160.

"Development of the past few years has been toward steam plants," he declared. "The trend has been toward lower construction costs and more efficient operation."

April 15, 1933

# THE TENNESSEE RIVER PROJECT: FIRST STEP IN A NATIONAL PLAN

## President Roosevelt Envisions the Development of Other Great Areas in a Program That Embraces a New Settlement of Lands

*Congress is now debating President Roosevelt's plan for the utilization of the Muscle Shoals power sources and the development of the Tennessee Valley area. The following article reveals the possibilities opened up by the proposed development and shows its relation to national planning.*

### By BENTON MacKAYE,
**Vice President, Regional Planning Association of America.**

"IN short, this power development [Muscle Shoals] leads logically to national planning. * * * It touches and gives life to all forms of human concerns." This epitomized President Roosevelt's historic message to Congress on April 10.

The President, in picturing for us the complete use of the Tennessee Valley—in calling thus upon the "vision of the pioneer"—takes the greatest step yet taken to meet the challenge to our country's future implied by Matthew Arnold when he said: "The test of your democracy will come with the exhaustion of your public lands."

Such time has come. The unreserved public lands are practically exhausted and a free farm out West is no longer an alternative for a job (or lack of job) back East. So Mr. Roosevelt proposes to do something about it—immediately in this emergency; he would enable Uncle Sam again to open up the country, not in the old way, but in a new way. How?

Let the national government undertake specific public works in a single river basin; and, if it is successful there, repeat the job in other regions. The region first chosen is the Tennessee Valley. "Envisioned in its entirety," says the President, the use of the Tennessee "transcends mere power development." And he sketches a larger picture. This picture has three parts: (1) Reforestation, (2) reclamation, (3) resettlement.

### Three Uses of the Forest.

Reforestation is much more than tree planting. Many people do not realize this, but Mr. Roosevelt does. Forest growth, he says, "should be thinned out to give the remaining trees a chance to grow." The President knows forestry. Indeed, the whole American forest east of the Mississippi should be treated to a vast process of thinning. Forests and mountains go together; the highest peaks east of the Rockies occur in country contiguous to this very Tennessee basin; and some ten national forest areas have been purchased on their

slopes. The highest of all—the Great Smokies—have been included in a national park. Thus all three uses of the forest are at hand—timber, recreation, protection or stream control.

This protective feature is vital—especially down there on the Carolina highland with its drenching rainfall (second heaviest on the continent). The protective forest cover on the mountain slope acts as a natural spongelike carpet, sopping up the rainfall and letting it ooze out again in gentle streamlets. Thus, the forest is a natural reservoir. Since protection forests, like timber forests, need thinning out and planting up, the President's forestation program fits into his Tennessee program.

Reclamation covers a multitude of nature's sins—especially her fickleness in supplying water for man's needs. Rivers are temperamental, their waters rising high or low, according to the hour's whim. Rainfall, and not the river, is, of course, responsible; and so it happens that large portions of the nation's areas are too dry or else too wet. Irrigation of the desert and drainage of the swamp form the

two main tasks of reclamation. In the valley of the Tennessee, as in the lower Mississippi, reclamation consists chiefly in the control of stream flow.

### Two Kinds of Stream Flow.

There are two kinds of stream flow to be controlled. One is the flow of water; the other is the flow of soil suspended in the water. This flow of soil comes from erosion of the land. Erosion cannot be stopped, for it is part of the geologic process, but it can be reduced by engineering means. To neglect these means is to stand by and watch good farm land slide needlessly into the water. "Thousands of acres are now in the Gulf of Mexico," says Senator Norris.

With stream flow, effective control begins at the source; it begins with the forest cover up on the mountain slope—the "natural reservoir." Next comes the man-made flood waters. A baker's dozen of these great storage tanks are already built on the upper branches of the Tennessee—on the Ocoee River, the Cheoah, the Pigeon, the French Broad, the Nolichucky. An-

other baker's dozen are mapped out for these same streams. Over on the Holston and Clinch Rivers more reservoirs are planned, the main series being on the latter stream above Cove Creek. The biggest "tanks" of all occur down stream: one near Chattanooga, the other held by the Wilson Dam at Muscle Shoals.

Resettlement is the final goal—to give the people in the great Eastern urban centres a chance for elbow room. This means living in towns of decently small sizes, which means decentralizing the manufacturing industry, which means the spread of cheap electricity. Each step is provided for in the Tennessee Valley; there is plenty of room for the towns (without crowding), and there is plenty of latent water horsepower—610,000 at Wilson Dam, 3,518,000 in the ten main projects on the river proper, 6,605,000 in the total projected system. All this involves three kinds of construction—towns, roads, power equipment.

### The Tennessee Valley Authority.

The legal machinery is contained in Senator Norris's bill—the "Tennessee Valley act of 1933." This puts the job in the hands of three men—a so-called "Tennessee Valley Authority." Its immediate duties relate to the power development at Muscle Shoals. One point of this development is cheap electric current; and the final means of delivering it is cheap transmission. To get this the authority would first take direct charge of generating the power at the shoals. Next it is empowered to build transmission lines and sell the current (at wholesale) to towns or farm cooperative groups. Also it may sell to private companies, but under a strict regulation of the ultimate rates to be charged. Thus appears to be settled the long-fought question of transmission.

The authority is directed to provide for sundry other utilities—fertilizer production, demonstration farms and laboratories, fixed nitrogen plants. The War Department will build a dam at Cove Creek. The President is directed, "from time to time," to recommend legislation in respect of reforestation, reclamation, resettlement.

What of the costs? A bond issue of $50,000,000 is authorized, to run forty years at 3 per cent. This would make a start only. The costs would depend, of course, on how far we cared to go. The President is reported to have said that he would like ultimately to place 200,000 men. At $500 per man per year the ultimate annual charge would be $100,000,000. Of this the reservoirs would take the lion's share, for they are expensive things. The Wilson Dam cost $47,000,000; the Cove Creek Dam is estimated at $34,000,000.

### Resettling the Country.

Reforestation, reclamation, resettlement, and the greatest of these comes last—the control of population and migration. To visualize

this (the big feature of the plan) we must see it in perspective. We all know about the Mayflower and Plymouth Rock, the covered wagon and that second great American migration led by the iron horse. But what about the third—that inflow from the rural areas to the big cities? It marked the social culmination of the generation just elapsed—the one between the two Roosevelts. The big cities, saturated by this "inflow," are beginning now to burst their bounds, and a definite "backflow" issues to the suburbs and beyond.

Mr. Roosevelt's vision has recognized this point. In his annual message of 1932 to the New York Legislature he said:

We seem to have established that the distribution of population during recent years has got out of balance, and that there is a definite overpopulation of the larger communities. * * * An immediate gain can occur if as many people as possible can return closer to the sources of agricultural food supply. This is not a mere "back-to-the-farm" movement. It is based on the fact that the pendulum has swung too far in the direction of the cities and that a readjustment must take place to restore the economic and sociological balance.

I am a great believer in the larger aspects of regional planning and in my judgment the time has come for this State to adopt a far-reaching policy of land utilization and of population distribution.

### A Part of National Planning.

What Governor Roosevelt said a year ago about New York, President Roosevelt says now about America. "Our nation has 'just grown,'" he says. "It is time to extend planning to a wider field. * * * If we are successful here [in the Tennessee Valley] we can march on, step by step, in a like development of other great natural territorial units."

To realize this we must look at some national geography. The Tennessee Valley is one of the constituent valleys of that far-flung Mississippi Basin which occupies two-fifths of the area of Continental United States. It is part of the headwater rim of the Mississippi Basin; it is one of five critical areas controlling in large measure the sources of the Father of Waters.

The others are the Pittsburgh-

Allegheny area, the Minnesota-Wisconsin forest area, the Columbia-Yellowstone area and the Colorado-Platte area. All these areas are "upstream" on the Mississippi drainage system. And on the upstream control of these five valleys depends in large measure the reclamation—downstream—of a sixth empire, namely, the fertile flood-plain of the lower Mississippi herself.

### An Intermountain Area.

The Tennessee is not only a member of the Mississippi family of valleys but also a member of another independent family of valleys; it is a member of that long string of intermountain areas collectively known among geographers as the "Great Appalachian Valley." This is also called the "great highway" —from Southland to Northland, from Chattanooga to Lake Champlain. Within a day's ride of this valley—and highway—lives half the population of the country.

The future of this great eastern lane is graphically prophesied by Professor J. Russell Smith. This future, he says, "seems to be plainly marked in the continuation of its present. Everywhere it is a region of beautiful landscape, healthful climate, fertile soil, with abundant supplies of raw materials. It will soon be supplied with electric power from mine-mouths and waterpower plants." He adds:

It seems to be plainly destined for a continued growth in manufacture which will dot it from end to end with a succession of small cities. These will have the great advantage of not becoming metropolises in size, and for that reason will have better opportunities to get food, raw material and space to live.

And what the Appalachian Valley is to the Atlantic Coast the Columbia-Sacramento Valley is to the Pacific Coast; this great lane flanks the Sierra-Cascade range from Los Angeles to Puget Sound.

Here, then, are a dozen belts and areas, related by natural geographic features, covering perhaps a fifth of the nation's acreage, which together constitute a realm of future settlement. Here indeed is a new "public domain." Here are the related lanes in the framework of a national planning—and the Tennessee Valley is strategic in the scheme.

April 16, 1933

# HUTCHINS DEFENDS THE 'BRAINS TRUST'

### Head of Chicago University Says Roosevelt's Advisers Give 'Honest Intelligence.'

#### INDEPENDENCE AN ASSET

#### Insull 'Travesty' Might Have Been Avoided, He Declares, if Professors Had Been Heeded.

A defense of President Roosevelt's "brains trust" and of professors generally was made before the luncheon of the Bond Club yesterday by Dr. Robert Maynard Hutchins, president of the University of Chicago, whose subject was, "The professor is sometimes right."

Declaring the professor was likely to be right because he pursued truth for its own sake and had no vested interests that he was struggling to protect, Dr. Hutchins said the professor was independent and free to exercise his reason even though it led him to criticize established institutions or policies.

"The most recent phase of the depression has come with the realization that after three-and-a-half years of psalm-singing, the boat is sinking more rapidly than ever and perhaps some new devices might be tried to see whether it can be saved," he declared. "Many of the new devices that are being tried originated with professors and some of them are being conducted under their personal supervision.

#### Held Especially Fitted.

"Now, for all I know, a great many things may be said against

these gentlemen. I know a few of them personally. I cannot speak of their social graces, their individual talents or their domestic habits. It may be that they are open to criticism in any or all of these important areas. But I do feel competent to pass on the principal, if not the sole, criticism I have heard since Mr. Roosevelt moved the government to Washington, and that criticism is that his advisers are professors.

"Now, it is precisely because they are professors that they have a contribution to make which neither politicians nor business men have yet offered, and as long as they remain professors and do not become politicians or business men, they will continue to make that contribution; and that contribution is the application of a clear, disinterested, honest, trained intelligence to the great problems that confront us. Such intelligence some politicians and business men possess. It is not the outstanding characteristic of their craft, nor can it be said that many of those who have ruled over us in the past ten years have given much evidence of it."

#### Tariff Bill Assailed.

Had his suggestions concerning professors been made four years ago, said Dr. Hutchins, they would have been regarded as "the grossest heresy." Those were the days, he said, when "the new era cast its rosy glow over the operations of practical men and when intelligence was a positive handicap to success," the days when professors who suggested that all was not well with society were classed as "reds" or "pinks."

"And yet, I am prepared to defend the proposition that the Insull travesty could have been avoided if the public had been in any mood to pay any attention whatever to the repeated warnings that issued from the universities in Chicago," he added. "More or less in this period all, or almost all, the professors of economics in America urged Mr. Hoover not to sign the Hawley-Smoot tariff bill. He signed it and gave new impetus to the world depression."

May 18, 1933

# CALLS SOCIALISM 'BRAIN TRUST' AIM

### Hatfield Asserts 'New Deal' Follows Ideas of Stalin, Mussolini and Hitler.

#### MARKET RIGGING CHARGED

#### Senator Says Speculators Are Gambling They Will Be Able to Unload Holdings on Public.

Special to THE NEW YORK TIMES.
WASHINGTON, May 30.—An assertion that the Roosevelt administration, guided by the "brain

trust," was "endeavoring to force socialism upon the American people under the guise of industrial democracy" was made by Senator Hatfield, chairman of the Republican Senatorial campaign committee, in a Senate speech this afternoon. In an attack upon the National Industrial Recovery Bill and other essentials of the Roosevelt program, he said:

"The 'new deal,' while it sings the praises of Jefferson and Jackson, is more in keeping with the preachings of Norman Thomas, Stalin, Mussolini and Hitler. Since March 4 we have had proposed by the Chief Executive, and the Congress has enacted, more out-and-out socialistic legislation than has ever been enacted in a similar period by any major power other than Soviet Russia."

The Senator said that Mordecai Ezekiel had "made an extensive study of Soviet Russia," obtained a

97

place "high in the councils of the Farm Board" and then joined the "brain trust."

### "Dictatorships" Attacked.

He declared it was "a strange co-incidence" that General Hugh S. Johnson, "dictator of American industry," has been closely associated with George N. Peek, "virtual dictator" of American farm interests.

"It is common knowledge that Professor Tugwell and his associates, Professors Moley, Berle, Ezekiel and others, seemingly have a controlling influence with the President," said Mr. Hatfield, "and,

through the influence of the White House, are able to force through the Congress legislative proposals of a character far different from that which might well be termed the American idea of voluntarism."

The "new deal," Senator Hatfield continued, is far different from expectations. "It has been turned over to a group of college professors," he said, and the "taxing power and right to engage in foreign alliances turned over to those representing international bankers."

President Roosevelt, the Senator continued, recently "apologized" over the radio for the "dictatorial powers" he possesses and suggested that Congress had "foisted" these powers upon him.

### Charges "Rigging" of Market.

"The President's statement was that misleading, and contrary to known and undisputed facts," Senator Hatfield went on. "So far as I can recall, since the inauguration of the 'new deal' on March 4, no legislation has yet been enacted which was not drafted by the 'brain trust' and sent to Congress from the White House, with the possible exception of the Glass banking bill.

"All the legislation wherein the Congress has created a dictatorship over our monetary system, or is considering the creation of dictatorships has emanated from the White House."

President Roosevelt has "virtually taken upon himself all political and economical power" in the United States, he declared.

Declaring that securities of key American industries have jumped "many millions of dollars" in the last forty days, Senator Hatfield asked who is responsible for "rigging the market."

"Bankers and speculators," he went on, "some of whom may be more conversant than others with the plans of those now in control of the government, to my mind are gambling that, with guaranteed profits to the few through exploitation of the many, they will be able to unload their holdings on the dear public at a later date with tremendous enrichment to themselves."

May 31, 1933

# THE SOCIAL ECONOMICS OF THE NEW DEAL

## Berle Interprets the Philosophy Behind the Program for Reconstruction Through Control of the Old Forces

*Last Sunday over the radio the President reported on the nation's reconstruction task, begun nearly eight months ago. The philosophy behind the administration's program is here interpreted by one who helped to formulate that program.*

### By A. A. BERLE JR.

THERE is no mystery about the economics of the New Deal. For several generations, governments ran their affairs on the theory that natural economic forces balance themselves out. The law of supply and demand would regulate prices. When there was too little supply, the price would go up, and this would automatically increase the supply. When there was too much, the price would go down, and this would automatically decrease the supply. The efficient producer would succeed, the inefficient would fail, and this would keep the productive capacity of the country about in line with the needs for consumption. When credit was needed, bankers would supply it; when too much credit had been extended, there was a period of general inflation cutting down the debt. All this was comprehended in the governmental theory of the time which was really based on the classical economics of Adam Smith.

A tremendous force came into the world in the middle of the nineteenth century. It is usually tied up with what is called the industrial revolution and the advent of large-scale production. But we know now that the actual forces released ran further than that.

The power and force of organization had come into economics. Originally this collected around great investments of capital in huge plants, such as railroads, steel companies and the like. But as the economic machinery adapted itself to the idea of great organizations to run these plants, it became possible to have great organizations only partly dependent upon such plants.

This has led to a revision in some of our economic thinking. No longer can we rely on the economics of balance to take care of human needs. The effect of organization will distort and delay the forces leading to a balance to a degree as yet unmeasured. A falling price does not mean a falling supply under an agricultural system plus a credit system so organized that when the price went down every one tried to produce more wheat, or more cotton or more sugar in order to get out of debt. A big inefficient plant does not shut down because it cannot make a profit. It reorganizes, cuts its debt to nothing, and goes right on. Then it has no interest charges to pay, and only a small investment. It can accordingly undersell a more efficient producer, and drive him into bankruptcy, too. And this is repeated all through the industry.

Only after the entire industry has been bankrupted, do inefficient plants actually begin to go out of business. This process may take fifteen or twenty years, during which time the capital, the labor, the customers, and the industry

generally, suffer from the effects of a disorganized and unsound condition.

The old economic forces still work and they do produce a balance after a while. But they take so long to do it and they crush so many men in the process that the strain on the social system becomes intolerable. Leaving economic forces to work themselves out as they now stand will produce an economic balance, but in the course of it you may have half of the entire country begging in the streets or starving to death.

\* \* \*

THE New Deal may be said to be merely a recognition of the fact that human beings cannot indefinitely be sacrificed by millions to the operation of economic forces accentuated by this factor of organization. Further, the mere process of organization which could create the economic mechanism can be invoked to prevent the shocking toll on life and health and happiness which readjustment under modern conditions demands.

Whatever the outcome, President Roosevelt will live in history as a great President if only for this one fact. He not only appreciated the situation, but had the courage to grapple with the cardinal economic problem of modern life. And he did so not in the spirit of hatred manifested by the red revolutionary or the black Fascist abroad, but in the typical American spirit of great generosity and great recognition that individual life and individual homes are the precious possessions;

all else is merely machinery for the attainment of a full life.

\* \* \*

YOU will find that the forces which the New Deal called into action roughly correspond to the organized forces which economists recognize as the senior controls of our present society. The first and the most important is the control of credit, banking and currency. This, the most important, the most delicate and the most complex, was in obvious collapse on March 4. Wisely, the legislation attending the banking holiday did not commit to any final solution; it is one of the problems with which the administration has yet to deal. The reason is not far to seek.

With five countries around us managing their currency, with the whole problem of the American price level then to be worked out, with the many aspects of that problem in vivid dispute, no one in his senses would have undertaken to lay down a definitive system. What was done was to gather into the hands of the administration many of the tools which could be used on a problem of this sort. It is after all a little naïve to assume that there could be any one lever in that vast machinery which would serve as the complete solution.

A second senior control lies in the tremendously concentrated domination of certain groups over industry. Now industry heretofore has been assumed to be an enterprise conducted for private profit, providing goods and services which the country needs. But it is a great deal more than that. It is one of the principal avenues by which the national income is distributed through the form of wages, dividends, bond interest and so forth. In this item wages are distinctly the largest factor.

Now distribution of the national income is something more than a problem in social welfare. America, in a most intense form, is struggling with a problem that is common to all countries which are highly developed industrially. This is the fact that no industrial civilization can function at all unless there is a tremendous body of people able and willing to buy the products of industry.

* * *

THE very process of building big factories means that there is a great output of goods which were formerly called luxuries, but which become necessities as the standard of living rises. In order to keep these plants going at all there have to be customers. Which means, when you carry it one step further, that there have to be people whose wages are high enough and steady enough to enable them to buy these goods. In the economist's jargon, it means that the national income has to be widely diffused. A national income of, say, eighty millions will not support an industrial civilization if 5 per cent of the country has most of it and 95 per cent divides the remnant. We got into exactly that position—we are there yet, for that matter—and it is one of the great obstacles to recovery.

This is, in political thinking, a new approach to the problem of wealth. The Communist has talked about having no property at all and distributing goods and services currently, because he thought of it in terms of social justice. Sociologists have talked about an evenly distributed income, on the theory that a large middle class, or rather, a nation of people of moderate means, formed the basis for a healthier national life. It remained for the hard-boiled student to work out the simple equation that unless the national income was pretty widely diffused there were not enough customers to keep the plants going; and as the plants shut down the wages shut down, too, and you became engaged in a vicious spiral in which there was less production, hence less wages, hence less income, hence still fewer customers, still less production, and so on down the scale.

We hit the bottom of that mad spiral some time last February, at which point roughly 40 per cent of all wage-earners were out of a job. At that time, as a necessary result, no factories had orders enough to carry on with; only a few railroads had traffic enough to pay their current bills, and the whole machinery threatened to fall into absolute collapse. To this problem the in-

coming administration addressed itself.

* * *

IT WAS conceived that by mobilizing industry through the National Recovery Administration and requiring it to meet the responsibilities of an income distributing group much could be done toward achieving the balance and distribution of income which is required to keep a system like ours afloat. When people talk of "creating purchasing power" what they really mean is that the national income goes not into stagnant pools of unneeded investment but into the hands of people who need goods.

Mobilization of this kind cannot be wholesale in scope; it has to be worked out industry by industry, in an intimateness of detail which can be coped with only by men thoroughly familiar with that industry. This accounts for the machinery of the National Recovery Administration. It involves, incidentally, a problem of education of a large order; for business men are not accustomed to work together, or to realize that if every one pursues his individual interest the result may be bankruptcy for all. I am not quite clear whether the hearings on national codes are not quite as important from the point of view of education as they are from the point of view of industrial organization.

The third and extremely important lever was grasped through the medium of the agricultural legislation—the first time in America that machinery has been devised to control production. We had the paradox that the more successful farming was, the more bankrupt was the farmer. And this in turn meant fewer markets for our industrial goods and ultimately unemployment in the cities. Prosperity to one section while another was in difficulties meant nothing; Mr. Roosevelt's now famous dictum that a country cannot endure "half boom and half broke" was an accurate bit of economic diagnosis as well as a brilliant phrase.

Still another of the senior controls is transportation. Through the various processes of regulation, we have held more control over railroads and transportation than over other parts of the national economy. It is plain, however, that the system was, and for that matter still is, badly askew. After conferences with the railroads themselves, the law creating a railroad coordinator was passed, with the object of setting up a nucleus of organization and at the same time providing sufficient "punch," so that the results of cooperation in railroading could be made available and could be passed on to the public either in the form of wages or in the form of lower rates or in the form of a solvent railroad; and preferably through the medium of all three.

* * *

AN effective bit of machinery was the Reconstruction Finance Corporation which, properly rejuvenated, became during the early days of the administration the focus of most of the private finance of the country. Jesse Jones, the chairman of that board, took on a job the like of which has not been seen in history; for, from the beginning of the bank holiday until well through into the Summer, the Reconstruction Finance Corporation under his leadership was the principal support of our entire fabric, both of long-term and of short-term finance.

I am aware of the many criticisms leveled at the Reconstruction Finance Corporation largely arising out of its early operations, when it was conceived principally as an aid to certain great railroads and banks. Under the philosophy of a new administration, however, it became an instrument for safeguarding and making available the banking and credit structure which is the life blood of all trade. For a period the Reconstruction Finance Corporation virtually took over the great bulk of the work normally done by Wall Street and by the financial centres throughout the country; and as it has completed job after job it has turned the situation back to the respective communities in far better shape than ever before.

The overpowering burden of debt with which the country was struggling as a result of the prosperous decade threatened, and, for that matter, still threatens to engulf much of the economic activity liberated as these various great mechanisms are brought into play. That problem is by no means solved; but I merely mention the Agricultural Credit Corporation, the Home Owners Loan Corporation and other similar institutions designed to take up part of this burden and to reduce it to manageable form.

As a necessary supplement there is the program of public works designed to inject as and when necessary (and it is necessary now) additional activity into the commercial system.

There are many more similar levers and controls, but space does not permit description of them all. It is enough to say that in the aggregate they aim at introducing a power of organization into the economic system which can be used to counterbalance the effects of organization gone wrong; and to make sure that the burdens of readjustment are equitably distributed, and that no group of individuals will be ground to powder in order to satisfy the needs of an economic balance.

* * *

THE overwhelming question today is, will this gigantic attempt to mold an individualist, capitalist system into a directed economic effort produce the result? Before answering that question, it is well to look at the alternative.

For myself, this alternative, drastic as it may sound, has far less terror than a general breakdown. Those of us who had the privilege of working on the original plan began with the assumption that what we needed most was a machine that worked. Whether it was rugged individualism, Fascism, Communism, Socialism, or what-not, made not the slightest bit of difference. Actually, the job was to satisfy the perfectly legitimate needs of a huge mass of people, all of whom were entitled to their right to live. If it cannot be done one way, it must be done another; but we may as well face with entire frankness what might have to be done should the present experiment fail.

A question has been asked which has not yet been answered. Every one is familiar with it. Why is it that with more food, more clothing, more housing, more luxuries, than we know what to do with, there are some 25,000,000 people in the United States who are hungry, naked, living most precariously, and with little more than the bare necessities of subsistence? Every civilized human being is asking that question; and the fact that there are millions of people to whom civilization offers nothing just now means that the question will go right on being asked until an answer is found.

Now there is an answer possible. If, let us say, the government of the United States, forgetting all about the Constitution, were to commandeer everything and every one tomorrow afternoon, it could make a program that would look something like this:

It would say to every department store, and small retailer, "You are now a government distributing office." It could say the same to every wholesaler, every jobber, every warehouse. It could say to every manufacturer of finished goods, and every supplier of raw material, "You are now a government production agency." It could say to every railroad, truckman and the like, "You are now a government transportation agency." It could say to every one working in any capacity, as president, as day laborer, or as roustabout, employed or unemployed, "You are now enrolled as a part of the government labor supply."

It could say at the same time, "All of you will now go back to work. You will produce until we tell you to stop. When we have more than enough of what you happen to be producing, we will give you a furlough, until we need some more." It could say to the miner, "You will produce copper, or coal, or iron"; to the manufacturer, "You will produce finished products and we will supply your requisitions for raw materials." It could say to the transportation agencies, "You will requisition what you need to run your railroad with, and you will transport as we direct." So far, this is very much what we do in war time.

* * *

BUT it would have to say something more than that. A government tackling a solution on these lines would have to say: "Nobody will be paid anything. Debts and interest are canceled. Instead of that, we will give to every one a red card entitling him to go to the nearest government distributing agency (for which you can read the department store, the little shop on the corner of Third Avenue, the drug store in the little town, the grocery shop you habitually deal with), and can get your share of possible bright pink underwear in the approved fashion-poster designs, and very-much-alive and wriggly soft-shell crabs. A garbage cart on its rounds may halt the traffic for ten minutes. But there is less impatient honking than when a taxicab uptown holds up the stream of motors for half a second.

Food shops are the principal thing, of course, with signs chiefly in foreign languages; there are also shops for household goods, clothing, electrical goods, radios, brass, candy. In the midst of this medley you may find a stretch of several blocks devoted principally to the diamond business. In the heart of what might be supposed to be a sort of lower-depths refuge of poverty this would be surprising. But the truth is that the deep east side is not a refuge of poverty. The outward aspect of squalor notwithstanding, it is really a thrift station on the way to a competence and riches. The squalor is less in the people you see, indeed, than in the wretched state of the decayed buildings, left over, perhaps, from as long ago as the days of those ship-building magnates over on the river. (Some of their mansions still linger out toward the end of East Broadway where it runs into Grand Street.)

The women of the oldest vintage in the deep east side sometimes wear queer wigs or shawls on their heads instead of hats. But the young women wear saucy little shapes exactly like the ones in the Fifth Avenue shop windows. Of a bright day—especially a holiday—there is an effect of a gala fashion parade of the younger set turned out in the latest mode from little hat to shiny patent leather pumps. This includes the young mothers who may be wheeling very grand capacious perambulators with the best appointments in the way of pink or blue blankets, and sometimes twins inside. The young men —on such occasions—are apt to wear what the overdressed young man wears almost everywhere. The tough guy with the long-visored cap is very little in evidence.

In the afternoon the streets overflow with children who are really amazingly well dressed, if not overdressed. Among them are many racial types from blond to brunette. It is not always easy to tag them with the right race tag. But the language they speak is the English of New York—not the language of any of the foreign countries or alien races which contribute to the melting pot: a curious composite which gives to the English of New York its peculiar accent and intonation—the tune the words are spoken to, in fact. It is a tune as characteristic of this city as the cockney is of London, and, like the cockney, always transforming itself.

* * *

SINCE so much of social life goes on out-of-doors, though in the street, there is a sort of tendency to a town-and-country mélange in the costume of the young folks. In the evening especially. Where the sidewalks lie between lines of pushcarts on the one hand and shops on the other, spilling over onto the pavement all sorts of things, including ice-filled tubs of fish, the footway is always a bit dank and clammy. Nevertheless, while the merchants and the elders are busy and noisy with their bargaining— or just patiently waiting for a customer—the girls use the market place as a promenade as if it were a prado somewhere or a boardwalk somewhere else. They move vivaciously, dark-eyed and bare-headed, in their frocks demure or gay, wearing sandals, with or without socks on their bare legs, regardless of the muck.

So much business is done on many of these streets that they are always a little dirty and rich in smells of garden truck, delicatessen, butcher stalls, fish shops. But that is after the ancient tradition of cities and especially seaports the world over. What stands out is that this part of New York is carrying on very much as if nothing had happened. In this part of town business is not paralyzed. On a busy Saturday market night, with everybody abroad and everybody mingling in the crowds of buyers and sellers, the impression is that here is pre-depression New York unchanged, even though here, as everywhere else, the Blue Eagles of the NRA are on display in the shop windows.

It is only when you walk in the broad daylight along the same streets—especially those far downtown—that you notice that what has happened uptown has happened here, too. Many shops are shut. Not a few are boarded up without even a "for rent" sign displayed. Whole buildings are empty of tenants in streets where the inhabitants used to be packed like sardines. However, if you look a little more closely you will see that most of these empty buildings are old rookeries which were so little fitted for human habitation that what has befallen them cannot be regarded as an unmixed evil.

* * *

HERE is another sign that the island of Manhattan really is losing population and that plans for the future must take account of that fact. These empty houses are found in still seemingly well populated quarters. Yet thousands of buildings in the territory we are surveying have been razed for the sake of letting in sun and air where for half a century was little of either. The great swaths of open space along Allen Street, between Christopher and Forsyth Streets, along Delancey Street and East Houston Street, where the city has cleared away blocks of tenements, have worked an extraordinary transformation in what was the very deepest jungle of the deep East Side.

The great open space between Chrystie and Forsyth, that used to pack them in Heaven knows how deep, is now a sun-bathed avenue wider than any other avenue we have—wider than the Champs Elysées—looking up toward the tall spike of the Chrysler Building. Traffic runs in the paved streets on each side. The rest is a bare level of open ground—a waste, if you will—used as a playground and at times a place for the mobilization of bread lines.

But the idea will intrude—especially in view of the steady decline in the population of Manhattan Island—that this great open space might easily serve the city of the future much better than anything in the housing line that could be set up there, however modern and sanitary.

# SAGA OF AMOS 'N' ANDY

## Review of Their Triumph as They Sign Off for Vacation——Amos Going to Alaska, Andy to Europe

### By ORRIN E. DUNLAP Jr.

IT'S a long road that has no turning, so Amos 'n' Andy after eight years on the air will sign off for their first vacation on Friday, the 13th, with Andy bound for Europe and Amos for Alaska. The "13" looms to them as a lucky day, the beginning of a two months' vacation, after which they will be back on the air Sept. 17 with many fresh ideas for their broadcast.

Mr. and Mrs. Charles J. Correll (Andy) have booked passage on the Bremen sailing from New York on July 17, and Andy says, on that voyage he'll be "restin' my brain." After a visit in England he will tour the Continent, but he has no definite itinerary mapped out.

Mr. and Mrs. Freeman F. Gosden (Amos) will take a trip through the Canadian Northwest and then go by steamer to Alaska, where Amos plans to do a lot of fishin' and "unlax."

### In the $100,000-a-Year Class.

Theirs has been an enviable record of success on the radio; in fact, it is referred to as a phenomenon the "psyrology" of which noted psychologists have attempted to explain. No other ethereal team has established such records. The 3,500,000 words which they have spoken into space is an achievement that puts them away out in front. Practically every popularity survey among listeners over the past few years gives Amos 'n' Andy the lead. Their blackface dialogue, their comic strip on the air night after night at the stroke of 7 o'clock, but recently at 7:45 P. M., put them in the $100,000-a-year class as radio actors.

While in reality only two performers will bid the microphone adieu for several weeks, an entire troupe will be missing from the unseen waves that criss-cross over America; the Kingfish will get a vacation, so will Brother Crawford, Madame Queen, Lightnin', Señorita Butterfly, Ruby Taylor, Rollin Weber, Henry Van Porter and a host of characters Amos 'n' Andy have created by the artistry of sound alone. By cleverly shifting their voices they have introduced more than seventy-five different characters; they have played each part themselves. This is an art.

They have revealed the power of radio by their simple, homespun, philosophy. With a great flare for showmanship they have mastered their art by expert use of such tools as sentiment, pathos, drama, honesty, cleanliness, humor and, last but not least, their everyday antics are human.

### A Comic Strip of the Air.

Their achievement is attributed to the same psychology that accounts for the popularity of the comic strip. There is no daily climax but a serial that is unraveled from day to day, each episode carefully prepared so that each presentation dovetails with the one of the previous broadcast. This enables the listener to keep track of the continuity in case he missed an episode. With a deft theatrical touch they briefly allude to what has gone ahead so the listener does not lose interest in them should he miss a broadcast or even a dozen. That is one of the wonders of Amos 'n' Andy technique. It is showmanship.

Mindful that the unseen audience, just like the movie audience, prides itself in being a few steps ahead of what is coming, Amos and Andy have never neglected this idea. It is one of their secrets of success; part of their formula. They prepare the broadcast script so the listener can create his own mental impression, so he can supply the imagination and the scenery. And whether the listener is a banker or a carpenter, a sailor or a lawyer, he invariably enjoys the show because he is apparently a trifle wiser than the two at the microphone, because he can "see what's coming"—and Correll and Gosden are glad the audience is "wiser" than they are. It is all so simple, and in the simplicity is found the keynote of a successful eight years in which they have written 1,892 episodes that have attracted many millions who have kept a rendezvous with them day after day.

### They Do All the Writing.

Every word they have written themselves, and so powerful has been their influence in America that they have been requested on several occasions to do a bit of missionary work while broadcast-

ing; during the depression they sought on several occasions to cheer up the nation, to promote a happy spirit in their broadcasts, to banish fear and to spread encouragement. Their power for good is said to be amazing to the nth degree.

Few probably realized their tremendous following until one night in 1929, when their time was changed from 11 P. M. to 7 P. M. An avalanche of complaints came by mail and by telegraph; telephone switchboards at the broadcasting stations were swamped with calls. WMAQ alone received 100,000 protests. The uprising was referred to as "the Amos 'n' Andy Rebellion." It was quickly quelled, however, by adopting the 7 o'clock period, but also by staging a repeat performance for Western listeners at 11 P. M. (Eastern time). That was a glorious day for "Amos Jones," who was once a tobacco salesman, and for "Andrew H. Brown," who was once a bricklayer. Radio changed their careers.

Success has never spoiled them. They are the same friendly Amos 'n' Andy that one met six years ago. Amos is always full of fun; Andy is the more serious, yet he has the twinkle of a comedian in his eye. He worries more than Amos, the carefree one of the two. For example, while on a visit to New York they were wined and dined every minute. Andy remarked that he would like to get some sleep; he complained that too much play might detract from their theatrical talents on the air. He was worried about the next script. But Amos assured him everything would work out all right.

Nevertheless, Andy said he didn't like too many festive "propolitions."

They made "The Fresh Air Taxicab Company of America, Incorpolated," a national institution. They made "The Mystic Knights of the Sea" an organization known in every city and hamlet as effectively as if the lodges were actually scattered across the continent. Many expressions have been introduced and popularized by them, revealing their originality and creative talents, such as "Ise regusted," "Is I Blue?" "Awah! Awah!" "I ain' gonna do it," "Check and double check," "Ain't dat sumpin'" and "Sho, sho."

### No Studio Visitors See Them.

They have adhered strictly to their studio rule of "No visitors allowed." Amos explained that an audience would embarrass them, spoil their technique. For example,

when he plays the rôle of Brother Crawford he bounces up and down on the chair. If an audience were watching he might be embarrassed at such silly antics and endeavor to act more naturally, but that would ruin the effect. And if an audience laughed at their gestures and contortions, that would be bad. In fact, Amos said Andy is so funny at times that he has to look the other way or else he might laugh when hilarity is not opportune.

Chicago is their centre of activity and the majority of their broadcasts come from that city, although when in New York or other cities they are put on the network without the audience being aware of where they are performing. Bill Hay is their announcer, and always has been on the job to tell the world that "Here they are!"

The tall, blond, curly-haired Amos was born in 1899 at Richmond, Va. The short, stocky, dark-haired Andy was born in 1890 at Peoria, Ill.

The year 1927 was one of honeymoon for them. Correll married Marie Janes in January of that year and Gosden wedded Leta Schreiber in June. Andy has no children, but Amos has two—Freeman Jr., born in 1928, and Virginia Marie, born in 1930.

A flare for acting, for showmanship, brought Correll and Gosden together. They clowned and clogged together. Then radio came along. "Just for the fun of it," they asked for an audition at WEBH, Chicago. That was in 1925, in the days when volunteer talent had a chance at the microphone. At WGN, Chicago, in 1926, they performed as Sam and Henry. That sent them up the ladder. Then at WMAQ as Amos 'n' Andy they began to win a widespread reputation. That was in March, 1928. Their idiosyncrasies of pronunciation were being quoted throughout the length and breadth of America, for soon they were on a nation-wide network. One Christmas they received 30,000 greeting cards.

It might well be said that they have lost themselves in their characters, for in visiting with them it would seem awkward to address Amos as Mr. Gosden or as Freeman; likewise, to refer to Andy as Mr. Correll or Charles. They are Amos and Andy, and as such millions of Americans will miss them for two months, yet all will be wishing them bon voyage and a pleasant respite from the mute microphone through which they have won countless friends and a national reputation as master showmen.

# 'EVERY MAN A KING' DRIVE BY LONG IS ON

## 'Kingfish' on the Air Appeals for Recruits for His 'Share Our Wealth' Campaign.

## AGAIN ATTACKS PRESIDENT

## Meanwhile, Square Deal Group Urges Louisiana Revolt to End His Grip on Legislature.

Special to THE NEW YORK TIMES.

WASHINGTON, Jan. 9. — In a radio address tonight Senator Long declared that there was no further hope from the Roosevelt policies, and urged the American people to join in the Long "Share our Wealth" and "Every Man a King" programs.

His predictions as to economic conditions in 1933 and 1934 had all come true, the Senator declared, justifying his saying "I told you so."

He added that 1,000,000 more men were out of work than a year ago, 5,000,000 more families were on the dole, and "the rich earn more, the common people less; the rich get hold of what is in the country and, in general, America travels on toward its route to ——."

Senator Long said he "begged and pleaded and did everything else under the sun" to "try to get Mr. Roosevelt to keep his word that he gave to us." He asserted that he had "warned the President" what would happen if the "promises" were not kept.

The administration has taken Federal patronage in Louisiana away from Mr. Long.

### He Recalls His Filibuster.

Speaking over a network of the National Broadcasting Company, Senator Long said that "whatever we have been able to do to try to hold the situation together during the past three years has been forced down the throat of the national administration."

"I held the floor in the Senate for days until they allowed the bank laws to be amended that permitted the banks in the small cities and towns to reopen," he went on. "The bank deposit guarantee law and the Frazier-Lemke farm debt moratorium law had to be passed in spite of the Roosevelt administration. I helped to pass them both.

"Hope for more through Roosevelt? He has promised and promised, smiled and bowed; he has read fine speeches and told any one in need to get in touch with him. What has it meant?

"We must now become awakened! We must know the truth and speak the truth. There is no use to wait three more years. It is not Roosevelt or ruin, it is Roosevelt's ruin."

### President's Promises Hit.

The Presidential promises Mr. Long described as:

"First: That the size of the big man's fortune would be reduced so as to give the masses at the bottom enough to wipe out all poverty; and

"Second: That the hours of labor would be so reduced that all would share in the work to be done and in consuming the abundance mankind produced."

Senator Long said Mr. Roosevelt "reiterated these pledges even after" he became President, and continued:

"When I saw him spending all his time of ease and recreation with the business partners of Mr. John D. Rockefeller Jr., with such men as the Astors, &c., maybe I ought to have had better sense than to have believed he would ever break down their big fortunes to give enough to the masses to end poverty.

"Maybe some will think me weak for ever believing it all, but millions of other people were fooled the same as myself.

"All the people of America have been invited to a barbecue. God invited us all to come and eat and drink all we wanted. He smiled on our land and we grew crops of plenty to eat and wear.

### "Feast" for America.

"He showed us in the earth, the iron and other things to make anything we wanted. He unfolded to us the secrets of science so that our work might be easy. God called: 'Come to my feast.'

"Then what happened? Rockefeller, Morgan and their crowd stepped up and took enough for 120,000,000 people and left only enough for 5,000,000, for all the other 125,000,000 to eat. And so many millions must go hungry and without these good things God gave us, unless we call on them to put some of it back.

"I call on you to organize share-our-wealth societies."

Senator Long closed his speech with this original verse:

Why weep or slumber, America?
Land of brave and true;
With castles, clothing and food for all,
All belongs to you.
Ev'ry man a king; ev'ry man a king;
For you can be a millionaire.
But there's something belonging to others,
There's enough for all people to share.
When it's sunny June or December too,
Or in the Winter time or Spring,
There'll be peace without end
Ev'ry neighbor a friend,
With ev'ry man a king.

*January 10, 1935*

---

# FARLEY DECLARES PROFIT MOTIVE SAFE

## President a Sensible Citizen Who 'Chases No Rainbows,' He Tells 1,000 Business Men.

## HE WARNS ON ALARMISTS

## Industry Cannot Be Crucified, He Asserts—Sees Recovery 'Job' About Half Done.

Assurance of the administration's support of the profit system, with no business man needing to "lie awake nights worrying about what is going to happen" as regards the government's policies, was expressed by James A. Farley, Postmaster General, in an address last night. He spoke to more than 1,000 business men, industrialists and financiers at the dinner of the Anthracite Club of New York in the Hotel Astor.

Economy, moderation and social service were the guiding principles of the Roosevelt administration, Mr. Farley said, as he reaffirmed recent statements by President Roosevelt and high officials of the government on the question of its determination to preserve the profit motive in American economic life.

Mr. Farley defended the administration's policy, the part played therein by the brain trust, his own operation of the Postoffice Department, and the government's unemployment relief program. He drew a picture of marked progress toward recovery and assured his audience that under the President's leadership the nation might look forward to complete economic and social rehabilitation.

### Getting Along "Pretty Well."

"Despite the gloomy views of people who for one reason or another are uncomfortable under present conditions, or who feel bound to find fault with whatever is done by the administration, this country is getting along pretty well," Mr. Farley said. "Business is improving.

"The railroads, the department stores, in fact every considerable industry reflects the advance. The job, of course, is not half done, but it will be done in a shorter time than most of you anticipate if the country does not listen to the voices of the alarmists, who seem to think that they are performing a service to themselves and to the nation generally by scaring people, without regard to the plain and available facts of the situation."

Reaffirming the administration's devotion to the existing economic system, Mr. Farley said it "could no more venture to take the profit motive out of industry and commerce, as some of the wildest assailants of the administration have suggested is its intent, than it could attempt to establish deliberately a wage scale below that which would afford a decent standard of living to the toiling population."

"It could no more crucify industry than it could permit agriculture to go into nation-wide bankruptcy," Mr. Farley emphasized. "If it did either of these things, the administration would be a failure."

### Job Not Yet Complete.

Mr. Farley declared that "there is not a man among you who is any more level-headed, any more practical than Franklin D. Roosevelt."

"He has stemmed the tide of hopelessness," he continued.

Proceeding to the question of government economy and administration of unemployment relief, Mr. Farley defended the method of public works and work relief in general as far more advantageous than the dole method of direct relief. Even though more expensive now, he argued, it gives the nation something tangible in accomplishment while preserving the morale and self-respect of the people.

Closing his address with a plea for confidence in the administration and recognition of its positive accomplishments, Mr. Farley said:

"I think you will all agree that a contrast between today and the day President Roosevelt came to the White House is cheering and not at all doleful. It ought not to be necessary for me to tell you that Franklin D. Roosevelt is a practical, sensible citizen who chases no rainbows."

Another speaker at the dinner was Ward M. Canaday, director of public relations for the Federal Housing Administration, who told of what it was doing as a part of the general recovery policies.

Charles Dorrance, president of the Pan Anthracite Collieries Company, presided.

*January 18, 1935*

# 52 Yes, 36 No

## The Court Loses

Eight years ago, when Detroit was bulging over its borders to make room for the hordes brought to the city by the booming motor car industry, an unknown priest was assigned by his Bishop to a poor and tiny parish in the suburb of Royal Oak. The voice of the priest, as he preached his first sermons, was heard only by the twenty-six families of his congregation. Last week that same voice was one of the mighty in the land; it contributed heavily to the Senate's defeat of the World Court.

The Senate voted 52 for adherence to the court, 36 against. Two-thirds, or 59, was necessary to put through the measure. The surprise result, a distinct setback to President Roosevelt was in considerable measure the product of a last-minute campaign of intensive anti-court propaganda. That's where the Rev. Charles E. Coughlin, pastor of the Shrine of the Little Flower at Royal Oak, came in.

Speaking over his usual network of twenty-nine radio stations, Father Coughlin had appealed to "every solid American" to save the nation from becoming "the hunting ground of international plutocrats."

He urged his hearers—"whether you can afford it or not"—to telegraph their Senators. That night and the next day Washington was deluged with wires. The waverers were won over, and the administration lost a contest it had expected to win with ease.

ATTACKER

Associated Press.
**Father Coughlin.**
*"I Appeal to Every Solid American to Keep America Safe for Americans."*

## And Also Huey Long.

The radio priest—whose parish now is building a magnificent limestone church, paid for by contributors who listen to his broadcasts—was not, of course, the sole cause of the President's defeat. But he did personify the vehement opposition. The old hatred of "entangling alliances," the antipathy caused by the present unrest in Europe, the anti-court campaign of the Hearst newspapers—all these were important factors. And, also, there was Huey Long.

The Louisiana Senator rushed back to Washington, despite the presence of revolt in his own province, and became the leading button-holer of the anti-court faction. He hurried about the floor, exhorting Senators on the doubtful list. Now a foe of Mr. Roosevelt, he took delight in baiting Senator Robinson, the President's spokesman.

The vote, taken on Tuesday, was received with a burst of applause. The President was unruffled by the defeat, and the general belief was that the effects of the setback would not be serious to his prestige. Mr. Roosevelt made no public comment. Others did:

*Senator Borah:* "Thank God!"
*Senator Johnson:* "Delighted."
*Elihu Root:* "I think the majority of the Senate which has been defeated under the two-thirds rule truly represents with the President the sincere conviction of the American people who hate war."
*Father Coughlin:* "Our thanks are due to Almighty God in that America retains her sovereignty."

February 3, 1935

# COUGHLIN TERMS NEW DEAL FAILURE

### Radio Priest Says It Dealt Cards Marked for High Finance and Big Business.

### DENOUNCES 'COMPROMISES'

### Condemns NRA, AAA and 'New Social System'—Leaders at Capital Stand on Record.

Special to THE NEW YORK TIMES.

DETROIT, Mich., March 3.—Asserting that "you cannot have a new deal without a new deck," the Rev. Charles E. Coughlin, radio priest, declared in his regular Sunday broadcast that every card dealt from the deck of the Roosevelt New Deal had been marked for "high finance" and "big business."

In a review of the two years since the inauguration of President Roosevelt, Father Coughlin said:

"Somehow or other the cards dealt by the New Deal contained the same joker, the same hidden cards, which were found in the old deal. This time, however, not only the aces of high finance were wild; the kings of big industry were also wild!"

Denouncing what he termed the "compromises" of the present administration, he continued:

"Big ownership and private financialism are still with us untouched, unhampered and unafraid.

"No government can hope to establish a new economic deal unless at every moment and at every move the arrogance of big ownership is deflated and the tyranny of private financialism is broken.

"Two years more of this policy which is associated with preserving big business and big finance will be remembered in American history as the sad experiment.

### Charges "Two Years of Failure."

"Big business and big finance were practically the only ones who really benefited from the New Deal, which for two long, dreary years has failed to realize its promises of driving the money changers out of the temple and of legislating against the concentration of wealth.

"The first two years of the New Deal shall be remembered as two years of compromise, two years of social planning, two years of endeavoring to mix bad and good, two years of surrender, two years of matching the puerile, puny brains of idealists against the virile viciousness of business and finance—two years of economic failure.

"The New Dealers themselves, recognizing that they have not produced results, have used the euphemistic term of 'experimentation' when everybody knows there was no need to experiment, when everybody knows there was need to drive the money changers from the temple.

"The New Deal has been inefficacious in giving the laboring classes the least semblance of a new deal."

Singling out various phases of the Roosevelt administration for criticism, Father Coughlin charged that it had "out-Hoovered Hoover" in assisting banks by buying their securities with public funds; that under its New Deal prices had risen faster than wages; that its NRA was a "farce," and that its AAA, curtailing farm production, was a "failure."

He denounced the administration's opposition to the "prevailing wage" amendment in the Work Relief Bill as the "unkindest cut of all" and said that paying less than prevailing wages would "translate a new deal into a raw deal."

Calling upon the administration to cease "treading the waters long since muddied by the greed of economic abuses" and to set out "with bold strokes for the shore where we can enjoy the abundance with which we are blessed," he said:

"I shall support with all my strength the economics of social justice and the conservation of the American standard of living which these social reformers are destroying as in this land of plenty they insult the intelligence of our population with their $50 a month wages and their programs of destruction which are associated with scarcity through the burning of wheat and the slaughtering of pigs."

Stating that he refused to "swallow the candy-coated pill of a social reform," Father Coughlin went on:

"Is it not evident that our government has been captured by a group of scientific social workers who preach to us that big, bad bankers and good, little laborers shall submit to a multiplicity of conventional regulations, each class retaining what it had under the old economy as they learn to habituate themselves to a strange admixture of fascism, of capitalism, of communism and of Americanism?

"I refer to a new social system where by intent if not by practice the Federal Government reserves for itself the right to enter into every phase of business—business which not only respects the development of public resources but business of the most private nature.

"I refer to the tendency to substitute undemocratic methods of government for the democratic usages and legally established institutions to which we have dedicated our destinies.

"I refer to the establishment of unnecessary bureaucracies which inordinately have transgressed the fundamental rights of State government.

"I refer to the indomitable determination to preserve the worst forms of plutocracy around whose throne this nation is subjected to live and move and have its being."

### "Compromise" as "Weakness."

"President Roosevelt has both compromised with the money-changers and conciliated with monopolistic industry," Father Coughlin concluded.

"This spirit of compromise has been the predominant weakness of our present leadership to such an extent that it has not disdained to hold out the olive branch to those whose policies are crimsoned with the theories of sovietism and international socialism.

"We cannot applaud a New Deal which, with all its chaotic implications, submits either to the supremacy of a financial overlord more obnoxious than King George III or to the red slavery of an economic Simon Legree more ruthless than the one confronted by a Lincoln.

"In the past there was no compromise. In the present there can be no compromise, if a new liberty, a further freedom, shall be born."

# RACKETS BAFFLE THE LAW

## Fear Silences the Victims of Oppression Which Reigns in Many City Trades

### By MEYER BERGER.

Once more there is much talk of "rackets." But the term does not mean anything any more, because the public keeps it between its teeth for instant application to any kind of enterprise, criminal, semi-legal or perfectly legal. And even public officials assigned to put down "rackets" don't know where to draw the line.

Ask a prosecutor how many rackets flourish in New York and he is apt to hand you the red book and the business directory for answer, then add the "snatch racket" (kidnapping), "the slot machine racket," "the dope racket," "the French pictures racket," "the labor racket," "fake accident racket," "fake portrait racket," "loan shark racket," "antique racket"—and so on, without end.

Most of these are old frauds and moss-hung forms of chiseling draped with the much-abused word that somehow or other seems to give a new meaning to them.

When you ask a public official, "How much do rackets cost New York every year?" you usually stump him. If he is honest he will admit he doesn't know. Some officials, though, will make a wild guess and get a warm glow from sensational headlines. Once a figure gets into print it will be used over and over again.

Police officials, prosecutors, chambers of commerce and trade statisticians keep uttering statements purporting to disclose how much money is lost by the public in the various "rackets," but actually they do not know. Of course, the sum must be tremendous, but one honest prosecutor admitted the other day that whether the city's loss is measured in millions or in billions, he couldn't tell.

### Group Affairs.

Outside of kidnapping, professional homicide and similar definitely criminal enterprises which have flourished since the beginning of time, most of the so-called "rackets" that draw extra funds from the thinned purses of the buying public are practiced by groups or associations that operate behind plate-glass windows where every one can see — in neighborhood stores, in the laundries, in the dye-

ing and cleaning shops, in the bakeries.

These business "rackets" all operate along pretty much the same lines and get their start, in most instances, in the same way. A price war starts and there is no law strong enough to stop it; at least, not soon enough to do any good. Then the merchants or shopkeepers, in desperation, take the fatal step. They invite the underworld leaders in, to get swift results.

Tricky lawyers are called in, too. No really important "racket" can exist without them. They draw up "membership contracts" and form associations with amusing gravity. These contracts are usually proof against legal attack.

The tradesmen or shopkeepers who enter such associations pay heavy initiation fees and monthly dues; very often a percentage of their gross receipts. The organizer, pocketing the money, then begins to "stabilize" the industry, whatever it may be. He does not use very subtle methods, but what he does is effective.

### Violent Reprisals.

The shopkeeper or tradesman who doesn't join the "association" finds his place made uninhabitable with noisesome chemicals dropped by some intruder. His windows are broken. Acids are dropped on his product. His drivers are slugged. Or some hard-faced stranger pays him a personal visit and breaks his nose.

In one case during the cleaning and dyeing "stabilization" in Brooklyn, one of the non-members of the association got a bill from the association for $2,020 after his home had been bombed. It turned out that it had cost the association that much to do the bombing job, which was listed on the books among "disbursement."

Attorney General John J. Bennett Jr. tried to get at the roots of that association to prevent it from strangling the industry. He found the victims scared; information had to be dragged from them. Then it developed that really honest and well-meaning men in the industry had actually invited the thug organizers to "stabilize" things.

Bakers got into a similar mess: tricky lawyers, underworld leaders with hard-knuckled men-at-arms,

regular dues, stench bombs, broken windows. In this case the Attorney General was able to get witnesses to convict two of the "organizers" for extortion. In most instances of business racketeering, though, the prosecutor is backed only by the comparatively weak laws aimed at unfair business competition.

### A Suggested "Cure."

John F. X. McGohey, Assistant Attorney General in charge of the Anti-Racket Bureau, was asked what might help stamp out the domination of industry by gangster-controlled associations.

"Codified regulation of intrastate industry might relieve the employer of the necessity of invoking strong-arm methods to preserve his interests against unfair competitors," was his answer. "With the law behind him, he could legally eliminate price-cutting. Then employers could operate on an equal footing and the racketeer would no longer find a fertile field for and ready market for his nefarious activities."

Mr. McGohey admitted, however, that that simple remedy would not be enough; it would merely make it harder for the thug organizer to muscle into industry. Business "rackets" by whatever name will probably bob up just as they always have throughout the ages.

### The "Labor Racket."

The plug-ugly and the slippery lawyer form a particularly vicious combination in the so-called "labor racket." It would be impossible to guess how many hundred of thousands of working men (and women, too) are cowed, browbeaten and betrayed to unscrupulous employers by fat-necked bullies posing as business agents. In many labor unions members dare not open their mouths to oppose the moves of the leaders. When they vote at a union election they quiver under the hard eyes of gun-toters and muscle men. If they work up enough courage to vote for one of their own choice they can expect a thorough mauling.

If they complain to the District Attorney their families are threatened. If they reach the point where they are willing to testify against their oppressors it may mean a one-way "ride."

Without the victim's testimony and without his complaints, public officials cannot send the bullying labor boss and his sluggers to jail. The unscrupulous labor boss knows that. And right there is the whole nub of gangster-dominated industry, gangster-dominated labor unions and gangster domination of all the rackets. It is rule by fear

# SOCIAL SECURITY: THE FOUNDATION

## The New Measure, Says Secretary Perkins, Is a Step Toward a Better Ordered Society

*In the following article the aims and purposes of the Social Security Act are set out by the Secretary of Labor. Miss Perkins was chairman of the President's Committee on Economic Security, which made the study leading to the introduction of the bill. She has been active for fifteen years in advocating such legislation and conducted a special study of European insurance systems for Mr. Roosevelt when he was Governor of New York.*

### By FRANCES PERKINS
#### Secretary of Labor

THE social security program, which has just been embodied in an act of Congress, represents a most significant step in our national development. It is a milestone in our progress toward a better ordered society, providing, as it does, protection against the loss of income due to unemployment, old age, and the death of the breadwinner. All this is in the interest of the national welfare.

If we are to maintain a healthy economy and thriving production, we need to maintain the standard of living of the lower-income groups in our population, who constitute 90 per cent of our purchasing power. The President's Committee on Economic Security, of which I had the honor to be chairman, in drawing up the plan, was convinced that its enactment into law would not only carry us a long way toward the goal of economic security for the individual, but also a long way toward the promotion and stabilization of mass purchasing power, without which the present economic system cannot endure.

That this intimate connection between the maintenance of mass purchasing power through a system of protection of the individual against major economic hazards is not theoretical is evidenced by the fact that England has been able to withstand the effects of the world-wide depression, even though her prosperity depends so largely upon foreign trade. English economists agree with employers and workers that this ability to weather adverse conditions has been due in no small part to social insurance benefits and regular payments, which have served to maintain necessary purchasing power.

\* \* \*

FEW legislative proposals have had as careful study, as thorough and conscientious deliberation, as that which went into the preparation of our social security program. This program is embodied in perhaps the most useful and fundamental single piece of Federal legislation in the interest of wage-earners in the United States.

It provides the majority of our people with a substantial measure of security in infancy and childhood, in economic crises of their working life, and in their old age. It will be one of the forces working against the recurrence of severe depressions in the future. We can, as the principle of sustained purchasing power in hard times makes itself felt in every shop and store and mill, grow old without being haunted by the spectre of a poverty-ridden old age or of being a burden on our children.

In its outlines it recognizes and covers a wide area of the social distress and maladjustment which has long been present in American life in times of plenty as in times of depression. The measure provides at present a modest degree of protection against known hazards. It is reasonable, and if it errs it is in the direction of safety—of taking on only known problems and making the original provision well within the capacity of our present business structure and outlook.

Growth of the program on these principles will inevitably and naturally take place as a response to the experience and testing which come only with the attempt of conscientious officers to make just and fair application of a new law. The vitality of legislation of this sort consists in its capacity for sound growth from orderly and solid foundations.

The passage of this act with so few dissenting votes and with so much intelligent public support is deeply significant of the progress which the American people have made in thought in the social field and awareness of methods of using cooperation through government to overcome social hazards against which the individual alone is inadequate. To socialize the costs of individual disasters which are unpreventable by the individual is a growing method in our highly complicated civilization.

\* \* \*

THE cost of social security will be comparatively small for some years to come. This was deliberately arranged by the committee for the President in order that the incidence of tax might be gradual, as business and workers would be paying this tax in the early years of recovery from depression and before the full prosperity level had been reached.

The act provides for Federal aid to the States for old-age assistance, mothers' pensions, public-health services and various other measures which have for their purpose the care of dependents or the reduction of destitution and dependency in future years. This Federal assistance will aggregate slightly less than $100,000,000 in the next fiscal year and will increase thereafter. Almost all of these grants will be made on condition that they are matched by the States.

It is an error to treat the Federal and State expenditures for these purposes as a new and additional cost. All State and local governments now spend money for all or many of these purposes. Also, in the near future, the policy under which State and local governments must resume responsibility for the care of their people unable to work on relief goes into effect. Their expenditures for these purposes will have to be greatly increased. Through the aid provided by the social security measure, the Federal Government will assist the States and local governments in the proper discharge of this function.

It is desirable that it should do so, not only to stimulate the States to undertake these very necessary social services but also for fiscal reasons. With the very wide differences which exist between States in per capita income and wealth, and the limited possibilities open to the State and local governments for securing revenues other than from property taxes, it is sound financial policy that a part of the costs for social services should be met by the Federal Government.

\* \* \*

SIMILARLY, the costs of unemployment compensation and old-age insurance are not actually additional costs. In some degree they have long been borne by the people, but irregularly, the burden falling much more heavily on some than on others, and none of such provisions offering an orderly or systematic assurance to those in need. The years of depression have brought home to all of us that unemployment entails huge costs to government, industry and the public alike.

Unemployment insurance will within a short time considerably lighten the public burden of caring for those now unemployed. It will materially reduce relief costs in future years. In essence, it is a method by which reserves are built up during periods of employment from which compensation is paid to the unemployed in periods when work is lacking.

It substitutes systematic for haphazard methods of providing income for the unemployed, and, while it will not eliminate entirely the need for work programs and direct relief, it should make these measures largely unnecessary except in major depressions or in communities where a particular industry is dying or moving away. Unemployment compensation may also be made a most effective weapon in stabilizing industry and reducing unemployment. Cooperation of government, business and labor will undoubtedly make rapid progress in this field.

The first tax which will be levied is that under the unemployment compensation title, which will amount to 1 per cent on payrolls for the calendar year 1936, 2 per cent the next year and 3 per cent thereafter. The contributory old-age annuity tax does not go into effect until Jan. 1, 1937. It amounts to only 1 per cent for the employer and 1 per cent for the employe on individual earnings up to $3,000 per year.

This rate increases gradually until by Jan. 1, 1949, more than thirteen years hence, the rate is 3 per cent for the employer and the same for the employe. Thus, even when these taxes go into full force and effect, they will amount to only 9 per cent, 6 per cent to be paid by the employer and 3 per cent to be paid by the employe.

The social security measure does not establish a Federal system of unemployment compensation, but makes it possible for the States to enact unemployment compensation laws, since by levying a tax upon all employers in the country against which a credit is allowed for contributions to State unemployment compensation funds it equalizes the cost between States with insurance laws and those without. This Federal tax is levied exclusively upon the employers, but the States are free to add other contributions.

* * *

A FEDERALLY administered old-age annuity system is the other major social insurance measure included in the act. Beginning in the year 1942, this will provide annuities at age 65 to substantially all workers other than those engaged in farm labor, private domestic or government service. These annuities will not be granted as a matter of public charity and will usually be more adequate than the pensions it is possible to provide to needy old people under the State old-age assistance laws. They will be earned annuities to which the recipients are entitled as a matter of right.

Taxes needed will prove no fearful burden on industry. What were the possible alternatives? Free pensions to the needy are very necessary, but during the past year it became doubtful whether we could maintain the principle that free pensions be given only to those old people without adequate means and without children able and willing to support them. It seemed reasonably likely that unless a contributory old-age insurance system was established this country would be driven to free pensions for all citizens who reach a specified age, regardless of need.

A pension of $30 per month to all those now over 65 would cost nearly two and one-half billion dollars, and within a generation the number of those who are over 65 will be doubled, as the proportion of older people in the country is tending to increase, according to all vital statistics.

Nor would we find it easy to stop at $30 per month or adhere to a 65-year age qualification once we came to free pensions for everybody. Contributory old-age insurance, as provided for in the social security measure, while it is costly, is not nearly so costly as its probable alternative— free pensions for all the many millions of old people in the country without regard to need.

* * *

THE social security legislation has been criticized because the Federal Government makes no contribution from general tax revenues to the costs of unemployment compensation and old-age benefits. This criticism overlooks the very large amounts the Federal Government has appropriated for work relief and the aid it will give to the States for the care of unemployables.

It is certainly justifiable that the government should at this time devote its contributions to the relief of those now destitute, rather than to the accumulation of reserve funds for the payment of unemployment compensation and old-age benefits in future years. The government will also in future periods of long depression participate in or maintain the work benefits that may follow cash benefits paid from reserves and thereby make its contribution at the time of greatest need when other payments to the fund are found to be lowered by the shrinkage of business volume.

The Federal Government also, in participation with State governments, will maintain old-age pensions for those indigent aged persons not covered by the age annuity section of the measure. Thus the government contribution from general taxation will be substantial and will serve to establish the Federal Government's continuing responsibility for proper administration and proper growth of a system of social security on an adequate and businesslike basis.

Like all pioneer legislation, the social security measure is not perfect, but it is essentially sound. It imposes no impossible financial burden, and it distributes the burden it does impose in at least a reasonably fair manner. It provides systematic income to those placed in personal jeopardy by most recognized social causes. While the degree of benefit may often be inadequate, it is at least as generous as that in other government systems.

Now that the social security program is assured, the States will have the opportunity to bring most of the nation's wage-earners under its benefits. New York, Washington, Utah, California and New Hampshire have passed unemployment insurance laws in recent months; Wisconsin's law is in ef-

fect. Thirty-three States have old-age pension statutes, and mothers' pension acts are in force in all but two States. I am convinced that the people of the different States favor the program designed to bring them greater security in the future and that their Legislatures will speedily pass appropriate laws so that all may help to promote the general welfare.

Federal legislation was framed in the thought that the attack upon the problems of insecurity should be a cooperative venture participated in by both the Federal and the State governments, preserving the benefits of local administration and national leadership. It was thought unwise to have the Federal Government decide all questions of policy and dictate completely what the States should do. Only very necessary minimum standards are included in the Federal measure, leaving wide latitude to the States.

* * *

WHILE the different State laws on unemployment insurance must make all contributions compulsory, the States, in addition to deciding how these contributions shall be levied, have freedom in determining their own waiting periods, benefit rates, maximum benefit periods, and the like. Care should be taken that these laws do not contain benefit provisions in excess of collections. While unemployment varies greatly in different States, there is no certainty that States which have had less than normal unemployment heretofore will in the future have a more favorable experience than the average for the country.

It is obvious that in the best interests of the worker and industry and society there must be a certain uniformity of standards. It is obvious, too, that we must prevent the penalizing of competitive industry in any State which plans the early adoption of a sound system of unemployment insurance, and provide effective guarantees against the possibility of industry in one State having an advantage over that of another. This the uniform Federal tax does, as it costs the employer the same whether he pays the levy to the Federal Government or makes a contribution to a State unemployment insurance fund. The amount of the tax itself is a relative assurance that benefits will be standardized in all States, since under the law the entire collection must be spent on benefits to unemployed.

The social security measure looks primarily to the future and is only a part of the administration's plan to promote sound and stable recovery. We cannot think of it as disassociated from the government's program to save the homes, farms, businesses and banks of the nation,

and especially must we consider it as a companion measure to the Work Relief Act, which does undertake to provide immediate increase in employment and corresponding stimulation to private industry by purchase of supplies.

* * *

WHILE it is not anticipated as a complete remedy for the abnormal conditions confronting us at the present time, it is designed to afford protection for the individual against future major economic vicissitudes. It is a sound and reasonable plan and framed with due regard for the present state of economic recovery. It does not represent a complete solution of the problems of economic security, but it does represent a substantial necessary beginning. It has been developed after careful and intelligent consideration of all the facts and all of the programs that have been suggested or applied anywhere.

The foundation has been laid. On it will be reared a structure through the experience of the years to come, which will prove a haven for the nation's wage-earners in times of economic distress and when they become old and feeble. It will be a refuge also for widows and dependent children. In achieving such results it will likewise benefit all employers and investors by promoting and stabilizing mass purchasing power.

During the fifteen years I have been advocating such legislation as this I have learned that the American people want such security as the new measure provides. It will make this great Republic a better and a happier place in which to live—for us, our children and their children. It is a profound and sacred satisfaction to have had some part in securing this great boon to the people of our country.

The privilege of participating with economists, business men, workers and socially minded people everywhere in the plans and details has been a gratifying one. But to one who looks consistently on the ability of a free people to use political technique for the solution of major problems of individuals with due regard to welfare and progress of the whole of society, the new revelation of the capacity of Congress to act quickly, conscientiously and scientifically, and of the intellectual courage and human insight of the President, has brought a renewal of faith in the possibilities of life in this great nation as broad as a continent.

## SAVINGS BANKS FEAR END OF THRIFT HABIT

### Social Security Program May Have Disastrous Effect, Bay State Group Is Told.

SWAMPSCOTT, Mass., Sept. 12 (P). The effects of the social security program will determine savings banking of the future, Carl M. Spencer, president of the Savings Bank Association of Massachusetts, said today at the annual meeting of 1,000 members of that organization.

After reporting that nearly 3,000,-000 depositors had placed more than $2,000,000,000 in savings banks in Massachusetts, Mr. Spencer said:

"But what of the Social Security Bill providing for old-age pensions and unemployment insurance? In my judgment, in the long run, this will prove of the most importance to us and indeed all the business of the country."

"The promise of pensions and unemployment insurance may do surprising things to the thrift habits of our people," he added. "In the future is there to be no use for savings banks except for temporary savings?"

Professor Neil Carothers of Lehigh University, addressing the meeting, said that "recovery measures of the government have retarded recovery in this country at least six months and probably a year." He predicted an inflationary price rise, but added that it would not be a "headlong, all destroying rise."

"There are already in this country," he said, "enough excess reserves and idle credit to finance a boom twice as great as the awful orgy of 1928-29. There is a definite danger the inflationary elements in our government, seeing the failure of their monetary policies so far, will rush into a final inflation that will destroy all the securities, equities and fixed incomes in the country."

## WORKERS AND FACTORY GO BACK TO THE LAND

Times Wide World Photo.

**Factory near Hightstown, N. J., built by the Resettlement Administration for Jersey Homesteads**

# PIONEERS DEDICATE RA FACTORY-FARM

### Take Over Jersey Homesteads With Speeches and Fashion Show as 2,000 Cheer.

### 'FEEL LIKE MILLIONAIRES'

### Garment Workers Who Rose From Slums Voice Faith in Cooperative Security.

**From a Staff Correspondent.**
HIGHTSTOWN, N. J., Aug. 2.—A little band of New York garment workers, pioneers in the quest for group security through cooperative effort, took over from the Federal Government today responsibility for the successful conduct of Jersey Homesteads, the experimental industrial and farm village built for them by the Resettlement Administration.

They dedicated themselves to the task with speeches and a fashion show at the formal opening of the steel and glass factory, which the RA put up at a cost of $95,000 and which will be the center of the in-

dustrial life of the community. Nearly 2,000 relatives and friends came in taxicabs, buses and automobiles to cheer the pioneers.

They did not look like visionaries —these men and women who had backed their faith in the economic and social future of the village with an initial investment of $500 a family.

Many of them came to the United States seeking a refuge from persecution and privation. They found homes in the "lung blocks" of the lower East Side, spent years hunched over machines in sweatshops and skyscraper lofts and slowly pulled themselves up to the humble luxury of flats in Brooklyn and the Bronx.

Now, installed in functional, one-story homes that seem to have climbed full-grown from the red dust of Monmouth County, they find themselves, as one of them put it today, "feeling like millionaires."

**Project Not Yet Complete**

Delays in the completion of the project have left no imprint on the confidence of the settlers. Of the 200 projected homes, only eight are completed and occupied. The factory is not yet equipped for work on a mass scale. But no note of these difficulties was allowed to intrude on the day's ceremonies.

With a sound truck blaring out a recorded version of "The Stars and Stripes Forever," the homesteaders marched to their seats at the front of the hall. They wore polo shirts, house dresses, slacks and checkered caps, but in their eyes was the expression of high resolve.

For two and one-half hours, while the temperature shot sky-

ward, they listened to oratorical estimates of the project's significance. They heard, too, a telegram from Rexford G. Tugwell, Resettlement Administrator, in which he said:

"Pressure of government business will prevent my being with you on Aug. 2. My best wishes go with you in this cooperative enterprise. From now on the success and repute of Jersey Homesteads will become more and more your responsibility. I am confident that you will meet it with courage, patience and determination."

Boris Drasin, president of the Workers Aim Cooperative Association, the name taken by the settlers, opened the meeting by declaring that the eyes of the world were focused on the project. Two of the younger pioneers, apparently unaware of the world's gaze, broke away from their parents at this point and romped about the runway erected for the fashion show. The speech was interrupted while the mothers recaptured them.

A chorus of youths sang the "theme song" of the colony. The refrain went like this:

Production, cooperation,
Freedom for every nation,
Here, there and everywhere,
This is our claim:
Workers' aim,
Workers' aim.

**Threefold Cooperation**

Benjamin Brown, "father" of the enterprise and co-author, with Mrs. Brown, of the song, disclosed that the trade name of the factory's products would be "Tripod."

"This stands," he explained, "for three types of cooperation—cooperation by agriculturists, cooperation by industrialists and cooperation by consumers. On this tripod will we not only bring back craftsman-

107

ship and pride of achievement, together with security, but we will bring back prosperity based on abundance and not on curtailment."

The cooperative village, Mr. Brown felt sure, was in harmony with the thought and principles of the framers of the Constitution. He heatedly denied that the project was expressive of any ism other than "common sense-ism."

"We defy any demagogue who may dare to say that this is not the American way," Mr. Brown declared. And the crowd cheered.

Other speakers included Dr. Eugene E. Agger, Assistant Resettlement Administrator; Mrs. Dorothy M. Beck, regional director of the RA, and Morris Rothenberg, Zionist leader.

The coats and dresses exhibited in the fashion show were made at the association's temporary factory at 246 West Thirty-eighth Street, Manhattan, and the finishing touches were applied on the sewing machines here last week. Seven models from New York, two of them members of the cooperative's regular staff, paraded across the factory floor wearing Fall and Winter outfits priced to wholesale at from $10.75 to $59.75. Buyers representing many large metropolitan concerns were in the crowd as guests of the settlers.

A flood of advance orders has piled up at the local factory, but officials were unable to predict accurately the extent to which work would get under way this week. Thirty-two sewing machines, eight hand pressers and two steam pressers have been installed. Twelve of the sewing machines are due to start tomorrow, but officials admitted that the actual beginning of operations might be postponed until Tuesday and maybe later.

# TOPSY-TURVYDOM

## Three Acts of Monkeyshines by Moss Hart And George S. Kaufman

### By BROOKS ATKINSON

AS soon as the laughter had subsided at the Booth Theatre on Monday evening and the audience had started to go home in a cheerful frame of mind the neighborhood intellectual began carping. After a droll and hilarious evening he is a dismal fellow to see. With a look of intellectual dissent in his eyes, he said that Mr. Hart and Mr. Kaufman had not explained how the Sycamore family could ride their hobby-horses so fantastically in a world dominated by rent, the price of foodstuffs and raw materials. And when Grandfather Vanderhof, snake-hunter, stamp-collector and avocationist-in-ordinary, genially advised the world never to work at anything that is distasteful, the neighborhood intellectual had been embarrassed by such a show of wishful thinking. The whole whirligig of humor and fancy seemed to him economically unsound.

\* \* \*

WELL, it is true. Probably Mr. Hart and Mr. Kaufman will acknowledge that their genial skit about a crack-brained Washington Heights family does not explain how a man can have his cake and eat it, too. Essie does make candy on the kitchen stove and her amiable husband carries it around to stores. together with slogans from Trotsky that he likes to print on his hand press. Alice is a banker's secretary, which is presumably a paid job; Grandfather has been drawing an income from real estate since 1901, and it may easily be that Mr. Sycamore sells a few of the fireworks which he and the former iceman exuberantly manufacture in the cellar. But there is no denying that the Sycamore circus is stuffed with deadheads. After eight years of tapping at a typewriter, which was delivered at the door by mistake several years ago, Mrs. Sycamore is still an unproduced playwright, and there is no income from xylophone playing in the dining-room, tap-dancing or dart-throwing. It is to be feared that neither the authors nor the characters in the play are boldly facing the grave facts of life.

\* \* \*

IN the circumstances, it will be necessary to look upon "You Can't Take It With You" as a gallimaufry of gambols and the best comedy these authors have written. They have never before written about such enjoyable people or treated them so tolerantly. I confess to being a little weary of the Broadway conquest by wisecrack which treats characters like pins in a bowling alley and knocks them down with deadly shots from skillful players. For good sportsmanship that game is a little too unequal to be wholly refreshing; the characters are doomed to a shaft of destructive wit the instant they appear on the stage. The characters in this new prank may be a little casual about the world of fact, but they are excellent coiners of fancy, and their home life is virtually ideal. With all the junk that clutters the dining-room and the irresponsible hospitality that warms it, the Sycamore household is so attractive that any one is likely to join it at any moment. The milkman stayed five years until he died; the iceman has already been there eight years, and Essie's husband is merely a likable lad who just happened in. No one can say that the Sycamores are snobs or climbers.

\* \* \*

TO extract the full jovial flavor of the Sycamore madness it is necessary to contrast them with conventional people and to invent a practicable crisis. All this the authors have accomplished as casually as though they were Sycamores themselves—by engaging the most sensible girl in the family to the handsome son of a pompous family and by dragging in the police under some plausible misapprehension. Put this down as the mechanics of popular playmaking. The banker's son is only a musical comedy cipher and the banker is merely he who gets persuaded. If you agree that there has to be some end to all this hobbledehoy moonshine, and a happy one into the bargain, you will not tax Mr. Hart and Mr. Kaufman with their lack of interest in important people. For they, too, have caught the contagion of Grandfather's benevolent relish of topsy-turvydom and all they want is that it may continue until bedtime. When the Sycamore jangle becomes a little madder than usual Grandfather leans blissfully back in his chair and says: "I hope I live to be a hundred." When the whole place hums with lunacy he goes further: "I've got to live to be a hundred and fifty." To the family Sycamore tree add the names of Mr. Hart and Mr. Kaufman and most of the light-headed theatregoers of the town.

\* \* \*

AT any rate, add the name of Henry Travers. After "The Good Earth" catastrophe of October, 1932, he fled to Hollywood, where he has been quietly acting in pictures. Before that, for about fifteen years, he had been one of the drollest comedians in the theatre. In the Shaw plays he was perfect—just ruminative enough to turn the cerebral handsprings of the master satirist. And now he is here again, pottering around placidly in the part of Grandfather, adjusting his glasses, speaking in the dry voice that gives dialogue pawkiness and common sense—withal a little breathless and uneasy as though he could not stand much more of it. Although Mr. Travers gives an impression of slumping down comfortably into a part, he really sets a part firmly on its feet.

\* \* \*

IN the present instance he is well matched by Josephine Hull whose homely comedy is in a related key, gasping, fluttery, egregiously middle class. And as the retired iceman here is our old friend Frank Conlan, whose mouth is always wide open in wonder at the oddities of the world. There is not a wise-cracker in the cast. But there are enough props to furnish a madhouse. For "You Can't Take It With You" is the perfect idiot's delight of the season, although, as the neighborhood intellectual points out, a little deficient in its economic interpretation of life.

# EXILES FROM THE DUST BOWL

## They Create a Grave Problem for California

By DOUGLAS W. CHURCHILL
LOS ANGELES

IN another decade a century will have passed since a man strode through the streets of San Francisco holding a bottle of yellow dust aloft and shouting, "Gold! Gold dust from the American River!" That cry rang across the world. It created a new empire. It took its toll from the farms, the factories and the marts of a nation; it lured hundreds of thousands from the farthest corners of the earth. In wagons, on horseback, behind teams of oxen, around the Horn by sailing ship, men fought and lived or died attempting to reach California that they might scoop up the powder in their hands and become rich.

Today a new army is on the march, out of the vast, dry bowl of the Southwest and on to California. Leaving ruin behind, the marchers come in dilapidated cars and decrepit trucks. Again it is dust that impels their migration. Instead of a lure, it is a parching, blinding, suffocating monster that has driven them from their homes. They have seen great black clouds sweep down on their land and leave it bare. In one respect only does their procession resemble the trek of almost 100 years ago. Like the pioneers, they have turned toward the Far West in hope. The Forty-Niners sought a fortune; the Argonauts of 1938 seek an existence.

In the years between, the movement did not stop; California has always held out a promise of a pleasanter life. But the recent droughts quickened the pace until now the number of refugees seeking livelihood in the State is estimated at 200,000. No accurate count of their number is possible since no check has been made on those who have left California.

THESE newcomers have scattered through the central valleys of California from the northern reaches of the Sacramento to the very door of Los Angeles at the end of the San Joaquin. Some of them have settled in camps on the great ranches, some are in lean-tos beside the irrigation ditches, some in the government resettlement camps. This Winter the problem their presence creates for State relief agencies and for the Federal Government becomes more acute than it has been at any time since the migration began in earnest two years ago.

Across the border they streamed, many of them with their few remaining possessions tied to their cars. High on the running boards were piled their moveable belongings. Cooking utensils, used on the march, rattled against the sides of the machines and tents were lashed across the engines' hoods. Possibly over the ragged top lay a mattress and resting on it a chicken coop containing all the livestock left by the searing winds. Inside the car were crowded six or seven or eight or nine men, women and children. Generally it was a single family. Sometimes, though, two neighbors pooled their resources and united in a common aim, to head for California, the golden.

In nearly every case the move was made in desperation. The refugees were farmers whose lands had been ravaged by the winds, or artisans and tradesmen from the towns that have suffered most in those parts of Oklahoma, Kansas, Texas, Colorado and New Mexico, in which the dust plague has taken its toll. Most started out with barely enough money for gas and food to reach the Coast; a few were fortified with extra dollars paid to them by government agents for the bony carcasses of cattle they had to kill. The dust, inadequate relief in their home districts and the hope of better things "beyond the mountains" all motivated the trek.

When Los Angeles and other California cities got wind of what was happening they became alarmed. Hordes of hungry were envisioned descending on the urban centers. Los Angeles stationed battalions of police along the California border in an effort to stem the tide. Thousands were frightened away or turned back. After the Attorney General objected to the blockade and when it appeared that the refugees sought work in the rich valleys rather than relief in the towns, the guard was withdrawn. The invaders arrived in increasing numbers and drifted through the State to become a part of its 90-year-old migratory labor system.

IN many cases they have come to be regarded by large ranch operators as a godsend. In California ranches are not simply farms. They are industrial concerns and their purpose is to grow and ship. A holding of 2,500 acres is ordinary. Thirty per cent of the large-scale agricultural operations in the United States are in the California valleys. Through purchase, merger and foreclosure, ownership of the land has been centralized in recent years and, although the area in the State under cultivation has not been increased since 1885, in the last five years holdings in excess of 1,000 acres have increased 37 per cent, while those under fifty acres have decreased. The key to profit on such large

ventures, California has found, is cheap labor and plenty of it.

THE State has always had an abundant supply. Development of the refrigerator car after the railroads were laid created a new demand for labor, but there were enough who had been failures at prospecting among the 350,000 gold-rush immigrants to provide the first army of migratory field and shed hands. It was a stopgap for them and they counted on nothing beyond a few weeks' work. But as season followed season, "fruit tramp" became the name of a trade and a calling for thousands.

Prior to 1860, 45,000 Chinese coolies had entered California to work in the mines. Racial troubles drove them out and they took to the railroads and eventually to the ranches. Labor contractors began playing the yellow against the white, an activity that kept wages at a minimum. This continued until the century's turn. By that time the Chinese had become less active or had saved enough money to return to China.

The Japanese followed and gave rise to what California called the "yellow peril." In 1907, 30,000 entered the port of San Francisco and they were rushed to the valleys to join those who had preceded them. Wily, shrewd, good farmers, they were not content to remain laborers for the whites and they bought land. Exclusion laws followed. As a result of the controversy, they colonized their own lands or moved to the cities.

The Mexicans were imported to take their place. Contractors found that these newcomers were happy with a dollar a day and they flooded the labor market. During the Twenties, when the first indications that the Mexicans were getting out of hand were observed, Filipinos were brought in, but they quickly became enamored of the cities and those who remained on the land centered their activities in the asparagus fields and the rice marshes.

THUS a new labor source was desired. The dust-bowl refugees seemed to be the solution. To replace the foreign-born migratories, these Americans—their names attest to their nativity—answer the need of large numbers of workers for the short periods when the crop is being harvested. They are better than the Chinese and Mexicans, because only the male members of those peoples worked in the fields. Like the Japanese, whole families—men, women and children—labor in fields and sheds, a family wage frequently being from $1.20 to $1.50 a day.

The refugees' prior condition, the luck they have upon reaching California and the advice of friends determine, to a large extent, their mode of living here. Roughly, they reach one of four levels. First are those who get into government camps, of which two out of a projected eight have been completed in the State, harboring from 1,500 to 3,000 migratories each. For 10 cents a day they are given a platform on which to pitch a tent, basic medical attention, sanitation and recreational advantages. They keep their children in school when they are not working, and make a bid for independence.

Those in the second stratum live in rented shacks for which they pay, on an average, $8 a month. Below this level are most of the ranch camps. Many of the ranchers would like to house all their workers, but on no ranch visited were there accommodations for more than a portion of the hands. Sanitary facilities are limited and water must be carried long distances.

The fourth and lowest group are the most distressing. They usually live in hovels on the banks of irrigation ditches beneath cottonwoods. Some have fragments of tents to which they have added fiberboard boxes or anything that gives a suggestion of shelter.

NO two elements in California view alike the refugees and the problems they have created. For the most part the city dwellers are oblivious of them. Not many of the refugees are seen in the urban centers. But Californians who are aware of them have pronounced feelings.

"They are robbing our residents of work and they present a critical relief problem this Winter," said a Los Angeles welfare official.

"They're lazy, no-account failures and they'd rather live on the county than work," exclaimed the owner of a 7,500-acre ranch. "Why, I've offered them land and they won't work it!"

"They're just the same as the rest of us, but their breaks were tougher," said the owner of a forty-acre ranch.

"They're criminals, radicals and un-American," charged a Chief of Police.

"They're broken, starving creatures," commented the assistant head of a public hospital. "They work when they can and when they are able. Some are diseased; all are undernourished."

"They could be one of the great assets of California if given land and the self-respect that goes with it," said a government agent in one of the resettlement camps.

The only apparent organized movement toward a solution is being undertaken by the Farms Security Administration, succes-tration, in cooperation with the California State Emergency Relief Administration. Construction of six tent colony camps has been undertaken. Two other camps, one at Marysville and one at Arvin, near Bakersfield, have been in operation for some time.

IN addition to the tents of Arvin, adobe houses suitable for the climate are being built. Each costs approximately $900 and is equipped with hot and cold water, electricity and ample land for a home garden. The rent is set at $8 a month. The first unit will house fifty families, each of which will be assigned a house for a year. Those who do not show that they are benefiting from the experiment will be supplanted.

The west slopes of the San Joaquin and Sacramento Valleys are being developed by the government as a great reclamation project and within three years a large fertile district is expected to begin producing. Some of the Federal men would like to see some of this land purchased by the government and sold to the migratories in small parcels. They believe that a two-acre plot with a house for each family would go far toward solving the problem. The land, they maintain, would give the settlers a living and possibly a little surplus during the season in which the men were not needed on the ranches. With their own produce and money earned from field and shed work, these people, it is held, would be-come self-sustaining middle-class farmers. They would, in turn, provide the ranches with a stable and high-class labor source and would improve the social and economic standing of the valleys.

ON a broader scale, the FSA plans to coordinate the efforts of several divisions in the Department of Agriculture to meet the difficulty at its source in the Great Plains area by developing "better land use and a sound program of mitigating the danger to land from dust storm and drought." More than 100 counties in Colorado, Kansas, New Mexico, Oklahoma and Texas are included in the area in which the program would operate.

Administrators point out that the first problems to be met were those of poverty and wind erosion and that the FSA, through its rural rehabilitation program, has made several thousand loans to distressed farmers for human and animal subsistence. The next step was to effect a change in the type of agriculture.

The storms that have swept the State in recent weeks have added to the misery and problems of the transients. The march of the nomads has continued throughout the Winter, and while the number of dust-bowl refugees has decreased thousands have been added to the transitory army. Snows have brought temporary relief to the arid lands, but the end of dust storms, and waves of migration, is not in sight.

# John Steinbeck's New Novel Brims With Anger and Pity

## "The Grapes of Wrath" Is a Deeply Felt Story of Landless American Migrants

THE GRAPES OF WRATH. By John Steinbeck. 619 pp. New York: The Viking Press. $2.75.

*By PETER MONRO JACK*

THERE are a few novelists writing as well as Steinbeck and perhaps a very few who write better; but it is most interesting to note how very much alike they are all writing. Hemingway, Caldwell, Faulkner, Dos Passos in the novel, and MacLeish in poetry are those whom we easily think of in their similarity of theme and style. Each is writing stories and scenarios of America with a curious and sudden intensity, almost as if they had never seen or understood it before. They are looking at it again with revolutionary eyes. Stirred like every other man in the street with news of foreign persecution, they turn to their own land to find seeds of the same destructive hatred. Their themes of pity and anger, their styles of sentimental elegy and scarifying denunciation may come to seem representative of our time. MacLeish's "Land of the Free," for instance, going directly to the matter with poetry and pictures—the matter being that the land is no longer free, having been mortgaged, bought and finally bankrupted by a succession of anonymous companies, banks, politicians and courts, or, for the present instance, Steinbeck's "The Grapes of Wrath," as pitiful and angry a novel ever to be written about America.

It is a very long novel, the longest that Steinbeck has written, and yet it reads as if it had been composed in a flash, ripped off the typewriter and delivered to the public as an ultimatum. It is a long and thoughtful novel as one thinks about it. It is a short and vivid scene as one feels it.

The opening scene is in Oklahoma, where a change in the land

110

is taking place that no one understands, neither the single families who have pioneered it nor the great owners who have bought it over with their banks and lawyers. As plainly as it can be put, Mr. Steinbeck puts it. A man wants to build a wall, a house, a dam, and inside that a certain security to raise a family that will continue his work. But there is no security for a single family. The cotton crops have sucked out the roots of the land and the dust has overlaid it. The men from the Bank or the Company, sitting in their closed cars, try to explain to the squatting farmers what they scarcely understand themselves: that the tenants whose grandfathers settled the land have no longer the title to it, that a tractor does more work than a single family of men, women and children put together, that their land is to be mechanically plowed under, with special instructions that their hand-built houses are to be razed to the ground.

This may read like a disquisition by Stuart Chase. 'There is, in fact, a series of essays on the subject running through the book, angry and abstract—like the characters, "perplexed and figuring." The essayist in Steinbeck alternates with the novelist, as it does with Caldwell and the others. The moralist is as important as the story-teller, may possibly outlast him; but the story at the moment is the important thing.

The most interesting figure of this Oklahoma family is the son who has just been released from jail. He is on his way home from prison, hitch-hiking across the State in his new cheap prison suit, picking up a preacher who had baptized him when young, and arriving to find the family setting out for California. The Bank had come "to tractorin' off the place." The house had been knocked over by the tractor making straight furrows for the cotton. The Joad family had read handbills promising work for thousands in California, orange picking. They had bought an old car, were on the point of leaving, when Tom turned up from prison with the preacher. They can scarcely wait for this promised land of fabulous oranges, grapes and peaches. Only one stubborn fellow remains on the land where his great-grandfather had shot Indians and built his house. The others, with Tom and the preacher, pack their belongings on the second-hand truck, set out for the

new land, to start over again in California.

The journey across is done in superb style, one marvellous short story after another, and all melting into this long novel of the great trek. The grandfather dies on the way, and then the grandmother. The son Noah stops at a river and decides to stay there. Without quite knowing it, he is the Thoreau in the family. A fine river, fish to catch and eat, the day and night to dream in: he wants nothing else. The little children have their fun along the road; wise little brats, they are growing up, secret and knowing. Tom and his brother take turns driving the truck, easing her over the mountains, grinding her valves, scraping the plugs: they are the mechanics. The sister, Rosasharn, christened for Rose of Sharon, expects to have her baby. Her husband disappears, aims to better himself in his own selfish way. The Joad family meet people coming and going, going to California from the Western States with hope and the orange handbills and a $75 jalopy; people coming from California embittered and broke, speaking darkly of deputies, double-crossing, 20 cents an hour and labor trouble. Those coming from California are going back to their native Oklahoma, Texas or Arkansas, to die starving in what had once been their homes, rather than die starving in a strange country.

Californians are not going to like this angry novel. The Joad family drive over the mountains, through the desert, the great valley, through Tehacapi in the morning glow—"Al jammed on the brake and stopped in the middle of the road. * * * The vineyards, the orchards, the great flat valley, green and beautiful, the trees set in rows, and the farm houses."

And Pa said, "God Almighty!"

*From a Painting by Stjernstrom.*

John Steinbeck.

The distant cities, the little towns in the orchard land, and the morning sun, golden on the valley. . . . The grain fields golden in the morning, and the willow lines, the eucalyptus trees in rows. . . . Pa sighed, "I never knowed they was anything like her,"—silent and awestruck, embarrassed before the great valley, writes Mr. Steinbeck, of even the children.

The beauty and fertility of California conceal human fear, hatred and violence. "Scairt" is a Western farmer's word for the inhabitants, frightened of the influx of workers eager for jobs, and when they are frightened they become vicious and cruel. This part of the story reads like the news from Nazi Germany. Families from Oklahoma are known as "Okies." While they

work they live in what might as well be called concentration camps. Only a few hundred are given jobs out of the thousands who traveled West in response to the handbills. Their pay is cut from 30 cents an hour to 25, to 20. If any one objects he is a Red, an agitator, a trouble-maker who had better get out of the country. Deputy sheriffs are around with guns, legally shooting or clubbing any one from the rest of the Union who questions the law of California. The Joad family find only one place of order and decency in this country of fear and violence, in a government camp, and it is a pleasure to follow the family as they take a shower bath and go to the Saturday night dances. But even here the deputy sheriffs, hired by the banks who run the Farmers Association, are poking in their guns, on the pretext of inciting to riot and the necessity of protective custody. The Joad family moves on through California, hunted by anonymous guns while they are picking peaches for 2½ cents a box, hoping only for a little land free of guns and dust on which they might settle and work as they were accustomed to. The promised grapes of California have turned into grapes of wrath that might come to fruition at any moment.

How true this may be no reviewer can say. One may very easily point out that a similar message has been read by the writers mentioned above, and that Mr. Steinbeck has done the same thing before. It is easy to add that the novel comes to no conclusion, that the preacher is killed because he is a strikebreaker, that Tom disappears as a fugitive from California justice, that the novel ends on a minor and sentimental note; that the story stops after 600 pages merely because a story has to stop somewhere. All this is true enough but the real truth is that Steinbeck has written a novel from the depths of his heart with a sincerity seldom equaled. It may be an exaggeration, but it is the exaggeration of an honest and splendid writer.

April 16, 1939

# SWING MUSIC HELD DEGENERATED JAZZ

## Grant Lays Its Popularity to Economic Conditions— Urges Rhumbas, Tangos

## 'CAPE COD CAPERS' SHOWN

## Dancing Teachers See Latest Routine—It Has Lateral Glides but No Hops

Swing music was characterized as "a degenerated form of jazz" and its devotees were described as "the unfortunate victims of economic instability" yesterday by Donald Grant, president of the Dancing Teachers Business Association, at the third annual convention of that organization at the Park Central Hotel.

"The current furore over swing dance music is a sign of our uncertain times," Mr. Grant declared. "Our young people, disturbed by uncertainties of their economic situation and wondering whether they will be on WPA or in a CCC camp tomorrow have found in swing neurotic and erotic expressions of physical activity. There is little or no display of natural grace in a good jitterbug."

### Advocates "Suave" Types

More "suave" types of dancing, particularly those to be found in the best tangos and rhumbas, were advocated by the head of the dancing teachers' association. He predicted that the popularity of swing will fade with the return of economic stability, and that young people as well as more mature adults will find in the more "stylistic" dances greater spiritual and physical satisfaction. The natural grace used in a good tango has a certain "feline" character about it that makes it not only beautiful to watch but much more satisfying to execute than any swing, Mr. Grant emphasized.

Every adult should take part in folk art, Mr. Grant believed. Folk-dancing brings with it an uplift of the spirit and helps to develop the personality to such an extent that frequently it may transform the whole individuality of a human being, he said.

Various dance authorities during the day emphasized dancing as an aid to muscular development and in encouraging natural poise, grace and coordination. Dancing, it was pointed out, will help to correct physical defects in children before such defects become permanent, even though such corrective measures may be impossible to obtain from calesthenics and competitive games.

### Dancing Aids Social Sense

Children who are fond of dancing develop a certain quickness of physical and mental reactions which also stands them in good stead in their school work, it was explained. Dancing was also recommended for the development of normal social sense in children, and the correction of abnormal shyness.

During the dance clinics, which were attended by the 400 dancing teachers from all parts of the country and Canada during the day, was an exhibition for the first time of a new dance called the Cape Cod Capers. The exhibition was by Donald Sawyer. The Cape Cod Capers, which may be performed in couples or in groups, consists principally of smooth lateral slides, without hops. The sliding steps are close to the floor, giving the dancers an appearance of natural gliding grace.

The convention will hold its annual business meeting today. One of the proposals the teachers are expected to consider is opposition to pending bills in Congress, particularly the Coffee-Pepper bill, which in the opinion of many of the teachers at the meeting may make the teaching of dancing "a political proposition."

July 27, 1938

# THE LEGION COUNTS TWENTY YEARS

By SAMUEL T. WILLIAMSON

IT makes no difference whether the landscape is rolling prairie, Southwestern vastness or chilly New England stone walls: everywhere in this country some things are the same. In every American settlement is at least one church, school house, town hall, chain store, filling station and American Legion hall.

Among more than 4,000,000 still living who served in the United States Army or Navy (or Marine Corps) during the World War, are slightly less than a million Legionnaires; and their posts are at almost every whistle stop. It wouldn't be Memorial Day, Fourth of July or Armistice Day without them. Politicians of both parties court them, Ph. D.'s examine them as social phenomena, chambers of commerce display symptoms of coronary thrombosis at their bonus campaigns, and left-wing comrades strain both larynxes and adjectives in expression of extreme distaste. The Legion is as American as tomato juice, chewing gum, drug-store sandwiches and cigarettes in packages of twenty.

It has grown up. It celebrates its twentieth birthday this week. The years have brought a change in the members who joined up in 1919 and the early Nineteen Twenties. Then most of them were ramrod-backed youngsters. They were yet to get their first jobs, or else were wondering about getting their old ones back. Today, shoulders have slumped forward, waistlines show greater expansion than chests; what hair remains worth shearing is turning gray. Some members are still worrying about jobs. Their children are growing up, and new grandfathers are more usual than new fathers. Legion squads are called out with greater frequency to fire three volleys over freshly dug graves, but another fifty years will pass before the Legion becomes a pathetic little remnant like the Grand Army of the Republic.

And it appears destined to have a different history from the G. A. R. The majority of Union veterans of the Civil War voted as they shot—the straight Republican ticket. G. A. R. and G. O. P. were inextricably entwined. No such propensity exists among the men who wear the Legion's blue overseas cap. The Legion has its own politics. Its State and national conventions are scarcely different from similar meetings of political parties—standards in the aisles, "demonstrations" for candidates, delegate hunts and trades and logrollings. Many a party politician has graduated from Legion affairs to public office. World War veterans comprise more than one-quarter of the membership of the House of Representatives. A score are United States Senators. The Legion has produced politicians, but it has been free from party politics. Every attempt of a political party to capture the Legion has been blocked by Legionnaires.

It has been that way since the beginning. The Armistice found 2,000,000 American soldiers in France, an equal number executing "squads right" in the United States, and 1,000,000 who wore sailor suits and squirmed every night into navy hammocks. In France everybody wanted to go home at once, but there was barbed wire to be rolled up, a Rhine bridgehead at Coblenz to be guarded. Technically the war was still on, for there was no telling whether the Germans would sign a peace.

The A. E. F. was as homesick as a boy on his first night at boarding school; and if it couldn't see the Statue of Liberty, it had heard a lot about Paris. Courts-martial were busy trying case after case of absence without leave. Company clerks, if they weren't in that status themselves, marked "A. W. O. L." on thousands of service records. Officers and men were as touchy as though they had hives. John Pershing wouldn't have been sure of the soldier vote for dog catcher.

Persons who didn't sleep well of nights feared what would happen when the soldiers were demobilized, and the specter of "bolshevism" Suzie-Q'ed over their blankets. They had heard of "soldiers' and sailors' councils" in other armies, and they wondered. As a matter of fact, although the A. E. F. was somewhat rough and forgetful of Sunday school lessons, it was no more bolshevistic than Bishop Manning. It merely wanted to go home.

There was no denying that morale was considerably frayed and that further unraveling must be stopped. Mere general orders could not assuage a Winter of discontent. The people at G. H. Q. took a leaf from civilian practice; they decided to call a conference. Twenty officers from ten infantry divisions and as many other units in the A. E. F. were summoned to Paris. They included Lieut. Cols. Bennett Champ Clark, Theodore Roosevelt, David M. Goodrich, Franklin D'Olier, Colonel William J. (Wild Bill) Donovan and Captain Ogden L. Mills. All were former civilians of prominence who held National Guard or Reserve commissions, and two days were consumed in telling regulars what was wrong with the army and what should be done in the way of less restriction, more leaves and programs of athletics, entertainment and study.

On Feb. 15, the night before the officers were to return to their commands, Roosevelt invited them to dinner. Until little cups of what the French fondly believed was coffee were passed, the guests were occupied with the A. E. F.'s favorite conversational exercise: their own division had won the war single-handed. Roosevelt interrupted these historical liberties with announcement that he had something on his chest. Steps would be taken at once to lift army morale, but what would happen when the soldiers returned to civilian life? He proposed a veterans' organization comprised of all—officers and men—who had served with the colors, at home or abroad, during the World War.

Although a few diners sought to attach their pet ideas to the project, the group agreed to put the whole question of a veterans' organization before a meeting to be held in Paris a month from then, a meeting of officers and men representing all elements of the A. E. F.

In the shadow of Eiffel Tower lay the gas house-shaped Cirque de Paris. There acrobats once allez-ooped and little white dogs walked on their hind legs and leaped through paper hoops, and there in the presence of the future King of the Belgians (who was chewing gum) Private J. J. Tunney, United States Marine Corps, was soon to win the light-heavyweight championship of the A. E. F. Five hundred officers and a like number of enlisted men were expected there March 15, 16 and 17. The thousand delegates arrived in Paris, but a third of them never reached the hall. Pressure of other engagements.

The virtuous two-thirds chose Lieut. Col. Clark (now United States Senator from Missouri) temporary chairman. Motion was made and carried that all matters of rank be waived during the caucus, and one bogy that the proposed veterans' organization would develop into an "officers-only" affair was definitely laid. Buck privates were entitled to the same voice as wearers of Sam Browne belts, and the men in hob-nailed hikers were not slow in expressing their minds. There were few reticences.

The committee on name failed lamentably to rise to the occasion. The best it could propose was "Legion of the Great War." Second choice was "Veterans of the Great War." Another high favorite was "Liberty League," and the commit-

tee's report was thrown to the wolves. Long after it was time for lunch, Maurice K. Gordon suggested "American Legion," which was adopted amid cries of "When do we eat?"

THE committee on constitution submitted a preamble beginning with a slight run of fancy: "We, the members of the Military and Naval Service"—fancy because, with the exception of a few Marines, all delegates to the caucus were soldiers. But on the last day of the session a lone sailor poked his head through the door. He looked surprised, said "I thought there was a show going on here," and immediately was made representative of "the naval service."

Roosevelt returned with a group to the United States to lay the groundwork for a meeting in St. Louis which should be a duplicate of the
Paris affair, while in France Colonel Milton J. Foreman of Illinois found himself "the temporary head of an interim committee of a proposed organization."

Which was as it should be. Few great organizations were as free of self-seeking founders as the Legion. The group of twenty officers at the Roosevelt dinner in February had deferred to a caucus of the A. E. F. at which enlisted men would be represented. And now the A. E. F. veterans left results of their three-day meeting to the verdict of the men at home.

EVERY State but one was represented by the 1,000 delegates who met in St. Louis on May 8. For six months the country had been "welcoming the heroes home" and now the heroes were a problem. For more than a year between 4,000,000 and 5,000,000 men had been taken out of productive work while others filled their places; now they wanted their old jobs back again. If they were united behind one leader, they could take things into their own hands. The St. Louis caucus gave the country its answer.

"The floor is open," said young Theodore Roosevelt, "for nomination for permanent chairman." The floor was of but one howling mind. It went crazy over "young Teddy." Then and there the American Legion might have committed suicide in willing to become a personal organization of a man who bore a magic name. Roosevelt was not without political ambition, and the temptation must have been enormous. "He rose to meet it superbly," Marquis James chronicles in his history of the Legion, "and guided the Legion for the last time it needed one man's guidance."

He declined nomination. He was elected unanimously. He declined to serve, was renominated, declined again. That clinched it, and later the caucus made sure that the Legion never could become a one-man organization by stipulating that the National Commander should serve for one year only and might not succeed himself.

THE Legion's next answer was to those who feared tha demobilized service men "were poisoned by radicalism." The caucus heard, then shouted down an earnest delegate from the Soldiers and Sailors Council. The Legion had shown that it would not be an officers-only group; now it refused to have any truck with an outfit that sought other class distinctions.

Finally the caucus quieted down to the one-two-three-fours of a constitution. Again it declined outside assistance. One delegate brought from New York a proposed draft written by the country's greatest constitutional lawyer, Elihu Root. It was masterly, but it left the veterans cold. A committee set to work upon a new draft. The committee emerged with a document containing a preamble that ranks with the most eloquent statements of American principles. No one hand produced it; the phrasing and thought came from twenty or thirty men, most of them young lawyers. But with that preamble the Legion went proudly to the country and to its comrades; and within eighteen months it had 800,000 members.

Today, twenty years later, that preamble seems more than ever worthy of attention and adherence, for it reads:

For God and country we associate ourselves together for the following purposes: To uphold and defend the Constitution of the United States of America; to maintain law and order; to foster and perpetuate a one hundred per cent Americanism; to preserve the memories and incidents of our association in the Great War; to inculcate a sense of individual obligation to the community, State and nation; to combat the autocracy of both the classes and the masses; to make right the master of might; to promote peace and good-will on earth; to safeguard and transmit to posterity the principles of justice, freedom and democracy; to consecrate and sanctify our comradeship by our devotion to mutual helpfulness.

THE first matter to which the Legion, with rapidly growing membership, gave its attention was the plight of the ex-service man. The Federal Government's

vocational training board was snarled in its own red tape. Likewise engulfed was the War Risk Insurance Bureau, with 300,000 unacted-upon cases before it. Congress was so bogged down that its leaders "deeply regretted" that legislation for care of the disabled must wait; but a Legion delegation boiled into Washington, with the result that within two days rules were suspended and the bill was passed setting up the Veterans Bureau.

Folks on Capitol Hill soon discovered in the Legion's legislative committee a persuasive force. The committee's Washington representative, who is still John Thomas Taylor, reaches Congressional ears with little difficulty, because legislators have found that his arguments are repeated in a flood of letters from their home districts. Contrasted with other lobbies, the Legion's Washington loboy is small. It knows what few pressure groups realize: That the voice of a home constituency is louder than all the noise of organized pilgrimages and marches on Washington.

FOR the first few months the young organization handled the bonus problem gingerly. Its first convention at Minneapolis declared veterans entitled to "an adjustment of compensation," which was referred "with confidence to the Congress" because the Legion "could not ask for legislation in its own selfish interests." But as the weeks of the next legislative session dragged on without action, the Legion lost its "confidence" in an unpersuaded Congress. It turned on the heat. Congressmen were toasted on both sides, and for four years the bonus ranked with prohibition as a subject impossible of discussion without loud words, bad names and high blood pressures. After two Presidential ve oes it was passed in the form of a twenty-year endowment policy. Hard times brought demands, not officially sponsored by the Legion, for a 50 per cent loan upon these policies in 1931; and by 1936 bonds were issued which veterans might cash for the remainder.

Legion insistence was behind successive appropriations for what is now the greatest government hospital system in the world —$150,000,000 worth of veterans' hospitals. Only once was the Legion lobby set back on its heels: the 1933 Economy Act took away much of what the Legion had pressed for, but another year came by and Congress restored most of it over a Presidential veto.

Thus far Legionnaires have not demanded pensions for all veterans; their present goal is annuities to widows and orphans.

A bad time would be in store for any one who should say that Legion legislative influence had helped to make it possible for some veterans to get more from their government than they gave to their country. In behalf of that influence it may be claimed that without the powerful voice of the Legion care for the disabled or rehabilitation of jobless veterans might have been mere pious promises.

THE Legion has given as well as compelled aid. The part that it plays in community undertakings depends considerably upon the quality of its local leadership. It has not been found wanting in rising to emergency responsibilities; in many a disaster the Legion has raced with the Red Cross to be first at the scene. As an organization it has taken part in no labor wars or strike-breaking activities.

Few persons realize the social welfare work undertaken by the veterans. Almost from the Legion's start it had a child-welfare program. Last year it had 30,000 volunteers at work among 320,000 needy children, and spent $4,000,-000. More than 3,000 Boy Scout troops are Legion-sponsored.

In fact, the Legion on parade and at play has been better known than the Legion at work. Its annual conventions capture a city like an invading army, but each year the horse-play tapers off. Maybe it's because the Legionnaires are now middle-aged. Maybe it's because they now take their wives and children with them; the Legion's women's auxiliary now numbers nearly a half million, and the six-year-old organization, Sons of the American Legion, with a monthly publication, The Legion Heir, has a membership of 60,000. For the Legion is becoming a family affair.

In times of need and distress it can be counted upon to do more than its part. It does not hesitate to say what it wants. No love is lost between it and comrades of the left wing who call those who don't like them "Fascists." But any one who has ever seen an American Legion convention with its accompanying didoes knows that Legionnaires would laugh themselves sick at the suggestion of wearing shirts all of the same color. They did once, and that's what's the matter with them.

# 61,808 FANS ROAR TRIBUTE TO GEHRIG

## Captain of Yankees Honored at Stadium—Calls Himself 'Luckiest Man Alive'

### By JOHN DREBINGER

In perhaps as colorful and dramatic a pageant as ever was enacted on a baseball field, 61,808 fans thundered a hail and farewell to Henry Lou Gehrig at the Yankee Stadium yesterday.

To be sure, it was a holiday and there would have been a big crowd and plenty of roaring in any event. For the Yankees, after getting nosed out, 3 to 2, in the opening game of the double-header, despite a ninth-inning home run by George Selkirk, came right back in typical fashion to crush the Senators, 11 to 1, in the nightcap. Twinkletoes Selkirk embellished this contest with another home run.

But it was the spectacle staged between the games which doubtless never will be forgotten by those who saw it. For more than forty minutes there paraded in review two mighty championship hosts—the Yankees of 1927 and the current edition of Yanks who definitely are winging their way to a fourth straight pennant and a chance for another world title.

### Old Mates Reassemble

From far and wide the 1927 stalwarts came to reassemble for Lou Gehrig Appreciation Day and to pay their own tribute to their former comrade-in-arms who had carried on beyond all of them only to have his own brilliant career come to a tragic close when it was revealed that he had fallen victim of a form of infantile paralysis.

In conclusion, the vast gathering, sitting in absolute silence for a longer period than perhaps any baseball crowd in history, heard Gehrig himself deliver as amazing a valedictory as ever came from a ball player.

So shaken with emotion that at first it appeared he would not be able to talk at all, the mighty Iron Horse, with a rare display of that indomitable will power that had carried him through 2,130 consecutive games, moved to the microphone at home plate to express his own appreciation.

And for the final fadeout, there stood the still burly and hearty Babe Ruth alongside of Gehrig, their arms about each other's shoulders, facing a battery of camera men.

All through the long exercises Gehrig had tried in vain to smile, but with the irrepressible Bambino beside him he finally made it. The Babe whispered something to him and Lou chuckled. Then they both chuckled and the crowd roared and roared.

### Late Rally Fails

The ceremonies began directly after the debris of the first game had been cleared away. There had been some vociferous cheering as the Yanks, fired to action by Selkirk's homer, tried to snatch that opener away from the Senators in the last few seconds of the ninth. But they couldn't quite make it and the players hustled off the field.

Then, from out of a box alongside the Yankee dugout there spryly hopped more than a dozen elderly gentlemen, some gray, some shockingly baldish, but all happy to be on hand. The crowd recognized them at once, for they were the Yanks of 1927, not the first Yankee world championship team, but the first, with Gehrig an important cog in the machine, to win a world series in four straight games.

Down the field, behind Captain Sutherland's Seventh Regiment Band, they marched—Ruth, Bob Meusel, who had come all the way from California; Waite Hoyt, alone still maintaining his boyish countenance; Wally Schang, Benny Bengough, Tony Lazzeri, Mark Koenig, Jumping Joe Dugan, Bob Shawkey, Herb Pennock, Deacon Everett Scott, whose endurance record Gehrig eventually surpassed; Wally Pipp, who faded out as the Yankee first sacker the day Columbia Lou took over the job away back in 1925, and George Pipgras, now an umpire and, in fact, actually officiating in the day's games.

At the flagpole, these old Yanks raised the world series pennant they had won so magnificently from the Pirates in 1927 and, as they paraded back, another familiar figure streaked out of the dugout, the only one still wearing a Yankee uniform. It was the silver-haired Earle Combs, now a coach.

### Old-Timers Face Plate

Arriving at the infield, the old-timers strung out, facing the plate. The players of both Yankee and Senator squads also emerged from their dugouts to form a rectangle, and the first real ovation followed as Gehrig moved out to the plate to greet his colleagues, past and present.

One by one the old-timers were introduced with Sid Mercer acting as toastmaster. Clark Griffith, venerable white-haired owner of the Senators and a Yankee himself in the days when they were known as Highlanders, also joined the procession.

Gifts of all sorts followed. The Yankees presented their stricken comrade with a silver trophy measuring more than a foot and a half in height, their thoughts expressed in verse inscribed upon the base.

Manager Joe McCarthy, almost as visibly affected as Gehrig himself, made this presentation and hurried back to fall in line with his players. But every few minutes, when he saw that the once stalwart figure they called the Iron Horse was swaying on shaky legs, Marse Joe would come forward to give Lou an assuring word of cheer.

Mayor La Guardia officially extended the city's appreciation of the services Columbia Lou had given his home town.

"You are the greatest prototype of good sportsmanship and citizenship," said the Mayor, concluding with "Lou, we're proud of you."

Postmaster General Farley also was on hand, closing his remarks with "for generations to come boys who play baseball will point with pride to your record."

When time came for Gehrig to address the gathering it looked as if he simply would never make it. He gulped and fought to keep back the tears as he kept his eyes fastened on the ground.

But Marse Joe came forward again, said something that might have been "come on, Lou, just rap out another," and somehow those magical words had the same effect as in all the past fifteen years when the gallant Iron Horse would step up to the plate to "rap out another."

### Gehrig Speaks Slowly

He spoke slowly and evenly, and stressed the appreciation that he felt for all that was being done for him. He spoke of the men with whom he had been associated in his long career with the Yankees—the late Colonel Jacob Ruppert, the late Miller Huggins, his first manager, who gave him his start in New York; Edward G. Barrow, the present head of baseball's most powerful organization; the Yanks of old who now stood silently in front of him, as well as the players of today.

"What young man wouldn't give anything to mingle with such men for a single day as I have for all these years?" he asked.

"You've been reading about my bad break for weeks now," he said. "But today I think I'm the luckiest man alive. I now feel more than ever that I have much to live for."

The gifts included a silver service set from the New York club, a fruit bowl and two candlesticks from the Giants, a silver pitcher from the Stevens Associates, two silver platters from the Stevens employes, a fishing rod and tackle from the Stadium employes and ushers, a silver cup from the Yankee office staff, a scroll from the Old Timers Association of Denver that was presented by John Kieran, a scroll from Washington fans, a tobacco stand from the New York Chapter of the Baseball Writers Association of America, and the silver trophy from his team-mates.

The last-named present, about eighteen inches tall with a wooden base, supported by six silver bats with an eagle atop a silver ball, made Gehrig weep. President Barrow walked out to put his arms about Lou in an effort to steady him when this presentation was made. It appeared for an instant that Gehrig was near collapse.

On one side of the trophy were the names of all his present fellow-players. On the other were the following touching inscription:

#### TO LOU GEHRIG

We've been to the wars together,
We took our foes as they came,
And always you were the leader
And ever you played the game.

Idol of cheering millions,
Records are yours by the sheaves,
Iron of frame they hailed you,
Decked you with laurel leaves.

But higher than that we hold you,
We who have known you best,
Knowing the way you came through
Every human test.

Let this be a silent token
Of lasting friendship's gleam,
And all that we've left unspoken,
Your pals of the Yankee team.

As Gehrig finished his talk, Ruth, robust, round and sun-tanned, was nudged toward the microphone and, in his own inimitable, blustering style, snapped the tears away. He gave it as his unqualified opinion that the Yanks of 1927 were greater than the Yanks of today, and seemed even anxious to prove it right there.

"Anyway," he added, "that's my opinion and while Lazzeri here pointed out to me that there are only about thirteen or fourteen of us here, my answer is, shucks, we only need nine to beat 'em."

Then, as the famous home-run slugger, who also has faded into baseball retirement, stood with his arms entwined around Gehrig's shoulders, the band played "I Love You Truly," while the crowd took up the chant: "We love you, Lou."

### All Tributes Spontaneous

All given spontaneously, it was without doubt one of the most touching scenes ever witnessed on a ball field and one that made even case-hardened ball players and chroniclers of the game swallow hard.

When Gehrig arrived in the Yankee dressing rooms he was so close to a complete collapse it was feared that the strain upon him had been too great and Dr. Robert E. Walsh, the Yankees' attending physician, hurried to his assistance. But after some refreshment, he recovered quickly and faithful to his one remaining task, that of being the inactive captain of his team, he stuck to his post in the dugout throughout the second game.

Long after the tumult and shouting had died and the last of the crowd had filed out, Lou trudged across the field for his familiar hike to his favorite exit gate. With him walked his bosom pal and teammate, Bill Dickey, with whom he always rooms when the Yanks are on the road.

Lou walks with a slight hitch in his gait now, but there was supreme confidence in his voice as he said to his friend:

"Bill, I'm going to remember this day for a long time."

So, doubtless, will all the others who helped make this an unforgettable day in baseball.

July 5, 1939

# Clubs Would Stir Patriotic Fervor

## City Federation Will Ask Use of National Anthem in Theatres and Schools

Intensification of patriotic fervor as a weapon against subversive influence in national life will be urged this week by the New York City Federation of Women's Clubs. Theatres and motion picture houses will be asked to provide a recording of "The Star Spangled Banner" as a prelude to all performances. The Board of Education will be solicited to make the singing of the national anthem the first order of every school day.

Mrs. Rudolph M. Binder, president, has put the emphasis of her administration on a program designed to exemplify the advantages of living in a democracy.

As chairman of American patriotism, Mrs. William H. Rowland of Larchmont will direct the effort for cooperation of motion picture theatres, as an instrument for reaching the public. With Mrs. Edward T. Herbert, chairman of motion pictures for the organization, she will visit New York representatives of producers who control the management of theatres.

"A start has been made in Brooklyn, where the flag is now being displayed on the screens of many theatres," said Mrs. Rowland. "Some are screening the words of our national anthem, and we hope to have every picture house help to make it better known and loved. It seems to us in the federation that the time to show our patriotism is right now, without waiting for a crisis to stir us.

"In Canada, England and France, the singing of the national anthem in normal times closes most gatherings and has been credited with solidifying patriotic sentiment.

"We will ask the Board of Education to introduce the singing of the hymn in the kindergartens—to let the children grow up with it. We hope to have it explained to them, its significance in their lives, its symbolism. It is now sung on occasion in some schools, but our hope is to make its use general."

The federation's resolution under which the campaign will be conducted credits the national anthem with engendering both courage and enthusiasm.

December 3, 1939

# FARMERS WARNED ON PRICE DEMANDS

## Wallace Asks Caution in Need of United America to Defeat Hitler and His Agents

## SAYS WE CAN SAVE WORLD

## But Only by Rapid Increase in Our Rate of Production, AAA Parley Is Told

Special to THE NEW YORK TIMES.

WASHINGTON, June 13—A plea to farmers to subordinate their economic group interests to the general welfare so that a united front may be presented against Hitlerism was made today by Vice President Wallace in an address at the final session of the conference of Agricultural Adjustment Administration committeemen.

"It is only the might of the United States that stands between Hitler and world domination," the Vice President asserted.

Warning against putting price considerations first, Mr. Wallace pleaded for the burying of politics and minor interests of all kinds. If the United States could increase production fast enough, he said, it might not only avert war for this country but a United America will greatly influence the course of some nations which have not yet taken sides in the conflict.

Cautioning against the possibility of subversive activities, Mr. Wallace asked that farmers report information of value to the Federal Bureau of Investigation.

"I believe that subversive forces will make tremendous efforts to bring about fires, strikes and airplane disasters," he said. "The hellish ingenuity of this crowd is beyond all description—take my word for that."

**Warns of Political Spirit**

The subordination of economic group interests to the nation's united defense effort is the attitude which, he said, will serve the farmers best for the next ten years, "not the greedy, grabbing, political spirit, which would reap a whirlwind later on."

"I am convinced that if we can demonstrate we are a united people, producing to the utmost of our ability, and that we are on our toes," he went on, "it is quite possible that we won't have to spill a million gallons of blood."

This can be accomplished, he said, only if the nation does not permit the propagandists to divide it.

"All of us know," he added, "that the dictators have been engaged in an undeclared war of propaganda against the United States for at least seven years. It has intensified enormously in the past two years. Thoughts are things — thoughts are bullets. That thought has been used by the dictator countries."

Secretary Wickard called for a continuation of the "war on greed." The farmers, he said, would lose their greatest asset, the good opinion of the public as a whole, if they attempted to use the government or any other instrument to obtain prices "above a just parity."

A report of the AAA Committee on Defense was unanimously approved by the conference.

"The defense effort must succeed," the report said. "The interests of any economic group must be subservient to it. Our national point of view must be animated and inspired by a willingness to give rather than a desire to take. As representing the farmers of the

nation in respect to the program of the Agricultural Adjustment Administration, we assure the people and the government of the United States of our full compliance with this policy."

**Tells How Gangsters Rose**

In stating that the people had gradually come to realize that they should help Britain to the utmost, even at the risk of getting into the war, the Vice President said he meant no reflection, "not one iota, on those splendid United States citizens whose ancestors came from Germany."

"With modern propaganda weapons it is very easy for gangsters to get control of respectable people," he cautioned. "When this gangsterism operates on a worldwide scale with all the machines of science at its disposal, it becomes necessary for democracy to organize itself as it has never been organized before. But we must organize sensibly, not hysterically."

He urged the committeemen to do what they could to mold public opinion along patriotic lines in their home areas, and to prepare the farm population for sacrifice, and for shifts in popular programs during the coming months.

The defense effort has been relatively painless for everybody up to the present, he said, "but we are rapidly coming into the time when we will all have to make sacrifices."

"Our production is around a billion dollars a month now," he said. "It will be about two billion a month a year from now."

Mr. Wallace said he had told thousands of people that the total debt position of the United States—Federal, local and private, was higher in 1929 than at the present time, but he had never seen this "simple fact" in a newspaper.

Probably the real criterion, he declared, is the ratio of interest payments to national income. He said that for 1941 the interest burden is about 6 per cent of the national income, as against about 7½ per cent in 1929.

June 14, 194

# CONGRESS ISOLATIONISTS FACE APPARENT DEFEAT

## Service Extension Likely as Once Ruling Bloc Fights as Minority

### By TURNER CATLEDGE

WASHINGTON, Aug. 2—Isolationists in Congress have been pushed from one reserve trench to another ever since the contest over repeal of the embargo provisions of the Neutrality Act in the Fall of 1939. Previous to that, except for a short interlude in 1931 when President Hoover rushed through

the original moratorium on interallied war debts, the group which proudly labels itself as "noninterventionists" in the present international crisis enjoyed some twenty years of bountiful political prosperity.

Starting with the defeat of the League of Nations Covenant to the Versailles treaty in 1919, their

ascendency was marked by the later rejection of the World Court protocol and other successes, and topped by a veritable field day in achieving the munitions investigation of 1935 and the consequent enactment of the original neutrality law. Their influence on foreign policy grew to be so irresistible that the Administration of Franklin D. Roosevelt, now regarded as perhaps the most dynamic internationally in the history of the Republic, found it prudent for the most part, or at least expedient, to "go along," and at times to take the lead in some of the projects of the isolationists.

### A Decided Minority

But today it is plain to see that the worm has taken a turn. Whether it is in substantiation of the theory that the United States, by virtue of its powerful position or the progress of science, cannot detach itself from the rest of the world, or whether the powers in Washington have deliberately pitched their course in an opposite direction from the so-called "traditional" foreign policy, the truth is that the men and women who espouse the isolationist point of view for this country find themselves in a decided minority at Washington.

The isolationists in Congress are quite a definitive group. Roll-call votes in the two houses on major war and defense measures which have come to test—changes in the Neutrality Act in 1939, the Selective Service training bill in 1940, the lease-lend measure and ship-seizure bills of 1941—have rather well established their personal identity, their geographical and sectional connection, as well as their voting strength. The forthcoming division on the service-extension legislation will hardly do more than confirm all of these.

Individually they are an able and personable lot. The greater number of their present constituencies are in the West and Middle West, with a scattering of representation from each of the other major geographical sections of the country. Their voting strength in the Senate ranges between twenty-five and thirty and in the House from 100 to 160, depending upon the partisan flavor of the measure under consideration.

## Sincerity of Views

At the root of the isolationist cause is a high degree of sincerity, which exponents of the opposite view all too often make the mistake of discounting. However rational the argument to the contrary, they believe sincerely and fervently that they are the keepers of what they consider the historical foreign policy of the United States, as handed down from the days of George Washington. They reject wholly the idea that new concepts of government in the world, or the advance of science, have nullified that policy or even call for its modernization.

It would be less than fair to deny that the philosophy sketched above is at the base of the isolationist movement which holds on so doggedly in the American Congress. It would be naïve to contend, however, that detached philosophy is the sole fuel for all the heat over the international situation on Capitol Hill. There is another element that is heavily involved. It is spelled p-o-l-i-t-i-c-s.

Regardless of the criss-crossing of party lines occasioned by specific war and defense measures, there still are persons in Congress who can see little good in whatever Mr. Roosevelt does, either in the domestic or foreign field. Certain of these have been moved to new suspicions—to bitterness and anger—by the President's activities in connection with the war.

## A Gamble on Reactions

But probably of equal importance on the political side of the picture is the "opportunistic" vote —the men and women who, short of more fundamental conviction on present problems of international relations, are gambling on the reactions which may come in this country with the restoration of peace in the world.

The Republicans in Congress are evidently linking their fortunes to opposing moves which favor one side against the other in the European war, while supporting measures aimed solely at strengthening domestic defense. The lease-lend bill, for instance, was opposed by 85 per cent of the Republicans in the House and 63 per cent in the Senate. When the Neutrality Act was revised in 1939, seven out of every eight Republican Representatives and three out of every four Republican Senators opposed lifting the arms embargo. Sixty-eight per cent of the Republican leaders in both houses have in the Senate voted against the Selective Service Training Bill.

Some of the outstanding Republican leaders in both Houses have repudiated the isolationist position which their party assumed after the last war and which a majority seem now to be following, and they are supported in their repudiation by Wendell L. Willkie, who, as the last Presidential candidate, is the titular head of the party.

There is no way adequately to appraise the isolationist contention that they are backed in their views and actions by the majority of the voting public. This contention is based primarily on the results of polls showing a majority of the people still opposed to the United States entering actively into war.

## Influence on Legislation

Even though, in the net, the Administration had its way with Congress during these last eighteen months, the isolationists have written many limitations into war and defense measures which the White House, yielding often to expediency, now finds distasteful and is trying to dissolve. They euchred both major parties into unequivocal statements against foreign wars in the platforms last year — statements which were expanded by the two principal candidates in the campaign that followed.

But even more than their direct influence on Congressional and party action, the isolationists have succeeded in creating and keeping alive the perplexing question of the weight of public opinion in the country. That question is today more restrictive on the actions of the responsible authorities in Washington than any combination of the limitations that have been written into law.

August 3, 1941

## THE RENDEZVOUS WITH DESTINY

The great winds of history blew the two gray ships together in the shadowy lanes of the North Atlantic. They met at some predetermined point of latitude and longitude, there in the narrowing moat between two hemispheres where enemy submarines stalked the convoys shuttling back and forth from the Arsenal to the Fortress. But wherever they met, it was also a predestined point. The passengers they carried to secret rendezvous at sea were not merely men with a flare for Aeschylean drama. They were not only statesmen staging an unprecedented conference at the climactic moment of a widening war. This is a war of personified forces, leaders performing as nations, human wills and passions blown up into storming armies —and Franklin Roosevelt and Winston Churchill incarnate in their own persons the force of democracy. In the play of would-be gods and self-elected giants, they are figures representing the only two great Powers left in the world that speak with human voices, in the name of people.

This meeting has dramatized that force. The dictators in their armored trains at the Brenner Pass are dwarfed into actors on a local circuit by this bold encounter on the Atlantic battlefield, the mighty materialization of hands-across-the-sea. Dwarfed likewise are the performances in other theatres. Hitler has gone to the Ukraine, says Rome, to draw the spotlight back to "the greatest battle in history." The first speech of Darlan as military dictator of France goes unheeded. Tokyo is silent. The reverberations of this meeting drown out all sounds. They are louder than the bombs in Chungking or the murmurs rising in France.

They are heard from the River Bug to the sullen fjords of Norway, from wavering Bangkok to Dakar and Teheran. No other act of Washington or London could notify the world so unmistakably that the two democracies are united by a common idea and are determined to pursue together to the end their common purpose.

Behind the President and the Prime Minister, in the background of the momentous decisions taken in the fields of policy and high strategy, there was a third power at this conference—the power of destiny. In the apocalyptic struggle that envelops the planet, the United States and Great Britain have no choice but to act together. This is the fate and the fact, the immense and inevitable fact of Anglo-American partnership that overshadows even the eight-point statement of war aims made by the two leaders. Yet this in itself is a document of great importance.

To regard it as mere window-dressing intended to hide some secret understanding, or to dismiss it as "empty" or "rhetorical" simply because it speaks in generalities and uses words that have been used before, is to misread and to undervalue a declaration whose significance derives from the very fact that it states the terms of Anglo-American cooperation. This is not an ordinary statement on the subject of "war aims" by Mr. Hull or Mr. Eden, or even by Mr. Roosevelt or Mr. Churchill. It is a joint declaration, without precedent in Anglo-American history, made formally by the leaders of the two English-speaking democracies in one of the great crises of history. This declaration will guide the efforts and measure the progress of the United States and the British Commonwealth of Nations until both the war and the peace are won.

\* \* \*

Two decisions of immense importance are implicit in the declaration. The first is concerned with the future of the German nation. Here the die has been cast against "dismemberment" as a method of maintaining peace. The German people are assured that once "the final destruction of the Nazi tyranny" has been accomplished, Britain and the United States "desire to see no territorial changes that do not accord with the freely expressed wishes of the peoples concerned." Hitler will denounce this assurance as a perfidious promise, made only to be broken. But to the extent that British and American statesmanship can make the good faith of their promise apparent to the German people, they will rob Hitler of his greatest weapon—the present belief of the German people that the outcome of this war means life or death for the German nation. And to the extent that Germany's power of resistance is broken by the enormous air superiority which Britain is certain to achieve, and the truth then dawns upon the German people that they cannot and will not win this war, the degree of their faith in this Anglo-American promise will become a factor of immediate political importance.

Along with this promise goes another commitment, even more sweeping in its implications. This is the assurance given to tormented and war-weary people in every corner in the world that the great power of Britain and the United States will be pooled in the work of post-war reconstruction. No mention is made in the eight-point declaration of a new League of Nations, or of any association like it. But in every line of the document, from its emphasis on "the fullest collaboration between all nations in the economic field" to its proposal for enforced disarmament—in the first instance, of those nations which have been the aggressors in this war—there is implied the creation of a post-war organization to maintain peace, with the United States a full partner in this effort.

This is the second great decision implicit in this historic Declaration of the Atlantic. It means that so long as the leadership of Franklin Roosevelt prevails, and so long as a great majority of the American people endorse his views on world affairs—as they do unquestionably today—the prestige and the influence and the resources of this country will be marshalled on the side of international law and order. This is the end of isolation. It is the beginning of a new era in which the United States assumes the responsibilities which fall naturally to a great World Power.

August 15, 194

# Westchester Town Scrap Drive Center

## Group Circularizes Families in Greenburg to Collect Metals and Foil

A drive to collect scrap metals for defense, which is being conducted by women of Greenville in Westchester County, took on added speed last week as a plan to make such collections popular nationally was announced by the OPM.

Heading the local drive is Mrs. Adam K. Geiger, who, as chairman of the Materials Conservation Committee, has distributed circulars on the campaign this Fall to more than 800 families in the town of Greenburg.

Householders have responded with tin and aluminum foil, worn kitchen utensils and other household articles made of rubber, cork or metals that can be reclaimed. The collection center is the Greenville Pumping Station, where discarded automobile batteries, wash boards, ice boxes, lamps and overshoes, usually lost to industry, will eventually be sold to scrap dealers.

The materials contributed will be sorted by the women themselves when the collection is completed this week. Proceeds from the sale will be divided between several war relief agencies. In a similar drive made last Winter the committee realized a total of 700 pounds.

To interest the younger members of the community in the need for the conservation of scrap materials during the emergency, the committee is preparing an educational drive among school children. Albert S. Allen, who acts as consultant in chemistry to the women, will speak for them on the subject of "Scarcity and Substitutes."

The committee's secretary is Mrs. Max Waldeau and its treasurer Mrs. Townsend L. Cannon. Other members are Mrs. Dana Caulkins, Mrs. Roland Gsell, Mrs. Daniel W. Keefe and Mrs. A. K. Eaton.

November 9, 194

# Press as a Unit Backs War on Axis

*Newspaper comment throughout the country is united in the view that the declarations of war force the United States into a long conflict, but they agree must end in victory. Excerpts from many newspapers follow:*

## NEW YORK CITY
### Predicts Ruin of Axis Trio
From The Herald Tribune

The Axis has delivered its combined attack upon our country, first, treacherously, with bombs and torpedoes at Oahu and in the Philippines; now, openly, with its own declarations, delivered in quick succession from Tokyo, Rome and Berlin. They have begun the war. The United States will end it, whether it takes two years or ten, whatever the cost in time or life or effort, and will end with it this monstrous evil of blood and tyranny which has now challenged the whole earth.

Hitler still talks about "his Europe" at a moment when he is forced to stake the survival of his Nazi "master race" upon the shaky Oriental imperialism of the Japanese. The dream of "Greater East Asia" is now linked to the wearied German war machine, already recoiling through the bitter snows of Russia. One cannot win now until all have won; equally, one cannot be beaten until all have been beaten, but that they must be and they will be. To that single end—to the end of total and unconditional victory over this colossal criminality—every last energy and last resource of every last American is now irrevocably pledged.

### Change in Totalitarian Methods
From The Sun

That Herr Hitler and his Charlie McCarthy down at Rome should have declared war on the United States surprises the average American citizen in one way only. It is unprecedented, almost a violation of totalitarian ethics, for Nazi Germany to declare war in this way. Its customary procedure is rather that which Japan so characteristically illustrated on Sunday last—to start raiding and bombing first and declare war afterward.

### "Great Day of Our Lives"
From The Post

The open declarations of war by Hitler and Mussolini today can only have the effect throughout America and in hundreds of millions of hearts around the world of inspiring a solemn confidence in the victory of right.

This Dec. 11, 1941, is the great day of our lives, perhaps surpassing all days in its vast import. The American people will accept it in complete consecration. Forward march!

### Expects Victory in Long War
From The Daily News

It looks to us like a long war and a tough one, but with an Allied victory waiting at the end of the rocky road. We think it is going to get worse before it gets better, and that all of us would be wise to steel our minds to that probability.

### "Russia to Be Heard From"
From The Brooklyn Eagle

With the declaration of war against the United States by Germany and Italy this morning the line-up in the Second World War is taking final form. Russia alone remains to be heard from.

We will hope that there is no hidden implication in Hitler's announcement that he has stopped his drive on Moscow for the Winter. For it would be a serious business if Russia did not openly line up with Britain and the United States in this war.

## BOSTON
### "Anticlimax" After Sunday
From The Herald

It is strange, but Nazi Germany's and Fascist Italy's declarations of war on us came as an anticlimax after Sunday's thunderous events.

The Senate and House took the news as the people of the nation did, not casually or complacently, but with a courageous determination to take on all the cutthroats at once.

## PHILADELPHIA
### Righteous Sword Unsheathed
From The Inquirer

America, arsenal of democracy and defender of human liberties, today stands with the sword of righteous anger unsheathed against the gangster forces of barbarism and destruction.

This is the hour of crisis, the hour of high resolve. Let us be loyal to the President, our leader. Let us have faith in America's destiny and our own strength.

## BALTIMORE
### Challenge to Industry, Labor
From The Sun

Do not let your mind be dominated by any question of diplomacy or of military and naval operations. Put your mind on the simple, massive, monumental fact that Hitler's challenge is a challenge to American industry and American labor. Go forth on this home front with every energy of minds and strong right arms. And damned be that man who thinks first of self!

## ATLANTA
### Must Wipe Out "Bestial Thing"
From The Constitution

So Germany and Italy have formally declared war against the United States. Which fact makes absolutely no difference. We have long realized that, if this world is to be a fit place for our children and their children's children, the bestial thing for which the Axis powers stand must be wiped from the globe.

## NEW ORLEANS
### Unmasking of Hitler
From The Times Picayune

By his war declaration against the United States, Hitler yesterday discarded the mask he has worn so long in the effort to trick the people of the Americas. Impartial historians of these times will record the conquest of the Western Hemisphere among his original aims and ambitions.

## DALLAS
### Job for Western Hemisphere
From The News

Into the invocation of the tripartite pact by Germany and Italy can be clearly read their responsibility for the attack made on this country last Sunday by Japan. Theirs is a tacit admission of authorship which the President had fully recognized in his address today. Well, we know now where we stand. Immediately the entire Western Hemisphere must be mobilized against this sinister threat from abroad.

## ST. LOUIS
### "Stark Reality" Faced at Last
From The Globe Democrat

The issue which this nation has disputed for many long and apprehensive months is now dissolved into stark reality. We are at war with Germany. We are at war with Italy. We are at war with Japan. We are committed to fight these gangsters with all our resources of men and weapons until they are exterminated. So be it. And may God grant us the strength to carry through.

## KANSAS CITY
### All-Out Production Now
From The Star

It's straight down the line of all-out production for America now, with not an hour lost or a useful plant idle or a needed man off the job. Our men in the military service and on lower pay cannot limit their hours. For them it is and will be a continuous alert and often a risk of their lives. In the greater security at home every person in some way must help to back them up.

## PITTSBURGH
### Cords of Confusion Broken
From The Post Gazette

Like Gulliver bound by a multitude of small cords, the United States has been bound down by its own confusion. Those cords are broken now. In the last four days, from the Japanese attack on Hawaii to the European developments yesterday, clarity has come to America. Two words are opposed and only one will survive. The final outcome is not in doubt.

## CLEVELAND
### War One of Materials
From The Plain Dealer

While in these early days of actual conflict we read the first official communiqués issued by the government in Washington with a great deal of concern because of the unfavorable news in the Far East, we need to be reassured by the fact that in increasing measure from this point forth the war will be one of materials and supplies.

## DETROIT
### Battle Against Bondage
From The Free Press

America knew, in Sunday's electric hour, that whether their war was declared or not, nazism and fascism were arrayed against us in battle line-up with the Japanese. America knew from that moment that it was we or they, on into the unforeseeable future—human freedom and decency locked in a death struggle against human bondage and barbarism.

## CHICAGO
### "Must Win War and Peace"
From The Tribune

We cannot afford to minimize the effort which must be made for the task which lies before us. Nor can we afford to dissipate our energies and our war effort by pointless alarms and excursions. We are now engaged in the greatest war ever fought by the American people. They must win it and win a peace which will protect them and their future.

## MINNEAPOLIS
### Courage and Sacrifice to Win
From The Star Journal

We have done too little and we have done it too late. Now the battle is on us. By unremitting application of the vigor and courage and sacrifice of free men, and with the aid of those who stand with us everywhere to fight for liberty, we can and will win.

## LOS ANGELES
### Sets New Kind of "Record"
From The Times

In their declaration of war Germany and Italy have established some sort of a record in that it is the first time in their history that any Axis nations have taken such a step without having made a treacherous and unwarned attack immediately in advance of it. Actually the state of war has existed for months. It started on May 21, when the Robin Moor was sunk.

## SAN FRANCISCO
### "Committed Without Limit"
From The Chronicle

Doubtless by this time we realize that it is serious, but do we appreciate how serious? We are now committed absolutely without limit. When you are boxing your seconds may throw in the sponge to save you from a too bloody knockout in the next round. When it is a business deal, you may compromise. But when it is this sort of a war you fight until you are dead, and then someone takes your place to fight until he is dead. You pay, if necessary, until you have paid your all, and then toil until you break, to pay still more.

### PORTLAND, ORE.
#### "Let None Be Pale"
From The Oregonian
Let us take for our model that young lieutenant of Truxton's gallant ship, the Constellation, who wrote "we would put a man to death even for looking pale aboard this ship." America—the greatest ship of state the world has known—is now a-sail, pressing for vic-

tory. Every man; with his wife and child, is called to post. And let none be pale.

### SEATTLE
#### Mussolini Still "A Stooge"
From The Post-Intelligence
From its outset World War II has been a Hitler war. In the early stages Mussolini served as a stooge for Hitler. In being allowed to make the war announcement he is still playing stooge though in truth his present position is more nearly that of a prisoner of the Nazi military machine. The lay of the cards is against the Axis at both its ends. And this government and this people are playing to win not an isolated engagement but the war.

December 12, 1941

## JOLLY LOAD OF 'SHARERS'

This windshield sticker shows a car owner's membership in the "4-in-1" group riding club, new national program of the American Legion. White arrows on the blue foreground point to a factory, home, school and business building from which the four car-sharing riders come.

# Nation Enters 'Car Sharing' Era to Make Its Tires Last

### By PHILIP B. COAN

All signs now point to the automobile's becoming a sociable drawing room on wheels. On a seat-for-seat basis, it is getting mighty popular. The driver is waving good-bye to his old habit of traveling alone, bored by the monotony of covering mile after mile with no company except the car radio.

Instead, he has a jovial group of friends —and fellow-riders beside him and in the back seat. The "gang" go to and from work together. They use Bill's car this week, Harry's next and so on. George, who has no car, "chips in" a little extra for expense.

While Bill takes every one in his car, Harry's wife takes the men's wives shopping. She brings the children to school and home again, if that is necessary. She is this week's taxi driver for the families. The other wives coordinate their plans to do all shopping at once and be ready when the driver calls.

There is no more saying "Oh, I must go back to the cleaner's with this dress I left at home."

### See the Carrots!

The car, of course, looks like a combination bus and delivery truck at the end of each shopping expedition. Tempers, too, after a hot morning of shopping, must be toned down and "coordinated"—like the shared driving. Relatively speaking, the situation holds high promise of fostering needed diplo-

macy in joint activities of neighbors.

Before schools closed, it will be remembered, one often saw a carload of shrieking children on the way home from school with a harried mother grimly controlling the car and herself. They were sharing, too. For some reason, maybe because the kids are just small adults, they are more silent going to school in the morning than coming home.

As a matter of fact, car sharing —also called the group riding plan or club and many other names— establishes a new outlook on motoring. That basic American institution, the automobile, is undergoing changes. Drivers are learning to know one another. Through proximity, they are taking the chips off their shoulders.

The old competitive challenge of the road is on the decline. Cars don't pass each other with a leer and a snort, like strange bulls in the same pasture. After all, how can you "get mad" at a load of people who are riding together just like your own group to save gasoline, tires and the cars themselves?

On a limited scale, group riding is as old as motoring. People always have traveled together by car. Only since wartime shortages of rubber and gasoline transportation developed and no new cars have been built has car sharing become a national program.

Factories engaged in war work acted early to adopt car-sharing in an organized fashion. Some plants went so far as to charge drivers using free parking areas 10 cents for each vacant seat. By that stratagem, a lone driver of a sedan paid 40 cents a day to park while he worked. He soon found riders.

More recently, the War Department's highway traffic advisory committee, the Office of Defense Transportation and the Office of Civilian Defense have taken active steps to make club riding general. The stumbling block in each central program was lack of an organization to tie up millions of drivers in car-sharing groups.

The latest program, being put forth by the American Legion through its more than 1,000,000 members in the United States at 12,250 Legion Posts in 11,700 communities, provides the means for reaching the motorists who are not riding together already.

Aiming particularly at neighborhood and community groups to make one car do the work of four and save the other three by sharing turns of weekly driving, the Legion's effort has the backing of the War Department and the ODT. Conversely, the plan is for "4-in-1 War Clubs" with four riders sharing one car.

All the group programs have one main aim—to save tires. Lightly loaded cars wear out near-

ly as much tire rubber as vehicles with full loads at the same time, it is necessary to keep cars running lest the nation be crippled by the lack of transportation.

### Finding 'Club Members'

Formation of "ride together" groups is easy, once pains are taken to find automobile users whose driving is similar in nature or can be dovetailed. For preliminary efforts, the groups might be called "get acquainted clubs." Neighborhood clubs form spontaneously without central control to aid them.

Industrial workers have the advantage there and made use of it under factory sponsorship. Workers on the same shifts and living near each other "shared" naturally. Sometimes working hours had to be changed for one man or another.

The men's cars can be seen going to and from plants today displaying a figurative "standing room only" sign. Some cars make fifty-mile trips each way daily daily with five men.

For commercial workers, small business employes and housewives the problem is more complex. The car-sharing plan now is reaching such groups to combine trips with similar origins and destinations. Soon Americans may find car-sharing every place from Skowhegan, Me., to Mecca, Calif.

# Vision, Not Hate, Will Win the War

### The hope of a better world, says J. B. Priestley, will provide 'the great unifying idea, the fast resolve' that ultimately will bring us victory.

**By J. B. Priestley,**
English Novelist and Essayist
LONDON *(By Wireless)*

EVERYBODY knows now that total war means a fight between whole populations. It also means that the people must be solidly behind the war effort. If the people do not believe in the war they cannot be coerced into creating the necessary effort. A perfunctory acquiescence will not do, as we saw in France. There must be determination and a willingness to make sacrifices with enthusiasm, and all else that goes with "high morale."

The problem then is how to heighten morale and then keep it up there. It is the problem that the French could not hope to solve, and that the Russians appear to have solved triumphantly. You in the United States and we in Britain come somewhere between the two. Our morale might be worse, but then again it could be much better.

What is the test? We can say that morale is high when people put the war first without any hesitation, when sectional interests vanish, when people are eager to serve the war effort in any capacity, when the government need no longer either bully or cajole its citizens into making the necessary sacrifices—when, indeed, those no longer seem like sacrifices.

It is a mistake to suppose that danger —heavy bombing or actual invasion—will automatically heighten morale. If the people's morale is bad, the presence of danger will make it worse. It is only when morale is good anyhow that it is heightened by the appearance of the enemy. Hitler took a chance on Russian morale being bad and therefore hoped to make it rapidly worse. But it was good, and his arrival only made it better.

Making people conscious of the war is no bad thing, but it is not the terrific morale builder that it is often imagined to be. Indeed, in my view, this business of slamming war into the public mind can easily be overdone and so defeat itself. To fill newspapers and magazines with war stories, to deafen radio listeners and motion-picture audiences with the roar of planes and battle of machine guns—this is all very well and may even be vitally necessary in the early days, but I fancy that the saturation point is soon reached. And in any event propaganda of this kind can never become the solid foundation of morale.

Neither can hate-the-enemy campaigns. I happen to dislike the Nazis intensely. I disliked them at a time when some of our loudest haters were still running across to Nuremberg and accepting the hospitality of those murderers. I have as much hatred for the devilish Nazi's system as it is possible for me to manufacture. But hate seems to me to make an uneasy and treacherous foundation for public morale.

To begin with, men filled with hate and not much else are not, in my view, in a sound psychological condition to make a great cooperative effort. They may begin hating each other. And their minds are not cool and unclouded. Fighting men especially should not be turned into screaming, slavering fanatics, for they will need their wits about them.

Then, again, in order to produce this hatred you have to give the enemy a gigantic build-up. Hitler becomes Lucifer, his fellow-gangsters so many giant demons. This is apt to play just the kind of tricks in the unconscious mind that the Nazis like. You are giving them the sort of magical prestige that cool common sense would instantly deny them. It is, in fact, playing their game. It is better to play our own game which they do not know how to play and so keep our heads to use our common sense and laugh sometimes.

WE cannot destroy nazism by creating a Nazi atmosphere on our side. If we are all going to stamp and scream and hate, then even if Hitler does not win, Hitlerism will have won. What Fascists hate and fear in democracy is its cool, critical and humorous common sense, and so if we say good-bye to that, we immediately begin to weaken ourselves. A Britain and a United States engaged in a huge, solemn hate campaign are no longer the hope of the world.

Probably most officials, both in the United States and Britain, would agree with what I have said about hate. "But all that is necessary," they will go on to say, "is for us to point out the terrible danger of Nazism, its urgent threat to all we hold dear and to declare our determination to rid the world of this pest, for public morale to be securely established."

IN other words, the negative aim—down with Hitlerism—ought to be sufficient. Perhaps it ought to be. But the fact remains that it is not sufficient. It seems to me that by announcing this negative aim you can raise morale to a certain useful level but can never get it any higher. And even at that useful level it is always in danger of sagging badly. If the enemy can persuade some sections of your peoples that he is not really a genuine menace to them—and much of his propaganda may be artfully directed toward that—then your national morale begins to crack. This negative aim does not do good in cementing the job.

Probably the chief trouble is that when you ask men to defend what they have, they are encouraged to remember rather than forget their sectional interests. They are not united in a new way. They may combine, but it will only be a surface combination, not a genuine fusion. Old habits will still prevail. Capital will still behave like capital, labor like labor. All pre-war suspicions and grievances will still be there lurking in the background. In spite of all the flag-waving and fuss there will have been no real change in the atmosphere.

"To get rid of the Nazis" only becomes a positive aim strong enough to make all men ready and eager to risk death, in a country actually occupied by the Nazis. It is one of the fatal weaknesses of the Hitlerites that they cannot make friends. No matter how smooth and polite they may be at first, very soon their tyranny and brutality come through; and then desire to be rid of these bullies and brutes begins to unite millions of folk who before knew no common aim. For this reason I disagree with those friends of mine who think that the people of the occupied countries need to be talked to in terms of frontiers and Constitutions and economic systems. All these people need be told is that food and freedom are on their way.

BUT if the enemy is not in the next village but across the sea somewhere, then I maintain that this negative aim is not good enough. It does not, in fact, raise morale to a high level. It does not even provide a secure foundation. What is needed, first of all, is the great unifying idea which must represent something clean outside fascism; which completely defies, because it completely repudiates, the Fascist's idea; which stands for a world wherein Hitlerism could never exist. People inspired by such an idea are well out of reach of enemy propaganda. Nothing that fascism says can touch them, for they are secure in their acceptance of an idea that completely outlaws fascism.

This is not an opinion that could be held only by an idealistic literary man. It is held by all persons who have any real insight into the nature of this conflict. Thus we find a military expert and critic of strategy, Captain Liddell Hart, declaring: "It is in the psychological sphere that this war may be decided. True leadership must provide creative ideas out of which a positive faith can be generated. To get the best out of men it is not enough to tell them that they must be ready to die in the last ditch. They must be given a new vision of the future. And a new hope."

Most people in Britain and the United States eagerly await a new vision of the future—a new hope. There are a few who don't, who are anxious not to be uprooted out of the old world. And I say that both in Britain and the United States we pay too much attention to those few, and are too tender toward them. I suggest that we would fight this war better without them so long as the many are newly inspired and united as never before. It is my belief that those few who cling to the pre-war world, which was a world that produced fascism, will never make good colleagues in a war to destroy fascism. Therefore, if they are beyond the reach of our unifying idea, they are no great loss. Let them sulk. What matters is that the people in general do not sulk, for only their enthusiastic cooperation can win the war.

It is a mistake to suppose that in our great democracies we can find in nationalism this great unifying idea. It no longer has the necessary driving force. Moreover, you really cannot square it with this war. The United Nations must be something more than united nations. They must represent a certain world view that completely excludes the Fascist idea. Whatever fascism really stands for must be repudiated by us. For example, if

fascism stands for the deliberate suppression and exploitation of the masses for the benefit of small power-seeking groups—and it does—then we must announce that we will allow no more suppressions and exploitation of the common people by anybody for any purpose.

Once men believe in such an idea, once they have hope and vision of the future, they can be united in a new way—to fight the war or do anything else required of them. If the idea leaves the past behind, then the people are encouraged to leave the past behind. Instead of regarding the war as a tiresome interruption in the settled order of things, they will see it for what it is—a new chapter in human history—a rather grim fresh start. They will soon forget their old sectional interests. The old habits will vanish. The whole atmosphere will be changed.

Next in importance for morale

Edmund Duffy in the OWI pamphlet, "The Unconquered People"

"Desire to get rid of the bullies and brutes unites millions in occupied countries who before knew no common aim."

"…is not enough to tell men they must be ready to die in the last ditch. They must be given a new vision of the future, and a new hope."

building comes the idea of a people's war. We are always being told that this is a people's war, but at least half the officials who tell us this do not behave as if they believed what they said. Frequently they go on to talk about the war as if it was some private property of theirs. (I am referring now to Britain and don't know what happens in the United States.) There is a tendency, especially on the part of Mandarins not famous for their brain power and weight of personality, to treat people as if they were children. Thus in Britain the news of any disasters are nearly always so shockingly handled that it is this treatment rather than the disaster itself that maddens the public.

AGAIN, people are always being told that everything is rapidly changing for the better, that the bad old world is gone for good, but I think many of them could do with more proof. Our Foreign Secretary has just told his constituents and the general public that the bad old world

is gone for good. But does his department, the Foreign Office, behave as if this statement were true? Is it in fact quite unlike the Foreign Office we once knew? What is it doing to prove that it has recently been born again? I don't say that it is doing nothing. I only declare that I, for one, do not know, and I should be much more impressed if the conduct of Mr. Eden's department proved the truth of his public utterances. In short, we could do with more action and less rhetoric.

For the rest, people should not be encouraged—as they often are by official speeches and pamphlets—to regard wartime life as their old ordinary life with most of the fun taken out of it. They should be encouraged to regard it as a dramatic adventure. (I think the United States is less likely to make this mistake than Britain.) The Russians appear to be masters of this technique, giving everything a tremendous dramatic build-up. Not long ago, in connection with an important radio feature, I wanted

three girls from war-factories and suggested that they should be chosen on some competitive basis. One official to whom the application had been made replied that he could do nothing because either he or his Ministry—I forget which —"disliked the competitive spirit." If British morale has never taken a nosedive—and it never has—no thanks are due this official and his friends.

Finally, as the war enters new phases, people should not only be told about these new phases but should be encouraged to regard their particular tasks and sacrifices in a new way. The same old appeals should not be made in the same old way. We should be made to feel that the world drama is the beginning of another act, and we should hear different music, see different lighting. Thus on the surface there should be plenty of variety. But below the surface as a solid foundation of the war effort there must remain unchanged the great unifying idea, the fast resolve, the vision of the future, the hope of the world.

October 18, 1942

# 'We Shall Hate, or We Shall Fail'

### If we do not hate the Germans now, says Rex Stout, we shall fail in our effort to establish a lasting peace.

**By Rex Stout**

Author, Chairman Writers' War Board

LOVE your enemies. Fight your enemies, shoot them, starve them, kill them, destroy their cities, bomb their factories and gardens — but love them! That may make sense to the Tuesday Evening Culture Club but not to me.

The Christian imperatives and ideals are the noblest expression of man's highest aspirations, but when men shrink from the hard necessities imposed upon them by human defects and stupidities by hiding behind the skirts of those imperatives and ideals, there is nothing noble about that. There is one imperative: thou shalt not kill. There is another: love your enemies. They are equally essential parts of a moral and philosophic whole. If I obey both of them, I may, sadly enough, be a highly impractical man, but at least I am a saintly man and deserve respect. If I violate one of them but insist that the other be adhered to, I am manifestly guilty of sanctimonious double talk and deserve no respect from any one whatever.

Some say that they admit it is impossible to love the Germans, but we must not hate them. That is worse than double-talk, it is plain nonsense. Either the hundreds of thousands of Germans we are preparing to kill deserve to be killed, or they do not. Apparently most Americans are agreed that they do, since most Americans favor a vigorous prosecution of the war. If we are not to kill them while loving them, and not to kill them while hating them, precisely what are our feelings supposed to be during the unpleasant operation? Are we expected to proceed with the bloody task in an emotional vacuum? Or in a state of benign (though murderous) detachment?

Not a pretty picture, that would be; not adherence to a Christian ideal, but assumption of a frigid and phony divinity, usurpation of the prerogatives of God Himself, which, I submit, in the light of current events, would be somewhat impertinent.

Shall we hate Germans? Each of us must answer that question for himself. But to kill them while pretending to love them is dishonest, to kill them and remain emotionally indifferent is abhorrent, and to kill them with an assumption of the attributes of God is inadmissible. As fairly decent and responsible human beings, we cannot and must not kill them unless we do hate them.

Some will say, indeed have said, listen to him, the fiend, he is trying to fill our breasts with blind and vindictive passion. That is one of the oldest tricks of the controversial acrobat, to pretend that your adversary doesn't mean what he is saying, he means something else. "Blind" and "vindictive" and "passion." It isn't a very good trick.

THERE are as many kinds of hate as there are kinds of love. There are people who hate dill pickles; that's the way they put it. There are people who hate labor, those who hate capital, those who hate President Roosevelt or noisy little children or Mr. McCormick of Chicago. The hate I am talking about is a feeling toward the Germans of deep and implacable resentment for their savage attack upon the rights and dignity of man, of loathing for their ruthless assault on the persons and property of innocent and well-meaning people, of contempt for their arrogant and insolent doctrine of the German master race.

If any one, agreeing with all that, wants to pick another word for it, I can't stop him; but, having consulted my dictionary, I call it hate. I see nothing admirable in aiding and abetting the death by violence of millions of fellow-beings but fleeing in repugnance from a four-letter word. I hate Germans, and am not ashamed of it. On the contrary, in view of what the Germans have done, and of what my countrymen are preparing to do to them, I would be profoundly ashamed of myself if I did not hate Germans.

I am not a born German-hater. In March, 1915, when a visiting British lecturer made biting remarks about the Germans, I arose and left the gathering because I thought he was intemperate and unfair. He wasn't. As I discovered later, I was grossly ignorant. The trouble was that the British hated the Germans not wisely but too little.

ADOLF HITLER is nothing to be surprised at. A close student of German history, if sufficiently acute, might in the year 1900 have predicted a Hitler as the culmination of the deep-rooted mental and nervous disease afflicting the German people. The adoration of force as the only arbiter, and skulduggery as the supreme technique, in human affairs, which is the essence of nazism, was fully expounded by Clausewitz over a century ago; and Clausewitz has been the political bible of four generations of German leaders. A people who dined on Clausewitz for 120 years was bound to have Hitler for dessert. And Hitler was bound to say, as he has said, "You can be a German or a Christian. You cannot be both."

He might as well have said Hindu or Moslem, instead of Christian. For what he meant was "You can be a German, or you can accept a code of morality. You cannot do both." That was implicit in Clausewitz. It has been stated or implied in a thousand ways by ten thousand Germans. Long before there were any Nazis, a German said a treaty was only a scrap of paper. Before Adolf Hitler was born another German, von Bülow, made a speech to a great audience assembled for a memorial performance of Beethoven's symphonies. He shouted, "To the meaningless French idealisms, Liberty, Equality and Fraternity, we oppose the German realities, Infantry, Cavalry and Artillery!" And the throng of Germans, gathered to honor Beethoven, applauded madly. Sieg heil!

By word, and by deed. After the last war there were well-meaning souls who tried to persuade us that the Germans had committed no atrocities. They will not find it so easy a job this time; there are too many millions of eyewitnesses, and too many thousands of documents already collected. This is condensed from a sworn affidavit now on file in London:

> On Nov. 11, 1939, at Torun in Western Poland, a window in a German barracks was broken at night by a stone. Twelve boys of from 11 to 16 years of age were taken into custody and immediately shot. The bodies of the victims remained where they fell for the whole of four days, in spite of pleas of relatives to remove them for burial.

This is from a German official report made in March, 1941, at Tyn, a town in Czechoslovakia:

> Josef Plodek, a mill-owner, was given grain to grind for German use. He removed a panful of the flour and gave it to a neighbor. Since it was discovered that his wife was an accomplice in the crime, they were both hanged.

THIS is from an affidavit made by a Russian civilian who was captured by the Germans and later escaped:

> Marching us to another prison camp, the Germans invented a game. One of them would order us to march by fours, while another ordered us to form by sixes. This naturally resulted in confusion, and then they would shout that we were disobeying orders and open fire on us. In this manner, on the day's march to Uman, sixty-four of us were killed.

Multiply those instances by a thousand, ten thousand—yes, it must be admitted, that is hateful. But can't we somehow squirm out of it?

There are the metaphysicians, both amateur and professional. The people who say, yes, we must hate injustice and cruelty and barbarism, that's all right, but we must not hate our fellow-beings.

That would be a remarkable stunt, and an extremely convenient one, if there were any man or woman alive capable of performing it. It is merely another trick with words.

What is "cruelty"? It is a word invented by men to describe a quality of a deed performed by a living creature upon another living creature. Any attempt to treat it as a thing in itself, to separate it in any way whatever, from the deed it was invented to describe, or from the person performing the deed, is tommyrot.

A man murders a child. You see him do it. You say you do not hate the man. Very well, then you have, to put it one way, an exceptionally developed power of detachment. But if you say you hate the "cruelty" but do not hate the man, what do you mean? You simply don't mean anything. You are talking drivel. If no one had ever invented any such word as "cruelty" (and for many thousands of years after man started to talk there were no abstract words), then what would you say? What did men say? Are we to assume that the mere invention of abstract words changed the structure of the human brain and men became miraculously capable of hating words instead of people?

No. A man who tells you he hates evil but not the doer of evil is kidding either you or himself, and in any case is gibbering.

IF we shall hate, shall we hate all Germans, everywhere? Shall we hate Mr. Schulz, who came to America thirty years ago at the age of 12, who now runs the grocery store at the corner of Sixth and Main and despises Adolf Hitler? To ask the foolish question is to answer it. No. Then if we are not to hate all Germans, everywhere, how do we go about the colossal job of picking and choosing?

I find no great difficulty. I hate all Nazi Germans. I hate all Germans who accept, either actively or passively, the doctrine of the German master race, the doctrine which permeated German thought long before Hitler was born, the doctrine by which the Germans justify their contempt of all other people and their domination of other countries by force. I hate all Germans who joined with the Nazis to bring that doctrine to its inevitable culmination of brutal disregard of the rights and dignities which distinguish a man from a beast. I hate all Germans who, reluctant to join the Nazis, nevertheless failed, through lack of courage or conviction, to prevent the Nazis from seizing power and plunging the world into this filthy swamp of destruction, misery and hatred.

**T**HOSE are the Germans I hate from the bottom of my soul. Ninety-nine per cent of them are in Germany. As to what proportion they are of all Germans in Germany I do not know and have no way of finding out.

In 1934 the German Minister of Education issued an order which contained a list of slogans to be permanently displayed on the blackboard of every schoolroom in Germany. One of the slogans read, "The Ten Commandments are the deposit of the lowest human instincts." There is, I suppose, no argument as to our opinion of the German minister or of the government which gave him his job. But what of the parents, all of them, who sent their children, day after day and year after year, to those schoolrooms and made no effective protest? Who did not, by force if necessary, by stealth if courage was lacking, invade those schools and make the blackboards clean? They have shown no squeamishness about invading the schools and homes and factories of all the rest of Europe. But day after day, year after year, they washed and dressed their children, fed them, and sent them to sit on their school benches facing that brazen denial of the very foundation of civilized society. Because the Germans are the master race! Phooey! Have they earned my hate? They have; they've got it.

Are we, then, to go on hating Germans forever! I hope not. It is not unreasonable to suppose that the disease of which the German nation is sick can in time be cured. It is likely, and perhaps regrettable, that the Poles and Greeks and Norwegians who have seen their loved ones murdered, tortured and goaded into suicide carry within them certain personal emotions of the kind that distort men's features and warp their minds. We have not had that experience. With us it is not a question of vengeance, vindictiveness, punishment, irremovable enmity. It is a question of facing realistically the ugly fact of the German doctrine—not the Hitler or the Nazi doctrine, the German doctrine—of the master race, and the resulting deep-rooted German attitude toward all other nations and peoples.

If we do not face it, and hate it with every drop of our blood, the chance is slim that we shall do what must be done to eradicate it. It will remain through our lives and, after we die, a menace to our children and grandchildren, an impassable barrier to the organization of a decent and workable world.

It is not true that if we hate the Germans now we are helping to fill a reservoir of hate-poison that will infect the future beyond all hope of antisepsis. On the contrary. If we do not hate the Germans now, we shall inevitably fail in our purpose to establish the world on a basis of peace. If we do not see the evil clearly enough to hate it as it deserves, which means, make no mistake, hating those who do or tolerate the evil, the temptation will be irresistible, at one point or another, to compromise with it instead of destroying it.

There never will be a world in which there is nothing and no one that is hateful. But it can be better than it is if we are sufficiently resolved to make it better. That resolution can be strong enough for its job only if it has emotional motivation and support in an uncompromising hatred for those evils with which there can be no truce, and for the people who are the champions of those evils, or the servants of the champions.

We shall hate, or we shall fail.

January 17, 1943

# 'Hate Is Moral Poison'

Professor Bowie repudiates the thesis of
Rex Stout, that we must hate the Germans
or we shall fail to make a lasting peace.

**By Walter Russell Bowie**
Professor of Practical Theology
Union Theological Seminary

**I**T was of the African Congo that Vachel Lindsay was thinking when he wrote his wild, exciting lines:

*Then I heard the boom of the blood-lust song*
*And a thigh-bone beating on a tin-pan gong.*

But nowadays it is not so much in Africa as here in America that the blood-lust song is beginning to echo, and that the "skull-faced, lean witch doctors" are finding a contemporary chorus.

"We Shall Hate, or We Shall Fail" that is the title of an article by Rex Stout, chairman of the Writers' War Board, in THE NEW YORK TIMES Magazine of Jan. 17. Then the subtitle goes on to say, "If we do not hate the Germans now, we shall fail in our effort to establish a lasting peace."

That is meant for patriotic fervor. Actually it is moral poison. If those words were listened to, they would twist this war away from any hope of a decent result, and turn it into a kind of frenzied dervish dance, or a voodoo incantation of the instincts of the jungle.

Mr. Stout ostensibly defines his terms. He says that by "hate" he means "a feeling toward the Germans of deep and implacable resentment for their savage attack upon the rights and dignity of man, of loathing for their ruthless assault on the persons and property of innocent and well-meaning peoples, of contempt for their arrogant and insolent doctrine of the German master race."

What those words *seem* to mean is a deep and implacable resentment against what Germany under its Nazi masters believes in and has done. In that judgment there appears to be discrimination, and therefore moral dignity. But Mr. Stout's argument runs to an indiscriminate ferocity. "I hate Germans and am not ashamed of it," he declares; and he will not be content until all the middle-aged gentlemen in their clubs and ladies at their knitting try to see how hard they can hate, "which means, make no mistake, hating those who do or tolerate the evil."

That is to say, not only what Germany now represents but "all Nazi Germans" must be hated. To "hate injustice, cruelty and barbarism" is not enough. Everybody who has been connected with these must be hated too. To hate the wrongs and "not hate our fellow-beings," says Mr. Stout, "would be a remarkable stunt and an extremely convenient one, if there were any person alive capable of performing it." But to suggest that there is any person alive capable of doing that would be "merely another trick with words."

That would be important, if true. But it is not true. What it says is that there is no possibility of fighting evil unless you fight vindictively. What it says is that a nation cannot espouse a great cause and carry it through victoriously unless the tom-toms of primitive passion keep beating louder and louder. That is as unsound in fact as it is atavistic in morals.

WHAT has a man been accustomed to who argues like that? Has he never happened to see a policeman—the actual everyday policeman who will pit his life at a moment's notice against crime and savagery, but who has never had it enter his head that in order to do that he must first work up an indiscriminate rage against every human being who has been a criminal and against all criminals' families besides? Has nobody ever suggested that there is such a thing as modern penology, and that the reason why its civilized process is different from the senseless rage of savages is precisely that civilized persons—judges, policemen, prison officials—do every day what Mr. Stout asserts that nobody is capable of doing? They do hate crime without losing the controlled intelligence which can discriminate among those who are classed as criminals.

BUT what has all this to do with war against the Nazis? it might be demanded. What is this but "another trick with words"? Well, it is not a trick with words; and it leads on directly to the question of war, and this particular war against Nazi Germany, and against Japan too, for that matter. Do men fight better by getting all frothed at the mouth with fury?

Look at England. Did the almost incredible courage of the little ordinary people of bombed London need to be kept up by harangues from hate-mongers? Most of them did not bother their heads about hating: they have sense enough and humor enough to keep their wits, and coolly to get on with the job. Now and then, it is true, some excited military leader in England and America does urge the inculcation of hate. An American general here at home exclaimed, "We must hate with every fiber of our being We must lust for battle." At one of the training centers in England there was a so-called hate room, with elaborate equipment to whip up the passions of men. When the news of that came out the Moderator of the Church of Scotland immediately protested and General B. C. T. Paget officially replied:

"Such an attitude of hate is foreign to the British temperament, and any attempt to produce it by artificial stimulus during training is bound to fail, as it did in the last war. Officers and NCO's must be made to realize the difference between the building up of this artificial hate and the building of a true offensive spirit combined with the will power which will not recognize defeat." And a high officer of the American forces, commenting on General Paget's instructions, wrote: "He exactly states my feeling, which has already been embodied in instructions issued to my officers * * * designated to strengthen the soldier's personal resolution in this great fight for liberty and decency in the world. Put forward the rightness and the importance of the cause."

FOR the most part, where is it that we hear so much about hate? Do we read of it in letters from the men at the battlefronts? Would we have it dinned into our ears if we were there? We would not. Of course, there is hot blood and the terrible instinctive impulse to kill rather than be killed. (That is the curse of war in any case.) But the real soldiers have an outlet for their emotions in costly courage; they have too much respect for men fighting like themselves on the other side to bother about emotional histrionics. That can be left to the professional pamphleteers who must get their emotional release in words.

Perhaps the pamphleteers were shocked when General Montgomery took the captured General von Thoma of the Africa Corps into his tent for breakfast; presumably what he should have done was to beat out his brains with a hatchet. On the day when these words are written there is in the newspapers an Associated Press picture of an Australian soldier putting his canteen to the lips of a wounded Japanese; presumably what he should have done was to strangle him. For to win the war, we must hate, hate all the time, hate everybody, hate as much as we can, and then learn to hate some more.

SO! How do people who talk thus get that way? Have they ever stopped to consider the picture they present? They might well look at the cartoon which the invincible British common sense and triumphant humor put on one of the pages of Punch. It was a drawing of a fat father and mother and a group of children sitting around a breakfast table, grimacing furiously; and it was entitled, "German family having its morning hate." Yes, if anybody has to have that sort of insanity, why not let it be the Germans? Hitler and Goebbels in their screaming frenzies can be crazier than we can.

"We shall hate, or we shall fail." There is one word used in the article which has those words for its heading which may appropriately be borrowed and used right here. "Tommyrot!" The truth is that wars are not won by dosing people up with a lot of synthetic hatred. They can be effectively lost that way, as Hitler will find out. This nation had better take its chance of winning, not by glandular virus, but by clear thinking, positive purpose and intelligently disciplined will.

AND suppose we did persuade everybody, the men at the front and the people at home, to do more hating. What would happen after the war? Is nobody to consider that? Hatred is not something that discharges itself upon one object and then conveniently disappears. It is a poison in the blood, an emotional debauch, which is not quick to disappear. People who should get the habit of hating all German Nazis, man, woman and child, would get so that they would just have to hate somebody. Like the drunkard, if they lose one bottle they will look for another; and if they can't have whisky, even wood alcohol will do. There may be plenty of demagogues in America after this war who would feed

A British soldier distributes food to a group of Axis prisoners, behind the fighting lines in North Africa.

people who had got the taste for hating with new brands of hate: race hatreds, class hatreds, religious hatreds.

On the same day when Mr. Stout's article appeared, there appeared in the news columns a statement by the Educational Policies Committee of the National Education Association. Even if "hatred of the enemy and desire for revenge" were inculcated among the fighting men, the committee said:

We especially deplore the cultivation of such traits among the younger children and others who are not likely to see military service. The spiritual casualties of war will be great enough and lasting enough without any help from the teaching profession.

We must certainly feel an intense aversion to the evil men who have betrayed their compatriots and who, by their vicious policies and wicked actions, have brought needless misery to so many innocent people. Nevertheless, intense and revengeful rancor toward the great mass of the people of the enemy countries is not likely to hasten our final victory. These violent and confused emotions, these malignant indictments of entire nations and races are the characteristic weapons of dictators. They are not suitable weapons for na-

tions conducting a great crusade for the extension of liberty and justice to all peoples everywhere in the world.

After the war, then what? Will the overthrow of Hitler and the Japanese warlords amount to anything? Will the accomplishment of that, and only that, be worth this war's horrible cost? Of course not. Their overthrow would at best do no more than clear the ground — clear the ground upon which slowly we may begin to shape the fabric of a world order conceived and built according to those principles of justice and human consideration which alone could make it fit to last. That kind of world cannot be created by men still stupid and truculent with the hangovers of deliberate hating. It will require men whose souls have been big enough to keep sober in a maddened time.

SOMETIMES we can see the truth when we get it in perspective—see the truth which we might not see at all when it is blurred by our own near passions. The real dignities of the mind and heart emerge, and other things which might have seemed desirable are revealed as near in-

decency. In our Civil War here in America there were plenty of people who preached hatred as though men's souls depended on it. Thaddeus Stevens, haranguing the Congress at Washington, shouted that it "must treat those States now outside of the Union as conquered provinces, and settle them with new men, and drive the rebels as exiles from this country."

In so far as Thaddeus Stevens had his way, the Civil War was carried on into a long aftermath of bitterness and sadistic vengeance. Against such men as Stevens— and sneeringly opposed and repudiated by him—stood the spirit of Abraham Lincoln, who said in his second inaugural:

"With malice toward none; with charity for all; with firmness in the right, as God gives us to see the right, let us strive on to finish the work we are in; to bind up the nation's wounds; * * * to do all which may achieve and cherish a just and lasting peace among ourselves, and with all nations."

LOOKING back upon these two types of men, can anybody

fail now to see which the nation is proud of and which it would want to forget? Does anybody doubt that all that is wholesome and strong in this united country is due to the fact that slowly the spirit of Lincoln prevailed and the spirit of hatred was repudiated?

The same truth invites us now. We do not need a new crop of Thaddeus Stevenses. We need men "with malice toward none, with charity for all," who shall be big enough in spirit to show us how to deserve, and then to create, "a just and lasting peace among all nations." For this great task which will confront us, we may well listen to the words which Philip Gibbs, most discerning among the front-line correspondents, wrote as he surveyed the First World War:

"Let us exorcise our own devils and get back to kindness toward all men of good will. * * * Let us seek the beauty of life and God's truth somehow, remembering the boys who died too soon. * * * By blood and passion there will be no healing. We have seen too much blood. We want to wipe it out of our eyes and souls."

January 31, 1943

# BETTER AND/OR WORSE

### By BOSLEY CROWTHER

PIQUED by an idle curiosity (and the grim urge to make a minor point), this corner was just now wondering how high has been the average in past years of the good and commendable pictures which have come along in Thanksgiving weeks. You might think the score would be sizable, considering the season's marked significance. At least, we thought it would be. So we checked back. Would you believe it: it has not. No more than one in five pictures which have graced the Thanksgiving fare in five years past have been of such notable consequence that you would care to write home about them. So we felt supremely elated at the thought that two of this past week's seven films were well above middling entertainment. A ten per cent gain! That's progress, folks.

You may thank the Warners for this benefaction. For it was they who turned out the two top films: "Casablanca," showing at the Hollywood, and "Gentleman Jim," at the Strand. Usually a studio doesn't so obviously compete with itself. Good films are not so abundant that they may be squandered recklessly. But in this particular instance the Warners are playing them smart. "Casablanca" is hot with the headlines and "Gentleman Jim" is an Errol Flynn film. Why shouldn't they be grateful for their fortune and share with the customers?

### Rick's Tricks

"Casablanca" is by far the better. In fact, it is a corking good show—a tough, romantic thriller of a sort which has distinguished this studio. But more than that—more than just a taut thriller—it is a moving and even heroic tale of a brave man's casual defiance of Nazi authority and insolence abroad. For this is the heartwarming story of Rick, the American proprietor of a hot cafe and clip casino in the "refugee port" of Casablanca (prior to recent events), and of the manner in which he makes it possible for an old love and her Czech husband to escape to a refuge in America, thus foiling the Nazis' evil designs.

That is the story in bare outline, but it doesn't tell the half of it. It doesn't tell, for instance, of the stunning performance of Humphrey Bogart as Rick—of his beautiful demonstration of cold conflict between his love for a woman and his sense of what is right. It doesn't tell of Ingrid Bergman's genuine and compassionate characterization of the girl, or of Conrad Veidt's embodiment of a Nazi colonel or Claude Rains's cunning Vichy cop. It doesn't tell of the soul-stirring moment when Paul Henreid, as the Czech patriot, starts the customers in a cafe to singing the Marseillaise to drown the Nazis' "Die Wacht am Rhein." It doesn't tell of the moods which are evoked when Dooley Wilson, as a Negro pianist, starts playing those old sentimental torch songs which sound so haunting in a smoke-filled cafe. It doesn't tell a thing of the pathos and the humor which have been artfully worked into this film by those Warner Gracchi, the Epstein brothers, and Howard Koch, who wrote the script. But that doesn't really matter, because you'll see it yourself if you know what's best.

*November 29, 1942*

# ZOOT SUITS BECOME ISSUE ON COAST

### By LAWRENCE E. DAVIES

LOS ANGELES, June 12—The zoot suit with the reat pleat, the drape shape and the stuff cuff has been the object of much amusement and considerable derision from Harlem to the Pacific during the last two or three years. Psychiatrists may have their own ideas about it, but, according to the reasoning of many newcomers to the armed service, especially hundreds of young sailors in this area, the zoot suit has become the symbol these last ten days of a fester on the body politic which should be removed by Navy vigilantes, if police will not or cannot do the job.

Adventures of the Navy boys in trying to accomplish their purpose have been watched with such interest in all quarters—bringing cheers from some and causing concern to others—that newspapers were snatched up eagerly on downtown street corners the other day when newsboys handling late afternoon and morning "bulldog" editions shouted:

"No more zoot suits!"

"Navy bans Los Angeles!"

### "Out of Bounds"

These headlines referred to the action of Rear Admiral David W. Bagley, commandant of the Eleventh Naval District, in placing this city under "temporarily restricted liberty for naval personnel." This means that only in special cases could sailors be at large in the city.

This greatly reduced, if it failed to stop altogether, clashes between small bands of zoot-suit wearers, chiefly of Mexican descent, and groups of Navy seamen out to retaliate for attacks on lone sailors or their girls by the pork-pie-hatted hoodlums.

To some persons who have watched the development of juvenile gangs, especially in Mexican areas of Los Angeles County, in the last few years, the spectacle here this month has not been surprising.

The "zooters," investigators report, are products of slum districts, are boys of 16 to 20 years who are not intellectually inclined as a rule, who enjoy notoriety and who are not amenable to parental discipline. There is insistence on every side that the problem presented by their scraps with the Navy is not intrinsically one of race; that it is merely unfortunate, that the wearers of the zoot suits are chiefly Americans of Mexican descent, along with some Negroes.

What is the outlook? Mayor Fletcher Bowron, Chief of Police C. B. Horrall and others, including some of the State investigators, working under the direction of Governor Earl Warren, are optimistic. They believe Los Angeles will calm down and police will be able to handle the situation, even with the Navy ban lifted. Others are not so sure. They see here a serious juvenile delinquency problem which must be handled realistically.

The Army, meanwhile, has entered the picture by warning soldiers against "riotous conduct" and "inciting to riot."

*June 13, 194*

---

## LET US HAVE PEACE

The six-year nightmare is over. The guns fall into silence. The war pilots have finished their missions. The young men who were marked for death will live. In every American home there must be thankfulness too deep for words, too profound to find full expression in the blowing of whistles, the ringing of bells and all the noise and tumult of the victory celebrations.

Soon now our fighting men can begin redeploying for peace, to resume the normal lives that were interrupted by war, to marry, to raise families, to take up the work of rebuilding the civilization that came so near destruction. It is now our obligation, in the words of Lincoln's second inaugural, "to bind up the nation's wounds; to care for him who shall have borne the battle, and for his widow and his orphan—to do all which may achieve and cherish a just and lasting peace among ourselves and with all nations."

One by one the aggressors have fallen under the avenging sword. Mussolini's Mare Nostrum is a free sea again. Hitler's boasted thousand years were reduced to a dozen. The Greater East Asia Co-Prosperity Sphere has gone the way of the dreams of the rulers of Babylon. The vision of democracy has been revived in Europe. The victors, in their absolute power, even hold it before the eyes of the broken masses of Germany. It is written into the peace terms given Japan. It flames before the faces of Asia's swarming millions.

The cave men, armed with every modern weapon save one, made their bid for world dominion. How nearly they achieved it we now know, and even on this day of victory and peace the thought sends a cold chill through every marrow. Had Hitler invaded an almost defenseless Britain after Dunkerque; had he given Rommel enough troops to reach Suez; had he broken into the Near East when he took Crete; had the Japanese seized the Hawaiian Islands instead of running away after the attack on Pearl Harbor; above all, had the secret of the atomic bomb been known to our enemies before we mastered it, the peace that has now come to the world might be a peace of cruel and endless slavery for the great majority of the human race.

They did not succeed. We can say, if we like, that it was not the will of God that they should succeed. But we had better also say that it was not the will of humanity, and that it is now the responsibility of the victorious nations, including our own democracy, to see to it that this menace shall not recur. And this means much more than guarding a single terrible weapon, the atomic bomb, from irresponsible possession. It means guarding against the destructive weapons of international jealousy, hate and fear.

The absolute victors in any previous war could make any peace settlement that seemed to their immediate advantage. They could arrange boundaries, secure raw materials, take possession of military and naval bases. Something like this may be done now. Something like it is being done. But it will have to be tested and judged as no peace settlement in history has been judged. It will have to meet the test and judgment of justice in the eyes of all mankind.

No temporary advantage and no satisfaction of revenge can safely be the guide in this peace. The time has arrived when righteousness is necessary to the safety of humanity. Justice to the conquered requires the punishment of guilty individuals. That punishment will be inflicted. But justice to the common people of the world requires a larger conception: justice to those who have died for this victory; justice to those who have suffered cruel injuries to win it; justice to the bereaved and sorrow-stricken; justice to those who are now children and those unborn.

Let us have peace. Let us have a true and enduring peace. Let us have a peace that gives hope to the innocent wherever they are found, even in enemy countries. Let us have a peace in which none need be afraid. Let us have a peace in which mankind can build happier and freer lives. Let us dedicate ourselves today to that sort of peace. None other can last. None other can save the world.

August 15, 1945

# Books of the Times

## By ORVILLE PRESCOTT

"THE NAKED AND THE DEAD,"* by Norman Mailer, is in many ways the most impressive novel about the second World War that I have ever read. It has faults and serious ones; but its total effect is overwhelming. Here as rarely before in print is the terrible urgency of battle, the chilling excitement, the stupefying exhaustion, the tension, fear and despair.

**Norman Mailer**

Here also is an amazingly deep penetration into the minds and hearts of men. For maturity of viewpoint, for technical competence and for stark dramatic power this book is an incredibly finished performance. It is a first novel by a young veteran of the Pacific war, who is only 25 years old. Mr. Mailer is as certain to become famous as any fledgling novelist can be. Unfortunately, he is just as likely to become notorious. In his effort to carry his realistic portrayal of men at war to the ultimate degree of authenticity he has wallowed in a grotesque and excessive fidelity to the coarseness of their language. In the middle of this outspoken century no normal adult has any illusions about the profanity and obscenity of soldier talk. But the nature of such talk can be suggested briefly in fiction without rubbing the reader's nose in it a thousand times. There is more explicitly vile speech in "The Naked and the Dead" than I have ever seen printed in a work of serious literature before. It is probably truthful reporting; but it is unnecessarily offensive and it is marvelously tiresome.

### Termed an Artistic Mistake

It is also, it seems to me, an artistic mistake. It clogs and defaces a fine and serious novel. It will prevent many persons from reading "The Naked and the Dead" who otherwise would do so. It will attract many other readers who never will appreciate the extraordinary merits of Mr. Mailer's book, but who always gather like vultures around the carcass of a reputedly sensational novel.

Once this most conspicuous attribute of "The Naked and the Dead" is dutifully recorded, it is a relief and a pleasure to forget it and to recall the real stature of Mr. Mailer's achievement. In the first place this is not just another novel about the horrors of war. Mr. Mailer has laid them on thickly, the ghastly injuries, the maggots and the rotting flesh; but his chief emphasis is on the character of a dozen men. What kind of men they were before they were landed on the jungle island of Anopei is shown in a series

*THE NAKED AND THE DEAD. By Norman Mailer. 721 pages. Rinehart. $4.

of long flashbacks obviously written by a conscientious student of John Dos Passos. What kind of men they became under the pressure of war is Mr. Mailer's central theme.

He develops it with brilliant self-assurance, with wonderful command of atmosphere and with a fine understanding of the relative importance of exterior and interior drama. The exterior adventures, the combat, the harrowing hardships of a fantastically dangerous jungle patrol, the clash of personalities, are all superbly described. One fairly hears the whine and ricochet of bullets, feels the terrible exhaustion that can reduce tough men to tears, shares their boredom and their fear.

But, engrossing as all this is, it is even more interesting to watch the deft way with which Mr. Mailer digs into his soldiers, into their ignorance, their prejudice, their pride, their fear of being afraid, their fear of each other as well as of the Japanese. The dozen men who shared the same climactic patrol were very different from each other; but most of them were alike in their lack of education, their impoverished homes, their concentration on liquor and sex, their suspicion of their wives and their callow cynicism.

### General Bedazzled by Power

Some of them had stronger nerves or stronger bodies than others. Some of them were more fundamentally decent. Others had greater physical courage. The top sergeant was coldly courageous, cruel and mean. His courage was an expression of his frustration in civilian life and his lust for power, for leadership, for command. The major general in charge of the whole Anopei campaign was a better educated and a far subtler man. But he, too, was bedazzled by power. Having more intelligence and a longer view than the brutal top sergeant, the general planned for the future and was a convinced Fascist.

There is such an abundance of fiercely dramatic and psychologically interesting material in "The Naked and the Dead" that sometimes it is difficult to see the woods for the trees, to discern just what is Mr. Mailer's own position. He seems to be fond of his foul-mouthed soldiers, to respect them as human beings. But his group picture of them is a bitter comment on American civilization. Likable, childlike, more than adequately brave, they still are frighteningly primitive, barren of ideas and ideals, a sad reflection on the social system that left them so intellectually immature.

But, even so, when the soldiers in "The Naked and the Dead" when they shout their anti-Semitism or malinger or murder prisoners are treated by Mr. Mailer as comparatively harmless products of their environment.

It is the general with his reasoned defense of fascism who seems to be the real object of Mr. Mailer's wrath and fear. But even the general is provided with a set of circumstances that do much to explain him. Perhaps Mr. Mailer, like so many of us, dislikes a world that can send ignorant men to die in tropical jungles, hopes for a better day and doubts that its approach is at all imminent.

May 7 1948

# Tough and Tormented,
# This Was the Army to Mr. Jones

FROM HERE TO ETERNITY. By
James Jones. 861 pp. New York:
Charles Scribner's Sons. $4.50.

## By DAVID DEMPSEY

WHEN a book is as commanding in its narrative power and grasp of character as this one, it bears comparison with the very best that is being done in American fiction today. "From Here to Eternity" is the work of a major new American novelist. To anyone who reads this immensely long and deeply convincing story of life in the peacetime army, it will be apparent that in James Jones an original and utterly honest talent has restored American realism to a pre-eminent place in world literature.

Mr. Jones' novel, set at Schofield Barracks, Oahu, covers the years before and up through Pearl Harbor. It is about men who are at peace with the world and at war with themselves, about their rivalries, frustrations, hates and loneliness; about their women; about all the sutlers of virtue and camp-followers of vice that surround what is called, in peacetime, the Standing Army—an army, curiously enough, that always seems to be seated.

All this and hell too, for the moral azimuth of the novel is straight down. Since there are no great loves arising out of the priapic preoccupations of the soldiers, nor any heroic redemptions out of their sins, we would be wiser to turn to Margaret Mead rather than Dante as a guide. Mr. Jones is concerned with the almost biological relationship between the individual and the group, with the totems and taboos and orgiastic rites of a race of moral primitives, with the emotional pressures that fill the vacuum of life in the peacetime army. He has succeeded brilliantly in showing us the forces that destroy men when they live lives of rootless expediency.

The central theme is nonconformism. Using the Golden Boy idea, the author follows the career of a soldier who would rather bugle than box. There are no regulations in the army that decree that a man must box, but there are human improvisations which can make it tough for him if he doesn't. These are known as The Treatment and Pvt. Robert E. Lee Prewitt, the novel's principal character—a man who once played taps at Arlington—gets The Treatment.

HIS efforts to hold out against it form a study in the disintegration of a soldier and—in Thoreau's sense at least—the making of a man. Unfortunately, rebellion becomes an end in itself (all but one of Mr. Jones' recalcitrants fall into this fallacy) and the cause is lost.

This is not to suggest that the novel is involved with an elaborate symbolism; the book gives us the essence of a soldier's life rather than the symbols. It is the really eloquent virtue of "From Here to Eternity" that Mr. Jones makes us believe in his people, from the brass hats to the brass checks. They are human within the subhuman anonymity of the military machine—Prewitt, the bugler; Warden, the First Sergeant who manages his company with the dedication of a saint while seducing his commanding officer's wife; Bloom, who makes the one successful outward adjustment and then commits suicide; Malloy, the philosophical rebel.

They are talking about Bloom's suicide and Malloy expresses his approval:

For every general in this world there have to be 6,000 privates. That's why I wouldn't stop any man from committing suicide. If he came up and asked to borrow my gun, I'd give it to him. Because he is either serious or else he's trying to maintain that illusion of freedom. If he was serious I'd want him to have it; if he was play-acting I'd want to call him * * * In our world, citizens, theres only one way a man can have freedom, and that is to die for it, and after he's died for it it dont do him any good. Thats the whole problem, citizens. In a nutshell.

Yet their tragedy consists not alone in being among the 6,000 privates, but in the recklessness of their lives, for which the army is no help.

"From Here to Eternity" is so uninhibited in its vocabulary, so outspoken in its descriptions that it is bound to shock. It is a book for adults. Mr. Jones uses profanity skillfully, as do most soldiers for whom swearing is a way of making endurable the unendurable. Yet the book's extreme naturalism gives it a special importance at this time, when much of our serious fiction has turned introspective and somewhat effeminate in quest of psychological rather than social relationships.

In its statement of the ultimate values of a soldier's life, "From Here to Eternity" may not be as profound as Robert Henriques' "No Arms, No Armour." Yet it will be read a long time for its minute and almost uncanny insight into army life, its pungent dialogue, its sheer narrative pull, its portrayal of the tenderness that sometimes is found beneath the crudest animal drives, its absence of mock heroics, its comic absurdities and irony and, above all else, its revelation of the perversity of human nature in the face of evil.

MR. JONES has obviously written out of his own experiences. A native of Robinson, Ill., and a graduate of the Robinson High School, he served five years in the Army, fought on Guadalcanal, where he was wounded, and witnessed the bombing of Pearl Harbor. At the time of his discharge he held the rank of private, having twice been reduced from (1) corporal and (2) sergeant.

Although his book ends shortly after the bombing of Pearl Harbor, it is a better "war" novel than those which have had war as a setting. Anyone who has ever worn the uniform of a soldier will recognize it as a definitive work, truer in its characterizations than "The Naked and the Dead," less theme-ridden than "The Young Lions" and "Act of Love," in every sense a work of heroic proportions.

In pushing forward the limits of naturalism while looking into the hearts of men, Mr. Jones does for our time what Stephen Crane did for his in "The Red Badge of Courage." There have been more subtly written books about the American soldier, and books with more finished, conscious technique, but none that has been written with more integrity, or with a surer grasp of its material.

Make no mistake about it, "From Here to Eternity" is a major contribution to our literature, written with contempt for the forces that waste human life, and out of compassion for men who find love and honor and courage in the lower depths, where they are less apparent but sometimes more enduring. Its author speaks to us across an ocean of unshared experiences but from a world of common values. He makes us care about his soldiers and caring about them, we care about humanity.

*Mr. Dempsey, a member of the Book Review staff, is a co-author of "Uncommon Valor," a book about Marine combat.*

## AMERICANS AGAIN MOVE OVER THE SEINE

Boy Scouts who represented this country at the world jamboree in Moissons, France, marching across the bridge at Rolleboise on Aug. 20 to commemorate the crossing made by our troops during World War II.

Associated Press

August 25, 1947

# CHAPTER 2

# Survival in the Atomic Age

*Atomic testing, August 1, 1946, at Bikini Atoll*

Courtesy The New York Times

# FINDS PAGANS NUMEROUS

## Peale Says They Constitute a Large Part of U. S. Population

Pagans constitute a large proportion of this country's population, the Rev. Dr. Norman Vincent Peale, rector of the Marble Collegiate Reformed Church, Fifth Avenue and Twenty-ninth Street.

Dr. Peale said that the "pagan" population was composed of persons who were normally Catholics, Protestants and Jews, "but for whom religion certainly is not a vital matter."

"They have long since lost their religious moorings," he asserted. "They seldom, if ever, go to church. The teachings of religion and the certainties of faith have grown dim and pallid in their lives. Their entire outlook is materialistic and sensual."

# Concerning Post-War Morals and the Excited Style

AN ESSAY ON MORALS. By Philip Wylie. xvi+204 pp. New York: Rinehart & Co. $2.50.

THE REDISCOVERY OF MORALS. By Henry C. Link. An American Mercury Book. 223 pp. New York: E. P. Dutton & Co. $2.50.

### By HOWARD MUMFORD JONES

AFTER World War I, we had Dadaism, Joseph Wood Krutch's "The Modern Temper" and Walter Lippmann's "A Preface to Morals." After World War II, we have Existentialism, Philip Wylie's "An Essay on Morals" and Dr. Link's "The Rediscovery of Morals," described as an "American Mercury Book," a phrase which places it somewhat right of center. Dadaism, dismissed by the current Britannica as having "no definite technique and no principles," exalted nonsense into a pastime, whereas the volumes by Krutch and Lippmann were serious volumes having definite principles and a bounding line. Existentialism, so far as one can get a glimpse of its real meaning, is an intellectually respectable philosophy of definite principles, but I confess that the two books by Wylie and Link leave me in a state of general confusion as to the intent and the tenets of their writers.

Mr. Wylie is a prodigious producer of words, some eighteen volumes being listed in the front matter of "An Essay on Morals," besides which one must count his newspaper columns and various other forms of communication. The subtitle of his "Essay" has the same prodigious size:

A science of philosophy and a philosophy of the sciences; a popular explanation of the Jungian theory of human instinct; a new Bible for the bold mind and a way to personal peace by logic; the heretic's handbook and text for honest skeptics, including a description of man suitable for an atomic age, together with a compendium of means to brotherhood in a better world and a voyage beyond the opposite directions of religion and objective truth, to understanding.

There you are. All for two dollars and a half.

A brochure sent out by Mr. Wylie's publishers concerning their author is cunningly entitled "God's Little Acher," but I cannot quite believe that the intricate ethical and intellectual problems of our age are to be solved in terms of slick journalism. Such an introduction does Mr. Wylie

*Abner Dean.*

**Philip Wylie.**

disservice—if his publishers wish us to take his book seriously. And his intent is serious. Unfortunately, as in the case of how many other moralists, Mr. Wylie is more expert at denunciation than he is at rebuilding.

He is rather violently anti-clerical; he seems to be also anti-national and pro-democracy, as who is not? Peace of mind and ethical balance, one gathers, are to come when we are all persuaded that we can live cleanly as splendid animals in the Jungian "collective unconscious," or instinct. But Mr. Wylie is far from clear as to how you know the collective unconscious when you meet it. And Mr. Wylie is thoroughly annoyed by those who do not live according to this scheme of values. So thoroughly annoyed, that one wonders if the collective unconscious is any less cantankerous than the church. For example:

There are other plagues of the human psyche; but this pair has principally sabotaged its peace. Because of them the human prospect is always uncertain and now more than ever. The world's inhabited by a rabble of two billion God-owned zealots and patriots who yearn for tranquillity as individuals, but insist that it must be arranged under special terms, and who struggle secretly in the meantime so that they will be able to annihilate each other in the event of major disagreement. The common patriot, Hindu or Hoosier, and the common big, Brahmin or Baptist, are madder powder-makers than all the merchants of death and the military men together.

This excited manner is, I fear, a poor recommendation for Mr. Wylie's moral system, for it is precisely the manner he denounces.

DR. LINK, most of whose pages are strewn with italic sentences, is honorably opposed to racial prejudice and would like to do something to end class conflict. This he thinks can be brought about if we will but return to some unshaken ethical code, preferably the Ten Commandments, which make, he thinks, for the dignity of man. The argument is impeccable; the only difficulty is how this miracle is to be brought about. Dr. Link seems sometimes to believe that legislation and the schools can be enlisted; but at other times he seems to think that educators and the law merely increase the evils he wants cured.

I think I should be more sympathetic with his volume if he were not so bound up with prejudice against communism in general and Russia in particular. He seems to equate absolute morality with free enterprise—and, therefore, strongly implies that communism is immoral. He is capable of writing: "What Hitler's 'Mein Kampf' is to racial conflict, the writings of Marx have for a hundred years been to class conflict," that is, a handbook for "arousing the baser passions of men." This is surely to throw the baby out with the bath. Whatever opinion one may have of "Das Kapital," it is a book of the severest intellectual discipline, product of a mind poles removed from the confused nonsense of "Mein Kampf." One's suspicion will not down that Dr. Link's ethical system is entirely relative to the morals of capitalism. Inasmuch as the morals of capitalism are precisely what is in question, Dr. Link, to be convincing, will have to avoid assuming what he must first prove; namely, that the economic order of the United States is that direct and absolute product of the moral law he thinks it ought to be.

The world is looking for clear, simple, and persuasive moral leaders. But neither on the basis of prose style nor philosophical system (so far as I comprehend them) does Mr. Wylie or Dr. Link supply the want.

# The Dissenter's Role in a Totalitarian Age

**The true prophet, the honest heretic are needed more than ever before, a chronic dissenter says.**

### By NORMAN THOMAS

DISSENTERS have played more than one role in history. At various times, at various places, and on issues big and little, they have been responsible for confusion, division and discontent. And for progress. Your true prophets have always been dissenters. Heretics have often been gravely in error. Nevertheless, as I am not the first man to observe, the heretic has always been the growing point in society. When he is repressed by force society stagnates. A virile society follows its true prophets and has better ways to deal with error than the club, the noose or the stake.

Prometheus, according to ancient legend, was punished by the gods for bringing fire as a gift to men. For that punishment I have always suspected that fearful men, slaves to the old ways, not jealous gods, were responsible.

Certainly in historic times the man with new ideas, not alone in religion and politics but in what we now call science, has rarely been honored by his own generation. "Your fathers killed the prophets and you have builded their tombs" is a judgment on us which was by no means completely altered either by the coming of Christianity or the advent of the modern scientific method. A few famous dissenters have been successful rebels and when success led them to power they have sometimes tasted the dregs of disillusion within its cup.

When one talks of dissenters, however, one is discussing a far more numerous company than the famous pathfinders and prophets who have proved themselves the leaders of men. The capacity of just plain folks for dissent is important. It is today an expression of the kind of courage upon which the very life of democracy depends.

THE menacing conflicts of our time are not between the individual prophet in high place or low and his prejudiced or apathetic neighbors. Increasingly they are between rival groups with different interests and ideologies, all of them inclined to act like mobs rather than fellowships of free men. Neither the Communist nor the Fascist deserves the honored name of dissenter. He is merely the docile but often fanatic slave to his own particular group and its leaders. He wants no true freedom of dissent. In this respect Communists and Fascists exaggerate a common failing. Most men want the freedom

**NORMAN THOMAS** has been Socialist party candidate for President six times. He is a writer and editor for various publications.

of which they talk for themselves so that they may advance their particular truth. If and when their group gets power, freedom becomes only a right to agree with them or docilely submit to their sway.

We Americans have visited harsh judgment upon Russians and Germans who assented to the practices of demagogues and dictators even when in their hearts they disapproved of them. We have seen very clearly what tragedy fell on Germany and mankind because there were so few bold dissenters, unknown soldiers of truth, in towns or villages when the Nazis were consolidating their power. Most of our written and spoken comment carries the implication that that sort of thing couldn't happen here in our America. Yet it does happen here whenever and wherever a community condones mob violence whether in Groveland, Fla., or in Westchester County, N. Y.

There was a grim and terrible warning in a story which received little notice in the press or radio. Only the other day, at long last, a persistent wife won from an honest judge freedom for her husband who had spent twenty-six years of his life in a state prison for a rape which he did not commit. The man was James Montgomery, a poor Negro worker of good repute. At a time and in a place—Illinois, not Georgia—cursed by the Ku Klux Klan, James Montgomery was accused of rape on the unsupported word of an eccentric woman who later was committed to an insane asylum. The frightening thing, it is now discovered, is that the police played along with the Klan and that the physician who examined the woman knew all along that no rape had been committed, and yet lacked courage to testify to the truth because he liked "a quiet life" and the Klan was strong. How often, one wonders, have he and his fellow-citizens in that Illinois community thanked God that they were not as other men, even these Germans?

The guilty silence of the physician and the overt hostility of the police in the Montgomery case represented the extreme antithesis to dissent, a conformity to the wishes of the powerful without regard to any values except safety and the poor satisfactions that belong to the members of the herd. Such things threaten any decent democracy.

PHILOSOPHERS have sometimes argued that the business of living in groups requires that most of our actions shall be traditional and habitual rather than reflective. The dissenter can be, indeed he

often has been, a crackpot or a fanatic. Every great religion is obliged to warn us against false prophets. On this basis the observer from the windows of his ivory tower (or the lesser security of an editor's office) may comfortably conclude that on the whole it is well that men do not change capriciously or follow every Pied Piper who may pipe them a tune. Yet clearly our danger is not from the honest dissenter but from the passions of the mob and those who manipulate it in the struggle for profit and power.

It may seem that I have been talking in melodramatic terms and that in our America the role of the dissenter is neither so necessary nor so dangerous as some of my illustrations and historical observations would imply. Thank God, it is true that for most of us dissent requires no super-human courage and that there is even some fun to be derived from it. Americans are kept in line by their own fears of what might happen far more than by the bitterness of what does happen.

THE list of dissenters even in America who have been held back in their trade or profession, or blacklisted altogether, who have faced hostile audiences or ugly mobs, who have known arrest or imprisonment is long, but it is very short compared with men who have been kept in line simply by fear of being different, or by determination to keep up with the Joneses. I speak against the background of some experience when I say that if dissenters rarely are troubled by the weight of income taxes in the higher brackets they by no means furnish a chief recruiting ground for relief rolls. If fame and fortune are not the usual rewards of dissent in America, neither is the poorhouse.

Trouble often comes not to the open dissenter but to one who is suspected of hiding the degree of his nonconformity. I have spoken with complete impunity before audiences of considerable size at times and in places where men were denied the right to speak, or whose meetings were badly disturbed, because they were suspected of socialism or some other heresy which they denied.

So I come to my own dissenting experience. The editor who suggested this article hinted that I might. With the natural egotism of every writer thus encouraged, let me record the fact that I have enjoyed my role as dissenter, only regretting my lack of success. More than once I have said that I would rather be right than be President, but was perfectly willing to be both. (Henry Clay, author of that much quoted sentiment, succeeded in being neither.)

I CERTAINLY have not run repeatedly for office out of any masochistic pleasure in recurrent defeat. I never ran merely to make a protest, which at times has value, or to be a "gadfly." (The only notable achievement of a gadfly, in my experience, was to make my horse run away.) A dissenter worth his salt never dissents just for the pleasure of being "agin' the Government." He dissents from the established rule, custom or theory, because, clearly or vaguely, he envisages something better which he positively desires for himself and his fellows. The religious dissenter believes that he has found a better road to heaven; the political dissenter, a better way of life upon earth. If he is to be useful his capacity for dissent must not be at the price of incapacity for constructive cooperation.

Assuredly, I never coveted the dubious honor of being the most often defeated candidate for high office in American history. Neither did I ever run with the expectation of election. I ran because of an honest conviction that by running I could, better than in any other way, further two related causes dear to my heart: the education of the public in democratic socialism and the realignment of American political parties so that our political divisions would be meaningful and we should have genuine party responsibility. I was, in other words, a dissenter from the old-line parties not so much because I disliked them as because I wanted something different.

IN respect to promoting a political realignment such as my heart desired, I have been a failure, and failure hurts. In respect to a certain degree of public education and a kind of indirect influence on the old parties, my failure was by no means so complete. I can honestly claim that something had been accomplished. And it is more than a pious platitude to say that in many respects the struggle is its own reward. In short, I have enjoyed life more as a dissenter than, so far as I can judge, many of my conforming friends and acquaintances — including some of those who have won elections. I have suffered no more than they from current — and damnable — smear techniques.

In my role of aging sage, bestowing advice—unasked—upon the young, I should not dare to promise them as good a life as I have found as a dissenter. I am gratefully and humbly aware of what fortune has done for me. But I would insist that to believe in something enough to stand on your own feet in its behalf, to feel that you are something more than a member of the herd, is a satisfaction transcending inescapable duty. You can find in it a real joy in life, especially if you hang on to a sense of humor. Yes, there's fun in trying to be the Joneses with whom others should seek to keep up.

THE editors of The Daily Worker, if for purposes of objurgation they read this article at all, will cry to high heaven that I have no right to speak as a dissenter; that I am and have been only a "capitalist lackey"; and that the real dissenters are those recently on trial and picket duty in Foley Square. Let me repeat that today your Communist is not so much a dissenter as an ultra-orthodox member of an opposing political church, subject in every respect to its discipline.

In the campaign of 1944 more than once Communists called on the Government to prevent me from speaking because I was a heretic or dissenter against the Government policy, which the Communists then vociferously approved, of winning lasting peace by total vengeance against Germans and appeasement of Stalin.

The Communists applauded the conviction of Trotskyite heretics under the very law under which their leaders have been convicted. Of all men, they have least use for the individual dissenter. As for their claim that their efforts at secrecy and their use of special party names are necessities because otherwise, in a cruel America, they would face loss of jobs or even imprisonment, that also is not true on the record.

AFTER the conclusion of Mitchell Palmer's "obscene anti-red raids"—the phrase is that of a conservative historian—of which raids the Communists were by no means the chief victims, there was a very high degree of political freedom in America until the "cold war" and Communist subservience to Stalin created an opposition which is often unwise and even hysterical. William Z. Foster lived with complete impunity in America and traveled unnecessarily on false passports for years after he had written the revolutionary book, "Towards a Soviet America," which he now says is obsolete.

To a very considerable degree the Communists have created a problem new in American history because they have deliberately flouted the established practice of American radicals from Colonial times on. That practice was not long-continued secret conspiracy, deceit and concealment, but a flamboyant honesty which, for instance, led the Wobblies of old to fill the jails in towns in which one or more of their comrades had been arrested. Your true dissenter loves the light and believes in the capacity of the

Norman Thomas—"Certain dissents are an essential condition of the life of mankind."

common man to walk in it when it is allowed to shine.

I SHOULD like to end this article on something other than a historic or explanatory note. Our democracy is in desperate need of intelligent and constructive dissenters. The particular dissent which haunts me day and night is against the notion that peace for my children and grandchildren can be guaranteed by the present race in arms.

For unnumbered centuries men have accepted the notion that peace can be had, or at least security, by preparing for war. But today, by every precedent of history and every rule of logic, there can be but one end of this armament race if we continue it: that is the war of the age of atomic bombs and bacteriological agents of destruction which are already possessed by both groups of potential belligerents.

Our technology has driven us to a new sort of war and gives a new significance to war. Yet we plod along, simply intensifying the sort of

arms race which in the past has led straight to the wars which nominally it was intended to prevent. Lasting peace requires much more than the end of the arms race. But there will be no peace without the end of our frantic competition in weapons of death. So long as our present rivalry continues, our minds will be too preoccupied, our emotions too absorbed, to be capable of the constructive thinking required for the conquest of hunger and a just and equitable rule of law in our one world.

While the arms race continues it is a mockery to talk of a successful attack upon poverty. Nations feel themselves obliged to spend from 20 to 50 per cent of their current budgets on getting ready for war. The British Labor Government has been denounced for its reckless extravagance in providing for social welfare. But all its expenditures for social welfare outside of education fall 34 million pounds short of what it is spending in the arms race on its current military commitments.

**A**LREADY so tied are we Americans to an arms economy that our fantastic military expenditures are even now hailed as a bulwark against depression. A proclamation of universal peace would mean economic panic except as we might rapidly substitute planning for life instead of planning for death.

There is no easy answer to this problem of armament in Stalin's world. Our immediate hope lies in the fact that such is the nature of atomic war that it is to everybody's interest, indeed, it has become almost a condition of survival, that conflict between democracy and totalitarianism be transferred from the realm of atomic war and preparation for it. This cannot and will not be done except as we banish war.

And yet so afraid are we of dissent from habitual reliance upon arms and yet more arms, so unable are we to match our boldness in physics with boldness in politics, that neither our Government nor people seems willing even to try the effect upon Governments and masses of men of a well-thought-out appeal for the universal end of the armament race, under supervision of the United Nations, with international arrangements for security.

**T**HE best that Secretary Acheson could do, when addressing the U. N., was to promise that his Government would contribute to confidence, and with its attainment would "play its full role in the regulation and reduction under effective safeguards of armaments and armed forces." Here is no mighty and passionate dissent calculated to warn men's minds and hearts that they walk the path to destruction. Here is instead a continued failure to make that beginning in sounding out the trumpet call which may yet stir men to the only way of life and safety.

We live in a time when certain dissents against mass folly have become an essential condition of the progress if not the very life of mankind. The most necessary of these dissents concerns the method of war; if its articulation is successful, it must drive us to cooperative action for peace.

# CHURCHES COUNCIL SETS SOCIAL CODE

## Adopts Christian Precepts Opposing Collectivism and Backing Free Enterprise

### By GEORGE DUGAN

A declaration of Christian principles and their relation to social and economic life was adopted yesterday by the policy-making General Board of the National Council of Churches of Christ in the U. S. A.

The 4,000-word declaration included thirteen "norms for guidance" in applying these principles to daily life. It rejected the socialization of production and gravely warned against the dangers of "collectivism." At the same time, it approved the democratic way of life and praised a responsible free enterprise system.

The document, which had been debated and revised many times in the last two years, was approved by a vote of 77 to 4. It is the National Council's first major statement on social and economic issues since its formation in 1950.

The interchurch organization represents thirty Protestant and Eastern Orthodox communions with a total membership in excess of 35,000,000 persons. The board meeting was held at the Brick Presbyterian Church, Park Avenue and Ninety-first Street.

Opposition to the document was spearheaded by a laymen's group within the council that contended, in essence, that the church should hew closely to the spiritual goals of religion and refrain from speaking out on political, social and economic issues that might tend to divide churchgoers.

The pronouncement, in rejecting socialized production, declared that "in some situations Christians have had the misconception that the one sure road to economic justice is the socialization of all major means of production."

"During periods of exploitation of large classes of the population and also in times of depression and unemployment," it said, "it was understandable that some Christians and others concerned about the welfare of the victims of the situation should regard every move toward increasing social control as an advance.

"Today we have enough knowledge of what happens under a thoroughgoing collectivism to realize that uncritical recourse to the state to remedy every evil creates its own evils. It may easily become a threat to freedom as well as to efficiency.

"The union of political and economic power is a dangerous road, whether it leads toward complete state control of economic life or toward control of the state by private centers of economic power. A wide distribution of centers of power and decision is important to the preservation of democratic freedom."

The declaration warned, however, against "another misconception" held by some Christians "that a maximum of individual economic freedom will by itself create the economic conditions that contribute to a good society."

"On the contrary," it asserted, "the weight of evidence shows that some use of government in relation to economic activities is essential to provide the environment in which human freedom can flourish."

### Answer to Totalitarians

In discussing the role of the church in its relation to society, the document made it clear that "from the Christian standpoint free democratic institutions are clearly superior to any form of totalitarianism." It added:

"But our way of life has been challenged by totalitarian philosophies and practices, especially communism, which are competing with it for the loyalty of men around the world."

The document was presented to the Board by Charles P. Taft, Cincinnati lawyer and chairman of the 121-member General Committee of the Department of the Church and Economic Life of the National Council. Mr. Taft described it later as a guide for denominations and local councils of churches.

The general board also adopted a resolution urging its constituent members to heed the call of President Eisenhower to pray for peace on Sept. 22.

A statement on the use of the hydrogen bomb was referred back to a committee for further study.

The board will meet again on Nov. 22 in Boston on the eve of the four-day third general assembly of the National Council.

# One Vote for This Age of Anxiety

**Our anxieties, an anthropologist declares, have replaced the fear and hunger of simpler societies and are signs of hope for a better world.**

### By MARGARET MEAD

WHEN critics wish to repudiate the world in which we live today, one of their familiar ways of doing it is to castigate modern man because anxiety is his chief problem. This, they say, in W. H. Auden's phrase, is the age of anxiety. This is what we have arrived at with all our vaunted progress, our great technological advances, our great wealth—everyone goes about with a burden of anxiety so enormous that, in the end, our stomachs and our arteries and our skins express the tension under which we live. Americans who have lived in Europe come back to comment on our favorite farewell which, instead of the old goodbye (God be with you), is now "Take it easy," each American admonishing the other not to break down from the tension and strain of modern life.

Whenever an age is characterized by a phrase, it is presumably in contrast to other ages. If we are the age of anxiety, what were other ages? And here the critics and carpers do a very amusing thing. First, they give us lists of the opposites of anxiety: security, trust, self-confidence, self-direction. Then, without much further discussion, they let us assume that other ages, other periods of history, were somehow the ages of trust or confident direction.

The savage who, on his South Sea island, simply sat and let bread fruit fall into his lap, the simple peasant, at one with the fields he ploughed and the beasts he tended, the craftsman busy with his tools and lost in the fulfillment of the instinct of workmanship—these are the counter-images conjured up by descriptions of the strain under which men live today. But no one who lived in those days has returned to testify how paradisiacal they really were.

CERTAINLY if we observe and question the savages or simple peasants in the world today, we find something quite different. The untouched savage in the middle of New Guinea isn't anxious; he is seriously and continually *frightened*—of black magic, of enemies with spears who may kill him or his wives and children at any moment, while they stoop to drink from a spring, or climb a palm tree for a coconut. He goes warily, day and night, taut and fearful.

As for the peasant populations of a great part of the world, they aren't so much anxious as hungry. They aren't anxious about whether they will get a salary raise, or which of the three colleges of their choice they will be admitted to, or whether to buy a Ford or Cadillac, or whether the kind of TV set they want is too expensive. They are hungry, cold and, in many parts of the world, they dread that local warfare, bandits, political coups may endanger their homes, their meager livelihoods and their lives. But surely they are not anxious.

FOR anxiety, as we have come to use it to describe our characteristic state of mind, can be contrasted with the active fear of hunger, loss, violence and death. Anxiety is the appro-

MARGARET MEAD is associate curator of ethnology at the Museum of Natural History in New York City. Her most recent book, "New Lives for Old," has just been published.

Age of Terror...

priate emotion when the immediate personal terror—of a volcano, an arrow, the sorcerer's spell, a stab in the back and other calamities, all directed against one's self—disappears.

This is not to say that there isn't plenty to worry about in our world of today. The explosion of a bomb in the streets of a city whose name no one had ever heard before may set in motion forces which end up by ruining one's carefully planned education in law school, half a world away. But there is still not the personal, immediate, active sense of impending disaster that the savage knows. There is rather the vague anxiety, the sense that the future is unmanageable.

The kind of world that produces anxiety is actually a world of relative safety, a world in which no one feels that he himself is facing sudden death. Possibly sudden death may strike a certain number of unidentified other people—but not him. The anxiety exists as an uneasy state of mind, in which one has a feeling that something unspecified and undeterminable may go wrong. If the world seems to be going well, this produces anxiety—for good times may end. If the world is going badly—it may get worse. Anxiety tends to be without locus; the anxious person doesn't know

whether to blame himself or other people. He isn't sure whether it is 1956 or the Administration or a change in climate or the atom bomb that is to blame for this undefined sense of unease.

IT is clear that we have developed a society which depends on having the *right* amount of anxiety to make it work. Psychiatrists have been heard to say, "He didn't have enough anxiety to get well," indicating that, while we agree that too much anxiety is inimical to mental health, we have come to rely on anxiety to push and prod us into seeing a doctor about a symptom which may indicate cancer, into checking up on that old life insurance policy which may

have out-of-date clauses in it, into having a conference with Billy's teacher even though his report card looks all right.

People who are anxious enough keep their car insurance up, have the brakes checked, don't take a second drink when they have to drive, are careful where they go and with whom they drive on holidays. People who are too anxious either refuse to go into cars at all—and so complicate the ordinary course of life—or drive so tensely and overcautiously that they help cause accidents. People who aren't anxious enough take chance after chance, which increases the terrible death toll of the roads.

ON balance, our age of anxiety represents a large advance over savage and peasant cultures. Out of a productive system of technology drawing upon enormous resources, we have created a nation in which anxiety has replaced terror and despair, for all except the severely disturbed. The specter of hunger means something only to those Americans who can identify themselves with the millions of hungry people on other continents. The specter of terror may still be roused in some by a knock at the door in a few parts of the South, or in those who have just escaped from a totalitarian regime or who have kin still behind the Curtains.

But in this twilight world which is neither at peace nor at war, and where there is insurance against certain immediate, downright, personal disasters, for most Americans there remains only anxiety over what may happen, might happen, could happen.

THIS is the world out of which grows the hope, for the

... Age of Anxiety.

first time in history, of a society where there will be freedom from want and freedom from fear. Our very anxiety is born of our knowledge of what is now possible for each and for all. The number of people who consult psychiatrists today is not, as is sometimes felt, a symptom of increasing mental ill health, but rather the precursor of a world in which the hope of genuine mental health will be open to everyone, a world in which no individual feels that he need be hopelessly brokenhearted, a failure, a menace to others or a traitor to himself.

But if, then, our anxieties are actually signs of hope, why is there such a voice of discontent abroad in the land? I think this comes perhaps because our anxiety exists without an accompanying recognition of the tragedy which will always be inherent in human life, however well we build our world. We may banish hunger, and fear of sorcery, violence or secret police; we may bring up children who have learned to trust life and who have the spontaneity and curiosity necessary to devise ways of making trips to the moon; we cannot as we have tried to do banish death itself.

Americans who stem from generations which left their old people behind and never closed their parents' eyelids in death, and who have experienced the additional distance from death provided by two world wars fought far from our shores are today pushing away from them both a recognition of death and a recognition of the tremendous significance for the future of the way we live our lives. Acceptance of the inevitability of death, which, when faced, can give dignity to life, and acceptance of our inescapable role in the modern world, might transmute our anxiety about making the right choices, taking the right precautions, and the right risks into the sterner stuff of responsibility, which ennobles the whole face rather than furrowing the forehead with the little anxious wrinkles of worry.

WORRY in an empty context means that men die daily little deaths. But good anxiety —not about the things that were left undone long ago, that return to haunt and harry men's minds, but active, vivid anxiety about what must be done and that quickly binds men to life with an intense concern.

This is still a world in which too many of the wrong things happen somewhere. But this is a world in which we now have the means to make a great many more of the right things happen everywhere. For Americans, the generalization which a Swedish social scientist made about our attitudes on race relations is true in many other fields: anticipated change which we feel is right and necessary but

Woodcut by Clare Leighton

difficult makes us unduly anxious and apprehensive, but such change, once consummated, brings a glow of relief. We are still a people who in the literal sense believe in making good.

# As Billy Graham Sees His Role

**Bringing his crusade to New York, the controversial, crowd-drawing evangelist calls himself a 'proclaimer': 'My job is simply to proclaim the Gospel.'**

**By STANLEY ROWLAND Jr.**

ON May 15, Madison Square Garden will open its doors for an event that has been under quiet but elaborate preparation for more than a year, that is being prayed for in groups across the world, that will continue for at least six weeks and perhaps more than four months, making exactly the same appeal night after night, six or seven nights a week, attracting people from as far as Canada and the South, building ever-increasing crowds—if a dozen other cities around the world are any indication—and featuring one man with a Bible.

It will be the first full-scale New York crusade of the Rev. William Franklin Graham, a 38-year-old evangelist known as Billy Graham to millions of supporters and critics. Born of a Presbyterian farm family in Charlotte, N. C., and now a Baptist who makes his home in Montreat, N. C., the evangelist is interdenominational in his preachings. The local crusade was initiated by the Protestant Council of the City of New York and is backed by churches of many denominations. Its pattern of events will be typical of all his crusades.

In action on the speaker's platform Mr. Graham loosens his tie and speaks with a clear urgency. He is a tall, commanding figure (6 feet 2 inches), and conviction seems to vibrate through his tense body. In firm, sweeping gestures, his arm goes straight out with finger pointing, then up with the fist clenched, then down in a short arc to the Bible on the podium as he drives a point home with a Biblical quotation. Sweat begins to glisten on his face.

THE words come in a rush, Bible verses and colorful descriptions of Eve, Joe Doaks and the shenanigans of Satan tumble headlong over one another, converging on one central point: repent, believe in the Lord Jesus Christ, and be saved. Again the big arm springs out, cupped hand seeming to take in the crowd as he describes through taut lips how Christ confronts the man in the street. Then, a little abruptly, his urgent words cease. In quiet tones he invites people to come forward and "receive Christ." They come. Subsequently, local volunteers, guided by the Graham staff, route them to churches of their choice.

Why do they step forward? Some observers write it off entirely to emotion. There are cases where this is probably important. However, Mr. Graham is not extraordinarily emo-

Evangelist in action—Billy Graham reads from the Bible in London's Trafalgar Square. "Conviction seems to vibrate through his tense body and sweeping gestures."

tional as evangelists go, at least some of his conversions do last, and a number of those who "decide for Christ" do so only after having returned thoughtfully for several nights.

Another explanation is supplied by reason and observation. Put a handsome, forceful speaker of obvious conviction before a crowd of 15,000 people, and it would be surprising if at least a few did not respond. Add the fact that a number go to a crusade meeting because they feel a lack in their lives, and the chances of response are increased. Then add the fact that Mr. Graham tells his hearers that they are not impersonal cogs in a machine but individuals with immortal souls cherished by God, and the chances of response are augmented once more in this "age of anxiety" or "conformity."

Mr. Graham insists that the reasons for lasting conversion are primarily religious. He says that the Holy Spirit rides with his words out to the audience. Some disagree. Others, who do agree, say that the Gospel carries within itself the power of conversion when proclaimed with real conviction, though the proclaiming may be done from various viewpoints by a priest, a theologian, or a Billy Graham.

Converts themselves usually explain in simple, personal terms of religious experience. During the London crusade, a doctor who went with binoculars to "see the circus" returned for five nights, then made his decision. "I gave my life to the Lord," was his blunt, simple explanation. A newspaper man went to "the show." After his conversion, he walked home five miles through the rain "trying to figure out what had happened to me." He and the doctor go on to tell of lives of new dedication and meaning.

Actually, Mr. Graham is simply doing with large-scale, thorough organization what other evangelists are doing with much less money and preparation. When he hits a city it is with guaranteed backing and extensive spadework beforehand. Then he digs in for a goodly stay. Big crowds make news, the publicity keeps hammering away, and gradually the crusade begins to permeate the city. In the midst of it all stands Billy Graham. Although clergymen and laymen have called him everything from a profiteering phony to a Christian knight in the shining armor of the Holy Spirit, the simplest description of him is also probably the most accurate: he is a proclaimer.

"The meaning of the word 'evangelist' is 'proclaimer,' a proclaimer of good news," Mr. Graham explained at the start of a recent interview. "My job is not to defend the Gospel; my job is simply to proclaim the Gospel, and to let the Spirit of God apply in the individual hearts."

HE returned again and again to this definition of his task in the course of a two-hour talk in his suite atop a lofty local hotel. The evangelist punctuated his remarks with brief, wholesome laughs and gestured occasionally, but rarely raised his voice. He spoke in the strongest terms of the Bible (he takes it on faith and quotes it whenever pressed) and publicity (his feelings are mixed).

His richly textured, medium dark gray suit with its narrow lapels hung with impeccable exactness; cuffs broke on shoe tops so precisely that one felt he feared lest he smack of the small town. Yet he needed a haircut; his almost blond hair was a little shaggy where it couldn't be seen in the mirror. And his formal black shoes badly needed a shine.

Glancing over the sunny rooftops, Mr. Graham explained why he considers this city the great challenge.

"It's the very complexity of New York City, with all its cultural and linguistic backgrounds," he said. "Actually the whole world looks to New York as the world capital. * * * To touch a city spiritually of an area of 12,000,000 people is a tremendous thing, especially where you have 58 per cent of the people that attend no church.

"I HAVE found a sense of discouragement and I think frustration on the part of many ministers here that I have not felt in other parts of the United States. I have come to have a great burden and I believe a sense of compassion for this city." As for the prospects at Madison Square Garden, he admitted: "Our type of crusade may not make a dent in New York. I think the greatest thing that will be accomplished is that possibly the entire city for a brief period will become God-conscious."

Then, likening himself to the sower in the Biblical parable of the seed that fell on fruitful and unfruitful ground, he waxed earnestly hopeful. "There are people in this city that I believe that God the Holy Spirit has been preparing for this crusade. When they hear the word of God, when they hear the Gospel preached, there is going to be an automatic response." But others, he said with a philosophical shrug, will "be over it next morning. We know that happens—Christ said it would happen."

HE leaned back in a low armchair and launched into a dissertation on financing.

"We have never sold anything but song books," he said, "and that is for the people right there, and we get nothing from that. The money goes to the local crusade. You see, they need $900,000 here for this crusade, and that money is handled entirely by the executive committee." He named several business men who have been signed up by local Protestant leaders and are under the chairmanship of George Champion, the president of the Chase Manhattan Bank. "They handle the money and I never see it, I don't get any of it, none of our team will receive any honorariums while here. They're entirely on salary from Minneapolis, Minn. [home of the Billy Graham Evangelistic Association, a non-profit corporation, supported by contributions, of which Mr. Graham is president]. I receive $15,000 a year as my salary." One-tenth goes as his tithe to the Baptist Church.

Hunching forward with elbows on knees, he hammered away on the subject of financial purity. He said that the "Billy Graham" buttons and whatnot that were hawked at the London crusade in 1954—and will probably appear here —were products of private firms trying to turn a fast buck. "We didn't sell them, we never had anything to do with it, in fact we never have anything to do with 90 per cent of what's made to go on," he insisted. This attitude contrasts with his approach in Los Angeles in 1949, when he first won national attention by converting a famous athlete and an infamous gambler, both of whom remain stanch Christians, and where he advertised himself as "America's Sensational Young Evangelist" in "Mammoth Tent Crusade" with "Dazzling Array of Gospel Talent."

REMINDED of this past, Mr. Graham looked a little pained. "That was in the early days before we had very many people coming to our meetings. And all the publicity is handled by local committees. There will be a tremendous amount of advertising here in the City of New York, for example, for this crusade, both by television and so forth, but there won't be any adjectives describing me." Then he leaned forward and blurted:

"My wife and I have lost our privacy, and I don't think anyone who has lost their privacy ever doesn't long to have it back. You don't realize what a priceless possession it is to be a private individual. To be looked at, to be stared at everywhere one goes, never to go to a restaurant without being looked at." He unfolded from the chair and took a restless turn around the room.

"THAT is one of the reasons that I left England, not to go back, at least in the last two years, because I felt there was too much of Billy Graham. I wanted the discussion to be around Christ." On his last night in London he packed Wembley Stadium with 120,-000 persons. In 1955 he spoke in various cities in Great Britain and on the Continent. His wife, Ruth, whom he met while they were undergraduates at Wheaton College, in Illinois, stays home in Montreat with their four children when Billy is off crusading. Last year he toured India.

The evangelist folded back into his armchair and explained how he had changed from a blunt critic of that country's policies to something of an apologist for Prime Minister Nehru. "I was critical of India because I didn't understand India, I didn't understand why Mr. Nehru takes some of the stands he takes until I went to India and saw for myself the terrible economic and social problems he must wrestle with, and that actually Mr. Nehru represents the Indian people in his pacifism and his neutrality. That gave me an understanding."

**T**HEN, almost in the tone of a young man who wants to share a discovery, he told what traveling had taught him about the racial issue. "I don't think it's a sectional problem at all, I don't even think it's an American problem. I think it's a world problem." He cited the caste system in India and diagnosed the Arab-Israel conflict as racial, then jumped back to his insistence upon racial integration at his meetings. Leaning forward, he warmed to the subject:

"I don't think it can be done altogether by preachments, though I shall certainly do my share of it. But it's going to have to be done by setting an example of love, as I think Martin Luther King [the leader of t. Montgomery bus boycott] has done in setting an example of Christian love. * * * Paul said there is neither Jew nor Greek, nor Scythian nor barbarian in Christ."

His role, he reiterated, is to face people with Christ—an exhausting business. "I try to be in bed nine hours every night. Billy Sunday used to stay in his pajamas all the time and I used to wonder why—that he stayed in bed so much—until I understood how

exhausting a thing it is to address a crowd of 15,000 or 20,000 people and try to get them to receive Christ." He continues, not because he fancies himself a preacher—

"I am not a great preacher, and people will be disappointed in my preaching"—but because "God has given me a gift, a gift of evangelism, and I couldn't deny that gift. Paul told Timothy, 'Stir up the gift that is within thee.'"

**M**R. GRAHAM plunged into his favorite topic: the Bible. He disowned the statement, quoted even by admirers, that at one time he was willing to give the exact dimensions of heaven, and readily admitted to passing through a period of Biblical skepticism some time ago. He declined to be classified as either fundamentalist or as anything approaching liberal, though he has sporadically been accused of both from opposite directions. At one

point he declared that the Bible is the inspired word of God, but not dictated by Him; at another point he asserted that Christ was God incarnate, and at still another he asserted that if Christ should appear today He would go on television because "the Bible says that when He comes back every eye shall see Him." Then, using the method of graphic analogy that runs through his sermons, he erected a defense for his variety of Biblicism.

"Suppose I take this Bible and say there're parts of it—let's suppose this—that are not inspired of God, that are not authoritative. All right, then I become the judge. And I sit up and I say, 'Well, this page is no good, I'll rip that one out.' He tore one hand through the air above his open Bible. "'I can't accept that.' Then I turn over here and I rip another one out. * * * And after a while I have about ten million different kinds of Bibles because one scholar says this and one scholar says that and one scholar says another, until after a while I have no authority.

"And I've talked to scores of ministers at this very point who have lost the authority in their message and their whole ministry has gone out the window because they're not sure what they can believe any longer. Well, to me, I would far rather settle it and say, 'By faith I accept it as God's inspired word.'" Scientific theories about the origin of the universe take as much, or more, faith to believe, he argued—"I mean, it's faith either way."

**T**O Mr. Graham this means an act of belief, not a pat

formula. "The Bible depicts the Christian life as a conflict and a battle and a warfare. I believe that when a person receives Christ and tries to live the Christian life that he immediately comes in conflict with various areas of his society and the people around about him because he is going against the current stream."

He pushed a palm through the air and forced his fist against it. "I mean, here's the stream coming this way and a true Christian is going this way. Well, immediately there's a conflict in every area"—fairly severe, it seemed from his gestures—"but Christ in the heart gives peace, and a great resource of power in the midst of these battles."

**T**HIS is the crux of Mr. Graham's beliefs: the battle against sin and the power of Christ. His easy, analogical reasoning, full of references to "ten million" of this and "scores" of that, has drawn the charge of superficiality from Christian thinkers. In his defense, it must be pointed out that he promises no cures or worldly success. He preaches an elementary, "hard" Gospel of sin and salvation.

"There will be no emotional outbursts" at Madison Square Garden, he promised. "When I give the invitation for people to receive Christ it will be so quiet you can hear a pin drop. It will be as holy and reverent a moment as you would have in any church in the worship service. And you will see people coming forward deliberately, quietly, reverently, thoughtfully, and many of their lives—the evidence will pile up for years to come—will have been transformed and changed in that moment."

# Text of Eisenhower's Farewell Address

*Following is the text of President Eisenhower's farewell address to the nation last night from Washington as recorded by The New York Times:*

Good evening, my fellow Americans:

First, I should like to express my gratitude to the radio and television networks for the opportunities they have given me over the years to bring reports and messages to our nation. My special thanks go to them for the opportunity of addressing you this evening.

Three days from now, after half a century in the service of our country, I shall lay down the responsibilities of office as, in traditional and solemn ceremony, the authority of the Presidency is vested in my successor.

This evening I come to you with a message of leave-taking and farewell, and to share a few final thoughts with you, my countrymen.

Like every other citizen, I wish the new President, and all who will labor with him, Godspeed. I pray that the coming years will be blessed with peace and prosperity for all.

Our people expect their President and the Congress to find essential agreement on issues of great moment, the wise resolution of which will better shape the future of the nation.

My own relations with the Congress, which began on a remote and tenuous basis when, long ago, a member of the Senate appointed me to West Point, have since ranged to the intimate during the war and immediate post-war period, and finally to the mutually interdependent during these past eight years.

### His Relations Good

In this final relationship, the Congress and the Administration have, on most vital issues, cooperated well, to serve the nation good rather than mere partisanship, and so have assured that the business of the nation should go forward. So my official relationship with the Congress ends in a feeling, on my part, of gratitude that we have been able to do so much together.

We now stand ten years past the midpoint of a century that has witnessed four major wars among great nations—three of these involved our own country.

Despite these holocausts America is today the strongest, the most influential and most productive nation in the world. Understandably proud of this pre-eminence, we yet realize that America's leadership and prestige depend, not merely upon our unmatched material progress, riches and military strength, but on how we use our power in the interests of world peace and human betterment.

Throughout America's adventure in free government, our basic purposes have been to keep the peace; to foster progress in human achievement, and to enhance liberty, dignity and integrity among peoples and among nations.

To strive for less would be unworthy of a free and religious people.

Any failure traceable to arrogance or our lack of comprehension or readiness to sacrifice would inflict upon us grievous hurt, both at home and abroad.

Progress toward these noble goals is persistently threatened by the conflict now engulfing the world. It commands our whole attention, absorbs our very beings.

We face a hostile ideology-global in scope, atheistic in character, ruthless in purpose and insidious in method. Unhappily the danger it poses promises to be of indefinite duration. To meet it successfully there is called for, not so much the emotional and transitory sacrifices of crisis, but rather those which enable us to carry forward steadily, surely and without complaint the burdens of a prolonged and complex struggle—with liberty the stake.

Only thus shall we remain, despite every provocation, on our charted course toward permanent peace and human betterment.

### Says Crises Will Continue

Crises there will continue to be. In meeting them, whether foreign or domestic, great or small, there is a recurring temptation to feel that some spectacular and costly action could become the miraculous solution to all current difficulties. A huge increase in newer elements of our defenses; development of unrealistic programs to cure every ill in agriculture; a dramatic expansion in basic and applied research—these and many other possibilities, each possibly promising in itself, may be suggested as the only way to the road we wish to travel.

But each proposal must be weighed in the light of a broader consideration; the need to maintain balance in and among national programs —balance between the private and the public economy, balance between the cost and hoped for advantages—balance between the clearly necessary and the comfortably desirable; balance between our essential requirements as a nation and the duties imposed by the nation upon the individual; balance between actions of the moment and the national welfare of the future. Good judgment seeks balance and progress; lack of it eventually finds imbalance and frustration.

The record of many decades stands as proof that our people and their Government have, in the main, understood these truths and have responded to them well in the face of threat and stress.

### New Threats Cited

But threats, new in kind or degree, constantly arise. Of these, I mention two only.

A vital element in keeping the peace is our military establishment. Our arms must be mighty, ready for instant action, so that no potential aggressor may be tempted to risk his own destruction.

Our military organization today bears little relation to that known of any of my predecessors in peacetime— or, indeed, by the fighting men of World War II or Korea.

Until the latest of our world conflicts, the United States had no armaments industry. American makers of plowshares could, with time and as required, make swords as well.

But we can no longer risk emergency improvisation of national defense. We have been compelled to create a permanent armaments industry of vast proportions. Added to this, three and a half million men and women are directly engaged in the defense establishment. We annually spend on military security alone more than the net income of all United States corporations.

Now this conjunction of an immense military establishment and a large arms industry is new in the American experience. The total influence—economic, political, even spiritual—is felt in every city, every state house, every office of the Federal Government. We recognize the imperative need for this development. Yet we must not fail to comprehend its grave implications. Our toil, resources and livelihood are all involved; so is the very structure of our society.

### Warning on Influence

In the councils of Government, we must guard against the acquisition of unwarranted influence, whether sought or unsought, by the military-industrial complex. The potential for the disastrous rise of misplaced power exists and will persist.

We must never let the weight of this combination endanger our liberties or democratic processes. We should take nothing for granted. Only an alert and knowledgeable citizenry can compel the proper meshing of the huge industrial and military machinery of defense with our peaceful methods and goals, so that security and liberty may prosper together.

Akin to, and largely responsible for the sweeping changes in our industrial-military posture has been the technological revolution during recent decades.

In this revolution research has become central. It also becomes more formalized, complex and costly. A steadily increasing share is conducted for, by, or at the direction of the Federal Government.

Today the solitary inventor, tinkering in his shop, has been overshadowed by task forces of scientists, in laboratories and testing fields. In the same fashion, the free university, historically the fountainhead of free ideas and scientific discovery, has experienced a revolution in the conduct of research. Partly because of the huge costs involved, a Government contract becomes virtually a substitute for intellectual curiosity.

For every old blackboard there are now hundreds of new electronic computers.

### Prospect of Domination

The prospect of domination of the nation's scholars by Federal employment, project allocations and the power of money is ever present, and is gravely to be regarded.

Yet, in holding scientific research and discovery in respect, as we should, we must also be alert to the equal and opposite danger that public policy could itself become the captive of a scientific-technological elite.

It is the task of statesmanship to mold, to balance, and to integrate these and other forces, new and old, within the principles of our democratic system—ever aiming toward the supreme goals of our free society.

### Time Element Involved

Another factor in maintaining balance involves the element of time. As we peer into society's future, we—you and I, and our Government— must avoid the impulse to live only for today, plundering, for our own ease and convenience, the precious resources of tomorrow.

We cannot mortgage the material assets of our grandchildren without risking the loss also of their political and spiritual heritage. We want democracy to survive for all generations to come, not to become the insolvent phantom of tomorrow.

During the long lane of the history yet to be written America knows that this world of ours, ever growing smaller, must avoid becoming a community of dreadful fear and hate, and be, instead, a proud confederation of mutual trust and respect.

Such a confederation must be one of equals. The weakest must come to the conference table with the same confidence as do we, protected as we are by our moral, economic and military strength. That table, though scarred by many past frustrations, cannot be abandoned for the certain agony of the battlefield.

Disarmament, with mutual honor and confidence, is a continuing imperative. Together we must learn how to compose differences—not with arms, but with intellect and decent purpose. Because this need is so sharp and apparent, I confess that I lay down my official responsibilities in this field with a definite sense of disappointment. As one who has witnessed the horror and the lingering sadness of war, as one who knows that another war could utterly destroy this civilization which has been so slowly and painfully built over thousands of years, I wish I could say tonight that a lasting peace is in sight.

Happily, I can say that war has been avoided. Steady progress toward our ultimate goal has been made. But so much remains to be done. As a private citizen, I shall never cease to do what little I can to help the world advance along that road.

### 'My Last Good Night'

So, in this, my last good night to you as your President, I thank you for the many opportunities you have given me for public service in war and in peace.

I trust in that you — that, in that service, you find some things worthy. As for the rest of it, I know you will find ways to improve performance in the future.

You and I — my fellow citizens — need to be strong in our faith that all nations, under God, will reach the goal of peace with justice. May we be ever unswerving in devotion to principle, confident but humble with power, diligent in pursuit of the nation's great goals.

To all the peoples of the world, I once more give expression to America's prayerful and continuing aspiration:

We pray that peoples of all faiths, all races, all nations, may have their great human needs satisfied; that those now denied opportunity shall come to enjoy it to the full; that all who yearn for freedom may experience its spiritual blessings, those who have freedom will understand, also, its heavy responsibility; that all who are insensitive to the needs of others, will learn charity, and that the sources—scourges of poverty, disease and ignorance will be made to disappear from the earth; and that in the goodness of time, all peoples will come to live together in a peace guaranteed by the binding force of mutual respect and love.

Now, on Friday noon, I am to become a private citizen. I am proud to do so. I look forward to it.

Thank you, and, good night.

## Topics of The Times

**Science and Its Duty to Man** It is a rather large order that the scientists have on their books after being lectured a bit the other night at St. Louis by the Columbia philosopher, Irwin Edman. Having just completed the agent of man's destruction, the atomic bomb, they must now turn to and manufacture some human happiness. It is an assignment we can all watch with interest.

Professor Edman is "frightened," and he suspects that the scientists are themselves, by the deadly accomplishments of science in the last five years. The use of science is a moral question, he told the Association for the Advancement of Science in a speech which, because of the pressure of unphilosophical news, largely escaped the attention of the New York press. He pointed out that despite all its contributions through the years, science had not always promoted man's "serenity and his joy."

**Finding Out the Facts** Dr. Edman would apply the habit of scientific approach to understanding of the world in which we live, and of ourselves, to discover what happiness consists of. He would thus hope to eliminate the sorrows that arise from a misunderstanding of where felicity lies. The scientific point of view would define the "scope and orbit of our possible good," and when candor and objectivity associated with the laboratory spirit became habitual with people when viewing their personal affairs and the affairs of society, illusory goods would no longer be sought after.

This is, then, a job of fact-finding, which is so popular in many realms today. It is a technique that stirs the imagination.

**How It Works at Home** For every man to apply the scientific method to a microscopic examination of his own condition and aspirations would, perhaps, call for a larger element of detachment than he could expect to develop in a short time. But he could, without too much straining, successfully apply it to his near-by kin.

Would the members of his family, for instance, be made happier if he as their head put his nose closer to the grindstone and brought home a larger pay check? Professor Edman will surely not object if we apply the scientific method to this mundane but universal problem. The answer, briefly, is no, as we shall show at once by a rapid review of the facts.

**Fiscal Things First** Take the wife first. She would, with more money in the weekly budget, want a larger home. But would this contribute to her happiness? No, it would add to her responsibilities, lengthen her working day, take her more frequently into crowded stores to shop for furnishings, tempt her to invite more week-end guests and inspire envy in the hearts of neighbors, all of which would react unfavorably on her peace of mind.

And now how about the little ones? More money would mean for Osbert, perhaps, private school and a regrettable deterioration in his presently overdeveloped sense of democracy, closer application to study, a loss of dear old friends in the public school, the wearing of a jacket, better attention to hair-combing and many other changes leading to his uneasiness and irritation. For little Gertrude the future would be fraught with equal danger. Dancing school, greater preoccupation with clothes, a hastening of precocity, premature dates with boys—that way, as everyone knows, lies trouble.

**But to the Grave** How easy this fact-finding is when you really get down to it, and how satisfying the results! It is obvious that a little practice produces the objectivity needed for self-examination, after all.

For the head of the house a larger pay check would start in motion a train of events and impulses leading only to sorrow for himself and those who cherish him. The greater pay must be earned by greater production, an economic axiom. Responsibilities would rain down from the boss in a never-ending deluge of anxieties. The nerves begin to strain. One pay rise leads to the yearning for another. The pace grows quicker. An earlier train is taken in the morning, a later at night. Lunch is brought in to eat at the desk. A dictating machine supplants the quiet pleasures of stenography. A little beauty vanishes from life. Soon madness, and the home is broken.

**Some Deeper Meanings** We are not at all sure that this is what Dr. Edman meant by applying the scientific method in the search for happiness. But we would serve badly his serious purpose and ours if we failed to express the hope, in all sobriety, that science will, in these fateful coming years, produce a happier world. There is little doubt that the scientist, in making the atomic bomb, awakened in himself a new, alarmed awareness that the laboratory is, whether he likes the idea or not, a moral force. He takes his place now beside the philosopher, the artist, the teacher, the man of God.

April 1, 194

# ATOM BOMB 'FEARS' HELD POLICY ISSUE

## Psychologists Assert America Has Alternatives of Isolation or Seeking Ban on War

### MILITARY SECRECY DECRIED

**By JOHN H. CRIDER**
Special to THE NEW YORK TIMES.

WASHINGTON, May 25 — A committee of prominent psychologists reported today that the greatest danger from the public fears engendered by the development of the atomic bomb was that they might lead Americans either to "escapist thinking," which would cause the people to minimize the dangers of the situation, or to desperation, causing them to take steps that could only result in war.

Constructively, the national and international fears stemming from the development of atomic energy are "not necessarily bad," the psychologists said, "for human fear releases great psychological energies."

From this aspect, the committee declared, "our first objective must be to mobilize a healthy, action-goading fear for effective measures against the real danger—war."

The report was prepared by the Committee on International Peace of the Society for the Psychological Study of Social Issues, a division of the American Psychological Association. Dr. David Krech of Swarthmore College is chairman of the committee.

### Study Asked by Atomic Scientists

The psychologists' study and report were requested by the Federation of American Scientists, comprising many of the scientists who worked on the production of the atomic bomb. The undertaking was described as unique as representing the first time that social scientists have been asked to collaborate with physical scientists on a major public problem, thus marking "a new departure in scientific cooperation."

"Public fear of the atomic bomb does stem from a real and frightful danger," the psychologists affirmed, adding: "This danger comes from the fact that there is no military defense against the atomic bomb."

Then they emphasized at once, their great hope, namely, that people's fear of the bomb would motivate the world to constructive measures to avert war.

But the "other kind of fear"—"the intangible, unhealthy fear"—they held to be a real threat to such constructive action. This kind of fear, they said, grows from the policy of secrecy, from military control of atomic energy, which identified it with war, and from "the intense rivalry among the nations for access to atomic power."

This kind of fear produces "a crippling feeling of ignorance, impotence and general insecurity," which leads people to act in an immature or helpless manner, or to become panicky and destructive, psychologists said.

The danger for us as a nation, their report went on, was that we will react in the same way as a mentally sick individual under similar fear motivation, either indulging in "escapist thinking," which would cause us to underestimate the dangers and take com-

146

fort in false hopes of "some defense against the bomb ... despite what the scientists say."

Or we may go in the other direction of militarism and isolationism, following a pattern that the psychologists called "the mental preparation which sets the stage for international conflict and violence."

This could only cause other nations also to be "ridden by fear and confusion," they said. Other peoples "can have little confidence in our intentions," they added, "when we continue to manufacture and stockpile bombs against vague future contingencies."

### Recommendations for America

Declaring that America has a "tremendous opportunity" because of its means of becoming "a unique influence," the psychologists recommended a six-point program for this nation, as follows:

"(1) The real danger of the atomic bomb —the possibility of another war—must be made clear to all of our people." Therefore, prevention of war must be "the goal of all our actions."

"(2) Serious and intelligent action must be taken to advance international friendship."

"(3) International control of atomic energy," as proposed by the State Department's "Lilienthal-Acheson report," must be undertaken as soon as possible.

"(4) We must stop making atomic bombs immediately" to remove suspicion of us abroad and a false sense of security at home.

"(5) An effective civilian control of atomic energy must be instituted by our country at once." The committee said military use of atomic energy increased both public ignorance and fears. It urged "a policy of maximum public candor rather than maximum secrecy."

"(6) "The possible benefits of atomic energy must be emphasized and developed." There should be, the committee said, "a free and vigorous program of research and engineering to turn this energy to the service of human welfare."

Serving with Dr. Krech on the committee were Dr. Richard Crutchfield of Swarthmore, Drs. Eugene Hartley and Gardner Murphy of the College of the City of New York, Dr. Theodore Newcomb of the University of Michigan, Dr. Ruth Tolman of Pasadena, Calif.; Dr. Godwin Watson of Columbia University, and Dr. Ralph White of Stanford University.

The Federation of American Scientists issued a statement on the forthcoming Navy-Army atomic bomb tests on the Bikini Atoll.

"The tests are purely military, not scientific," the Federation's statement said. "Scientists expect nothing of scientific value, and little of technical value to peace time uses of atomic energy, as a result of these tests."

"Scientists are cooperating in these tests at the request of their country's armed forces, although they do so with heavy hearts, and without enthusiasm," it went on.

"Scientists seek by education to teach men that they must abandon atomic weapons to preserve civilization, but we must recognize that it may take an atomic war to teach them a lesson."

The statement added that the number of ships destroyed would not be the best standard for judging the effect of the bomb. They urged that the actual atomic strength of the Bikini blast be announced, and stated that "the deep under-water tests of next year will be far more important than the tests planned this spring."

May 26, 1946

# 'The Real Problem Is in the Hearts of Men'

### Professor Einstein says a new type of thinking is needed to meet the challenge of the atomic bomb.

#### By ALBERT EINSTEIN
*In an Interview With Michael Amrine*

*As Chairman of the Emergency Committee of Atomic Scientists, with headquarters at Princeton, N. J., Professor Einstein recently invited public support for "a nation-wide campaign to let the people know that a new type of thinking is essential if mankind is to survive and move to higher levels." Here Professor Einstein gives his ideas on how to meet the threat of the atom bomb.*

MANY persons have inquired concerning a recent message of mine that "a new type of thinking is essential if mankind is to survive and move to higher levels."

Often in evolutionary processes a species must adapt to new conditions in order to survive. Today the atomic bomb has altered profoundly the nature of the world as we knew it, and the human race consequently finds itself in a new habitat to which it must adapt its thinking.

In the light of new knowledge, a world authority and an eventual world state are not just *desirable* in the name of brotherhood, they are *necessary* for survival. In previous ages a nation's life and culture could be protected to some extent by the growth of armies in national competition. Today we must abandon competition and secure cooperation. This must be the central fact in all our considerations of international affairs; otherwise we face certain disaster. Past thinking and methods did not prevent world wars. Future thinking *must* prevent wars.

MODERN war, the bomb, and other discoveries or inventions, present us with revolutionary circumstances. Never before was it possible for one nation to make war on another without sending armies across borders. Now with rockets and atomic bombs no center of population on the earth's surface is secure from surprise destruction in a single attack.

America has a temporary superiority in armament, but it is certain that we have no lasting secret. What nature tells one group of men, she will tell in time to any other group interested and patient enough in asking the questions. But our temporary superiority gives this nation the tremendous responsibility of leading mankind's effort to surmount the crisis.

Being an ingenious people, Americans find it hard to believe there is no foreseeable defense against atomic bombs. But this is a basic fact. Scientists do not even know of any field which promises us any hope of adequate defense. The military-minded cling to old methods of thinking and one Army department has been surveying possibilities of going underground, and in wartime placing factories in places like Mammoth Cave. Others speak of dispersing our population centers into "linear" or "ribbon" cities.

Reasonable men with these new facts to consider refuse to contemplate a future in which our culture would attempt to survive in ribbons or in underground tombs. Neither is there reassurance in proposals to keep a hundred thousand men alert along the coasts scanning the sky with radar. There is no radar defense against the V-2, and should a "defense" be developed after years of research, it is not humanly possible for any defense to be perfect. Should one rocket with atomic warhead strike Minneapolis, that city would look almost exactly like Nagasaki. Rifle bullets kill men, but atomic bombs kill cities. A tank is a defense against a bullet but there is no defense in science against the weapon which can destroy civilization.

OUR defense is not in armaments, nor in science, nor in going underground. Our defense is in law and order.

Henceforth, every nation's foreign policy must be judged at every point by one consideration: does it lead us to a world of law and order or does it lead us back toward anarchy and death? I do not believe that we can prepare for war and at the same time prepare for a world community. When humanity holds in its hand the weapon with which it can commit suicide, I believe that to put more power into the gun is to increase the probability of disaster.

REMEMBERING that our main consideration is to avoid this disaster, let us briefly consider international relations in the world today, and start with America. The war which began with Germany using weapons of unprecedented frightfulness against women and children ended with the United States using a supreme weapon killing thousands at one blow.

Many persons in other countries now look on America with great suspicion, not only for the bomb but because they fear she will become imperialistic. Before the recent turn in our policy I was sometimes not quite free from such fears myself.

Others might not fear Americans if they knew us as we know one another, honest and sober and neighbors. But in other countries they know that a sober nation can become drunk with victory. If Germany had not won a victory in 1870, what tragedy for the human race might have been averted!

We are still making bombs and the bombs are making hate and suspicion. We are keeping secrets and secrets breed distrust. I do not say we should now turn the secret of the bomb loose in the world, but are we ardently seeking a world in which there will be no need for bombs or secrets, a world in which science and men will be free?

While we distrust Russia's secrecy and she distrusts ours we walk together to certain doom.

THE basic principles of the Acheson-Lilienthal Report are scientifically sound and technically ingenious, but as Mr. Baruch wisely said, it is a problem not of physics but of ethics. There has been too much emphasis on legalisms and procedure; it is easier to denature plutonium than it is to denature the evil spirit of man.

The United Nations is the only instrument we have to work with in our struggle to achieve something better. But we have used U. N. and U. N. form and procedure to outvote the Russians on some occasions when the Russians were right. Yes, I do not think it is possible for any nation to be right all the time or wrong all

the time. In all negotiations, whether over Spain, Argentina, Palestine, food or atomic energy, so long as we rely on procedure and keep the threat of military power, we are attempting to use old methods in a world which is changed forever.

No one gainsays that the United Nations Organization at times gives great evidence of eventually justifying the desperate hope that millions have in it. But time is not given to us in solving the problems science and war have brought. Powerful forces in the political world are moving swiftly toward crisis. When we look back to the end of the war it does not seem ten months—it seems ten years ago! Many leaders express well the need for world authority and an eventual world government, but actual planning and action to this end have been appallingly slow.

PRIVATE organizations anticipate the future, but government agencies seem to live in the past. In working away from nationalism toward a supra-nationalism, for example, it is obvious that the national spirit will survive longer in armies than anywhere else. This might be tempered in the United Nations military forces by mixing the various units together, but certainly not by keeping a Russian unit intact side by side with an intact American unit, with the usual inter-unit competition added to the national spirit of the soldiers in this world enforcement army. But if the military staffs of the U. N. are working out concrete proposals along these lines, for a true internationally minded force, I have yet to read of it.

Similarly, we are plagued in the present world councils over the question of representation. It does not seem fair to some, for example, that each small Latin-American nation should have a vote while much larger nations are also limited to one vote. On the other hand, representation on a population basis may seem unfair to the highly developed states, because surely great masses of ignorant, backward peoples should not carry as much voice in the complicated technology of our world as those with greater experience.

Fremont Rider in an excellent book, "The Great Dilemma of World Organization," discusses the idea of representation on the basis of education and literacy—number of teachers, physicians,

and so on. Backward nations looking forward to greater power in the councils of men would be told, "To get more votes you must earn them."

THESE and a hundred other questions concerning the desirable evolution of the world seem to be getting very little attention. Meanwhile, men high in government propose defense or war measures which would not only compel us to live in a universal atmosphere of fear but would cost untold billions of dollars and ultimately destroy our American free way of life— even before a war.

To retain even a temporary total security in an age of total war, government will have to secure total control. Restrictive measures will be required by the necessities of the situation, not through the conspiracy of wilful men. Starting with the fantastic guardianship now imposed on innocent physics professors, outmoded thinkers will insidiously change men's lives more completely than did Hitler, for the forces behind them will be more compelling.

BEFORE the raid on Hiroshima, leading physicists urged the War Department not to use the bomb against defenseless women and children. The war could have been won without it. The decision was made in consideration of possible future loss of American lives—and now we have to consider possible loss in future atomic bombings of *millions of lives*. The American decision may have been a fatal error, for men accustom themselves to thinking a weapon which was used once can be used again.

Had we shown other nations the test explosion at Alamogordo, New Mexico, we could have used it as an education for new ideas. It would have been an impressive and favorable moment to make considered proposals for world order to end war. Our renunciation of this weapon as too terrible to use would have carried great weight in negotiations and made convincing our sincerity in asking other nations for a binding partnership to develop these newly unleashed powers for good.

THE old type of thinking can raise a thousand objections of "realism" against this simplicity. But such thought ignores the *psychological realities*. All men fear atomic war. All men hope for benefits from these new powers. Between the realities of man's

true desires and the realities of man's danger, what are the obsolete "realities" of protocol and military protection?

During the war many persons fell out of the habit of doing their own thinking, for many had to do simply what they were told to do. Today lack of interest would be a great error, for there is much the average man can do about this danger.

This nation held a great debate concerning the menace of the Axis, and again today we need a great chain reaction of awareness and communication. Current proposals should be discussed in the light of the basic facts, in every newspaper, in schools, churches, in town meetings, in private conversations, and neighbor to neighbor. Merely reading about the bomb promotes knowledge in the mind, but only talk between men promotes feeling in the heart.

Not even scientists completely understand atomic energy, for each man's knowledge is incomplete. Few men have ever seen the bomb. But all men if told a few facts can understand that this bomb and the danger of war is a very real thing, and not something far away. It directly concerns every person in the civilized world. We cannot leave it to generals, Senators, and diplomats to work out a solution over a period of generations. Perhaps five years from now several nations will have made bombs and it will be too late to avoid disaster.

IGNORING the realities of faith, good-will and honesty in seeking a solution, we place too much faith in legalisms, treaties, and mechanisms. We must begin through the U. N. Atomic Energy Commission to work for binding agreement, but America's decision will not be made over a table in the United Nations. Our representatives in New York, in Paris, or in Moscow depend ultimately on decisions made in the village square.

To the village square we must carry the facts of atomic energy. From there must come America's voice.

This belief of physicists promoted our formation of the Emergency Committee of Atomic Scientists, with headquarters at Princeton, N. J., to make possible a great national campaign for education on these issues, through the National Committee on Atomic Information. Detailed planning for world security will be easier when negotiators are assured of public understanding of our dilemmas.

"Harnessing the atom."

Then our American proposals will be not merely documents about machinery, the dull, dry statements of a government to other governments, but the embodiment of a message to humanity from a nation of human beings.

SCIENCE has brought forth this danger, but the real problem is in the minds and hearts of men. We will not change the hearts of other men by mechanisms, but by changing *our* hearts and speaking bravely.

We must be generous in giving to the world the knowledge we have of the forces of nature, after establishing safeguards against abuse.

We must be not merely willing but actively eager to submit ourselves to binding authority necessary for world security.

We must realize we cannot simultaneously plan for war and peace.

When we are clear in heart and mind—only then shall we find courage to surmount the fear which haunts the world.

June 23, 1946

# SCIENTISTS TO BAR 'DESTRUCTIVE' AID

## Group Organizes to Foster Moral Responsibility for Work to Benefit Mankind

By Religious News Service.

HAVERFORD, Pa., Sept. 17—A group of scientists and engineers who propose "to foster throughout the world a tradition of personal moral responsibility for the consequence for humanity of professional activity," formed the Society for Social Responsibility in Science at a meeting here.

The group said it would emphasize "constructive alternatives to militarism" by pledging its members to "abstain from destructive work" and by devoting themselves to constructive efforts.

Victor Paschkis of Neshanic Station, N. J., director of an engineering research laboratory of Columbia University, was elected president.

Mr. Paschkis said that scientists had "usually omitted all the social and moral aspects of their work in their decisions as to what problems to tackle." He explained that the new society's members were exceptions to this tendency and that they traced their "heterodoxy" back to Leonardo da Vinci's invention of a submarine which he refused to describe publicly "lest man put it to evil purposes."

As a present-day example of "scientific conscience," Mr. Paschkis cited Norbert Weiner, founder of the new scientific field, cybernetics, "who recently refused to put his knowledge at the disposal of the armed forces of this country."

Regional, foreign and functional units of the new Society will be organized, it was announced. English, German and Swiss scientists have expressed interest in joining the society.

One of the group's projects will be the operation of an employment service which will bring together scientists and employers who do not wish to engage in war work.

Other officers of the society are: Vice president, William F. Hewitt Jr., of Washington, physiologist at Howard University School of Medicine; secretary treasurer, Vincent Cochrane of Middletown, Conn., biologist at Wesleyan University; members of the council: Leonard Dart, physicist for the American Viscose Corporation, Marcus Hook, Pa.; Theodore B. Hetzel, of the engineering faculty at Haverford College; Franklin Miller, Jr., physicist at Kenyon College, Gambier, Ohio; William T. Scott, physicist at Brookhaven National Laboratory, Long Island, N. Y., and at Smith College, Northampton, Mass., and James G. Vail of Media, Pa., past president of the American Institute of Chemical Engineers.

September 18, 1949

149

# The Atom and the Scientific Mind

**If we are to maintain our lead in research it is vital that we understand how scientists work.**

*By WALDEMAR KAEMPFFERT*

IN much less time than was generally predicted, Soviet Russia has produced an atomic bomb. How good a bomb it is, how many others have been produced, how many the Russians may be expected to turn out per year, how their methods compare with ours—these are matters for the military and political leaders to ponder. For it is now clear that the cold war between East and West has become more than ever a struggle of science. In that struggle it is essential for Western science to keep its lead in the field of atomic fission.

This grim necessity points up questions of tremendous importance to our future. They have to do with science and the work of scientists in a democratic society that is fighting for survival. Are we making the best use of our scientific brains? Are conditions more favorable for science than in Russia? How is Western science faring in its unaccustomed role of serving major military and political needs? How are those dissimilar things known as the "scientific mind" and the "military mind" getting on together?

Such questions call for an examination of the nature of science and of the scientific man. Fortunately, we learned something of these matters during the war, and the experience has been used with profit.

Before the task of developing an atomic bomb was assigned to them, the scientists had been free to discuss their work, and they had taken orders from nobody. But with the establishment of the Manhattan project the Army gave the orders. It forbade free discussion even within the walls of laboratories engaged in nuclear research for the Government. It tried to compartmentalize physicists, chemists and biologists, so that no man could either receive or give information of technical importance. In the resulting clash of the so-called "scientific mind" with the so-called "military mind" the scientific mind won.

Dr. Leo Szilard, one of the key physicists who worked on the atomic bomb, testified before the House Committee on Military Affairs in October, 1945, that "we had to choose between obeying orders and sabo-

taging or slowing down our work," with the result that "we used common sense in place of obeying rules." So the nuclear physicists and the chemists broke Army rules flagrantly. With the last shot of the war they packed up and returned to their universities.

WHEN the Atomic Energy Commission was created after the war it ran into this inherited trouble. Physicists, chemists and engineers had to be organized anew. Profiting by wartime experience, it was wisely decided that the scientific mind must have its way. This does not mean that there is no plan and no organization, but it does mean that the scientific mind is free—at least so far as the creative theorists at the top are concerned.

Consider what is meant by the "scientific mind." It might be supposed that last summer's Congressional hearings conducted at the instigation of Senator Bourke B. Hickenlooper into the "incredible mismanagement" of the Atomic Energy Commission by David Lilienthal would have thrown some light on how scientists' minds function, since the main work of the commission is essentially scientific. But it did not, because Senator Hickenlooper delved largely into irrelevancies.

Had the inquiry been conducted properly it would have brought out from the scientists who work for the commission the important fact that the "scientific mind," as such, is a romantic fiction. There is no more a scientific mind than there is a cobbler's mind or a farmer's mind. What the phrase connotes is a scientific *method* of experimenting, analyzing and appraising phenomena—a method that takes nothing for granted and cannot be bound by nonscientific rules. This is a principle learned by thousands of students every year.

WHETHER or not the scientific method is applied correctly depends on aptitudes which are inborn and on attitudes which are acquired through education and experience. Of the attitudes, the most important is objectively—the subjugation of prejudices, preferences, hopes, fears, emotions in general. The thing that counts is what the spectroscope proclaims or what the thermometer indicates.

When we talk of the scientific mind we mean this com-

bination of method, aptitudes, attitudes and objectivity. There is no harm in using the phrase so long as we remember what it stands for.

"God give me strength to face a fact though it slay me," prayed Thomas Huxley. The implications of the scientific mind—this combination of aptitudes and attitudes—have never been stated more tersely or effectively.

HOW does the "scientific mind" work? It is plain that Huxley was right in implying that scientists are not always willing to face facts, to discard cherished beliefs. It is also plain that what is good experimenting in one case is not necessarily good in another. In other words, there are scientific methods—not just one scientific method. But all scientific methods have objectivity as a common characteristic.

The distinguishing mark of a good scientist is his honesty and his sense of duty to the world and to his work. He scrupulously gives credit to the men who preceded him and blazed the trail that he is following, and he holds nothing back. In the whole history of science there are very few instances of deliberate deception, and these were quickly discovered and denounced. A scientist may have his jealousies and his ambitions, and he may even stoop to intrigue in order to gain an advantage for himself. But in the end his work must speak for itself. The sharpest minds in the world judge it. No trickery can escape them long.

THERE is much of the artist in the great creative scientist. Both scientists and poets are filled with wonder as they behold the glory of a sunset or the unfolding of a flower. The sunset loses none of its mystery for the scientist if he knows the part that atmospheric diffraction plays in it, and he never ceases to marvel at the billions of stars that seem like luminous dust on his photographic plates. Such conceptions as Newton's laws of motion, Darwin's origin of species, Einstein's doctrine of relativity have a grandeur that

WALDEMAR KAEMPFFERT has covered scientific news for forty years and has been The Times science editor for twenty years. Among his books in this field is "Science Today and Tomorrow."

marks only great epics or some of Beethoven's last music.

Both scientists and poets are interpreters of the cosmos. The scientist analyzes samples of the universe—a rock, the leaf of a tree, the light of a distant star—and the poet states as eloquently as he can how the universe affects him and what his reaction to the universe is. Perhaps it is because they have this interest in the universe in common that so many scientists are given to quoting poetry.

Poets would be willing to muse and write lyrics in an attic, provided they were assured of a modest living. So it is with the great, creative scientists, the men who devote their lives to fundamental research. If they are willing to work for a fraction of what they could earn in business it is because of the excitement, the sense of adventure that the exploration of the unknown always arouses.

A STUDENT of the late Sir J. J. Thomson once asked that Titan of physics: "Why is it, professor, that you earn only a few hundred pounds a year in the Cavendish laboratory of Cambridge, whereas stock brokers make thousands of pounds a year?" To which Thomson replied: "That's exactly as it should be. See the nasty work they have to do."

To ask a scientist of Thomson's stature to develop a metal that would stand the terrific erosion to which the blades of a steam-turbine are subjected would be like asking Shakespeare to write for $5,000 each the advertisements that sang the praises of a breakfast food.

What is $25,000 a year compared with making a discovery that means the conquest of tuberculosis or cancer? What are all the inventions ever made compared with the release of energy from the atom? What are television and rocket planes compared with a discovery that tells us how life was created and how it evolves from protoplasmic slime into man?

Sometimes a scientist is overwhelmed by the implications of his own discovery. It is said that Newton was unable to finish the simple calculation that verified his laws of gravitation because he saw in advance what the result would be. A lesser mind, Halley's probably, had to complete the calculation. It is because of this exciting sense of adventure that so many scientists reject offers of industrial salaries that run into five figures.

PERHAPS it is because he is so much of an idealist that in the popular mind the scientist cuts an almost comic figure when he attempts to deal with social and political issues. The conception is baseless. Some heavy thinking was done on the international control of atomic energy by nuclear physicists, and, though many of them plumped for a world government, impractical in the present temper of the Soviet Union and the Western democracies, they were an aid in developing the ideas that were eventually incorporated in the Acheson-Lilienthal report and the Baruch proposal. The social and political thinking of scientists is no better and no worse than that of leaders in business, professors of literature, engineers or well-educated farmers.

Partly because of their acquired objectivity scientists turn a Marxian proposal this way and that, so view it in all its aspects, and sometimes accept it. The communistic argument appeals to younger scientists. This thinking augurs that under capitalism science developed in a haphazard fashion, with the physical sciences far outstripping the biological sciences because profits and military advantage obviously lie in engineering and chemistry but not in botany, paleontology or oceanography.

IF the state decides to abandon the profit and military motive and to advance science on all fronts, which is what Russia claims to be doing, society must be the gainer in the end. The old definition of science as knowledge derived by methods of observation, experiment and calculation and subject to verification by practical tests is still good, but according to the communistically minded, it is applicable only to a small portion of knowledge and action, as in astrophysics or biochemistry. Or, as Julian Huxley puts it, "science is not the disembodied sort of activity that some people would make out, engaged in the abstract task of pursuing the universal truth, but a social function intimately linked up with human history and human destiny."

It is easy to understand why a convert to communism accepts the broad conception of science as a social instrument, but not why he so willingly casts aside the freedom of thought, expression and action on which he insists as essentials in scientific research. This leaning toward what is

still called "radicalism" is nothing new. Darwin and Wallace were followers of Robert Owen, August Comte and Saint Simon, predecessors of Karl Marx. But in those days no one suggested that a scientist would have to think as a totalitarian state dictated.

It is this freedom to think—to pursue lines of inquiry and draw objective conclusions regardless of social dogmas—that chiefly distinguishes the Western attitude toward science and the men of science. It is one of the chief differences between the Western approach and the Soviet approach to science.

IN the United States freedom in science is so essential that in the laboratories of great corporations good research scientists will resign unless it is granted. A wise director knows that without it there is no initiative, no enthusiasm.

Dr. K. H. Hickman started the investigation that culminated in his remarkable process of whirling vitamins out of fish-liver oils, in the Eastman Kodak Company; Dr. R. R. Williams made his first attempts at isolating vitamin B-1 in the Bell Telephone Laboratories; a Nobel Prize winner worked for several years at his private theory of the atom at his corporative employer's expense. If one of these unruly hirelings of corporations makes only one important discovery in ten years, the profits may run into the tens of millions.

Warned by what happened at Oak Ridge under Army rule, the Atomic Energy Commission allows its laboratories and the university professors who conduct research on its behalf in their own institutions a latitude that business men would not tolerate in their offices. The beneficiaries of this latitude are primarily the top men who are engaged in fundamental research with no thought of practical results. No orders are given to these privileged high priests. They may be "asked" to consider problems in theoretical physics, chemistry or biology. If there is no enthusiastic response the director does not insist. Below these top scientists are physicists, engineers and biologists who do take orders and who are concerned with practical solutions—problems that may originate in the armed forces or in the minds of laboratory directors. The Atomic Energy Commission exercises little direct control over its own labo-

ratories and none over those of its contractors.

UNLESS the atmosphere of the laboratory suits a top research scientist, unless his colleagues are congenial, unless he can discuss his technical difficulties with them, he is so unhappy that eventually he resigns. So in all atomic research laboratories supported by the commission there are seminars, colloquia, lectures, free discussions. Members of the research staff visit other laboratories or attend scientific meetings in distant cities.

Distinguished physicists, chemists, engineers and biologists are welcomed. They bring news of the outer scientific world and arouse interest in new procedures. The publication of results that have no military value is encouraged.

With this freedom, with this seeming lack of management direction, how is the policy of the AEC to be appraised? By its results. These results were set forth by Dr. Oppenheimer in testimony before the Joint Congressional Committee on Atomic Energy. "Better weapons have been developed and tested, and production of materials has been substantially increased and assured and a sound and forward-looking program has been established," are the words in which he expressed his appraisal and approval. All of which indicates what can happen when the scientific mind is given free play and management is reduced to such low terms that it looks like no management.

DOES it then necessarily follow that Russian science, subjected to the Kremlin's dictates and living in fear of purges if its investigations lead it astray from the party line, is incapable of matching the achievements of free science in the West? That is a difficult question to answer, but there is good reason to believe that the Russian scientists do not follow the party line.

Research scientists do their work, but in presenting their results they indicate how they were reached by reasoning in the approved Marxian way—that is, the way of material dialecticism. Although Newton knew nothing of the Marxian mode of reasoning, a Russian believer in it would have no difficulty in showing, three centuries after the event, just how it could have been reached and even was reached, in his opinion, in the Marxian way.

The question of Soviet science involves two major factors. One is the actual extent to which Russia's top theoretical scientists are curbed by political considerations. The other involves Russia's totalitarian organization of the mechanics of science to reach a given goal.

We are made aware from time to time that Soviet scientists are excoriated in Pravda for reaching un-Marxian conclusions. The case of genetics, the science of heredity, has given ample proof of that, and some of the leading Soviet geneticists have disappeared from the scene because of their nonconformity.

Earlier in the year it was learned from on high that such "mysticism" as the quantum theory and Heisenberg's principle of uncertainty were anti-Marxian. The Politburo wants the atomic model of the nineteenth century, though it is as out of date as the high-wheel bicycle and though a belief in it would never have aided physicists in devising a uranium or a plutonium bomb.

To the extent Soviet science has succeeded—and it has succeeded greatly in many lines—it has done so not because of Marxism, as Marxists claim, but in spite of Marxism. Nevertheless, there is reason to believe that in certain fields of science not directly related to Marxist social doctrine the leading scientists are allowed considerable leeway. The Kremlin is, after all, pragmatic. Until recently it did not let finer points of doctrine seriously handicap development in such a crucial field as atomic fission, which explains why an atomic bomb was achieved.

The second factor, the effective organization of scientific manpower and equipment to achieve a certain goal, does much to explain Soviet success in the atomic field. Nor is this the paradox it may seem in the light of the preceding discussion of American scientific freedom. For this organization applies to the vast and detailed jobs of research and production where organization is also required in America. It

## FREEDOM

In Schenectady, N. Y., the story is told that when a sign that read "No Smoking" was tacked up in a General Electric Laboratory, the late Dr. Charles P. Steinmetz walked out. He could not think and work without a long cigar in his mouth. When the sign came down Steinmetz walked in again.

may restrict certain lines of investigation which prove productive under a free science, but it can certainly get results when applied to a particular problem.

How, then, can American science be assured of success in the atomic race with Russian science? The answer, I believe, lies in retention of the present freedom of investigation and discussion coupled with greater teamwork and planning in "fundamental" research. The latter will not necessarily hamper essential freedom. It all depends on how it is done.

What is needed is some means of voluntarily pooling scientific knowledge to a greater extent than is now available. We need a National Science Foundation with broad powers to survey the whole field of science, find gaps in our knowledge and fill them. It should be flexible, so as to utilize contributions to knowledge from whatever source, but it should be able also to direct investigation toward the knowledge that is lacking. The over-all plan should be kept in mind when research grants and contracts are to be made. There would be no compulsion, but there would be greater efficiency.

This, in my opinion, is the only way American science can be geared to the great effort in atomics without losing its freedom and the material benefits stemming from freedom. By such means we would avoid the weaknesses of totalitarian science while gaining the strength that comes from organization.

# TRUMAN ORDERS HYDROGEN BOMB BUILT FOR SECURITY PENDING AN ATOMIC PACT; CONGRESS HAILS STEP; BOARD BEGINS JOB

## HISTORIC DECISION

### President Says He Must Defend Nation Against Possible Aggressor

### SOVIET 'EXPLOSION' CITED

His Ruling Wins Bipartisan Support on Capitol Hill—No Fund Request Due Now

**By ANTHONY LEVIERO**
Special to THE NEW YORK TIMES.

WASHINGTON, Jan. 31—President Truman announced today that he had ordered the Atomic Energy Commission to produce the hydrogen bomb.

The Chief Executive acted in his role of Commander in Chief of the Armed forces, ordering an improved weapon for national security. Thus, from the domestic standpoint, he removed the question of producing the super-weapon as an issue that might be argued on moral grounds.

As for international statecraft, Mr. Truman, by treating the hydrogen bomb as an addition to the American armory, also removed it as an issue that might be interpreted as an advanced threat or inducement in seeking international control of atomic weapons.

Nevertheless, Mr. Truman said that his perseverance in providing for national defense would be matched by his efforts to seek international control of atomic weapons.

### New Phase of Atomic Age

In his announcement, Mr. Truman regarded the hydrogen bomb as a progressive outgrowth of United States production of the uranium-plutonium atomic bomb. He put it this way: the commission was "to continue its work on all forms of atomic weapons, including the so-called hydrogen or super-bomb."

His use of the word "continue" was understood to imply that with national security the over-riding consideration, the chief factor guiding his decision was whether it was practicable to make the weapon. Scientists have said that it is.

In effect, the President's decision, which won wide acclaim in Congress, marked the advent of a new phase of the atomic age and a surge ahead of Russia in the race to retain military ascendancy.

The bombs that visited destruction on Hiroshima and Nagasaki split the atom. The new bomb would fuse atoms instead, but with a power 100 to 1,000 times greater than the improved fission bombs that have been developed since the Japanese cities were struck.

### The President's Statement

The President made his decision known in the following brief statement:

"It is part of my responsibility as Commander in Chief of the armed forces to see to it that our country is able to defend itself against any possible aggressor. Accordingly, I have directed the Atomic Energy Commission to continue its work on all forms of atomic weapons, including the so-called hydrogen or super-bomb. Like all other work in the field of atomic weapons, it is being and will be carried forward on a basis consistent with the over-all objectives of our program for peace and security.

"This we shall continue to do until a satisfactory plan for international control of atomic energy is achieved. We shall also continue to examine all those factors that affect our program for peace and this country's security."

On Capitol Hill when news of the Chief Executive's decision was received there, Republicans and Democrats joined in approving it. This bipartisanship boded well for Congressional backing of the new project, though it was said in informed quarters that Mr. Truman would not request funds for it at this time.

The Joint Congressional Committee on Atomic Energy held a previously scheduled meeting about an hour after the President's statement came out, and its chairman, Senator Brien McMahon, Democrat, of Connecticut, said that it had approved Mr. Truman's decision. He added that the committee would now proceed with meetings in which the implementation of the hydrogen bomb program would be studied.

Louis Johnson, Secretary of Defense, who had been in Mr. Truman's office today, would say no more than that "the President's statement speaks for itself." The view of the professional soldier was expressed by an anonymous but high-ranking officer speaking in the absence of Gen. Omar N. Bradley, Chairman of the Joint Chiefs of Staff. He said:

"This is one of the gravest decisions the United States has ever had to make, but it had to be done."

Mr. Truman was as undramatic in making his announcement as he was last Sept. 23 when he disclosed that Russia had achieved an atomic explosion — a development that clearly showed that our absolute dominance in atomic weapons was virtually ended. The President was not in his office when the historic statement came out. He was lunching at Blair House, the official residence.

It was 1:55 P. M. when Miss Genevieve Irish of the White House staff walked through the lobby of the Executive Offices and into the press room, crying "press." White House reporters hurried into the office of Charles G. Ross, the press secretary. He requested that none should leave the room until each had a copy of the mimeographed statement that he held in his hands. He does not make such a request unless the subject is momentous.

### Truman Preferred Secrecy

Mr. Truman's decision was a direct result of the discovery in September of the Russian explosion. After it was established beyond doubt that the Soviet Union had accomplished atomic fission, he called in David E. Lilienthal, chairman of the Atomic Energy Commission, and asked what should be done about holding this country's lead in atomic weapons.

Mr. Lilienthal, who is to resign about Feb. 15, was reported to have reminded the President of the possibility of producing the hydrogen super-bomb and asked if he wished to go head with it. Thereupon Mr. Truman sought the advice of Mr. Lilienthal as well as of the three other leading officials concerned—Mr. Johnson, General Bradley and Dean Acheson, Secretary of State.

It was learned that the President would have produced the hydrogen bomb in secrecy, as most military weapons have been in the past, except for the great debate over it that erupted last November and has continued since.

Mr. Truman was represented as feeling that while the new weapon was particularly destructive, this country should have kept its development secret so as to retain the element of surprise as an additional measure of security.

The President sought to discourage discussion of the new type of bomb after Senator Edwin C. Johnson, Democrat, of Colorado, said in a television broadcast that this country was making considerable progress in developing an atomic bomb 1,000 times deadlier than the one dropped on Nagasaki.

J. Howard McGrath, Attorney General, and Senator McMahon were called to the White House on Nov. 25 and urged by Mr. Truman to prevent leaks on data so vital to national security.

Informed sources characterized as ludicrous published estimates that it would take $2,000,000,000 to $4,000,000,000 to produce the hydrogen bomb. The figure would be nearer $200,000,000, it was said, since this country's vast, well-developed atomic plants and "know-how" would be used in its production. In this respect, it was added, the United States retained a great advantage over Russia.

Because the work could be undertaken by the Atomic Energy Commission with its present resources, officials said, no new funds would be needed immediately. The work could be carried on with present appropriations and plants until advanced stages were reached.

February 1, 1950

# BOMB REFUGE HERE FOR 4,000 PLANNED

## Big Office Structure Will Be City's First to Incorporate Atomic Age Shelter

### By LEE E. COOPER

An atomic bomb shelter — described as the first structural recognition by skyscraper builders here of the perils of the nuclear age—will be built into the lower levels of the blockfront office edifice that will rise soon at 260 Madison Avenue.

Plans for the new building, made public yesterday by the owners and their agents, disclosed that the sub-basement space was being planned in accordance with the latest advice received from leading atomic scientists to provide what is considered the maximum possible protection against the bomb. Consultation between these experts and engineers for the project has led to the adoption of an unusual design for the below-grade accommodations. These call for floors, ceilings and walls sturdy enough, it is believed, to withstand anything but a direct bomb hit.

The steel and concrete supports of the proposed shelter will be so constructed as to hold up even if the building above it collapses in an air raid.

The protected area will cover about 24,000 square feet to give a temporary haven for as many as 4,000 persons. This is believed to be the maximum number of tenants and visitors to be expected at any one time.

Equipment will be installed to permit reverse ventilation that would suck air out of the shelter for fifteen to twenty minutes as a protection against deadly radiation in the outside air just after a nuclear explosion.

Special emergency exits will be provided for escape in case the regular entrances are closed by the blast. As a further precaution, storage space for valuables will be available on the second sub-basement level.

Spokesmen for Calman J. Ginsberg of 80 Broad Street, president of the building group, said the cost of the added protection would be considerably less than had been expected because the shelter was incorporated in the original plans instead of as an expensive afterthought.

They estimated that the twenty-one-story structure, which will contain 373,000 square feet above the ground floor, would represent an investment of $15,000,000. In normal times the bomb shelter will be utilized as parking space for 125 automobiles.

Excavation work will begin immediately on the site of 29,000 square feet on the west side of Madison Avenue between Thirty-eighth and Thirty-ninth Streets. Plans have been filed through Sylvan Bien, architect, completion of the building is likely within a year.

The major part of the land formerly was held by the late George F. Baker, of The First National Bank, and was purchased by the builders through Brown, Harris, Stevens, Inc., who will be agents. Mortgage financing has been arranged by Ivor B. Clark, Inc., broker, with the Metropolitan Life Insurance Company.

The plot originally excluded the southwest corner of Madison Avenue and Thirty-ninth Street, occupied by a four-story building owned and used by the Visiting Nurse Service of New York. This corner had been given to the Visiting Nurse Service by the family of the late Jacob H. Schiff, in his memory, and at first was considered unobtainable. It was Mr. Clark who finally arranged the purchase that rounded out the site. The sellers have taken temporary quarters at 598 Madison Avenue.

The front of the new building will be of glass and aluminum in a pattern somewhat like that utilized for the United Nations headquarters. Instead of rising perpendicularly to its full height it will have a series of setbacks starting at the tenth floor.

The sides and back of the edifice will be of white stone masonry with windows in the form of continuous strips of glass running horizontally around these three walls. The facade of the ground floor will be of black polished granite. Other features will include air-conditioning, fluorescent lighting and acoustical ceilings.

Basement parking service will include acceptance and delivery of tenants' automobiles at the street entrance. To help cut traffic congestion and as a convenience to car owners, a free station wagon service will be provided for garage tenants for short trips.

August 20, 1950

---

# ATOM BOMB FEARS MINIMIZED BY U. S.

## Civil Defense Office Booklet 'Bible' on Protection, Hits Myth of 'Super' Explosive

### By PAUL P. KENNEDY
Special to The New York Times.

WASHINGTON, Oct. 28—A thirty-two-page booklet assuring the public that it can live through an atom bomb raid without the aid of a Geiger counter, protective clothing or special training was issued today by the Civil Defense Office of the National Security Resources Board.

The booklet, described as "John Citizen's Bible on Atomic Attack Protection," will have an initial distribution of several hundred thousand copies. Ultimately it is planned to place a copy of it in every home in the United States and its Territories.

While the treatise, compiled with the cooperation of several Federal agencies including the Atomic Energy Commission, does not attempt to detract from the seriousness of the atom bomb, it devotes considerable space to breaking down what it terms "myths" about atomic energy. These so-called "myths," the booklet says, center largely about the effects of radiation and "the wild talk of 'super-super bombs.'"

"Injury by radioactivity does not necessarily mean you are doomed to die or be crippled," the booklet says. It also points out that the children of survivors of the Nagasaki and Hiroshima attacks are normal.

### Damage of Bombs Weighed

Those survivors of the atom blast who were temporarily unable to have children because of radiation now are having children again.

As for the super or hydrogen bomb, the booklet says:

"A modern atomic bomb can do heavy damage to houses and buildings roughly two miles away. But doubling its power will extend the range of damage to only about two and one-half miles. In the same way, if there were a bomb 100 times as powerful, it would reach out only a little more than four and one-half, not 100 times as far."

The double-page center of the booklet, containing "six survival secrets for atomic attacks," is, according to Civil Defense Office officials, the most important part of the work. It is arranged so as to be easily detached from the booklet, and the reader is advised to "remove this sheet and keep it with you until you've memorized it."

### Six Rules for Survival

The six rules for survival as presented are:

1. TRY TO GET SHIELDED: If you have time, get down in a basement or subway. Should you unexpectedly be caught out-of-doors, seek shelter alongside a building or jump in any handy ditch or gutter.
2. DROP FLAT ON GROUND OR FLOOR: To keep from being tossed about and to lessen the chances of being struck by falling and flying objects, flatten out at the base of a wall, or at the bottom of a bank.
3. BURY YOUR FACE IN YOUR ARMS: When you drop flat, hide your eyes in the crook of your elbow. That will protect your face from flash burns, prevent temporary blindness and keep flying objects out of your eyes.
4. DON'T RUSH OUTSIDE RIGHT AFTER A BOMBING: After an air burst, wait a few minutes, then go to help fight fires. After other kinds of bursts wait at least until lingering radiation has some chance to die down.
5. DON'T TAKE CHANCES WITH FOOD OR WATER IN OPEN CONTAINERS: To prevent radioactive poisoning or disease, select your food and water with care. When there is reason to believe these may be contaminated, stick to canned and bottled things if possible.
6. DON'T START RUMORS: In the confusion that follows a bombing, a single rumor might touch off a panic that could cost you your life.

### Chances of Escape Studied

A person's chance of escaping alive when within one-half mile of the center of an atomic explosion would be one to ten, according to the booklet's calculations. It continues, however, that "from one-half to one mile away, you have a 50-50 chance."

Further calculations agree that: "At points from one to one and one-half miles out, the odds that you will be killed are only fifteen in 100. At points from one-half to two miles away, deaths drop all the way down to only two or three out of each 100. Beyond two miles, the explosion will cause practically no deaths at all."

The booklet assures the public that "your chances of surviving an atomic attack are better than you may have thought."

It says that in the City of Hiroshima, slightly more than half the people who were a mile from the atomic explosion are alive. At Nagasaki, it adds, "almost 70 per cent of the people a mile away from the bomb lived to tell their experiences."

### Advice Is Given on Risks

It is emphasized throughout the booklet that all calculations of death and injury risks are based on the premise that there has been no advance warning of a bomb attack.

To lessen the risk of injuries from a blast, the booklet advises falling flat beside a wall or ducking under a bed or a table.

"When you fall flat to protect yourself from a bombing," it is advised, "don't look up to see what is coming. Even during the daylight hours, the flash from a bursting A-bomb can cause several moments of blindness if you're facing that way."

More than half of all bombing injuries, the booklet says, are the result of being bodily tossed about or being struck by falling and flying objects. About 30 per cent of the injuries at Hiroshima and Nagasaki were the result of flash burns from the atom bomb's light and heat, it adds.

October 29, 195

# Two Military Problems

## Eisenhower Held Facing Ultra Secrecy and Moral Laxity That Impair Defense

### By HANSON W. BALDWIN

Two military problems, both intangibles, that faced Eisenhower, the general, confront Eisenhower, the President, as he takes office today.

Both problems have increased in magnitude and have become more pressing with time. Both are of fundamental importance to the military services and yet both transcend the military. Their solutions, or the lack of them, will establish the national climate that, in turn, determines the health of the armed services.

One of these problems is the problem of security, the classification and restriction of material relating to the national defense.

War and the preparations for it are so total today that the excuse of "military security" can be, and often has been, invoked to screen and hide all sorts of information. The trend toward over-classification and ultra secrecy has become more and more pronounced, and in many ways security restrictions today are self-defeating.

Secrecy has never meant security but far too often has cloaked weaknesses. Representative government cannot insist upon corrective action unless it knows the facts and today facts are hard to come by, due to censorship at the source—in the Government itself.

The most dramatic and frightening example of this trend is in the field of new weapons. Civilian defense, an important part of the defense set-up, has failed to receive adequate public support, in large measure because of the ultra secrecy with which all atomic developments have been guarded by the Government.

#### Apathy of Public Noted

Toward this and many other crucial defense problems of the atomic age the public is apathetic. A type of fatalism, of shifting responsibility to Government shoulders for decisions the individual citizen should make, has influenced American public opinion.

Only strong and enlightened Government leadership can penetrate the subconscious of American public opinion with the frightful facts of such a new weapon as the hydrogen bomb. President Truman made a start in this process with his reference to the hydrogen age in his farewell address, but far more facts are needed before public and Congressional consciousness is sufficiently aroused

to legislate wisely on defense problems in the hydrogen age.

The second problem—related in one sense to the first—is what Wesley C. Clark, associate dean of the School of Journalism at Syracuse University, has called the "moral tone of the nation," which is established in so major a measure by the example of Washington. Just how greatly the deterioration in the country's moral tone has affected the armed services is perhaps best shown by a talk Lieut. Gen. Willis D. Crittenberger, retired, until recently Commanding General of the First Army, delivered to his officers on Governors Island last November.

#### Concern Voiced by General

"I am very much concerned," General Crittenberger said, "over a series of recent incidents which have tended to lower the Army of the United States in the esteem of the public.

"* * * Derelictions run all the way from misappropriation of public funds, falsification of accounts, gambling in violation of regulations and state and Federal laws, bigamy, drunkenness and deceit to violations of honor and decency. * * * The very character of our Army has been unassailable through the years, because of its high moral fiber and strong sense of duty. To note now any deviation from these high purposes which the Army personifies should be the cause for genuine alarm."

Yet that "genuine alarm" has been expressed frequently by others among the more discerning and more courageous of our military leaders.

The officer corps of the services, greatly expanded in numbers, do not possess today the same high standards of service, of duty, of honor that once motivated them. There has been a growth in the services, as well as in the nation, of the easy doctrine that "it's all right if you get away with it." Morale and esprit have suffered as the standards of leadership have declined.

Yet the services can be no better than the nation from which they spring. General Eisenhower will have the heavy responsibility of awakening the people from the comforting illusion that what you don't know won't hurt you, and at the same time of restoring the "moral tone of the nation."

---

# FAMILY PLAN URGED FOR CIVIL DEFENSE

## Mrs. Howard, the Acting Chief, Calls Program Best Chance for Maximum Survival

Special to THE NEW YORK TIMES.

WASHINGTON, Aug. 29—Mrs. Charles P. Howard, acting Civil Defense Administrator, urged today greatly increased "down-to-earth, home-by-home" civil defense protection through a "family action program."

This plan is expected to be widely taken up by women's clubs and parent-teachers associations in their fall programs.

Mrs. Howard said that civil defense studies indicated that short of some new national plan for warnings far in advance and orderly mass evacuation of target areas, the best chance for maximum survival rested with family-unit preparedness.

She pointed out that whereas a vast improvement in the destructive powers of atom weapons might have turned the mass shelters that were effective in the last war into death traps, the Nevada atomic bomb experiments last March had indicated that basement and backyard shelters could save many lives.

#### Some Mannequins Survived.

Mannequins placed in various small types of basement and ground shelters in and near two houses survived the Nevada experiments. Mannequins in family groups on the above-ground floors were part of the general wreckage and would, if alive, have been killed or injured.

Instructions on how to make the various types of home shelters tested in the blast have been published in an eighty-six page booklet for the use of civil defense technicians. The shelters range in cost from a $40 wooden lean-to shelter protecting four persons to a $1,000 (labor cost included) reinforced concrete basement exit shelter for six.

For the individual householder, three pamphlets tell how to build the shelter-type of his choice. Their titles—"Lean-To Shelters," "Corner Room Shelter" and "Outdoor Shelters."

Mrs. Howard emphasized, however, that any shelter-building program should be supplemented by the "Family Action Exercises," which the Civil Defense Administration has worked out for protection in an emergency.

#### More Funds Available

At present there are only 5,000 advance copies on this booklet, but Civil Defense officials said enough new funds now were available to print 100,000 copies.

Outlined are family exercises in six fields:

1. Preparing your shelter.
2. What to do when an alert warning sounds.
3. Safeguarding your home against fire.
4. Home fire-fighting.
5. What to do if some one is trapped.
6. Safe food and water in emergencies.

Mrs. Howard said it was not necessary for any one to delay getting started on these exercises. Any family can begin by eliminating the obvious fire-traps around the home, she added. However, she emphasized that no snap course was offered.

Each family, Mrs. Howard declared, was supposed to conduct its own evacuation drills to its own scientifically stocked shelter, complete with a three-day supply of food and safe drinking water.

#### Bomb Shelter Paid Off

Mrs. Howard recalled that maintaining a well-stocked bomb shelter in her own home in Beacon Street, Boston, had paid off in an emergency.

"Our family was off on a vacation trip when we received a phone call saying our house had been set afire by an incendiarist," she said.

"By the time we arrived home, it was completely gutted by a three-alarm type of fire. Then we looked for the bomb shelter, and I heard some one exclaim, 'My gosh, it is there!' We had a lot of work to do inspecting the extent of the damage, and since all utilities were cut off, we opened up the emergency supply of bottled spring water, and made a meal on the Sterno stove from our canned goods and sat in the ruins and ate it."

The Civil Defense Administration, Mrs. Howard said, is now working on a very complete home defense handbook that will include advice on emergency sanitation and home feeding. It also will suggest the extent to which car radios, which are not cut off when electric power systems fail, can be used in receiving warnings.

---

January 20, 1953

August 30, 1953

# A Civil Defense Impasse

## Problem Viewed as Unresolved as New Rand Report Differs With Gaither Study

### By HANSON W. BALDWIN

The controversial problem of civilian defense is once again emphasized, but by no means solved, with the publication of a Rand Corporation study on "Non-Military Defense."

The Rand Corporation is a private organization. Under contract, it conducts both classified and unclassified research projects for the United States Air Force and other Government agencies. It also sponsors with its own funds research projects in public welfare matters and national security projects.

| News Analysis |
|---|

Its "Report on a Study of Non-Military Defense" represents its own private study, but it has attracted unusual attention because of the corporation's past extensive researches in the national security field.

The study investigated civil defense in all its aspects, including foreign policy implications, shelters, evacuation; radiation and fall-out; food, agriculture and water, and economic recuperation.

None of the report was based on classified information.

Its conclusions differed from others dealing with the same subject.

The most striking feature of the Rand report is the qualified nature of its conclusions. It declares that "there are more promising possibilities for alleviating the disaster of a nuclear war than have been generally recognized.

### Possibilities Listed

"There appear," it further said, "to be possibilities of providing inexpensive fall-out protection for people outside blast areas, of constructing [effective] blast shelters, of carrying out strategic or tactical evacuation," of countering the radiation hazard, of providing food and reconstructing destroyed industrial capital.

"Some hypothetical non-military defense systems that have been examined," the report said, "seem to be capable of saving tens of millions of lives in the face of conceivable enemy attacks."

The operative words in these optimistic conclusions are the qualifying ones, possibilities, appear and seem. The report explicitly states that "each of these possibilities is at present surrounded by considerable uncertainty, with respect to both performance and cost."

"Accordingly, the principal policy suggestion stemming from this study," the report declares, "is that the United States ought to undertake a serious research, development and planning program in the field of non-military defense.

"It does not appear sensible to embark on a comprehensive non-military defense program now without such prior research. An ill-considered program could be costly, threatened with obsolescence, and inconsistent with other important elements of national defense."

The reports suggests a $200,000,000 budget, spread over two or three years, for such a program of research, development and planning.

The Rand report thus conflicts strongly with the recommendations of some Government panels, which based their conclusions upon classified material.

The so-called Gaither Committee prepared a secret report for the National Security Council, only the highlights of which have been unofficially reported to the public. This committee is known, however, to have urged an immediate start on an extensive fall-out shelter program.

The committee was named for its chairman, H. Rowan Gaither Jr.

### Fundamentally Different

Thus two studies of civilian defense, each conducted by competent experts, have arrived at fundamentally different conclusions.

One, the Rand group, is optimistic about the possibilities of civil defense but advocates further studies before major expenditures. The other, the Gaither committee, declares that the necessary studies have been made and that it is essential that major expenditures of about $5,000,000,000 annually be authorized immediately.

The Administration appears to have made its choice despite the discrepancy of these views. It recommended to the last session of Congress an expenditure in the current fiscal year of $13,150,000 for construction of prototype shelters, architectural and engineering research and to "provide the stimulation necessary for the American people to make [their] own preparations for fall-out protection."

The amount was less than urged by the Rand report.

Congress, however, paid only token attention to the Administration's recommendation. It appropriated $2,500,000 for an adult education program, apparently intended to persuade the public to build its own shelters, and $2,000,000 for radiological instruments. Nothing was voted for prototype shelters, surveys, or studies.

Thus these actions and the widely varying views of two distinguished bodies leave the problem of civil defense about where it has been since the first test of a hydrogen weapon—"neither fish nor flesh nor good red herring."

## Shelter Controversy

A major national debate over fall-out shelters has developed since Premier Khrushchev revived the Berlin crisis and resumed nuclear testing.

Advocates of an extensive shelter program contend that shelters could save many lives. The argument is that, while a nuclear bomb would kill everybody in the impact area, people outside the area could survive if they had protection from the immediate radioactive fall-out that would follow the blast.

Many persons however, see shelters as useless. In this view most of the people in shelters would be incinerated or suffocated by the heat effects of the bombs, and those who survived would emerge into hopeless devastation.

Federal policy has not yet crystallized. President Kennedy has urged individuals to "act" on building shelters for themselves, and he won from Congress an appropriation of $207,000,000 to identify public buildings suitable for shelters and put supplies in them. He has also indicated that the Administration would have more to say on shelters.

# Truman's Aims Seen Based On Freedom of Enterprise

## His Foreign Policy Connected With Ideals Announced at Baylor University

### By RUSSELL PORTER

President Truman's message to Congress last Wednesday, formulating a new foreign policy of world-wide defense of democracy against communism, gains added significance when read against the background of his Baylor University address in the preceding week. "There is one thing Americans value even more than peace," said the President at Baylor. "It is freedom—freedom of worship, freedom of speech, freedom of enterprise."

He went on to state a fundamental tenet of the American way of life that many seem to have failed to understand, to have forgotten or to have discounted. That is that the first two of these freedoms are related to the third. Throughout history, he pointed out, freedom of worship and freedom of speech have been enjoyed most frequently in those societies that have accorded a considerable measure of freedom to individual enterprise.

Although this aspect of the Truman policy has been subordinated naturally in most comment to the more immediate military and diplomatic implications, it seems to this observer to contain the basic truth of that for which we are taking our stand and how we can best defend it successfully.

The sum and substance of it appears to be that we are standing for individual liberty, even at the risk of war, and are proposing a long-term program based upon freedom of individual enterprise as the means to save the United States and the rest of the civilized world from totalitarian tyranny or barbarism.

Global and incalculable are the ramifications and repercussions of this policy. It illustrates to perfection the interdependence, especially in the air age and the atomic age, of foreign and domestic issues, economic and political problems, free enterprise and democracy.

Its impact upon the daily life of every American citizen will be enormous, regardless of war or peace. Every major public issue is affected—industrial peace vs. class warfare, high tariffs vs. low, the balanced budget, tax cuts and debt reduction vs. Government spending; free markets vs. Government controls.

The Communist fifth column in the Congress of Industrial Organizations, in the press and elsewhere undoubtedly will redouble its agitation for strikes and slowdowns—for civil war, if possible—in order to interfere with the production and transportation of goods to Greece, Turkey and other countries which later may come within the protection of Pax Americana. This would merely follow the precedent that our native Communists set during the Nazi-Soviet pact.

Moreover, the needs of labor for higher wages and of management for higher earnings might both be increased by a substantial rise in the cost of living and the costs of production due to the new policy. This would come from further large Government spending and shipments of American food, clothing and manufactured goods sufficient to prolong the period of serious shortages of goods and high prices that still exists in this country.

Such developments would tend to increase frictions in labor-management relations and to step up inflationary pressures at a time when, it had been hoped, the national economy could be stabilized at a more reasonable price level without risking a serious depression.

This tendency has shown up in recent weeks as a result of Government buying of wheat for export and speculation in the grain pits. If it continues, it may destroy the country's hopes of controlling the post-war boom well enough to keep it from eventually collapsing in a major depression, with widespread business failures and mass unemployment.

Renewed agitation for Government spending and controls could then be expected. It might all very well end in the breakdown of free enterprise and democracy and the very triumph of totalitarianism that we are seeking to forestall.

### Calculated Risks

But public opinion obviously regards these as calculated risks, necessary to take in order to avoid the greater evil. The President's extension of the Monroe Doctrine and the Good Neighbor policy to a first line of defense in the Mediterranean clearly has majority public approval, as indicated by editorial comment. The election returns and public-opinion polls have demonstrated beyond all doubt that the people are determined to keep the American way of life, whatever the cost may be.

But this raises the questions how these costs and risks may be minimized. Most Americans seem to agree that we must help others from falling into the bottomless pit for both their own sake and ours. With each country that is engulfed, the danger comes closer to us. But how can we make sure that we do not fall in ourselves or let others, going under themselves, pull us in with them?

Labor-management cooperation and government leadership comparable to that which we enjoyed during the war seem to be required. We need to release the dynamic qualities of free enterprise at home and abroad from restrictions which keep it from functioning at its utmost efficiency. Increased productivity of men and machines can give us the volume production essential to meet the crisis without undermining the national economy through perpetuating higher prices and shortages. We need another "miracle" of production at home such as we had in the war—without a "boom-bust" cycle.

The situation is more or less similar in the international field. We need reservations and conditions which not only will keep our gifts and loans from being wasted or used to sabotage our way of life, but also will enable us to prevent reactionary ruling classes and doctrinaire Utopians from nullifying our efforts to teach the "secret" of American prosperity to peoples who seek our aid.

This need not imply either intervention in the internal affairs of other countries or a crusade to impose our way of life upon them. But it does call for cooperation and a realization that cooperation is a joint effort.

There is actually no "miracle" or "secret" involved, but merely the liberty of the individual to live, work and produce in freedom, enjoying the fruits of his labor in accordance with his free competitive ability and will to work, under a system of law which is fair to all, without being oppressed or exploited by either private monopoly or state tyranny.

Under "Pax Americana," production is the door to world peace and prosperity, and free enterprise is the key.

March 16, 1947

# What Is Loyalty?  A Difficult Question

## For it touches both civil liberties and the right of government to protect itself.

### By ARTHUR M. SCHLESINGER JR.

WE have heard a good deal in recent months about loyalty and Americanism. Spokesmen on one side proclaim that the American way of life is in imminent danger from any one who questions the eternal rightness of the capitalist system. Spokesmen on the other side proclaim that a sinister witch-hunt is already transforming the United States into a totalitarian police state.

The situation cries out for a little less hysteria and a little more calm sense. A calm survey surely reveals two propositions on which we can all agree: (1) that Americanism is not a totalitarian faith, which can impose a single economic or political dogma or require a uniformity in observance from all its devotees; but (2) that a serious problem for national security has been created by that fanatical group which rejects all American interests in favor of those of the Soviet Union.

In other words, the disciples of the Un-American Activities Committee and the leadership of the American Legion must be reminded that Americanism means something far richer and deeper than submission to their own collection of petty prejudices; and civil libertarians who honestly fear a witch-hunt must be reminded that in an imperfect world of spies and traitors a Government must be conceded the right of self-protection. We see here an inescapable conflict between civil liberty and national security, and we must face up to the problem of resolving the conflict.

WHAT is Americanism? To get quickly to what its loudest exponents seem to regard as its basic point—private enterprise—there is nothing un-American about criticizing the capitalist system. Let us reveal the hideous secret: capitalism was not handed down with the Ten Commandments at Sinai. The Constitution of the United States does not ordain the economic status quo. It can well be argued that there is nothing in our fundamental law to prevent Congress from socializing all basic industry tomorrow; there is certainly nothing in our state laws to prevent public ownership.

Are we to assume that revelations concerning the sacrosanctity of private capitalism have been vouchsafed to the NAM and to the Republican party which were denied to the Founding Fathers?

ARTHUR M. SCHLESINGER JR. teaches history at Harvard University and is the author of the Pulitzer Prize-winning study, "The Age of Jackson." He has written for many publications on social and political questions in America.

More than this, the basic tradition in American democracy—the tradition associated with such names as Jefferson, Jackson, Wilson and the two Roosevelts—has been a fight on behalf of the broad masses against the economic excesses of capitalism and against the political aspirations of the business community.

It is even hard to argue that assertion of the right of revolution is un-American. According to that once-respected document, the Declaration of Independence, when a government becomes injurious to life, liberty and the pursuit of happiness, "it is the right of the people to alter or to abolish it and to institute new government, laying its foundation on such principles and organizing its power in such form as to them shall seem most likely to effect their safety and happiness."

JAMES WILSON, one of the fathers of the Constitution and perhaps a greater authority on it than the chairman of the Un-American Activities Committee, declared: "A revolution principle certainly is, and certainly should be taught as a principle of the Constitution of the United States." Surely no one like Congressman Rankin, who holds Gen. Robert E. Lee and his colleagues in pious veneration, has much ground for stickling at the thought of armed rebellion.

This insistence on the infallibility of capitalism and on the heresy of change finds no sanction in the usages of the American democratic tradition. It reaches its pinnacle of imbecility in such episodes as the attack on the film "The Best Years of Our Lives" as Communist-minded because it makes

> fun of the American business man, or in the standards employed by the Un-American Committee in their current Hollywood investigation. What havoc the rigid identification of Americanism with business worship would wreak upon the history and traditions of our country! Yet this very identification pervades altogether too much of the popular campaign against communism. Many conservatives are happily pouncing upon the Communist scare as an excuse for silencing all critics of business supremacy.

BUT those who believe that the agitation over communism is only a pretext for purging liberals—that this is a repetition of A. Mitchell Palmer and the red raids—are themselves

mistaking a part for the whole. Times have changed a good deal since A. Mitchell Palmer. In 1919 the U.S.S.R. was a torn and struggling nation with its back to the wall. Today Soviet totalitarianism is massive, well-organized and on the march. Its spies and agents are ubiquitous. We face here not just a figment of the reactionary imagination but a proved problem for the security of free nations.

Experience by now must have exposed the illusion that it is possible to work with Communists or fellow-travelers—with persons whose loyalties are signed, sealed and delivered elsewhere. President Gonzales Videla of Chile and Joe Curran of the National Maritime Union have presented only the most recent case histories. One may still wonder perhaps whether the divergence of political loyalties really goes to the length of espionage. Again the record is clear. Herbert Morrison, hardly a reactionary, has borne testimony, for example, to the cases of Communist espionage which came to him as British Home Secretary at a time when Britain and Russia were fighting allies.

"IT may be said that all countries spy, and it may be that they do," Morrison observed. "But there is a grave difference between the ordinary spying of the professional spy * * * and espionage through a political organization." The documents of the Canadian spy case report the techniques of Communist political corruption in fascinating and indisputable detail—in particular, the use of the "study group" as a way of feeling out the degrees of political fanaticism.

The national Communist parties and their front organizations provide, in fact, a unique means of getting, recruiting and testing potential agents. Morrison has stated one result of these tactics—his discomfort at the thought of "sitting in the same cabinet where members of the American Communist party were participating in our discussions with access to secret documents." That discomfort must continue wherever in government agencies, Communists or their allies or dupes have access to classified materials.

It would be rash to assume that Moscow has its intelligence networks operating in every country except the one it has repeatedly named as its chief enemy — the United States. Certainly the American Communist party has made no secret of its belief that the United States should always follow the Soviet lead. As recently as September, 1947, Political Affairs, the American Communist theological organ, made its usual references to the "fact" that "the policies of the Soviet Union before, during and since the anti-Axis war, have corresponded to the best interests of the American people."

In view of such repeated declarations, it becomes increasingly difficult to see how even Henry Wallace can continue saying, "The very few Communists I have met have been very good Americans." The presumption becomes overwhelming that the U.S.S.R., through the NKVD, its underground Communist cells and its front organizations, is commissioning agents to penetrate the "sensitive" branches of the Government, particularly the State Department, the Department of National Defense and the Atomic Energy Commission.

Let us then admit that a real danger exists. But the solution is surely not, on the one hand, to fire every one suspected of liberal leanings, nor, on the other, to fire only avowed and open Communists. The solution is rather to construct some means of ridding the security agencies of questionable characters, while at the same time retaining enough safeguards to insure against indiscriminate purges.

Discharge in advance of an overt act may seem a rough policy. Yet the failure to discharge suspicious persons may well imperil national security; it certainly would lead to the use of precautionary measures, such as wire-tapping and constant shadowing, which would bring the police state much nearer. Let us recall for a moment the situation in 1938. Obviously Nazis, their conscious fellow-travelers and soft-headed Americans who conceived Germany to be a much misunderstood nation

had no business in the State Department; and liberals were correct in demanding their dismissal in advance of overt acts. I cannot see why this same principle does not apply today to the fellow-travelers of a rival totalitarianism.

Have we, in fact, a witch-hunt today? We must first discriminate between the wishes of some members of Congress and the intentions of the Executive. The most shocking actions of the Administration —notably the President's executive order, the State Department's loyalty code and some of the recent firings— have doubtless been motivated in great part by a desire to head off more extreme action from Congress. Yet, this very process of appeasing the worst element in Congress has led to the compromise of principles which cannot be properly compromised in a democracy. Appeasement has produced throughout the Executive Branch an atmosphere of apprehension and anxiety that is fatal to boldness in government.

We may agree that this picture can be overdrawn—that Communist propaganda in this country is working overtime to paint Washington as a terror-ridden police state. Presumably on the basis of such overwrought stories, Harold Laski can write in The New Statesman and Nation, "America is in the grip of an hysterical witch-hunt that is as ugly in its character as it is fantastic in its proportions." we can only admire the effectiveness of the propaganda campaign. Indeed, one atrocity story went so far in claiming that all readers of liberal magazines would fall under suspicion that the rumor boomeranged in the shape of cancellations flowing into the magazine offices.

The New Republic then made haste to state editorially, as it had not bothered to do before, that the subscribers were unnecessarily agitated and were only victims of "the new war of nerves." Both the Civil Service Commission and the Federal Bureau of Investigation, the two agencies that probe the loyalty of Federal employes, flatly deny asking questions about the reading habits of government employes."

Yet the executive order and the State Department code are inexcusably defective. In particular, the recent action of the State Department

in denying most of those discharged both the right to a hearing and the right to resignation without prejudice betrays a state of mind going beyond the requirements of security and entering the realm of persecution. The department must be able to terminate employment on suspicion; this can be done in a number of ways; but the department cannot be allowed to stigmatize individuals and wreck lives on suspicion.

One may understand the travail of people trying to frame security regulations with the hot breath of Parnell Thomas and John Rankin on their necks; but the results go too far in waiving traditional procedural guarantees. The final result can only be to enthrone the narrow, bureaucratic conformist at the expense of the courageous and independent public servant— and at the ultimate expense of the belief in human dignity which purports to be the main objective of our foreign policy.

Still, honest civil libertarians might better devote themselves, not to blanket abuse of any attempts to meet the problem but to the construction of alternatives which would better secure individual rights while still permitting the Government to deal effectively with the grim dangers of foreign espionage. As Herbert Morrison once said, "It is easier to criticize Governments fighting this business of espionage than to be that Government that has to fight the espionage."

The first constructive step, perhaps, would be to make a clear distinction between the rights of an American citizen and the rights of a government employe in a security agency. The private political views of a Hollywood writer, for example, hardly seem to be the proper consideration of the United States Government or a committee of Congress. An American citizen clearly must be protected in his right to think and speak freely—as a Communist, a Fascist or whatever he wants; but no rule of the Constitution or of common sense requires the State Department to employ him.

Obviously the security agencies must be distinguished, not only from the citizenry at large, but from the rest of the Government. In doubtful cases the security agency rather than the individual must receive the benefit of the doubt —but it would be dangerous to

extend this principle, say, to the National Park Service. The kind of nonsense embodied in the Rees bill and similar congressional proposals involves a shocking infringement of civil liberties—and one which no consideration of national security can justify.

The second step would be to hedge round the process of dismissal from security agencies with much firmer procedural safeguards. At some point in the process full power to summon witnesses and to weigh evidence must be concentrated. That point plainly must be, not the investigative agency, but a government review board to which all persons dismissed on security grounds can appeal. That board must acquaint the accused with the charges and permit him the protection of counsel. It must be able to obtain from the FBI full data concerning the reliability of the evidence; the situation is intolerable where the administrator must act on the basis of statements from informants identified only by letters, numbers or FBI code-names.

The board must have the further power to interrogate these informants. The problem of permitting the accused to confront the informants, however, is not so simple as it sounds. Espionage breeds counter-espionage; and government counter-espionage agencies simply cannot unveil their agents at every demand of a defense attorney. Where the evidence by itself is substantial, the review board cannot be expected to require confrontation. But, where the evidence is tenuous, the board must have the power of confronting the accused with the accuser. If the FBI does not think the case important enough to risk blowing a counter-espionage chain, it must choose between the chain and the conviction.

Such a system imposes heavy responsibility upon the review board. It should be composed of men of the caliber of Learned Hand, Owen J. Roberts, Francis Biddle, Zechariah Chafee Jr.— men whose devotion to civil liberties is beyond cavil. Born in the conflict of principle between civil liberty and national security, it must realize that both principles are in its keeping. It must resolutely defend individuals against the pressure of Congress and the hysterical press, because surrender to that pressure will deprive the United States of the kind of people who gave it momentum in the past.

IT must strengthen administrators in the fight to prevent witch-hunting from spreading any further through the executive branches the black taint of fear which discourages independence and originality of thought. It must just as resolutely reject the curious modern doctrine that prosecution of Communists or fellow-travelers in any circumstances is a violation of civil liberties.

The press has an equal responsibility, for the final safeguard against injustice lies in the appeal to public opinion. The Washington Post, for example, has done a notable job in the nation's capital in guarding against the violation of civil liberties. In this connection it is interesting to note that, except for the courageous Miss Yuhas, none of the victims of the alleged reign of terror in the State Department has yet availed himself of the opportunities proferred to set forth his case in the press.

The situation imposes a special responsibility, too, I think, upon the American left. Liberals who complain when Parnell Thomas fails to distinguish between liberals and Communists should remember that too often they have failed to make that distinction themselves. History by now has surely documented that distinction to the point of surfeit; the attack on the free Socialist parties in the recent Belgrade manifesto is only the most recent example of the deadly Soviet hostility to the non-Communist left.

THE liberal movement in this country must reject the Communists as forthrightly as the British Labor party has rejected them; it must not

squander its energy and influence in covering up for them. This is the dictate of strategy as well as principle. Whatever conservatism may say about Wilson Wyatt or Leon Henderson and Americans for Democratic Action, or about such labor leaders as Walter Reuther and David Dubinsky, it cannot combat them by smearing them as fellow-travelers.

But the situation imposes just as grave a responsibility upon American conservatives. They must remember that the only criterion for disloyalty is superior loyalty to another country, and that reservations about the capitalist system or skepticism concerning the wisdom of the business community are by themselves no evidence at all of external loyalties. The essential fight in Europe today, for example, is between socialism and communism; and socialism has many supporters and sympathizers in this country who are resolutely anti-totalitarian. If the leadership of this country were to be confined to men endorsed by the business community, then the United States would be doomed once more to that morass of confusion and failure into which business rule has invariably plunged us through our history.

THERE is no easy answer to this conflict of principles between civil liberty and national security. The practical results thus must depend too much for comfort upon the restraint and wisdom of individuals. This responsibility becomes only one aspect of the great moral challenge which confronts us. If we cannot handle this conflict of principle soberly and responsibly, if we cannot rise to the world crisis, then we lack the qualities of greatness as a nation, and we can expect to pay the price of hysteria or of paralysis.

# FILM MEN ADMIT ACTIVITY BY REDS; HOLD IT IS FOILED

### Sam Wood Lists Writers by Name as Communists and Says Group Seeks Rule

### SOME CONTRACTS DROPPED

### Jack Warner Tells Congress Inquiry Ousted Workers Had Un-American Views

**By SAMUEL A. TOWER**
Special to THE NEW YORK TIMES.

WASHINGTON, Oct. 20—While they conceded the presence of a core of persons of "un-American" or reputed Communist leanings in the film industry, principally among screen writers, three Hollywood producers asserted today that Communist efforts to penetrate the movies had been checkmated in their productions and that the bulk of the industry was overwhelmingly patriotic.

The three producers, Louis B. Mayer, president of Metro-Goldwyn-Mayer; Jack Warner, vice president of Warner Brothers, and Sam Wood, an independent, were the first day's witnesses as the House Committee on Un-American Activities opened an inquiry into "alleged Communist influence and infiltration in the motion-picture industry."

In the course of the testimony, Mr. Wood, president of the Motion Picture Alliance for the Preservation of American Ideals, a recently-formed Hollywood organization, denounced a group of screen writers and directors specifically by name as unquestioned Communists, serving, in his view, as "agents of a foreign power." He maintained that "a tight disciplined group of Communist party members and party-liners" had been and still was endeavoring to gain control of the industry.

**Rejects Move for Quashing**

Mr. Warner, carefully shunning the term "Communist," testified that Warner Brothers had failed to renew the contracts of almost a dozen writers because they held what he considered "un-American" views.

Mr. Mayer acknowledged the presence of two or three reputed

Communists in his company, but stated that the reports were not proved, that nothing subversive had ever been contributed by them and that M-G-M, through examination and re-examination of its productions, had never put out any movies containing anything alien to American doctrines.

The committee refused to take up a motion to quash the subpoenas that it had issued against nineteen Hollywood figures, directing them to appear as witnesses.

The motion was brought before the committee by Robert W. Kenny, former Attorney General of California, and Bartley C. Crum, San Francisco attorney, acting in conjunction with four other lawyers in behalf of the group of nineteen, some of whom were subsequently named by the producers.

Representative J. Parnell Thomas, Republican, of New Jersey, the committee chairman, directed the two attorneys, who presented their motion as the hearings began, to make it next week, when their clients would be summoned to testify. In the meantime the committee took the brief under consideration.

**Wood Lists Several Names**

Mr. Wood, an independent producer and director of thirty years' experience in the industry, has made such films as "For Whom the Bell Tolls," "Saratoga Trunk," "Kitty Foyle" and "Ivy." He asserted that the Communists and their sympathizers, although "a small proportion," were constantly seeking to gain control of segments of the industry and to spread their influence either by pro-Communist contributions or by touches inimical to the United States.

Speaking as a member of the Screen Directors Guild, he charged John Cromwell, Irving Pichel, Edward Dymtryk, Frank Tuttle and another whose name he could not recall with trying to "steer us into the red river."

Under questioning as to the activities of screen writers, he alleged that Dalton Trumbo, Donald Ogden Stewart and John Howard Lawson held Communist leanings.

"Is there any question in your mind that Lawson is a Communist?" he was asked.

"If there is I haven't any mind," he replied.

While wholeheartedly in favor of uprooting "the conspiratorial group" seeking to subvert the screen, Mr. Wood warned of the danger of censorship in such efforts, along with the danger of violation of freedom of expression.

"Those people are so well organized that they would go to town and put their people in control of the censorship," he said.

November 2, 1947

In response to a question about financial contributions to the Communist cause in Hollywood, Mr. Wood stated that "substantial" contributions were made, calling attention to a recent rally at which Katharine Hepburn, the actress, appeared and $87,000 was raised. This money "didn't go to the Boy Scouts," he added.

Mr. Warner, emphasizing that anything subversive was culled from his studio's productions, admitted that there had been some infiltration into the movie capital of individuals whose outlook he regarded as "un-American."

Despite repeated questions by Robert E. Stripling, the committee's chief investigator, he steadfastly avoided the term Communist, submitting that he had encountered, principally among his writers, those seeking to incorporate into film productions ideas that he regarded as "un-American."

The producer's testimony of last Spring, taken in Hollywood by a subcommittee under Chairman Thomas, was read. In this Mr. Warner stated that he had failed to take up the contracts, because of lack of sympathy with their views, of Irwin Shaw, Clifford Odets, Alvah Bessie, Gordon Kahn, Guy Endore, Howard Koch, Ring Lardner Jr., Robert Rosson, Emmett Lavery, Albert Maltz, Sheridan Gibney, Julius and Philip Epstein, John Wexley, Dalton Trumbo and John Howard Lawson.

In his testimony today Mr. Warner declared that he had reconsidered and that he felt, in retrospect, that the names of Messrs. Endore, Gibney and J. and P. Epstein should be deleted from the list.

He stood by his previous testimony that 95 per cent of those holding "un-American" views were writers. He reiterated that he had never seen a Communist, to his knowledge, and explained that his attitude toward the writers was based on what he regarded as "slanted" lines and writing that "I consider un-American doctrine."

Mr. Mayer told the committee that the Communists were unable to get "a single thing" in M-G-M productions because they were checked and rechecked by himself, his readers, his editors and his producers.

Asked if there were any Communist writers in his studio, he testified that he had heard three mentioned in this category, Dalton Trumbo, Donald Ogden Stewart and Lester Cole, but that he had never seen any Communist propaganda in their work.

Mr. Mayer observed that M-G-M counsel had informed him that the studio, if it attempted to discharge an employe for communism, would have to prove it or be liable for damage suits. In response to questions he said that he would not employ anyone holding a dues card from the Communist party.

Along with Mr. Warner and Mr. Wood, Mr. Mayer favored action to make the Communist party an illegal organization.

The M-G-M head then read a spirited statement defending his studio and the industry and particularly the production of the film, "Song of Russia," which committee representatives described as containing Communist propaganda.

"Like others in the motion picture industry," he declared, "I have maintained a relentless vigilance against un-American influences. If, as has been alleged, Communists have attempted to use the screen for subversive purposes, I am proud of our success in circumventing them.

"The motion picture industry employs many thousands of people. As is the case with the newspaper, radio, publishing and theater business, we cannot be responsible for the political views of each individual employe. It is, however, our complete responsibility to determine what appears on the motion picture screen.

"The Communists attack our screen as an instrument of capitalism. Few, if any, of our films, ever reach Russia. It hates us because it fears us. We show too much of the American way of life, of human dignity, of the opportunity and the happiness to be enjoyed in a democracy.

"More than any other country in the world, we have enjoyed the fullest freedom of speech in all means of communication. It is this freedom that has enabled the motion picture to carry the message to the world of our democratic way of life."

While acknowledging that the criticized movie, "Song of Russia," was friendly to Russia, Mr. Mayer emphasized that it was produced in an effort to aid the war, at a time when the Russian situation at Stalingrad was desperate and our national leaders were pleading for all-out support for our wartime ally.

Differing with the star of the movie, Robert Taylor, who has testified before the subcommittee that the picture was "Communist propaganda," Mr. Mayer contended that the final script of the film was little more than a musical boy-and-girl romance featuring a Russian setting and the music of Tchaikovsky.

Because the script of the movie was changed to eliminate references to Soviet farm collectivism— "I don't preach any ideology except Americanism and I don't even preach that. I let it speak for itself"—Mr. Mayer explained that the late Frank Knox, then Secretary of the Navy, had put off Mr. Taylor's enlistment in the Navy to allow him to complete the delayed film.

Reminding the committee of a number of films produced by M-G-M to support the war effort, including "Mrs. Miniver," which "was rushed into release at the urgent request of the United States officials to meet the rising tide of anti-English feeling that followed the fall of Tobruk," Mr. Mayer recalled further:

"The United States Army Signal Corps made 'The Battle of Stalingrad,' released in 1943, with a prologue expressing high tribute from President Roosevelt, our Secretaries of State, War and Navy, and from Generals Marshall and MacArthur."

After Mr. Mayer had read reviews of "Song of Russia" from THE NEW YORK TIMES, The New York Herald Tribune, The Washington Post and other newspapers, describing the film as a harmless musical film containing more things American than Russian, the committee's chief investigator summoned Ayn Rand, Russian-born novelist and author of a recent best-seller, "The Fountainhead," to the stand.

The novelist, who testified that she had left Russia in 1926 and was under contract to write film productions, denounced "Song of Russia" as a vehicle of Communist propaganda full of distortions and inaccuracies and an outright falsification of Russian life as she knew it.

Mr. Warner asserted that "there is not a Warner Brothers picture that can fairly be judged to be hostile to our country, or communistic in tone or purpose," and cited many movies produced by that studio furthering the American way of life and ideals. He similarly rejected committee allegations that the studio's production of "Mission to Moscow" contained Communist propaganda.

It followed faithfully the book written by Joseph E. Davies, former Ambassador to Russia, he stated when challenged as to its accuracy, and added that it was designed to further our war effort by encouraging Russia at a time when it was feared the Soviet Union might withdraw from the war.

Mr. Thomas, opening the hearings, read a statement asserting that "there is no question that there are Communists in Hollywood" and said his committee was trying to determine the "extent" of penetration.

October 21, 1947

# PLAYWRIGHT SAYS, 'GO EAST, YOUNG MAN'

### By IRWIN SHAW

*(Playwright, author and critic who was called "un-American" in testimony before the House Un-American Activities Committee.)*

BEING a writer these days is a complicated business. You are liable to wake up one morning and see by the headlines that Jack Warner has proclaimed to a Congressional committee that you are "un-American" and that he has fired you for trying to inject "un-American doctrines" into the work you did for his studio. You read further and learn that Mr. Warner has declared that un-American writers are those who propagandize for the overthrow of the Government of the United States by force. Mr. Warner is asked to prove nothing and he leaves in a bright burst of publicity, with the blessing of the committee.

You wait for the committee to call you to answer these charges. But nothing happens. New names are plastered across the headlines and when you make a statement to the press categorically calling Mr. Warner's accusations false, your denial never seems to reach the same number of people who read the original charge in the headlines. Then you begin to see that men are being accused, tried and condemned these days in a manner that is beyond the reach of any normal procedure of law, and you begin to wonder about the other nuggets of information the committee has unearthed.

I have some nuggets of my own, all of them documented by communications between the Warner Brothers Studio and my agents. The first is that Warner Brothers never fired me. I wrote one script for them, in 1941, which the studio did so badly I felt forced to take my name from it. Mr. Warner liked this script so much that he offered me a contract for three more pictures, at almost twice the money (the contract is in my possession) and an official of the studio complained that Mr. Warner was very indignant with me for refusing to sign the contract. (I went into the Army instead, and perhaps Mr. Warner feels that dodging German shells in France in preference to writing for Adolphe Menjou represents a dangerous un-American attitude.)

Last April a leading producer of Warner Brothers, who knows my work and my politics, asked me to do an anti-Communist picture for that studio. I turned this down to work on a novel which I am still engaged on.

Just two weeks ago, three days before Mr. Warner defamed me in Washington, his studio, through my agent, called me from Hollywood to ask me to do a scenario of Gogol's "The Inspector General" for them.

Aside from the fact that Mr. Warner was never asked to produce the one script which I had done for him and point out the "un-American" doctrine in it, these other facts seem to add up to an irresponsibility that might just as well do damage to any other American citizen, picked at random, whose name happened to cross Mr. Warner's mind while he was on the witness stand.

It is an example of the sick temper of our times that I feel forced to announce that I have never for a moment entertained the notion of overthrowing the Government of the United States; that I am not "un-American," which apparently is Mr. Warner's way of saying "Communist." I am not and have never been a Communist, and have fought the Communists in the American Veterans Committee and have been elected on the so-called anti-left wing slate to the council of the Authors League of America. I re-gret to say that I have found the endless bickering of the Screen Writers Guild so boring that I have given up attending meetings.

As a citizen unjustly denounced in his nation's capital, I must say that I am alarmed by the committee's procedure. But as a worker in the theatre, I feel all this may do us a world of good.

### Silver Lining

From the point of view of the theatre, there is reason for exhilaration in the denunciation of a batch of movie writers by the Thomas committee. The committee has kindly singled out the best of the Western crop to excoriate and it is possible that these writers may be so disgusted by the shabby manner in which their employers, for whom they have earned so many millions of dollars, have cowardly thrown them to the Congressional wolves, that they may turn their backs on Hollywood and devote their considerable talents once more to the theatre, to the theatre's enduring profit.

As for myself (and I am ruefully aware of the doubts in the minds of my critics as to my value to the craft of Shakespeare and Euripides)—I hope to collect such a large penalty from Mr. Warner for the surprising things he said about me that I shall be able to sit back and write, at my well-upholstered leisure, another dozen plays, one of which, at least, may be worth the necessary dogged effort of such prolonged creation. It is true that I wrote only one scenario in the last five years (story conferences would have been difficult for a Pfc in Africa and Normandy), but that took six months out of my life and who knows what sudden fire of inspiration might have swept through me if I had spent that time writing for Cornell rather than Blondell?

The theatre has a great deal to offer to the embattled artists whom the timid giant of the Pacific has permitted to be cited for contempt of Congress. Their politics will be judged and criticized here, but only the politics in their work, not the politics of the organizations to which they belong. They will be damned if their third act falls flat, but not for the fact that in 1937 they gave $10 to an organization which was setting up a blood bank for Loyalist soldiers who were wounded fighting Italian troops outside Madrid. They may fail to get their work produced here, but not because in 1938 they aided a writer of incidental music to escape the gas ovens of Dachau. Their plays may be damned and they may starve to death on Broadway, but not because in 1942 they joined Gen. George Marshall, Franklin Roosevelt and Winston Churchill in praising the Russians.

### Broadway Treatment

From time to time they will be harshly criticized, and from all points of the compass (a lady on the Nation, for example, contemptuously lumped John Hersey and me together as slick defenders of the Luce notion of the bourgeois American century, and I no longer have the courage to read the bitter strictures on my work in the New Masses), but as each script comes along producers will read it on its own merits, coldly asking themselves, "Will it make a dollar?"

There are many things wrong with our theatre, but it has the rough American honesty of an institution in which ideas are legal tender. So I say "Come back, children, come back to Broadway. Leave Vine Street, leave the movie scenarios in which the bankers must all be sweet and the poor must all be happy, to Lela Rogers. Leave the real movie making to the French, the Italians and the British, who have demonstrated they have the courage to present life as it is, and not as a political committee thinks it ought to be. Leave Hollywood now, because the masters of Hollywood have defended you poorly and too late. Leave in disgust today and you will return in triumph tomorrow, because the movie producers will look at their dwindling bank balances and cry, out of the tragic depths of their pocketbooks, 'We need you. Make your own terms!'"

November 2, 1947

---

# Ten Film Men Cited for Contempt In Overwhelming Votes by House

### By JAY WALZ
#### Special to THE NEW YORK TIMES.

WASHINGTON, Nov. 24—The House approved overwhelmingly today citations for contempt of Congress against ten Hollywood personalities who refused last month to tell the Committee on Un-American Activities whether they were members of the Communist party.

The first of the cases, against Albert Maltz, a writer credited with "Destination Tokyo," resulted in a vote of 346 to 17 for the citation, thus turning the case over to the United States Attorney for prosecution. One Republican and the sole American Labor member of the House voted with fifteen Democrats in opposition.

The second case, that of Dalton Trumbo, another motion-picture writer, was decided in a standing vote of 240 to 15. The remaining eight cases were handled in rapid-fire order without debate and by voice vote. These concerned Samuel Ornitz, John Howard Lawson, Ring Lardner Jr., Lester Cole and Alvah Bessie, writers; Herbert Biberman, a director-producer; Edward Dmytryk, director, and Robert Adrian Scott, a writer and producer.

Attorney General Tom C. Clark said tonight that he had asked the United States District Attorney, Morris Fay, to prosecute the ten witnesses accused of contempt, adding that "the authority of the Congress must be maintained."

A court conviction of contempt of Congress carries a maximum punishment of one year in jail and a $1,000 fine.

Chairman J. Parnell Thomas of the House committee brought in the unanimous recommendation of the Un-American Activities group that the ten "hostile" witnesses be cited, and told House members that the men had utterly defied the committee in its effort to delve into subversive activities in this country.

Each of the cases was introduced with the presentation by Mr. Thomas of a formal report of the witness' appearance before the committee. These reports, as presented to the House, contained quotations from their testimony showing that none had answered directly the question: "Are you now, or have you ever been, a member of the Communist party?"

Some had also declined to state, on constitutional grounds, whether they belonged to the Screen Writers Guild.

When the witnesses declined direct answers to these questions, they were excused from the witness stand without further testimony. Most of the witnesses, described by the committee as "hostile" or "unfriendly," had come with prepared statements, which Chairman Thomas refused to let them present.

Leading off the debate on Mr. Maltz's case, Mr. Thomas promised that his committee had staged "only the beginning" of a drive against Communists in the motion-picture industry. He said it was "ridiculous" for the ten witnesses and their supporters to think that the committee had no right to inquire into their political affiliations.

"The Constitution was never intended to cloak or shield those who would destroy it," he said. He added that the Communist party was in no sense a political party, but "a conspiracy to overthrow the Government of the United States."

"We have been called to Washington to sit in special session to appropriate billions of dollars to stop the floodtide of communism from sweeping all of Europe," Mr. Thomas continued. "What a paradox if that same Congress cannot inquire into the activities of a

Communist conspirator in the United States, whose first allegiance is to a foreign government."

Mr. Thomas and fellow committee members insisted throughout the afternoon that the contempt citations were based on the refusal of the witnesses "to answer the most pertinent question that we could ask."

The committee chairman declared, however, that the ten witnesses had not been picked at random, but were subpoenaed "because our investigation had disclosed that they were Communists or had long records of Communist affiliation and activities."

Opponents of the citations contended vigorously that Mr. Thomas' committee had conducted its inquiry illegally by violating the constitutional rights of free speech and thought.

Representative Herman Eberharter, Democrat, of Pennsylvania, who was first to speak against the citations, said the House had the choice of supporting either the Thomas committee, or free speech.

"We cannot do both," he said.

The Pennsylvanian added that he felt the committee was trying not to destroy a subversive threat, but to control the motion-picture industry. If Congressional committees were to try men, they should do it "in the American tradition," he said, holding that the men facing citation had not received rights from the committee which they would have received in a trial court.

Representative Chet Holifield, Democrat, of California, who also voted against the citations, said the House, in upholding the Un-American Activities Committee, was "treading on dangerous grounds," and was stepping into a 'quicksand which will engulf our liberties."

Representative Vito Marcantonio, American Laborite of New York, attacked the Thomas committee's procedure as unconstitutional.

Representative Helen Gahagan Douglas, Democrat, of California, announced that she was introducing a bill to modify drastically committee procedures "to adequately safeguard individual rights."

Committee supporters, however, contended that committee procedures in the recent hearings had been both constitutional and fair.

Representative Richard B. Vail, Illinois Republican, said each of the ten witnesses had conducted himself "in full accord with standard Communist practice long established."

Representative Claude I. Bakewell of St. Louis was the only Republican who voted against citing Mr. Maltz.

The fifteen Democrats were Representatives Eberharter, Holifield and Douglas, Emanuel Celler of New York, Arthur G. Klein of New York, John A. Blatnik of Minnesota, Sol Bloom of New York, John A. Carroll of Colorado, F. R. Havenner of California, Walter B. Huber of Ohio, Frank M. Karsten of Missouri, Thomas E. Morgan of Pennsylvania, Joseph L. Pfeifer of New York, Adam C. Powell Jr. of New York and George G. Sadowski of Michigan.

On the only roll call vote taken, 209 Republicans and 137 Democrats favored citing Mr. Maltz for contempt.

### Accused Group Makes Reply

HOLLYWOOD, Calif., Nov. 24 (P)—The ten screen personalities cited by the House issued a joint statement expressing the opinion that "the Thomas-Rankin committee succeeded today in having the Congress cite the Bill of Rights for contempt."

"Nevertheless," the statement added, "the people and the press of the country have expressed almost unparalleled opposition to this committee, which pretends to defend America by calling the Ku Klux Klan an acceptable organization. This opposition will ultimately determine this issue.

"The next test is in the office of the Attorney General. Since there is no expectation that the Supreme Court will uphold the Thomas committee, it is hoped that the Attorney General will stand with the Constitution and will refuse to permit the citation to proceed to the courts.

"We are gratified that seventeen members of Congress were not stampeded by the irresponsible lies and charges with which Thomas and Rankin attempted to justify these citations.

"The assertion that a Congressional committee can act as prosecutor, judge and jury, and thus destroy a citizen's character and livelihood, threatens every teacher, writer, publisher, scientist, and every church and trade union member in America.

"We are confident that these seventeen votes in Congress reflect the increasing determination of the American people to abolish this corrupt committee. The United States can keep its constitutional liberties or it can keep the Thomas committee. It can't keep both."

# Movies to Oust Ten Cited For Contempt of Congress

## Major Companies Also Vote to Refuse Jobs to Communists—'Hysteria, Surrender of Freedom' Charged by Defense Counsel

The motion picture industry, in an action unprecedented in American industrial fields, voted unanimously yesterday to refuse employment to Communists and to 'discharge or suspend without compensation" the ten Hollywood figures who have been cited for contempt of Congress.

This step was taken at the end of a two-day meeting of fifty leaders in the industry at the Waldorf-Astoria Hotel. Virtually the entire industry was represented, including the major studios and the independents, through the Motion Picture Association of America, the Association of Motion Picture Producers and the Society of Independent Motion Picture Producers.

In a statement issued by Eric Johnston, president of the first two of these groups, and Donald M. Nelson, president of the independents, it was declared that the new policy was "not going to be swayed by hysteria or intimidation." It promised that an atmosphere of fear in Hollywood would not be created and innocent persons would be protected.

The groups also called on Congress to enact legislation to help all American industry "rid itself of subversive, disloyal elements." They declared that Hollywood has produced nothing "subversive or un-American" and defended the work and loyalty of the industry during war and peace.

The film executives' action brought immediate protests from the chief counsel of the ten men in Washington, from the men themselves in Hollywood and from liberal groups. Mr. Johnston's statement was denounced as "hysteria" and a proof that the film industry has been "stampeded into surrendering" its freedom.

Yesterday's decision here followed similar steps taken by separate companies in the film industry. Last Thursday Twentieth Century-Fox decided to dispense with the services of acknowledged Communists or of any employes who refused before any Congressional committee to answer questions as to whether they were Communists. Two weeks ago RKO-Radio Pictures announced it would not employ "known Communists."

### Text of Statement

The text of yesterday's statement follows:

"Members of the Association of Motion Picture Producers deplore the action of the ten Hollywood men who have been cited for contempt of the House of Representatives. We do not desire to prejudge their legal rights, but their actions have been a disservice to their employers and have impaired their usefulness to the industry.

"We will forthwith discharge or suspend without compensation those in our employ, and we will not re-employ any of the ten until such time as he is acquitted or has purged himself of contempt and declares under oath that he is not a Communist.

"On the broader issue of alleged subversive and disloyal elements in Hollywood, our members are likewise prepared to take positive action. We will not knowingly employ a Communist or a member of any party or group which advocates the overthrow of the Government of the United States by force or by any illegal or unconstitutional methods.

"In pursuing this policy, we are not going to be swayed by hysteria or intimidation from any source. We are frank to recognize that such a policy involves dangers and risks. There is the danger of hurting innocent people. There is the risk of creating an atmosphere of fear. Creative work at its best cannot be carried on in an atmosphere of fear. We will guard against this danger, this risk, this fear.

"To this end we will invite the Hollywood talent guilds to work with us to eliminate any subversives; to protect the innocent; and to safeguard free speech and a free screen wherever threatened.

### Help of Congress Asked

"The absence of a national policy, established by Congress with respect to the employment of Communists in private industry, makes our task difficult. Ours is a nation of laws. We request Congress to enact legislation to assist American industry to rid itself of subversive, disloyal elements.

"Nothing subversive or un-American has appeared on the screen. Nor can any number of Hollywood investigations obscure the patriotic services of the 30,000 loyal Americans employed in Hollywood who have given our Government invaluable aid in war and peace."

Mr. Johnston was reluctant to amplify the statement, saying, "It speaks for itself, it's very clear." When asked whether the phrase,

163

"We will not knowingly employ a Communist," referred to both present and future employes, he declared:

"That phrase is perfectly clear. 'Not employ' means you are not going to have some one in your employment. I assume that's what the language means."

Asked about the distinction between discharging and suspending without pay the ten cited for contempt, Mr. Johnston said:

"That is a legal matter, having to do with the statutes of the State of California. I believe that our purpose is to suspend, not to discharge."

One of the Hollywood executives attending the meeting was Dore Schary, vice president in charge of production for RKO, who had told the House Committee on Un-American Activities during the Hollywood investigation that he would not discharge an employe because he was a Communist.

"The decision was unanimous," Mr. Schary said after yesterday's meeting. "What I told the Un-American Activities Committee was my own personal view. However, I also stated that the ultimate policy would have to be made by the president of RKO. That policy has now been established. As an employe of the company, I will abide by the decision."

Others attending the meeting were former Secretary of State James F. Byrnes and Paul V. McNutt, among the industry's counsel; Nicholas M. Schenck, president of Loew's, Inc.; Barney Balaban, president of Paramount Pictures; J. Cheever Cowdin, chairman of the board of Universal Pictures; Jack Cohn, vice president of Columbia Pictures; Spyros Skouras, president of Twentieth Century-Fox; Nate Blumberg, president of Universal; Harry Cohn, president of Columbia; Ned Depinet, executive vice president of RKO; Samuel Goldwyn and Walter Wanger, independent producers, and many others important in the industry.

The ten men cited for contempt were Albert Maltz, Dalton Trumbo, Samuel Ornitz, John Howard Lawson, Ring Lardner Jr., Lester Cole and Alvah Bessie, all writers; Herbert Biberman, a director-producer; Edward Dmytryk, a director, and Robert Adrian Scott, a writer and producer.

Their chief counsel, Robert W. Kenny, said yesterday in Washington that the announcement, along with the statement by Chairman J. Parnell Thomas of the Un-American Activities Committee that he would publish a list of films con-

## AFTER VOTING TO REFUSE EMPLOYMENT TO COMMUNISTS

The New York Times

Leaders of the motion picture industry at the Waldorf-Astoria Hotel yesterday. Left to right, front: Gradwell G. Sears, president of United Artists; Barney Balaban, president of Paramount; Eric Johnston, president of the Motion Picture Association of America; Nicholas M. Schenck, president of Loew's, and Jack Cohn, vice president of Columbia. Left to right, rear: Ned Depinet, executive vice president of RKO; Nate Blumberg, president of Universal, and Sam Schneider, vice president of Warner Brothers.

taining Communist propaganda, "proves that any appeasement by the motion-picture industry is only an invitation to further attack."

**Sees Censorship Achieved**

"To surrender to the demand for discrimination against individuals means that the real objective of the committee — censorship — has been attained," Mr. Kenny declared.

"The ten witnesses who upheld the proposition that the Thomas committee had no right to invade the realm of ideas, whether manifested by speech, writing or association are truly the defenders of a free screen—not Mr. Johnston and his associates. Despite the producers' willingness to abandon them at this time, only by the defense these men are presenting can a free and prosperous film industry be maintained. The Thomas committee does not respect the Bill of Rights, but the Producers Association goes one step further and apparently takes the position that a man is guilty until he is proven innocent.

"I am confident the courts will rule in our favor. The Constitution is the same document that it always was despite the present hysteria."

Mr. Thomas, according to The

Associated Press, called the executives' action "a constructive step and a body blow to the Communists." He added that, while the committee would help the film industry in every way to oust the Communists, "our hearings and exposures will continue."

Another protest came here from Dr. Harlow Shapley of Harvard University, chairman of the Arts, Sciences and Professions Council of the Progressive Citizens of America. He telegraphed to Mr. Johnston that "to yield to hysteria by establishing blacklists and purges would be a betrayal of the trust of the American people."

November 26, 1947

# 90 GROUPS, SCHOOLS NAMED ON U. S. LIST AS BEING DISLOYAL

## Clark Cites Communist Party, 'Totalitarians, Fascists' to Guide Federal Agencies

### 3 NEW YORK SCHOOLS HIT

#### These Are Among 11 Classed as Adjuncts of Soviet—Klan and Film Body Accused

**By LEWIS WOOD**
Special to THE NEW YORK TIMES.

WASHINGTON, Dec. 4—A list of about ninety organizations of questioned loyalty to the United States, prepared under direction of Attorney General Tom C. Clark, was made public tonight by the special board now examining the loyalty of Federal Government employes.

The groups were designated by the Attorney General as "totalitarian, fascist, Communist, or subversive." In preparing the long calendar, Mr. Clark followed the Executive Order of President Truman, who set up the loyalty board some weeks ago.

Out of the long list, thirty-three associations were, with few exceptions, named for the first time, in addition to eleven schools which the Attorney General designated as adjuncts of the Communist party.

Included in the thirty-three groups were organizations such as the Communist party and its divisions; the Ku Klux Klan; Hollywood Writers Mobilization for Defense; Veterans of the Abraham Lincoln Brigade, and the National Council of American-Soviet Friendship.

Three of the schools which Mr. Clark held to be communistic are in New York City: George Washington Carver School, Jefferson School of Social Science, School of Jewish Studies.

The list compiled by Attorney General Clark is now being circulated by Seth W. Richardson, chairman of the loyalty board, to the heads of various Government departments and agencies, so it can be ascertained whether any Government employes are members of the organizations.

However, the mere fact of membership will not be proof of disloyalty. Quoting President Truman on this point, Mr. Richardson said his board agreed with the President that membership was simply one piece of evidence which might or might not be helpful in reaching a conclusion on a particular case. And Mr. Clark strongly stated:

"Guilt by association has never been one of the principles of our American jurisprudence. We must be satisfied that reasonable grounds exist for concluding that an individual is disloyal. That must be the guide."

Attorney General Clark told Mr. Richardson that the list was drawn up as the result of FBI investigation, the recommendations of Department of Justice officials, and "my subsequent study of the recommendations of all."

The Attorney General said also that the list did not represent a complete or final docket.

"For example," he wrote, "a number of small and local organizations are not listed. As to many organizations not named, the presently available information is insufficient to warrant a final determination as to their character.

"Others, presently innocuous, may become the victims of dangerous infiltrating forces and, as a consequence, become proper subjects for designation. New organizations may come into existence whose purposes and activities are in conflict with loyalty to the United States."

#### Further Lists May Come

Further lists would be submitted if investigation warranted such action, he stated.

The loyalty board was set up by an executive order of President Truman, also requiring the Department of Justice to supply the board with:

"The name of each foreign or domestic organization, association, movement, group or combination of persons which the Attorney General, after appropriate investigation and determination, designates as totalitarian, fascist, communist, or subversive, or as having adopted a policy of advocating or approving the commission of acts of force or violence to deny others their rights under the Constitution of the United States, or as seeking to alter the form of government of the United States by unconstitutional means."

Opening witnesses appeared today before the District of Columbia grand jury now investigating the cases of the ten Hollywood writers and executives who refused to tell the House Un-American Activities Committee whether they were members of the Communist party.

## Doctrine of Violence Laid to Reds In U. S. by Thomas Group's Report

**By JOHN D. MORRIS**
Special to THE NEW YORK TIMES.

WASHINGTON, May 11—The House Committee on Un-American Activities presented today what it called documentary proof that the Communist party of the United States and its leaders advocated the Government's overthrow by force and violence.

In a unanimously-approved, 160-page report, the committee concluded that the threat to national security of "the continued, almost unrestricted operation of such a movement within our own borders should be obvious to everyone."

It called on the Administration for "vigorous enforcement" of existing laws to curb communist activities, "without further delay."

"To hesitate any longer will be to sacrifice our national security," the committee asserted.

Chairman J. Parnell Thomas said the report, together with a similar one issued last year to prove that the Communist party of the United States was an agent of a foreign power, showed conclusively that Communists in this country were resorting to subversive activity to accomplish their purposes.

He said the two reports provided the most effective argument possible for passage of the Mundt-Nixon bill to curb communistic activities, which the House is due to take up Thursday.

The Congress of Industrial Organizations meanwhile called for defeat of the measure on the ground that it "seriously threatens the existence of bona-fide labor unions and because it sweeps aside civil rights guaranteed to every American by the Constitution."

In today's report, the House committee quoted extensively from Marx, Engels, Lenin and Stalin to show the doctrine of forceful and violent overthrow of anti-Communist governments to be a "basic premise" of their teachings.

To prove that these teachings constituted "the credo of the Communist party, U. S. A., the committee presented similar documentary evidence in the form of excerpts from party publications and statements of Communist leaders in this country.

"The chairman of the American Communist party, William Z. Foster, is on public record as endorsing such revolutionary tactics despite his recent disavowals," the report held.

The committee also said the United States Communist party had supported and defended, without a single deviation, "the ruthless measures of foreign Communist parties to overthrow their legally constituted governments by force and violence."

"In other words," it stated, "what the Chinese or Greek Communists are doing today is what the American Communists plan to do tomorrow under similar circumstances."

The committe accused the Communists of deliberately promoting confusion regarding their belief in the violent overthrow of the United States Government "in order to lull the American people into a false sense of security and to avoid prosecution under the law."

It pointed out that two laws now on the statute books provide fines and jail penalties for persons advocating the violent overthrow of the Government and require the registration of foreign-controlled organizations having such aims.

"A vigorous enforcement of both laws, based on the true character of the Communist party, should be instituted by the executive branch of the Government without further delay," the committee said.

December 5, 1947

May 12, 1948

# RED 'UNDERGROUND' IN FEDERAL POSTS ALLEGED BY EDITOR

## IN NEW DEAL ERA

### Ex-Communist Names Alger Hiss, Then in State Department

**WALLACE AIDES ON LIST**

### Chambers Also Includes Former Treasury Official, White— Tells of Fears for His Life

**By C. P. TRUSSELL**

Special to THE NEW YORK TIMES.

WASHINGTON, Aug. 3 — An "underground" Communist organization, led by men at key posts of government and operating to infiltrate the whole establishment with its party members, was described to the House Committee on Un-American Activities today by an admitted former Communist, Whittaker Chambers, who said he served as a courier for the group.

Mr. Chambers, now a senior editor of Time magazine, swore that this organization, which he viewed as a forerunner of the Soviet spy rings testimony of which has shaken Washington recently, had these leaders:

Alger Hiss, former director of special political affairs in the State Department, executive secretary of the Dumbarton Oaks conversations and secretary general of the San Francisco Conference at which the United Nations charter was written. Mr. Hiss accompanied President Franklin D. Roosevelt to Malta and the Yalta conference in 1945 and the following year was a principal adviser to the American delegation at the first session of the United Nations General Assembly at London. He is now president of the Carnegie Endowment for International Peace, in New York.

Donald Hiss, a younger brother of Alger Hiss, who held posts in the State and Agriculture Departments.

#### Former NLRB Secretary Named

Nathan Witt, former general secretary of the National Labor Relations Board, who resigned in 1941 after eight years of service. He is now practicing law in New York.

Lee Pressman, who held posts as assistant general counsel in the Agricultural Adjustment Administration under appointment by former Secretary Henry A. Wallace; general counsel for the Works Progress Administration by appointment of the late Harry L. Hopkins, and general counsel of the Resettlement Administration under Rexford G. Tugwell. Later Mr. Pressman was general counsel for the Congress of Industrial Organizations and the CIO's Steelworkers' Organizing Committee. He is now associated with Mr. Wallace's Progressive party.

John J. Abt, who from 1933 to 1935 was chief of litigation for the AAA, an assistant general counsel for the WPA in 1935, chief counsel for the Senate (La Follette) Civil Liberties Investigating Committee in 1936 and 1937 and special assistant to the Attorney General in 1937 and 1938. Mr. Abt was accused last Saturday by Miss Elizabeth T. Bentley, confessed courier for the alleged Soviet spy ring, as being a member of the "Perlo group" of that organization.

#### War Production Board Aide

Victor Perlo, formerly with the War Production Board, the alleged head of one of several espionage groups about which Miss Bentley testified.

Charles Kramer, also described as Charles Kravitzky, who was identified as counsel to special Senate labor problems committees under the chairmanships of Senators Claude Pepper of Florida and Harley M. Kilgore of West Virginia. Mr. Kramer was said by committee attachés to be now associated with the Progressive party.

Henry Collins, formerly in the Agriculture Department, at whose apartment the meetings of the organization described by Mr. Chambers were said to have been held.

Meanwhile William W. Remington, formerly with the War Production Board and now in the Department of Commerce, told a Sen-

ate committee that he had never given confidential information to Miss Bentley, whose revelations inspired the current Congressional inquiries.

Testimony that he had knowledge of some aspects of the atomic bomb project brought from the witness a statement that he "did not give it to Miss Bentley or mention it to a single soul." He asserted that what he knew was "nothing very much."

As Mr. Chambers testified before the House group, dramatically at first as he told of risks in quitting Communist affiliation and discipline, and later with great calm, the name of Harry Dexter White, former Assistant Secretary of the Treasury, was brought into his story. Mr. White was named by Miss Bentley as one of those who had supplied "information" to the espionage organization. She explained that she never had received information from him direct. The former assistant secretary, in informal rebuttal, has described her testimony concerning him as "fantastic" and "shocking."

Today, Mr. Chambers described him as a willing and cooperative "fellow traveler" with the group of which he testified and, as it was asked whether Mr. White was a Communist party member, added:

"I cannot say whether he was a member. But he certainly was a fellow traveler so far within the fold that his not being a party member would have been a mistake on both sides."

"But," interposed Representative F. Edward Hebert, Democrat, of Louisiana, "Mr. White has called the charges against him 'fantastic' and 'shocking.'"

"After my testimony," Mr. Chambers responded, "he will have to find some more adjectives."

#### Once Feared for His Life

Mr. Chambers, a quiet, heavy-set man who spoke so softly that at times committee members requested him to repeat what he had said, explained that his was an old story, although it had not come into the open before. He joined the Communist party in 1924, he said, and in 1937 "repudiated Marx's doctrines and Lenin's tactics." For a year, he added, he lived in fear of personal harm being done him. He slept during the day, hidden out, and at night stayed awake with a gun handy. He had told his story "to the Government," Mr. Chambers continued, and had "sound reason for supposing that the Communists might try to kill me."

Although he had given his story to the State Department "almost exactly nine years ago"—two days after Hitler and Stalin signed their pact—nothing had been done about it, Mr. Chambers said.

To get the story to the Government, he added, he went to the White House. Through Isaac Don Levine, editor of Plain Talk, he said, the late Marvin McIntyre, then a secretary to President Roosevelt, was told that he was willing to talk. Mr. McIntyre, the witness testified, referred him to A. A. Berle, then Assistant Secretary of State. Mr. Berle is now the head of the Liberal party of New York, which was formed in

1944 when the American Labor party was taken over by the Left Wing.

"When I told Mr. Berle my story," Mr. Chambers said to the committee, "he indicated great excitement. He said, 'we absolutely must have a clear Government service, as we are faced with a possibility of war.'

"I was surprised, a long time afterward, when I checked up, that nothing had been done about it.

"I went to Washington and reported to the authorities that I knew about the infiltration of the United States Government by Communists. For years international communism, of which the United States Communist party is an integral part, had been in a state of undeclared war with this republic.

"I regarded my action in going to the Government as a simple act of war, like the shooting of an armed enemy in combat. I was one of the few men on this side of the battle who could perform this service.

"The heart of my report consisted of a description of the apparatus to which I was attached. It was an underground organization of the United States Communist party developed, to the best of my knowledge, by Harold Ware, one of the sons of the Communist leader known as 'Mother Bloor.'

"I knew it at its top level, a group of seven or so men, from among whom, in later years, certain members of Miss Bentley's (alleged wartime espionage) organization were apparently recruited.

"The head of the underground group at the time I knew it was Nathan Witt. Later, John Abt became the leader. Lee Pressman was also a member of this group, as was Alger Hiss who, as a member of the State Department, later organized the conference at Dumbarton Oaks, San Francisco, and the United States side of the Yalta conference.

"The purpose of this group at that time was not primarily espionage. Its original purpose was the Communist infiltration of the American Government. But espionage was certainly one of its eventual objectives. Let no one be surprised at this statement. Disloyalty is a matter of principle with every member of the Communist party.

"The Communist party exists for the specific purpose of overthrowing the Government, at the opportune time, by any and all means, and each of its members, by the fact that he is a member, is dedicated to this purpose."

Mr. Chambers contended that the Washington group, while apparently functioning in the pattern of Harold Ware, was really in the hands of one "J. Peters," who, he said, used many party names. He identified this functionary as being a former member of the Russian agricultural commissariat who had come into this country by means of an illegal passport.

The witness also said that Peters had explained to him "how easy it was to get false passports." The system, he added, was to have Communist party researchers posing as genealogical students seeking information at the New York Public Library pick out the names of American babies born on convenient dates and use their names and birth records for passport procurement. Peters, he said, got into the country under the name of "Isadore Boorstein," and added that he also was known as "Goldberg," which Mr. Chambers had heard was the "real name."

As committee attention focused on Alger Hiss who, when he left the State Department late in 1946, was described by Dean Acheson, Undersecretary, as one who had served "with outstanding devotion and ability," Mr. Chambers said he had "tried to get Mr. Hiss away from the Communists," but had failed."

Mr. Chambers said that he went to the Hiss home at what he viewed as "a considerable personal risk." While he awaited the return of Mr.

Hiss, he testified, Mrs. Hiss attempted to make a telephone call which he assumed was "to other Communists." He said that she "hung up" as he approached closely enough to hear what might be said.

"When Hiss came home," he told the committee, "I tried to persuade him to break away from this group. He cried when we separated, but he said something about 'the party line' and wouldn't break with the party."

Mr. Chambers testified that he also had endeavored to call Mr. White, the former Assistant Secretary of the Treasury and its former director of monetary research, away from association with the group he accused. He asserted that "developments" had indicated that he had "failed."

Mr. White, according to Mr. Chambers, had been picked by the group as one who might "go

places" in the administration and thus aid the infiltration movement. What the Communist organization was looking for, he said, was a group of "the elite" in government, that would encourage Communist infiltration.

"So it was decided," Mr. Chambers testified, "to add people who were not previously in the apparatus. One was Mr. White."

"These," he said, "were an elite group which, it was believed, would **rise to posts in Government and** thus make their positions more valuable to the party."

"Would you say," asked Representative Hebert, "that Mr. White was an unwitting dupe?"

"I would hardly say 'unwitting'," Mr. Chambers answered.

"Did he know what he was being used?" Mr. Herbert persisted.

"I would scarcely say 'used'," Mr. Chambers said. "He was willing."

August 4, 1948

## Microfilms in Pumpkin At the Chambers Farm

Special to THE NEW YORK TIMES.

WASHINGTON, Dec. 3— Microfilms which the House Un-American Activities Committee described as definite proof of an extensive espionage ring were produced from a hollowed-out pumpkin, Robert E. Stripling, the committee's chief investigator, said tonight.

He said that when investigators talked with Whittaker Chambers under subpoena last night at his farm near Westminster, Md., Mr. Chambers led them to a spot behind the farmhouse. There he showed them a pumpkin. He then lifted a cut-out lid and pulled out the microfilms.

December 4, 1948

# HISS GUILTY ON BOTH PERJURY COUNTS; BETRAYAL OF U.S. SECRETS IS AFFIRMED; SENTENCE WEDNESDAY; LIMIT 10 YEARS

## JURY OUT 24 HOURS

### Verdict Follows a Call on Judge to Restate Rulings on Evidence

### CHAMBERS STORY UPHELD

### Defendant Is Impassive—His Counsel Announces That an Appeal Will Be Taken

**By WILLIAM R. CONKLIN**

Alger Hiss, a highly regarded State Department official for ten of his forty-five years, was found guilty on two counts of perjury by a Federal jury of eight women and four men yesterday.

Nearly twenty-four hours after receiving the case, the jury reported its verdict at 2:50 P. M. The middle-aged jurors had begun their

**Alger Hiss leaving Federal Building.**

deliberations at 3:10 P. M. on Friday after ten weeks of testimony in the second perjury trial.

By convicting Hiss on both counts, the jury found that he had betrayed his trust by passing secret State Department documents to Whittaker Chambers. The former courier for a Communist spy ring was the Government's key witness against the former official. The verdict meant that the jury believed Mr. Chambers and the corroborating evidence produced by the Government.

The convicted defendant faces maximum penalties of five years' imprisonment and a $2,000 fine on each count, a combined total of ten years and $4,000. Federal Judge Henry W. Goddard continued his bail at $5,000 and set Wednesday at 10:30 A. M. for sentencing. Sentence will be passed in the same thirteenth floor courtroom of the United States District Court where Hiss was tried.

### Lapsing of Espionage Charge

The case of "The United States of America versus Alger Hiss" rested on a two-count perjury indictment. Thomas F. Murphy, Government prosecutor, had taxed Mr. Hiss with treason and espionage against his country. However,

any possible prosecution for espionage had been ruled out by a three-year statute of limitations, which conferred immunity after March, 1941.

Hiss was thus brought to trial on one count of perjury for denying that he ever gave secret documents to Mr. Chambers. The second count charged perjury for denying that he had seen the ex-Communist after Jan. 1, 1937. The Government contended that the documents were passed in February and March, 1938.

By its verdict the jury upheld the Government's contention that Priscilla Hiss, 46-year-old wife of the defendant, had typed copies of the documents for Mr. Chambers on the Hisses' Woodstock typewriter.

Mr. Chambers had told the jury that he had been a paid functionary of the Communist party in Washington and had collected secret information for Russia from 1935 to April, 1938.

### Basis Laid for Appeal

Claude B. Cross and Edward C. McLean, defense attorneys, would not say at first whether they would appeal the verdict. They had established a basis for an appeal by taking exception to a part of the charge of Judge Henry W. Goddard.

"There won't be any statement," Mr. McLean said. "I do not wish to discuss the possibility of an appeal now. There is just no statement." But later Mr. Cross said that "you can be sure the verdict will be appealed."

After the jury had convicted on both counts, Mr. Murphy asked that Hiss' bail of $5,000 be increased in conformity with the custom for "all convicted defendants." After Mr. Cross protested, Judge Goddard permitted Hiss to remain at liberty under the same bail. Mr. Cross said he would make some motions on Wednesday, the day set for sentencing.

Should defense attorneys file an appeal, it would act as an automatic stay of sentence. If an appeal should reach the United States Supreme Court, it was considered a foregone conclusion that Justices Felix Frankfurter and Stanley H. Reed would disqualify themselves. Both appeared at the first trial as character witnesses for Hiss, but were absent from his second trial.

In his first trial, which began on May 31 and ended on July 8, Hiss failed to win vindication from a jury. After hearing testimony for six weeks, the jury of ten men and two women deadlocked at eight to four for conviction. The second trial began on Nov. 17, took ten weeks and ended on its fortieth court day with the verdict.

United States Attorney Irving H. Saypol commended Mr. Murphy and his associates for the presentation of the Government's case.

"The verdict of the jury demonstrates that Mr. Murphy has vindicated justice," he said. "My personal and official commendations go to him and to the members of my staff, including Clarke S. Ryan, Assistant United States Attorney; Thomas J. Donegan, special assistant to the Attorney, General, and the Federal Bureau of Investigation."

Asked for his comment, Federal Prosecutor Murphy said:

"My job was to present the facts to an American jury, and it was their job to decide the facts. By their verdict this issue has now been permanently decided. I want to take the opportunity to thank sincerely all the men who have worked so hard and so long with me on this case."

**Final Instruction of Jury**

The jury, scheduled to resume deliberations at 10 o'clock yesterday morning, arrived at 9:20. At 10:31 the jurors asked Judge Goddard to reread parts of his charge on reasonable doubt, circumstantial evidence, corroborative evidence, and the relation of these factors to each other. They listened to the reading from 10:44 to 10:55 o'clock.

After luncheon, 12:55 to 2:08 P. M., the jury filed in with its verdict at 2:48. Two minutes later the verdict was on the record and Mr. Cross had polled the jury without changing the result. The jury was out a total of 23 hours 40 minutes, with 9 hours and 13 minutes spent in actual deliberations.

Hiss steadfastly refused comment on the outcome of the case, maintaining his silence until he left Foley Square with his wife in a friend's car at 3:23 o'clock. Like his wife, he had taken the verdict stolidly.

Hiss is the plaintiff in a $75,000 libel suit filed in November, 1948, in Baltimore against Mr. Chambers. The suit is based on the fact that Mr. Chambers called Hiss a Communist on a nation-wide broadcast.

Judge Goddard in his charge to the jury said the outcome of the perjury trial might well affect the decision in the libel suit. The Baltimore action has been deferred pending the outcome of the perjury trial here.

# Hiss, Coplon and Law

The United States Court of Appeals for the Second Judicial Circuit (Vermont, Connecticut and New York) last week decided appeals in two of the great post-war "spy" cases. In the case of Alger Hiss the decision was: Judgment affirmed. In the case of Judith Coplon the decision was: Conviction reversed.

## THE HISS CASE

Alger Hiss, center of the most important of all the "spy" cases, has spent almost all of his time for many months working with attorneys on his appeal. He has had no job. Friends have contributed to help him press his case. Others who never knew his name have come forward with money, too, explaining that they want to help him meet the costs of an appeal which they think he should make.

Hiss was convicted and sentenced to five years in prison last January for perjury in connection with espionage charges made against him by Whittaker Chambers. The decision on appeal, agreed to unanimously by Judges Harris B. Chase, Augustus N. Hand and Thomas W. Swan, dealt chiefly with two questions—evidence and trial errors.

*Evidence.* In perjury cases Federal law requires two witnesses to the crimes charged, or one with substantiation. Chambers was the only witness to make the essential charges against Hiss; substantiating evidence consisted of papers which Chambers said Hiss had given him for transmission to Russia, and the typewriter on which the papers were typed. The defense claimed that Chambers could not be believed because he was a "psychopathic liar," and that the supporting evidence was insufficient. The court, finding for the Government, held that Chambers' credibility was a matter for the jury to decide and that the other evidence was ample for a perjury conviction.

*Errors.* The defense objected to parts of the trial judge's charge and said he had allowed the Government too much leeway in presenting its case. The Court of Appeals found no reversible errors.

After the decision was announced, Hiss said: "I reaffirm my innocence." He will now make a final appeal to the Supreme Court. He has asked permission, pending its decision, to remain free in $10,000 bail.

## THE COPLON CASE

Miss Coplon, a former Justice Department employe, and Valentin Gubitchev, a Russian who worked for the United Nations, were convicted in New York last March on an espionage charge—conspiring to transmit United States Government papers to Russia. Each was sentenced to fifteen years in prison. In return for foregoing an appeal Gubitchev was allowed to return to Russia. Miss Coplon appealed.

The Court of Appeals panel which heard Miss Coplon's case—Chief Judge Learned Hand and Judges Thomas W. Swan and Jerome N. Frank—agreed unanimously: "The guilt is plain." But the court ruled that her conviction was illegal on two grounds:

(1) Her arrest was illegal because F. B. I. agents who made it had no warrant, and Government papers found in her handbag at the time should not have been admitted as evidence. Federal law permits F. B. I. agents to arrest and search a suspect without warrant if "there is a likelihood of his escaping before a warrant can be obtained." But the court found that the Government had not shown that likelihood.

(2) Much of the evidence in the trial apparently was obtained by wiretapping, which is illegal under Federal law. The Government admitted agents had tapped Miss Coplon's wires but said taps were used only to corroborate advice from a "confidential informant." The Government would not identify the informant and the Court said it was not convinced of his existence.

The Court recommended a new trial in which the Government might offer some more proof on the likelihood of Miss Coplon's case and on its informant. Miss Coplon is under conviction on a separate espionage charge tried in Washington. An appeal is now being considered by the Court of Appeals there.

## Protests Block Robeson as Guest On Mrs. Roosevelt TV Program

A scheduled appearance by Paul Robeson on Mrs. Franklin D. Roosevelt's television program has been "indefinitely postponed" and probably will be canceled, the National Broadcasting Company said last night.

The singer was to participate next Sunday afternoon in a discussion of "The Position of the Negro in American Political Life." This was announced last Sunday afternoon at the close of the program, "Today With Mrs. Roosevelt."

An N. B. C. spokesman said that thirty telephone calls of protest had been received at the network Sunday night, and that the number of objections had risen to "between two and three hundred" by last night.

The decision to postpone the program, N. B. C. said, was made by Mrs. Roosevelt's son Elliott and Martin Jones, its co-producers. They were said to have feared that Mr. Robeson's appearance might "confuse the issue" by focusing major attention on a controversial personality. As a substitute topic, "The Foreign Policy of the U. S. A." has been selected.

Charles R. Denny, executive vice president of N. B. C. said:

"We are all agreed that Mr. Robeson's appearance would lead only to misunderstanding and confusion, and no good purpose would be served in having him speak on the issue of Negroes in politics. The announcement that Mr. Robeson would be a participant in the discussion was premature and I cannot understand why it was made."

The announcement was "premature," the spokesman said, because the program, which is carried on a sustaining basis, had not been cleared with the broadcasting company. He stressed, however, that the producers had made the postponement voluntarily.

Others originally slated to participate in the program were Representative Adam Clayton Powell of New York, and Perry Howard.

## Reds Infiltrate Town in Wisconsin To Deride Mock May Day Seizure

Special to THE NEW YORK TIMES.

MOSINEE, Wis., April 30—In sequel to infiltration last night by real Communist agents this paper mill town of 1,400 prepared tonight to be "taken over" tomorrow by mock Communists in a May Day Americanism demonstration sponsored by the Wisconsin American Legion.

Plans were completed tonight in the two-story brick American Legion headquarters off Main Street and in the offices of The Mosinee Times for a "pageant" starting around dawn.

In the pageant the community will succumb to a mock seizure by "Communists," will see its constituted government and clergy deposed for the day and will participate in the triumph of democracy at an evening rally, when the "Communists" doff their masks and resume their identity as Legionnaires and civic leaders.

The townspeople tonight are in a festive mood, betokening their whole-hearted support of the demonstration.

An unscheduled development was the distribution last night of Communist literature on the doorsteps of the town's homes and business places. An estimated 600 packets of the literature were disseminated.

Probably not more than two persons made the distribution, according to Paul Theilen, state director of publicity for the Legion.

[At Milwaukee, according to The Associated Press, Fred Bassett Blair, Communist state vice chairman, said that several party members from the Mosinee area distributed the literature.]

Residents found on their doorsteps mimeographed sheets signed "The Communist Party of Wisconsin," copies of The Sunday Worker and a four-page brochure entitled "For Peace." The copies of the Worker were dated April 9, 16 and 23.

The mimeographed sheets were headed "So this is supposed to be communism—says who?" They went on to answer this question in part as follows:

"The boss—the guy who owns the mills.

"American Legion big shots—who do what the mill owners tell them to. They are the ones who try to get you mixed up in their dirty work.

"Stool pigeons—who are payed plenty by the mills for lying and double crossing labor unions and other organizations."

Tomorrow's pageant will be directed by a committee of local townspeople under the general chairmanship of Frances F. Schweinler, editor of The Mosinee Times, a weekly.

As part of the demonstration, The Times will publish tomorrow a four-page, adless issue of "The Red Star," printed on red paper and purveying "Communist propaganda."

Benjamin Gitlow and Joseph Zack Kornfeder, former Communists, have charge of the technical direction of the pageant.

Plans call for a "cadre" of Mosinee civic leaders to "seize" Mayor Ralph Kronenwetter and Police Chief Carl Gewis at their homes in the morning and "arrest" the town's clergymen, whose churches will be "padlocked." The power house of the paper mill and other key buildings will be "seized."

### "Commissariat" to Be Set Up

Posters identifying them as 'Commissariat of Public Information" and so on will be affixed to the town's public buildings and edicts will be published closing the library and other civic institutions. Slogans on the order of "Religion is the opium (sic) of the people" will be posted.

At 9:15 A. M. a parade will get under way for "Red Square," where a mass rally is to be held at 9:30.

Mayor Kronenwetter will be "forced" to issue a statement turning over administration of the community to Mr. Gitlow as "Secretary of the Communist Party of the United Soviet States of America" and Mr. Kornfeder as "Chairman of the Council of Peoples' Commissars" or "Supreme Commissar."

Civics classes at the high school will expose their pupils to Communist ideology during the day.

"Rationing" will be in effect at the stores.

Among the props of the demonstration will be a barbed wire "concentration camp."

The "occupation" will end with another rally at 8 P. M., in which, after the day's "invaders" unmask, there will be a program showing the triumph of democracy. The keynote speech of the evening rally will be by Charles L. Larson of Port Washington, state American Legion commander, who will speak on "Americanism."

Observers tonight did not anticipate any untoward developments in the presentation of the pageant tomorrow. Any concentration of persons sizable enough to start a serious counter demonstration would be easily noticeable in a town so small as this, they pointed out. It was generally believed that those who distributed Communist literature last night were still in town tonight.

Mr. Theilen, who is from Milwaukee, said that the idea for the pageant originated with John A. Decker of Milwaukee, a member of the State Legion Policy Committee, and himself. He added that Mosinee was chosen for its site because of Mr. Schweinler's interest in Legion affairs and its suitability in size and location.

Mosinee, on the Wisconsin River, is thirteen miles south of Wausau and 180 miles northwest of Milwaukee. A predominantly Republican community, its principal industry besides the paper mill is farming. The Mosinee Times normally comes out on Wednesday and is nonpartisan editorially.

# John S. Service Is Ousted; Diplomat's Loyalty 'Doubted'

### By WALTER H. WAGGONER
Special to THE NEW YORK TIMES.

WASHINGTON, Dec. 13—The State Department dismissed John Stewart Service tonight on the advice of the Government's top loyalty agency that there was "reasonable doubt" as to the foreign service officer's loyalty.

The Civil Service Commission's Loyalty Review Board found that Mr. Service, a career diplomat for eighteen years, had raised doubt as to his loyalty by making "intentional and unauthorized disclosure" of classified documents. It said it had uncovered no evidence that Mr. Service had been a member of the Communist party or of any other organization which had been listed as subversive by the Attorney General.

The Loyalty Review Board, set up by President Truman last year to be the final arbiter of loyalty questions, reversed the State Department's own Loyalty Security Board, which six times had found Mr. Service free of any suspicion of disloyalty. The Review Board is headed by Hiram Bingham, former Republican Senator from Connecticut.

Mr. Service has been working in the State Department's Office of Operating Facilities, an administrative and housekeeping unit without access to classified material, since being recalled from India for investigation in March, 1950.

### "Amerasia" Case Cited

That investigation and an almost continuous inquiry into charges against Mr. Service since then had been provoked by Senator Joseph R. McCarthy, Republican of Wisconsin, who made the foreign service office one of the targets of his attacks against what he called Communists in the State Department.

The principal basis for the Loyalty Review Board's unfavorable decision was Mr. Service's role in the so-called Amerasia case of 1945, when classified official reports were made available to the magazine of that name.

The Loyalty Review Board's letter telling Secretary of State Dean Acheson of its findings stated only that "reasonable doubt" had been raised as to Mr. Service's loyalty.

In its announcement tonight, however, the State Department included also the opinion of its own Loyalty Security Board, which, in 8,500 words, set down the reasons for having cleared Mr. Service on six previous occasions.

It found that Mr. Service had "clearly committed two serious indiscretions" by turning over classified reports and other information to Philip J. Jaffe, Russian-born American citizen who was co-editor of Amerasia.

The department's loyalty unit, nevertheless, concluded that the material made available by Mr. Service contained nothing "harmful to the national security" and that it did not form a basis for finding Mr. Service disloyal.

Amerasia, now defunct, was published in New York. It dealt with Far Eastern affairs. Six persons were arrested after raids on its offices revealed secret documents. Mr. Jaffe was fined $2,500, and Emmanuel S. Larsen, an alleged associate, $500 on charges of possessing secret Government documents. The other defendants were cleared. Later Senator McCarthy charged a "whitewash."

The State Department's announcement of Mr. Service's dismissal said the decision by the President's Loyalty Review Board "is based on the evidence which was considered by the department's board and found to be insufficient on which to base a finding of 'reasonable doubt' as to Mr. Service's loyalty or security."

### Service Issues Statement

Mr. Service, on learning of the board's action, issued this statement:

"The Loyalty Review Board's decision is a surprise, a shock and an injustice. I am not now and never have been disloyal to the United States.

"The board expressly states that is does not find me disloyal. What is has done is base a 'reasonable doubt' on a single episode which occurred six and a half years ago which has been freely admitted by me and known to all responsible quarters since that time and for which I have been tried and unanimously acquitted at least nine times.

"That episode involved discussing normal and proper background information with a journalist whom I believed and had every reason to believe at the time to be nothing more than the editor of a reputable, specialist magazine dealing with the Far East.

"The selected background information which I gave him did not adversely affect or even deal with the national interests of the United States, nor did it come within the meaning of regulations defining the classifications 'secret and confidential.'

"The information involved was known, or at least available to, all of the American correspondents in China. The only thing that kept these facts about China from an uninformed American public was a foreign censorship. The same information had been used repeatedly by me, with official approval, in discussing the situation in China with other writers and researchers in the United States.

"I am confident that my record of eighteen and a half years' service to the American Government and the testimony of the many people who have worked with me during that period will support me in my conviction that there is no doubt of my loyalty."

### Was Cleared Seven Times

Altogether, Mr. Service had been cleared of disloyalty charges seven times since the Amerasia case. The chronology of those inquiries follows:

In August, 1945, a grand jury investigation of the Amerasia case cleared Mr. Service with a "no true bill," in effect finding that the charges of having transmitted classified material to unauthorized persons had not been substantiated.

The State Department's Loyalty Security Board, under the direction of Gen. Conrad E. Snow (Reserve), a New Hampshire Republican, then cleared Mr. Service on these dates: Jan. 18, 1949; March 1, 1950; Oct. 6, 1950; March 7, 1951; June 11, 1951; and, after the standards had been changed from "reasonable grounds" for finding a person disloyal to "reasonable doubt" of his loyalty, finally on July 31, 1951.

The State Department's loyalty unit submitted its final report on Mr. Service to the Loyalty Review Board Sept. 4, for what is known as a "post-audit," or review. On Oct. 9 the Civil Service Commission Board again took up the case and returned its verdict today.

In effect, the State Department this evening stood by its favorable decisions. Its announcement called attention to the fact that the department's loyalty unit, "while censuring Mr. Service for indiscretions, believed that the experience Mr. Service had been through as a result of his indiscretions in 1945 had served to make him far more than normally security conscious."

Mr. Service denied repeatedly that he ever had been a Communist or friendly to communism. The report of the Loyalty Review Board appeared to support him on that point.

The foreign service officer also had won the respect and friendship of his associates and superiors holding influential posts in the State Department.

In a statement replying to Senator McCarthy, John E. Peurifoy, then Deputy Under Secretary of State and now Ambassador to Greece, declared on March 16, 1950:

"Here, in the person of Jack Service, we have an able, conscientious, and—I say again, as I've already said many times before—a demonstrably loyal foreign service officer, a veteran of seventeen years with the department, and one of our outstanding experts on Far Eastern affairs."

On that occasion Mr. Peurifoy bitterly reported that orders had gone out to Mr. Service, en route to a new assignment as First Secretary in the United States Embassy in India, to return to Washington "to face another 'loyalty probe.'"

### China Career Examined

The report of the Loyalty Review Board, dated yesterday, reviewed Mr. Service's career in China in 1944 and said that "we have in the file no sufficient evidence to support a doubt on the question of loyalty."

It stated similarly that a review of the entire file "also satisfied us that no reasonable doubt concerning the employe's loyalty arises from his activities while assigned to the staff of General MacArthur in Tokyo."

In connection with Mr. Service's participation in the Amerasia case, set down in some detail in the agency's report to the State Department the Civil Service Commission loyalty board found its ground for "reasonable doubt."

"To say that his course of conduct does not raise a reasonable doubt as to Service's own loyalty," the board concluded, "would, we are forced to think, stretch the mantle of charity much too far.

"We are not required to find Service guilty of disloyalty, and we do not do so, but for an experienced and trusted representative of our State Department to so far forget his duty to his trust as his conduct with Jaffe so clearly indicates, forces us with great regret to conclude that there is reasonable doubt as to his loyalty. The favorable finding of the Loyalty Security Board of the Department of State is accordingly reversed."

### Was Born in China

Mr. Service, born in China of American parents forty-two years ago, joined the United States foreign service in 1933 at the age of 24 as clerk in the United States Consulate in Yunnanfu.

He remained in China for the diplomatic service until May, 1945, when he was assigned to the State Department here. Then he was named political adviser to General MacArthur in September of that year; was moved to Wellington, New Zealand, in July, 1946; returned briefly to the State Department in 1948; went to Calcutta as counselor in November, 1949; and was then assigned as counselor of the embassy in New Delhi, a post he never reached.

Mr. Service is married and has three children.

# The Freedom to Search for Knowledge

**This is indispensable to the educator's work, and it must be preserved against unjustified assaults.**

### By ROBERT M. MacIVER

THERE has never been so much commotion over the freedom of the scholar or the educator as there is in this country today. In the past there has indeed been less, much less, academic freedom—for in the ages of authority it was at best a very limited affair. But never in modern times has there been so massive and many-sided an assault upon it. Many of these assaults have been repelled, but more than a few have succeeded. All across the country there are groups that, under one banner or another, are seeking to limit it. Dozens of organizations are "investigating" it, including at present three Congressional bodies. There is not a single important institution of learning that has not been the object of some accusation concerning it. There is scarcely a college or university president who has not run into some troubles over it.

What is this academic freedom? What is its importance? Why is there so much concern over it? These things need to be explained, for the people are being misled about these questions, and even some educators are by no means sufficiently alert to the situation.

Academic freedom means the freedom of the educator to do his proper work, to fulfill his function, to render to his society the special service that he has to offer. His work is to learn and to teach, and this is what every genuine scholar wants above all to do. That is what he is appointed to do. That is what the institution of learning is for. Here lies its unique function, its primary mission in society.

EVERY major type of social organization has its own unique function which requires an appropriate range of freedom to fulfill. The church aspires to one. The family another. So also the academy, the college or the university. Academic freedom then is the freedom of the men of the academy, the faculty members, within their various areas of competence, in the field of learning and teaching.

Observe that this freedom is not the freedom to express opinions on any matter under the sun. In a democratic country that is the freedom of the citizen. What we're talking about is a special form of freedom derived from a special function—the freedom proper to the member of a particular profes-

ROBERT M. MacIVER, sociologist, is making a study of intellectual freedom for the American Academic Freedom Project at Columbia.

sion, without which the calling is perverted and falsified and the service it renders is betrayed. Just as the medical man needs a particular area of freedom for his work, or the man of law, so does the man of the academy.

The effort to seek and impart knowledge means a limit to the control of any external authority over the institution of learning. Where this freedom exists, no authority can say: "This is the truth, this is what you must teach." Or: "This is the truth; if your investigations lead you to doubt it or to deny it, you must refrain from doing so."

It is the freedom to reach conclusions through scholarly investigation. It does not imply the freedom to *act* according to your conclusions, if such action is against the law. It is emphatically not a freedom to conspire to overthrow government or to incite others to do so. But it embraces the freedom of the serious student of government to reach and express conclusions regarding its nature and regarding the good or evil results of this or that form of government.

Academic freedom is at the same time a high responsibility. It is not a privilege possessed by an academic guild. It is not a concession granted by a government or by a community to an enclave of scholars. It is claimed as a necessity, not a luxury; as a condition of service, not as a social award. As we shall presently see, it is a fundamental condition of a free society.

SOME enemies of this freedom say: "We are perfectly willing to let the teacher do his job. His job is to impart information—we don't in the least want to interfere with that. What we object to is when the teacher throws his weight around and starts indoctrinating his students. That's not his business. By all means let him give the students any knowledge he has, but let him keep to the facts and keep his valuations out of it. We don't pay him to teach values, especially values contrary to our own."

This sounds plausible—perhaps even reasonable. But let us see how it works out. Suppose, for example, you are a teacher of English literature. What would confining yourself to "the facts" mean? What sort of understanding would you convey of a play of Shakespeare or, say, Walt Whitman's poems if you confined yourself to "the facts"? Would it not deaden any incipient interest the student might have, or at the least deaden his interest in you, unless you did a bit of interpretation?

And if you do that, you are no longer giving "the facts."

Or suppose you are an economist and you're talking about inflation. Would you reel off changing index numbers and stop there, or would you analyze inflation as a problem? If the latter, are you confining yourself to "the facts"? Are you even steering clear of "values"?

Or you are a sociologist, and you're discussing, say, a housing shortage in some part of the country. But why call it a shortage? A shortage is not a "fact" but a conclusion you believe to be borne out by the evidence. And why deal with it at all if you're eschewing values altogether? The facts are of interest because they have meaning for us. If you exclude the meaning your teaching is dead. If you include it you cannot altogether exclude values.

HE who seeks knowledge is seeking the connections between things. He is not interested in mere detached items of information. He wants to find out how things are related. His mere opinions do not count and he should not foist them on his students. But he should be free to express any conclusions he reaches as a result of his study in his own field, explaining how he reaches them. His conclusions may be faulty, but

there is no other road to knowledge. Nor is there any other way to education since the teacher is out to train the student's mind, not to load his memory with undigestible "facts."

This, then, is the freedom the scholar needs, the freedom that is now on the defensive. Why is it important? Why does it matter much to anyone but the scholar? Why should the people, too, be concerned if this freedom is threatened or abridged?

ACADEMIC freedom is important to us all because knowledge is important, because the search for knowledge is important, and because the spirit of the search for knowledge is most important of all.

That knowledge is important needs no telling. Knowledge is power and knowledge is opportunity. Knowledge alone enables the "frail reed," man, to make nature serve his purposes. On knowledge alone can intelligent policy be based and successful action be carried through.

The search for knowledge has again a value outside of the direct rewards it brings. Anything we know, we know only in part, and many things we think we know are not knowledge.

At one time men knew the earth was flat and that the heavenly bodies revolved around the earth. Until recently Newtonian physics, itself a tremendous advance, was the last word in knowledge. But there is never a last word. To the seeker after truth all horizons are eternally open. He is the enemy of all the hard, proud dogmatisms that fasten on the minds of men and breed intolerance and sharp division between group and group, between people and people, between nation and nation.

The business of the university is not so much the guardianship of knowledge as the search for knowledge, the keeping open of the intellectual horizon. This service is invaluable. The one institution supremely dedicated to the spread of enlightenment is the institution of learning. Its individual members have interests and prejudices and passions like other men. They go wrong like other men. But together, each in his own field, they seek for knowledge, and thus the institution is redeemed. It is the belief in the supreme importance of the freedom to seek knowledge which unites them.

Without that belief and its triumphant vindication in our colleges and universities the right of a man to think for himself, to inquire, to have his own opinions, would lack any sure foundation. Democracy, in a world of incessantly whirling propaganda, would have no strong defense. And civilization, what remained of it, would become no more than a mesh of techniques designed

"We can trust Americans when they understand the alternatives. That is the way of the institution of learning."

for the enslavement of body and mind, as it was in Hitler's Germany, as it is in Soviet Russia.

ONLY the spirit that animates the endless search for knowledge can save us from these things. This spirit must continue to flourish outside our universities as well as within their walls. It is the same spirit that keeps the press free. It is back of the democratic willingness to let the views of every group be decently heard. It is the spirit that repudiates the right of the state or the church or any other bodies to establish a censorship over the expression of opinion or the freedom of inquiry.

It is now endangered. In every society there are always those who, fearful for their interests or secure in their dogmatisms, are ready to suppress or to control the search for knowledge. In ours today they have found a formidable new weapon.

Under the guise of protecting us from communism they employ a Communist technique to further their own interest to acquire political capital or economic advantage. They brand as "red" or "pink" or "subversive" or at the least "un-American" everything they happen to dislike, whether it be progressive education or state hospitals or anti-discrimination laws or social insurance or a policy toward China different from their own or Keynesian economics or the United Nations.

THE real danger besetting academic freedom—and indeed the fundamental freedom of thought, opinion, and inquiry in every form—comes from the misdirection of legitimate fears of communism and the deliberate exploitation of those fears. Communism has at this stage no influence whatever in our institutions of learning, and even in the heyday of the Thirties its influ-

ence was insignificant in the great majority of these institutions.

The danger in this direction is grossly exaggerated—for whatever purposes. Attacks on academic freedom have increased on the specious ground that faculties need protection from Communist infiltration. Our colleges are perfectly capable of protecting themselves. Beyond that, these institutions (as the writer can report from personal knowledge) have shown the light to more than a few students who came to them as Communists and there learned the error of their way.

Misguided legislative bodies and pressure groups—such as the Broyles Commission in Illinois—have wanted to pass laws to expel from our colleges any Communist student. Nothing could be more stupid —or more alien to the democratic way. We can trust Americans when they understand the alternatives. That is the way of the institution of learning.

WE cannot defend democracy abroad if we undermine our own at home. It is the free world—or rather the freedom of all mankind—that America is now called upon to guard. But our defense of it will be vain if it is not undertaken in the spirit as well as in the name of democracy.

There is the fear of the darkness and there is the fear of the light. The Soviets have chosen the darkness, the darkness of thought control, and so they fear our light. And because they would impose it on the rest of mankind, we must fear their darkness. But if we should come to fear alike the darkness and the light, the light of freedom of thought, then indeed we are undone.

# ROSENBERGS EXECUTED AS ATOM SPIES AFTER SUPREME COURT VACATES STAY; LAST-MINUTE PLEA TO PRESIDENT FAILS

## SIX JUSTICES AGREE

### President Says Couple Increased 'Chances of Atomic War'

By LUTHER A. HUSTON
Special to THE NEW YORK TIMES.

WASHINGTON, June 19—President Eisenhower and the Supreme Court refused today to save Julius and Ethel Rosenberg from death in the electric chair.

The high court vacated the stay granted to the atomic spies on Wednesday by Justice William O. Douglas. It upheld the legality of the death sentence imposed by Federal Judge Irving R. Kaufman.

Less than an hour after the court had announced its verdict, President Eisenhower refused Executive clemency for the second time. He had denied a similar petition on Feb. 11.

"I can only say that, by immeasurably increasing the chances of atomic war, the Rosenbergs may have condemned to death tens of millions of innocent people all over the world," the President said. "The execution of two human beings is a grave matter. But even graver is the thought of the millions of dead whose deaths may be directly attributable to what these spies have done."

He was convinced, the President said, that the Rosenbergs had received "the fullest measure of justice and due process of law."

"When in their most solemn judgment, the tribunals of the United States have adjudged them guilty and the sentence just, I will not intervene in this matter," the President declared.

#### Vinson Reads Court's Ruling

The prevailing opinion setting aside Justice Douglas' stay of execution was read by Chief Justice Fred M. Vinson and was concurred in by Associate Justices Stanley F. Reed, Robert H. Jackson, Harold H. Burton, Sherman Minton and Tom C. Clark.

## Their Death Penalty Carried Out

**Julius Rosenberg**

Associated Press
**Ethel Rosenberg**

Justices Douglas and Hugo L. Black dissented. Justice Felix Frankfurter announced neither a concurrence nor a dissent. In a brief separate opinion he said the questions raised were "complicated and novel" and that he felt the application of the Attorney General for revocation of the stay should not be disposed of until more time had been afforded for study and argument. He promised to set forth more specifically in due course the ground for this position.

Also read from the bench were a concurring opinion by Justice Clark, in which he was joined by Justices Vinson, Reed, Jackson, Burton and Minton, and a concurring opinion by Justice Jackson, also joined by the five other members of the majority.

These actions by the President and the highest judicial tribunal of the land blighted the hopes of lawyers for the Rosenbergs that their clients might by some last-minute dispensation be saved from the electric chair. Nevertheless, the attorneys carried the fight into the last hour of the Rosenberg lives.

Even after the court had turned them down, the lawyers sought another justice to grant a stay of execution. In succession their pleas were rejected by Justice Black, Burton and Frankfurter.

Finally abandoning the court, Emanuel H. Bloch, principal attorney for the spies, sent a telegram and a letter to the White House and sought a personal interview with the President.

All of those desperately earnest last-minute efforts were unavailing.

The letter Mr. Bloch sent to the White House was written by Mrs. Ethel Rosenberg to the President from "Women's Wing—C. C. (condemned cells)" in Sing Sing prison. It was dated June 16.

#### Follows Mrs. Oatis' Example

Mrs. Rosenberg said she had been moved to write the President many times "during the two long and bitter years I have spent in the death house at Sing Sing." The success of Mrs. William Oatis in obtaining the release of her husband from a Czechoslovakian prison by writing a letter to the President of that country, enabled her to overcome the shyness "the ordinary person feels in the presence of the great and famous."

Mrs. Oatis, the wife of an Associated Press correspondent who was imprisoned in Prague for espionage, wrote a letter to President Antonin Zapotocky, who pardoned

her husband. Mr. Oatis was released May 16.

"It is chiefly the death sentence I would entreat you to ponder," Mrs. Rosenberg wrote to President Eisenhower. "I would entreat you to ask yourself whether that sentence does not serve the ends of 'force and violence' rather than an enlightened justice."

She entreated the "affectionate grandfather, the sensitive artist, the devoutly religious man" to offer to God "a simple act of compassion" by sparing the lives of herself and her husband for their two sons.

The telegram that Mr. Bloch sent to the White House, requesting a new hearing on a plea for clemency, was received by Bernard Shanley, special counsel to President Eisenhower, and transmitted to the Department of Justice.

As these last-minute moves to save the Rosenbergs were going on pickets marched before the White House carrying banners demanding that the lives of the Rosenbergs be spared. On several occasions they were derided by persons driving past in automobiles or buses.

#### Heavy Guard at White House

Uneasiness on the part of the authorities was marked by especially heavy police details in the White House vicinity.

When Mr. Bloch appeared at the White House gates at 7:43 P. M. to seek a personal interview with the President the pickets broke into cheers. Corp. William J. McCarthy of the White House police, refused to let him enter the grounds.

Mr. Bloch acknowledged that he had no appointment with anyone in the White House and the policeman said he had no authority to admit him without an appointment.

Mr. Bloch asked if he could use the telephone in the police box at the gate to call Sherman Adams, assistant to the President, or James C. Hagerty, White House Press Secretary, to ask for an appointment. The officer told him he would have to use a public telephone down the street.

Later Murray Snyder, assistant White House Press Secretary, read to reporters this statement concerning Mrs. Rosenberg's letter:

"The President has read the letter. He states that in his conviction it adds nothing to the issues covered in his statement of this afternoon."

That was a reference to the President's earlier statement rejecting the plea for clemency.

Corporal McCarthy accepted some material that Mr. Bloch asked if he could leave at the gate, and the lawyer then walked west on Pennsylvania Avenue. The material included the letter from Mrs. Rosenberg and a copy of the majority opinion of the Supreme Court.

The prevailing opinion of the six Justices was brief, of the type known as a per curiam opinion. This designates an opinion not signed by the Justice who wrote it. It was reported that Justice Jackson wrote it, but it was read from the bench by the Chief Justice.

The justices looked grim as they ascended the bench. Their expressions indicated that the conferences at which the decision was hammered out might have been strenous, perhaps bitter.

Justice Black said, in his dissenting opinion, that he did not know of any previous instance where stays granted by an individual justice during a court vacation had been set aside by the full court before the next regular term.

Justice Douglas had granted the stay because, he said, the question whether the provisions of the Atomic Energy Act, passed in 1946, superseded the Espionage Act of 1917, as far as the power of the District Judge to impose the death penalty was concerned, raised a substantial point of law that the courts should decide. A death sentence imposed under the Atomic Energy Act without a recommendation of that sentence by a jury would be illegal.

The majority opinion of the court said:

"We think the question is not substantial. We think further proceedings to litigate it are unwarranted. A conspiracy was charged and proved to violate the Espionage Act in wartime. The Atomic Energy Act did not repeal or limit the provisions of the Espionage Act."

Justice Douglas' dissenting opinion was sharply worded and sometimes impassioned. He stuck by his guns.

After recalling that the legal question of the applicability of the Atomic Energy Act to the Rosenbergs' case had "deeply troubled" him before he issued the stay so that he felt the court should decide a point never before presented to it, Justice Douglas said:

"Before the present argument I knew only that the question was serious and substantial. Now I am sure of the answer. I know deep in my heart that I am right on the law. Knowing that, my duty is clear."

### Penalty For Giving Atom Data

There could be no doubt, the Justice asserted, that the death penalty was imposed upon the Rosenbergs because of their disclosure of atomic secrets.

"The cold fact is," he wrote, "that the death sentence may not be imposed for what the Rosenbergs did unless the jury so recommends."

One of the questions raised in arguments and in motions filed with the court was the power of the full court to vacate Justice Douglas' order. Robert L. Stern, acting Solicitor General, had argued for the Government that the court had that power.

Justice Black, however, did not agree. In his dissenting opinion he said that he had "found no statute or rule of the court which permits the full court to set aside a mere temporary stay entered by a justice in obedience to his statutory obligations."

Justice Black agreed with Justice Douglas that the sentences were improperly imposed. He said the Atomic Energy Act "appears to have taken the death sentencing power from the District Judges, in cases of atomic energy espionage, except where juries recommend a death sentence."

The justice further felt that the court should have taken more time to consider the legal complexities involved and he thought the court should have passed upon the question of whether the Rosenbergs had had a fair trial.

"It is not amiss," he said, "to point out that this court has never reviewed this record [of the trial] and has never affirmed the fairness of the trial below. Without an affirmance of the fairness of the trial by the highest court of the land, there may always be questions as to whether these executions were legally and rightfully carried out."

When all the opinions and dis-

sents had been read, Mr. Bloch moved that a stay be granted to afford sufficient time for an appeal for executive clemency. Fyke Farmer, the lawyer who had raised the point upon which Justice Douglas granted the stay, made a motion that the Court hear oral arguments on the power of the full Court to override the stay.

Mr. Farmer of Nashville, Tenn., and another attorney, Daniel G. Marshall of Los Angeles, had been engaged to enter the case by Irwin Edelman of Los Angeles, a free-lance writer and pamphleteer. Judge Kaufman had refused to hear the two men, describing them as "interlopers," but Justice Douglas considered their arguments on Tuesday.

The motions by Mr. Bloch and Mr. Farmer were denied by the Supreme Court. The justices retired to their conference room, but when they returned a short time later the Chief Justice announced their decision. He said that Justice Black had dissented to both rulings of the court.

The nine black-robed jurists looked even more grim as they announced their final rulings in a case that had been before them seven times, in one form or another. The Crier proclaimed that the special term, called on application of Attorney General Herbert Brownell Jr., to consider Justice Douglas' order, was adjourned.

Silently the justices turned away from the bench, not to return until Oct. 5, and the last judicial episode in the Rosenberg case was over.

June 20, 1955

# PRESIDENT CHIDES M'CARTHY ON 'FAIR PLAY' AT HEARINGS; SENATOR DEFIANT IN RETORT

## OFFICERS UPHELD

### Eisenhower to Bar Any Humiliation of Them —Praises Zwicker

**By W. H. LAWRENCE**

Special to THE NEW YORK TIMES.

WASHINGTON, March 3—President Eisenhower and Sena-

tor Joseph R. McCarthy clashed today in a struggle that might have lasting effects on the unity of the Republican party.

The President led off at a packed news conference with a moderately critical statement about the "disregard for standards of fair play" in some instances by Congressional committees.

He said his Administration would not tolerate personal humiliation of any officer or Executive Department employe

testifying before Congressional committees or elsewhere.

Senator McCarthy replied with a statement in sharper tone within the hour. He declared that "if a stupid, arrogant or witless man in a position of power apppears before our committee and is found aiding the Communist party, he will be exposed."

The exchange also left the two men contradicting each other on the Wisconsin Senator's authority to challenge the wisdom of John Foster Dulles, the Secretary of

State, in stripping personnel authority from Scott McLeod, State Department security chief.

The President said this was Mr. Dulles' responsibility alone and that of no one else. Senator McCarthy said his Committee on Government Operations had a legal directive to examine carefully any reorganization proposal, and would look into the changes at the State Department.

**Other Developments**

The McCarthy controversy

dominated President Eisenhower's twenty-six-minute news conference, which was attended by 256 reporters, but there were these other developments:

¶The President reiterated his opposition to a Federal Fair Employment Practices Commission with punitive powers or compulsory power, but he upheld the right of James P. Mitchell, the Secretary of Labor, to advocate other views. He declared he did not wish to have a bunch of yes-men around him.

¶He expressed regret at the tragic events on Capitol Hill when five House members were wounded by Puerto Rican Nationalists, but he absolved the masses of Puerto Rico from responsibility for such a deed.

¶He expressed anew his opposition to any excise (sales) tax cuts beyond those recommended by George M. Humphrey, the Secretary of the Treasury, but withheld a threat to veto any measure that went beyond his recommendations.

¶He gave new emphasis to the Red Cross fund raising campaign by saying the need for the Red Cross work among armed forces personnel had been increased, rather than reduced, by the truce in Korea.

¶He disclosed that the Administration had been studying for more than a year a proposal to outlaw the Communist party as such but had not surmounted yet constitutional barriers to such action.

¶He believed the 2,427 persons who resigned or were dismissed under the security program during the final seven months of 1953 were bad security risks. He had never said they were subversives, and he agreed there might be merit in a suggestion they be termed "undesirables."

¶He promised definite action this week on requests for higher tariffs on imported wool, but declined to reveal his decision at this time.

The President pinned his hopes for future "fair play" by Congressional committees investigating communism on "the conscience of America," which was, he said, reflected in Congress.

## Encourages Rules Changes

He gave encouragement to rules changes proposed by the Republican leadership in the Senate designed to curb one-man investigations such as have been conducted by Senator McCarthy and others. But the word from Capitol Hill late today was that this effort was bogging down.

The tone of Senator McCarthy's response to what was generally regarded as a mild statement by the President surprised many members of Congress.

A Democratic Senator asked whether "this open declaration of war requires approval by the Senate."

There was a strong conviction that Senator McCarthy had deliberately asserted his leadership of the Republican "right wing" in challenging the President directly. Middle-of-the-road Republicans were disturbed and silent.

Senator McCarthy made no effort to conceal that he was disputing the President directly.

General Eisenhower had admitted "serious errors" in the Army's handling of an honorable discharge for Maj. Irving Peress, a New York dental officer who declined, on constitutional grounds governing possible self-incrimination, when asked by Senator McCarthy about his Communist associations. The President attributed the Peress situation, in part, to laws on commissions for doctors and dentists.

Senator McCarthy said he was facing "an unprecedented mudslinging" attack because he had dared to bring to light "the cold, unpleasant facts about a Fifth Amendment Communist Army officer who was promoted, given special immunity from duty outside the United States and finally given an honorable discharge with the full knowledge of all concerned that he was a member of the Communist party."

"It now appears," he added, "that he [Major Peress] was a sacred cow of certain Army brass."

Included in the original McCarthy typewritten statement, but deleted from it by pencil marks before it was released, was the following sentence:

"Far too much wind has been blowing from high places in defense of this Fifth Amendment Communist Army officer."

The President expressed confidence in the "complete loyalty" of the military service and had high praise for Brig. Gen. Ralph W. Zwicker, Camp Kilmer, N. J., commandant, who was termed by Senator McCarthy unfit for command. Major Peress received his discharge at Camp Kilmer.

To General Eisenhower's assertion that he would permit no humiliation of officers or others testifying, Senator McCarthy made his comment, that he would continue to expose "stupid, arrogant or witless" men found to be aiding the Communist party. The Senator added, that the fact that such a person "might be a general, places him in no special class, as far as I am concerned."

The President expressed the hope that the average American's love of fair play would bring about fair play in all inquiries into communism.

"When the shouting and the tumult dies," Senator McCarthy replied, "the American people and the President will realize that this unprecedented mudslinging against the committee by extreme Left Wing elements of press and radio was caused because another Fifth Amendment Communist in Government was finally dug out of the dark recesses and exposed to public view."

While President Eisenhower stressed the grave nature of the problem confronting the country in exercising vigilance against subversive penetration without adopting unjust and unfair methods, Senator McCarthy called the Peress case controversy "this silly tempest in a teapot."

"Apparently the President and I agree on the necessity of getting rid of Communists," said Senator McCarthy. "We apparently disagree only on how we should handle those who protect Communists."

There was no formal reaction at the White House to Senator McCarthy's reply to the President, but it was made plain in other Administration quarters that the battle that opened this morning was far from over.

The President emphasized repeatedly that while it was the responsibility of the Executive Branch to remove subversives from Government, he was not challenging the right of Congress to inquire and investigate into every phase of our public operation.

President Eisenhower said he expected the Republican members to assume primary responsibility for proper practices, and he was glad to report assurances from Senator William F. Knowland of California, the Floor Leader, that "effective steps are already being taken by the Republican leadership to set up codes of fair procedure."

In asserting his own leadership, the President said his legislative recommendations now before the Congress "deserve the undivided and incessant attention of the Congress, of the Executive branch, of the public information media of our nation, of our schools and even of our churches."

"I regard it as unfortunate," he added, "when we are diverted from these grave problems, of which one is vigilance against any kind of internal subversion—through disregard of the standards of fair play recognized by the American people."

The President was asked about suggestion by Senator McCarthy on establishing special labor camps for alleged Communists in the armed forces. He said the problem was under study at the Defense Department.

Charles E. Wilson, Secretary of Defense, said in a letter to Senator Leverett Saltonstall of Massachusetts, chairman of the Senate Armed Services Committee, that the study was being made "a matter of urgency."

The President was asked about Senator McCarthy's charge that Army officers had "coddled Communists."

He replied that originally he had meant to say something about this allegation in his formal statement, but he had deleted it because the statement was getting too long.

March 4, 1954

# M'CARTHY CHARGES ARMY 'BLACKMAIL,' SAYS STEVENS SOUGHT DEAL WITH HIM; 'UTTERLY UNTRUE,' SECRETARY REPLIES

### Senator's Data Report Stevens Asked Navy, Air Force Inquiry

**By W. H. LAWRENCE**
Special to THE NEW YORK TIMES.

WASHINGTON, March 12—Senator Joseph R. McCarthy today angrily charged the Army with attempted blackmail in an effort to stop his exposure of Communists. Army authorities promptly declared the assertion was "fantastic."

Fighting desperately and almost alone to save his political prestige and the job of his chief counsel, Roy M. Cohn, the Wisconsin Republican struck back at the Army's documentary report issued yesterday.

The Army report charged the Senator and Mr. Cohn with threats and pressures to obtain favored treatment for Pvt. G. David Schine, a former unpaid committee consultant.

Republicans and Democrats on the Senate Permanent Subcommittee on Investigations joined in demanding a prompt, full inquiry into Mr. Cohn's conduct, and his removal if the Army charges were sustained. Senator McCarthy refused to call a meeting of the full subcommittee today, but indicated one might be held Tuesday.

A bitter exchange of statements between the Army and Senator McCarthy also stirred new criticism of Robert T. Stevens, Secretary of the Army, but he replied, "Positively not," when asked if he contemplated handing in his resignation.

#### Stevens Denies Charges

In his broadside at the Army, Senator McCarthy charged that Secretary Stevens, trying to stop investigations of Army Communists, had suggested to him that the committee "go after the

Associated Press Wirephoto

**DENIES ARMY CHARGE:** Roy M. Cohn, chief counsel for subcommittee headed by Senator Joseph R. McCarthy, left, as he denied at a news conference yesterday that he used improper influence with Army on behalf of Pvt. G. David Schine, former subcommittee consultant.

Navy, Air Force and Defense Department instead."

He said Mr. Stevens had agreed with a suggestion by John G. Adams, counselor of the Department of the Army, that the Army would provide the committee with leads to "plenty of dirt" in the other military services.

Secretary Stevens promptly responded that this statement was "utterly untrue."

"Anyone who knows me would realize that such a charge is fantastic," the Secretary declared.

"During the year it has been my privilege to serve as Secretary of the Army, my interest in, and cooperation with, the Navy and Air Force has been widely

known throughout those two splendid services. Anything in these services which seemed to me to need attention has been called to the notice of the other Secretaries and they have done the same thing for me. * * *"

#### McCarthy Backs Cohn

Mr. Cohn, flatly denying any improper intervention on behalf of Private Schine, also said he had no intention of resigning, and Senator McCarthy declared he would fight to the last ditch to keep him on the committee staff.

"There is only one man the Communists hate more than Roy Cohn," the Senator said. "That's J. Edgar Hoover."

As of late today Senator Mc-

Carthy was Mr. Cohn's only outright defender among the seven subcommittee members, who, regardless of party, said they meant for the committee and not its chairman to pass on staff qualifications.

Mr. McCarthy asserted he had known for some time of the existence of the Army report, released late yesterday, and that Mr. Adams had used it as long ago as Jan. 22 in an attempt to "blackmail" him into calling off his investigations into the Army.

"No investigation by me will ever be ended by threats of blackmail," said Senator McCarthy.

Mr. Adams declared the charges were "fantastic and false" and pointed out that Senator Mc-

Carthy had lodged no complaint against him with the Secretary of the Army.

From the long-range standpoint of possibly curbing Senator McCarthy in the future and reforming the methods of operation by his committee, the most significant development of the day, perhaps, was the united front other committee members developed in demanding the fullest inquiry into Mr. Cohn's conduct.

The last to join in criticism of Senator McCarthy was his old friend and supporter, Senator Everett M. Dirksen, Illinois Republican, who became angry when the chairman suddenly and without warning canceled a scheduled meeting of the four Republican committee members this afternoon.

Senator Charles E. Potter, Michigan Republican, led off early this morning with a demand for an immediate committee meeting. He declared that the Army report carried "most shocking charges."

"Assuming the information is accurate," Senator Potter said, "Mr. Cohn should be removed immediately. If the information is without foundation, however, then in all fairness to Mr. Cohn and the subcommittee, the facts should be ascertained without delay."

The three Democrats on the subcommittee—Senators John L. McClellan of Arkansas, Henry M. Jackson of Washington and Stuart Symington of Missouri—followed with a declaration that they believed the Cohn-Schine affair should receive priority over all committee business and be dealt with promptly.

## Cohn Story Asked

Senator Karl E. Mundt, South Dakota Republican, said, "if the report released by the Army is completely accurate, I believe Cohn erred sufficiently so that prompt action should be taken by our committee." He added that "like any other citizen who has been accused, Roy Cohn is entitled to present his side of the story to the committee."

Senator Dirksen also was angered by Senator McCarthy's charge of "blackmail" against the Army. He said this violated an agreement among the Republicans to withhold comment on the Army report until it had been studied carefully by them.

The Illinoisan went on to say that the Republican members as a whole, and not Senator McCarthy alone, had to take responsibility for staff members.

"I do mean to meet it," Senator Dirksen said. "There will be no fooling about it. The matter has gone far enough."

All the demands for disciplinary action were aimed at Mr. Cohn, and there was not, as yet, any suggestion in any quarter that the Senate itself might censure Senator McCarthy for his part in allegedly trying to get favored treatment for Private Schine.

Senator McCarthy made no effort to consult with other members of his subcommittee before he joined Mr. Cohn in a joint press conference defense of themselves and renewed assault on Secretary Stevens and the Army.

Neither did he provide other committee members with copies of the staff memoranda he handed to the press to support his allegations that the Army was bringing improper pressure on him through its treatment of Private Schine as "a hostage."

Senator McCarthy made no effort to conceal his anger as he struck back at the Army and denied any effort on his part to obtain any different treatment for Private Schine than was given any other draftee.

Mr. McCarthy did admit that he had suggested to Secretary Stevens that Private Schine receive an assignment in the New York area to study alleged pro-Communist material in West Point textbooks and Army indoctrination courses.

He defended this action today, contending it still would be a good idea to get a team of six or seven Army men with Private Schine's training and background to make such a study.

## Report Common Knowledge

The Army report that stirred Washington and aroused Senator McCarthy's anger had long been in preparation, and knowledge of its existence was common in Washington. It was understood to have been one of the weapons Secretary Stevens was ready to use in his counter-attack on Senator McCarthy in the most recent controversy.

But it was kept in the files when the Army Secretary bowed to Senator McCarthy's demand that he provide Army officers as witnesses who had any part in promoting or discharging honorably Maj. Irving Peress. Major Peress was the New York dental officer who received an honorable discharge after he had declined, on constitutional grounds against self-incrimination, to tell the Army or Senator McCarthy whether he had been a Communist.

Mr. Cohn sat at Senator McCarthy's left as he praised and defended his young staff aide, declaring he would believe him before he would accept the report of Mr. Adams to the Army.

"I do say the statements to the effect that improper pressure was exerted by us are a lie," Mr. Cohn said in response to questions. "I do say I didn't say I would wreck the Army. I never threatened any one or did any other such absurd thing. I think [Frank] Carr [committee staff director] was present at the meeting at which it was supposed to have been said and will bear me out."

In striking back at the Army's forty-four-numbered section report, released yesterday, Senator McCarthy made public ten separate memoranda from Mr. Carr and Mr. Cohn making serious charges against Secretary Stevens and Mr. Adams.

Senator McCarthy called attention to an unsigned report, presumably from Mr. Carr, on a session at the Pentagon Nov. 6, 1953, attended by the five main principals—Messrs. Stevens, McCarthy, Carr, Cohn and Adams.

In that McCarthy subcommittee report, it was said that Secretary Stevens had asked for and received a report on the evidence the McCarthy subcommittee intended to produce in its planned hearings about alleged subversion in the Army Signal Corps at Fort Monmouth, N. J.

The memorandum declared:

"Stevens said that if we brought out everything, he would have to resign. He said he had been in office for ten months and would have to take responsibility.

"He said that they were particularly worried about us seeking to identify those who were responsible for not acting to get rid of Communists and security risks in the Army, and who ordered their reinstatement.

### 'Plenty of Dirt'

"Mr. Stevens asked that we hold up our public hearings on the Army. He suggested that we go after the Navy, Air Force and Defense Department instead. We said first of all we had no evidence warranting an investigation of these other departments.

"Adams said not to worry about that, because there was plenty of dirt there, and they would furnish us with leads. Mr. Stevens thought this was the answer to his problem.

"We said this was not possible because we have already planned our next investigation which was one of subversion in defense plants handling Government and military contracts. He asked us why we did not start on that.***"

There was another memorandum, dated Dec. 9, from Mr. Cohn to Senator McCarthy declaring that Mr. Adams, "following up the idea about investigating the Air Force," had called to report he had collected "specific information for us about an Air Force base where there were a large number of homosexuals."

### Trade of Data Cited

"He [Mr. Adams] said that he would trade us that information if we would tell him what the next Army project was that we would investigate," Mr. Cohn wrote.

In a statement late today, Mr. Stevens did not deny he had told Senator McCarthy he might have to resign. When asked about this omission, he said he would "stand on his statement."

The Army Secretary and Mr. Adams did deny they had tried to direct the Senator's attention toward other military services and that they had offered to help him find "leads."

The Army report released yesterday dealing with the Nov. 6 meeting dealt with the Fort Monmouth situation in one line, saying that this was the "principal subject of discussion" at the luncheon.

The report then went on to chronicle in some detail requests by Senator McCarthy and Mr. Cohn that Mr. Schine receive a New York assignment when he entered the Army and that he be made available to the committee from time to time while he was undergoing basic training.

There was agreement on the latter point in the new memorandum released by Senator McCarthy today.

Another unsigned memorandum "for the files," dated Nov. 17, was released by Senator McCarthy concerning a luncheon conference he had had on that date with Secretary Stevens at the Merchants Club in New York.

According to this memorandum, Secretary Stevens told Senator McCarthy he had been "badly misquoted" in the press when he denied at a news conference that there was any evidence of espionage at Fort Monmouth.

"At this meeting," the McCarthy memorandum continued, "Stevens again said he wished that we could get onto the Air Force and the Navy and the personnel employed directly by the defense establishment instead of continuing with the Army hearings."

The Army account of the same meeting contains no mention of the luncheon table discussion. It said that Secretary Stevens gave Senator McCarthy and members of his staff a ride in his airplane to Maguire Air Force Base, adjoining Fort Dix. It said Private Schine received a pass that evening to see Senator McCarthy and subcommittee staff members.

On Dec. 9, Mr. Carr wrote to Senator McCarthy saying that he was "getting fed up with the way the Army is trying to use Schine as a hostage to pressure us to stop our hearings on the Army."

"Again today John Adams came down here after the hearings and using clever phrases tried to find out, 'what's there in it for us' if he and Stevens did something for Schine," said Mr. Carr's report.

"He refers to Schine as our hostage or the hostage whenever his name comes up. It was made clear that as far as I was concerned, I don't personally care what treatment they gave Schine, and that as far as I was concerned, he was in the Army.

"I did say I thought it wasn't fair of them to take in out on Schine, because we were investigating the Army, or to keep using it to try to stop our investigations.

"I told him the only contact we were authorized to have with him about Schine was on investigations committee business. * * * I am convinced that they will keep right on trying to blackmail us as long as Schine is in the Army.

"Even though they said he deserved the commission, they didn't give it to him because of the left-wing press, and they keep trying to dangle proposed small favors to him in front of us."

### 'He Is Baiting Roy'

The Army report of Dec. 9 said that Mr. Cohn had approached Mr. Adams to seek information about Private Schine's prospective assignment but had broken off the conversation by turning his back on the Army representative when he was told that "Private Schine was going to be handled the same as any other private soldier."

Another of Mr. Carr's memoranda to Senator McCarthy dated Jan. 15 suggested that the Senator might speak "in a friendly way" to Mr. Adams because "he is baiting Roy pretty much lately on the 'hostage' situation." Mr. Carr forecast, "it's going to lead to trouble."

One of the more serious charges against Mr. Adams was made in a very brief memorandum of Mr. Cohn to Senator McCarthy dated Jan. 14.

"Adams said this was the last chance for me to arrange that law partnership in New York which he wanted," Mr. Cohn said. "One would think he was kidding, but his persistence on this subject makes it clear he is serious. He said he had turned down a job in industry at $17,500, and needed a guarantee of $25,000 from a law firm."

Mr. Adams entered a general denial of the charges against him, and, in response to a specific question whether he had sought a New York law firm offer through Mr. Cohn, responded, "I'll stand on my original statement."

Senator Potter said his advice was "to put Cohn and Adams under oath" before the subcommittee and to seek the facts. He said they should be heard first in closed session, and then in public.

There was some doubt about how soon such a confrontation might be arranged. Senator McCarthy went to Wisconsin on a week-end speaking trip this afternoon, and Senator McClellan, the ranking Democrat, started for Arkansas on a similar mission. Senator McCarthy is expected back Monday, but plans to leave again on Wednesday for a speaking trip that will take him to Chicago, Milwaukee, and

Oklahoma City during the remainder of the week.

Senator McClellan will not return until Monday night or Tuesday. That makes it likely that the subcommittee will, at most, agree on a procedure of investigation next week, but will not be able to schedule either open or closed investigative sessions before the following week. •

While Senator McCarthy has no objection to one-man hearings conducted by himself, it is most unlikely he would agree to any hearings on the Cohn-Schine case during his absence for a speech-making tour.

**Another Inquiry Suggested**

There was a suggestion today by Senator Estes Kefauver, Tennessee Democrat, that the Senate Armed Services Committee investigate the Cohn-Schine case and the allegations of preferen-

tial treatment given by the Army under pressure.

But Senator Leverett Saltonstall, Massachusetts Republican and committee chairman, said he felt the issue was one for Senator McCarthy's committee to settle itself.

He declared the main interest of his committee, at its scheduled March 18 meeting, was to see if new legislation was required to handle the problem of Communists drafted into the Army.

A public demand that Mr. Stevens resign because he had given special favors to Private Schine was made by Representative Charles R. Howell, New Jersey Democrat. He said the Army report was "a shocking indictment" not alone of Mr. Cohn but also of Secretary Stevens. The Secretary, he said, owed the public an immediate explanation of his actions.

March 13, 1954

# Q. and A.

## In Army v. McCarthy

Out of the massive record of the case of Army v. McCarthy (33 hours of sessions held, 10 witnesses heard, 160,000 words of testimony taken) these broad impressions have emerged:

*First,* that there were differences between Senator Joseph R. McCarthy and Secretary of the Army Robert T. Stevens as early as last October over the Senator's hunt for subversives in Army installations.

*Second,* that Secretary Stevens made numerous accommodations to the Senator's wishes during that investigation and at the same time tried to persuade the Senator to call off his hearings and leave it to the Army to conduct its own inquiry and report to him.

*Third,* that Senator McCarthy and his counsel, Roy M. Cohn, repeatedly sought special treatment for their former colleague, G. David Schine, both before and after his induction into the Army last Nov. 3.

*Fourth,* that the Army went out of its way to accommodate the Senator in the matter—formally by ordering that Schine be given frequent off-the-post passes to help on "committee business" and informally by allowing him personal advantages on the post that privates normally don't have.

*Fifth,* that the Army declined to make the major accommodations that were sought in the Schine case—he did not get a commission nor a special assignment in the New York area, allegedly sought after his induction.

### Charges and Counter-Charges

All these factors are directly related to the fundamental issues in the extraordinary spectacle that is now

unfolding in the Caucus Room of the Senate Office Building in Washington, D. C. The charge—by the Army—is that Senator McCarthy and his staff made the Army a special target for investigation in reprisal for the Army's refusal to grant either a commission or a special assignment to Schine. The counter-charge—by Senator McCarthy—is that the Army used Schine as a "hostage" as part of an effort to "blackmail" the Senator into calling off his Army investigation. Behind these specific allegations there lay the whole controversy that revolves around the Senator and the issue his name symbolizes—a controversy that on many occasions has backwashed to the White House.

These fundamental questions were largely overshadowed in the hearings last week. There were wordy wrangles over procedure, and speeches frankly directed at the millions watching on TV. There were meanderings down by-paths that might or might not lead to telling disclosures. For long stretches the testimony turned back on itself —to questions, for example, about why the McCarthy office "doctored" a photograph it submitted in evidence. Over much of the testimony hung warnings of the consequences of perjury.

In the nation it was plain that public interest in the controversy was intense. But there was also impatience that the central facts were slow in emerging. And particularly among Republican politicians there was deep dismay over the spectacle being presented to the nation and the world of the U. S. Government deeply embroiled within itself at a critical stage in world affairs.

## The Monmouth Affair

The hearings last week developed —with new twists and turns each

day — the strangely intertwined story of G. David Schine and the question of security at Fort Monmouth. Army testimony two weeks ago had traced—and the McCarthy side did not contradict—the essential narrative of the efforts by the Senator and Mr. Cohn to get Mr. Schine first a commission and then assignment to the New York area. When committee counsel Jenkins resumed his cross-examination on Monday morning he quickly took up the Fort Monmouth strand.

The Monmouth affair began last summer. While it was going on, it was presented in piecemeal fashion —largely through press briefings by Senator McCarthy of what went on in closed hearings. Behind the scenes, however, there was constant maneuvering between Senator McCarthy and Secretary Stevens' office. Much of this maneuvering came out in testimony last week. This is the chronological story—put together from press accounts at the time and the testimony last week.

On Aug. 19, the Army began new investigations—as required by President Eisenhower's April 27 security order—of all civilian employes at Fort Monmouth whose files contained derogatory information. That day it suspended one employe.

On Aug. 31 the McCarthy committee interrogated three Signal Corps employes in the New York area. The Army was soon aware that Senator McCarthy was planning an investigation into Monmouth. On Sept. 29, the Army suspended five more employes at Monmouth.

On Oct. 2, Mr. Cohn and Mr. Francis Carr, director of the committee staff, complained to Secretary Stevens that personnel at Monmouth had been ordered not to talk with them. Secretary Stevens testified that in their presence he had phoned Maj. Gen. Kirke B. Lawton,

Monmouth commander, and told him to cooperate with the committee.

On Oct. 8, Senator McCarthy began a series of one-man secret hearings at the Federal Court House in Foley Square, New York. These hearings lasted for over a month. Frequently after the hearings the Senator would call in the press for a briefing in which he would make large charges and give dark hints of things to come. These are some of the things he said:

It has all the earmarks of extremely dangerous espionage. If it develops, it may envelop the entire Signal Corps. (Oct. 12.)

We have completely convincing testimony that some of the top secret missing documents * * * did turn up in the eastern zone in Berlin. (Oct. 14.)

A top Communist undercover agent * * * [has been] in telephone contact [with the radar center as recently as a week ago.] (Nov. 6.)

### Issue Over Lawton

On Oct. 14 Secretary Stevens and General Lawton came to New York for the hearings, accompanied by John G. Adams, Army counsel as of Oct. 1. Secretary Stevens left after a short time. After the hearing, Senator McCarthy talked with General Lawton in Mr. Adams' presence. Later Senator McCarthy told the press that General Lawton was waging "a vigorous campaign to clean up the mess he found when he took over at Fort Monmouth."

Cross-questioning last week threw new light on this meeting. According to an account given Counsel Jenkins by Senator McCarthy, General Lawton said he had not suspended anyone in twenty-one months until the previous two weeks. As to why there had been no suspensions during that period, the testimony indicated that the general pointed to Mr. Adams and said:

"There is one reason." This was an exchange in the testimony:

JENKINS: Do you recall that [General Lawton] was asked * * *: "Did Secretary Stevens ever direct you not to make any suspensions on your own initiative?" * * * [and that] General Lawton's reply was, in substance, "I would rather not answer; I am working for Secretary Stevens."

STEVENS: That I am not familiar with. * * * I had given instructions that our field commanders were to exercise their own judgment * * *.

Evidently General Lawton had moved fast after he began. Twenty-seven were suspended in October. Counsel Jenkins asked whether this was the "result of the McCarthy investigations." The reply was:

STEVENS: My answer to that * * * would have to be no * * * [but] it is probably true that as a result of this committee's activities some of those suspensions took effect sooner than they otherwise would have.

## Stevens Cooperates

If General Lawton was cooperating with the committee in October, Secretary Stevens himself was doing everything possible not to antagonize the Senator or his staff. He had resisted all efforts to have Mr. Schine—who was to be inducted on Nov. 3—assigned to the New York area, but he had agreed that Schine should be made available for committee work, providing it did not interfere with his training.

By the end of October, however, Secretary Stevens had become extremely "exercised" over the headlines Senator McCarthy was making with his briefings on "espionage" at Fort Monmouth.

Mr. Stevens was in something of a dilemma. He felt that Senator McCarthy was misrepresenting the situation at Monmouth, and that morale was suffering. On the other hand, he felt he must cooperate with the Senator. The President himself had set that pattern. Repeatedly the President had said that he was not going to be put in the position of criticizing Congress and that it had the right to conduct such investigations as it found necessary.

The concern Mr. Stevens was feeling was brought out in a surprise move by Counsel Jenkins at the start of Thursday's hearings. He produced a memo, dictated in his presence a few minutes before by General Lawton. It read:

Adams asked Lawton by phone, "I hope you can see your way clear to withdraw certain cases which you have recommended for removal as bad security risks."

LAWTON: I would not. Let the Secretary take the responsibility.

Under rigorous cross-examination, Secretary Stevens said he could not recall such a conversation and had not ordered Mr. Adams to make such a request. Then he made this statement:

STEVENS: I did not want to have a stampede started that would re-

sult in the wholesale suspension of people on the basis of guilt by association. * * * On the thirty-first of October I talked with General Back, the Chief Signal Officer, and * * * I said * * * that I wanted to be sure that * * * General Lawton * * * did not move * * * without sufficient information on which to justify those suspensions. * * * I think against that background it could be entirely possible that I might have talked to Mr. Adams, I might even conceivably have said, "John, perhaps you had better call General Lawton."

By Nov. 6, Mr. Stevens was so concerned that he asked Senator McCarthy to come to lunch at the Pentagon. Messrs. Cohn, Carr and Adams were present. Cross-examination brought out this picture of the meeting:

STEVENS: At the Nov. 6 luncheon when the Fort Monmouth thing was discussed, I said I didn't like this constant hammering in the headlines of the Army because I thought it gave a picture * * * of considerable espionage * * * which was not in accordance with the facts. I therefore wanted to handle this job myself * * * [and] make progress reports to Senator McCarthy * * *.

Senator McCarthy was not moved by this appeal. On Nov. 13 Mr. Stevens had a press conference. He said, bluntly the Army had found no evidence of "current espionage" at Monmouth. Three days later Messrs. Cohn and Carr visited him at the Pentagon. Mr. Stevens gave this account of the meeting:

STEVENS. Mr. Cohn indicated that Senator McCarthy was very mad and felt that I had double-crossed him * * * I said that I was sorry * * * and I enquired where he was and found he was in New York, and I said I would go to New York.

At a joint press conference the next day, Nov. 17, Mr. Stevens said that in speaking of "no current espionage," he was referring only to the Army's investigation.

The Senator simply announced he would start public hearings in New York the next week. They began Nov. 24. Army counsel Adams attended. During the day Secretary Stevens called him and asked him to tell the Senator that he was considering relieving General Lawton of his command. Mr. McCarthy—according to Mr. Stevens' testimony—was "distressed." General Lawton was not relieved.

During the public hearings, Senator McCarthy called only one present Monmouth employe, who denied any Communist ties. On Dec. 10 he said he had "no real hope" of proving espionage at Monmouth, and that "it is not our function to develop cases of espionage." The hearings ended on Dec. 17.

Last week Secretary Stevens gave this accounting on the suspensions at Monmouth:

Suspended ................... 35
Restored to duty with full clearance ................... 1
Restored to non-sensitive duty pending further investigation. 9
Resigned ................... 3
Still under suspension awaiting final action ...............22

Mr. Stevens said that none were suspended for espionage.

Of the thirty-five suspended, the McCarthy committee had interrogated twenty-five. In only one case, Mr. Stevens said, the McCarthy committee had turned up "minor" derogatory information not already supplied the Army by the F. B. I.

---

## The Other Issues

The flood of testimony that swirled around the central issue last week had to do with tangential and secondary questions of motives and credibility of witnesses; good faith and bad faith, and of the "ground rules" of the investigation itself. These were the questions that made most of the spot news and that had Senators, attorneys, witnesses and the public by turns fascinated and exasperated:

### THE 'DOCTORED' PHOTOGRAPH

Senator McCarthy maintains that the Army's complaints of "improper" pressure for Schine are made in bad faith because at the time the pressure was supposed to have taken place Mr. Stevens was on friendly terms with Schine. To support his point the Senator claims that last November the Army Secretary asked to have his picture taken with the private. Last week this issue caused an uproar not only over the picture question itself but also over the credibility of several of the witnesses.

Mr. Stevens, questioned by Mr. Jenkins last Monday, said he might have suggested a picture of several people including Schine, but he hadn't ever asked for one alone with Schine. Then Mr. Jenkins produced the famous picture—Stevens and Schine alone. A murmur rose in the committee room. The Army Secretary floundered in confusion.

Next morning Army Counsel Welch struck back with a charge that the picture had been "doctored." He brought in another print which showed that the picture originally was a group photograph with Stevens, Schine, Col. Jack Bradley and part of a fourth man. The effect was electric. Mr. Jenkins indignantly announced that his picture had been furnished him by the McCarthy staff with "no intimation, no insinuation * * * that [it] had in any wise been changed or altered." Then began the long wrangle over who had changed the picture and why.

## Five Witnesses

Five members of the McCarthy staff took the witness stand in turn—Mr. Cohn, Private Schine, George Anastos, Mrs. Frances Mims and James N. Juliana. It was the

first appearance of Messrs. Cohn and Schine, the two young men at the heart of the controversy. Mr. Cohn was a nimble, fast-talking witness. He made long speeches praising the McCarthy staff. At one point even Senator McCarthy told him: "Just stick to this testimony."

Private Schine had an easy manner and a quick smile. His answers were punctuated with "Sirs." He apologized for not remembering small details like who on the McCarthy staff was present at a dinner three nights before when a picture —"a different picture"—was discussed. He did recall that he had eaten a butterscotch sundae. When Senator McCarthy protested that Mr. Jenkins was "badgering this Army private," Schine said he didn't mind.

From what the five McCarthy witnesses said, this much was clear: After the group photograph was taken last fall near Fort Dix, Private Schine asked the Air Force photographer to send him a copy. The picture he got showed him between Mr. Stevens and Colonel Bradley; the fourth man had been "cropped," or deleted. Mr. Schine hung it in his office. Mr. Cohn saw it there. Before the current hearings opened, Mr. Cohn told Mr. Jenkins there was available a picture of Schine and Stevens. (Later Cohn testified he hadn't recalled whether or not a third man was in it but didn't think it had "the slightest importance.") Mr. Jenkins asked for the picture Cohn described. Private Schine delivered his picture to the McCarthy staff. Mr. Juliana had a photostat made of it—but without Colonel Bradley. As to why he had changed the picture, Mr. Juliana testified:

I was under the instructions, we can call them, by Mr. Cohn and/or Mr. Jenkins that I was to blow up this picture and to make available to Mr. Jenkins a picture of Mr. Schine and Secretary Stevens. * * * I was under instructions to furnish a picture of only the two individuals.

There the affair of the altered photograph now stands.

### SCHINE'S TREATMENT

The Army charges that McCarthy staff "sought by improper means to obtain preferential treatment" for Mr. Schine. The McCarthy staff charges that the Army held Schine down and used him as "a club" against the subcommittee.

Mr. Schine did not get the most important favors sought—a commission, among other things. But from a series of lengthy cross-examinations of Mr. Stevens it seemed plain that Private Schine had received a good many privileges ranging from "not doing his proper quota of K. P. duty" to getting "an unusually large number of leaves and absences." The testimony suggested that he acted as a "big shot"; he was said to have told a lieutenant his mission was to "modernize the American

Army." But the significance of the exchanges was not so much how Private Schine was treated as why he was treated that way. On this question there were three main views expressed.

Mr. Jenkins said he felt that "If [Schine] were accorded preferential treatment, it is some evidence that [the McCarthy staff asked for it]." He also indicated that "these special dispensations for Schine" might have been made by the Army "for the purpose of appeasing Senator McCarthy * * *."

## Denies Appeasement

Secretary Stevens flatly denied trying to "appease" anyone. He said he hadn't found out about Private Schine's privileges until long after they were given, and that he had not ordered them. He said the McCarthy subcommittee staff wanted Private Schine made available for certain work and he, Stevens, had cooperated by ordering "that Private Schine was to be made available [given leaves and passes] for subcommittee work * * * and for no other purpose, provided

it did not interfere with [his] training."

Senator McCarthy's strategy was to belittle the favors Schine had received and to underscore instead the fact that he was not promoted. This was one exchange:

McCARTHY: Don't you think, actually, * * * that this is all ridiculous in the extreme [to be] trying to find out why a private in the Army was successively promoted until he is finally up to the very top position of private?

STEVENS: Well, I think you would like to have had him something other than a private.

### PROCEDURAL WRANGLE

Before the hearings started, the committee agreed on certain rules of procedure. In examining witnesses, Mr. Jenkins would have unrestricted right of cross-examination. When he finished, each of the seven committee members and each of the two sides to the dispute would have ten minutes apiece. Then the circle would begin over again until everyone had asked all the questions he wanted. Testimony could be interrupted for points of

order—objections to violations of rules or immaterial or irrelevant testimony.

From the outset these rules have had the effect of slowing down the pace of the hearings. There are nine cross-examiners, with no limit to the number of go-rounds with each witness. Senator McCarthy has made the most of his own opportunities as cross-examiner. And the sound that has recurred more than any other in the hearings is the booming of the Senator's voice through the microphones saying, "Mr. Chairman * * * Mr. Chairman * * * Mr. Chairman."

## Senator's Interruptions

So far Mr. McCarthy has raised nearly twice as many "points of order" and interruptions as all the other questioners combined. Most of the "points of order" he has not attempted to justify. It has been apparent—he has said so on many occasions—that he is intent upon contradicting hostile testimony immediately it is given lest it go unchallenged too long in the minds of the TV watchers.

Chairman Mundt has frequently ruled the McCarthy interruptions out of order, but without great effect. Last week, however, Mr. Mundt appeared to be growing more and more exasperated. On Wednesday, for example, the Senator raised a "point of order," and then challenged a part of Mr. Stevens' testimony. Chairman Mundt reprimanded him for "spurious points of order." This exchange took place:

McCARTHY: I do intend to interrupt whenever I find flagrant dishonesty on the part of a witness.

McCLELLAN: If we're all going to make speeches, I'm going to make one too.

MUNDT: * * * [The] rules are very clear that there are to be no interruptions at any time except on points of order * * *.

McCARTHY: I don't think anyone can accuse me of interrupting unnecessarily.

Friday Senator McCarthy warned that he felt the committee was changing the "ground rules" and threatened that if it continued, he would "insist upon resuming my place upon the subcommittee."

May 2, 1954

# ARMY-M'CARTHY VERDICTS PUT BLAME ON BOTH SIDES; WATKINS SILENCES SENATOR

## COHN IS ASSAILED

### Majority and Minority Hit Counsel—Stevens' 'Vacillation' Scored

**By C. P. TRUSSELL**
Special to The New York Times.

WASHINGTON, Aug. 31—The Army-McCarthy battle of charge and counter-charge that ran through thirty-six days of April-to-June televised hearings ended tonight with both sides sharing censure.

The Republican majority of Senator Joseph R. McCarthy's own panel, the Senate Permanent Subcommittee on Investigations, cleared the chairman of operat-

ing directly to force the Army to bestow special favors on G. David Schine, the subcommittee's unpaid chief consultant, after Mr. Schine had been drafted.

However, the majority found that the Wisconsin Republican had permitted Roy M. Cohn, chief counsel of his investigating group, and perhaps others to make things uncomfortable for the Army if Mr. Schine did not get special privileges.

The three Democratic members in a minority report said Senator McCarthy "merited severe criticism" along with Mr. Cohn for actions in Mr. Schine's behalf.

#### Stevens Criticized

Robert T. Stevens, Secretary of the Army, who faced many days of sharp questioning, was held by the Republicans of the subcommittee to have been "beyond reproach." However, to these words of comfort were added a criticism that Mr. Ste-

vens had dealt in "placation," "appeasement" and "vacillation" in handling Mr. Cohn in particular.

The four Republicans who signed the majority report were Senators Karl E. Mundt of South Dakota, who served as chairman of the special investigation; Everett M. Dirksen of Illinois; Charles E. Potter of Michigan, and Henry C. Dworshak of Idaho.

The Democratic minority was composed of Senators John L. McClellan of Arkansas, Henry M. Jackson of Washington, and Stuart Symington of Missouri.

Senator Potter filed a separate report in which, speaking for himself, he was much more critical of all concerned than was the general tenor of the majority's findings. Senator Dirksen also filed an indivdual report saying the Army charges against Senator McCarthy had not been proved.

Senator McClellan, in a brief statement, said he was "grati-

fied" that the Democratic members had been able to reconcile differences on minor points and submit a joint report, not separate and independent views. The majority report ran to about 2,000 words, while the Democrats let theirs extend to about 7,800.

These reports released today had been culled from more than 1,000,000 words of testimony supplemented by supporting exhibits.

#### The Majority Points

The Republican majority of the special committee concluded:

¶That the charge of improper influence on behalf of Private Schine had not been established as a deliberate and personal act of Senator McCarthy, but that he should have displayed "more vigorous discipline in stopping any member of his staff" from attempting such a move.

¶That Mr. McCarthy appeared to have known about such activities and to have condoned them.

¶That Mr. Cohn was "unduly persistent and aggressive" on behalf of Mr. Schine without any curbs being applied by Senator McCarthy.

¶That the Fort Monmouth, N.J., inquiry, still largely in controversy, was not a part of a possible plan to get Army favors for Mr. Schine.

¶That Secretary Stevens and John G. Adams, Army Counsellor, did try to bring about a termination or deferment of the Fort Monmouth investigations in one backstage maneuver or another

¶That when matters subject to Congressional investigation were apparent, the Army's spokesmen were "derelict" in not introducing immediate protest against the committee's alleged interest in and pressures for Mr. Schine.

## Democrats Milder

The report of the Democrats seemed milder at many points than those made jointly or individually by Republicans. The Democratic report held that Mr. McCarthy had "fully acquiesced in and condoned" the "improper actions" of Mr. Cohn.

"For these inexcusable actions," the report added, "Senator McCarthy and Mr. Cohn merit severe criticism" on the ground that they had sought preferential Army treatment for Private Schine.

The Democrats also rebuked Secretary Stevens and Mr. Adams for following the line of "appeasement."

It was the duty of Secretary Stevens, as the head of the Army, the Democrats contended, to report immediately any instance in which pressure had been invoked to urge the department to depart from its system of impartial treatment to all of its human components.

Herein, it was held, the Secretary "demonstrated an inexcusable indecisiveness."

The principal issues of the long and sensational inquiry were these:

¶Did Senator McCarthy, Mr. Cohn and Francis P. Carr, the subcommittee's executive director, use the investigating arm of the Senate in an effort to secure preferential treatment for Mr. Schine?

¶Did Mr. Stevens seek to use Mr. Schine as a means to halt or deter investigation of certain activities of the Army by the McCarthy subcommittee?

## Two Discarded Issues

Other issues entered the picture. Senator McCarthy was accused of using "vehement language" and "browbeating" Brig. Gen. Ralph W. Zwicker, commandant of Camp Kilmer, as he questioned him in closed session.

One discarded issue was the propriety of Senator McCarthy's presentation as evidence of excerpts of a report by the Federal Bureau of Investigation—held to be "top secret"—for public view. Another was Mr. McCarthy's contention that employes or officials in executive departments should turn over to his committee information "in the public inter-

est" that remained classified as matter still under security order.

The Republicans of the subcommittee held that these were extraneous matters, even though their importance might be great. As assigned to the specific Army-McCarthy dispute, they held such matters were beyond their jurisdiction and should be handled as routine of the investigations subcommittee when it returns to its assigned tasks.

## On Future Investigations

The majority made several specific recommendations dealing with the conduct of committee personnel and with future procedures of Congressional investigations. Among them were:

¶That no unpaid staff members be used.

¶That committees adopt a rule against unauthorized contacts between staff members and policy-forming officials of the Executive Branch on matters not specifically involved in committee proceedings.

¶That hearings outside Washington be authorized by majority vote and that at least two members attend.

¶That investigating committee chairmen supply members with a weekly summary of staff activities.

¶That a Senate Judiciary subcommittee study what data the Executive Branch is justified in denying Congress.

In his report Senator Dirksen alleged, in effect, that the Army never would have filed charges against the investigating group if Senator McCarthy had not served notice that he was going to subpoena members of the Army loyalty and screening board. Mr. McCarthy served this notice as he was pursuing the case of Maj. Irving M. Peress, an Army dentist who received an honorable discharge after refusing to answer questions concerning alleged Communistic sympathies.

Senator Potter contended that while the subcommittee was investigating the Army, Mr. Cohn exerted his full pressure as chief counsel of the subcommittee to obtain favors for Private Schine. Senator McCarthy knew what was going on, he stated, but instead of stopping it, continued to praise and express confidence in Mr. Cohn and the work he was doing. That, he held, was giving Mr. Cohn a free rein.

## Dirksen Cites Chronology

Mr. Dirksen focused on the Army's own "chronology of events," the basis of its twenty-nine charges against Senator McCarthy and members of his staff. The chronology covered more than a year, during which, the Senator contended, luncheons, dinners, prize fights, theatre tickets and other signs of harmonious companionship — not suspicion and recriminations—were the order of the day.

It was four months after Mr.

Schine joined the subcommittee staff, Mr. Dirksen held, that the first alleged improper effort was made to obtain for him, as a prospective draftee, an Army commission. Mr. Schine did not get a commission, he said, but there was no complaint about Mr. Cohn's attempt to get him one.

Four hours later, Mr. Dirksen declared, the committee first began to formalize its inquiry to Fort Monmouth. Mr. Schine was drafted about a month after that.

Not until last January, Senator Dirksen emphasized, did the subpoena issue arise, accompanied by the first indication that the Army was to open fire on the subcommittee. At that time, the Senator said, the Army began compiling its "chronology," which developed into formal charges in April.

Senator Dirksen contended that the review of monitored telephone calls to, from and within the Pentagon "impels" a conclusion that Secretary Stevens "entertained no belief of improper means or influence on the part of Senator McCarthy or his staff."

One call in particular, the Senator stated, demonstrated that Secretary Stevens was "fully acquainted with every facet and angle of the Schine story." He declared that in this telephonic conversation Mr. Stevens had said: "* * * I don't have a lot of stuff so far as my contact with Joe or the committee is concerned."

## Potter's Conclusions

Senator Potter concluded, in brief, that:

¶Secretary Stevens handled charge and counter-charge through days of questioning in a way suggesting "lack of competency," "bewilderment" and a record of "vacillation and appeasement" while under pressure for favors to be granted Mr. Schine. Meanwhile the Secretary strongly supported charges intending to defer or terminate investigations at Fort Monmouth, with the Schine case developments as weapons to fight off further inquiry.

¶Mr. Schine, lacking professional investigative training and being of "questionable value" to the subcommittee, knew of the imminence of his induction not long after Mr. Cohn had got him his post as a volunteer and unpaid chief consultant of the subcommittee.

¶Mr. Cohn's activities on the part of Mr. Schine impaired the effectiveness of legislative inquiries into the operations of the Executive Branch and subtracted from public confidence in Congressional investigations.

¶Mr. Carr, an F. B. I.-trained investigator, who became executive director of subcommittee programs, was junior to Mr. Cohn in service and appeared to be acceding to Mr. Cohn's wishes. What-

ever protests he entered were "feeble."

¶Mr. Adams, the highest legal authority in the Department of the Army, appeared to share the Secretary's hope that the Fort Monmouth investigation could be deterred, and to act accordingly in his back-stage discussions with committee spokesmen.

## McClellan's Statement

Senator McClellan in his statement commenting on the report said:

"Because of the highly controversial nature of the issues and the personalities involved, this has been one of the most unpleasant public services I have ever had to perform. Throughout the hearings and in writing this report, I have tried to be fair and just to all of the principles to this controversy. In considering and writing this report, there was present at times the natural inclination to say as little as possible, or to say more than might be necessary, or to so phrase it in language that might be susceptible of varied interpretations—in other words, to say a lot that might mean nothing.

"Speaking for the Democratic members of the subcommittee, however, we were able to reconcile such minor differences as may have existed among us, and it is gratifying to me that we have been able to submit a joint report and not separate and independent views. We have recorded our findings in terms we trust that are temperate and judicious and that are based upon and sustained by the record of the proceedings before us."

Three of the principals withheld comment this evening.

Senator McCarthy declared he would have nothing to say tonight.

Secretary Stevens left word at the Pentagon that he had "no comment at this time."

Mr. Adams said he planned to spend the evening at Griffith Stadium watching a baseball game between the Washington Senators and the Detroit Tigers. "I will have nothing to say about the report, in whole or in part, until I've had an opportunity to read it," he declared.

## People Judge, Says Cohn

Mr. Cohn issued the following statement last night:

"The American people have seen and heard what took place at these hearings. They are the jury. Their decision is what counts. And they have given me tremendous support in this controversy and in my work on the prosecution of Communists and spies.

"It is now apparent that anyone who associates himself with the cause of exposing atheistic Communist infiltration has to contend not only with the smears of Communists but with partisan politics as well."

# FINAL VOTE CONDEMNS M'CARTHY, 67-22, FOR ABUSING SENATE AND COMMITTEE; ZWICKER COUNT ELIMINATED IN DEBATE

## REPUBLICANS SPLIT

### Democrats Act Solidly in Support of Motion Against Senator

**By ANTHONY LEVIERO**

Special to The New York Times.

WASHINGTON, Dec. 2—The Senate voted 67 to 22 tonight to condemn Joseph R. McCarthy, Republican Senator from Wisconsin.

Every one of the forty-four Democrats present voted against Mr. McCarthy. The Republicans were evenly divided—twenty-two for condemnation and twenty-two against. The one independent, Senator Wayne Morse of Oregon, also voted against Mr. McCarthy.

In the ultimate action the Senate voted to condemn Senator McCarthy for contempt of a Senate Elections subcommittee that investigated his conduct and financial affairs, for abuse of its members, and for his insults to the Senate itself during the censure proceeding.

Lost in a day of complex and often confused parliamentary maneuvering was the proposal to censure Senator McCarthy for his denunciation of Brig. Gen. Ralph W. Zwicker as unfit to wear his uniform.

This proposal was defeated by a parliamentary device that avoided a direct vote on the merits of the issue. Inquiry among influential Senators indicated they considered the Zwicker proposal a dilemma they wished to avoid.

#### Amendment Substituted

They said they wished to censure because the facts warranted it. If they failed to do so, they believed large elements of the public would feel the Senate took notice of offenses only against itself and not against ordinary citizens.

But also if they did censure for this, then Senator McCarthy could exploit the decision, contending he was being punished for his effort to expose former Maj. Irving Peress, the Army dentist who was promoted and honorably discharged, and who was denounced by Mr. McCarthy as a "Fifth Amendment Communist."

Mr. McCarthy's denunciation of General Zwicker, who was commanding officer at Camp Kilmer, N. J., when Dr. Peress was discharged, occurred when the Senator interrogated General Zwicker on the question of who had promoted Dr. Peress.

The direct test on the Zwicker issue was avoided by the substitution of the amendment to condemn Senator McCarthy for having insulted the Senate during his censure trial.

#### McCarthy Loses Three Tests

Thus in its final form the resolution of condemnation was in two parts, covering the offenses against the Elections subcommittee and its members in the first part, and against the Senate in the second. Three test votes were all lost by Mr. McCarthy before the final condemnation.

First was a motion to table the Zwicker proposal, made by Senator Styles Bridges, Republican of New Hampshire, the president pro tem of the Senate, who assumed the leadership of the effort to save Mr. McCarthy yesterday.

Such a motion, if it had succeeded, might have led to a situation that would have prolonged the debate.

But amid signs that the Zwicker issue would have tough sledding, Senator Wallace F. Bennett, Republican of Utah, served notice that if Mr. Bridges' move were defeated he would attempt to substitute for the Zwicker issue his amendment for abuse of the Senate. The significance of this was that an amendment by substitution would require no time out for debate.

Then the voting proceeded. The motion to table was defeated 55 to 33. Mr. Bennett's motion to substitute passed by 64 to 23 and in the next vote his amendment was adopted by the same tally.

The final vote placing Mr. McCarthy under moral condemnation by the Senate came at 5:03 P. M.

The moment of decision was something of an anti-climax after days of emotional and bitter debate. It was punctuated by mocking laughter from the hard core of Mr. McCarthy's adherents.

The accused Senator was present, but he was not led to the bar of the Senate to hear any punishment. Instead Mr. Bridges arose from the coterie in the vicinity of Mr. McCarthy and asked Vice President Richard M. Nixon if the word "censure" appeared anywhere in the resolution in its final form.

Laughter from Senator William E. Jenner, Republican of Indiana, and one of Mr. McCarthy's most vociferous supporters, resounded through the chamber. Senator McCarthy was grinning. Senator George W. Malone, Republican of Nevada, standing by Senator Jenner, was laughing, and so was Senator Herman Welker, Republican of Idaho, sitting beside Mr. Jenner, who all through the debate made the running defense for Mr. McCarthy.

Mr. Jenner guffawed loudly again as Mr. Nixon, after examining the text with a clerk, announced the word "censure" was absent. The document used the word "condemned" in each of its two parts, it was explained.

"Then it is not a censure resolution," said Mr. Bridges, who by virtue of his office presides over the Senate when Mr. Nixon is absent. He also asked if condemnation was censure.

#### Fulbright Reads Definitions

"The resolution does concern the conduct of the junior Senator from Wisconsin," replied the Vice President. "The interpretation must be that of the Senator or any other Senator."

Then Senator J. William Fulbright, Democrat of Arkansas, rose with Webster's International Dictionary before him and read definitions of condemn and censure amid general laughter. Senator Jenner, without asking for the floor said, "Let's do it over again. Let's do a retake."

Senator Bridges then remarked that this was "peculiar censure" to discover after all the time and expense of a special Senate session that the resolution did not contain the word "censure."

Senator Fulbright asserted that Senator Welker had attached a more serious meaning to "condemn" than to "censure." Earlier today in one of his impassioned speeches Mr. Welker had said, "You don't censure a man to death, you condemn him to death."

Senator Arthur V. Watkins, Republican of Utah, who was chairman of the special committee that recommended censure, then said that in the last censure proceeding, twenty-five years ago, the word "censure" was not used but that the resolution had stated that "such conduct is hereby condemned."

"The point I wanted to make," said Senator Watkins, "is that it is the historical word used in censure resolutions."

Then Mr. Jenner asked for the floor in the usual parliamentary way, this time to remark, grinning, there was some confusion and "do you suppose we could do it all over again?"

Senator Welker rose to comment on definitions and referred to the censure proceedings as a "mock court."

Shortly afterward Senator McCarthy left. He had been in the Senate chamber only briefly, coming in after the final roll-call on the ultimate vote had started. He said "present" instead of voting on the issue that is bound to have a marked effect on his political career.

Later, outside the chamber, reporters asked him if he felt he had been censured.

"Well, it wasn't exactly a vote of confidence," replied Mr. McCarthy, who was still wearing his right arm in a bandage for the bursitis that had interrupted the censure proceedings for ten days.

"I'm happy to have this circus ended so I can get back to the real work of digging out communism, crime and corruption," he continued. "That job will start officially Monday morning, after ten months of inaction." He was referring to a coming inquiry into alleged Communists in defense plants.

He had referred to the session as a "lynch party"—one of the remarks for which he was condemned in the Bennett amendment—and was asked if he felt he had been "lynched."

"I don't feel I have been lynched," he replied.

He expressed his disappointment that the Democrats had voted "straight down the party line, even though they had declared before it started that this was to be a judicial proceeding."

Among Democrats the view was that he might have received a number of their votes if he had not condemned the whole Democratic party some months ago as "the party of treason."

Mr. McCarthy said after referring to the "circus" that he felt no different than he had last night. That is when he had referred to the censure proceeding as a "farce" and a "foul job."

Shouting objections, Senator Jenner opposed an amendment by Senator Edwin C. Johnson, Democrat of Colorado, and vice chairman of the censure committee, that would have placed the Senate on record in the censure resolution as being against communism and determined to investigate subversion relentlessly.

"You're not going to gild the lily now," shouted Senator Jenner. "The record has been made and you are going to stay with it."

He declared that the Democrats had permitted Communists to steal Government secrets through infiltration of the Government.

Senator Price Daniels, Democrat of Texas, then made an eloquent plea, proposing that the resolution be amended to state that the resolution should not be construed to limit the investigative powers of the Senate, especially as to any Communist conspiracy.

He said he wanted to do this to counter the McCarthy charge that the Communist party had reached into the Senate to make a censure committee "do the work of the Communist party."

"I want to make them [the Communists] unhappy and they will be unhappy if you will permit this amendement to be adopted," said Mr. Daniels to Mr. Jenner. "We will be able to say to the world that the allegation is untrue that the Communist party instigated this."

Vice President Nixon ruled that under a consent agreement between the two parties neither the Johnson nor the Daniel amendment could be accepted because it was not germane to the issue of censure.

**Flanders Retracts One Point**

Toward the end of the Senate session, which adjourned sine die for this year at 7:10 P. M., Senator Ralph E. Flanders, Republican of Vermont, who had sponsored the original censure motion, said he would stand by all the speeches he had made against Senator McCarthy except that he would like to apologize for a passage in a speech of last March, when he had likened Mr. McCarthy to Hitler.

He also asked unanimous consent to strike the passage from whatever volumes of The Congressional Record remained unbound, but Senator Welker made the single objection that prevented this.

Senators McCarthy, Welker and Jenner have threatened to file counter censure resolutions against Senators Flanders, Fulbright and Morse, who had filed the specifications for the McCarthy censure action. They gave no indication of their plans, and adjournment of the Senate tonight would compel them to wait until the next session.

But Senator Jenner threatened Mr. Flanders with a subpoena if he did not appear before some committee to testify about any relations he might have had with Owen Lattimore.

Mr. Lattimore is a former State Department consultant and professor at Johns Hopkins University who is under indictment on a charge of perjury in a Congressional hearing on his alleged Communist associations.

General Zwicker, now with combat troops in Japan, was criticized by a few McCarthy adherents today as an arrogant and evasive witness against the contrary evidence of the censure committee, which had called him as a witness.

He had a great many champions, though, even among some Senators who said they would not vote for censure in his case, though they deplored the treatment he had received.

Senator Herbert H. Lehman, Democrat of New York, was among those urging censure in the Zwicker incident. The view of this group was that it would be notice to the country that the Senate was interested only in the offenses against itself but cared nothing for abusive treatment of ordinary citizens.

Senator A. S. Mike Monroney, Democrat of Oklahoma, declared that failure to censure on this count would be notice to the public that the Senate was "a privileged class." He asserted the Zwicker incident was a prime example of how Senator McCarthy indiscriminately abused heroes of the United States and Communists.

Senator Monroney also said failure to censure on this count would be notice that it was all right to place wire taps and intercept mail and telephone calls of teachers, professors, private citizens, whether it was constitutional or not, but that it was not all right to do so in the case of the ninety-six Senators.

It would also amount to saying, he added, that "We are sacrosanct, we are going to disregard the constitutional guarantees."

His allusion here was to the charge by Senator McCarthy that the Elections subcommittee that had investigated his conduct and finances in 1952 had kept a undercover watch on his mail and telephone calls.

Mr. McCarthy contended this was illegal, but the debate brought out yesterday that the subcommittee had been investigating the charge that Senator McCarthy was using money sent him by the public to fight communism to speculate on a commodity exchange.

Senator Charles E. Potter, Republican of Michigan, a Silver Star Army veteran who lost both legs in combat, said he also favored censure in the Zwicker case.

Senator Irving M. Ives, Republican of New York, defeated in the race for Governor in the recent election, kept silent on the McCarthy issue all through the debate, but voted against Mr. McCarthy.

However, whenever Senator Watkins made the pro forma motions to reconsider each vote— a technicality needed to make it final—Senator Ives each time made the necessary motion to table.

# THE CHRONOLOGY IN M'CARTHY CASE

### Dispute Over Senator Started With 1950 Speech on Reds in State Department

Special to The New York Times.

WASHINGTON, Dec. 2—Following is a chronology of events in the recent emergence of Senator Joseph R. McCarthy as a "controversial figure" from his Wheeling, West Va. speech on "Communists in the State Department"ing, W. Va., speech on "Conduct today by the United States Senate:

Feb. 9, 1950—Speech in Wheeling stated that there were 205 (later 57) Communists in the State Department.

March 8, 1950—Investigation of McCarthy charges begun by Tydings subcommittee of Senate Foreign Relations Committee.

July 17, 1950—Tydings subcommittee submitted report stating that McCarthy charges against the State Department were "a hoax and fraud." Senators Lodge and Hickenlooper in minority report called inquiry "superficial and inconclusive" and charged that it "lacked impartiality."

June 14, 1951—Senate speech on General of the Army George C. Marshall stated that General Marshall was "steeped in falsehood" and "has recourse to the lie whenever it suits his convenience."

Aug. 3, 1951—Gillette elections subcommittee report on the 1950 Maryland Senatorial campaign submitted. Report stated that Senator McCarthy and his staff were a "leading and potent force" in the campaign. The tactics used against Senator Tydings were described as "* * * destructive of fundamental American principles."

Sept. 28, 1951—Senate Rules Subcommittee on Privileges and Elections began hearings under S. Res. 187 incorporating charges by Senator Benton that Senator McCarthy "has committed perjury and has practiced calculated deceit" and proposing his ouster.

March 26, 1952—Filed $2,000,000 libel and slander suit against Senator Benton.

June 3, 1952—Privileges and Elections subcommittee decided to conduct parallel inquiries under S. Res. 187 and S. Res. 304 incorporating Senator McCarthy's countercharges concerning Senator Benton's finances, campaign tactics, record on subversion and labor practices.

Nov. 4, 1952—Re-elected for second Senate term.

Jan. 2, 1953—Privileges and Elections subcommittee submitted report. Criticized Senators McCarthy and Benton but made no recommendations. Charged that Senator McCarthy had "deliberately set out to thwart the investigation."

December 3, 1954

March 21, 1953—Opposed confirmation of Charles E. Bohlen as Ambassador to Russia. Charged Secretary of State Dulles had made "untrue" statement concerning Mr. Bohlen's security clearance.

March 30, 1953—Harold E. Stassen states Senator McCarthy was "undermining" Administration efforts to stop trade with Communist countries. The McCarthy committee staff earlier had negotiated an agreement with a group of Greek shipowners in London in which the shipowners pledged not to engage in trade with Communist nations.

April 2, 1953—President Eisenhower suggests that Mr. Stassen might have meant to use "infringement" rather than "undermine" in describing Senator McCarthy's action.

May 5, 1953—Charged that "30,000 to 40,000 books by Communists and fellow-travelers" were in overseas libraries.

July 8, 1953—State Department issued policy statement on books in overseas libraries reaffirming the fact that the content of the book and "its special usefulness in terms of our overseas needs" would be the basis of selection.

July 8, 1953—Senator McCarthy, according to Maj. Gen. Niles Reber, then chief of legislative liaison for the Army, tells General Reber he is interested in "obtaining" a direct Army commission for G. David Schine, who faces a draft call.

Aug. 19, 1953—Army orders its first suspension of a Fort Monmouth civilian employe on security charges.

Aug. 31, 1953—Senate Permanent Subcommittee on Investigations starts closed-door hearings on Signal Corps employes in New York.

Sept. 8, 1953—Army Secretary Stevens meets with Senator McCarthy for the first time. Mr. Stevens, according to his own testimony, arranged the interview upon reading news reports of a "disturbing situation," which Senator McCarthy said he had found among personnel at Fort Monmouth.

Oct. 12, 1953—Mr. McCarthy, in press conference on Monmouth hearings, tells reporters that the case has the "earmarks of dangerous espionage."

Oct. 13, 1953—Secretary Stevens, at Senator McCarthy's suggestion, attends a dinner given by Mr. Schine's parents at a New York hotel.

Oct. 14, 1953—Mr. McCarthy tells the press, "we have completely convincing evidence that some * * * top-secret missing documents [from Fort Monmouth] did turn up in the Eastern [Russian] zone of Berlin."

Oct. 16, 1953—Attorney General Brownell announced that investigation of Senator McCarthy's finances had revealed no evidence of any violation of fraud or election laws.

Nov. 3, 1953—Mr. Schine inducted into the Army as a private and is assigned to Fort Dix, N. J., for basic training.

Nov. 13, 1953—Secretary Stevens issues a report on the Army's own investigation of alleged subversives at Fort Monmouth, saying there is no evidence of "current espionage."

Nov. 24, 1954—Criticized Administration for not stopping trade with Communists.

Dec. 3, 1953—Urges persons who agree with him on trade with China to write or wire the President.

Dec. 3, 1953—Mr. McCarthy opens investigation of case of Maj. Irving Peress, dentist at Camp Kilmer, N. J. An Army personnel board had received, six months before, a recommendation for Captain Peress' discharge on grounds that he had refused to answer loyalty questions. Since then, Captain Peress, in a separate action, had been automatically promoted from captain on the basis of age and professional experience.

Dec. 30, 1953—Army decides to discharge Major Peress.

Jan. 1, 1954—Urges defeat of any Congressional candidate not on record against aid to nations trading with Communists.

Jan. 30, 1954—Major Peress, questioned by Senator McCarthy at a hearing, refuses to answer most questions, citing the Fifth Amendment.

Feb. 2, 1954—Major Peress honorably discharged.

Feb. 18, 1954—Senator McCarthy questions Brig. Gen. Ralph W. Zwicker, Major Peress' former commandant at Camp Kilmer, and when he refuses to answer certain questions on ground that

loyalty investigation rules forbid it, Senator McCarthy says General Zwicker is "unfit to wear [the Army] uniform."

March 5, 1954—Dropped suit against former Senator Benton.

March 9, 1954—Senator Flanders charges Senator McCarthy has become "one-man party" and is "doing his best to shatter" Republican party.

March 11, 1954—Army charges in report prepared for some members of Congress and "leaked" to the press that members of Senator McCarthy's staff had threatened "to wreck the Army" unless special treatment was given to their former colleague, Private Schine.

March 12, 1954—Senator McCarthy, in countercharge, says Army tried to "blackmail" him into calling off his investigations of the Army.

March 16, 1954—Senate investigating subcommittee votes to air the entire McCarthy-Army controversy in open hearings.

April 14, 1954—Army files with subcommittee its formal charges against Senator McCarthy and Roy M. Cohn and Francis Carr, aides of Senator McCarthy.

April 20, 1954—McCarthy group files countercharges, including an accusation that the Army's campaign was designed by Assistant Defense Secretary H. Struve Hensel to stop subcommittee investigation of Mr. Hensel for "misconduct and possible law violation," while in a high Navy Department post in the last war. Mr. Hensel called the charge a "barefaced lit."

April 22, 1954—Hearings on the Army - McCarthy controversy begin.

June 17, 1954—Hearings end, after thirty-six days of testimony.

July 18, 1954—Senator Flanders urges Senate to back his motion to censure Senator McCarthy.

July 30, 1954—Debate on Senator Flanders' motion to censure Senator McCarthy begins.

Aug. 2, 1954—Senate votes, 75 to 12, to form select Senate committee to weigh censure motion.

Aug. 5, 1954—Committee named by Vice President Nixon.

Aug. 6, 1954—Senator Watkins named chairman.

Aug. 9, 1954—Public hearings set

for Aug. 30. Senator McCarthy granted right to cross-examine any witness but only one person will be able to examine any given witness.

Aug. 24, 1954—Senator Watkins issues statement cataloguing charges.

Aug. 31, 1954—Army-McCarthy subcommittee issues four reports on hearings.

1. By majority (Senators Mundt, Dirksen, Potter, Dworshak). Clears Senator McCarthy of operating directly to force Army to give special favors to Private Schine; finds that he should have been more vigorous in stopping staff members, especially Mr. Cohn, from attempting to exert improper influence for Private Schine; that he apparently knew of such attempts and condoned them; that Mr. Cohn was "unduly persistent and aggressive" on Private Schine's behalf and was not curbed by Senator McCarthy; that Mr. Stevens and John G. Adams, his aide, sought to defer or end Fort Monmouth inquiry.

2. By minority (Senators McClellan, Symington, Jackson). Senator McCarthy and Mr. Cohn merit "severe criticism" for actions in Private Schine's behalf; that Senator McCarthy "fully acquiesced in and condoned" improper actions by Mr. Cohn; that Mr. Stevens and Mr. Adams followed the line of appeasement.

3. By Senator Potter, a separate report more critical of principals.

4. By Senator Dirksen, a separate report finding Army charges against Senator McCarthy were not proved.

Aug. 31, 1954—First day of hearings on motion to censure.

Sept. 13, 1954—Last day of censure hearings. (Nine days of hearings.)

Sept. 24, 1954—Senator Watkins announces committee report completed. Senate to convene Nov. 8.

Sept. 27, 1954—Watkins committee unanimously recommends censure on three of five categories.

Nov. 8, 1954—First day of Senate debate on censure resolution. Senate votes approval of censure resolution after rejecting successive efforts to dilute or erase condemnation of Wisconsin Senator.

December 3, 1954

# Where Government May Not Trespass

## The clamor of McCarthyism has faded away. But, says a noted historian, a dangerous drift is taking place toward Federal controls in the realm of ideas.

### By HENRY STEELE COMMAGER

THE climate of freedom has cleared, to some degree at least, in the last two years—thanks in good part to the integrity and wisdom of our courts—and the nightmare of McCarthyism is receding into

the past to join similar aberrations ranging from the Alien and Sedition Acts of 1798 to the Red hysteria of the Twenties.

But while the overt threat to freedom is less urgent, a new and, in some ways, more serious threat has developed. This is the threat of gov-

ernmental control over ideas. It is more serious because it is less ostentatious and does not therefore excite alarm. It affects groups and interests unorganized and unable to protect themselves. It threatens not merely a temporary departure from sound constitutional practices but a fundamental revolution in the constitutional system itself; it also threatens the most precious of all our interests, our intellectual and spiritual integrity.

The framers of our constitutions, state and national, differed on the question of what authority government should exercise, but they were almost unanimous on the question of what authority government should not exercise. All of them—Jefferson and Hamilton, Madison and John Adams, Paine and Wilson—agreed that there were some things no government could do. And if we ask what were these things —what was the area over which government had no authority whatsoever —the answer is plain. It is the answer written into bills of rights, state and Federal alike. Government had no authority over the realm of ideas and their communication—religion, speech, press, assembly, association and so forth.

The reason that control over these matters was denied to government is equally plain. It was not out of any peculiar tenderness for preachers or writers or editors or critics. It was because the kind of governments that the framers were setting up—governments resting on the consent of the people and run by the people—simply could not work unless churches, press, universities, political parties and private associations were free to inquire, discuss and criticize. This is not a sentimental consideration, but a tough-minded one. If government controls access to and dissemination of information, there is no true freedom, and without freedom we will fall into error that may be irremediable.

WHAT we have witnessed since the second World War, and more particularly in the last four or five years, is the entry of government into areas heretofore thought immune from governmental invasion. The danger is not — as the President and many state Governors argue — that the Federal Government has taken on new responsibilities in the realms of social security or hydroelectric power, public health or housing. These developments we can take in our stride. If they prove to be mistaken or misguided, they can be reversed. What is ominous is that government — chiefly, though not exclusively, the Federal Government — has invaded the area of ideas and their communication. It has moved, steadily and stubbornly, into control of activities traditionally—and constitutionally—immune from such control.

This is not, let it be said at once, the result of a conspiracy, or of lust for power, any more than the growth of Federal control over such matters as conservation, agriculture, banking and transportation was the product of a conspiracy or lust for power. Nobody,

HENRY STEELE COMMAGER is Professor of American History at Amherst College.

apparently, wants it this way, and nobody in authority is prepared to admit that it is happening. Almost everybody talks about the necessity of less control in certain areas and, for example, the return to the states of oil lands goes on apace. But in the realm that really counts—the realm that will be decisive of the kind of government we have in the future—Federal assumption of authority increases.

LET us look at this process of growing controls in the realm of ideas, and let us note the way in which local governments and private groups, ordinarily hostile to controls, supinely acquiesce in and adopt Federal practices and standards. First, there is the approval of the "security" program, which President Truman inaugurated, and which has expanded under Mr. Eisenhower. I am not concerned here with the wisdom or the ethics of the program itself, with its monstrous abuses, with its palpable inefficiency. What I am concerned with is, rather, the way in which its operation puts control over political and social ideas in the hands of government. The Attorney General's list, for example—a list to which the Wright Commission on Government Security would now give clear legality and permanence— establishes Federal standards of desirable and undesirable organizations. It is a list which state after state has adopted—and expanded; it is a list which local communities, and even private organizations, have hastened to accept as a standard for employment, or even for the purchase of library books or of works of art.

THUS New Yorkers who look with dismay on the invasion by the Federal Government of slum clearance are quite prepared to accept a list prepared by some bureaucrat in Washington as a valid test for the hiring of teachers. Thus Texans who are ready to fight at a new Alamo against Federal control of tidelands oil or of natural gas are quite ready to accept what amounts to Federal standards of what books should be in their libraries and what pictures should hang in their art museums.

Consider the furor over those who take refuge in the First or Fifth Amendment, or who refuse to "cooperate" with Congressional committees. Some states require by law that all those

in public employment "cooperate" with investigating committees; others punish by deprivation of their jobs those who, for one reason or another, take refuge in the First or Fifth Amendment, thus punishing where the law itself does not punish. Everywhere the result is the same: local standards are influenced or determined by decisions, or

merely attitudes, radiating from Washington.

A SECOND example of the growth of Federal authority in the realm of ideas is the exercise of control over foreign travel. Time was when Americans did not need passports for travel abroad. Then they came to be used purely as statements of identification and formal requests for courtesy from other nations. The use of the passport and the visa as a mark of approval or disapproval is something new in our history, and it is fraught with danger.

If the right to travel abroad is to depend on the subjective judgment of some subordinate in the State Department as to whose travel is "in the interests of the United States," there is an end—in theory, at least—to freedom of travel. Who determines what are the interests of the United States? Who determines whether a particular passport applicant meets these murky criteria? If everyone who expects to travel must so comport himself as to satisfy the notions of Federal bureaucracy about political ideas, associations and activities, control over travel may well become a powerful instrument for Federal control of thought.

NOR does this principle operate only in the denial of passports. When the State Department assumes responsibility to decide that it is, or is not, in the interest of the United States for a particular person to go abroad, it follows in logic that those who are permitted to travel travel in the interests of the United States. This is, perhaps, the logical assumption behind Mr. Dulles' recent announcement that newspaper men are, in a sense, instruments of national policy.

A third area of Federal control is science. We know from our own experience, and from the experience of Germany and Italy, how important it is to national security and progress that science be free. But we know, too, that the pressures on science and scientists to be "instruments of national policy" is heavy, and growing. The concern of the Government with the whole area of nuclear physics, for example, is too obvious to elaborate, and it is obvious, too, that the Government must maintain security regulations in such areas of scientific investigation. This in itself assures extensive Federal control over important realms of science.

Another factor making for governmental control of science is, of course, the power of the purse. It is in the interest of the Government to subsidize research in university and private laboratories; such subsidy almost inevitably carries with it some measure of direction and supervision.

But what this means is that in large and important areas scientists are no longer free agents, but subject to governmental pressure. They are committed to projects not always of their own choosing, and sometimes to the neglect of pure research of the greatest value. Universities that accept Federal subsidies find themselves accepting, too, Federal supervision over their faculty members, their research assistants, even over the uses to which their findings may be put. This is not only the negation of the function of the university, it is an enormous accretion to Federal authority. Those who oppose Federal aid to school construction but accept Federal supervision of scientific research are indeed straining at a gnat and swallowing a camel.

A FOURTH major area of Federal authority is education. An important part of American nationalism has been the absence of statism, and one thing that has contributed most powerfully to this is that education has never been subject to national control. Even those who advocate Federal aid to school building or to school lunch programs, or Federal scholarship aid, balk at suggesting Federal control over the content of education itself. Yet, indirectly, the Federal Government is moving steadily toward the exercise of such controls, and many state and local governments are enthusiastically supporting the policy. Thus teachers who belong to organizations on some Congressional "list" are in danger of dismissal; teachers who refuse to "cooperate" with Congressional committees lose their jobs; teachers who advocate policies currently unacceptable to the State Department—the recognition of Communist China, for example—find themselves in hot water — though the water is not quite so hot now as it was a year or two ago.

STUDENTS, too, must be careful what organizations they join, and even what books they read. Those who expect to enter the civil service or who are candidates for officer training have had fair warning: their careers may depend on obscure standards established by obscure officials in Washington.

There is a drift toward Government control even in the field of religion, long thought immune. This has come indirectly, in the pressures of the Velde committee, the operation of the security program, the activities of the customs and post office censors. The spectacle of the Velde committee attacking Bishop Oxnam because it disapproved a pamphlet sent out by the Methodist Church to its missionaries, or of the Customs Office holding up literature advocating pacifism, is one to give grave concern to those who cherish the traditional separation between church and state in America. Even more ominous is the attempt of a Congressional committee to dictate policy to the Religious Society of Friends, the Quakers.

CLOSELY connected with education and religion is the work of the foundations, and here the pressure of Federal control is peculiarly dangerous. The argument advanced by the Cox, the Reece and the Walters committees to justify their investigations into the operations of the Ford and other foundations is at once simple and delusive. It is that because they enjoy tax exemption Government has a right to inquire into their activities —into the substance, as well as the administration and financing, of their work. On the basis of this theory the committees saw fit to inquire into the social and political philosophies of recipients of awards, into the interest and direction of scholarly programs.

No more specious theory has ever been advanced than that tax exemption authorizes government to inquire into the ideas of every church. If this is true, it is equally true that tax exemption to religious bodies authorizes Government agencies to pass on the content of every sermon preached in every church, or into the doctrines taught in theological seminaries. If it is true, it is equally true that tax exemption authorizes government to investigate what is taught in the classrooms of state and private universities—a theory actually advanced by the Attorney General of New Hampshire, only to be rejected by the Supreme Court with the contempt which it merited. Once establish the theory that tax exemption authorizes Federal supervision of ideas, as distinct from overt actions, and there is an end to freedom for intellectual or spiritual activities.

ONE of the most dangerous areas of Federal control is that occupied by the press: a term which embraces books, magazines and newspapers alike. No one in America needs to be convinced of the quintessential importance of freedom of the press, yet in recent years we have witnessed a series of developments which, collectively, seriously curtail our access to information through the press.

These pressures are exercised in many ways, some subtle, some ostentatious. There is the kind of pressure that was implicit in the effort to intimidate Mr. James Wechsler of The New York Post. There is the kind of pressure involved in the prolonged denial of passports to newsmen who wish to go to China, a policy now at last reversed. There is the pressure that comes from denial of information, or from classification of information as secret.

This policy of the denial of information is one that has grown to ominous proportions in recent years. It has, indeed, been elevated into a principle, which we may designate, after its formulator, the Philip Young Doctrine of "the inherent non-availability of information." Not only sensitive Government departments —the Department of Defense or the Atomic Energy Commission—now have censorship officers, but almost every department; even the Civil Service Commission and the Department of Agriculture find it necessary to establish internal censorship. If agencies of the national Government can influence or intimidate the press, or can control the flow of information through the press, we will have taken a long, and dangerous, step toward authoritarianism.

THESE examples by no means exhaust the list. There is pressure for Federal supervision, direct or indirect, over the films, the theatre, the radio and television. There is pressure—through the policies of the State Department—on art and music. Refusal to underwrite a traveling art exhibit or symphony orchestra because of the political beliefs of the artists involved, squints toward what we have hitherto escaped: official standards of orthodoxy in the arts. All these developments are not only threats to freedom; they are threats to local autonomy and to grass-roots democracy.

The most notable example of centralization in the realm of civil liberties is, of course, the Fourteenth Amendment of 1868. This, the most important amendment ever added to the Constitution, worked a revolution in the relations of state and Federal governments to the rights of persons. In effect, it nationalized the liberties of men, throwing over them the protective mantle of the Federal Government. For, whereas the original Bill of Rights had been designed to protect men against Federal tyranny, the Fourteenth Amendment was designed to protect men against state tyranny. For a long time ineffective, this function of the Fourteenth Amendment took on vitality in the Nineteen Twenties, when the Supreme Court began to hold that its due process clause in effect incorporated the guarantees of the first eight amendments, and began to apply it energetically to state denial or impairment of civil and political liberties.

RECENT civil rights legislation is designed to give effect to the guarantees of the Fourteenth Amendment and—where voting is involved—of the Fifteenth as well.

This is, of course, Federal centralization, and it is a centralization that affects the realm of ideas and their communication. The Fourteenth Amendment is not a recent development, but constitutionally almost ninety years old, and almost venerable; only its more energetic application is relatively new. It differs fundamentally from recent legislative and administrative invasion of the realms of civil and personal rights in that it is designed to enlarge, not to circumscribe, the exercise of those rights; to facilitate, not to hamper, the communication of ideas. Its application is not, in short, centralization of the control of ideas, but the use of the Federal authority to frustrate such control.

Those who fear the Leviathan state direct their fears, and their defenses, almost entirely to the political and economic realms, just as those who are determined to maintain private enterprise think of it almost entirely in economic terms. But the growth of economic centralization, mistaken as it may be, is of *relatively* minor importance, as the concept of private enterprise as an economic institution is of *relatively* minor importance. The real danger is not to economic enterprise, but to intellectual enterprise. And the real danger of governmental authority is in the intellectual realm.

ONCE allow the state to invade the areas of thought—

scholarship, science, the press, the arts, religion and association, and we will surely have statism. It will be too late, then, to protect invasion of the economic realm. Those who fear the Leviathan state—and

all who are steeped in the American tradition must fear it—should resolutely oppose it where it is most dangerous —namely, in the realm of the mind and spirit of men. Once we get a government strong

enough to control men's minds, we will have a government strong enough to control everything.

November 24, 1957

# SECURITY PROCEDURES REFLECT CALMER ERA

## New Government Program Shows Diminished Communist Specter

### By ANTHONY LEWIS
#### Special to The New York Times.

WASHINGTON, Feb. 20—The change in this country's attitude on issues of internal security was illustrated today by President Eisenhower's establishment of new industrial security procedures.

For the first time in any Government security program since World War II, the presumption will be that suspects are entitled to confront and cross-examine their accusers. The use of confidential informants is to be the exception, not the rule.

The new program does provide for use of secret evidence in specified circumstances. But the burden will be on the secourity officers to persuade a high official—in the end, the head of the department—that such evidence must be used.

The industrial security revision is merely the latest evidence of calm on the Communist issue. The excitement and tension that existed as recently as half a dozen years ago have relaxed gradually but considerably and the actual restrictions imposed on individuals in the name of fighting communism are surely diminished also.

### Change in Hollywood

Even so timorous an institution as Hollywood has been affected. In recent weeks two producer-directors, Otto Preminger and Stanley Kramer, have been so bold as to hire—under their own names—writers denounced by the House Committee on Un-American Activities.

A run-down of the various areas in which concern for internal security has manifested itself indicates that tensions have eased across the board.

The various security programs — covering Government employes, for example, as well as defense plant workers—have been affected by a succession of Supreme Court decisions. The first of these, in 1956, limited the Government employe program to sensitive jobs.

Last June, in the case of William L. Greene, the court found that neither Congress nor the President had clearly authorized industrial security procedures without rights of confrontation.

Today's executive order is designed to close the gap left by the Greene case.

### Excesses Ended

Quite apart from the courts, the worse excesses of the security programs—the kind uncovered in the early days of the Eisenhower Administration — have been eliminated administratively. The dragging in of irrelevancies, the labeling of young men because of their mothers' associations, the interminable proceedings—all these seem no longer to exist, at least in extreme form.

A 1957 Supreme Court case laid down a strict standard of proof for the Government under the Smith Act of 1940. The court said that Communists could be convicted only for inciting people to act against the Government, not for "theoretical advocacy" of the Government's overthrow. The Justice Department has accepted this standard and has not asked Congress to toughen the law.

A drastic change has taken place, of course, in the effect of Congressional committees on American life. It is hard even to remember now how the whole Executive Branch quivered, up through 1954, when Senator Joseph R. McCarthy snapped his fingers.

The House Committee on Un-American Activities is still active, and individuals are still being subpoenaed. But the volume of its business, and certainly the size of the newspaper headlines that affect the

public atmosphere, are sharply reduced.

Congress went so far last summer as to repeal the non-Communist oath provision of the Taft-Hartley Act as ineffectual. It is being pressed hard now to remove a similar provision from the National Defense Education Act,

### Communist Oath

A few years ago it would have been inconceivable that Congress would repeal a loyalty oath of this kind. The possibility that it will do so now is indicative of how the Communist issue has lost its political steam.

The political contrast between 1960 and 1952 or 1954 is perhaps the most striking of all. In 1952 the Republican candidate for Vice President referred to the Democratic Presidential candidate as "Adlai the appeaser * * * who got a Ph.D. from Dean Acheson's college of cowardly Communist containment."

Through the early years of the Eisenhower Administration, its high officials rode the Communist issue for all it was worth. Herbert Brownell Jr., then Attorney General, charged that former President Truman had knowingly promoted a Communist spy in the Government.

The Administration issued regular totals of the security risks it said it had forced out of Federal jobs—figures that were used vigorously by Vice President Nixon in the 1954

campaign, but which were later admitted to be false or misleading.

Why, then, has the atmosphere changed so much?

The general reason is surely the slow, inscrutable working of the American political system. The excesses of Senator McCarthy and others eventually caused a reaction. The scientific and intellectual communities were outraged at injustice in the security programs. The public at large became surfeited with the Communist issue.

The 1954 election result was itself a repudiation of extremist tactics. After that election, with Senator McCarthy's harassing power gone, the Administration stopped trying to ride the whirlwind. The Communist issue was scarcely mentioned in the 1956 campaign, and Administration officials have deliberately tried to play down internal security matters since then.

The Supreme Court has clearly played a role also. Its decisions have focused the country's moral discontent about excesses in the fight against communism. Thus the Watkins case of 1957, though later shown to be narrow in its legal significance, pointed up the need for rudimentary fairness in Congressional investigations.

Beyond that the high court has forced the Executive Branch to re-examine matters it had taken for granted. That is just what happened in the industrial security case. Officials were forced, for the first time, to consider carefully the interests of the individual and weigh those against governmental need

Of course, the picture is not entirely rosy. The law still requires the deportation of aliens for having joined the Communist party years before party membership was a ground for deportation, and the Supreme Court has upheld the statute. The vast mechanism of the security programs is intact and still subject to grave abuse. Undoubtedly Americans still feel somewhat reluctant to join some organizations, or to express radical thoughts. But 1960 is a long way from 1954.

February 21, 1960

## TEACHING OF CHILD IN SPENDING URGED

### All Youngsters Should Learn About Money Early in Life, Symposium Holds

**By CATHERINE MACKENZIE**

The extent to which money affects the present-day family whose living is earned rather than "made," and the importance of giving children real experiences in handling money at home and at school were points discussed by specialists in a symposium released yesterday by the Child Study Association of America, 221 West Fifty-seventh Street.

Dependence on money as a source of family security is a major change in our economy since grandfather's day when the family lived off the land and children were an asset and not an expense, according to A. J. Altmeyer, chairman, Social Security Board, Federal Security Agency.

He reviews the new family outlook on money in terms of new risks posed by sickness, death or disability of the breadwinner and compares this changed scene with an earlier period when relatives and neighbors helped out in emergencies. Significant figures on earnings and savings are included in this appraisal of money and family security now published in the winter 1945-46 issue of Child Study Quarterly.

It is against this background of change, and its effect on the family that early lessons in handling money are urged by Sidonie Matsner Gruenberg and Helen G. Sternau. Children must learn about money earlier, they say, because children actually use money sooner, and because the lessons learned in the family help to shape their outlook on giving and receiving, on spending and saving.

Suggesting that a regular allowance should be looked on as an educational device, the authors point out that some foolish spending is inevitable as children learn, and that an allowance should not be given or withheld as a form of "discipline."

Figuring costs of supplies and of labor, checking inventories and actual handling of money in definite amounts and accounting for it are among the school experiences described by Charlotte Biber Winsor, instructor at New York University and at the Cooperative School for Teachers. In a school described, she states that groups of children from the age of 8 years up were responsible for some school enterprise such as the postoffice, the supply store, the printing press.

Boys and girls aged 13 who undertook to administer the school lunchroom learned the ins and outs of making a budget, estimating costs and including overhead and, the author submits, gained experience over and above those of drill in arithmetic. The relative value of money and the social as well as the financial responsibility involved in its use are some of the values seen by the author in these ventures of group earning and spending by children.

## Parents Cautioned Against Attempting To Teach Manners to Children Too Soon

Parents make a mistake in trying to teach good manners to very young children, Miss Cornelia Goldsmith, director of the day-care unit of the New York City Department of Health, Bureau of Child Hygiene, declared yesterday.

Discussing "How Children Develop Through Group Experiences" in a lecture series sponsored by Ivriah in the Hotel Barbizon-Plaza, Miss Goldsmith cautioned against parents "rushing" their children with imposed ideas before the youngsters are capable of absorbing them.

"We stress manners when we want a good report from our neighbors," Miss Goldsmith told 100 mothers at the lecture. Urging parents first to "set up an environment a child would share," she said that arbitrarily imposing good manners on a child could create a feeling of dishonesty by establishing an "artificial veneer." The child with too thick a layer of veneer will act one way and feel another, she explained.

Miss Goldsmith asserted that too many 2-year-olds are being sent to nursery schools before they are ready for group living. "We are taking the 2-year-old group too much for granted," she declared, pointing out that they "need guidance." The average 3-year-old is ready for group experience, the nursery educator said.

Miss Goldsmith also challenged the "don't do that" type of child education. She said that this method "is heard in too many classrooms of the city. Children should be allowed to make mistakes," she contended. "That's how we learn."

With many nursery schools conducting full-day programs for children, she advocated along with group play programs some "screened-off cubby-holes" where children could get away by themselves sometimes just to be and think alone.

She also asserted that children living in crowded New York City need country experience, too, and she deplored the fact that summer vacations are obtained chiefly by "very poor" or "very rich" children. She expressed the hope that "some day thoughtful schools will have a country and a city place for children."

Mrs. William Heller, chairman of Ivriah's child development seminar, presided.

March 2, 1946

February 5, 19

# Dodgers Purchase Robinson, First Negro in Modern Major League Baseball

**THE DODGERS ACQUIRE A NEW INFIELDER**

**By LOUIS EFFRAT**

Jackie Robinson, 28-year-old infielder, yesterday became the first Negro to achieve major-league baseball status in modern times. His contract was purchased from the Montreal Royals of the International League by the Dodgers and he will be in a Brooklyn uniform at Ebbets Field today, when the Brooks oppose the Yankees in the first of three exhibition games over the week-end.

A native of Georgia, Robinson won fame in baseball, football, basketball and track at the University of California at Los Angeles before entering the armed service as a private. He emerged a lieutenant in 1945 and in October of that year was signed to a Montreal contract. Robinson's performances in the International League, which he led in batting last season with an average of .349, prompted President Branch Rickey of the Dodgers to promote Jackie.

The decision was made while Robinson was playing first base for Montreal against the Dodgers at Ebbets Field. Jackie was blanked at the plate and contributed little to his team's 4-3 victory before 14,282 fans, but it was nevertheless, a history-making day for the well-proportioned lad.

### An Inopportune Moment

Jackie had just popped into a double-play, attempting to bunt in the fifth inning, when Arthur Mann, assistant to Rickey, appeared in the press box. He handed out a brief, typed announcement: "The Brooklyn Dodgers today purchased the contract of Jackie

Jackie Robinson being congratulated by Clay Hopper, manager of the Montreal Royals, at Ebbets Field yesterday after it was announced that the Brooklyn club had purchased the Negro from its farm team.

*Associated Press*

Roosevelt Robinson from the Montreal Royals."

Robinson will appear at the Brooklyn offices this morning to sign a contract. Rickey does not anticipate any difficulty over terms.

According to the records, the last Negro to play in the majors was one Moses Fleetwood Walker, who caught for Toledo of the American Association when that circuit enjoyed major-league classification back in 1884.

The call for Robinson was no surprise. Most baseball persons had been expecting it. After all, he had proved his right to the opportunity by his extraordinary work in the AAA minor league, where he stole 40 bases and was the best defensive second baseman. He sparked the Royals to the pennant and the team went on to annex the little world series.

Robinson's path in the immediate future may not be too smooth, however. He may run into antipathy from Southerners who form about 60 per cent of the league's playing strength. In fact, it is rumored that a number of Dodgers expressed themselves unhappy at the possibility of having to play with Jackie.

### Robinson Is "Thrilled"

Jackie, himself, expects no trouble. He said he was "thrilled and it's what I've been waiting for." When his Montreal mates congratulated him and wished him luck, Robinson answered: "Thanks, I'll need it."

Whether Robinson will be used at first or second base is not known. That will depend upon the new manager, yet to be named by Rickey.

Rickey, in answer to a direct query, declared he did not expect trouble from other players, because of Robinson. "We are all agreed," he said, "that Jackie is ready for the chance."

Several thousand Negroes were in the stands at yesterday's exhibition. When Robinson appeared for batting practice, he drew a warm and pleasant reception. Dixie Walker, quoted in 1945 as opposed to playing with Jackie, was booed on his first turn at bat. Walker answered with a resounding single.

If, however, Robinson is to make the grade, he will have to do better than he did against the Brooks. Against Ralph Branca, Jackie rolled meekly to the mound, walked and then popped an intended sacrifice bunt into a double play. At first base—a new position for him —he handled himself flawlessly, but did not have a difficult chance.

April 11, 1947

## AT THE THEATRE

### By BROOKS ATKINSON

Arthur Miller has written a superb drama. From every point of view "Death of a Salesman," which was acted at the Morosco last evening, is rich and memorable drama. It is so simple in style and so inevitable in theme that it scarcely seems like a thing that has been written and acted. For Mr. Miller has looked with compassion into the hearts of some ordinary Americans and quietly transferred their hope and anguish to the theatre. Under Elia Kazan's masterly direction, Lee J. Cobb gives a heroic performance, and every member of the cast plays like a person inspired.

\* \* \*

Two seasons ago Mr. Miller's "All My Sons" looked like the work of an honest and able playwright. In comparison with the new drama, that seems like a contrived play now. For "Death of a Salesman" has the flow and spontaneity of a suburban epic that may not be intended as poetry but becomes poetry in spite of itself because Mr. Miller has drawn it out of so many intangible sources.

It is the story of an aging salesman who has reached the end of his usefulness on the road. There has always been something unsubstantial about his work. But suddenly the unsubstantial aspects of it overwhelm him completely. When he was young, he looked dashing; he enjoyed the comradeship of other people—the humor, the kidding, the business.

In his early sixties he knows his business as well as he ever did. But the unsubstantial things have become decisive; the spring has gone from his step, the smile from his face and the heartiness from his personality. He is through. The phantom of his life has caught up with him. As literally as Mr. Miller can say it, dust returns to dust. Suddenly there is nothing.

*"I'm tired to the death. I couldn't make it. I just couldn't make it."*—Lee J. Cobb, who is tuckered out from an unproductive day on the road, conveys the sad news to Mildred Dunnock in a scene from "Death of a Salesman."

\* \* \*

This is only a little of what Mr. Miller is saying. For he conveys this elusive tragedy in terms of simple things—the loyalty and understanding of his wife, the careless selfishness of his two sons, the sympathetic devotion of a neighbor, the coldness of his former boss' son—the bills, the car, the tinkering around the house. And most of all: the illusions by which he has lived—opportunities missed, wrong formulas for success, fatal misconceptions about his place in the scheme of things.

Writing like a man who understands people, Mr. Miller has no moral precepts to offer and no solutions of the salesman's problems. He is full of pity, but he brings no piety to it. Chronicler of one frowsy corner of the American scene, he evokes a wraith-like tragedy out of it that spins through the many scenes of his play and gradually envelops the audience.

\* \* \*

As theatre "Death of a Salesman" is no less original than it is as literature. Jo Mielziner, always equal to an occasion, has designed a skeletonized set that captures the mood of the play and serves the actors brilliantly. Although Mr. Miller's text may be diffuse in form, Mr. Kazan has pulled it together into a deeply moving performance.

Mr. Cobb's tragic portrait of the defeated salesman is acting of the first rank. Although it is familiar and folksy in the details, it has something of the grand manner in the big size and the deep tone. Mildred Dunnock gives the performance of her career as the wife and mother—plain of speech but indomitable in spirit. The parts of the thoughtless sons are extremely well played by Arthur Kennedy and Cameron Mitchell, who are all youth, brag and bewilderment.

Other parts are well played by Howard Smith, Thomas Chalmers, Don Keefer, Alan Hewitt and Tom Pedi. If there were time, this report would gratefully include all the actors and fabricators of illusion. For they all realize that for once in their lives they are participating in a rare event in the theatre. Mr. Miller's elegy in a Brooklyn sidestreet is superb.

February 11, 1949

# The 'Terribly Normal' Class of '52

### By PENN KIMBALL

THE class of 1952, taking leave of the sheltering elms during these bright June days, looks on the world with an air of sad resignation and incurable hope. Neither mood deserves to be mistaken for the capital sins so often ascribed to alternating generations of American youth. This year's senior is no starry-eyed idealist. He's not a curled-lip cynic either. He is, in most respects, just terribly normal—a condition, all the same, his terribly normal elders may find upsetting to contemplate.

**PENN KIMBALL** of The Times Sunday staff belongs to the Princeton Class of 1937 and recently attended Yale and Columbia.

Military service is uppermost in the mind of the average boy graduating from college this month, although the tension and jitters that went with former draft uncertainties have subsided. The draft is accepted, with no show of zeal, as part of "the system," but the senior is at least relieved to know where he stands. He appears, to the interested observer, to be adjusted, fatalistic perhaps, about the immediate prospect of spending the next two or three years of his life in uniform.

He seems, furthermore, to be looking right through those years as pioneers might let their gaze skip past a desolate foreground to fix on purple mountains beyond. The important departure from this analogy is that the graduating student appears to be staring stark, straight ahead, rather than upward. He talks about exploring plateaus, not peaks. His life goals—even as expressed by those who do not identify themselves as "draft bait"—are modest and practical, though not the shallow and single-minded pursuit of economic security that many of us off campus have been led to believe.

In terms of long-range but somewhat unadventuresome objectives, then, the class of '52 might be described as self-confident and optimistic. It is self-confident as regards individual ability to surmount the knotty problems of starting late on both a career and a family, both of which are denied the majority right away by the pressure of circumstances. It is optimistic that the world situation in general will somehow work itself out, at least in no worse fashion than the era of strain and simmering conflict which is all that the class of '52 has ever known anyway throughout the thinking span of its whole adolescence.

For the class of 1952, be it recalled, was born two decades ago in the darkest years of economic depression. Pearl Harbor, in this instance, fell upon the consciousness of fifth-grade children. As high school students, this generation watched the sun break out briefly, only to be eclipsed almost at once by post-war ideological strife. Then, with the close of sophomore year in college, came Korea.

IN the memory of these youngsters, only Franklin D. Roosevelt and Harry S. Truman have ever been President; the New Deal or Fair Deal is all they have ever seen in Washington. Social security, big government, foreign aid, the cold war against communism—all of these are as commonplace, and as taken for granted, as T-shirts or crew cuts. A lot of seniors will be voting for the first time this fall, but the issues of their formative age have largely been decided, it seems, without the help of passionate debate in the quads.

This strikes one as odd when viewed against the American tradition of rebellion and revolt on the campus—one recalls the "lost" generations and hot-bloods of the Twenties and Thirties who talked in contemptuous tones of the way previous generations had fumbled the ball. Panty raids and spring riots notwithstanding, this crop of seniors rates itself on the phlegmatic side, blaming the hovering "dead spot" of future military duties for casting a pall on their boyish enthusiasms.

Whatever the reason, the college visitor finds the class of '52 sober without being earnest, quizzical rather than questioning, pretty strong-minded and pretty sophisticated. It is, on the whole, a very likable lot, disarmingly frank and surprisingly urbane. If this generation nurses a complex at all its vice is an almost excessive balance, an overpowering care not to commit its emotions too deeply to anything.

These generalities, rashly advanced on a topic always hot to the touch, are based on a few talks with some representative members of the graduating class at Columbia College. The New York City school last week awarded degrees to some 527 young survivors of a class which arrived on Morningside Heights four years ago at the same time as a brand-new university president named Dwight David Eisenhower.

"I DON'T care how much they talk to you about geology and geography," Eisenhower declared to the class of '52 that first September, "but I hope

EXAMS END for 527 members of the class of '52 advised as freshmen by Columbia President Dwight D. Eisenhower not to let a day go by "that you don't enjoy life."

the day never goes by that you don't have some fun, that you don't enjoy life. • • • I know what it means to a human being to believe that he has done something that day that is worth while."

**The advice,**

making allowances for changing times and circumstances, seems to have stuck in the minds of the class. And the recipients, making allowances for the local peculiarities which exist in all institutions of learning, are possibly not too far off the broad pattern of college seniors elsewhere. "On the whole, I suppose our bunch is quite ordinary," says Columbia's 1952 class president, Ira Hoffman, "but we think of ourselves as a little more open-minded, though a lot more narrow in ambition, than when we came in. We have a good sense of humor; most of us don't take anything too seriously and all of us are wondering when we'll ever get set."

COLLEGE administrators point out that these seniors are not just a little younger than the ex-G. I.'s who passed through the educational system just ahead of them (only eighteen Columbia seniors this year were still studying under the G. I. Bill). Gone with the old khakis and new babies, says a Columbia dean, is "an emotional lift and buoyancy on the campus. In comparison to the returned veteran, these 21-year-olds seem singularly lacking in high spirits and enthusiasm."

Faculty members also report a big change in their classes: "Getting back to normal has meant finding once more that our students lack experience by which to link their classroom courses with the outside world. The class of '52 has been more insulated, more passive in the aggregate than its immediate predecessors."

What do Columbia seniors say of themselves? A composite impression of their main spheres of interest might produce this:

### THE DRAFT

"Most of us expect to lose our educational deferments and revert to 1-A in the draft at the end of June. But nobody is sure. A lot of us really don't believe in educational deferments on principle, but as long as they're offered you can't blame us for trying all the angles that are within the rules. Our dope is that the local boards are waiting for us to graduate to stick us at the top of their list, so, if

there are any commission deals kicking around, we want to get in on them. Military service is just so much time out of our lives. We want to get it over with—as painlessly as possible. We're all thinking and planning about what we'll do when we get out.

"Nobody thinks our group is having it any rougher than other generations before. The hardest thing on us is that the draft has been hanging over our heads for so long; it hit the others before they thought too much about it. After we found out we could finish college, we more or less took it in stride. Now we are operating back on a week-to-week basis again, especially those who are aiming for a professional school in the fall."

### THE WAR

"No, we don't think in terms of combat during our military hitch. Maybe we just don't want to think about it that way. The truth is that the war in Korea seems very remote; very few in our circle of friends have been touched by it. A lot of us, those without older brothers maybe, can't remember much about the last war, when it comes to that, except as Boy Scouts in salvage drives. Our own impression is that things will continue to muddle along much as they have—for another ten or fifteen years. It's all so much bigger than we are."

### MARRIAGE

"Our generation of girls is ready for marriage, but the boys don't feel very marriage-minded with no income and a few years in the Army staring them in the face. A few seniors who have been going steady for a long time are getting married after graduation. One reason is that the girls are saying: 'It's June—or never.' It's quite a problem. Some of us didn't invite our best girls to Senior Week; it just didn't seem fair to keep them on the string.

"We want to get married all right, but we want to do it when we can afford to be definitely thinking of a family. We couldn't take the step now without depending on help from the girl's family or our own parents. A lot of us don't want to do it that way. So we refuse to get serious and try to play things so we don't get tied up. When the time comes, there's a lot to think about besides an emotional kick. A guy has to think of his wife and family as a business asset, too, and analyze his girl's good points and bad points

from that point of view as well as considering looks and intelligence."

### JOBS

"The minority who got their military service out of the way between high school and college are sitting pretty, of course. But the big companies seem willing to hire the draft eligibles, even if only for a month or two. The offers range from $250 to $350 a month, including the training period, but we try to look behind that starting salary. Sure, we'd like to latch on to something before the draft catches up with us, but we're looking for opportunity, too.

"WE don't want the company where we think we might get lost in the shuffle. We don't want to get bogged down with too much emphasis on seniority. We want to be able to advance as fast and as far as our ability will let us. We want something with a little satisfaction, a sense of performing a service in it, if we can, something that gets some respect in our home community.

"We're not indifferent to the dough—far from it. But just money or fancy security plans aren't what we're after. Maybe there isn't much we can do about changing the world. Nobody can stop you from working at something you like, though, and making a contribution to your own small group or profession and winning some recognition that way."

If politics, religion, international affairs, Government corruption and similar subjects are not reported here in eloquent, youthful phrases, the reason offered is that the college seniors of 1952 do not volunteer to declaim in that way on those issues. That is not the same thing as saying the class of '52 is indifferent to intellect, for conversation in dorms at Columbia is liberally sprinkled with Plato, T. S. Eliot and other learned references to the compulsory course in Humanities A. And the evidence is strong that the pendulum is swinging away from purely sensate values among our college kids, tabloid accounts to the contrary notwithstanding.

THE night before classes ended this year, it is true, a noisy crowd of Columbia undergraduates besieged the girls' dormitories of near-by Barnard College by the light of torches and fireworks. After carrying off assorted bits of underwear (most of them

thrown out the windows by co-operative females) the rioters started fires in public waste-baskets, set off stench bombs and cannon crackers, demonstrating for two hours before fifteen radio cars, fifty patrolmen and a police emergency truck carried the battle. An eminent columnist, surveying the wreckage, concluded that this form of spring madness was probably a throwback to the days when knights wore delicate tokens from their ladies on the outside of their armor.

Columbia seniors, more realistically, mark the occasion as a testimonial to the suggestive power of mass-circulation magazines, and contend that the crowd was swelled by a lot of neighborhood kids. The fact of the matter, they report, is that very few young collegians showed much taste for direct encounter with Barnard girls, and contented themselves with shouting and singing. "In other years we let off steam by throwing water containers and lighted paper out the window," says Class President Hoffman. "We're a little ashamed of the panty raid; it was so unoriginal."

The moral tone of the class of '52, according to Columbia's dean of students, Nicholas McKnight, has been "pretty high and pretty sober, with no indication of an eat-drink-and-be-merry attitude." Senior Winston Fliess, a pitcher on the varsity baseball team and an active fraternity man, observes: "We watched the G. I.'s in the classes ahead, and I think the reaction of a lot of us was in the direction of being a little less crude on dates and around the fraternity house. I don't know if our morals are any better than theirs, but at least the fellows are more discreet now. We don't want to be Boy Scouts, but we don't want to be hoodlums either."

ALTHOUGH Columbia has seen its share of political ferment through the years, the class of '52 by its own testimony is pretty apathetic, especially for a Presidential year. "These fellows have a lot more confidence, maybe, in their elders than our generation ever showed," a professor remarks. "Politics seems to touch very few." Max Frankel, former undergraduate editor of The Spectator, the campus paper, says "I think perhaps we are not quite as conscious as college graduates may once have been of becoming leaders in society. Politically, I don't believe this class will swing the national balance very much, either way."

A strike against the college administration by C. I. O.-organized cafeteria and maintenance workers this spring, an event which in former times might have aroused Columbia undergraduates to a boil, was regarded with bland indifference by all except tiny minorities aligned on each side of the dispute. Not a lecture was missed; not a class postponed. Bill Wallace, a strapping football tackle with a B average, thinks young folks "are as interested in liberal causes as they ever were, but they worry more now whether their own economic position as a college man is going to keep its value."

WALLACE, who expects to be drafted soon, talked to rep-

resentatives of twenty companies this spring about his own economic future. Five small concerns backed away when they heard about his draft status, and he wasn't interested in four others. Of the other eleven, nine made concrete job offers, and several took him on expense-paid tours of their home plants.

He didn't take the highest bid, or the surest future. "I think if a man has ability and wants to work he doesn't have to worry too much about security. He can make his own security." He chose a training program in insurance salesmanship, because "I think I'll get the feeling that I'm producing something that might do somebody some good, and I like the idea of being my own boss."

If this sounds unusual,

there's James Hurley, who has had lots of job offers because he performed his military service after finishing high school and also acquired some business experience running the student laundry agency at Columbia. Hurley nearly signed up with a carpet company at $300 a month, then backed down at the last minute. "I decided I would rather do what I want to than just make money, and the thing that I'm interested in is prison reform."

LAWRENCE GROSSMAN, former managing editor of The Spectator, hopes to make law school this fall if he isn't drafted. "I want to be a good lawyer and a credit to the profession, but I don't feel a driving ambition to get to the top. This class may possibly feel

frustrated by our inability to do anything about the big picture. It's a big job for us just to get ourselves and our own family and our own career going; it's too frightening a proposition to try to think in terms of tackling problems of a lot of other people, too. We're all looking for a peaceful life and a quiet life, within the bounds of our personal philosophy, among people we like. We figure we'll make our contribution to soci ..y in the way we lead our inc.. idual lives."

There it is, the class of '52, already sounding a little like its own twenty-fifth reunion, perhaps. So hard-headed, so analytical, so down-to-earth and, very possibly, feeling a trifle alone and abandoned. Safe now in the wide, wide world.

*June 8, 1952*

## WOMEN SPENDERS TOP THE MEN—EVEN AT 13

Starting as early as the age of 13, women begin to outspend men. Lester Rand, president of the Youth Research Institute, declared yesterday.

Reporting on the results of a recent national survey of the spending habits of 3,500 persons between the ages of 10 and 18, Mr. Rand attributed a part of this first spending spurt to the young women's first purchases at cosmetic counters.

In the opinion of the young men interviewed, this is only the beginning for the female spender, "with things becoming worse as the girls get older," Mr. Rand said. The institute specializes in studying the tastes, attitudes and opinions of persons under 25.

Average weekly earnings and allowances are included, as well as average weekly expenditures, the latter exclusive of those for clothes and food. Outstanding items purchased are listed, varying from chewing gum and newspapers to records and hobby equipment.

The survey indicates there can be little doubt this is "the biggest spending crop of youngsters ever produced in this country," and that "today's parents lavish more upon their children than in any other generation," Mr. Rand observed.

### Suburbia

Unlike their counterparts of the Nineteen Twenties, modern suburbanites want to "keep down with the Joneses"—that is, to be no more or no less conspicuous in their buying habits than their neighbors. This is one of the findings of a study by Fortune magazine, which also revealed that the United States suburban market now comprises 30,000,000 people with an average income of $6,500. This is 70 per cent higher than that of the rest of the nation. Suburbia, the publication also learned, has centered its customs and conventions on the needs of children and has geared its buying habits to them. It has kept whole industries busy making equipment for outdoor living; helped double the use of raiment woven of the once lowly denim, and caused the sales of sports shirts to overtake those of dress shirts. As for the future, Fortune estimates that by 1960 there may be 40,000,000 people in "moneyed, middle-class Suburbia — provided that there is no serious recession, that taxes are reduced and that productivity continues to rise as it has been rising since 1947."

# BIG FIELD OPENED BY HOME ARTISAN

### $4 Billion Sales in Prospect in 1954 as Result of Trend Back to Family Circle

**By ALFRED R. ZIPSER Jr.**

Americans will spend almost $4,000,000,000 this year on products they spurned or bought in negligible quantities only a few years ago.

The booming new market—or markets—spring from the flight of families from motion picture theaters, night clubs and other often costly outside activities back to the pleasures of home.

Psychologists and high-priced market analysts have various theories to account for the fact that the American as well as the Englishman now considers his home his castle. Some say that television is the principal agent in the revival of real family life that seemed almost extinct in the Roaring Twenties, Depression Thirties and War-Torn Forties. Others maintain the phenomenal increase in the number of new families and babies in recent years is the principal factor.

Groups of business men have no theories about the Stay-At-Home Fifties. They are too busy making money hand over fist as a result of demand for their products used in the home or for some purpose that contributes to family life.

The principal beneficiaries this year will be manufacturers and storekeepers who serve the seemingly insatiable "do-it-yourself" market. This is expected to run to about $3,500,000,000 in 1954.

As early as 1948, millions of veterans, established in new homes, found they could not watch television all the time. The family dwelling needed repairs or improvements. The first impulse was to call a carpenter or other craftsman. These persons offered to do the wanted jobs at prices far higher than the happy home owner could pay or else told him that they might get around to the work three weeks from some odd Wednesday.

The man who pays the family bills, sometimes called the head of the house, retired to his basement and undertook what he thought was a dreary chore. He found that few things compare with the satisfaction felt when gazing at a more than acceptable product turned out with one's own hands. A new market was born.

Manufacturers who make electric saws, drills and other power equipment and stores that sell them are hard put to keep up with orders from the growing legions of "cellar mechanics." Paint manufacturers report that the bulk of their sales are made to people who paint their own homes.

### Paint Industry Sees Trend

The paint industry, quick to see the trend early in the game, has not only promoted home painting vigorously but has simplified it to the point where any-

*April 3, 1953*

*October 27, 1953*

193

one not mentally deficient can do it successfully.

The home owner in the suburbs has found that he does not have to lay out a week's pay in a fancy New York night club to be entertained. He has discovered that a neighborhood party in his own finished basement can be twice as much fun.

The asphalt and plastic floor and wall tile industry and lumber and plywood operators stand ready to help him at a price. Their cash registers tinkle at a more than satisfactory pace. Lumber producers and yards have come to depend more and more on purchases by home craftsmen.

The renaissance of home life has poured dollars into businesses that are considered "big" by their officials but would be considered small by any minor vice president of the United States Steel Corporation. One of these is the home games industry.

Five years ago this industry took in about $6,000,000, according to Robert B. M. Barton, president of Parker Brothers, Inc., and a former president of the Toy Manufacturers of the U. S. A.,

Inc. This year the total volume should be more than $24,000,000, he predicted.

Others in the home games industry say Mr. Barton's predictions are as conservative as his nature. They are convinced that $55,000,000 worth of home games will be sold this year.

Mr. Barton says his concern is the world's largest manufacturer or "publisher" of proprietary games for the home. He defines proprietary games as those that require some skill on the part of the player. His company markets about 200 adult games, including Monopoly, Keyword and Clue.

The suppliers of these proprietary games get new ones from two sources, Mr. Barton reported. They maintain their own development departments, which come up with new games. Also, they take a new rough idea of an inventor and "edit" it so that it is marketable. The companies then put a price on it and sell it through stores. The inventor receives royalties from sales. This procedure makes them "game publishers," Mr. Barton said,

since they work exactly like book publishers.

Inventors of new home games are flourishing. Some months, Mr. Barton's company gets as many as 100 new ideas from hopeful game designers seeking to cash in on growing demand.

Another group of small business men flourishing as a result of the return to the home are manufacturers of equipment used for picnics and other outdoor gatherings of the family unit. A typical example is the Hamilton Metal Products Company.

In November of 1947 the company had $90 in the bank and $90,000 outstanding in accounts payable and payroll charges. Its two principals Herbert Piker, president, and his brother, Myron Piker, executive vice president, were afraid the end was in sight.

Myron, who describes himself as "absolutely the worst officer in the United States Naval Reserve during World War II," hated to see the 41-year-old family metal working enterprise founded by his father fail. It had floundered around making lunch boxes, fisherman's metal con-

tainers, tool boxes and similar products without much success until the crisis in 1947.

On borrowed money, the Piker brothers took a carefully insulated metal box and hired an industrial designer to cover it with plastic tartan designs. They called their products Skotch Koolers and promoted them widely as ideal picnic refrigerators. The doleful financial straits of 1947 now are a half-forgotten nightmare.

Thousands of families, finding that picnics are not necessarily family events that went out with the bustle, have bought the items Hamilton turns out. Last year the company earned more than $4,800,000. This year it is shooting for a minimum of $7,000,000.

Most of the money being poured out by people who make their homes the center of their lives is being garnered by many small companies like Hamilton and Parker Brothers. But big companies like United States Plywood, Johns-Manville, Aluminum Corporation of America are beginning to devote more and more attention to reaching the home market.

*March 7, 1954*

---

# A Critique On Freud

EROS AND CIVILIZATION. A Philosophical Inquiry into Freud. By Herbert Marcuse. 277 pp. Boston: The Beacon Press. $3.95.

### By CLYDE KLUCKHOHN

THIS remarkable book deals with "the fatal dialectic of civilization." Does the very progress of civilization lead to the release of increasingly destructive forces? On the whole, this was the conclusion of Freud and of many of his more orthodox followers. The "revisionists" (Erich Fromm, Karen Horney, Harry Stack Sullivan and others), have taken a different position, but Herbert Marcuse argues that this group has bogged down in circular reasoning. "In shifting the emphasis from the unconscious to the conscious [he writes], from the biological to the cultural factors, they cut off the roots of society in the instincts and instead take society at the level on which it confronts the individual as his ready-made 'environment,' without questioning its origin and legitimacy."

In other words, the Neo-Freudians have no "independent variable." Their social criticisms are directed against surface phenomena, and they accept basic premises which are ac-

tually local in time and space as unchangeable reality. This reviewer agrees that the "revisionists" are more superficial and far more culture-bound than they have alleged Freud to be. In spite of the European origins of Fromm and Horney, their theories bear the trademark "made in America" to a much greater extent than Freud's really carry the label "a product of bourgeois Viennese culture."

MR. MARCUSE, author of "Reason and Revolution," maintains that there is a hidden trend in Freud's thought, that he obtained insights which were and have remained tabooed in psychoanalysis for socio-historical reasons. Freud emphasized the recurrent cycle: domination-rebellion-domination, failing to see that the second domination is not simply a repetition of the first one. And his judgment was culturally relative in the important respect that he identified the "performance principle" as *the* reality principle.

Mr. Marcuse calls the second part of his book "Beyond the Reality Principle," pointing out that Western civilization "has attained a level of productivity at which the social demands upon instinctual energy to be spent in alienated labor could

be considerably reduced." This could make possible a new relation between the instincts and reason which would underlie a nonrepressive culture. This note is explicit in Freud when he interprets being in terms of Eros. Culture, as in the early stages of Plato's philosophy, is conceived as the free self-development of Eros rather than as repressive sublimation.

"BEYOND the performance principle" means largely the restoration of the esthetic dimension to its proper place in human life. Esthetics lies between sensuousness and morality and contains principles valid for both realms. The erotic reconciliation or union of man and nature can be found only in the esthetic attitude where order is beauty and where work is play. The esthetic liberation of the senses, far from destroying civilization, would give civilization a firmer basis and enhance its potentialities. "The desublimation of reason is just as essential a process in the emergence of a free culture as is the self-sublimation of sensuousness."

Nor, if sexuality be transformed into Eros, would the sex instincts reverse the constructive trends of civilization. Rather, Mr. Marcuse proposes a spread rather than an explosion of libido—a spread over private

and social relations "which bridges the gap maintained between them by a repressive reality principle."

Time is the deadly enemy of Eros. But if our thinking went beyond the reality principle, it could center upon images of a free future rather than a dark past. Mr. Marcuse, however, is no naïve utopian. He writes:

"But even the ultimate advent of freedom cannot redeem those who died in pain. It is the remembrance of them, and the accumulated guilt of mankind against its victims, that darken the prospect of a civilization without repression."

Philosophical critiques of psychoanalysis have been rare. Almost all of those that have appeared hitherto have been either undisguised attacks or, equally evidently, defenses. This one takes psychoanalysis seriously but not as unchallengeable dogma. "Eros and Civilization" is a stirring book and a cheering (though in no sense naïve) book. Except for Ernest Jones' two notable books on Freud and his life, this strikes the reviewer as the most significant general treatment of psychoanalytic theory since Freud himself ceased publication.

*Mr. Kluckhohn, a noted anthropologist, wrote "Mirror for Man" and other books.*

*November 27, 1955*

# The Freudian Revolution Analyzed

**Here, on the centenary of his birth, is a discussion of how and why the influence of Freud pervades so much of our culture.**

### By ALFRED KAZIN

IT is hard to believe that Sigmund Freud was born 100 years ago to-day. Although Freud has long been a household name (and, in fact, dominates many a household one could mention), his theories still seem too "advanced," they touch too bluntly on the most intimate side of human relations, for us to picture Freud himself coming out of a world that in all other respects now seems so quaint.

Although Freud has influenced even people who have never heard of him, not all his theories have been accepted even by his most orthodox followers, while a great many of his essential ideas are rejected even by many psychoanalysts. In one sense Freud himself is still battling for recognition, for because of the tabooed nature of the materials in which he worked and the unusually speculative quality of his mind, Freud still seems to many people more an irritant than a classic.

On the other hand, Freud's influence, which started from the growing skepticism about civilization and morality after the First World War, is now beyond description. Freudianism gave sanction to the increasing exasperation with public standards as opposed to private feelings; it upheld the truths of human nature as against the hypocrisies and cruelties of conventional morality; it stressed the enormous role that sex plays in man's imaginative life, in his relations to his parents, in the symbolism of language.

It is impossible to think of the greatest names in modern literature and art—Thomas Mann, James Joyce, Franz Kafka, T. S. Eliot, Ernest Hemingway, William Faulkner, Pablo Picasso, Paul Klee—without realizing our debt to Freud's exploration of dreams, myths, symbols and the imaginative profundity of man's inner life. Even those who believe that original sin is a safer guide to the nature of man than any other can find support in Freud's gloomy doubts about man's capacity for progress. For quite other reasons, Freud has found followers, even among Catholic psychiatrists, who believe that Freud offers a believable explanation of neurosis and a possible cure, and so leaves the sufferer cured to practice his faith in a rational way. Many psychologists who disagree with Freud's own materialism have gratefully adopted many of Freud's diagnoses, and although he himself was chary about the psychoanalytical technique in serious mental illness, more and more psychiatrists now follow his technique, or some adaptation of it.

For no other system of thought in modern times, except the great religions, has been adopted by so many people as a systematic interpretation of individual behavior. Consequently, to those who have no other belief, Freudianism sometimes serves as a philosophy of life.

FREUD, a tough old humanist with a profoundly skeptical mind, would have been shocked or amused by the degree to which everything is sometimes explained by "Freudian" doctrines. He offered us not something that applies dogmatically to all occasions, but something useful, a principle of inquiry into those unconscious forces that are constantly pulling people apart, both in themselves and from each other.

Freud's extraordinary achievement was to show us, in scientific terms, the primacy of natural desire, the secret wishes we proclaim in our dreams, the mixture of love and shame and jealousy in our relations to our parents, the child as father to the man, the deeply buried instincts that make us natural beings and that go back to the forgotten struggles of the human race. Until Freud, novelists and dramatists had never dared to think that science would back up their belief that personal passion is a stronger force in people's lives than socially accepted morality. Thanks to Freud, these insights now form a widely shared body of knowledge.

IN short, Freud had the ability, such as is given to very few individuals, to introduce a wholly new factor into human knowledge; to impress it upon people's minds as something for which there was evidence. He revealed a part of reality that many people before him had guessed at, but which no one before him was able to describe as systematically and convincingly as he did. In the same way that one associates the discovery of certain fundamentals with Copernicus, Newton, Darwin, Einstein, so one identifies many of one's deepest motivations with Freud. His name is no longer the name of a man; like "Darwin," it is now synonymous with a part of nature. This is the very greatest kind of influence that a man can have. It means that people use his name to signify something in the world of nature which, they believe, actually exists. A man's name has become identical with a phenomenon in nature, with a cause in nature, with a "reality" that we accept—even when we don't want to accept it. Every hour of every

day now, and especially in America, there are people who cannot forget a name, or make a slip of the tongue, or feel depressed; who cannot begin a love affair, or end a marriage, without wondering what the "Freudian" reason may be.

NO one can count the number of people who now think of any crisis as a *personal* failure, and who turn to a psychoanalyst or to psychoanalytical literature for an explanation of their suffering where once they would have turned to a minister or to the Bible for consolation. Freudian terms are now part of our thought. There are innumerable people who will never admit that they believe a word of his writings, who nevertheless, "unconsciously," as they would say, have learned to look for "motivations," to detect "compensations," to withhold a purely moralistic judgment in favor of individual understanding, to prize sexual satisfaction as a key to individual happiness, and to characterize people by the depth and urgency of their passions rather than by the nobility of their professions.

For much of this "Freudian" revolution, Freud himself is not responsible. And in evaluating the general effect of Freud's doctrines on the modern scene, especially in America, it is important to distinguish between the hard, biological, fundamentally classical thought of Freud, who was a determinist, pessimist, and genius, from the thousands of little cultural symptoms and "psychological" theories, the pretensions and self-indulgences, which are often found these days in the prosperous middle-class culture that has responded most enthusiastically to Freud.

THERE is, for example, the increasing tendency to think that *all* problems are "psychological," to ignore the real conflicts in society that underlie politics and to interpret politicians and candidates—especially those you don't like —in terms of "sexual" motives. There is the cunning use of "Freudian" terms in advertising, which has gone so far that nowadays there's a pretty clear suggestion that the girl comes with the car. There are all the psychologists who study "motivations," and sometimes invent them, so as to get you to buy two boxes of cereal where one would have done before.

There are the horrendous

movies and slick plays which not only evade the writer's need to explain characters honestly. but, by attributing to everybody what one can only call the Freudian nightmare. have imposed upon a credulous public the belief that it may not be art but that it is "true"—that is, sex —and so must be taken seriously. And, since this is endless but had better stop somewhere, there are all the people who have confused their "urges" with art, have learned in all moral crises to blame their upbringing rather than themselves, and tend to worship the psychoanalyst as God.

The worst of the "Freudian revolution" is the increasing tendency to attribute all criticism of our society to personal "sickness." The rebel is looked on as neurotic rather than as someone making a valid protest. Orthodox Freudians tend to support the status quo as a matter of course and to blame the individual for departing from it. Freud himself never made such a mistake, and no one would have been able to convince *him* that the Viennese world around him was "normal."

The identification of a military group, or a class, or a culture, with an absolute to which we must all be adjusted at any price is a dangerous trend. And the worst of it is that to many people psychoanalysts now signify "authority." so that people believe them on any and all subjects.

On the other hand, the greatest and most beautiful effect of Freudianism is the increasing awareness of childhood as the most important single influence on personal development. This profound cherishing of childhood has opened up wholly new relationships between husbands and wives, as well as between parents and children, and it represents—though often absurdly overanxious — a peculiar new tenderness in modern life. Similarly, though Freud's psychology is weakest on women, there can be no doubt that, again in America, the increasing acknowledgment of the importance of sexual satisfaction has given to women an increasing sense of their individual dignity and their specific needs.

**B**UT the greatest revolution of all, and one that really explains the overwhelming success of Freudianism in America, lies in the general insistence on individual fulfillment, satisfaction and happiness. Odd as it may seem to us, who take our striving toward these things for granted, the insistence on personal happiness represents the most revolutionary force in modern times. And it is precisely because our own tradition works toward individual self-realization, because private happiness does seem to us to be both an important ideal and a practical goal, that Freudianism has found so many recruits in this country.

Freud himself made his initial effect in the most traditional, the most rational, the most human kind of way: he wrote books; he presented evidence; he made claims and gave proofs. People read and believed. Many more did not read, and most of those who read Freud's first great work, "The Interpretation of Dreams," did not believe any of it. But, after all, very few books ever have a decisive effect on the world. In Freud's case, what counts is that some of the people who read, and believed what they read, were so stirred that they went on to change other minds.

The only kind of change in life which means anything— because it transforms everything in its path — is that which changes people's thinking, their deepest convictions, that which makes them see the world in a different way. This does not happen often, and it is the effect of Freud's books and clinical papers, radiating from a small circle of fellow-doctors in Vienna, that made Freud's influence so impressive. Only the power of truth can explain it. For everything was against him.

**H**E was a Jew in the obsessively anti-Semitic culture of Imperial Austria. He was working with names for things —*id, libido, superego, Oedipus complex, infantile sexuality*— that required a special effort, a "suspension of disbelief," as Coleridge would have said, to believe in. Freud insisted that he had not looked for this kind of material.

He had been an extraordinarily able neurologist, was the greatest authority in Europe on children's paralyses, had independently discovered the anesthetic properties of cocaine, but in his usual fashion had impatiently gone on to other experiments before he could get independent credit for his discovery. Far from being flighty in scientific matters, he had been thoroughly

"A tough old humanist with a profoundly skeptical mind"—This photograph of Freud was made in London in 1938, the year before his death.

trained by the prevailing school of physiology to think of the body as a machine, and in his own thinking he was a rigorous, old-fashioned rationalist whose only religion was science itself.

Freud even claimed that the evidence for his theories had been forced on him. But this was not quite true, either. Even when we remember Freud's rigid scientific training and his own utter honesty, it has to be made clear—not as a criticism of his method but as a characterization of his genius—that Freud was a "plunger," a highly speculative mind. It was the extraordinary combination of patience and daring, of method and radically new insight, that made him great.

THOUGH his old teacher and colleague, Joseph Breuer, came upon the famous example of hysteria in a woman which was the first clinical source for the book they wrote together—"Studies in Hysteria," which is technically the first document in psychoanalysis— Breuer soon took alarm from the dangerously "sexual" interest of the material and withdrew. Freud went on: working alone, he pieced together, in his own thinking, the whole set of sexual motivations that no one else had faced so bluntly or had systematized so closely into a whole new field of active cause-and-effect in the inner life of human beings.

It was this kind of comprehensive insight, backed up on the one hand by the utmost boldness in thinking out his material to its logical conclusion, and on the other by an extraordinary literary gift for persuading readers of the reality of what he was writing about, that led to Freud's effect on so many intellectuals, starting in the exciting years just before the first World War.

FREUD'S work appealed to the increasing regard for individual experience that is one of the great themes of modern literature and art. The sensitiveness to each individual as a significant register of consciousness in general, the artistic interest in carrying human consciousness to its farthest limits—it was this essential side of modern art that Freud's researches encouraged and deepened. He brought, as it were, the authority of science to the inner prompting of art, and thus helped writers and artists to feel that their interest in myths, in symbols, in dreams

was on the side of "reality," of science, itself, when it shows the fabulousness of the natural world.

Even if we regret, as we must, the fact that Freud's influence has been identified with a great many shallow and commercially slick ideas, the fact remains that if Freud's ideas appealed generally to the inwardness which is so important to modern writers and artists, it was because Freud thoroughly won his case against many aggressive but less intelligent opponents.

The people whose lives were changed by such masterpieces as "The Interpretation of Dreams," "The Psychopathology of Everyday Life," "Three Contributions to the Theory of Sex," "Totem and Taboo," were honestly convinced that Freud spoke the truth. They saw in Freud that passionate conviction of the reality of his theories that is the very stamp of genius, and as they read, they were prepared to give up other convictions—a sacrifice that caused some of them the deepest anguish, but which their conviction of Freud's utter truthfulness and objectivity made necessary.

NOW, if we look back for a moment, the impact of these theories seems all the more remarkable in view of the natural human tendency to suspect, to limit and to derogate sexual experience. What Freud proclaimed above all else was that "nature," which is nearest to us in the erotic side of man, and which culture and society are always pushing away as unworthy of man's "higher" nature, has constantly to be brought back into man's awareness. Freud saw in man's sexual instinct a force of profound natural urgency, a whole system of energies, which could be repressed and forgotten and pushed back into the unconsciousness only at the cost of unnecessary strain and even of self-destructiveness.

Yet far from preaching "sexuality" itself at any cost, Freud admitted that "civilization" requires the repression or at least the adaptation of sexuality. Civilization as we know it, Freud said, had been built up on man's heroic sacrifice of instinct. Only, Freud issued the warning that more and more men would resent this sacrifice, would wonder if civilization was worth the price. And how profoundly right he was in this can be seen not only in the Nazi madness that drove him as an old man out

of Vienna, that almost cost him his life, but in the increasing disdain for culture, in the secret lawlessness that has become, under the conformist surface, a sign of increasing personal irritation and rebelliousness in our society. More and more, the sexual freedom of our time seems to be a way of mentally getting even, of confused protest, and not the pagan enjoyment of instinct that writers like D. H. Lawrence upheld against Freud's gloomy forebodings.

For Freud the continuous sacrifice of "nature" that is demanded by "civilization" meant that it was only through rationality and the conscious awareness that maturity could be achieved. Far from counseling license, his most famous formula became—"Where id was, ego shall be"—the id representing the unconscious, the ego our dominant and purposive sense of ourselves. However, consciousness meant for Freud an unyielding insistence on the importance of sexuality. And it was just on this issue that, even before the first World War, his movement broke apart.

Jung went astray, as Freud thought, because he was lulled by the "mystical" side of religion; Adler, through his insistence that not sex but power feelings were primary. Later, Harry Stack Sullivan and Erich Fromm tended to emphasize, as against sex, the importance of personal relatedness to others, and nowadays many psychoanalysts tend to value religion much more highly than Freud ever could. But the root of the dissidence was always Freud's forthright insistence on the importance of sexuality and his old-fashioned, mid-nineteenth-century positivism. For Freud always emphasized the organic and the physical rather than the social and the "cultural."

In fact, it is now possible to say that it is precisely Freud's old-fashioned scientific rationalism, his need to think of man as a physical being rather than a "psychological" one, that explains the primacy of Freud's discoveries. Psychoanalysis, especially in America, has become more interested in making cures than in making discoveries, and it is significant that there has been very little original thought in the field since Freud.

FREUDIANISM has become a big business, and a very smooth one. The modern Freudian analyst, who is overbusy and who rather complacently uses his theory to explain everything, stands in

rather sad contrast to that extraordinary thinker, Sigmund Freud.

Perhaps it is because Freud was born a century ago that he had the old-fashioned belief that nothing—not even a lot of patients—is so important as carrying your ideas beyond the point at which everybody already agrees with you. Nowadays everybody is something of a Freudian, and to many Freudians, the truth is in their keeping, the system is complete. But what mattered most to Freud was relentlessly carrying on the revolution of human thought.

*May 6, 1956*

## MALE 'RAT RACE' DECRIED

### 'Suicidal Cult of Manliness' Is Blamed for Early Deaths

CHICAGO, Jan. 17 (UP)—The medical director of a large industrial concern blamed the "suicidal cult of manliness" for the "rat race" in which many American men find themselves today.

Dr. Lemuel C. McGee, Wilmington, Del., of the Hercules Powder Company, writing in the American Medical Association publication, Today's Health, said the average lifetime of men was about four years less than that of women, mainly because of the stress under which men live.

A "little common sense" could eliminate many of the tensions and stresses, providing a healthier and longer life, Dr. McGee said.

"The American male has been indoctrinated, with the philosophy that he must live, work and play at a dizzy pace; that he can and should wade through all emotional and physical situations without flinching and without reflection," he explained.

Dr. McGee said every man and boy must live within his own resources of physical and mental strength, but many fail to do so because of the "cult of manliness."

*January 18, 1957*

# Retired Persons Flock to Florida For Life in Sun at Modest Cost

### By MERRILL FOLSOM
MIAMI.

Yankees with moderate retirement incomes are settling at a record pace in Florida for the twilight years of their lives.

Homes without stairs, door sills, sidewalk curbs, unwieldly kitchens, troublesome furnaces, heavy taxes or big financial worries are mushrooming.

New housing developments as large as 92,000 acres each are rimming the glittering Gold Coast, the tranquil Gulf shores, the Everglades, the palmetto plains of the 30,000 lakes, and the undulating countryside of the citrus belt.

The sun doesn't always shine in the Sunshine State. The ground is often too swampy, the mosquitoes too voracious and the snakes too numerous. So the new havens are not entirely a heaven for the multitude of elderly persons who account partly for the state's population increase of 3,000 a week.

But the gardens bloom and the tarpon bite all year. The newcomers are enjoying the carefree subtropical life.

Couples who once heard from the resort ballyhooers that they should not come to Florida with less than $50 a day are finding this year that they can live in modest comfort on $160 to $200 a month, counting everything that two persons in good health require.

The other day a man of 65 paid a $35 bill with six checks —from Social Security, company pension, stock dividend and the contributions of two sons and a daughter. Not many years ago he would not have had only th children's money.

Problems of geriatrics, sociology, medicine, economics and community development are finding answers in the pensioners' new lives. Varied but related answers are evolving from these types of new Florida homes for the retired:

¶Three hundred thousand completed or planned one-level concrete block houses that are plentiful in the $7,000-$10,000 range and often run to $25,000, on plots commonly 80 by 125 feet, close to man-made waterways.

¶Sumptuous big hotels of yesteryear that are unable to compete with glamorous new hostelries and are being converted into gay-but-not-gaudy, share-the-work hotels for the elderly.

¶Colonies of ultramodern, tiny homes built with union and fraternal funds from the North for pensioners and convalescents—self-sufficent colonies with fishing piers, golf courses, swimming pools, recreation halls, theatres and do-it-yourself shops.

The developments generally are not posted as retirement centers. "The pensioners get mad as hell if we treat them as old people," says Thomas A. Ferris, an official of the Mackle Company, one of the biggest builders in Florida.

### Accent on Ease

But the builders adhere to one-level designs, avoid floor obstacles, put ovens at eye level, install electric dishwashers, provide ample wall heaters, put seats in bathtubs and use floors that are easy to clean.

One company sold $350,000 worth of small homes on one day last month. Purchasers included a nurse in Tokyo and an engineer in Arabia, each looking forward to a first trip to Florida.

Key Biscayne, a former coconut grove south of Miami, was attached to the mainland five years ago by a causeway. A considerable amount of retirement housing has risen there, and the tip of the key was sold for $9,500,000 last month for another development.

Keys on the overseas highway to Key West are being expanded for homes by use of bulkheads and muck pumped from the sea.

Home purchasers include many of the 150,000 persons who have been living in trailer camps and on boats. Their Cadillacs belie their apparent penury.

Although old people predominate, the young are numerous in colonies near the Air Force bases at Homestead and Cocoa, and in counties that big corporations recently "found." The Florida Development Commission welcomes the balance, as pensioners often balk at paying for the building of new schools and roads.

Tourists still are the backbone of the Florida economy, 6,500,000 of them a year spending $1,200,000,000. But a new community conscience is growing with the arrival of Glenn L. Martin's $100,000,000 guided missile factory at Orlando, a $42,000,000 Pratt & Whitney engine plant at West Palm Beach, an $80,000,000 Chemstrand factory at Pensacola, and 163 other major industries for 18,500 employes.

Sam T. Dell Jr., a Gainesville lawyer and the new chairman of the Florida Development Commission, said the state welcomed the newcomers, would try to get jobs for them but would insist on the growth being orderly.

"We don't want another era of people coming so fast they have to sleep on billiard tables at $7 a night," Mr. Dell said. "And we don't want people being romanced into coming without funds and then becoming welfare cases."

He reported that the state was canceling $100,000-a-year expenditures in farm journals to lure small farmers from the Midwest, as they could no longer compete with machine-operated farms of 4,000 acres.

Mr. Dell conceded that two persons could live in the retirement colonies on $160 a month and "be as happy as pigs in the sun." But, he added, "I wouldn't care to do it." He hopes for more $30,000 homes on three-acre plots.

### One Couple's Budget

Here is the budget of an elderly couple who bought a $6,526, two-bedroom house at Pompano Beach Highlands, using $390 cash and a Federal Housing Authority mortgage:

| | |
|---|---:|
| Mortgage charges and taxes | $44.00 |
| Electricity, heat and water | 17.50 |
| Groceries | 35.00 |
| Automobile | 12.00 |
| Barber and beauty shop | 5.00 |
| Lawn fertilizer and insecticides | 5.00 |
| Shrubbery and plants | 3.00 |
| Entertainment | 6.00 |
| Newspapers and magazines | 5.00 |
| Personal insurance | 10.00 |
| Brooms, dishes and other replacements | 10.00 |
| Church | 4.00 |
| Fraternal organizations | 2.00 |
| Total | $158.50 |

Fishing, the main hobby of the pensioners, supplemented the food budget. Little new clothing was needed. The couple did not bet on the races, although most of their neighbors did—and lost.

The real estate tax is complex. The state grants a homestead exemption on the first $5,000 of an assessed valuation. The state's pari-mutuel share of bets at the horse and dog tracks and the jai-alai frontons is so huge that it pays much of the school and government expenses. Eleven counties have no tax for current expenses, and in the fifty-six others the levy is generally low.

In Gainesville, a university town, a $20,000 house that would be taxed $600 a year in New York pays only $180. Sometimes a new waterworks, however, carries a tax rate sky high.

The pensioners welcome the absence of income and inheritance taxes in Florida but find to their dismay that they must pay a small levy on stocks.

Cooperative apartments are having a big boom this winter, but a six-room suite in a waterfront building can cost $25,000.

One of the greatest phenomena is the new life being pumped into the faltering old hotels of Miami Beach.

The Floridian, a fashionable gambling mecca and convention center thirty years ago, had bad times for the last eleven years. Then Michael Sossin and two associates converted it into a hotel for persons 75 to 95 years old.

The idea has suddenly become so popular that 22,000 persons in all states are seeking the Floridian's accommodations for 480. At rates beginning at $100 a month, a person receives a room, private bath, meals, college courses, handicraft instruction, games and the use of an Olympic-size swimming pool. The residents must make their own beds and perform other hotel chores.

Mr. Sossin was best man at three weddings of his "children" in the last two weeks. He is pleased, except that the newlyweds too often leave on honeymoons and buy a bungalow.

The Boulevard, Chesterfield and Helene Hotels at Miami Beach have been similarly converted. So have others as far north as Daytona Beach.

Salhaven is a new 670-acre community of the Upholsterers Union of North America that will open this month. It has risen from palmetto swamps at Jupiter, near West Palm Beach on the inland waterway.

Named for Sal B. Hoffmann, president of the union, Salhaven cost $5,000,000. It will be a retirement and convalescent village for union members from all parts of the nation. Ultimately it will accommodate 2,000.

Thirty completed buildings at Salhaven include an adminstration building, auditorium, medical center, cafeteria, educational building, social hall, do-it-yourself shops and housekeeping cottages. Each cluster of cottages has its own swimming pool.

The rent for one-bedroom cottage for two persons at Salhaven, including all utilities and medical services, is $50 a month. A single person pays $35. Leaders in industry serve on the board of directors with union officials.

Thirty-five labor unions are negotiating for clusters of homes for members at Charlotte Harbor on the Gulf. So are clergymen's organizations.

At Clermont, retired postmen have shares in orange groves that pay 8 per cent interest. They live near by. St. Cloud has so many veterans of all wars back to the Spanish-American that pay day at the post office resembles mobilization day. Winter Park has colonies of retired university professors and administrators.

March 10, 1957

# Values for Children—Who Sets Them?

## By DOROTHY BARCLAY

A YOUNG University of Pennsylvania psychologist, Dr. Eugene Galanter, set a group of parents on its collective ear recently by suggesting that in the not too distant future moral values could—and perhaps should—be taught by machine. Meanwhile, he suggested, with home and school having pretty well abdicated the responsibility, advertising agencies might as well do the job.

Traditionally, Dr. Galanter pointed out, values have been determined and passed along by various segments or forces in society as a whole—the aristocracy, the church, the schools, the government, the home. Since the moral and ethical values of both young people and their traditional mentors seem incredibly muddled today, he implied, why not let industry or labor, or both, through the medium of advertising, take over the job?

We have found it extremely difficult to judge, even in personal conversation, whether Dr. Galanter spoke with his tongue in his cheek. His statements, however—provocative in the extreme—served an extremely valuable purpose, in our opinion. They needled practically every parent who heard them into thinking hard about his own values and considering just how his youngsters were developing, or absorbing, their own standards.

The group which sponsored the meeting—the Parents Association of the Oak Lane Country Day School of Temple University—had been pretty provocative itself in setting the theme for discussion. "Today is the day of the big sell," they said. "Does our materialistic culture threaten our values?" This whole matter of values, indeed, is currently one of the most talked about in the parent education and child development fields.

What are sound values for today's youngsters? How can values be taught? Indeed, can they be taught at all? If so, should they be? Should one generation impose its values on another, or should children be free to develop their own values in line with changing times and customs?

QUESTIONS like these are ones that very few parents have the opportunity to ponder at length. As Dr. Dale B. Harris, director of the University of Minnesota's Institute of Child Welfare, put it recently: "To be a parent is to be in action; to be in action is to make choices—not to consider issues philosophically." Yet the very business of making choices, as Dr. Harris pointed out, depends on values, and the choices parents make will, in all likelihood, transmit to children a more accurate summation of parental values than all the verbal philosophizing of a lifetime.

Children, then, absorb values from the examples of adults and develop values for themselves in the process of making decisions in real life situations. Does this mean that parents should not do anything active about this important phase of development? As we've suggested above, there are those who seem to think so. They are not concerned that commercial interests, as Dr. Galanter suggested, will fill the void they leave. Given freedom and love, they hold, each child will find the "right" way for himself and will be the stronger for having come to it on his own.

Two speakers recently, however, have taken strong issue with this comfortable point of view. We've already mentioned Dr. Harris, who presented his ideas at the institute for workers in parent education sponsored by the Child Study Association of America. The other was Dr. Alfred L. Baldwin, head of the department of child development and family relationships at Cornell University.

Many values seem so completely accepted as right and desirable—at least at the lip-service stage—that one might well wonder what all the shouting is about. Responsibility, fairness, self-reliance, unselfishness, cooperation, respect, courage, friendliness, honesty, truthfulness, perseverance — the list of homely virtues could go on and on.

CONFUSION arises, however, when the child who has been urged to be generous, cooperative and fair finds, as he sometimes does, that there are certain very definite rewards in being "first," a position he can achieve sometimes only by a few sharp practices. Similarly, the youngster who has had responsibility and self-reliance set as valued standards may find himself in confusion when he discovers that he must work doubly hard to take up the slack left by companions who have found an easy way out from some commitment.

Standing quietly aside and letting youngsters make their own decisions in such cases is sometimes exactly the right thing to do. In Dr. Baldwin's opinion, however, such passivity is not to be advised as a standard course of action. "The parent must remember," he declared, "that merely to refrain from imposing one's own values on the child is not to assure that he will develop his own. The parent who does not strongly endorse, even demand, the values he does feel are important may actually be transmitting weakness of faith in all values. In attempting not to hamper the development of the child's own values, the parent may stunt the growth of any value commitment."

DR. BALDWIN'S point of view would seem to be supported by the evidence of some long-term research reported by Dr. Harris. Current follow-up interviews with some 200 children who had been members of special pre-school study groups twenty-five to thirty years ago indicate that those whose parents followed extremely permissive methods—not only allowing, but expecting, them at early ages to weigh alternatives and make their own decisions—are today inclined to lack focus, to be indecisive, to be seeking for something they know not what.

"Parenthood," Dr. Harris declares, "must be positive. It must commit itself to standards and maintain these standards in the presence of children." Parents' consistently expressed choices, reinforced by the discussions they have with their children, represent the most effective way of getting the idea across that "the universe is a place which requires a stand, a commitment, in order for any activity to develop purposefully."

# THE MIDDLE CLASS MOCKED AS 'BLAND'

## Anthropologist Finds Culture of U.S. in Conformity With Hamburger as Symbol

**By AUSTIN C. WEHRWEIN**
Special to The New York Times.

CHICAGO, Dec. 27 — The American middle class has a "puritanical and bland" culture that is symbolized by hamburgers, peanut butter and tomato soup, Prof. Martin B. Loeb said today.

"The word spicy has become a synonym for sexy," he added.

Professor Loeb, who is from the University of California at Los Angeles, was one of 500 anthropologists attending the annual meeting of the American Anthropological Association at the Palmer House.

He said that the American middle class, with its "packaged" way of life, had become the core of this country's culture. The core standards, he added, were "almost official."

It is, he conceded, a very solid culture. But he said the core was ridden by "conformity-anxiety" and its characteristic words were "nice" and "not nice."

Professor Loeb's remarks were made at a news conference in advance of a panel discussion, "A Look at American Culture," where he covered the same ground. The panel chairman was Prof. Solon T. Kimball of Columbia University, who was also at the news conference.

### Soviet Seen in Parallel

Professor Kimball told the news conference that Soviet rulers were trying to impress on the Russians, with police state force, a culture that paralleled that of the American middle class in its prudery and stress on progress through technology.

Hewing to the same line, Prof. John P. Gillin of the University of North Carolina, another panel member, presented a paper that said the basic American view was mechanistic. Americans, he asserted, put high value on progress, ingenu-

ity, efficiency and precise measurement of cleanliness.

The other member of the panel was Prof. Conrad M. Arensberg of Columbia University.

Professor Loeb said the American core was uniform in all sections of the country. He said its values—cleanliness, regularity, respectability and conformity—were virtually official because they were taught in church and school.

This is how he pictures the typical core family, which, he added, probably lives in a suburb:

It has two heads of the household, the mother, who discusses, and the father, who can exercise a veto. The mother may work, but apologetically, with the explanation that she does so to give the children advantages—such as dancing school.

This core family has a picture window with a lamp in it. But picture windows are for looking into, not for looking out of. The family is not deeply religious, but is religious in the sense that it thinks it is a good thing to go to church.

The goal for the son is to take business administration in college and become a junior executive. The aim is the sure thing, whereas in the upper classes it is the big chance.

### Religion and Living

Prof. Leslie White of the University of Michigan said in a paper that religion was an expression of general living conditions.

"A cultural system that can launch earth satellites can dispense with gods entirely," he added.

The Jewish-Christian tradition stemmed from a pastoral culture that pictured "the Lord as my shepherd," he said.

"Commercialism introduces bookkeeping in heaven with a recording angel to set down debits and credits," Professor White declared.

Profs. John W. M. Whiting and John L. Fischer of Harvard University said in a paper that it was too early to form a complete theory of religion. "We can say, however, that so far research indicates that religion springs from anger and fear rather than peace and love," they said.

Prof. Harry Hoijar, University of California at Los Angeles, was named association president for 1958. He succeeds Prof. E. Adamson Hoebel, University of Minnesota.

December 28, 1957

---

# *Social Life Makes Supermarket Just a General Store With Carts*

**By JOSEPH G. HERZBERG**

Although it has no cracker barrel to dip into, today's supermarket is, consciously or no, merchandising a highly attractive commodity—a community's social life. The bigger and brassier a supermarket grows, the more it resembles, at least in a customer's social habits, the old general store.

Where once the farm women came to town to visit together as they bought supplies, now busy suburban wives use the supermarket as a communications center. They catch up with the news, settle unfinished business and not infrequently arrange a swap.

Supermarket sales experts should know what a good thing they have here. It gets to be a tiresome day for a woman who must ferry her husband to the morning train, get the children off to school, feed the animals, straighten the house and wrack her brains for something a bit unusual for dinner. There isn't even much time for a chat over the telephone with an equally distracted friend.

Here the supermarket comes in. Any pleasant moments taken out for just plain gabbing can be counted as shopping time and won't rest heavily on a housewife's conscience.

### The Grapefruit Corner

In one supermarket, the women always manage to swing their shopping carts around what they call Grapefruit Corner. This is the spot just beyond butter, eggs and cheese, where traffic slows down and where a shopper who dawdles is sure to collect a friend whose tongue has been just as restlessly silent since the morning household hubbub quieted.

The two at Grapefruit Corner light cigarettes and as they chat the group grows to four or five.

"You ladies want chairs?" ask one of the check-out girls passing by.

The manager, covering up his male inability to break up a potential bottleneck, smiles weakly at his own pallid question: "Who's on the pan now."

Quite likely no one is on the pan. These housewives have a lot of other things to talk about —mutual friends none have seen for a long time, school problems with the children, everybody weak with colds, the way the town has been growing, the manner in which newcomers have taken over local groups.

Town government is not neglected either. If it is not taken up at Grapefruit Corner, there is always the dedicated and determined one who, between looking for the vanilla or rummaging for a larger jar of bread-and-butter pickles, spots

an acquaintance and sings out:

"Don't forget the town meeting tomorrow night. We need every vote. It's for the children, you know."

### The Male Side

Before any man assumes a feeling of superiority about all this, he should look at himself on Saturdays. Men appear with shopping lists and then pursue crazy courses through the aisles looking for items that are naturally next to the last one just picked up. In their meanderings, they run into old friends, too, and they have their cigarettes and chatter.

They don't know about Grapefruit Corner but set up roadblocks in the aisles and if shopping carts were automobiles no insurance company would take the risk. "Man shopper" is the supermarket equivalent of the highway's "woman driver."

A wife, when she becomes entangled in a Grapefruit Corner kaffee klatsch, must be careful to watch out for her husband if he has volunteered to shop with her. Uninterested in the nature of the conversation, he wanders off and when his wife finally collects him, she learns that her chatting has had a major effect on the budget.

Her wandering partner has amused himself by picking up a few extra cans of salted nuts, a cheese he has always wanted to taste, imported biscuits for the cheese, a small jar of caviar he knows will taste equally good with the biscuits and a tin of imported pumpernickel that should make a likely partner for either the cheese or the caviar.

With a child, a housewife can be firm and order her young one to put back those chocolate bars because there's enough candy in the house already and besides think of your teeth, but a man after all must at least be given the appearance of retaining his dignity and freedom of choice. (That will cost the housewife even more; with all those tasty things nothing goes so well as a dry martini—with imported gin, of course.)

Even at the checkout counter, the conversations opened at Grapefruit Corner keep on. A woman shouts across from one counter to another:

"Oh, Ann, I forgot to ask you if you knew of anybody in the market for electric trains?"

And the reply:

"Not me, but if I hear of someone, I'll call you. You know somebody interested in a pair of boy's figure skates? Size 1."

January 2, 195

## Rock-and-Roll Called 'Communicable Disease'

HARTFORD, Conn., March 27 (UP)—A noted psychiatrist described "rock-and-roll" music today as a "communicable disease" and another sign of adolescent rebellion."

Dr. Francis J. Braceland, psychiatrist in chief of the Institute of Living, called rock-and-roll a "cannibalistic and tribalistic" form of music. He was commenting on the disturbances that led to eleven arrests during the week-end at a local theatre.

It is insecurity and "rebellion," Dr. Braceland said, that impels teenagers to affect "ducktail" haircuts, wear zoot-suits and carry on boisterously at rock-and-roll affairs.

Six of those arrested were fined from $15 to $25 yesterday in Police Court. One hundred more were ejected from the theatre.

March 28, 1956

## FAMILY FUN FOUND CHANGED SINCE '40

### U. S. Reports Movies Giving Way to TV, Active Sports and Betting on Rise

#### By BESS FURMAN
Special to The New York Times.

WASHINGTON, April 23 — Does your family play the ponies? Do you and the children bowl or sail, putter around the garden, dabble in hi-fi or get most of your amusement from television and radio?

These are some of the amusements that have come up in popularity in the years since 1940, according to a study released today of the American family and its fun.

The study was made by home economists of the Department of Agriculture, using statistics compiled by the Department of Commerce.

The most striking change has been the decline of the movies and the rise of television. In 1940 the movies took 20 per cent of the family recreational budget; in 1955 they took only 10 per cent. In this period the "radio, TV, records, musical instruments" category of expenditure rose from 14 per cent to 23 per cent.

This was more than the American family spent on movies at any time.

Only two items other than movies in the recreational list declined when 1955 expenditures were compared (in 1955 dollars) to those in 1940. Spending for books and maps was 3 per cent less. Spending for spectator sports was 1 per cent less.

Spectator amusements, including movies, theatre, opera and spectator sports, dropped 19 per cent.

But spending for commercial amusement in which the spender takes part—bowling, skating and golf—increase 34 per cent between 1940 and 1955.

The report said:

"Greater interest in types of recreation in which the consumer can participate is also indicated by the big increase in the amount spent for durable pleasure equipment like boats, aircraft, bicycles and other wheel goods, golf clubs and durable toys."

Flowers, seeds and potted plants were given a listing in the recreation category. These went up from $3 per capita in 1940 to $4 in 1955.

Listed, too, were "pari-mutuel net receipts," which went up from $1 in 1940 to $3 in 1955. The report explained:

Because the analysis was made in the Department of Agriculture the findings are published in Rural Family Living although they are also applicable to city families.

April 24, 1957

# DISNEYLAND REPORTS ON ITS FIRST TEN MILLION

### By GLADWIN HILL

LOS ANGELES—On the last day of 1957 Disneyland tallied its 10,000,000th visitor. The total represents an average of some 10,000 visitors a day, 365 days a year, since the suburban amusement park's opening on July 18, 1955. The patronage betokens an impressive array of records in the field of entertainment and recreation.

In a short time the park has become the biggest tourist attraction in California and the West, among the biggest in the nation. Its annual patronage, for instance, exceeds not only that of Grand Canyon National Park, but of Grand Canyon, Yosemite and Yellowstone National Parks combined—three of the most popular attractions in the country. And the volume is not just attributable to Disneyland's proximity to the nation's third largest city. More than 40 per cent of its visitors are from outside California.

#### The Disney Secret

What is the secret of Disneyland's success?

Many factors have entered into it. But to pinpoint a single element, it would be imagination—not just imagination on the part of its impresarios, but their evocation of the imagination of the cash customers.

Walt Disney and his associates have managed to generate, in the traditionally raucous and ofttimes shoddy amusement-park field, the same "suspension of disbelief" which has been the secret of theatrical success down the corridors of time.

Everybody knows that relationships behind the footlights are simulated, that beneath a clown's ridiculous visage there is a human face, that Snow White is only a two-dimensional figure projected on a screen.

Similarly on Disneyland's popular African-River boat ride, a hard-bitten realist could point out that the boat is obviously on a track, that the jungle is a planted one, and that the animals and savages are mechanical. No F. B. I. man is needed to detect that another "river," which floats the big sternwheeler Mark Twain, meanders no more than a couple of city blocks; or that throughout the

Rocket Trip to the Moon one's seat is firmly anchored to the ground.

The point is that nobody wants to shatter illusions.

Theatrical artistry has been brought to bear so cleverly that the gates of Disneyland simply bar out the everyday world. Within the gates the park's entrance mall — the "Main Street" of 1900 America—leads to a circular array of realms of imagination. These are the tropical Adventureland, a pioneer-days Frontierland, a medieval Fantasyland, and a futuristic Tomorrowland. Once within them, the visitor indulges eagerly in that most ancient of games: "Let's pretend."

### Grown-Ups, Too

Disneyland is not a new dictatorship of juvenile fancy, imposed on hapless grown-up escorts. In fact, its patronage runs a steady ratio of more than three adults to every child. Not infrequently a compartment on one of the miniature streamlined trains can be seen occupied by a solitary oldster, lost in imagination. Visiting Russians have abruptly dropped their studied taciturnity to ride gleefully behind the bars of the Monkey Wagon on the toy circus train, heedless of any diplomatic repercussions. Parents scramble through the caves, tunnels, tree-house and stockade of Tom Sawyer's Island as avidly as their children.

While practically anyone who wants to go canoeing can do it fairly close to home any time, at Disneyland people line up to pay 35 cents for a few minutes paddling along the man-made vest-pocket "Mississippi." But this is in an Indian war canoe, with real Indians, bow and stern, controlling the exertions of a score of amateur paddlers at a time. Imagination again.

In the theatre the vital ingredient is not realism, but a blending of the real with the imaginary. The entertainer invites the audience to meet him half way. This is what has been successfully achieved at Disneyland.

Of the $21,000,000 that has been spent on the park, perhaps half or more has gone into details which average producers would not trouble about. The purpose is to make a compelling impact on the patrons' imagination.

Major facilities, from buildings to rolling-stock, are made in carefully reduced scales, ranging from five-eighths to a quarter of life-size—a constant reminder that one is playing a game. Illusion prevails even when fantasy is momentarily abandoned for conventional amusement-park rides like the whip and the merry-go-round.

A stagecoach ride through Disneyland's fabricated desert is not just motion and scenery. The stagecoach is so authentic in construction, appurtenances and decorations that it could serve tomorrow in a John Ford movie. It challenges even adult sophisticates to imagine they are bucketing across the plains a century ago.

### Faithful Replicas

Disneyland's four scaled-down railroad lines are faithful replicas, even to the mechanical parts of the locomotives. The stern-wheeler Mark Twain, even though kept on course by an underwater mechanism, could take to the real Mississippi tomorrow. One hundred and eight feet long, and weighing 125 tons, it was made by a ship-building company and is propelled by its own engines and paddle wheels.

The attendants who man the "Mississippi" keel-boats are different in mien, costume and pattern from the men who handle the African river boats. The animals along the river banks are realistic enough for a zoological exhibit, and are animated imaginatively. Some do no more than flick a tail or an ear—and through such restraint, seem all the more plausible. In "Autopia," the miniature cars course freeways so carefully scaled that a twelve-mile-an-hour whirl beside a neophyte young driver engenders, without much imagination, all the excitement of a real-life highway adventure.

A typical Disneyland feature is avoidance of unwieldy crowds even when hundreds of people are waiting at an attraction. This is accomplished by fences and railings which double back and forth in maze patterns, preventing crowding and without policing.

The park, covering sixty acres, was designed to handle 60,000 visitors a day comfortably. The record day's crowd, last August, was 36,566.

Attendants at the attractions are courteous, efficient and unobtrusive. The park's staff, varying with busy seasons, ranges from 1,400 to 2,000.

Disneyland started out as a $16,000,000 enterprise, in which Walt Disney Productions had only a minority interest, in company with other partners and commercial concessionaires. Now the Disney corporation owns 65.52 per cent and American Broadcasting Company-Paramount Pictures the rest. The park is basically the same in format as when it opened, but an additional $5,000,000 has been spent on a continuing program of modifications and additions.

The original orange-grove tract, in Anaheim, twenty-two miles south of Los Angeles, was 240 acres. An additional eighty-seven acres has been bought, although eighty of the reserve acres are still in oranges. Of the sixty acres in the amusement area proper, eighteen at the outset were vacant, elaboration of facilities has taken up four of these.

Major additions since the opening have included Tom Sawyer's Island in the middle of the river, reached by barge; and the Skyway, an aerial bucket-tram running for nearly a quarter of a mile across the park, seventy-five feet above the ground.

### Most Popular

The Mark Twain's ten-minute circuits of the river hold the individual-attraction traffic record, with an aggregate of 3,883,000 passengers. The Rocket Trip to the Moon—a concession of Trans-World Airlines which is possibly that company's most profitable operation — ranks high, with an attendance record of some 2,680,000. In this, passengers in the vibrating hull of a simulated rocket experience a trip through space around the moon, through sound effects and motion pictures ingeniously translated into images on observation screens fore-and-aft.

Of the score of free displays in the park, by far the most popular is the futuristic all-plastic house opened last summer by the Monsanto Chemical Company and collaborating manufacturers. An unending line of visitors from morning until long after dark has run up an attendance total of some 1,260,000 viewers already.

There are now thirty-six individual rides and other pay attractions in the park. Admissions range from 10 to 50 cents each. With a brace of kids, the potential outlay looks formidable, but the cost of a family expedition—which is not the sort of thing anyone would undertake weekly or even monthly—is brought within moderate limits by ticket books. These cover park admission and fifteen attractions, enough, by the writer's personal test, for a full day's round of the best the park has to offer, and cost $4 for adults, $3.50 for 12-to-17-year-old "juniors," and $3 for younger children. This is about a 25 per cent discount off individual-attraction prices.

A smaller book, covering ten attractions and encompassing the cream, sells for $3, $2.50 and $2 respectively. Thus a family of four can put in a full and, curiously enough, not exhausting day at Disneyland for around $15, aside from food. The park is dotted with snack bars and restaurants of various

Ward Allan Howe

**VOYAGE—The Mark Twain cruises down the river.**

sizes with full meals from $1 up.

Admission to the park and to attractions also can be bought individually. General admission is 90, 70 and 50 cents for the three age brackets.

## No Liquor Here

No alcoholic beverages are sold in the park. Good restaurant, coffee shop and bar facilities, along with overnight ac-commodations, are available at the Disneyland Hotel, a separately owned but collaborative $10,000,000 enterprise just outside the park. It has an assortment of hotel- and motel-type rooms and suites, starting at $10 for two and $16 for a family of four in one room. There are many motels along the near-by Santa Ana Freeway, and in Anaheim, and downtown Los Angeles is only a half hour's drive up the freeway.

Within the next few months, the last two traffic lights on the freeway route between Los Angeles and Disneyland, will be eliminated. There is also bus and helicopter service to the park.

Disneyland is open every day in the year, from 10 A. M. to 7:30 P. M. during the winter, and until 10 P. M. or later in the summer.

The park's attendance during its first year totaled 3,604,351. The second year it increased 13 per cent to 4,072,043. At the present rate, it will register a comparable increase by its third year-end in July. By comparison, the three aforementioned national parks in 1956 had an aggregate of 3,605,359 visitors.

The average Disneyland visitor, it is reckoned, spends five hours and forty minutes in the park, and $2.79, exclusive of food.

February 2, 1958

# Adults Urged To Aid Child For I.Q. Test

PARENTS have a right, in fact a responsibility, to coach their children for intelligence tests.

This is the opinion of a New York City teacher, David Engler, who presents his point of view—a highly controversial one in professional circles—in a new book, "How to Raise Your Child's I. Q." (Criterion Books).

In an interview, Mr. Engler explained the basis of his thinking and discussed some parental concerns and questions stimulated by the book: Is it actually possible to raise an I. Q.? If so, should it be done? How can it be done?

In answering the first question, Mr. Engler noted that psychologists long have debated the precise definition of "intelligence." Differences have been equally sharp over the best ways to measure it, whatever it is.

It may not be possible, Mr. Engler conceded, to increase a child's basic potential in the intellectual sphere. The I. Q. test, he said, cannot plumb the depths of basic potential; it can only measure its surface indications. It is largely a test of what a child has learned, he maintained.

### 'Tampering' Is Upheld

How adequately a child will function on such a test and how well equipped he is to perform in a way that will reveal his full capabilities can be influenced by his surroundings and experiences, Mr. Engler said. Therefore, I. Q. ratings can be raised in many instances, he declared.

Even though it may be possible to influence prospective I. Q. ratings, parents have asked Mr. Engler whether it is safe to "tamper" in such matters. Mr. Engler believes it not only is safe but also sensible. The importance of such efforts, he said, lies in the overdependence of some school administrators on the ratings made in such tests.

Classifying children for educational purposes on the basis of I. Q. alone never has been approved by specialists but, Mr. Engler held, it is a method increasingly relied on in overcrowded school systems. The I. Q., he said, should be but one factor considered in evaluating a child. He noted, however, that it was the tendency of many busy school administrators to rely on it routinely as a handy one-figure summing-up.

In such cases, the difference of just a few points may determine whether a child is selected for an "enrichment" class or, at the other extreme, placed with "slow learners." The effects of such placement can be accentuated with time, Mr. Engler said, for "it does not take a child long to sense I. Q.-based distinctions and live up—or down—to them." Therefore, he contended, it is both right and proper for parents to do all they reasonably can to insure their children's best performance on I. Q. tests.

What should they do? For the most part, Mr. Engler's recommendations differ little from suggestions frequently given for achieving a pleasant, stimulating family life. In support, he pointed to research indicating that children from impoverished homes, or those neglected or ignored by adults, consistently rated low on intelligence tests. When they remain in such a setting, their ratings may even drop with time.

However, similar children moved to pleasanter, more stimulating surroundings, and cared for by loving and interested adults, frequently show marked increases in I. Q. within a relatively short time.

### Emotional State a Factor

Moreover, Mr. Engler noted, a rating on a specific intelligence test can be influenced not only by the child's intellectual ability but also by his emotional state at the time of testing, his motivation and his morale.

Ironically enough, his performance also can be influenced by the skill and competence of the tester. Too often, Mr. Engler contended, the tests by which a child is judged in school are given by teachers inexperienced in the testing technique, in a distracting setting and under conditions of tension.

The youngster most likely to succeed in such a situation is the one able to meet unusual conditions with youthful poise, one respectful but not fearful of adults and one willing and accustomed to follow directions accurately. He is a child with self-confidence, initiative and a readiness to try new things.

Qualities such as these are developed from early childhood, Mr. Engler said, and spring from the quality of the relationship the child has with his parents. Discipline and guidance, which combine gentle firmness and control with steadily expanding freedom, are highly important, he said. Going on family trips, being read to, talked with and listened to by adults and having opportunities to play freely with stimulating toys and equipment will prepare a child to tackle with confidence the kinds of questions and problems he will be asked to work out on intelligence tests.

The concluding section of Mr. Engler's book includes samples of test forms. An imaginative parent, he said, could work out from these samples little games with words or pictures. These would familiarize a youngster with the sort of thing he will be asked to do and sharpen his thinking along the lines likely to help the most.

January 20, 1959

# PRISONERS OF THE MORE ABUNDANT LIFE

THE STATUS SEEKERS: An Exploration of Class Behavior in America and the Hidden Barriers That Affect You, Your Community, Your Future. By Vance Packard. 376 pp. New York: David McKay Company. $4.50.

### By A. C. SPECTORSKY

IN his new book, Vance Packard, the author of "The Hidden Persuaders," explores the viselike grip in which each of us is held by his place in the national pecking order. He takes issue with those who claim that postwar prosperity has rendered us virtually a one-class people, a vast middle class enjoying (or wallowing in) a flood of material plenty. On the contrary, he claims, the very prosperity which, as part of the American dream, was supposed to free us from class differences, has frozen the social classes and made it increasingly difficult to move upward. Mr. Packard states his case and then proves it—methodically and devastatingly. Woven through his portrait of a rigid class system is evidence that millions of Americans — those who strive to rise and those who accept their status with meekness or resignation—suffer as human beings because of it, and hence we as a nation suffer.

Mr. Packard lacks the grace and wit of a Russell Lynes; he does not possess the creative insights of a David Reisman, the corrosive passion of John Keats aroused, or the originality of investigators like W. Lloyd Warner and Robert and Helen Lynd. He is, rather, the excellent and painstaking reporter, and his book is journalism of the highest rank, an ordered compendium of his own researches and the findings of dozens of sociologists and investigators, with his interpretations and opinions clearly identified as such.

THE earlier chapters of "The Status Seekers" are mainly for the benefit of those who—in so far as reading sociological studies of post-war America is concerned—came in late. Mr. Packard lists ten changes in the national economy that "represent a transformation in a nation's way of life." These include the spectacular increase in individual wealth, the graduated income tax, the lessening of contrasts in the material life of rich and poor, the increase in geographical mobility with its attendant frequent need to re-establish status in new groupings (more than 25,000 families move and face new neighbors every day), the trend toward bigness and bureaucracy (Parkinson's Law proliferating organization men), the fragmentation of work and specialization in job function, and mass produced and socially homogeneous suburban communities replacing village and town.

*Mr. Spectorsky is the author of "The Exurbanites" and other studies of American life.*

Out of these changes, the author says, has come a new class system that splits the traditional middle class in two. The great chasm, as he sees it, is in this class; the diagram of our society he proposes comprises five horizontal layers, with the Real Upper Class and the Semi-Upper Class constituting the Diploma Elite. After them—and on the other side of the chasm—are the Supporting Classes: the Limited-Success Class, the Working Class and the Real Lower Class.

There is a second stratification in our society which the author sees as vertical rather than horizontal. This might be called ethnic classification, determined by recency of arrival on the local scene, national background, religion, pigmentation. Vertical and horizontal strata form a sort of grid, providing boxes into one of which each of us fits.

Having established his framework, the author starts pinning us, his specimens, to it for social dissection. Our homes first occupy his attention. He sees them as supplanting the car as the favored status symbol—partly because today anyone can own the "best" car via installment purchase. Symbols of status and class striving (antiques to denote a past, books to suggest education, gold-plated bathroom fixtures to signify wealth, etc.), rather than the desiderata of good living, determine the choice of the houses and furnishings most of us buy. The same holds for our choice of address. Each change in domicile is a new social beachhead. In a mobile nation of strangers people shun variety and "seek their own kind," thus reinforcing the homogeneity within communities. This situation is abetted by the fact that in seeking a "good" address, one must be found that is not so good as to render an insecure upward striver uncomfortable or attract unfavorable attention from his betters.

Mr. Packard now directs our attention to what he calls "totem poles of job prestige," powerful factors in fixing status in the public mind. The criteria by which one is assigned his place in the job-prestige hierarchy are quite brilliantly described and analyzed, as is status within the large corporate structure and the ways in which it is established and assigned. Mr. Packard goes on to prove (as others have done before him) that status may be discerned in U and non-U behavior patterns in speech, drinking, dining, games, pastimes, entertainment and magazine reading.

THE most private aspects of our lives are also fixed by class status. Kinsey revealed that sexual behavior varies from class to class. Packard draws on Kinsey and then goes further. He discusses the class line where male dominance of the family shifts to female dominance. He demonstrates that cross-class marriages are a poor risk, that dating across more than one class line is rare and frowned upon—though boys may date down one class without loss of status—and that vertical (ethnic and religious) stratifications are even more rigidly determinant in dating and marriage than horizontal stratifications.

Friendships, too, are seen to be increasingly controlled by status. It is not news that "consciousness of kind" makes people more at ease within the confines of status groupings. But the virtual vanishing of social situations that cut across classes (seen, for example, in the widespread withdrawal of the diploma élite from fraternal organizations) is news, as is the diminution in democratic sociability and its replacement by the planned guest list that preserves or enhances status. Who may invite whom, and which invitations to accept, have become burning questions in a status-dominated society in which even notions of what constitutes a good time are governed by class membership: the Real Upper party is generally relaxed, though it may be formal; the Semi-Uppers compete in food and décor; the Limited-Success class likes organizational parties—church suppers, club get-togethers, etc.; working class socializing is generally restricted to kin and neighbors, and home entertaining in the lower working class is almost entirely restricted to kin groups, with men and women splitting up.

Status and striving for status in clubs and lodges are explored, as are the protocols and perils of debuts and cotillions. Religion is shown to be shot through with status stratification—with two notable exceptions: the Roman Catholic Church and, recently (in the special area of desegregation) the Congregational Church. Highest in status and per capita wealth are Episcopalians. In descending status order, we next have Presbyterians, Congregationalists, Unitarians, Methodists, Lutherans, Baptists — and "others." Even our politics tend to be determined by status factors within ourselves, rather than by issues. Thus, says the author, one of a candidate's toughest problems is to win a combination of status groups in his electorate — "by such acts of symbol manipulation as eating pizza pies."

Education — starting in the cradle—is next considered. The author shows us how it inculcates class differences from birth, not only in schooling but in such less obvious matters as whether father or mother is the disciplinarian, and whether corporal or psychological punishment (the withdrawal of love) dominates in home training. Schools and colleges, fraternities and clubs, faculties and curricula are examined in terms of their status and their status-fixing roles. It is not a cheering study.

THE picture that emerges from Mr. Packard's book is one of greater and greater rigidity, of lonely and hopeless striving, of compulsive preoccupation with material symbols of success in lieu of genuine achievement, of resignation, the death of aspiration and, in the supporting classes, job boredom.

The author concludes this fascinating and disturbing book with his own recommendations for achieving a happier, more fruitful society within a reasonable status system. These include a discussion of techniques for establishing interclass communication and understanding, and proposals for "widening the gates to opportunity" via changes in our educational system and our corporate hiring practices. Mr. Packard makes excellent sense—which is no indication whatever that his recommendations will be acted upon.

"The Status Seekers" may not be as obviously sensational as "The Hidden Persuaders"—though its tone of wide-eyed wonder (real, or feigned for the reader's sake) at its own revelations might superficially make it seem so. But it is a far more important work.

*Drawing by Chas. Addams. ©1958 by The New Yorker Magazine, Inc.*
"You're right. That's **exactly** what they look like."

May 3, 1959

# In Defense of Romantic Love

*Is it a disease peculiar to those who are too young in heart?*
*Or is it the essential ingredient that makes the magic in marriage?*

By MORTON M. HUNT

AS the nation's institutions of higher learning begin their academic year, some thousands of sociologists and professors of family life are taking up again their crusade

MORTON M. HUNT is the author of "The Natural History of Love," an alternate Book-of-the-Month Club choice for November.

against an insidious and malign philosophy to which youth is perennially attracted—romantic love. Well over seven hundred universities and colleges are now offering courses in courtship, marriage and the family, and the instructors who teach them are, almost to a man, hostile to romantic love, holding it to be a deception, a danger, and even a disease.

In rare moments of jocularity, some of them sneeringly refer to it as "cardiac-respiratory love," but most of the time they soberly belabor it with case histories, assail it with statistics, and lay siege to it with random samples. Their avowed aim is to convince their students that it is a sickly fantasy, best abandoned as soon as possible in favor of "mature love" or "conjugal love," a sensible, realistic emotion. They speak and write of romantic love in terms like these:

"Only those people who do not know each other intimately can feel romantic."—Magoun, "Love and Marriage."

"Romantic love is a relationship of remoteness and adoration. Psychically it is attuned to persons who are emotionally adolescent and insecure."—Winch, "The Modern Family."

"[Romantic love] is like a drug. * * * Fortunately, its power can be more easily broken than that of drugs. Time and common sense * * * frequently restore even the violently afflicted to sanity—and happiness."—Baber, "Marriage and the Family."

There have, of course, always been people who spoke ill of romantic love. Francis Bacon acidly maintained that, of all the really great persons in history, "not one * * * hath been transported to the mad degree of love." Jonathan Swift termed it "a ridiculous passion which hath no being but in play-books and romances." H. L. Mencken dismissed it airily as a "state of perceptual anesthesia." But all this was only philosophic rodomontade; it waited upon modern sociology and anthropology to dignify the attack with the name of science.

**M**ARGARET MEAD lived with the Arapesh of New Guinea in the Nineteen Twenties, and with the Samoans somewhat later; her writings clearly implied that these peoples, who possessed nothing akin to the Western concept of romantic love, were happier and healthier without it. Similar reports came in from field workers in Tahiti, Rhodesia, and a score of other areas. Finally, in 1936, anthropologist Ralph Linton summarized the feelings of the social-science *avant-garde* in these classically sarcastic words:

"All societies recognize that there are occasional violent attachments between persons of opposite sex, but our present American culture is practically the only one which has attempted to capitalize on these and make them the basis for marriage. * * * Their rarity in most societies suggests that they are psychological abnormalities to which our culture has attached an extraordinary value just as other cultures have attached extreme values to other abnormalities. The hero of the modern American movie is always a romantic lover just as the hero of the old Arab epic is always an epileptic."

Ever since, this has been the prevailing view of most social scientists, a considerable number of whom have earned their Ph. D.'s by attacking some tenet or practice of romantic love.

And just what *is* this psychological abnormality of which they would cure us with the psychotherapy of cross-cultural studies and statistics? There is no satisfactorily rigorous definition of it, but as one sociologist writes, "In sociology it has been cus-tomary to apply the term 'romantic' to a kind of love characterized by idealization of the love-object and by its inaccessibility." From these fundamental characteristics stem the other qualities—its power and intensity, its bittersweet joy, its picturesque, poetic, or strange circumstances, its over-valuation of physical appeal, to which the lover ascribes all manner of spiritual and mental values.

**T**YPICALLY, the romantic lover has only to see the right girl the first time and something deep within him vibrates, or perhaps melts, or even rings like a bell. She may be a stranger across a crowded room, but somehow he *knows*. It does not matter that he is, say, a middle-aged French exile with half-breed children, and she an ignorant young girl from Little Rock, Ark., for love not only ignores such obstacles but thrives upon them.

The course of romantic love, however, does not run smoothly; there are always obstacles, separations, conflicts. The lovers yearn, despair, toss on their beds sleepless, walk alone in the moonlight, write notes and tear them up, think vaguely about renouncing everything or committing suicide. For the value of the world now depends upon the beloved: he (or she) is perfect, wonderful, and unique, and without him (or her) the world and life are worthless.

In this condition of wretched happiness and miserable joy, the romantic lovers want only one thing—to link their lives forever. They expect that when they marry, all problems will be solved, all wants and needs fulfilled. They will need no others, being sufficient unto themselves; they will be perennially entranced, continuously happy, their life an endless succession of mountain-top picnics, candle-lit dinners, love-filled nights.

But their love is always tender rather than lusty; as seen in the advertisements in magazines for young women, the handsome husband, faultlessly dressed, hovers adoringly over his wife after dinner, gallantly lighting her cigarette while she smiles prettily up at him. Every day is a date for two; there are no dirty dishes, cranky children, or unpaid bills.

Such is the general picture of romantic love, perpetuated in movies, fiction, and advertising, against which the anti-romantics have been waging warfare with their surveys and analyses. They accuse it of misdirecting young people in their choice of mates, of leading them to expect of marriage something unreal and nonexistent, of creating desires that can never be fulfilled, of blocking the development of satisfactory married love.

**T**HEY therefore term it a major cause of divorce, and have even turned their masses of statistics into marriage pre-

Romantic love, say sociologists, means that he (she) is ideal and inaccessible.

diction tests which show, to the second decimal place, that every difference between the cultural backgrounds of the lovers, be it in their education, religion, or social status, decreases the chances of happy marriage and lasting love. Indeed, by a logical extension of their arguments—though they never make it—the ideal mate for each man would be his sister.

The sociologists are not alone in condemning romantic love and viewing its consequences with alarm. Some psychoanalysts side with them; Lawrence Kubie, for instance, declares that "being in love is an obsessional state which, like all obsessions, is in part driven by unconscious anger," and Theodor Reik calls love "a reaction-formation to envy, possessiveness and hostility." Many marriage counselors consider any love affair between people of dissimilar backgrounds a form of retribution against one's parents.

In sum, the anti-romantics feel that romantic love is an antiquated, non-functional and immature (or perhaps neurotic) pattern that poisons the minds of the young and prevents them from experiencing that richer and healthier variety, mature or conjugal love.

And now, one wants to know, what *is* this marvelous thing, conjugal love? Here begins a mystery. It is easy to piece together the picture of romantic love, and to describe the actions and fancies of lovers of that stripe; but of conjugal love and lovers there is hardly a scrap of description to be found.

Search as you will in the writings of the anti-romantics, you cannot find any clear portrait of the thing. Some of the advocates of conjugal love

The realist school says romance is lost for those who know each other well.

speak of it in terms of "adjustment" and tabulate the average months or years needed for a man and woman to adjust to each other in religious matters, sexual matters, and so on. So treated, conjugal love sounds like a truce reached after exhaustion on the battlefield.

OTHERS equate it with companionship — though this quite fails to distinguish the love of people of different sexes from the friendship of men for each other; there is, happily, a difference. Still others discuss conjugal love in terms of "habit formation" and "accommodation to a standardized pattern of living, working and playing together"; this sounds unpleasantly like basic military training.

Psychologist A. H. Maslow of Brandeis University, lauding the intimacy and freedom of self-expression possible in mature conjugal love, says that in it "there is much less tendency to put the best foot forward * * * [or hide] physical defects. * * * There is much less maintenance of distance, mystery and glamour." Like much of the writing on the subject, this tells us what conjugal love is not rather than what it is; one might even be pardoned for wondering if anything recognizable as love exists within the state of so-called conjugal love.

It is no surprise, therefore, to find some of the critics of romantic love admitting plainly that love really has nothing to do with marriage, or should not have. Dr. Ernest van den Haag of New York University recently told a New York Times reporter:

"Love is a passion, and the literal meaning of passion is 'suffering.' It is the tension between desire and fulfillment. As love becomes fulfilled, it ceases to exist. * * * Marriage, on the other hand, is a very serious matter. It is rational, very legal, and quite public. It is, in fact, based on the temporary nature of love, and was designed by society to compel people to continue to live together long after their ardor has cooled."

CLEARLY, the opponents of romantic love would like to rid us of a disease most of us have found enjoyable and important, and are offering us instead a condition of health that will be good for us, and no pleasure whatever. But how valid, how fruitful, how meaningful have the teachings of the anti-romantic been? Is it helpful to cultivate adjustment, rather than love, within marriage?

Curiously enough, it is among the educated and intelligent stratum of Americans, who strive for adjustment hardest, that the incidence of infidelity grows with each year of marriage, reaching a peak in the late thirties, just when conjugal love should have become totally mature and satisfying. Although the libido slowly diminishes in intensity, the emotional hungers would seem to increase, or to be increasingly unsatisfied.

But a far graver defect in contemporary anti-romanticism is its internal inconsistency, which makes its directives conflicting and unworkable. Most of the anti-romantic marriage analysts admit that romantic love is, in our society, the only functioning method of mate selection; they further admit that it holds bride and groom together long enough to permit them to build permanent ties. Yet at the same time they counsel young people *against* choosing mates on the basis of romantic ideas, and even urge them to expel these feelings and ideas from their marriages as rapidly as they can. The late Willard Waller, a sociologist of considerable influence, actively advocated measured doses of quarreling early in marriage "to liquidate the effects of the romantic complex." Neither he nor any of his followers ever had the scientific good grace to follow up this suggestion and see what results it yielded.

WHAT has been passed off as a theory based on scientific method is, therefore, so tangled in its own contradictions that one may suspect the method has been used wrongly. But where and how? Maybe in the use made of cross-cultural comparisons. Romantic love is absent from Samoan life, and the Samoans are the better off therefor, but how does that prove that urbanized Americans, with no tribal and intimate community life, can likewise thrive without it? Quite possibly we would be as badly off without it as they would be without the outrigger canoe.

Or perhaps the scientific method has come unglued because it has rated kinds of love in terms of adjustment, assuming adjustment to be good without first proving it so. Americans have a rich cultural heritage that shapes their thinking and feeling, and that has stressed achievement, success, independence, freedom and other so-called Puritan values rather than adjustment. There are no scientific grounds for believing that adjustment is better in any absolute sense than our native values—or if there are, the anti-romantics have never bothered to demonstrate them.

OR perhaps the scientific method has foundered on a misuse of terms. Romantic love is not merely folly, adolescence, unreality and dreaming, but much more. The medieval knights and ladies who first introduced it into Western culture made basic changes in the nature of the relationship between men and women: sex grew tender and somewhat inhibited; lovers became devoted and loyal servants of each other; women were raised from their demeaned status and were idealized and worshiped. All of these characteristics of romantic love were absorbed into Western marriage, which has ever since been inescapably romantic in nature.

Furthermore, modern men and women have the notion that romantic love improves one's character and therefore has ethical value. Without it, they believe, life is barren, selfish and worthless, and until one has loved, his character is incomplete and imperfect. This, however, is a quintessentially romantic view of love as the medieval founders of it stated continually. "Oh, what a wonderful thing is love," wrote Andreas Capellanus in 1175 or thereabouts, "which makes a man

shine with so many virtues and teaches everyone, no matter who he is, so many good traits of character!"

Even the anti-romantics believe this, though they hide the ethical content behind the inability to love conjugally as a sign of immaturity (which is the equivalent of *bad* and the opposite as a sign of maturity (which is the equivalent of *good*).

WHO can quarrel with this? Yet it exposes the weakness of anti-romanticism as nothing else: the very people who identify romantic love as the *opposite* of conjugal love also describe conjugal love in terms borrowed from the romantic tradition.

Granted that the more unrealistic and foolish aspects of romantic love can be hurtful, if carried beyond adolescence, still the over-all attack on romantic love may be even more hurtful. The anti-romantics are salesmen of the humdrum in place of the wonderful; they are advocates of pain-reducing adjustment rather than emotional satisfaction. To "liquidate the effects of the romantic complex" is to rob marriage of much of its major function in the present era.

For what is that function? Not the breeding of warriors or farm hands. Not the maintenance of a dynastic name. Not the establishment of an economic unit that will produce food and clothing. Modern man can buy all the goods and services he needs for cash, and he has no compelling urge to continue a clear-cut family line. But the more our society becomes urban, mobile, fluid, and subject to rapid change, the more he needs warmth, reassurance, a sense of belonging, enduring friendship, and certainty of affection.

ALL these, combined with sex and expressed in part through it, are what he seeks in marriage. A studied liquidation of romantic values can only weaken it, blunt its purposes, and make it dull and unsatisfying. It is not so dreadful of us to continue hungering for romantic love after we marry; it is only dreadful if the marriage itself cannot appease that hunger.

So it is the larger forces of history and industrialism that have increased the need of the individual for those more basic and important components of romantic love we have just spelled out. Yet even the more superficial and seemingly foolish side of romantic love has a certain value in modern marriage, and ought t wholly to be abandoned to the teenagers.

Perhaps it seems immature to the psychologists for anyone to maintain illusions of physical attractiveness before his mate, but is it loving and generous to cease doing so? Each of us needs to feel capable of winning the love of someone desirable and attractive; the maturity that scorns this is the maturity of the saint or the corpse. To make the effort to seem attractive in the eyes of one's love partner is not just vanity and immaturity, but a form of thoughtfulness and generosity toward him or her.

Perhaps excessive idealization of a scarcely known person is ridiculous, and even harmful. But a small dollop of idealization of one's mate —seeing him or her as a little

handsomer, kinder, or more gifted than he really is—contributes to the satisfaction of both parties, and makes each a little more satisfied than he ought, in hardheaded realism, to be. The effort of each partner to meet the other's emotional needs and to do services for the other is unquestionably gratifying to both, and therefore important to the maintenance of the union.

Perhaps it is both undesirable and impossible to maintain a romantic aura throughout all the days and years of marriage. But those married people who can create it for themselves at appropriate times, with candlelight, wine, soft music and all other suitable appurtenances, will find their married love-making continually satisfying. It becomes dull only for those who discard, as unnecessary, the esthetic and mood-inducing

circumstances, and who wonder afterward, as the pathetic cliché has it, why the magic has gone out of their marriages.

No reasonable person will deny that the adolescent and fictional variety of romantic love is unsuited to adult life, and that a heavy diet of it may misguide and harm some young people. But there is an even greater danger in condemning all romantic values and trying to root them out of marriage—the danger that we may weaken its structural ties and render it unrewarding. It may be virtuous to strive for maturity, but, because one is virtuous, shall there be no more cakes and ale?

*September 27, 1959*

*September 27, 1959*

## FAMILY PRIDE LINKED TO CHARGE ACCOUNT

ST. LOUIS, Nov. 8 (AP)— Today's American family is the best educated ever, but also the most insecure. It is the most experienced, but the most nervous. It is the most adaptable, the most mobile and the most married, but it is also the least stable.

These views were offered tonight by Dr. Jessie Harris, dean emeritus of the College of Home Economics at the University of Tennessee. She spoke at a dinner meeting preliminary to the annual convention of the American Association of Land Grant Colleges and State Universities.

The old values of family life have changed, Miss Harris declared. Thrift is out of style, she said, and families now rate themselves by their charge accounts rather than their bank accounts.

In earlier years, she noted, the family had a large dwelling and produced much of what it needed. Today, she continued, the average family dwelling is small and convenient. Couples marry younger and raise their families earlier. The mother usually has her last child at the age of 26 and six years later is ready to follow the rest of the family into the workaday world.

*November 9, 1959*

# CURTAIN OF SOUND

## It Is Being Draped Over Every Aspect of Life

By HOWARD TAUBMAN

A CHAIN of apartment houses in Brooklyn is planning to feed music into its lobbies and laundries twenty-four hours a day, seven days a week and presumably twelve months a year. The idea is to provide a backdrop to the social and workaday noises that go with apartment-house life.

Is this progress? Somebody seems to think so. It is certainly regarded as a plus factor in the real estate business. Muzak, an estimable organization that pipes music into a host of places, reports that it is providing musical atmosphere to nearly 300 apartment projects throughout the country. Evi-

dently an amenity of this sort is considered a valuable extra by competing apartment developments.

One is accustomed to soft music in certain restaurants. It is not uncommon to encounter music, though not played softly, in supermarkets. Some hotels have it going incessantly in their elevators.

The notion that we must have a pretty musical backdrop for so many of our ordinary activities is not a new one. The radio and long-playing disk have put continuous music within everyone's reach, and countless people have taken advantage of this boon granted by a mechanical age.

### Need For Mist

It is a boon, of course, if you cannot bear the workaday noises of your home or the outside world without a beneficent mist of music. There are people who cannot study, read, masticate or make conversation unless they have appealing sounds in the background. A few are so desperate that they do not ven-

ture out for a walk in the park without a small radio clutched in their hands to provide them with music. How wise they are to arm themselves in advance; otherwise, heaven forfend, they might have to hear the song of a bird or the cry of a child without any ameliorating tune as a shield.

For people of this sort there is no problem of being part of a captive audience. They rejoice in a world filled with constant musical backdrops. They do not feel their privacy or freedom is invaded if the whirr of a high-speed washing or drying machine is set off neatly by "Pomp and Circumstance." Electrical appliances have taken the drudgery out of getting the laundry done, and now music turns it into enchantment. Hallelujah for the forward march of the twentieth century! The mind boggles at what the twenty-first will produce. Shall our descendants be whirling in space tuned to some disk jockey on earth to be sure they do not hear the music of the spheres?

But what's wrong? Serious statistical studies have shown that music can function like a stimulant or tranquilizer. Do you want to keep your factory crew from becoming bored with the routine of the assembly line? A lively waltz or a martial march will revive flagging interest. Do you want to soften a patient's pain when you drill his tooth? A gentle nocturne may lull the stab of a hurt nerve?

Who can object to the use of music in combating fatigue or easing discomfort? Who can find fault with the employment of a practical aid in such vital matters as commerce and medicine? No one, not even a stiff-necked believer in the significance of music as a profound and affecting expression of the human adventure. All he would ask is that a clear distinction be made between music as a backdrop and music as a form of communication.

### Machines Multiplying

Such a distinction ought to be taken for granted. But we live in a world in which, despite the "population explosion" about which we hear so much these days, machines multiply much faster than human beings. Add to the overabundance of sound-producing equipment an increasing capacity to amplify and project sound, and you are exposed almost without letup to a musical backdrop for the workaday social — and unsocial — noises.

Some of the background music, you may be told, is often of high caliber. But that is a service neither to the music nor to the listener, for a work of art deserves undivided attention. If a composition is truly meaningful, how is it possible to absorb it without unremitting concentration?

Don't think that everyone who attends performances in the concert hall and opera house has made the transition to full attention from the random listening one is likely to do when music is used as a backdrop. How often do you see people busily reading their program notes while a symphony is being played? How often do eyes wander to the boxes while something memorable is developing in the score?

Listening needs a conscientious effort. This column recalls remarking some years ago in a review of a difficult, new work that it demanded energy from the listener. A reader promptly wrote to question the use of the word energy in so queer a context.

But energy is precisely the word. Good music of any kind, whether it be a symphony, an opera, a quartet or a work for jazz band, merits the full concentration of the listener. Indeed, its rewards are likely to be in direct ratio to the amount of effort one invests in the listening.

## Attractive Gloss

In a society like ours, which tends to put an attractive gloss over so many of our concerns, there is a built-in disposition to make everything palatable and it follows that agreeable combinations of melody, harmony and rhythm will be turned into pervasive sweeteners. The habit of inattention, so mischievous in

art as in politics, is thus encouraged. In music it can be disastrous.

In recent weeks the air has been heavy with carols and other Christmas music. Most of us are thoroughly familiar with the lovely songs of the season, and we need not stop all our normal tasks to give them our energetic attention. But would they not say much more to us if we listened to them with our minds and hearts fully alert to the depth and richness of their meaning? Were they designed to be a backdrop for workaday noises? Are we so fearful and lonely that we must hang our lobbies and laundries with curtains of music?

January 3, 1960

# A COLLEGE PROBLEM

## Margaret Mead Takes Issue With Trend; College Officials Split

### By FRED M. HECHINGER

"Here Comes the Bride" has joined the more traditional list of college songs. Married students are no longer an oddity on American campuses.

That the academic world is concerned about the marriage problem was underlined last week when the alumni magazines of Dartmouth, Simmons College, Smith and a number of other institutions featured an article by Margaret Mead, the anthropologist, who asked "Is College Compatible With Marriage?"

Miss Mead answers her own question with a resounding "no." She warns: "Before we become too heavily committed to this trend, it may be wise to pause and question whether it endangers the value of undergraduate education as we have known it."

To Miss Mead the undergraduate campus should be a world in which young men and women may be free "in a way they can never be free again, to explore before they settle on the way their lives are to be lived."

She fears that "a new barbarism" is forcing young people to marry too soon. The blame is placed on "mothers who worry about boys and girls who don't begin dating in high school"; on "student-made rules about exclusive possession of a

girl twice dated by the same boy"; on employers who look for "a settled married man"; on the idea of marriage as a free pass to adulthood.

### Solid Trend

The problem with Miss Mead's criticism is that it fights windmills. Nothing short of a drastic change in the present American social and economic pattern, such as a major depression, is likely to stop the trend toward earlier marriage. The only allies she will find today are the small men's and women's colleges. Only the strongest among them can take active steps to discourage marriage.

Miss Mead deplores student marriage as an enemy of the "as-if world" of the secluded campus. The fact is that the car, vocational pressures and restlessness have already transformed so much of campus life, even without marriage, that it may be asked whether Miss Mead's premise itself lives in an "as-if world." Unfortunately, facts are facts—even when they are unfortunate.

What are Miss Mead's major academic objections?

(1) Married students have no chance "to find themselves in college because they have clung to each other so exclusively. They often show less breadth of

vision as seniors than they did as freshmen."

(2) Help from both sets of parents "perpetuates their immaturity."

(3) College served only as a place to get a degree and find a mate.

(4) If the girl gives up her own academic interests, either before or immediately after her graduation, to support the husband's graduate studies, she undermines her intellect and underlines his dependence.

What about the maturity of the veterans of the G. I. Bill of Rights? Miss Mead says they confirm her point: they had earned their stipend in the country's service. They were not "dependent."

Miss Mead charges that "college presidents have joined the matchmakers."

Not all college presidents agree. Thomas C. Mendenhall of Mount Holyoke, criticized "prevailing mania for early marriage."

### Reaction Divided

A spot check of college spokesmen found the colleges sharply divided.

Thaddeus Seymour, dean of the college at Dartmouth, pointed to the high proportion of married students whose wives must discontinue their own education. The college's policy is one of "toleration but not accommodation or encouragement," he said.

Helen L. Russell, dean of students at Smith College, feels that "one thing at a time is much better for the college student, especially at a time when academic competition is so keen." But she concedes that the situation may be better at large co-educational universities where both marriage partners

may attend college at the same time, living normal lives.

This seems to put in focus the dividing line of opinion. Arwood S. Northby, dean of students at the University of Connecticut, simply deplored that his institution lacked the money for married student housing and thus may deter many students from applying.

Tom King, dean of students at Michigan State University, pointing to 3,000 married undergraduates, said the university had provided housing for them since 1946 and praised their academic performance. "College has always been a marriage market," he said.

### Here to Stay

Clearly, the married student is here to stay—welcome or not. Dr. Gladys Meyer, associate professor of sociology at Barnard, who is preparing a reply to Miss Mead's article, says "whatever we may think, it won't reverse the trend toward earlier marriages." The problem, she adds, is new only in the East, particularly in the Ivy League and the women's colleges. In the Midwest and Far West, there have always been some happily married students, including her own parents, who "put each other through" college in the 1890's.

Miss Mead, the anthropologist, probably knows that she cannot alter the mores of the modern American tribe; Miss Mead, the philosopher and educator, nevertheless feels it her duty to save some students from the tyranny of tribal custom. Such rear-guard action may at least protect those students who would prefer "to play the field" — intellectually and romantically—but are in fear of being marked as social failures.

March 20, 1960

## EDUCATOR WARNS ON TOGETHERNESS

### Teachers' Parley Here Told Independence Is Better Than Belonging

**By GENE CURRIVAN**

The teaching of "togetherness" was assailed yesterday by a leading educator.

Dr. Francis H. Horn, president of the University of Rhode Island, said the theory was unsound. He said he favored self-reliance.

Dr. Horn addressed the annual spring conference of the Eastern States Association of Professional Schools for Teachers at the New Yorker Hotel.

"We have had enough of this togetherness," Dr. Horn declared, noting that togetherness was one of the themes of the forthcoming White House Conference on Children and Youth. He was referring to one of the "pledges" the conference will make to children—"We will help you strengthen your sense of belonging."

#### 'Unstability' Seen

Dr. Horn contended that reliance on belonging or togetherness instead of independence led to "emotional unstability."

Teachers and students from the association's eighty member institutions also heard Lawrence G. Derthick, United States Commissioner of Education. He offered a vigorous defense of the nation's education system, which he said had "no counterpart on earth." He said that this nation's best schools were without peers anywhere, but he complained that there were too many poor ones.

Schools must be concerned with character as well as intellect, he said. He agreed to some extent with Rear Admiral Hyman G. Rickover, who favors emphasis on scholastic achievement, but Mr. Derthick added, "We don't want to cross bridges built by engineers without character."

In his criticism of "togetherness," Dr. Horn said children should be taught "not to want to belong, not to lean on others, even on members of one's family."

#### Community Concept Scored

Dr. Horn, who is also a former president of Pratt Institute, held that the old concept of the community was an anachronism today.

"If we are to develop a sense of belonging to the community, a phrase used by educators," he asserted, "it should be directed to establishing an attitude of belonging to the world community."

"The child of today being prepared for tomorrow's world," he declared, "should be taught above all to consider himself primarily as a member of the human race, to recognize that every man is his brother, that his neighbor is not the man next door but the man everywhere regardless of the color of his skin, his ethnic background, his religious convictions or indeed the nature of his cooking or his plumbing."

March 26, 19

# Portrait of A Mobile Nation

## Americans are more and more on the go. What has spurred this wanderlust?

**By DAVID BOROFF**

COMMENTING on the so-called "reverse freedom riders" at a recent press conference, President Kennedy observed that interstate migration was commonplace and that 25 per cent of our population had moved across state lines in the last decade. The President, as usual, was well-informed. There is little doubt that Americans are a restlessly peregrinating people. In their mid-century phase, mobility has become an organic part of the American style of life. But how much are they on the move? Who are the people who do the moving? What effect does this mobility have on American life? And what does it portend?

According to the 1960 Census, 44.7 million people were born in a state other than that of their 1960 residence. And nearly half (47.3 per cent) of 159 million Americans 5 years of age and older were living in a different house from the one they occupied five years earlier. Of the 75 million movers, 47.5 million remained in the same county. Of the 27.7 million who moved to a different county, almost half (13.6 million) remained in the same state, while 14.1 million moved to another state. On average, approximately 3 per cent of the population moves across state lines every year.

From these statistics, a few general considerations emerge. First, although Americans do move around a good deal, the highways are not exactly choked with people fleeing their native heaths. The vivid sense of a nation on the move may have more to do with our psychic tempo than with population shifts. (According to reliable estimates, Americans spent $58.4 billions—almost one-tenth of the gross national product—just in traveling from one place to another last year.)

SECOND, the folklore of the times, which statistical and sociological evidence so often refutes, has proved to be true for a change. The West is the fastest-growing part of the country by far; the Northeast, which is to the West what England is to America in terms of stability, is the most settled part of the country. And the South actually is undergoing a serious drain of population and can ill afford its latest adventure in population leakage.

Mobility, the all-American sport, cuts across class and racial lines. Both rich and poor get around—although higher-income groups naturally do more of it. (Mobility also increases with the educational level.) Low-income groups tend to move more from residence to residence in the same locality while those with higher incomes shift more between counties. And despite the widely publicized Negro exodus from the South, whites have a higher rate of inter-county migration (6.8 per cent against 4 per cent). Negroes, however, have a substantially higher rate of movement within counties (18.4 per cent against 12.2 per cent).

THE national wanderlust seems to follow a clearly defined age cycle. Mobility is at its height late in adolescence and in early adulthood. For both sexes, the peak is between 21 and 22 years of age, when 40 per cent of that age group actually moves. Young families also move around a great deal but tend to settle down as their children reach high school. (In one study, the mobility rate was twice as high in cases where the head of the family was under 35 as in those where he was 35 to 44.) Suspended during the middle years, mobility picks up again with retirement.

Although we are a nation of migrants, there has always been some ambivalence of feeling about mobility. In the country's early days, those who moved West were generally people without property—drifters and subsistence farmers. Theirs was a migration

DAVID BOROFF has, since 1960, participated in the new mobility by shifting from a job as lecturer in English at Brooklyn College to an associate professorship at N. Y. U.

**RESTLESS**—With 75 million of us living in different dwellings from those of five years ago, the moving van, not the vine-covered cottage, may become the symbol of our domestic idyll.

around (similar to the three-year tour of duty of the armed forces).

What are the effects of these changes in family location? So many of our national pieties—family stability, the need for roots, the grace and wholesomeness of the settled community — would seem to be threatened by this restless moving in and out. The moving van, rather than the vine-covered cottage, may well become the symbol of our domestic idyll. As in so many other developments in the nation's life, the effects are both good and bad, but what is most striking is the American genius for accommodating the inevitable.

THERE have been some unhappy consequences of mobility. Roughly half of all American counties are losing population. For the most part, this is accompanied by sagging morale, reduced job opportunities and a further exodus of the most energetic members of these communities. The decline of America's rural culture is one of the sad casualties of our forward-driving age.

Family life has also undergone a change. The so-called "extended family"—embracing relatives as well as parents and children—has disintegrated with the dispersion of its units. (One sociologist has argued that with ease of travel and quick, inexpensive telephone communication, the extended family has held its own on a modified basis; but this thesis is highly doubtful.) On the other hand, the mobile family generally makes a tough, resourceful unit as the stressful experience of moving causes it to draw together. An Air Force wife summed matters up: "The family now provides all the security."

Along with these changes, there is a weakening in family continuity and memories. One executive pointed out that in moving, it is always the trunk in the attic full of heirlooms and frivolous souvenirs that gets left behind. Another Air Force wife remarked ruefully about this attrition of property: "They say that three moves are the equivalent of one fire."

BUT what saves the day for middle-class migrants is that so many of their counterparts in other places are also on the move. There is a vast army of

born of desperation—and as early as 1850, long before the dawn of formal demography, the United States Census was compiling figures about interstate movement. In the settled parts of the country, however, the approved mode was to stay where one was born.

The great divide between the relative immobility of the Nineteen Thirties, when the depression paralyzed movement (despite the saga of the Okies), and our own freewheeling time was World War II. The country had never before experienced such a vast population upheaval. Nor was there any return—despite war-spawned fantasies of quiet and stability—to the status quo. The effect of war was to open windows on other parts of the country —indeed, on the world. And this uprooting was accelerated by the G. I.

Bill in the post-war period which sent ex-G. I. students to every corner of the country. America was really on the move.

IN recent years, however, there has been a curious reversal in the complex pattern of population shifts. At the very time when mobility—formerly associated with the dispossessed—was becoming less attractive to working-class people increasingly anchored by their new prosperity, it became part of the life-style of the socially aspirant middle class. For middle-class people, the prime motive in moving to another part of the country is, of course, job improvement. And as corporations become larger and more ramified, the usual career pattern involves a good deal of shifting transient executives, engineers, academic people and officers in the armed forces on its way up. (Certain communities like Levittown, Pa., and Park Forest, Ill., are simply way stations on the career escalator.)

**UPHILL RACE**—Career migrants are in competition not only at work but up and down the social scale.

What this means, very simply, is that an executive and his family can move from the Northeast to the Middle West—and even the South—without having to make too strenuous an adjustment. There is now what might be called an "interchangeable community." The world of the middle-class executive or professional has been homogenized. And even the purchase of a house does not imply a permanent commitment—for the owner well knows that if he is transferred out, there will be someone else transferred in to whom he can sell the house.

The true focus of loyalty for middle-class migrants, therefore, is not their community but their profession, corporation or academic discipline. The General Motors executive is at home anywhere for his corporation is everywhere. The same is true of the Army, Navy or Air Force officer. Wherever he goes he will find a ready-made community. As a much-traveled corporation wife expressed it: "In the old days, it used to take two years before your neighbors accepted you. Today, there are always new friends waiting for you."

**H**OW do middle-class people feel about this enforced mobility? By and large, they submit to it cheerfully. "I don't like it but I take it in my stride. It's part of the deal," an executive remarked. Shifting around has become the normal style and the man who remains fixed in a post increasingly rare. "In many companies," a personnel man observed, "if you don't accept the first job change you're dead." At the Air Force Academy, a group of officers, assigned for a three-year tour, joked about the registrar, a permanent assignee. They suggested that there was a place in the post cemetery reserved for him.

Although executives and professionals go where corporate winds blow them, they generally prefer to move from a smaller center to a larger. The favored areas are the West Coast and the Northeast—with the San Francisco Bay area and New York as first choices. Southerners, despite their *mystique* of blood and soil, are as prone to move as the next man but differ in that they piously express the intention of returning South eventually.

The corporation executive's wife often has a good deal to say about moving, although she, too, accepts dislocation as part of the game. If she doesn't, her husband had better beware. "Some men aren't as strong at home as they are

**YOUTH AND AGE**—Wanderlust is at its peak in the 21-22 age group, but slows down in the middle years.

**NEW MIGRANTS**—In the old days, those who were on the move were mostly people without property. Today, mobility is increasingly part of the life-style of the aspiring middle class.

in the office," an executive in a management consultant firm said disapprovingly. "We try to deal with executives with the strength to resist their wives."

The concerns of the wife are likely to be different from those of her husband. She worries about the kind of community she is moving to, its schools and, increasingly, its cultural opportunities. ("Executives seem to marry women with a bent for the humanities," a personnel man said wryly.) Many, despite the prevailing folklore, shun a corporation-centered social life and move out of the unofficial compound to make other friends.

How does moving around influence child-rearing? There is a scare psychology which attributes juvenile delinquency and emotional unrest to mobility, but sociologists largely agree that moving need not present severe problems. Where the fabric of the family is strong, where parents are not themselves ridden with anxiety, there need be no serious emotional dislocations. The same is true of marriage. Moving merely intensifies already existing strains and stresses. It does not create them.

Career migrants generally have little anxiety about the education of their children. They are less inclined to move, however, once their youngsters have entered high school. ("Our children are reaching the age where they ought to have roots".) Panic about college admission plays a part, and there is often the fear that a high-school boy or girl on the move will be cheated out of the pleasure and benefit of extracurricular life.

**B**UT even in education, mobility has become respectable. Professors, formerly cloistered and sedentary types, are as much on the move as their corporate counterparts. It is part of the career pattern of the able academic to tea    in a number of colleges.    . if he is worth his salt, he may be invited, after he has tenure, to serve as a visiting professor or even to roam farther afield with the aid of foundation grants.

Among students, it is no longer a symptom of academic instability to transfer from school to school. It is viewed as a proper way of extending one's educational horizon. And Junior Year Abroad is not a form of expatriation but simply a classroom overseas.

Other kinds of middle-class mobility are also shaping the American outlook. Travel habits have broadened enormously since World War II. Places previously deemed inaccessible to all but the very rich are now within reach of most middle-class people. And they are now more likely to spend their vacations on the move than in settling down at one resort. The motel—the bedroom on the run—has become a fixed part of the American landscape.

Abroad, the pattern is the same. An innkeeper in the Austrian Tyrol recently observed that her American guests were noteworthy for their restlessness. "Germans or Italians will stay for a week or two," she remarked, "but Americans are on their way within a few days. They even move around from room to room within the *pension*."

ONE would imagine that this crisscrossing of the country—and of the world—by vast numbers of people would tend to diminish provincialism—and to some extent it does. In recent years, for example, small-town newspapers have scuttled much of their local gossip in favor of national and international news. But, in another sense, a new provincialism may be spreading. The supermarket in a new town offers the same wares as the one the newcomers left behind. The new P. T. A. has virtually the same agenda as the old, television programs are relentlessly unchanging and neighbors

**ALLEGIANCE** — Moving about, the family gives its loyalty not to a community but to a profession or business.

range predictably from the helpful to the insupportable.

Although one would assume that the broadening experiences of a change of scene would neutralize prejudice, the effects are modified by the fact that middle-class migrants are moving not only in space but up and down the social ladder. Such people, allegedly,

are more susceptible to group fears than more static types. Those on the way up are looking nervously over their shoulders for fear of being overtaken while those on the way down resent the inheritors of their former good fortune.

A recent study by sociologists Fred Silberstein and Melvin Seeman, however, reveals that a key factor is whether the migrant is primarily interested in his work or in status. If he is nervously attuned to status, then he will be more susceptible to prejudice.

IN general, uprooting is no longer the trauma it used to be—although there are, of course, many migrants to whom the experience is still disruptive and painful. The tens of thousands of Negroes who move from the South are still actors in a painful drama of exclusion and deprivation. Cities suffer, too, in the two-way traffic by which middle-class elements depart and deprived elements move in.

But mobility is another aspect of the openness of American society and, as such, it is healthy. Its effect will be to make Americans more at home in their own country and in the world. At the same time, it entails a further shrinkage of cultural and ethnic differences. Local provincialism may diminish, therefore, but there is the danger that the growing uniformity of American life which mobility encourages may replace it with an encircling *national* provincialism.

August 26, 1960

# Put It on the Cuff

### By ELLEN D. STRUHS

RECENTLY the Board of Governors of the Federal Reserve System lifted most of the wartime controls on installment buying and all of the restrictions on retail charge accounts. From now on an increasing number of people will be putting their purchases on the books and paying for them by the easy-payment plan. "Now that the lid is off, the American consumer will go into debt faster than he ever did before," one New York expert has predicted.

## CHARGE IT—

The "charge it, please," transaction is an old American custom. More than 60,000,000 retail customers, ranging from our richest millionaires to families of moderate circumstances, buy on credit. It has been estimated that in the post-war years the total volume of business done in retail stores will hit a peak of 75 billion or perhaps even 100 billion dollars a year. And of this amount more than 25 billion will be done on a credit basis—through charge accounts and installment buying.

A shopping convenience for the customer, credit buying also adds dignity to the business transaction—no filthy green stuff changing hands and no waiting around for the credit manager to approve a personal check. Business men like to extend credit because it encourages heavier buying. People who charge their purchases buy twice as much as cash customers, statisticians figure; yet the loss from bad accounts in normal years has never been more than one-half of 1 per cent.

## RESTRICTED—

The history of charge and installment buying in this country goes back to the early Eighteen Hundreds when Cowperthwait & Sons of New York City first sold furniture on a credit plan. About 1850 the Singer Sewing Machine Company adopted the same plan for marketing its products. And some time around 1875 pianos became one of the common products sold on installments. Rapidly the plan spread to all types of goods, until it covered practically everything from automobiles to diamond rings.

Around the turn of the present century charge accounts in retail and department stores were still limited mainly to wealthy patrons—the so-called "carriage trade," who preferred not to be encumbered by money on their persons. Soon after the first World War, however, department stores began to extend the same privilege to the rank and file of customer. Now anyone with a good credit rating can "put it on the cuff" with the credit manager's blessing.

## SUBTERFUGE—

While the great majority of applicants for credit are trustworthy, there are exceptions. Sometimes a woman who plans to leave her husband will "load up," buying to capacity at all stores where she has a charge account. When unusually heavy purchases are made the stores promptly notify the Credit Bureau. Husbands who have suffered a domestic crisis frequently guard against such spending sprees by inserting a notice in the papers: "My wife having left my bed and board, I will not be responsible for any of her debts."

Occasionally, someone tries to capitalize on a charge account. One young lady bought a new fur coat each Friday for three successive weeks, only to return each coat on the following Monday morning. An astute credit manager put two things together and deduced correctly that the young lady was using her charge account to keep warm at the football games. On her next trip he turned a polite thumbs-down on her "purchase."

## CHANGE OF HEART—

There was one prominent stockbroker who had often and publicly declared that he didn't believe in charge accounts and would not permit his wife to open one. Then one day the credit managers of all the large department stores in the city received letters asking them to extend charge privileges to the broker's wife. Tactfully the credit managers notified the broker, who admitted that he was responsible. It was his wife's birthday, he explained, and he wanted to surprise her with a charge account in every department store in New York.

### Banking Comics

The staid American Bankers Association has adopted colored comic books as a promotional device by which its members may develop thrift and a knowledge of banking services among children, as well as adults, it was disclosed yesterday. According to John B. Mack Jr., deputy manager of the association's advertising department, the comic book "Peter Penny and His Magic Dollar" will be made available to banks for distribution to their customers. "It's an effort to use a new medium to convey banking's story to children and adults," Mr. Mack explained. "Grown-ups read comics too." Adding a further note of social significance, he pointed out that it was important for children to know about the services available to them and their families by their home town banks, "not only for the purpose of developing potential business but also for the more important reason that banks, as one of the chief exponents of personal initiative and private enterprise, are now in the front battle line in the struggle between freedom and totalitarianism."

# MORE COMPLAINTS ON ADS ARE NOTE

## Better Business Bureau Fin Closer Competition Brings Greater Exaggeration

### By BRENDAN M. JONES

Sharpened competition h brought during the last six mont a large increase in the number complaints received by the Natio al Better Business Bureau on exa geration and misrepresentation advertising, Kenneth B. Willsc the bureau's operating manag disclosed here last week.

Most of the complaints conce misleading statements on valu and prices, Mr. Willson said. "A reflect unmistakable signs sharpening competition, and, b cause of a tendency to imitatic and reprisal in competitive adve tising, this condition could easi develop into an epidemic," added.

Along with this rise in cor plaint, Mr. Willson said, there al has been a substantial increase requests for the bureau's servic from both business and the publi The national bureau and the grea er number of local bureaus are no better equipped to serve busine because of extra facilities, grov ing experience and a well-train staff, he noted.

### Not Misleading in Entirety

"Generally, advertisements reputable media are not mislea ing if read in their entirety by person of reasonable intelligenc Mr. Willson stated. "Howeve superficial impressions made large-type copy, without the adc tional qualification of statemen in smaller type, are often the chi causes of misleading and confu ing reactions to many advertis ments. In the words of a rece decision by United States Supren Court Justice Black, 'laws a made to protect the trusting well as the suspicious.'"

Discussion of a competitor product in a disparaging mann violates the bureau's basic policie Mr. Willson continued. "In fac any comparisons to a competitor product is treading on dangerou ground," he said.

A conspicuous example of th type of advertising recently h

appeared in rival claims on new tires. One notable case was an advertisement in which a competitor's manner of presenting, point by point, the merits of his tire was duplicated for the purpose of alleging weaknesses, point by point, in the type of tire featured.

In the matter of "low" price claims, a large super-market chain prominently advertised that it offered the lowest food prices in any of its stores' "neighborhoods." Rival ads appearing in the same newspapers carried lower prices or identical articles. However, the chain had stated it would immediately reduce its prices when evidence of lower ones was brought to its attention.

## Impossible to Meet Claims

The BBB, Mr. Willson asserted, is opposed to claims by merchants that they continually undersell competitors. Usually such claims are inaccurate because they are impossible of fulfillment, the bureau's policy states. It is also considered impossible for the advertisers even though he uses checkers, to have accurate and complete knowledge of other prices, the bureau maintains. Sweeping claims of "lowest" prices, listing only a small percentage of specific reductions, creates, in the bureau's view, a false impression and is therefore misleading.

Another recent development, one in which value is misrepresented, is in the advertising of "special" combinations of articles, notably in drug items. A specific instance is that in which a well-known men's toilet article is offered in combination with a related article. The advertising states that the well-known item has a certain "retail value." This is added up with the "retail value" of the combination item, and the sum cut to a sales price about 40 per cent lower. Ads only a month or two older show that the well-known article was long sold at a price more than 40 per cent below the "retail value" claimed for it in the combination offer.

Still another version of this is to offer an established product, possibly a hair tonic, in combination with a new article, perhaps a cream or a rinse. An inflated value" is claimed for the unknown item, added to that of the established article, and then magnanimously slashed by 40 or 50 per cent.

The practice of the BBB in such cases is to notify the advertiser and urge a cessation of the claims, Mr. Willson said. If this is unsuccessful, all firms in the same trade are circularized on the subject.

# AD WRITERS ASSAIL IMMATURE APPEAL

## Industry to Fight Any Return to Practices That Shattered Public Faith in Thirties

### By BRENDAN M. JONES

The steadily mounting barrage of criticism in recent months against a revival of crass "huckstering" techniques in advertising was described by key agency officials last week as evidence that the industry's leaders are determined to fight any disinterment of practices that shattered public faith in advertising during the Thirties.

A survey of opinion produced the general conclusion that renewed competition and lack of originality are responsible for this current dusting-off of old tricks. However, not all of the criticism has been aimed at sharp and shady abuses. Much has struck at what apparently is a congenital trait of the trade—overworking of superlatives, and building of a dream world where soap rules destiny.

In commenting on this, Dr. Vergil D. Reed, associate director of research for the J. Walter Thompson Company, recommended a study of census figures which, he said, show a marked increase in the number of high school graduates. J. D. Cunningham, partner in the Newell-Emmett Company, who is regarded as one of the best copy writers in advertising, asserted that more progressive advertisers are moving out of the "twelve-year-old" market, in favor of more informative, definitely educational approaches to what they recognize as a wiser, harder-to-sell consumer.

The burden of attacks on what another official termed the "inefficiency" of advertising, is that the "twelve-year-old" market, if it ever did exist, is obviously the least lucrative for most advertisers. Buying power for major commodities does not go with lack of brain power, it is pointed out.

### Jingles Sell Soap

Despite the validity of these criticisms, another opinion held, there is still a large school of thought based on the principle that contests, jingles and kindergarten appeals does sell such products as candy, soda pop and soap. In the "mass" market, it is contended, these techniques build sales.

Among those who have assailed immature, unrealistic and exaggerated styles of advertising in growing number since the turn of the year, a counter-critic noted, are some who have been guilty of the faults they now deplore. Perhaps, because of this, they are in the best position to realize their present ineffectiveness, he commented.

More solid than all the "soul searching," an official of the National Better Business Bureau said, is the recent decision of the United States Supreme Court in ruling a puzzle contest misleading. Many advertisers and agencies, he added, still are just beginning to grasp its significance. Major points of this decision were:

"Advertisements as a whole may be completely misleading although every sentence is literally true," and "people have a right to assume that fraudulent advertising traps will not be laid to ensnare them."

# OUTPUT HELD HIGH IN AUTO INDUSTRY

## Companies Raise Production Schedules to Meet Demand While Other Lines Slump

DETROIT, July 16 (UP)—The automobile industry is puzzling over what is keeping the new car market at dizzying heights when some other industries have hit a slide. All major makers and most of the independent companies are shoving production schedules higher and higher to meet the demand for cars.

Some sales resistance is appearing in the high-priced auto field and lesser known makers are having to go out and "sell" their cars, but in the main the pace has not slackened.

There appear to be two reasons for high level prosperity in the auto field when some other industries are in doldrums. One of them is that the industry underestimated the backlog demand built up by auto vacuum during the war. The other is that post-war Americans more than ever have been educated to want a car.

Just before the war a Federal survey showed that 3,100,000 persons a year planned to buy cars. The latest survey showed that 3,600,000 persons wanted a new model in their garage.

And despite production of about 11,000,000 cars since the war, the highways still are clogged with more than 15,000,000 that are at least eight years old, 5,000,000 of them in the 10 to 12-year-old class.

Bank deposits show the public still is well heeled. The average American has trimmed large luxury items from his buying list, observers believe, but has left a new car in the "what I want next" classification.

The R. L. Polk Company, automotive statistical agency, estimated every three and one-half Americans owned an automobile to lead the world in per capita ownership.

While making cars as fast as assembly lines can turn them out, auto manufacturers are wondering how long their bonanza will last. Henry Ford 2d, president of the Ford Motor Company, recently predicted a return to a buyer's market this winter. Other experts also see a late fall buying slump.

But makers have two remedial shots-in-the-arm that could perk up a dragging market. One of them is price cuts. Right now producers have no inclination to reduce price tags when they can sell cars as fast as they roll off the line.

Reports of forthcoming new models are prevalent. As soon as there is a definite slump in sales reported by retailers, producers will offer sleek new cars to tempt the public's pocketbook.

## Young Fry's Cowboy Urge Builds Thriving Industry

The desire of American children to become "pistol totin'" cowboys and cowgirls has built up a multi-million dollar industry in the last seven years.

According to Stanley Breslaw, president of Carnell Manufacturing Company, more than 160,000,000 pistol and holster sets have been sold since 1944. The company is among the country's largest producers of this item. In 1944 there were ten concerns making the sets. The 1950 count showed 268.

March 2, 1951

## F. T. C. ENDS INQUIRY ON VIDEO CHILD ADS

Special to The New York Times.

WASHINGTON, March 7—The Federal Trade Commission today dropped its investigation into "child appeal" television advertisements with the reservation that it would reopen the inquiry "if future facts should warrant."

The commission announced that it had accepted written assurances from twenty-two manufacturers and their advertising agency, Ruthrauff & Ryan, Inc., of New York, that in the future they would not resort to advertising of "similar import."

The advertisements appeared last November in most major daily newspapers. The commission began an investigation Nov. 21, prompted by complaints from many parents and educational institutions.

According to the commission, the advertisements implied that a child would be handicapped from an educational standpoint and his morale would suffer unless there were a television set in his home. They were published under the heading "There Are Some Things a Son or Daughter Won't Tell You!"

March 8, 1951

## Fun Now—Pay Later

Under the "Fun Now—Pay Later" vacation loan program introduced by National Airlines, Inc., a vacationer may borrow cash from his bank or credit union to cover the cost of the trip, meals and incidental expenses plus clothing and sporting equipment. Special arrangements between the airline and the Industrial Bank of Commerce of New York have been worked out to insure preferred handling of applications for vacation loans by travelers taking one of the airlines' packaged "Piggy Bank" vacations this summer. Both applications for loans and information on the budget vacations to Miami Beach, Havana, Nassau, Jamaica or Mexico City, can be obtained either through National or direct from the bank.

May 5, 1951

# About Woman's Crowning Glory

### You can prefer a blonde but marry a brunette, and it's the same girl —thanks to today's dyes.

#### By MARYBETH WEINSTEIN

MANY a woman, like many a tree, is turning gold or russet-topped almost overnight. Autumn is always the hair colorists' busiest season but this year they're booked solid and a spot check on druggists shows do-it-yourself color kits are doing well, too.

Though the brunette has not—yet—joined the buffalo as a vanishing American, blondes and redheads are becoming far more common here than they used to be. Except for Scandinavia, where over 80 per cent of the people are blond, natural blondes are rather rare, and the natural redhead

**EGYPTIANS,** to be fashionably dark, wore black wigs or applied kohl to their hair.

belongs to an enviable 5 per cent even in Scotland, the country that, according to the British Medical Journal, has the highest ratio of redheads in the world. The enticement of real scarcity, however, may someday result in a muchness of ersatz; movie stars will have to be mousy to be different.

Our heightened local color began in 1950, with the introduction of home coloring products. Women who had longed to swing a drastic bottle at an unkind heredity or at age but were afraid to try a dye or tint (both as

**MARYBETH WEINSTEIN** of The New York Times Magazine is still a natural brunette, who hasn't yet let color go to her head.

216

ermanent as anything can be to something that won't stop growing) found they could experiment first with hair make-up (a diluted tint that leaves no line of demarcation) or rinses which can be shampooed out at will). And this, says Michel of Paris—of New York—has been a boon to professionals, not because of botched jobs, as one might think, but because some kits serve as a starter toward more unabashed transformations, for which many women prefer the beauty parlor to their own.

Though seasonal enthusiasm (ermines and mountain hares change for winter, too) and new techniques may explain the current increase in artifice, they do not plumb the urge itself. The first motivation is a perverse conviction, not strictly female, that change—whether it be the color of hair or the position of the waistline or in other societies, the slant of the head or the stretch of the neck—is ipso facto an improvement. The root of this anthropological leveler is discontent.

Ancient Egyptians, to be darker, used kohl on their own hair or wore black wigs. Sooty-haired Assyrians, to be lighter, sprinkled their locks with yellow dust. Yellow-haired Germans used a caustic soap to make their hair red. Redheaded Saxons preferred a delicate blue. And so on into the twentieth century when we read that an African tribe not long ago discovered that chlorophyll toothpaste makes a fetching green hair coloring and that in the sophisticated United States women spent over $18 million last year for home coloring kits alone.

OTHER stimuli include the it's-too-early-to-change-now feeling that hits the prematurely gray who would rather dye than submit to age but would rather die than admit it, and the it's-too-late-to-change-now whip that keeps women, once they've done the brummagem deed, enslaved to keeping it done. Marie Antoinette may have belonged to the first group. Legend has it that her hair went white overnight during her imprisonment. Certainly David's sketch of the queen as a haggard and white-haired prisoner contrasts sharply with other portraits and descriptions. A less romantic explanation is that in prison she lacked not only her powdered wigs but also her secret dyes.

In the it's-too-late group, Lucrezia Borgia is a perfect example. Affianced to Alfonso d'Este as a ravishing blonde —which she was, according to a painting by Pinturicchio, but which she wasn't in an anonymous portrait at times and according to scholars who point out that her father was exceptionally swarthy—Lucrezia managed to arrive at Ferrara, the home of the Estes, a little late but as golden-blond as the legend that preceded her. She had, however, been forced to stop

five times on the journey from Rome, for five elaborate shampoos.

Another coloring motive is the desire to look coddled and expensive. Women who fall into this group generally choose shades like platinum, silver or champagne blond, shades that not only sound expensive but are expensive and demand plenty of leisure, too. It can take five one-hour sessions for a brunette to become a silver blonde and a three-hour touch-up every ten days to stay one. To women who dread even a seasonal shearing, all this sitting time strongly suggests a streak of masochism as well—but evidently to the women who want to glitter when they walk and to the men who pay their bills, costly hair is as satisfying personally and impressive socially as a sustained tan in the wintertime.

AS a major motivation for feminine vanity, men are generally overrated. There probably are a few women who, if they haven't got a man to wash right out of their hair, will wash something into it in hopes; but they're rare. The beau who raves about Monroe if his girl is a brunette is merely nudging the inevitable.

Importers in imperial Rome, for example, did a thriving business selling lye soap and blond hair from Germany to dark patrician ladies despite the protests of the gentlemen. (Writers who contend that women's fashions, albeit in a contrary sort of way, reflect women's desire to attract and please men would probably insist that these ladies knew that harlots had once been required to wear blond wigs. Nonetheless. . . .) Ovid scolded his mistress: "Did I not tell you to leave off dyeing your hair? Now you have no hair left to dye." The poet Martial satirized the fad: "The golden hair that Galla wears/ Is hers: who would have thought it?/ She swears 'tis hers, and true she swears,/ For I know where she bought it."

That times may change but women never is made plain much later in Samuel Pepys' husbandly lament: "March 13, 1665—This day my wife begun to wear light coloured locks, quite white almost, which, though it makes her look very pretty, yet, not being natural, vexes me, that I will not have her wear them."

Fashion affects the colors women choose as well as the fad itself. Although blond hair has always been considered beautiful, as an ideal to be achieved by artifice it went into eclipse with Rome. The Middle Ages were the dark ages indeed, unless blondness was

**BLONDE?** — Lucrezia Borgia had to stop five times for touch-ups on the way to meet her groom.

God's good gift. But when Renaissance self-expression set in, dark Italian beauties again began practicing their own alchemy ("All the women of Venice * * * doe use to anoint their haire with oyle * * * then sit in some sunshining place," wrote an astonished English visitor).

In our own country, however, Puritans that we are, it was not until Lily Langtry and Lillian Russell were added to the blond tradition of Venus, Helen of Troy and company, that a few proper brunettes surreptitiously took to the bottle of peroxide. Jean Harlow broke down the rest of our reserve.

Red hair, however, was never envied until rather recently. The associations that cling to redheads—quick in anger, smoldering in love—associations considered alluring these neurotic days, made having red hair a torment in the past. In the Middle Ages it was apocryphally assigned to the sinners Jezebel, Judas and Mary Magdalene. Even for the brief period when Elizabeth I's red hair inspired sycophantic ladies to experiment with red dyes, red hair remained not quite respectable. In the era of the Victorians it was much too eye-catching for their otherwise gaudy taste.

IN the early Nineteen Hundreds, however, the impact of the auburn-haired diva, Adelina Patti, along with the advent of the green motoring veil, so flattering to redheads, gave red hair new glamour. Today, thanks to Technicolor, chemistry and motives afore-mentioned, red hair and red glints are not only respectable, they're big business. There's even a local dress shop, "The Red Headed Woman, Inc."

Since there are dolls now with hair that little girls can tint, the future for hair coloring seems established. It is hoped, however, that women of our day will heed the warning of history: blue and violet and pink were the latest thing in Paris just before the Revolution and when hair blueing first became popular here in the late Twenties— well, no need to go into *that.*

Drawings by Susan Perl.

October 23, 1955

217

# $71 BILLION FOOD CONSUMED IN U. S.

## Gain of 5% Made in a Year —Time-Saving Groceries in Enormous Demand

### By JAMES J. NAGLE

Americans chewed their way through about $71,000,000,000 worth of food last year, or 5 per cent more than in 1955.

The authority for that statement is Paul S. Willis, president of the Grocery Manufacturers of America, who said that of the total, $45,000,000,000 was sold by supermarkets and the corner grocery store. The balance was accounted for by institutions, restaurants, roadside stands, milk and bread routes.

The shift to convenience foods continued last year and was speeded by more and more women finding employment outside the home. For example, a selection of representative time-saving groceries showed a sales increase four times as large as their unprocessed counterparts, Mr. Willis said.

### Eating Habits Change

Changed eating habits also aided in sending dollar figures upward. According to the Department of Agriculture, Americans are now eating more of such relatively high-priced foods as beef, processed fruits and vegetables, poultry, eggs and dairy products. They are eating less potatoes and bread.

Sales of frozen foods also are rising. Last year, it is estimated frozen food sales topped $2,400,-000,000, a 10 per cent gain.

Total production of frozen foods last year was about 9,000,-000,000 pounds, according to the National Frozen Food Distributors Association. Of the total, about 1,500,000,000 pounds was in frozen vegetables. Frozen meats moved up to 325,000,000 pounds from 250,000,000 while prepared foods such as complete dinners and pies increased 20 per cent to 750,000,000 pounds.

Consumers continued to show their loyalty to the strongly advertised brands of groceries, Mr. Willis said. These accounted for 75 per cent of the sales of forty-one food commodities covered by the Nielsen Food Index.

Despite the growth of supermarkets, independent retail grocers working together in voluntary chains and retailer-cooperatives remained very much in the picture.

A study by the American Institute of Food Distribution revealed that sales of such grocers exceeded $15,500,000,000 in 1955 and were even higher last year.

January 2, 19

# REVOLVING CREDIT MAKES BIG GAINS

## But Increase in Installment Sales by Stores Raises Several Questions

## A RETURN TO BANKING?

## Rise May Force Merchants Back Into Role That They Have Been Dropping

### By ALBERT L. KRAUS

The charge plate may prove almost as handy as the marriage license for this year's June brides.

For, thanks to a growing kind of installment charge account, not only the ring and the furniture but the invitations, the trousseau, the wedding gown and even the cake can be bought now and paid for later in installments over periods of six to twelve months.

Known to the trade as revolving credit, this kind of credit is the most rapidly growing innovation in the consumer credit field. This growth raises these questions:

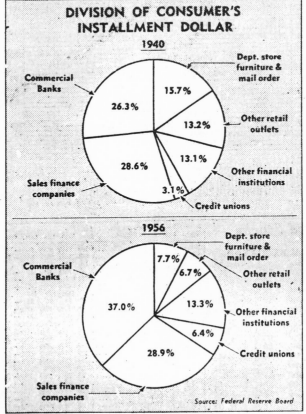

**DIVISION OF CONSUMER'S INSTALLMENT DOLLAR**

**1940**

Commercial Banks 26.3%
Sales finance companies 28.6%
Dept. store furniture & mail order 15.7%
Other retail outlets 13.2%
Other financial institutions 13.1%
Credit unions 3.1%

**1956**

Commercial Banks 37.0%
Sales finance companies 28.9%
Dept. store furniture & mail order 7.7%
Other retail outlets 6.7%
Other financial institutions 13.3%
Credit unions 6.4%

Source: Federal Reserve Board

The New York Times                    May 26, 1957

Role of merchants as bankers, measured by their share of consumer installment credit, has declined in recent years.

¶Will store operators be forced to return to the banking business, a field they have been withdrawing from steadily since World War II?

¶Will the sale and production of myriad items that comprise the bulk of department store sales—soft goods and smaller household wares—be stimulated? In the rapid rise of installment credit in recent years, these items have barely held their share of the consumer's dollar, while durable goods, particularly automobiles, have increased their share sharply.

¶Will customers be tempted to overbuy and will the delinquencies increase?

### Earlier Plans Failed to Grow

Revolving credit, offered today under a dozen variations, is an outgrowth of the thirty-sixty-ninety-day, coupon book and cash store installment plans of the depression of the Nineteen Thirties. These failed to grow because they were promoted for second-rate credit risks—persons who could not qualify for charge accounts.

Only since stores began several years ago to promote revolving credit to regular charge-account customers has this kind of account mushroomed. At first, customers were limited to fixed dollar ceilings, with a fixed number of months to pay.

Today, under the plan gaining general acceptance, any credit-worthy customer can open a charge account. She can pay in thirty days and avoid a service charge. Or she can pay over six, eight, ten or twelve months as she chooses—at a fixed monthly rate of interest, usually 1 or 1½ per cent.

218

Prompt payers benefit from the fact that the cost of carrying delinquent accounts is charged directly to the late-paying customer and not added to the merchandise mark-up.

Unlike traditional installment sales contracts, the revolving credit account is not limited to single big ticket items such as refrigerators and television sets. Instead, a customer can buy anything a store has to offer, adding to her purchases from month to month. Payments are figured by dividing the balance outstanding each month by the number of months in which she chooses to pay and adding interest.

Most stores, however, continue to offer traditional installment credit—with longer terms—on big ticket items.

Unlike most other kinds of consumer installment credit, the security of a revolving charge lies not in the collateral—for none is required—but in the credit worthiness of the customer, her good name and the store's willingness to accept her as a risk.

The growth of revolving credit accounts raises the possibility that store operators may be forced back into the banking business. Before World War II, department stores, mail order houses, furniture stores and other retail outlets held about 29 cents of every dollar of consumer installment debt outstanding. At the end of last year they held 14.4 cents.

However, store owners don't like to think of themselves as bankers. "We're merchandise men, not money men," one commented last week.

From the store owner's point of view, the great value of revolving credit is the possibility of moving more merchandise. It can be, according to one statement, the catalyst that turns consumer impulses into sales while the impulses are still alive.

At the same time, the question has been raised whether liberal promotion of installment and revolving credit plans hasn't converted some stores from sellers of goods to sellers of money.

Kenneth P. Mages, a New York accountant, told a National Retail Dry Goods Association credit conference recently that many stores offering revolving credit had a greater portion of current assets tied up in accounts receivable than in inventory. A store doing $83,000 a month in revolving credit sales on a six months' plan, for instance, always has $500,000 tied up in receivables.

### Depends on Banks

Under such conditions, he observed, store operators must pay as much attention to the way they buy money as to the way they buy merchandise. He urged that they explore the possibility of selling receivables to banks.

Whether the stores are forced back into the banking business depends largely on how the banks take to the unsecured receivables. Over the years retailers have prided themselves on the fact that their experience with unsecured charge accounts has been better than the experience of other credit originators whose paper has been backed by collateral.

But they concede that the newness of the revolving credit plans makes it difficult to say whether this favorable experience will continue.

A. L. Trotta, manager of the N. R. D. G. A.'s credit management division, says that there are indications that the most liberal kinds of revolving credit accounts may be contributing to a substantial increase in receivables. Also, he says, customers may misunderstand the charts printed in their monthly statements and interpret them as authorization to charge up to the maximum amount shown, resulting in overbuying.

Revolving credit, he notes, has broadened the base of potential credit customers, many of whom have never before had charge accounts. This has increased credit information costs, bad debt losses, collection costs and credit overhead.

All these things are items the banks probably would want to weigh carefully before entering full scale into the purchase of revolving credit paper.

What effect the growth of revolving credit may have on the sale of department store items, particularly soft goods, is equally unpredictable.

The Federal Reserve Board in a recent study of consumer installment credit concluded that the growth in the share of the consumer's dollar spent on automobiles since World War II was not caused by installment credit—but probably could not have occurred without it.

In contrast, the use of credit to finance other durable goods purchases increased in the same years but the share of the consumer dollar spent on such items did not.

Similarly, the growth of revolving credit in itself probably cannot stimulate soft goods sales. But it provides a fertile ground for strong sales efforts.

May 26, 1957

# Do Installments Peril the Economy?

**A Congressional specialist on credit discusses the nation's huge time payment debt and its possible effects on the recession.**

### By JOSEPH C. O'MAHONEY

WASHINGTON.

NOW that the recession is officially here, we may finally get an answer to the troublesome question of whether installment credit has gotten too high. It is no secret that Americans' installment debt, or the amount of money people still owe for things they have bought on time, has risen spectacularly in recent years—from about $9 billion in 1948 to a peak of more than $34 billion last December.

I hope that the answer to this question is not a dramatically catastrophic one; I hope that repossessions and failures to meet time payments won't snowball the economic downturn by dumping used consumer goods onto a declining market. Time will tell, but

JOSEPH C. O'MAHONEY, Senator (D.), from Wyoming, was the first chairman of the Joint Senate-House Economic Committee and is at present one of its members.

clearly that possibility is with us, for consumer credit can curl our economic hair.

To combat the recession, Washington advisers call for a restoration of confidence. It must be remembered that confidence and credit are not synonymous. A credit system which is extended to the breaking point, by no down payments and eons in which to pay, will destroy confidence and ruin sound government.

A clue to the danger we face lies in the fact that installment spending for "consumer durables"—the big things like cars, refrigerators, TV sets —began dropping in January and may well be contributing to the recession. It is my personal hunch that this is the proof that people had overextended themselves on installment purchases and have had to retrench; it also serves to reinforce my feeling that

now is an important time to take a keen look at the whole installment segment of the economy and to act to prevent future excesses.

The fact that many anti-recession moves are being aimed at the consumer to stimulate buying does not affect this situation. Certainly in an economy that is already sick, it does not help to stimulate it with phony buying—purchases without any cash payment by people whose income and jobs are in jeopardy. Efforts to stimulate sound installment purchases, using, for example, extra income from an excise tax cut as a down payment, are all to the good, of course, but such buying would in no way be dampened by sound consumer credit regulation anyway.

In recent years, several of my Sena-

219

torial colleagues, Republicans as well as Democrats, have shared apprehension over the installment credit situation. We have watched the growth of this form of money lending, and we know that it alone was largely untouched by the anti-inflation credit restraints exerted by the Federal Reserve Board until very recently on the other major sectors of the money market. We also know that installment credit, based on steady employment and payrolls rather than tangible collateral, may prove to be built on quicksand in a declining economy.

Now I, for one, feel strongly that a healthy consumer credit market is essential to our mass-production economy and the well-being of our people, and that it is a national responsibility to see that it is soundly based. Therefore, before I discuss the dangers in the present situation and what ought to be done to correct things, let me make plain just how important installment credit is as a force for growth in the economy.

WHEN the average person steps into his gleaming new car to drive into the country the chances are he will be traveling in a vehicle he calls his own but which, in fact, belongs to the seller. As he whirls along the highways, he views clusters of new homes from which television aerials spring like trees in a grove; to most of them a debt tag is attached. And if this average driver were to step into any of these houses, he would find all kinds of luxurious items—dishwashers, clothes dryers, furniture, even the jewelry in madam's bureau—in use and unpaid for, bought "on time."

Homes equipped with inventions for taking the drudgery out of housework, speedy automobiles, the gadgets of modern living, even world tours on a pay-later basis—all these, and more, sold on credit, have helped raise to record proportions the total output of the American economy.

Nothing illustrates this better than the automobile industry. The 4,000 automobiles manufactured in this country in 1899 were sold only to the very rich. When they were brought within the reach of the common man, first by Henry Ford and his concept of mass production, and then by installment selling, the total output was fantastically multiplied.

AS car sales increased, the whole national economy benefited. New markets were made not only for steel and copper and zinc, but for glass, for fabrics, for rubber and a vast multitude of commodities without which the automobile could not be made. New jobs were created not only for those operating the machine tools on the production line but also for those who built the tools and supplied the raw materials which go into every car.

Clearly, the rise of the installment credit technique for increasing retail sales has been as important as the general use of commercial credit in the healthy expansion of our fundamental production and distribution capacity.

After all, business cannot be conducted on a cash basis.

Generally, however, the credit which makes economic growth possible is the confidence of society that those who borrow money *have* the assets to repay the loan. In most lending operations, the assets of the borrower—blue chip

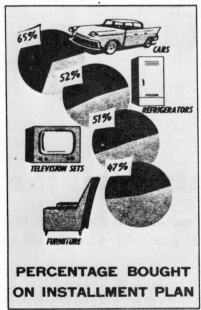

**PERCENTAGE BOUGHT ON INSTALLMENT PLAN**

Almost two-thirds of all motor cars and about half of all TV sets, refrigerators and pieces of furniture are bought on installment plans.

securities, real property, the inventory or stock of a corporation, and the like—are put up as collateral for the loan. They are the guarantee to the lender that, come what may, he can get most of his money back out of the possessions already owned by the borrower. This commitment also tends to make the borrower more cautious.

IN this fundamental respect installment credit is different. Here the confidence of the lender rests upon the belief that the borrower *will have* the assets to pay up in the future, when the time comes to pay the installments. The only collateral posted by the buyer is the article he is purchasing and this is not really his, since in most cases, he buys on a "conditional sale" and title does not pass to him until his final installment payment is made.

In substance, then, credit for a "time" purchase is granted by the lender in the faith that the buyer's income will remain steady enough to meet regular payments for twelve, twenty-four or even thirty-six months; his security is the article sold—the television set or automobile or washing machine—which drops enormously in value the minute it leaves the retail store. No lender of commercial credit—say, mortgage money—accepts so ephemeral a guarantee for his largesse.

For this very reason, the risk taken by the installment credit lender is greater than in most other business loan operations. His interest charges, naturally, are likely to be greater, too.

And this leads me to stress the noteworthy fact that installment credit was unrestricted by the "tight money" policy pursued by the Federal Reserve Board for more than two years as a weapon to discourage inflation. The instrument for tight money policy is the power of the Federal Reserve Board to raise or lower basic interest rates, that is, to set a minimum price on the cost of borrowing money. Many commercial borrowers could and often have deferred new funding operations when the high cost of money made the transaction too expensive to be profitable.

THE installment buyer does not measure things that way. Here we have an individual driven by the desire (self-generated or inspired by zealous salesmen) for some new possession. He pays little or no attention to the rate of interest he is paying or whether it might be absurdly high in relation to the cost of the article or his need for that article. His sole concern is whether the monthly payments seem to fit within his income, and, of course, he presumes his income will not shrink in the coming months.

This lack of buyer-resistance to high interest rates at the consumer-goods level has in effect negated the tight money policy in this sector of the economy; installment credit has remained "easy money." By the same token, installment credit is untouched now that the tight money policy has been dropped. Psychologically, the relaxed monetary atmosphere may tempt installment sellers to offer even "easier" terms—smaller down payments and longer time periods—but this probably will not add appreciably to the already swollen installment credit lists.

Consumer credit is now a far larger sum than all the cash in circulation. It is, in my view, a sum so enormously important in the nation's economy that the question of its soundness (i. e., the probability that all the huge debt will be repaid in full) becomes a national issue.

Has the consuming public over-extended itself?

This is a frightening question. Let us look for a minute at the reasons why it arises especially in the consumer credit field.

(1) By and large, the individual consumer determines for himself how much debt he can carry. Most installment sales retailers and their finance companies make no real effort to find out whether the buyer about to sign an installment contract might already have a dangerous percentage of his pay check committed to other credit purchases. Even if they find a big commitment, the chances are they will go ahead with the new conditional sale anyway.

(2) In many instances, the financing, because of the risk, is at usurious interest rates. The usury laws apply to loans of money. Since installment credit results from the sale of goods, legal ceilings on interest rates are lacking and the uninstructed purchaser pays rates that are in higher brackets than he often realizes.

As an example of this, let me cite a recent credit offer made by a very reputable retail store. A housewife who wishes to make a major purchase may agree with the store's credit people that she can afford monthly payments of, say, $20. The store then grants her

The sixty-two million American workers carry an average installment load of $537.

credit to purchase ten times that amount of goods, or $200 worth. Each month, she pays her $20 plus a "service charges" of 1½ per cent on the remaining balance; but she is also entitled to maintain her debt to the store at $200 and make $20 worth of new purchases each month to be paid for later. If she does this, she continues paying 1½ per cent a month on the balance—for an annual interest rate of 18 per cent.

(3) The rise of the credit finance company, although a worthy institution in many ways, presents another difficulty. Today, a great deal of in-

stallment credit money is loaned, not by the seller of the article, but by a separate company in business solely to lend money. In effect, these credit companies pay the retailer for the article you purchase; you pay the credit company. Under this system, the company, seeking to make a profit on its operations, charges a very high interest rate.

RECENTLY, a Federal Reserve Board study of consumer installment credit found that automobile dealers pass on to finance companies more than 95 per cent of the debt on the cars they sell, and that retailers in other fields pass on nearly half of their customers' debts.

(4) More important than the high interest rate is the fact that the system relieves the retailer of any responsibility for the soundness of his sale. And this, in turn, is an open invitation for the irresponsible, fast-talking, fly-by-night dealer.

Senator A. S. (Mike) Monroney, chairman of a subcommittee of the Senate Interstate and Foreign Commerce Committee on automobile marketing practices, declared during hearings last year that "it was freely admitted that many destructive sales tactics were practiced by the 'fringe' of the industry, and that while only a small percentage of the trade engaged in 'gyp' methods, 'phony' advertising, 'packed' prices and misleading offers, these things had a demoralizing effect on the automobile industry as a whole." Even the ethical majority is being badly squeezed because dealers must pay cash for their stock and sell on credit, with diminishing profit margins.

THE automobile industry is not alone in offering what can only be described as wildly unsound credit terms, but it presents some striking examples:

" '58 Model
No fixed down payment
Your old car is all you need to offer"

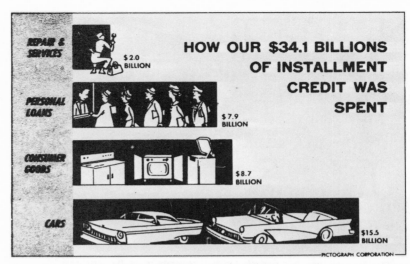

HOW OUR $34.1 BILLIONS OF INSTALLMENT CREDIT WAS SPENT

REPAIR & SERVICES — $2.0 BILLION
PERSONAL LOANS — $7.9 BILLION
CONSUMER GOODS — $8.7 BILLION
CARS — $15.5 BILLION

PICTOGRAPH CORPORATION

Automobile buying, through bank financing or other methods, accounts for 45 per cent of the total debt, with consumer goods and loans making up nearly all the rest.

HOW INSTALLMENT DEBT VARIES WITH FAMILY INCOME

| INCOME PER YEAR | FAMILIES WITH INSTALLMENT DEBT | NO INSTALLMENT DEBT |
|---|---|---|
| UNDER $1,000 | 16% | 84% |
| $1,000-2,000 | 30% | 70% |
| $2,000-3,000 | 40% | 60% |
| $3,000-4,000 | 50% | 50% |
| $4,000-7,500 | 61% | 39% |
| $7,500-10,000 | 55% | 45% |
| OVER $10,000 | 35% | 65% |

The proportion of families owing installments rises from 16 per cent of those in the lowest group to 61 per cent of those in the $4,000-$7,500 group, then declines.

"Drive home the No. 1 Deal
* * * even if you still owe on
your present car!"

Even in 1955, according to the Federal Reserve, "30 per cent of those credit buyers of new cars who had also bought the traded-in car on credit had debt still outstanding on the car they traded in." It is doubtless true that many individuals are capable of taking on new debts before retiring old ones, but when this becomes a practice it would certainly seem to be a warning of difficulties around the corner.

(5) The final element I want to stress is that the installment purchaser represents a segment of society at the bottom of the income scale. He is among those most likely to be laid off when jobs get scarce, and least likely to have any financial reserves. Into

SHOPPERS—Americans who buy products by time payments raised the installment debt from $9 billion in 1948 to a peak of more than $34 billion at the end of 1957.

this group fall the young people from 18 to 24 who are caught up in the desire to possess the conveniences and luxuries of the present era—and have no first-hand knowledge or recollection of the Great Depression after 1929.

So, in sum, this is our situation: by the latest figures available, there is a little more than $33 billion in credit outstanding, backed largely by faith in steady employment at a time when unemployment is rising, assumed largely by people who never knew the Great Depression, unregulated by the Federal Government because its users pay no attention to interest rates, and uncontrolled by normal market caution because the sellers (or lenders) take no responsibility for the soundness of the loans.

Up to now, there seems to have been little concern, either in the Government or private business, for the dangers inherent in all this. For example, the United States Chamber of Commerce reported recently to the Federal Reserve Board that of approximately 4,000 business men who replied to a questionnaire, about 50 per cent thought consumer credit might be "too high" for safety, and yet 70 per cent opposed any Federal regulations because "ours is a time of peace."

The Federal Reserve Board itself, having recently completed an exhaustive study of the consumer credit situation at the request of the President, concluded that regulation or control was not needed, even though its chairman, William McC. Martin, previously had agreed that "stand-by control powers" might be advisable. The board

seems to have been persuaded by such hoary arguments as: "Self-regulation is a sufficient protection against abuse," "The people should have the right to spend their own money as they please," and, finally, "The law of supply and demand will take care of any excesses."

In other words, this kind of problem isn't the Government's business except in time of war. Why shouldn't it be, if maintenance of a stable economy is—and it is—the Government's business?

WHAT should the Government do, particularly now that it is realized that Soviet Russia is waging economic war against us? What kind of control or regulation should we have? The answer is simple—re-establishment of the legal authority behind the old World War II "Regulation W." This authority would enable the Federal Government to require a *minimum* down payment on any installment purchase, based on a percentage of the selling price, and a *maximum* length of time in which the debt must be paid off. The fact that the monthly payments would be higher —over a shorter period—would make the buyer more keenly aware of the debt he was assuming. Also, the requirement of some down payment would be an effective brake on many an irresponsible consumer (and on the salesman tempting him) because it would force him to have some hard cash on hand.

These devices would quickly put installment credit on a basis that the nation could know was sound. They might, at least initially, curtail install-

ment purchasing. But those who argue that, in a declining economy, nothing should be done that might cut down consumer buying, I would say simply this: "Regulation W" restraints need not lead to a measurable reduction in consumer purchasing if the installment credit market is already soundly based. If, as I suspect, the base is weak, it is far better for the national economy to cut back in an orderly fashion to a healthy market than to go on to a catastrophic collapse of a phony market.

Obviously, few factors are more important to the economic stability of the country than the continued ability of the installment debtor to meet his debt. In the past few months there have been distressing signs that installment credit collections are becoming more difficult. We are told that banks are beginning to find a higher ratio of delinquency among debtors.

These are symptoms of trouble, of termites eating away at the basic support of our economic structure. It is the clear job of Congress to study the situation and pass legislation that will give the Government the power it needs to step in.

At this stage, I am personally uncommitted on the question of whether the Government's power to issue credit regulations should be mandatory or permissive; whether the power should be granted to the Federal Reserve or to some other agency. This can be determined after hearing the experts and assessing the attitudes of those who would administer the controls. I am also not prepared to state just what the terms should be, whether one-fifth to one-third down and fifteen months to pay, as under the final stage of "Regulation W," or some other combination.

In any case, I can only hope that the present recession does not cause the market supported by installment credit to collapse before Congress can enact a protective law.

IN candor, I do not think such a catastrophe is impending unless we refuse to act. Delay can be disastrous. I believe even the threat of it should force immediate action to save the great American consuming public from the blandishments of irresponsible supersalesmen and from the excesses of its desires for the luxuries of modern living. On the basis of past experience, I am sure that Congressional interest in this vital matter will be nonpartisan.

These are not times of peace and prosperity. They are times of scientific, military and economic conflict on a level mankind has never before experienced. The "cold war" in which we are engaged, especially with a domestic recession in progress, can be more dangerous than any of the brush wars some of our military men talk about. The survival of the system of private ownership is the issue of our time; we cannot afford to risk its stability.

# Resurvey of 'Hidden Persuaders'

**A critic of huckster methods shifts his concern to consumers; it is time, he says, to re-examine our materialistic set of values.**

*Just a year ago, a book called "The Hidden Persuaders" appeared. It attracted immediate attention, reached The New York Times best seller list on June 2 and has been there in all but two subsequent weeks. This is something of a phenomenon. In the following article, the author of "The Hidden Persuaders" restates his argument, reviews the controversy he stirred up and adds a postscript to his thesis.*

### By VANCE PACKARD

"THE HIDDEN PERSUADERS" was a protest against the growing interest professional persuaders are taking in techniques which promise to manipulate the public. Increasingly, they are eschewing rational appeals to us in favor of appeals carefully baited to trigger desired responses at the subconscious level. To this er , they are drawing upon the insights of social scientists and psychiatrists who, in a great many cases, have cooperated with the persuaders in pinpointing subconscious motives which can be tapped. Many of these efforts at motive-tapping are being made beneath the level of our awareness.

The greatest use of depth techniques is being made in the field of commerce, to influence our consuming habits. Although this so-called scientific approach to the consumer at his emotional level is still in the groping stage, it already has been used in campaigns where, in total, billions of dollars worth of goods have been involved. Many of the nation's largest marketers of consumer goods have been involved in these attempts.

On a more modest scale (because of more limited budgets) publicists, fund-raisers and political campaign managers have been exploring possible ways—throug'. a dredging of our motives—to engineer our consent to their projects or to engineer our enthusiasm for their candidates. We see political candidates being groomed as father images, and political managers seeking to condition the public with techniques inspired by Pavlov's famous experiments in conditioning dogs to respond to given stimuli.

IN the field of marketing the following techniques for subconscious selling are, I wrote, most commonly used:

(1) Create an image for a product that triggers a favorable response with the consumer because it has an "affinity" for an important aspect of his own personality.

(2) Present a product in such a way that it offers to satisfy a hidden need of the consumer, such as need for security or power.

(3) Offer the consumer relief from his feelings of guilt or anxiety concerning a product. The problem of calming these hidden reservations is said to be an important consideration in marketing billions of dollars worth of self-indulgence and labor-savings products today.

(4) Present a product in such a way that it seems especially appropriate for the consumer's particular social class, sex or ethnic group.

(5) Offer the consumer status enhancement if he buys the product (i.e. the long car, the costliest perfume, the suburban home.)

(6) Create dissatisfaction in the consumer's mind with a product he already owns (which may still be completely satisfactory from a functioning standpoint) so that he will feel a "need" to buy a new model.

(7) Finally, create a mood on the part of the public that encourages people to give vent to their whims and mollify their ids. Techniques for promoting impulse buying in supermarkets are being perfected. Marketers are being admonished to reassure consumers that the hedonistic approach to life is the moral one and that frugality and personal austerity are outdated hangovers of Puritanism.

These techniques are subject to scrutiny first of all on the ground of validity. There has been a great deal of overacceptance on the part of marketing enthusiasts of "motivation research." The clients often fail to examine the research tools being used on their behalf or the caliber of the staffs of the professional firms doing the research. Furthermore they often have failed to subject the findings of motivational analysis to conventional testing for confirmation.

MORE important, the techniques are subject to scrutiny on the ground of morality. Some of the techniques, certainly, have constructive or relatively harmless application. Many, however, do raise ethical questions of a most disturbing nature.

I referred to those that invade the privacy of our minds by playing upon our frailties, those that deliberately encourage irrational behavior, and those that seek to reshape our national character in the direction of self-indulgent materialism. Both the professional persuaders (advertising men, publicists, etc.) and the cooperating

scientists need, I felt, to develop codes of ethics which would cover the kinds of projects that can be condoned and those that cannot be condoned.

That, in gist, is what I conceived my book to be about.

The response to "The Hidden Persuaders" apparently reflects an increasing uneasiness on the part of the public concerning the growing role and influence of these professional persuaders in American life.

An analysis of criticisms of the book by advertising and marketing people reveals these as their major objections:

(1) The book was "malicious." (I wasn't aware of any malice but won't argue the point.)

(2) The book contained nothing new to advertising men. One critic pointed to such pre-Madison Avenue "manipulators" as Tom Paine, Harriet Beecher Stowe, Voltaire and Demosthenes. Another stated: "This psychology stuff is nothing new." (The "newness" of what is going on is the massive recruitment of social scientists to guide the manipulators.)

(3) I had been oversold on the effectiveness and potency of motivational research. A market researcher charged that I had "tumbled unsuspectingly" into the more "lurid" wing of market research and said I had recited with too much trust the "tricks, devices and formulas" of the motivational analysts.

MY main defense is that the efficacy of the techniques described was not, frankly, my principal concern. Techniques can be perfected, and these, I repeatedly stressed, were in their infancy. My concern was with the fact that these techniques, whatever their present validity, were *even being attempted* on the public. The public, I felt, should be put on notice. I still feel so and, were I writing the book today, would go further.

Since the book appeared the economic climate in America has changed in some unsettling ways. Several months ago we began experiencing an economic recession despite the best efforts of the industrial persuaders, hidden or other-

223

**OUTLET FOR OUTPUT**—"We need constructive outlets for our productivity if we are to escape consuming for consumption's sake—outlets such as educational facilities and elimination of urban blight." Above, a new Connecticut school; below, a New York City housing project

wise, to move our goods as fast as our economy could produce them. Warehouses became uncomfortably crowded with the products of our excess capacity. The long, fat, chrome-crusted automobile, our prime status symbol, became the victim of rather widespread disenchantment.

APPROXIMATELY simultaneously Russian satellites began streaking overhead and inspired a great many Americans to begin re-examining the materialistic values by which our society has increasingly been living.

In the field of marketing, meanwhile, the trend toward subconscious selling reached something of a nadir with the unveiling, as I had predicted, of so-called subliminal projection. That is the technique designed to flash messages past our conscious guard.

These developments, plus my own further reflections, have caused me to shift my main area of concern from the manipulators to the climate that has produced them. Today I see their efforts as symptoms of the strain our system is undergoing. Our system itself, which has been impelling us more and more to conform to a materialistic set of values, needs examining, I now see, along with the symptoms.

Our leaders, from the President down, are admonishing us to "buy" more. What we buy is not as important, seemingly, as the mere fact that

we buy. A New York newspaper recently headlined the fact that a "rise in thrift" was "disturbing" the Administration. In one United States city a forty-five-voice choir has been admonishing the public over the airways, seventy times a day, with a jingle which ends: "Buy, buy something that you need today."

The really critical problem, as I now perceive it, is this: We as a nation face a set of conditions unique in the history of mankind. In the past man has always had to learn to live with his wants. His world was geared to scarcity. Today the challenge is for man to develop and expand his wants. He is being urged and admonished, here in America, to become more and more self-indulgent in order that he may live comfortably with the ever-greater abundance provided by the fantastic, and constantly soaring, productivity of our automated factories and mechanized farms. We all face not merely the opportunity but the necessity of learning to live like sultans or our system, as presently geared, will languish.

OUR gross national product has soared more than 400 per cent since 1940. It shot past $400,000,000,000 in 1956 and some economists have predicted it may reach $600,000,000,000 by the mid-Sixties if our economy remains reasonably healthy.

In order to consume the

greatly stepped up output indicated by such a growth our population must, according to the estimate of one leading advertising executive, increase its consumption by an amount "nearly equal to the entire growth of the country in the 200 years from colonial days up to 1940." Consequently, he warned, the American people must be persuaded to expand much further their wants and needs, and quickly.

The relentless, if wondrous, growth of productivity in America is forcing a change in the major preoccupation of the men in America's executive suites, from producing the goods to selling them. The problem of selling all the goods our rapidly expanding economy can turn out when working near its ever-expanding capacity is each year becoming more challenging. It is producing signs not only of indigestion on the part of the public but unhealthy signs of straining on the part of the professional persuaders charged with moving the goods.

I SHOULD stress that the overwhelming majority of advertisements we see today are still simply informative, and often charmingly so. Nevertheless, there has been in the past five years a growing fascination in marketing circles with strategies for subconscious selling through national mass media such as television. The straining shows itself in the willingness to adopt strategies which would play upon hidden weaknesses

or encourage people to behave in non-rational ways.

Perhaps the most-frightening manifestation of this straining is the widespread adoption of marketing strategies based on the creation of "psychological obsolescence" or "planned obsolescence" of adequately functioning products we already own (cars, refrigerators, home furnishings, etc.).

A FEW weeks ago The Associated Press carried an article citing a number of industries in which this marketing strategy has been attempted and stated: "Advocates of planned obsolescence say it is basic to the modern American economy." It quoted others who disagreed. Financial columnist Sylvia F. Porter cites a leading industrial designer as charging: "One of the causes of the recession is the refusal of our people to be seduced any longer by planned obsolescence. * * * Legitimate improvements yes, but this Roman orgy of obsolescence merchandising must come to an end. * * *" Could it be that the public wants improved function more than "style"?

All this straining to keep the sales charts rising is responsible, too, for proposals in marketing circles that Americans should be constantly encouraged to modify their moral reservations toward a hedonistic (or "live it up") attitude toward life.

AMERICA has indeed become a nation on a tiger. We are being urged to consume simply to meet the needs of the productive process. That process, as theologian Reinhold Niebuhr has pointed out, threatens to enslave our culture, and force us toward an ever more luxurious style of living. What does our growing absorption with the consumption of goods — and our constant enticement at every turn by sales messages —do to the quality of life?

This necessity of learning to live with a prodigious economic plant presents us with a problem of enormous complexity.

I suspect it will increasingly absorb our attention in coming decades. Certainly any acceptable solution must assure reasonably full employment of our people. And we certainly need a stable economy. But the non-material well-being of the consumer-citizen deserves thoughtful consideration, too.

Americans, certainly, should all pitch in and help consume their way out of this recession, as governmental and industrial leaders are urging. They are offering no other alternatives. But the leaders should be urged to start some long-range thinking on this problem.

Our nation, perhaps, will need to find constructive outlets for our productivity if we are to escape the fate of consuming for consumption's sake. We may, for example, find it advisable to attempt finally to expand in a dramatic way our badly neglected and overcrowded health and educational facilities, and to eliminate our hundreds of square miles of urban blight.

Meanwhile, we should look to the non-material well-being of our people. Perhaps young Americans can be encouraged in our schools and colleges to gain a better perspective on possessions in relation to other life satisfactions. Perhaps they can be encouraged, through education, to develop

coherent philosophies of life, philosophies which do not begin and end with self-indulgence.

FINALLY, if marketers persist in devising strategies to invade the privacy of our minds, we should begin training our younger people to protect their privacy. An awareness of the techniques being attempted is itself a defense.

To sum up, the monumental problem we seem to face is that of working out a spiritually tolerable relationship between our fabulous, dynamic economy and our free people.

May 11, 1958

# Advertising: Mirror or Molder of Values?

**By PETER BART**

Does advertising subvert the nation's values or merely reflect them?

Some critics have argued that the relentless drum-beat of advertising encourages materialism and induces people to buy things they do not really need.

An article in the October issue of The Journal of Marketing, however, takes the opposite view. It is the nation's value system that shapes advertising rather than the other way around, the article argues.

"Whether we like it or not we are a materialistic people," the article states. "And a steadily rising standard of living is one of our most cherished goals. The truth of the matter is that the critics of advertising are not really criticizing advertising; they are criticizing the American value system itself."

The article was written by Alan Zakon, lecturer in marketing at the University of California, Los Angeles, and Thomas Petit, professor of economics and director of the Breech School of Business Administra-

tion, Drury College, Springfield, Mo. The Journal of Marketing is published by the American Marketing Association.

The authors emphasize that an unfortunate misunderstanding has arisen concerning "the causal relationship between advertising and the value system." Critics have observed the rising materialism of our society and the growing volume of advertising and have concluded that the latter causes the former.

But this is not the case, according to Messrs. Zakon and Petit. "Sociologically speaking

it would be impossible for advertising to be in conflict with the value system," they write. "It is the value system which determines the nature and significance of social institutions like advertising, not the other way around."

Advertising, they emphasize, provides a vivid means of expression for the materialistic, "consumption-oriented" value system that has taken root in this country. There may be a lot wrong with this sytem, but advertising should not take the rap for it, the two professors conclude.

October 19, 1962

## 200,000,000th Auto Is Produced by Detroit

DETROIT, Dec. 11 (UPI) —The car, once a costly luxury but now a necessity in the American way of life, reached a milestone today when the United States Auto industry built its 200,000,000th motor vehicle.

The event passed quietly. There was no fanfare or ceremony as the record car pulled from an assembly line. No one knew where it was built.

The Automobile Manufacturers Association said the exact hour and place of the 200,000,000th vehicle could not be determined since more than 35,000 cars and trucks were scheduled to be produced today in 25 plants around the country.

Eight million vehicles of the record total were built this year as the industry recorded its best year since 1955. The last 25,000,000 were built in three and one half years—from June, 1959.

December 12, 1962

---

# Personal Finance: Yule Season Again

### By RICHARD RUTTER

More than 15 million Americans are playing Santa Claus to themselves this year well before Christmas.

These are the members of the ubiquitous Christmas Clubs now in effect at more than 10,000 banks and savings institutions. Throughout this month the members are receiving a festive $1.85 billion in checks from their clubs.

It is, of course, money they have put in painstakingly week by week during the last year—and, so they are actually paying themselves back. It's hardly a gift, but it is a handy source of year-end funds to purchase gifts and pay other nonholiday expenses.

The concept of the Christmas Club originated in 1910. A year later less than 100 small and medium-sized banks were offering the service—for that is basically what they consider it—and the average individual's yearly accumulation was $18.50 a year. The growth in membership since then is obvious, although the average account still is probably $100 or less.

The plan is simple. Anyone who joins a Christmas Club signs an agreement to make a regular weekly deposit for 50 weeks. The amount is up to the saver—it can be 50 cents, $1, $2, $3, $5, $10, and, in some cases, as much as $20.

Each year's club comes to an end in November when the savings checks are mailed out. There is, of course, nothing to prevent a person from redepositing a part or all of his savings into next year's club and the accumulation process then begins all over again.

As a rule, the money put into a club account can be withdrawn at any time. Some commercial banks exact a penalty, however, for early withdrawal before the full 50-week period of payments has been completed.

Partial withdrawals before the expiration of the 50 weeks generally are not allowed. It is either leave it all in or take it all out.

Often employes in a company join a Christmas Club together. One member is delegated to take the weekly payments and coupon books and make the deposits for the group. Naturally, the savings institutions encourage this.

Christmas Club, a corporation, is the organization that sponsors most club plans and supplies coupon books and promotional material to participating institutions.

•

It made a recent survey to determine just why people join a club. The corporation found that 46 per cent joined because "it gives me money for Christmas gifts just when I need it most." About the same percentage emphasized the fact that they would not have saved the money otherwise.

Other reasons that were given were: the ease of putting aside a small sum each week; a convenient method of saving for taxes and insurance, and the freedom from worry about unpaid bills after holiday spending ends.

A breakdown of where this year's Christmas Club money will go shows: 38 per cent, or $703 million, will be used for Christmas purchases; 31 per cent, or $573.5 million, will go into savings or investment of a one kind or another; 13 per cent, or $240.5 million, has been earmarked to pay local and Federal taxes; 6 per cent, or $111 million, will go toward cleaning up yearend bills, and 12 per cent, or $222 million, is for miscellaneous expenditures.

•

On the surface, it would appear that there could be little to criticize about Christmas Clubs. Actually, there has been some criticism. The banks and other institutions pay no interest whatsoever on the funds that pile up in the clubs each year. Meanwhile, banks can, presumably, use this money, often a sizable amount, as they see fit —to make loans at interest or for profitable investments.

This point was underscored officially last year when Louis J. Lefkowitz, Attorney General of New York State, proposed a law that would require the payment of at least nominal interest on club accounts.

The proposal was discussed with bank representatives, who expressed strong opposition, and nothing has been heard of it since.

The banks for their part, at least those who want to discuss the matter, insist that it costs them to offer the club accounts as a service.

One large New York Savings bank made a cost-accounting survey two years ago. It showed that in the 16,037 club accounts it was carrying, the average paid-up deposit at the end of 50 weeks was $66.75.

"On this basis," an official said, "we operate the club at a loss. Any use we could make of the accumulated funds would not cover the cost of handling the thousands of individual transactions each week, keeping records, mailing checks, supplying promotional material and so forth."

•

This bank and others regard the club service as sort of a "loss-leader." It creates extra traffic to the bank and often results in many club members opening savings accounts and taking advantage of other services.

At least one major savings bank, which welcomes Christmas Club members and also pays 1 per cent interest on completed accounts, specializes in signing up numerous employes of a company and then persuading them to switch—en masse—over to payroll-savings plans. The end result is a sizable flow of steady new business for the bank.

And the fact remains that a Christmas Club, in effect, is a type of "forced savings" for the small or medium-bracket wage - earner who may not have the discipline to put aside a like sum every week on a fixed schedule.

Christmas Club, the corporation, reports that 28.8 per cent of club members are 24 years old, or younger (accounts can be opened in the name of minors). Fully half of all participants are less than 35.

It is a savings means, apparently, that has a strong appeal to the younger portion of the population. And that those who sign up are not exactly affluent is attested to because almost two-thirds of all members pay $2 or less a week into their accounts.

November 11, 1965

# TV TRANSFORMING U.S. SOCIAL SCENE; CHALLENGES FILMS

### Its Impact on Leisure, Politics, Reading, Culture Unparalleled Since Advent of the Auto

### MOVIE TRADE OFF 20-40%

### But 'Good' Pictures Still Draw Crowds—Inflation a Factor —Hollywood Weighs Plans

#### By JACK GOULD

Television, in commercial use for only a little more than five years, is influencing the social and economic habits of the nation to a degree unparalleled since the advent of the automobile.

The now familiar dipole aerial perched on the rooftop symbolizes a fundamental change in national behavior: The home has become a new center of interest for the most gregarious people on earth.

Reports by correspondents of THE NEW YORK TIMES in more than 100 cities, towns and villages over the country show that the impact of pictures sent into the living room is being felt in almost every phase of endeavor.

The ability of television to conquer time and distance together, permitting millions of persons to see and hear the same person simultaneously, is having its effect on the way the public passes its leisure time, how it feels and acts about politics and government, how much it reads, how it rears its children and how it charts its cultural future. The country never has experienced anything quite like it.

#### Inflation Plays a Role

The rise of television also has put the spotlight on corollary factors that are contributing to a shifting pattern of preferences in diversion. The inflationary spiral, especially the high cost of food, is working to the advantage of television as almost every community, even those without TV, reports a major decline in spending for "luxury" items.

The immediate consequence is increased activity, ranging from frantic self-appraisal to costly promotional outlay, among those who are competing for a share of the individual's budget of time and money. And the catalyst in the new era of intensified competition is society's powerful unknown: The continuous free show available upon the flicking of the switch of a television set.

What happens when the screen lights up in the home and the public curtails its spending is demonstrated graphically in the case of motion pictures.

Attendance at theatres has dropped 20 to 40 per cent since the introduction of television, according to reports from THE TIMES correspondents. Many film distributors believe the national decline is roughly 35 per cent.

In contrast, representative cities that do not have television report business is holding up well and attribute at most a 10 per cent decline to the higher cost of living.

There have been theatre closings—seventy in Eastern Pennsylvania, 134 in Southern California, sixty-one in Massachusetts, sixty-four in the Chicago area and at least fifty-five in metropolitan New York. The New York Film Board of Trade said that in the last six weeks there had been perhaps thirty closings, some only for varying periods in the warm-weather season.

Many cities reported film houses going on part-time schedules to a far greater extent than in any other summer.

But any assumption that the film industry faces extinction is contradicted by numerous other considerations.

Many of the theatres that were closed were outmoded buildings in distressed neighborhoods and could be considered normal business casualties. In addition, there have been many new houses that, in some cases at least, actually have added to the total seating capacity in a community.

Especially significant, however, is the number of drive-in theatres, where customers can avoid parking charges, baby-sitter fees and traffic congestion, and can dress as they please. These have increased by 800 in the last year, bringing the total to about 3,000. And almost all report a booming trade.

#### Quality Films Stressed

Exhibitors in every part of the country emphasized that pictures of quality or those boasting a fresh personality were doing a good business and were immune to TV's inroads. "The Great Caruso," "Born Yesterday" and "All About Eve" were among those repeatedly cited.

In pleading with Hollywood for an improved product, exhibitors lost much of the hesitancy that had marked their answers on the status of business at the box-office. Here are some sample observations:

Washington: "You can't charge for mediocrity any more when everybody can get it at home for nothing."

San Francisco: "Quality counts. That's the story."

New Orleans: "The good picture still packs 'em in."

Richmond: "Before the war movie-going was a habit. Now people come only when they really want to see a picture."

The plight of the theatre owners is borne out by specific reports of TIMES correspondents. TV was mentioned invariably as a contributory cause, but living costs and picture quality also received strong emphasis.

#### TV's Effect on Theatres

Here are representative reports from cities having television stations:

| City | Effect on Box-office Since TV |
|---|---|
| **EAST** | |
| Boston (2 stations) | 25-40% off |
| Providence (1) | 25-40% off |
| New Haven (1) | 10-40% off |
| New York (7) | 10% on Broadway, 20-40% in neighborhood |
| Philadelphia (3) | "Definite inroads"; "bad" |
| Wilmington (1) | "Slump in business" |
| Baltimore (3) | "Off sharply" |
| Washington (4) | "Definite drop" |
| Syracuse (2) | 50% off |
| Schenectady (1) | "TV unquestionably hurt" |
| Binghamton (1) | "Badly hurt" |
| Utica (1) | 30% off |
| Rochester (1) | "Drop in attendance" |
| Buffalo (1) | "Hit hard" |
| Pittsburgh (1) | 15% off |
| Lancaster (1) | "At least 25%" |
| Johnstown (1) | "Big drop" |
| **MIDWEST** | |
| Cleveland (3) | 25-35% off |
| Columbus (3) | "Noticeable drop" |
| Detroit (3) | 18-25% off |
| Grand Rapids (1) | 12-20% off |
| Lansing (1) | 20-40% off |
| Milwaukee (1) | "Poor attendance" |
| Minneapolis-St. Paul (2) | 20% off |
| Chicago (4) | 20-40% off |
| Kansas City (1) | 15% off |
| St. Louis (1) | "Definite effect, cutting attendance" |
| **SOUTH** | |
| Richmond (1) | "Downward trend" |
| Atlanta (2) | "Operators blame TV" |
| Birmingham (2) | "Badly hurt" |
| Jacksonville (1) | 5% off |
| New Orleans (1) | "Not noticeable—only one station" |
| Memphis (1) | 10-20% off |
| Nashville (1) | "Decline in attendance" |
| **SOUTHWEST** | |
| Houston (1) | "Slight crimp" |
| San Antonio (2) | "Very definitely cut" |
| Fort Worth (1) | "Fallen off sharply" |
| Oklahoma City (1) | "Effects uncertain" |
| **WEST** | |
| Los Angeles (7) | 25-40% off |
| San Francisco (3) | 5-10% off |
| San Diego (1) | 40% off |
| Seattle (1) | 15-20% off |
| Salt Lake City (2) | "Sluggish box office" |
| Phoenix (1) | "Not much effect" |
| Albuquerque (1) | "No sustained cut" |

Business in the suburbs outside the major cities reflected the general trend, except in the case of drive-ins. Population shifts—new housing developments having a preponderance of young families with no teen-agers to baby-sit—and parking facilities were factors.

In the New York area, Stamford, Conn., reported a decline running up to 50 per cent; Passaic-Clifton, N. J., 25 per cent; Patchogue, L. I., 20 per cent; Peekskill, N. Y., 25 per cent, and Englewood, N. J., 10 to 25 per cent.

#### Non-Video Areas Report

By contrast with returns from cities with television, the box-office situation in non-video cities varies substantially. For example:

| City | Box-office Business |
|---|---|
| Portland, Me. | "Attendance o. k." |
| Portland, Ore. | "Same as last year—some cases perhaps off 10 per cent" |
| Austin, Tex. | "Same as year ago" |
| Fargo, N. D. | "Business down slightly, but still good" |
| Denver | "Slightly higher" |
| Little Rock | "Virtually no change" |

That the American public is feeling the "squeeze" between rising costs and rising taxes likewise is borne out in reports from local theatre owners and business men:

Oklahoma City: "An occasional sirloin steak for the whole family is a hell of a lot more entertainment than it used to be."

Newark: "We're in some kind of a recession; people haven't got the money."

Seattle: "It costs about $5 for a couple to attend a movie. Two 94-cent tickets with all the taxes, parking expense, cup of coffee or dish of ice cream and then the baby-sitter."

Memphis: "The people are fearful; they don't know what's going to happen."

Chicago: "A lot of people are still paying for the hard goods bought during the rush after the start of the Korean war."

Isolated and highly tentative reports — from Erie, Pa.; New Brunswick, N. J.; Miami, Syracuse, White Plains, N. Y., and Dallas—give the first hints that veteran video viewers are beginning to resume the movie-going habit after a steady dose of TV. Business shows signs of leveling off, it is reported, and in some instances there is a slight upward trend at the box office.

"The housewife sooner or later is going to get fed up staying in the house day and night," remarked one exhibitor in Westchester County.

But the average theatre owner across the country has his fingers crossed and many correspondents reported persistent rumors that more closings could be expected. Granting that inflation is an important influence adversely affecting attendance, it was noted that many persons now were looking at television as a replacement for "movie night." That is what is new.

#### Hollywood's Big Problem

If the local theatre is acutely aware of television, the capital of the film industry, Hollywood, thinks of little else at the moment. Though a variety of causes are responsible, the gross revenues of the eight major film companies have declined from $952,000,000 in 1947 to $861,000,000 in 1950. Retrenchment is the order of the day on the West Coast.

In 1947 the average craft union employment in the Hollywood film industry was 18,400 persons and the average monthly payroll was $7,000,000.. By 1950, the average employment was down to 13,600 and the payroll to $5,600,000, but some of the slack has been taken up in production of films for video. Reductions in executive personnel as well as among actors, writers and directors appear inevitable, it was noted, and there will be further economies in production schedules. All indications, however, point to maintenance of the volume of picture output.

Production of films especially for television is a growing business in Hollywood, and seems certain to increase. According to one source, film footage for TV was being produced n May at a rate of 988 hours a year, compared with 855 hours of feature films for theatre showing.

Hollywood's difficulty is that it isn't geared to what the television sponsor can pay for a film. In this connection several of the smaller companies — Republic, Monogram and Lippert—have made arrangements to release their backlog of films by agreeing to make a new musical sound track that will benefit the American Federation of Musicians. Other producers have hesitated to release their old films lest they offend their primary customers, the theatre exhibitors.

Of increasing importance to both Hollywood and its exhibitors is theatre television, whereby video images are projected directly on the large-size screen. The recent box-office success in theatre television's pick-up of the Joe Louis-Lee Savold fight, which the home TV audience did not see as it happened, has stimulated interest. By fall perhaps more than 100 houses will have theatre TV equipment and will be in a position to outbid an advertising sponsor on home video.

Theatre TV, in turn, has led to a consideration of subscription television for the home, a system under which the viewer would have to pay if he wished to view "unscrambled" pictures. Paramount Pictures has invested in one coin-operated device and, with some reluctance, other producers have cooperated with the Zenith Radio Corporation's box-office method known as "Phonevision." In New York later this year there may be further tests of another method called "Skiatron."

### Speculation on "Marriage"

A matter for major speculation has been the possibility of "a marriage" between TV and Hollywood. While many deals have been rumored periodically, the only concrete development has been the contemplated merger of the American Broadcasting Company with United Paramount Theatres, which is a theatre chain and is not to be confused with the producing concern, Paramount Pictures, Inc.

But overshadowing all other considerations in the relationship between television and the motion-picture world is the fact that television is still only in its relatively early stages of development.

Today 107 stations are operating in sixty-three cities, within range of roughly 62 per cent of the country's population. Of the sixty-three cities, however, only twenty-four have between two and seven stations, and a choice of TV programs generally has been a prerequisite for the medium to exercise its full impact on competitive media. The remaining thirty-nine TV cities have only one station each.

For the last two years there has been a "freeze" on the construction of new television stations, which to some extent has provided the film industry with a chance to catch its breath. But the plans of the Federal Communications Commission envisage ultimately perhaps 2,000 stations serving several hundred communities.

Military priorities and many other factors may affect TV's expansion, but the motion picture business none the less has reason to worry. Television's major strides still lie ahead.

### Waiting Across 1,500 Miles

Milton Buhr of Saskatoon, Sask., in the western part of Canada, has a 100-foot television aerial in his backyard and a modern set. His only trouble so far is that he hasn't seen a program; the nearest station is 1,500 miles away.

"I'm going to be ready," he explained.

### Reaffirming of "Progress"

Twenty-five years ago Volmer Dahlstrand, president of the Milwaukee Federation of Musicians, complained to a theatre owner about the movies hurting the employment of pit orchestras.

"This is progress," replied the operator, curtly.

A few weeks ago the two men met and the theatre owner complained about television hurting his business.

"That's progress," replied Mr. Dahlstrand happily.

### As One Medium to Another

In Kansas City, Mo., movie houses are plugging their pictures on television while knocking the medium in their advertising statements.

A typical "ad" will describe the picture to be shown and close with this sort of announcement:

"Only the giant motion picture screen can present the true grandeur and magnificence of . . . etc."

June 24, 195

# Why Millions Love Lucy

## In the comical trials of Lucy and Ricky Ricardo TV audiences recognize the exasperation and warmth of their own lives.

### By JACK GOULD

LAST week's signing of a record $8,000,000 contract to keep "I Love Lucy" on television another two years was economic confirmation of the obvious. The weekly TV adventures of Lucille Ball and her husband, Desi Arnaz—"andor" Lucy and Ricky Ricardo—clearly are not susceptible to the usual mundane standards of appraisal. By every reasonable criterion they are something very special.

Not since the heyday of the fifteen-minute broadcasts of "Amos 'n' Andy," which back in the Nineteen Thirties brought American home life to a halt every evening, has a program so completely caught the interest and affection of the public. "I Love Lucy" is probably the most misleading title imaginable. For once all available

*JACK GOULD, radio and television editor of The Times, has followed the Ball-Arnaz rise in video since they made their debut.*

statistics are in agreement: millions love Lucy.

"I Love Lucy" is as much a phenomenon as an attraction. Fundamentally, it is a piece of hilarious theatre put together with deceptively brilliant know-how, but it also is many other things. In part it is a fusion of the make-believe of the footlights and the real-life existence of a glamorous "name." In part it is the product of inspired press agentry which has made a national legend of a couple which two years ago was on the Hollywood sidelines. In part it is the fruit of the perennial unpredictability of show business.

But whatever parts make up the whole of "I Love Lucy," the most trenchant fact is that week after week upwards of 40,000,000 persons tune in Lucy and Ricky at 9 o'clock (Eastern Time), on Monday evening. What makes them do it? What has Lucy got?

THE distinction of "I Love Lucy" lies in its skillful presentation of the

basic element of familiarity. If there is one universal theme that knows no age limitations and is recognizable to young and old, it is the institution of marriage—and more particularly the day-to-day trials of husband and wife. And especially on television, which plays to the family circle sitting in its own home, it is the single story line above all others with which the audience can most readily identify itself.

"I Love Lucy" has no monopoly on the humor inherent in marriage; the idea is as old as the theatre itself and television channels are cluttered with rival shows rather pathetically hoping that the "Lucy lightning" will strike. But what seems to escape most of these imitations is the extraordinary discipline and intuitive understanding of farce that gives "I Love Lucy" its engaging lilt and lift.

Miss Ball and Mr. Arnaz always know what they are about. Every installment of "I Love Lucy" begins with a plausible and logical premise. Casually the groundwork is laid for the essential motivation: Lucy vs. Ricky. Only after a firm foundation of credibility has been established is the element of absurdity introduced. It is in the smooth transition from sense to nonsense that "I Love Lucy" imparts both a warmth and a reality to the slapstick romp which comes as the climax. The viewer has a sense of being a co-conspirator rather than a spectator in completely unimportant yet amusing high jinks.

"I Love Lucy," in other words, is marriage projected in larger-than-life size but never so distorted that it loses its communion with the viewer at home. By the art of delightful exaggeration Lucy and Ricky put marriage in sharp focus.

As sheer farce, "I Love Lucy" has the fragility of this form of make-believe, and what the show would be without Miss Ball is a prospect about which no one should think. Unquestionably, she is the unrivaled top TV comedienne of today, a complete personality blessed with a very real and genuine comic artistry. How she was ever wasted as a sexy glamour girl in the motion pictures passes all understanding anywhere except Hollywood.

Miss Ball's gifts are those of the born trouper rather than the dramatic school student. First and foremost is her sense of timing; in this respect she is the distaff equivalent of Jack Benny. Maybe it is a roll of her big eyes. Maybe it is the sublime shrug which

housewives the world over will understand. Maybe it is the superb hollow laugh. Maybe it is the masterly double-take that tops the gag line. Whatever it is, it comes at the split-second instant that spells the difference between a guffaw and a smile.

But the most durable and recognizable quality conveyed by Miss Ball—perhaps it is the real heart of "I Love Lucy"—is wifely patience. Whatever the provocation or her exasperation, she is always the regular gal and the wonderful sport. On stage and off, Miss Ball is a person.

MR. ARNAZ, alias Ricky, is a success story in himself. Before TV he was known primarily as an orchestra conductor. The very qualities which presumably hampered his advance at that pursuit were turned to advantage on "I Love Lucy."

His rather marked accent and his unprofessional style of performing were wisely left alone. The result was a leading man far removed from the usual stereotyped stage husband. It was a case of awkwardness being recognized as an asset. Today—after two seasons in his role—Mr. Arnaz is rapidly becoming a competent actor.

As Ethel and Fred Mertz, the landlords, neighbors and friends of the Ricardos, Vivian Vance and William Frawley consistently turn in performances that are veritable cameos of resignation to the unpredictable ways of Lucy and Ricky. Would that the supporting casts of most other TV shows were half as good!

Probably no event in recent theatrical history has occasioned as much national suspense as the birth of a son to Lucille and Desi. By careful advance filming of the script the TV Ricardos also welcomed a new arrival. The two events managed to coincide on the same day because the child was delivered by Caesarean section. But it was plain luck that the birth of a boy happened to be exactly as called for in the script.

THE expected birth of a child, including the mother's obvious condition, seldom, if ever, has been used as the basis for an extended comedy series. There were a number of protests. But most viewers welcomed the tasteful and tactful handling of the sequences and certainly the humorous side was recognized by every parent. And, unlike so many shows that stand still, doing the same thing over and over again, "I Love Lucy" now has a limitless supply of comedy material in bringing up the child.

Perhaps that's the explanation of why millions do like "I Love Lucy." It's very human—and so are we.

Lucille Ball and Desi Arnaz play a comedy scene on "I Love Lucy."

March 1, 1953

# FAMILY OF 11 FAILS TO 'STRIKE IT RICH'

## Couple and 9 Children Arrive on Relief Check, Are Sent Home at $50 Cost to City

A destitute family of eleven from Port Deposit, Md., arrived here by bus at 5 A. M. yesterday with a tragic story they hoped to tell on the radio-television program "Strike It Rich."

They never spoke to anyone from the show; they cost the city $50.36; seven and a half hours later they were on a train bound for their home, and Welfare Commissioner Henry L. McCarthy warned that his department would no longer "be responsible for any indigent fortune-seekers."

The family, consisting of Michael Jaskulski, 45 years old, his pregnant wife, and nine children ranging from 1 to 17, spent their last relief check to come to New York. Led by the father, who speaks poor English and reads and writes only a little, the family gathered, confused, in the West Fiftieth Street Capitol Greyhound Bus Terminal.

Mr. Jaskulski carried a piece of yellow paper. On it, written by a neighbor, was the story of the Jaskulskis' plight. It was addressed to Warren Hull, master of ceremonies of "Strike It Rich."

### Two Children Unable to Walk

It told of the broken-down house in which the Jaskulskis lived without electricity or running water, of the leaking roof, of two of the children unable to walk since birth, and of the clothing, food and shelter the family needed.

The Travelers Aid Society representatives in the terminal notified the Welfare Department after the Jaskulskis arrived. They were taken to the department's Special Services Welfare Center at 630 Ninth Avenue.

The department telephoned the Maryland relief agency, which authorized New York to send the family back to their home in Port Deposit, thirty miles northeast of Baltimore. The Jaskulskis have been on relief in Port Deposit for the last six weeks.

Welfare Department representatives piled the family in two taxicabs and took them to Pennsylvania Station. Tickets costing $30.36 were bought on a train; $16 was given to the father. Of this amount, he spent $10 for sandwiches, coffee and milk. Another $4 was spent by the city for taxis to take the family to the center from the bus terminal and then to the railroad station.

The trip to New York had cost the Jaskulskis $17. They had $2 left when they arrived. When they left they still had this $2 and $6 left over from the welfare funds.

Commissioner McCarthy warned that other needy families arriving with hopes of getting on "Strike It Rich" would get no aid from the city. He said the department had provided for such indigents for two and a half years, but "we're not going to do it any more."

The "Strike It Rich" program disavowed responsibility, saying that "we keep telling people not to come here but there's nothing we can do to stop them."

*March 9, 1954*

---

# MAN IN THE STREET

## The Public Often Can Outshine TV Stars

### By JACK GOULD

THE past week in television has reaffirmed one of the most elementary yet most often ignored principles of good television: there's no people like non-show people. The TV that deals with actuality, with real unglamourized people behaving as themselves, is still the most fascinating TV of all.

Though "The $64,000 Question" is one of the most cleverly contrived shows of many a year, the program's success rests in great measure on its ability to capitalize on the TV medium's unique power: to hold the mirror up to life as it is revealed spontaneously before a viewer's eyes. This is the uncanny wizardry of TV, totally different from either stage or screen; yet it is amazing how infrequently this magic is put to fruitful use.

Long after "The $64,000 Question" has disappeared and been forgotten, it is just possible that the quiz show will have succeeded in persuading TV producers that they have overlooked their most obvious yet inexhaustible supply of material: people.

### Curiosity

Watching Gino Prato, the cobbler, decide how far he should go in pitting his knowledge of opera against a fortune was the intriguing come-on of "The $64,000 Question" for the last month. But what also made Prato an entrancing figure overnight was his own personality, modesty, pluck and intelligence. A nobody, in short, turned out to be a warm and intriguing guy.

Curiosity about other people, about new persons one may meet, is a fundamental human instinct, and it is the nature of video to sharpen it. Yet, if there are programs that do endeavor to satisfy this curiosity, there are only too many that miss their opportunity, either wholly or partly.

Take quiz shows in particular. Run down the list. One sees for the most part the same chronically familiar set of faces, the rather specialized group of individuals who likely as not are celebrities in TV and not any place else. Some are fine, but why not a new tack for a change?

In a country of 160,000,000 the woods must be filled with Gino Pratos, Mrs. Kreitzers and Patrolman O'Hanlons. Why not, for a change, some rotating panels of everyday people who are new to the viewer? For that matter, let's bring back something on the order of "Information Please" with Gino Prato, Mrs. Kreitzer and Patrolman O'Hanlon for a starting panel. Phooey on the celebrities! They're not needed so much in the TV age. TV can make its own, if it only will, and in the process impart some added and continuous excitment to viewing fare.

TV errs grievously in its tendency to make its guests fit into some predetermined studio mold; what TV needs is the freshness and element of the unexpected from the outside world. A small yet meaningful illustration is John Daly's habit of answering for the participants on "What's My Line?"

Except in absolutely necessary cases he should let the guest take over completely. Since Mr. Daly is a sound reporter, after the game is over couldn't he probe a little into the lives of the non-celebrity guests? The guests often are interesting persons, but a viewer hardly gets to know them.

Surely every viewer can recall one of TV's most common occurrences: An absorbing person is on the screen; then the TV interviewer sits there with egg on his face and doesn't know what question to ask next. If the video prima donnas could forget their own magnetism and do a little reportorial digging, they would find a gold mine in many a John Doe.

What applies to quiz shows also applies to discussion programs in many instances. The majority of the participants on these presentations are Congressmen, officials and authorities.

### Vox Populi

But there are others, too, in the United States who have opinions on life. Just once couldn't there be a discussion on a pressing national interest by a farmer from Kansas, a factory worker in New England, a professor from New Orleans and a doctor from Los Angeles? Television is being expertized almost to death. It would be a novel experience to hear more often what the people think, to expand to a half-hour what a show such as "Today" often does in abbreviated style.

Television complains continually that it doesn't know where its material will come from next and in desperation repeats itself ad nauseam. Yet, meanwhile, it overlooks the bottomless reservoir of intelligent people in the world who could be brought to the home screen with their varied faces, personalities, viewpoints and backgrounds. With a little imagination they could be used in limitless formats. All that's required is the interest and willingness to go out and find them. They're certainly t ere.

*August 14, 1955*

# TV QUIZZES GET A NEW AUDIENCE

## But Congress Sees A Different Show

**By RICHARD F. SHEPARD**

In March, 1957, the big-money quiz craze now being studied by a Congressional committee reached a crescendo on television. On Sunday there was "The $64,000 Challenge." On Monday, one gasped as Charles Van Doren crashed through the rating ceiling on "Twenty-One." As an appetizer on Tuesday the viewer had "The Big Surprise," just on its way out as its $100,-000 top awards were being dwarfed by the competition. Later that night, there was the granddaddy of the isolation booth genre, "The $64,000 Question." The rest of the week, the contestants went off to recharge the brain cells and the nation debated the merits of the questions and the size of the taxes on the winners.

But most of the drama lay ahead. In August last year, on a quiet Saturday afternoon, the Columbia Broadcasting System suddenly announced that "Dotto," a comparatively minor-league morning quiz, was being dropped then and there. Within a week, rumors that the answers were rigged were widespread. Soon another complainant came forth with charges against "Twenty-one." In New York, the District Attorney and a grand jury investigated the charges. The jurymen handed up a presentment but Judge Mitchell D. Schweitzer impounded the findings and refused to make them public, holding that the document made accusations without providing a forum for denials.

### Now Congress

Last week the House Special Subcommittee on Legislative Oversight began hearings on the fixing of quiz shows. The disclosures repeated many of the New York City investigation findings. But the cause of their investigation had disappeared. The last of the big quizzes expired on television last November.

Rarely has any type of show gained such attention as did the quizzes during their three-year lifespan. The idea was to take

Martha Holmes.

Charles Van Doren.

Associated Press

Herbert Stempel.

a contestant of some wit or humor and startle viewers by his tremendous fund of knowledge on subjects that he would seem least likely to know.

And so there trooped past

home screens a long parade of elderly housewives who knew the Bible by heart; a 10-year-old boy whose grasp of science amassed for him nearly $250,-000; an Army depot clerk, a veritable human filing cabinet, who topped that sum; another youngster who won $100,000 by knowing the ins and outs of the stock market, a jockey who knew art, a clergyman who answered questions on love stories and a showgirl who knew astronomy.

### Worldwide Fad

The virus had spread abroad to Great Britain, Italy and even the Soviet Union (where it didn't really catch on). But despite the dazzling aspect of the size of the awards, the quizzes were not individually expensive shows to produce. In comparison with even modest filmed half-hour dramas, they were modestly budgeted. A contestant amortized his prize money over weeks of appearances during which he won nothing. There were only a few professional performers and musicians on regular salary and the backdrop was always the same, an isolation booth or two, a machine that selected the question and a bank official who supervised the checks in return for a bank plug on the air.

During the Washington hearings, the question of ethics arose. It was not so much whether illegality was involved, but many people, including the Congressmen, worried about the morality of priming the contestants with answers and stage directions, such as when to mop the brow, wet the lips and otherwise demonstrate a brain-throbbing absorption in the problem before them.

There were several views expressed. Some observers, in and out of television, equated it with a P. T. Barnum tactic that took in a gullible public but left it satisfied. In addition, they felt, viewers had not lost or been hurt since the show was free entertainment, theirs merely for a flick of the dial. Even losing contestants went away with more than they had when they started.

On the other hand, many felt that a farce had been perpetrated upon the public and that some step should be taken to prevent a recurrence. The mother of one contestant said that "any parent would be outraged when their child had been deliberately led to be deceptive."

The comparison with wrestling was inevitable. Still a big draw on television, wrestling is presented as an exhibition and few fans let their knowledge that it is staged interfere with their enjoyment.

### Quiz Show Future

People in television today have mixed feelings about the future of the quiz. All agree that television quizzes are out as long as Congressional quizzes are on. But looking ahead, it is debatable whether they will ever return even when the investigations are only half-remembered. The following two views polarize the opinions.

Mark Goodson, a partner in Goodson-Todman Productions, feels that the big-money quiz has had it. His organization has never entered the field, although it has been spectacularly successful with such panel and audience participation shows as "What's My Line," "The Price Is Right" and "I've Got a Secret."

"The big chance show lasting week after week is gone," says Mr. Goodson. "It's dead and doomed. You could only watch a certain number of people sweating each week. If you had the world series three times a week, you'd get bored with it."

Michael H. Dann, C. B. S. vice president in charge of network programs in New York, takes a different view. "The networks would have no objection to new quizzes, if they fulfill certain basic requirements. But we believe that there has to be an awful lot of entertainment appeal before they get on the air. Anything spontaneous has a basic appeal. The quiz shows may never again reach the heights they occupied, but that's a good thing. Perhaps there was an excess of them from the point of view of balanced scheduling. But as soon as a good idea comes up, it will be considered."

# VAN DOREN ADMITS LYING, SAYS TV QUIZ WAS FIXED; LOSES HIS COLUMBIA POST

## COACHING BARED

### Teacher Fears He Has Done Disservice to All in Education

**By WILLIAM M. BLAIR**
Special to The New York Times.

WASHINGTON, Nov. 2 — Charles Van Doren confessed today that he had lived a lie for three years.

The 33-year-old Assistant Professor of English told the Congressional investigators he had deceived his family, his lawyer and the friends he had made through television by concealing his deep involvement in a fixed nationally televised quiz show.

He told of coming to the conclusion only recently that "the truth is the only thing with which a man can live."

He recited in detail how he had been given questions and answers in advance and coached on how to act in his fourteen appearances on the defunct quiz program "Twenty-one."

### Had Cash Guarantee

He testified he had been guaranteed specific amounts of money, starting at $1,000, and how an arrangement had been made for him to lose in a "dramatic manner" so that he won $129,000.

Mr. Van Doren told of private conferences, where he was told not only the questions he would be asked but how to make the answers more dramatic by hesitating and by answering part out of the regular order.

He said he had been talked into the rigging on the ground that his appearance would be a service to "the intellectual life, to teachers and to education in general."

"In fact," he added, "I think I have done a disservice to all of them."

### Would 'Reverse' His Life

He said he first denied knowledge of any fixing because he hated to betray the "faith and hope" of "millions" of friends and associates in teaching.

"I would give almost anything I have to reverse the course of my life in the last three years," he said.

His one hour and thirty-five minute appearance on the witness stand today attracted one of the largest crowds ever to attend a Congressional hearing.

Only about 500 persons, however, were able to gain admittance to the Caucus Room of the Old House Office Building, the scene of many of the subcommittee's often tumultuous hearings.

Several hundred persons lined up in the corridors but failed to get into the high-ceilinged room with its Corinthian columns and long curving dais where the House members sat. More than 100 persons stood two and three deep in the rear of the big room.

Mr. Van Doren, with his lawyer, Carl J. Rubino, beside him, faced the members on the dais. Behind him were more than 100 newspaper, radio and television reporters and the public spectators, most of them women.

### Father Is Pleased

Among the spectators were his wife, Geraldine Ann, who had answered his fan mail, and his father, Mark Van Doren, the poet. After his son's testimony, the elder Mr. Van Doren told a reporter: "I feel wonderful. This is the happiest day of my life."

With one exception, members of the house panel commended Mr. Van Doren for his "soul-searching confession." Their commendation drew applause from spectators.

The exception was Representative Steven B. Derounian, Republican of Nassau County, who asserted he could not agree with his colleagues. "I don't think an adult of your intelligence ought to be commended for telling the truth," he said. The youthful-appearing witness flushed.

After he left the stand, the House subcommittee turned its attention to alleged fixing on two other quiz shows, "The $64,000 Question" and "The $64,000 Challenge."

It was understood that the subcommittee probably would have as witnesses later this week at least one of the youngsters who won big stakes on a quiz show. Representative Oren Harris, Democrat of Arkansas and chairman of the subcommittee, announced that Xavier Cugat, the orchestra leader, and John Ross, manager of Patty Duke, an 11-year-old contestant who appeared on "The $64,000 Challenge," would appear tomorrow.

### Testifies Distinctly

Mr. Van Doren wore an oxford gray suit and dark figured tie. He appeared composed and a smile flicked across his face as he talked briefly after his arrival with Mr. Harris.

On the witness stand, a slightly raised wooden platform, Mr. Van Doren hunched over, his arms on the table on which he placed a prepared statement. He spoke distinctly and clearly into a microphone of the public address system needed for the acoustically poor room.

Mr. Van Doren testified that he had been coached for his appearances on "Twenty-one" in 1956 and 1957 by Albert Freedman, producer of the program. Mr. Freedman has been indicted by a New York County grand jury on charges of perjury for denying that the program was fixed.

Under questioning, Mr. Van Doren said that at one time Mr. Freedman had told him he was going to be the first quiz show contestant to win more than $100,000.

He quoted Mr. Freedman as saying: "Charlie, I think I ought to have $5,000 of that money."

"He never mentioned it again and nothing was ever done about it," Mr. Van Doren said. He went on that he did not think Mr. Freedman had meant "that the way it sounds."

"I think he blurted it out without thinking about it," he added.

### Describes Deception

Mr. Van Doren told how he had become a part of the deception on "Twenty-one" before he had appeared on the program. Mr. Freedman, he testified, called him to his apartment and told him that Herbert M. Stempel of Forest Hills, Queens, then the "champion," was unpopular and that the program was suffering in the public eye.

Mr. Freedman asked him, he said, as a favor to "agree to an arrangement" to tie Mr. Stempel and increase the entertainment value of the show.

He said he asked that he be permitted to go on the show "honestly" but Mr. Freedman said that was "impossible." It was then, he went on, that Mr. Freedman emphasized the "great service" he would do for intellectual life.

As a result of this meeting, he went on to tie Mr. Stempel three times on his first appearance under the coaching of Mr. Freedman and become the new champion on Dec. 5, 1956.

He said that thereafter he sought several times to be released but it was not until the end of January, 1957, that Mr. Freedman agreed to let him stop. But some time elapsed before "it could be arranged," he said, and it was not until the night of March 11, 1957, that he "lost" to Mrs. Vivienne Nearing, New York lawyer. She defeated him in the first game that night.

He missed on the question of the name of the King of the Belgians, a miss that brought protests in that country. Today, Mr. Van Doren told newsmen he had known about 80 per cent of the questions he was asked even without having the answers, but the name of King Baudouin had honestly escaped him.

It was not clear whether he was supposed to lose on that question or another one, but Mr. Freedman had told him he would lose that night.

Much of the questioning by subcommittee members dealt with whether N. B. C. had ever asked him if he had been fixed.

Subcommittee members bore down on whether any officials of N. B. C., which carried "Twenty-one," had ever asked him if the program had been manipulated or had urged him to tell the truth before the grand jury or go to Washington and tell of the rigging.

Mr. Van Doren said that two N. B. C. vice presidents had asked him to testify after the subcommittee invited him to appear voluntary last month. He identified them as James Stabile, vice president in charge of TV programs, and David Levy, vice president in charge of talent negotiations.

Beyond that, he said, no one had asked him to tell the truth. He said he had not, up to that time, told anyone at N. B. C. the whole truth nor had he told his own lawyer.

He also said, in response to questions, that he knew of no investigation that N. B. C. had made of the fixing once the scandal broke.

There also was discussion of the situation with the sponsors of the program, Pharmaceuticals, Inc., he said.

N. B. C., he testified, insisted that he send a telegram to the subcommittee demanding "the right to come down and testify." This demand, he said, was made on the night of Oct. 6 in a con-

Associated Press Wirephoto

**TELLS OF QUIZ FIXING: Charles Van Doren, former contestant on TV show "Twenty-one," appearing before the House Special Subcommittee on Legislative Oversight.**

ference that lasted from 7 P. M. to 12:30 A. M. with Mr. Stabile, Mr. Levy and others.

He said he drafted the telegram, which was approved by the N. B. C. officials. The wire denied he had received questions and answers or otherwise participated in the fixing of "Twenty-one." The subcommittee immediately invited him to appear.

It was then, he said, on Oct. 8, that "I did not know what to do."

He went on that Columbia University had offered him a week's leave of absence "and I simply ran away."

"I was running from myself," he said in his statement.

"I realized I had been doing it for a long time. I had to find a place where I could think, in peace and quiet. I knew I could not lie anymore, nor did I want to."

He related how he and his wife "drove aimlessly from one town to another" in New England "trying to come to some conclusion." But, he added, "I could not face up to what I had done."

He said he spent the following week "trying hopelessly to find a way out." There was no way, he said. "But even though my mind knew there was none I could not face the prospect emotionally."

## "Truth Is Always Best"

He said he often had considered the "one way out," which was to "simply tell the truth."

"But as long as I was trying to protect only myself and my own reputation, and, as I thought, the faith people had in me, I could not believe that way was possible," he said.

"I was beginning to realize what I should have known before, that the truth is always the best way, indeed it is the only way, to promote and protect faith."

He said his father had told him this "even though he did not know the truth in my case."

Mr. Van Doren glanced up at the subcommittee members before continuing to tell of how "in the end a small thing tipped the scales."

This "small thing," he went on, was a letter he received from a woman, a complete stranger to him. She had seen him on N. B. C.'s "Today" program with Dave Garroway and "said she admired my work there."

## Decides to Confess

"She told me the only way I could live with myself, and make up for what I had done. * * * was to admit it, clearly, openly, truly," he related. "Suddenly, I knew she was right. And this way, which had seemed so long the worse of all possible alternatives, suddenly became the only one."

He told of telephoning his lawyer the following morning of his decision to tell the truth. The lawyer's reply was: "God bless you."

There was almost complete silence as Mr. Van Doren finished his statement with these words and turned with a smile to Mr. Rubino.

Representative Harris led off the round of compliments to the young teacher. Robert W. Lishman, the subcommittee's chief counsel, joined in commending Mr. Van Doren for the "soul - searching fortitude you have displayed here today."

During his testimony Mr. Van Doren disclosed that Mr. Lishman and Robert Goodwin, a staff lawyer, had tried during the House investigation "to make me see that my folly was leading me in deeper and deeper, but I persisted in it."

## Calls Himself "Foolish"

"Foolish," "folly," "incredibly naive" were among the words and phrases Mr. Van Doren used several times throughout his testimony to describe his actions. He said he had written his eighteen-page statement without help except that he had shown it to his lawyer.

As the hearing ended, Mr. Harris said he wanted to echo the "God bless you" of Mr. Rubino and said that he hoped the country would derive benefit from his "unfortunate experience."

"I didn't think that I would ever thank this committee," Mr. Van Doren responded. He went to thank the members and staff, and concluded: "I hope I will never do that thing again."

After the hearing, Mr. Van Doren told reporters that "I feel better than I have for three years." A woman spectator pushed through the crowd to ask for an autograph. He gave it and then posed with his wife, who kissed him.

His wife, he said, did not know the full extent of his part in the fixing until Oct. 17. It was at that time he told his family of his participation and of the moral and mental struggle he related for the subcommittee.

He also returned to the office of District Attorney Frank S. Hogan and Assistant District Attorney Joseph Stone to recant his grand jury testimony. Mr. Stone has been an official observer at the hearings here.

Asked if he ever thought of the "cowardly way out," he replied: "Well, not really." Pressed whether he considered suicide, he said: "Oh, never very seriously. I want to live very much. I love life very much." He said also that he had thought of going to Brazil.

He told newsmen that most of his money had been eaten up in taxes and for lawyers' fees. He also said he had no plans to return the money.

After the hearing, he moved outside the hearing room to face a battery of cameras and lights. His wife and father slipped out through the door he had entered, down a side corridor, and into the street outside by a stairway.

# TV INQUIRY RAISES ISSUE OF PERJURY OVER QUIZ RIGGING

## Former Executive at Revlon and Head of Company Deny Any Complicity

## FEDERAL ACTION URGED

## President Voices Dismay— He Demands Clean-Up of 'This Whole Mess'

**By WILLIAM M. BLAIR**
Special to The New York Times.

WASHINGTON, Nov. 4 — House investigators raised the question of perjury today after a former executive of Revlon, Inc., had sworn he did not know that two nationally televised quiz shows were rigged.

The testimony of Martin Revson, former executive vice president of the New York cosmetics concern, was in direct conflict with that of three television producers and a former Revlon official, who had sworn that sponsors directed the rigging of the shows.

Fresh testimony on the rigging of "The $64,000 Question" and "The $64,000 Challenge" came tonight. Shirley Bernstein, associate producer of "The $64,000 Challenge," swore in an affidavit that she understood instructions for the fixing had come from Revlon.

The often-heated denials of Mr. Revson brought demands from two Republican House members that the Attorney General investigate the case.

### President Dismayed

President Eisenhower told his press conference today that the fixing had dismayed and bewildered him. He added: "Nobody will be satisfied until this whole mess is cleared up."

The chief officers of the Columbia Broadcasting System and the National Broadcasting Company were scheduled to appear tomorrow morning to tell what the networks knew of the rigging and what they have done since the disclosures. They are Dr. Frank Stanton, president of C. B. S., and Robert Kintner, president of N. B. C.

Representative Oren Harris, Democrat of Arkansas and subcommittee chairman, said he hoped to wind up the hearings with the testimony of the networks heads. However, an informed subcommittee source said the House investigators probably would continue to delve into the TV problem and resume hearing later.

The House panel also heard testimony in tonight's session of how an Allentown, Pa., department store paid $10,000 in cash to place an employe on "The $64,000 Question" and gain publicity for the store.

Earlier, Representatives John B. Bennett of Michigan and Steven B. Derounian of Long Island had joined in proposing that the Attorney General look into the possibility of perjury.

Mr. Bennett said outside the hearing room that he thought there was a clear case of perjury in the conflicting testimony presented to the House Special Subcommittee on Legislative Oversight. Mr. Derounian said, "The Attorney General should take it up and do something about it."

Charles Revson, president of Revlon and the brother of Martin, also testified that he was unaware of any rigging or control of the shows, which were carried by the Columbia Broadcasting System.

In her sworn deposition, Miss Bernstein said she understood "completely" that she was receiving instructions from Revlon on how quiz show matches should come out. Her testimony was read by Richard N. Goodwin, special consultant to the House panel, who questioned her during the investigation of the fixing.

Miss Bernstein is the sister of Leonard Bernstein, conductor of the New York Philharmonic Orchestra. She now is associated with C. B. S. in the production of a dramatic program.

The fixing, she said, was done at the request of Steven B. Carlin, executive producer of "The $64,000 Challenge," which was owned by Entertainment Productions, Inc.

Mr. Carlin, and Mert Koplin, producer of the show, testified yesterday on the pressure they had been put under by the sponsors to control contestants and to assure that certain contestants would win or lose.

Another sworn deposition read into the record today was from George Abrams, former vice president in charge of advertising for Revlon. He said that "the producers carried out the sponsors' wishes most of the time as expressed" in weekly meetings of company officials, advertising agency representatives and producers.

Martin Revson also made an accusation of conspiracy against Mr. Carlin and Mr. Koplin.

" I feel that Mr. Carlin and Mr. Koplin entered into a conspiracy against me," he told Representative Walter Rogers, Democrat of Texas, under questioning.

"As far as Mr. Abrams is concerned, he has more knowledge of producers than I have," Martin Revson added.

### Investigation Begun

Mr. Abrams' testimony, taken in New York last Monday, set off the excitement that led to the demands for a Department of Justice inquiry. A general investigation of the quiz scandals by Attorney General William P. Rogers already is under way at the direction of President Eisenhower.

Miss Bernstein's deposition was taken Oct. 5, immediately prior to the opening of public hearings by the House subcommittee.

In questioning her, Mr. Goodwin asked: "Was it your complete understanding from the start that you were receiving instructions from the sponsor as to how a match should come out?"

"Yes, completely," she replied. "There were many meetings with the sponsor where Mr. Carlin would come back white with anger."

Asked if Mr. Carlin ever told her directly that the sponsor had sought a particular outcome of a match on "The $64,000 Challenge," she answered: "Yes, often I would say 'Why do it this way?' Mr. Carlin would say that it was not his wish, but the sponsor wanted it that way."

"By sponsor, he meant primarily Revlon?" Mr. Goodwin asked.

"Yes, I was given to understand that we had little or no interference from the Lorillard people."

The P. Lorillard Tobacco Company was co-sponsor of the "Challenge."

The practice of getting questions and answers from the bank where they were purportedly deposited to guard their integrity was just a dramatic device she said. She had a key to the safe at the Chase Manhattan Bank of New York, she added, and she and her assistant "would go down to get the questions."

Another witness, James D. Webb, president of C. J. LaRoche and Co., Inc., New York advertising agency, also disputed testimony of the producers and Mr. Abrams. He said that until he read the testimony of Xavier Cugat, band leader who told how he had been coached, "I never suspected there was any dishonesty in these shows."

He said he had attended some of the weekly meetings described by the producers and that they had never given him "the slightest reason" to believe the shows were dishonest.

His agency handled a part of Revlon's total advertising account. Other agencies also had Revlon accounts.

Representative Bennett drew from Mr. Webb the information that his agency received between $230,000 and $240,000 in commissions from Revlon. It was the agency's fourth largest account.

Also read into the record was an interoffice memorandum written by Al Ward of the New York advertising agency of Batten, Barton, Durstine & Osborn to Robert L. Forman, executive vice president of the agency. It concerned the first "$64,000 Question" show that appeared on June 8, 1955. The memo was obtained from Revlon files.

In it Mr. Ward mentioned that the show had the "slight ring of a plugged nickel" and mentioned "rigging." It also said that Louis G. Cowan, then head of entertainment productions, had made a telephone call after the show and had remarked, "Fellows, we're in."

Martin Revson asserted that Mr. Cowan, now vice president of the C. B. S. Television network, was an "honest man" and that he had "no thought of rigging" at that time "as 'rigging' is used today."

Mr. Cowan has denied that any controls were used on "The $64,000 Question" at its inception. He left it about seven weeks after it went on the air.

Under questioning by Robert W. Lishman, chief counsel to the subcommittee, Martin Revson said he had never known that the New York District Attorney wanted to question him until recently or that he was wanted for an appearance before the New York grand jury that investigated the quiz shows for nine months.

"I was away in Hawaii," he said.

"Did you think it was your duty to go down and enlighten him?" he was asked.

"No, sir," the witness replied.

Martin Revson said he left Revlon in April, 1958. The TV quiz shows, he said, had helped Revlon to increase its sales of $33,604,000 in 1954 to $110,363,000 in 1958. The 1958 figures included $15,000,000 in shoe polish.

### Denies Knowledge

He answered "absolutely not!" to a question whether he knew of any controls used on the two quiz shows.

"If we had," he said, "we would have dropped the shows immediately."

He also said he was "shocked and surprised" to learn that Mr. Koplin had anything to do with the questions asked on the shows. He thought, he said, that they were made up by Dr. Bergen Evans, Professor of English at Northwestern University, whom he said he did not know.

The show producers, he asserted, had denied on three occasions that the shows were controlled by asking questions of contestants within their area of knowledge or by other means.

Once, he said, he complained that another quiz show, "The Big Surprise," carried by N.B.C., was a direct copy of "The $64,000 Question" and that he had heard that contestants on "The Big Surprise" had received answers. That show also was owned by Entertainment Productions, headed by Harry Fleischman.

The producers told him, he said, "that anything that happened on 'Big Surprise' couldn't happen on the $64,000 show."

**Teddy Nadler Discussed**

A memorandum on one of the weekly meetings, dated Jan. 31, 1957, and put into the record, read: "There was a discussion of the possibility of Teddy Nadler being champion throughout the proceedings."

Martin Revson said that he did not see anything wrong with that and added that the discussions at the weekly meeting ranged over all the problems of the shows, from ratings to the personalities of contestants.

"We never discussed how long a contestant would stay on the show," he asserted. "I want to make that clear!"

At this point, Mr. Bennett asked him, "If Mr. Abrams contradicted your testimony, would you be surprised?"

"He would tell the truth as he saw it under oath," Mr. Revson replied.

Mr. Bennett then began to tick off, point by point, Mr. Abrams' deposition, pausing occasionally to ask "Is that true?"

Looking directly at Mr. Bennett, the witness shook his head after each point and repeatedly said, "Not true."

The Abrams testimony said that at the weekly meetings, "if a contestant was interesting, it was generally the concensus of opinion that he should continue on the show."

"If he was dull," it added, "we would suggest to the producer that it would be desirable that the contestant not continue in the future.

"We understood that the technique used for controlling the destiny of a contestant was to employ questions ranging from 'tough' to 'easy' based on the producers' knowledge of the expertness of the contestant in certain areas within his chosen category as determined in their screening operation."

**Evans' Status Questioned**

Representative Peter L. Mack of Illinois also made the suggestion that Northwestern University in his own state should consider the role of Dr. Evans. It

was an obvious allusion to the dropping of Charles Van Doren as an English professor by Columbia University, after the big-money winner of the show "Twenty-one" testified he had been fed questions and answers throughout his fourteen weeks on that N.B.C. show.

Mr. Revson asserted "absolutely, it was" possible for Dr. Evans to have been connected with the show and not know about any fixing.

Charles Revson also denied ever expressing at the weekly meetings any hope that certain contestants would ever win or lose. He said he seldom attended the meetings and left that part of Revlon operations to his brother.

He said the later departure of Martin from the company was "a personal matter" and "if you allow me to keep it out, I would appreciate it." He made the request after being asked whether he and his brother had had a "falling out." He described the situation with his brother as an "understanding."

Asked why he had not acted more vigorously when the reports of TV riggings began to circulate in 1957 and 1958, he said, "If I had had a report I could hang my hat on, I would have done something."

**Revson Questioned**

He told of being "fed up" with quiz shows last year and of making arrangements to get out of both 64,000 programs.

In November, 1958, he said, the contract with Entertainment Productions was terminated. He said the organization was paid $255,000, of which $90,000 was paid by Revlon, $90,000 by Lorillard, and $75,000 by CBS.

Representative Walter Rogers, Democrat of Texas, asked Charles Revson a few moments before he left the stand whether he considered Revlon among the millions of Americans who were "victims of the same fraud."

"Yes, sir," Mr. Revson responded.

"Then, don't you think you ought to return the money you got from increased sales of your

**Revision Questioned**

"I wouldn't know how to answer that," Mr. Revson said.

"I wonder how you intended to right the wrong done to the American people," Mr. Rogers pressed.

"We have never given any thought to that," Mr. Revson said.

"You're not even thinking of planning to give the money back," Mr. Rogers went on.

Mr. Revson said, "there's no

basis for it," and added, "I don't follow you."

"I don't follow you either," Mr. Rogers replied.

In tonight's session, Max Hess, owner of the Hess Brothers Department Store of Allentown, testified that he had made many payments to get advertising "plugs" on TV shows and mention by newspaper columnists.

He said he had made so many payments he couldn't recall them all, but recalled that he had made such payments for "plugs" on the Kate Smith TV show and another program featuring Dunninger, the "mindreader."

He said he also had paid $1,000 each to Bob Considine and Jack O'Brian, Hearst newspaper columnists. Asked what these payments were for, Mr. Hess replied that they had "come up to the store and made a visit; it was goodwill."

Mr. Lishman, the subcommittee chief counsel, asked if he would characterize the "plug" payments as "commercial bribery." Mr. Hess said: "No. This is a business. Certain people in New York do nothing but 'plug' work."

Mr. Hess made no mention of any plugs by Mr. Considine or Mr. O'Brian in their newspaper columns.

David Gottlieb of Allentown, a former employe of the store, testified that he had made the $10,000 payment to get a store employe on "The $64,000 question" to Elroy Schwartz of Cowan Enterprises, Inc., which owned the show at that time.

Cowan Enterprises, headed by Louis G. Cowan, now vice president of C.B.S. Television, sold out his quiz-show interests when he moved to the network, and it became Entertainment Productions, Inc.

Mr. Gottlieb said that he had at first offered Mr. Schwartz a smaller amount to get Kenneth Hoffer on the show. He said he believed it was $1,000 or $2,000. But Mr. Schwartz complained, he said, that the payment was not large enough for "services requested."

He gave Mr. Schwartz $5,000 in cash at Lindy's Restaurant in New York on Aug. 9, 1955, he testified. Mr. Hoffer went on the program the same day. Two or three days later, he related, he handed over $5,000 more in "an envelope." This also took place in New York, he said.

**Considine Issues Statement**

Mr. Considine, who writes for the Hearst Headline Service,

said last night: "I've appeared in many places in my life. This is just another appearance. I've made hundreds of personal appearances."

"I mentioned Hess' store in one of my columns in what I considered a newsworthy way, just as I've mentioned Saks' Fifth Avenue and Gimbels and other newsworthy stores or organizations that I've heard of. On that particular occasion when I was in Allentown, I mentioned what an attractive arrangement the city had in placing flowers around lampposts.

"I mentioned that Hess' store had an interesting display of exotic foods like that in the S. S. Pierce store in Boston. I also called on the local paper carrying my column. I'm happy to mention any item of interest that is newsworthy. It had nothing to do with plugs."

Jack O'Brian, television columnist of The New York Journal-American, said last night:

"About four or five years ago I appeared on a television program sponsored by Mr. Hess on a Philadelphia station. There were other columnists on the show and I understand we were all paid the same amount—$1,000. We discussed TV personalities, such as Eddie Fisher, who is a Philadelphia boy.

"I also appeared at the store and was introduced to a number of people there, apparently to promote the show.

"If Mr. Hess tried to imply he paid $1,000 for plugs in my column, I never mentioned him in my column until I exposed the $10,000 pay-off this man made to get someone on 'The $64,000 Question.'

"There was nothing secret in my appearance. I was paid for my appearance, as I've been on several other TV shows."

**Bank Explains Role**

A spokesman for the Chase Manhattan Bank said last night that the producers of "The $64,000 Challenge" had rented a safe deposit box from the bank. During the run of the show, he said, the questions were kept in the box for the week preceding the Sunday night television presentation.

Because of the publicity value, the spokesman continued, the bank permitted one of its officers to appear on the program while the questions were being handed over to the master of ceremonies.

He said that the bank "was amazed as everyone else" on hearing the charges that the show was rigged.

# Reaction to the Van Doren Reaction

**The willingness of many Americans to condone a professor's lapse from truth, another professor says, reveals not compassion but our society's moral obtuseness.**

### By HANS J. MORGENTHAU

THE facts of the Charles Van Doren case are spread on the record. More important than these facts is the nation's reaction to them. That reaction is reason for the gravest concern and deserves the most careful analysis.

The Van Doren case is a great event in the history of America in a dual sense. It brings to the fore certain qualities of American society, known before but perhaps never disclosed with such poignancy, and it poses a moral issue that goes to the very heart of American society. In what America says about Van Doren, the moral fiber of America itself stands revealed. By judging Van Doren, America bears judgment upon itself.

This is not a case of political or commercial corruption, such as the Tweed, Teapot Dome or Insull scandals. Pecuniary corruption in the political and commercial spheres must be expected. For since the ultimate value of these fields is power, and wealth is a source of power, the possibility of pecuniary corruption is built into these spheres, however great or small the incidence of actual corruption may be in a particular period of history. Many politicians and businees men are uncorrupted, and some are uncorruptible, but they are all, by the very nature of their occupations, on familiar terms with corruption, encountering it even if they do not touch it.

Public reaction to political and commercial corruption is as predictable as the incidence of corruption itself. The familiarity of the fact evokes complacency, especially since many an onlooker preserves his virtue only for lack of opportunity to sin. The public rises in indignation only when the magnitude of the outrage exceeds the customary, when corruptive practices run counter to the political and commercial mores—which are indifferent to some offenses, such as implicit bribery, but condemn others, such as open blackmail—or when a prominent member of the other party or of the competition has been caught.

The moral issue that political and commercial corruption raises is but the general issue of human fallibility. The best we can hope and strive for is

---

**HANS J. MORGENTHAU** has taught at several universities. He is currently on leave as professor of political science at Chicago to serve as a member of the Johns Hopkins Center of Foreign Policy Research, in Washington.

to restrict its manifestations and mitigate its evil.

THE Van Doren case poses a different, more profound issue. It arose in a sphere whose ultimate value is neither power nor wealth but truth. The professor is a man who has devoted his life to "profess," and what he is pledged to profess is the truth as he sees it. Mendacity in a professor is a moral fault which denies the very core of the professor's calling. A mendacious professor is not like a politician who subordinates the public good to private gain, nor like a business man who cheats. Rather, he is like the physician who, pledged to heal, maims and kills. He is not so much the corrupter of the code by which he is supposed to live as its destroyer.

It is in view of the nature of the deed that the reaction of American society must be judged. The issue must be met head-on. There is no room for a Pontius Pilate washing his hands in skeptical abstention.

That is why the reactions of a considerable segment of the public cause the greatest concern. Of the nine members of the House of Representatives who heard the testimony, five addressed Van Doren in laudatory terms, "commending" and "complimenting" him and expressing their "appreciation."

Two Congressmen expressed the hope that he would not be dismissed from his positions at Columbia University and the National Broadcasting Company, and the chairman of the committee delivered a peroration predicting "a great future" for him. Only one member of the committee openly disagreed with the commendation of his colleagues. But even he did not convey awareness of the real issue, the scholar's special commitment to the truth.

Nor did the comments of most of Van Doren's students, as reported by the press. One expressed "faith in him as a man" and called him "a fine gentleman"; another thought that "what he did was not wrong"; a third called the acceptance of his resignation "very unfair." A petition bearing the signatures of 650 students demanded that he be rehired. None of the students whose reactions were recorded showed the slightest inkling of the moral issue raised by the case. Nor did many editorials and letters to newspapers.

HOW is this perversion of moral judgment, often praising what deserves to be condemned, and at best remaining indifferent to the real issue, to be explained? The explanation of Con-

gressional reaction is simple. The five members of Congress who approved Van Doren applied the general standards of political behavior to the academic sphere. They saw the Van Doren case as though it were just another instance of political corruption to be dealt with tolerantly, understandingly, even approvingly once the culprit had come clean and returned to the fold of fairly honest politicians.

However, the complacency of the politicians points to a deeper issue, a moral dilemma woven, as it were, into the very fabric of our American democracy.

This is the dilemma between objective standards of conduct and majority rule, between compliance in thought and deed with standards which are true regardless of time and place, and accommodation to the standards prevailing in a particular society in a particular time and place.

America was founded upon the recognition of certain self-evident truths which men do not create but find in the nature of things. Yet American society—and, more particularly, American democracy—has lived increasingly by conforming to whatever values appeared to be accepted by the élite or the majority of the moment. Mr. Justice Holmes' famous dictum, "* * * I have no practical criterion [with regard to laws] except what the crowd wants," is the classic expression of that resolution. It is also expressed in one Congressman's hope that Columbia University would not act "prematurely," but would wait to judge public reaction to Van Doren's statement.

THE objective standards which constitute the moral backbone of a civilized society are here dissolved. What a man ought or ought not to do becomes determined not by objective laws immutable as the stars, but by the results of the latest public opinion poll. A man who gets into trouble because he is temporarily out of step with public opinion needs only to slow down or hurry up, as the case may be, in order to get back into line, and all will be right again with him and the world. Moral judgment becomes thus the matter of a daily plebiscite, and what is morally good be-

OPEN YE THE GATES
THAT THE RIGHTEOUS NATION WHICH KEEPETH THE TRUTH
MAY ENTER IN

Inscription on a gate at Harvard.

comes identical with what the crowd wants and tolerates.

The moral illiteracy of the students is less easily explained. Students, so one would like to think, are apprentices in that noble endeavor of discovering and professing the truth, not yet compelled by the demands of society to compromise their convictions; they must look at a mendacious professor as a student of the priesthood looks at a priest who blasphemes God. How is it possible for a young man of presumably superior intelligence and breeding, predestined to be particularly sensitive to the moral issue of truth, to be so utterly insensitive to it?

These youths were born with a moral sense as they were born with a sense of sight. Who blinded them to the moral standards by which they —at least as students—are supposed to live?

The answer must be sought in the same sphere that produced Van Doren himself: the academic world. There is pro-found meaning in the solidarity between Van Doren and his students. While public opinion has pinned responsibility on television, advertising, business or teachers' low salaries, nobody seems to have pointed to the academic system which taught both teacher and students.

A system of higher education, dedicated to the discovery and transmission of the truth, is not a thing apart from the society which has created, maintains and uses it. The academic world partakes of the values prevailing in society and is exposed to social pressures to conform to them. Its very concept of what truth is bears the marks of the relativism dominant in American society, and, by teaching that kind of truth, it strengthens its dominance over the American mind.

Yet even commitment to this kind of truth is bound to come into conflict with the values and demands of society. The stronger the trend toward conformity within society and the stronger the commitment of the scholar to values such as wealth and power, the stronger will be his temptation to sacrifice his moral commitment to truth for social advantage. The tension between these contradictory commitments typically results in a compromise.

**O**N the one hand, it keeps the scholar's commitment to the truth within socially acceptable bounds—he exempts, for instance the taboos of society from investigation. On the other hand, it restrains social ambitions from seriously interfering with the scholar's search for a truth cautiously defined. In the measure that truth is thus limited, the search for it is deflected from its proper goal and thereby corrupted.

At the extreme ends of the academic spectrum, one finds two small groups. One is subversive of the truth by telling society what it wants to hear. The other is subversive of society by telling it what it does not want to hear.

Contemporary America offers enormous temptations to join the first group—that is, not only to corrupt the truth but to betray it. In the process, the academic world tends to transform itself into a duplicate of the business and political worlds. To the temptations of wealth and power held out by government, business and foundations, the scholar has nothing to oppose but his honor committed to a truth which for him, as for society, is but a doubtful thing. The step from corruption to betrayal is big in moral terms but small in execution.

**W**HAT difference is there between receiving $129,000 under false pretenses from government, business or a foundation, which has become almost standard operating procedure, and receiving the same amount under false pretenses from a television sponsor? The difference lies not in moral relevance but in the technique. Van Doren and his students were formed by a world which condones the betrayal of truth for the sake of wealth and power, provided the academic amenities are preserved.

In the world of Van Doren American society beholds its own world, the world of business and politics, of wealth and power. It cannot condemn him without condemning itself, and since it is unwilling to do the latter it cannot bring itself to do the former. Instead, it tends to absolve him by confusing the virtues of compassion and charity for the actor with the vice of condoning the act. Yet. by refusing to condemn Van Doren, it cannot but condemn itself. For it convicts itself of a moral obtuseness which signifies the beginning of the end of civilized society.

# SOME GOOD IS SEEN IN QUIZ SCANDALS

## State Education Head Urges Moral Re-examination— Camp Plan Is Backed

### By LEONARD BUDER
Special to The New York Times.

ROCHESTER, N. Y., Nov. 23 The State Education Commissioner declared tonight that the recent television scandals had underscored the need for schools to give special attention to the development of moral and spiritual values.

The Commissioner, Dr. James E. Allen Jr., said the quiz-show scandals had actually done some good by forcing the country to re-examine its moral values.

Dr. Allen expressed "shock and sorrow" that a teacher had been involved in the scandals and dismay over the fact that some segments of the public had not seemed concerned over the disclosures.

"It is reasonable to wonder as to which is more scandalous --the scandals themselves or the indifference, apathy, tolerance and amusement with which the revelations have been received by some," he said.

The Commissioner's mention of a teacher was a reference to Charles Van Doren, who was on the Columbia University faculty at the time he appeared on the rigged television quiz "Twenty-one." carried by the National Broadcasting Company. Mr. Van Doren has since been dismissed by the university.

Dr. Allen addressed the annual dinner at the Hotel Manger of the State Teachers Association. which is holding its House of Delegates meeting here.

## 'HATE HIS SIN'

The fact that what Charles Van Doren did is condoned by so many is a serious judgment upon the morals of our country. And the wrong becomes magnified by the fact that it was committed by a man whose calling it is to "profess" the truth.

However, there is an important aspect to this question that Mr. Morgenthau did not go into. Many of the persons who spoke up on behalf of Mr. Van Doren were speaking up on behalf of the man and not the wrong. They believed that he had come to grips with the seriousness of his offense and that in the future he would act in a moral way. As a Christian minister I can most easily put this in theological language. Many of those who spoke up for Mr. Van Doren love him as a sinner, but hate his sin. They believe that he has repented, confessed his sin and has become a new person. Thus he deserves our forgiveness.

REV. J. LAWRENCE AINSWORTH.
Jeffersonville, N. Y.

## 'DOUBLE STANDARD'

Professor Morgenthau says the "ultimate value" of politics is power; wealth is a source of power, therefore the possibility of pecuniary corruption is built into politics. (What is meant by ultimate value is never explained. Would Professor Morgenthau judge Hitler and Roosevelt merely by the amount of power they possessed or by the use they made of it?) However, says he, in the teaching profession the ultimate value is neither power nor wealth but truth.

Professor Morgenthau's double standard leads to strange results. It follows from his theory that an insignificant university instructor must behave more circumspectly than a statesman whose conduct may affect nations.

Surely this is a distorted perspective. Is it not about time that we applied to politicians the same standards of pecuniary and intellectual honesty that we apply to doctors, clergymen and even Professor Morgenthau's fellow teachers? JAMES S. OTTENBERG.
New York.

Growth of Opinion—"Before very long mass psychology will be recognized as the most important of all sciences from the standpoint of human welfare."

# The Science To Save Us From Science

## If we are to attain a stable society we must understand people's minds, says a philosopher.

### By BERTRAND RUSSELL

LONDON.

SINCE the beginning of the seventeenth century scientific discovery and invention have advanced at a continually increasing rate. This fact has made the last three hundred and fifty years profoundly different from all previous ages. The gulf separating man from his past has widened from generation to generation, and finally from decade to decade. A reflective person, meditating on the extinction of trilobites, dinosaurs and mammoths, is driven to ask himself some very disquieting questions. Can our species endure so rapid a change? Can the habits which insured survival

BERTRAND RUSSELL, philosopher, has written a score of books on subjects ranging from "The ABC of Atoms" (1923) to "A History of Western Philosophy" (1945). He is associated with Trinity College, Cambridge.

in a comparatively stable past still suffice amid the kaleidoscopic scenery of our time? And, if not, will it be possible to change ancient patterns of behavior as quickly as the inventors change our material environment? No one knows the answer, but it is possible to survey probabilities, and to form some hypotheses as to the alternative directions that human development may take.

The first question is: Will scientific advance continue to grow more and more rapid, or will it reach a maximum speed and then begin to slow down?

The discovery of scientific method required genius, but its utilization requires only talent. An intelligent young scientist, if he gets a job giving access to a good laboratory, can be pretty certain of finding out something of interest, and may stumble upon some new fact of immense importance. Science, which was still a rebellious

force in the early seventeenth century, is now integrated with the life of the community by the support of governments and universities. And as its importance becomes more evident, the number of people employed in scientific research continually increases. It would seem to follow that, so long as social and economic conditions do not become adverse, we may expect the rate of scientific advance to be maintained, and even increased, until some new limiting factor intervenes.

It might be suggested that, in time, the amount of knowledge needed before a new discovery could be made would become so great as to absorb all the best years of a scientist's life, so that by the time he reached the frontier of knowledge he would be senile. I suppose this may happen some day, but that day is certainly very distant. In the first place, methods of teaching improve. Plato thought that students in his academy would have to spend ten years learning what was then known of mathematics; nowadays any mathematically minded schoolboy learns much more mathematics in a year.

In the second place, with increasing specialization, it is possible to reach the frontier of knowledge along a narrow path, involving much less labor than a broad highway. In the third place, the frontier is not a circle but an irregular contour, in some places not far from the center. Mendel's epoch-making discovery required little previous knowledge; what it needed was a life of elegant leisure spent in a garden. Radio-activity was discovered by the fact that some specimens of pitchblende were unexpectedly found to have photographed themselves in the dark. I do not think, therefore, that purely intellectual reasons will slow up scientific advances for a very long time to come.

There is another reason for expecting scientific advance to continue, and that is that it increasingly attracts the best brains. Leonardo da Vinci was equally pre-eminent in art and science, but it was from art that he derived his greatest fame. A man of similar endowments living at the present day would almost certainly hold some post which would require his giving all his time to science; if his politics were orthodox, he would probably be engaged in devising the hydrogen bomb, which our age would consider more useful than his pictures. The artist, alas, has not the status that he once had. Renaissance princes might compete for Michelangelo; modern states compete for nuclear physicists.

There are considerations of quite a different sort which might lead to an expectation of scientific retrogression. It may be held that science itself generates explosive forces which will, sooner or later, make it impossible to preserve the kind of society in which science can flourish. This is a large and different

question, to which no confident answer can be given. It is a very important question, which deserves to be examined. Let us therefore see what is to be said about it.

Industrialism, which is in the main a product of science, has provided a certain way of life and a certain outlook on the world. In America and Britain, the oldest industrial countries, this outlook and this way of life have come gradually, and the population has been able to adjust itself to them without any violent breach of continuity. These countries, accordingly, did not develop dangerous psychological stresses. Those who preferred the old ways could remain on the land, while the

more adventurous could migrate to the new centers of industry. There they found pioneers who were compatriots, who shared in the main the general outlook of their neighbors. The only protests came from men like Carlyle and Ruskin, whom everybody at once praised and disregarded.

It was a very different matter when industrialism and science, as well-developed systems, burst violently upon countries hitherto ignorant of both, especially since they came as something foreign, demanding imitation of enemies and disruption of ancient national habits. In varying degrees this shock has been endured by Germany, Russia, Japan, India and the natives of Africa. Everywhere it has caused and is causing upheavals of one sort or another, of which as yet no one can foresee the end.

The earliest important result of the impact of industrialism on Germans was the Communist Manifesto. We think of this now as the Bible of one of the two powerful groups into which the world is divided, but it is worth while to think back to its origin in 1848. It then shows itself as an expression of admiring horror by two young university students from a pleasant and peaceful cathedral city, brought roughly and without intellectual preparation into the hurly-burly of Manchester competition.

Germany, before Bismarck had "educated" it, was a deeply religious country, with a quiet, exceptional sense of public duty. Competition, which the British regarded as essential to efficiency, and which Darwin elevated to an almost cosmic dignity, shocked the Germans, to whom service to the state seemed the obviously right moral ideal. It was therefore natural that they should fit industrialism into a framework of nationalism or socialism. The Nazis combined both. The somewhat insane and frantic character of German industrialism and the policies it inspired is due to its foreign origin and its sudden advent.

Marx's doctrine was suited to countries where industrialism was new. The German Social Democrats abandoned his dogmas when their country became industrially adult. But by that time Russia was where Germany had been in 1848, and it was natural that Marxism should find a new

home. Stalin, with great skill, has combined the new revolutionary creed with the traditional belief in "Holy Russia" and the "Little Father." This is as yet the most notable example of the arrival of science in an environment that is not ripe for it. China bids fair to follow suit.

Japan, like Germany, combined modern technique with worship of the state. Educated Japanese abandoned as much of their ancient way of life as was necessary in order to secure industrial and military efficiency. Sudden change produced collective hysteria, leading to insane visions of world power unrestrained by traditional pieties.

These various forms of madness — communism, nazism, Japanese imperialism — are the natural result of the impact of science on nations with a strong pre-scientific culture. The effects in Asia are still at an early stage. The effects upon the native races of Africa have hardly begun. It is therefore unlikely that the world will recover sanity in the near future.

The future of science—nay more, the future of mankind—depends upon whether it will be possible to restrain these various collective hysterias until the populations concerned have had time to adjust themselves to the new scientific environment. If such adjustment proves impossible, civilized society will disappear, and science will be only a dim memory. In the Dark Ages science was not distinguished from sorcery, and it is not impossible that a new Dark Ages may revive this point of view.

The danger is not remote; it threatens within the next few years. But I am not now concerned with such immediate issues. I am concerned with the wider question: Can a society based, as ours is, on science and scientific technique, have the sort of stability that many societies had in the past, or is it bound to develop explosive forces that will destroy it? This question takes us beyond the sphere of science into that of ethics and moral codes and the imaginative understanding of mass psychology. This last is a matter which political theorists have quite unduly neglected.

Let us begin with moral codes. I will illustrate the problem by a somewhat trivial illustration. There are those who think it wicked to smoke

tobacco, but they are mostly people untouched by science. Those whose outlook has been strongly influenced by science usually take the view that smoking is neither a vice nor a virtue. But when I visited a Nobel works, where rivers of nitro-glycerine flowed like water, I had to leave all matches at the entrance, and it was obvious that to smoke inside the works would be an act of appalling wickedness.

This instance illustrates two points: first, that a scientific outlook tends to make some parts of traditional moral codes appear superstitious and irrational; second, that by creating a new environment science creates new duties, which may happen to coincide with those that have been discarded. A world containing hydrogen bombs is like one containing rivers of nitro-glycerine; actions elsewhere harmless may become dangerous in the highest degree. We need therefore, in a scientific world, a somewhat different moral code from the one inherited from the past. But to give to a new moral code sufficient compulsive force to restrain actions formerly considered harmless is not easy, and cannot possibly be achieved in a day.

As regards ethics, what is important is to realize the new dangers and to consider what ethical outlook will do most to diminish them. The most important new facts are that the world is more unified than it used to be, and that communities at war with each other have more power of inflicting mutual disaster than at any former time. The question of power has a new importance. Science has enormously increased human power, but has not increased it without limit. The increase of power brings an increase of responsibility; it brings also a danger of arrogant self-assertion, which can only be averted by continuing to remember that man is not omnipotent.

The most influential sciences, hitherto, have been physics and chemistry; biology is just beginning to rival them. But before very long psychology, and especially mass psychology, will be recognized as the most important of all sciences from the standpoint of human welfare. It is obvious that populations have dominant moods, which change from time to time according to their circumstances. Each mood has a corresponding ethic. Nelson inculcated these ethical principles on midshipmen: to tell the truth, to shoot straight, and to hate a Frenchman as you would the devil. This last was chiefly because the English were angry with France for intervening on the side of America. Shakespeare's Henry V says:

*If it be a sin to covet honor,*
*I am the most offending*
*soul alive.*

THIS is the ethical sentiment that goes with aggressive imperialism: "honor" is proportional to the number of harmless people you slaughter. A great many sins may be excused under the name of "patriotism." On the other hand complete powerlessness suggests humility and submission as the greatest virtues; hence the vogue of stoicism in the Roman Empire and of Methodism among the English poor in the early nineteenth century. When, however, there is a chance of successful revolt, fierce vindictive justice suddenly becomes the dominant ethical principle.

In the past, the only recognized way of inculcating moral precepts has been by preaching. But this method has very definite limitations: it is notorious that, on the average, sons of clergy are not morally superior to other people. When science has mastered this field, quite different methods will be adopted. It will be known what circumstances generate what moods, and what moods incline men to what ethical systems. Governments will then decide what sort of morality their subjects are to have and their subjects will adopt what the Government favors, but will do so under the impression that they are exercising free will. This may sound unduly cynical, but that is only because we are not yet accustomed to applying science to the human mind. Science has powers for evil, not only physically, but mentally: the hydrogen bomb can kill the body, and government propaganda (as in Russia) can kill the mind.

In view of the terrifying power that science is conferring on governments, it is necessary that those who control governments should have enlightened and intelligent ideals, since otherwise they can lead mankind to disaster.

I CALL an ideal "intelligent" when it is possible to approximate to it by pursuing it. This is by no means sufficient as an ethical criterion, but it is a test by which many aims can be condemned. It cannot be supposed that Hitler desired the fate which he brought upon his country and himself, and yet it was pretty certain that this would be the result of his arrogance. Therefore the ideal of "Deutschland ueber Alles" can be condemned as unintelligent. (I do not mean to suggest that this is its only defect.) Spain, France, Germany and Russia have successively sought world dominion: three of them have endured defeat in consequence, but their fate has not inspired wisdom.

Whether science—and indeed civilization in general—can long survive depends upon psychology, that is to say, it depends upon what human beings desire. The human beings concerned are rulers in totalitarian countries, and the mass of men and women in democracies. Political passions determine political conduct much more directly than is often supposed. If men desire victory more than cooperation, they will think victory possible.

BUT if hatred so dominates them that they are more anxious to see their enemies killed than to keep their own children alive, they will discover all kinds of "noble" reasons in favor of war. If they resent inferiority or wish to preserve superiority, they will have the sentiments that promote the class war. If they are bored beyond a point, they will welcome excitement even of a painful kind.

Such sentiments, when widespread, determine the policies and decisions of nations. Science can, if rulers so desire, create sentiments which will avert disaster and facilitate cooperation. At present there are powerful rulers who have no such wish. But the possibility exists, and science can be just as potent for good as for evil. It is not science, however, which will determine how science is used.

Science, by itself, cannot supply us with an ethic. It can show us how to achieve a given end, and it may show us that some ends cannot be achieved. But among ends that can be achieved our choice must be decided by other than purely scientific considerations. If a man were to say, "I hate the human race, and I think it would be a good thing if it were exterminated," we could say, "Well, my dear sir, let us begin the process with you." But this is hardly argument, and no amount of science could prove such a man mistaken.

BUT all who are not lunatics are agreed about certain things: That it is better to be alive than dead, better to be adequately fed than starved, better to be free than a slave. Many people desire those things only for themselves and their friends; they are quite content that their enemies should suffer. These people can be refuted by science: Mankind has become so much one family that we cannot insure our own prosperity except by insuring that of everyone else. If you wish to be happy yourself, you must resign yourself to seeing others also happy.

Whether science can continue, and whether, while it continues, it can do more good than harm, depends upon the capacity of mankind to learn this simple lesson. Perhaps it is necessary that all should learn it, but it must be learned by all who have great power, and among those some still have a long way to go.

March 19, 1950

## MUSEUMS DEMAND FREEDOM FOR ARTS

Manifesto on Modern Work Cites Its Broad Influence, Defines Exhibitor's Role

### DIVERSITY TERMED VITAL

Two Institutions Here, One in Boston Join in Rejecting 'Narrow Nationalism'

Three museums whose interests center on modern art issued yesterday a joint statement affirming their belief in the necessity of expression in the arts, and defining their function as objective surveyors presenting an impartial review of the contemporary scene.

The document was drawn up by the Museum of Modern Art and the Whitney Museum of American Art in New York, which have formed a program of coordinated activity for the future, and the Institute of Contemporary Art in Boston. In the past few years the Boston Institute has been collaborating with the Modern Museum in exchange exhibitions.

The signers were Rene D'Harnoncourt, director; Alfred H. Barr Jr., director of museum collections, and Andrew C. Ritchie, director of painting and sculpture, all of the Modern Museum; Hermon More, director, and Lloyd Goodrich, associate director, of the Whitney; and James S. Plaut, director, and Frederick S. Wight, director of education of the Boston institute.

#### MUSEUMS' MANIFESTO

The statement follows:

This statement is made in the hope that it may help to clarify current controversial issues about modern art, which are confusing to the public and harmful to the artist. Its object is not to bar honest differences of opinion, but to state certain broad principles on which we are agreed.

The field of contemporary art is immensely wide and varied, with many diverse viewpoints and styles. We believe that this diversity is a sign of vitality and of the freedom of expression inherent in a democratic society. We oppose any attempt to make art or opinion about art conform to a single point of view.

We affirm our belief in the continuing validity of what is generally known as modern art, the multiform movement which was in progress during the opening years of the twentieth century and which has produced the most original and significant art of our period. We believe that the modern movement was a vital force not only in its pioneer phases, but that its broad, everchanging tradition of courageous exploration and creative achievement is a force today, as is proved by the continuing capacity of the younger generation of artists to embody new ideas in new forms.

At the same time we believe in the validity of conservative and retrospective tendencies when they make creative use of traditional values. We do not assume that modernity in itself is any guarantee of quality or importance.

We believe that a primary duty of a museum concerned with contemporary art is to be receptive to new tendencies and talents. We recognize the historic fact that the new in art, as in all other creative activities, is appreciated at first by a relatively small proportion of the public; almost all the art of the past hundred and fifty years now generally accepted as good was originally misunderstood, neglected or ridiculed not only by the public but by many artists, critics and museum officials.

### Merit Versus Acceptance

We place in evidence the careers of Blake, Turner, Constable, Delacroix, Corot, Millet, Courbet, Manet, Whistler, Monet, Cézanne, Renoir, Rodin, Gauguin, van Gogh, Eakins, Ryder, not to mention the leaders of the twentieth century. We also recognize that some artists of unquestionable merit never become popular, although their work may eventually have a widespread influence. We therefore believe that it is a museum's duty to present the art that it considers good, even if it is not yet generally accepted. By so doing, we believe, the museum best fulfills its long-range responsibility to the public.

We believe that the so-called "unintelligibility" of some modern art is an inevitable result of its exploration of new frontiers. Like the scientist's innovations, the procedures of the artist are often not readily understood and make him an easy target for reactionary attack. We do not believe that many artists deliberately aim to be unintelligible, or have voluntarily withdrawn from the public. On the contrary, we believe that most artists today desire communication with a receptive audience.

The gap between artist and public, in our opinion, has been greatly exaggerated; actually the public interest in progressive art, as proved by attendance at exhibitions and by attention in the popular press, is larger than at any previous time in history.

We believe in the humanistic value of modern art even though it may not adhere to academic humanism with its insistence on the human figure as the central element of art. Art which explores newly discovered levels of consciousness, new concepts of science and new technological methods is contributing to humanism in the deepest sense,

by helping humanity to come to terms with the modern world, not by retreating from it but by facing and mastering it.

We recognize the humanistic value of abstract art, as an expression of thought and emotion and the basic human aspirations toward freedom and order. In these ways modern art contributes to the dignity of man.

Contrary to those who attack the advanced artist as anti-social, we believe in his spiritual and social role. We honor the man who is prepared to sacrifice popularity and economic security to be true to his personal vision. We believe that his unworldly pursuit of perfection has a moral and therefore a social value. But we do not believe that unreasonable demands should be made on him. Though his spiritual energy may be religious in the broadest sense, he should not be asked to be priest or saint. Though his art may symbolize discipline or liberty, he cannot be asked to save civilization.

### Reject Narrow Nationalism

Believing strongly in the quality and vitality of American art, we oppose its definition in narrow nationalistic terms. We hold that American art which is international in character is as valid as art obviously American in subject-matter. We deplore the revival of the tendency to identify American art exclusively with popular realism, regional subject and nationalistic sentiment.

We also reject the assumption that art which is esthetically an innovation must somehow be socially or politically subversive, and therefore un-American. We deplore the reckless and ignorant use of political or moral terms in attacking modern art.

We recall that the Nazis suppressed modern art, branding it "degenerate," "bolshevistic," "international" and "un-German"; and that the Soviets suppressed modern art as "formalistic," "bourgeois," "subjective," "nihilistic" and "un-Russian"; and that Nazi officials insisted and Soviet officials still insist upon a hackneyed realism saturated with nationalistic propaganda.

We believe that it is not a museum's function to try to control the course of art or to tell the artist what he shall or shall not do; or to impose its tastes dogmatically upon the public. A museum's proper function, in our opinion, is to survey what artists are doing, as objectively as possible, and to present their works to the public as impartially as is consistent with those standards of quality which the museum must try to maintain.

We acknowledge that humility is required of those who select works of art, as it is of those who create them or seek to understand them.

We believe that there is urgent need for an objective and open-minded attitude toward the art of our time, and for an affirmative faith to match the creative energy and integrity of the living artist.

# SPEAKING OF BOOKS

### By J. DONALD ADAMS

THE question recently raised here, whether there is a fundamental conflict between the values set up by science and those which we think of as nourished by the arts, is one that seems to interest many readers of this column. Some of them think that I have overstated the case for the existence of such a conflict, and I should like to give space to certain thoughtful comments which have been made. My correspondents are particularly concerned with the contention of William Macneile Dixon, which I quoted, to the effect that there is a necessary choice for us all between placing our trust in purely rational processes or in what he referred to as "the inner vision, the intimations of the soul."

"I believe it dangerous," writes Benjamin F. Holme Jr., "to say that these two forms of human endeavor (science and art) are irreconcilable. What the artist must do is no less important than what the scientist does; both activities are in the final analysis directed toward a common goal. The appearance of irreconcilability has developed largely because of our failure to integrate properly. The need of the present age is not for a further cleavage between the intellect and the spirit—a cleavage which, indeed, is responsible for most of our perplexities today—but rather for a synthesis of the two."

THERE need be, he continues, no "choice" between the spirit and the intellect. "In fact, there must be no choice. We have reached the point from which further progress is impossible without a pooling of all our faculties. It seems to me, therefore, that the responsibility of the artist is much greater than

you imply, for without him the scientist and the rest of humanity are lost. A modern artist's endeavor must be to understand, to inform and enlighten the mind of the scientist. And in order to do this he must to a certain extent become a scientist himself."

But it seems to me that such a synthesis is precisely what Professor Dixon had in mind. When he presents us with a choice he is not discrediting what has been and can be won by rational processes. As he himself says elsewhere, "No one in his senses will attempt to diminish the glory of modern science." But he is saying that these processes are not sufficient in themselves; the choice I believe he demands of us is that we shall not elect to abide by them alone. And surely there can be no question that the tendency to put complete trust in the intellect is one that has gained great strength in the modern world.

FROM George A. McCauliff comes these observations: "It is true that science ignores an area of reality more vast than that which it investigates; that the special province of art is precisely what science prefers to deny. The difficulty, however, seems to lie in the fact (1) that science unwittingly hobbles itself and art unwittingly kicks against the goad of science, and (2) that science of its own nature cannot *prove* anything more than art is intended to prove anything.

"It would seem that reality is vulnerable to a third method of attack—a method which can be welcomed both by science awakened to its limitations and by art conscious of its inadequacies. It is not fashionable in these days to write a suprarational faith which does not contradict reason. Nevertheless the fact of such a faith is undeniable—a faith indeed given but none the less rational. Until science realizes that whatever obtusely attacks faith undercuts science; until art realizes that whatever exalts art at the expense of truth poisons art at its source; until religion realizes that whatever attacks reason undermines faith, men will remain more fundamentally divided than the atom in the act of fission—fission possibly more interesting as a symbol than as a fact."

SCIENCE, remarks Mr. McCauliff, "at its best, can offer only the uncertainty of uncertainty and that art which attempts to build action on esthetics courts failure both in action and esthetics. Religion which holds knowledge in contempt, whether quantitative knowledge as discovered by science or qualitative knowledge as revealed by art, is untrue to itself. What matters everywhere and at all times is truth regardless of by whom perceived or by what methods determined.

"It is the present duty of science to acknowledge the existence of a world closed to the scientific method. It is the duty of art to probe that invisible world under the impulse of the intuitive drive. It is the heavy duty of religion fundamentally to recognize that the unity of truth first demands the end of divisions, the elimination of sects. After that perhaps a start could be made, for it is the further duty of religion properly to educate science and art for the reception of a given faith which can open up an infinite world in which present differences are presently resolved, in which creative energy can be poured out for the good of mankind and—dare it be whispered in the twentieth century!—for the glory of God. Of course, the prospects for such a transformation of values in our times are, shall we say, rather less than many."

# 'ANONYMOUS' ART

## One of the Problems That Confronts Our Extreme Abstract Painting

### By HOWARD DEVREE

THE recent emphasis on extreme abstraction — the nonobjective or nonfigurative art which has proved so controversial in the last few years—raises questions which go to the very basis of artistic expression. Anyone who has visited big group shows in the last five or ten years must have noticed that there is a great similarity in much of the work.

In a recent Whitney annual, a group which included several artists stood before two pictures that by coincidence of hanging had been placed side by side. Each had a large dark form like a blown-up calligraphic symbol against a light background and members of the group were arguing whether the names of the painters of these over-large and rather empty compositions had been accidentally interchanged.

### Anonymous or Personal

It is this anonymous aspect of some of the extreme abstraction which raises many questions and has grave implications for the future of our painting. For it has been the contention of the more avowed partisans of abstract expressionism that the opposite is true—that this work reveals a very personal reaction to our time. The advances of science, the permeation of the new psychology since the doctrines of Freud became a part of general consciousness, and the unease of the artist facing the confusions of a divided world have all been cited as factors in this new painting. The very personal subjective nature of the art has been stressed.

A whole new jargon has developed in the writing about this extreme abstraction. With the human figure and other representational elements wholly removed from the canvas, many painters have turned to color as expressive in itself. Shapes and the tensions between them, or color relations, are put forward as sufficient in themselves. Some painting has been called visual music.

A generation or two ago Vernon Lee and others were interested in relating color to sounds: scarlet or yellow was soprano, purple bass. But people react differently to color, and the fixing of such values in a pseudo-science of course proved impossible.

### Types of Abstraction

One may group certain types of expression within the non-objective field: symbols against primarily blank backgrounds; free floating color shapes; geometrical use of color forms; an all-over color organization deriving frequently from cubism; lyrical use of color frequently suggestive of landscape or marine themes; linear mazes from the "drip" or automatic approach, and so on. But within each of these groups the similarity is pronounced, the anonymity creeps in and the identity of the artist and what he has to say is lessened. There is a dehumanization effected which is at the other pole from an artist's individuality of expression. When pictures are numbered like prisoners instead of titled, anonymity can go no farther.

There are many kinds of anonymity—the anonymity of archaic Greek or Egyptian sculpture; the anonymity of a medieval craftsman by his identification with a group working on a cathedral in a common purpose; the anonymity of much near-Eastern art in which figure and scene were excluded for stylized motifs as in rugs and pottery. But this last is essentially an art of sheer decoration, dependent on color and stylization, static. This is the danger, the blind alley which, it seems to me, confronts much of the nonobjective or expressionist-abstract work of today. Color and color relations or the interplay of forms may help to establish a mood, but is that by itself enough?

There have been in the last year or two distinct signs that the artists themselves feel that much of this work is not suf-

ficiently satisfying. Perhaps the first visible evidence of this unrest came with deKooning's show entitled "Woman." The problem for many of the nonobjective painters was how to introduce figurative or landscape elements without abandoning all they had done. But ever since the de Kooning show the figure has been making tentative appearances, and efforts have been noted to increase the suggestive power of the abstract painting —to suggest, however remotely, landscape, a season, a submarine impression, the dynamics of figures in motion, the flickering effect of light in a forest and other approaches to communication in its widest sense. The burden of interpretation is still left largely to the beholder, but greater effort at conveying the sense of something more than a mood through color or shapes alone begins to be evident.

Even so stanch a champion of modern art as Herbert Read, who tends to stress education and the social background of art, has felt that "the greater part of American painting is merely a tidy doodling, devoid of sensuous harmony or elegance. . . . Such art is popular, I suggest, because it is a perfect mask—a form of communication that, like the carefully worded 'press release' issued by statesmen, tells the public precisely nothing. It is the art-form of a society directed by its neuroses toward anonymity and uniformity." (The Philosophy of Modern Art; Meridian Books.)

Harsh words and overstated, to be sure. But while talking of science, the time-space continuum and other matters, have not some of our painters forgotten the old maxim in physics that to every action there is an equal and contrary reaction? Our native romanticism was easily led on into expressionism which in various ways tied up with abstraction. Let us hope that the reaction will not carry that infusing element of romanticism back to Alma Tadema, the Greek revival, Bouguereau and other insipidities through the national tendency to swing from one extreme to another. In the courageous experiment, the laboratory work, the development of technique, the extension of the boundaries of what can be stated—all of which are clearly evident in the best of the work produced—there is too much that is valuable for the future to be lost.

March 18, 1951

February 20, 1955

# ART ALSO SERVES

## It Shares With Science the Duty of Creating a Complete Culture

### By BROOKS ATKINSON

IT'S a story as old as the country. In America art lies outside the main stream of national life. The American artist has less prestige and influence than he has in Europe and even in the Soviet Union, where an artist is as respectable as an engineer.

Let's concede at the outset that in the last half century American art has shaken off the provincialism that hung over it until about the time Mencken and Nathan started to apply their impudent bastinadoes. Especially today there is an expanding interest in and curiosity about art throughout the country. No one can watch the development of the New York stage without believing that by and large art is recognized and appreciated. O'Neill's "The Iceman Cometh," Chekhov's "Uncle Vanya" and "The Threepenny Opera" by Weill, Brecht and Blitzstein have had astonishingly long runs, supported by theatregoers who love art.

But a culture in which art flourishes only within its own bailiwick is not complete. In a new volume entitled "Tragedy" (Cornell), the late Henry Myers asserts that there are two essential ways of looking at man in relation to the universe: "one from within, the other from without." Art, looking from within, brings illumination to the individual and releases him from "his lonely island in the sea of his isolation." Science, viewing him from the outside, measures him by objective standards.

"The poet and the scientist are not rivals," Professor Myers concludes, "but equal and trustworthy partners in the task of teaching man, through insight, to see others as he sees himself, and, through objectivity, to see himself as others see him." In a sound democratic society, based on the integrity of the individual, Professor Myers regarded both points of view as imperative. For society—the mass—is composed of individuals, and no society can be wholesome if the individuals are not individually fulfilled.

### Technology

There is not much doubt that art is a poor second to science in the total life of the nation. People in general have more confidence in the objective measurements of the scientific point of view than they have in the insights, passions, aspirations and wonder of the poets. Our civilization is technological, derived from scientific research. People are manipulated as statistics. From the objective point of view man does not amount to much. He is the prisoner of his heritage, environment and physical, social and economic needs. Who is Carl Sandburg in comparison with General Motors?

Some great things have been accomplished by American techniques. The standard of living has risen sensationally. We live much better than our forebears, not only in more comfort but in better health. As consumers of everything, including education, we have compiled a series of statistics that are phenomenal. If it is true that no one goes hungry in this country, a great milestone has been reached in the history of the race. Research, management, organization, mass techniques in general have built a society that looks fabulous, it is so well equipped and efficient.

But it does not satisfy every need. We cannot build mental hospitals fast enough to look after those who have succumbed to psychic disorders. The common life that ought to be enjoyed and sustained by everyone is marred by juvenile delinquency, riots against Negro school children in the South, vilification of nonconformists, distrust and suspicion of neighbors and other forms of hysteria that derive largely from lack of human understanding. This is the area where insight is needed, and this is the area where our civilization is out of balance. We know the price of everything but we are not much concerned with its value.

### Conscience

"Life without inquiry is not worth living," Plato declared. The artist is the one who inquires from the inside—from the inside of his own mind, from the inside of the minds of the characters he creates in literature and painting. He performs research, too, and contributes conscience and feeling to total enlightenment.

Why does Willy Loman destroy his life in "Death of a Salesman"? Because he chooses ideals that are alien to his character. He blindly accepts the myths of success—leaning on external things rather than the strength of his own being. That is what Arthur Miller contributed to the public conscience. Why does Blanche DuBois go to pieces in "A Streetcar Named Desire"? Because she tries to conform to social standards that have no relationship to her experience. That is what Tennessee Williams contributed to public awareness.

Since the artist is only one man in a world populated by millions, he cannot give the cosmic answers that solve all problems. He is subject to the errors and limitations of the human species. But he works from the inside to bring men together in human understanding. Taking life out of the humdrum and the mechanical, he gives it flashes of meaning. After a lifetime devoted to painting, John Sloan could say triumphantly: "Art brings life to life." It widens horizons and relieves loneliness. Even in its most elementary forms, it is an antidote to the dullness of civil life.

In a democracy it is imperative that we understand each other from the inside, as well as the outside, for we have to make the ultimate decisions together. We have to resolve the many into the one. There is nothing more democratic than a theatre audience in which several hundred people of all kinds and conditions sit down together all evening, and lose their identities in the presence of a play they believe in. After the curtain has fallen they disperse to their hundreds of individual homes and circles. But they take away a common experience that moves out through their lives in concentric circles.

They and the people of the theatre have been practicing democracy without knowing it, and helping to found a civilization. It's as good a service as a new automobile. It's as essential as anything else produced in America.

*September 30, 1956*

# CONGRESS AND ART

## Recent Sessions Active In Cultural Matters

### By ROSS PARMENTER

COMPARED with previous Congresses, last year's Eighty-fourth did well by the arts. By passing the International Cultural Exchange and Trade Fair Participation Act it committed the Federal Government to supporting American musicians and other artists in serving as goodwill ambassadors abroad. Having won this much, Congressional advocates for Government aid to the arts are now concentrating their efforts on a little help for music and the other arts at home.

Their campaigns are moving on three levels. One is a drive merely to get the Government to admit that it should support the performing arts in America. A second is to try to get those arts some modest appropriations. The third is to free the arts of prejudicial legislation.

This last, of course, means taxation. And it is one of the repeated charges of those who deplore our official attitude to the arts that we actually tax the very arts that Governments abroad vote money to support.

The present Congress is the Eighty-fifth. In the just completed first session, cultural campaigns did not make much headway. In the matter of tax relief, though, some tangible steps were taken. On July 31 the House voted to remove the excise tax on children's phonograph records selling for 25 cents or less. And on Aug. 5 the House voted to reduce the so-called cabaret tax from 20 per cent to 10 per cent.

It might be argued that the kiddies' record tax did not cut very deeply into our cultural life. It might also be argued that dine-and-dance places do not add materially to our culture. But they do employ musicians, and the American Federation of Musicians has been fighting for two years for the repeal of what it calls "this job-destroying tax."

The Federation holds, and there are others who would agree, that anything that helps the employment of musicians ultimately helps culture. Cutting this particular tax in half, it is believed, will be helpful because, having lost out in the motion-picture houses, the vaudeville theatres and the radio stations, the majority of Amer-

244

ican musicians earn their living playing in dine-and-dance places.

House action on only these two taxes might seem a very small achievement for an eight-month session. Yet the general tone among backers of arts legislation is one of optimism rather than of discouragement.

They point out that President Eisenhower used his personal influence to establish the international exchange program, and in his 1955 State of the Union address he flatly stated that "the Federal Government should do more to give official recognition to the arts." In addition, there are more Senators and Representatives in Congress who are pressing arts bills than there ever have been.

Even a casual examination of the arts legislation in the hopper, however, is enough to show that most of it might be classed merely as "foot-in-the-door" legislation. The Government post that is being urged for the top man in the arts is a case in point.

Those who remember the Pepper-Coffee Bill in 1938 for a Federal Bureau of Fine Arts may recall that at that time many were pressing for a cabinet post for a Secretary of Fine Arts. Now the aim is for nothing so exalted. The goal of the bill that Representative Frank Thompson Jr. has introduced is the appointment of an Assistant Secretary of State for International Cultural Relations.

## Advisory Group

There is no longer any talk of a Department of Fine Arts. Perhaps experience has shown that such a thing is beyond possibility at present. What is being worked for is an advisory institution that will make recommendations on the appropriate role of the Federal Government in fostering the arts and the manner in which Federal responsibilities toward the arts can best be discharged. It has been described variously as a commission and a council.

President Eisenhower, in recommending such an institution in his 1955 State of the Union message, called for a Federal Advisory Commission. Mr. Thompson's bill favoring it also calls for a "commission." So do two other bills. But four of the bills favoring it call for a "council." There is agreement that the commission or council should be under the Department of Health, Education and Welfare.

A bill for such an advisory institution was passed in the Senate in the last Congress. This gives hope that on a second time round such a bill will

get through both houses, perhaps early next year. Some people feel cynical about the creation of a commission to make studies of matters already studied. What they say existing art bodies need are appropriations. Yet even the cynics favor the bills because the texts agree in stating this principle:

"The encouragement of the arts, while primarily a matter for private and local initiative, is an appropriate matter of concern to the United States Government."

There is a bill that does ask for an appropriation. It is the one Senator Jacob K. Javits introduced calling for a United States Arts Foundation. It asks for $2,500,000 for the foundation's first year of operation. From this money, financial assistance would be given to non-profit groups concerned with the performing arts. It would be available for them to provide instruction; also, if they were touring units, to enable them to go where they could not afford to go otherwise.

Other cultural bills have been proposed with a variety of purposes. They include provision of a permanent home for the National Collection of Fine Arts in the Patent Office Building; medals for civilians who have done distinguished work, including work in the arts, and the addition of representatives of music and the theatre to the 47-year-old Commission of the Fine Arts. The commission advises on the artistic embellishment of the District of Columbia, as well as on Federal monuments elsewhere.

## Roll of Honor

Those Congressmen who have been particularly active working for legislation to help music and other arts surely deserve a small listing in a roll of honor. Everyone agrees that Representative Thompson deserves to head the list. He's a Democrat. Other Democrats who are fostering arts legislation are Emanuel Celler, Aime J. Forand, Edith Green, Eugene J. McCarthy, Adam Clayton Powell Jr., James E. Murray and Henry S. Reuss. Active Republican Representatives are Carroll D. Kearns and Stuyvesant Wainwright.

Senator Hubert H. Humphrey of Minnesota is conceded to be the Senate leader. He's a Democrat too; as are Senators Clinton P. Anderson, Paul H. Douglas, William J. Fulbright, Thomas C. Hennings Jr. and John J. Sparkman. The Republican Senators most active for the arts are Mr. Javits, Karl E. Mundt and Alexander Wiley.

September 8, 1957

# President Names 15 Trustees For National Cultural Center

Special to The New York Times.

WASHINGTON, Jan. 29 — President Eisenhower announced today the names of fifteen trustees from the public for the National Cultural Center.

Many of them are business men. There are a few bankers, former diplomats and society leaders. There are no artists, or musicians on the list.

The announcement was accompanied by protests from Representative Frank Thompson Jr., Democrat of New Jersey, one of the authors of the law designed to create a center of the performing arts here. He charged that Sherman Adams, formerly the Assistant to the President, had forced Herbert May, Pittsburgh industrialist, off the list of trustees to put Ralph Becker, Washington lawyer, on it.

The only members of the thirty-member board not appointed are the three from the House. If a fund drive is successful, the center will be built in the Foggy Bottom area of the capital. The cost is expected to be at least $25,000,000.

Mr. Adams resigned following disclosures that he had accepted gifts from Bernard Goldfine, Boston industrialist.

The White House made no immediate reply to Representative Thompson's statement.

The trustees named were:

For two-year terms — Mr. Becker; Mrs. Jouett Shouse, vice president of the National Symphony Orchestra; Henry C. Hofheimer 2d of Norfolk, Va., building materials executive.

For four years — Philip M. Talbott, president of the Woodward & Lothrop department stores here and currently president of the United States Chamber of Commerce; Floyd D. Akers, Cadillac dealer here; John J. Emery, Cincinnati industrialist.

For six years — Winthrop W. Aldrich of New York, former United States Ambassador to Britain; Mrs. George Garrett, wife of the former Minister to Ireland; Daniel W. Bell, Washington banker and former Under Secretary of the Treasury.

For eight years — Dr. Ralph J. Bunche, Under Secretary General of the United Nations; Mrs. Norman Chandler, wife of the publisher of The Los Angeles Times and Robert W. Wood of Midland, Tex., engaged in the oil industry.

For ten years — L. Corrin Strong, former Ambassador to Norway; John Nicholas Brown of Providence, R. I., counting house executive and former assistant secretary of the Navy, and Frank H. Ricketson, Denver theatre owner.

January 30, 1959

245

# RAND Corporation Furnishes Brain Power for the Air Force

### By BILL BECKER
#### Special to The New York Times.

SANTA MONICA, Calif., May 21—RAND is a four-letter word meaning "think." There are some, however, who believe RAND means defense, security and any deep-dish research project nobody else has time for.

All of these definitions may become acceptable to future crossword-puzzle makers. At present RAND ranks as one of the United States' most potent and least-known reservoirs of brain-power.

RAND planners did much of the early work on Tiros I, the weather-forecasting satellite. A RAND man recently discovered a high-energy source hovering over the North Pole. Almost weekly, some RAND scientist writes or delivers a paper of lasting value.

The RAND Corporation is a nonprofit institution, which has been called "the Air Force's think factory." It began in 1946 as an Air Force civilian research and development project—hence the name RAND — and 90 per cent of its work is still done for and supported by the Air Force.

But the scope of the work ranges from farthest-out space to the bottom of the sea. Problems of peaceful coexistence and missile-era strategy are paramount, but not all-consuming, considerations in this $5,000,000 Brainsville-by-the-Sea.

Here 500 scientists and 400 aides pursue their studies in a thought-provoking atmosphere overlooking the Pacific. Protected by security measures as strict as the Pentagon's, sport-shirted scientists informally develop theories and recommendations that tomorrow may become the nation's basic defense policies.

"Get the best brains and turn them loose on the problems of the future."

### Foundation Lent Support

That, in essence, was the instruction given by the late Gen. H. H. Arnold and his aides to F. R. Collbohm and a nucleus staff of six engineers recruited from the Douglas Aircraft Company.

Douglas gave a home to the research project in its formative years. The RAND Corporation was established in 1948, with financial support from the Ford Foundation. Mr. Collbohm is president of the corporation, which is governed by a board reading like a "Who's Who" in science, industry and education.

RAND's two-story, California-modern headquarters, opposite the Santa Monica City Hall, was built in 1952. Before that, the growing scientfic complex had mushroomed through seven old buildings and security was becoming a problem.

There is no such thing as a casual visitor at RAND. Visits are by specific appointment and all visitors are tagged by plant security officers in the reception lobby. Badges are good for one visit only and must be returned.

Wastebaskets are carefully checked and contents burned nightly as in the Pentagon. Classified papers must be locked up in safes overnight, and security officers continually remind overly absorbed scientists of the fact. There is a double-check patrol at the end of each day.

One absent-minded mathematician who had trouble remembering to lock his safe file is now working elsewhere. However, RAND executives say there has been no breach of security thus far.

The think factory is open twenty-four hours a day. Some deep thinkers find the night most conducive to their cerebrations. Each man or woman is allowed to work out his own schedule to the extent feasible.

RAND has about thirty women scientists. Perhaps the foremost is Mrs. Hildegarde Kallmann Bijl, German-born upper-air physicist who was an American delegate to the convention of the Committee on Space and Aeronautical Research last year at Nice, France.

Operating on an Air Force budget of $13,500,000 annually, RAND also conducts research for the Atomic Energy Commission, the National Aeronautics and Space Administration and the Defense Department's Advanced Research Projects Agency. Six per cent fee on contracts is earmarked for RAND's own research.

### Five Divisions

The work falls into five divisions — engineering, economics, physics, mathematics and social sciences. On any given project, a research team may consist of scientists from any or all divisions.

The flexibility and initiative that RAND encourages makes recruiting relatively simple. RAND attracts the cream of scientific graduate schools despite offering new Ph. D's less than $10,000 a year, considerably below the going scale in industry.

To some extent, RAND gets the visionary type who, in the words of one close observer, "wouldn't be caught dead in a factory or aircraft plant."

The average age of the scientific staff is 37, with division heads generally older. However, Dr. Richard Latter, physics chief, is only 37. Dr. Latter was a member of the United States negotiating team at the Geneva atomic conference in 1959.

The engineering division is the largest and has the widest scope, covering such fields as aeroastronautics, electronics and planetary sciences.

Typical of the younger leaders at RAND is Robert W. Buchheim, 35-year-old head of the aeroastronautics department. The program he directs seeks, among other things, new metals for missiles and improved defense systems against constantly improving intercontinental weapons.

Mr. Buchheim is one of a number of RAND men who feel the Soviet Union's missile lead is serious.

"Perhaps we are behind to stay until the race goes away," he commented tersely. He meant the space race, not the human.

A Yale graduate and a Doctor of Philosophy, Mr. Buchheim was project engineer for the Snark missile guidance system at North American Aviation before joining RAND in 1954. He edited and had a large part in completing a space handbook for Congress that has become a standard reference.

Richard Bellman, a wide-ranging mathematician, is the Renaissance man type. He is the founder of dynamic programming, a mathematical theory of decision-making with the aid of highly sophisticated computers. The theory is applicable in economics and engineering.

Together with Robert Kalaba of RAND and Dr. John Jacquez of the Sloan-Kettering Institute, he is now trying to construct a mathematical model of the action of various drugs that might be used in cancer chemotherapy.

Mr. Bellman, 39, a New Yorker who has taught at Princeton and Stanford, has been affiliated with RAND for twelve years. He has written four books, five monographs and 250 scientific papers, several on game theory. One mathematician's delight is titled, "Some Two-Person Games Involving Bluffing."

War games play an important part in RAND formulations. Game theories frequently evolve into doctrines of military strategy. Playing games simulating attack conditions provides answers to such problems as how to supply threatened fighter bases around the globe, and how to defend cities against bomber or missile strikes or even satellite bombings.

The mathematics division, concerned largely with computer development, is not as large as it once was. Many of the mathematicians and computer technicians are with System Development Corporation, which split off from RAND to work on the air defense warning system for the Air Force.

System Development, also a nonprofit organization, started with thirty employes, now has 3,500 workers and its own independent plant. It offers its computer services and analyses to military contractors.

The economics division helps to keep the Air Force within budget bounds. Studies to improve the air material system fall to a logistics department headed by C. J. Zwick, former Harvard economist.

From a book-lined office decorated with abstract modern paintings, Mr. Zwick directs a staff of efficiency experts who advise the Air Force on how to save money and manpower. An inventory shows that the Air Force has $14,000,000,000 worth of spare parts throughout the world.

A major project for the future is missile base conversion, rated a $20,000,000-a-year problem.

RAND specialists, particularly engineers and economists, are constantly on the move, consulting with Air Force heads in the Pentagon and at bases everywhere. RAND also maintains a staff of thirty in Washington and has a reserve of 300 consultants.

The average thinking man's salary at RAND is about $15,000. Most old-timers think twice before leaving.

Physicists and social scientists probably have the most leeway. In semi-cloistered cubicles, they pursue elusive tangents in an atmosphere as rare as that of the Institute for Advanced Study.

Their studious reading of journals, papers and books from all over the world, followed by reflection and discussion with colleagues, occasionally results in some sharp updating of theory and policy by Washington politicians, not just the Air Force.

## Art Takes Second Place

### Harper's Article Points Up Difference Between U. S. and European Attitudes

#### By BROOKS ATKINSON

AMONG many penetrating comments on "The State of the Theatre" in the current Harper's, Arthur Miller makes some marginal remarks about the state of the artist in America. He is using the word "artist" to include writers, musicians, painters and all people concerned with the arts.

"The artist is hard put to reassure himself that his occupation is anything but trivial," Mr. Miller remarks to Henry Brandon, who has written the interview. No American writer, Mr. Miller declares, can regard himself as "spokesman for the national spirit," as French and Russian writers can: "In a word, we have no status except that we are makers of entertainment, or heavy thinkers, or earners of big money."

• 

Success in the arts is recognized as any kind of worldly success is recognized here. But the arts in themselves are not commonly regarded as a basic part of the national culture. It never occurred to anyone in this country to arrange national funerals for Eugene O'Neill and Sinclair Lewis, like the national funerals for Stanislavsky in Russia and André Gide in France.

Although the arts have increasing importance throughout the nation, they have never acquired the national respect they have in England, France, Germany, Norway, Sweden and Russia. Official patronage of the arts is alien to our tradition.

We lack a tradition perhaps because, as a nation, we were overwhelmed with problems of survival in the early days. At a time when the arts were patronized by kings, queens and persons of influence in England and Europe, Jamestown was founded by colonists sent over from England by a company of investors and merchants; and Plymouth and Massachusetts Bay were colonized by Separatists and Puritans, who regarded the arts as wicked.

The immediate need was for farmers, fishermen, sailors, masons, blacksmiths, carpenters and artisans—not artists. There was a less tangible but very critical need: It was for statesmen. Fortunately, the country bred enlightened statesmen when thought and political guidance were most urgent. If Franklin and Jefferson had lived in a more stable society, they might have devoted all of their energies to the arts. What they wrote in their leisure or on public order (like the Declaration of Independence) proves that they would have excelled in any tellectual or artistic enterprise.

Many of our seventeenth-and eighteenth-century buildings, both private and public, show that early Americans had an instinct for form and beauty. But books, paintings, theatre and music were hardly more than a polite veneer brought from England. Primitive American paintings portray hard, graceless people in hard, graceless pictures.

During those preliminary centuries, there was certainly some anti-intellectualism and disdain for art. William Penn cautioned his children that "much reading is an oppression of the mind and extinguishes the natural Candle."

In one of his "Letters From an American Farmer," St. John de Crèvecour remarked:

"We enjoy in our woods a substantial happiness which the wonders of art cannot communicate."

An educated Frenchman, comfortably established in Pennsylvania, de Crèvecour was bemused by the spectacle of poor Europeans hacking freedom and independence out of the American forests. He was satisfied to see all the energy, both intellectual and physical, directed towards the founding of a republic. There is no disposition here to take exception to his choice.

• 

What happened in the seventeenth and eighteenth centuries does not account for the twentieth-century fact that the arts have a relatively insignificant place in the American civilization. But it does remind us that, at the time when England had Shakespeare and France had Molière, we were delving and spinning, like Adam and Eve.

Now that the elementary labors are finished, the arts exist. Their vitality depends upon the ability they have to examine critically the American way of life. At present, as Mr. Miller says, the artist does not occupy a recognized place in our society. Few people think of him as a spokesman for America equal to the heads of giant corporations.

November 11, 1960

# The Nation's Culture: New Age for the Arts

**In the development of new institutions, says the White House Special Consultant on the Arts, lies one of "the best assurances of true progress" for the country.**

#### By AUGUST HECKSCHER

EVERYONE knows that the arts in America are booming. Statistics in abundance exist to prove it. To be sure, it is always a little disconcerting when we begin to ask what lies behind the statistics. So many millions of good books are bought. Are they read? Are they read with discernment and understanding? So many millions of Americans own musical instru-

AUGUST HECKSCHER *serves as Special Consultant on the Arts to the White House. He is director of the Twentieth Century Fund.*

ments. True: but one can't help wondering how many of these are actually played—to say nothing of played well. In too many households an unused violin remains in the closet, the symbol of a mother's hopes and a young boy's rebellion: or the piano stands more as an impressive object than an actual source of music.

Yet when all has been said in the way of caution or disparagement, the fact remains that numbers *are* important. The United States today is in the midst of a vast quantitative expansion of its cultural life. Where so much is

happening, at least some of it must be good. Where so many books, records, and musical instruments are being bought, some of them must certainly be put to effective use.

In the older biographies one often read of the child finding his way into his father's library. The volumes there stood staidly upon the shelves, dustcovered in a dusty and dark room. Yet the youth made his entrance into a world hitherto unknown, and afterwards the memory of those long afternoons stood out as adventures into far lands. In somewhat the same way children of the present generation perhaps enter, through byways their elders have neglected or misused, into the enchantment of the arts.

THE fashion has been to decry "mass culture." Indeed the temptation to do so recurs almost every time we sit for any length of time before a television set or subject ourselves to the kind of vulgarity spawned by the "gray areas" of the modern city. It is not original and authentic ugliness which is most distressing in these encounters. It is not absolute badness of taste or style, but the sense that something potentially good has been corrupted and weakened. The inevitable question arises whether excellence can be transmitted to a vast population without debasing it. From that sobering question critics of modern culture have gone on to indict nearly everything that is being done, or could be done, to develop the arts in a highly industrialized society.

These critics have on their side not only a good deal of troubling evidence but the major consideration that the experiment upon which America has embarked has never yet been proven capable of success. We actually do not know whether a society such as our own, with its material abundance and its growing leisure for all parts of the population, can attain to a true appreciation of fineness and excellence in the esthetic sphere. It is an open question. But at least I would insist that it is open.

The chance exists that we may come out into a period of creativity and enjoyment such as no other nation has quite known—not a period characterized by the imitative and traditional qualities of folk art, nor by the withdrawn beauties of an aristocratic patronage, but by the liveliness, the sense of innovation, variety and vigor which goes with democracy at its best. That is at least a chance worth cultivating.

IN my own case I am often depressed by what I see or hear in today's crowded and noisy environment; but I am almost invariably exhilarated when I think of what is going on at the core of things. Men and women are building themselves new forms of human habitation—cities on a scale never hitherto believed practicable. They are preparing for themselves and their children a life without the unremitting toil which has for so many countless centuries limited man's possibilities. They are opening up new universes of knowledge and action.

In all these vast, sometimes half-understood enterprises, the arts are bound to play a crucial role. They alone can humanize the great community of tomorrow, can provide a focus for the free days and years of the new leisure, can interpret and make meaningful the areas which science opens up. The outward scene must be brought in the end into at least a rough conformity with the values which the arts foster and encourage.

With this degree of hopefulness, let us now look at some of the manifestations of our present cultural life. Two things stand out: the high level of individual attainment among artists and creators in virtually all fields, and the general improvement in popular taste. That the United States has painters, sculptors, musicians and architects of the first rank, no one can deny. Men and women in other countries seeking the most novel and significant developments in these fields look to the United States. An exhibition by Calder or Tobey (to name only two of those whose work has won plaudits abroad) creates news and excitement, the way the latest developments in the Paris art field did for so long.

AT the same time, on the popular level, taste has noticeably improved. When the average person builds a house, furnishes a room, buys himself possessions or expresses delight in some vista or experience, he reflects—to a degree rare even a few years ago—a liking for what is light, simple and humanly scaled. Commercialism is continually reintroducing into the goods and gadgets of the market place a certain embellishment and exaggeration; and that part of the public which aspires to keep up with fashion succumbs to the lure. It may even be (which Heaven forbid) that we shall see a reversion to chrome and something like tailfins in our automobiles.

But beneath these aberrations the general tendency seems to be toward simplification and good design. The public has understood, vaguely and at long last, the basic esthetic of the machine; from its clothes to its landscapes it accepts and desires a kind of happy repetition, emphasizing the real differences that come from use and not the false distinctions that are superimposed.

THE achievements of the individual artist and this heightening of the level of taste on the part of the public are not matched in the United States of today by the kinds of institutions which can bring artist and public together. It is troubling that so many of our singers, for example, go abroad for employment, and so many of our potential playwrights and composers give themselves to other, and often secondary, forms of expression. It is disturbing that the level of design which the people expect in their homes and offices should so often be at odds with what they permit in the public environment. It is almost as if they felt they had no voice and no influence in the shaping of their cities or in the control of the debris that runs along so many of the highways.

The American people have been slow to recognize that artistic and cultural expression is closely related to the vitality of institutions. Education needs schools: so the collection of art needs museums; the development of actors and playwrights needs an effective organized theater. The same Americans who are hungry for a more intense esthetic experience have been hesitant to take stock of the economic and structural needs of their cultural life.

They have acted as if the instability, the discontinuity and often the actual poverty of their cultural institutions were tolerable—and perhaps even a good thing. The artist, it was said, prospered in a garret; might not the museum or the opera company prosper in the same way if it were not allowed to be too sure where its next dollar was coming from? Without making a generalization about the relation between poverty and the creativity of the individual, it can surely be said that a down-at-the-heel institution does not promote the most effective artistic expression.

IN the same way, Americans have been reluctant to admit that the progress of the arts is in any way related to democratic procedures or to governmental action. A badly designed post office is surely as much a matter of legitimate citizen concern as a badly drafted law. Stating the matter positively, a landscape or cityscape shaped so as to be pleasing to the eye and spirit should be as much a matter of civic pride as a smoothly functioning legislature. In other countries the people have had much more strongly than here the feeling that the outward community is their own—that they have made it and that it rests in their keeping.

We seem instinctively to act as if hostile and uncontrollable forces were at work in altering the world we live in. They are tearing down the old buildings; they are flooding the countryside with seas of asphalt. The democratic "we" hardly comes into play where esthetic factors are involved.

The next stage in our cultural development may well see a change in these attitudes. We are beginning to look with fresh insight upon the institutions which nurture and foster the arts. We recognize them as precious—vessels through which the genius of the individual artist is given form and expression. Research groups are beginning to examine the sources of their economic support. The men who are responsible for their future make plans on a scale fitted to the contribution which these cultural institutions make to the community. Haphazard standards of management are giving way in many areas to a professional, and often highly imaginative, approach.

AT the same time it begins to seem clear that these institutions have relations at many levels and in many different forms to the public and to government. American experience has provided us with examples of municipal, state and federal support for the arts; it has shown us mixtures between public and private contributions of every conceivable variety. The task now before us is to give prevalence to those methods of support which effectively meet existing public needs—to examine with a open mind the role of the government as it expresses itself from the local to the Federal levels. There are precedents for using public funds to pay for the buildings in which the arts are presented. There are precedents for having the states or cities directly engage the services of orchestras or theatrical groups, and precedents (though rarer) for direct subsidies. •

If the citizens over the next decade or so could take an active interest in the planning of their cities, in the design of public buildings, in the esthetic quality of housing and road building, if they could exert themselves to preserve what is of lasting value in their architectural heritage, they would go far toward bridging the gap which so generally exists between their private and their public worlds.

THE present weakness of our cultural institutions is nowhere more striking than in the performing arts. Museums and libraries, though often impoverished, have achieved a large measure of stability and continuity. Opera and ballet companies by comparison seem doomed to a perpetual battle for their lives. Symphony orchestras (which we classify among the performing arts) have frequently the support of the most public-spirited and wealthy groups in the communities across the country; yet even they face each year the problem of matching a deficit by passing the hat and hoping for the best. Meanwhile the musicians exist at what can scarcely be called a living wage, playing for short seasons and keeping busy the rest of the year through a variety of jobs not always related to their vocation.

These institutions, nevertheless, seem viable and seaworthy compared with the theater. Here, in a striking way we observe the gulf that exists between the talent of creative individuals and the poverty of the organization through which the talent should reveal itself. The United States has certainly not been deficient in aptitudes for the theater—in the skills of playwrights, actors, directors, scene designers and the rest. Yet the commercial theater on Broadway is diminishing each year in the number of productions and consequently in the variety and scope of its performances.

THE Off-Broadway theater becomes increasingly subject to the same high costs and general inflexibility which are affecting the big houses. Children are growing up over wide areas of the country without ever having seen a live performance or experienced the unfolding of a great play.

In the universities, in amateur and semi-professional groups in the smaller cities, and slowly in a few outstanding repertory companies in New York and across the country, the foundations of a new theatrical tradition are being laid. Actors are getting experience; the playwrights are starting to see new opportunities. Audiences are learning again what it is to watch the lights go up on the great stage and illusion become more real than life itself.

In the development of new institutions which herald fresh life for the performing arts as a whole—in the prospect of a completed and flourishing Lincoln Center and a National Cultural Center in Washington—we see one of the best assurances of true progress of all the arts.

# Sociologist Warns on 'Big-Brotherism'

**By NATALIE JAFFE**
Special to The New York Times

SAN FRANCISCO, April 14 —In a benevolent, scientific disguise, the age of big-brotherism is fast approaching with possibly disastrous consequences only dimly recognized by researchers and the public, a mental health meeting here was told today.

Apparently in the interests of social welfare and scientific knowledge, "an ugly alliance may be developing between legal-electronic surveillance, scientific research and Government dossiers," according to Dr. Orville G. Brim Jr., a prominent sociologist who is president of the Russell Sage Foundation of New York.

Dr. Brim participated in one of several sessions on surveillance, testing and the right of privacy that were held today during the American Orthopsychiatric Association's 43d annual meeting.

At the various sessions, behavioral scientists from different fields agreed independently that the growth of psychological tests, personality questionnaires, electronic surveillance and social research presented dangers that fell into these categories:

¶The control of an individual's future by the existence of a "government dossier bank" that would contain test and questionnaire results, possibly erroneous personal references and out of date health, police and welfare records.

¶The emotional damage that might be done by forcing an individual to reveal or to learn things about himself that he would rather keep hidden.

¶The distortion of values among a whole generation of scientists who pride themselves on using deceit in experiments with human beings who are considered merely experimental objects.

The creation of a central agency that would pool all the public records on each citizen —Dr. Brim dubbed it the "government dossier bank"—may be only two years away, he said. A Government commission recently recommended the formation of a data pool, which would be operated either by a separate agency or the Bureau of the Census.

"There is no doubt that we can run the society better with this information," Dr. Brim said, "but doing this must be in conflict with all our fears of having privacy invaded."

Alan F. Westin, a professor of law at Columbia University, predicted even greater growth for "surveillance technology." In addition to wiretapping and closed-circuit television, he mentioned personality testing, "truth serums," brain wave analysis, voice recording and the increasing exchange of information among public agencies.

The existence of a "dossier bank" could unfairly affect a person's life chances several speakers noted, both because an individual changes throughout his life and because the original material might be faulty.

A professor of law in the audience at one session recalls the hundreds of detailed questionnaires he had been asked to fill out on former students.

"My verdict on the emotional adjustment of a student I saw only in class may affect him for the rest of his life," he said. "It's damned unfair."

CHAPTER **3**
# Prosperity

*ew neighborhood rises in a suburb*

*rtesy The New York Times*

# National Purpose: Stevenson's View

## The Pursuit of Truth and Rewards for Intellect Are Proposed

### by ADLAI E. STEVENSON

It is not too difficult, I think, to state the classic goals and purposes of American society. We probably cannot improve on the definition of our Founding Fathers: "to form a more perfect Union, establish justice, insure domestic tranquillity, provide for the common defense, promote the general welfare and secure the blessings of liberty."

Add Tom Paine's words—"My country is the world"—to give our goals universal application. and we have distilled the essence out of all the rhetoric about the freedom and the democratic self - government for which we proudly stand.

But the difficulty is that aims in the abstract mean little. A society is measured by what it does, and no Fourth of July oratory will make its purposes great if in fact they are small, or change them into a moving element in the world's passionate dialogue of destiny if they are meager and private and unconcerned.

We have therefore to look at our noble purpose of freedom (and surely no one would deny that it is the organizing principle of American life) in terms of the concrete, practical content which Americans give to the concept.

As one might expect in a free society, we find at once that freedom itself has many meanings and has implied different things to different people at different times in our national life. In fact, one can observe something of a rhythm in the nation's mood, a swing from one definition of freedom almost to its opposite, recurring regularly throughout the almost 200 years of our independent history.

### The Private Aspect

The first mood reflects the *private* aspect of freedom—the right of men to choose their own ideas and pursuits, to be free from the arbitrary interventions of government, to "do what they like with their own."

Many early immigrants escaped the arbitrary restraints of governments in Europe and came to set their money and their wits to work in the new climate of freedom. This sense of the link between "freedom" and private business has indeed been so strong that at some periods they have been virtually equated, as when Calvin Coolidge thus defined the American purpose:

"The business of America is business."

But equally freedom has had its *public* aspect as the organizing principle of a new kind of society. In the Declaration of Independence, the basic charter of the modern world, the picture is of a great civic order in which governments, deriving their authority from the consent of the governed, help to secure the inalienable preconditions of the good life: equality before the law and in human respect, life, liberty and, most precious yet intangible of rights, the pursuit of happiness.

This positive vision of society in which public authority plays its essential part in bettering the lot of all citizens was as inherent as freedom itself in the vision of our founders and philosophers.

But what do we find? Never before in my lifetime—not even in the days of Harding and Coolidge—has the mystique of privacy seemed to me so pervasive. The face which we present to the world, especially through our mass circulation media, is the face of the individual or the family as a high consumption unit with minimal social links or responsibilities—father happily drinking his favorite beer, mother dreamily fondling soft garments newly rinsed in a wonderful new detergent, the children gaily calling from the new barbecue pit for a famous sauce for their steak.

### The Poles of Energy

There is no inevitable contradiction between these public and private aspects of American society. Indeed, they are the essential poles of energy in a vigorous social order.

Without individual decision and inventiveness, without widely dispersed centers of authority and responsibility, the social order grows rigid and centralized. Spontaneity withers before the killing frost of public conformity. Individual citizens with all their varied relationships, as parents, neighbors, churchgoers, workers, business men, are reduced to the single loyalties of party and state.

In this century we are not likely to underestimate that danger. We have seen free societies destroyed in this way by totalitarians of both the right and the left.

Yet the pursuit of private interest and well-being does not, as the Eighteenth Century sometimes naïvely believed, automatically add up to the well-being of all. The strong pursuit of *my* interest can override the vital interests of others, if nature, health, energy and property have weighted the odds in my favor. Social evils pile up when little more than unchecked private interest determines the pattern of society.

At best, the result is a "pressure group" state in which each organized group jostles for its own interests at the expense of the weak, the isolated or the unorganized. At worst, the power and influence of the few can violate the fundamental rights and decencies of the many, as they did in the long survival of human slavery and in the long resistance of industry to child labor laws and minimum wages.

In our own prosperous days a new possibility has arisen: that the many can smugly overlook the squalor and misery of the few and tolerate, in the midst of unparalleled plenty,

The New York Times

"A NEW POSSIBILITY," writes Mr. Stevenson, "has arisen: that the many can smugly overlook the squalor and misery of the few and tolerate, in the midst of unparalleled plenty, ugly slums * * * and second-class citizenship."

ugly slums, rural destitution and second-class citizenship.

It is the often mediocre and sometimes intolerable consequences of unchecked private interest that have led to the reassertion, at regular intervals in American history, of the primacy of public good.

Sometimes the swing occurs because evil has become so obtrusive that only vigorous public action can check it in time. The conviction that the spread of slavery endangered the Union itself helped precipitate the Civil War. The demoralization of the entire economy after 1929 led to the experiments and reforms of Roosevelt's New Deal. Sometimes the swing seems to occur in response to subtler promptings. Early in this century, for instance, under Theodore Roosevelt and Woodrow Wilson, it was not imminent social collapse but disgust at the smash-and-grab materialism which was devouring America that aroused people once more to demand the restatement of America's public purposes and a new vision of the common good.

Whatever the reasons for America's recurrent swing in emphasis from private interest to public responsibility, it has always had a significant external consequence. It has aroused both in America and in the world at large the sense, eloquently expressed by our greatest statesmen, that the American experiment has significance far beyond its own frontiers and is in some measure a portent for all mankind.

### Working Model Needed

Today I don't suppose anyone will deny that mankind is in acute need of a convincing working model of a free society. Never in human history has there been an epoch of such profound and sudden social upheaval on so universal a scale. Never has the working model of tyranny made such claims for its own effectiveness; never has monolithic discipline attacked so savagely what it calls the pretentions of the free way of life. The whole of human society has become plastic and malleable in the flames of social revolution.

Thus there has never been a time when the public aspect of American liberty as the organizing principle of a great order has needed to be more studied and stressed.

### It Is Not All

No doubt many of the world's peoples want and mean to get a lot more of this. But it is not all they want, and they have to look hard to find the balancing picture of America's wider purposes and to learn that high private consumption is not our ultimate aim of life, nor our answer to all man's evils and disorders in a time of breath-taking social change.

For all these good "things" do not solve the problems of urban decay and congestion. Behind the shining child in the advertisement lurks the juvenile delinquent in the run-down slum. Nor does high consumption guarantee to America's children the teachers or the schools that should be their birthright. It does nothing to end the shame of racial discrimination. It does not counter the exorbitant cost of maintaining good health, nor conserve the nation's precious reserves of land and water and wilderness.

The contrast between private opulence and public squalor on most of our panorama is now too obvious to be denied. Yet we still spend per capita almost as much on advertising to multiply the private wants of our people as we do on education to enable them to seek a fuller, wiser and more satisfying civic existence.

Nor is this imbalance simply a matter of drift and the unmeant consequence of our fabulous new opportunities for wealth creation. It is in real measure the result of considered and deliberate government policy.

Except for defense, American public expenditure today is proportionately lower than it was in 1939. And while we raise a cheer at the fact that we are spending less, let us also remember that this means a relative decline in support for such basic needs as schooling, research, health, small income housing, urban renewal and all forms of public services—local, state and federal—at a time when there has been steadily more income to spend on every private want, or unwant.

With the supermarket as our temple and the singing commercial as our litany, are we likely to fire the world with an irresistible vision of America's exalted purposes and inspiring way of life?

Even where public spending has been high, for defense and economy aid, our performance has been more defensive than indicative of freedom's positive purposes. We have stressed so much our aim of stopping communism for our own security that self-interest has often contaminated our generous aid programs. And even in the vital field of military security, the Administration's concern for the citizen as a private consumer rather than as a mature, responsible American who will accept the unpleasant facts about his country's safety, leaves one with the lurking suspicion that budgetary considerations, rather than the stark needs of strategy, are determining our defense effort.

### Stirring of New Vitality

In short, at a time of universal social upheaval and challenge, our vision of our own society seems to be of limited social significance. An air of disengagement and disinterest hangs over the most powerful and affluent society the world has ever known. Neither the turbulence of the world abroad nor the fatness and flatness of the world at home are moving us to more vital effort. We seem becalmed in a season of storm, drifting through a century of mighty dreams and great achievements. As an American I am disturbed.

It is arguable that after the shocks and rigors of the Nineteen Thirties and Nineteen Forties, we as a nation needed a period of relaxation, though I would note that the Russians and the Chinese, after far greater shocks, have had no opportunity for a cozy nap. Now, however, we have had our rest, and I sense the stirring of a new vitality, possibly the beginning of that traditional swing of the political pendulum away from private pursuits to a concern for the nation's broader purposes.

I am persuaded that he who speaks clearly to the Americans of their social responsibilities, as well as their private wants, will now command a more attentive hearing. I believe the old idea of America and its

The New York Times

"FROM EVERY LARGE URBAN CENTER," the author says of urban life, "the suburbs spread out and out*** commuters jam the city approaches and a strange half life of divided families and Sunday fathers is growing up."

government as a positive instrument for the common weal is being restored once again after all the cheap sarcasm about "bureaucracy" and "creeping socialism."

And if a change of mood and attitude toward our public needs and institutions is in fact on the way, I do not think there can be much question about the fields in which the new sense of responsibility must quickly go to work.

At home we must ask ourselves again what quality of life we want, both public and private, as citizens of this great republic. Education and the arts are the starting point, for it is only here that the citizens of tomorrow can learn to demand and live a fuller life. A respect for excellence and a sense of discipline in the attainment of knowledge are virtues not just because the Russians pioneered the space age and photographed the other side of the moon, but because the new society that technology is building demands a grasp and competence among the mass of citizens undreamed of in earlier civilizations.

By education and the arts we mean something more than better school buildings, higher teachers' salaries and more scholarships for the intelligent. We mean a reorientation of our ideals and tastes, the strenuous stretching of mental and artistic talent, the exaltation of excellence above social approval, and of mental achievement above quick material success.

We mean, in short, new standards of respect and reward for intellect and culture. And we mean more stable financing for basic research, more concern for advancing knowledge for its own sake. We mean cooperation with other communities of scholars and creative thinkers, as in the International Geophysical Year, in order that our pursuit of truth may be an adventure we share with all mankind. And we mean that the pursuit of truth in itself is the highest activity of man.

Here, then, in all its ramifications of expense, of standards, content and opportunity, is a top priority for a great new America and a national purpose few would dispute.

## Our Urban Life

I would include not far below a reconsideration of our urban life. We are adding a city the size of Philadelphia to our population every year. From every

large urban center the suburbs spread out and out, without shape or grace or any centered form of civic life. Many are so built that they are the slums of tomorrow. Meanwhile town centers decay, racial divisions destroy harmony, commuters jam the city approaches and a strange, half life of divided families and Sunday fathers is growing up.

If we accept both the fact of our rapid growth in population and the fact that most people will live in cities, we can begin a serious attack upon our congested, ugly, inconvenient metropolitan sprawls. We can create the preconditions of a good urban life that could become a new model for an urbanizing world.

Restoration of compassion is a clumsy way to describe another great embracing national purpose. In the past, evils and miseries have been the driving force of majority discontent. But now, for the first time in history, the engine of social progress has run out of the fuel of discontent. We have therefore to mobilize our imagination, our personal sense of indignation, if we are to act on the conviction that gross poverty, curable illness, racial indignity, mental disease and suffering in old age are a disgrace amidst the surrounding luxuries, privileges and indulgence of such a wealthy society as ours.

## Must Go Beyond

And here our top priorities must reach beyond our shores. For it is not chiefly in America or in the fortunate North Atlantic basin that the world's miseries are to be found. On the contrary, we confidently predict a doubling and tripling of our high living standards. But in Asia, Africa and Latin America live scores of millions who, on present forecasts, may have no such expectations.

This disparity in living standards between the rich and the poor is as great a threat to peace as the arms race, and narrowing the gap is as imperative as arms control.

Our aid programs should therefore be designed not primarily to counter communism, though they will do this too, but to create conditions of self-respect and self-sustaining growth in economies still behind the threshold of modernization.

The needs are so staggering

that to achieve this will demand not only the greatest intelligence, perseverance and financial enterprise, private and public, but also a much broader cooperation and joint effort with other advanced nations.

If we accept this as fundamental American foreign policy, not on a year-to-year basis but for the next critical generation, we shall develop the perspective and staying power to reach real solutions, not doles, handouts, bad debts—and dislike.

## Landmarks Vanishing

And in so doing, we shall do more than set the processes of modernization in healthy motion. I believe that this is the chief way open to us to extend our vision of "a more perfect union" to all mankind.

It is a commonplace that in a world made one by science and the atom the old national boundaries are dissolving, the old landmarks vanishing. We can't have privacy and the hydrogen bomb too.

A workable human society has to be fashioned and we must start where we can—by setting up the institutions of a common economic life, by employing our wealth and wisdom to spark the growth of production in poorer lands, by working together with like-minded powers to establish the permanent patterns of a workable world economy.

In this way we can hope to establish one of the two main preconditions of peaceful human society — economic solidarity and mutual help.

The other precondition of peace—and this, of all priorities, is our highest—is our unwavering search for peace under law which, in our present context, means controlled and supervised disarmament. Only a disarmed world offers us security worth the name any longer.

I do not believe, even now, that the world accepts the idea that genuine disarmament is America's primary, public purpose. We talk of peace and our devotion to it. But there is far more hard, unremitting effort in the task than speeches or protestations or journeys, however distant.

What seems to be lacking is sincere and sustained dedication to this goal and unwearying pursuit by our highest officers, military and civilian. There is a widespread impression that the United States is "dragging its feet."

I believe that the American people are prepared to face the cost, the rigors, the efforts and the challenge which are involved in recovering the public image of a great America. The cost in physical terms—in hard work, in discipline, in more taxes if need be—is hard to estimate precisely.

Any arms control would release resources. Our growing gross national product will certainly provide wider margins out of which vital public expenditures could be met. But if the cost is higher than our present level of public spending, I frankly believe that education and health for our children, dignity and beauty in our civic lives, and security and wellbeing in the world at large are more important than the "things" which might otherwise have priority.

But still more important is America's need to face squarely the facts about its situation. If freedom is really the organizing principle of our society, then we cannot forget that it is not illusion, propaganda and sedatives, but truth, and truth alone, that makes us free.

## Entails Hard Choices

Under the influence of the politics of sedation and the techniques of salesmanship, I believe that in recent years self-deceit has slackened our grip on reality. We have tended to shirk the difficult truth and accept the easy half-truth. Perhaps it is always that way. As the old humorist Josh Billings used to say:

"As scarce as truth is, the supply has always been in excess of the demand."

But we know from our own lives that reality entails hard choices and disappointments: that it measures real achievement not in terms of luck but in terms of difficulties overcome. I don't believe our national life can follow any other pattern.

No preordained destiny decrees that America shall have all the breaks and soft options. Neither greatness nor even freedom lies that way. So we must surely return to the reality principle, to the bracing, invigorating, upland climate of truth itself. I think we are ready now to move forward into the rigors and glories of the new decade with open eyes, eager step and firm purposes worthy of our great past.

# ROCKEFELLER FUND PRODS U.S. ON AIMS

## Report Asks Leadership to Seize Initiative in the 'Cold War' From Communists

### By RUSSELL PORTER

The Rockefeller Brothers Fund called yesterday for strong American leadership to define the national purpose and wrest the initiative in the "cold war" from the Communists.

The fund issued a report expressing confidence that democracy could survive in peace and freedom if it had proper leadership. Hesitation to supply this leadership, it held, betrays failure to understand the inherent resources of the democratic system.

The report urged long-range planning, the setting of definite goals, centralized controls at many points and constant military readiness against possible Communist aggression. It also said the public should be told the facts necessary for an "honest and fearless" discussion of the issues of war and peace.

### Political Aspects Cited

The fund was headed by Nelson A. Rockefeller until his election as Governor. He was succeeded as fund president by his brother, Laurance S. Rockefeller.

The fund is a philanthropic organization set up by the late John D. Rockefeller Jr. He gave it $59,000,000 in his lifetime and left it half of the bulk of his $150,000,000 estate when he died last May. The fund is administered by nine trustees, including Governor Rockefeller, his four brothers and one sister.

The report appeared likely to have political repercussions. It was in some respects reminiscent of statements made by Governor Rockefeller before he made his peace pact with Vice President Nixon on the eve of the Republican convention.

In that pact the Governor and Mr. Nixon agreed on fourteen key points for inclusion in the Republican platform. Thereafter Mr. Rockefeller endorsed Mr. Nixon for the Republican nomination for President.

In pre-convention statements the Governor had seemed to imply criticism of President Eisenhower for failure to provide strong leadership against the Communists in the "cold war."

### Sixth in Report Series

The report is entitled "The Power of the Democratic Ideal." It is the sixth in a series, "America at Mid-Century," prepared by the fund's special studies project. This project was organized in 1956 to assess major problems likely to confront the United States in the next ten or fifteen years.

The current report brings the series to an end.

A spokesman for the fund said the current report was intended to set its previous reports in a philosophical background and serve as a capstone for the entire series. The earlier reports dealt with specific questions of foreign policy, national defense, national and foreign economic policy, and education. In general they advocated more forceful policies than the Eisenhower Administration has followed.

The current report deals with whether American democracy can act with "the force, resolution and imagination necessary to meet the problems it faces in the second half of the twentieth century."

"We are sobered as we reflect on the tasks to be performed," the report said, "yet confident in the power of the democratic idea to help us perform these tasks and maintain our liberties.

### Communist Peril Noted

"One of the most perplexing problems of the cold war is how to deal with the efforts of the international Communist apparatus. The perplexity arises from the skillful use by this apparatus of democratic symbols and machinery to subvert democratic processes.

"The American Communist party is too insignificant to be a present danger, but the total international apparatus of communism is powerful and is always ready to use underhanded methods. Toughness and realism are required to deal with this conspiracy.

"If fundamental democratic values are to be preserved, however, restraint is also necessary. The excesses of various loyalty programs illustrate this aspect of the problem. When Government clearances require the individual to prove his loyalty, a basic democratic postulate is ignored."

The report also urged restraint in restricting public information on military and foreign affairs.

### Challenge Outlined

"These problems bring us to the underlying issue that the present crisis raises for American society," it went on. "Democracies are not warlike. Large military budgets, recurrent alarms and excursions, a state of prolonged international tension are all foreign to the normal climate of freedom.

"Many of the practices this state of affairs requires, such as centralized controls at many points, long-range planning and the maintenance of a constant state of military readiness, have not been habitual in the United States. It is natural that they should be employed reluctantly and that the belief should persist that a democracy cannot do more than respond to the initiatives taken by its enemies."

The report said this belief was incompatible with the wealth, past and resources of the United States. It said citizens of this and other democracies had repeatedly proved their ability to pull hard together when the purpose was clear.

"But for the long pull that must now be made, this purpose must be defined by leadership," the report went on. "And the support for this definition of our national purpose will have to be won in the way that enduring support for any policy must be achieved in a democracy—by honest and fearless exploration of the issues conducted on the premise that a democracy's citizens want to listen to reason and deserve to be told the facts.

'Hesitation in setting this process in motion reveals only a failure to understand the inherent resources of the democratic system."

The report said modern democracies had shown they could outlast other social systems but that today they faced problems rising from scientific, technological and economic changes.

Democratic citizens of prosperous countries, it went on, must develop new sensibility and personal ethics to meet new needs and demands for educational opportunities, economic progress, individual freedom and racial equality, both nationally and internationally.

It said the present generation of Americans should clarify and strengthen their democratic tradition, as a world-wide test tube for democratic principles. They must, it went on, "demonstrate their power to generate visions, set programs in motion and kindle the hopes of people elsewhere."

"At the greatest moments in the American past, Americans had an image before them of what free men, working together, could make of human life," the report said.

"The great question that the present generation of Americans will answer is whether the American democratic adventure will continued and renewed, and whether American life can be lit by a sense of opportunities to be seized and great things to be done.

"This report is an effort to indicate that the problems America faces today, although they are heavy, are not burdens but invitations to achievement."

### Old and New Business

The report said Americans had important unfinished business to attend to in strengthening their educational system, in developing television and other mass communications as a source of public information, and in eliminating racial barriers.

It said political leaders should satisfy the "human impulse to idealism" with "definite programs of action." These, it went on, would give the people "a sense that large projects are under way and that they are part of some significant and enduring human enterprise."

The report held that all citizens in democracy should have the opportunity to join or refuse to join groups but that none of these groups must exercise monopolistic power.

"As the social democratic parties of western Europe now seem to agree," it went on, "the state cannot be the only employer in the community; its power over the individual must be checked by the existence of other possible employers.

"Similarly the individual must be protected against private employers by his union and by the state, and his rights must also be protected within his union by the action of the state or other appropriate means."

The report said an essential of democracy was "vigorous and independent activity of private citizens possessing sources of power and wealth that lie outside the government sector.

"It is a mark of a free society," it went on, "that it draws a line between the areas that are subject to state control or legal coercion and those in which the private judgment of individuals or voluntary groups will prevail."

### Readjustment Urged

Whether the American democratic system can satisfy the hopes that it has set loose in the world, the report said, depends on its inherent resources and its ability to readjust to today's "radically changed environment."

It said the practical problem was to protect and reinforce the power that individuals could bring to bear on their environments.

"The purposeful reorganization of our cities to provide neighborhoods that will encourage people to meet and work together is one example of what can be done," it went on.

It said an entirely new kind of society was emerging in the United States.

### Leisure Not Enough

"An unprecedented proportion of the population will be in schools," it went on. "A steadily growing proportion will live to what was once known as old age; young, middle-aged and old will have more leisure than all but a privileged few have enjoyed in the past, and they will have more to buy and consume.

"The vista is exciting, but it will bring issues that have never troubled any nation on so vast a scale. In such a world, more than ever before, a society should be able to offer its members something better than a life of mere accumulation and of sensation without commitment."

The report said the influence of American democracy abroad would depend largely on "the discrimination and sense of purpose that America shows in using its wealth—the way it allocates its resources, the shape it gives to its civilization."

### Leadership and Support

The report said that the solution of today's problems depends on "the quality of the men who occupy positions of leadership, the information and resources available to them, the cirmumstances in which they work, and the support they receive from their fellow citizens."

"When there is weakness in democracy, it does not lie in the process by which democracy reaches its decisions," the report went on. "It lies in the values held by the individuals who take part in these decisions —in what they hold dear and in what they regard as right and wrong."

The current report ties together the fund's earlier reports. In its foreign - policy report, issued last December, the fund said the over-all objective of United States foreign policy should be a peaceful world based on "separate political entities acting as a community."

Such as international community, it held, should be open to all states, including Communist, that refrained from trying to impose their way of life on others. It urged a "candid recognition" of the "realities" of the position of Communist China and warned against letting "emotion or difference in ideology" close the door on better relations with the Chinese people.

### Curb on Soviet Asked

The foreign - policy report called for strengthening the Atlantic community and for a coordinated program by the United States to improve conditions in Latin America.

It held that the United States could not permit Communist states to extend their rule, could not abandon West Berlin, could not allow West Germany to fall into the Soviet orbit, and could not dissolve the North Atlantic Treaty Organization.

The fund's first report, issued in January, 1958, urged heavy increases in military spending and a broad reorganization of the defense establishment to prevent the world balance of power from shifting to the Soviet bloc.

Another report advocated a new trade system in the free world, based on regional groups without economic barriers, designed to lead eventually to political and social as well as economic cooperation. Without such a system, it held, underdeveloped areas would be vulnerable to Soviet economic warfare.

The report on domestic economic policy recommended a ten-year plan for a 5 per cent annual rise in Gross National Product—total value of goods and services—to nullify announced Soviet plans to overtake the United States standard of living.

A report on education called for an overhaul of the United States educational system to give equal opportunities for the fullest development of all. It said Federal aid would be needed unless there was a thorough overhaul of state and local tax systems to make the necessary funds available for educational reform.

The current report was prepared under the direction of an over-all panel of which Laurance Rockefeller was chairman. Other members were:

Adolf A. Berle Jr., senior partner, Berle, Berle & Brunner; Professor of Law, Columbia University.

James A. Perkins, vice president of the Carnegie Corporation of New York, was chairman of the writing committee for the report. Dr. Charles Frankel, Professor of Philosophy at Columbia University, was its principal author.

Other members of the writing committee were Lewis Galantiere, counselor of the Free Europe Committee; August Heckscher, director of the Twentieth Century Fund, and Pendleton Herring, president of the Social Science Research Council.

# KENNEDY ASSURES TEXAS MINISTERS OF INDEPENDENCE

## Says He'd Quit Presidency if Unable to Withstand Any Church Pressure

### By W. H. LAWRENCE
Special to The New York Times.

HOUSTON, Tex., Sept. 12—Senator John F. Kennedy told Protestant ministers here tonight that he would resign as President if he could not make every decision in the national interest "without regard to outside religious pressures or dictates."

Senator Kennedy's address, to the Greater Houston Ministerial Association, was televised throughout Texas.

It constituted an affirmation of his belief in the separation of church and state. It was also his answer to critics who have sought to mobilize anti-Catholic sentiment against him by contending he would not resist church pressure on major issues.

"I do not speak for my church on public matters," Senator Kennedy declared, "and the church does not speak for me.

### Would Ignore 'Pressures'

"Whatever issue may come before me as President — on birth control, divorce, censorship, gambling, or any other subject—I will make my decision in accordance with what my conscience tells me to be the national interest, and without regard to outside religious pressures or dictates."

Public officials, the Senator said, should not request or accept instructions on public policy directly or indirectly from the Pope, from the National Council of Churches, or from any other ecclesiastical source seeking to impose its will on the general public.

Mr. Kennedy said, "No power or threat of punishment could cause me" to deviate from the national interest.

September 8, 1960

"But if the time should ever come—I do not concede any conflict to be even remotely possible — when my office would require me to either violate my conscience or violate the national interest," Senator Kennedy said, "then I would resign the office; and I hope any conscientious public servant would do the same."

Mr. Kennedy also struck at the group of Protestant clergymen, led by the Rev. Dr. Norman Vincent Peale, that has questioned his ability to withstand Roman Catholic pressures if he were President. Dr. Peale is minister of the Marble Collegiate Church in New York.

Such groups, Mr. Kennedy said, are working to "subvert" the declaration, in Article VI of the Constitution, that there shall be no religious test of office. They should be out openly working for repeal of Article VI, he said, rather than trying to change it by indirection.

The speech represented a major effort by Senator Kennedy to meet the religious issue head on. In it, he also continued to try to draw back into the Democratic party a segment of its membership, particularly in the South and the Midwest, that has made known its unwillingness to vote for a Catholic.

### Asks Judging of Record

Mr. Kennedy asked voters to judge him on his public record from fourteen years of Congress. This record, he said, included his "declared stands against an Ambassador to the Vatican, against unconstitutional aid to parochial schools, and against any boycott of the public schools." He pointed out he had gone to public schools himself.

He said he believed equally that no Catholic prelate should tell a President how to act and that no Protestant minister should tell his parishioners how to vote.

"This is the kind of America I believe in," he asserted, "and this is the kind of America I fought for in the South Pacific, and the kind my brother died for in Europe. No one suggested then that we might have a 'divided loyalty,' that we did 'not believe in liberty' or that we belonged to a disloyal group that threatened the 'freedoms for which our forefathers died.'"

The quotations Mr. Kennedy cited were from the manifesto of the Peale group, which calls itself the National Conference for Religious Freedom.

### Controversy Recalled

One passage in Senator Kennedy's speech bore on a controversy with another clergyman, the Rev. Dr. Daniel Poling, a Baptist and former unsuccessful Republican candidate for Mayor of Philadelphia. The issue involved in the controversy has been widely used against the Democratic nominee.

It concerns his not participating in 1947 in the dedication of the Chapel of the Four Chaplains. The chapel is an interfaith memorial in the Temple Baptist Church in Philadelphia.

It honors four Protestant, Catholic and Jewish chaplains who perished together on a Navy ship during World War II, giving up their chances of survival in favor of others. One of the victims was Dr. Poling's son.

Dr. Poling has asserted that Mr. Kennedy was forced by pressure from the late Dennis Cardinal Dougherty to decline an invitation he originally had accepted.

Senator Kennedy explained before the National Press Club last January that he canceled his appearance when he learned that the chapel was in a Protestant church. Thus, he said, the Catholic altar could not be consecrated under the tenets of his church, which does not participate with other faiths in religious ceremonies.

### Basis of Objection

Mr. Kennedy said that had he been invited as an individual or as a member of the House of Representatives, he would have gone and his church would have interposed no objections.

He was quoted by his campaign assistants last Thursday on the same incident.

"I was invited by the Rev. Dr. Poling," he said, "to attend the dinner in connection with the financial drive to build the Chapel of the Four Chaplains." I was happy to accept.

"A few days before the event, I learned, as the Rev. Dr. Poling describes in his book, that I was to be the spokesman for the Catholic faith. I was not being invited as a former member of Congress or as an individual, but as an official representative of a religious organization.

"I further learned that the memorial was to be located in the sanctuary of a church of a different faith. This is against the precepts of the Catholic Church."

The Senator alluded to this issue tonight when he said that the President of all the people should "attend any ceremony, service or dinner his office may, appropriately, require of him— and whose fulfillment of his Presidential oath is not limited or conditioned by any religious oath, ritual or obligation."

September 13, 1960

# Text of Kennedy's Inaugural Outlining Policies on World Peace and Freedom

*Following is the text of President Kennedy's Inaugural Address at Washington yesterday, as recorded by The New York Times:*

Vice President Johnson, Mr. Speaker, Mr. Chief Justice, President Eisenhower, Vice President Nixon, President Truman, Reverend Clergy, fellow citizens:

We observe today not a victory of party but a celebration of freedom—symbolizing an end as well as a beginning—signifying renewal as well as change. For I have sworn before you and Almighty God the same solemn oath our forebears prescribed nearly a century and three-quarters ago.

The world is very different now. For man holds in his mortal hands the power to abolish all forms of human poverty and all forms of human life. And yet the same revolutionary beliefs for which our forebears fought are still at issue around the globe— the belief that the rights of man come not from the generosity of the state but from the hand of God.

We dare not forget today that we are the heirs of that first revolution. Let the word go forth from this time and place, to friend and foe alike, that the torch has been passed to a new generation of Americans—born in this century, tempered by war, disciplined by a hard and bitter peace, proud of our ancient heritage—and unwilling to witness or permit the slow undoing of those human rights to which this nation has always been committed, and to which we are committed today at home and around the world.

Let every nation know, whether it wishes us well or ill, that we shall pay any price, bear any burden, meet any hardship, support any friend, oppose any foe to assure the survival and the success of liberty.

This much we pledge—and more.

### A Pledge to Allies

To those old allies whose cultural and spiritual origins we share, we pledge the loyalty of faithful friends. United, there is little we cannot do in a host of new cooperative ventures. Divided, there is little we can do—for we dare not meet a powerful challenge at odds and split asunder.

To those new states whom we welcome to the ranks of the free, we pledge our word that one form of colonial control shall not have passed away merely to be replaced by a far more iron tyranny. We shall not always expect to find them supporting our view. But we shall always hope to find them strongly supporting their own freedom —and to remember that, in the past, those who foolishly sought power by riding the back of the tiger ended up inside.

To those peoples in the huts and villages of half the globe struggling to break the bonds of mass misery, we pledge our best efforts to help them help themselves, for whatever period is required—not because the Communists may be doing it, not because we seek their votes, but because it is right. If a free society cannot help the many who are poor, it can not save the few who are rich. To our sister republics south of our border, we offer a special pledge—to convert our good words into good deeds—in a new alliance for progress—to assist free men and free governments in casting off the chains of poverty. But this peaceful revolution of hope cannot become the prey of hostile powers. Let all our neighbors know that we shall join with them to oppose aggression or subversion anywhere in the Americas. And let every other power know that this hemisphere intends to remain the master of its own house.

### Support for U. N.

To that world assembly of sovereign states, the United Nations, our last best hope in an age where the instruments of war have far outpaced the instruments of peace, we renew our pledge of support— to prevent it from becoming merely a forum for invective —to strengthen its shield of the new and the weak—and to enlarge the area in which its writ may run.

Finally, to those nations who would make themselves our adversary, we offer not a pledge but a request: that both sides begin anew the quest for peace, before the dark powers of destruction unleashed by science engulf all humanity in planned or accidental self-destruction.

We dare not tempt them with weakness. For only when our arms are sufficient beyond doubt can we be certain beyond doubt that they will never be employed.

But neither can two great and powerful groups of nations take comfort from our present course—both sides overburdened by the cost of modern weapons, both rightly alarmed by the steady spread of the deadly atom, yet both racing to alter that uncertain balance of terror that stays the hand of mankind's final war.

So let us begin anew—remembering on both sides that civility is not a sign of weakness, and sincerity is always subject to proof. Let us never negotiate out of fear. But let us never fear to negotiate.

Let both sides explore what problems unite us instead of belaboring those problems which divide us.

### Arms Control Urged

Let both sides, for the first time, formulate serious and precise proposals for the inspection and control of arms—and bring the absolute power to destroy other nations

under the absolute control of all nations.

Let both sides seek to invoke the wonders of science instead of its terrors. Together let us explore the stars, conquer the deserts, eradicate disease, tap the ocean depths and encourage the arts and commerce.

Let both sides unite to heed in all corners of the earth the command of Isaiah—to "undo the heavy burdens . . . [and] let the oppressed go free."

And if a beachhead of co-operation may push back the jungles of suspicion, let both sides join in creating a new endeavor—not a new balance of power, but a new world of law, where the strong are just and the weak secure and the peace preserved.

All this will not be finished in the first 100 days. Nor will it be finished in the first 1,000 days, nor in the life of this Administration, nor even perhaps in our lifetime on this planet. But let us begin.

In your hands, my fellow citizens, more than mine, will rest the final success or failure of our course. Since

this country was founded, each generation of Americans has been summoned to give testimony to its national loyalty. The graves of young Americans who answered the call to service surround the globe.

Now the trumpet summons us again—not as a call to bear arms, though arms we need—not as a call to battle, though embattled we are—but a call to bear the burden of a long twilight struggle year in and year out, "rejoicing in hope, patient in tribulation"—a struggle against the common enemies of man: tyranny, poverty, disease and war itself.

Can we forge against these enemies a grand and global alliance, north and south, east and west, that can assure a more fruitful life for all mankind? Will you join in that historic effort?

In the long history of the world, only a few generations have been granted the role of defending freedom in its hour of maximum danger. I do not shrink from this responsibility

—I welcome it. I do not believe that any of us would exchange places with any other people or any other generation. The energy, the faith, the devotion which we bring to this endeavor will light our country and all who serve it—and the glow from that fire can truly light the world.

And so, my fellow Americans: ask not what your country can do for you—ask what you can do for your country.

My fellow citizens of the world: ask not what America will do for you, but what together we can do for the freedom of man.

Finally, whether you are citizens of America or citizens of the world, ask of us here the same high standards of strength and sacrifice which we ask of you. With a good conscience our only sure reward, with history the final judge of our deeds, let us go forth to lead the land we love, asking His blessing and His help, but knowing that here on earth God's work must truly be our own.

*January 21, 1961*

# We Have Changed—and Must

**A historian reviews the profound transformation our nation has known, and charts some lines of development for the future.**

### By HENRY STEELE COMMAGER

WE are in the midst of changes, at home and abroad, as far-reaching in their implications, and in their demands upon us, as any we have experienced in the past. Some of these flow from scientific and technological developments connected with the harnessing of atomic energy, desalinization and the redistribution of water, automation, and so forth; some are the consequences of the new world pattern created by the emergence of Africa and Asia into modernity. Some are created by—or perhaps just required by—the growth of population, cities and the welfare state.

This is an old story, yet one that is ever new. How extraordinary, we assure each other, the changes that we have experienced, the changes that our society has experienced: from the horse and buggy to the automobile; from the railroad to the jet airplane; from dependence on the vagaries of weather to reliance on oil heating and air-conditioning; from stage shows to

television; from old-fashioned guns to atomic missiles. The list is inexhaustible.

A good many of us never get much further in our contemplation of these changes than an expression of astonishment and—usually, though not always—of gratification that it should be our fortune to live in a civilization so mechanized and improved.

YET these changes, far-reaching as they doubtless are, and fascinating, too, are almost purely quantitative. Certainly since the industrial revolution each generation has experienced them—and almost always with comparable excitement. It is a pretty safe prediction that each future generation will continue to experience them. Let us not disparage them. They add immensely to the interest of life; they maintain the economy; they excite the imagination; they give an illusion of progress and, in some instances—

medicine, for example—the reality. But they are not, in fact, very surprising. If they did *not* materialize—that would be really surprising. Nor are they, in any intellectual sense, deeply interesting, for they are the commonplace of growth and of time.

There is a second category of change that is more interesting and more significant, but, again, not particularly puzzling. I refer to those changes, often basic and far-reaching, which are brought about by shifts in the economy or in the political machinery. These changes are for the most part self-explanatory.

Thus, for example, the passing of thrift: a product of inflation and of the welfare state. Thus the changing position of the military: a product of two World Wars, of dependence on the military for survival, and of the shift in the center of gravity of the military itself from the battlefield to the factory and the laboratory. Thus the passing of the myth that rural life was somehow morally superior to urban life: with the population three-fourths urban or suburban, and the countryside itself largely urbanized, and the advantages of urban life so plain, it is inevitable that philosophy should adjust itself to fact.

These and similar changes in the mechanics of life do not present any serious challenge to the understanding.

THE really interesting changes are not so much in material circumstances, or in the machinery of life, but in habits of thought and conduct, in manners and morals, in sentiment and taste. In the long run these may well be the most important, as well, for they dictate, or at least condition, changes in the economic and material arrangements of society. What is more, they are irresistibly interesting, for they do not lend themselves to easy explanation, but challenge and baffle our understanding.

Let us look at a few examples of these changes.

First, consider the growth of humanitarianism. Our great-grandparents —say, a century ago—were at least as virtuous, as religious, as kindly and humane, as we are. Yet they tolerated, nay, took for granted, what we would consider monstrous inhumanity of man to man—and to woman and to child, too. They took for granted that those who were unable to pay their debts should languish in prison for months and sometimes for years. They condemned the feeble-minded to imprisonment in wretched cells, chained them to walls, beat them for their failings and starved them, too: the whole story can be read in Dorothea Dix's famous report of 1842.

THEY allowed little children to work twelve hours a day in factories and mills. They inflicted brutal punishments on prisoners and seamen—flogging, for example—and they assumed, too, that teachers would keep order in school rooms by the liberal use of the rod. They condemned immigrants to life in miserable hovels that were breeding places for vice and crime and disease. South of the Mason-Dixon line, Christian men and women not only tolerated the enslavement of Negroes, but counted the "peculiar institution" a positive blessing for all concerned.

All this has changed. Public opinion no longer permits children to work in factories, no longer tolerates mistreatment of prisoners and the feeble-minded, and has done away with flogging in the Navy and the schoolroom. And even the most intransigent of White Citizens Councils would be appalled at the suggestion of reviving Negro slavery.

Or consider the change in the position of women. A century ago it was taken for granted that while women were morally superior to men they were intellectually—and in almost all other ways inferior. Like children, they were to

be seen but not heard. The London meeting of the World Anti-Slavery Convention broke up because the British would not permit lady abolitionists to participate as delegates!

Women were allowed to work long hours in factories, but not to practice law or medicine, or to preach. The Army did not even want them as nurses in the Civil War. Married women had, in effect, no rights that their husbands need respect: no right even to their children. Everywhere the double standard of morality was taken for granted. As for politics, as late as 1912 intelligent men were gravely prophesying the disintegration of society and the collapse of morality if women were so much as allowed to vote!

IN less than a century all this changed. The double standard gave way to the single. Women today not only control their own property, but the major part of the wealth of the nation. They are not allowed to work long hours, or at night, or for less than minimum wages, but there is no profession from which they are barred, and few which they do not adorn. And none of the dire consequences of their participation in politics has materialized.

Or look to a quite different, but no less significant, development, the growth of tolerance in the past century or two—a short period, after all, in human history. From time to time we are alarmed, and justly, by manifestations of intolerance in our society—by anti-Semitism or anti-Catholicism, by racism in the South, by McCarthyism, by dangerous pressures for intellectual and social conformity. But if we look back over a period of a a few centuries what is most impressive is the steady growth of tolerance—in religion, above all, but in politics and society as well.

TIME was when every nation had a State Church and, what is more, enforced conformity to it by rope and fire. Nor did governments tolerate dissent in the political realm. In the seventeenth and eighteenth centuries, and even in the nineteenth in some countries, political dissent was silenced as fiercely as religious.

Criticism of the King, or of the State, was commonly treated as seditious libel. As late as 1663 William Twyn was drawn and quartered for "imagining" the death of the King, and a few years later Judge Jeffreys sent the noble

Algernon Sidney to the gallows for writing an unpublished manuscript advocating republicanism. Persecution persisted through the eighteenth century and into the nineteenth in England: as late as 1850 Catholics could not attend, nor nonconformists teach, at Oxford or Cambridge.

Nor were our own forefathers much more tolerant. The Puritans of Massachusetts Bay drove out Roger Williams and Anne Hutchinson, and persecuted Quakers and "witches" as did the rulers of Virginia. During the Revolution patriots decreed death for Loyalists, and conveniently confiscated their property, and not long after the Revolution Congress made it a penal offense to write or publish anything that was designed to bring the President or the Congress "into contempt or disrepute."

A generation or so later Southerners zealous to end all discussion of Negro slavery banned magazines and newspapers, burned books, purged libraries, silenced teachers and preachers who agitated the slavery issue. In 1834 a mob in Charlestown, Mass., burned an Ursuline convent; a jury acquitted the mob leaders and the state refused to compensate the Catholic church for the destruction of its property.

In 1837 a mob in Alton, Ill., killed the abolitionist Elijah Lovejoy and destroyed his press. The following year a Philadelphia mob burned Pennsylvania Hall to the ground because abolitionists held meetings there.

CLEARLY the climate of opinion has changed. There is no active religious intolerance in England or in the United States now, no suppression of political discussion or even of social nonconformity. Who would have thought, at a time hardly more than a century ago when mobs were burning Catholic convents, that it would ever be possible to elect a Catholic to the Presidency?

The most baffling of all changes are changes in taste —whatever that elusive word may mean. An infallible way to induce gaiety and a comfortable sense of superiority is to show pictures of bathing costumes of the Eighteen Nineties, or of domestic architecture and interior decoration in the days when the stained-glass window, the rubber plant and the antimacassar were the epitome of good taste.

HOW does it happen that our grandparents took delight

in architecture with turrets and towers and spires and fretwork and stained-glass; that our grandmothers filled their parlors with potted palms, hung heavily tasseled velvet draperies between rooms, and put paper fans in the highly decorated black marble fireplaces? Why did they turn away from the simple and dignified architecture of the Federalist period or of the Greek Revival toward the pseudo-Gothic, the pseudo-Italian and the pseudo-Queen Anne?

Will our grandchildren be as repelled by—or amused by— our glass office buildings, our ranch houses, our functional furniture and our decorative austerity? Beauty, we know, is in the eye of the beholder; why is it that the eyes of each generation reflect such different visions of beauty?

Look, finally, to a major social change — the change in the attitude toward work and toward play. For three hundred years—that is, almost up to our own time—Americans took work for granted and, what is more, looked upon it as a blessing.

Benjamin Franklin's Poor Richard spoke not only to his own generation but to future generations in his many admonitions to be up and doing: "Diligence is the mother of good-luck;" "God gives all things to industry, then plough deep while sluggards sleep;" "The used key is always bright;" "Industry pays debts;" "The sleeping fox catches no poultry;" "There will be sleeping enough in the grave"—these and dozens of others were household axioms for two centuries.

NOT only in Puritan New England and Quaker Pennsylvania, but everywhere in the country, in the South and along the frontier as well, it was assumed that work was the destiny of man and that it was on the whole a good destiny. Few Americans of the past were disturbed by long hours of labor; few gave thought to vacations; and the cliché "Relax!" had not yet entered the language. Play was well enough for children— though even children were admonished that Satan found mischief for idle hands—but when boys and girls had passed the age of 12 they were expected to work like their elders.

Only in the last generation has work come to seem the exception rather than the rule, something to be avoided rather than something to be

259

embraced. The ideal of our time is "relaxation." The coffee break and the cocktail hour, the long summer vacation, the ski week-end, the winter trip to the Caribbean; the cult of sports and of games, the evenings devoted to bowling or to television; the rise of the country club to the position of a national institution — all these reflect the American mania for play.

NOR is this merely a response to automation or to labor-saving devices. The rich of earlier generations had their labor-saving devices as well: cheap labor and slave labor; but that did not persuade them to try to make their lives a perpetual vacation, or free them from a sense of responsibility to work to the limit of their capacity.

How account for these, and similar, changes in moral habits and manners and taste? We cannot explain them but we can, in a sense, bound them, as we used to bound states or countries in old-fashioned geography.

Change is a phenomenon of a highly civilized society. The American Indian, the Aztec and the Inca did not change, nor did the Hindu or the Bedouin during the past three or four centuries. It is a phenomenon of the modern world: there was, apparently, very little change, or interest in change, before the Renaissance.

Change appears to be associated with three major modern institutions—the city, the machine, and democracy. Certainly it proceeds more rapidly and more easily in industrialized economies than in agricultural. It is associated with cities—the very climate of city life encourages experimentation, as well as indifference to tradition and to the past. It is related to education because education presumably opens minds to new ideas; and to democracy because democracy enlists the average man in the affairs of his society and thereby encourages discussion.

THESE characteristics—industrialization, urbanization, education, democracy — are peculiarly prominent in American society. Historically, Americans have been the people most tolerant of, indeed enthusiastic about, change. That process of uprooting and transplanting which was the settlement of America is the obvious and dramatic manifestation of this. But it is in the realm of society, economy and politics that Americans proved themselves most resourceful, most ready to challenge the traditional and embark upon new enterprises.

They challenged the notion that men were to be governed by kings and nobles and priests, and set up the first large-scale experiment in self-government. They challenged the principle that church and state were two sides of the same shield and that each was essential to the support of the other, and set up a state without a state church.

They challenged the age-old notion that society was divided into classes whose position was part of the cosmic system—"untune that string, and hark what chaos follows" — and they inaugurated an experiment in a classless society. They challenged the notion that colonies were always subordinate to a mother country and designed for exploitation, and were the first people to do away with colonialism altogether.

THERE is no such thing as standing still; to cling to the past, or try to preserve the status quo intact, is to go backward. Change does not necessarily assure progress, but progress implacably requires change. If our society is to flourish and prosper, it should encourage both institutions and practices that facilitate change: above all, the growth of education and of free discussion.

Education is essential to change, for education creates both new wants and the ability to satisfy them. It inspires at once that discontent for existing conditions and that faith in improvement which are essential to progress; and it provides the technical skills that enable us to achieve the goals we set ourselves.

Also, if we are to progress by evolution rather than by revolution, we need to encourage free discussion with no quantitative or qualitative limits. Those who fear change instinctively try to suppress the give-and-take of free discussion. They delude themselves that they can achieve security and maintain things as they are by smothering curiosity, blocking inquiry and silencing criticism.

But that policy has never assured either peace or security, unless it is the peace of stagnation or the security of death, and inevitably it drives discontent underground. We have experience of this in our own history. Thus, leaders of the Old South deluded themselves that they could somehow maintain slavery by preventing any discussion of it, thereby imposing on the people of the South a uniform pattern of thought and conduct.

OF course, all they did was to drive discussion not so much underground as North, and to force those who hoped to ameliorate the great evil of slavery into drastic and violent measures. They did not save the institution — perhaps they could not — but they made sure that its liquidation would come about through violence; they did not save their society, but brought about its destruction.

There is no assurance that education and freedom will in fact enable us to solve those tremendous problems that loom upon us or assure a peaceful and prosperous future to mankind. But this is certain: that without education and freedom it will be impossible to solve these or any problems.

By LAWRENCE E. DAVIES
Special to The New York Times.

SAN FRANCISCO, Jan. 29—— The independent thinker was a hero at a four-day international symposium ending here today at the University of California Medical Center.

He received hearty thumps on the back during discussions by American and European experts of the basic theme, "Control of the Mind." The independent thinker was warned, however, that conformity was a powerful and growing attribute of modern society.

The view that, "operationally," neither Western nor Communist culture wants persons to be free was suggested by Dr. Carl R. Rogers of the University of Wisconsin. He said that for the most part society was "extremely fearful and ambivalent of any process which leads to inner freedom."

"Nevertheless," he said, "it is my conviction that rigidity and constriction are the surest road to world catastrophe, and that one of the major hopes for the future is that, through education, we might utilize our knowledge to develop flexible, adaptive, creative individuals

April 30, 1961

who are in the process of learning to be free."

### Women Are Conformers

Dr. Richard S. Crutchfield, a University of California psychologist, reported that experiments tended to show women to be greater conformists than men. He said the young conformed more than the old. He found that among his test subjects military officers on the average conformed more than research scientists or architects.

Dr. Crutchfield gave tests to 600 persons, five at a time. He isolated them in cubicles and told them to answer questions, flashed on a screen, only after they had seen the answers given by the four other subjects flashed on another screen.

The replies actually were his own, and on critical items he deliberately made them wrong to test the independence of the subjects.

Industry was also advised to free itself of personality tests that have come into widespread usage in the recruitment and promotion of employes.

Dr. S. Rains Wallace, a psychologist and director of the Research Life Insurance Agency Management Association in Hartford, Conn., called most such tests worthless.

### Violinist Speaks Mind

He said a "biographical data blank" had shown itself to be far more fruitful than its "more glamorous and publicized competitors." It consisted, he said, of "a series of questions about matters of perceived fact in the individual's past, ranging from age, last year's income, number of dependents, etc., to how the respondent spent his vacation last summer, or whether his current job gives him enough security."

Joseph Szigeti, the violinist, one of the final day's speakers, criticized conformity in the field of music. He decried audiences made up of passive, not active, hearers.

"Not only must we resign ourselves to his [the passive hearer's] presence in the audience but we must also recognize that he has an influence on the taste of the time," Mr. Szigeti said.

# Conspicuous Consumers

IS ANYBODY HAPPY? A Study of the American Search for Pleasure. By Norman M. Lobsenz. 190 pp. New York: Doubleday & Co. $4.50.

By SAMUEL T. WILLIAMSON

ACCORDING to some recent occupants of the list or Page 8 of the Book Review we Americans are a status-seeking, hidden - persuaded, nation of sheep. This best-seller tendency to mental flagellation suggests exploration by a Vance Packard for the reasons for the popularity of the Vance Packard type of indictment of a whole nation.

Now comes another one-man jury which examines the "unalienable" right, as declaimed in the Declaration of Independence, to the pursuit of happiness, and Norman M. Lobsenz's indictment is that Americans have no time for happiness because they are too busy pursuing it. That pursuit, he finds, has become a gigantic rat race. "What has happened in the last thirty years?" he asks. "Why could our fathers, who worked fifty-four hours a week, find time to relax while we run around like a chicken with its head cut off?"

"Conspicuous consumption" was one manifestation of the leisure class which Thorstein Veblen held in such polysyllabic contempt. But virtually the whole population has become conspicuous consumers. Gadgets, gimcracks and "conversation pieces" clutter garages, kitchens, tool sheds, living rooms and everywhere but non-existent attics. Forty billion a year is spent in pursuit of pleasure, a sum equivalent to national outlay for defense. A billion is spent for outdoor swimming pools and a quarter of that sum for women's bathing suits.

AS a result, Veblen's leisure class has become "a leisure mass" for which there is no leisure. "Have fun" is a typical leave-taking phrase, "Our public personalities wear only one expression: a grin." And in the "conspiracy against relaxation" and the "compulsion to be eternally occupied with something or another" as seen by Mr. Lobsenz, there isn't much fun to be had or to smile over.

One Lobsenz chapter examines "pleasures of the senses." Supermarket shelves lined with "Quick-This" and "Minit-That" contribute to the "rape of the taste buds." A generation of "joyless poseurs" has given us "geometric nightmares of modern art and architecture." Melody and harmony are "lost altogether in the dissonance of 'computer music.'"

If Mr. Lobsenz draws a long bow, he tips his arrows with the tart phrase, and we may have fun reading his easily debatable contention that we aren't having fun.

# COURT'S DECISION STIRS CONFLICTS

## Prayer Ban Draws Comment From 3 Ex-Presidents

By ALEXANDER BURNHAM

The Supreme Court's ruling on Monday against official prayers in New York State public schools reverberated across the nation yesterday.

Churchmen, laymen and three former Presidents of the United States expressed opinions for and against what promises to be one of the most controversial decisions since the court ruled on school desegregation in 1954.

Most comments appeared to be against the decision. Declarations of support seemed to come mainly from Jewish groups, civil liberties organizations and some Protestant organizations.

In some quarters the court was denounced. Others praised the decision. And some state officials said they would defy the ruling. Roman Catholic opinion was particularly strong in opposition to the court's decision.

On Long Island, where the controversy had its beginnings, a school official declared that several defiant school boards in Nassau County indicated they would retain the Board of Regents' prayer, which the court had decided, was unconstitutional.

Former President Harry S. Truman declared that "the Supreme Court, of course, is the interpreter of the Constitution." However, former President Herbert Hoover, in a rare comment on a ruling by the court, called for Congressional action.

"The Congress should at once submit an amendment to the Constitution which establishes the right to religious devotion in all governmental agencies— national, state or local," he said.

Mr. Hoover added that the court's decision represented "a disintegration of a sacred American heritage."

In Gettysburg, Pa., former President Dwight D. Eisenhower said that "I always thought that this nation was essentially a religious one." He added:

"I realize, of course, that the Declaration of Independence antedates the Constitution, but the fact remains that the Declaration was our certificate of national birth. It specifically asserts that we as individuals possess certain rights as an endowment from our common creator—a religious concept."

## Does Not Elaborate

General Eisenhower did not elaborate.

Indicative of the defiance of the court's action expressed in some quarters around the country was the statement yesterday by William A. Bruno, a trustee of the Hicksville, L. I., school board and a leader in the conservative movement in Nassau County. A number of school boards in the area, he said, had indicated they intended to retain the Board of Regents' prayer.

Mr. Bruno added that if plans failed in Congress to make an official school prayer legal, he would prepare an alternate prayer for use in the school district that would mention God.

"Let's see what the Supreme Court will do about that," he added.

Mr. Bruno said "it looks like" Robert Welch, the head of the John Birch Society, "had the right idea in asking for the impeachment of the Supreme Court."

Mr. Bruno apparently was referring to a long-standing demand by Mr. Welch for the impeachment of Chief Justice Warren.

Robert S. Hoshino, president of the school board for the Levittown School District, the largest on Long Island, termed the decision a victory for communism.

"Levittown will not vote out the Regents' prayer," he said.

Criticism of the Supreme Court's decision by dignitaries of the Roman Catholic church continued yesterday following Monday night's denunciations by Cardinals Spellman and McIntyre. Cardinal Spellman had said he was "shocked" and Cardinal McIntyre called the ruling "scandalizing" and one that "puts shame on our faces, as we are forced to emulate Mr. Khrushchev."

Cardinal Cushing of Boston said yesterday that the court's ruling was fuel for Communist propaganda.

He declared "it is ridiculous to have a motto like 'In God We Trust' on our coins and to begin legislative sessions with a chaplain's prayer and at the same time prevent children from opening classes with public school prayer."

"You can imagine to what extent the Communists will use that decision as propaganda means," he told 1,200 delegates assembled at the sixteenth biennial Ecclesiastical Congress of the Greek Orthodox Archdiocese of North and South America in Boston.

Bishop Walter P. Kellenberg of the Roman Catholic Diocese of Rockville Centre, L. I., declared, "I am astounded that the men who are leading judicial figures of our country have shown themselves to be confused concerning the 'establishment of religion' and religion itself.

"These are two distinctly different things. This apparent misunderstanding on the part of our judges about the 'establishment of religion' (a state church) and the virtue of religion is most disturbing. Our founding fathers placed the no-establishment clause in the Constitution to guarantee freedom of religion and religious practice, as well as to foster the growth of God-fearing men as members of the newly found republic which has now become our great United States."

In Boston, an editorial was prepared for publication this week in The Pilot, the oldest Catholic newspaper in the United States, asking whether the decision would bring other future changes.

### Theme of Editorial

The editorial will say, in part: "Are we approaching the day, enunciated by Justice Douglas, when the prayer that opens our legislatures and courts, the verses of our national anthem and the inscriptions on our coins, celebration of Thanksgiving and Christmas day, as well as many other religious references traditional in American life, must be cast rudely and permanently aside?

"Are these matters so essentially offensive to the minority groups as to have their public observance prohibited? Must every public religious reference be routed out of American life to please the secularists?"

The ruling, the weekly will say, is "a stupid decision, a doctrinaire decision, an unrealistic decision, a decision that spits in the face of our history, our tradition and our heritage as a religious people."

The ruling, the weekly added, "clearly dramatizes the unreal-

ity and futility of following a course of public policy and public law which is based on the clamorous and constant protestation of a well-organized and litigious minority."

J. Irwin Miller, president of the National Council of the Churches of Christ in the U.S.A., and the Rev. Dr. Roy G. Ross, general secretary, released a joint statement yesterday asserting that "the Supreme Court bears the responsibility for interpreting the laws of our country."

"However," the statement added, "this does not relieve the churches, the schools and individual citizens from the imperative need for finding, within the letter and spirit of the laws of the land, ways to recognize the importance of religion to a healthful culture and to emphasize the strong religious convictions which have been the foundation of our nation."

Rabbi Julius Mark, president of the Synagogue Council of America, expressed support for the ruling.

In Washington, Dr. C. Emanuel Carlson, executive director of the Baptist Joint Committee on Public Affairs, said he was not disturbed by the elimination of "required prayers" from schools because he had never felt that recital of such prayers had any real religious value for children.

George E. Rundquist, executive director of the New York Civil Liberties Union, called the decision a "major step forward for the strengthening of religious freedom."

Elsewhere in the nation there were signs of disagreement with the decision on a state level.

The Superintendent of Education in Alabama, for example, said he believed schools should keep religious practices "regardless of what the Supreme Court says."

Attorney General Daniel McLeod of South Carolina said prayers in his state were up to the classroom teachers.

On Long Island, forty-six superintendents of sixty-one school districts said that their schools practiced some form of daily prayer or meditation.

Eighteen of the superintendents said they had no choice but to comply immediately to the ruling; twenty said they would wait for a school board policy meeting before making up their minds, and eight said they would resist.

# Is God Dead, Or Is It Man?

"Factors arising in the sexual life represent the nearest and practically the most momentous causes of every single case of nervous illness." — SIGMUND FREUD, 1898.

"Many neurotic conflicts are ultimately determined by cultural conditions." — KAREN HORNEY, 1939.

In the nearly 70 years since Freud developed his theory of the libido—that man's nature and conduct are primarily shaped by his instinctual, usually sexual, desires and drives — the psychoanalytic movement which he fathered has become one of the major influences on modern life. But the movement has been fractionalized by dissenting views and emphasis among Freud's one-time disciples.

One of the most influential of the "neo-Freudian" schools is the group that follows the teachings of the late Dr. Horney in emphasizing the cultural rather than the instinctual basis for neuroses. Among the initial members of the group was Dr. Erich Fromm. Although he has since diverged from strict adherence to the Horney teachings, Dr. Fromm—now 66—is one of the leading exponents of cultural and environmental factors in shaping the human psyche.

Last week Dr. Fromm took a look at the modern American and found that he is suffering from a neurosis not traceable mainly to the Oedipus complex but to the headlines, the advertisements and the TV programs that are his daily fare. Addressing 2,500 social workers, psychologists and psychiatrists at the 43d annual meeting of the American Orthopsychiatric Association in San Francisco, Dr. Fromm declared:

"A man sits in front of a bad television program and does not know that he is bored; he reads of Vietcong casualties in the newspaper and does not recall the teachings of religion; he learns of the dangers of nuclear holocaust and does not feel fear; he joins the rat race of commerce, where personal worth is measured in terms of market values, and is not aware of his anxiety. Ulcers speak louder than the mind.

"Theologians and philosophers have been saying for a century that God is dead, but what we confront now is the possibility that man is dead, transformed into a thing, a producer, a consumer, an idolator of other things."

Psychiatrists, suggested Dr. Fromm, should concentrate on "the pathology of normalcy—the drive to conform."

# JOHNSON REVIEWS LIFE IN AMERICA AND FINDS IT GOOD

## Brings Audience of Jaycees to Feet in Comparing U.S. With Rest of the World

## NOTES SOME PROBLEMS

## But President Finds Much to Praise — He Deplores the Impact of Dissent

**By MAX FRANKEL**
Special to The New York Times

BALTIMORE, June 27 — President Johnson roused an audience of young men and women to their feet here today with a passionate defense of "the things that are right with America" and, incidentally, with his Administration and policies.

Confronted by the most enthusiastic crowd he had faced in a long time — 5,000 members of the Jaycees, formerly Junior Chambers of Commerce, and their wives from all parts of the country — Mr. Johnson piled paean upon paean and statistic upon statistic to compare life today and life in the "good old days" and life in America with life everywhere else.

### Calls for Leadership

"If you forget everything else I say, please remember this when you go back to your own community to provide them with the leadership that I want to provide you — that I'm trying so hard to provide you," the President asserted, making most of his points off the cuff.

"You say to them that it's not absolutely essential; it is not a prerequisite; it's not required that you tear our country down and our flag down in order to lift them up."

The response was deafening. The young businessmen, aged 21 to 36, and clad in wildly colored vests and hats, were on their feet, cheering, whistling and cranking sirens. There had been a four-minute ovation at the start and the clapping barely stopped between the President's thoughts.

There was applause for the praise of patriotism and for the scorn for critics. There was applause for the decision to meet with Soviet Premier Aleksei N. Kosygin and for the asserted result of a better understanding of the respective Soviet and American motivation and commitments.

There were cheers for the modestly phrased request for support of the war in Vietnam —"to the extent that you can give it." And there were cheers for the view that the fight for "self-determination" in Asia is really a fight for the right to live that the United States asks for Israel—"for all the nations of the Middle East, and not just for some of them."

### Theme and Purpose

If the President had a theme in commenting on all his concerns from health to Holly Bush, it was that criticism and complaint should not be allowed to drown out great sacrifice and achievement.

If the President had a purpose, it was to tie together his problems and policies at home and abroad in a rationale that seems destined to become the leitmotif of his bid for re-election next year.

If he had any doubts, the crowd may well have begun to dispel them.

Mr. Johnson denied with some heat that the war in Vietnam was causing cutbacks in spending for education and for the poor.

"Well, that's just not true," he said. "That's just not so."

When he became President, the United States was in Vietnam "but we had no poverty program," Mr. Johnson said. More money will be spent on poverty this year than on Vietnam, he insisted, and the amount is being increased by 25 per cent "without tucking tail and running in Vietnam."

Mr. Johnson kept stressing that many problems remained and that solutions were often hard to find. But he kept pouring forth the statistics that showed Americans to be the best fed, best paid and best educated of peoples that are the envy of the world.

Even the slums about which something must be done, he said, are "in a luxury class for the masses of some other countries."

The President said it was "good that we have a system where we can freely talk about what's wrong," but he deplored the impressions often created by dissent. A dozen protestors in the Pentagon get elaborate and dramatic coverage, he said, while nothing is said about the 10,000 young Americans who volunteered their services and their lives at the Pentagon's enlistment centers in the same week.

"Unfortunately, a student carrying a sign, or a protester wearing a beard, or an attention-seeker burning a draft card in front of a camera, can get more attention and more billing than all 10,000 of these volunteers," the President said.

"So we will continue to have those [who] visit the Pentagon to speak their minds and we will continue to have those [who] visit the enlistment stations to give their lives, but let's keep the two in perspective."

Mr. Johnson dealt simply, but from the audience's reaction effectively, with his foreign policy message. In Saigon, as in the Sinai, as at the Holly Bush mansion conference with Mr. Kosygin in Glassboro, N. J., and in the Appalachia poverty program, he said, it was the United States' purpose to assist men in their "struggle to make their own future and to secure their little families."

He met with the Soviet leader, the President said, because in the family of nations the two strongest have the greatest responsibilities.

"For my part and for our nation, that responsibility involves helping other nations to choose their own futures, as they see it," he added, saying he had made clear this motivation and that degree of commitment to the Soviet leader.

The President concluded by noting that he was not too concerned about differences with other nations. Though some are great, all but a few can be reconciled, he remarked.

"But I am concerned," he added, "that every boy and girl and that every man and woman that enjoys citizenship and freedom and prosperity and the blessings of this land know what they have and are determined to build upon it, to improve it, and by all means to keep it."

# Topics: 'Things Fall Apart; the Center Cannot Hold . . .'

**By ROBERT F. KENNEDY**

As 1967 came to an end, E. B. White observed in a Topics column on this page that all Americans seemed to be asking the same questions: "What happened? What went sour? What did I do wrong? Who's to blame?"

President Johnson speaks of a mood of "restlessness." Cabinet officers and commentators, poets and protesters tell us that America is deep in a malaise of the spirit, discouraging initiative, paralyzing will and action, dividing Americans from one another by their age, their views and the color of their skin.

## Direction of the Country

Demonstrators shout down Government officials and the Government drafts protesters. Anarchists threaten to burn the country down, and some have begun to try—while tanks have patrolled American streets and machine guns have fired at American children. Our young people—the best educated and comforted in our history—turn from the Peace Corps and public commitment of a few years ago to lives of disengagement and despair, turned on with drugs and turned off America.

Indeed, we seem to fulfill the vision of Yeats: "Things fall apart; the center cannot hold;/ Mere anarchy is loosed upon the world."

This is a year in which we elect a President. Yet it is a year for us to examine not only the candidates but also the country; to ask not only who will lead us but where we wish to be led; to look not only to immediate crises but also to the nature and direction of the civilization we wish to build.

For the many roots of despair all feed at a common source. We have fought great wars, made unprecedented sacrifices at home and abroad, made prodigious efforts to achieve personal and national wealth. Yet we ourselves are uncertain of what we have achieved and whether we like it.

Our gross national product now soars over $800 billion a year. But that counts air pollution and cigarette advertising, and ambulances to clear our highways of carnage. It counts special locks for our doors, and jails for the people who break them. It includes the destruction of the redwoods, and armored cars for the police to fight riots in our cities. It counts Whitman's rifle and Speck's knife and television programs which glorify violence the better to sell toys to our children.

## Our Intangible Wealth

Yet the gross national product does not allow for the health of our youth, the quality of their education or the joy of their play. It does not include the beauty of our poetry or the strength of our marriages, the intelligence of our public debate or the integrity of our public officials. It measures neither our wit nor our courage, neither our wisdom nor our learning, neither our compassion nor our devotion to country.

It measures everything, in short, except that which makes life worth while; and it can tell us everything about America—except why we are proud to be Americans.

Children are starving in Mississippi, idling their lives away in the ghetto and committing suicide in the despair of Indian reservations. No television sets —not even 70 million of them —can bring us pride in that kind of wealth.

Nor are we taking pride in our place in the world. Once we thought, with Jefferson, that we were the "best hope" of all mankind. But now we seem to rely only on our wealth and power.

So half a million of our finest young men struggle, and many die, in a war halfway around the world; while millions more of our best youth neither understand the war nor respect its purposes, and some repudiate the very institutions of a Government they do not believe. There is something basically and terribly wrong in the spectacle of young Americans, however few, dodging the draft in Canada or deserting to Sweden.

Our power is enormous, the greatest the world has ever seen. Yet, as we see old allies pulling back to their shores, and old alliances dissolving in quarrels, we sense that even America cannot act as if no other nation existed, flaunting our power and wealth against the judgment and desires of neutrals and allies alike. We wonder if we still hold "a decent respect to the opinions of mankind"—or whether, like Athens of old, we will forfeit sympathy and support alike, and ultimately our own security, in the single-minded pursuit of our own goals and objectives.

### The '68 Elections

Finally, we sense that as individuals we have far too little to say or do about these issues, which have swallowed the very substance of our lives. We have discovered that private accomplishment or affluence affords no escape from the perils and plagues that afflict the nation—and that these questions are far too important to be entrusted to remote leaders.

We search for answers to specific problems; but more than this, we seek to recapture our country. We have not yet discovered how to do it. That, perhaps, is what troubles these long nights of our national spirit. And that is what the 1968 elections must really be about.

---

*Mr. Kennedy is United States Senator from New York.*

February 10, 196

## Conviction Lacking

To the Editor:

In his Feb. 10 column on your editorial page, Senator Robert F. Kennedy quotes Yeats's "The Second Coming": "Things fall apart; the centre cannot hold;/ Mere anarchy is loosed upon the world."

Descriptive as this is of our present situation, it would have been even more appropriate had Senator Kennedy gone on to finish the verse, especially in view of his refusal to challenge President Johnson for the nomination. "The blood-dimmed tide is loosed and everywhere/The ceremony of innocence is drowned;/The best lack all conviction, while the worst/Are full of passionate intensity."

ROBIN and GEORGE LAKOFF
Cambridge, Mass., Feb. 10, 1968

## Silent Senator

To the Editor:

It was with great sympathy that I read your "Topics" of Feb. 10 until I realized that its author was Robert Kennedy. The words rang hollow from a man who professes such concern for the deepening crises, one which may be by now irreversible, and yet refuses to expose himself to a course of action backing this concern aside from writing learned articles and delivering speeches of the same ilk.

It seems to me a reasonable assumption that another four years of leadership which has given impetus, if not birth, to such a devaluation of the American spirit and ideal may see the end of America in terms of its viability and freedom.

To wait four or even eight years for the political occasion to be more propitious seems ludicrous, because the heir intended may ultimately be without a province to govern.

Mr. Kennedy is, I fear, no different from the rest of us sidewalk superintendents, except for the quantity of rhetoric which conceals active pursuit and conviction to his ideals and sensibilities.

SAMUEL J. MANN
Clifton, N. J., Feb. 12, 1968

February 17, 1968

February 23, 196

# The Revolution of the Joneses

**Trends in various areas of our life are building toward a radically new America: one nation indivisible—and middle-class.**

By BRUCE BLIVEN

AN amazing social revolution is taking place in the United States. Everyone talks about this revolution, but to feel its impact one should, like me, have been born in the Administration of Benjamin Harrison and have observed the changes it has made —and is still making.

Here are some of the things that have happened since I first began to notice the world around me, sixty-odd years ago:

The family income of American workers (allowing for fluctuations in the value of money) has increased more than two and a half times.

Three of every five Americans now own their homes, as opposed to one in three.

The work week has been reduced by at least twenty hours, or about one-third, and production per man-hour has tripled.

Women, formerly one-fifth of all wage-earners, now constitute one-third.

The proportion of high-school graduates has increased ten times, and of college graduates, seven times.

With 6 per cent of the world's population and 7 per cent of the land, we are producing more than one-third of the world's goods.

When the century began, there was —in spite of all the Fourth of July oratory to the contrary—a well-defined class structure in this country. At the base of the pyramid were the working class and most of the farmers; together, they were practically identical with "the poor." Above them was the much smaller middle class and, above it, the wealthy, far smaller still. Each of these sections of the population had its own culture and characteristics; each was uneasy if thrown into social contact with either of the two others.

Today, the scene is greatly altered. I don't want to paint the picture with false brightness; class distinctions still exist to some degree, as do artificial snobbery and exploitation of the disadvantaged. Yet, as far as the externals of living are concerned, most of us really are beginning to approach the classless society we were always supposed to be.

The cultural revolution is even more striking than the economic one. Sociologists used to divide our society, especially in the long-settled Northeast, into six groups—upper upper, lower upper, upper middle, and so on; today, for most of the country these divisions are not very realistic as cultural classi-

fications. A parallel sophistication index has been noted by Russell Lynes and others, dividing us into various types of high-, middle- and lowbrow; but here again, the influence of mass communications is blurring the lines of demarcation. More than has ever been true of any other large country in modern times, we are a homogenized population.

The new American society is centered upon the middle-income group, or what used to be called the lower-middle class. Its family earnings begin at about $4,000—the point at which discretionary, or luxury buying, begins—and ends, roughly, at $10,000. Above it, the upper-middle class shades off imperceptibly into the wealthy. But the middle-income group is significant as a classification only in a financial sense; culturally, it is rapidly becoming the common denominator of almost the whole nation.

THE working class is moving up from below, both financially and culturally. The rich are also taking on the protective coloration of the middle-income group, partly because of high income and inheritance taxes, partly because what Veblen called conspicuous consumption has gone out of fashion. It isn't only the automobile that is disappearing as a status symbol (vide the amazing success of the new compact cars); all the outward symbols of wealth are becoming less defined. When it is the height of fashion for the sons and daughters of the millionaires to throng college campuses dressed in dungarees like working stiffs, you may be sure our attitude has changed perceptibly.

The speed of these changes continues to increase. In the past decade, the median income has risen about 50 per cent—from $3,300 to $5,050. At the end of the Second World War, in spite of high war wages, about a quarter of the population was still earning less than $1,000; today, one-half of these have moved up into the $1,000-$2,000 bracket. The lowest two-fifths of the population has gained by 114 per cent, and the next two-fifths by 100 per cent; fringe benefits, many of them obtained through union contracts, make these gains even larger. By contrast, the top fifth of the population has gained 59 per cent and the top one-twentieth, 38 per cent.

THE middle-income group is the "anchor man" in our economy. The Internal Revenue Bureau tells us that in 1957 the 26,000,000 taxpayers in that

group had an adjusted gross income of about $156 billion, well over half of the nation's total of individual incomes, now somewhat in excess of $280 billion. The 30,000,000 with incomes of less than $4,000 earned about $62 billion; the 3,500,000 with more than $10,000 received roughly the same amount— about $64 billion. (Of the really rich— $100,000 and over—there are about 23,000, with total incomes of about $4.3 billion before taxes. The old gibe of the Marxists—that 20, or 10 per cent of the population owns 80, or 90 per cent of the wealth — is certainly not true today, if it ever was.)

What are the members of the middle-income group like today? What are they doing, and thinking?

I have had an exceptional opportunity to study them first-hand since, for several years, I have been living in California, in the midst of a vast welter of new suburban

developments. As everyone knows, California is the paradise of the middle class. Every new pattern of living occurs a little earlier here than anywhere else, and it seems to emerge a little larger than life-size.

*We are moving to the suburbs.* In the nation as a whole, about 15,000,000 people have moved out of the cities since the end of the Second World War, increasing the suburban population by one-half.

The total in the suburbs will almost double in the next fifteen years. Suburban incomes usually begin a little above $4,000 and shape upward to the wealthy.

IT is a familiar story that the move to the suburbs has left the big cities increasingly to the slum dwellers and wrought havoc with the city tax structure. The move is also creating problems in the suburbs; the new communities are growing so fast that neither the physical nor the social organization can keep up. It is hard to get the new migrants to take a proper interest in local government, or to vote bond issues for necessary new public services.

*We are losing our inferiority complex.* Those who formerly belonged to the working class are rapidly shedding the remnants of the discomfort they felt when brought into social contact with the middle-in-

265

come group. This is partly because they have money in their pockets, partly because they now know considerably more about what middle-class living is like.

The public schools have contributed to this understanding, as have new media of communication—above all, television, which offers, amid its mediocre dramas, some irresistibly authentic portrayals of "how the other (middle) half lives."

*We are upgrading ourselves culturally.* For generations, the passion of Americans for self-improvement has been one of the wonders of the world. This phenomenon is at its height in the middle-income group today. Our three million college students (they will number six million long before the end of this decade) are without precedent. With a population about three and one half times that of Great Britain, we have 1,800 colleges and universities to her fifteen.

**M**ASS communication is, again, a potent force in this area, both for good and bad. It brings us millions of comic books, but also millions of color reproductions of the world's great masterpieces of painting. It offers jukebox and rock 'n' roll, but it also provides hi-fi sets through which the greatest compositions are heard in millions of homes.

While much routine fare on television is sorry stuff, some of it opens wonderful windows on the world. Olivier's "Hamlet" was probably seen by more people in a single showing than saw the play "live" in all the theatres of the world from Shakespeare's day to this. A majority of our third of a billion paperback books are still at a pretty low level but, again, Shakespeare's plays sell more than a million copies annually. The proliferation of new, quasi-amateur orchestras and theatres across the country is itself an amazing story.

To be sure, some of our new cultural gloss is superficial, but the point is that it pleases those who possess it and helps remove any lingering shyness *vis-à-vis* those higher in the social scale.

*We are playing new family roles.* With the disappearance of domestic servants, replaced by a multitude of labor-saving devices and products, including packaged, prepared foods, has come a change in the division of household labor. The husband and father has to help in a lot of chores his grandfather would have considered beneath him.

**I**T is a truism to say that "the head of the household" is no longer the sort of petty autocrat that Clarence Day Sr. represented to his son—a type known to millions of households sixty years ago. New insights into psychology and a new philosophy of education have destroyed the old image. While the reduction of the family tyrant to the status of mother's helper has some bad aspects, it has good ones, too. And anyhow, dictators are going out of fashion—on the national and every other scale.

*There are fewer tired business men.* Our social evolution has caused a tremendous decrease in the relative number of independent enterprises; the trend today is toward salaried employment with big public or private institutions. Elderly employers, not yet reconciled to this change, complain that young applicants for positions now seem more interested in old-age pensions and other fringe benefits than they are in chances to fight their way to the top.

This makes for a new "togetherness" as the center of interest for the husband and father shifts from his place of work to his family. Margaret Mead has remarked that, instead of the tired business man in the home, we now have the tired family man in the office.

*We get a little more conservative.* As our income rises, and especially as we move to the suburbs, we tend to become more conservative politically. In the anonymity of the big city even the corporation employe can be somewhat to the Left without causing anyone to look askance, but in the goldfish bowl of the suburbs, the story is different; in some of them, it takes real courage to register as a Democrat, or to sympathize publicly with trade unions.

Social upgrading also brings some alteration in church membership, to the advantage of the Episcopal church as opposed to some other types of Protestantism thought to carry fewer connotations of social acceptance.

\* \* \*

**T**HE sociologists, of course, are wringing their hands about many aspects of the new middle class, especially in its suburban manifestations. They say our moral fiber is rotted with easy living and that our young men would not fight to defend their country (the same comment was heard shortly before both the First

and Second World War). They report we are "other-" and not "inner-" directed, which suggests that there was a time —perhaps a hundred years ago?—when this was not true.

They worry because the new suburban developments are filled with young couples of approximately the same age whose children miss any contact with the old. (The alarmists forget that the whole American continent, from the Alleghenies westward, was settled by bands of people of whom this was pretty true.)

They are gloomy over our obsession with television, the number of broken homes (which helps to produce juvenile delinquency), the use of the automobile by adolescents to escape into a world of their own, the rat-race of more and more installment buying, and the fate of the cities abandoned by so many of their most useful and solid citizens.

**W**HILE I'm usually ready to wring a hand with anybody, I can't share wholly in the pessimism of these observers (some of whom are intellectuals repudiating their own middle-class origins and, given the chance, would make equally disparaging reports on Paradise). We certainly have plenty of troubles in this country—and shall continue to have them, human nature being imperfect—but my own observation makes me feel that many of the criticisms of the way most Americans now live refer to conditions that are temporary or exaggerated.

Conformism, as I have suggested, is not a new phenomenon; what is new—and hopeful—is the fact that we now bother to take note of it. The high divorce rate is regrettable, just as it is also regrettable when unhappy people who dislike each other are forced for any reason to remain married. But this problem is more serious among the very rich and the very poor than in the middle bracket.

Installment buying has its dangers, but it is also the foundation of our current prosperity, and there were shiftless, incompetent people, and lots of them, before installment buying was ever invented. More than 95 per cent of the American middle class is demonstrably a good credit risk.

**J**UVENILE delinquency is alarming, and exists to some extent in the middle-class

suburbs, but its real home is in the slums of the big cities. Again, 95 per cent is a good figure for the proportion of young people who behave.

Television presents difficulties, especially in regard to children; but the wild prophecies that school work would be wrecked and the next generation illiterate, heard a decade ago, have all faded away. Dr. Wilbur Schramm, director of the Institute for Communication Research at Stanford University, writes in **TV Guide:** "None of the studies of the effect of television on children has come up with any evidence of a simple and direct effect that was very important \* \* \* Television seems to send children to the first grade with larger vocabularies; it fills their heads with a wide assortment of information, some of which is useful and some not \* \* \*.

"The British anthropologist Geoffrey Gorer warns us that each time in our century when mass communications have got a new medium, the older people have blamed the new medium for the defects they find in the younger generation. You were corrupted by radio, your parents probably said, and I was ruined by Deadwood Dick."

**I**T is true that the exodus from our big cities is creating a bad problem; but the only real answer is to make the metropolis attractive enough to bring back the middle class, or a substantial part of it. (Some countermovement is already beginning to appear.) The great advantages the city possesses in art museums, music, libraries, hospitals, and other necessities and amenities will again exert their appeal, if we can make real progress in solving the problems of living space, smog, noise, dirt, traffic congestion, crime and vice (to be sure, a tall order).

In short, with all the troubles that still hang over our heads, the American middle class is, I believe, the most resourceful, adaptable and resilient large group anywhere in the world, with the highest standards in all fields that have ever characterized any major section of the population in any big country. Always allowing for a minority of malcontents, its members are happy where they are, they don't want to go anywhere else, they don't believe they are in trouble and, until somebody invents a still better way of life, they are here to stay.

# The Loved One Is in the Slumber Room, Laid Out in Style

THE AMERICAN WAY OF DEATH. By Jessica Mitford. 333 pp. New York: Simon & Schuster. $4.95.

### By RICHARD GILMAN

"IT seems I am dying beyond my means," Oscar Wilde is reported to have said on his death-bed. The remark might have served as a prefatory quotation for Jessica Mitford's splendidly uninhibited account of American funeral practices, had she not found one much more devastating — although anything but consciously witty — by the executive secretary of the National Funeral Directors Association, Howard C. Raether. "Funerals," Mr. Raether announces in the delicious if ultimately harrowing rhetoric which Miss Mitford calls upon throughout in order to let the funeral people hang themselves, "Funerals are becoming more and more a part of the American way of life."

The two quotations define the scope of Miss Mitford's witty, sane and sardonic book—qualities that will surprise no one who remembers her best-selling autobiography, "Daughters and Rebels." It is about the high financial cost of dying in America and the immeasurably greater human cost of maintaining a way of death which, in its unspeakable ugliness, its self-deception, sentimentality and perversion of the most fundamental attitudes toward existence, has never been approached by any other society, however technically "backward."

A few years ago an article on the funeral business in the Roman Catholic magazine Jubilee commented that "the whole industry has been moving steadily beyond the reach of satire." Miss Mitford is aware of this (she remarks that Evelyn Waugh's "The Loved One" is by now a piece of understatement), but since she rightly feels that some humor is necessary in view of the subject, she proceeds, as I said, to let the perpetrators of the outrage satirize themselves. They do a magnificent job.

EVERYONE will have his own favorites, but these are mine:

An undertaker defending the high cost of funerals: "So then you've got a slumber room tied up for three days or more. Right there's a consideration: How much would it cost you to stay in a good motel for three days? Fifty dollars or more, right?"

A salesman for a crematorium explaining the new desirability of outside crypts for ashes: "It's all part of the trend toward outdoor living."

An item from the catalogue of the Practical Burial Footwear Company of Columbus, Ohio: "The No. 280 reflects character and station in life. It is superb in styling and provides a formal reflection of successful living."

The same company, Miss Mitford tells us, also offers the Ko-Zee, with "soft cushioned soles and warm, luxurious slipper comfort, but true shoe smartness." And there is another outfit that has a line of "hostess gowns" and "brunch coats" for women who wish to be fashionably dead. What is so unspeakable in all this is not so much the fact of hucksterism — there are salesmen for everything in America, salvation included — but the extent of the campaign by which the American funeral industry has succeeded in obliterating the distinction between death and life, their pretence that the body after death is somehow still involved in the ugliest and most trivial pursuits of the living.

The process is most directly seen in its semantic aspect, the substitution of a set of euphemisms for the old straight-forward vocabulary of death. Undertaker has become "mortician" or "funeral director" (or, incredibly, "grief therapist"), corpse is "loved one" or "Mr. (Mrs., Miss) Blank," coffin is "casket," hearse is "casket coach" or "professional car," flowers are "floral tributes," cremated ashes are "cremated remains" or simply "cremains," cemeteries are "memorial parks" or "memory gardens." And then there are "slumber" and "reposing" rooms, and "calcination," the "kindlier" method of cremation.

Beneath the verbal screen is the unbelievably sordid and rapacious world of the physical procedures. Miss Mitford spends a long chapter on the prices of funerals, detailing the methods by which funeral directors, impelled by their high overheads and fantastic range of unnecessary services, charge as a universal policy all that the traffic will bear, cajoling, shaming or tricking their bewildered and helpless customers into spending everything that can be extracted from them. And she stresses that such practices are not confined to unscrupulous operators, but are endorsed and given elaborate justification by the industry itself. "A funeral is not an occasion for the display of cheapness," intones the National Funeral Service Journal. "It is . . . an opportunity

*Painting by Byron Thomas. Collection Mr. and Mrs. John McDill.*
"Cemeteries are 'memorial parks' or 'memory gardens'."

for the display of a status symbol which, by bolstering family pride, does much to assuage grief."

The book is full of such revelations, and I can only cite a few. It is common practice, Miss Mitford says, for morticians to draw aside clergymen who have accompanied families to the funeral parlor, in order to prevent them from exerting influence toward the purchase of an inexpensive, simple coffin. It is also common practice for crematoria to discourage the taking away of ashes for scattering or private display—something that would eliminate the revenues from "perpetual care" of urns—and this is often done by deliberately failing to use enough heat to pulverize the bones, thus leaving large, unpleasant fragments to deal with.

Perhaps the most shocking revelation concerns the question of embalming. The American funeral depends, as nowhere else, on this process by which the corpse is rendered "lifelike," cosmetized into the monstrous simulacrum of the person the bereaved knew. This is in the interest of "displaying" the corpse, which in turn is in the interest of those extravagant satin-lined coffins.

Miss Mitford here accuses the industry of its most direct deceitfulness. In no state, she says, is embalming required by law (except in rare cases involving transportation of a body), but invariably funeral directors assert that it is, embalm as a matter of course and frequently over-ride the wishes of the deceased or his family in the matter. Their defense on sanitary grounds is wholly unsupported by public-health authorities, and their plaintive plea that it is a consolation to the survivors has backing neither in psychiatry nor in the most ordinary human experience.

THE funeral people are, it

would seem, a much misunderstood group. They see enemies everywhere, enemies, moreover, which by opposing their activities are menacing the American way of life. "Religion, avarice and a burning desire for social reform" are the incongruous triumvirate which the National Funeral Service Journal sees at the head of the plotters.

They are bitterly opposed to anything that threatens their profits or their self-esteem, either directly or by a critique of the perversions they have introduced into our treatment and contemplation of death. If anything else is needed to give the show away it is their paranoiac reaction to the growth of Memorial Societies, the cooperative movement for inexpensive, unostentatious funerals which Miss Mitford describes as one of our only hopes for sanity and dignity in the matter. (A directory of these is included in an appendix.)

Until the beginning of the century, Miss Mitford says, the American funeral was simple "to the point of starkness, the plain pine box, the laying out of the dead by friends and family who also bore the coffin to the grave." But the people of the modern funeral industry—desperately wanting to be respected and loved, claiming a tradition for their abominations which is entirely nonexistent, dizzily wheeling in the contradictions between their rhetoric and their practices—are certain to jump out of their skins at this calm, deadly, unsparing recital of their follies and abuses. Meanwhile the book may help the rest of us to begin moving toward that maturity in regard to death, or at least to its public face, which almost every other society today possesses as a fundamental mark of being civilized.

## Clergymen of 3 Faiths Join in Growing Assault on Prices and Practices

### FAVOR SIMPLE DIGNITY

## Undertakers and Florists Defend Ceremonies— Score Mitford Book

### By HOMER BIGART

Undertakers, long-suffering butts of satire, sarcasm and wisecracks, are now squirming under a new and formidable assault.

The assault is being pressed by the clergy. Tired of the minor role to which they are often relegated at funerals, clergymen of the three major faiths are demanding reform.

They demand a curb on what they call the neo-pagan corpse worship of the modern funeral. Never keen on embalming, cosmetology, fancy coffins and other frills of funerary art, they want a return to simple, inexpensive and austere rites.

Their campaign, which has agitated both undertakers and florists, is receiving considerable impetus from a savagely witty and well-documented exposé by Jessica Mitford.

Having rejected such suggested chapter titles as "The High Cost of Leaving," "Mourning Becomes Expensive," "Remains to Be Seen," "A Funny Thing Happened on the Way to the Mausoleum" and "Dig that Crazy Grave," Miss Mitford scores by understatement in her book "The American Way of Death."

In the opinion of most reviewers, she effectively exposes the commercialization, the unnecessary extravagance and the maudlin deception of the modern funeral.

### Undertakers Counterattack

Angrily, the undertakers have questioned Miss Mitford's motives. From his seat in Evanston, Ill., Wilber M. Krieger, managing director of the National Selected Morticians, concluded that Miss Mitford was

trying to substitute the American funeral service "with that practiced in Communistic countries such as the Soviet Union."

"Is the author a practicing member of any church—an active member of any church?" demanded Dr. Charles M. Nichols, educational director of the National Selected Morticians. Dr. Nichols has written a review of Miss Mitford's book which was published by Simon & Schuster, for the trade. He found her unfair, "a master at the false innuendo," a "propagandist" for memorial societies that advocate cheap funerals.

"Life would be pretty drab without ritual," commented George Goodstein, counsel for the New York State Funeral Directors Association. "I won't say her thinking is abnormal—it's unique. She just doesn't believe in ceremony. Most people do. That's why there are christenings, bar mitzvahs, wedding receptions and funerals."

### 'World Runs on Sentiment'

"The dames that write these books—they don't want to hear anything good," complained Herbert J. Herrlich, president of Frank E. Campbell, "The Funeral Church, Inc."

Mr. Herrlich recalled that a "pipsqueak" clergyman had once told him that funerals contained too much maudlin sentiment. He said he had replied: "If you kill sentiment, you're a dead pigeon. The world runs on sentiment."

But the clergy seem overwhelmingly on the side of Miss Mitford. For years they have been saying in their religious publications that a man's worth is not measured by the expense of coffin or by the quantity of floral tributes.

In a few weeks, the National Council of Churches' Department of Church and Economic Life will begin a study of funeral and burial costs. The Rev. Dr. Cameron P. Hall, executive director of the department, said the inquiry had been suggested by a layman.

He said he had no doubt there was "a lot of paganism" in modern funerals and added: "We ought to educate people in the Christian attitude toward death."

Dr. Hall recalled how when he was the pastor of Christ Presbyterian Church at 344 West 36th Street, terribly poor families would emerge from their slum dwellings to ride to the cemetery in Cadillacs. He found "a grim humor in the disproportionate elegance" of the funeral.

"These families hardly attained a minimum standard of living, yet all the savings of the breadwinner went into excessively costly funerals," Dr. Hall said. "Obviously these people were suffering from feelings of guilt as well as grief. Their armor was down; their judgment was numbed."

Across Morningside Heights, in the library of the Cathedral Church of St. John the Divine, a staff member cautioned, "Not all undertakers are charlatans; some are conscientious and sincere." But he said he was appalled by the chicanery of others, and he told a macabre story of an early encounter with the trade in Southern California.

"During my first assignment in Pasadena," recalled the Rev. Dr. Howard A. Johnson, Canon Theologian of the cathedral, "I was called to a nearby memorial park.

### Pine Box or Paraphernalia

"I entered this outfit expecting to see a corpse laid out. Instead, a marcelled receptionist with a toothy smile said: 'Mrs. McAdoo will see you.'" This sounded weird, because Mrs. McAdoo had died the preceding day.

"She led us into a sort of boudoir, replete with dressing table, combs, etc. Mrs. McAdoo [Canon Johnson was using a fictitious name] was lying on a canopied bed in negligee."

"I stalked out of there and said I'd never conduct a funeral in that place."

Canon Johnson deplored some of the ads in the morticians' journals. He found "Eternity Rest" mattresses particularly offensive for implying that death was just a big, interminable sleep. Miss Mitford, in her book, had also cited Ko-Zee slippers, "hostess gowns," "brunch coats", Bra-Form, Post Mortem Form Restoration and the Beautyrama Adjustable Soft-Foam Bed.

Canon Johnson said he could see no sense in this paraphernalia of "gracious dying." A pine box without any upholstery is good enough for him, he said.

He recalled a nice couple, well-to-do, who bought pine boxes and kept them in the attic for 20 years.

### 'Shocked Silence'

"The man died first," Canon Johnson said. "I remember showing the undertaker that stout pine box. He stood there for a moment, staring in shocked silence.

"Finally he exclaimed: 'But no mattress!'

"I said: 'Can you give me one good reason why a mattress is required?' He couldn't."

Canon Johnson said funerals in Southern California were remarkably uninhibited in vulgarity. One family wanted "Beautiful Dreamer" played at a funeral; another favored "Tumbling Tumbleweed." He knew of a millionaire who insisted that his wife be buried wearing a $30,000 pearl necklace.

Canon Johnson is opposed to embalming, except when required by climate or local law. (No state in the United States requires embalming.) He insists that the coffin be closed during the funeral service as required in all Episcopal churches.

"The closed coffin gives no opportunity to the cosmetologist to display his skill," Canon Johnson said.

He also likes the almost universal use by Episcopalians of the pall, a large blanket that goes over the coffin. This represents the essential democracy of the church, he explained, for if the coffin is covered no one can tell whether it is a pine box or a $5,000 bronze work.

### Floral Tribute a Waste?

Flowers at a funeral are "just a colossal waste," he said, the blooms often shrivelled by the end of the service. Canon Johnson said Episcopal churches "tried to make the florists a little happier by suggesting to the family that memorial flowers be placed on the altar for 'X' number of years."

Cremation was favored by the Rev. Thomas K. Thompson, executive director of the National Council of Churches' Department of Stewardship and Benevolences. The senselessness of an elaborate coffin would be more easily apparent, he thought, if the family knew it would contain the body for only a day or so and then be slid into the crematory.

It is "bad Protestant religion" to squander money, whether on cars, boats, houses or expensive funerals, Mr. Thompson added. He suggested that funeral services be held in churches, rather than private funeral chapels; that the coffins be closed; that instead of spending money on fancy coffins, embalming, cosmetics and flowers the money be used for scholarships, medical research or other work "dear to the heart of the deceased."

Mr. Thompson said that burial associations should be encouraged. These associations, like the Community Funeral Society of the Community Church, 40 East 35th Street, are an extension of the cooperative movement—they seek less expensive service.

Finally he proposed that clergymen regain control of the service. "This," he predicted, "will meet great resistance from funeral directors and florists."

The Rev. Dr. Donald S. Harrington, pastor of the Community Church, reported that his Funeral Society, now 18 years old, had grown steadily despite opposition from the undertaker associations.

The society's least expensive funeral costs $195 plus New York City sales tax. The cost includes a pine coffin, any required preparation of the dead (no embalming), conveyance to crematory within 24 hours after death, and cremation. There is no viewing of the remains.

Roman Catholics and Jews have added their voices to criticism of modern funeral practices. Three years ago, Jubilee, a nationally distributed Roman Catholic monthly, accused undertakers of charging exorbitant prices to the poor. The article condemned the viewing of prettied-up corpses: "Modern embalming, featuring 'that alive look' has enabled corpses to look more and more like window-display mannequins."

### The Catholic View

Subsequently the Canadian Register, official organ of the Catholic Church Extension Society, ran an editorial advising readers to consult the Toronto Medical Society, "a group of citizens who decided four years ago to encourage simplicity, dignity and moderate expense in funeral arrangements."

This provoked James O'Hagen, editor of Canadian Funeral Service, to ask several Archbishops: "Is it official policy of the Catholic Church to approve 'cheaper' funerals simply to save money, no matter the loss to human dignity?"

A reply came from the Apostolic Delegate, the Most Rev. Sebastiano Baggio. The Archbishop proposed that the funeral directors make "an 'agonizing reappraisal' not only of price structures but also of pagan customs and trappings that have crept into the industry."

"The alternative," he added, "may well be that Christian communities, in their dissatisfaction, will set up cooperatives to operate according to the dictates of Christian conscience and to their means."

### Rabbinical Guide

The Jews are traditionally opposed to any ostentation at funerals. A "funeral guide" recently published by the Joint Funeral Standards Committee of the Rabbinical Council of America and the Union of Orthodox Jewish Congregations of America notes that: "Flowers and music have no place at the Jewish funeral service. Embalming and viewing are contrary to Jewish law. Interment should not be unduly delayed."

The dead are to wear traditional white burial shrouds "symbolizing that all men are equal before their Creator." The casket is to be wooden.

"But they don't say 'cheapest wood,'" exclaimed Mr. Goodstein of the New York State Funeral Directors Association. "And the shroud can be expensive!"

### Funeral Customs Defended

To the Editor of The New York Times:

Homer Bigart's recent news article on funeral customs was anything but objective.

It is not valid to relate the average expenditure for funerals to the cost of funerals. They are vastly different things. The first discloses the amount that people have chosen to pay for what they evidently felt was desirable. The necessary cost, however, can be far below the expenditure, for every reputable mortician offers a full range of fees to meet every need—plainly priced and readily available, including all services and casket—usually from about $200 up. And it probably would surprise Mr. Bigart to know how often we serve without fee or any hope of payment.

Studies by our organization based on 358,489 funerals show an average expenditure for the funeral director's complete service of $707.35, with 56 per cent below $600 and only 12 per cent over $900.

It is indeed regrettable that Mr. Bigart's attack attempts to indicate a cleavage between the clergy and the funeral director when none exists except in rare and isolated instances. Further inquiry would have shown that most clergymen feel we perform a valuable service.

The families are striving to express their grief, their personal sense of the appropriate, as best they can in the harrowing, tragic days of a most complex religious, social and emotional crisis. They need all the help, encouragement and sincere interest that anyone can give them — not criticism for failure to conform to something of which they have no knowledge or experience.

I strongly defend the right of the memorial society person to have what he wants and any reputable funeral director will provide it for him whether he belongs to a society or not—as little as he wishes, for a fee that is equitable.

And I just as strongly defend the right of everyone else to have that which is most meaningful and satisfying to them, provided it be within the teachings of their church, if they have one. But I just as strongly deny the right of either group to inflict their personal prejudices on the other. Grief is personal and regimentation is not right.

W. L. BUSTARD,
President, National Selected Morticians.
Casper, Wyo., Sept. 20, 1963.

# CHILDREN OF AGED CAN END SUPPORT

## New Law Puts Responsibility on Authorities, Relieving Hard-Pressed Relatives

## CITY EXPECTED TO SAVE

## With No More Investigations and Court Costs, Expense Can Be Offset, Aide Says

**By NATALIE JAFFE**

Thousands of needy old people are being informed this month that the law no longer requires their children to support them—and the response from both generations seems to be one of great relief.

"I know I'm morally responsible for my mother, but the financial responsibility has been terrible — I'm 73 years old and I've never had a decent apartment of my own," said the son of a 95-year-old resident at the Menorah Home in Brooklyn.

The director of the 420-bed, nonprofit home reported that her elderly residents were "so relieved that their children would now be free to take a vacation, get a new car, or give the grandchildren some extras."

And the head of a commercial nursing home on Long Island said his patients "feel more secure."

"They don't have to worry whether the payment will come or not," he said.

### Obscure Law Used

The change in the law governing "responsible relatives" stems from little-known provisions in Title 19 of the Federal Government's Medicare program and the recently adopted state law passed to take advantage of the program.

The Federal law eliminated the requirement that children be responsible for their parents' medical bills, and the state law extended that exemption to all kinds of support.

Under previous state law, relatives held responsible for support and medical payments included spouses for each other, parents for children under 21 and adult children for their parents.

Earlier this month the city's Welfare Department sent word of the change to all nursing homes, hospitals and homes for the aged here. A notice will accompany every welfare check on July 16. And several nonprofit homes for the aged said they were notifying all families whose support of their parents was known to be a financial hardship.

Welfare officials said there was no way of knowing how many of the 50,000 welfare clients over 65 years of age were being supported in part by their children, or how many new applicants for public assistance would result from the rule change.

### No Way to Get Figures

A review of several surveys made during the last five years, however, indicated that at least 2,000 elderly New Yorkers would be immediately affected. Many more, who have not applied for welfare to protect their children from investigation, pursuit and extra financial burdens, can be expected to apply now, officials agreed.

Welfare Commissioner Mitchell I. Ginsberg, who discussed the new law in a recent interview, called it "one of those rare creatures — a rule that achieves a social good and doesn't cost money."

The additional cost to the city, which will now pick up the bills previously paid by children, will be offset by savings in investigation and court costs, Mr. Ginsberg said.

### Many Cases Go to Court

Thousands of welfare applications have been denied each year after lengthy investigations that found relatives able to pay. And several hundred cases a year are taken to court.

An applicant for welfare is routinely examined to see if he has any relatives who might be held responsible for his support, under a strict formula determining ability to pay.

For example, a $10,000-a-year man with a wife and two children — the cut-off income for a family of four was $5,600 a year — was required to pay half the difference between those two figures, or $2,200, toward his parent's support.

"That bite every year has really been hard on middle-income families, and the old people felt very guilty about it, too," said Mrs. Millie Felder, director of the Menorah Home.

The directors of commercial nursing homes were less enthusiastic about the new law.

"This, in combination with Medicare and Title 19, is going to drive us right out of business," declared Irwin R. Karassic, director of the Metropolitan New York Nursing Homes Association. "There will be no more private patients," he said.

*June 21, 1966*

# *Books of The Times*

## Looking Darling, and Just Looking
### By ELIOT FREMONT-SMITH

THE BEAUTIFUL PEOPLE. By Marylin Bender. Illustrated. 320 pages. Coward-McCann. $6.95.

NEW YORK: The New Art Scene. Photographs by Ugo Mulas. Text by Alan Solomon. 341 pages. Holt, Rinehart & Winston. $19.95.

ONCE upon a time, society was "high," fashion was haute couture (and for ladies only), and both were accepted as properly the pursuits of aristocrats, who, whatever their private behavior, could expect to be treated publicly with a certain amount of mannerly awe. Then—according to Marylin Bender, a fashion and society reporter for The New York Times—came Mrs. Kennedy. "Jackie Has the Knack of Looking Darling," cooed a headline in Woman's Wear Daily, and no one was displeased.

Of course, Mrs. Kennedy didn't revolutionize the concepts of fashion and society all by herself. The revolution was already well under way, and merely waiting for an idol. The main forces of the revolution were identifiable in the nineteen-fifties: the growth of a financially independent, present-oriented and pan-national youth culture; the decline of an aristocracy defined by the services once exclusively available to it (the "jet set" in its final phase), and the development of instant communication and—it follows, as evening follows late afternoon—instant publicity. As Miss Bender briskly puts it: "In mass culture, it ain't what you do but the way that you do it. Shadow is more real than substance. Fashion is a tool in the frantic effort to prove personal and commercial merit." And, she might have added, to make the two indistinguishable.

### A Marriage of Convenience

The theme of "The Beautiful People"—the title is Vogue's concoction for those it and the rest of the fashion media choose to publicize—is the marriage of fashion and a redefined, free-swinging, youth-adulating society in the nineteen-sixties. Miss Bender calls it a marriage of convenience, in which socialites gain free publicity, clothes at wholesale prices and Modish escorts, and fashion designers gain almost free publicity, entrée to the social whirl and modish girls to escort. The result, she says, "is more and more commotion about less and less dress."

But this is only half the story, and along the way in "The Beautiful People," Miss Bender examines the other half—the breakdown of class in fashion, the new androgyny (though she pooh-poohs any new or pernicious deviant influence), the rise of male fashion and of specialized fashion services that make the beauty parlor as dated as Dobbin, and the displacement of beauty as such as a fashion goal.

Now the idea is simply to have "a look"; it doesn't matter what the look is as long as it seems deliberate and attracts attention—the right people's attention, of course, the right people being fashion editors, artists, certain politicians, film people, public intellectuals, culture mongers (the jacket of the book is a large photo of Lincoln Center) and hippie, Mod, pop, New Left, underground, discothèquing, "flower children" and perhaps even flaming youth, or reasonable facsimiles thereof.

Many of these people are named, which is O.K. except that the specifics may give a wrong impression of non-replicability; the leading fashion designers and moguls are examined at some length. Miss Bender knows the scene and writes with caustic good humor (a reverent book would be the antithesis of chic today), and, though only the most desperately out-of-it eager and name-hunters will stick with it all the way, it is an entertaining work of current cultural history.

### The Paper Autocracy

Of the future, Miss Bender writes that hemlines may go up or down, but "women's clothes will never regain what they have lost—intricate construction, for one thing." On paper dresses, though, she does have a comforting word for the status-conscious: "No need to worry that such a democratic dress—one that absolutely anyone can afford—will destroy the fashion élite. The woman of wealth and social contacts can commission an artist to create a special paper dress for a special event, then donate it to a museum, provided the garment hasn't deteriorated on the dance floor." Which would have its own fascination as a Happening, no more or less wicked than, say, Andy Warhol's finding art in the banal, and vice versa, which did occur on his parallel route to fame. You see, everything is camp: everything is serious. Today, a torn paper dress. Tomorrow an opening at the Castelli gallery.

With a genuflection to creative intent, work and Dada history, this is the emphasis of "New York: The New Art Scene," a hefty, pretentious tour through the studios of 15 fashionable, mostly popish, New York artists for those who haven't so far been invited. Alan Solomon's text is lucid enough; Ugo Mulas's photographs are giant-sized and display the artists at what seems an important part of their work: having their pictures taken.

No harm in that: there's enough publicity to go around, and Christmas is approaching. But the volume may also seem to illustrate, for disenchanted viewers, a quotation from Hilton Kramer, The Times's art critic: "The more minimal the art, the more maximum the explanation." Significantly—and what isn't in the swinging sixties?—the quotation appears not in "New York: The New Art Scene," but in "The Beautiful People." Beautiful.

*September 15, 1967*

# What Makes Norman Run

MAKING IT. By Norman Podhoretz. 360 pp. New York: Random House. $6.95.

**By FREDERIC RAPHAEL**

"LET me introduce myself," begins Norman Podhoretz, with what sounds like the peremptory diffidence of a man who needs no introduction. And, indeed, everyone who is anyone knows Norman Podhoretz, right? The editor of Commentary, the Intellectual's Intellectual (never out of the top six), the Symposiast's Symposiast, the man who not only helped to put Jewish writing squarely on the map of American literature but also, for a season and more, threatened to push almost everything else off it (leaving room, Gore Vidal WASPishly complained, for only one O.K. goy, who presumably wasn't Gore Vidal).

Podhoretz's success story—for what else can "Making It" be?—may not seem very stunning to those who judge these things by general fame or large financial fortunes. He tells, when the dust has settled and the names have dropped, a modest enough tale. He has made neither a million nor a millionairess (so far as we know) but in terms of the quality of his achievement, the caliber of the brains who recognize his brains, he has graduated in one of the toughest schools in the world—the New York Literary Establishment—and one which is merciless in its rankings.

What makes Norman run and, more important, what Norman now suddenly perceives makes most of them run, are those two very American urges, the wish to be somebody and to make a buck. No surprises there, surely? But Podhoretz is dealing with a section of the community and a particular specimen—himself—which has systematically repressed these common desires. The intimacy of his book has something of that quality of finally released confession that the analyst's couch is supposed to turn on. The freshness of its account of Brooklyn youth and Manhattan maturity, of Army life and editorial infighting (how good a book, by the way, it makes Wilfrid Sheed's "Office Politics" seem) is due more to the driving personal heed which Podhoretz has to exorcise his own personal demons than because it breaks any fundamentally new ground.

Reading the book I was often reminded of Marcel Marceau's famous mime in which he plays a clown being suffocated by the smiling mask he wears. The Egghead (I use the slightly dated term to lock Podhoretz in the persona he is so much at pains to discard) suffers from the converse affliction: amused, he must frown; delighted, he must groan; tickled, he must weep. No sign of happiness must show through the tragic mask. What, in heaven's name, is there to enjoy in a world where bad art constantly drives out good and where paths of glory lead but to Reader's Digest condensa-

tions? Such, roughly, was—and to some extent remains—the ideology of the Critical Family in whose uxorious but Savonarolan fraternity every Bright Young Man longed so ardently to be numbered, in the days when the young Mr. P. (as Saul Bellow, nettled by honest words about "Augie March," was disposed to abbreviate him) first uncapped his prize-winning pen.

Savonarola's name (like Heaven's) has a real pertinence here; for the Western intellectual, despite his liberated assumptions, is still the prisoner of a vocabulary (a tradition, since that is what a tradition is) loaded with theological concepts and theocratic bias. Fancifully, it might be argued that the eclipse of Savonarola—idea no less than actual incendiary—was engineered only at the cost of a compromise: art was suffered to revive, but only so long as it agreed to be wedded, at least in its classiest aspects, to the apparatus spiritual. (The C.I.A. has nothing to teach the Church about the technique of infection with benign cultures.) Secularization came in, but we still whisper in museums.

It was against this shotgun sublimity that D. H. Lawrence sublimely rebelled, but the modern movement, reindoctrinated by the Flaubertian spell, continued to think of writing as a vocation and persecuted its heretics, enshrined its saints and anathematized its schismatics. F. R. Leavis, one of the key influences on Podhoretz and other brilliant contemporaries, is perhaps better understood (for what he is, rather than what he says, of course) as the last in a great line of English sermon-writers. Between High Priests and Higher Critics there lies a distinction only of rituals and scripture.

Nowhere in the whole of his frank and honest book is Podhoretz more frank and honest than in those passages where he recounts his frantic aspirations to belong to divine circles; he is the very opposite of Groucho Marx — eager to join almost any club that's prepared to have him as a member. I don't mean that Podhoretz has no standa. is, but that any standards, as long as they were high, set him a target he felt he had to meet. Up! Up! Up! Must he write as turgidly as Leavis? Must he have the "tragic sense of life" mandatory with the New York incrowd? Must he drain the Rahvs' martinis to the dregs? All of these things and many, many more he earnestly, humbly set himself to do as he served his novitiate for one Holy Order after another.

Whence this docile, high-stepping brilliance? Born of immigrant parents and raised in Brooklyn, Podhoretz was brought up to be a Jew, whatever that meant. What it meant, his father was not sure, his own practice being inconsistent, typical of that generation which lacked fervent religious conviction while remaining fervently convinced of the importance of being *recognizably* Jewish. The early sections of "Making It" are tactfully and touchingly revealing of the fearful ambitions of Podhoretz's family, who simultaneously goaded their scintillating son toward the all-embracing American dream of success and tried to keep him true to a concept of Jewishness which his education and success itself were bound to lead him to find both socially narrow and intellectually unendurable.

How hard he tried to serve two masters! All the time he was stepping out at Columbia College, learning the vocabulary of the "Christian" tradition under the eyes of enlightened Jews like Lionel Trilling and Moses Hadas, his feet remained bandaged, so to speak, by the tight restraints wished upon him by the Jewish Seminary he still felt himself obliged to attend and where, through sheer force of habitual endeavor, he tottered on to become the star pupil. So does the "brilliant" child, the apple of his mother's eye, postpone the pain (to others and to himself) of radical decisions by the exercise of "pure" cleverness. Nothing is more ironic than the reputation for "maturity" and seriousness which this postponement earns.

Podhoretz speaks elsewhere of all the young men of the 1940's and 50's who skipped adolescence and, marrying young, bid fair to break out in all the usual spotty symptoms somewhere in their thirties. Had he himself in mind? "Making It" is an act of calculated shamelessness; as those who marry too young break their bonds in the hope of regaining their lost opportunities for promiscuity, so Podhoretz breaks his icons to recover his lost freedom to enjoy himself. Sexually, he has few regrets, thanks to the warm ministrations of a Rabbi's daughter, but that tragic mask, buckled so long over any joyous expression, has rubbed blisters he cannot any longer suffer in silence. Intellectually, he has managed a long marriage between his wide culture and his Jewish heritage. Commentary, recognizably Jewish and yet widely read and assimilated as a journal of ideas, has given him an emancipated home where he has been comfortable and, like a model of the liberal parent, simultaneously a trusted elder and one of the boys.

Norman Podhoretz.

Photograph by Tim Kantor.

HE says that someone once said of him that he had a superego like a horse; well, he has allowed it to ride him damned nearly into the ground. Now he has decided to unhorse his horse and to proclaim, to confess, to shout out—what? Well . . . that he likes things! And by that I don't mean that he has decided to dole out more raves or change his mind about "Augie March," but that, quite literally, he has come to realize what pleasure there is in pleasure, how sweet is the smell of success. The taste for real estate has long been one of the appetites prudent Jews have repressed (Stephen Birmingham's "Our Crowd" is full of crude examples) and I suspect that the timing of Podhoretz's confession has to do with the new sense of security in and of commitment to the American scene felt by the sons and grandsons of the first-generation immigrants. To abstain from the possession of property and the enjoyment of wealth is no longer a sign of solidarity or of allegiance to higher values. It is simply, like celibacy since Freud, the token of an unused life.

Podhoretz's proclamation of the vitamin-charged deliciousness of the fruits of this world involves, however, something beyond the revelation that room service hath charms, though one passage of defiantly crude stridency does indeed show him nauseatingly over-reacting to the joys of a bell push. (To discover the sophisticate suddenly doe-eyed is, to me, quite reassuring, but dough-eyed is going too far.) I suspect that "Making It" seems so fresh, so miraculously right for the times, because Mr. Podhoretz, ever adroit at scenting the coming climate, is not only telling his own sad story with attractive wit and self-mockery but also presaging a far more fundamental assault on the whole metaphysical and social basis of the Artistic Life. A straw in the wind is the ad for the new magazine Avant-Garde, in which the vanguard is persuasively redefined as, among other gaudy things, "wildly hedonistic." Mr. Eliot, thou shouldst be living at this hour!

The position which Podhoretz is abandoning is no longer commanding; like a crusader castle, it lords it over a route less often traveled than overflown. We no longer, let me suggest, look to critics with the same servility; their right to stop and search is no longer absolute: we want to get on, not to be received among the garrison. (Though no one objects if they cheer us on our way.) The resurgence of the movies, as everyone's medium, a medium which largely postpones judging until *showing* has been completed, suggests that the whole structure of our presuppositions may be on the point of subversion.

THE young, it might be held, no longer want to make girls (or even It): they want to make movies. Film bypasses conceptualization and so renders much less vital the office of the analyst, the evaluator. (I take this to be at least a part of Susan Sontag's case Against Interpretation.) Experience need no longer pass through the morally fine sieve of language but can get through, in unreduced forms, with the aid of a visual (and *heard*) "vocabulary" which is uncontaminated by the detritus of the ages. We are burdened with a cultural superego which no analytic system can unship, since new analyses systematically trade new superegos for old. (People now feel guilty about not having sexual problems, a meta-Freudian predicament if there ever was one.)

Let's not lose our heads: if we can now claim to "know more" than the Old Party Members and the deluded Bright Young Men, of whom Podhoretz is a paradigm, it is because, as Eliot said in another context, it is them that we know. Podhoretz has "allowed himself to be fully known" and so may give the key to the B.Y.M. of the next generation, which will allow them to shuck the iron mask of premature intellectual good taste and join in the common pursuit of self-knowledge and self-expression. "Making It" is at once a warning and a model.

January 7, 1968

# A Strange Kind of Simplicity

By NORA EPHRON

TWENTY-FIVE years ago, Howard Roark laughed. Standing naked at the edge of a cliff, his face gaunt, his hair the color of bright orange rind, his body a composition of straight, clean lines and angles, each curve breaking into smooth, clean planes, Howard Roark laughed. It was probably a soundless laugh; most of Ayn Rand's heroes laugh soundlessly, particularly while making love. It was probably a laugh with head thrown back; most of Ayn Rand's heroes do things with their heads thrown back, particularly while dealing with the rest of mankind. It was probably a laugh that had a strange kind of simplicity; most of Ayn Rand's heroes act with a strange kind of simplicity, particularly when what they are doing is of a complex nature.

Whatever else it was, Howard Roark's laugh began a book that has become one of the most astonishing phenomena in publishing history. "The Fountainhead" by Ayn Rand was published on May 8, 1943, by the Bobbs-Merrill Company, at the then-staggering price of $3. Its author, a Russian émigré with a Dutch-boy haircut, had written the 754-page book over a period of seven years, six months of which were spent hanging around an architect's office learning the lingo of the profession Howard Roark was to romantically exemplify. The book was turned down by 12 publishers; the editor-in-chief of Bobbs finally bought it over the objections of his publisher.

In the years since, "The Fountainhead" has sold over 2.5-million copies in hard and soft cover. Bobbs-Merrill, which is about to issue its 32nd printing, a 25th-anniversary deluxe edition that will sell for $8, calls it "the book that just won't stop selling." Along with Miss Rand's other blockbuster, "Atlas Shrugged" (1957), it forms the theoretical basis for the Rand philosophy known as Objectivism. New American Library considers the two books the prize possessions of its paperback backlist. "Once or twice a year, we reissue these books," said Ed Kuhn, former editor-in-chief of N.A.L. who recently became publisher of the World Publishing Company. "And I'm not talking about a printing of 10,000. These books are reprinted in runs of 50,000 and 100,000 copies. What this means is that every year, 100,000 new people read 'The Fountainhead'—a new

generation of readers every five years. Other than with Fitzgerald and Hemingway — and I couldn't even say Faulkner and Sinclair Lewis— this just doesn't happen."

"The Fountainhead" is the story of Howard Roark, modern architect, and his fight for integrity, individualism and ego-fulfillment against the altruistic parasites who believe in Gothic architecture, and more important, against the near-heroes who do not believe the fight can be won. It is also the story of Roark's thoroughly peculiar love affair with one Dominique Francon (whose body is also a clean composition of straight, clean lines and angles, notwithstanding the fact that conventional curves might have been better). Miss Francon is first attracted to Roark while he is working splitting rocks in a granite quarry on her property; she is raped by him on page 219 of the new deluxe edition and page 209 in the paperback. When she discovers, somewhat later, that he is the only architect whose work she admires, she sets out to protect him from disappointment by making certain no one ever gives him a job. She marries two men just to tick him off. "Dominique is myself in a bad mood," Miss Rand has said.

The book ends in a blaze of ego when Roark blows up a housing project he has designed after details of it have been altered; he is ultimately acquitted; and he marries Dominique. They live happily ever after, one supposes, in a steel and glass house.

When "The Fountainhead" was published, almost every critic who reviewed it missed the point — that the welfare of society must always be subordinate to individual self-interest. Rather than dealing with this theme of ego, most of the reviewers treated it as a Big Book, and treated it badly. The reviewer for The New York Times called it "a whale of a book about architecture" and thought it overwritten and melodramatic. Wrote the critic for Architectural Forum, "The architecture profession, may the Lord protect it, has at last been made a background for a novel. According to its publishers, 'The Fountainhead' will do for architects what 'Arrowsmith' did for doctors. Though we do not recall precisely what 'Arrowsmith' did for doctors, it seems likely that 'The Fountainhead' may do a lot less for the architects."

Like most of my contemporaries,

I first read "The Fountainhead" when I was 18 years old. I loved it. I too missed the point. I thought it was a book about a strong-willed architect — Frank Lloyd Wright, my friends told me — and his love-life. It was the first book I had ever read on modern architecture, and I found it fascinating. I deliberately skipped over all the passages about egotism and altruism. And I spent the next year hoping I would meet a gaunt, orange-haired architect who would rape me. Or failing that, an architect who would rape me. Or failing that, an architect. I am certain that "The Fountainhead" did a great deal more for architects than Architectural Forum ever dreamed: there were thousands of fat, pudgy non-architects who could not get dates during college because of the influence "The Fountainhead" had on girls like me.

In any case, about a year after I read the book, I sat in on a freshman orientation seminar which discussed the book (among other novels it was suspected incoming Wellesley girls had read) and was shocked to discover:

That Howard Roark probably shouldn't have blown up that housing project.

That altruism was not bad in moderation.

That the book I had loved was virtually a polemic.

That its author was opposed to the welfare state.

I also learned, though not in the seminar, that architects were, for the most part, nothing like Howard Roark.

I recently reread "The Fountainhead," and while I still have a great affection for it and recommend it to anyone taking a plane trip, I am forced to conclude that it is better read when one is young enough to miss the point. Otherwise, one cannot help thinking it is a very silly book. ("Atlas Shrugged," the saga of a group of Roark-like heroes who go on strike, move to a small Atlantis somewhere in Colorado, and allow the world to go to pot in their absence, is not a silly book. It is a ridiculous book. It is also quite obviously a book by an author whose previous work readers have missed the point of. It is impossible to miss the point of "Atlas Shrugged." Nevertheless, it is a book that cannot be put down, and therefore probably should not be picked up in the first place.)

"*The Fountainhead* was only an overture to ATLAS SHRUGGED," Miss Rand has written, emphasizing the disparity between the two books

Ayn Rand.

by italicizing the one and capitalizing the other. The philosophy of Objectivism that assumes such pollinating proportions in the latter was only blossoming in the former—though according to Rand's official biography, it had begun to develop in Miss Rand shortly after her birth.

Ayn (rhymes with pine) Rand was born in 1905 to Jewish parents in Petrograd. "I know they call it Leningrad now," she said years later, "but I still call it Petrograd." She grew up loving the romantic fiction of Victor Hugo, hating Communist ideology and denouncing God. In 1926, after a Chicago relative offered to sponsor her passage to the United States, Miss Rand joyfully left for New York. As she sailed into Manhattan, she once recalled, "There was one skyscraper that stood out ablaze like the finger of God, and it seemed to me the greatest symbol of free men. . . . I made a mental note that some day I would write a novel with the skyscraper as a theme." The tallest skyscraper at that time was the elaborately Gothic Woolworth building.

In the 17 years that elapsed between her vow and its execution, Miss Rand, among other things, lived at the Studio Club in Hollywood, was an extra in the film "King of Kings," wrote motion picture scenarios, stuffed envelopes, waited on tables, and married Frank O'Connor, a painter, who is not to be confused with the short-story writer. (His paint-

ing of a skyscraper under construction adorns the cover of the deluxe edition of "The Fountainhead.") In 1934, she and her husband moved to New York; in 1936, her first novel, "We the Living," was published, and her play, "The Night of January 16," a melo-drama, ran seven months on Broadway. And she set to work—in architect Ely Jacques Kahn's office—on her new book.

By late 1940, she had completed one-third of the manuscript, then entitled "Second-Hand Lives," and been rejected by 12 publishers. When funds ran out, she went to work as a reader at Paramount Pictures; there she showed her book to the late Richard Mealand, Paramount story editor. Mealand, who loved it, showed it to Archibald Ogden, editor-in-chief of Bobbs; Ogden, who loved it, sent it to Indianapolis to Bobbs-president D.L. Chambers; Chambers, who hated it, sent it back with orders not to buy it. "I do not care much for allegories myself," he wrote. "I presume you will not wish to proceed further with your negotiations." Ogden wrote back: "If this is not the book for you, then I am not the editor for you." To which Chambers wired: "Far be it from me to dampen such enthusiasm. Sign the contract." Miss Rand signed — and received a modest $1,000 advance.

THE final manuscript—75,000 words shorter than Miss Rand had written it—continued to displease Chambers. He suggested that the book be cut in half. Without telling Ogden, he ordered the first printing cut from 25,000 copies to 12,000 and insisted it be printed from type: there was no point in making plates for a book that would clearly never sell out its first printing.

And of course it did. "The Fountainhead" — the title was changed at Ogden's suggestion —has become known in the trade as the classic cult book. The classic book that made its own way. "It was the greatest word-of-mouth book I've ever been connected with," said Bobbs-Merrill's sales manager William Finneran. "Over the years we spent about $250,000 in advertising it, and we might as well have plowed it back into profits for all the good it did us." Six slow months after publication — and its purchase by Warner Brothers for a film that starred Gary Cooper and Patricia Neal — sales began to build; ultimately, the book appeared on the best-seller list 26 times through 1945. "I did not know that I was predicting my own future," Ayn Rand once wrote, "when I described the process of Roark's success: 'It was as if an underground stream flowed through the country and broke out in sudden springs that shot to the surface at random, in unpredictable places.'"

As it happened, the places were not all that unpredictable. According to Finneran, the book first began to sell in small cities. A bookstore owner in Detroit told his customers he was not interested in their business unless they bought the book. A friend of the public library in Cleveland demanded that the library buy 25 copies of it. A lady in Minneapolis gave it to all her friends and later claimed total credit for the book's sales. "It started out with people in their 30's emerging from the Depression," said Finneran, "and I think if you put them through a computer you'd find they were people who have read three books in their whole lives, other than books they had to read in business, and the other two were 'Gone With the Wind' and 'Anthony Adverse.'"

By 1950, an unorganized cult of Rand enthusiasts — none of whom, by the way, had missed the point — was at loose in the land. Miss Rand

Gary Cooper in a scene from the film version of "The Fountainhead."

was then living in a house built by Richard Neutra in the San Fernando Valley, where she had moved six years earlier to write the script of "The Fountainhead." (The movie, released in 1949, was not financially successful, but Miss Rand loved it. Not a line of her script was altered. "She told me she would blow up the Warner Brothers lot if we changed one word of her beautiful dialogue," said producer Henry Blanke. "And we believed her. Even Jack Warner believed her. He gave her a cigar.") There, she

received a letter from a U.C.L.A. psychology student named Nathaniel Branden asking about the philosophical implications of her novel. Branden became her disciple—and since his family name is Blumenthal it is probably no coincidence that his adopted name contains his mentor's last name (as well as ben—as in son of?). When he, his future wife Barbara and the O'Connors moved to New York a year later, Branden became the organizer of a group of Rand devotees who met every Saturday night at Miss

Rand's East 30's apartment. They were known as the Class of 1943, after The Book's publication date, and Miss Rand referred to them as "the children."

In 1957, after "Atlas Shrugged" was published by Random House, Branden opened the Nathaniel Branden Institute and has since graduated 25,000 students schooled in the principles of Objectivism: that individualism is preferable to collectivism, selfishness to altruism, and 19th-century capitalism to any other kind of economic system. Those beliefs, which run loose through "The Fountainhead" and run amuck in "Atlas Shrugged," are expounded by Miss Rand and Branden in The Objectivist Newsletter, which has 60,000 subscribers. Objectivists occasionally smoke cigarettes with dollar signs on them. They quote Howard Roark. Like John Galt, the Roark of "Atlas Shrugged," Branden is an unabashed capitalist and bills his organization as "profit-making." Miss Rand is said to wear a gold dollar-sign brooch.

One would have liked to ask Miss Rand about that brooch, but she does not give interviews to non-sympathizers. One would have liked to ask her a number of other questions: how she feels about "The Fountainhead"'s continuing success, how she reacts when she thinks of the people in publishing who said it would never sell, what she does when she opens her royalty checks. Presumably, Ayn Rand laughs. ∎

# The Unknown And Unseen

THE OTHER AMERICA: Poverty in the United States. By Michael Harrington. 191 pp. New York: The Macmillan Company. $4.

### By A. H. RASKIN

BEHIND the glittering facade of America's "affluent society" lies a ghetto of loneliness and defeat populated by the poor. It is an invisible land, even though it has millions of inhabitants and its streets are often those we walk. It is a modern poor farm for the rejects of the economy and of society—men, women and children maimed in spirit and dragging out their lives at levels beneath those necessary for human decency.

This is the angry thesis of Michael Harrington's study of poverty in a nation that prides itself on having built the highest standard of living in the world and on having done most to assure economic justice for all its people. Mr. Harrington, who began being angry ten years ago when he was ministering to Bowery derelicts as a member of the staff of The Catholic Worker, makes no pretense to detachment. His book is a scream of rage, a call to conscience. He considers it scandalous that so much social misery should survive in a nation with a technology adequate to provide every citizen with a decent life.

His study is not meant as a dissent from the thesis so illuminatingly expounded by John Kenneth Galbraith in "The Affluent Society" that our economic thinking must now be geared to solving the problems of opulence rather than those of want. Mr. Harrington cheerfully embraces the Galbraith notion that today's poor are the first minority poor in history, the first poor not to be seen and thus the first poor the politicians can afford to ignore. But he has no sympathy for Mr. Galbraith's belief that what we have left in the way of poverty can be overcome by an individual case approach or by attacking "islands" of unemployment or social neglect.

His skepticism stems from a conviction that the structure of our welfare state, with its hitching of public and private social-security systems to wages, is calculated to provide the least help for those who need it most. He estimates—and the basis for his estimates is likely to draw violent challenge from less impassioned analysts—that 40 million to 50 million Americans now live as

Photograph by David Gahr.
"An alien in an affluent society."

internal aliens in a society bent on forgetting their existence.

In this quarter of the population he puts the needy, aged and the sick, the workers rendered useless by technological change, the unskilled in an industrial netherworld exempt from minimum-wage protection, the undereducated adolescents stripped of aspiration, the uprooted farm workers now equally unwelcome in urban slums, the victims of racial discrimination and a broad range of other economic outcasts.

Handicapped by lack of schooling and lack of skills they stand not to benefit by automation and other industrial progress but to experience a deepening of exile. Not only do they not share in the fruits of the higher productivity improved technology permits but they find themselves further disadvantaged by the freeze-out of the unskilled and semiskilled work on which they once relied.

TO Mr. Harrington, there is a culture of poverty that makes the poor different from the rich in ways that transcend money. "Everything about them from the condition of their teeth to the way they love is suffused and permeated by the fact of their poverty. * * * They need an American Dickens to record the smell and texture and quality of their lives. The cycles and trends, the massive forces, must be seen as affecting persons who talk and think differently."

Mr. Harrington does his best as stand-in for Dickens, with strong overtones of Jeremiah. He writes with sensitivity and perception as well as indignation. The Council of Economic Advisers might say, with justice, that he has overdrawn his case as to both the size and intractability of the problem. That is no indictment. The chroniclers and celebrants of America's upward movement are plentiful; it is good to be reminded that we are still a long way from the stars. Without the will to see through the wall of affluence and recognize the brotherhood of the impoverished stranger on the other side, we are unlikely to muster the corrective energy essential to render false this parting Harrington thrust:

"At precisely that moment in history where for the first time a people have the material ability to end poverty, they lack the will to do so. They cannot see; they cannot act. The consciences of the well-off are the victims of affluence; the lives of the poor are the victims of a physical and spiritual misery."

April 8, 196

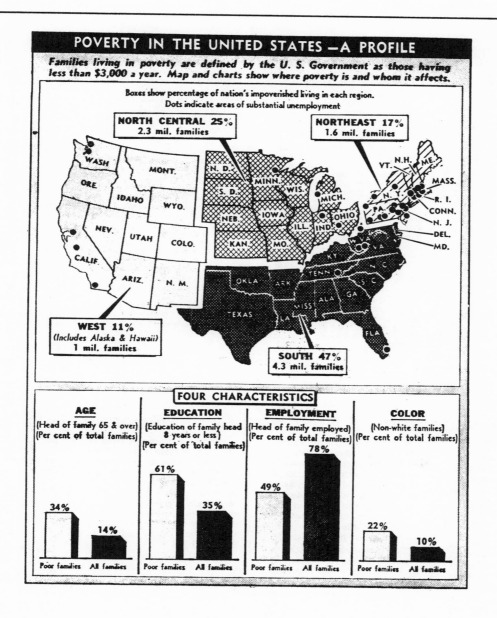

## POVERTY IN THE UNITED STATES —A PROFILE

Families living in poverty are defined by the U. S. Government as those having less than $3,000 a year. Map and charts show where poverty is and whom it affects.

Boxes show percentage of nation's impoverished living in each region.
Dots indicate areas of substantial unemployment

**NORTH CENTRAL 25%**
2.3 mil. families

**NORTHEAST 17%**
1.6 mil. families

**WEST 11%**
(Includes Alaska & Hawaii)
1 mil. families

**SOUTH 47%**
4.3 mil. families

### FOUR CHARACTERISTICS

**AGE**
(Head of family 65 & over)
(Per cent of total families)

Poor families 34%
All families 14%

**EDUCATION**
(Education of family head 8 years or less)
(Per cent of total families)

Poor families 61%
All families 35%

**EMPLOYMENT**
(Head of family employed)
(Per cent of total families)

Poor families 49%
All families 78%

**COLOR**
(Non-white families)
(Per cent of total families)

Poor families 22%
All families 10%

August 16, 1964

# Campaign Issues

## Positions of Nominees Differ Sharply On Poverty and Medical Care of Aged

### By JOHN D. POMFRET
Special to The New York Times

WASHINGTON, Oct. 29—It is the nature of politics that the campaigners exaggerate each other's position. This has certainly been the case in the current campaign with respect to the issues of Social Security, welfare policy and poverty.

Were one to believe their Republican detractors, President

**News Analysis**

Johnson and, even more so, his Vice-Presidential running mate, Senator Hubert H. Humphrey, are wild-eyed radicals bent on turning the country into a Socialist state.

And were one to believe the

Democrats, Senator Barry Goldwater is a heartless fellow untouched by the sufferings of the poor, the sick, the aged and the helpless.

Yet, even allowing a substantial discount for campaign hyperbole, one of the interesting facets of this campaign is that in the broad area of Social Security and welfare policy the voters are being offered a choice, not an echo.

Consider, for example, two specific issues, poverty and medicare.

President Johnson recently declared that he would make enactment of a medical insurance plan for the aged under Social Security the first item on his legislative agenda if re-elected.

Senator Goldwater is flatly opposed to medicare. On Sept. 1 he made a cross-country flight from Phoenix, Ariz., to Washington to vote against medicare in the Senate.

#### Dispute on Poverty Plan

Mr. Johnson considered his $1 billion antipoverty measure, passed by the last session of Congress, to be an essential element of his domestic program.

Mr. Goldwater denounced this, too, later calling it a "hodgepodge of handouts" and a "worthless nostrum." He accused Mr. Johnson of trifling with human misery to get votes.

With respect to the Social Security system itself, the issue is not so clearly drawn. Although the Democrats have implied that Mr. Goldwater would abolish it, he has never taken such a position and, apparently recognizing that to be so identified is extremely damaging politically, has taken pains to deny repeatedly the Democrats' allegation.

Just what Mr. Goldwater would like to see happen to the Social Security system, however, is not entirely clear.

He used to say it should be made voluntary. He abandoned this some time ago and now says he wants to see it strengthened. But he has not said in detail just how, although in the past he has voted for raising benefits.

Mr. Goldwater sees the system as providing a basic floor of economic protection, but says it should never be allowed to replace individual savings and private retirement and insurance plans.

### Decries 'Intervention'

His enthusiasm for private solutions — or those undertaken by state and local governments, as opposed to the Federal — is most clearly evident in the general welfare field.

Here is what the Arizonan said last month:

"We in the Republican Administration shall never abandon the needy and the aged. We shall never forsake the helpless. We understand their problems in our hearts.

"But we know that a true and lasting solution of these problems cannot be found in degrading, capricious and politically motivated handouts from the White House. It must ultimately be found in a thriving and compassionate economy and in programs principally handled by the levels of government closest to the people.

"Prudence requires that we proceed slowly and steadily in withdrawing the central government from its many unwarranted interventions in our private economic lives."

Mr. Goldwater has also suggested that most of the people who lack jobs or education owe their position to low intelligence or low ambition. He has declared that a trend toward "handouts and circuses" is threatening the nation with a fate comparable to that of Rome or ancient Egypt.

Last month he linked "welfare state" social theories to rising crime rates.

"If it is entirely proper for government to take from some to give to others," he told a rally at Minneapolis, "then won't some be led to believe that they can rightfully take from anyone who has more than they?"

### Johnson's Views

In sharp contrast, the Johnson Administration believes that more often than not poverty and unemployment are the results of social and economic circumstances—for example, racial discrimination, the accident of having been born into poverty, and technological change — rather than the personal deficiencies of the poor or the jobless. Furthermore, the Administration believes that the Federal Government has a responsibility to do something in this area.

President Johnson told a labor convention last Spring:

"Some have criticized me for taking from the haves and giving to the have-nots. Well, I want you to read me loud and clear. When Secretary [of Defense Robert S.] McNamara can eliminate an obsolete military base that is a have in our old budget, I'm not going to hesitate to let Sargent Shriver use it to save a have-not, perhaps a delinquent school dropout, from 50 years of waste and want."

And more recently:

"Giving a man a chance to work and feed his family and provide for his children does not destroy his initiative. Hunger destroys initiative. Hopelessness destroys initiative. Ignorance destroys initiative. A cold and indifferent government destroys initiative."

The issue, then, seems clearly drawn between the two national tickets.

The Johnson Administration believes the Federal Government should undertake a wide range of social welfare programs to help the poor and the aged.

Mr. Goldwater would rely primarily on private efforts, supplemented by state and local government programs, keeping the role of the Federal Government to a minimum.

October 30, 19

# Washington: A Just and Compassionate Society

By JAMES RESTON

WASHINGTON, March 16—At no time since the New Deal, and probably not even then, has this country had such a clear sense of Government purpose on the home front as it has today.

President Johnson may not achieve a Great Society in his time—few men in history can claim that—but he is working toward a just and compassionate society with remarkable vigor, skill and success.

His equal voting rights message is only the latest evidence of the fact. Long before he ever came into the White House, he maintained that the vote was the key to the emancipation of the American Negro.

Assure this, he insisted when he was in the Senate, and eventually most of the other grievances of the Negro in the South would be met by politicians who would have to consider the rights of all voters, black and white.

### Johnson's Strategy

Five years ago it would never have occurred to Lyndon Johnson to propose that Federal registrars should be empowered to assure Negro voting when local officials barred the way, but he has always insisted that equal voting was the best answer to the Negro's problems.

This, however, is only one aspect of a larger Johnson strategy. He has clearly identified his targets: ignorance, poverty, disease and crime. His strategy is to attack these problems as if they were epidemics threatening the health of the entire society, and his tactic is to strike at the highest possible moment of public attention.

This is what he did with the voting message. He waited out his critics. He let the television clips of the riots in Selma make their own impression on the whole country. He allowed the demonstrations and appeals for counteraction to build up, and then dramatized his response with perhaps his most eloquent speech before the television cameras and the Congress.

### The Art of Timing

His timing has been superb. For a generation and more, while the nation has been preoccupied with foreign policy, the problems of the home front have accumulated. There is scarcely a community or an institution that has not been transformed or felt the need of transformation in this convulsive period since the war.

It is only now, however, that a massive effort has been put in train to deal with the vast expansion of the nation's population, the decline in its facilities and standards, the gap between its rich and poor.

Without an informed order of priorities, without a plan of action, and without a shrewd knowledge of the House and Senate, however, the present program of education, medical care, manpower retraining, law enforcement, housing and urban development, and equal voting rights would be in trouble on Capitol Hill.

Now the prospect for this entire legislative program is good, and for a variety of reasons. Imaginative fiscal and tax policies have kept the economic boom going and provided new money to finance new social programs. The White House has been used as an educational forum to dramatize the condition of the schools and the poor.

A new class of vigorous young Negroes has captured the revolution of their people and forced their problems on the conscience of the rest of the nation and, ironically, Alabama and Mississippi have made their contributions too.

For without their vicious and extreme opposition, carried into homes across the nation by the new instruments of communication, public opinion might still be indifferent to the Negro revolt.

President Johnson's contribution has been to channel all these emotions and struggles into legislation at the right moment, and in this he has had the help of an effective young home-front Cabinet and staff, centering on Vice President Humphrey, Bill Moyers in the White House, Attorney General Nicholas deB. Katzenbach, and Secretaries Wirtz at Labor, Celebrezze at Health, Education and Welfare, Udall at Interior and Freeman at Agriculture.

### The Contrast at State

The contrast of the home front with policy and direction on the foreign front is startling and instructive. The President's goals and priorities are clear at home. They have been defined and broadcast to the nation in a remarkable series of speeches and messages to the Congress, and this is precisely what has been lacking in the foreign field.

For lack of an over-all strategy, Saigon has become the major capital of the State Department's world, the Gulf of Tonkin larger than the Atlantic, Vietnam more important than Europe or Latin America.

Overseas, the problem is clearly more difficult, for the President cannot control and sometimes cannot even influence the actions of other nations, but it needs a sense of strategy and purpose as well, and the President has demonstrated on the home front what can be done with an orderly plan.

March 17, 19

# Prosperity Is Not Enough

The United States, in the ordering of its domestic affairs, continues to offer to the world the curious spectacle of private affluence in the midst of public poverty. The economy is booming, profits and wages are rising, and the stock market makes new highs; but public services are starved for funds.

The nation's schools, hospitals, libraries, museums, parks and charitable agencies are short of fully trained professional employes. Buildings are overcrowded and salaries are low. In New York City, the problem of staffing schools in Harlem and other slum areas is critical. In Oklahoma, teachers are contemplating what would be, in effect, a statewide boycott because of chronically low salaries.

Many small towns across the nation are desperate to recruit doctors who will serve as general practitioners, and the doctor shortage is worsening. Yet all the while the sales of air-conditioned luxury automobiles, of mink coats, of gourmet foods and imported vintage wines steadily rise.

Economists have long been familiar with these stark contrasts between what they call the public and the private sectors of the economy. Their concerns entered the general stream of national political debate in the late nineteen-fifties. The Rockefeller Fund reports called attention to the accumulation of unfilled national needs. President Eisenhower reacted to the growing uneasiness by appointing a Commission on the National Purpose. The Kennedy "New Frontier" and the Johnson "Great Society" programs developed out of this same ferment.

Halfway through this decade, however, the country has not yet made much actual progress in overcoming these deficiencies. The antipoverty and Federal education programs are only now getting under way. Other programs under consideration in Congress show some promise of helping to close the gap.

But there are disquieting signs that the President and Congress do not fully comprehend the dimensions of the problem or are unwilling to face up to them. One such sign is Mr. Johnson's espousal of luxury excise tax reduction. Reducing such taxes in the way proposed doesn't do much to improve or enlarge essential public services. Another such sign was the resistance within the House Public Works Committee to undertaking an effective—and necessarily expensive—water pollution program. The Federal Government, like the states, has tried to evade action on railroad passenger service, which steadily deteriorates.

The moral of these prosperous years is plain: prosperity is not enough. Private spending and private initiative cannot clear the smoggy air, clean the polluted rivers or abolish the hideous slums. More money in private pockets cannot teach a child, police a dark street or enable an overworked doctor to be two places at once. If the national purpose of a just, compassionate and truly free society is to be achieved, the President, the Congress and an informed electorate must see to it that the public needs of the national community are fully met. They are not being met now. The nation's priorities are still out of order.

May 23, 1965

# SLUM DWELLERS FOUND EXPLOITED

## Government and Business Accused of Manipulation

### By NATALIE JAFFE
Special to The New York Times

ATLANTIC CITY, May 27— Life in the slums is characterized by the lawlessness of private businessmen and government agencies even more than by that of the slum dwellers, several sessions of the National Conference on Social Welfare were told today.

"The lawless manipulation of the poor by the private trader and the allegedly benevolent government agency has accomplished the very exploitation and harassment of the poor it was intended to prevent," according to Edward V. Sparer, legal director of Mobilization for Youth in New York.

"There has been a tendency on the part of the bar, and the social workers, too, to look for cures for mistreatment in new legislation," he said in an interview. "The emphasis should not be on new laws, but on getting out to use the ones we've got."

In an earlier session, William Stringfellow, a white lawyer who has practiced in Harlem for many years, said that most of his colleagues declined to represent the poor "because their cases have been regarded as vulgar, offensive and unimportant."

As a result, he said, "the law has completely failed to deal with the multitude of cases, complaints and causes of action of the poor for so long that the multitudes of ordinary citizens now distrust the law as a significant instrument of social change."

Both lawyers emphasized the urgent need for advocates to secure due process for poor persons whose daily lives are controlled by public institutions. Examples of this institutional control were given by Richard A. Cloward, professor of the Columbia University School of Social Work and research director of Mobilization for Youth. He said:

"The Department of Welfare controls subsistence levels, the Housing Authority controls access to housing, school-suspension hearings control who stays in school. These are semi-judicial, administrative tribunals making decisions that are just as important as court decisions concerned with the deprivation of liberty.

"Yet we have no lawyers who know about welfare regulations, eviction proceedings or school suspensions. The only way to keep large institutions responsive to the people they serve is to insure that the client has resources to redress his grievances."

The legal staff of four at Mobilization for Youth, Mr. Sparer said, has recently handled these typical cases:

That of the 40-year-old mother who slept with her four children for several nights in tenement hallways after the local welfare office refused emergency assistance; that of the young man about to be dismissed from his job for defaulting on installment payments under a contract he never signed; that of two Puerto Rican brothers, 17 and 18 years old, evicted from a public-housing project after their only relative's death, because of a rule against minors holding leases.

May 28, 1965

# Great Society: What It Was, Where It Is

By CLAYTON KNOWLES
Special to The New York Times

## Federal Domestic Role Has Increased Tenfold in the Johnson Era

WASHINGTON, Dec. 8 — "Dick Nixon is going to be taking over a government one hell of a lot different than the one he left in January, 1961."

These words, spoken by a departing White House aide, dramatize the change in the Federal domestic role in the last five years because of Lyndon B. Johnson's Great Society program.

Joseph A. Califano Jr., President Johnson's man Friday in nurturing the Great Society, said in an interview that President-elect Richard M. Nixon would find that a tenfold growth had occurred in governmental activities designed to "make life better for all Americans."

**45 Then, 435 Now**

"There were about 45 domestic social programs when the Eisenhower Administration ended," Mr. Califano said. "Now there are no less than 435."

As the Johnson Presidency nears an end, it is possible to look at the Great Society with some perspective and examine a few of its programs.

The larger government role described by Mr. Califano involves more than new laws, though they are counted in the hundreds. Much of the change stems from a new direction of old programs, imparted either by Congressional or administrative action, to meet broader objectives.

Topsy-like at times, the program has grown in many directions, though authorizations and funding were often cut well below Administration requests. A drumfire of criticism frequently attended a grudging acceptance of principle.

It was said that inflation watered down the dollar value of benefits to the poor, that waste and duplication threatened achievements, that over-promises created problems bigger than those up for solution.

Conservatives urged that the Federal obligation be discharged through general area grants to the states for programs developed at the state level.

The enormous cost of the war in Vietnam limited the amount that could be spent on the social programs. The fact that the war was being accelerated while the Great Society program was being developed made what progress there was all the more remarkable.

Many of the new programs have virtually become household words — Medicare, model cities, the Job Corps, the war on poverty, truth in lending, Head Start and Upward Bound.

**Programs Redirected**

Others, such as the insured mortgage loan program of the Federal Housing Administration that spawned the nation's suburban growth, are now being redirected to the cities.

To put a price tag on the vast, somewhat amorphous Great Society is difficult, though it is clear that it represents a national commitment entailing billions of dollars.

Excluding Social Security payments, Mr. Califano estimates that the Great Society is a $25.6-billion enterprise, compared with the $9.9-billion social budget of 1960 and $12.9-billion of 1963. If Social Security costs are included, he says, $49-billion is being spent today against $22-billion eight years ago.

This turnabout in national policy on the homefront, signaled in a speech by President Johnson at University of Michigan commencement exercises on May 22, 1964, constitutes a recognition of mushrooming urban problems as an essential matter of Federal concern.

Though a descendant in many ways of the New Deal, Fair Deal and New Frontier, the Great Society established a new approach to problems that accented working relationships with the region, the state and the city more than direct Federal aid to the individual.

In five years, something of a national consensus has developed in support of comprehensive aid to cities. The recognition is now general that the cities, lacking a broad tax base other than real estate, do not have the resources to meet the many problems in a nation 70 per cent urbanized.

Even an economic conservative such as Representative Gerald R. Ford of Michigan, House Republican leader, acknowledges that huge Federal outlays are needed to meet the urban crisis. He argues only that the money go directly to the states in "broad problem area grants."

President Johnson described the Great Society as "a challenge constantly renewed" in his University of Michigan speech.

"The Great Society rests on abundance and liberty for all," he said. "It demands an end to poverty and racial injustice, to which we are totally committed in our time. But that is just a beginning.

"The Great Society is a place where every child can find knowledge to enrich his mind and enlarge his talents. It is a place where leisure is a welcomed chance to build and reflect, not a feared cause of boredom and restlessness. It is a place where the city of man serves not only the needs of the body but the desire for beauty and the hunger for enrichment.

"It is a place where man can renew contact with nature. It is a place which honors creation for its own sake and for what it adds to the understanding of the race. It is a place where men are more concerned with the quality of their goals than the quality of their goods."

Threaded through the address ran the promise of a broad attack on the problems of the poor and underprivileged — housing, education, equal rights and equal opportunity — as well as a drive for environmental improvement — conservation, beautification, clean air and clean water — that would benefit all.

The programs that emerged can be grouped under general headings despite constant interaction among elements in different categories, particularly in the cities.

The highlights of the Great Society, by general category:

### CITIES

ANTIPOVERTY CAMPAIGN: Begun in 1964 with the Economic Opportunity Act and a one-year authorization of just under $1-billion, stepped up greatly in later years with the Department of Health, Education and Welfare, the Department of Labor and the Department of Housing and Urban Development, set up in 1965, increasingly involved.

TRANSPORTATION: Urban mass transportation acts of 1964 and 1966.

MODEL CITIES: Act of 1966 proposing grants to cities, supplemental to those available from other Federal sources, to fight urban problems in the most blighted areas, including housing, health, education, jobs, welfare, transportation and public facilities. Funded with $312-million in the fiscal year 1968. Its appropriation has been doubled for the coming year.

RENT SUPPLEMENTS: Started in 1966 to provide better housing for low-income families, funded far below Administration requests.

CRIME CONTROL: Safe Streets and Crime Control Act of 1968, providing block grants to improve state and city law enforcement.

### CIVIL RIGHTS

SEGREGATION: Act of 1964 outlawing discrimination in hospitals, restaurants, hotels and employment; authorizing shutoff in Federal aid used in a discriminatory manner.

VOTING: Act of 1965 protecting voting rights at the national, state and local level.

HOUSING: Act of 1968 protecting civil rights workers and initiating fair housing requirements nationally.

COMMUNITY RELATIONS: Transfer of the Community Relations Service from the Commerce to the Justice Department.

### CONSERVATION

WATER POLLUTION: Water Quality Act of 1965 and the Clean Water Restoration Act of 1966, under which $5.5-billion in grants have been made for water purification and sewage treatment plants.

AIR POLLUTION: Clean Air Act and Air Quality Acts of 1965 and 1967 seeking air cleansing through regional grants.

WASTE: Solid Waste Disposal Act of 1965.

ROADS: Highway Beautification Act of 1965 to cover 75 per cent of the cost of removing roadside eyesores.

RECREATION: Urban beautification under the urban renewal act, including the creation of vest pocket parks in congested areas.

PARKS: Expansion of the

national park system by 2.2-million acres.

## CONSUMER PROTECTION

MEAT: Meat Inspection Act of 1967, requiring states to enforce Federal standards or yield to Federal inspection.

POULTRY: Poultry Inspection Act of 1968.

FABRICS: Establishment of Product Safety Commission in 1967 to study dangerous household products and flammable fabrics amendments to a 1953 act directing the Secretary of Commerce to fix safety standards in clothing.

FARM PRICES: Food Marketing Commission set up to study farm-to-consumer prices.

TRUTH IN LENDING: Act of 1968 requiring dollar-and-cents accounting of actual costs under "easy credit" and other financing plans.

PACKAGING: Fair Packaging and Labeling Act.

ELECTRONICS: Hazardous Radiation Act designed to reduce possible harmful effects of television and other electronic house devices.

TRAFFIC: Traffic and Highway Safety Act setting standards to be met by manufacturers for automobile safety.

## EDUCATION

ELEMENTARY SCHOOLS: Elementary and Secondary Act of 1965, strengthened in 1966, providing stepped-up aid to 100 per cent in 1970 for quality education, including text books for public and private schools, with a $9.2-billion authorization for the next two years.

HIGHER EDUCATION: Act of 1965 providing liberal loans, scholarship and facility construction money.

TEACHER CORPS: Act of 1965 to train teachers.

AID TO POOR: Educational Opportunity Act of 1968 to help poor go to college.

ADULT EDUCATION: Act of 1968.

## JOB OPPORTUNITY

TRAINING: Manpower Development and Training Act of 1964 to qualify persons for new and better jobs.

JOB CORPS: Economic Opportunity Act of 1964 setting up Job Corps, Neighborhood Youth Corps and new careers programs.

BUSINESS: Job Opportunities in the Business Sector, which, under the leadership of the National Alliance of Businessmen, seeks 500,000 jobs for hard-cored unemployed.

APPALACHIA: Program of 1965 seeking economic development and jobs in 11-state economically depressed area.

WAGE: Increase in minimum wage by 35 cents to $1.60.

## HEALTH

MEDICARE: Set up in 1965, insurance for 20 million citizens at 65 under the Social Security system to cover hospital and doctor costs.

MEDICAID: Act of 1965, providing medical care for the needy, with 7.7 million people in 43 states now getting aid.

DOCTORS TRAINING: Health Professions Act of 1963-65 seeking to train 1,700 doctors.

NURSES TRAINING: Act of 1964, which has already provided 65,000 loans for schooling.

MENTAL HEALTH: Program of 1965-66, providing centers for treatment and training.

IMMUNIZATION: Program for preschool children against polio, diphtheria, whooping cough, tetanus and measles, under which, for example, the annual incidence of measles dropped from 450,000 in 1963 to 62,000 last year.

HEALTH CENTERS: Heart, cancer and stroke regional centers.

CHILD HEALTH: Improvement and Protection Act of 1968 for prenatal and postnatal care.

### Climate Ripe

Much of all this legislation had been sought for years, and when Mr. Johnson took office after the assassination of President Kennedy, the climate was apparently ripe for breakthroughs.

President Johnson moved quickly, and kept up the pace after the landslide election in 1964 brought him large majorities in the House and Senate.

Negro rioting in the slums in 1966, capped by a Republican gain of 47 seats in the still-Democratic House, slowed the Great Society.

The election strengthened the Southern Democrat-conservative Republican coalition that had repeatedly blocked many of these projects in the past.

The Administration sought $662-million for the fiscal year 1968 ending last June 30 to fund the model cities program. It got $312-million. It sought $1-billion for 1969 and got $625-million.

However, observers considered it significant that a modest expansion of the Great Society was nevertheless made during the 90th Congress.

While noting that the Vietnam war intensified during the developing stages of the Great Society, Wilbur J. Cohen, Secretary of the Department of Health, Education and Welfare, said recently that the choice was "not between guns and butter."

"There is a third factor—quality of life," he said. "It is a decision every American must face. A third of our families have two or more cars, 15 million of us own yachts. There is a lot of money for liquor and cigarettes. We've

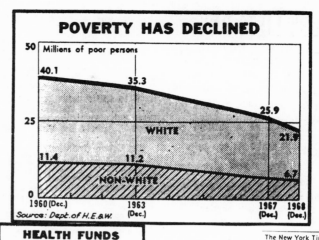

## POVERTY HAS DECLINED
Millions of poor persons

40.1 · 35.3 · 25.9 · 21.9

WHITE

11.4 · 11.2 · NON-WHITE · 6.7

1960 (Dec.) · 1963 (Dec.) · 1967 (Dec.) · 1968 (Dec.)

Source: Dept. of H.E.&W.

The New York Times
Dec. 9, 1968

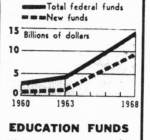

### HEALTH FUNDS
—— Total federal funds
- - - New funds

Billions of dollars

1960 · 1963 · 1968

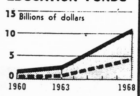

### EDUCATION FUNDS
Billions of dollars

1960 · 1963 · 1968

### FUNDS FOR CHILDREN AND YOUTH
Billions of dollars

1960 · 1963 · 1968

### FUNDS FOR AGED
Billions of dollars

1960 · 1963 · 1968

### FUNDS FOR POOR
Billions of dollars

1960 · 1963 · 1968

Source: Dept. of H.E.&W.

got the money but we've got to establish our priorities."

He said that "the United States can eliminate poverty in the coming decade and go on to assure adequate income for the overwhelming majority of Americans."

### The Poverty Line

Mr. Cohen noted that since 1960 the Government had "lifted 18 million out of poverty." He defined the poverty line as $3,300 annually for a city family of four. Still below the poverty level are 21.9 million Americans.

There are other Administration claims of progress, such as 10.5 million jobs created in seven and a half years, salaries and wages up 72 per cent in the period, corporate profits after taxes up 61 per cent, three record years with unemployment below 3.8 per cent, the Federal education budget up $12-million, $5.5-million spent for housing and community development.

Many impartial observers find it hard to disagree with most claims, which are accompanied with details on the job still to be done.

During the recent national campaign, Mr. Nixon did not reject any significant facet of the Great Society but at various times suggested that the drive for a better America could be achieved more effectively by other means.

He favored, for example, tax incentives to draw business more actively into the campaign against poverty and related programs.

But the country will probably have to wait until the new President's inaugural address Jan. 20 for a clearer idea of the course of the Great Society.

December 9, 1968

# COURT LIFTS BAN ON 'ULYSSES' HERE

## Woolsey Holds Joyce Novel Is Not Obscene—He Finds It a Work of Literary Merit.

### IGNORES SINGLE PASSAGES

#### His Judging of Volume as a Whole, Not in Isolated Parts, Establishes a Precedent.

James Joyce's "Ulysses," a novel which has been banned from the United States by customs censors on the ground that it might cause American readers to harbor "impure and lustful thoughts," found a champion yesterday in the United States District Court.

Federal Judge John M. Woolsey, after devoting almost a month of his time to reading the book, ruled in an opinion which he filed in court that "Ulysses" not only was not obscene in a legal sense, but that it was a work of literary merit.

Under the ruling the book will be published here in unexpurgated form on Jan. 20 by Random House. It will contain an introduction especially written for it by Joyce and also the full decision of Judge Woolsey, which was considered here to establish a precedent in an interpretation of "obscenity."

Judge Woolsey held in brief that single passages could not be isolated from a literary work in determining whether or not the work as a whole was pornographic.

He defended Joyce's purpose in writing "Ulysses" and suggested that attacks against the book had been occasioned because "Joyce has been loyal to his technique and has not funked its necessary implications."

The court, expressing its own reaction to a reading of the book found it to be "brilliant" and at the same time "dull." It had not been "easy to read," he noted, nor had it been clear in all places, though in other places it was thoroughly intelligible.

#### No "Dirt for Dirt Sake."

"In many places," Judge Woolsey wrote, "it seems to me to be disgusting," but nothing, he added, had been included in it as "dirt for dirt sake."

Before announcing his decision Judge Woolsey noted that he had read the whole book and had given special attention to passages singled out by the government as objectionable.

"I am quite aware," he concluded, "that owing to some of its scenes 'Ulysses' is a rather strong draught to ask some sensitive though normal person to take. But my considered opinion, after long reflection, is that whilst it many places the effect of Ulysses on the reader undoubtedly is somewhat emetic, nowhere does it tend to be an aphrodisiac.

"'Ulysses' may, therefore, be admitted into the United States."

Judge Woolsey directed that a copy of the book which the custom censors had seized as it entered this port from Europe be surrendered to Random House, Inc., the assignee. Samuel C. Coleman, Assistant United States Attorney, who brought the matter to the court's attention, said that the decision, in his opinion, was a masterpiece and "thoroughly wholesome."

Judge Woolsey began his opinion by saying that he believed "Ulysses" to be "a sincere and serious attempt to devise a new literary method for the observation and description of mankind."

He explained that in arriving at his conclusions he had also weighed the merits of other books of the same school. He described these books as "satellites of 'Ulysses.'"

#### Holds Purpose Not Obscene.

The principal question he had to solve, the court suggested, was whether or not Joyce's purpose in writing the book had been pornographic.

"In spite of its unusual frankness," he wrote, "I do not detect anywhere the leer of the sensualist. I hold, therefore, that it is not pornographic.

"In writing 'Ulysses' Joyce sought to make a serious experiment in a new if not wholly novel literary genre.

"Joyce has attempted—it seems to me with astonishing success — to show how the screen of consciousness with its ever-shifting kaleidoscopic impressions carries as it were on a plastic palimpsest not only what is in the focus of each man's observation of the actual things about him, but also in a penumbral zone residua of past impressions, some recent and some drawn up by association from the domain of the subconscious.

"The words which are criticized as dirty are old Saxon words known to almost all men, and, I venture to many women, and are such words as would be naturally and habitually used, I believe, by the types of folk whose life, physical and mental, Joyce is seeking to describe.

"If one does not wish to associate with such folks as Joyce describes, that is one's own choice."

December 7, 19

# The Evolution Of the Movie Kiss

## It has passed through startling phases since its casual discovery in the silent film era.

### By BOSLEY CROWTHER

To some people a kiss is a greeting; to most it is a form of caress—but to the people who make our Hollywood movies it is just a sure-fire theatrical device, durable and unfailing. The custard pie, once a fixture, is almost obsolete. The slug-fest, though still employed for rough work, has limited application and is crude. Even the "chase," a standard fitting in film carpentry through the years, is less used in modern construction. But the kiss is here to stay.

One reason for its cinematic popularity is that the kiss is always in process of evolution; it is never static. For proof there is Alfred Hitchcock's recent picture, "Notorious," in which he tested his theory that people make love even when their thoughts wander to mundane things. In a now-famous scene the hero and heroine, Cary Grant and Ingrid Bergman, brush each other's faces with their lips, never precisely kissing, but never really doing anything else. And most of the time one is talking on the telephone and the other is planning a chicken dinner. It was a bit of artistic romancing that poses a challenge to Hollywood. New and more exotic ways of kissing must be invented.

The kiss on the screen has exerted a singular fascination almost since the beginning of movies as a popular graphic art. At that it was casually discovered. Among the first episodic pictures made for the antique movie-viewers—pictures of such gay, abandoned things as Annie Oakley shooting clay targets and Sandow hoisting heavyweights—the producers, Raff and Gammon, came up with a "sleeper," as we say. It was a close-up of a lady and a gentleman indulging in a big kiss.

That was all. The lady and the gentleman were May Irwin and John C. Rice, who were then (1896) starring in a successful stage play, "The Widow Jones," in which there occurred what some considered a sensational kissing scene. It was this scene which was enacted before the Edison camera, all in thirty seconds at most, and today it has all the appearance of good, clean, comical fun. But to the gawking, impressionable patrons of the wondrous new shadow machine it was a thrilling and shocking experience. Something new had been discovered.

And even a Hollywood genius can now see the reason why. On the stage the kiss is an objective thing as observed at comparative distance by the third-person audience. But on the screen, with the benefit of the close-up, which takes the audience right into the embrace—plus all of the other cinema techniques employed to establish the mood—the kiss can be made as immediate and emotionally climactic as if it were being placed upon the willing observer's lips.

Even the most blasé observer is barely insulated against the movie kiss. That was the startling discovery made with the May Irwin-John C. Rice kiss. Audiences suddenly went for it with overwhelming inquisitiveness. Ladies observed the performance in delicious embarrassment; gentlemen came away from it with self-conscious smirks. And persons of more pious disposition regarded it with horrified distress. "The Kiss," which was what the title tagged it, was the movies' first bait for censorship. Terry Ramsaye, the early screen's historian, quotes a bluenose in prophetic words: "Magnified to Gargantuan proportions, it is absolutely disgusting. Such things call for police interference."

Since that earliest exhibit, which had no story around it and no point (other than to demonstrate an action), the kiss has enjoyed a mad career as a principal participant in the story-telling revels of the screen. And the manner and style of its employment have undergone considerable change. Indeed, in the exercise of kissing, as displayed on the screen for fifty years, may be traced not only the character of our entertainment but also our general romantic attitudes and mores.

For instance, in the earliest silent flickers the kiss was still a fitful affair, hasty and paroxysmic. An actor would grab an actress, plant a quick, explosive smack on her lips and then jump away with such dexterity that you'd think he had caught an electric shock. The close-up, despite the famous precedent, was seldom and sparingly employed, and there was little or none of the locking in heavy embraces that later came to vogue. Actually, the cameras and projectors of that period were spasmodic in their speed, and the kiss was still a wee bit too intimate for elaborately detailed display.

However, in the years succeeding America's entry into World War I revolutionary things began to happen in the field of film romance, and the kiss broke out of moral bondage into licentious anarchy. Whether the screen merely reflected the so-called "freedom" of the times or helped inspire it is a question you can argue for years. In any event, the movies cut loose with some mighty love scenes.

That was the period of the fabulous "great lovers" of the screen—such bashless and baroque exhibitionists as Antonio Moreno, Rudolph Valentino and John Barrymore, not to mention John Gilbert, who was probably the classiest kisser of them all. It was the period of the highly complicated and prolonged embrace.

Memorable and significant from that period is the graphically symbolic kiss which Mr. Moreno and Alice Terry engineered in "Mare Nostrum" (1926). It was boldly and candidly patterned to imitate the tentacular grip of an octopus which the two characters in the story had watched in an aquarium. And some of the kisses of Valentino were classics in this line—although it always has been a wonder why the actresses didn't have their backs thrown out of joint. For the general technique of Valentino was to open with a modified half-nelson hold, from

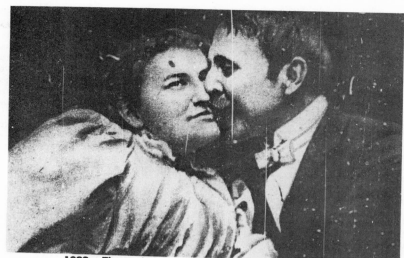

1896—The movies' first kiss—May Irwin and John C. Rice.

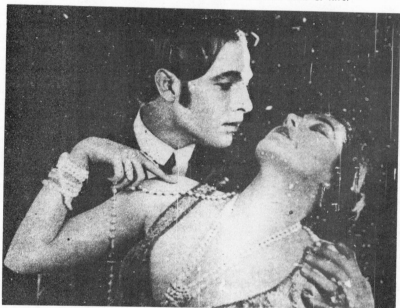

1922—The "baroque" kiss—Rudolph Valentino and Nita Naldi.

1946—The "blunt and graphic" kiss—Humphrey Bogart and Lauren Bacall.

which position he would bend his collaborator into a sectional pretzel shape and there suspend her for several seconds as he lingeringly pressed his lips to hers.

The catch-as-catch-can kiss was further perfected and elaborated upon by Mr. Gilbert, especially when he was teamed with Greta Garbo in their silent films. In these particular exhibits the close-up was used so studiously that sometimes the faces of the lovers seemed to be observed through a magnifying glass. And at times their positions were so novel that it appeared Mr. Gilbert must be hanging from a chandelier.

**W**ITH the advent of sound a marked change in screen kissing began. Something had been added which considerably affected the kiss. In the silent pictures ardor and passion had to be shown in the originality of the "clinches," but the talkies made possible a brand of communication with the lips that was not confined to the kiss. Now the characters could tell one another how they felt—and they did!

Coincidentally, there was shaping a parallel social change. The abandoned physicality of the Twenties, manifested by "flaming youth" and the exercise known as "necking," was becoming decidedly de trop. Youth—and their elders—were displaying a little more maturity and sophistication in their romance. The athletic kiss of the movies was recognized as a phony thing. The depression, which pulverized prosperity, helped to deflate the movie kiss.

At the same time the growing popularity of gangster pictures, with their tough attitude toward "dames," decreed that the kiss should be a rugged, realistic affair. The famous episode in which Jimmy Cagney smeared a grapefruit across Mae Clark's face instead of giving her a morning kiss marked an eye-opening turn on the screen. From that violence on, females were liable to slugs as well as kisses.

**A**ND—perhaps most influential—the famous film Production Code, which made movie, "morals" mandatory, came into being and took a firm stand on the kiss. "No excessive or lustful kissing"—that's what the Code decreed, thus putting it up to the authorities to pass on each separate display. With this peril of censorship threatening their efforts, the movie "clinchers" came down to earth. "Keep one foot on the floor"—a tacit dictum governing love scenes—was the order which had to be observed.

**I**T may be of social significance that the kiss has had an artistic renascence on the screen within the past few years, with the physical details of kissing quite bluntly and graphically revealed. This more recent style was marked for distinguished attention in "Lifeboat" a couple of years back. The evidence in this particular instance was an uncommonly hungry embrace which Tallulah Bankhead clamped upon John Hodiak while rocking about in a lifeboat in a violent storm.

Since that particular kiss there have been several which have occasioned some lifting of critical brows—especially the one which Humphrey Bogart and Lauren Bacall did in "To Have and Have Not." A sort of preliminary touching of lips was displayed by the two, with Miss Bacall showing disappointment of the most obvious sort. But, after a studious and leisurely walk around Mr. Bogart, she locked with him again and drew back after several seconds with the husky remark, "It's better when you help."

This sort of kissing became so extravagant on the screen —even in such virtuous little stories of marital happiness as "Claudia and David"—that it naturally came to the attention of the guardians of the Production Code. And it is whispered in Hollywood that the word went out to "clean up the kissing—quick." Certain local communities have their views on the manner of kissing, too. The pressing of lips against a lady's throat or shoulders is primly labeled "unconventional kissing"—and is banned.

**K**ISSING—as proved by "Notorious" — has unlimited horizons when used by imaginative directors. And the screen may be entering a phase of highly ingenious variations upon an old and familiar act. To be sure, the juvenile devotees of "horse opera" frown upon the kiss as a "sissified" thing for their heroes and, until recently, the Japanese did not tolerate it in their movies. (Some reactionaries still hold out for cooing doves and other limp symbolizations.) But how much ice do you think is cut by a few small boys and Orientals? Long live the kiss! And it will!

The film industry has revised and relaxed its code of morals and taboos for the first time since the code was adopted in 1930.

This action was announced yesterday by Eric Johnston, president of the Motion Picture Association of America, at a conference held at the association's headquarters, 28 West Forty-fourth Street.

The action on the code came after almost a year of study and countless consultations by a committee of film company executives appointed by Mr. Johnston. The revisions go into effect immediately.

The regulations are known familiarly as the "Hays Code" because of their adoption while the late Will H. Hays was president of the association.

Specific changes include elimination of the absolute prohibition against the handling of subjects having to do with illicit narcotics practice, prostitution, abortion and kidnapping. Two previous taboos that are continued unqualifiedly are those against showing sex perversion and venereal disease, including social hygiene.

Miscegenation, which formerly was listed as a special subject to be "treated within the careful limits of good taste," now may be handled at the producer's discretion.

The new code also stresses that the use of derogatory racial appelations should be avoided. Previously the code instructed producers to "take cognizance" of the fact that such terms were offensive to movie patrons.

In approving certain portrayals of abortion, illicit narcotics practice, prostitution and kidnapping, the modernized code is specific in its qualifications.

For example, the scrapped section regarding abortion declares that it is "not a proper subject for theatrical motion pictures." The new view in part is that the subject "shall be discouraged, shall never be more than suggested, and when referred to shall be condemned.

It must never be treated lightly or made the subject of comedy."

The new regulations against the portrayal of prostitution declare that "the methods and techniques of prostitution and white slavery shall never be presented in detail, nor shall the subjects be presented unless shown in contrast to right standards of behavior." Formerly the subjects had to be treated "within the careful limits of good taste."

The new code, Mr. Johnston declared, was "neither tighter nor looser than the old one," but more modern. He added that it still adhered to the idea of high moral standards and was still unequivocally against movies glorifying "crime, wrongdoing, evil or sin."

Scenes of actual childbirth, formerly prohibited in fact or in silhouette, now, together with surgical operations, are permitted to be treated "with discretion, restraint and within the careful limits of good taste."

The subject of narcotics traffic, formerly forbidden, is clarified with an expanded list of specifications governing the presentation. This theme was a controversial one on several occasions, particularly in the case of the screen version of "The Man With the Golden Arm." This picture never received a Production Code seal and was shown extensively without it.

The code also took a stronger stand against cruelty and brutality than before. It banned all "detailed and protracted" presentations of physical violence, torture and abuse.

In response to questions about "Baby Doll," a controversial feature due to open here next week, Mr. Johnston said that the revisions were made "with no specific movie in mind." Recently, the Roman Catholic National Legion of Decency condemned the picture and added that while it had received a Production Code seal of approval, it nevertheless was "an obvious violation" of the code.

The code continues to uphold the sanctity of marriage and the home. It says that "adultery and illicit sex, sometimes necessary plot material, shall not be explicitly treated, nor shall they be justified or made to seem right and permissible."

The code was written in 1929 by the late Rev. Daniel J. Lord, a Roman Catholic, and Martin Quigley Sr., publisher of The Motion Picture Daily and The Motion Picture Herald.

# POST OFFICE'S BAN ON 'CHATTERLEY' IS UPSET BY COURT

### Lawrence Book Not Smut, Judge Bryan Decides— Summerfield Chided

**By DAVID ANDERSON**

The United States Post Office ban on "Lady Chatterley's Lover," the novel by D. H. Lawrence, was upset here yesterday by Federal Judge Frederick vanPelt Bryan.

Judge Bryan ruled that the mail restriction imposed last April by Postmaster General Arthur E. Summerfield was "illegal and void." The judge, who read the unexpurgated edition of the romance twice, held it was not obscene.

He said:

"To exclude this book from the mails on the grounds of obscenity would fashion a rule which could be applied to a substantial portion of the classics of our literature. Such a rule would be inimical to a free society."

He also noted in his thirty-page decision that it was the first time a book of comparable standing had been charged with violating the obscenity statutes since the late Federal Judge John M. Woolsey had ruled in favor of James Joyce's "Ulysses" in 1933.

#### A Significant Book

The court made the following points:

¶ "Lady Chatterley's Lover" must be considered against its background and in the light of its stature as a significant work of a distinguished British novelist.

¶ The Postmaster General had no special competence qualifying him to render an informed judgment as to what constituted obscenity within the meaning of the law. This, it was held, must be left for the courts. Judge Bryan explained later: "I did not pass on whether Mr. Summerfield had the power or discretion but, assuming that he did, whatever he did must be reviewed by the courts. He could take temporary, not final, action."

¶ It is essential to a free society that the severest restrictions be placed upon barriers to the flow of ideas.

¶ Language in the book that shocks some readers is not, except in a few rare instances, inconsistent with character, situation or theme. Fine writing and descriptive passages of beauty leave no doubt of its literary merit.

On April 30 the Acting New York Postmaster, Robert K. Christenberry, on orders from Washington, held up 20,000 circulars of Readers' Subscription, Inc., announcing a new edition of the novel published here by Grove Press, Inc. The edition was first published in Italy in 1928.

Two weeks later a Post Office departmental hearing was held and a final decision passed on to Mr. Summerfield. He found on June 11 that the Grove edition was "obscene and nonmailable," together with the circulars issued by the book club. The Government, in the case before Judge Bryan, sought a summary judgment affirming the ban while the publishers and distributors had sued to upset it.

Judge Bryan set noon today for an order releasing "Lady Chatterley's Lover" from the postal ban. United States Attorney S. Hazard Gillespie said the question of an appeal would be considered.

The story of Constance Chatterley, which has interested or revolted readers for more than thirty years, had until this year never been published here. The current edition is the third version written by Lawrence; it was printed in Italy and authorized in France during his lifetime.

Judge Bryan justified his decision on the ground that there was nothing sensational about the book's promotion today and that it was, indeed, a major literary event carried out by serious-minded men. He cited the First Amedment to the Constitution, guaranteeing freedom of the press.

He stressed the viewpoint that such a work should not be judged by excerpts or passages deemed sensational but rather as a whole. Mr. Summerfield, it was said, must have found parts of it "offensive" and on this basis condemned it entirely.

Grove Press welcomed the decision for demonstrating that "a great book is not obscene, for disavowing the right of the Post Office to censor, for protecting the right of a serious publisher to issue books without the threat of confiscation and prosecution" and because it discouraged "other self-appointed censors."

Arthur H. Rosenthal, president of the Readers' Subscription, a book club, termed Judge Bryan's action "historic" for terminating "the role of the Postmaster General as a literary referee." It was, he said, "inconceivable" that the content of "Lady Chatterley's Lover" could "so unhinge the judgment of a Cabinet officer." Book censorship by administrative decree, Mr. Rosenthal concluded, is a great danger.

The New York Civil Liberties Union praised the "devastating" opinion of Judge Bryan. Mr. Summerfield, it asserted, "went far past the standards set down by the United States Supreme Court and other Federal courts in determining how allegedly obscene material shall be judged."

# HOLLYWOOD EXPOSED

## Industry in Dilemma Over Inclusion Of Nude Scenes for U.S. Viewers

### By MURRAY SCHUMACH

HOLLYWOOD.

ANY month now some New York art house may advertise "unexpurgated" Hollywood films. Posters may lure moviegoers with: "See the original. Exactly as shown to enraptured audiences in London, Paris and Rome."

This possibility is not too far - fetched. Increasingly Hollywood is spicing its pictures with a few naked or seminaked women for the foreign market. For the American theaters, alternate shots are filmed in which the ladies wear bits of clothes at strategic places or else the camera is less revealing.

Generally, the producers of these pictures are silent about their double standards of moviemaking. They may seek publicity by provoking a synthetic controversy with the Production Code Administration, the movie industry's self-censoring agency. But the foreign version with nudes is a secret.

### Bare Facts

Recently, Martin Ransohoff, Metro - Goldwyn-Mayer's most active producer, admitted that when his latest film, "The Americanization of Emily" is shown in Europe, it will have three nude sequences that are not in the American version. They were deleted to get a seal of approval from the Production Code Administration.

Though Mr. Ransohoff has irritated many moviemakers here who suspect his motives, he has performed a service by his frankness. When he called for a re-examination of the entire motion picture code, the Bible of the industry, he was expressing the opinion held privately by many of his colleagues. When Mr. Ransohoff asks for a poll of the producers and executives on this subject, he is inviting a frank expression of opinion. When he suggests nudity has become a weapon of unfair competition by foreign moviemakers, he is merely saying in public what is said in private in Hollywood. How much Mr. Ransohoff is motivated by his desire for publicity for his movie or himself is less important than the issues he brings into the open.

### Ignored "Censor"

Without investigating the criteria of art—and many Hollywood producers and directors are scornful of critical praise bestowed on foreign films—the fact is that nudity is not unusual in European pictures. American producers are justified in assuming that European morality is not offended by filmed nudity. Then why, they ask, is it wrong to include nudity in American pictures abroad?

What many American movie executives and producers conveniently forget is that every European country has classification. Thus, the American films, with the nudes restored, will not be shown to youngsters in European nations. Producers here may complain that the code prevents them from making such pictures as "Never on Sunday," or "Room at the Top," or "La Dolce Vita." But they do not add that none of these pictures may be shown to children in Europe.

When those films were made it was understood they would be, in truth, for adult audiences.

The movie industry wants the increased freedom without increased responsibility. The Motion Picture Association of America is opposed to any sort of classification, voluntary or governmental. Its motto is: Let the parents beware. Its only concession has been to increase from 30,000 to 60,000, the number of green sheets it prints as a guide to parents.

### What's "Adult"?

The position of the movie industry is obvious. It is fearful that classification will hurt its box office in this country. It wants the freedom to make "adult" movies. but it does not want to limit such movies to adults. Nor does the industry have the honesty to say that it sees nothing wrong with allowing children to see all movies. Yet nearly all of this nation's good directors favor voluntary classification.

Inherent in any discussion of Hollywood's desire to make "adult" films is the question of modernizing the motion picture code. Mr. Ransohoff wants the code made more flexible, so that there can be allowances for the over-all content of the pictures and the intent of the producer. He thinks the ban on nudity should be ended. In its place he wants nudity judged on the basis of "good taste." He used to oppose any kind of classification. Now he concedes that some films are not for children.

The American movie industry is being forced to face the same reality as Mr. Ransohoff. If it wants the artistic freedom of European moviemakers, then it should be willing to pay the price of voluntary classification. Either that or follow the example of Walt Disney, who has no trouble whatever abiding by the code.

---

# 100 FIGHT ARREST OF LENNY BRUCE

## Arts Leaders Protest, Citing Violation of Free Speech

### By THOMAS BUCKLEY

Nearly 100 persons prominent in the arts charged yesterday that the arrest here of Lenny Bruce for indecency violated Constitutional guarantees of free speech.

The text of the statement and the list of signers was released yesterday by the Committee on Poetry, an organization established to protest legal repression of creative activities. It is headed by Allen Ginsberg, the poet.

The entertainer was arrested in April while performing at a Greenwich Village cafe. A grand jury had handed up a true bill charging that his act was obscene after hearing a tape recording made by plainclothes men.

He is now at his home in Los Angeles, where a similar charge against him was dismissed last week. Mr. Bruce has also been arrested for obscenity in Chicago, and in other cities for the asserted possession of drugs.

The 38-year-old performer, who is decribed in the statement as a social satirist "in the tradition of Swift, Rabelais and Twain," uses not only the fourletter words but also the lessfrequently heard 10-letter and 12-letter ones in his monologues on religion, the civil rights fight and the battle of the sexes.

### 'Intended as Satire'

Acknowledging this, the statement went on to say that the words were used "within the context of his satirical intent and not to arouse the prurient interests of his listeners."

The protest adds, "It is up to the audience to determine what is offensive to them; it is not a function of the police department of New York or any other city to decide what adult private citizens may or may not hear."

"Whether we regard Bruce as a moral spokesman or simply as an entertainer, we believe he should be allowed to perform free from censorship or harassment," it states.

Among the signers were Dr. Reinhold Niebuhr, professor emeritus at Union Theological Seminary; Lionel Trilling, professor of English at Columbia

March 29, 1964

University; Eric Bentley, head of the university's drama department; Arnold Beichman, chairman of the American Committee for Cultural Freedom, and Dwight Macdonald, the critic and social historian.

Novelists who signed the statement were Norman Mailer, James Jones, William Styron, Terry Sothern, Harvey Swados, John Updike, Gore Vidal, Joseph Heller, Henry Miller, Elizabeth Hardwick and James Baldwin.

Among the poets were Lawrence Ferlinghetti, John Hollander, Cecil Hemley, Kenneth Koch, Robert Lowell and Peter Orlovsky.

Professor Trilling said he had never attended one of Mr. Bruce's performances but had read transcripts of them. He said that he was most interested in defending the principals of free speech and that he found Mr. Bruce "a very remarkable and pointed satirist."

### 'Impressed and Depressed'

Mr. Beichman said that he was both "impressed and depressed" by Mr. Bruce, but that this view was irrelevant, as was any judgment as to whether it was necessary for the comedian to use language that is still seldom heard in mixed company.

"I just don't think the police should be impowered to censor words," he said. "It's a matter of principle. For me, there hasn't been a comedian since W. C. Fields."

sMr. Macdonald said he was not so much concerned with the free-speech issue as with the fact that Mr. Bruce's monologues provided "what is genuinely a criticism of our society."

"He uses rough language, but he uses it in a witty, sophisticated and parodic way," he said.

Dr. Niebuhr, reached by telephone at his summer home in Stockbridge, Mass., said that he had signed the statement after hearing about the case from close friends.

"I have never seen Mr. Bruce or read anything about him," the renowned theologian said.

Speaking for himself at his Lower East Side apartment, Mr. Ginsberg, who returned to New York in February after spending a year and a half in India, said that the arrest of Mr. Bruce was part of a pattern of harrassment of the avant-garde.

He cited the closing of coffeehouses at which poets gathered to read their works and the conviction on Friday of Jonas Mekas, the cinema theorist and filmmaker, on charges of exhibiting an obscene movie, "Flaming Creatures."

# SPEAKING OF BOOKS: Sex and the Novel

### By LEON EDEL

LITERARY historians will probably record that the novel in the English-speaking world devoted some three or four decades of the 20th century to liberating itself from rooted inhibitions until finally it was able to say anything and everything—print all the forbidden words, describe all the forbidden scenes, devote itself as minutely to the carnal side of man as the old novelists did to man's spiritual side. The battle with censorship is far from ended, but the old puritanisms have been vanquished. The word "reticent" is obsolete—at least in fiction. Yet no one seems able to draw a dividing line between what is pornography and what is "realism." In the tumult, certain literary and esthetic questions are being ignored.

The history of the sexual "liberation" of the novel is complex, but it can be stated in its simplest terms. The naturalists on the Continent led the way. Later came the "literalists"—like James Joyce, who was determined to put four-letter words into print. In his wake D. H. Lawrence wrote minutely, lyrically (and with a churchly solemnity) about the physical side of love. He, in turn, opened the way for Henry Miller's rowdy genital chronicles. It is wrong to say, however, that these novelists "discovered" sex. What they did, as a result of the limitations of Joyce's imagination and Lawrence's phallic compulsiveness was to write about it without the old-time indirection, and often with much less subtlety and charm than their predecessors.

In the process we have had a kind of dehumanization of sex in fiction. There are sexual encounters in Zola which have more truth in them than any D. H. Lawrence described—and also more humanity. Zola wrote of sex as a natural part of life; Lawrence wrote as if all his adults were naughty children defying prudish parents. The French writers moreover treated sex where it was relevant; some of our novelists introduce it without regard to the logic of their story. One feels indeed that they often resort to the bedroom because it is an easy way to avoid writing about life in other rooms, and about the complexity of man. One can understand a storyteller describing in a novel how a character brushes his teeth; some persons brush them with considerable effect; but one would protest if the novelist gave us a tooth-brushing performance every few chapters. Yet bedroom scenes are often grimly repeated, as if there were a special virtue in chronicling every encounter.

In the old novels—say in Trollope—the central question was whether the hero and heroine would ever reach the bedroom. The getting there was the story. Love endlessly frustrated, endlessly seeking resolution, kept the old novels alive. The quest for the bedroom led to revelation of man's idiosyncrasies, and the mysteries of human relations; and when the ending was reached the reader did not need to be told what would ensue. Today's novels begin often where the old ones ended. Then they have nowhere to go—save back in to the bedroom. And we seem to remain there an unconscionably long time. V. S. Pritchett has said that D. H. Lawrence's cult of sex was "a disaster to descriptive writing," and that Lawrence is "responsible for the fact that no living writer has any idea of how to write about sexual love." Equally true is the same critic's observation that "the ecstasies of sexual sensation are no more to be described than the ecstasies of music which they resemble."

To be sure, this is no reason for not trying. Novelists have sought for 200 years to capture moments of passion and of ecstasy, when they have not written about the hearty and cheerful side of sex. But they have usually been most successful when they have captured not the joys of the flesh but the deprivation, ambiguity, guilt, self-indulgence and self-doubt. Imagine being a spectator to the love-making of Dimmesdale and Hester, of Anna and Vronsky, of Isabel and Osmond! They would be ordinary naked creatures, participating in an age-old choreography. As it is, they are larger than life; and they are eternal. It is the things left unsaid in novels that stir our imagination, as well as the things said. Some of our novelists nevertheless write as if they must record everything, to the tying of the last shoelace.

The revolt against the Victorians ended long ago. The extremists have had their little day. Thus far they have impoverished the novel rather than enriched it. By their excesses they have made it a dull affair; one finds in it always the expected, rather than the unexpected. In the trivial, passionless, mechanical attitude toward sex, there may be a reflection of the emptiness between men and women in our time. There still exist, nevertheless, the values Faulkner invoked in his Nobel Prize speech at Stockholm. The novel, when it recovers from its embeddedness, is almost certain to take heed.

# FILM CENSORSHIP IN STATE IS UPSET

## High Court Says, in Effect, That Procedures Here Are Unconstitutional

### By JOHN D. POMFRET
Special to The New York Times

WASHINGTON, March 15—The Supreme Court today held, in effect, that New York State's movie censorship procedures were unconstitutional.

The Court reversed a New York Court of Appeals decision reinstating a ruling by state censorship authorities refusing a license for the exhibition of a Danish movie, "A Stranger Knocks," unless two scenes it deemed to be obscene were cut. The scenes depicted sexual intercourse.

In its brief order, the Supreme Court did not actually say that New York's movie licensing procedures are unconstitutional. But it pointedly cited, without comment, its decision on March 1 in a similar case involving Maryland's movie censorship law.

In that case, the Court held Maryland's movie censorship procedures to be an unconstitutional restraint on free expression on several grounds that appear to apply to the situation in New York.

The Court said in the Maryland case that "a noncriminal process which requires the prior submission of a film to a censor avoids constitutional infirmity only if it takes place under procedural safeguards designed to obviate the dangers of a censorship system."

The Court laid down these procedural rules to govern prior censorship:

¶The burden of proving that a film should not be shown must rest on the censor.

¶Final restraint can be imposed only after judicial review; the censor's determination cannot be final.

¶There must be assurance of swift judicial review.

The Court held that Maryland's law met none of these standards.

Under the New York State procedure, the administrative ruling of the censor is final unless the person who wants to show the film appeals it to the state courts. Thus the burden of proving that a movie should not be shown does not rest with the censorship authorities. Further, their decision is final unless appealed.

The appealing party has 20 days in New York to file a petition for review with the State Supreme Court, and the censoring agency has eight days to reply. The appealing party can seek to speed this procedure by asking the court for an order directing the censorship authorities to show cause at a hearing within 24 hours why they should not be directed to issue a license. But in neither case is there any time limit within which the Court must rule.

### Legal Fight Called Costly

The Trans-Lux Distributing Corporation, which sought to circulate "A Stranger Knocks," said that the record in the case "abundantly demonstrates the substantial deterrent effect of New York's cumbersome and elaborate licensing system."

"Confronted with the lengthy and costly proceedings necessary to secure the right to exhibit a film (assuming ultimate success on the merits)," Trans-Lux added, "a distributor or an exhibitor is strongly motivated to cut a film rather than to litigate." •

Trans-Lux first sought a license to show "A Stranger Knocks" in March 1963. The Motion Picture Division of the State Education Department declined to issue it unless the two scenes it said were obscene were cut.

On June 27, 1963, the State Board of Regents sustained the determination of the Motion Picture Division.

Trans-Lux appealed to the Appellate Division of State Supreme Court, which held on Nov. 21, 1963, that the film was not obscene and that the license should be issued.

The Board of Regents then appealed to the State Court of Appeals. This court ruled 4 to 3 on March 26, 1964, that the film was obscene and was not entitled to a license unless the scenes were cut.

The Court said that "a filmed presentation of sexual intercourse, whether real or simulated is just as subject to state prohibition as similar conduct if engaged in on the street."

The United States Supreme Court, in its action today, apparently did not intend any ruling on whether the movie was obscene. The Maryland case, which it cited, involved a movie that everyone agreed was not obscene. In that case, the exhibitor had shown the movie without first applying for a license, as required by Maryland law, and was prosecuted.

The Court today also did not appear to intend its action to be taken as holding movie censorship statutes to be unconstitutional simply because they require movies to be submitted for censorship before showing.

It did not strike down the requirement for prior submission in the Maryland case, but said instead that such a requirement must be surrounded by safeguards.

In another action today, the Court refused to take a case in which it was asked to strike down the New York statute solely on the ground that a requirement for prior submission for censorship of a firm was unconstitutional.

In this case, the Gate Film Club was not permitted by the owner of a theater in New York City to show films because of a threat by the State Motion Picture Division to prosecute if the club did not first get the required licenses.

The United States District Court dismissed the club's petition for a hearing by a three-judge court on the ground that the Supreme Court had decided the issue of prior licensing in 1961. It was this dismissal that the Supreme Court refused to review today.

The court in its opinion in the Maryland case indicated one censorship procedure that it considers acceptable. This is New York's injunctive procedure to prevent the sale of obscene books.

That procedure postpones any restraint on sale until a judicial determination of obscenity following notice and an adversary hearing. The law provides for a hearing one day after the issue is joined and the judge must hand down his decision within two days after the hearing ends.

---

# Pulp Sex Novels Thrive as Trade Comes Into Open

### By PAUL L. MONTGOMERY

The pulp sex novel, once considered the preserve of pasty-faced men in shabby overcoats, has emerged from underground to become an $18 million-a-year business.

This year, by conservative estimate, the burgeoning industry will produce 500 lurid titles exploring Lesbianism, nymphomania, male homosexuality, sado-masochism, fetishism, incest and other pursuits that used to be treated primarily in medical journals.

In the well-ordered dirty-bookstores, of which there are now a dozen in midtown Manhattan, special sections are set aside for the most popular categories of aberrance. The largest emporium displays 1,000 titles, ranging from "Address for Sex" to "Wife Traders."

Much of the expanded market, however, has come from other outlets. Racks of the sex paperbacks blossom these days in many cigar and candy stores, and even some drugstores. They are a profitable item.

To some, the ready availability of the prurient indicates progress toward American maturity in matters sexual. Others, including the censorship groups and most churches, do not agree.

"A veritable floodgate of obscenity [has been] opened in the last 12 months in the form of obscene pocket books, magazines and greeting cards, to such an extent that it is unbelievable," the Mayor's Citizens Antipornography Commission reported recently.

There are few on either side of the argument, however, who would deny that the increasing number of sex novels are badly written, joyless, repetitious and twisted in their emphasis on the sneaky and the abnormal. It is difficult not to regard many of the outpourings of extravagant language and soaring passion as boring, if not comical.

Even those who write and publish the works feel they are engaged in a less than noble profession.

March 16, 1965

### Frustration a Factor

One commercial writer who has produced a number of the pulps says he writes "by and large for men who are afraid of women." He believes that men buy such books to feel superior to the heroines, who are either sexually insatiable, inclined toward Lesbianism, or aggressively given to other unattractive practices. Thus the book buyer, the writer says, "feels he's not really missing a lot in relating so poorly to women."

The editor of a leading line of sex books believes his audience is primarily made up of "frustrated men." The books, he says, allow such men to "transfer their guilt feeling about their inadequacies from themselves to the women in the book." Lesbianism is the most popular theme at present, he believes, because the reader "gets two immoral women for the price of one."

The writers of the pulp novels get a flat rate averaging $750 or $1,000, although some smaller concerns pay much less. It takes about two weeks to complete a book.

According to one editor, many of the men, and the few women, who write sex books have enough talent to move on to better things, but very few do. On the whole their lives are disorderly and speculative; few have families or live outside the large cities.

### 3 Classes of Publishers

The publishers fall generally into three classes. First there are the three middle-of-the-road ones — Midwood Books and Lancer Books, both of 185 Madison Avenue, and Beacon Publishers, 808 Third Avenue. A second class, which produces slightly more sensational items, are the dozen or so concerns in Chicago, Detroit and on the West Coast.

The third group, which is responsible for what the trade calls "the very rough stuff," consists of fly-by-night operators. These are men, generally of unsavory character and long experience in the trade, who conduct their business wherever there is space for their suitcase.

The suitcase operators generally begin by assembling two or three manuscripts, though they are not above stealing stories that have been printed by others. They get them printed cheaply, usually in a run of 50 or 60 thousand. The books appear with an imprint like "An Atlas Book" but have no publishers' name or address. They then sell their output to a distributor for about half the cover price and move on.

The fly-by-night product is selectively distributed — that is, it goes only to "trustworthy" outlets. Most of it is available in the midtown stores.

### Suggestion Emphasized

The more respectable concerns put out a polished product, long on suggestion but short on actual prurient content. Larry Shaw, the editor of Lancer Books, says he judges manuscripts "on whether the writer has a story to tell aside from sex." Readers of the concern's Domino Books—the sex book line—would be "really disappointed if they are looking for pornography," Mr. Shaw says.

The 10 Domino Books for August and September include seven that judging from the covers, have a Lesbian theme. The others, the covers say, are about a "desperately wanton woman," an "untamed, man-crazy temptress" and a "Manhattan apartment overflowing with warmly wanton girls."

Mr. Shaw notes that there are fewer and fewer taboos to be observed in sex books. "The censors have suffered several setbacks nationally," he says. "Our main problems now are the local level."

Until two or three years ago, nymphomania was the most popular theme for the pulp paperbacks. Since then, however, Lesbianism has gained the ascendancy, although it appears now to be losing ground to male homosexuality. Books about sado-masochism and fetishism, generally involving secluded castles, bullwhips, tight leather suits and spike-heeled boots, have also become popular.

### Selling Tricks Used

The preparation of the final package is regarded in the trade as a high art. The key elements are a lurid cover painting—generally costing $200 or $300—spicy blurbs on the front and back covers and the first inside page, and a suggestive title.

Some title words apparently have a hypnotic effect on buyers. One compilation of current books includes "Flesh Avenger," "Flesh Drunk," "Fleshpot," "Flesh Castle," "Flesh Cousins," "Flesh Fancy," "Flesh Hunt," "Flesh Prize," "Flesh Town," "Flesh Village," and "Flesh Whip."

The manuscripts are also carefully edited. Some writers get carried away and have to be toned down from anatomical specificness to general suggestiveness. Most concerns remove all profanity. It is not considered to be in good taste.

Four-letter words, which are common in serious fiction, are carefully avoided, because they are considered to have an anti-erotic effect on readers. One sex book writer who was asked if he used obscenity in his stories replied "Good God, no—that's dirty."

Because a lot of the buying of pulp books is on impulse, most publishers try to get some mention of sex in each paragraph. In this way, the casual browser will be caught up in the product no matter where he opens the book.

The last task is to give the book a message. This practice is based on a Supreme Court ruling defining obscenity as material "utterly without redeeming social importance."

A letter to writers from one sex book publisher discusses the matter in depth. "Essentially, we are interested in publishing adult novels exploring Lesbian or heterosexual love as it applies to our society today," the letter begins.

Then comes the message:

"The attitude of Society towards all the plot ingredients should be carefully considered. Whatever is frowned upon by Society should not, obviously, be advocated in the plot. For example, in stories dealing with Lesbianism, whether or not the characters ultimately decide to practice Lesbianism is less important than their realization that such practice would result in financial, social, emotional and-or psychological problems which would offset the advantages they might find in Lesbianism. Therefore, if they did decide to practice it, they would be doing so with full knowledge that their lives would not be completely happy."

### 1963 Ruling Recalled

Actually, in a 1963 ruling, State Supreme Court Justice J. Irwin Shapiro shifted the ground of the argument somewhat. His decision is regarded as a landmark by both civil libertarians and dirty-book publishers.

Justice Shapiro ruled that pulp sex novels, while "profane, offensive, disgusting and plain unvarnished trash," still "have a place in our society."

"There are those who, because of lack of education, the meanness of their social existence or mental insufficiency, cannot cope with anything better," he argued. "Slick-paper confessions, pulp adventure and comic-book type of magazines provide them with an escape from reality.

"In an era of bikinis, which reveal more than they conceal; of cinemas, which show females swimming in the nude — one must conclude that these books, in the mores of these days, do not constitute hard-core pornography. Coarse they are, but so is much in our civilization."

### Low Printing Costs

The books cost from 5 to 7 cents a copy to print. Shipping, which is absorbed by the publisher, comes to another penny. The publisher generally realizes about half the cover price, which can range from 50 cents to $1. The other half is divided between distributor and retailer. Press runs range from 50,000 copies for the small concerns to 100,000 for the large ones.

The estimate for the sex book industry's annual income of $18 million, a conservative figure, is reached by multiplying the year's harvest of titles (500) by an average press run (60,000) and an average price (60 cents).

Retailers can increase their profits, however, by blacking out the original cover price and raising it a quarter. When this is done, the book is generally wrapped in cellophane to give it an extra illicit look and to discourage aimless browsing.

After the distributor, the last step in the production is the retailer. These are generally a group of tight-lipped, harassed men who must bear the brunt of police raids, fines and pressures from censorship groups.

"I'm a businessman," the owner of one midtown store says. "If these creeps want to buy those books, I can't stop them. I don't even think about it; I just sell."

As he spoke, a group of purchasers milled around in the shabby "Gentleman's Section," pawing the products. Every once in a while the clerk would say mechanically, "All right, pick 'em out, pick 'em out— you can read them at home."

### Few Get Rich

It is generally agreed in the trade that only a very few distributors and publishers have grown rich from the dirty-book trade. Most in the business seem perpetually to be on the ragged edge of existence. "The only ones this business is good for are lawyers," one writer says.

There is no evidence that the pulp business is slackening. The writers and publishers continue to turn out the product, although some do it reluctantly.

Recently, a man in a respectable profession was appalled to find that a friend of his who writes dirty books under a pseudonym had dedicated one of them to him. He called the writer on the phone.

"How come," he asked, "you put my name in the book when you won't even use your own?"

"I should put my name on a book like that?" the writer replied.

# HIGH COURT RULES ADS CAN BE PROOF OF OBSCENE WORK

### Backs Ginzburg Conviction and 5-Year Term—Cites 'Titillating' Promotion

### 'FANNY HILL' PLEA WINS

### Bench Also Upholds Verdict Against Yonkers Producer of 'Sadistic' Material

**By FRED P. GRAHAM**
Special to The New York Times

WASHINGTON, March 21—By a vote of 5 to 4, the Supreme Court upheld today the obscenity conviction of Ralph Ginzburg, publisher of "Eros" and other erotic literature, and decided that "titillating" advertising could be proof that the advertised material was obscene.

The Court also affirmed, by a 6-to-3 vote, the conviction of Edward Mishkin of Yonkers; N. Y., on charges of publishing material admitted to be "sadistic and masochistic."

The two cases were the first in which the Supreme Court had held publications to be obscene.

In a third decision the Court reversed, by a 6-to-3 vote, a Massachusetts ruling that the 18th century novel "Fanny Hill" was obscene. However, it held that the state could still find the book obscene if its advertising and promotion led to that conclusion.

## Court Is Divided

A capacity audience of lawyers and other spectators heard Justice William J. Brennan Jr. read the decisions. Six other justices filed 11 additional opinions as the Court split widely in the three cases.

Lawyers expressed surprise at the introduction of advertising and promotional material as a crucial factor in determining obscenity.

Previously, the Court had adhered to the obscenity test it announced in 1957 in Roth v. United States:

"Whether to the average persons, applying contemporary community standards, the dominant theme of the material taken as a whole appeals to prurient interest."

## Other Grounds Stated

In addition, the Roth test required a finding that the material be "patently offensive" and "utterly without redeeming social value."

Justice Brennan insisted today that the Court was not abandoning this test, which can be applied by an inspection of the material itself.

However, by ruling that in a close case a court may decide on the basis of the publisher's motives, as revealed by his advertising, Justice Brennan seemed to be adding a new element to the obscenity equation.

He said that Ginzburg's promotion of the three publications involved — Eros, "The Housewife's Handbook on Selective Promiscuity," and Liaison—had been permeated by the "leer of the sensualist."

The publishers, Justice Brennan further said, "boasted that they would take full advantage of what they regarded as unrestricted license allowed by law in the expression of sexual matters."

Justice Brennan's voice rang as he denounced "those who would make a business of pandering to the widespread weakness for titillation by pornography."

Justice William O. Douglas, who has consistently opposed all censorship, said that the new ruling condemned an ancient advertising technique. He said:

"The advertisements of our best magazines are chock-full of thighs, ankles, calves, bosoms, eyes, and hair. to draw the potential buyers' attention to lotions, tires, food, liquor, clothing, autos, and even insurance policies."

Justice Brennan singled out for criticism the practice of publicizing the fact that a book had been previously banned. And his wording cast doubts upon the use of bosomy book jackets, spicy book advertisements, and suggestive blurbs on movie theaters' marquees.

## Ruling Surprises Lawyers

The Ginzburg decision surprised lawyers. It had been widely assumed that the Justices accepted his appeal, not because it presented any novel legal points, but because they thought that the five-year sentence and $28,000 fine for sending obscene matter through the mails were too harsh.

The Justice Department had hinted in its brief that the Court might throw out the conviction without arguments. At the oral arguments its lawyer, Paul Bender, conceded that 75 to 90 per cent of the material the Government routinely seeks to suppress is more objectionable than Eros.

Justice Brennan was joined in the Ginzburg opinion by Chief Justice Earl Warren and Justices Tom C. Clark, Abe Fortas and Byron R. White. Dissenting opinions were filed by Justices Douglas, Hugo L. Black, John M. Harlan and Potter Stewart.

Justice Stewart revealed a new side of his judicial philosophy by taking an anticensorship stand almost as militant as the Court's long-standing censorship foes, Justice Black and Douglas.

Justice Stewart said that none of the publications were "hard - core" pornography — which he described as filth so blatant that it was obvious to all—so they could not constitutionally be censored. Short of hard - core pornography, the First Amendment protects all publications from censorship, he said.

In the case of "Fanny Hill,"

formally known as "John Cleland's Memoirs of a Woman of Pleasure," Justice Brennan said that the Massachusetts ruling must be reversed because it had admitted that the book had a "modicum of literary and historical value."

He emphasized that under the Roth test, a publication must be utterly without redeeming social value, but said this could be true of "Fanny Hill" if it were found to be "exploited by panderers."

Chief Justice Warren and Justice Fortas joined in this opinion. Justices Black, Douglas and Stewart concurred because they believed that none of the publications involved in today's decisions were obscene.

Justices White, Harlan and Clark dissented.

Justice Harlan said that states should be given wide latitude to set obscenity standards, even if it resulted in "Fanny Hill's" being banned in Massachusetts and allowed in other states.

## Couldn't 'Stomach' Book

Describing himself as no "shrinking violet." Justice Clark said he nevertheless could not stomach "Fanny Hill," and cited its contents in detail to prove that it should be banned.

The Mishkin case involved a three - year jail sentence and $12,000 fine for publishing tracts known by booksellers as "spanking" or "bondage" books. His lawyers admitted that the books were "sadistic and masochistic" but denied that they were obscene under the Roth test because they did not appeal to the prurient interest of average people. He said they appealed only to perverted people.

The Court ruled that when material was designed for a deviant sexual group, it was obscene if it appealed to the prurient interest of members of that group.

Sidney Dickstein of Washington argued for Ginzburg.

Charles Rembar of New York argued for G.P. Putnam's sons, publishers of "Fanny Hill." William I. Cowin, assistant attorney General of Massachusetts, argued for the state.

Emmanuel Redfield of New York argued for Mishkin. H. Richard Uviller, assistant district attorney of New York City, argued for the state.

March 22, 1966

# TV: Chipping Away at Well-Entrenched Taboos

## Liberal Trend Reflected by 'Never on Sunday'

### By JACK GOULD

THE liberalized mores of today's society were reflected Saturday night in the back-to-back scheduling of the American League pennant race and the motion picture "Never on Sunday," starring Melina Mercouri.

Once upon a time, probably only a few years ago, the idea of adjacent scheduling of a crucial baseball contest and the sophisticated story of an engaging prostitute would have brought the roof down on the head of the National Broadcasting Company.

●

But in the late 1960's any alarms over the prospect of little leaguers in the home audience being prematurely exposed to the adult facts of life failed to materialize, even after the sportcasters in Detroit strenuously urged one and all to stay tuned for "a very funny film."

Throughout Saturday morning and afternoon, N.B.C. in New York received a handful of calls objecting in general to the TV presentation of the ingratiating Illya of the streets of Piraeus. But while the Detroit Tigers were busily losing the second half of the double-header to the Los Angeles Angels, there were more than 200 telephone inquiries from worried viewers as to whether the account of the lady who insisted on resting on the seventh day would be jeopardized by the length of the baseball game.

●

N.B.C. deferred the picture's start to about 6 minutes after 9 P.M. on Channel 4 to give full coverage to both the national pastime in Detroit and the oldest profession in the Greek port.

The network presentation of Miss Mercouri's celebrated performance as the cooperative enchantress of the waterfront, which reached the Midwest just after 8 o'clock, was one more indication of how the candid themes of the films are now reaching the masses in their living rooms.

●

Already this season the Columbia Broadcasting System has carried "The Apartment," the Jack Lemmon vehicle on the accommodation of extracurricular executive needs, and the only discernible repercussion was an eminently satisfactory program rating. On Channel 2's Saturday night late show, a new movie called "Some May Love" included a sequence on genteel adultery; the rival show on Channel 7, incidentally, was "Lolita."

The paradox is that in shows expressly produced for TV there continues to be the traditional concern over the preservation of blandness to suit all age groups. Matters of sex, let alone hints of extramarital relationships, are skirted like the plague. Physical violence—the Indian tribes and professional football players with fragile knees that may be wiped out by midseason—is a safer alternative.

Moreover, the feature-length films of bolder moment carry built-in security for TV network officials: They were not produced by them, which means there is room at the top for passing the buck, and they have passed the test of acceptability in theaters.

●

But expanded permissiveness of TV is evident in many other ways. When Eric Hoffer, the West Coast waterfront philosopher, used the phrase "son of a bitch" in his recent interview with Eric Sevareid on C.B.S., it was neither cut out nor, apparently, widely noticed.

The same freedom from restraint was not accorded by C.B.S. to Pete Seeger, however, when the last verse of one of his folk songs was inferentially critical of President Johnson's handling of the Vietnamese war.

Even a hippie may have gulped once over the American Broadcasing Company's Saturday night showing of "The Dating Game"; a boy and a girl of 8 years or less won a week's chaperoned trip to Hawaii.

Johnny Carson is the adroit master at extracting a laugh from the conversation that veers toward sex; the same deadpan conveys an understanding of a remark's possible second meaning without inviting the censor's blipping, of the tape. Mr. Carson's program undoubtedly has contributed to the new permissiveness; he has quipped that he can remember the time when not even a pause could be described as pregnant.

●

It is on the independent stations in New York that conversational candor is most marked, notably on the shows of Alan Burke, David Susskind and Mrs. Helen Gurley Brown. The old broadcasting taboos have virtually all been struck down on everything from free love, homosexuality and Lesbianism to the specifics of drug addiction, divorce and alleged Negro anti-Semitism.

Where legitimate permissiveness ends and commercialized sensationalism begins could be an incipient controversial issue facing TV Yesterday a group preferring to remain anonymous wrote this writer that it would boycott advertisers participating in shows whose moral values it condemned.

But this does not negate the obvious fact that TV is now at least as outspoken as the print media and, as the networks buy even more recent films, the trend will very likely increase.

*October 2, 1967*

# Vietnam Blues

### By TOM PHILLIPS

OPPOSITION to the Vietnam war in this country has produced sit-ins, teach-ins, sleep-ins, walkouts, vigils, fasts and hundreds of marches over the past few years. As might be expected, it has also produced some songs, from both the under-30 generation and the veteran folksingers of the American left.

At this point, none of the songs is widely known, largely because most radio and TV stations will not touch this kind of material. Pro-war songs about Vietnam are usually considered acceptable for the air waves, and two have been commercial hits: Sgt. Barry Sadler's "Ballad of the Green Berets" and Pat Boone's "Wish You Were Here, Buddy." But the only protest songs to make the pop charts have been generalized antiwar pieces, such as Barry McGuire's "Eve of Destruction."

However, quite a few protest songs specifically about Vietnam have been recorded, and many have been printed in two New York-based magazines, Broadside and Sing Out!. Two of them have also made the newspapers in recent months, both as a result of disputes over censorship.

PETE SEEGER, America's premier protest singer, ended 17 years on the broadcasting industry's blacklist last Sept. 10, when he appeared on the Smothers Brothers Comedy Hour. But the next day he complained loudly that the song he considered his "most important statement" had been cut out of the program. The song was "Waist Deep in the Big Muddy"—a parable, very plainly about the politics of escalation:

*It was back in nineteen forty-two*
*I was part of a good platoon.*
*We were on maneuvers in Looziana*
*One night by the light of the moon.*
*The captain told us to ford a river*
*And that's how it all begun* ——
*We were knee deep in the Big Muddy*
*But the big fool said to push on.*

The sergeant protests as they go deeper and deeper,

291

but the captain tells him not to be a "nervous Nellie" and insists they can make it across. They don't:

*All of a sudden, the moon clouded over*
*We heard a gurgling cry.*
*A few seconds later the captain's helmet*
*Was all that floated by.*
*The sergeant said, "Turn around, men,*
*I'm in charge from now on"——*
*And we just made it out of the Big Muddy*
*With the captain dead and gone . . .*

At the end, Seeger spells out the meaning:

*. . . every time I read the papers*
*That old feelin' comes on*
*——*
*We're waist deep in the Big Muddy*
*And the big fool says to push on.*[1]

It was this final verse that apparently raised objections from the Columbia Broadcasting System's programing executives. Seeger says he was asked to do the song without it, but that he refused, and the whole number was then cut. Ironically, the verse really serves little purpose so far as the meaning is concerned; the song's reference to Vietnam is certainly clear without it.

Another censorship dispute this summer involved Joan Baez, the leading lady folksinger of the New Left. In August, the Daughters of the American Revolution refused to let Miss Baez perform in the D.A.R.'s Constitution Hall in Washington because of her views on the war. She then took the show outdoors and sang "Saigon Bride" before a nonpaying crowd of about 30,000 at the foot of the Washington Monument.

This is by far the most widely circulated of the songs. It is in Miss Baez's latest album, which is moving up the best-seller charts. It sold about 150,000 copies in its first month alone, which is more than twice the sales total for any other album with an anti-Vietnam war song in it.

"Saigon Bride" is quietly sad and pessimistic, really more of a lament than a protest. On the record it opens

with a dirgelike block of chords, played by a brass section. The protagonist in the lyrics is a soldier, presumably a South Vietnamese, leaving for the war:

*Farewell, my wistful Saigon bride,*
*I'm going out to stem the tide.*
*A tide which never saw the seas,*
*It flows through jungles, round the trees.*
*Some say it's yellow, some say red.*
*It will not matter when we're dead.*
*How many dead men will it take*
*To build a dike that will not break?*
*How many children must we kill*
*Before we make the wave stand still? . . .*[2]

**B**ESIDES being the most publicized (or least unpublicized) of the protest songs, "Big Muddy" and "Saigon Bride" are probably the most thoughtful and responsible of the opposition pieces written to date. Both are serious approaches to the moral and political questions raised by the war, and their arguments are rational and sophisticated.

Most of the other protest songs fall much more clearly into the category of straight propaganda: the dominant tone is sarcasm, ranging from barbed humor to all-out venom. One of the bitterest and most direct is by a grandmother from Berkeley, Malvina Reynolds, long a writer of popular protest songs. It's called "Napalm":

*Luci Baines, did you ever see that napalm?*
*Did you ever see a baby hit with napalm?*
*When they try to pull it loose*
*Why the flesh comes, too,*
*And that's the way they do with that napalm. . . .*[3]

Another frontal assault that also focuses on the napalm issue is a new and as yet unreleased song by the leading "underground" rock group, the Fugs. The Fugs' work is a kind of synthesis of avant-garde pop music with neo-

Beat poetry—and the lyrics to this one are distinctive for their free verse and vivid imagery. "War Song" starts off as a rock 'n' roll travesty:

*Strafe them creeps in the rice paddy daddy ,*
*didi womp didi womp. . . .*
But it doesn't stay funny for long:
*The vultures drool on the skush*
*hissing drops of blood*
*burn inside the smashed babe's face*
*o napalm rotisserie!*
*cook the world a TV dinner*
*The earth drinks blood*
*WAR WAR WAR*
*the meat goes to war. . . .*

**T**HERE are also some funny songs about the war, although the output here has dwindled and the humor has grown blacker as the conflict has escalated. One of the cleverest is Tom Paxton's 1965 satire, "Lyndon Johnson Told the Nation," in which Lyndon Johnson tells the nation:

*Have no fear of escalation,*
*I am trying everyone to please,*
*Though it isn't really war*
*We're sending fifty thousand more*
*To help save Vietnam from the Vietnamese. . . .*[5]

An early song by the Fugs is also in a light, if bloody, vein:

*. . . if you don't kill them first*
*then the Chinese will,*
*If you don't want America to play second fiddle,*
*Kill, kill,*
*KILL FOR PEACE!*[6]

There's probably more opportunity for humor in a domestic issue that's inextricably bound up with the war—namely, the draft, and how to avoid it. The first standard in this field, "Draft Dodger Rag," was written more than two years ago by Phil Ochs. In it, the young antihero tells the Man:

*I'm only eighteen*
*I got a ruptured spleen*
*and I always carry a purse*

*I got eyes like a bat*
*and my feet are flat*
*and my asthma's getting worse. . . .*[7]

A newer work on the same theme is "Alice's Restaurant," by Arlo Guthrie, a rising young musician and writer who happens to be the son of the legendary folksinger Woody Guthrie. Most of the song is a long monologue, and the scene is that building on Whitehall Street where they "inject you, inspect you, detect you and infect you." This draftee hopes to get out with the maniacal-behavior ploy, so they send him upstairs to the psychiatrist:

[spoken] *he said 'what's wrong with you?' I said 'Shrink, I wanna kill, I wanna kill . . . I wanna see blood and gore—and veins and muscles—in my hands! Rip flesh, eat dead burnt bodies. I wanna kill kill kill KILL!' And he started chantin' with me, and he got up on the desk, and he was yellin' 'kill KILL.' And he pinned a medal on me and sent me down the hall—said 'YOU'RE OUR BOY!'*[8]

One of the latest antidraft songs is a favorite in the Black Power movement, and this one doesn't mince words. It has been recorded with a commercial-sounding rock-'n'-roll background and sounds like something from the top 40 until you catch the lyrics:

*I ain't going to Vietnam*
*The Vietcong's just like I am.*
*I ain't going to Vietnam*
*Cause the U.S. Army is the Ku Klux Klan.*
*UP TIGHT*
*THAT'S RIGHT*
*I ain't gonna go*
*HELL NO!*[9]

**O**NE thing that's missing from this collection is a song that could serve as a theme for the movement, a rallying cry of the kind that's been common in movements with wide support on the American left. Thirty years ago the labor movement had "We Shall Not Be Moved"; in the fifties, "Down by the Riverside" was sung almost ceaselessly at ban-the-bomb rallies. Only two years ago, thousands of civil-rights activists were locking arms and singing "We Shall Overcome" on TV newscasts nearly every night.

These songs have been car-

[1] ©1967 Melody Trails, Inc., New York. Used by permission.

[2] From "Saigon Bride" words by Nina Dusheck music by Joan Baez. ©1967 Robbins Music Corp. and Chandos Music Company.
[3] Words and music by Malvina Reynolds. ©1965 by Schroder Music Co.

[4] ©1967 Heavy Metal Music. Used with permission.
[5] ©1965 Deep Fork Music, Inc. Used by permission.
[6] ©1966 Heavy Metal Music. Used with permission.
[7] ©1964 by Appleseed Music, Inc., 200 W. 57th St., New York.

[8] ©1966, 1967 by Appleseed Music, Inc.
[9] Used with permission of the authors.

ried over to the anti-Vietnam war movement, but they've lost most of their original power, partly because everyone knows they're second-hand, and partly because they don't quite fit the subject matter. No one has come up with anything as clear, simple and inspirational as those old standards, and probably no one will.

The issue itself is far from clear and simple, and the opposition today ranges from liberal Republicans favoring the enclave theory to teen-age Bolsheviks who want to send grenades to the Vietcong. It would be hard to write a song that everyone could sing in good conscience.

More important, the people in this movement have no goal in mind as inspiring as the emancipation of the working-man or the American Negro, or an end to war in the abstract. All that most of them want is an end to what they consider a national disgrace. As a result, the songs are sometimes satiric, sometimes sorrowful and sometimes indignant, but the tone is always negative.

**N**EVERTHELESS, there is reason to expect that the musical output will keep pace with the war, and if escalation continues, the tone of

protest songs would become even more bitter. This has certainly been the trend.

It is interesting to look back at one of the first war protest songs, Phil Ochs's "Talking Vietnam," which was recorded in 1964 when the U.S. military commitment in Vietnam was still on the "adviser" basis. Washington's policy comes in for some broad satire:

[spoken]

*. . . training a million Vietnamese to fight for the wrong government and the American way. . . .*

but the war itself is treated almost whimsically, more as a stupid mistake than a moral outrage. The only villains di-

rectly mentioned are Madame Nhu and the ghost of President Diem:

*. . . families that slay together stay together. . . .*[10]

Three years later, such mild chiding is very much out of style. Nobody "jabs" at the Administration these days; it's more like a bomb for a bomb. ∎

---

[10] © 1964 by Appleseed Music, Inc.

**TOM PHILLIPS,** a member of The Times news staff, frequently writes on pop and folk music.

October 8, 1967

# Why Do They Laugh at 'G' Movies?

**By VINCENT CANBY**

**N**OT long ago I attended a sneak preview of a new film in a local theater, filled mostly with patrons who did not know the name of the film they were about to see. Before the credits, there appeared on the screen a card announcing that the film about to be shown had been rated "G," suggested for general audiences. The people in the theater groaned, and then laughed in good-natured recognition of themselves as closet sophisticates.

The Motion Picture Association of America's film rating system was one year old only yesterday, but already we've come to feel that any movie rated "G" couldn't possibly be of interest to any-

one over the age of 5. Quite often we're right. But that doesn't necessarily mean that the "X" films are likely to be more worthy of attention, as anyone who has unwittingly wandered into a film like "de Sade" can testify.

For better or worse—and I'm inclined to think it's for the better — the film rating system exists, principally as a service to the public. Because it is a service to the public first, and to the industry (which is trying to keep the censors off its back) second, I don't think it can do much harm.

**According to figures supplied by the MPAA, the seven film rating administrators (six of whom operate in plush**

offices over a Rexall super-drugstore in downtown Hollywood, the other man in New York), rated 435 films in the period from Nov. 1, 1968, through Oct. 27, 1969. Of these, 139 were "G"; 170 were "M," suggested for mature audiences, parental discretion advised; 101 were "R," restricted, persons under 16 not admitted unless accompanied by a parent or adult guardian; and 25 were "X," persons under 16 not admitted.

This first year of film ratings has not been without bizarre incident. There was, for example, the curious case of John Frankenheimer's "The Gypsy Moths," which, when it played its first domestic engagement at the Radio City

Music Hall here, was rated "M." It's now revealed that some footage that was eliminated from the film for the Hall engagement has been put back (in scenes of what originally seemed to be a rather tepid striptease) and the rest of the country will see the film with an "R" rating. Henry Hathaway's "True Grit," which the Code Administration originally rated "M," was cut slightly so that it could play the Hall with a "G" rating, Frank Perry's "Last Summer" opened here and was reviewed as an "X" film. Later, footage was cut from the climactic rape scene and the picture was given an "R."

Just this week the Rating Administration announced

that it had given an "R" rating to Henri-Georges Clouzot's "La Prisonniere," which deals explicitly and unpleasantly with masochism and voyeurism, and an "X" to Bo Widerberg's "Adalen 31." I can only assume that "Adalen" was found to be more dangerous than the Clouzot film because it's very humanistic, has a couple of nude scenes and treats sex with tenderness and humor.

This type of hassling over "exposure" — a nipple here, a buttock there, perhaps some fleeting shots of private parts —is demeaning to everyone concerned—to the filmmaker, to the audience (which can never be quite sure just what or whose version of a film it is seeing), as well as to those men who make their living trying to decide how to categorize individual films. (Jack Valenti, the president of the MPAA, reported this week that the Code's rules were being changed to prevent this sort of gratuitous, opportunistic rating and re-rating procedure.)

Ideally, of course, there should be no rating systems and no censorship. I not only question the qualifications of the Production Code people who are responsible for carrying out the present rating system ("They're neither gods nor fools," says Valenti, humbly), but wonder if there really is anybody who is qualified for the job. I also question a system that seems more concerned with keeping us sexually pure, and with pretending that 14- or 15-year-old kids have never seen certain parts of their own bodies and never heard certain four-letter words, than with somehow controlling the uses and representations of violence in films.

Built into any system that attempts to classify films on what are essentially technical grounds, rather than artistic grounds, is a sort of institutionalized fetishism. The classifiers spy some pubic hair or hear a dirty word and they spring into action, either by persuading the filmmaker to cut the offending scenes or by classifying the film upwards in a way that must limit the film's audience. They are concerned with segments, seldom the entire work. They function as isolationists.

All of this is true and depressing, and I'm sure that the rating system must inhibit some good filmmakers, while prompting others to test the outer limits of acceptability. On the pragmatic level, however, I'm not so sure that this is really so terrible. Moviemakers working within the Hollywood establishment have always been subject to inhibitions, mostly economic. The inhibitions prompted by the new rating system are so much less severe than those that were operative under the old Code that I believe the com-mercial Hollywood filmmaker today may have more freedom than he has ever had. I also believe that if the system has done nothing but to neutralize efforts to impose local, state and Federal censorship, it has performed at least one extremely important service.

The existence of the rating system has also allowed the production of certain commercial films that I doubt would ever have been attempted before. John Schlesinger's "Midnight Cowboy" ("X") was conceived and produced before the rating system went into effect, but it seems highly unlikely that it ever would have been released in its present form had it not had the protection of the system that provides that children can be denied entry to certain films. The box-office successes of "Midnight Cowboy" and "I Am Curious (Yellow)" have shown that it's possible to make sizable profits from "X" films, even when, as a matter of course, many exhibitors refuse to play them.

The last 12 months have also proved that "X" films are not automatic money-makers. The first film to be so rated last year, Jack Cardiff's "Girl on a Motorcycle," was such a box-office disappointment that the distributors cut it to obtain an "R" rating. Even then, it continued to be something of a small disaster area.

Nobody yet seems to know how well the ratings are being enforced at theater box offices, although I understand that the National Association of Theater Owners is making some sort of survey of this matter. Perhaps the strangest criticism being leveled at the rating system is the sort that blames the system for the existence of the films being rated. Such criticism, I think, can only be made by people who live in cocoons. Mores in conventional movies, like the mores in all of the other arts, in politics and personal behavior, have been coming apart for some time now.

The implementation of a film classification system happened to coincide with several of the more spectacular examples of the new movie morality. With or without ratings, "I Am Curious (Yellow)" would have been released in this country. The way was paved by a Federal Court of Appeals and by that tireless prophet of his own time, Andy Warhol, whose "The Chelsea Girls" started the whole thing, officially.

The film rating system isn't going to change our society or the trend toward an increasing permissiveness in the arts. I'd guess only a major political upheaval could do that. It does, however, offer some guidelines, which, though often odd and imperfect, may be of help to that most confused and anxious of citizens, the moviegoer-parent.

November 2, 1969

# Agnew Says TV Networks Are Distorting the News

## Accuses Some Commentators of Bias and Calls on Viewers to Complain— Criticizes Harriman's Paris Role

### By E. W. KENWORTHY
#### Special to The New York Times

WASHINGTON, Nov. 13—Vice President Agnew accused the television networks tonight of permitting producers of news programs, newscasters and commentators to give the American people a highly selected and often biased presentation of the news.

In a speech released here and delivered in Des Moines, Iowa, before the Mid-West Regional Republican Committee, the Vice President called upon the American people to "let the networks know that they want their news straight and objective."

Mr. Agnew urged television viewers to register "their complaints" by writing to the networks and phoning to local stations.

Thousands of Americans immediately responded to the

Vice President's invitation by calling the networks and many newspapers and venting their views on the media's handling of the news.

The Vice President's speech was vigorously defended and denounced. In some cities, such as Dallas, television stations reported that most callers supported Mr. Agnew's views. In other cities, such as New York, the reaction was more mixed.

In addition to attacking the networks, the Vice President also denounced the Johnson Administration and W. Averell Harriman, the former United States peace negotiator in Paris, for the "concessions" that he asserted had been made to the North Vietnamese.

During the 10 months that Mr. Harriman was chief negotiator, Mr. Agnew said, "the United States swapped some of the greatest military concessions in the history of warfare for an enemy agreement on the shape of a bargaining table."

Mr. Agnew did not say what the "concessions" were.

Negotiations over the shape of the table took place after the end of the bombings of North Vietnam, Nov. 1, 1968, and were completed in mid-January.

The Vice President's press secretary, Herbert Thompson, said that he did not know what concessions the Vice President had in mind. He contended that Mr. Agnew would not have made the statement without substantive information to back up his charges.

Mr. Agnew said that Mr. Harriman, who had commented on the President's Vietnam speech two weeks ago over the American Broadcasting Company's network, was apparently under "heavy compulsion to justify his failures to anyone who will listen," and "the networks have shown themselves willing to give him all the time he desires."

At the conclusion of his speech, Mr. Agnew seemed to challenge the networks to carry his speech nationally. He said that every elected leader depended on the television media and yet "whether what I have said to you tonight will be heard and seen at all by the nation is not my decision, it is not your decision, it is their decision."

The three networks accepted the challenge. They all carried the speech live. In New York their regular news programs moved up to clear time for Mr. Agnew's address.

In an interview in the cur-

rent U.S. News & World Report, Mr. Agnew sharply criticized the press, saying that he sometimes thought those writing for the papers, especially the "big-city liberal media, were "about the most superficial thinkers I've ever seen."

In his Des Moines speech, Mr. Agnew said that the American people would be right in refusing to tolerate in Government the kind of concentration of power that had been allowed in the hands "of a tiny and closed fraternity of privileged men, elected by no one, and enjoying a monopoly sanctioned and licensed by Government."

As a particularly flagrant example of what he called the biased reporting of "self-appointed analysts," the Vice President cited the treatment of the President's speech on Vietnam two weeks ago.

Most of the commentators, he said, expressed "in one way or another, their hostility to what he had to say," and "it was obvious that their minds were made up in advance.'

Expanding his criticism to cover also the producers of the programs, the Vice President said:

"To guarantee in advance that the President's plea for national unity would be challenged, one network trotted out Averell Harriman for the occasion."

"When the President concluded," Mr. Agnew went on, "Mr. Harriman recited perfectly. He attacked the Thieu Government as unrepresentative; he criticized the President's speech for various deficiencies; he twice issued a call for the Senate Foreign Relations Committee to debate Vietnam once again; he stated his belief that the Vietcong or North Vietnamese did not really want a military takeover of South Vietnam . . ."

"Every American," Mr. Agnew declared, "has a right to disagree with the President of the United States, and to express publicly that disagreement. But the President of the United States has a right to communicate directly with the people who elected him, and the people of this country have the right to make up their own minds and form their own opinions about a Presidential address without having the President's words and thoughts characterized through the prejudices of hostile critics before they can even be digested."

In recent weeks Mr. Agnew has drawn both criticism and praise for the pungency of his language as he has characterized Vietnam war critics as "an effete corps of impudent snobs" and demonstrations against the

war as "a carnival in the streets."

There has been much speculation here on whether the President has encouraged, or at least not disapproved, the Vice President's recent speeches.

There were some who thought that the President was encouraging Mr. Agnew to play the "point of the spear," as Mr. Nixon did in the early years of the Eisenhower Administration.

There were others who believed that Mr. Agnew was acting on his own.

But there seemed little question that in his attack on the networks Mr. Agnew was expressing the resentments of the White House. Several White House officials have made no secret of their anger at the way at least one network handled the commentary after the President's speech.

Gerald Warren, the assistant White House press secretary, said that neither the President nor the press office had seen the text of Mr. Agnew's speech. Mr. Warren said that there would be no immediate comment from the White House.

Asked for comment tonight on Mr. Agnew's criticism of him, Mr. Harriman said:

"I don't think that the statement deserves serious comment. All I can say is that I'm glad to be included with the television news media, which I feel, by and large are trying to do a conscientious job of keeping the American public informed on many subjects of national interest."

An examination of what Mr. Harriman said as a guest commentator for A.B.C. suggests that he was not explicitly critical of the President.

He began by saying, "I'm sure you know that I wouldn't be [so] presumptuous [as] to give a complete analysis of a very carefully thought-out speech by the President of the United States. I'm sure he wants to end this war and no one wishes him well any more than I do."

### Not Seeking Censorship

Mr. Harriman went on to say that his approach to the problem differed in some ways from that of the President, and gave his reasons. But he concluded by saying: "There are so many things we've got to know about this, but I want to end this by saying I wish the President well, I hope he can lead us to peace. But this is not the whole story that we've heard tonight."

Mr. Agnew said that he was not asking for Government censorship of the networks. He was, he said, simply asking whether the commentators

themselves were not censoring the news.

"The views of this fraternity," he said, "do not represent the views of America. That is why such a great gulf existed between how the nation received the President's address — and how the networks reviewed it."

While not proposing censorship of television commentary, Mr. Agnew seemed to suggest that the networks had not the same claim to First Amendment rights as the newspapers.

The situations were not identical, Mr. Agnew said, because television has more impact than the printed page, and because the networks have a near monopoly and the viewers have little selection, whereas a man who does not like a newspaper's views or news handling can switch to another paper.

---

### The Public Responds
By JOSEPH P. FRIED

Thousands of Americans accepted last night Vice President Agnew's invitation to express their views on the television networks' handling of the news.

In phone calls to the networks and to many newspapers that began just after the Vice President's speech was broadcast, Mr. Agnew's remarks were both defended and denounced.

In some cities, such as Dallas, most callers supported Mr. Agnew's views, according to The Associated Press. In New York and other cities, the reaction appeared to be more mixed.

But there was no doubt, from the emotional response on both sides, that Mr. Agnew had touched a sensitive nerve in the American people.

Mary Procter, a Brooklyn clerk, said in a phone call to The New York Times:

"I'm heartily in favor of everything that he said.

"I think the entire speech exactly the way it should have been and I'm neither a Bircher or a right winger—I just want to be a good American."

Sidney Unger of New Rochelle, president of the Kord Manufacturing Company in the Bronx, said in a call to The Times:

"I was horrified by the Agnew speech. It reminded me of speeches of Hitler before he got into power and he was brainwashing the German people against opinions that were against him."

### 'I'm No Kook'

Another pro-Agnew statement came from a caller who identified himself as Joseph Ercolano of Ozone Park in Queens.

"I'm no kook," he said. "I'm against the war and for the moratorium. But I do not believe there is a broad representative viewpoint either in the newspapers or on TV. There is only the extreme right of The Daily News and the extreme left of The Times and The Post.

Another anti-Agnew response was voiced by a caller who identified herself as Mrs. Milton Jucovy of Great Neck. "I'm terribly distressed at the speech and frightened," she said. "It seems that totalitarian government is taking over here.

Generally, pro-Agnew callers lauded the Vice President for speaking out against what they described as slanted news by a small group of broadcasters and newspaper writers who, the callers contended, did not represent the true views of most Americans.

And many critics of the Vice President asserted that his views were more suited to an official of a dictatorship that would control broadcasters than to a leader of democracy.

About 40 calls came to The Times in the three hours after Mr. Agnew's speech was broadcast. About half supported him and half opposed him.

The National Broadcasting Company reported that, in the first hour after the broadcast of the speech ended here, it had received 614 calls favoring Mr. Agnew's views and 554 opposing them.

Both the American Broadcasting Company and the Columbia Broadcasting System reported receiving hundreds of calls at their New York offices after the broadcast of the speech, but said they had no immediate tally on the number for and against the Vice President.

# Pornography in U.S.: A Big Business

**By STEVEN V. ROBERTS**
Special to The New York Times

LOS ANGELES, Feb. 21—Pornography has become big business in America. In a nation founded by Puritans, there has developed a huge and often shadowy industry devoted to the exploitation of sex.

Using the techniques of modern business, from mass production to mass distribution, the pornography industry makes a variety of books, magazines, movies, records, photographs and "sexual devices." Its customers are millions of Americans every week.

There appear to be two main reasons for this explosion of erotica. The Supreme Court has, over the last decade, deemed most pornography legal. Only so-called "hard core" pornography, or "obscenity," is considered illegal, although local interpretations vary.

"Obscenity," says Stanley Fleishman of Los Angeles, one of the nation's best known lawyers in the field, "is a matter of geography."

More importantly, the sexual revolution in America—and around the world—has made people more tolerant. Public opinion polls still say that more than three-quarters of the population want stricter laws against pornography. But the pressure to suppress erotica has waned considerably in the era of the miniskirt and the coed college dormitory.

The annual volume of the pornography business is difficult to estimate. Some observers have said $2-billion; most experts put the figure at closer to $500-million. But what is not disputable is the industry's tremendous recent growth.

Five years ago about 90 theaters around the country showed "sexploitation" movies or "skin flicks." Now there are more than 600, and the number is growing weekly.

Some have abandoned seedy downtown areas for the suburbs; many are clean and respectable looking, with ad-mission prices as high as $5 in big cities. But these theaters are not limited to metropolitan areas. "Skin houses" have opened recently in cities as varied as Litchfield, Conn.; Augusta, Ga., and Girard, Ohio.

"Adult bookstores" have managed to enjoy a similar prosperity. Only nine such stores existed in Los Angeles several years ago, most of them on Main Street, which is similar to New York's 42nd Street.

Today, there are more than 90 bookstores here catering to sex, and 20 of them are in the suburban San Fernando Valley. Six new stores have opened in Houston in the last year. Atlanta has more than a dozen, and New York, which along with Los Angeles produces almost all the pornography in the country, now has more than 200.

Probably the fastest segment of the pornography business is mail order. While several large companies dominate the market, more than 500 operators offer through the mail material ranging from color film to artificial sex organs.

Last year the Post Office Department in Washington received 232,070 complaints from people who had received unsolicited advertising for pornography. The total was up almost 100,000 from two years ago. When the mail-order business started several years ago, sellers used specialized lists to solicit customers. Then some enterprising operators in Los Angeles started taking names at random out of phone books. At the same time, the ads started to include pictures of the merchandise.

### Detailed Films

The most explicit material is still available only in major cities. In San Francisco, for instance, which has 25 sex-oriented movie theaters, several have recently started to show detailed films of actual oral and genital copulation.

In St. Louis, stores openly display magazines showing female genitalia in such detail that they look like gynecological textbooks. Many stores are selling a book with Danish photographs that portray several techniques of sexual inter-course. The price of the book is $4.75.

There are still towns, of course, where Playboy magazine is considered dirty. One recent issue was confiscated in Concord, N. H. But in most medium-sized cities, that is, with more than 100,000 population, a knowledgeable buyer can find films and magazines showing frontal nudity.

In bigger cities, the most popular purveyor of pornography is the "adult bookstore," a veritable supermarket of erotica for every taste and price range. Most of them are dingy storefronts, with the windows painted black or covered with wrapping paper for privacy.

Inside, the books and magazines are arranged on crude racks according to subject matter: heterosexual, homosexual, lesbian, bondage and flagellations, bestiality and foot fetishism. Films and sexual devices are often displayed near the cashier, who will sometimes provide such illegal material as stag films on request.

### Arcades Are Popular

A popular attraction in many stores is the "arcades," a collection of jukebox-like machines that for a quarter show a film that lasts about a minute.

The cardinal rule in an adult bookstore seems to be silence. Patrons tend to stand as far away from one another as possible while perusing the merchandise. Any untoward movement and they start like frightened deer. The only sound, as one observer in Madison, Wis., put it, "is the jingle of the cash register."

Why is pornography good business? Who buys it and why? The answers cannot be precise, but there is general agreement within the industry that the bulk of its customers are middle class, middle-aged men and white-collar and blue-collar workers.

Hyman's Book Store in Des Moines, Iowa, reports that its most consistent customers are the doctors, lawyers and dentists from nearby office buildings. The owner of the Monument Square Smoke Shop in Portland, Me., said: "My customers include all kinds, but there are plenty of businessmen who come in and carry out the books in their briefcases."

Few buyers of pornography like to talk about it. "I enjoy it," is virtually the universal reason given for buying it. But the issue is more complex.

"Most of the buyers are lonely, frustrated men who use

this to stimulate themselves," said one bookstore owner. A theater owner from Long Island said, "Basically, we are all voyeurs."

## Other Reasons Given

Pornography is not used only for solitary gratification.

"Many guys come in here and say they want something that will turn their wives on," said a book dealer in Hollywood. "Sometimes they're rather pathetic. 'What can I do?' they ask me. 'Why won't she respond to me?'

"But I also get some sophisticated couples who want to know what's happening. I had a girl the other day who came in and bought two magazines for her husband as a present."

Just about every producer agrees that young people make very poor customers. "Kids today look on sex as a participant sport, not a spectator sport," said David Friedman, a major sex movie producer.

"If a kid wants to see a naked woman, he tells his girl friend to take her clothes off. He doesn't have to see my movies. When they do come, they come to laugh. They think it's camp."

Some producers fear that when the younger generation grows up, the markets for pornography will diminish. But others are not so sure.

"These kids will get old, too," said one with a chuckle. "When they get to be 40 they'll do less acting and more looking."

How does a pornographer get started in the business? In the early 1950's, for example, Bill Hambling was publishing science fiction magazines in Chicago. His friend, Hugh Hefner, tried to borrow money from him to start a magazine called Playboy.

"Hef," Bill Hambling said sagely, "you can't sell sex to the American people."

Several years later, Mr. Hambling re-evaluated his judgment. He brought out a magazine called Rogue, which included, among other things, a foldout, color photograph of an undressed young lady. Soon he branched out into book publishing.

Today, Mr. Hambling is the president of Greenleaf Classics of San Diego, and he can laugh at the chance he missed to own part of Playboy. Greenleaf publishes 36 new paperback titles every month, with a print run of 30,000 a title, or a total of one million books. Almost every one has a single subject: sex.

Sex publishers do not talk readily about economics but the average book costs about 25 cents to produce. If it car-

ries a cover price of $2 the publisher sells it to the distributor for $1.

Mr. Hambling's office is in a plush new building the company owns and is decorated with modern art. The publisher dresses sharply, drives a new car and greets people with a direct manner that is almost military in its crispness.

"When I first started, we published a book about Harry Truman and the Prendergast machine," Mr. Hambling recalls. "I thought it was great, and I set up a $10,000 advertising budget. The book lost $40,000. A few years later, we did a big book about Vietnam, with an introduction by Senator Fulbright. It laid the biggest egg of the year.

"But when we brought out "Candy," people were lined up to buy it. I was as stupid as any publisher who thinks he can create a market. I can't make you want to read anything; all I can do as a publisher is exploit your need. I've never lost money on a sex book —that should be some indication of what the public wants."

## Theaters Change Policy

The movie business is similar; dozens of general theaters, faltering under the impact of television, have switched to sexual fare. The change is often dramatic.

Leroy Griffith, a theater owner in Miami, said: "I built a brand new theater and played The Sound of Music," and I lost money. I switched to an adult policy, and the first week I made $4,000.

Pornography is a highly competitive and specialized industry. Take the magazine field, for example. The heart of the business is the photography, and editors must constantly keep up to date or risk losing their share of the market.

"At first we tried to put out things we thought were in good taste," one editor said. "Then I saw what the others were doing, and it made our stuff look like Mother Goose. I thought they couldn't get away with it, but my salesmen came in and said we were getting returns from all over the country. So we had to keep up. You can't make a living selling buggy whips."

One marked change in the pornography business is the girls who pose for the photographs. According to officials in New Orleans, once a center for illicit pornography, most models 20 years ago were prostitutes.

Today, the girls are different. They are usually wanderers in a big city, lost and penniless, who may sleep with many men but seldom accept money for

this. That is particularly true in Los Angeles, where many young people are attracted by the warm weather, the glamour of Hollywood or the promise of a hippie life style.

"The simple and most important reason is that they're looking for bread," said the manager of an agency that specializes in nude models. "If they have a rent payment due, and they need decent money fast, this is one of the few legal ways they can get it.

"A girl doesn't need references or skills—just a good body—and she can get the money right away. Most of the girls who come in here are too lazy to hold down a regular job. This is easy money— $50 a day—and they have no inhibitions about taking their clothes off. A few are rebelling against their parents, or the Puritanic ethic, but not many."

The book business is somewhat different. While magazines are still vying for explicitness, there are few descriptions of sex acts that have not been written about many times. Thus, the premium is placed on originality. There is a joke around the industry that the man who can dream up a new fetish will strike it rich.

Several years ago the booming segment of the market was books about homosexuals. Little had been written about the subject before, and homosexuals bought nearly everything that came out, no matter how badly done. Now the market has leveled off. The best selling stories today involve wife swapping, with a hint of group sex and bisexuality. Greenleaf has a whole line devoted to the subject.

## Writer's Pay is Low

Certain topics have always sold well, however, including stories about nurses and stewardesses. "Most men take a plane and here's this pretty girl who's very nice to him, and his fantasies start whirling," explained one writer.

The pay for sex novels is usually very low, about 1 or 2 cents a word. Thus, for a typical 50,000-word manuscript, a writer might get from $500 to $1,000. Nevertheless, publishers receive 10 times as many manuscripts as they can use.

They come from out-of-work television and movie writers, teachers, insurance salesmen, aspiring novelists who need rent money while they do their "serious" work. Only about 10 per cent of the authors write sex books full time.

One who did — until he switched to mysteries last year —was Victor Banif, the author of more than 100 steamy paper-

backs over the last five years. Mr. Banif, who grew up on a farm in Ohio, was working as a Government clerk in 1964 when he decided to try writing full time. He recalled:

"I had done a lot of writing in school, and I gave myself a year to make it. I took the approach of being a commercial writer. I wanted to make money at it, and sex books seemed a good way to do that."

He works on a strict schedule: $100 a day. If he is getting $700 for a book, he works a week, but he has done some in three days. He does not even retype his first draft.

## 'Sin, Suffer, Repent'

"Once you learn the basic formula, it's easy," he said. "The best example is the confession novel: sin, suffer, repent. Most sex books were confession stories, but now they're getting a little wilder."

One thing that doesn't sell is humor. "The editors think humor takes the sex out of a book," he said.

Most people in the pornography industry admit that most of the books they publish are junk. Many editors do not even read the stories, especially if they know the writer's work. The major changes made in most manuscripts involve spelling and punctuation.

Nevertheless, the sex books have sold so well that many of the major publishing houses are copying the style. "When Irving Wallace's new book came out," said a large publisher, "one of our editors cracked, 'That's formula No. 6 we abandoned four years ago.'"

Competition from the legitimate industry is even fiercer in movie making. The line between the "sexploitation" movies and some "major" films has blurred beyond recognition.

The "sexploitation" or "nudie" industry started about 10 years ago with "The Immoral Mr. Teas," a movie about a man who finds a pair of eyeglasses that allow him to see through clothing. The director, Russ Meyer, a former Army combat photographer, invested $24,000 and grossed more than $1-million.

## Double Their Money

Mr. Teas started a rash of low budget, poor quality films with plots out of True Romances and as much skin as possible. Around the industry, large breasts are known familiarly as "ticket sellers," and sell they did. The average producer could at least double his money on most pictures with little trouble.

The "nudie" films are facing tough competition. The major studios often show as much skin as they do and sometimes more. So independent film makers have started making movies that include close-ups of male and female genitalia and some sex play. They do not have even the pretense of a plot. Mostly shot in 16-millimeter, these films are shown publicly in several big cities and are spreading rapidly.

Despite the competition from legitimate publishers and movie studios, the pornography business is thriving more than ever. The police here have some evidence that the Mafia thinks the business is good enough to be a target of muscling in. But most pornographers are independent entrepreneurs who started with very little and built up huge businesses.

"Some people say we're part of the Communist conspiracy," joked one movie maker, "but we're really classic American capitalists."

The basic law governing pornography was enunciated by the Supreme Court in the Roth case of 1957. In that case, the Court ruled that obscenity was not protected by the First Amendment guarantee of freedom of speech.

But the Court went on to define obscenity in this manner: To be obscene the material, taken as a whole, must appeal primarily to the purient interest, must go significantly beyond accepted community standards, and must be utterly without redeeming social value.

Applying this test, the Court has gradually widened the definition of material that is not obscene. The process has been accelerated by publishers and film makers who constantly bring test cases on franker and franker material. In addition, the courts have established numerous procedural safeguards to protect pornographers from police harassment.

As a result, the police across the country have complained that these rules seriously hamper their ability to control pornography. Donald Shidell of the Los Angeles Police Department vice squad said: "The courts have created so much utter chaos and so many restrictions that they have almost legalized obscenity."

Many legal experts agree with Mr. Shidell and say that the Supreme Court is moving toward standards under which virtually anything will be permitted for adults.

The Court has upheld laws, however, that prohibit the sale of pornography to minors. It has also said that "pandering."

or advertisements that promote material as obscene, can be held against a defendant.

The most controversial legal area today involves the burgeoning mail-order business. Citizens receiving unsolicited advertisements have inundated the post office with complaints, and 200 bills have been introduced in Congress to curb the flow of unwanted erotica.

At present, a person can request that a company take his name off its mailing list, and if the company fails to do so, it can be prosecuted. But mailing lists circulate among so many different operators that the law is not very effective.

According to public opinion polls, the nation continues to be adamantly opposed to pornography. A recent Gallup Poll reported that 85 per cent of the people want stricter laws regarding mail-order solicitation, and 76 per cent want tighter restrictions on street sales.

Organized groups such as Citizens for Decent Literature continue to denounce the spread of "smut," and politicians regularly take up the cause—particularly at election time.

But perhaps the most telling expression of public opinion is recorded by the cash register. "If the public practiced what it preached, we would be out of business tomorrow," said Paul Mart, a noted "sexploitation" film maker.

A major question that remains unanswered about pornography is its effect on people. To its opponents, it "erodes the moral fiber" of the country and can lead to sexual assaults and similar crimes.

Most scientists in the field field agree that no conclusive evidence is available. But the research that has been done indicates that pornography seldom leads to criminal acts and might even be helpful in some cases.

In any case, the trend in America today is toward allowing individuals to decide for themselves what they should read and see. President Nixon tacitly admitted this last spring when he sent a message to Congress on obscenity.

"When indecent books no longer find a market," the President said, "when pornographic films can no longer draw an audience, when obscene plays open to empty houses, then the tide will turn. Government can maintain the dikes against obscenity, but only people can turn back the tide."

On that basis, the people show little inclination to turn back the tide—or the clock.

# Storm Brews Over Report On Smut

WASHINGTON — When King Edward III picked up the Countes of Salisbury's garter in 1348, he issued a royal opinion on obscenity: "Evil to him who thinks evil." Since then and before, states, mayors, chiefs of police and boards of censors have tried to draw the obscenity line, saying that all to this side is, all to that is not.

Edward drew the line at the knee, others at the ankle. It has shifted as often and erratically as the hems of fashion.

Last week, the Presidential Commission on Obscenity and Pornography gave its opinion that the line is imaginary, like the Equator.

The commission announced its anticipated conclusions at a news conference on Wednesday:

(1)—For willing adults, there is nothing that must be labeled obscene, "no warrant for continued governmental interference with the full freedom of adults to read, obtain or view explicit sexual materials."

(2)—"The sale of sexual material to young persons" should be regulated by law.

(3)—Most emphatically, we need "a massive sex education effort aimed at all segments of the society, adults as well as children . . . on the issues regarding obscenity and pornography."

The commission — academicians, lawyers and clergymen— was formed by President Johnson in 1968 and headed by William B. Lockhart, dean of the University of Minnesota Law School.

Its conclusions—none unanimous, but each supported by at least 12 of the 18 members— drew public rebuttal from Charles H. Keating Jr., a Cincinnati lawyer appointed by President Nixon, and the Rev. Morton A. Hill, president of a New York anti-obscenity group called "Morality in Media." Others—the Rev. Winfrey C. Link of Nashville; Thomas C. Lynch, Attorney General of California; Rabbi Irving Lehrman of Miami Beach and Mrs. Cathryn A. Spelts of the South Dakota School of Mines—dissented in whole or part.

Mr. Keating, who said he was the "only ordinary citizen" on the commission, said its recommendations could lead to "paganism and animalism." He did not define his terms.

The difficulty of such definitions has taxed men for centuries.

In 1957, the Supreme Court narrowed judicial interest to "hard-core" material and set the first specific test for the obscene: "Whether to the average person, applying contemporary community standards, the dominant theme . . . taken as a whole appeals to the prurient interest."

The test did imply that hardcore pornography could and should be universally banned, but in 1969 the Court, in Stanley v. Georgia, made a drastic modification: Persons in the privacy of their homes could read and look at whatever they wished.

The President's commission presented studies and conclusions in its 873-page report.

The studies, which Mr. Lockhart said he considers the basic contribution, establish much that everyone knew: Sex today is presented publicly, graphically, explicitly and with variety.

The majority concluded that there was no evidence that sexual materials "play a significant role" in causing "social harm."

And there was some mildly surprising incidental information: "Adult" book publishing is not very profitable and "adult" bookstore customers are, overwhelmingly, "white, middle-class, middle-aged, married males dressed in business suits."

The major recommendations—that willing adults should be allowed to follow their bent and that children and the unwilling should be protected—follow the decisions of the courts.

Chairman Lockhart suggested that the results of the effort would be substantial, although not immediate.

One immediate result was apparent. The subject is of intense, if possibly limited, political interest.

Dissenter Keating said he was certain that had President Nixon named all the commission members, the results would have been dramatically improved.

White House Press Secretary Ronald L. Ziegler and Attorney General John N. Mitchell publicly disavowed the recommendations, and Robert H. Finch, Mr. Nixon's close political adviser, said that "in common with what I believe to be the overwhelming majority of American people, I challenge and condemn such counsels of irresponsibility."

The feelings of the majority are a matter of speculation. A commission survey showed that only 2 per cent of the population considered the traffic in erotic material one of the nation's three most pressing problems. The survey was challenged by the dissenters, and, at any rate, people may be more concerned about war, racial conflict and the economy and still be concerned with what they consider smut.

It is most unlikely that legislation to implement the recommendations will be passed by Congress this session, or even the next. The advantage now is with the attackers, particularly in the next few weeks. Mr. Finch and the Administration can hardly lose votes by denouncing the Johnson appointees as promoters of "utter license in the area of behavior and morality."

Democrats who might wish to defend are aware that no one was ever elected running as the pornographer's friend.

—TOM KELLY

October 4, 1970

# White House Drafts Tough Rules On Contents of TV Programing

### By ALBIN KREBS

The White House has drafted tough new legislation that would hold individual television stations accountable, at the risk of losing their licenses, for the content of all network material they broadcast, including news, entertainment programs and advertisements.

The draft legislation was interpreted by some broadcasting officials here as the Nixon Administration's boldest effort so far to equip the Government with a strong legal means of keeping broadcasters in line economically and ideologically.

The proposed legislation would supplant regulations of the Federal Communications Commission—sometimes loosely enforced—that govern the operations of TV stations and the networks that supply them with more than 60 per cent o their broadcast material.

The existence of the draft legislation, and the intention of the Administration to introduce it in Congress early next year, without substantial change, were revealed yesterday by Clay T. Whitehead, director of the White House Office of Telecommunications Policy.

In a sharply worded speech at a luncheon of the Indianapolis chapter of Sigma Delta Chi, the professional journalism fraternity, Mr. Whitehead, the ranking White House adviser in the field of broadcasting, condemned "ideological plugola' in network news reporting and said local stations would have to bear responsibility for such matter carried over their facilities.

"When there are only a few sources of national news on television, as we now have, editorial responsibility must be exercised more effectively by local broadcasters and by network management," Mr. Whitehead said.

"Station managers and network officials who fail to act to correct imbalance or consistent bias in the networks—or who acquiesce by silence—can only be considered willing participants, to be held fully accountable . . . at license renewal time.

Associated Press

**Clay T. Whitehead speaking in Indianapolis.**

"Who else but management can or should correct so-called professionals who confuse sensationalism with sense and who dispense élitist gossip in the guise of news analysis?"

The bite of Mr. Whitehead's remarks led some sources in broadcasting to speculate that the Administration was renewing the controversy begun two years ago with Vice President Agnew's attacks on the networks.

Mr. Whitehead denied at an earlier news conference that the draft legislation was intended as a vindictive assault on the networks, and described it as designed to force broadcasters to take more responsibility for what goes into American homes by television.

### 'Plain Apoplectic'

Tom Chauncey, president of TV station KOOL in Phoenix, Ariz., said, "I'm just plain apoplectic. If Whitehead really means this, we might as well be living in the Soviet Union. This would mean censorship of news and entertainment, the Government telling us what to broadcast and telling the people what they should see or hear.

"Washington wants to put the onus on the individual stations, make us afraid to broadcast what the networks feed us. I'd far rather hear Agnew raising hell; at least he's only talking. Whitehead is talking about actually passing oppressive laws."

A spokesman for the National

Broadcasting Company said the plan as reported by Mr. Whitehead "seems to be another attempt to drive a wedge between television stations and the networks." A spokesman for the American Broadcasting Company said, "We are concerned that Mr. Whitehead's remarks may represent an obstacle to the continued good relationship between the networks and local stations." Spokesmen for the Columbia Broadcasting System declined comment.

"It's been easy for broadcasters to give lip service to the uniquely American principle of placing broadcasting power and responsibility at the local level," Mr. Whitehead said. "But it has also been easy—too easy—for broadcasters to turn around and sell their responsibility along with their audiences to a network at the going rate for affiliate compensation.

"The ease of passing the buck to make a buck is reflected in the steady increase in the amount of network programs carried by affiliates between 1960 and 1970 . . . The average affiliate still devotes over 61 per cent of his schedule to network programs."

He accused local stations of exercising little responsibility for the programs and commercials "that come down the network pipe."

"Local responsibility is the keystone of our private enterprise broadcast system operating under the First Amendment protections," Mr. Whitehead said, "but excessive concentration of control over broadcasting is as bad when exercised from New York as when exercised from Washington. When affiliates consistently pass the buck to the networks, they're frustrating the fundamental purposes of the First Amendment's free press provision."

The Administration draft, he said, establishes two criteria the individual station must meet before the F.C.C. grants a license renewal:

"First, the broadcaster must demonstrate he has been substantially attuned to the [viewer's] needs and interests in all his programs, irrespective of whether those programs are created by the station, purchased from program suppliers or obtained from a network.

"Second, the broadcaster must show that he has afforded reasonable, realistic and practical opportunities for the preservation and discussion of conflicting views on controversial issues."

"These requirements have teeth," said Mr. Whitehead. He added that the proposed standards "should be applied with particular force to the

·large TV stations in our major cities, including the 15 stations owned by the TV networks." The F.C.C. allows each network to own five television stations.

The proposed laws would make it incumbent on the local stations to demonstrate continuing responsibility for what gets on TV screens. "They can no longer accept network standards of taste, violence, and decency in programing," Mr. Whitehead said.

There is no area where station management responsibility is more important than news, he went on, adding:

"When a reporter or disk jockey slips in or passes over information in order to line his pocket, that's plugola. And management would take quick corrective action. But men also stress or suppress information in accordance with their beliefs. Will station licensees or network executives also take action against this ideological plugola?"

# What Are We To Think of 'Deep Throat'?

**By VINCENT CANBY**

TRYING to write honestly about pornographic films is like trying to tie one's shoe while walking: it's practically impossible without sacrificing stride and balance and a certain amount of ordinary dignity, the sort one uses with bank tellers who question a signature. Almost any attitude the writer adopts will whirl around and hit him from the other side. The haughty approach ("It's boring") has long-since been suspected as evidence of a mixture of embarrassment and arousal. The golly-gee-whiz style ("They've gone as far as they can go!") is patently untrue, while to make fun of pornography is to avoid facing the subject at all. To call it a healthy development is another vast oversimplification that refuses to acknowledge that it may be fine for some people, and quite upsetting for others.

Then, too, to suggest that pornography degrades the audience as well as the performers assumes a familiarity with all of the members of all audiences that I, for one, do not have. It even ignores what little evidence I do have about the production of the films. Not long ago, a director of several porno films, a seriously bearded young man with an interest in Cinema, told me he was never aware of any of his performers feeling degraded. "They do it because they enjoy it and because it's an easy way to make money—I think in that order. They're also exhibitionists. The camera turns them on. The women as well as the men. Sometimes, at the end of the day, they don't want to stop."

It's difficult to write honestly about pornographic films, but it's getting easier, largely, I think, as a result of all of the publicity given to "Deep Throat," including the recent, widely covered Criminal Court trial here to determine whether or not the film is obscene. With an early assist ("The very best porn film ever made") from Al Goldstein, the editor of Screw Magazine who isn't exactly stingy with his superlatives (a few months later he was quoted as saying that " 'Bijou' tops 'Deep Throat' "), "Deep Throat" has become the most financially successful hard-core pornographic film ever to play New York. According to Variety, which now regularly reviews porno films as a service to the film trade and gives weekly box-office reports on their business, "Deep Throat," made in Florida on a budget of $25,000, has grossed more than $650,000 at the New Mature World Theater here since it opened last June. (The New Mature World Theater is, incidentally, the former World Theater, on 49th Street near Seventh Avenue, which, in its old immature days, used to play films like "Open City" and "Shoe Shine.")

For reasons that still baffle me, "Deep Throat" became the one porno film in New York chic to see and to be seen at, even before the court

300

case, even before Earl Wilson wrote about it.

When I went to see it last summer, mostly because of the Goldstein review, I was so convinced of its junkiness that I didn't bother writing about it. Still uncertain, I went back to see it again last Sunday. The large afternoon crowd sat through what seemed like at least a half-hour of porno trailers (which may be better pornography than narrative features since they're nothing but climaxes), plus Paul Bartel's fairly amusing, non-porno short, "The Naughty Nurse," as well as an old Paramount cartoon, a G-rated, absolutely straight, violence-without-sex cat-and-mouse thing, in order to experience the dubious achievements of "Deep Throat," which runs 62 minutes. Although the audience last Sunday was a good deal more cheerful and less furtive than the one with which I first saw it, the film itself remains junk, at best only a souvenir of a time and place. I'm sure that if "Deep Throat" hadn't caught the public's fancy at this point in history, some other porno film, no better and maybe no worse, would have.

As for "Deep Throat," its pleasures — its powers to arouse — are not inexhaustible, or, at least, they are very exhausted once one gets over the wonder and surprise at the accomplishments of its

heroine, Linda Lovelace. The frame of the film — Linda's search for sexual fulfillment once she learns that fellatio is her thing — provides little room for the kind of satire that some critics have professed to see in the movie. Its few dumb gags, not including a rather funny title song, cannot disguise the straight porno intent of what has been reported to be the film's "seven acts of fellatio and four of cunnilingus."

At the risk of sounding like the usual bored critic (which I certainly wasn't the first time around), I must say "Deep Throat" is much less erotic than technically amazing. How does she do it? The film has less to do with the manifold pleasures of sex than with physical engineering.

It's possible — but only if one really tries — to make "Deep Throat" sound more significant than it is. You can argue that Linda in her way is a kind of liberated woman, using men as sex objects the way men in most porno films are supposed to use women. But that's straining to make a point that is very debatable. You can also argue, as Arthur Knight did at the trial here, that Linda and her friends show us that there's more than one way to have sex. It's almost as if he saw the film in the position of a missionary.

All of these arguments can be made — and, I suppose,

they should be made — to defend the film against censorship laws that are, academically speaking, wrong. I say academically because I'm about to put myself in a corner that can't be reasonably defended: the laws are wrong but the film isn't worth fighting for. The necessity to prove a film totally without redeeming social value in order to get an obscenity conviction is, to my way of thinking, absurd. Everything created in this era — good, bad and pornographic — is or will be of social interest (my definition of social value), hence it's rather idiotic to have adults arguing this point back and forth in court. Expert witnesses, who defended "Deep Throat" against the charges made possible by fuzzy laws, wind up, in effect, by acknowledging the validity of the laws. In defending the film the way they do, they become parties to the foolishness of the established order.

They've been co-opted, which is, I understand, the only way to fight the laws, but I think they might have second thoughts about attempting to prove their points by citing "Deep Throat" as "more professional, more cleverly and amusingly written" than others. Professor Knight even went on about the "clarity and lack of grain" in the photography.

We are living on the other side of the looking glass. Bad films are correctly defended for the wrong reasons. "Deep Throat" is described in terms that would not demean Henry Miller.

What may be worse, the film is prompting a whole new flood of inexpert, very biased writing about pornography, including this piece and other rather tortured articles elsewhere. The New York Review headed its recent contribution "Hard to Swallow," and at least two writers I've read have made bad puns on the fact that while most people are curious about porno films, they're too yellow to see them, in reference, of course, to the Swedish film of 1969 that a lot of hysterical people said was pornographic and went as far as films could go. Both claims turned out to be false.

The only possible way to write about porno films, I suspect, is to be so autobiographical that the reader gets a fair idea of the sexual orientation of the writer, of his each little quiver during the showing of the film. This, however, makes necessary a kind of journalism that few of us are equipped to practice well. When it isn't practiced well, we are apt to get the dopey film critic-confessionals that reverse the usual way of doing things. They intrude the critic's privacy upon the public.

# Too Much Murder—Or Not Enough?

### Movies, radio and comic books raise an issue concerning the mind of the child.

#### By GERTRUDE SAMUELS

FOR some time there have been all kinds of efforts to give children greater "protection" from their most popular sources of entertainment—radio, movies and the comic magazines.

One radio system has voted to ban mystery and crime during early evening hours (though paradoxically continuing soap operas by day) on the ground that horror shows are harming children's minds. Groups like the Schools' Motion Picture Committee and the churches are vigorously pushing movies "suitable for children between the ages of 8 and 14," and criticizing parents who send their offspring to neighborhood movies without regard to whether Donald Duck or Dracula is showing.

Educators, psychiatrists and parents are also troubled about the 100-odd comic magazines which sell 40 million copies monthly to an estimated 90 per cent of children. To many adults the antics of such characters as Superman, Cosmo the Cat, Captain Marvel and Señor Tamale hold four-dimensional horror—visual, psychological, social and cultural. For instance, in a recent strip a tough asks "Percy" (who looks about 7), "How'd ya like to make an easy ten bucks?" and three picture panels later one reads: "Haw, Haw! What a dope! He doesn't know that the tin box holds stolen deposits from the Foist National Bank."

Do children need to be "protected" from such influences? Protection, as we understand it today, was inconceivable fifty years ago. Then the word was applied to the dependent, the neglected and the maltreated child. Normal youngsters were brought up on a simple principle: children should not be overindulged and should be seen and not heard.

TODAY we realize that children do not become constructive citizens by reaching an "age of reason." The seeds of maturity—values, tastes, humor, in short, character—have been planted in early childhood, and the way those seeds are nurtured by outside influences—the emotional growth—may affect not only the individual child's future but that of society.

So, looked at in terms of what children think and feel and, as Coleridge significantly put it, of the pictures their "eyes make * * * when they are shut," such diversions as movies, radio, comics and even fairy tales become serious contend-

GERTRUDE SAMUELS, a Times staff member, interviewed child psychologists, school officials and various other authorities for this article.

ers for that most precious human treasure—children's minds.

The basic question is: Do children need this exposure to violence, red-blooded adventure and the argot of criminals as part of their natural process of "growing up"?

Many, experts say that they do.

They believe that children need some release for their fears and hostilities. They escape from the "dullness" and routine of everyday living into a magic world where heroes and villains come to grips, where they can identify themselves with the hero. Piloting their own plane, riding the swiftest horse, shooting with perfect marksmanship, gives them a harmless outlet for their aggressive feelings. These experts argue that through the suspense, action and hostility of radio and movie programs children "work off" tendencies toward anti-social behavior and juvenile delinquency. If as a result children seem to express much more fear, anxiety and hatred, they say, this is a signal to look for the real causes—fear of adults or their environments—instead of blaming the media.

"CHILDREN must have this kind of vicarious adventure," said Josette Frank of the Child Study Association, consultant to a national comics group, adviser on the Superman and Hop Harrigan radio programs, and the mother of two radio-loving youngsters. "Normal children not only can 'take' it—they need it. This is partly because of the intense pleasure which they get out of it—remember when you were a child?—and partly because it helps them to handle their own fears. Some children frighten themselves deliberately and enjoy that experience; apparently, it fills some needs which no other activity can fill. Other children need a hate object on which they can pour out their frustrations.

"It's not hard to understand why children escape to a world of cowboys, G-men, sea captains and flying wonders, and, if they're girls, of beautiful, struggling heroines who always bring the evil-doer to justice. Modern homes don't expect children to be as useful as children of fifty years ago. Moreover, their reasons for listening are their own. Let's not call their having fun, wasting time."

ANOTHER who endorses this trend of thought is Dr. S. Harcourt Peppard, child psychiatrist and acting director of New York's Bureau of Child Guidance. Scoffing at radio criticisms, Dr. Peppard feels that children's programs must "have enough suspense, fantasy and aggression" or the child "will get his satisfaction elsewhere."

"Prohibition will not suffice," Dr. Peppard said in a recent symposium. "If this happens, parents will lose the opportunity for developing a sound relationship based on mutual confidence. There are two basic criteria for judging children's programs. First, they should give children pleasure. And second, offer constructive outlets for suspense, adventure and aggression."

The opposing school of thought takes this view:

Children are born with primitive capacities for anger, fear, hate, it is true. But they have other tremendous talents and capacities—for humor, for learning good social skills, for music and sports. The emphasis on violence and horror has come along because of a lack of these other things. Thus children are willfully being "underprotected" when they are exposed regularly to violence and not to those aspects of radio, movies and comics which nurture their better nature.

On the view that crime, love-making, murder and cheap language give children an outlet for their aggressiveness, a way of "letting off steam" leaving them relaxed and content, Professor Arthur T. Jersild of Teachers College in his well-known book, "Child Psychology," observes: "This theory is a very inviting one. Unfortunately, there is a lack of convincing scientific evidence as to whether or to what extent the average child derives benefit from the movies, radio programs and comics in keeping with the theory."

THIS view finds vigorous support from Dr. Frank J. O'Brien, Associate Superintendent of Schools for New York in charge of the Division of Child Welfare, a psychiatrist, and the father of four children.

"We are concerned with children's mental health," said Dr. O'Brien. "We know that stimulation of undesirable emotions have far-reaching bodily as well as emotional effects on children. A great many children feel insecure anyway and are desperate for affection and attention in their homes. For example, take 15-year-old Jimmy who belonged to a gang and got into trouble. I asked him, 'Jimmy, don't you get sick and tired of going to the principal's office?' 'No,' he said, 'because all the fellas see me.' Children like these—and they are in all economic groups —who live in a loveless environment or who have no sense of security or belonging are thrown back on fantasy.

"When that happens the symptoms can be very grave. They have all kinds of sicknesses, suffer with their dreams and carry those nightmares over into their daily lives. We run a great and terrible risk in exposing children to these undesirable emotions."

He swung around impatiently in his chair. "Why on earth don't we *give* the kids something constructive to get excited about?"

**I**T is this apparent vacuum —the lack of constructive movies, radio programs and comics — which troubles all who criticize the media. Dr. Rudolf Arnheim of the New School for Social Research calls it "lack of motivation," saying: "Society today is essentially uninterested in what is happening in civilization and unconcerned with the deeper aims of life. Therefore it is in need of motives. Lacking them, we get vicarious emotions."

Professor Jersild, in his office-study at Columbia University, added: "The indictment must be shared by parents and schools. We waste our children. Movies, comics, radio have been the creatures, not the creators, of this culture. They merely capitalize on this appetite for violence and unreality. But by catering to this interest, they in a sense cultivate it, because the more time is filled with violence, the less time there is for other things."

There is one common meeting ground for experts on both sides of the question. Fairy-tales, they feel, are in a class by themselves. The reason why fairy tales have survived, they say, is that they symbolize supposed truths and provide children with harmless drama into which they project some of their feelings.

**B**UT one does not have to rely on the adult authorities for an evaluation. The children themselves give the story—in two ways.

First, they tell it by their actions, especially in that fascinating laboratory, the Saturday movie matinee. I went to a matinee recently at the Museum of Natural History with an 8-year-old Dick Tracy fan in whose career I have a more than passing interest. Admission was free, and the big auditorium was packed with 5-to-16-year-olds. For an hour and a half we watched a thrilling story of how the pre-Columbus Ojibway tribe lived, ate, hunted caribou, fell in love, fought their battle with the Arctic snows and survived. When the lights went on, the children's faces revealed a healthy sense of vicarious achievement.

At another matinee uptown the movie "Kiss of Death" was showing. Children of all ages yelled, laughed, screamed and applauded at the sadism of one character who threw an old, crippled woman in her wheelchair down a flight of stairs.

**A**ND the children tell it in words. I visited several classes in both high-income and low-income neighborhoods and the principal and teachers put direct questions to the children. The economic status made little difference; answers were virtually the same. The unabashed answers and criticisms revealed astonishingly how much the children themselves understood the problem.

For example, to the question, "What kind of movies and radio programs do you like best?" the majority of answers was "comedy," one 16-year-old girl rising to her feet with the qualification, "But good comedy." The older girls' preferences went to "comedies, plays and the hit song parades." Many of the children said that radio and movie programs were the only entertainment they had. A large number said that they preferred to listen to music and quiz programs, but "there aren't enough for us." Almost all said they would rather be doing other things than listening to the radio or going to movies —sports, reading, driving; a few preferred concerts.

These comments were typical of the boys:

"I like murder—just for the thrill of it!"

"I like ghost stories and Inner Sanctum mysteries."

"I like Superman and Jack Armstrong because they aren't really murders but you try to figure out what's going to happen the next day."

"Stories themselves don't bother me, but on Suspense I hear that bell going all night."

"I want to be kept on pins and needles."

"I have to listen to the murder mysteries because after I go to bed my mother listens to every one and I can hear them."

**F**INALLY, I popped some of my questions to my favorite 8-year-old during the Children's Hour — the hour when Dick Tracy, Superman, Terry and the Pirates, Jack Armstrong and Sky King usher in the twilight for many of the nation's 32,000,000 youngsters.

"Tell me," I got in during a pause in "Death Comes to a Lumber Camp," "do you like that stuff?"

"Like it?" he yelled. "Of course. I love it."

"Well," I persisted, "does it make you want to go out and kill a man, like that Sky King or Dick Tracy?"

"They don't kill anyone," he said emphatically. He turned up the radio louder. "Of course, it doesn't make me want to kill anyone. It's just fun." Then he had a second thought. "Maybe you wouldn't think so. You're a girl."

**W**HILE it is impossible to tell conclusively how much of a problem all this presents to parents, the best guess is that they're not worrying too much. Many seem to think that children's outdoor interests are still supreme and that their offspring wouldn't dream of giving them up for a mere radio program, movie or comic magazine. They take the long view — that the average child who lives in an atmosphere of love, understanding and give-and-take can absorb stimulants without harm.

The basic feeling of all experts is that mothers shouldn't expect radio, movies and comics to raise their children for them. They've got to know their own children, many say. If a child is nervous, extra-sensitive or timid, or if he has a low intelligence quotient, parents should consult their own common sense and set up some reasonable controls.

What parents generally would like to see is the extension to movies and comics of the standards adopted by the Radio Council for Children's Programs: Be entertaining; be dramatic, with reasonable suspense; be of high artistic quality and integrity; stress human relations for cooperative living; stress intercultural understanding and appreciation.

But then, they add wistfully, why not give adults a break, too?

# KENNEDY IS AS HE RIDES IN JOHNSON SWORN

## Gov. Connally Shot; Mrs. Kennedy Safe

### President Is Struck Down by a Rifle Shot From Building on Motorcade Route— Johnson, Riding Behind, Is Unhurt

**By TOM WICKER**

Special to The New York Times

DALLAS, Nov. 22—President John Fitzgerald Kennedy was shot and killed by an assassin today.

He died of a wound in the brain caused by a rifle bullet that was fired at him as he was riding through downtown Dallas in a motorcade.

Vice President Lyndon Baines Johnson, who was riding in the third car behind Mr. Kennedy's, was sworn in as the 36th President of the United States 99 minutes after Mr. Kennedy's death.

Mr. Johnson is 55 years old; Mr. Kennedy was 46.

Shortly after the assassination, Lee H. Oswald, who once defected to the Soviet Union and who has been active in the Fair Play for Cuba Committee, was arrested by the Dallas police. Tonight he was accused of the killing.

### Suspect Captured After Scuffle

Oswald, 24 years old, was also accused of slaying a policeman who had approached him in the street. Oswald was subdued after a scuffle with a second policeman in a nearby theater.

President Kennedy was shot at 12:30 P.M., Central standard time (1:30 P.M., New York time). He was pronounced dead at 1 P.M. and Mr. Johnson was sworn in at 2:39 P.M.

Mr. Johnson, who was uninjured in the shooting, took his oath in the Presidential jet plane as it stood on the runway at Love Field. The body of Mr. Kennedy was aboard. Immediately after the oath-taking, the plane took off for Washington.

Standing beside the new President as Mr. Johnson took the oath of office was Mrs. John F. Kennedy. Her stockings were spattered with her husband's blood.

Gov. John B. Connally Jr. of Texas, who was riding in the same car with Mr. Kennedy, was severely wounded in the chest, ribs and arm. His condition was serious, but not critical.

The killer fired the rifle from a building just off the motorcade route. Mr. Kennedy, Governor Connally and Mr. Johnson had just received an enthusiastic welcome from a large crowd in downtown Dallas.

Mr. Kennedy apparently was hit by the first of what witnesses believed were three shots. He was driven at high speed to Dallas's Parkland Hospital. There, in an emergency operating room, with only physicians and nurses in attendance, he died without regaining consciousness.

Mrs. Kennedy, Mrs. Connally and a Secret Service agent were in the car with Mrs. Kennedy and Governor Connally. Two Secret Service agents flanked the car. Other than Mr. Connally, none of this group was injured in the shooting. Mrs. Kennedy cried, "Oh no!" immediately after her husband was struck.

Mrs. Kennedy was in the hospital near her husband when he died, but not in the operating room. When the body was taken from the hospital in a bronze coffin about 2 P.M., Mrs. Kennedy walked beside it.

Her face was sorrowful. She looked steadily

# KILLED BY SNIPER CAR IN DALLAS; IN ON PLANE

**John Fitzgerald Kennedy**
**1917-1963**

Henry Grossman

Presidential jet. Mrs. Kennedy then attended the swearing-in ceremony for Mr. Johnson.

As Mr. Kennedy's body left Parkland Hospital, a few stunned persons stood outside. Nurses and doctors, whispering among themselves, looked from the window. A larger crowd that had gathered earlier, before it was known that the President was dead, had been dispersed by Secret Service men and policemen.

### Priests Administer Last Rites

Two priests administered last rites to Mr. Kennedy, a Roman Catholic. They were the Very Rev. Oscar Huber, the pastor of Holy Trinity Church in Dallas, and the Rev. James Thompson.

Mr. Johnson was sworn in as President by Federal Judge Sarah T. Hughes of the Northern District of Texas. She was appointed to the judgeship by Mr. Kennedy in October, 1961.

The ceremony, delayed about five minutes for Mrs. Kennedy's arrival, took place in the private Presidential cabin in the rear of the plane.

About 25 to 30 persons—members of the late President's staff, members of Congress who had been accompanying the President on a two-day tour of Texas cities and a few reporters —crowded into the little room.

No accurate listing of those present could be obtained. Mrs. Kennedy stood at the left of Mr. Johnson, her eyes and face showing the signs of weeping that had apparently shaken her since she left the hospital not long before.

Mrs. Johnson, wearing a beige dress, stood at her husband's right.

As Judge Hughes read the brief oath of office, her eyes, too, were red from weeping. Mr. Johnson's hands rested on a black, leather-bound Bible as Judge Hughes read and he repeated:

"I do solemnly swear that I will perform the duties of the President of the United States to the best of my ability and defend protect

at the floor. She still wore the raspberry-colored suit in which she had greeted welcoming crowds in Fort Worth and Dallas. But she had taken off the matching pillbox hat she wore earlier in the day, and her dark hair was windblown and tangled. Her hand rested lightly on her husband's coffin as it was taken to a waiting hearse.

Mrs. Kennedy climbed in beside the coffin. Then the ambulance drove to Love Field, and Mr. Kennedy's body was placed aboard the and preserve the Constitution of the United States."

Those 34 words made Lyndon Baines Johnson, one-time farmboy and schoolteacher of Johnson City, the President.

## Johnson Embraces Mrs. Kennedy

Mr. Johnson made no statement. He embraced Mrs. Kennedy and she held his hand for a long moment. He also embraced Mrs. Johnson and Mrs. Evelyn Lincoln, Mr. Kennedy's private secretary.

"O.K.," Mr. Johnson said. "Lets get this plane back to Washington."

At 2:46 P.M., seven minutes after he had become President, 106 minutes after Mr. Kennedy had become the fourth American President to succumb to an assassin's wounds, the white and red jet took off for Washington.

In the cabin when Mr. Johnson took the oath was Cecil Stoughton, an armed forces photographer assigned to the White House.

Mr. Kennedy's staff members appeared stunned and bewildered. Lawrence F. O'Brien, the Congressional liaison officer, and P. Kenneth O'Donnell, the appointment secretary, both long associates of Mr. Kennedy, showed evidences of weeping. None had anything to say.

Other staff members believed to be in the cabin for the swearing-in included David F. Powers, the White House receptionist; Miss Pamela Turnure, Mrs. Kennedy's press secretary, and Malcolm Kilduff, the assistant White House press secretary.

Mr. Kilduff announced the President's death, with choked voice and red-rimmed eyes, at about 1:36 P.M.

"President John F. Kennedy died at approximately 1 o'clock Central standard time today here in Dallas," Mr. Kilduff said at the hospital. "He died of a gunshot wound in the brain. I have no other details regarding the assassination of the President."

Mr. Kilduff also announced that Governor Connally had been hit by a bullet or bullets and that Mr. Johnson, who had not yet been sworn in, was safe in the protective custody of the Secret Service at an unannounced place, presumably the airplane at Love Field.

Mr. Kilduff indicated that the President had been shot once. Later medical reports raised the possibility that there had been two wounds. But the death was caused, as far as could be learned, by a massive wound in the brain.

Later in the afternoon, Dr. Malcolm Perry, an attending surgeon, and Dr. Kemp Clark, chief of neurosurgery at Parkland Hospital, gave more details.

Mr. Kennedy was hit by a bullet in the throat, just below the Adam's apple, they said.

This wound had the appearance of a bullet's entry.

Mr. Kennedy also had a massive, gaping wound in the back and one on the right side of the head. However, the doctors said it was impossible to determine immediately whether the wounds had been caused by on bullet or two.

## Resuscitation Attempted

Dr. Perry, the first physician to treat the President, said a number of resuscitative measures had been attempted, including oxygen, anesthesia, an indotracheal tube, a tracheotomy, blood and fluids. An electrocardiogram monitor was attached to measure Mr. Kennedy's heart beats.

Dr. Clark was summoned and arrived in a minute or two. By then, Dr. Perry said, Mr. Kennedy was "critically ill and moribund," or near death.

Dr. Clark said that on his first sight of the President, he had concluded immediately that Mr. Kennedy could not live.

"It was apparent that the President had sustained a lethal wound," he said. "A missile had gone in and out of the back of his head causing external lacerations and loss of brain tissue."

Shortly after he arrived, Dr. Clark said, "the President lost his heart action by the electrocardiogram." A closed-chest cardiograph massage was attempted, as were other emergency resuscitation measures.

Dr. Clark said these had produced "palpable pulses" for a short time, but all were "to no avail."

## In Operating Room 40 Minutes

The President was on the emergency table at the hospital for about 40 minutes, the doctors said. At the end, perhaps eight physicians were in Operating Room No. 1, where Mr. Kennedy remained until his death. Dr. Clark said it was difficult to determine the exact moment of death, but the doctors said officially that it occurred at 1 P.M.

Later, there were unofficial reports that Mr. Kennedy had been killed instantly. The source of these reports, Dr. Tom Shires, chief surgeon at the hospital and professor of surgery at the University of Texas Southwest Medical School, issued this statement tonight:

"Medically, it was apparent the President was not alive when he was brought in. There was no spontaneous respiration. He had dilated, fixed pupils. It was obvious he had a lethal head wound.

"Technically, however, by using vigorous resuscitation, intravenous tubes and all the usual supportive measures, we were able to raise a semblance of a heartbeat."

Dr. Shires said he was "positive it was impossible" that President Kennedy could have spoken after being shot. "I am absolutely sure he never knew what hit him," Dr. Shires said.

Dr. Shires was not present when Mr. Kennedy was being treated at Parkland Hospital. He issued his statement, however, after lengthy conferences with the doctors who had attended the President.

Mr. Johnson remained in the hospital about 30 minutes after Mr. Kennedy died.

The details of what happened when shots first rang out, as the President's car moved along at about 25 miles an hour, were sketchy. Secret Service agents, who might have given more details, were unavailable to the press at first, and then returned to Washington with President Johnson.

## Kennedys Hailed at Breakfast

Mr. Kennedy had opened his day in Fort Worth, first with a speech in a parking lot and then at a Chamber of Commerce breakfast. The breakfast appearance was a particular triumph for Mrs. Kennedy, who entered late and was given an ovation.

Then the Presidential party, including Governor and Mrs. Connally, flew on to Dallas, an eight-minute flight. Mr. Johnson, as is customary, flew in a separate plane. The President and the Vice President do not travel together, out of fear of a double tragedy.

At Love Field, Mr. and Mrs. Kennedy lingered for 10 minutes, shaking hands with an enthusiastic group lining the fence. The group called itself "Grassroots Democrats."

Mr. Kennedy then entered his open Lincoln convertible at the head of the motorcade. He sat in the rear seat on the right-hand side. Mrs. Kennedy, who appeared to be enjoying one of the first political outings she had ever made with her husband, sat at his left.

In the "jump" seat, directly ahead of Mr. Kennedy, sat Governor Connally, with Mrs. Connally at his left in another "jump" seat. A Secret Service agent was driving and the two others ran alongside.

Behind the President's limousine was an open sedan carrying a number of Secret Service agents. Behind them, in an open convertible, rode Mr. and Mrs. Johnson and Texas's senior Senator, Ralph W. Yarborough, a Democrat.

The motorcade proceeded uneventfully along a 10-mile route through downtown Dallas, aiming for the Merchandise Mart. Mr. Kennedy was to address a group of the city's leading citizens at a luncheon in his honor.

In downtown Dallas, crowds were thick, enthusiastic and cheering. The turnout was somewhat unusual for this center of conserva-

tism, where only a month ago Adlai E. Stevenson was attacked by a rightist crowd. It was also in Dallas, during the 1960 campaign, that Senator Lyndon B. Johnson and his wife were nearly mobbed in the lobby of the Baker Hotel.

As the motorcade neared its end and the President's car moved out of the thick crowds onto Stemmonds Freeway near the Merchandise Mart, Mrs. Connally recalled later, "we were all very pleased with the reception in downtown Dallas."

## Approaching 3-Street Underpass

Behind the three leading cars were a string of others carrying Texas and Dallas dignitaries, two buses of reporters, several open cars carrying photographers and other reporters, and a bus for White House staff members.

As Mrs. Connally recalled later, the President's car was almost ready to go underneath a "triple underpass" beneath three streets — Elm, Commerce and Main—when the first shot was fired.

That shot apparently struck Mr. Kennedy. Governor Connally turned in his seat at the sound and appeared immediately to be hit in the chest.

Mrs. Mary Norman of Dallas was standing at the curb and at that moment was aiming her camera at the President. She saw him slump forward, then slide down in the seat.

"My God," Mrs. Norman screamed, as she recalled it later, "he's shot!"

Mrs. Connally said that Mrs. Kennedy had reached and "grabbed" her husband. Mrs. Connally put her arms around the Governor. Mrs. Connally said that she and Mrs. Kennedy had then ducked low in the car as it sped off.

Mrs. Connally's recollections were reported by Julian Reade, an aide to the Governor.

Most reporters in the press buses were too far back to see the shootings, but they observed some quick scurrying by motor policemen accompanying the motorcade. It was noted that the President's car had picked up speed and raced away, but reporters were not aware that anything serious had occurred until they reached the Merchandise Mart two or three minutes later.

## Rumors Spread at Trade Mart

Rumors of the shooting already were spreading through the luncheon crowd of hundreds, which was having the first course. No White House officials or Secret Service agents were present, but the reporters were taken quickly to Parkland Hospital on the strength of the rumors.

There they encountered Senator Yarborough, white, shaken and horrified.

The shots, he said, seemed to have come from the right and the rear of the car in which he was riding, the third in the motorcade. Another eyewitness, Mel Crouch, a Dallas television reporter, reported that as the shots rang out he saw a rifle extended and then withdrawn from a window on the "fifth or sixth floor" of the Texas Public School Book Depository. This is a leased state building on Elm Street, to the right of the motorcade route.

Senator Yarborough said there had been a slight pause between the first two shots and a longer pause between the second and third. A Secret Service man riding in the Senator's car, the Senator said, immediately ordered Mr. and Mrs. Johnson to get down below the level of the doors. They did so, and Senator Yarborough also got down.

The leading cars of the motorcade then pulled away at high speed toward Parkland Hospital, which was not far away, by the fast highway.

"We knew by the speed that something was terribly wrong," Senator Yarborough reported. When he put his head up, he said, he saw a Secret Service man in the car ahead beating his fists against the trunk deck of the car in which he was riding, apparently in frustration and anguish.

## Mrs. Kennedy's Reaction

Only White House staff members spoke with Mrs. Kennedy. A Dallas medical student, David Edwards, saw her in Parkland Hospital while she was waiting for news of her husband. He gave this description:

"The look in her eyes was like an animal that had been trapped, like a little rabbit—brave, but fear was in the eyes."

Dr. Clark was reported to have informed Mrs. Kennedy of her husband's death.

No witnesses reported seeing or hearing any of the Secret Service agents or policemen fire back. One agent was seen to brandish a machine gun as the cars sped away. Mr. Crouch observed a policeman falling to the ground and pulling a weapon. But the events had occurred so quickly that there was apparently nothing for the men to shoot at.

Mr. Crouch said he saw two women, standing at a curb to watch the motorcade pass, fall to the ground when the shots rang out. He also saw a man snatch up his little girl and run along the road. Policemen, he said, immediately chased this man under the impression he had been involved in the shooting, but Mr. Crouch said he had been a fleeing spectator.

Mr. Kennedy's limousine—license No. GG300 under District of Columbia registry—pulled up at the emergency entrance of Parkland Hospital. Senator Yarborough said the President had been carried inside on a stretcher.

By the time reporters arrived at the hospital, the police were guarding the Presidential car closely. They would allow no one to approach it. A bucket of water stood by the car, suggesting that the back seat had been scrubbed out.

Robert Clark of the American Broadcasting Company, who had been riding near the front of the motorcade, said Mr. Kennedy was motionless when he was carried inside. There was a great amount of blood on Mr. Kennedy's suit and shirtfront and the front of his body, Mr. Clark said.

Mrs. Kennedy was leaning over her husband when the car stopped, Mr. Clark said, and walked beside the wheeled stretcher into the hospital. Mr. Connally sat with his hands holding his stomach, his head bent over. He, too, was moved into the hospital in a stretcher, with Mrs. Connally at his side.

Robert McNeill of the National Broadcasting Company, who also was in the reporters' pool car, jumped out at the scene of the shooting. He said the police had taken two eyewitnesses into custody—an 8-year-old Negro boy and a white man—for informational purposes.

Many of these reports could not be verified immediately.

## Eyewitness Describes Shooting

An unidentified Dallas man, interviewed on television here, said he had been waving at the President when the shots were fired. His belief was that Mr. Kennedy had been struck twice—once, as Mrs. Norman recalled, when he slumped in his seat; again when he slid down in it.

"It seemed to just knock him down," the man said.

Governor Connally's condition was reported as "satisfactory" tonight after four hours in surgery at Parkland Hospital.

Dr. Robert R. Shaw, a thoracic surgeon, operated on the Governor to repair damage to his left chest.

Later, Dr. Shaw said Governor Connally had been hit in the back just below the shoulder blade, and that the bullet had gone completely through the Governor's chest, taking out part of the fifth rib.

After leaving the body, he said, the bullet struck the Governor's right wrist, causing a compound fracture. It then lodged in the left thigh.

The thigh wound, Dr. Shaw said, was trivial. He said the compound fracture would heal.

Dr. Shaw said it would be unwise for Governor Connally to be moved in the next 10 to 14 days. Mrs. Connally was remaining at his side tonight.

## Tour by Mrs. Kennedy Unusual

Mrs. Kennedy's presence near her husband's bedside at his death resulted from somewhat unusual circumstances. She had rarely accompanied him on his trips about the country and had almost never made political trips with him.

The tour on which Mr. Kennedy was engaged yesterday and today was only quasi-political; the only open political activity was to have been a speech tonight to a fund-raising dinner at the state capitol in Austin.

In visiting Texas, Mr. Kennedy was seeking to improve his political fortunes in a pivotal state that he barely won in 1960. He was also hoping to patch a bitter internal dispute among Texas's Democrats.

At 8:45 A.M., when Mr. Kennedy left the Texas Hotel in Fort Worth, where he spent his last night, to address the parking lot crowd across the street, Mrs. Kennedy was not with him. There appeared to be some disappointment.

"Mrs. Kennedy is organizing herself," the President said good-naturedly. "It takes longer, but, of course, she looks better than we do when she does it."

Later, Mrs. Kennedy appeared late at the Chamber of Commerce breakfast in Fort Worth.

Again, Mr. Kennedy took note of her presence. "Two years ago," he said, "I introduced myself in Paris by saying that I was the man who had accompanied Mrs. Kennedy to Paris. I am getting somewhat that same sensation as I travel around Texas. Nobody wonders what Lyndon and I wear."

The speech Mr. Kennedy never delivered at the Merchandise Mart luncheon contained a passage commenting on a recent preoccupation of his, and a subject of much interest in this city, where right-wing conservatism is the rule rather than the exception.

Voices are being heard in the land, he said, "voices preaching doctrines wholly unrelated to reality, wholly unsuited to the sixties, doctrines which apparently assume that words will suffice without weapons, that vituperation is as good as victory and that peace is a sign of weakness."

The speech went on: "At a time when the national debt is steadily being reduced in terms of its burden on our economy, they see that debt as the greatest threat to our security. At a time when we are steadily reducing the number of Federal employes serving every thousand citizens, they fear those supposed hordes of civil servants far more than the actual hordes of opposing armies.

"We cannot expect that everyone, to use the phrase of a decade ago, will 'talk sense to the American people.' But we can hope that fewer people will listen to nonsense. And the notion that this nation is headed for defeat through deficit, or that strength is but a matter of slogans, is nothing but just plain nonsense."

November 23, 1963

## Queens Woman Is Stabbed To Death in Front of Home

A 28-year-old Queens woman was stabbed to death early yesterday morning outside her apartment house in Kew Gardens.

Neighbors who were awakened by her screams found the woman, Miss Catherine Genovese of 82-70 Austin Street, shortly after 3 A.M. in front of a building three doors from her home.

The police said that Miss Genovese had been attacked in front of her building and had run to where she fell. She had parked her car in a nearby lot, the police said, after having driven it from the Hollis bar where she was day manager.

The police, who spent the day searching for the murder weapon, interviewing witnesses and checking automobiles that had been seen in the neighborhood, said last night they had no clues.

March 14, 1964

# TV CALLED FACTOR IN SLAYING APATHY

## Psychiatrist Gives Views on Witnesses in Queens

A confusion of fantasy with reality, fed by an endless stream of television violence, was in part responsible for the fact that 37 Queens residents could passively watch a murder taking place, a psychiatrist said yesterday.

The psychiatrist, Dr. Ralph S. Banay, addressed about 100 persons at a symposium on violence conducted at the Barbizon-Plaza Hotel by the Medical Correctional Association, of which he is president.

"We underestimate the damage that these accumulated images do to the brain," Dr. Banay said. "The immediate effect can be delusional, equivalent to a sort of post-hypnotic suggestion."

The killing took place in the early morning hours of March 13 on a well-lighted sidewalk in front of an apartment building in Kew Gardens. The victim was Miss Catherine Genovese, a night-club hostess who lived near by.

**Screams Unanswered**

Two weeks later the police announced that their investigation had disclosed that 38 persons saw the three knife attacks over more than 30 minutes that led to the woman's death. Despite Miss Genovese's repeated screams for help, the police said, no one went to her aid. A telephone call to the police was made by one woman only after the victim was dead.

The police disclosures of public apathy in the face of murder shocked the city, and led to many attempts to explain it.

Dr. Banay suggested yesterday that the murder vicariously gratified the sadistic impulses of those who witnessed it.

"They were deaf, paralyzed, hypnotized with excitation," he declared, "fascinated by the drama, by the action, and yet not entirely sure that what was taking place was actually happening."

Dr. Banay, who is professor of forensic psychiatry at Manhattan College, interpreted the readiness of the 37 persons to admit to the police that they had failed to act as an attempt through confession to purge the guilt that their enjoyment of the sight had aroused.

"Persons with mature and well-integrated personalities would not have acted in this way," he said.

Another speaker, Dr. Karl Menninger, the director of the Menninger Foundation in Topeka, Kan., touched on the same theme when he said that "public apathy [to crime] is itself a manifestation of aggressiveness."

**Encouraged by Many**

Noting that lawless behavior was tacitly encouraged in many ways, he added, "Crime has too much vicarious usefulness to society to be readily eliminated."

Dr. Walter Bromberg, a consultant in the defense of Jack Ruby, who was convicted of killing Lee Harvey Oswald, urged that a central registry be established for persons suffering from epilepsy and related diseases and that they be required to undergo treatment. Dr. Bromberg is clinical director of Pinewood Sanitarium in Katonah, N. Y.

Another psychiatrist, Dr. Maier I. Tuchler of Phoenix, said that parents often encouraged delinquency in their children to gratify their own antisocial impulses. He said the problem was intensified in a rapidly changing, rootless society.

In a related paper on the family as "the breeding ground of violence," Dr. Lidia Kopernik stated that a study of prisoners' families in Pennsylvania found that only one of 98 could be regarded as a well-adjusted unit.

# Study of the Sickness Called Apathy

## By A. M. ROSENTHAL

IT happens from time to time in New York that the life of the city is frozen by an instant of shock. In that instant the people of the city are seized by the paralyzing realization that they are one, that each man is in some way a mirror of every other man. They stare at each other—or, really, into themselves—and a look quite like a flush of embarrassment passes over the face of the city. Then the instant passes and the beat resumes and the people turn away and try to explain what they have seen, or try to deny it.

The last 35 minutes of the young life of Miss Catherine Genovese became such a shock in the life of the city. But at the time she died, stabbed again and again by a marauder in her quiet, dark but entirely respectable, street in Kew Gardens, New York hardly took note.

It was not until two weeks later that Catherine Genovese, known as Kitty, returned in death to cry the city awake. Even then it was not her life or her dying that froze the city, but the witnessing of her murder—the choking fact that 38 of her neighbors had seen her stabbed or heard her cries, and that not one of them, during that hideous half-hour, had lifted the telephone from the safety of his own apartment to call the police and try to save her life. When it was over and Miss Genovese was dead and the murderer gone, one man did call—not from his own apartment but from a neighbor's, and only after he had called a friend and asked her what to do.

THE day that the story of the witnessing of the death of Miss Genovese appeared in this newspaper became that frozen instant. "Thirty-eight!" people said over and over. "Thirty-eight!"

It was as if the number itself had some special meaning, and in a way, of course, it did. One person or two or even three or four witnessing a murder passively would have been the unnoticed symptom of the disease in the city's body and again would have passed unnoticed. But 38—it was like a man with a running low fever suddenly beginning to cough blood; his friends could no longer ignore his illness, nor could he turn away from himself.

At first there was, briefly, the reaction of shared guilt. Even people who were sure that they certainly would have acted differently felt it somehow. "Dear God, what have we come to?" a woman said that day. "We," not "they."

For in that instant of shock, the mirror showed quite clearly what was wrong, that the face of mankind was spotted with the disease of apathy—all mankind. But this was too frightening a thought to live with and soon the beholders began to set boundaries for the illness, to search frantically for causes that were external and to look for the carrier.

There was a rash of metropolitan masochism. "What the devil do you expect in a town, a jungle, like this?" Sociologists and psychiatrists reached for the warm comfort of jargon—"alienation of the individual from the group," "megalopolitan societies," "the disaster syndrome."

People who came from small towns said it could never happen back home. New Yorkers, ashamed, agreed. Nobody seemed to stop to ask whether there were not perhaps various forms of apathy and that some that exist in villages and towns do not exist in great cities.

GUILT turned into masochism, and masochism, as it often does, became a sadistic search for a target. Quite soon, the target became the police.

There is no doubt whatsoever that the police in New York have failed, to put it politely, to instill a feeling of total confidence in the population. There are great areas in this city—fine parks as well as slums—where no person in his right mind would wander of an evening or an early morning. There is no central emergency point to receive calls for help. And a small river of letters from citizens to this newspaper testifies to the fact that patrols are often late in answering calls and that policemen on desk duty often give the bitter edge of their tongues to citizens calling for succor.

There is no doubt of these things. But to blame the police for apathy is a bit like blaming the sea wall for springing leaks. The police of this city are more efficient, more restrained and more responsive to public demands than any others the writer has encountered in a decade of traveling the world. Their faults are either mechanical or a reflection of a city where almost every act of police self-protection is assumed to be an act of police brutality, and where a night-club comedian can, as one did the other night, stand on a stage for an hour and a half and vilify the police as brutes, thieves, homosexuals, illiterates and "Gestapo agents" while the audience howls in laughter as it drinks Scotch from bootleg bottles hidden under the tables.

**T**HERE are two tragedies in the story of Catherine Genovese. One is the fact that her life was taken from her, that she died in pain and horror at the age of 28. The other is that in dying she gave every human being — not just species New Yorker — an opportunity to examine some truths about the nature of apathy and that this has not been done.

Austin Street, where Catherine Genovese lived, is in a section of Queens known as Kew Gardens. There are two apartment buildings and the rest of the street consists of one-family homes— red-brick, stucco or wood-frame. There are Jews, Catholics and Protestants, a scattering of foreign accents, middle-class incomes.

On the night of March 13, about 3 A.M., Catherine Genovese was returning to her home. She worked late as manager of a bar in Hollis, another part of Queens. She parked her car (a red Fiat) and started to walk to her death.

Lurking near the parking lot was a man. Miss Genovese saw him in the shadows, turned and walked toward a police call box. The man pursued her, stabbed her. She screamed, "Oh my God, he stabbed

me! Please help me! Please help me!"

Somebody threw open a window and a man called out: "Let that girl alone!" Other lights turned on, other windows were raised. The attacker got into a car and drove away. A bus passed.

The attacker drove back, got out, searched out Miss Genovese in the back of an apartment building where she had crawled for safety, stabbed her again, drove away again.

The first attack came at 3:15. The first call to the police came at 3:50. Police arrived within two minutes, they say. Miss Genovese was dead.

**T**HAT night and the next morning the police combed the neighborhood looking for witnesses. They found them, 38.

Two weeks later, when this newspaper heard of the story, a reporter went knocking, door to door, asking why, why.

Through half-opened doors, they told him. Most of them were neither defiant nor terribly embarrassed nor particularly ashamed. The underlying attitude, or explanation, seemed to be fear of involvement—any kind of involvement.

"I didn't want my husband to get involved," a housewife said.

"We thought it was a lovers' quarrel," said another woman. "I went back to bed."

"I was tired," said a man.

"I don't know," said another man.

"I don't know," said still another.

"I don't know," said others.

On March 19, police arrested a 29-year-old business-machine operator named Winston Moseley and charged him with the murder of Catherine Genovese. He has confessed to killing two other women, for one of whose murders police say they have a confession from another man.

**N**OT much is said or heard or thought in the city about Winston Moseley. In this drama, as far as the city is concerned, he appeared briefly, acted his piece, exited into the wings.

A week after the first story appeared, a reporter went back to Austin Street. Now the witnesses no longer wanted to talk. They were harried, annoyed; they thought they should keep their mouths shut. "I've done enough talking," one witness said. "Oh, it's you

again," said a woman witness and slammed the door.

The neighbors of the witnesses are willing to talk. Their sympathy is for the silent witnesses and the embarrassment in which they now live.

Max Heilbrunn, who runs a coffee house on Austin Street, talked about all the newspaper publicity and said his neighbors felt they were being picked on. "It isn't a bad neighborhood," he said.

And this from Frank Facciola, the owner of the neighborhood barber shop: "I resent the way these newspaper and television people have hurt us. We have wonderful people here. What happened could have happened any place. There is no question in my mind that people here now would rush out to help anyone being attacked on the street."

Then he said: "The same thing [failure to call the police] happens in other sections every day. Why make such a fuss when it happens in Kew Gardens? We are trying to forget it happened here."

A Frenchwoman in the neighborhood said: "Let's forget the whole thing. It is a quiet neighborhood, good to live in. What happened, happened."

**E**ACH individual, obviously, approaches the story of Catherine Genovese, reacts to it and veers away from it against the background of his own life and experience, and his own fears and shortcomings and rationalizations.

It seems to this writer that what happened in the apartments and houses on Austin Street was a symptom of a terrible reality in the human condition—that only under certain situations and only in response to certain reflexes or certain beliefs will a man step out of his shell toward his brother.

To say this is not to excuse, but to try to understand and in so doing perhaps eventually to extend the reflexes and beliefs and situations to include more people. To ignore it is to perpetuate myths that lead nowhere. Of these the two most futile philosophically are that apathy is a response to official ineptitude ("The cops never come on time anyway"), or that apathy is a condition only of metropolitan life.

Certainly police procedures must be improved—although in the story of Miss Genovese all indications were that, once called into action, the police machine behaved perfectly.

**MURDER SPOT**—Here, behind an apartment building in Kew Gardens, Catherine Genovese was killed, while 38 witnesses did nothing.

As far as is known, not one witness has said that he remained silent because he had had any unpleasant experience with the police. It is a pointless point; there are men who will jump into a river to rescue a drowner; there are others who will tell themselves that a police launch will be cruising by or that, if it doesn't, it should.

Nobody can say why the 38 did not lift the phone while Miss Genovese was being attacked, since they cannot say themselves. It can be assumed, however, that their apathy was indeed of a big-city variety. It is almost a matter of psychological survival, if one is surrounded and pressed by millions of people, to prevent them from constantly impinging on you and the only way to do this is to ignore them as often as possible.

Indifference to one's neighbor and his troubles is a conditioned reflex of life in New York as it is in other big cities. In every major city in which I have lived—in Tokyo and Warsaw, Vienna and Bombay—I have seen, over and over again, people walk away from accident victims. I have walked away myself.

Out-of-towners, and sometimes New Yorkers themselves, like to think that there is something special about New York's metropolitan apathy. It is special in that there are more people here than any place else in the country—and therefore more people to turn away from each other.

**F**OR decades, New York turned away from the truth that is Harlem or Bedford-Stuyvesant in Brooklyn. Everybody knew that in the Negro ghettos, men, women and children lived in filth and degradation. But the city, as a city, turned away with the metropolitan brand of apathy.

This, most simply, consists of drowning the person-to-person responsibility in a wave of impersonal social action.

Committees were organized, speeches made, budgets passed to "do something" about Harlem or Bedford-Stuyvesant—to do something about the communities. This dulled the reality, and still does, that the communities consist of individual people who ache and suffer in the loss of their individual prides. Housewives who contributed to the N.A.A.C.P. saw nothing wrong in going down to the daily shape-up of domestic workers in the Bronx and selecting a maid for the day after looking over the coffle to see which "girl" among the Negro matrons present looked huskiest.

Now there is an acute awareness of the problems of the Negroes in New York. But, again, it is an impersonal awareness, and more and more it is tinged with irritation at the thought that the integration movement will impinge on the daily personal life of the city.

Nor are Negroes in the city immune from apathy—toward one another or toward whites. They are apathetic toward one another's right to believe and act as they please; one man's concept of proper action is labeled with the group epithet "Uncle Tom." And, until the recent upsurge of the integration movement, there was less action taken within the Negro community to improve conditions in Harlem than there was in the all-white sections of the East Side. It has become fashionable to sneer at "white liberals" — fashionable even among Negroes who for years did nothing for brothers even of their own color.

**I**N their own sense of being wronged, some Negroes of New York have become totally apathetic to the sensitivities of all other groups. In a night club in Harlem the other night, an aspiring Negro politician, a most decent man, talked of how the Jewish shopkeepers exploited the Negroes, how he wished Negroes could "save a dollar like the Jews," totally apathetic toward the fact that Jews at the table might be as hurt as he would be if they talked in clichés of the happy-go-lucky Stepin Fetchit Negro. When a Jew protested, the Negro was stunned—because he was convinced he hated anti-Semitism. He did, in the abstract.

Since the Genovese case, New Yorkers have sought explanations of their apathy toward individuals. Fear, some say—fear of involvement, fear of reprisal from goons, fear of becoming "mixed up" with the police. This, it seems to this writer, is simply rationalization.

The self-protective shells in which we live are determined not only by the difference between big cities and small. They are determined by economics and social class, by caste and by color, and by religion, and by politics.

**I**F I were to see a beggar starving to death in rags on the streets of Paris or New York or London I would be moved to take some kind of action. But many times I have seen starving men lying like broken dolls in the streets of Calcutta or Madras and have done nothing.

I think I would have called the police to save Miss Genovese but I know that I did not save a beggar in Calcutta. Was my failing really so much smaller than that of the people who watched from their windows on Austin Street? And what was the apathy of the people of Austin Street compared, let's say, with the apathy of non-Nazi Germans toward Jews?

Geography is a factor of apathy. Indians reacted to Portuguese imprisoning Goans, but not to Russians killing Hungarians.

Color is a factor. Ghanaians reacted toward Frenchmen killing Algerians, not toward Congolese killing white missionaries.

Strangeness is a factor. Americans react to the extermination of Jews but not to the extermination of Watusis.

There are national as well as individual apathies, all inhibiting the ability to react. The "mind-your-own-business" attitude is despised among individuals, and clucked at by sociologists, but glorified as pragmatic national policy among nations.

**O**NLY in scattered moments, and then in halting embarrassment, does the United States, the most involved nation in the world, get down to hard cases about the nature of governments with which it deals, and how they treat their subject citizens. People who believe that a free government should react to the oppression of people in the mass by other governments are regarded as fanatics or romantics by the same diplomats who would react in horror to the oppression of one single individual in Washington. Between apathy, regarded as a moral disease, and national policy, the line is often hard to find.

There are, it seems to me, only two logical ways to look at the story of the murder of Catherine Genovese. One is the way of the neighbor on Austin Street — "Let's forget the whole thing."

The other is to recognize that the bell tolls even on each man's individual island, to recognize that every man must fear the witness in himself who whispers to close the window.

# Tenants Form Security Patrols

## 2 City Groups Active

### By JOHN SIBLEY

Two large groups of apartment dwellers have taken measures in recent days to protect themselves against muggers, purse - snatchers, rapists and burglars.

In Delano Village, a development of seven buildings housing 1,800 families in North Harlem, tenants are setting up their own patrols. Men equipped with billy clubs and walkie-talkie radios, working in pairs, stand tricks of one or two hours between 4 P.M and 1:30 A.M.

On Manhattan's West Side, leaders of tenant groups in a dozen apartment houses organized to find ways of making their buildings more secure. Nearly everyone who attended the organizational meeting told of recent crime in his own building.

These moves were not isolated. In growing numbers, frightened and angry citizens have been banding together to protect themselves against criminal attacks.

The trend gained wide attention last spring when Hasidic Jews in the Crown Heights section of Brooklyn began patrolling the area in radio cars. They acted after a number of their people were beaten and mugged, in most cases by hoodlums from the nearby Bedford-Stuyvesant section

The police view the situation apprehensively. Commenting yesterday on the tenant patrols in Delano Village, Deputy Commissioner Walter Arm said:

"If they feel they need additional protection within the project, that's their business. But we don't condone police action by any group except the police."

Mr Arm said he hoped the citizen-guards would not act beyond their authority. Asked whether the police would cooperate with the tenants, he replied:

"We'd like them to cooperate with us. They can do the most good by giving us quick information if trouble breaks out."

In Delano Village, the night patrols have been organized so far on a building-by-building basis. The development occupies a tract bounded by 139th and 143d Streets and Fifth and Lenox Avenues.

Last Thursday 200 tenants of 60 West 142d Street met in the building's recreation room and agreed to contribute $1 a family to equip the patrols. Sixty men volunteered to stand regular tours of duty; since then 15 more men have volunteered.

Altogether, the volunteers make up one-third of the men in the building.

Wade Hudson, a Transit Authority worker who serves on the tenants' steering committee, said yesterday the group was working out a regular schedule for the patrols. He said his building's group would meet this week with representatives from other buildings to coordinate the program.

Charles Axelrod, president of the corporation that owns and manages Delano Village, voiced qualified approval of the tenant patrols. The corporation employs eight private policemen. Two or three at a time patrol the entire project.

"We could have 100 men, and it still wouldn't be enough," Mr. Axelrod said. "These characters who snatch purses and molest women are nothing new to this area.

"The rents that are being paid here do not cover the security force. As a matter of fact I'm not even required to have a security force. So I'm glad to see the tenants form a committee. I hope it'll do some good."

In the other situation, a group of tenants from buildings along West End Avenue and Riverside Drive met Thursday night in the apartment of Frederick Fried, a writer, of 875 West End Avenue, at 103d Street.

Among them was State Senator Constance Baker Motley, who lives in the building.

As they chatted before the formal meeting began, the tenant leaders exchanged accounts of muggings in unguarded elevators and basement laundry rooms, and of burglars prowling roofs and fire-escapes.

They agreed that crime had increased in their section of the city since the recent rise in the cost of heroin. Narcotics addicts were blamed for most of the trouble.

Mrs. Motley told the group:

"I certainly hope this is the beginning of a permanent organization. This kind of problem can only be attacked on a neighborhood basis.

"Ultimately we may need legislation requiring landlords to have manned elevators or doormen. The landlords are going to oppose it, and some tenants will oppose it, too.

"Rent increases would probably be necessary. But we can't have it both ways."

The meeting listened attentively to Robert Schur of 203 West 90th Street, the building in which a lawyer named Leonard Simpson was killed last June 17, allegedly by an addict.

Mr. Schur reported that after the murder in an unguarded elevator, men in the building began taking turns standing guard duty in the lobby until midnight. The tenants hired a doorman for the midnight-to-dawn stint.

Mr. Schur urged the group to join his tenants' association in a program to educate apartment dwellers in protective measures and to push for legislation.

He produced a "tenants security check list" that had been distributed in his building. It contains such warnings as: "Never buzz back to your front door unless you are sure the visitor is safe; never permit outsiders to enter the front door with you; never enter the elevator alone with any stranger."

He said his group was seeking legislation that would require among other things:

¶Automatic locks and intercommunication system at the main entrance to buildings that have no doormen.

¶Locks on every entrance to apartment buildings.

¶Floodlighting of alleys and courtyards.

The group agreed to hold a second meeting this week that would bring in tenant leaders from other buildings in the area

In a related development earlier this month, the United Nations began using its uniformed security guards to escort late-working women employes to nearby points where they can get taxis.

December 14, 1964

---

# Bar Leader Finds High Court Too Lenient in Criminal Cases

## Fears Recent Rulings Have Tipped Scales at Expense of the Public's Safety

### By EDITH EVANS ASBURY

The president of the American Bar Association said yesterday that there was growing reason for the belief that recent Supreme Court decisions had tipped the scales of justice too far in favor of criminals at the expense of the public's safety.

As a result, Lewis F. Powell Jr., the A.B.A. president, said, "there are valid reasons for criminals to think that crime does pay, and that slow and fumbling justice can be evaded."

Mr. Powell, a Richmond attorney, addressed the annual meeting of the New York State Bar Association at the headquarters of the Association of the Bar of the City of New York, at 42 West 44th Street.

He cautioned that it was "unproductive and destructive to criticize the court itself" for performing its "historic function" of "protecting the constitutional rights of the individual against alleged unlawful acts of government."

However, the Supreme Court decisions that have, in recent years, strengthened the rights of accused persons have rendered the task of law enforcement more difficult at a time when crime is increasing at an alarming rate, he said.

"The right of society in general, and of each individual in particular, to be protected from crime must never be subordinated to other rights," Mr. Powell asserted.

"There is a growing body of opinion that the rights of law-abiding citizens are being subordinated. The pendulum may have swung too far in affording rights which are abused and misused by criminals."

Mr. Powell said there was a 10 per cent increase in crime in 1963 over the previous year and the trend continued in 1964 with a 13 per cent increase in the first nine months.

"The nature of the crimes committed is also disturbing," he continued, "with crimes of violence continuing to increase.

"The single most shocking statistic, documented in F.B.I. reports, is that since 1958 crime has been increasing five times faster than the population growth," he added.

Despite the annual cost in money and human misery, Mr.

313

Powell said the American public seems apathetic about the crime situation.

"In a country which is said to stand on the threshold of the Great Society," Mr. Powell declared, it is incongruous that in some urban areas law-abiding citizens are unsafe in their homes and denied the privilege of using public streets and parks for fear of their personal safety.

### 'We Must Act Now'

This fear signifies a breakdown in the primary responsibility of government, which is "the duty to protect citizens in their persons and property from criminal conduct—whatever its source or cause," Mr. Powell said.

"Society cannot await the millennium when crime will lying causes have been removed," Mr. Powell said. "We must act now."

A major program to develop national standards for the administration of criminal justice was undertaken recently by the A.B.A. under the chairmanship of Chief Judge J. Edward Lumbard of the United States Court of Appeals for the Second Circuit.

The project, expected to require three years and cost $750,000 will consider "the entire spectrum of criminal justice," Mr. Powell said.

Another encouraging sign of attention to the problem of maintaining the proper balance between individual rights and the rights of the public, Mr. Powell said, is the new Office of Criminal Justice within the Department of Justice.

Also, he continued, Governor Rockefeller recently proposed "an imaginative anticrime program for New York," including a new penal code and a new school of criminal justice.

A number of other states are also re-examining their criminal codes, he said.

The State Bar Association elected Sidney B. Pfeifer of Buffalo, president, replacing Orison S. Marden of New York City. It also elected C. Everett Shults of Hornell as secretary and re-elected Robert C. Poskanzer of Albany treasurer.

# NEWS OF THE WEEK IN LAW

## War on Crime

### By JOHN D. POMFRET

President Johnson this week proposed the first step in what could become an enormously significant Federal program to improve state and local law enforcement.

This was the most important aspect of a Presidential message to Congress that asked as well for legislative action to aid Federal law enforcement efforts and announced a Presidential commission to make the most intensive study of crime since the Wickersham report of 25 years ago.

Mr. Johnson's message reflected public uneasiness at the growing number of brutal and senseless crimes that have made many city dwellers apprehensive about walking their streets at night—and in some neighborhoods even during the day.

The day before it went to Capitol Hill, the Federal Bureau of Investigation reported an increase of 13 per cent in serious crimes in 1964. Proportionally, rape and assault went up the most.

Solving and preventing crime of this kind—"crime in the streets"—is primarily the function of state and local law enforcement officials.

### Low Prestige

Yet in many communities, policemen are overworked and underpaid. Their prestige is low and their equipment poor. They are poorly trained. Correctional facilities and methods are inadequate. Local courts are clogged and inefficient.

To begin remedying this situation, the President has proposed that the Attorney General be authorized to make grants to establish or enlarge programs and facilities to provide professional training and related education for state and local law enforcement personnel.

Experimental projects to develop methods of making cities safer would also be made possible. Areas with high crime rates might be saturated with police, for example, to see whether that was an effective remedy. Modern communications and alarm techniques might be tried out.

The amount budgeted for the first year of the program —$10 million—is a token. Discussion is under way on whether, if Congress approves the program, the money should be spread around widely or concentrated in just a few cities to see what can be done on an intensive basis.

### Decision Reached

No one connected with developing the proposal thinks that i will solve all the problems of local and state law enforcement agencies. But they hope that at least the program may begin to show the way and eventually result in a major upgrading of the skill and professional caliber of law enforcement officials.

The proposal does not tackle at all one major problem confronted by state and local law enforcement agencies. This is the lack in most states of any centralized statewide control over law enforcement and the plethora of police jurisdictions—each beholden only unto itself.

In most states, the state's attorney general has no authority over local district attorneys, who are usually elected, jealous of their autonomy and sometimes have political ties that impinge on the vigorous discharge of their duty.

Had the Administration undertaken to sort out this problem, however, it would have created for itself a large political issue that would almost certainly have ended the chance of enactment of other aspects of the program.

In fact, the Administration has been careful to propose only the sort of limited Federal assistance to state and local enforcement agencies that it gives in other fields.

In the Federal area, Mr. Johnson's discussion of the central problem—how to combat organized crime—was couched in generalities.

"It has become an entrenched national industry. It embraces gambling, narcotics, stock and bankruptcy fraud, usurious loans, or corruption of public officials or labor-management relations."

The Justice Department will propose a series of specific measures to give it better weapons with which to wage its continuing war on the crime syndicate, or Mafia.

In fact, it asked for the first measure this week—a

new law making interstate arson activity a Federal crime.

It will also seek once more

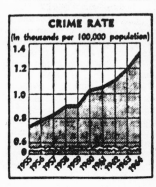

a law that would allow its investigators to tap telephones under court order for limited periods to gather information about certain serious criminal activity. Private wire-tapping would be banned. State and local authorities would also be able to wiretap provided they met the same standards that would be established for Federal authorities. And evidence so obtained would be admissible in court.

The department also will seek an extension of immunity provisions that now exist in some 55 other statutes to the anti-racketeering laws. This would enable the department to skirt the Fifth Amendment ban on self-incrimination by granting immunity from prosecution to certain witnesses. If they still refused to testify, they could be punished for contempt of court.

There is no plan at present, however, to seek to create any major new Federal offense.

Government experts, mindful of the difficult legal problems that have confronted the Justice Department at almost every turn in enforcing the statute making membership in the Communist party a crime, are not persuaded that such a step would be helpful.

They think that the law as it stands is probably sufficient for the job, but that the problem lies in cracking the crime syndicate's curtain of silence, enforced on pain of death. Hence, the interest in wire-tapping legislation and, to a lesser extent, extension of the immunity provisions.

# 16 ON DEATH ROW SHOW LITTLE JOY

## Concerned More With Ball Game Than Penalty Bill

### By McCANDLISH PHILLIPS

Word that the death penalty had been abolished for most crimes in New York State was received joylessly, almost without comment, in the death house at Sing Sing late yesterday afternoon.

In the place where it would seem they would care the most —a few yards from the electric chair that has taken 614 lives since 1891—the men seemed to think little of the news.

The New York Mets were playing the Cubs at Chicago and the game was piped in by radio loudspeaker to the long corridor of the death house at Ossining. At 5 minutes before 5 o'clock, the sportscast was cut off for a bulletin: Governor Rockefeller had signed the bill abolishing the death penalty in most cases.

Then there was silence. The baseball broadcast came back on.

### 'No Discussion at All'

"There was no demonstration, no cheering, no yelling at each other," Warden Wilfred Denno said by telephone a few minutes later. "There was no discussion at all. It may sound incredible, but they seemed more interested in the ball game."

In the 10 minutes following the bulletin, a guard heard only one comment. "It takes a relief off my mind," he quoted a condemned man as having said.

There are 20 men condemned to death in New York, but four of them are temporarily out of Sing Sing for various legal hearings, so only 16 were present yesterday when the news came.

Having discussed it with their lawyers, the men knew that the bill made no provision for men already condemned to death in the state. Mr. Denno thought that was one reason for their phlegmatic attitude. The reaction was about the same when the Legislature passed the abolition bill, Mr. Denno said.

The men knew, too, that three of their number were "cop killers" exempt from the terms of the new law.

There have been many years in which 15 to 20 persons were executed at Sing Sing, but none of the condemned men yesterday felt himself in the immediate shadow of the antique instrument of legal death. The most recent electrocution came on Aug. 15, 1963, and none is now scheduled.

### Tennessee Cases Recalled

"I think life imprisonment is the greater punishment than death," the warden said. "When Governor [Frank G.] Clement of Tennessee went in a few months ago and commuted the death sentences of condemned men to 99 years, we heard comments here like, 'I wouldn't want my sentence commuted to 99 years.'"

"In one sense, your troubles are over" when you go to the chair," the warden said.

The Rev. Luther K. Hannum, the Protestant chaplain at Sing Sing, known as Doc Hannum, had a similar comment. He will retire in August after 25 years service, and in that time he has walked to the chair with condemned men 68 times.

"From 75 to 80 per cent of the men who have gone to the electric chair have preferred death to spending the rest of their lives in prison," he said.

### A Separate Building

The death house is a separate brick structure in the southwest corner of the high-walled prison compound at Ossining on the Hudson River.

The men are held in solitary confinement in 8-by-12-foot cells that stretch along one side of the corridor, so that no cell faces any other. Each cell has three steel walls with a cage-like front, and each has a light fixture on the ceiling, an iron cot, a backless stool and a sink with a cold-water tap.

As to whether the death penalty is a deterrent to murder, Warden Denno said:

"You'll never know what's in anybody's mind. Only time will tell whether fellows who use imitation pistols or unloaded pistols in robberies when they could have got real ones would have used real ones if they hadn't been thinking about the risk of murder.

"You ask them about it and we hear them say, 'We didn't want anybody to get nervous or jittery and shoot someone. We didn't want to get the chair.' In those cases we know it was a deterrent."

Warden Denno said he thought the streets of New York City would now be the main testing ground of whether or not capital punishment had restrained some from wanton shooting.

*June 2, 1965*

# ONE NIGHT ON A KANSAS FARM

IN COLD BLOOD: A True Account of a Multiple Murder and Its Consequences. By Truman Capote. 343 pp. New York: Random House. $5.95.

### By CONRAD KNICKERBOCKER

THE plains of western Kansas are even lonelier than the sea. Men, farm houses and windmills become specks against the vast sky. At night, the wind seems to have come from hundreds of miles distant. Diesel-engine horns echo immensity. During the day, one drives flat out through shimmering mirages. Highways all roll straight to the point of infinity on a far horizon. Tires click; tumbleweed rustles; Coca-Cola signs endlessly creak.

On the Indian summer night of Nov. 14, 1959, two criminals visited this haunting geography. With a knife and a 12-gauge shotgun, they robbed and murdered a man and his wife and their son and daughter. The deed filled the scene. It echoed through the lives of all who lived

*Mr. Knickerbocker is a critic and writer who knows the Kansas plains.*

nearby, rushing toward some appalling, mysterious point of psychic infinity. It made haggard men out of the guardians of order. Eventually, through a fluke almost as gratuitous as the killing itself, they captured the murderers. On an April night last year, as rain beat on the roof, the two were hanged in a chilly warehouse in the corner of the yard of the Kansas State Penitentiary at Lansing.

To the Midwestern newspaper reader, the crime and its aftermath, while awful enough, were not especially astonishing. Spectacular violence seems appropriate to the empty stage of the plains, as though by such cosmic acts mankind must occasionally signal its presence. Charlie Starkweather, accompanied by his teen-age lover, killed 10 people. George Ronald York and James Douglas Latham murdered seven. Lowell Lee Andrews, the mild, fat student with dreams of becoming a Chicago gunman, dispatched his father, mother and older sister with 21 bullets. Last May, Duane Pope, a clean-cut

young football player, shot four people (three of them fatally) who were lying face down on the floor of a rural bank in Nebraska. Multiple murder is one of the traditional expressions of youthful hostility.

To Truman Capote, the killings in western Kansas seemed less commonplace. Already he had explored beyond the lush settings and moonlit characters that had made him famous. The very forms of novel and short story seemed to him increasingly inadequate to the weird dynamics of the age. "Breakfast at Tiffany's" was a bon-bon, but in "The Muses Are Heard," with its improbable cast of Negro performers and Russian and American culturati, he demonstrated that reality, if heard out patiently, could orchestrate its own full range. He did not intend to be merely the novelist-as-journalist, writing diversionary occasional pieces. He had already done all that in "Local Color." In the completer role of novelist-as-journalist-as-artist, he was after a new kind of statement. He wanted the facts to declare a reality that transcended reality.

He went west, to Kansas City, to Garden City and Holcomb, Kan., the hamlet where the murders took place. With the obsessiveness of a man demonstrating a profound new hypothesis, he spent more than five years unraveling and following to its end every thread in the killing of Herbert W. Clutter and his family. "In Cold Blood," the resulting chronicle, is a masterpiece—agonizing, terrible, possessed, proof that the times, so surfeited with disasters, are still capable of tragedy.

The tragedy was existential. The murder was seemingly without motive. The killers, Perry Smith and Richard Hickock, almost parodied the literary anti-hero. Social dropouts filled with nausea, disillusioned romantics, they were the perfect loners. Their relationship, if not physical, was spiritually homosexual, similar to the exalted *Freundschaft*, bound in blood, of SS brothers. Smith, the archetypal underground exile, had the usual existential loathing of the body; he hated his crushed legs. Chewing aspirin and drinking root beer, he daydreamed in his crushed heart of a Mexican beach paradise with treasure under the sea. At night, sometimes afflicted with enuresis, he dreamed of a giant yellow bird that would lift him to salvation. Sometimes his captors saw in him the violence and power of a maimed jungle animal. Hickock, on the other hand, was nothing, merely the kid next door gone totally wrong. He was only charming while unloading hot checks on clothing salesmen. One of his weaknesses was little girls, and to the end he loudly asserted he was "a normal."

The Clutters made especially poignant victims. It was not that they wanted killing, but their lives, like so many of their countrymen's, rigid, solidly reliant on the grace of affluence, denied the possibility of evil and thus were crucially diminished. Mr. Clutter tolerated no drinkers among those who worked on his farm. He ate apples in the morning and bought everything by check. The wax on the floors of his $40,000 house exuded a lemon scent. His daughter, Nancy, lovely and virginal, baked pies and attended 4-H Club meetings. Once, her father caught her kissing a boy, but she could never marry him because he was a Catholic. His son Kenyon made

Photograph by Mike Smith.

Truman Capote.

good things with his hands in the basement workshop. Mrs. Clutter, the pious Bonnie, afflicted with deathly cold shivers and fits of anxiety amid the sunny bounties of a Kansas farm, was the only discordant element in this American dream. Finally they knew terror, and the knowledge in Mr. Capote's words becomes heartbreaking.

The crime confronted the townsfolk of Holcomb with their own isolation. Neighborliness evaporated. The natural order seemed suspended. Chaos poised to rush in. They distrusted and came to suspect not terrible strangers, but themselves. At the trial, struck mostly silent, they gaped. A squadron of psychiatrists, about the best we can produce in the way of a tragic chorus, emphasized the banality and dehydration of the current articulations of motive. "Paranoid orientation," they said. "Schizophrenic reaction. Severe character disorder."

Perry Smith, on the other hand, had mastered the true modern vocabulary. He spoke with the nightmare logic of all the socially and emotionally dispersed: "I thought he was a very nice gentleman. . . . I thought so right up to the moment I cut his throat."

There are two Truman Capotes. One is the artful charmer, prone to the gossamer and the exquisite, of "The Grass Harp" and Holly Golightly. The other, darker and stronger, is the discoverer of death. He began the latter exploration as a very young man in his first novel "Other Voices, Other Rooms" and in such stories as "Master Misery," "The Headless Hawk" and "A Tree of Night." He has traveled far from the misty, moss-hung Southern-Gothic landscapes of his youth. He now broods with the austerity of a Greek or an Elizabethan.

As he says in his interview with George Plimpton, he wrote "In Cold Blood" without mechanical aids—tape recorder or shorthand book. He memorized the event and its dialogues so thoroughly, and so totally committed a large piece of his life to it, that he was able to write it as a novel. Yet it is difficult to imagine such a work appearing at a time other than the electronic age. The sound of the book creates the illusion of tape. Its taut cross-cutting is cinematic. Tape and film, documentaries, instant news, have sensitized us to the glare of surface and close-ups. He gratifies our electronically induced appetite for massive quantities of detail, but at the same time, like an ironic magician, he shows that appearances are nothing.

"In Cold Blood" also mocks many of the advances (on paper) of anti-realism. It presents the metaphysics of anti-realism through a total evocation of reality. Not the least of the book's merits is that it manages a major moral judgment without the author's appearance once on stage. At a time when the external happening has become largely meaningless and our reaction to it brutalized, when we should "Jump!" to the man on the ledge, Mr. Capote has restored dignity to the event. His book is also a grieving testament of faith in what used to be called the soul.

# When the Cops Were Not 'Handcuffed'

By YALE KAMISAR

ARE we losing the war against crime? Is the public getting a fair break? Has the pendulum swung too far to the left? Do the victims of crime have some rights, too? Are the courts handcuffing the police?

If there were a hit parade for newspaper and magazine articles, speeches and panel discussions, these questions would rank high on the list. Not only are they being raised with increasing frequency, but they are being debated with growing fury.

Last year, probably the most famous police chief in the United States, William H. Parker of Los Angeles, protested that American police work has been "tragically weakened" through a progressive "judicial takeover." These are strong words, but Boston District Attorney Garrett Byrne, then president of the National Association of District Attorneys, easily topped the chief with the cry that the Supreme Court is "destroying the nation." (Despite this rant, Mr. Byrne has since been appointed to the President's newly established National Crime Commission, which has been assigned the task of making a systematic study of the entire spectrum of the problems of crime.)

This year, Michael J. Murphy, former Police Commissioner of New York, is the leading contender for anti-Supreme Court honors. Mr. Murphy's pet line is: "We [the police] are forced to fight by Marquis of Queensberry rules while the criminals are permitted to gouge and bite."

Not infrequently, one who dares to defend the Court, or simply to explain what the Court is doing and why, is asked which side he is on: the side of law and order—or the side of the robber, the dope peddler and the rapist. Any defense of the Court is an attack on the police. And any attack on the police (to quote Mayor Sam Yorty of Los Angeles, and he is not alone) is an "attack on our American system," perhaps even part of "a world-wide campaign by Communists, Communist dupes and sympathizers."

TODAY, the course of the Court is clear. Once concerned with property rights much more than with human liberty, it is now, as Anthony Lewis wrote several years ago, "the keeper, not of the nation's property, but of its conscience." If that role constitutes lending aid and comfort to the criminal element, then the Court is guilty.

As Judge Walter Schaefer of the Illinois Supreme Court pointed out in his famous Holmes Lecture of a decade ago, however, many of those safeguards of criminal procedure which we now take for granted came surprisingly late. Whether a state had to appoint counsel for an indigent defendant was a question which did not confront the Court until 1932, and it held then that counsel had to be provided only when the defendant was facing a possible death sentence. Whether the state could convict a defendant on the basis of a coerced confession was an issue first presented to the Court in 1936, and all the Court was asked to do then was ban confessions extracted by brutal beatings.

WHAT was it like in 1910 and 1920 and 1930 when the effectuation and implementation of criminal procedural safeguards were pretty much left to the states themselves? What was it like in the days when, as Dean Erwin Griswold of the Harvard Law School recently pointed out, "some things that were rather clearly there" (in the Constitution) had not yet "been given the attention and effect which they should have if our Constitution is to be a truly meaningful document"? Or, if you prefer, what was it like in the "good old days" before the Supreme Court began to mess up things?

In 1910, Curtis Lindley, president of the California Bar Association, declared the need for an "adjustment" in our criminal procedures "to meet the expanding social necessity." "Many of the difficulties," he continued, "are due to an exaggerated respect for the individual. . . ." He proposed (1) that a suspect be interrogated by a magistrate and, if he refused to answer the inquiries, that the state be permitted to comment on this fact at the trial; and (2) that the requirement of a unanimous verdict of guilty be reduced to three-fourths, "except possibly in cases where infliction of the death penalty

is involved." This, he pointed out, would still "give the defendant three-fourths of the show."

The following year, 1911, in a hard-hitting Atlantic Monthly article entitled "Coddling the Criminal," New York prosecutor Charles Nott charged that "the appalling amount of crime in the United States compared with other civilized countries is due to the fact that it is generally known that the punishment for crime in America is uncertain and far from severe." Where lay the fault? According to Nott, the two law-enforcement obstacles which had to be cleared were the protection against double jeopardy and the privilege against self-incrimination.

Eight years later, Hugo Pam, president of the Institute of Criminal Law and Criminology, also addressed himself to the "crime problem" one which had been greatly aggravated by "the advent of the automobile." As he viewed the situation in 1919, "the boldness of the crimes and the apparent helplessness of the law have embittered the public to the extent that any advance in treatment of criminals save punishment is looked upon with disfavor." Law-enforcement officials, he noted, "have repeatedly charged that in the main these serious crimes have been committed by people on probation or parole." It followed, of course, that there was a strong movement afoot to curtail or completely repeal these provisions.

THE following year, 1920, and again in 1922, Edwin W. Sims, the first head of the newly established Chicago Crime Commission, added his voice to the insistent demands "for action" that would reduce crime. He had the figures: "During 1919 there were more murders in Chicago (with a population of three million) than in the entire British Isles (with a population of 40 million)." Moreover, the prosecution had obtained only 44 convictions as against 336 murders. The situation called for strong words and Mr. Sims was equal to the occasion:

"We have kept on providing criminals with flowers, libraries, athletics, hot and cold running water, and probation and parole. The tender solicitude for the welfare of criminals publicly expressed by social workers conveys to 10,000 criminals plying their vocation in Chicago the mistaken impression that the community is more interested in them than it is in their victims. . . .

"There has been too much mollycoddling of the criminal population. . . . It is time for plain speaking. Murderers are turned loose. They have no fear of the police. They sneer at the law. It is not a time for promises. It is a time for action. The turning point has come. Decency wins or anarchy triumphs. There is no middle course."

If Edwin Sims were still in fine voice today, he would be much in demand. At home and on the road, he would probably outdraw even Messrs. Byrne, Murphy and Parker. About all Sims would have to do would be to strike "social workers," insert "Supreme Court," and maybe add a paragraph or two about recent Supreme Court decisions. But his era, I repeat, was 1920.

The nineteen-twenties were troubled times. In speaking of the need for a National Crime Commission. The New Republic of Aug. 26, 1925, declared: "It is no exaggeration to assert that the administration of criminal justice has broken down in the United States and that in this respect American state governments are failing to perform the most primitive and

most essential function which society imposes on government." At about the same time, the great criminologist Edwin H. Sutherland reported: "Capital punishment has been restored in four states since the war, and in many places there is a strenuous demand for the whipping post. . . . Crime commissions are recommending increased severity and certainty of punishment."

**B**Y 1933, the public had become so alarmed at an apparent increase in professional criminality that a U.S. Senate investigating committee, headed by Royal S. Copeland of New York, scoured the country for information which could lead to a national legislative solution.

The Detroit hearings brought out that the murder rate in the United States was nine times higher than in England and in Wales, "where they have basically the same Anglo-Saxon institutions," and even twice as high as Italy's, "the home of the Mafia, the 'Black Hand.'" In New York, a witness solemnly declared that "the crime situation in this country is so serious that it approaches a major crisis in our history, a crisis which will determine whether the nation is to belong to normal citizens or whether it is to be surrendered completely to gangster rule."

In Chicago, drawing upon his 20 years of experience as a lawyer, prosecutor and municipal judge, a witness concluded that "there is entirely too much worry, consideration and too many safeguards about the criminal's constitutional rights." He recommend-

ed for the Senate committee's consideration Illinois's new "reputation vagrancy law, which provides that all persons who are reputed to habitually violate the criminal laws and who are reputed to carry concealed weapons are vagrants." "Under this law," he reported, "we have harassed and convicted . . . numerous mad dogs of the West Side." (The following year, the Illinois Supreme Court struck down the law as unconstitutional.)

Senator Copeland told assembled witnesses of his desire for "a frank expression of opinion, no matter how critical you may be of existing institutions." Most of the witnesses were equal to the challenge.

A Maj. Homer Shockley urged that "constitutional and statutory guaranties, applicable to the average citizen, be suspended by special court procedure for the person who is known to be an habitual criminal . . . or who habitually consorts with criminals, to the end that the burden of proof of innocence of any fairly well substantiated charge be squarely placed on the accused; that he be tried without the benefit of a jury; and that, if convicted, all of his property and wealth be confiscated except such portion as the accused can prove were honestly gained by honest effort." The presumption of innocence is "fair enough" for the normal person, but not "for the dirty rat whom everybody knows to be an incurably habitual crook."

(Lest the major be peremptorily dismissed as a nonlegally trained commentator, it should be noted that two years earlier the dean of a Middle Western law school was reported to have advocated the establishment of a commission empowered to convict persons as "public enemies" and fix terms of their removal from society without convicting them for any specific offense, as historically required.)

**C**ITING Toronto, where whippings were said to have broken a wave of jewelry-store stick-ups, another witness at the 1933 hearings, New York Police Commissioner Edward Mulrooney, came out for 30 or 40 lashes to be applied at the time a criminal entered prison, others every six months thereafter.

Lewis E. Lawes, the famous warden of Sing Sing prison, exclaimed: "Strip our hysteri-

cal reaction in the present emergency and what have you? A confession that our agencies are not keeping step with crime, are falling short of their mark. Yesterday it was robbery, today it is kidnapping, tomorrow it will be something else. With every new crime racket will come a new hysteria." After delivering these refreshingly sober remarks, Warden Lawes proceeded to disregard his own advice:

"I think I am a liberal, but at the same time, in case of war I would fight for the country, and this is war. I believe if they do not have some form of martial law against this particular group [racketeers and kidnappers] that there will come in . . . lynch law and from lynch law they will have the martial law. . . . It seems to me that this is a war to be stamped out quickly and could be stopped in 60 days if all the authorities get together honestly and let the public know exactly what they are doing. . . . If I were Mussolini I could do it in 30 days."

Even renowned defense attorney Sam Liebowitz, honored "to be called upon to speak from the viewpoint of the criminal lawyer," seemed to get into the swing of things. He proposed a "national vagrancy law," whereby if a well-dressed crook "cannot give a good account of himself" to a police officer who spots him on the street or in his Cadillac "you take him into the station house and question him, and then take him before a judge. The judge says, 'Prove you are earning an honest living.'

"No honest man need rebel against a thing like that," contended the great criminal lawyer. "If you are earning an honest dollar, you can show what you are doing. . . . It is the crook that sets up the cry of the Constitution, and the protection of the Constitution, when he is in trouble."

Detroit prosecutor Harry Toy agreed that "a national vagrancy act—we call it a public-enemy act—is a wonderful thing." Mr. Liebowitz had assumed that a national vagrancy act would require an amendment to the privilege against self-incrimination, but the Detroit prosecutor insisted that such an act "could be framed under the present Federal Constitution as it now stands." (His own state's "public-enemy" law was held unconstitutional by the Michigan Supreme Court a few months later. The following

year New Jersey made it a felony, punishable by 20 years' imprisonment, to be a "gangster"; the U.S. Supreme Court struck the law down in 1939 on the grounds of vagueness and uncertainty.)

Chicago Municipal Court Judge Thomas Green plumped for an amendment to the Fourth Amendment permitting searches of persons "reputed" to be criminals and to be carrying firearms. The reason the framers of the Constitution stressed personal liberty, he explained, was that "there were no gangsters" then. "I think personal liberty is a wonderful thing," he hastened to add, "but today the man who takes advantage of personal liberty is the gangster, the gunman, the kidnapper."

**V**IRTUALLY every procedural safeguard caught heavy fire in the Senate hearings. One witness called "the right to the 'shield of silence'" (the privilege against self-incrimination) "the greatest stumbling block to justice and incentive to crime in all common-law countries." Another maintained that "the present provisions against self-incrimination were intended to protect the citizen against the medieval methods of torture, and they have become obsolete in modern life."

A report of the International Association of Chiefs of Police listed as "contributing factors to our serious crime problem . . . the resort to injunctions, writs of habeas corpus, changes of venue, etc., all with a view of embarrassing and retarding the administration of justice." The "founders of the Republic," it was argued, "never intended that habeas corpus and bail should be granted to a thug or serious thief."

Judge William Skillman of Detroit Criminal Court, known as "the one-man grand jury," maintained that permitting the state to appeal an acquittal "would do much to insure to society, represented by the state, a fair break in the trial of a lawsuit" because "the so-called 'former jeopardy clause' . . . has many times been used as a shield by a weak or timid or even a venal judge." Capt. A. B. Moore of the New York State Police proposed that an "expert adviser" or legally trained "technician" sit with and retire to the jury room with the jury "to advise them [on] those technicalities that had been implanted in their

**DEATH ON 42D STREET**—The body of a gunman lies on the pavement. Many officials complain that recent court rulings have encouraged crime.

minds by a very clever attorney."

So much for the teens and twenties and thirties, the so-called golden era when the U.S. Supreme Court kept "hands off" local law enforcement.

When Chief Parker warns us in our time that "the police . . . are limited like the Yalu River boundary, and the result of it is that they are losing the war just like we lost the war in Korea," I wonder: When, if ever, weren't we supposedly losing the war against crime? When, if ever, weren't law enforcement personnel impatient with the checks and balances of our system? When, it ever, didn't they feel unduly "limited"? When, if ever, will they realize that our citizens are free *because* the police are "limited"?

When an official of the National District Attorneys Association insists in our time: "This country can no longer afford a 'civil-rights binge' that so restricts law-enforcement agencies that they become ineffective and organized crime flourishes," I wonder: When, if ever, in the

opinion of law-enforcement personnel, could this country afford a "civil-rights binge"? When, if ever, wasn't there a "crime crisis"? When, if ever, weren't there proclamations of great emergencies and announcements of disbelief in the capacities of ordinary institutions and regular procedures to cope with them?

When Chicago's famous police chief, O. W. Wilson, stumps the country, pointing to the favorable crime picture in England, and other nations "unhampered" by restrictive court decisions, and exclaiming that "crime is overwhelming our society" (at the very time he is accepting credit in Chicago for a 20 per cent drop in crimes against the person). I am reminded of a story, apocryphal no doubt, about a certain aging promiscuous actress. When asked what she would do if she could live her life all over again she is said to have replied: "The same thing—with different people."

I venture to say that today too many law-enforcement spokesmen are doing "the

same thing—with different people." They are using different crime statistics and they are concentrating on a different target—the Supreme Court rather than the state courts, parole boards, social workers and "shyster lawyers"—but they are reacting the same way they reacted in past generations.

They are reconciling the delusion of our omnipotence with the experience of limited power to cope with the "crime crisis" by explaining failure in terms of betrayal. To borrow a phrase from Dean Acheson, they are letting a "mood of irritated frustration with complexity" find expression in "scapegoating."

Secretaries and ex-Secretaries of State know almost as much about scapegoating as Supreme Court justices. If the task of containing or controlling "change" in Africa or Asia is beyond our capabilities, to many people it means simply, or at least used to mean simply, that the State Department is full of incompetents or Communists or both.

Here, as elsewhere, if things seem to be going wrong, but there is no simple and satisfactory reason why, it is tempting to think that "the way to stop the mischief is to root out the witches."

Crime is a baffling, complex, frustrating, defiant problem. And as James Reston once pointed out in explaining Barry Goldwater's appeal to millions of Americans: "The more complicated life becomes, the more people are attracted to simple solutions; the more irrational the world seems, the more they long for rational answers; and the more diverse everything is, the more they want it all reduced to identity."

As the Wickersham Report of 1931 disclosed, the prevailing "interrogation methods" of the nineteen-twenties and thirties included the application of the rubber hose to the back or the pit of the stomach, kicks in the shins and blows struck with a telephone book on the side of the victim's head.

These techniques did not stem the tide of crime. Nor did the use of illegally seized evidence, which most state courts permitted as late as the nineteen-forties and fifties.

Nor, while they lasted, did the "public-enemy" laws, or the many criminal registration ordinances stimulated by the Copeland hearings.

IF history does anything, it supports David Acheson, who, when U. S. Attorney for the District of Columbia (the jurisdiction which has borne the brunt of "restrictive" court rules), dismissed the suggestion that "the crime rate will go away if we give back to law-enforcement agencies 'power taken from them by Federal court decisions'" with the assurance that "the war against crime does not lie on this front. Prosecution procedure has, at most, only the most remote casual connection with crime. Changes in court decisions and prosecution procedure would have about the same effect on the crime rate as an aspirin would have on a tumor of the brain."

Unfortunately this speech was not given the publicity it deserved. Nor were the refreshingly cool, thoughtful remarks of the new Deputy Attorney General, Ramsey Clark, who last August pointed out:

"Court rules do not cause crime. People do not commit crime because they know they cannot be questioned by police before presentment, or even because they feel they will not be convicted. We as a people commit crimes because we are capable of committing crimes. We choose to commit crimes. . . . In the long run, only the elimination of the causes of crime can make a significant and lasting difference in the incidence of crime.

"But the reduction of the causes of crime is a slow and arduous process and the need to protect persons and property is immediate. The present need for greater protection . . . can be filled not by . . . court rulings affirming convictions based on confessions secured after hours of questioning, or evidence seized in searches made without warrants. The immediate need can be filled by more and better police protection."

Chief Parker has expressed the hope that in searching for answers to our crime problem the new National Crime Commission "not overlook the influencing factor of the judicial revolution." The greater danger is that too much attention will be paid to this "revolution."

Critics of the courts are well represented, but not a single criminologist or sociologist or psychologist sits on the 19-

man commission. These are conspicuous omissions for a group asked "to be daring and creative and revolutionary" in its recommendations. These are incredible omissions for those of us who share the views of the Deputy Attorney General that "the first, the most pervasive and the most difficult" front in the war on crime "is the battle against the causes of crime: poverty, ignorance, unequal opportunity, social tension, moral erosion."

BY a strange coincidence, the very day the President announced the formation of the Crime Commission, the F.B.I. released new figures on the crime rate—soaring as usual—and J. Edgar Hoover took a sideswipe at "restrictive court decisions affecting police prevention and enforcement activity." And at their very first meeting, last September, the commission members were told by Mr. Hoover that recent court decisions had "too often severely and unfairly shackled the police officer."

Probably the most eminently qualified member of the President's Commission is Columbia Law School's Herbert Wechsler, the director of the American Law Institute and chief draftsman of the recently completed Model Penal Code, a monumental work which has already had a tremendous impact throughout the nation. The commission would have gotten off to a more auspicious start if, instead of listening to a criticism of recent court decisions, its members had read (or reread) what Mr. Wechsler, then a young, obscure assistant law professor, once said of other crime conferences in another era of "crisis" (those called by the U. S. Attorney General and a number of states, including New York, in 1934-36):

"The most satisfactory method of crime prevention is the solution of the basic problems of government—the production and distribution of external goods, education and recreation. . . . That the problems of social reform present dilemmas of their own, I do not pretend to deny. I argue only that one can pay for social reform as a means to the end of improved crime control what can also be said for better personnel but cannot be said for drastic tightening of the processes of the criminal law—that even if the end should not be achieved, the means is desirable for its own sake."

November 7, 1965

## HIDDEN ARSENALS FOUND ON COAST

### By PETER BART
Special to The New York Times

LOS ANGELES, July 2 — Policemen in nearby Riverside last week went to the home of a steel company laborer named Jack B. Tomlin to investigate reports that he owned an unregistered machine gun.

The police say they found not just a gun but a private arsenal consisting of dynamite, booby traps, machine guns and some solid-fuel rocket propellant.

Incredibly, discoveries of caches of weapons and explosives are recurring with increasing frequency in Southern California. Six arsenals have been detected in the last month and more than a dozen in the last year.

Thomas C. Lynch, attorney general of California, said that some of the discoveries clearly involved weapons that belonged to or were destined for what he described as extremist private armies operating in the state—the Minute Men and the California Rangers among them.

"The situation represents a continuing threat to the peace of the community," he said.

The detection of these illegal private weapons hoards has helped to dramatize a much broader problem that is worrying authorities in Southern California—the tremendous increase in the quantity of legal hand guns in the possession of ordinary citizens.

The Watts riots of last summer first set off a buying wave and this pace has not slackened in the year since the riots. According to official estimates, more than 31,000 hand guns will be sold in Los Angeles this year, enough to arm two infantry divisions.

"The potential for danger is awesome," The Los Angeles Times said in an editorial this week.

While ordinary citizens acquire most of their guns through regular commercial outlets, three Southern California Representatives demanded this week a full-scale investigation into the possibility that the extremist groups might have found yet another secret channel for acquiring weapons en masse.

The Representatives demanding an investigation were Charles H. Wilson, John Tunney and Thomas Rees, all Democrats from Southern California.

Their concern was touched off by the assertions of David De Mulle, one of the men arrested for having a private weapon hoard. He said that a substantial amount of the arms and explosives had been abandoned by the Army after military maneuvers.

De Mulle, who was charged with possession of TNT, tear gas, smoke grenades and other weapons in his small apartment, said that extremist groups and "gun nuts" simply cruised the desert after Army maneuvers and picked up vast quantities of discarded weapons.

Although military clean-up crews are supposed to clear weapons from the areas, De Mulle said that there were always plenty of weapons around after they leave. Some men are still finding weapons left over from Operation Desert Strike, a maneuver in 1964 that involved 100,000 troops, he said. He also said that he had once seen a truck painted with swastikas cruising the desert looking for weapons.

The Army promptly replied that its clean-up crews carefully picked up all material after each maneuver.

De Mulle made his charges after police had found TNT, tear gas, smoke grenades and other materials in his apartment. De Mulle allegedly was a friend of Tomlin, the steel company laborer.

Investigators said they did not believe that either Tomlin or De Mulle were members of extremist groups. However, one official said that police were investigating the connections of another unidentified man, the son of a wealthy local businessman, who had concealed scores of hand grenades and other weapons in his backyard. This man is believed to be affiliated with the militant National States' Rights party, whose members affect military ranks and uniforms.

Among other paramilitary organizations that maintain "private armies" in the state, the official said, are the Minute Men, the American Nazi party, the California Rangers and the Christian Defense League.

The activities of private armies in California have been inhibited by the passage of a law that went into effect last September. It bans formal training exercises by paramilitary groups. Since that time the training maneuvers reportedly have been shifted to Arizona and Nevada and the once-garrulous leaders of the armies have gone underground.

Of all the groups the Minute Men probably attract the most attention. Law enforcement officials estimate its state membership at between 500 and 1,000.

Members of the organization are urged to join the National Rifle Association and to form rifle clubs, thereby qualifying to purchase Army rifles and hand guns at less than market prices.

The Minute Men's handbook urges members "to have on hand as many hand and rifle grenades as possible."

July 3, 196

320

# On the Wild Side

HELL'S ANGELS. A Strange and Terrible Saga. By Hunter S. Thompson. 278 pp. New York: Random House. $4.95.

By LEO E. LITWAK

IN 1965 the Attorney General of the State of California distributed a report on the Hell's Angels Motorcycle Club to law enforcement agencies throughout the state, urging that all measures be taken to contain the menace of this élite outlaw organization.

According to the Lynch report, the 450 members of the club had a record of 874 felony arrests, 300 felony convictions, more than 1,000 misdemeanor convictions. The report held that there would have been an even more extensive record but for the Angels' practice of intimidating witnesses.

The criminal actions listed by the Lynch report ranged from the terrorization of rural communities to the theft of motorcycle parts. Included were detailed charges of attempted murder, assault and battery, malicious destruction of property, narcotics violations and sexual aberrations. Investigating officers further reported that "both club members and female associates seem badly in need of a bath."

It was a picture of alarming menace. Depraved hoodlums — unmanageable, incorrigible, vindictive and organized — roamed the California highways in stripped down Harley-Davidson motorcycles. They were dressed like pirates, with full beards, a ring in one ear, shoulder-length hair, an embroidered winged skull on the backs of their sleeveless denim jackets, Iron Crosses on their chests, swastikas on their helmets. These weren't the teen-agers of the usual urban gang, but adults, ranging in age from the early 20's to the mid-40's. They could strike anywhere in the state, and they didn't fear the police. The underground in which they were lords seemed dark, rancid, impenetrable.

Hunter Thompson entered this terra incognita to become its cartographer. For almost a year, he accompanied the Hell's Angels on their rallies. He drank at their bars, exchanged home visits, recorded their brutalities, viewed their sexual caprices, became converted to their motorcycle mystique, and was so intrigued, as he puts it, that "I was no longer sure whether I was doing research on the Hell's Angels or being slowly absorbed by them." At the conclusion of his year's tenure the ambiguity of his position was ended when a group of Angels knocked him to the ground and stomped him.

Without denying that the Angels are violent, unpredictable and dangerous, Thompson regards the Lynch report as vastly exaggerating their menace and misrepresenting their life in crime. "There was a certain pleasure," he writes, "in sharing the Angels' amusement at the stir they created."

According to Thompson, the membership is in the neighborhood of 100, not 450 as the report claimed. The failure to get convictions had less to do with the intimidation of witnesses than with the baselessness of the complaints. Police harassment was responsible for the large number of misdemeanor convictions. Thompson, noting the relatively insignificant part the Angels play in California crime statistics, is amused at the disproportionate publicity they have secured. He argues that publicity saved the club from extinction. Prior to the Lynch report, club fortunes were on the wane. The Lynch report called the Angels to the attention of national media and with the "publicity breakthrough" they again flourished. Thompson, in a tone of exuberant irony reminiscent of Mencken, comments, "In a nation of frightened dullards there is a shortage of outlaws."

The underworld Thompson reveals to us is a more familiar terrain than the shadowy nightmare world of the Lynch report. He doesn't find an effective criminal conspiracy, nor does he see an organization grounded in Nazi ideology. He draws a picture of desperate men, without status and— despite their motorcycles — without mobility. He traces their origins to the Okies and Arkies and hillbillies who migrated to California during the Depression. He finds the literary prototype of their ancestor in the protagonist of Nelson Algren's "A Walk on the Wild Side," Dove Linkhorn. Most Angels are uneducated. Only one Angel in 10 has steady work; "Motorcycle outlaws are not much in demand on the labor market." The world demands skills they have no chance of acquiring; "They are out of the ball game and they know it."" They have no future; "In a world increasingly geared to specialists, technicians, and fantastically complicated machinery, the Hell's Angels are obvious losers, and it bugs them."

They survive in various ways. According to Thompson, a few have steady work, some pander, some steal, some live off their ladies. Some are married and faithful to their wives. Others have a predilection for gang

Hell's Angels during their Bass Lake run, July 4, 1965: An Angel on his chopper and, right, Skip, from Richmond, Calif., combs the hair of a fellow Angel, Buck, a member of the San Francisco Gypsy Jokers Club.

Photographs by Bob Grant.

love. What they share is a guiding concern to be "righteous Angels" and a love for motorcycles. An Angel is quoted as saying, "We don't lie to each other. Of course that don't go for outsiders because we have to fight fire with fire."

Thompson describes the attitude of a Hell's Angel to outsiders as follows: "To him they are all the same — the running dogs of whatever fiendish conspiracy has plagued him all these years. He knows that somewhere behind the moat, the Main Cop has scrawled his name on a blackboard in the Big Briefing Room with a notation beside it: 'Get this boy, give him no peace, he's incorrigible, like an egg-sucking dog.'"

Mounted on his bike, he assumes a dignity he often lacks on foot. The high-speed trip described by Thompson is akin to the psychedelic trip made on LSD. The Angel has small chance of assuming the role of hero save in a fantasy trip. "Most Angels . . . are well enough grounded in the eternal verities to know that very few of the toads in this world are Charming Princes in disguise. The others are simply toads, and no matter how many magic maidens they kiss or rape, they are going to stay that way."

Vindictive at being toads, they invert the ethic of Prince Charming. The initiation ceremony of an Angel centers on the defiling of his new uniform and emblem. "A bucket of dung and urine will be collected during the meeting, then poured on the newcomer's head in a solemn baptismal." They never wash their soiled colors. They mock the courtly love of Prince Charming with gang love. Instead of the gentlemanly duel they subscribe to the principle of All on One. They don't seek justice in dispensing punishment. Rather, the response is always one of total retaliation. "If a man gets wise, mash his face. If a woman snubs you, rape her. This is the thinking, if not the reality, behind the whole Angel's act."

The Angel rejects precautions, whether riding a motorcycle or entering a brawl. "They inhabit a world in which violence is as common as spilled beer." The Angel has been injured so often that he is indifferent to pain. "This casual acceptance of bloodletting is a key to the terror they inspire in the squares . . . It is a simple matter of having been hit or stomped often enough to forget the ugly panic that nice people associate with a serious fight." The "reality behind the Angel's whole act" is that most of the damage is inflicted on themselves. An average of four die violently each year.

The easy acceptance of violence lends to Thompson's account a cartoon quality. We observe Angels brutalizing themselves and others and somehow we expect them to recover as quickly as the cartoon cat and mouse. It's not that Thompson doesn't give us a vivid picture of brawls and orgies. His language is brilliant, his eye is remarkable, and his point of view is reminiscent of Huck Finn's. He'll look at anything; he won't compromise his integrity. Somehow his exuberance and innocence are unaffected by what he sees.

Dirty Ed is laid flat by a two-foot lead pipe, but he gets up and drives away on his motorcycle. Terry the Tramp is stomped by the Diablos, a rival gang, but he still manages to make the Labor Day run. We see a mass assault on a compliant lady during a party; the dancing continues. A 7-foot Negro invades the Angel clubroom. He is overwhelmed, cast down, kicked in the face and belly, dumped in the parking lot. He gets up and walks to the ambulance. During Thompson's last interview with a group of Angels, he is suddenly struck from behind, then from all sides. He is knocked down and stomped. He is almost done in by a "vicious swine trying to get at me with the stone held in a two-handed Godzilla grip." He gets to a hospital unaided.

Because the Hell's Angels have lacked a focus for their hostility, their violence has been undirected. However, those who observe the trappings — the swastikas and Iron Crosses — have wondered if there might not be in them the raw material out of which Brown Shirts are made. This suspicion seemed confirmed when, in the fall of 1965, a group of Hell's Angels attacked an anti-war rally at the Oakland-Berkeley boundary, an assault which put them into direct conflict with the radical left in neighboring Berkeley.

"The attack was an awful shock to those who had seen the Hell's Angels as pioneers of the human spirit, but to anyone who knew them it was entirely logical. The Angels' collective viewpoint has always been fascistic. They insist and seem to believe that their swastika fetish is no more than an anti-social joke, a guaranteed gimmick to bug the squares, the taxpayers — all those they spitefully refer to as 'citizens.' . . . If they wanted to be artful about bugging the squares they would drop the swastika and decorate their bikes with the hammer and sickle. That would really raise hell on the freeways . . . hundreds of Communist thugs roaming the countryside on big motorcycles, looking for trouble."

However, the threat to disrupt all future anti-war demonstrations didn't materialize. A visit from poet Allen Ginsberg and novelist Ken Kesey served to pacify the Angels and there has been no recent sign of political direction.

Hunter Thompson has presented us with a close view of a world most of us would never dare encounter, yet one with which we should be familiar. He has brought on stage men who have lost all options and are not reconciled to the loss. They have great resources for violence which doesn't as yet have any effective focus. Thompson suggests that these few Angels are but the vanguard of a growing army of disappropriated, disaffiliated and desperate men. There's always the risk that somehow they may force the wrong options into being.

# POLL FINDS CRIME TOP FEAR AT HOME

### Gallup Reports Issue Leads List of Domestic Problems

Special to The New York Times

PRINCETON, N. J., Feb. 27—Crime and lawlessness are viewed by the public as the top domestic problem facing the nation for the first time since the beginning of scientific polling in the mid-thirties, according to the latest Gallup Poll.

Next to Vietnam, this is the issue that almost certainly will have a powerful influence on the vote in November.

The growing concern in this country over crime and lawlessness reflects the actual crime rate, which, according to a recent F.B.I. report, is going up nearly nine times as fast as the population.

Crime topped the list when people were asked a subsequent question about problems facing their own community. Even other pressing local problems, such as crowded schools, transportation and high taxes, take second place.

Three persons in ten (31 per cent) admitted to being afraid of going out alone at night in their neighborhood. Among women and persons living in the largest cities, the figure jumped to about four in ten.

One person in five (19 per cent) said he had had to call upon the police during the last 12 months.

Some of the reasons given were for less serious matters—one woman asked the police to get a cow off her front lawn—but many were of a serious or potentially serious nature. The reason most frequently given for calling the police was theft or robbery.

Gallup Poll interviewers working in over 800 communities of all sizes first asked this question:

"What do you think is the most important problem facing this country today?"

The Vietnam war was cited most often (by 53 per cent of respondents) but in terms of domestic or national problems, the remainder of the responses divided as follows:

1. Crime and lawlessness (including riots, looting, juvenile delinquency).
2. Civil rights.
3. High cost of living.
4. Poverty.
5. General unrest in nation.

This question was asked next: "What is the most important problem facing this community today?"

Crime and lawlessness were mentioned nearly twice as often as any other local problem. The order was as follows:

1. Crime and lawlessness.
2. Education: crowded schools, poor quality of education.
3. Transportation, parking, traffic.
4. High taxes.
5. Unemployment.
6. Lack of community service programs.
7. High cost of living.
8. Racial problems.
9. Slums, overcrowded housing.
10. Poor local government.
11. Sanitation: garbage, sewage.
12. Lack of cultural, recreational facilities.
13. Lack of religion, ethics.

The next question in the series: "Have you yourself had to call upon the police for any reason during the last 12 months?"

The following results were based on the 19 per cent who replied in the affirmative:

1. Theft, robbery.
2. Vandalism.
3. Trespassers, prowlers.
4. Troublesome, drunken neighbors.
5. To report parking, traffic violations, accidents.
6. Assault.
7. Problems, injuries in respondent's household.
8. Home and community maintenance problems.
9. Problems with dogs, other animals.

February 28, 1968

# Is America By Nature A Violent Society?

## "Lawlessness Is Inherent In the Uprooted"

### By HANNAH ARENDT

Political scientist; university professor New School for Social Research; author of, among other books, "On Revolution"

IT is highly doubtful that we know anything about the natural character of societies, but it seems evident that a country inhabited by a multitude of ethnic groups cannot even be said to possess that nearest equivalent to natural traits which is called "national character." If "like attracts like" is as natural for human society as that birds of a feather flock together, one could even say that American society is artificial "by nature." Still, it seems true that America, for historical, social and political reasons, is more likely to erupt into violence than most other civilized countries. And yet there are very few countries where respect for law is so deeply rooted and where citizens are so law-abiding.

The reason for this seeming paradox must probably be looked for in the American past, in the experience of establishing law against lawlessness in a colonial country—an experience which culminated, but was not ended, with the foundation of a new body politic and the establishment of a new law of the land in the American Revolution. For it was a similar experience that came into play in the colonization of the continent as well as in the integration of the many waves of immigrants during the last century. Each time the law had to be confirmed anew against the lawlessness inherent in all uprooted people.

I think that another peculiarity of American society is more relevant to the present situation. Freedom of assembly is among the crucial, most cherished and, perhaps, most dangerous rights of American citizens. Every time Washington is unreceptive to the claims of a sufficiently large number of citizens, the danger of violence arises. Violence—taking the law into one's own hands—is perhaps more likely to be the consequence of frustrated power in America than in other countries.

We have just lived through a period when opposition to our bloody imperialist adventures—voiced first on the campuses, on chiefly moral grounds, and supported by an almost unanimous verdict of highly qualified opinion in the country at large—remained not only without echo but was treated with open contempt by the Administration. The opposition, taught in the school of the powerful and nonviolent civil-rights movement of the early nineteen-sixties, took to the streets, more and more embittered against "the system" as such. The spell was broken, and the danger of violence, inherent in the disaffection of a whole generation, averted, when Senator McCarthy provided in his person the link between the opposition in the Senate with that in the streets. He said himself that he had wanted "to test the system," and the results, though still inconclusive, have been reassuring in some important respects. Not only has popular pressure enforced an at least temporary change in policy; it has also been demonstrated how quickly the younger generation can become dealienated, jumping on this first opportunity not to abolish the system, but to make it work again.

The factor of racism is the only one with respect to which one could speak of a strain of violence so deeply rooted in American society as to appear to be "natural." "Racial violence was present almost from the beginning of the American experience," the splendid Report on Civil Disorders has put it.

This country has never been a nation-state and therefore has been little affected by the vices of nationalism and chauvinism. It has dealt rather successfully with the obvious dangers of domestic violence inherent in a multinational social body by making adherence to the law of the land, and not national origin, the chief touchstone of citizenship and by tolerating a considerable amount of mutual discrimination in society. But nationalism and racism are not the same, and what has worked with regard to the disruptive forces of the former has not worked with regard to the destructive force of the latter.

In the North, where I think the problem is more acute than in the South, we deal with a group uprooted through recent migration and hence no less lawless than other immigrant groups in their initial stages. Their massive arrival in recent decades has hastened the disastrous disintegration of the big cities, to which they came at a time when the demand for unskilled labor rapidly declined. We all know the consequences, and it is no secret that racist feeling among the urban population is today at an unprecedented high. It is easy to blame the people; it is less easy to admit the fact that, as things are handled now, those who stand most to lose and are expected to pay by far the greatest part of the bill are precisely those groups who have just "made it" and can least afford it. Impotence breeds violence, and the more impotent these white groups feel the greater is the danger of violence.

Just as "power checks power" (Montesquieu) so violence breeds violence. Unlike nationalism, which is normally limited by a territory and therefore admits, in principle at least, the existence of a "family of nations" with equal status for each, racism always insists on absolute superiority over all others. Hence, racism is humiliating "by nature," and humiliation breeds even more violence than sheer impotence.

The Negro violence we are witnessing now is political to the small extent that it is hoped to dramatize justified grievances, to serve as an unhappy substitute for organized power. It is social to the much larger extent that it expresses the violent rage of the poor in an overaffluent society where deprivation is no longer the burden of a majority and hence no longer felt as a curse from which only the few are exempt. Not even the violence for its own sake, preached by extremeists—as distinguished from the rioting and looting for the sake of whisky, color television and pianos—is revolutionary, because it is not a means to an end: No one dreams of being able to seize power. If it is to be a contest of violence, does anybody doubt who is going to win?

The real danger is not violence, black or white, but the possibility of a white backlash of such proportions as to be able to invade the domain of regular government. Only such a victory at the polls could stop the present policy of integration. Its consequences would be unmitigated disaster—the end, perhaps not of the country, but certainly of the American Republic. ∎

## "Spontaneous, Sporadic and Disorganized"

### By RICHARD HOFSTADTER

Professor of American history, Columbia

THERE is a small semantic trap in asking whether America is "by nature" a violent society. "By nature" suggests the possibility of an unchangeable national character. In this I do not believe. But I do think that America, by history and by habit, has been a violent society.

Americans seem to me to show a surprising tolerance of violence and a remarkably passive acceptance of the probability that it will recur. The feebleness of our efforts at gun control, even in the face of the grave crisis that is upon us, is an illustration of this passivity. But the distinctive thing about American violence is that it has been spontaneous, sporadic and disorganized. Traditionally, Americans were always strongly antimilitarist. What this meant was not that they had a penchant for pacifism but simply that they did not like standing armies—that is, they were against *institutional* militarism.

Again, it has long seemed to me that the case of the American labor movement is quite pertinent to this theme. As the laboring classes of the industrial world go, ours has been relatively lacking in class-conscious militancy, but no national labor history is so heavily marked by violent struggles in which lives and property were destroyed.

Race has always provided a background for violent conflict, whether in Indian wars, slave insurrections, lynchings or race riots. The race riots of 1919 were as formidable, though not as numerous, as the ghetto riots we have experienced in the last few years. The week-long Chicago riot of 1919, one of a number in the postwar period, left 15 whites and 23 Negroes dead, and 537 injured. The hiatus in major riots that occurred between the Detroit, Harlem and Los Angeles riots of 1943 and the riots of 1964 may have caused us to forget the frequency of this kind of violence in our history. But we are unlikely to forget it so readily again.

The historical catalogue of American violence is a formidable one. Mob action was already a force of some importance in the political life of colonial America. It goes on from there: a number of fitful rebellions, the long, ruthless struggle with the Indians, our slave insurrections, our filibustering expeditions, our burned convents and mobbed abolitionists and lynched Wobblies, our Homesteads, Pullmans and Patersons, our race lynchings, race riots and ghetto riots, our organized gangsterism, our needless wars.

There seems to be more truth than we care to admit in the famous dictum of D. H. Lawrence that (I am quoting from memory) "the essential American soul is hard, isolate, stoic and a killer." It exists, oddly enough, along with a remarkable tenderness about life under certain circumstances. It also exists along with a great readiness to declare ourselves for law and order, to admonish against violence, so long as we are not expected to do anything about it. We have, now, a mountain of fresh sermons against violence, but any zealot, any maniac, can still buy a gun if he has the price. This is one of the sacred rights of American manhood, and it will be hard to give it up, even after we have suffered within the span of a few years the murders of two cherished public men, and even after the black nationalists, in *their* quest for manhood, have started to take their cue from the whites. ∎

## Reagan, Scoring Courts, Links Shooting to Permissive Attitude

Special to The New York Times

SACRAMENTO, Calif., June 5—Gov. Ronald Reagan of California attributed the shooting of Senator Robert F. Kennedy today to a growing permissiveness in the nation.

Mr. Reagan attributed this permissiveness in part to the courts and also to a growing attitude "that says a man can choose the laws he must obey, that he can take the law into his own hands for a cause, that crime does not necessarily mean punishment." He went on:

"This attitude has been spurred by demagogic and irresponsible words of so-called leaders in and out of public office and it has been helped along by some in places of authority who are fearful of the wrong but timid about standing for what is right.

"In so doing they have thrown our nation into chaos and confusion and have bred a climate that permits this ultimate tragedy.

**Avoids Answering Questions**

"This nation can no longer tolerate the spirit of permissiveness that pervades our courts and other institutions."

Mr. Reagan, who is considered a Republican Presidential possibility, read his statement to his regular news conference, then departed abruptly without answering questions, leaving his press aide to reply to newmen's queries.

His communications director, Lyn Nofziger, and press secretary, Paul Beck, in a sometimes heated exchange with newsmen, both refused to say who were the leaders that the Governor was attacking.

Mr. Beck said, "I think the statement speaks for itself. I'd rather leave it to you to interpret."

Mr. Nofziger interjected, "We're just not going to get in a position of calling names or making accusations against certain people in this country."

When a reporter said, "You've already done that," Mr. Nofziger replied, "All right, then, we'll stand on the statement."

**Declines to Elaborate**

Another newsman asked if the Reagan statment was meant to reflect partly on Senator Kennedy himself. Mr. Nofziger answered, "You'll have to draw your own conclusions, because the statement is there, and we do not intend to go beyond it."

In his statement, the Governor also declared that the permissiveness he was denouncing would not be tolerated in California.

"This administration will lend aid and support to our local governments and to all those who need and request it," Mr. Reagan said. "We will not stand by and see the institutions of a free people destroyed by those who claim it is being done in the name of freedom.

"This is not a sick society, but is a society that is sick of what has been going on in this nation."

Mr. Reagan reiterated his sympathy for the Senator, his family and for the other victims of "this senseless, savage act."

He also announced he had sent a message of condolences to Mrs. Kennedy.

June 6, 1968

**Paper Stops Dick Tracy**

GREENSBORO, N.C., June 12 (AP) — The Greensboro Daily News has canceled its Dick Tracy and Little Orphan Annie comic strips because of what the paper described as their "constant exploitation and advocacy of violence." Little Orphan Annie has run continuously in The Daily News since 1926, and Dick Tracy since 1939.

# Topics:
## On the Shooting of Robert Kennedy

**BY ARTHUR MILLER**

Is it not time to take a long look at ourselves, at the way we live and the way we think, and to face the fact that the violence in our streets is the violence in our hearts, that with all our accomplishments, our spires and mines and clean, glistening packages, our charities and gods, we are what we were—a people of violence?

Lincoln, Garfield, McKinley, John F. Kennedy, Martin Luther King, Medgar Evers—plus the line going into a sad infinity of lynched men, of men beaten to death in police cells, of Indians expropriated by knife and gun, of the Negro people held in slavery for a century by a thousand small armies dubbed chivalrous by themselves who long ago enchained black labor and kept black mankind from walking in freedom—Robert Kennedy's brain received only the latest fragment of a barrage as old as this country.

### The Unanswered Poor

Here is a Congress literally face to face with an army of poor people pleading for some relief of their misery—a Congress whose reply is a sneer, a smirk and a warning to keep order.

Here is a people that would rather clutch hatred to its heart than stretch out a hand in brotherhood to the black man and the poor man. That is why there is violence. It is murderous to tell a man he cannot live where he wishes to live. It is murderous to tell a woman that because she has borne a child out of wedlock that she cannot eat, nor the child either.

### TV Success Standard

There is violence because we have daily honored violence. Any half-educated man in a good suit can make his fortune by concocting a television show whose brutality is photographed in sufficiently monstrous detail. Who produces these shows, who pays to sponsor them, who is honored for acting in them? Are these people delinquent psychopaths slinking along tenement streets? No, they are the pillars of society, our honored men, our exemplars of success and social attainment.

We must begin to feel the shame and contrition we have earned before we can begin to sensibly construct a peaceful society, let alone a peaceful world. A country where people cannot walk safely in their own streets has not earned the right to tell any other people how to govern itself, let alone to bomb and burn that people.

What must be done? A decent humility, not cynicism. Our best cards are finally being called. Thomas Jefferson, a slaveholder, wrote the promise he could not keep himself and we must now keep it. "Life, Liberty and the Pursuit of Happiness." The pursuit of happiness is impossible for millions of Americans.

Let us take the thirty billion from the war, and let us devote the same energy and ingenuity we have given to war and apply it to wiping out the disgrace of poverty in this richest of all nations. Let us feel that disgrace, let us feel it for what it is, a personal affront to each of us that cannot be permitted to stand.

We are two hundred millions now. Either we begin to construct a civilization, which means a common consciousness of social responsibility, or the predator within us will devour us all.

It must be faced now that we are afraid of the Negro because we have denied him social justice and we do not know how to stop denying him.

We are afraid of the poor because we know that there is enough to go around, that we have not made it our first order of business to literally create the jobs that can and must be created.

We are afraid of other countries because we fear that they know better how to satisfy the demands of poor people and colored people.

We are afraid of ourselves because we have advertised and promoted and sloganized ourselves into a state of contentment, when we know that desperate people surround us everywhere and we do not know how to break out of our contentment.

We are at war not only with Vietnamese but with Americans. Stop both. We are rich enough to wipe out every slum and to open a world of hope to the poor. What keeps us? Do we want peace in Vietnam? Then make peace. Do we want hope in our cities and towns? Then stop denying any man his birthright.

### Social Justice—Or the Gun

Because America has been bigger on promises than any other country, she must be bigger by far on deliveries. Maybe we have only one promise left in the bag, the promise of social justice for every man regardless of his color or condition.

Between the promise and its denial—there stands the man with the gun. Between the promise and its denial stands a man holding them apart—the American. Either he recognizes what he is doing, or he will take the final, fatal step to suppress the violence he has called up.

Only justice will overcome the nightmare. The American Dream is ours to evoke.

*Mr. Miller is the well-known American playwright.*

---

## View of U.S. from Vietnam

To the Editor:

In view of the recent violence in our nation, the assassinations of Dr. Martin Luther King and Robert F. Kennedy, the riots in the large urban areas, the looting, burning and killing, it seems that our armed forces should be back at home, trying to protect our decent citizens.

However, we also have a job to do here in Vietnam. In view of this, and the fact my tour in Vietnam is nearing its end, I have extended my tour, as I see nothing in the States worth coming back to.

MATTHEW T. LEWIS
Second Class Petty Officer
U.S.N.
Vietnam, June 8, 1968

# VIOLENCE REPORT DECLARES NATION IS 'BLOODY-MINDED'

## Panel Finds a Tradition of Using Force Obscured by 'a Historical Amnesia'

## CAUSE NOT PINPOINTED

## Presidential Group Asserts Trouble Persists in the U.S. but Declines Elsewhere

**By JOHN HERBERS**
Special to The New York Times

WASHINGTON, June 5 —A study group of scholars appointed by a Presidential commission told Americans today that they had become a "rather bloody-minded people in both action and reaction."

The National Commission on the Causes and Prevention of Violence issued, without comment, the work of a study group appointed last August to evaluate the history and foreign parallels of contemporary violence in this country.

The 22-chapter report, issued on the anniversary of the assassination of Senator Robert F. Kennedy, was ordered by the commission last August in an effort to help bring about a better understanding of the use of violence in domestic affairs.

The 13-member commission was appointed by former President Johnson after Senator Kennedy had been shot in Los Angeles while campaigning for the Presidency.

### A Panel of Scholars

Participating in the study were historians, political scientists, anthropologists, lawyers, psychiatrists, psychologists, and sociologists, many of whom wrote chapters of the report.

The study was directed by Dr. Hugh Davis Graham, associate professor of history at Johns Hopkins University, and Dr. Ted Robert Gurr, assistant professor of politics at Princeton University. They wrote a conclusion.

The report, the first broad study of its kind, documents in great detail a violent tradition in America, with various interest groups using violence to gain their ends. But the co-directors said in a conclusion to the study that this had been obscured by "a kind of historical amnesia."

"Probably all nations share this tendency to sweeten memories of their past through collective repression," they said, "but Americans have probably magnified this process of selective recollection, owing to our historic vision of ourselves as a latterday chosen people, a new Jerusalem."

This might explain why many Americans have been shocked at the violence of the 1960's, acknowledged by the authors of the study to be one of the nation's most violent eras.

Most other Western nations share the tradition for violence, the study showed, but what remains to be explained is why violence persists in the United States while it has diminished in other countries.

"The first and obvious answer is that some fundamental grievances in the United States have not only gone unresolved but have intensified in recent years," the authors said.

A less obvious answer, they said, is that "the myth of the melting pot" has obscured the fact that the United States is made up of a myriad of ethinic, national, religious, regional, and occupational groups involved in competition and conflict.

Throughout history, virtually all groups involved have used violence both for protection and to promote their causes, the study showed.

"Almost every major act of violence in our history, whether public or private, has antagonized one group at the same time that it satisfied another," the authors said, adding:

"The grievances and satisfactions of violence have so reinforced one another that we have become a rather bloody-minded people in both action and reaction. We are likely to remain so as long as so many of us think violence is an ultimate solution to social problems."

Charles Tilly, professor of sociology at the University of Toronto, contributed a long chapter on the European tradition and concluded that "historically, collective violence has flowed regularly out of the central political processes of Western countries.

"Men seeking to seize, hold, or realign the levers of power have continually engaged in collective violence as part of their struggles," he continued. "The oppressed have struck in the name of justice, the privileged in the name of order, those in between in the name of fear."

The odd thing, Mr. Tilly said, is how quickly people forget.

"When Lincoln Steffens visited London in 1910, he found distinguished members of Parliament convinced that England was on the brink of revolution as a result of the angry strikes of the time.

Richard M. Brown, professor of history at the College of William and Mary, wrote that although there was general alarm at the urban violence of today "the fact is that our cities have been in a state of more or less continuous turmoil since the Colonial period."

During the American Revolution, Mr. Brown said, both sides adopted the operational philosophy that the end justifies the means.

"Thus given sanctification by the Revolution, Americans have never been loathe to employ the most unremitting violence in the interest of any cause deemed to be a good one," he wrote.

The report contains 350,000 words.

The authors said that although the report should provide "substantial insights" into the causes and character of violence in America, "we have yet to understand fully how civil peace is created and maintained.

"But at least," they added, "we know that it is possible, for Americans and other people have done so before."

June 6, 1969

# We Can Expect More Atticas

**By WILLIAM J. GOODE**

The Attica bloodshed demands an answer to the anguished question our politicians keep asking, "What is wrong with our sick society?"

All the killings at Attica, whether of guards or prisoners, are tragic; we should all feel compassion for those killed, and for their families and friends. But these killings are, in a larger sense, a symptom of much deeper problems in our nation. Literally hundreds of studies over the decades have reported findings that prove our nation as a whole, like our prison systems, pursues policies that generate more violence. Consequently, we can expect more such killings in the future.

I do not believe that strong statement is political at all, for it is based on data from good sociological research:

(1) In any social system—whether a nation, a conquered country, a gang, a prison, or a family—violence breeds violence. If you use violence to control people, they will hate you and will use it themselves when they get the chance.

(2) If you strip away from a human being the very fundamentals of his humanity—sex and love, meaningful work, and freedom from arbitrary violence—as American prisons do—then he will see at once that there is no point to "improving himself in prison," for as long as he is there he can win back none of them.

All of the organizations that have been successful in changing men's

327

hearts, such as the Catholic orders, West Point in its prime, or medical schools, inform their members that their old selves must be thrown away, but they offer in return a higher dignity through belonging to the new organization: meaningful work, human acceptance, and fraternal solidarity. We do the reverse in our prisons; we take all these things away.

(3) All social order and obedience to authority rests basically on legitimacy, on people's belief that the system is fundamentally decent, fair, honorable, and protective to its members. If leaders blatantly lie in order to persuade the people, they destroy credence, faith, and legitimacy. Both respectable citizens and prisoners withdrew some of their support of the system when they learned that they were fed lies: The Attica prisoners did not slash the throats of the guards, did not castrate them, did not even have guns, and apparently the attacking lawmen killed both prisoners and guards.

(4) If you don't want violence between guards. who are almost all white and prisoners who are mostly black, you must bring in more black guards. Their presence keeps the racism of the white guards in some check, and lowers their eagerness to use force. The prisoners, in turn, are less inclined to use force and indeed are more likely to feel that both black and white guards have some sympathy with them.

(5) If you want to gain the loyalty of some prisoners, to persuade many that their best interests lie in reforming themselves, to convince most that violence is a poor policy, you must consult with them on almost all the problems of running the prison. Dozens of studies have shown that arbitrary rule is ineffective, administration without participation is unwise, rule by fiat is destructive.

Again, I repeat: These statements are not political propaganda. They have been confirmed by many studies in a vast range of different settings—prisons, families, corporations, imperial colonies, and nations. Perhaps they prove no more than really wise men have always known, and sociological research was not needed to prove them. If so, it is high time we listened to those wise men.

September 20, 197

## Lumpenhippies and their guru

# The Family

The Story of Charles Manson's
Dune Buggy Attack Battalion.
By Ed Sanders.
412 pp. New York:
E. P. Dutton & Co. $6.95.

### By ROBERT CHRISTGAU

"The Family" is the first complete, authoritative account of the career of Charles Manson. A small-time thief, forger and pimp who was paroled after seven years in prison at the dawn of San Francisco's 1967 Summer of Love, Manson, hirsute and acid-eyed, was charged with the Tate-LaBianca murders less than three years later. In January, 1971, he was convicted of these seven murders. He must still stand trial for two oth-

Robert Christgau writes the Rock & Roll & column for The Village Voice and teaches in the Integrated Studies program at Richmond College, C.U.N.Y.

ers—one of them, according to author Ed Sanders, a hideous torture experiment—and is implicated in many more.

"The Family" tells how an ambitious petty criminal focused some cunning amateur psychology on particularly vulnerable examples of the mass alienation of California's youth Bohemia, and created a "family" of disciples bound together by a macabre synthesis of antisocial pathology and communal ideals. Combining calculated alterations of tenderness and violence with awesome sexual stamina and a line of pseudo-guru babble, he attracted a following of pathetic young women whose sexual favors helped him move his band of lumpenhippies through various crash scenes. He used drugs and sex for blackmail and mind control, developed a doom philosophy influenced by the satanist cults that flourish around Los Angeles, and prepared his disciples for racial Armageddon, which they all believed was imminent, with a battalion of stolen dune buggies equipped with booty acquired on stolen credit cards. The murders that resulted from this run-

away obsession with violence seem inevitable in retrospect.

The outline of this story has been known for quite a while—sometimes reliably, sometimes not. Ed Sanders has solidified it, filling in particulars and verifying rumors. Manson's close relationship with hip Hollywooders like record and television producer Terry Melcher and Beach Boy rock star Dennis Wilson, now minimized by the principals, is fully described. His occult connections are detailed. The crimes and their solutions are recounted with great care for sequence and consistency. Sanders's research occupied a year and a half of his life; tens of thousands of pages of data were organized into some 50 subject files and dozens of chronological files. All the allegations he reports have been checked against known facts, and for the most part he refused to use any information that didn't come from at least two separate individuals. This work was extraordinarily difficult, requiring auxiliary investigators and even disguises. Since most of Manson's associates are partisans of violence, it was also dangerous.

So why did Sanders bother? The

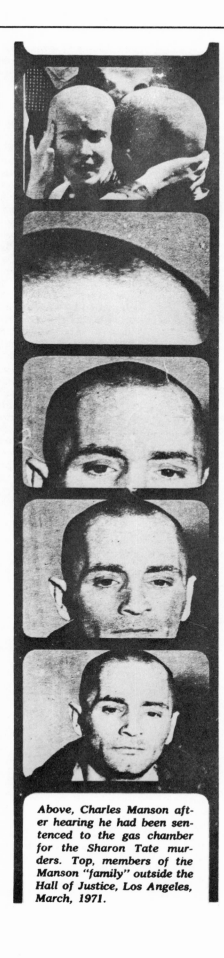

*Above, Charles Manson after hearing he had been sentenced to the gas chamber for the Sharon Tate murders. Top, members of the Manson "family" outside the Hall of Justice, Los Angeles, March, 1971.*

money accrued is certain to be matched by the pain, and Sanders is by profession a poet, not a reporter. The answer is that, despite his taste for what he calls "a quiet life of poetry and peace," Sanders has found himself impelled, by esthetic and ethical commitments that are often indistinguishable, into a series of progressively more public manifestations. In 1961 he was one of the pacifists who attempted to board a nuclear submarine in a seminal act of passive resistance that seemed aberrant at the time. In 1962 he founded "A Magazine of the Arts" whose title could not even be reproduced in a newspaper. But he ended up on the cover of one of Life's hippie issues in 1967, the leader of a successful and influential rock group called the Fugs. The Fugs gave way almost imperceptibly to active support of the pop-hip politics of Yippie and Chicago 1968, which Sanders immortalized last year in a mock-heroic novel, "Shards of God."

It was a natural step for Sanders to concern himself with Manson, one of the culminations of America's public romance with the hippies. Like Manson, Sanders was into sex, dope, the occult and the downfall of straight society. Both his Fugs monologues and "Shards of God" were full of references to jelly orgies, titanic mind-warps and arcane rituals. Of course, many of these references were ironic, overstated metaphors that weren't intended literally. But metaphors have content — Sanders really does believe in expanded sexuality, sacramental and recreational psychedelics, and non-rationalistic modes of knowing—and irony is a sophisticated tool. What could Sanders do when a would-be groupie actually brought a jar of jelly to a Fugs concert—send her back for the Skippy? Such misunderstandings are inevitable when avant-gardism is transformed into a mass movement. This is a liability that long-haired criminals like Charlie Manson and who knows how many other punk charismatics can exploit.

In the age of the new togetherness, it isn't just the good guys who get together. In "The Family," Sanders states this problem once and never makes the point again: "the flower movement was like a valley of thousands of plump white rabbits surrounded by wounded coyotes. Sure, the 'leaders' were tough, some of them geniuses and great poets. But the acid-dropping middle-class children from Des Moines were rabbits."

Sanders doesn't dwell on this idea because his narrative is almost compulsively free of what in a more literal context he refers to as "horse dooky." He refuses to philosophize, psychoanalyze or make excuses. "The Family" is nothing more than a chronological arrangement of all those facts, apparently written direct from the files, rapidly. True, the diction is characteristic Sanders Americanese — in all his work he has a way of coming up with hyphenated coinages like "bunch-punching," "murder-fated" and "hell-creep," and he is fond of words like "tycoon" and "sleuth"— and he will occasionally add a jarring note of boyish sarcasm to some especially grisly disclosure by ending the paragraph with a brief "far out" or "oo-ee-oo." But the book is determinedly non-written. There is no theorizing, and no new journalism either — no fabricated immediacy, no reconstructed dialogue, no arty pace.

This data-mania is itself an anti-middlebrow avant-garde ploy. Sanders Is quite capable of normal prose and fictional technique, and had he deemed the effort worthy he probably could have made "The Family" into something like "In Cold Blood" or even "The Boston Strangler," but he represents a sensibility that has pretty much rejected such devices and his book is truer and more exciting for it. His terse notebook style, avoiding comment and ignoring conventional standards of rhetoric, functions as a deliberate artistic choice. Although he may mention in passing that arrests for possessing a harmless euphoriant or for "felonious breast-feeding" can be expected to spark dangerous resentment, he clearly feels that the facts about Manson and his followers speak for themselves, and that they are horrible beyond explanation.

The intensity of this feeling, which reflects Sanders's commitment to nonviolence, is the greatest virtue of an excellent book. The Manson case engendered much confusion in the ranks of hip. A distressing minority—represented at its most extreme by Weatherwoman Bernardine Dohrn (who cited the murders as revolutionary acts before going underground) and, more reasonably, by those who suspect a frame-up—were unwilling to believe that a long-haired minstrel could also be a racist and male supremacist who used dope and orgasm and even some variety of love to perpetuate his own murderous sadism. In his coverage of the trial for the Los Angeles Free Press, Sanders did his best to protect Manson's presumption of innocence, and he was severely critical of anti-hippie hysteria among straight journalists, but his own research convinced him who was how guilty and ought to convince anybody.

Guilt is definitely the word. Sanders believes that, for whatever reason, the plump white rabbits in Manson's entourage have become "crazed with the willingness to mur-

*Ed Sanders.*

der" and must be separated from society. His portrayal of Sharon Tate and associates, on the other hand, while tinged with the deep disdain of a genuine psychic voyager for ruling-

class dabblers, is temperate. He doesn't conceal their connections with big-time dope and with the occult, but he does withhold damaging but irrelevant information "in respect for the memory of the innocent slain."

The murderers are guilty and their victims were innocent—after years of rationalization and hip irony, such a formulation has a refreshing moral directness. Let others fulminate over co-optation by rich straights. Sanders knows that for the most part the co-opters are only contemptible, and he will return to oppose the death-creeps who rule this society some other time. For now, he is horrified by the satanist coyotes who battle the forces of Yippie for the soul of the disaffected young—the sexist bikers, the cults that traffic in animal and (it would appear) human sacrifice. In order to say this, Sanders has done nothing less than risk his own life, for that's how serious he believes the enemy within to be, and who knows enough to gainsay him? It is only fitting that such a risk should produce such a terrifying book. ■

# The Godfather

## By WILLIAM V. SHANNON

WASHINGTON, July 31—The announcement that production will soon begin on a movie called· "The Godfather—Part Two" must surely rank as the most depressing cultural event of 1972.

This revolting film, already a box office success, is apparently to be mined for another thick profit. I can imagine the series now—"Return of the Godfather," "Son of the Godfather," "The Godfather in Las Vegas," "The Godfather in Miami Beach," and so stretching on into profitable infinity.

In one of its aspects, "The Godfather" is part of the growing pornography of violence. Having done about all they can to make sexual intercourse explicit and boring on the wide screen, the movie makers are now in the process of acquainting everyone with the many varieties of violence. Murder by submachine gun is still a hardy favorite. "The Godfather" teaches some new lessons in murder such as How to Garrot Your Brother-in-Law. These are in addition to examples of persons being murdered while starting a car, having a massage, paying a causeway toll, going through a revolving door and eating spaghetti.

With startling close-ups, vivid death ageny sequences and technicolor blood spurting everywhere, these new-style movie murders do manage to hold audience attention. By the end of movie, however, when the new Godfather presides over the murders of the heads of the New York underworld's "Five Families" as well as two or three miscellaneous enemies (I lost count), these deaths are becoming mechanical and meaningless.

A few years of such pictures will succeed in making the most gruesome and vivid murders as tedious as a nudist film. In reaching that impasse, the movie industry will have further degraded the taste and coarsened the sensitivity of millions of people, including the vulnerable young.

Any person of religious sensibility can only find the film's exploitation of a child's Baptism profoundly offensive. To juxtapose the preparation for multiple murders against the words of the Priest claiming the child for Christ is to trivialize the most important of the Christian sacraments.

It is as offensive as the scene in that much overpraised film, "The Graduate," in which the hero uses a crucifix to jam the church door. And in both films, these crude gestures are used to make an artistic point which is already abundantly clear.

In "The Godfather," the exploitation of Catholic rituals and Italian customs — in the wedding and funeral scenes as well as the Baptism—is part of the biggest cultural ripoff that any commercial promoters have gotten away with in years. "The Godfather" stereotypes Italian-Americans as gangsters or as the half-admiring, half-fearful pawns of gangsters. The authentic details of how a bride receives money gifts at a wedding or how spaghetti is cooked only give credibility to that central lie about Italian-Americans.

The film flatters Italian males by stressing their toughness and sexual prowess. But to what purpose? To end with a hero, the young Godfather, who is—by any decent human standard—a monster. Some flattery.

As an American of Irish ancestry, it seems to me that Italian-Americans ought to dislike the picture intensely. There was a time much earlier in this century when the Irish dominated the underworld. In 1931, Warner Brothers started the modern genre of gangster films with "Public Enemy" starring James Cagney as an Irish-American gangster. The Hays Office censorship of those days did not permit murders to be depicted in morbid detail, but Cagney came through quite as tough and nasty as the Corleone Brothers. In one famous scene he slammed a grapefruit into his wife's face at the breakfast table.

When John O'Hara wrote "Butterfield 8" in 1935 he had the hero complain bitterly that Hollywood cast actors like Cagney as the perfect gangster type because the tough young Irishman fit Protestant America's stereotype of an outlaw.

But by that time the Irish were already a dwindling force in organized crime, and the stereotype faded. Indeed, one of the best things that ever happened to the American Irish was that they were muscled out of the mobs by hungrier, more ruthless competitors. Otherwise, some Irish-American stockbrokers and advertising men who now sedately ride the commuter trains and shake their heads over the morning newspaper at the latest misdeeds of the Mafia might themselves be Gaelic versions of Michael Corleone.

No one denies that a few Italian-Americans are gangsters. To that extent, "The Godfather" rests on a substratum of fact. But for the millions of Italian-Americans who are not gangsters, the success of this film raises an enormous cultural obstacle. It retards their efforts to overcome this dark legacy from the past and to establish positive heroes for their children to emulate.

Events have consequences, and the consequences of "The Godfather" cannot be good for Americans of Italian or non-Italian ancestry.

*William V. Shannon is a member of the editorial board of The Times.*

August 1, 1972

331

# CHAPTER 4

# Protest

# 'Equal Protection'

## Court Bans Segregation

*Now, therefore, I, Abraham Lincoln, President of the United States, by virtue of the power in me vested * * * do order and declare that all persons held as slaves * * * are, and henceforward shall be, free * * ***

In the ninety-one years since Lincoln's Emancipation Proclamation, there have been many efforts to reconcile the reality of the bi-racial system in the South with the American ideal of equality for all men. The Negro has scored many gains and segregation has often been decried as a blot on the nation's conscience. But the bi-racial system has continued as an accommodation to habit, tradition and political necessity.

Last week the Supreme Court cut through to the heart of the problem and issued a historic judgment for racial equality. Unanimously the nine high court Justices ruled that enforced segregation of Negro children in public schools violated the Constitution.

Before the decision was issued there had been dire threats of violence in the South if the Court ruled against segregation. Yet it was received with general calm. Last week attention turned to the vast task of translating the decision into educational fact.

## The Background

When the War Between the States ended, the North was hell-bent on proving that "all men are created equal" and forcing the South to accept it. A strongly Republican Congress pushed through the "Reconstruction Amendments" — the Thirteenth, to abolish slavery; the Fourteenth, to give the Negro full citizenship rights and "equal protection of the laws"; the Fifteenth, to give him the right to vote.

But the South was steeped in the tradition of "white supremacy." It fought bitterly to halt and then turn back the surge toward full emancipation. During the Reconstruction Era, the Southern states enacted legislation providing that in schools, colleges, hospitals, libraries, restaurants, trains, buses, places of amusement and all other public places, Negroes must be segregated from whites.

### 'Separate but Equal'

Gradually, reluctantly, the rest of the nation accepted the racial wall as the price for bringing the South back into the Union. The culmination of this period of accommodation came in 1896 when the Supreme Court devised the famous "separate but equal" doctrine which had the effect of sanctioning segregation. In a case involving public transportation, the Court ruled that segregation did not violate the "equal protection" clause of the Fourteenth Amendment provided equal public facilities were made available to both Negroes and whites.

At the time, the "separate but equal" dictum aroused opposition from all sides. Northerners endorsed Justice John Harlan's sharp dissenting words: "Our Constitution is color-blind." Southerners, for their part, bitterly resented what appeared to be a judicial effort to force Negro equality down their throats. Nonetheless, the "separate but equal" doctrine provided a meeting-ground for the South and the Constitution, and for this practical reason it survived for half a century.

World War II launched a new era in the battle over the status of the Negro. Industrialization of the South had already given impetus to the demands for better Negro education. The assignment of Negro draftees to racial units in the armed forces sharpened their resentment against segregation. The courts were flooded with suits attacking the validity of various segregation laws. During this period the Supreme Court did not discard the "separate but equal" doctrine, but it interpreted "equality" in increasingly broad terms. Negroes won many decisions—against the all-white primary; against restrictive covenants forbidding the sale of property to Negroes; against segregation in public carriers in interstate commerce; against segregated state university graduate schools on the ground that even if a Negro graduate school had "equal" physical facilities, it could not offer its students "equal" professional contacts and prestige.

In December, 1952, came the broadest challenge to racial discrimination. The Supreme Court was asked to outlaw segregation in the field in which it is most widely enforced—public education. Seventeen states and the District of Columbia require segregation in public elementary and high schools and four states permit it. About 40 per cent of the nation's public elementary and high school children— a total of 8,200,000 whites and 2,-530,000 Negroes—are required to attend segregated schools. The specific cases presented to the Supreme Court involved four states—South Carolina, Virginia, Delaware and Kansas—and the District of Columbia, but the future of all segregation states hung on those cases.

## The Decision

The Court was acutely aware of the significance of the issue before it. After six months of study, the Justices announced they wanted the cases reargued. Last December rearguments began. Attorneys for the Southern states contended that when Congress and the states adopted the Fourteenth Amendment, they "did not contemplate" the abolition of segregation in public schools; that the Supreme Court seven times had upheld the validity of the "separate but equal" doctrine; that the Constitution gives each state "sole power to educate its citizens." Attorneys for the Negro children and for the Federal Government argued that the intent of the Fourteenth Amendment was to strike out segregation; that it deprived the states "of any power to make racial distinctions"; that the "separate but equal" doctrine was not valid because separation in itself denotes inequality.

### Warren Reads Verdict

The nine Justices who heard these arguments included five who were appointed by President Franklin D. Roosevelt, three by President Truman, and the Chief Justice, Earl Warren of California, whom President Eisenhower appointed. Three of the nine were from segregated states. Some were regarded as "liberal," some as "conservative."

The South and the anti-segregation forces eagerly awaited their decision. For the past three months on Mondays—the Court's decision day—the marble-columned Supreme Court chamber has been crowded with reporters. Last Monday, after three minor opinions were announced, the crowd began to dwindle. Then a court officer told news men, "Reading of the segregation decisions is about to begin." They poured back into the chamber. Chief Justice Earl Warren began reading.

In many respects the decision was unusual. It was unanimous, and on important issues the Court frequently is split. It was short—only 1,500 words. It was couched in layman's English, without resort to legalisms. And it emphasized moral and sociological factors more than legal arguments.

### No Answer in History

The decision said the court had searched history to find the answer to the case and had failed because there have been so many changes since the Fourteenth Amendment was adopted and since the "separate but equal" doctrine was proclaimed. It said:

We cannot turn the clock back [to Nineteenth Century standards and conditions]. We must consider public education in the light of its * * * present place in American life * * * Today it is a principal instrument in awakening the child to cultural values * * * in helping him to adjust normally * * *. We come then to the question presented: Does segregation of children in public schools solely on the basis of race, even though the physical facilities * * * may be equal, deprive the children of the minority group of equal educational opportunities? We believe that it does.

The key factor the Court considered was the effect of school segregation upon Negroes. The decision said:

To separate them from others of similar age and qualifications solely because of their race generates a feeling of inferiority as to their status in the community that may affect their hearts and minds in a way unlikely ever to be undone.

The old "separate but equal" dictum was discarded in these words:

Separate educational facilities are inherently unequal.

Negro correspondents in the Court chamber listened with tears in their eyes. The Negro newspaper, The Amsterdam News, called the decision "The greatest victory for the Negro people since the Emancipation Proclamation."

## The Future

The Court has not yet decreed how or when public school segregation is to be ended. The Justices said that because of the "wide applicability" of the decision, they wanted to hear arguments on the question of what procedures should be followed and by whom. When the Court convenes next fall, attorneys for both sides will discuss possible ways of implementing the ruling.

The problems of implementation are enormous. There are the psychological problems of the adjustment of Southern society to what will ultimately be an entirely new pattern. There are the practical and financial questions of what to do with two sets of schools and two sets of teachers. There are the legal questions of whether the Federal courts have power to formulate decrees that would alter state laws or whether the states themselves must devise the remedies.

Last week it was plain that years would pass before some of these problems are solved. Meanwhile, there are many ways in which the South could circumvent the spirit of the decision—by gerrymandering school districts (as the North has done in a number of areas) for example, or by running white schools as private associations.

Nevertheless the feeling is that gradually school segregation will disappear. To some extent this feeling stems from the reaction to the decision. Before it was announced, many Southerners had threatened to abolish the whole public school system rather than accept mixed education. But there were few such threats last week. Gov. Herman Talmadge declared that "Georgians will fight for their right * * * to manage their own affairs" but other Southern Governors, while critical of the Supreme Court, tempered their views. Gov. James F. Byrnes of South Carolina said although he was "shocked" he felt the South should "exercise restraint and preserve order."

### Congress Cautious

In Congress, reaction was cautious as both parties tried to anticipate the political effects. The Republican National Committee pointed with pride to the decision and said the Republicans were "leading the fight for human equality." The Democrats noted that eight of the nine Justices were Democratic appointees. Neither party is expected to claim credit for the decision in the South.

Most areas of the country outside of the South warmly applauded the Court for reaffirming the principles of democracy and re-enforcing the ideal of equality. There was also praise for the Court's decision to take its time about formulating decrees, and for the Justices' unanimity — which many persons attributed to the influence of Chief Justice Warren. In the North, and especially in Negro circles, there was no disposition to minimize the difficulties of implementing the ruling, or the possibilities for evading it, or the fact that segregation in many other fields is still legal in some states. But there was no doubt as to the tremendous impact of the decision to strike at racial intolerance at its starting point—among children at school.

May 23, 1954

## BUSES BOYCOTTED OVER RACE ISSUE

### Montgomery, Ala., Negroes Protest Woman's Arrest for Defying Segregation

MONTGOMERY, Ala., Dec. 5 (AP)—A court test of segregated transportation loomed today following the arrest of a Negro who refused to move to the colored section of a city bus.

While thousands of other Negroes boycotted Montgomery city lines in protest, Mrs. Rosa Parks was fined $14 in Police Court today for having disregarded last Thursday a driver's order to move to the rear of a bus. Negro passengers ride in the rear of buses here, white passengers in front under a municipal segregation ordinance.

An emotional crowd of Negroes, estimated by the police at 5,000, roared approval tonight at a meeting to continue the boycott.

Spokesmen said the boycott would continue until people who rode buses were no longer "intimidated, embarrassed and coerced." They said a "delegation of citizens" was ready to help city and bus line officials develop a program that would be "satisfactory and equitable."

#### Released Under Bond

Mrs. Parks appealed her fine and was released under $100 bond signed by an attorney, Fred Gray, and a former state president of the National Association for the Advancement of Colored People, E. D. Nixon.

Mr. Gray and Charles Langford, another Negro lawyer representing the 42-year-old department store seamstress, refused to say whether they planned to attack the constitutionality of segregation laws affecting public transportation.

The Supreme Court in Washington already has before it a test case against segregation on buses operating in Columbia, S. C. The United States Court of Appeals in Richmond, Va., has ruled in this case that segregation must be ended. If the Supreme Court sustains the decision, the effect will be to outlaw segregation in all states and cities.

Mrs. Parks was charged first with violating a city ordinance that gives bus drivers police powers to enforce racial segregation. But at the request of City Attorney Eugene Loe, the warrant was amended to a charge of violation of a similar state law. The state statute authorizes bus companies to provide and enforce separate facilities for whites and Negroes. Violation is punishable by a maximum fine of $500.

Other Negroes by the thousands, meanwhile, found other means of transportation or stayed home today in an organized boycott of City Lines Buses, operated by a subsidiary of National City Lines at Chicago.

The manager, J. H. Bagley, estimated that "80 or maybe 90 per cent" of the Negroes who normally used the buses had joined the boycott. He said "several thousand" Negroes rode the buses on a normal day.

December 6, 1955

# PRESIDENT SENDS TROOPS TO LITTLE ROCK, FEDERALIZES ARKANSAS NATIONAL GUARD; TELLS NATION HE ACTED TO AVOID ANARCHY

## EISENHOWER ON AIR

### Says School Defiance Has Gravely Harmed Prestige of U. S.

**By ANTHONY LEWIS**
Special to The New York Times.

WASHINGTON, Sept. 24—President Eisenhower sent Federal troops to Little Rock, Ark., today to open the way for the admission of nine Negro pupils to Central High School.

Earlier, the President federalized the Arkansas National Guard and authorized calling the Guard and regular Federal forces to remove obstructions to justice in Little Rock school integration.

His history-making action was based on a formal finding that his "cease and desist" proclamation, issued last night, had not been obeyed. Mobs of pro-segregationists still gathered in the vicinity of Central High School this morning.

Tonight, from the White House, President Eisenhower told the nation in a speech for radio and television that he had acted to prevent "mob rule" and "anarchy."

#### Historic Decision

The President's decision to send troops to Little Rock was reached at his vacation headquarters in Newport, R. I. It was one of historic importance politically, socially, constitutionally. For the first time since the Reconstruction days that followed the Civil War, the Federal Government was using its ultimate power to compel equal treatment of the Negro in the South.

He said violent defiance of Federal Court orders in Little Rock had done grave harm to "the prestige and influence, and indeed to the safety, of our nation and the world." He called on the people of Arkansas and the South to "preserve and respect the law even when they disagree with it."

#### Guardsmen Withdrawn

Action quickly followed the President's orders. During the day and night 1,000 members of the 101st Airborne Division were flown to Little Rock. Charles E. Wilson, Secretary of the Defense, ordered into Federal service all 10,000 members of the Arkansas National Guard.

Today's events were the

335

climax of three weeks of skirmishing between the Federal Government and Gov. Orval E. Faubus of Arkansas. It was three weeks ago this morning that the Governor first ordered National Guard troops to Central High School to preserve order. The nine Negro students were prevented from entering the school.

The Guardsmen were gone yesterday, withdrawn by Governor Faubus as the result of a Federal Court order. But a shrieking mob compelled the nine children to withdraw from the school.

President Eisenhower yesterday cleared the way for full use of his powers with a proclamation commanding the mob in Little Rock to "disperse."

At 12:22 P. M. today in Newport the President signed a second proclamation. It said first that yesterday's command had "not been obeyed and willful obstruction of said court orders exists and threatens to continue."

The proclamation then directed Charles E. Wilson, Secretary of Defense, to take all necessary steps to enforce the court orders for admission of the Negro children, including the call of any or all Arkansas Guardsmen under Federal command and the use of the armed forces of the United States.

Later in the afternoon the President flew from Newport to Washington, arriving at the National Airport at 4:50 o'clock.

He began his broadcast speech with this explanation of the flight:

"I could have spoken from Rhode Island, but I felt that, in speaking from the house of Lincoln, of Jackson and of Wilson, my words would more clearly convey both the sadness I feel in the action I was compelled to take and the firmness with which I intend to pursue this course. * * *"

It was a firm address, with some language unusually strong for President Eisenhower.

"Under the leadership of demagogic extremists," the President said, "disorderly mobs have deliberately prevented the carrying out of proper orders from a Federal court. Local authorities have not eliminated that violent opposition."

The President traced the course of the integration dispute in Little Rock. He noted especially that the Federal Court there had rejected what he called an "abrupt change" in segregated schooling and had adopted a "gradual" plan.

"Proper and sensible observance of the law," the President said, "then demanded the respectful obedience which the nation has a right to expect from all the people. This, unfortunately, has not been the case at Little Rock.

"Certain misguided persons, many of them imported into Little Rock by agitators, have

insisted upon defying the law and have sought to bring it into disrepute. The orders of the court have thus been frustrated."

The reference to "imported" members of the mob was seen as a sign that the Federal Bureau of Investigation had information, obtained through agents in Little Rock, on the organization of yesterday's violence.

The President tried to make it plain that he had not sought the use of Federal power in Little Rock, nor welcomed it. Rather he suggested that as Chief Executive he had no choice.

"The President's responsibility is inescapable," he said at one point. At another he said that when the decrees of a Federal court were obstructed, "the law and the national interest demanded that the President take action."

"The very basis of our individual rights and freedoms," he said, "is the certainty that the President and the Executive Branch of Government will support and insure the carrying out of the decisions of the Federal Courts, even, when necessary with all the means at the President's command.

"Unless the President did so, anarchy would result.

"There would be no security for any except that which each one of us could provide for himself.

"The interest of the nation in the proper fulfillment of the law's requirements cannot yield to opposition and demonstrations by some few persons.

"Mob rule cannot be allowed to override the decisions of the courts."

The President appeared fit and vigorous when he stepped into his White House office tonight to face a battery of news and television cameras.

His face showed the ruddiness of the outdoors exercise he has been enjoying on the golf links.

The President, who wore a gray single-breasted suit with blue shirt and tie, spoke calmly and his voice, after setting a steady deliberate pace, rose only occasionally as he sought emphasis for certain words and phrases.

It rose on the word "firmness" when he spoke of his course in this grave situation, and "mob" when he referred to the perpetrators of the Little Rock violence, and "agitators" he said were brought in from the outside.

At either side on the wall on either side of him as he spoke hung portraits of the four leaders whom the President has stated he regards as the greatest American heroes—Benjamin Franklin, George Washington, Abraham Lincoln and Robert E. Lee.

But in his thirteen-minute address tonight, General Eisenhower mentioned only Lincoln.

September 25, 1957

# NEGROES IN SOUTH IN STORE SITDOWN

## Carolina College Students Fight Woolworth Ban on Lunch Counter Service

GREENSBORO, N. C., Feb. 2 (UPI)—A group of well-dressed Negro college students staged a sitdown strike in a downtown Woolworth store today and vowed to continue it in relays until Negroes were served at the lunch counter.

"We believe since we buy books and papers in the other part of the store we should get served in this part," said the spokesman for the group.

The store manager, C. L. Harris commented:

"They can just sit there. It's nothing to me."

He declined to say whether it was the policy of the store not to serve Negroes.

The Negroes, students at North Carolina Agricultural and Technical College here, arrived shortly after 10 A. M. and sat at two sections of the lunch counter.

At 12:30 P. M., the group filed out of the store and stood on the sidewalk in this city's busiest downtown street. They formed a tight circle, threw their hands into a pyramid in the center and recited the Lord's Prayer.

The spokesman said that "another shift" of students would carry forward the strike and it would continue "until we get served."

### School Suit Is Filed

Meanwhile, a school integration suit sponsored by the National Association for the Advancement of Colored People was filed in Federal court here against the Chapel Hill School Board.

The suit was brought on behalf of a minor Negro, Stanley Boya Vickers, by Thomas Lee Vickers and Lattice Vickers, his parents. They ask that the child be assigned to Carrboro Elementary School, which is said to be nearer his home than Northside Elementary School he now attends.

The suit says Northside Elementary is "a facility maintained and operated solely for Negroes."

White children living at distances are assigned to Carrboro, the suit states.

"These white children are plaintiff's natural playmates and, in fact, during nonschool hours he does play with them," the suit declares.

The plaintiffs describe the suit as a class action.

February 3, 1960

# 1,000 Negroes Join March in Alabama

### By CLAUDE SITTON
Special to The New York Times.

MONTGOMERY, Ala., March 1—A thousand Negro students prayed and sang the National Anthem today on the steps of the first capital of the Old Confederacy in a peaceful protest against segregation.

Neither the police nor white hoodlums, one of whom attacked a Negro woman with a miniature baseball bat last week-end, attempted to interfere.

High state officials watched from the entrance to the building, which now serves as Alabama's capitol, with an occasional muttered comment.

The likelihood remained that at least some of the demonstrators would be punished. Gov. John Patterson has strongly implied that their leaders should be expelled from Alabama State College, an all-Negro institution. He had called initially for the expulsion of all involved.

Today marked the one-month anniversary of the passive resistance movement, which began with the lunch counter "sit-in" in Greensboro, N. C., and later spread into Virginia, Florida, South Carolina, Tennessee and Alabama.

### Orderly March Urged

The students gathered at 8:45 A. M. on the Alabama State College campus. One of their leaders, Elroy Embry, warned that "if anyone thinks that they cannot be orderly they can help us better by staying here."

Then they set out on the march of more than a mile to the stately Colonial building on a hilltop overlooking downtown Montgomery. The students came silently by two's as white-helmeted motorcycle policemen roared ahead of the column or sat watchfully along the way.

It was Mardi Gras day in Alabama and capitol offices were closed. The students lined up thirty-five abreast on the white marble steps at the front entrance just below the spot where Jefferson Davis took the oath of office as President of the Confederate States of America ninety-nine years ago.

At a word from one youth, they bowed their heads and said The Lord's Prayer in unison. Then the students sang "The Star Spangled Banner."

The students re-formed into a column of two's and marched back to the campus where they were dismissed by a leader. The demonstration had lasted for twenty-five minutes.

March 2, 1960

# VANDERBILT ACTS TO HEAL BREACH

## Agrees to Allow Expelled Student to Graduate— Divinity Dean Dropped

Special to The New York Times.

NASHVILLE, June 13—Vanderbilt University today approved settlement of a three-month controversy over a Negro divinity student's expulsion on faculty terms it rejected last week.

In a statement Chancellor Harvie Branscomb said:

"This matter is now closed, and except for necessary details will not be further discussed."

Under terms of the settlement plan the divinity student, the Rev. James M. Lawson, will be allowed to obtain his degree at Vanderbilt, either by taking written examinations without re-enrolling or by transferring to Vanderbilt credits he is expected to receive at Boston University, where he is now studying. He must act by Sept. 15.

### Dean Nelson Is Out

The Chancellor also accepted the resignation of Dean J. Robert Nelson of the Divinity School, effective Aug. 31, but relieved him of his duties immediately.

The eleven other Divinity School faculty members who resigned with Dean Nelson in protest against Mr. Lawson's expulsion will be allowed ten days to withdraw their resignations.

The dispute between the faculty and the university administration grew out of a negotiating session between leaders of the sit-in campaign to obtain desegregation of lunch counters in Nashville and city officials.

The university expelled Mr. Lawson, who was accused of having urged students to flout local ordinances.

Most divinity faculty members were out of town. However, Arthur L. Foster, Assistant Professor of Pastoral Theology, expressed doubt that Mr. Lawson would be "willing to return to a campus where Dean Nelson has been unjustly discredited."

### 'Invites Us to Crawl'

Emphasizing that he was giving only his personal reaction, he added:

"Furthermore, this proposal puts upon us the onus of withdrawing our resignations within ten days and in effect invites us to crawl back."

Dr. Branscomb reiterated that Mr. Lawson had not been expelled for participating in the sit-in protests "but because of his commitment to an active program of civil disobedience."

"Vanderbilt University stands on the principle that racial progress in the South must be based on obedience to law," he said. "There cannot be one principle for whites and a different one for Negroes.

"The law has been the basis for much of the Negro's progress in the past and is the guarantee of their continued progress. The university will not desert this principle, whatever the difficulties."

In Boston, Mr. Lawson said he would withold comment until officially notified by the university.

June 14, 1960

# VIOLENCE FLARES IN JACKSONVILLE

## 50 Injured as White Gangs Clash With Negroes— 16-Year-Old Stabbed

By United Press International.

JACKSONVILLE, Fla., Aug. 27—Angry bands of club-swinging whites clashed with Negroes in the streets of downtown Jacksonville today.

At least fifty persons were injured. A white youth was stabbed and two Negroes suffered minor bullet wounds. Patrolmen armed with shotguns and threatening to use fire hoses succeeded in dispersing most of the crowd of 3,000 that gathered in the downtown area.

However, there were reports of incidents far into the night, particularly in Negro districts and outlying areas.

### Streets Blocked

The police said they had one unconfirmed report that a Negro woman was cruising streets in a panel truck urging Negroes, over a loudspeaker, to stand up for their rights.

Streets in several sections of the downtown area where crowds had gathered earlier were blocked.

The Florida National Guard was ordered to stand by in case the situation grew worse, according to William Durden, administrative assistant to Gov. LeRoy Collins. He said, however, that Jacksonville authorities had advised him that there was no immediate need for troops.

Jacksonville officials said they had more than 200 city, county and state policemen on duty. They said sixty-two persons had been arrested on charges ranging from disorderly conduct to inciting to riot. Forty-eight were Negroes and fourteen whites.

Officers at the police complaint desk estimated that about fifty had suffered injuries ranging from slight to serious in the beatings and fights. The Duval Medical Center said two Negro youths, 12 and 18, had received minor bullet wounds.

Police Inspector Emmett Lee said the shootings had allegedly occurred when a small group of Negroes threw bottles at a white man riding past in a car in a suburban neighborhood. The man was reported to have stopped the car and opened fire with a pistol.

Three other Negroes were beaten by bands of whites in the downtown disorders.

A white taxi cab company employe, identified as Wayne Heidler, was burned when four Negro men hurled potash in his face as he stopped his car for a red light in a Negro section, the police said.

The racial unrest broke into the open today after repeated sit-in demonstrations at two downtown variety stores.

Yesterday a hair-pulling scuffle occurred between a white and Negro woman in front of one of the stores and several other white women were knocked to the pavement.

Whites, armed with baseball bats, ax handles and heavy walking sticks began gathering in the downtown area about mid-morning. Some carried Confederate flags. About noon a handful of Negroes appeared and several approached the crowd of whites.

Three were beaten before the police managed to rescue them.

The whites then discovered another small band of Negroes along a side street. They rushed the Negroes, who momentarily stood their ground and then turned and ran.

Mayor Haydon Burns said at midafternoon that the situation appeared to be under control in the downtown section. But small crowds continued to form in various other areas and Police Inspector W. L. Bates said isolated fights were occurring "all over town."

A hospital spokesman at Duval Medical Center estimated twenty persons or more—both Negroes and whites—had been treated for cuts, bruises and other injuries.

The 16-year-old white youth who was stabbed was taken to St. Luke's Hospital in serious condition with a wound in the left chest.

The hospital identified him as William Howard Pellham of Jacksonville. He told attendants he had been stabbed by a Negro man who had stopped his car in a suburban area.

One of the white men passed out mimeographed sheets signed by the "Segregation Forces of Duval County."

The leaflets said: "We have warned the merchants of Jacksonville with lunch counters that if they allow our Florida laws to be flounted (sic) we will immediately institute a county-wide boycott against any establishment guilty of such acts."

A white segregation leader said hurried calls had been made to anti-Negro factions throughout the city last night. He estimated sixty local whites and an undetermined number of Ku Klux Klan and White Citizens Council members from South Georgia and neighboring towns were among those who met this morning downtown and at a small city park between Woolworth's and Cohen's.

August 28, 1960

337

**By CLAUDE SITTON**
Special to The New York Times.

JACKSON, Miss., May 24—Twenty-seven "Freedom Riders" were arrested and jailed today after coming here from Montgomery, Ala., in buses under armed military escort.

No violence resulted from the attempts of the two groups to challenge segregation in bus terminals, despite rising racial tension that produced a series of riots in Alabama in the last ten days.

Mississippi National Guard officers reported that a threat had been made to dynamite the first bus as it crossed the state line. The threat was not carried out.

#### Served at Lunch Counter

Some of the twenty-five Negroes and two white persons in the two groups made successful demands for service at the lunch counter in the white waiting room of the Trailways Bus Terminal in Montgomery before leaving there.

However, four of the first group were arrested when they sought to enter white rest rooms in the station here after their arrival at 3:55 P. M. Eastern daylight time. The eight others were seized inside the white men's rest room a few minutes later.

The bus carrying the other demonstrators pulled into the terminal at 6:47 P. M. Three minutes later, all fifteen had been arrested. They had lined up in front of the entrance to the terminal's white cafeteria and had refused the demand from Police Capt. J. L. Ray that they leave.

All were charged with breach of the peace in refusing to obey an officer. They were held in lieu of bonds totaling $1,000 each of the two charges. Before leaving the Alabama capital, their leaders had vowed that the demonstrators would remain in jail rather than post bond or pay a fine.

Jack Travis, the city Prosecutor, said that they would probably be tried Friday. They face a maximum penalty of fines amounting to $700 and ten months imprisonment.

# 27 BI-RACIAL BUS RIDERS JAILED IN JACKSON, MISS., AS THEY WIDEN CAMPAIGN

United Press International Telephoto

**MISSISSIPPI BUS STATION:** Busload of "Freedom Riders" arrives at Jackson, Miss., from Montgomery, Ala. National Guardsmen and police were on duty to prevent disorder.

#### Riot Charges Dropped

The first twelve arrested were also charged with inciting to riot but this charge was dropped later.

The Supreme Court has ruled that a state cannot enforce segregation in any form of transportation. The court has also found that interstate waiting rooms in terminals may not be segregated. In a ruling this term, it decided also that a private restaurant in an interstate terminal designed to serve interstate passengers could not be segregated.

Among those arrested was James Farmer, national director of the Congress of Racial Equality of New York. C. O. R. E., as the organization is popularly known, started the Freedom Ride the first week of May in Washington.

The original destination was New Orleans. However, the C. O. R. E. demonstrators, most of whom were non-Southerners, returned to their homes after a bus was burned in Anniston, Ala., and they had been attacked there and again in Birmingham.

#### Seen Off by Dr. King

Other demonstrators, members of Nashville's Student Nonviolent Committee, resumed the campaign last Wednesday and finally boarded a bus for Montgomery Saturday.

The Rev. Dr. Martin Luther King Jr., principal leader of the "nonviolent action" espoused by the students, saw them off in Montgomery this morning. He said he expected that there would be Freedom Riders on many of the buses leaving Montgomery within the next few weeks.

The buses carried no general riders—only the Freedom Riders, about twenty newsmen and some Guardsmen, who rode part of the time with bayonets fixed.

The big Vista View red and white Trailways buses that carried the demonstrators halfway across Alabama and into Mississippi passed up all stations on the way. This led to a controversy on the first bus. One of the demonstrators accused Lieut. Col. Gillespie V. Montgomery of "degrading and inhumane" treatment in refusing to halt for a rest stop.

The first party pulled out of the Montgomery terminal at 9:12 A. M. After the escort of National Guardsmen and highway patrolmen was changed at the state line, the Rev. C. T. Vivian, 36 years old, of the Cosmopolitan Community Church of Nashville, Tenn., approached the Mississippi officer and made his request to stop. The colonel said that he did not have authority to stop the bus.

"This is degrading us," the minister asserted after the National Guardsman ordered him to return to his seat.

#### Refused Second Time

Mr. Vivian returned to speak with Colonel Montgomery twenty-five minutes later and said it was imperative that he and others among the Freedom Riders be allowed to make a rest stop. He was again refused permission.

The route taken by the buses —United States Route 80— leads through the heart of the Black Belt, an area of dark soil and a large Negro population. Militant segregationists hold the reigns of power throughout much of this strip and race relations have made relatively little progress.

Jackson is the modern capital of segregation, the home base of the Citizens' Council movement, which wields strong influence in state governmental affairs.

Mississippi's Governor, Ross R. Barnett, campaigned on a platform of unrelenting opposition to desegregation and pledged to go to jail if necessary to prevent its coming.

Nevertheless, the councils, Mr. Barnett and leading citizens urged here that there be no repetition here of the violence that broke out in Alabama. A front-page editorial today in The State Times probably represented the sentiments of many Mississippians.

The newspaper's editor, Oliver Emmerich, said that the Freedom Riders had failed in Georgia, Virginia, North and South Carolina because they did not "obtain their objective to stir up violence." He continued:

"When the 'Freedom Riders' reach Mississippi we do not want them to have their efforts crowned with success. Their ob-

jective is to make the headlines. They want to stir up violence. The more violent the people, the more successful their campaign. Theirs is a grandstand play, and we should receive it as such.

"* * * We must recognize this is a test for Mississippi. We urge our people to show restraint in the face of these unwanted visitors who seek to besmirch Mississippi's good name."

Dr. King held a brief prayer meeting for the Freedom Riders in Montgomery before they were escorted to the bus station by National Guardsmen. When they arrived, the street on which the terminal is located had been blocked off by 250 soldiers with bayonets fixed and rifles held high.

Maj. Gen. Henry V. Graham, the State Adjutant General, took personal command of the operation. He said that 1,000 Guardsmen had already taken up positions along the route to the Mississippi line. Floyd Mann, the State Commissioner of Public Safety, also was on hand.

### Ride Not 'a Valid Test'

Before the bus pulled out, Dr. King told newsmen that the Freedom Riders would not consider this ride "a valid test" of bus desegregation and expressed hope that one day such precautions would not be necessary.

General Graham boarded the bus and warned the one white and eleven Negro demonstrators and some twenty newsmen that "this could be a hazardous trip." He noted that Gov. John Patterson had ordered him and Mr. Mann to prevent any trouble and he said that none was expected.

"We wish you—sincerely—a good trip," he said, smiling, and left the bus to take his position in the command car.

Forty-one vehicles, including sixteen highway patrol cruisers each carrying three combat-equipped National Guardsmen and two troopers, accompanied the bus.

A squad of city motorcycle policemen headed the column to the city limits, where the patrol cruisers took over with their red dome lights flashing.

As Fred Stokes, the 25-year-old driver, drove the bus over the bridge across the Alabama River, the riders sang a sit-in song to the Calypso tune of "Day O."

Freedom, give us freedom,
Freedom's coming and it won't be long.

Three L-19 reconnaissance planes and two helicopters circled overhead.

A farmer following a motorized cultivator raised one hand as the bus passed and thumbed his nose.

As the convoy passed through Selma at 10:33 A. M., a roughly dressed group of whites shouted curses and threats.

At the rear of the bus, the Rev. James M. Lawson, pastor of the Scott Chapel Methodist Church of Shelbyville, Tenn., and one of Dr. King's leading disciples, conducted a workshop on "nonviolent action."

"If we get knocked down too often, let's kneel together where we are," he told the eleven others at one point.

The convoy made several stops at isolated spots along the highway.

Sixty miles from the Mississippi line the bus passed through another community, most of whose populace turned out to see the show. A white man stuck out his tongue at the passing bus and a Negro woman across the street smiled and waved, her fingers reaching out as if to touch the vehicle.

At Demopolis, Ala., another white man shook his fist and a hard object struck the side of the bus. Others in the crowd along the highway jeered and shouted curses.

The Alabamans turned the bus over to a much smaller escort of Mississippi National Guardsmen and highway patrolmen at 2:10 P. M. The Mississippians were under the command of Maj. Gen. W. P. Wilson.

The city police here had cleared the Trailways Terminal of spectators and had stationed fifty men inside and outside. Three German shepherd police dogs imported from Vicksburg were held on leashes in front of the station.

The New York Times        May 25, 1961

**The 27 bus riders who left Montgomery, Ala. (1) for New Orleans (3) were held in Jackson, Miss. (2).**

# 3,000 TROOPS PUT DOWN MISSISSIPPI RIOTING AND SEIZE 200 AS NEGRO ATTENDS CLASSES; EX-GEN. WALKER IS HELD FOR INSURRECTION

## SHOTS QUELL MOB

### Enrolling of Meredith Ends Segregation in State Schools

**By CLAUDE SITTON**
Special to The New York Times

OXFORD, Miss., Oct. 1—James H. Meredith, a Negro, enrolled in the University of Mississippi today and began classes as Federal troops and federalized units of the Mississippi National Guard quelled a 15-hour riot.

A force of more than 3,000 soldiers and guardsmen and 400 deputy United States marshals fired rifles and hurled tear-gas grenades to stop the violent demonstrations.

Throughout the day more troops streamed into Oxford. Tonight a force approaching 5,000 soldiers and guardsmen, along with the Federal marshals, maintained an uneasy peace in this town of 6,500 in the northern Mississippi hills.

[There were two flareups tonight in which tear gas had to be used, United Press International reported. A small crowd of students began throwing bottles at marshals outside Baxter Hall where Mr. Meredith was housed. They were quickly dispersed by tear gas. Soldiers also broke up a minor demonstration at a downtown intersection.]

**200 Are Seized**

The troops seized approximately 200 persons.

They were seized in the mobs of students and adults that besieged the university administration building last night and attacked troops on the town square this morning.

Among those arrested was former Maj. Gen. Edwin A. Walker, who resigned his commission after having been reprimanded for his ultra-right-wing political activity. He was charged with insurrection.

The university's acceptance of Mr. Meredith, a 29-year-old Air Force veteran, followed Gov. Ross R. Barnett's retreat from his defiance of Federal court orders that the Negro be enrolled.

The 64-year-old official, a member of the militantly segregationist Citizens Councils, had vowed he would go to jail if necessary to prevent university desegregation.

Mr. Meredith's admission marked the first desegregation of a public educational institution in Mississippi. It reduced the Deep South bloc of massive-resistance states to two — Alabama and South Carolina.

Although the step brought an apparent end to the most serious Federal-state conflict since the Civil War, its cost in human lives and bitterness was the greatest in any dispute over desegregation directives of the Federal courts.

Two men were killed in the rioting, which broke out about 8 o'clock last night after Mr. Meredith had been escorted onto the campus by the marshals.

The victims were Paul Guihard, 30 years old, a correspondent for Agence France Presse, and Ray Gunter, 23, a jukebox repairman from nearby Abbeville, Miss.

The number of injured could not be determined definitely. But Mr. Guthman told newsmen 25 marshals had required medical treatment. One of them, shot through the neck, was reported in critical condition.

A military spokesman said 20 soldiers and guardsmen had been injured, none of them seriously.

Dr. Vernon B. Harrison, director of the Student Health Service, said between 60 and 70 persons, including some marshals, had been treated at the university infirmary.

Others who were wounded or were burned by exploding tear-gas grenades obtained aid from local physicians or from Army doctors who moved into the infirmary last night.

**Corps Chief in Command**

Lieut. Gen. Hamilton Howze, commander of the 18th Airborne Corps, arrived here from Fort Bragg, in North Carolina, to take over the field command. The corps includes the 82d and the 101st Airborne Divisions.

Lieut. Col. Gordon Hill, Army public information officer here, said General Howze was accompanied by his corps command. There were reports that other units of the two famed airborne divisions were moving into the area.

The general's presence indicated that a major build-up of Army troops was under way here, in Columbus, Miss., and at Memphis.

General Howze took over command from Brig. Gen. Charles Billingslea, assistant commander of the Second Infantry Division, Fort Benning, Ga.

Mr. Guthman said Federal forces were prepared to remain as long as necessary.

"Our mission is to see that the orders of the courts are enforced," he said.

Asked if the mission included the preservation of order in the town, he replied:

"I think we have a duty to maintain law and order."

The toll of property damaged included five automobiles and a mobile television unit that were burned.

**Garden Ripped Up**

Bricks, lumber and other building materials were stolen from a construction site and used as missiles or roadblocks. The rioters ripped up the garden of a home in their search for brickbats and commandeered a fire engine and a bulldozer.

A hard core of 70 to 100 youths, most of whom appeared to be Ole Miss students, touched off the riot. They were soon joined by students from other universities and colleges in this area.

Youths and men from Lafayette County, of which Oxford is the seat, and from surrounding counties joined the fray.

Some members of the mob wore jackets from Mississippi State University, at Starkeville, and Memphis State College, in Memphis.

Members of the Ku Klux Klan and similar racist groups in Alabama and northern Louisiana reportedly had threatened to join the opposition against Mr. Meredith's enrollment.

**State Charge Denied**

In briefing newsmen, Mr. Guthman flatly denied assertions by state officials that Chief United States Marshal James J. P. McShane had precipitated the riot by ordering use of tear gas prematurely.

The Justice Department spokesman said tear gas had been used only after the students had showered the marshals with rocks and one deputy had been struck with an iron

WALKER IS STOPPED BY TROOPS: Former Maj. Gen. Edwin A. Walker is detained
by soldiers near the courthouse in Oxford. He was turned over to U.S. marshals and is
being held in $100,000 bail on charges stemming from his role in Sunday's campus riots.

Associated Press
ASSUMES COMMAND:
Lieut. Gen. Hamilton Howze.

pipe, which left a deep dent in his helmet.

A force of 200 state troopers, used by Governor Barnett to block one of Mr. Meredith's three previous attempts to register, stood by on and around the campus last night. The troopers made no effort to break up the mob at the administration building, called the Lyceum. Some made it plain they sided with the students.

The troopers pulled back from the riot scene shortly after 9 o'clock, leaving the marshals to defend themselves.

The action was authorized by State Senator George Yarborough of Red Banks, the President pro tem of the Senate and Governor Barnett's official representative on the campus.

"We had been assured by the Governor that the state police would assist us in maintaining law and order," Mr. Guthman said.

The besieged marshals, commanded by Chief Marshal McShane and Nicholas deB. Katzenbach, Deputy United States Attorney General, held their redoubt at the Lyceum until shortly after midnight.

They got reinforcement then from Troop E, Second Reconnaissance Squadron, 108th Armored Cavalry, of the Mississippi National Guard.

The first unit of combat military policemen called up by the President did not arrive until 4:30 this morning. This was

Company A of the 503d Military Police Battalion, from Fort Bragg, N. C.

Other troops poured into Oxford by truck and by plane. They included the 716th Military Police Battalion, which came overland from Fort Dix, N. J.; the 720th Military Police Battalion from Fort Hood, Tex.; the Second Battle Group, Second Infantry Division, from Fort Benning, Ga., and the 31st Helicopter Company from Jacksonville, N. C.

The Mississippi National Guard units sent here included the 108th Armored Cavalry Regiment from Tupelo and the Second Battle Group, 155th Infantry, from Amory.

A detachment of the 70th Engineering Battalion from Fort Campbell, Kentucky, operated a "tent city" for the marshals 15 miles north of here, in the Holly Springs National Forest.

The unit included medical and communications specialists from the 101st Airborne Division.

The 101st had been ordered to Little Rock, Ark., in September of 1957 by President Eisenhower to put down rioting and to enforce Federal court desegregation orders directing the admission of nine Negroes to Central High School.

The first military policemen to arrive helped the marshals and National Guardsmen repel a final assault on the Lyceum at 5 A. M. Barrage after bar-

rage of tear gas and smoke grenades drove back the howling mob, whose strength had dwindled from a peak of 2,500 to 100.

It was difficult to estimate the number of persons who actually took part in the riot. Acrid clouds of smoke and tear gas billowed across the front of a campus area called the Grove, a tree-shaded oval in front of the Lyceum.

Virtually all the street lights were shot out or broken by rocks early in the evening. Observers edging as close to the action as the tear gas and prudence would permit got a view of shadowy forms racing back and forth behind Confederate battle flags.

The rioters cranked up the bulldozer twice and sent it crashing driverless toward the marshals. Both times it hit trees and other obstructions that stopped it before it reached their ranks.

Shouting members of the mob raced the fire engine back and forth through the trees and strewed links of hose across the Grove. At one point the engine careened down the asphalt drive only a few feet from the marshals, who peppered it with blasts from their tear-gas guns.

Several persons were burned as canisters of tear gas struck them or exploded near them.

**Snipers Fire in Darkness**

Snipers operated under the cover of darkness, aiming blasts

of birdshot and pistol and rifle fire at the marshals and others.

Mr. Guihard received a bullet wound in the back. Mr. Gunter was shot in the forehead.

A sniper fired three quick shots at Karl Fleming, a reporter in the Atlanta bureau of Newsweek magazine, but the bullet struck the doorway of the Lyceum.

Other newsmen were attacked and beaten. Gordon Yoder, a Telenews cameraman from Dallas, and Mrs. Yoder were set upon by the mob. State troopers rescued them.

A group of teen-agers and a few men massed on the town square before the three-story Lafayette County Courthouse about 9:30 A. M. today. Many of them wore gray caps bearing Confederate battle flags.

They took up positions on the southeast corner of the square, facing two platoons of military policemen on the southwest corner. About a third of the M.P.'s were Negroes.

The youths began hurling bottles at the soldiers, drawing lusty cheers from adult bystanders when they scored a hit. The soldiers remained in ranks.

The platoons fixed bayonets, formed two wedges and scattered the assailants. But the mob returned and began tossing bottles and rocks at the soldiers again.

The M.P.'s donned their gas masks, formed in a line and moved across the square, throwing tear-gas grenades. The youths retreated.

The mob returned again, and squads of eight to ten soldiers chased them back along the streets, firing rifles over their heads. This broke up the mob.

Business establishments that had opened this morning closed their doors hurriedly. Except for the troops, the square was deserted at noon.

October 2, 1962

# Books of The Times

By SHELDON BINN
Special to The New York Times.

NEW YORK.

"You must put yourself in the skin of a man . . ." writes James Baldwin as he seeks to translate what it means to be a Negro in white America so that a white man can understand it.

Despite the inherent difficulties of such a task, his translation in his latest book, "The Fire Next Time," is masterful. No matter the skill of the writer, and Mr. Baldwin is skillful, one can never really know the corrosion of hate, the taste of fear or the misery of humiliation unless one has lived it. Only James Meredith knows what it really means to be James Meredith. But if the actuality cannot be known, it can be related.

**James Baldwin**

On one level it can be related so the listener becomes more or less curious, mildly interested and intellectually aware of what he is hearing.

On another and higher level, it can be related so the listener becomes virtually part of the experience, intensely feels the hurt and pain and despair, and yes, even the hope. The listener can be transformed, as far as words will take him, into the skin of the teller. Out of his own pain and despair and hope, Mr. Baldwin has fashioned such a transformation.

He has pictured white America as seen through the eyes of a Negro.

## A Bitter Picture

What he has drawn will not sit well with even some whites who count themselves as friends of the Negro. But he has not written this book of two essays to please.

THE FIRE NEXT TIME. By James Baldwin. 120 pages. Dial. $3.50.

Mr. Binn is a member of the staff of The New York Times.

"The brutality with which Negroes are treated in this country simply cannot be overstated, however unwilling white men may be to hear it," he writes.

Thus he has written from a heart which has felt a unique kind of hurt and a brain which has desperately sought hope in face of what often seems to be the merciless logic of despair. He has fashioned his plea to America out of the past he has known, from the ferment of the present and the possibilities of the future.

One possibility is grim, as the book's title suggests. It is taken from a prophecy recreated from the Bible in a song of a slave:

*"God gave Noah the rainbow sign,*
*No more water, the fire next time!"*

This is the text of the message of Mr. Baldwin's two essays. One is a short "Letter to My Nephew on the One Hundredth Anniversary of the Emancipation" which originally appeared in The Progressive in Madison, Wis. The other, a longer article, is entitled "Down at the Cross, a Letter from a Region of My Mind." It appeared last year in The New Yorker.

Mr. Baldwin pleads: "If we—and I mean the relatively conscious whites and the relatively conscious black, who must, like lovers, insist on, or create, the consciousness of others—do not falter in our duty now, we may be able, handful that we are, to end the racial nightmare, and achieve our country, and change the history of the world."

Otherwise, the next time fire.

He opens the longer essay with the story of his experiences as a youth in Harlem when he "fled into the church" out of the despair of his existence. His heart guides his pen. His experience tells the tale in staccato clarity.

He wonders why God "if His love was so great, and if He loved all His children, why were we, the blacks, cast down so far?"

He says, switching from visceral to intellectual inspiration, that Christianity has operated with "unmitigated arrogance and cruelty." He writes of the "remarkable arrogance that assumed that the ways and morals of other were inferior to those of the Christians . . ."

But if the facts he adduces are damning, his transcendent hope remains. He says we must not ask whether it is possible for a human being to become truly moral.

"I think we must *believe* it is possible," he writes.

Mr. Baldwin recounts a meeting he had with Elijah Muhammad, a leader of the Nation of Islam movement which would have the Negroes form a separate nation in America.

Muhammad, he says, has been able to do what generations of welfare workers and committees and resolutions and reports and housing projects and playgrounds have failed to do: "To heal and redeem drunkards and junkies, to convert people who have come out of prison and keep them out, to make men chaste and women virtuous . . ." How? By telling the Negroes that God is black, that all black men belong to Islam, that they have been chosen. This is a dream that thousands carry away after they have heard the Muslim minister.

Mr. Baldwin writes: "The white God has not delivered them, perhaps the black God will."

## He Scorns Vengeance

Vengeance is not an unnatural desire of the oppressed. But Mr. Baldwin rejects it and therefore rejects Muhammad's approach. Glorification of one race and the debasement of another, he says, is a recipe for murder.

Mr. Baldwin is proud of his race, of those who have been able to "produce children of kindergarten age who can walk through mobs to get to school." He says the "Negro boys and girls who are facing mobs today come out of a long line of improbable aristocrats—the only genuine aristocrats this country has produced."

And again, torn between reality and hope, he pleads for Americans to reject the delusion of the value placed in the color of skin. He admits what "I am asking is impossible," but adds that human history, and American Negro history in particular, testifies to the prepetual achievement of the impossible.

He has sounded a warning and a hope. Men of good will must hope his hope is well founded.

## Mississippi Victim Lived With Peril in His Job

**By EMANUEL PERLMUTTER**

Medgar W. Evers, who was killed yesterday, knew that his position as field secretary for the National Association for the Advancement of Colored People in Jackson, Miss., was a dangerous one.

In 1961, when he applauded a courtroom defendant in a sit-down proceeding, a policeman beat him over the head with a revolver.

When he was 14 years old, a friend of his father's was lynched for allegedly insulting a white woman. Mr. Evers never forgot the sight of the murdered man.

In a television interview with a reporter for the Columbia Broadcasting System that was recorded on June 28, 1962, and rebroadcast in part last night, he related occasions on which

### Evers Knew Racial Violence From the Age of 14—Often Attacked and Threatened

he was warned by anonymous telephone callers that they would blow up his home and that "I had only a few hours to live."

"I remember distinctly one individual calling with a pistol on the other end, and he hit the cylinder and of course you could hear it was a revolver," he recalled.

"He said, 'This is for you.'

"And I said, 'Well, whenever my time comes, I'm ready.' "

Mr. Evers also recalled that in 1958, when he boarded a bus in Meridian, Miss., and refused to sit in a segregated rear seat, the local police took him to the station house for questioning. When he went back to the bus and sat in a front seat again, a white man punched him in the face.

In an interview 10 days ago in his Jackson office, Mr. Evers said calmly:

"If I die, it will be in a good cause. I've been fighting for America just as much as the soldiers in Vietnam."

The previous night, a fire bomb had been hurled onto the carport of his home. It caused no damage.

Despite the assaults and threats to his life, Mr. Evers continued his efforts to register Negroes to vote and to organize demonstrations against segregation.

The husky 37-year-old Negro, who still had the solid body of the varsity football player he was in his youth, was born on July 2, 1925, in Decatur, Miss. He attended elementary and high school in Newton County, Miss., and entered the United States Army in 1943.

After the war, he enrolled at Alcorn Agricultural and Mechanical College in southwestern Mississippi, majoring in business administration. For a few years after graduation, he worked as an insurance salesman. He joined the N.A.A.C.P. in 1952 and became a member of its staff in 1954.

He was married to Myrlie Beasley on Dec. 24, 1951. They were the parents of two sons, Darrell K., 10 years old, and James Van Dyke 3d, 3, and a daughter, Reena D., 8.

White officials with whom he dealt considered him an effective organizer. They described him as a reasonable and dependable man.

*June 13, 1963*

# 00,000 MARCH FOR CIVIL RIGHTS 'N ORDERLY WASHINGTON RALLY; PRESIDENT SEES GAIN FOR NEGRO

## ACTION ASKED NOW

### 10 Leaders of Protest Urge Laws to End Racial Inequity

**By E. W. KENWORTHY**
Special to The New York Times

WASHINGTON, Aug. 28

More than 200,000 Americans, most of them black but many of them white, demonstrated here today for a full and speedy program of civil rights and equal job opportunities.

It was the greatest assembly for a redress of grievances that this capital has ever seen.

One hundred years and 240 days after Abraham Lincoln enjoined the emancipated slaves to "abstain from all violence" and "labor faithfully for reasonable wages," this vast throng proclaimed in march and song and through the speeches of their leaders that they were still waiting for the freedom and the jobs.

#### Children Clap and Sing

There was no violence to mar the demonstration. In fact, at times there was an air of hootenanny about it as groups of schoolchildren clapped hands and swung into the familiar freedom songs.

But if the crowd was good-natured, the underlying tone was one of dead seriousness. The emphasis was on "freedom" and "now." At the same time the leaders emphasized, paradoxically but realistically, that the struggle was just beginning.

On Capitol Hill, opinion was divided about the impact of the demonstration in stimulating Congressional action on civil rights legislation. But at the White House, President Kennedy declared that the cause of 20,000,000 Negroes had been advanced by the march.

The march leaders went from the shadows of the Lincoln Memorial to the White House to meet with the President for 75 minutes. Afterward, Mr. Kennedy issued a 400-word statement praising the marchers for the "deep fervor and the quiet dignity" that had characterized the demonstration.

#### Says Nation Can Be Proud

The nation, the President said, "can properly be proud of the demonstration that has occurred here today."

The main target of the demonstration was Congress, where committees are now considering the Administration's civil rights bill.

At the Lincoln Memorial this afternoon, some speakers, knowing little of the ways of Congress, assumed that the passage of a strengthened civil rights bill had been assured by the moving events of the day.

But from statements by Congressional leaders, after they had met with the march committee this morning, this did not seem certain at all. These statements came before the demonstration.

Senator Mike Mansfield of Montana, the Senate Democratic leader, said he could not say whether the mass protest would speed the legislation, which faces a filibuster by Southerners.

Senator Everett McKinley Dirksen of Illinois, the Republican leader, said he thought the demonstration would be neither an advantage nor a disadvantage to the prospects for the civil rights bill.

The human tide that swept over the Mall between the shrines of Washington and Lincoln fell back faster than it came on. As soon as the ceremony broke up this afternoon, the exodus began. With astounding speed, the last buses and trains cleared the city by midevening.

At 9 P.M. the city was as calm as the waters of the Reflecting Pool between the two memorials.

At the Lincoln Memorial early in the afternoon, in the midst of a songfest before the addresses, Josephine Baker, the singer, who had flown from her home in Paris, said to the thousands stretching down both sides of the Reflecting Pool:

"You are on the eve of a complete victory. You can't go

343

**VIEW FROM THE LINCOLN MEMORIAL:** The scene during the march looking toward the Washington Monument

United Press International Telephoto

**VIEW FROM THE WASHINGTON MONUMENT:** Marchers assembling around Reflecting Pool at the Lincoln Memorial

Associated Press

wrong. The world **is behind you.**"

Miss Baker said, **as if she** saw a dream coming true before her eyes, that "this is the happiest day of my life."

But of all the 10 leaders of the march on Washington who followed her, only the Rev. Dr. Martin Luther King Jr., president of the Southern Christian Leadership Conference, saw that dream so hopefully.

The other leaders, except for the three clergymen among the 10, concentrated on the struggle ahead and spoke in tough, even harsh, language.

But paradoxically it was Dr. King—who had suffered perhaps most of all—who ignited the crowd with words that might have been written by the sad, brooding man enshrined within.

As he arose, a great roar welled up from the crowd. When he started to speak, a hush fell.

"Even though we face the difficulties of today and tomorrow, I still have a dream," he said.

"It is a dream chiefly rooted in the American dream," he went on.

"I have a dream that one day this nation will rise up and live out the true meaning of its creed: "We hold these truths to be self-evident, that all men are created equal.'

### Dream of Brotherhood

"I have a dream . . ." The vast throng listening intently to him roared.

". . . that one day on the red hills of Georgia, the sons of former slaves and the sons of former slave-owners will be able to sit together at the table of brotherhood.

"I have a dream . . ." The crowd roared.

". . . that one day even the State of Mississippi, a state sweltering with the heat of injustice, sweltering with the heat of oppression, will be transformed into an oasis of freedom and justice.

"I have a dream . . ." The crowd roared.

". . . that my four little children will one day live in a nation where they will not be judged by the color of their skin but by the content of their character.

"I have a dream . . ." The crowd roared.

". . . that one day every valley shall be exalted, every hill and mountain shall be made low, the rough places will be made plain, and the crooked places will be made straight, and the glory of the Lord shall be revealed and all flesh shall see it together."

As Dr. King concluded with a quotation from a Negro hymn

—"Free at last, free at last, thank God almighty"—the crowd, recognizing that he was finishing, roared once again and waved their signs and pennants.

But the civil rights leaders, who knew the strength of the forces arrayed against them from past battles, knew also that a hard struggle lay ahead. The tone of their speeches was frequently militant.

Roy Wilkins, executive secretary of the National Association for the Advancement of Colored People, made plain that he and his colleagues thought the President's civil rights bill did not go nearly far enough. He said:

"The President's proposals represent so moderate an approach that if any one is weakened or eliminated, the remainder will be little more than sugar water. Indeed, the package needs strengthening."

Harshest of all the speakers was John Lewis, chairman of the Student Nonviolent Coordinating Committee.

"My friends," he said, "let us not forget that we are involved in a serious social revolution. But by and large American politics is dominated by politicians who build their career on immoral compromising and ally themselves with open forums of political, economic and social exploitation."

He concluded:

"They're talking about slowdown and stop. We will not stop.

"If we do not get meaningful legislation out of this Congress, the time will come when we will not confine our marching to Washington. We will march through the South, through the streets of Jackson, through the streets of Danville, through the streets of Cambridge, through the streets of Birmingham.

"But we will march with the spirit of love and the spirit of dignity that we have shown here today."

In the original text of the speech, distributed last night, Mr. Lewis had said:

"We will not wait for the President, the Justice Department, nor the Congress, but we will take matters into our own hands and create a source of power, outside of any national structure, that could and would assure us a victory."

He also said in the original text that "we will march through the South, through the heart of Dixie, the way Sherman did."

It was understood that at least the last of these statements was changed as the result of a protest by the Most Rev. Patrick J. O'Boyle, Roman Catholic Archbishop of Washington,

who refused to give the invocation if the offending words were spoken by Mr. Lewis.

The great day really began the night before. As a half moon rose over the lagoon by the Jefferson Memorial and the tall, lighted shaft of the Washington Monument gleamed in the reflecting pool, a file of Negroes from out of town began climbing the steps of the Lincoln Memorial.

There, while the carpenters nailed the last planks on the television platforms for the next day and the TV technicians called through the loudspeakers, "Final audio, one, two, three, four," a middle-aged Negro couple, the man's arm around the shoulders of his plump wife, stood and read with their lips:

"If we shall suppose that American slavery is one of the offenses which in the providence of God must come but which having continued through His appointed time, He now wills to remove. . . ."

The day dawned clear and cool. At 7 A. M. the town had a Sunday appearance, except for the shuttle buses drawn up in front of Union Station, waiting.

By 10 A. M. there were 40,-000 on the slopes around the Washington Monument. An hour later the police estimated the crowd at 90,000. And still they poured in.

Because some things went wrong at the monument, everything was right. Most of the stage and screen celebrities **from New York and Hollywood who were scheduled** to begin entertaining the crowd at 10 did not arrive at the airport until 11:15.

As a result the whole affair at the monument grounds began to take on the spontaneity of a church picnic. Even before the entertainment was to begin, groups of high school students were singing with wonderful improvisations and hand-clapping all over the monument slope.

Civil rights demonstrators who had been released from jail in Danville, Va., were singing:

Move on, move on,
Till all the world is free.

And members of Local 144 of the Hotel and Allied Service Employes Union from New York City, an integrated local since 1950, were stomping:

Oh, freedom, we shall not,
we shall not be moved,
Just like a tree that's
planted by the water.

Then the pros took over, starting with the folk singers. The crowd joined in with them.

Joan Baez started things rolling with "the song"—"We Shall Overcome."

Oh deep in my heart I do believe
We shall overcome some day.

And Peter, Paul and Mary sang "How many times must a man look up before he can see the sky."

And Odetta's great, full-throated voice carried almost to Capitol Hill: "If they ask you who you are, tell them you're a child of God."

Jackie Robinson told the crowd that "we cannot be turned back," and Norman Thomas, the venerable Socialist, said: "I'm glad I lived long enough to see this day."

The march to the Lincoln Memorial was supposed to start at 11:30, behind the leaders. But at 11:20 it set off spontaneously down Constitution Avenue behind the Kenilworth Knights, a local drum and bugle corps dazzling in yellow silk blazers, green trousers and green berets.

Apparently forgotten was the intention to make the march to the Lincoln Memorial a solemn tribute to Medgar W. Evers, N.A.A.C.P. official murdered in Jackson, Miss., last June 12, and others who had died for the cause of civil rights.

The leaders were lost, and they never did get to the head of the parade.

The leaders included also Walter P. Reuther, head of the United Automobile Workers; A. Philip Randolph, head of the American Negro Labor Council; the Rev. Dr. Eugene Carson Blake, vice chairman of the Commission on Religion and Race of the National Council of Churches; Mathew Ahmann, executive director of the National Catholic Conference for Interracial Justice; Rabbi Joachim Prinz, president of the American Jewish Congress; Whitney M. Young Jr., executive director of the National Urban League, and James Farmer, president of the Congress of Racial Equality.

All spoke at the memorial except Mr. Farmer, who is in jail in Louisiana following his arrest as a result of a civil rights demonstration. His speech was read by Floyd B. McKissick, CORE national chairman.

At the close of the ceremonies at the Lincoln Memorial, Bayard Rustin, the organizer of the march, asked Mr. Randolph, who conceived it, to lead the vast throng in a pledge.

Repeating after Mr. Randolph, the marchers pledged "complete personal commitment to the struggle for jobs and freedom for Americans" and "to carry the message of the march to my friends and neighbors back home and arouse them to an equal commitment and an equal effort."

# BIRMINGHAM BOMB KILLS 4 NEGRO GIRLS IN CHURCH; RIOTS FLARE; 2 BOYS SLAIN

## GUARD SUMMONED

### Wallace Acts on City Plea for Help as 20 Are Injured

**By CLAUDE SITTON**
Special to The New York Times

BIRMINGHAM, Ala., Sept. 15—A bomb severely damaged a Negro church today during Sunday school services, killing four Negro girls and setting off racial rioting and other violence in which two Negro boys were shot to death.

Fourteen Negroes were injured in the explosion. One Negro and five whites were hurt in the disorders that followed.

Some 500 National Guardsmen in battle dress stood by at armories here tonight, on orders of Gov. George C. Wallace. And 300 state troopers joined the Birmingham police, Jefferson County sheriff's deputies and other law-enforcement units in efforts to restore peace.

Governor Wallace sent the guardsmen and the troopers in response to requests from local authorities.

Sporadic gunfire sounded in Negro neighborhoods tonight, and small bands of residents roamed the streets. Aside from the patrols that cruised the city armed with riot guns, carbines and shotguns, few whites were seen.

#### Fire Bomb Hurled

At one point, three fires burned simultaneously in Negro sections, one at a broom and mop factory, one at a roofing company and a third in another building. An incendiary bomb was tossed into a supermarket, but the flames were extinguished swiftly. Fire marshals investigated blazes at two vacant houses to see if arson was involved.

Mayor Albert Boutwell and other city officials and civic leaders appeared on television station WAPI late tonight and urged residents to cooperate in ending "this senseless reign of terror."

Sheriff Melvin Bailey referred to the day as "the most distressing in the history of Birmingham."

The explosion at the 16th Street Baptist Church this morning brought hundreds of angry Negroes pouring into the streets. Some attacked the police with stones. The police dispersed them by firing shotguns over their heads.

Johnny Robinson, a 16-year-old Negro, was shot in the back and killed by a policeman with a shotgun this afternoon. Officers said the victim was among a group that had hurled stones at white youths driving through the area in cars flying Confederate battle flags.

When the police arrived, the youths fled, and one policeman said he had fired low but that some of the shot had struck the Robinson youth in the back.

Virgil Wade, a 13-year-old Negro, was shot and killed just outside Birmingham while riding a bicycle. The Jefferson County sheriff's office said "there apparently was no reason at all" for the killing, but indicated that it was related to the general racial disorders.

Another Negro youth and a white youth were shot but not seriously wounded in separate incidents. Four whites, including a honeymooning couple from Chicago, were injured by stones while driving through the neighborhood of the bombing.

The bombing, the fourth such incident in less than a month, resulted in heavy damage to the church, to a two-story office building across the street and to a home.

#### Wallace Offers Reward

Governor Wallace, at the request of city officials, offered a $5,000 reward for the arrest and conviction of the bombers.

None of the 50 bombings of Negro property here since World War II have been solved.

Mayor Boutwell and Chief of Police Jamie Moore expressed fear that the bombing, coming on top of tension aroused by desegregation of three schools last week, would bring further violence.

George G. Seibels Jr., chairman of the City Council's police committee, broadcast frequent appeals tonight to white parents, urging them to restrain their children from staging demonstrations tomorrow. He said a repetition of the segregationist motorcades that raced through the streets last Thursday and Friday "could provoke serious trouble, resulting in possible death or injury."

The Rev. Dr. Martin Luther King Jr. arrived tonight by plane from Atlanta. He had led Negroes, who make up almost one-third of Birmingham's popu-

Associated Press Wirephoto
**AFTER BLAST:** Rescue workers examine debris outside Negro church in Birmingham

346

United Press International Telephoto

**READY FOR TROUBLE**: Alabama state troopers congregate in front of Birmingham's City Hall after being called in from all over the state to reinforce the city police.

Associated Press

**ROWD GATHERS**: Policemen move in to disperse crowd of Negroes outside the bombed Church

lation, in a five-week campaign last spring that brought some lunch-counter desegregation and improved job opportunities. The bombed church had been used as the staging point by Negro demonstrators.

**Curfew Plan Rejected**

Col. Albert J. Lingo, State director of Public Safety and commander of the troopers, met with Mayor Boutwell and the City Council in emergency session. They discussed imposition of a curfew but decided against it.

The bombing came five days after the desegregation of three previously all-white schools in Birmingham. The way had been cleared for the desegregation when President Kennedy federalized the Alabama National Guard and the Federal courts issued a sweeping order against Governor Wallace, thus ending his defiance toward the integration step.

The four girls killed in the blast had just heard Mrs. Ella C. Demand, their teacher, complete the Sunday School lesson for the day. The subject was "The Love That Forgives."

During the period between the class and an assembly in the main auditorium, they went to the women's lounge in the basement, at the northeast corner of the church.

The blast occurred at about 10:25 A.M. (12:25 P.M. New York time).

Church members said they found the girls huddled together beneath a pile of masonry debris.

**Parents of 3 Are Teachers**

Both parents of each of three of the victims teach in the city's schools. The dead were identified by University Hospital officials as:

Cynthia Wesley, 14, the only child of Claude A. Wesley, principal of the Lewis Elementary School, and Mrs. Wesley, a teacher there.

Denise McNair, 11, also an only child, whose parents are teachers.

Carol Robertson, 14, whose parents are teachers and whose grandmother, Mrs. Sallie Anderson, is one of the Negro members of a biracial committee established by Mayor Boutwell to deal with racial problems.

Addie Mae Collins, 14, about whom no information was immediately available.

The blast blew gaping holes through walls in the church basement. Floors of offices in the rear of the sanctuary appeared near collapse. Stairways were blocked by splintered window frames, glass and timbers.

Chief Police Inspector W. J. Haley said the impact of the blast indicated that at least 15 sticks of dynamite might have caused it. He said the police had talked to two witnesses who reported having seen a car drive by the church, slow down and then speed away before the blast.

September 16, 1963

# Malcolm X Shot to Death at Rally Here

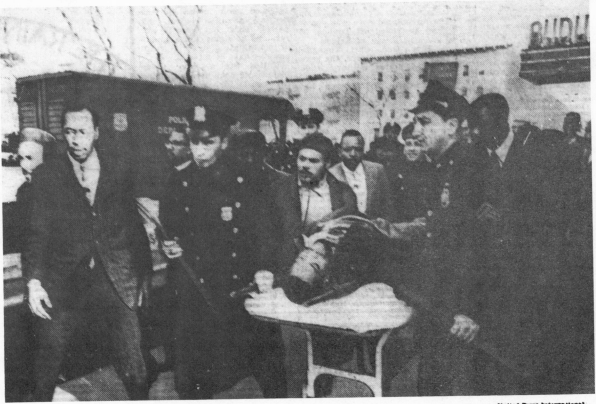

Malcolm X being taken to hospital from Audubon Ballroom yesterday after he was shot while addressing a meeting

## Malcolm Knew He Was a 'Marked Man'

**By THEODORE JONES**

"I live like a man who's already dead," Malcolm X said last Thursday in a two-hour interview in the Harlem office of his Organization for Afro-American Unity.

"I'm a marked man," he said slowly as he fingered the horn-rimmed glasses he wore and leaned forward to give emphasis to his words. "It doesn't frighten me for myself as long as I felt they would not hurt my family."

Asked about "they," Malcolm smiled, shook his head, and said, "those folks down at 116th Street and that man in Chicago."

The references, Malcolm quickly confirmed, were to his former associates in the Black Muslim movement and to Elijah Muhammad, the organizer and head of the movement. Before Malcolm X left the movement 18 months ago, he

was the minister of the Black Muslims' Harlem mosque at 116th Street and Lenox Avenue.

"No one can get out without trouble," Malcolm continued, "and this thing with me will be resolved by death and violence."

Why were they after him? "Because I'm me," he replied.

But realizing that was not enough to say, he pushed into an almost endless flow of sentences.

"I was the spokesman for the Black Muslims," he said. "I believed in Elijah Muhammad more strongly than Christians do in Jesus. I believed in him so strongly that my mind, my body, my voice functioned 100 per cent for him and the movement. My belief led others to believe.

"Now I'm out. And there's the fear if my image isn't

shattered, the Muslims in the movement will leave. Then, they know I know a lot. As long as I was in the movement, anything he [Elijah Muhammad] did was to me by divine guidance."

Malcolm said that he knew many things that made him a "dangerous man to the movement."

"But I didn't want to harm anyone or the movement when I got out," he added. "But I had learned to disbelieve, sir, and Mr. Muhammad knew that I would fight against him if I did not believe and he threatened."

The man, who was once the dynamic spokesman for the Black Muslims, suddenly leaned forward and began watching the traffic at Seventh Avenue and 125th Street through the large picture window of his private office in the Hotel Theresa. He began talking again, but this time he spoke as if there was only the battered mahog-

any desk and the rusted, three-section filing cabinet in the small room.

"I know brothers in the movement who were given orders to kill me," he said slowly, nodding his head and rubbing his small goatee. "I've had highly placed people within tell me, 'be careful, Malcolm.'"

"The press gives the impression that I'm jiving about this thing," he said, turning, but not accusing his visitor. "They ignore the evidence and the actual attempts."

How did Malcolm see the future and his feud with the Black Muslims?

"I have no feud with the Black Muslims, sir. This is a one-sided thing. Those that have done violence are fanatics who think they are doing the will of God when they go and maim and cripple those who left the movement."

Those who left the movement, Malcolm continued, "have not been involved in violence against those within," adding: "I believe in taking action, but not action against black people. No, sir."

What about the comments by people in Harlem that now they do not know where Malcolm X stands? Is it possible to change so suddenly?

He smiled, opened his black suit jacket, and began rubbing his fingers along the black sweater vest he wore underneath.

"I won't deny I don't know where I'm at," he said with a boyish grin. "But by the same token how many of us put the finger down on one point and say I'm here."

"I know that I'm 1,000 per cent against the Ku Klux Klan, the Rockwells and any organized white groups that are against the black people in this country," he said, in reference to Lincoln Rockwell, leader of the Nazi party in the United States, and such groups as the Citizens Council.

Then assessing his present situation, he observed:

"I feel like a man who has been asleep somewhat and under someone else's control. I feel what I'm thinking and saying now is for myself. Before, it was for and by the guidance of Elijah Muhammad. Now I think with my own mind, sir."

## Malcolm X's Sister Says He Was "Living in Fear"

BOSTON, Feb. 21 (AP)—Malcolm X's older sister said tonight her brother knew he was marked for death.

Mrs. Ella Mae Collins, proprietor of a rooming house in the city's South End, said she spent yesterday with her brother in New York and he had told her: "They are after me. They won't rest until they get me."

Mrs. Collins said her brother, who she described as 'living in fear,' carried a gun as he walked about in his room yesterday and had kept peering through drawn window shades.

# FREEDOM MARCH BEGINS AT SELMA; TROOPS ON GUARD

### 3,200 Take Part in Protest as 54-Mile Rights Walk to Montgomery Starts

### DR. KING HAILS MISSION

### Envisions 'a New Alabama' and 'a New America'— Crowd's Mood Festive

**By ROY REED**
Special to The New York Times

SELMA, Ala., March 21 — Backed by the armed might of the United States, 3,200 persons marched out of Selma today on the first leg of a historic venture in nonviolent protest.

The marchers, or at least many of them, are on their way to the State Capitol at Montgomery to submit a petition for Negro rights Thursday to Gov. George C. Wallace, a man with little sympathy for their cause.

Today was the third attempt for the Alabama Freedom March. On the first two, the marchers were stopped by state troopers, the first time with tear gas and clubs.

The troopers were on hand today, but they limited themselves to helping Federal troops handle traffic on U.S. Highway 80 as the marchers left Selma.

### Soldiers Line Highway

Hundreds of Army and federalized National Guard troops stood guard in Selma and lined the highway out of town to protect the marchers. The troops were sent by President Johnson after Governor Wallace said that Alabama could not afford the expense of protecting the march.

The marchers were in festive humor as they started. The tone was set by the Rev. Ralph D. Abernathy, top aide to the Rev. Dr. Martin Luther King Jr. in the Southern Christian Leadership Conference, as he introduced Dr. King for an address before the march started.

"When we get to Montgomery," Mr. Abernathy said, "we are going to go up to Governor Wallace's door and say, 'George, it's all over now. We've got the ballot.'"

The throng laughed and cheered.

### Seven Miles Covered

The marchers, a large majority of them Negroes, walked a little over seven miles today.

Governor Wallace is not expected to be at the State Capitol when the marchers arrive at the end of their 54-mile journey. An aide has said that he will probably be "in Michigan, or someplace" making a speech Thursday.

Not enough buses could be found to escort 2,900 of the 3,200 marchers back to Selma tonight in line with a Federal Court order limiting the number to 300 along a two-lane stretch of highway.

The authorities feared for the safety of those returning to Selma. Justice Department officials finally arranged with the Southern Railway for a special train of the Western Railway of Alabama to take them back. The Western is a subsidiary of the Southern.

### Johnson Praised

Highway 80 narrows from a four-lane to a two-lane road about five miles past the point where the marchers stopped tonight. It widens to four lanes again as it approaches Montgomery.

In his talk at the start of the march, Dr. King praised President Johnson, saying of his voting-rights message to Congress last Monday: "Never has a President spoken so eloquently or so sincerely on the question of civil rights."

Then he turned to the crowd in front of Browns Chapel Methodist Church, the thousands of whites and Negroes from Alabama and around the country who were congregated for the march, and said:

"You will be the people that will light a new chapter in the history books of our nation. Those of us who are Negroes don't have much. We have known the long night of poverty. Because of the system, we don't have much education and some of us don't know how to make our nouns and verbs agree. But thank God we have our bodies, our feet and our souls.

"Walk together, children, don't you get weary, and it will lead us to the promised land. And Alabama will be a new Alabama, and America will be a new America."

Dr. King's sense of history, if not his optimism, seemed well-placed. The Alabama march appears destined for a niche in the annals of the great protest demonstrations.

The march is the culmination of a turbulent nine-week campaign that began as an effort to abolish restrictions on Negro voting in the Alabama Black Belt and widened finally to encompass a general protest against racial injustice in the state.

The drive has left two men dead and scores injured. Some 3,800 persons have been arrested in Selma and neighboring communities.

The march got under way at 12:47 P.M., 2 hours 47 minutes late, after a confused flurry of last-minute planning and organizing.

The marchers reached the first night's campsite, 7.3 miles east of Selma, at 5:30. When they got there they found four big tents pitched in a Negro farmer's field.

Leading the march with Dr. King were Dr. Ralph J. Bunche, United Nations Under Secretary for Special Political Affairs; the Right Rev. Richard Millard, Suffragan Bishop of the Episcopal Diocese of California, and Cager Lee, grandfather of Jimmie Lee Jackson, the young Negro killed by a state trooper last month at Marion, Ala.

Also among the leaders were John Lewis, president of the Student Nonviolent Coordinating Committee; Deaconess Phyllis Edwards of the Episcopal Diocese of California; Rabbi Abraham Heschel, professor of Jewish mysticism and ethics at the Jewish Theological Seminary in New York; Mr. Abernathy, and the Rev. Frederick D. Reese, a Negro minister from Selma, who is president of the Dallas County Voters League.

### 2,000 Spectators

About 2,000 white and Negro spectators watched the procession leave town. That was 4,000 fewer than Army Intelligence had predicted.

About 150 whites watched in silence as the march turned from Alabama Avenue and headed down Broad Street toward Edmund Pettus Bridge. A white man hoisted his young son to his shoulder to give the lad a better view. Several persons snapped pictures.

Brig. Gen. Henry V. Graham, a National Guard officer, commanded all Federal troops on the scene, including the Regular Army military policemen. General Graham, a tall, square-jawed man, stood in the middle of Pettus Bridge wearing a helmet as he directed the operation.

Two state trooper cars led the procession across the bridge. In the lead car was Maj. John Cloud, the man who directed the rout, with tear gas and nightsticks, of 525 Negro

# The Big Parade: On the Road to Montgomery

The Rev. Dr. Martin Luther King Jr. leads marchers from Browns Chapel Methodist Church in Selma. He is flanked by the Rev. Ralph D. Abernathy, left, and Dr. Ralph J. Bunche, U.N. Under Secretary. Paul R. Screvane, New York City Council President, is third in line behind Dr. King. Mrs. Constance Baker Motley, Manhattan Borough President, is beside him. Mrs. Ruby Hurley, Southeastern Secretary of the N.A.A.C.P., is behind Mr. Abernathy.

marchers near the foot of the same bridge two weeks ago.

The marchers passed the site of the bloody incident without signal, except for a reminder from a white heckler.

It was to protest the officers' rout of the first marchers that the Rev. James J. Reeb, a white Unitarian minister from Boston, came to Selma with scores of other clergymen. While he was here, Mr. Reeb was fatally beaten by a band of white men on March 9.

The heckler held up a sign as the procession left Pettus Bridge early this afternoon. It read, "Too bad, Reeb."

A few feet away, another white spectator held a sign saying, "I hate niggers."

### More Hecklers

More whites heckled from a railroad embankment running along the highway. They apparently were upset over the way the marchers were carrying a United States flag. They were carrying it upside down, the position of the distress signal.

On down the road, three cars painted with anti-Negro slogans passed in the south section of the fou lane highway. One car, with a Mississippi license plate, bore the words "Meridian, Miss., hates niggers." A Confederate flag flew from the radio aerial. The lettering on another car said, "Go home scum."

Back in town some 20 stragglers ran up Broad Street toward the bridge with knapsacks bouncing on their backs, trying to catch the procession, which had already disappeared over the bridge. The marchers walked on the left side of the highway.

The Federal presence was everywhere, even in the air. About a dozen planes and helicopters, many of them manned by military personnel, flew over the procession constantly.

John Doar, head of the Civil Rights Division of the Justice Department, walked to one side at the head of the march, watching.

Maj. Gen. Carl C. Turner, Provost Marshal General of the United States Army, was on the scene as the personal representative of the Army Chief of Staff, Gen. Harold K. Johnson.

By radio, Federal agents reported minute by minute to the Justice Department and the Pentagon in Washington.

M.P.'s guarded every crossroad, leapfrogging in Jeeps to stay ahead of the march.

There was one report of violence. An unidentified white minister riding in an advance car was said to have been attacked by four white men when he got out of the car on the side of the road.

A spokesman for the marchers said the minister had been struck on the face once and knocked to the ground but had not been seriously hurt.

Today's leg of the journey

**RESPITE ALONG U.S. 80:** Civil rights marchers relax on median strip during the first leg of their 50-mile hike to Montgomery, where they will press for Negroes' rights.

tered along the highway on the outskirts of the city.

At Craig Air Force Base, five miles east on Highway 80, a dozen big Army trucks could be seen from the road. They were filled with armed troops.

The temperature was 2 degrees above freezing when people began gathering in Sylvan Street this morning. The sun came out brilliantly, and by 11 A.M. the temperature was up to 42 degrees.

The marchers were out in everything from shirtsleeves to heavy coats. One elderly Negro wore a dress Air Force topcoat and a heavy wool headpiece that covered his head, throat and most of his face.

Paul R. Screvane, president of the New York City Council, showed up in a suit and blue overcoat. He and Mrs. Constance Baker Motley, Manhattan's Negro Borough President, joined the milling crowd in front of Browns Chapel at mid-morning.

was cut short four miles by a court injunction obtained by a white landowner who did not want the marchers camping overnight on his land. A Negro tenant had agreed to let them camp there.

The march leaders found a new campsite. The Negro farmer's field where they slept tonight is about a quarter of a mile south of the highway.

The field is about 500 yards from the New Sister Springs Baptist Church. It was at the church that the marchers returning to Selma tonight boarded rented Greyhound buses and numerous automobiles that shuttled them to the railway loading point about a mile from the campsite.

Most of those who left the march this way spent the night, as many had spent previous nights, with Negro families in Selma.

Some will remain in Alabama and rejoin the march Thursday, the final day. Leaders of the march hope to arrive at Montgomery in impressive numbers.

The military authorities are concerned about protection for the marchers at night. Show business personalities such as Harry Belafonte and Lena Horne are scheduled to entertain the group every night. The officials fear that outsiders may come to the camps to see and hear the entertainers, and that troublemakers may infiltrate at the same time.

A military spokesman said the troops had no authority to search cars for weapons.

Although the weather was relatively warm for the beginning of the march, the temperature dropped below freezing.

The coming of the troops to Selma has produced none of the crushing grimness of the Federal presence that characterized the Government's intervention at Little Rock, Ark., in 1957 and Oxford, Miss., in 1962.

The main difference is that troops were used in the earlier instances to suppress violence already out of hand, or threatening to get out of hand, while they were brought here to prevent violence.

Most of Selma's whites today went about their Sunday morning business, which is church, and only a few bothered with the commotion on Sylvan Street.

About 30 whites gathered at Broad Street and Alabama Avenue at midmorning to wait for the march to go by. The march was late, as expected, and while they waited half a dozen spectators joshed with the four armed military policemen stationed there.

The state and local authorities have repeatedly urged Alabama whites to stay away from U.S. Highway 80 while the march is in progress.

Early this morning, two or three armed M.P.'s were deployed at each intersection on the march route in the city. More were strung out along Highway 80 on the other side of Edmund Pettus Bridge. Several state troopers were scat-

**Marchers on U.S. 80 after crossing Edmund Pettus Bridge**

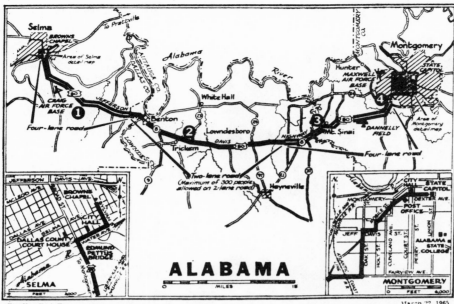

March 22, 1965

**MARCH ROUTE:** Demonstrators left Browns Chapel Church in Selma and marched to New Sister Springs Church (1), near where 300 camped. They were to stop overnight Monday at a farm (2), Tuesday at a church (3), and Wednesday at the City of St. Jude (4), a Catholic institution serving Negroes. From there they planned to continue until Thursday to the Capitol in Montgomery, where the march will end. The farm and the church on the route were not identified for security reasons.

Mr. Screvane explained why he was there.

"We came to represent Mayor Wagner and, we hope, the people of New York in what we consider to be a just cause," he said.

Dozens of union officials and clergymen came in today and joined the hundreds of ministers and students and civil rights workers already here.

A fresh college group arrived, 33 students and three professors from Canisius College, a Roman Catholic institution in Buffalo, N. Y. A sign thrust up from the group said, "Civil Man Wants Civil Rights."

Early today, plans for the march were still being hammered out. At 8 A.M., 400 or 500 persons milled in the street.

Milling has become the style of the movement in recent weeks, and the character of the milling has changed as hundreds of whites from the North, East and West have come into town to add their protest to the Negro's. The outsiders mill with a greater air of purpose.

The marchers who showed up very early today in front of Browns Chapel were from the hard core of the movement. Others did not begin to appear on Sylvan Street until the sun was high.

The Alabama Freedom March has a long history, as the leaders see it. The Rev. Andrew Young, executive assistant to Dr. King in the Southern Christian Leadership Conference, told reporters last night that the whole Alabama project went back to the Birmingham church bombing of 1963 in which five Negro children were killed.

"At that time," he said, "we began to ask ourselves, 'What can we do to change the climate of an entire state?'"

The Black Belt movement began that year. The Student Nonviolent Coordinating Committee moved into Selma, which calls itself queen of the Alabama Black Belt—the swath of rich, dark soil and heavy Negro population across south-central Alabama—and began holding meetings and demonstrations.

Dr. King and the Southern Christian Leadership Conference came here last January and put the Selma movement on the map.

**FEDERAL PROTECTION:** Soldiers, prepared to prevent trouble,

posted along the line of march outside Selma

March 22, 1965

# 2,000 TROOPS ENTER LOS ANGELES ON THIRD DAY OF NEGRO RIOTING; 4 DIE AS FIRES AND LOOTING GROW

## YOUTHS RUN WILD

### Violence Spreads to City's White Areas— Shots Exchanged

**By PETER BART**
Special to The New York Times

LOS ANGELES, Saturday, Aug. 14—Two thousand heavily armed National Guardsmen moved into Los Angeles last night to battle rioters in the burning and looted Negro area.

The Guardsmen were under orders to use rifles, machine guns, tear gas and bayonets in support of a battered contingent of 900 policemen and deputy sheriffs.

Four persons were killed in the rioting yesterday, including three Negroes and a police officer. Thirty-three police officers had been injured, 75 civilians seriously injured, and 249 rioters had been arrested. This morning violence spread to white areas.

Gangs of Negroes appeared last night in various parts of Los Angeles County, up to 20 miles from the riot scene. One group of about 25 Negroes started tossing rocks in San Pedro in the harbor area, while another group appeared in Pacoima, a Negro community in the San Fernando Valley. Police units dispersed these groups.

**Gun Fire Exchanged**

The National Guardsmen were being brought into the riot zone early this morning in small convoys led by jeeps with machine guns mounted on them. The convoys contained one or two troop carriers. One Guard unit opened machine-gun fire for 10-minutes on a gang of Negroes who then fled down the street. One Guardsman said the rioters fired with pistols and at least one rifle. No one was apparent-

ly hit. The Guardsmen continued to penetrate the riot area.

"They've got weapons and ammo," one Guard spokesman said. "It's going to be like Vietnam."

Indications in other areas were that the Negroes were dispersing in the face of the reinforcements and were reforming in other areas.

**Fire Out of Control**

A National Guard spokesman said that besides the 2,000 men in the area, thousands more were on their way.

The Guard, he said, plans to "hit them and make them stop."

Riflemen will have bayonets fixed and ammunition will be readily available, he said.

"They will pursue the bands of rioters in detachments, operating in convoys led by jeeps with machineguns on them," he said.

Throughout the Negro section, crowds numbering in the thousands were chanting, "White devils what are you doing here?"

At one point the Negro rioters charged Oak Park Hospital, where many of those injured and wounded in the riots were being treated. The hospital locked its fire doors and the rioters left after shattering its front windows.

Officials reported that they had abandoned efforts to halt a fire sweeping a three-block section after Negroes hurled fire bombs and rocks at the fire fighters. Negro youths later took complete control of another two-block area and set 15 fires to homes and stores.

As the rioting continued to penetrate north and east toward white neighborhoods, police sound trucks went up and down the streets warning residents to stay in their homes and lock their doors.

The first fatality came last night, when a deputy sheriff, Ronald E. Ludlow, 27 years old, died in the emergency room at St. Francis Hospital in Lynwood. He had been shot in the stomach.

Later, the police reported an unidentified Negro in his mid-30's had been found dead of bullet wounds on a street not far from the riot area.

The police said the third and fourth deaths were a Negro looter, who was shot dead at 28th Street and Central Avenue and a demonstrator who was shot dead at 97th and Figueroa.

As many as 14 fires were raging on one street alone—103d Street in Watts—and it was believed that not a single business in that commercial center would remain intact. Most of the stores are believed owned by whites.

The rattle of gunfire was heard increasingly in the Negro section during the hot, smoggy evening as the police confronted roving bands of rampaging Negroes.

The Negroes, in three days and nights, have looted uncounted stores, overturned and burned more than 150 automobiles and set over 100 fires.

The 150-block section of Los Angeles last night took on the pearance of a war zone with men crouching in the shadows, streets littered with debris or completely torn up, store windows broken and scorched and a pall of smoke hanging over the area.

No accurate tally of injuries was possible, since many of the injured Negroes have remained within the riot area.

Ambulances attempting to penetrate the area have been met with a shower of rocks and occasional Molotov cocktails—bottles of gasoline with wicks.

The rioting started Wednesday night after a routine drunken-driving arrest near the predominantly Negro Watts section of Los Angeles. It was resumed Thursday night when some 7,000 Negroes took to the streets.

After a lull, rioting flared again yesterday morning with hundreds of roving Negro gangs spilling over into surrounding areas. Last night the police estimated as many as 7,000 Negroes again were on the streets.

Sociologists were divided on the causes of the riots. Some blamed Negro resentment over civil rights strife in the South, while others cited a lack of communication between the whites and Negroes.

Unlike many race riots, the south Los Angeles melee has no main combat front.

"It's guerrilla warfare," said Chief of Police William H. Parker. As the night wore on the warfare seemed to be shifting steadily north toward downtown Los Angeles.

Helicopters operated by the police and by radio and television stations covering the riots were repeatedly fired upon by Negroes on the ground.

The police late in the evening opened fire on a menacing mob of 1,000 rioters two miles northwest of the point of the first rioting.

The fire department estimated loss from fires at over $10 million.

Several Negroes exchanging gunfire with police emerged from the garage carrying a wounded woman. One of the Negroes waved a white flag.

In a nearby area, police escorted some 40 employes, many of them white, from a factory after receiving phone calls that their plant had been surrounded by rioters.

**Asked for Guard in Morning**

Chief Parker asked for National Guard support at 10:30 yesterday morning but it was not until 5:05 P.M. that the order was signed by Lieut. Gov. Glenn M. Anderson, acting for vacationing Gov. Edmund G. Brown.

Chief Parker and other city officials angrily denounced the delay in calling up the Guard.

The units mobilized are from the 40th Armored Division of the National Guard, which was scheduled to go to summer camp this weekend.

The fire situation was reported critical. One six-block area was engulfed by several fires. A dress manufacturing company, several markets and countless other shops were in flames.

One Fire Department spokesman said his engines had been able to reach only a few fires.

An orange pall of smoke hung in the sky above south Los Angeles this morning as more than 30 major fires raged out of control. One of the biggest fires leveled the Friendly Furniture Company factory and quickly spread to five nearby Negro homes. Firemen said they could not as yet reach most of the fires because rioters greeted the fire engines with Molotov cocktails and rocks.

Mayor Samuel Yorty tonight said it might be several days

353

before the situation is in complete control. The riots were being spearheaded by "the criminal element" he said.

Witnesses described the scene inside the riot zone as "terrifying" and "hysterical." One Negro merchant said a pack of shrieking Negro teen-agers suddenly hurtled into his store. Within minutes he said they had looted the store and set it afire.

Another Negro merchant, J. W. Heath, said clusters of Negroes were standing around the street deciding which stores to attack.

One Negro who was seen leaving the riot area said he had been hiding in his apartment for two days never daring even to turn on the lights. He said he had seen Negroes making Molotov cocktails outside his window.

At one point the rioters tried to storm a police station but were beaten off. They inflicted considerable damage on a post-office in the Watts area.

One clerk said, "I've been in this neighborhood for years and I couldn't recognize a single face among those boys."

A Negro handyman who was eating a snack at Foxies Freeze near the riot zone remarked:

"Most of these rioters are young toughs from all over the city who don't have anything better to do."

Scores of homeowners and apartment dwellers in the area were phoning police asking to be evacuated from the neighborhood. A center for hundreds of refugees was set up in a church near the riot zone.

There were several cases of Negroes saving the lives of white victims. Bishop R. J. Morris, a Methodist minister, ignored angry threats from Negroes to rescue a teen-age couple whose car had been stoned and who had been badly beaten by the mob.

"Go back to your church," one rioter warned.

"I'm going to help these young people," the minister replied. He drove off with them in his car.

Mrs. Michele LeGrave, a 21-year-old white woman, was rescued by a Negro motorist after her car was stoned and she was forced to abandon it.

The rioters were reported to be setting fires, then standing in the street to stone fire equipment that tried to get to the scene.

One Negro with a stream from his garden hose tried to extinguish a roaring fire in four stores on Avalon Boulevard, central street in the rioting.

Witnesses at the riot scene described a bizarre atmosphere.

"Everything seems calm for a

Associated Press Wirephotos

**FIRE:** Smoke rises from fires set by rioters in Watts area. They burned out of control.

**DESTRUCTION:** Overturned burned-out autos block the street after second day of riots

moment, then suddenly there's a pack coming down on you," a Negro minister said. "Surging mobs turned up unexpectedly at the 77th Street police station tossing rocks and other debris and then rushed away when police with rifles took up positions outside the station.

One Negro told of a band of armed Negroes that went from store to store tossing bricks through windows and looting the contents. All the men carried pistols or rifles, he said, and the group appeared to be led by a huge woman who was carrying several bricks.

Among the injured was Dick Gregory, the Negro comedian, who was shot Thursday night while trying to calm the crowd.

He termed the outbreak "the worst riot I've ever seen."

Mr. Gregory was hit in the thigh as he pleaded with rioters to disperse. After being wounded he rose to his feet and shouted. "You shot me once, now get off the streets!" No one obeyed.

Mr. Gregory was taken to the hospital, treated for a minor wound and then returned to the riot area.

Mr. Gregory was just one of scores of Negroes who have been injured in the rioting. Many of the rioters apparently are not interested in the race of their targets.

The riots already have produced bitterness. One Roman Catholic organization, Catholics

United for Racial Equality, called on Pope Paul VI to oust James Francis Cardinal Mc-Intyre, Archbishop of the Los Angeles Diocese, on the ground that he had "contributed to the current racial outbursts."

The Cardinal, meanwhile, said he was "grieved that the splendid spirit and high moral integrity of the Negro people in our beloved city is being besmirched by the happenings of recent days." He termed the riots "unjustified."

The guardsmen are commanded by Col. Irving J. Taylor. The Second Brigade has 1,000 officers and men from Burbank, Inglewood, Glendale, Long Beach and Santa Ana.

August 14, 1965

# The Call Of the Black Panthers

By SOL STERN

SAN FRANCISCO.

IN early May, front pages across America carried the illustrated story of an "armed invasion" of the California Legislature by a group of black men known as the Black Panther Party for Self Defense. What actually happened that day in Sacramento was something less than the beginning of a Negro insurrection, but it was no less important for all that: The appearance of the gun-bearing Panthers at the white Capitol was a dramatic portent of something that is stirring in the Northern black ghettos.

By any yardstick used by the civil-rights movement, the Panther organization is not yet very important or effective. The Panthers' political influence in the Negro community remains marginal. The voice of the Panthers is a discordant one, full of the rhetoric of revolutionary violence, and seemingly out of place in affluent America. But it is a voice that ought to be studied. Like it or not, it is increasingly the voice of young ghetto blacks who in city after city this summer have been confronting cops with bricks, bottles and bullets.

THE Panthers came to Sacramento from their homes in the San Francisco Bay Area not to "invade" or to "take over" the Legislature, but simply to exercise their right to attend a session of the Legislature and to state their opposition to a pending bill. The bill was, and is, intended to impose severe restrictions on the carrying of loaded weapons in public —a practice not prohibited by present law so long as the weapons are unconcealed. Since the Panthers have been in the habit of carrying loaded weapons at rallies and public meetings, they regarded the legislation as aimed at them in particular and at black people in general. The only thing that was unusual about their lobbying junket is that they brought their loaded guns with them.

The Panthers arrived in hot, dry, lifeless Sacramento and descended on the Capitol with M-1 rifles and 12-gauge shotguns cradled in their arms, .45-caliber pistols visible on their hips, cartridge belts around their

SOL STERN is assistant managing editor of Ramparts magazine.

waists. Up the white steps and between the classic marble pillars they marched, in two columns, young, black and tough-looking in their leather jackets, boots and tight-fitting clothes. As they marched grimly down the immaculate halls, secretaries and tourists gaped and then moved quickly out of the way. By the time they were halfway down the corridor, every reporter and cameraman in the building had gathered; they stayed in front of the Panthers, moving backward, snapping pictures as they went.

THE Panthers, though all were experts on firearms legislation, did not know their way around the building; they followed the reporters and cameramen who were backing toward the legislative chamber. Instead of veering off toward the spectators' galleries, the group flowed right into the Assembly, past guards who were either too startled or simply too slow to stop them.

Actually, it was the photographers, moving backward, who were the first to move through the large oak doors at the rear of the chamber. The Speaker, seeing the commotion, asked the guards to "clear those cameramen." By the time the legislators realized what was happening behind them, most of the group of cameramen and Panthers had been moved out of the chamber. Outside in the corridor, the guards took some guns away from the Panthers—but since the Panthers were not breaking any law, they had to return them. The Panthers read their statement of protest to the reporters and television cameramen, and left. That would have been all, except for a car that broke down.

A Sacramento police officer spotted the armed Panthers at the gas station at which they stopped for repairs, and sent out a hurried call for reinforcements. This time, the Panthers were arrested on a variety of charges, including some stemming from obscure fish-and-game laws. After they had been in jail overnight, the Sacramento District Attorney changed all the charges; 18 members of the group, now out on bail, await trial for disrupting the State Legislature—a misdemeanor—and for conspiracy to disrupt the Legislature—a felony.

As lobbyists, the Black Panthers

are not very effective; but then, the Panthers did not really care much whether the gun bill passed or not. Their purpose was to call attention to their claim that black people in the ghetto must rely on armed self-defense and not the white man's courts to protect themselves.

THE adventure at the Capitol assured the passage of the gun legislation, however, and it will soon be signed into law—welcome news to Bay Area police chiefs, who have been frustrated ever since the Panthers first started carrying their loaded weapons in public. In Oakland, across the bay from San Francisco, the police have not waited for the new legislation; they regularly arrest armed Panthers, usually on charges of brandishing a weapon in a threatening manner. The Panthers insist that this is merely harassment, but they have tactically retreated and usually now leave their guns at home.

For the Panthers, their guns have had both real and symbolic meaning —real because they believe they will have to use the guns, eventually, against the white power structure that they charge is suppressing them; symbolic because of the important political effects they think that a few blacks, openly carrying guns, can have in the black community.

"Ninety per cent of the reason we carried guns in the first place," says Panther leader Huey P. Newton, "was educational. We set the example. We made black people aware that they have the right to carry guns."

Only seven years ago, when the head of the Monroe, N. C., chapter of the National Association for the Advancement of Colored People proposed that Negroes should shoot back when armed bands of white rednecks start shooting up the Negro section of town, he set off a furor in the national civil-rights movements and turned himself into a pariah. Robert Williams, eventually charged with kidnapping in what his supporters insist was a frame-up, ultimately left America for Cuba and then China, a revolutionary in exile. It was a short time ago; much has happened in black America since the simple proposal of armed self-defense could provoke so much tumult.

THE Black Panther Party for Self Defense was organized principally by 25-year-old Huey Newton and 30-year-old Bobby Seale. Newton

355

looks younger than his years, is tall and lithe, with handsome, almost sculptured features. His title is Minister of Defense, while his darker and more mature-looking friend, Seale, is the chairman. The Minister of Defense is preeminent because, they say, they are in a condition of war. "Black people realize," Newton says, "that they are already at war with the racist white power structure."

Being at war, they are reluctant to give out strategic information about the internal workings of their organization. As they put it, quoting Malcolm X: "Those who know don't say and those who say don't know." Outside estimates of their membership run anywhere from 75 to 200, organized into small units in the various black communities in the Bay area. Each unit has a captain; the captains, along with Newton, Seale and a treasurer, make up an executive committee which sets basic policy for the entire organization. The Panthers get out their message of armed self-defense to the black communities through a biweekly newspaper, and on Saturdays there are outdoor street rallies.

On a sunny Saturday at the end of June, two such rallies were scheduled. The first was on San Francisco's Potrero Hill, at a nearly all-black housing project composed of decaying World War II barracks that should have been torn down years ago. Desolate and windy, the project overlooks an industrial section of the city jammed between Potrero Hill and the Bay. It is an ugly and depressing place.

By the time Huey Newton and Bobby Seale arrive from the other side of the Bay, there are about 30 young blacks milling around at the rally site, a dead-end street which serves as a parking lot in the middle of the development. Newton and Seale do not seem disappointed at the turnout. Seale turns over a city garbage can, stands on it and announces that the rally will begin. A half-dozen curious children come running over as the bloods gather. Some women poke their heads out of windows overlooking the street. There is not a white face in sight, nor a policeman, unless someone in the crowd is an undercover agent.

Seale explains the Black Panther Party for Self Defense and the significance of its name. It was inspired, he says, by the example of the Lowndes County Freedom Organization in Alabama, which first adopted the black-panther symbol. That symbol, Seale says, is an appropriate one for black people in America today. "It is not in the panther's nature to attack anyone first, but when he is attacked and backed into a corner, he will respond viciously and wipe out the aggressor."

Seale then introduces the Minister of Defense; Huey Newton provides a 15-minute capsule history of the Negro struggle in America, and then begins to relate it to the world revolution and to the example of the people of Vietnam. "There were only 30 million of them," Newton says of the Vietnamese, "but first they threw out the Japanese, then they drove out the French and now they are kicking hell out of the Americans and you better believe it, brothers." Black people can learn lessons from the fight of the Vietnamese, Newton continues; black people in America also must arm themselves for self-defense against the same racist army. "Every time you go execute a white racist Gestapo cop, you are defending yourself," he concludes.

**W**HEN Seale returns to the garbage-can platform, the crowd is already with him, shouting "That's right" and "You tell it" as he speaks.

"All right, brothers," he tells them, "let's understand what we want. We have to change our tactics. Black people can't just mass on the streets and riot. They'll just shoot us down." Instead, it is necessary to organize in small groups to "take care of business." The "business" includes among other things "executing racist cops."

Graphically, Seale describes how a couple of bloods can surprise cops on their coffee break. The Negroes march up to the cop and then "they shoot him down—voom, voom —with a 12-gauge shotgun." That, says Seale, would be an example of "righteous power." No more "praying and bootlicking." No more singing of "We Shall Overcome." "The only way you're going to over-

come is to apply righteous power."

Seale tells the young crowd not to be impressed by the fact that Negroes are only an 11 per cent minority in America. "We have potential destructive power. Look around at those factories down there. If we don't get what we want, we can make it impossible for the man's system to function. All we got to do is drop some cocktails into those oil tanks and then watch everything go."

No one in the crowd questions the propriety of the Black Panther program. One man says that it sounds O.K. but it's all talk and the trouble is that, when it's time for action, "most of the bloods cut out." Seale says that's true, but "we have to organize."

While a few of the bloods take membership applications and give their names to the local captain, Seale and Newton jump into a car and race across the Bay Bridge to the second rally in Richmond, 20 miles away on the east side of the bay, just north of Berkeley. Only the surroundings are different: It is a ghetto of tiny homes and rundown cottages with green lawns and carports. The rally is held on the lawn of George Dowell, who joined the Panthers after his brother Denzil was shot and killed by the police. Denzil Dowell's body was riddled with six shotgun pellets. The police say he was shot trying to escape after he was caught breaking into a store. The Panthers and many of the people in the neighborhood say simply that he was murdered.

During the rally George Dowell patrols the fringes of the small group, carrying a loaded .30-.30 rifle. Another Panther stands on the Dowell roof, demonstrating the loading of a shotgun with a 20-inch barrel — a gun which Bobby Seale tells the group he recommends highly.

Driving away from the rally, a tired Huey Newton jokes with a pretty girl who is his date that evening. She is a member of the Panthers, and has her hair done African style. She says that Richmond reminds her of Watts, where she grew up; the people in Richmond, she adds, are very warm and friendly. Newton agrees.

Asked whether the talk at

rallies about killing cops is serious, Newton replies that it is very serious. Then why, he is asked, stake everything, including the lives of the Panthers, on the killing of a couple of cops?

"It won't be just a couple of cops," he says, "when the time comes, it will be part of a whole national coordinated effort." Is he willing to kill a cop? Yes, he answers, and when the time comes he is willing to die. What does he think is going to happen to him?

"I am going to be killed," he says with a smile on his face. He looks very young.

**T**O Oakland's chief of police, Robert Preston, the Panthers are hardly worth commenting upon. "It's not the police but society that should be concerned with groups such as this," said Preston, displaying a cool response to the Panthers that perhaps masks a deeper concern. On second thought, Preston said: "They have on occasion harassed police and made some efforts to stir up animosity against us, but they are not deserving of any special treatment. They have made pretty ridiculous assertions which don't deserve to be dignified by anyone commenting on them."

Some of Preston's men on the beat were less reluctant to voice their gut reactions to the Panthers. One of them issued a series of unprintable epithets; another, giggling, suggested, "Maybe those guys ought to pick their best gunman and we pick ours and then have an old-fashioned shoot-it-out."

Despite Huey Newton's fatalism, the Panthers are not simply nihilistic terrorists. When confronted by the police and placed under arrest, as they were in Sacramento, the Panthers have so far surrendered their guns and submitted peacefully. If cops are to be shot—and there is no reason to question the Panthers' willingness to do this—it will be part of a general plan of action which they hope will force revolutionary changes in the society. The Panthers see the white cops in the ghetto as a "foreign occupying army" whose job is to prevent that change by force.

Reflecting on the outbreaks in Northern ghettos recently,

Huey Newton said, "They were rebellions and a part of the revolutionary struggle, even though incorrect methods were used. But people learn warfare by indulging in warfare. That's the way they learn better tactics. When people go into the streets in large numbers they are more easily contained. We ought to look to historic revolutions such as Vietnam and learn to wear the enemy down. The way to do that is to break up into groups of threes and fours."

The Panther program calls for the black community to become independent and self-governing. The Negro community in which the Panthers held their second rally that Saturday is an unincorporated part of Contra Costa County; the Panthers are organizing a petition drive that would put the question of incorporation on the ballot. If they should succeed, they will accomplish by legal means one of the goals for which they say they are ultimately willing to engage in violence—removal of the white man's government from the black community.

LIKE most revolutionaries, the leaders of the Black Panthers do not come from the bottom of the economic ladder. Huey Newton could have escaped from the ghetto, if he had wanted to. He went to the integrated and excellent Berkeley High School, and eventually spent a year in law school. Bright but rebellious, he had numerous run-ins with the authorities (he always remembers them as "white authorities") in high school before he finally was graduated, to go on to Merritt College, a small, rundown two-year institution on the fringes of the Oakland ghetto. That was in the early nineteen-sixties, when Merritt had become a kind of incubator of Negro nationalism.

Both Newton and Seale, who also attended Merritt, remember the time as an exciting period of self-discovery for scores of young Oakland blacks. They would cut classes and sit around the nearby coffee shops, arguing about the black revolution, and reading the classics of black nationalism together.

Both Seale and Newton joined their first organization during that period: a group called the Afro-American Association, which advo-

cated black nationalism and stressed Negro separateness and self-improvement. Seale and Newton both became disillusioned with the group because they felt it did not offer anything but some innocuous cultural nationalism. (The group still functions, led by a lawyer named Donald Warden, whom Seale and Newton scoffingly refer to as a "hard-core capitalist.")

After they had left the Afro-American Association, there was a period of political uncertainty for both Seale and Newton. At one point, Newton was tempted to become a Black Muslim; he had great respect for Malcolm X, but could not "accept the religious aspect." There was also a period of "hustling on the streets" for Newton and frequent arrests for theft and burglary. "But even then I discriminated between black and white property," he says.

EVENTUALLY came a year in the county jail on an assault-with-a-deadly-weapon conviction. In jail, again, there was the confrontation with white authority. Newton led riots and food strikes—for which he was placed in solitary confinement. In Ala-

MINISTER OF DEFENSE—A poster issued by the Black Panthers of the San Francisco Bay Area shows Huey P. Newton. He is considered pre-eminent in the movement because, he says, "black people realize they are already at war with the racist white power structure."

meda County at the time this constituted a unique and degrading form of punishment. The solitary cells were called "soul breakers" by the Negro prisoners. Each was totally bare, without even a washstand. The prisoner was put into it without any clothes and slept on the cement floor. In the middle of the cement floor was a hole which served as a toilet. The prisoners did their time in blocks of 15 days, after which they were allowed out for a shower and some exercise before going back in again.

Newton took it as a challenge. The "white bulls" were out to break him, and he had to resist. He made sure that when they opened the door to his cell he would be doing push-ups. It was also a time for thinking, since there was nothing else to do.

"I relived my life," he says. "I thought of everything I had done. And I realized some new things in that jail. I viewed the jail as no different from the outside. I thought about the relationship between being outside of a jail and being in, and I saw the great similarities. It was the whites who had the guns who controlled everything, with a few Uncle Tom blacks helping them out."

For Newton, as for Malcolm X, the prison experience only confirmed his hostility to the white world and made him more militant. Outside, Newton and Bobby Seale hooked up again and began to talk about the need for a revolutionary party that would represent the black masses and the ghetto youth unrepresented by other civil-rights groups.

"We began to understand the unwritten law of force," says Bobby Seale. "They, the police, have guns, and what the law actually says ain't worth a damn. We started to think of a program that defines and offsets this physical fact of the ghetto. I view black people in America as a colonial people. Therefore we have to arm ourselves and make the colonial power give us our freedom."

San Francisco's Hunters Point riot of last summer galvanized Newton and Seale into action. They viewed the disorganized half-hearted attempts of the Negroes to fight back against the cops as a waste. A new strategy was needed. After the riots

Marcus Garvey.

Mao Tse-tung.

**Panthers' Heroes**

they moved around the Bay Area talking to groups of bloods and gangs from the ghettos. The young bloods would ask Seale and Newton: "Tell us how we are going to do something. Tell us what we are going to do about the cops." The answer was the Black Panthers.

"THE dream of the black people in the ghetto is how to stop the police brutality on the street," says Bobby Seale. "Can the people in the ghetto stand up to the cops? The ghetto black isn't afraid because he already lives with violence. He expects to die any day."

To someone who is not black, the issue of police brutality and police malpractice in the ghetto cannot be disposed of by checking a sociologist's statistics or the records of police review boards. It remains, an unrecorded fact that lurks in unlit ghetto streets, in moving police cars, in the privacy of police stations. It is recorded in the eyes of the young Negroes at Black Panther rallies who do not even blink when the speaker talks of "executing a cop"; it is as if every one of them has at least one memory of some long unpunished indignity suffered at the hands of a white cop.

To these young men, the execution of a police officer would be as natural and justifiable as the execution of a German soldier by a member of the French Resistance. This

W. E. B. Du Bois.

Malcolm X.

**REQUIRED READING**—The writings of these four are considered the standard works on revolution by the Black Panthers, and must be studied by the party's recruits.

is the grim reality upon which the Panthers build a movement.

To the blood on the street, the black man who can face down the white cop is a hero. One of the early tactics of the Panthers was the "defense patrol." Four Panthers, armed with shotguns, would ride around in a car following a police car in the ghetto. If the police stopped to question a Negro on the street, the Panthers with their guns drawn would get out and observe the behavior of the

police. If an arrest was made, the Panthers would try to raise the money to bail the Negro out.

On the basis of such acts, new members were recruited, taught the rudiments of the law on search and seizure, the right to bear arms and arrest procedure, and introduced to the standard works of militant black revolution: Frantz Fanon, Malcolm X, W. E. B. Du Bois, Marcus Garvey. Currently, Panthers are reading and digesting Mao Tse-tung's Little Red Book. Seale and

**CHAIRMAN**—Bobby Seale of the Black Panthers. "The ghetto black isn't afraid to stand up to the cops," he says, "because he already lives with violence. He expects to die any day."

Newton admit that the rank and file of the Panthers, many of whom are members of street gangs, are not sophisticated politically, but insist that they are "wise in the ways of power."

To Newton and Seale the identification with world revolution is a serious business. They see the United States as the center of an imperialist system which suppresses the worldwide revolution of colored people. And, says Newton: "We can stop the machinery. We can stop the imperialists from using it against black people all over the world. We are in a strategic position in this country, and we won't be the only group rebelling against the oppressor here."

If the Panthers are no more than a tiny minority even among militant Negroes, it does not seem to affect their revolutionary fervor. Theirs is a vision of an American apocalypse in which all blacks are forced to unite for survival against the white oppressors. Newton puts it this way: "At the height of the resistance they are going to be slaughtering black people indiscriminately. We are sure that at that time Martin Luther King will be a member of the Black Panthers through necessity. He and others like him will have to band together with us just to save themselves."

IN the meantime, all is not smooth among the black militants. The Panthers have had running feuds with other black nationalist groups, one of them a Bay Area group which has also used the name "Black Panthers," and which has been attacked by Newton and Seale for its overly intellectual approach and for its unwillingness to carry guns in the open. "Cultural nationalists" is the epithet that Newton and Seale use for black nationalists who they claim never try to develop grass-roots support in the ghetto community, but are content to live in an intellectual milieu of black nationalism.

In turn, the Panthers have been criticized for their provocative and public actions by other black militants. One Negro leader in the area said privately, "These cats have just been playing cowboys and Indians." But opinions among black leaders are sharply divided on the subject. When asked about the Panthers on a recent trip to the Bay Area, H. Rap Brown, the new national chairman of the Student Nonviolent Coordinating Committee, had only favorable things to say about them. "What they're doing is very important," said Brown. "Black people are just begin-

ning to get over their fear of the police and the Panthers are playing an important role in helping them to surmount that fear." (Eleven days ago, Brown was arrested on charges of inciting Negroes to riot in Cambridge, Md.)

How does the ordinary, nonpolitical Negro respond to the Panthers? Consider, not because he is representative, but for the quality of the reaction, 22-year-old Billy John Carr, once a star athlete at Berkeley High School. Carr lives in Berkeley's Negro ghetto, has a wife and child now, and tries to keep his family together with sporadic work as a laborer. He has never been a member of any political organization and knows the Panthers only by reputation. Of the Panthers he says: "As far as I'm concerned it's beautiful that we finally got an organization that don't walk around singing. I'm not for all this talking stuff. When things start happening I'll be ready to die if that's necessary and it's important that we have somebody around to organize us."

The Sacramento incident clearly won the Panthers grudging respect and put them on the map in the ghetto. Recently, when traditional civil-rights organizations and Negro politicians in California organized what they called a "Black Survival Conference," the Panthers were invited to speak and got an enthusiastic response.

Are the Panthers racists? Both Huey Newton and Bobby Seale deny it. "Black people aren't racists. Racism is primarily a white man's problem," says Seale, perhaps begging the question. Whatever the root causes of American racism, there *are* Negroes in the society who simply hate whites as a matter of principle, and would commit indiscriminate violence against them merely for their color. The violent rhetoric of the Panthers — which pits the black man against the white cop — undoubtedly fans such feelings.

Yet the fact is that the Panthers, unlike certain other black nationalist groups, have not allowed themselves to indulge in baiting the "white devil." They are race-conscious, they are exclusively "pro-black," but they also seem conscious of the dangers of simple-minded antiwhite hostility.

Though the Panthers will not allow whites to attend their membership meetings, they have had friendly relations with groups of white radicals in the area. They participated in a meeting with leaders of the San Francisco "hippie" community, in which common problems were discussed. The hippies had been concerned about trouble with young Negroes in the area who were starting fights and harassing the hippies. "We went around and told these guys that the hippies weren't the enemy, that they shouldn't waste their time on them," says Newton.

THE Panthers' relations with the local chapter of S.N.C.C., which has a number of whites in it, have been friendly. Terry Cannon, a white member of the editorial board of The Movement, a newspaper affiliated with S.N.C.C., and long a Bay Area activist, sees the Panthers' initial action as necessary. "The Panthers have demonstrated something that was very much needed in Northern cities," says Cannon. "They have effectively demonstrated that the black community is willing to defend itself."

Though they claim to have started chapters in Los Angeles, Harlem and elsewhere in the North, the Panthers remain pitifully small in numbers and their organizational resources meager. Frequent arrests have brought severe financial strain in the form of bail money and legal fees—and police harassment is certain to continue. If the Panthers increasingly "go underground" to escape such pressures, they will find it that much more difficult to broaden their contact with the rest of the black community.

But to write off the Panthers as a fringe group of little influence is to miss the point. The group's roots are in the desperation and anger that no civil-rights legislation or poverty program has touched in the ghetto. The fate of the Panthers as an organization is not the issue. What matters is that there are a thousand black people in the ghetto thinking privately what any Panther says out loud. ∎

August 6, 1967

# MARTIN LUTHER KING
# A WHITE IS SUSPECTED;

## GUARD CALLED OUT

### Curfew Is Ordered in Memphis, but Fires and Looting Erupt

**By EARL CALDWELL**
Special to The New York Times

MEMPHIS, Friday, April 5—The Rev. Dr. Martin Luther King Jr., who preached nonviolence and racial brotherhood, was fatally shot here last night by a distant gunman who then raced away and escaped.

Four thousand National Guard troops were ordered into Memphis by Gov. Buford Ellington after the 39-year-old Nobel Prize-winning civil rights leader died.

A curfew was imposed on the shocked city of 550,000 inhabitants, 40 per cent of whom are Negro.

But the police said the tragedy had been followed by incidents that included sporadic shooting, fires, bricks and bottles thrown at policemen, and looting that started in Negro districts and then spread over the city.

#### White Car Sought

Police Director Frank Holloman said the assassin might have been a white man who was "50 to 100 yards away in a flophouse."

Chief of Detectives W. P. Huston said a late model white Mustang was believed to have been the killer's getaway car. Its occupant was described as a bareheaded white man in his 30's, wearing a black suit and black tie.

The detective chief said the police had chased two cars near the motel where Dr. King was shot and had halted one that had two out-of-town men as occupants. The men were questioned but seemed

**THE REV. DR. MARTIN LUTHER KING Jr.**

Associated Press

to have nothing to do with the killing, he said.

#### Rifle Found Nearby

A high-powered 30.06-caliber rifle was found about a block from the scene of the shooting, on South Main Street. "We think it's the gun," Chief Huston said, reporting it would be turned over to the Federal Bureau of Investigation.

Dr. King was shot while he leaned over a second-floor railing outside his room at the Lorraine Motel. He was chatting with two friends just before starting for dinner.

One of the friends was a musician, and Dr. King had just

asked him to play a Negro spiritual, "Precious Lord, Take My Hand," at a rally that was to have been held two hours later in support of striking Memphis sanitationmen.

Paul Hess, assistant administrator at St. Joseph's Hospital, where Dr. King died despite emergency surgery, said the minister had "received a gunshot wound on the right side of the neck, at the root of the neck, a gaping wound."

"He was pronounced dead at 7:05 P.M. Central standard time (8:05 P.M. New York time) by staff doctors," Mr. Hess said. "They did everything humanly possible."

Dr. King's mourning associ-

ates sought to calm the people they met by recalling his messages of peace, but there was widespread concern by law enforcement officers here and elsewhere over potential reactions.

In a television broadcast after the curfew was ordered here, Mr. Holloman said, "rioting has broken out in parts of the city" and "looting is rampant."

Dr. King had come back to Memphis Wednesday morning to organize support once again for 1,300 sanitation workers who have been striking since Lincoln's Birthday. Just a week ago yesterday he led a march in the strikers' cause that ended in violence. A 16-year-old Negro was killed, 62 persons were injured and 200 were arrested.

Yesterday Dr. King had been in his second-floor room—Number 306—throughout the day. Just about 6 P.M. he emerged, wearing a silkish-looking black suit and white shirt.

Solomon Jones Jr., his driver, had been waiting to take him by car to the home of the Rev. Samuel Kyles of Memphis for dinner. Mr. Jones said later he had observed, "It's cold outside, put your topcoat on," and Dr. King had replied, "O. K., I will."

#### Two Men in Courtyard

Dr. King, an open-faced, genial man, leaned over a green iron railing to chat with an associate, Jesse Jackson, standing just below him in a courtyard parking lot.

"Do you know Ben?" Mr. Jackson asked, introducing Ben Branch of Chicago, a musician who was to play at the night's rally.

"Yes, that's my man!" Dr. King glowed.

The two men recalled Dr. King's asking for the playing of the spiritual. "I really want you to play that tonight," Dr. King said, enthusiastically.

The Rev. Ralph W. Abernathy, perhaps Dr. King's closest friend, was just about to come out of the motel room when the sudden loud noise burst out.

Dr. King toppled to the concrete second-floor walkway. Blood gushed from the right jaw and neck area. His necktie had been ripped off by the blast.

# IS SLAIN IN MEMPHIS; JOHNSON URGES CALM

"He had just bent over," Mr. Jackson recalled later. "If he had been standing up, he wouldn't have been hit in the face."

**Policemen 'All Over'**

"When I turned around," Mr. Jackson went on, bitterly, "I saw police coming from everywhere. They said, 'where did it come from?' And I said, 'behind you.' The police were coming from where the shot came."

Mr. Branch asserted that the shot had come from "the hill on the other side of the street."

"When I looked up, the police and the sheriff's deputies were running all around," Mr. Branch declared.

"We didn't need to call the police," Mr. Jackson said. "They were here all over the place."

Mr. Kyles said Dr. King had stood in the open "about three minutes."

Mr. Jones, the driver, said that a squad car with four policemen in it drove down the street only moments before the gunshot. The police had been circulating throughout the motel area on precautionary patrols.

After the shot, Mr. Jones said, he saw a man "with something white on his face" creep away from a thicket across the street.

Someone rushed up with a towel to stem the flow of Dr. King's blood. Mr. Kyles said he put a blanket over Dr. King, but "I knew he was gone." He ran down the stairs and tried to telephone from the motel office for an ambulance.

Mr. Abernathy hurried up with a second larger towel.

**Police With Helmets**

Policemen were pouring into the motel area, carrying rifles and shotguns and wearing riot helmets.

But the King aides said it seemed to be 10 or 15 minutes before a Fire Department ambulance arrived.

Dr. King was apparently still living when he reached the St. Joseph's Hospital operating room for emergency surgery. He was borne in on a stretcher, the bloody towel over his head.

It was the same emergency room to which James H. Meredith, first Negro enrolled at the University of Mississippi, was taken after he was ambushed and shot in June, 1965, at Her-

nando, Miss., a few miles south of Memphis. Mr. Meredith was not seriously hurt.

Outside the emergency room some of Dr. King's aides waited in forlorn hope. One was Chauncey Eskridge, his legal adviser. He broke into sobs when Dr. King's death was announced.

"A man full of life, full of love and he was shot," Mr. Eskridge said. "He had always lived with that expectation—but nobody ever expected it to happen."

But the Rev. Andrew Young, executive director of Dr. King's Southern Christian Leadership Conference, recalled there had been some talk Wednesday night about possible harm to Dr. King in Memphis.

Mr. Young recalled: "He said he had reached the pinnacle of fulfillment with his nonviolent movement, and these reports did not bother him."

Mr. Young believed that the fatal shot might have been fired from a passing car. "It sounded like a firecracker," he said.

In a nearby building, a newsman who had been watching a television program thought, however, that "it was a tremendous blast that sounded like a bomb."

There were perhaps 15 persons in the motel courtyard area when Dr. King was shot, all believed to be Negroes and Dr. King's associates.

Past the courtyard is a small empty swimming pool. Then comes Mulberry Street, a short street only three blocks away from storied Beale Street on the fringe of downtown Memphis.

**Fire Station Nearby**

On the other side of the street is a six-foot brick restraining wall, with bushes and grass atop it and a hillside going on to a patch of trees. Behind the trees is a rusty wire fence enclosing backyards of two-story brick and frame houses.

At the corner at Butler Street is a newish-looking white brick fire station.

Police were reported to have chased a late-model blue or white car through Memphis and north to Millington. A civilian in another car that had a citizens band radio was also reported to have pursued the fleeing car and to have opened fire on it.

The police first cordoned off an area of about five blocks around the Lorraine Motel, chosen by Dr. King for his stay here because it is Negro-owned. The two-story motel is an addition to a small two-story hotel in a largely Negro area.

Mayor Henry Loeb had ordered a curfew here after last week's disorder, and National Guard units had been on duty for five days until they were deactivated Wednesday.

Last night the Mayor reinstated the curfew at 6:35 and declared:

"After the tragedy which has happened in Memphis tonight,

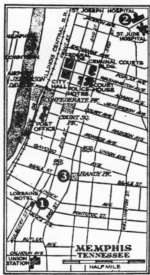

The New York Times          April 5, 1968

**AREA OF THE MURDER: (1) Motel where the shooting occurred; (2) hospital where Dr. King died, and (3) famed Beale Street, scene of demonstrations.**

for the protection of all our citizens, we are putting the curfew back in effect. All movement is restricted except for health or emergency reasons."

Governor Ellington, calling out the National Guard and pledging all necessary action by the state to prevent disorder, announced:

"For the second time in recent days, I most earnestly ask

the people of Memphis and Shelby County to remain calm. I do so aagin tonight in the face of this most regrettable incident.

"Every possible action is being taken to apprehend the person or persons responsible for committing this act.

"We are also taking precautionary steps to prevent any acts of disorder. I can fully appreciate the feelings and emotions which this crime has aroused, but for the benefit of everyone, all of our citizens must exercise restraint, caution and good judgment."

National Guard planes flew over the state to bring in contingents of riot-trained highway patrolmen. Units of the Arkansas State Patrol were deputized and brought into Memphis.

Assistant Chief Bartholomew early this morning said that unidentified persons had shot from rooftops and windows at policemen eight or 10 times. He said bullets had shattered one police car's windshield, wounding two policemen with flying glass. They were treated at the same hospital where Dr. King died.

Sixty arrests were made for looting, burglary and disorderly conduct, chief Bartholomew said.

Numerous minor injuries were reported in four hours of clashes between civilians and law enforcement officers. But any serious disorders were under control by 11:15 P.M., Chief Bartholomew said. Early this morning streets were virtually empty except for patrol cars riding without headlights on.

**Once Stabbed in Harlem**

In his career Dr. King had suffered beatings and blows. Once—on Sept. 20, 1958—he was stabbed in a Harlem department store in New York by a Negro woman later adjudged insane.

That time he underwent a four-hour operation to remove a steel letter opener that had been plunged into his upper left chest. For a time he was on the critical list, but he told his wife, while in the hospital, "I don't hold any bitterness toward this woman."

In Memphis, Dr. King's chief associates met in his room after he died. They included Mr.

**WHERE IT HAPPENED:** Memphis police standing on the balcony of the Lorraine Hotel in Memphis, where the Rev. Dr. Martin Luther King Jr. was fatally shot last night.

**LED MARCH ON WASHINGTON: Dr. King** speaking to the marchers from steps of Lincoln Memorial on Aug. 28, 1963.

Young, Mr. Abernathy, Mr. Jackson, the Rev. James Bevel and Hosea Williams.

They had to step across a drying pool of Dr. King's blood to enter. Someone had thrown a crumpled pack of cigarettes into the blood.

After 15 minutes they emerged. Mr. Jackson looked at the blood. He embraced Mr. Abernathy.

"Stand tall!" somebody exhorted.

"Murder! Murder!" Mr. Bevel groaned. "Doc said that's not the way."

"Doc" was what they often called Dr. King.

Then the murdered leader's aides said they would go on to the hall where tonight's rally was to have been held. They wanted to urge calm upon the mourners.

Some policemen sought to dissuade them.

But eventually the group did start out, with a police escort.

At the Federal Bureau of Investigation office here, Robert Jensen, special agent in charge, said the F. B. I. had entered the murder investigation at the request of Attorney General Ramsey Clark.

Last night Dr. King's body was taken to the Shelby County morgue, according to the police. They said it would be up to Dr. Derry Francisco, county medical examiner, to order further disposition.

April 5, 1968

## In Pursuit Of 'Kicks'

ON THE ROAD. By Jack Kerouac. 310 pp. New York: The Viking Press. $3.95.

**By DAVID DEMPSEY**

THIRTY years ago it was fashionable for the young and the weary—creatures of Hemingway and F. Scott Fitzgerald—simply to be "lost." Today, one depression and two wars later, in order to remain uncommitted one must at least flirt with depravity. "On the Road" belongs to the new Bohemianism in American fiction in which an experimental style is combined with eccentric characters and a morally neutral point of view. It is not so much a novel as a long affectionate lark inspired by the so-called "beat" generation, and an example of the degree to which some of the most original work being done in this country has come to depend upon the bizarre and the off-beat for its creative stimulus Jack Kerouac has written an enormously readable and entertaining book but one reads it in the same mood that he might visit a sideshow—the freaks are fascinating although they are hardly part of our lives.

The story is told—with great relish—by Sal Paradise, a young college student who satisfies, through his association with a character named Dean Moriarity, his restlessness and search for "kicks." Moriarity, a good-natured and slap-happy reform-school alumnus, is pathologically given to aimless travel, women, car stealing, reefers, bop jazz, liquor and pseudo-intellectual talk, as though life were just one long joy-ride that can't be stopped. He is Mr. Kerouac's answer to the age of anxiety—and one of the au-

*Mr. Dempsey is a freelance writer and critic of fiction.*

thor's real accomplishments is to make him both agreeable and sympathetic.

THROUGH Moriarity we meet his three wives. We are also introduced to a dope addict, a poet—and an assortment of migratory decadents whose playground is the vast American subcontinent of cheap lodgings, saloons, broken-down cars, cross-country buses and all night restaurants. Moriarity's continual roaming is interrupted only by a half-hearted attempt to find his alcoholic father. The incessant and frenetic moving around is the chief dynamic of "On the Road," partly because this is one of the symptoms of "beatness" but partly, too, because the hot pursuit of pleasure enables Mr. Kerouac to serve up the great, raw slices of America that give his book a descriptive excitement unmatched since the days of Thomas Wolfe.

Unlike Wolfe, Nelson Algren or Saul Bellow (there are trace elements of all three writers here). Mr. Kerouac throws his characters away, as it were. His people are not developed but simply presented; they perform, take their bows and do a handspring into the wings. It is the difference between a vaudeville act and a play. The hedonism, the exquisite pointlessness of Moriarity's way of life is not so much the subject of "On The Road" as a sightseeing device.

The non sequiturs of the beat generation become the author's own plotless and themeless technique—having absolved his characters of all responsibility, he can absolve himself of the writer's customary attention to motivation and credibility. As a portrait of a disjointed segment of society acting out of its own neurotic necessity, "On The Road" is a stunning achievement. But it is a road, as far as the characters are concerned, that leads nowhere—and which the novelist himself cannot afford to travel more than once.

## COOL CATS DON'T DIG THE SQUARES

THE HOLY BARBARIANS. By Lawrence Lipton. Illustrated. 318 pp. New York: Julian Messner. $5.

**By HARRY T. MOORE**

IN the Nineteen Fifties America has been besieged from within by bearded men in green berets and sandals and by women in Levis made up like German silent-film actresses, a self-styled Beat Generation speaking in a jam-session slang and caught up in a tarantism of jazz. The group, not a large but a loud one, has put on a lively show. Because some of them have claimed to be artists, even important artists, the question comes up as to how good their product is, apart from the floor show itself. Since literature is the broadest area of their art activity, the inquiry can take place there, and the writing that has come out of the very exclusive "hipster" colonies can be related to that of young writers on the outside.

One of the important pieces of evidence will be this new book by Lawrence Lipton. It is a thorough and vigorous partisan study of the so-called Beatniks, not a formal chronicle but a series of anecdotes, case histories and sometimes perilous claims, accompanied by a helpful and entertaining glossary of "cat" idiom. Mr. Lipton, who conducts a jazz-canto workshop, is a kind of father-confessor to the Venice (Calif.) congregation. He knows the hipsters there and in their big-city groups: Bovarys escaping from dull marriages, business men doing the Gauguin, girls fleeing from parents who are either too far to the right or the left, and college boys who have discovered that their classrooms promote the values of the "squares," those successors to what used to be called the bourgeoisie.

IT'S a world the Beat Generation never made, but they assume an unalienable right to act up in it. To Mr. Lipton they represent the barbarians who have appeared at times of crisis in civilization—these are holy barbarians because this is a spiritual crisis and they "come, not with the weapons of war, but with the songs and ikons of peace."

What Mr. Lipton calls their disaffiliation is not of course complete; though

*Mr. Moore, author of two critical biographies of D. H. Lawrence, teaches modern American and British literature at Southern Illinois University.*

they are non-political they resemble the Communists in at least one thing, in expecting civil rights in a society they disrespect. Some of them even play the squares' unemployment insurance for all it's worth. The hipsters are no more than kissing cousins to the juvenile delinquents, Mr. Lipton says; if some of the Beatniks are shoplifters, they at least aren't switch-knife killers. As to morals, they observe few of the conventional type, though many of these cats are married and remain monogamous, and even bring up children in their colonies. Most of the floating girls there are sexually available or, as this book puts it, free-wheeling chicks with no cover charge.

Deviates are welcome as "the *beatest* of the Beat" because illegal sex is a supreme defiance of the squares. Horse (heroin) may be bad, but Mr. Lipton defends tea (marijuana) as harmless and not habit-forming and, when the roaches (butts) are socially passed around, as essentially creative. Well, most of us squares are still not going to be convinced that marijuana is our dish of tea.

There is much else in this book, but Mr. Lipton might have profitably given more space to a description of the religious manifestations: he never for example quite makes it plain how a slowly and painfully acquired discipline such as Zen could possibly be absorbed in haste by these unquiet Westerners throbbing to jazz. He is at his best, in sketch and dialogue, as a kind of Boswell of the Beatniks, with his portraits of mine-run cats as well as of some of their heroes, including a comic report of Allen Ginsberg reciting his poem "Howl" in Los Angeles and stripping in order to show a heckler he wasn't "afraid."

Beyond sketch and anecdote, there is the other consideration glanced at earlier: How seriously can we take the work of the minority of hipsters who are attempting to produce something creative? This is a question they try to squelch, even before it can be raised, by sneering at its dependence upon English literature standards (for squares only). Mr. Lipton finds that the fifteen "Mid-Century American Poets" of John Ciardi's anthology "can't swing with the beat because they are too conscious of every word they put on paper." But mere clamorous assertion that the Beatniks' "spontaneity" brings their verse alive doesn't necessarily bring it alive in contrast with that of these other poets. Perhaps, like jazz, the finest effects of Beat poetry can't be written down, and it is true, as Mr. Lipton says, that the verse of the hipsters he quotes gains when read aloud. Nevertheless, as the centuries have shown, the force of true poetry can be conveyed in print; even the best poems of these hipsters are no more than watered-down 1912 Pound.

MR. LIPTON grants less attention to the Beat prose writers, who, he thinks,

*Photograph by Austin Anton from "The Holy Barbarians."*
**Painter-sculptor Ben Talbert and wife listen to jazz on their hi-fi in Venice, Calif.**

haven't developed so far as the poets. Novelists such as Anatole Broyard, R. V. Cassill and John Clellon Holmes write in too conventional a style to please him. He finds this fault also in Jack Kerouac's "The Dharma Bums," which he further thinks is weakened because it contains "too much of Hallelujah I'm a Buddha." Certainly Mr. Lipton is right in finding the wilder prose of Kerouac's "The Subterraneans" better suited to Beatnik subject-matter, and further right in saying that the prose of the book improves when read aloud.

Whatever critics of either camp think of Kerouac, he has the ability to transform attitude into myth, and this is one of the reasons why he is the hipsters' strongest point of comparison with the younger non-beat novelists. He stands up against them more firmly than, for example, Ginsberg, Lawrence Ferlinghetti and Stuart Z.

Perkoff stand up against such "mid-century" stars as Robert Lowell, Karl Shapiro and Richard Wilbur.

One point which soon manifests itself in comparison between hipsters and other young writers is that the cats lack humor. They could use an Art Buchwald. They seem, particularly in their novels, unable to view with detachment, or indeed with any sense of amusement, their own determined ultra-bohemianism, their own grim conformities. It may be true, as Mr. Lipton says,

that they have a holy-idiot quality, and certainly they often behave as if they are playing an elaborate prank on society, but for all this they display none of the zany fun that characterizes so much of the work of non-Beatnik writers such as Saul Bellow, Vance Bourjaily, Truman Capote and

Calder Willingham. Humor of course doesn't have to be part of a novel or poem, but an awareness of it often helps the writer in his orientation to his material.

Orientation of various kinds has always been an important consideration for authors, never more so than today, when young writers have the actual problem of living in a society whose dominant values they largely suspect. In a smaller way, such problems have existed in the past, when a Tolstoy, a Voltaire and a Ruskin expressed their dissatisfactions without going to the underworld extremes of a François Villon. Today the problem seems more wide-ranging and intense, when most of our young writers find so much to dislike: the hidden persuaders, the power élites and the other-directed types of popularized sociology seem almost as abhorrent to them as the cold-war situation. But the best of the newer authors, while not celebrating the present condition of society, don't sever themselves from it: they even accept many of its norms. Three recent, apparently quite different novels bear this out: Herbert Gold's "The Man Who Was Not With It" (1956); Bernard Malamud's "The Assistant" (1957), and Dennis Murphy's "The Sergeant" (1958).

It must be said at once that these three books have excellent reputations: for their statements about life, their vigor of language and their development in depth, they were rated higher

---

## From Lipton's Beat Glossary

**BREAD**—Money, as in "Could you lay some bread on me?" meaning lend or give some money.

**CAT**—The swinging, sex-free, footloose, nocturnal, uninhibited, non-conformist genus of the human race.

**COOL**—Said of anything that sends you, whether cool jazz or a cool chick.

**COP OUT**—To settle down, go conventional, in the sense of "sell out" or "cop a plea." In some circles you may be charged with copping out if you shave off your beard.

**DIG**—Understand, appreciate, listen to, approve of, enjoy. Do you dig me, man?

**FLIP**—Anything from a fit of high enthusiasm to a stretch in the laughing academy (mental institution).

**GAS**—Supreme, tops, the most. A gasser.

**GONE**—The most, the farthest out. If you go far out enough you're gone—"out of this world."

**HIPSTER**—One who is in the know. A cool cat.

**PAD**—A cat's home is his pad.

**POT (or pod)**—Marijuana. Also called tea and at various times and places, muta, muggles, the weed.

**SQUARE**—Conformist, Organization Man, solid citizen, anyone who doesn't swing and isn't with it. Also called Creep and Cornball.

**WITH IT**—If you're in the know you're with it. If you ain't with it, man, you ain't nowhere no how.

---

by most critics than Kerouac's fast-moving but essentially flat-structured novels. "The Man Who Was Not With It," "The Assistant" and "The Sergeant" have distinctly dissimilar backgrounds — carnival, grocery, army—yet the young man in each of the stories struggles, against rough obstacles, toward normality. Bud in Herbert Gold's novel breaks away from both heroin addiction and the jangling life of the carnival; Frank in "The Assistant" overcomes among other things his tendency toward thievery; Tom in Dennis Murphy's book frees himself at last from the evil dominance which he has let the sergeant establish over him.

**A**LTHOUGH the goal of each of these protagonists is love and marriage in the world the Beatnik scoffs at, they do not seek for a gray-flannel orthodoxy or for a Marjorie Morningstar ideal of suburban conformity. These Gold, Malamud and Murphy stories have no pat solution; the struggles of Bud, Frank and Tom toward some kind of adjustment occur at levels deeper than those found in soap opera novels. And, as Herbert Gold's hero at the last says of himself, his wife and his child, "We will not—and cannot—pull our son out of the way of our own hard times. They go on. There's a good and with it way to be not with it, too."

This last idea is expressed in Beatnik idiom: the term "with it" even appears in Mr. Lipton's glossary. But this complication of nonconformity and conformity will hardly appeal to the hipsters, who want a rigorous simplification in such matters, for they are in their own way organization men. This is a point to be remembered by young writers who might be tempted to believe that Beatnik colonies harbor the secret of modern existence.

# 4 Beatles and How They Grew

## Peoplewise

### By JOHN A. OSMUNDSEN

Even before they return as promised to their native England, they have set minds across the United States to wondering what the uproar was all about.

They—the Beatles, of course —were seen and heard by, and conquered, millions of Americans.

How, people are asking, could four mop-headed, neo-Edwardian-attired, Liverpudlian-accented, guitar-playing, drum-beating, "little boys" from across the ocean come here and attract the immense amount of attention they did by stomping and hollering out songs in a musical idiom that is distinctly American?

Ask a typical Beatle fan— female, in her early teens—and she will say it is because:

"They're so keee-oot."

Or because:

"They're different! They're just so different!"

Adults, some but not all of whom view the Beatles somewhat cynically, are likely to say that the craze sprang from the high-powered promotion that the performers received before their arrival and throughout their stay.

Social scientists agree with both the adult and teen-age views but note that, no matter how effective the promotion of the Beatles may have been, the public response to them was real and deserves a deeper probe for its origins within the needs and attitudes of the Beatlemaniac himself.

Practically every standard explanation in the book has been offered by psychologists and psychiatrists for Beatlemania. The Beatles, these analyses say, serve as symbols of:

¶Adolescent revolt against parental authority.

¶Status that comes from belonging to a group, in this case, of other Beatlemaniacs.

¶Sex, both from the supposed erotic nature of the Beatles' music and the way they perform it and from the appeal they seem to have to the "mother instinct."

¶Success by persons who are seen as fellow teen-agers (although none of the Beatles are under 21) and as underdogs who came from the wrong side of the tracks and have made good.

¶The frenetically felt urgency for having a good time and living life fast in an uncertain world plagued with mortal dangers.

### Deeper Reason Seen

Any or all of those explanations of Beatlemania may be more or less correct, in the opinion of a young Barnard College sociologist whose shoulder-length brown hair tends to flop Veronica Lake-fashion over one eye and who remembers attending a "Hit Parade" broadcast in the midst of girls her own age who shrieked and swooned into their bobby socks over Frank Sinatra.

But she thinks the most important answers to the Beatlemania question run much deeper than sex and status. She believes, moreover, that the phenomenon could serve as an ideal subject for a sociological study of the dynamics of fads and crazes and of social stratification.

The sociologist's name is Renee Claire Fox. She is an assistant professor of sociology at Barnard, but her researches have taken her as far away in the last two years as Belgium, where she studied the conduct of medical research and the scientists who do it, and the Congo.

Although those experiences do not qualify her as an expert on such matters as Beatlemania, her general sociological training has given her insight into the kinds of questions that could be asked about such a phenomenon.

In fact, she has developed a theory to explain Beatlemania and last week even explored ways of testing it as an exercise for students in the course on sociological research that she teaches.

Dr. Fox's theory is essentially this: The wide range of the Beatles' appeal stems from their personification of many forms of duality that exist in our society.

The Beatles, she says, constitute a treasure trove of such dualities.

For example, she explains, they are male and yet have many feminine characteristics, especially their floppy hairdos. They also play the dual roles of both adults and children. And they appear to be good boys who nevertheless dress and pose as bad ones—London's Teddyboys.

Their fancy, Edwardian clothes suggest a sort of sophistication that, Dr. Fox believes, contrasts further with their "homespun" style of performance.

### Poor Boys Make Good

Much has been made of their poor, lower-class backgrounds in Northern England. Yet they are accepted by the upper crust, having attracted the auspicious attention of the Queen Mother, Princess Margaret, Mrs. Nelson A. Rockefeller and President Johnson, the latter through a statement by White House Press Secretary Pierre Salinger.

Nor is this all. The Beatles, in their personal appearances, sing and play but seldom can be heard above the shrieks of the audience, and so they almost play the role of mimes. In addition, Dr. Fox observes, the four are both an audience for their own antics, and for those of their cavorting, screaming audience, acting, as it were, a play within a play.

"There is a Chaplinesque quality to their style." Dr. Fox said. "They convey the image of absurd little men in an absurd, big world, bewildered but bemused by it at the same time."

### Adults Are Fans, Too

The Barnard social scientist observes that here, as in England, the appeal of the Beatles is not confined to girls in their teens and younger, but spreads to boys and to many adults of both sexes.

She says she thinks that at least part of the attraction for adults lies in the Beatles's realistic attitudes toward their own success and their eventual eclipse.

In the Beatles, Dr. Fox believes, people see four basically nice young boys who project some of the same contradictions that exist in many Americans, who are having a wonderful time at the acceptable expense of both themselves and their audiences, who have expressed their gratitude for this fling and who have promised a graceful adjustment to the time when the party will be over.

It would seem, to paraphrase W. C. Fields, that someone who possesses all those qualities can't be all bad, no matter what some parents have been driven to think.

February 17, 1964

# ORGANIZED HIPPIES EMERGE ON COAST

## Civic Group and Two Papers Make Admirers Fear Loss of Desire for Nothing

**By MARTIN ARNOLD**
Special to The New York Times

SAN FRANCISCO, April 30 —The hippies are becoming more and more organized. They have two newspapers and a civic association.

If this trend continues the hippies won't be hippies anymore, hippie admirers feel, and this city's Haight-Ashbury section, the hippie capital, will turn into just another Bohemian quarter like North Beach here or East Village in New York.

Villagers are for things: noninvolvement in Vietnam and Negro civil rights. Hippies are for nothing. "Why can't I stand on a street corner and wait for nobody? Why can't everyone?"

Or, as Claude Haywood, a married 21-year-old hippie with shoulder length hair, said, "The world is going to chew you up, so why bother? Just wait until it does." Mr. Haywood migrated here from New York four years ago.

Hippies almost always refer to Negroes as "spades."

They have no malicious intent, but they don't dig the civil rights movement. David Simpson, 26, a hippie who came here from Chicago four years ago, summed it up this way: "The Negroes are fighting to become what we've rejected. We don't see any sense in that."

Mr. Simpson, a college graduate, has nearly shoulder-length blond hair. He wears a large gold earring and, around his head, a light blue cloth band. It holds in place on his forehead a stuffed parakeet—the tail of which curls along the ridge of his nose. He calls himself "Bird" and is somewhat typical of the Haight-Ashbury hippies.

### 'Experiments in Living'

"We're trying various experiments in living. I'm getting a new pad. Nine of us will move in, and see how it works out," he explained.

Haight-Ashbury is a lower middle-class section of San Francisco. Its residences are mostly three- and four-story homes that have been converted into apartment houses, as the brownstones were converted in New York.

Most of the area's residents have learned to live with the 15,000 or so hippies for neighbors. But despite the hippies' almost total noninvolvement there are some things hippies do actively like, and these bother not only their neighbors but the San Francisco police as well.

Hippies like LSD, marijuana, nude parties, sex, drawing on walls and sidewalks, not paying their rent, making noise, and rock 'n' roll music.

Earlier this week, music was blasting from an apartment window overlooking the intersection of Haight (pronounced Hate) and Ashbury Streets. Before long, several hundred hippies were dancing to it in the street.

When the police arrived, the hippies, who are usually nonviolent, showered them with fruit and vegetables. About 50 of the hippies were rounded up and carted off in paddy wagons but all but 16 were let go.

There are two philosophical trends in hippiedom, and as the hippies become organized, those who adhere to one or the other hippie concept tend to become less tolerant of the other.

The old-line hippies are definitely religious in a general sense. "God is Love," is the basic tenet of their subculture. They whisper that to passers-by on the street, are always calm and friendly, and they will demonstrate their love for humanity by throwing flowers at the police who harry them. Flowers and bells are their cross and crown.

These hippies publish a newspaper, The Oracle, which is illustrated with psychedelic pictures. It contains articles that feature no news, but essays on loving one another.

Younger hippies, however, have a slightly different "thing" or way of life, which was summed up by one of them this way: "Think what you want, but the number one rule is that you can't force your thing on other people."

They also operate a newspaper, the Communication Company, which publishes mimeographed tracts for the hippies.

The Communication Company was started in January and has already put out more than 500 communications. It operates out of the top floor of a three-story apartment, in which members of the staff smoke grass, or marijuana; take LSD trips together, and sleep on mattresses on littered floors.

The company has run out of rent money, so eviction proceedings have started. However, the company does own three mimeograph machines, an electronic copier and a hi-fi set.

"It will take two months before we go through the courts," one staff member said. "We'll have two months of free living. That's part of our thing anyhow. We're teaching people how to survive, be fed and clothed, without having any money."

Because the daily use of drugs is such a common part of life in Haight-Ashbury, one of the most popular items put out by the Communication Company is called "The Dope Sheet." It is a four-page, single-spaced text on how to use drugs, particularly LSD, and advises the hippies to take their first "trip" with "someone who is wiser and/or more experienced than you—someone you trust, who should be able to answer whatever questions you may be able to ask."

The sheet notes that "one of the reasons hippies are so fond of [American] Indians is that acid [LSD] dissolves our European conditioning and turns us into temporary Indians."

This affinity for Indians is reflected in the style the hippies affect. Many wear ponchos. Bells and beads and even seeds around their necks are common. One young hippie from Westport, Conn., wears a bicycle chain around his neck. He has no home, but wanders nightly from place to place looking for an apartment to "crash"—that is, sleep in.

All pure hippies, both boys and girls, have long and dirty hair. And though many of them work—a number of them are postmen—and have cars, they do not like to pay their bills, so often is the water shut off in their pads, making it difficult for them to wash.

The Haight-Ashbury hippies differ from residents of other Bohemian centers in that they have a strong communal sense. A number of them recently have formed what they call a "survival school." This was set up to teach young would-be hippies how to survive without money. Another group is called the Diggers, and it is the hippies' civic association.

The Diggers have set up a free store with racks and piles of used clothing that people can have free. It is not uncommon to see mothers outfitting their small children in the free store, being as picky and choosy among the dirty clothes and shoes as they would in a regular department store.

The Diggers also give out free luncheons—mostly leftover food donated by nearby restaurants. People are encouraged to come into the free store and paint psychedelic pictures on their clothing or dance, or neck, or do anything they want.

The other day a small group of hippies was sitting around a coffin in the store discussing jazz.

While the hippies insist they love just about everyone, nobody here loves the hippies. But they have become a tourist attraction, and traffic jams are not uncommon in Haight-Ashbury as people drive slowly through the area gawking at the hippies, who have, for example, put dimes in the parking meters and lain in the parking space on the street.

One bus line has put on a daily tourist tour billed as the "Hippie Hop" through the "Sodom" of Haight-Ashbury.

The city fears a possible mass migration of would-be hippies to the area this summer from all over the country. The hippies themselves keep frightening the city establishment by predicting that 100,000 teenagers will flock here this summer to become hippies.

*May 5, 1967*

## 30 Seized in Philadelphia As 2,500 Stage a 'Be-In'

PHILADELPHIA, May 14 (AP)—About 2,500 "hippies" and "teeny-boppers" gathered in front of Independence Hall this afternoon for what was billed as a "Happy Un-Birthday Be-In."

Some 30 members of the crowd were hauled off by the police after an incident that ended in the blocking of a police car.

James Kennedy of the Police Juvenile Aid Division said the brief sit-in around his unmarked police car began when he attempted to take a youth to the police station for questioning in connection with suspected possession of marijuana.

A crowd gathered around the car and a girl yelled, "Down, everybody, down," and they sat down, a newsman on the scene said.

The "be-in" was described as a gathering organized for unorganized activity.

*May 15, 1967*

# At a Commune for Diggers Rules Are Few and Simple

### By STEPHEN A. O. GOLDEN

Galahad is a 21-year-old who, until early last December, lived in Kansas City. He now lives in the East Village and operates a commune, an apartment where anyone can stay for a night, a week or as long as he likes.

Galahad, as he is usually known, is a digger; a hippie who survives with no noticeable income. Although hippies hold occasional jobs, all of the 20 to 30 people who live in the commune are diggers. The rent each month on the apartment, on 11th Street between Avenues B and C, is $36. Galahad is never quite sure how they get together the money for the rent, but somehow it is delivered to the landlord on time each month.

There are some rules, however, about living in the apartment. According to Galahad, no drugs or alcohol are allowed, no one is allowed in under the influence of either, and no one is to have anything to do with any girl under 18 years old.

The police, who arrested 38 hippies Tuesday night in Tompkins Square on charges of being disorderly, are also a sore point with Galahad. He says they have "busted" or raided his apartment "about 30 times" in the last two and one-half months, a figure his lawyer, John Mage, agrees with.

Last Wednesday night the police came in—without a warrant, Galahad said—and arrested eight persons from his commune on charges of "impairing the morals of a minor," a 15-year-old girl who ran away from her home in Queens.

When Galahad found out, he went to the Ninth Precinct Stationhouse on East Fifth Street to complain. The police arrested Galahad, charged him with impairing the morals of a minor, and let the others go. The police would not comment on the case.

Galahad, whose real name is Ronald Johnson, was arraigned in Night Court and placed under $1,000 bond. His friends called WBAI-FM, a station that occasionally takes up social or political causes, and they broadcast the case history of Galahad's apartment. Jerome Epstein, a graduate assistant in physics at New York University, heard the broadcast and came to bail out Galahad because "I've seen similar cases of police harassment and I don't like it."

The American Civil Liberties Union is studying the case. Paul Chevigny, a lawyer for the organization, said, "We are preparing papers on behalf of Galahad."

Mr. Mage, Galahad's own lawyer, whose office is at 225 West 86 Street, is working with the A.C.L.U. on the case.

Galahad has also filed a complaint with the Police Review Board about the raids. Joan Klippel, a policewoman and an investigator for the Review Board, said the complaint had been filed, but would not comment on it—because the case was under investigation.

A hearing was set for Monday, but when Galahad arrived, he found over 50 of his friends at the court waiting for him. They were sitting about the courthouse, chanting Buddhist hymns.

The hearing was put off until June 15.

The day after the court hearing, Galahad and about 20 other diggers went to the stationhouse on Fifth Street with buckets of paint and brushes and offered to paint the dirty walls of the police station. They were thrown out.

"I noticed the walls were dirty and I wanted to help out," Galahad later explained.

Capt. Joseph Fink, commander of the Ninth Precinct, said the police "couldn't let just anyone paint the walls—matters of liability."

### Offer to Wash Cars

Another time the commune residents offered to come to the stationhouse once a week and clean up and wash the radio cars. Galahad said the police "told me to shut-the-hell-up."

From time to time Galahad has returned to their parents minors who have strayed into the East Village and sought shelter in the commune.

One such parent, Mrs. Selma Donnelly, the mother of a 13-year-old boy from Queens, came to the commune Saturday night with Galahad's wallet, which he had left at her home when he took her son home. She put $5 in it "because you paid for the carfare to get him home."

"Thanks for my wallet," Galahad said.

"Thanks for my son," Mrs. Donnely replied.

There is also a radio and a television set in the commune, both the gifts of grateful parents.

The TV set was a gift from a textile executive in New Jersey, whose 14-year-old daughter, Nicki, had been talked into returning home by Galahad. He then panhandled enough money for two bus tickets to New Jersey, rode out with her and then hitchhiked home.

### Gives Parents Advice

The radio was a gift from the mother of a 15-year-old boy from the Bronx.

Each time Galahad takes a youngster home, he talks with the parents, telling them "what was wrong, why the kid left, what he doesn't like and what they can do."

One of the mothers verified this, saying: "I've had no trouble at all with Celia since Galahad talked with us." She said that Galahad had "made sense to all of us." The parents of another child said much the same thing.

Galahad won't talk much about his past. He grew up in Kansas City where his father was "a foreman" and his mother was "just a housewife." He once said his father was an Indian.

"I was raised in a church—I've got papers to prove it," he said, adding he still believed very strongly in God. Late last year he left home and went to New Orleans where he met Groovy, a youth who is now one of his closest friends. They came to New York three months ago and set up the commune.

### Just Walk In and Ask

The commune operates on a simple basis. If a person needs a place to sleep or stay awhile, all he does is walk in and ask. The apartment belongs to anyone who is in it.

Runaway—he will be 19 soon—lives there. All anyone knows about him is that he is Runaway and that at 8 P.M. last Saturday he had lived in the commune for a month. He won't say where he's from.

Kitty lives there sometimes. Kitty is 19 and she used to live in Miami Beach before she came to New York April 1. She is a pretty girl with hair dyed blonde, a high-pitched giggle and an easy smile. When she doesn't live in the commune she stays in the apartment above.

Kelly and Groovy live there. No one knows much about Groovy or Kelly except that most of the time, they—like the others—wear no shoes. Neither one likes to talk much about "the time before the commune." "Many hippies drop their family names and adopt such names.

Galahad said "someone called me 'Galahad' one day and it stuck."

No one in Galahad's commune is sure how they get money or food, but they know they never steal and that there is always food in the refrigerator.

"When Groovy and I first hit town," Galahad explained, "we didn't have a place to stay. Somebody put us up in a bookstore overnight. I really saw that something had to be done, I mean people can't just come to town and not have any place to sleep and take a bath and change clothes."

"First thing we did was rent this pad and open it up. People find out about it. Anyone's welcome."

How do people find out about the commune? Nearly everyone in the East Village and most people in the West Vil-

lage (the diggers call that the West Side) know Galahad and where he lives.

The Psychadelicatessen (a store on Avenue A near 11th Street that sells various symbols of the hippie generation, such as shimmery stickers and incense) has a list of "open pads" throughout the country.

In addition to Galahad's apartment, the list includes places in Colton, Calif., San Francisco's Haight-Asbury, the hippie capital of the world (the hippies call it Hashbury), and Detroit.

"Nothing wrong happens in the commune," Galahad said. "Kitty can come in, strip and take a bath. No one cares and no one really stares at her."

### Bananas Allowed

"Banana hash is the only thing we allow in," he said in explaining the commune's rules on drugs. Banana hash is the baked scraping of a banana peel that is smoked to induce a "high" described as similar to the effects of marijuana. It is not illegal.

"The cops can't bust [arrest] you for being under the influence of a banana or for possesion of a banana."

A recent study by the Food and Drug Administration found that smoking banana skin scrapings had no narcotic effect on humans.

Galahad said he does take LSD outside his apartment, and once, when he did, he climbed to the roof of his six-story building and walked along the ledge.

Galahad was asked why he let the 15-year-old girl into the apartment.

"I'm not breaking any of God's laws," Galahad said simply. "I'm breaking man's laws and some of them are wrong. I believe that J. C. will take care of us."

"God is the only one who makes laws you can't break. Some of man's laws are stupid," Galahad said. "That 15-year-old girl was much safer in the commune than she would be on East 11th Street at midnight."

### God Is the Answer

Galahad doesn't talk about Love as the be-all and end-all as do many of the other East Village hippies. His answer to all of that is God.

Although Galahad's rules do not allow addictive drugs or marijuana in the pad, LSD and marijuana are very much a part of the scene with Galahad and his diggers. But they use them only outside the apartments, according to Galahad.

Taking LSD "is almost like you were in a little glass bubble looking out and freaking on all the people," Kitty said.

"You die and then you are reborn as a child," Skip said. "We're all really like children."

Galahad and Kitty said they were taking a trip on "acid" (LSD) on Saturday, but they would not go back into the commune until the effect had worn off.

**Galahad, 21, walks along the parapet of six-story building, oblivious to the sheer drop, while high on LSD**

At the police station Captain Fink said he "wouldn't know. couldn't answer" about the number of times the police have entered Galahad's commune or whether they had warrants.

"I know that not only our patrolmen, but our detectives have entered the apartment, as have the narcotics squad," he said. "The narcotics bureau found no drugs in Galahad's apartment.

"We have no intention to violate anyone's civil rights or impair his right to assemble," the captain said.

Galahad thinks differently.

"They don't like the diggers," he said, "because we don't have short hair and we don't wear shoes and we don't have jobs. They just don't want us around.

"But J. C. guards this place and us. He won't let anything bad happen. It's got to work. We have a beautiful thing here —something I don't want to see disappear."

June 1, 1967

# The Two Worlds of Linda Fitzpatrick:

**By J. ANTHONY LUKAS**

The windows of Dr. Irving Sklar's reception room at 2 Fifth Avenue look out across Washington Square. A patient waiting uneasily for the dentist's drill can watch the pigeons circling Stanford White's dignified Washington Arch, the children playing hopscotch on the square's wide walkways and the students walking hand in hand beneath the American elms.

"Certainly we knew the Village; our family dentist is at 2 Fifth Avenue," said Irving Fitzpatrick, the wealthy Greenwich, Conn., spice importer whose daughter, Linda, was found murdered with a hippie friend in an East Village boiler room a week ago yesterday.

Mr. Fitzpatrick spoke during a three-hour interview with his family around the fireplace in the library of their 30-room home a mile from the Greenwich Country Club.

For the Fitzpatricks, "the Village" was the Henry James scene they saw out Dr. Sklar's windows and "those dear little shops" that Mrs. Fitzpatrick and her daughters occasionally visited. ("I didn't even know there was an East Village," Mr. Fitzpatrick said. "I've heard of the Lower East Side, but the East Village?")

But for 18-year-old Linda —at least in the last 10 weeks of her life—the Village was a different scene whose ingredients included crash pads, acid trips, freaking out, psychedelic art, witches and warlocks.

If the Fitzpatricks' knowledge of the Village stopped at Washington Square, their knowledge of their daughter stopped at the unsettling but familiar image of a young, talented girl overly impatient to taste the joys of life.

Reality in both cases went far beyond the Fitzpatricks' wildest fears—so far, in fact, that they are still unable to believe what their daughter was going through in her last weeks.

It is perhaps futile to ask which was "the real Linda" —the Linda of Greenwich, Conn., or the Linda of Greenwich Village. For, as The New York Times investigated the two Lindas last week through interviews with her family and with her friends and acquaintances in the Village, it found her a strange mixture of these two worlds, a mixture so tangled that Linda probably did not know in which she belonged.

The last weeks of Linda's life are a source of profound anguish for her parents. The forces at work on young people like Linda are the source of puzzlement for many other parents and of studies by social workers and psychologists, as they seek to understand the thousands of youths who are leaving middle-class homes throughout the country for the "mind expanding drug" scene in places like Greenwich Village.

Until a few months ago, Linda—or "Fitzpoo," as she was known to her family and friends—seemed to be a happy, well-adjusted product of wealthy American suburbia.

"Linda is a well-rounded, fine, healthy girl," her mother, a well-groomed blonde in a high-collared chocolate brown dress, said during the interview in Greenwich. Throughout the interview Mrs. Fitzpatrick used the present tense in talking of her daughter.

### Attended Good Schools

Born in Greenwich, Linda attended the Greenwich Country Day School, where she excelled in athletics. She won a place as center forward on the "Stuyvesant Team," the all-Fairfield County field hockey team, and also gained swimming and riding awards. She went on to the Oldfields School, a four-year college preparatory school in Glencoe, Md.

A blonde tending to pudginess, she never quite matched the striking good looks of her mother, who as Dorothy Ann Rush was a leading model and cover girl in the thirties, or of her elder sister, Cindy.

At country club dances, Linda often sat in the corner and talked with one of her half-brothers; but, apparently more interested in sports and painting than dancing, she never seemed to mind very much.

According to her family, Linda's last summer began nor-mally. In mid-June she returned from Oldfields after an active year during which she was elected art editor of the yearbook. She spent several weeks in Greenwich, then left with the family for a month in Bermuda.

### Vacations With Family

"The family always takes its summer vacations together; we always do things as a family," said Mr. Fitzpatrick, a tall, athletic-looking man in a well-tailored gray suit, blue tie and gold tie-clip. "Sometimes we went to Florida, sometimes to the Antibes, but for the past few summers we've rented a house in Bermuda. This time it was at Paget."

The family included seven children—Linda and 9-year-old Melissa ("Missy) from this marriage; Perry, 32; Robert, 30; Carol, 27, and David, 25, from Mr. Fitzpatrick's first marriage, which ended in divorce; and Cindy from Mrs. Fitzpatrick's first marriage, which also ended in divorce. But this time only Linda and Missy accompanied their parents to Ber-muda, while Cindy and her husband joined them later for 10 days.

As the Fitzpatricks remember it, Linda spent "a typical Bermuda vacation"—swimming in the crystal ocean; beach parties on the white sands; hours of painting; occasional shopping expeditions to town.

### 'The Girl We Knew'

On July 31 the family returned to Greenwich, where Linda spent most of August. Again the family insists she was "the girl we knew and loved."

They say she spent most of her time painting in the studio in the back of the house. But she found plenty of time for swimming with friends in the large robin's-egg-blue pool, playing the piano, and sitting with Missy.

"Linda and Missy were terribly close," their mother said, biting her lip. "Just as close as Cindy and Linda were when they were younger."

If Linda went to New York during August, the family said,

Linda Fitzpatrick at 17 wore her hair long. It was cut shortly before her death. This photo was made in 1966.

# Greenwich, Conn., and Greenwich Village

it was "just a quick trip in and out—just for the day."

### The 'Village' Version

Friends in the Village have a different version of Linda's summer.

"Linda told me she took LSD and smoked grass [marijuana] many times during her stay in Bermuda," recalls Susan Robinson, a small, shy hippie who ran away last May from her home on Cape Cod. "She talked a lot about a fellow who gave her a capsule of acid [LSD] down there and how she was going to send him one."

Susan and her husband, David, who live with two cats and posters of Bob Dylan, Timothy Leary, Allen Ginsberg and D. H. Lawrence in a two-room apartment at 537 East 13th Street, first met Linda when she showed up there some time early in August.

The Robinson apartment served this summer as a "crash pad"—a place where homeless hippies could spend the night or part of the night. Scrawled in pencil on the tin door to the apartment is a sign that reads: "No visitors after midnight unless by appointment please." It is signed with a flower.

"Linda just showed up one evening with a guy named Pigeon," Susan recalls. "She'd just bought Pigeon some acid. We were fooling around and everything. She stayed maybe a couple of hours and then took off."

### Flying on Acid

"But we liked each other, and she came back a few nights later with a kid from Boston. She turned him on, too [gave him some LSD]. She was always doing that. She'd come into the city on weekends with $30 or $40 and would buy acid for people who needed some."

David Robinson, a gentle young man with a black D. H. Lawrence beard who works in a brassiere factory, recalls how Linda turned him on on Aug. 22. "We went to this guy who sold us three capsules for $10 apiece," he said. "She put one away to send to the guy in Bermuda, gave me one and took one herself. She was always getting burned [purchasing fake

LSD] and that night she kept saying, 'God, I just hope this is good.' We were out in the Square [Tompkins Park] and we dropped it [swallowed it] right there. Forty-five minutes later — around midnight — we were off.

"We walked over to a pad on 11th Street just feeling the surge, then over to Tompkins Park, then to Cooper Union Square, where we had a very good discussion with a drunk. By then we were really flying. She was very, very groovy. At 8 A.M. I came back to the pad to sleep, and Linda took the subway up to Grand Central and got on the train to Greenwich. She must still have been flying when she got home."

That weekend in Greenwich, Mrs. Fitzpatrick was getting Linda ready for school. "We bought her almost an entire new wardrobe," she recalled, "and Linda even agreed to get her hair cut."

For months Mr. Fitzpatrick had complained about Linda's hair, which flowed down over her shoulders, but Linda didn't want to change it. Then at the end of August she agreed. "We went to Saks Fifth Avenue and the hairdresser gave her a kind of Sassoon blunt cut, short and full. She looked so cute and smart. Hardly a hippie thing to do," Mrs. Fitzpatrick said.

The first day of school was only 11 days off when Linda went to New York on Sept. 1. When she returned to Greenwich the next day, she told her mother she didn't want to go back to Oldfields. She wanted to live and paint in the Village.

### A Surprise for Family

"We couldn't have been more surprised," Mrs. Fitzpatrick said, fingering her eyeglasses, which hung from a gold pin at her left shoulder.

"Linda said her favorite teacher, who taught English, and his wife, who taught art, weren't coming back. She just adored them—when they went to Europe she just had to send champagne and fruit to the boat—and she couldn't face going back to school if they weren't there.

"What's more, she said there wasn't anything else she could learn about art at Oldfields. They'd already offered to set up a special course for her there, but she didn't want more courses. She just wanted to paint. She thought she'd be wasting her time at school."

Mother and daughter talked for nearly two hours that Saturday morning of the Labor Day weekend. Then Mrs. Fitzpatrick told her husband, who at first was determined that Linda should finished school.

### Reluctant Consent Given

"But we talked about it with all the family and with friends all through the weekend," Mr. Fitzpatrick recalls. "Finally, on Sunday night, we gave Linda our reluctant permission, though not our approval." Linda left for New York the next morning and the family never saw her alive again.

"After all," her mother put in, "Linda's whole life was art. She had a burning desire to be something in the art world. I knew how she felt. I wanted to be a dancer or an artist when I was young, too."

The Fitzpatricks' minds were eased when Linda assured them she had already made respectable living arrangements. "She told us that she was going to live at the Village Plaza Hotel, a very nice hotel on Washington Place, near the university, you know." her mother said.

"'I'll be perfectly safe, mother,' she kept saying. 'It's a perfectly nice place with a doorman and television.' She said she'd be rooming with a girl named Paula Bush, a 22-year-old receptionist from a good family. That made us feel a lot better."

### A Room at 'The Plaza'

The Village Plaza, 79 Washington Place, has no doorman. A flaking sign by the tiny reception desk announces "Television for Rental" amidst a forest of other signs: "No Refunds," "All Rents Must Be Paid in Advance," "No Checks Cashed," "No Outgoing Calls for Transients."

"Sure I remember Linda," said the stooped desk clerk. "But Paula Bush? There wasn't no Paula Bush. It was Paul Bush."

Ruffling through a pile of stained and thumb-marked cards, he came up with one that had Linda Fitzpatrick's name inked at the top in neat Greenwich Country Day School penmanship. Below it in pencil was written: "Paul Bush. Bob Brumberger."

"Yeh," the clerk said. "She moved in here on Sept. 4, Labor Day, with these two hippie guys, Bush and Brumberger. They had Room 504. She paid the full month's rent —$120—in advance. Of course, she had lots of other men up there all the time. Anybody off the street—the dirtiest, bearded hippies she could find."

### 'She Was Different'

"I kept telling her she hadn't ought to act like that. She didn't pay me any attention. But you know she never answered back real snappy like some of the other girls. She was different. She had some-

**VILLAGE FRIENDS: David and Susan Robinson in their East Village apartment.**

The New York Times

thing—I don't know, class. The day she checked out—oh, it was about Sept. 20—I was out on the steps, and as she left she said, 'I guess I caused you a lot of trouble,' and I said, 'Oh, it wasn't any trouble, really.'"

"You want to see the room? Well, there are some people up there now, but I think it'll be O.K."

The elevator was out of order. The stairs were dark and narrow, heavy with the sweet reek of marijuana. A knock, and the door to 504 swung open. A bearded young man took his place again on the sway-backed double bed that filled half the room. The young man and three girls were plucking chocolates out of a box.

Against one of the light green walls was a peeling gray dresser, with the upper left drawer missing. Scrawled on the mirror above the dresser in what looked like eyebrow pencil was "Tea Heads Forever" (a tea head is a marijuana smoker) and in lighter pencil, "War Is Hell." Red plastic flowers hung from an overhead light fixture. The bathroom, directly across the hall, was shared with four other rooms.

"Would you like to see Linda's room?" her mother asked, leading the way up the thickly carpeted stairway. "That used to be her room," she said, pointing into an airy bedroom with a white, canopied bed. "until she began playing all those records teen-agers play these days and she asked to move upstairs so she could make all the noise she wanted."

On the third floor Mrs. Fitzpatrick opened the red curtains in the large room. "Red and white are Linda's favorite colors; she thinks they're gay," Mrs. Fitzpatrick said, taking in the red and white striped wallpaper, the twin beds with red bedspreads, the red pillow with white lettering: Decisions, Decisions, Decisions."

Orange flashed here and there—in the orange and black tiger on the bed ("that's for her father's college, Princeton; we're a Princeton family") and in the orange "Gs" framed on the wall. athletic awards from Greenwich Country Day School.

On the shelves. between a ceramic collie and a glass Bambi. were Edith Hamilton's "The Greek Way" and Agatha Christie's "Murder at Hazelmoor." Nearby were a stack of records, among them Eddie Fisher's "Tonight" and Joey Dee's "Peppermint Twist." In the bright bathroom hung blue and red ribbons from the Oldfields Horse Show and the Greenwich Riding Association Show.

"As you can see, she was such a nice, outgoing, happy girl," her mother said. "If any-

thing's changed, it's changed awfully fast."

Downstairs again, over ginger ale and brownies that Cindy brought in from the kitchen, the Fitzpatricks said they had been reassured about Linda's life in the Village because she said she had a job making posters for "Poster Bazaar" at $80 a week.

"Later she called and said she'd switched to a place called Imports, Ltd., for $85 a week and was making posters on weekends. She sounded so excited and happy," Mrs. Fitzpatrick recalled.

Nobody The Times interviewed had heard of a store called Poster Bazaar. At 177 Macdougal Street is a shop called Fred Leighton's Mexican Imports, Ltd., where, the records show, Linda worked for $2 an hour selling dresses for three days—Sept. 11, 12 and 13. On the third day she was discharged.

"She was always coming in late, and they just got fed up with her," a salesgirl said. Although Linda was given a week's notice, she left on Sept. 14 for a "doctor's appointment" and never came back.

*A Try at Panhandling*

Before she left, she asked the manager not to tell her parents she had been discharged, if they called. The manager said the parents did not call after Linda had left, although there had been one call while she was working there.

David Robinson said Linda supported herself from then on by "panhandling" on Washington Square. "She was pretty good at it," he said. "She always got enough to eat."

Linda may have had some money left over from what her mother gave her before she left ("I gave her something," Mrs. Fitzpatrick said, "I thought she was going to be a career girl"), although she never had very much those last weeks.

Yet, David recalls, Linda frequently talked about making big money. "She had a thing about money. Once she told me she wanted to get a job with Hallmark cards drawing those little cartoons. She said she'd make $40,000 a year, rent a big apartment on the Upper East Side and then invite all her hippie friends up there."

**Experimenting With Art**

"We're a great card-exchanging family," Cindy said. "Whenever the occasion arose—birthdays, holidays, illnesses—Linda would make up her own cards and illustrate them with cute little pictures of people and animals."

From a pile on the hall table, Cindy picked out a card with a picture of a girl and an inked inscription, "Please get well

'cause I miss ya, love Linda XOX." In the same pile was a Paris street scene in pastels, two forest scenes made with oils rolled with a Coke bottle, several other gentle landscapes. "Linda was experimenting with all sorts of paints and techniques," Cindy said.

"You want to see some of the paintings she did down here?" asked Susan Robinson. as she went to a pile of papers in the corner and came back with five ink drawings on big white sheets from a sketching pad.

The drawings were in the surrealistic style of modern psychedelic art: distorted womens' faces, particularly heavily lidded eyes, dragons, devils, all hidden in a thick jungle of flowers, leaves and vines, interspersed with phrases in psychedelic script like, "Forever. the Mind," "Flyin High," "Tomorrow Will Come."

"Linda was never terribly boy crazy," her mother said. "She was very shy. When a boy got interested in. her, she'd almost always lose interest in him. She got a proposal in August from a very nice boy from Arizona. She told me, 'He's very nice and I like him, but he's just too anxious.' The boy sent flowers for the funeral. That was thoughtful."

The Robinsons and her other friends in the Village said there were always men in Linda's life there: first Pigeon, then the boy from Boston, then Paul Bush.

Bush, the 19-year-old son of a Holly, Mich., television repairman, is described by those who knew him here as "a real drifter, a way-out hippie." He

carried a live lizard named Lyndon on a string around his neck. Bush, who says he left New York on Oct. 4, was interviewed by telephone in San Francisco yesterday.

*The Nonexistant 'Paula'*

"I met Linda at the Robinsons about Aug. 18 — a few days after I got to town," he recalls. "We wandered around together. She said her parents bugged her, always hollered at her. . . . So I said I'd get a pad with her and Brumberger, this kid from New Jersey.

"She said she'd tell her parents she was living with a girl named Paula Bush, because she didn't want them to know she was living with a man. That was O.K. with me. I only stayed about a week anyway, and Brumberger even less. Then she brought in some other guy. I don't know who he was, except he was tall with long hair and a beard."

This may have been Ed, a tall hippie who the Robinsons saw with Linda several times in mid-September. Later came James L. (Groovy) Hutchinson, the man with whom she was killed last week.

Toward the end of September, Susan Robinson says, Linda told her she feared she was pregnant. "She was very worried about the effect of LSD on the baby, and since I was pregnant, too, we talked about it for quite a while."

**Father Inclined to Doubt**

"I don't believe Linda really had anything to do with the hippies," her father said. "I remember during August we were in this room watching a C.B.S. special about the San Fran-

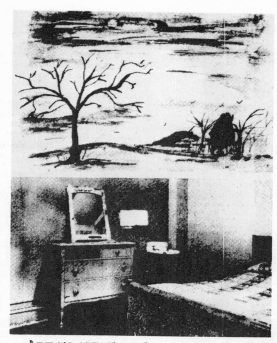

LINDA'S ART: Shown here are three of works provided by David and Susan Robinson, East Village friends. Drawings were done, they said, while Linda Fitzpatrick lived in room, center, in Village Plaza on Washington Place, and was a user of LSD. The drawings contain such psychedelic inscriptions as "Flyin High," in the drawing on the left, and "Love," in one on right. The picture of the naked trees and house was on back of the drawing at right. Written above mirror in Linda's room were several mottos. One of them said "War is hell." Another, referring to smoking marijuana, said "Tea heads fore ever." Linda was said to have left the hotel sometime around Sept. 20.

cisco hippies. I expressed my abhorrence for the whole thing, and her comments were much like mine. I don't believe she was attracted to them."

However, Linda's half-brother, Perry, recalls that during August Mr. Fitzpatrick also read a story about Galahad, a New York hippie leader, and expressed his "disdain" for him. Linda mentioned casually that she had met Galahad and that she understood he was "helping people," but her father let the remark pass, apparently considering it of no significance.

Her friends say Linda was fascinated by the scene in the Haight-Ashbury section of San Francisco. In late September she apparently visited there.

Susan Robinson recalls that she did not see Linda for some time in late September and that suddenly, on Oct. 1, Linda turned up at her pad and said she had been to Haight-Ashbury. "She said she stayed out there only two days and was very disappointed; that it was a really bad scene; that everybody was on speed [a powerful drug called methadrine]. She said she got out and drove back."

In the first week of October, the Fitzpatricks got a postcard postmarked Knightstown, Ind., a small town 30 miles east of Indianapolis. Mrs. Fitzpatrick did not want to show the card to a visitor because "it was the

last thing I've got which Linda touched." But she said it read roughly: "I'm on my way to see Bob [her brother, who is a Los Angeles lawyer]. Offered a good job painting posters in Berkeley. I love you. I will send you a poster. Love, Linda."

Also in the first week of October a girl who identified herself as Linda telephoned her brother's office in Los Angeles but was told he was in San Francisco. She never called back.

When Linda saw Susan on Oct. 1 she told her she had met two warlocks, or male witches, in California and had driven back with them.

"This didn't surprise me," Susan said. "Linda told me several times she was a witch. She said she had discovered this one day when she was sitting on a beach and wished she had some money. Three dollar bills floated down from heaven.

"Then she looked down the beach and thought how empty it was and wished there was someone there. She said a man suddenly appeared. She was always talking about her supernatural powers. Once she was walking on a street in the Village with this girl Judy, and she stumbled over a broom. 'Oh,' she told Judy, 'this is my lucky day. Now I can fly away.'"

"Linda told me she met these two warlocks out there and that

they could snap their fingers and make light bulbs pop. She said one of the warlocks took her mind apart and scattered it all over the room and then put it together again. Ever since, she said, she felt the warlock owned her."

'That's Not True'

"One of the newspapers said Linda was interested in Buddhism and Hinduism and all that supernatural stuff," Cindy said. "That's not true at all. I don't think she ever even knew what it was."

Last Friday a self-styled warlock who said he was one of the two who drove Linda back to New York was interviewed in the Village. The warlock, who called himself "Pepsi," is in his late 20's, with long, sandy hair, a scruffy beard, heavily tattooed forearms, wire-rim glasses and long suede Indian boots.

"My buddy and I ran into Linda in a club in Indianapolis called the Glory Hole," Pepsi said. "We took Linda along. You could see right away she was a real meth monster—that's my name for a speed freak, somebody hooked on speed.

"We were two days driving back. We got in on Oct. 1, and she put up with me and my buddy in this pad on Avenue B. She was supposed to keep it clean, but all she ever did all day was sit around. She had this real weird imagination, but

she was like talking in smaller and smaller circles. She was supposed to be this great artist, but it wasn't much good. It was just teeny bopper stuff—drawing one curving line, then embellishing it.

A Lot of Potential

"It sounds like I'm knocking her. I'm not. She was a good kid, if she hadn't been so freaked out on meth. She had a lot of, what do you call it—potential. Sometimes she was a lot of fun to be with. We took her on a couple of spiritual seances, and we went out on the Staten Island Ferry one day at dawn and surfing once on Long Island."

Pepsi saw Linda at 10 P.M. Saturday Oct. 8 standing in front of the Cave on Avenue A with Groovy. She said she'd taken a grain and a half of speed and was "high." Three hours later she and Groovy were dead—their nude bodies stretched out on the boiler room floor, their heads shattered by bricks. The police have charged two men with the murders and are continuing their investigation.

"It's too late for the whole thing to do us much good," her brother Perry said on Saturday after he had been told of her life in the Village. "But maybe somebody else can learn something from it."

# Political Activism New Hippie 'Thing'

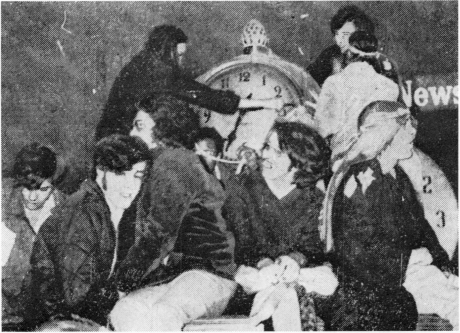

United Press International

Hippies sitting on the information center in the main concourse at Grand Central Terminal early yesterday. Hands were torn from clock faces, and slogans daubed on dials.

By MICHAEL STERN

An invasion of Grand Central Terminal by 3,000 chanting youths that was transformed from a spring be-in to a militant antiwar demonstration early yesterday morning may have signaled a new turn in the hippie movement toward activism in politics and the arts.

The organizers of the be-in — the Youth International Party — said they had planned the affair as a gathering of youths to share songs, popcorn, jellybeans and love for humanity.

But the gathering became a disorderly rally in which the youths chanted anti-draft slogans and painted antiwar messages on the walls until they were shoved out of the terminal by wedges of police of the Tactical Patrol Force.

The police, who charged into the youths swinging their nightsticks, reported later that 57 persons had been arrested on charges ranging from felonious assault and criminal mischief to resisting arrest and disorderly conduct.

Two of the arrested youths were hospitalized with concussions, five policemen were injured and two others reported themselves sick.

The meaning of the hippie phenomenon has long been in dispute. Last summer, at the height of the Tompkins Square troubles, it was thought by many observers that hippies were alienated, disorganized and often troubled youths who were against the mainstream values of American life, but for nothing in particular

## Days Were Aimless

Living on what they could scrounge from family, friends and middle-class oglers who went to the East Village to be titillated, they spent their aimless days "doing their thing," which chiefly involved introspection aided by drugs, meditation, exotic religion and music.

This year, on the eve of a new influx of youths on spring and summer school holidays, Greenwich Village and East Village policemen, clergymen and social workers, and self-styled spokesmen for the hippies, have said that they sense a new feeling of involvement on the part of youth.

"Many of the kids we had down here last summer are going into politics," said Inspector Joseph Fink, commander of the East Fifth Street police station. "They sense a real alternative in the McCarthy and Kennedy candidacies."

The Rev. Michael Allen, rector of St. Mark's in the Bowery on East 10th Street, said:

"The stereotype hippies never really existed in great numbers. What we have down here are several thousand alienated youths—most of them college dropouts—who wear their hair long, but who hold jobs or are trying to write or do something. They are dissenting from American values by withdrawing, but they are very much involved in life."

Allen Ginsberg, the bearded poet, guru and culture hero of many hippies, denies that being a hippie ever meant complete withdrawal from life. "These people are simply seeking another form of social cooperation," Mr. Ginsberg said in an interview.

"They are trying to start a utopian society in the midst of a locked-in technological society," he said. "That is something beautiful. It realy is a return to earlier American values, to the idea of Thoreau and Whitman that the individual is a state higher than the state."

## A Sense of Urgency Felt

Keith Lampe, a 36-year-old former newspaperman and college English teacher who is a leader of the Youth International Party, said he could feel "a special sense of urgency and involvement" among Village youths.

"They have the feeling that the next six or eight months can make a real difference in the United States, in stopping the war in Vietnam and in the Presidency," he said.

But another leader of the Y.I.P., Mrs. Abby Hoffman, said yesterday that she doubted that many hippies were going to get involved in the campaigns of Senator Robert F. Kennedy or Senator Eugene McCarthy.

Both Mr. Lampe and Mrs. Hoffman are involved in planning the Y.I.P.'s Festival of Life, scheduled for August in Chicago while the Democratic National Convention is in session there.

"It will be a demonstration of an alternative way of life," Mrs. Hoffman said, "a six-day living experience in a park in Chicago, with free food, tents, theater, underground newspapers and lots of rock bands and folk singers."

Mr. Lampe called the Chicago festival "a cultural alternative to the Democratic Death Convention."

While the aims of hippies are hard to define precisely, the outward manifestations of the movement are fully visible on St. Mark's Place and Second Avenue in the East Village and along Macdougal Street in Greenwich Village.

In increasing numbers as the spring nights get warmer, bearded, long-haired young men wearing bits of cast off military uniforms, beaded headbands and bell necklaces, and tangle-haired girls in long skirts, leather jackets and winter-stained boots throng those streets.

## Dress Not Conclusive Proof

Though adult residents and visitors to those neighborhoods assume that all young people in such bizarre dress are hippies, this is far from the truth.

Separating the real from the make-believe hippies among the thousands of young people who are living in the shabby, cheap apartments of the Lower East Side is an impossible task, but some adults who come in contact with them believe that the numbers of real hippies are declining.

The death of Linda Fitzpatrick, the Greenwich, Conn., girl who was slain in an East Village cellar last October, shocked and frightened many would-be hippies, according to Inspector Fink.

Newspaper reports of the possibility of genetic damage caused by use of LSD, the mind-altering drug, turned many others away from the hippie life, said Father Allen of St. Mark's Church.

But both Father Allen and Capt. Brian Figueroa of the Salvation Army believe many left to return to college and will be back in May or June as soon as their classes are ended.

"We expect just as many this summer as we had last year," said Captain Figueroa as he showed a visitor around the Army's shelter for homeless youth's at the Bowery and East Third Street.

The shelter, formerly a mission for alcoholics, and a coffeehouse called the Answer on Macdougal Street are the Salvation Army's chief contact points with runaway youths who are attracted to the Village by the hippie life.

"Many of the kids are just in trouble at home and are trying to get away," Captain Figueroa said. "But others think they can lead a life of free sex, or get drugs or escape responsibilities down here. We try to show them a better way."

Of 86 boys and girls who have been taken into the Army's Bowery shelter since Jan. 1, Captain Figueroa said all but one had gone home to work out problems with their families. The exception was a boy who was not wanted at home and knew it. He has been enrolled in school here until a

more permanent arrangement can be made for him.

Father Allen reported that the arts program at his church that is supported by a grant from the Federal Department of Health, Education and Welfare is attracting several hundred youths who had gone to the East Village after having dropped out of college.

The St. Mark's program includes a drama workshop, filmmaking and a poetry workshop that meets six evenings a week and publishes a monthly journal.

Father Allen left his church at the corner of Second Avenue for a sabbatical last summer and returned to find many of the streets around his church filled with young panhandlers.

St. Mark's Place is the street where most of them do their begging.

This kind of life is becoming increasingly hard in the East Village, according to shopkeepers and adult residents. A man who runs a clothing shop on St. Mark's Place and asked not to be identified said, "the police keep chasing them and fewer come back each week."

"By summer, I hope they are all gone," he added.

Mr. Lampe, the Youth International Party leader, said the hope of many hippies to live freely was being frustrated all around the country by police harassment. "It makes us all angry," he said. "It makes us feel we have to resist."

The Grand Central Terminal spring festival, he said, was an attempt to "give everybody a celebration because we felt we needed it after all the arrests this winter for draft resistance. It was going to be like a spring tonic."

Mr. Lampe said that almost spontaneously the anti-war chant, "Hell, no, We Won't Go," began and was picked up in many parts of the domed terminal hall.

Mrs. Hoffman said members of Mayor Lindsay's staff had been told in advance of the party's plans, but had neither sanctioned the demonstration nor asked that it be called off.

"If they had wanted to stop us, they could have had the police shut the doors," Mrs. Hoffman said. "But when we got there and saw all the others we thought, 'How beautiful,' they're letting us do it."

The police said the throng of youths began entering the terminal shortly before midnight. They marched back and forth through the concourse singing songs, chanting slogans and releasing hundreds of colored balloons, which floated slowly toward the midnight-blue vaulted dome of the ceiling.

A little after 1 A.M., firecrackers began exploding over the heads of the police and the demonstrators. Then a band of youths climbed on the roof of the information booth and be-

gan spinning the hands of the four-faced clock. The hands of the clock were broken off and the slogan "Peace Now" and other sayings were painted on the clock faces.

The police began moving in wedges toward the demonstrators, nightclubs swinging, pushing them toward the side exits. Many youths were knocked to the ground. When the crowd had been thinned, the police pulled back and left the others to leave by themselves. The terminal was cleared by 4:15 A.M.

Although the police reported only two injuries requiring hospitalization, another person, Ronald Shay, a 22-year-old laboratory assistant from Baltimore, was admitted to Roosevelt Hospital with large lacerations on both of his arms.

Don McNeill, a staff member of The Village Voice, who was covering the event for his paper, said that the police had slammed his head against a glass door so hard he had to have five stitches taken to close the wound. Mr. McNeill said he was wearing his press card pined to his coat when he was pushed by the police.

More than 100 men from the Manhattan South Task Force and the Tactical Patrol Force were assigned to the station. They were under the command of Chief Inspector Sanford D. Garelik.

*March 24, 1968*

# LOVE IS DEAD

**By EARL SHORRIS**

SAN FRANCISCO.

A 19-YEAR-OLD BOY, tall and blond and very thin, with crooked teeth and a delicate, girl child's face, wipes his nose on his poncho, hitches up his rucksack and thumbs his way out, away from the Haight. He is leaving because, he says: "Leary is a fake. The underground newspapers are fake. Lot

of the young kids are fake. Maybe the Diggers aren't fake—maybe.

"I've had six bad trips; the last time I was turning into the sidewalk. Pellets [LSD] don't scare me, though. I'll keep dropping them. It's the cops, wearing black gloves, four of them coming from each direction on both sides of the street, busting everybody. You've got to show ID to the cops and you have to leave your ID at the distributing office to get newspapers to sell. I might go to Colorado or West Virginia; I know somebody there with a cabin."

He doesn't know what day it is and he can't remember whether his parents live in India or Denver. He had pneumonia four times during his stay in the Haight-Ashbury district. He thinks he has been there for seven months, but he knows he left home two years ago and went directly to

EARL SHORRIS, a San Francisco novelist, is the author of "Ofay," published this month.

the Haight. It is more than he can cope with to reconcile the dates.

THE hippie movement is over. In January, the Human Be-In drew a crowd estimated at 10,000 to San Francisco's Golden Gate Park. On Oct. 6, the funeral which was to mark a hippie death-and-rebirth ceremony, staged and publicized by many of the same people, drew fewer than a hundred of the lingering faithful.

The alternative to the "computerized society" has proved to be as unsatisfactory to its adherents as the society that gave birth to it. The hippie philosophy, in which Buddha reads Tarot cards, Confucius is an astrologer and Hesse peddles acid, was incapable of sustaining a mass movement. With the help of LSD it quickly turned inward, and the possibility of a hippie community was lost, for a community of solipsists, each "doing his own thing," is a contradiction without hope for synthesis. The notion of order grew out of

375

observation of organized society; it was not imposed upon it. The political animal described by Aristotle, thrust into a disordered hippie community, must adopt a life style contrary to his nature, which over a protracted period is unendurable.

Without a viable, unifying philosophy, the hippies became prey to disease, commercialism, publicity, teeny-boppers, boredom, one another and the psychopathic criminals who found them the easy underbelly of the white middle class. The motorcycle gangs and the junkies prowl Haight Street in San Francisco. In the East Village of New York the "plastic" hippies come home from their uptown jobs to be mugged and robbed. The murder of Linda Fitzpatrick and James L. (Groovy) Hutchinson was shocking, but the East Village hipsters knew it, or something like it, was coming. The mixture of large quantities of middle-class whites, angry blacks and drugs had been seething for months; the explosion was, if anything, overdue.

Hostility is not now uncommon among the hippies themselves. Knives have appeared. The children in the streets no longer ask; they demand. Four newly arrived hippies were sitting on the sidewalk in the Haight. One was begging "small change" from tourists. Two others were busy with piercing the left ear of the fourth. They were too young to grow beards and too fresh from home to have long hair. Their blue jeans were dirty and their feet were bare. One of them called out to a passing tourist: "Want to see us pierce his ear?" The tourist smiled and continued walking. The young hippie snarled after him: "How would you like me to put a hole in your ear?"

Superspade, who sold drugs to hippies, was recently murdered, put in a cloth bag and thrown off a cliff north of San Francisco. The confessed hippie murderer of another drug peddler was arrested with his victim's arm in his possession. A San Francisco hippie film maker sent this message to his Los Angeles counterpart: "If you come into the Haight, we'll smash your cameras and bust your head." Those hippies who do not attach some mystical significance to these events have begun to wonder if the term "Love Generation" is a misnomer.

It is not easy for a hippie to be filled with love. Life in the movement has been disillusioning for most of them. Macrobiotic diets, instead of prolonging life, make one more susceptible to disease. The hippie life perverts middle-class values rather than exorcising them. The dream of nirvana dies quickly. Bad trips lead to suicide, murder or madness. Good trips lead to a mushy brain. Lucy is in the sky with zircons.

A worker in the Hip Job Corps explained: "I left the East Village two months ago because everything went sour for me. I was all up in the air and when I came down my feet were pointing toward California, so I came out here to a commune that's on a farm. That wasn't any good, so I came to the Haight. A lot of the people I was told to look up here had left. A different kind of people are here. The spirit has changed. The people here now are running away, looking for someplace to hide. I think I might go to Big Sur."

BOREDOM, perhaps more than any other single factor, appears to have brought about the moribund state of the movement. Turning inward, many of the hippies apparently found there wasn't enough there to sustain them. They went to kicks instead, but marijuana experiences become repetitive, Methedrine is a drug with vicious side effects, there is no variety in total sexual promiscuity even for the few who are able to attain it, and the example of Timothy Leary, fear of the bad trip and publicity about the permanent damage that may be done by LSD limit the number of trips they dare to take.

A psychiatrist described the LSD pattern in a woman patient: "When she took LSD she had a very good experience. She believed she communicated with God. During the experience and immediately afterward, she felt a heightening of life. Within a short time, however, her life returned to the normal pattern, and she became depressed. The further she got from the period of ecstasy, the more depressed she became."

The moment of ecstasy has also passed for the hippies. The promises of the hippie life were illusory. Sex in the hippie world belongs to the seniors; the freshmen just arrived from Connecticut and Minnesota find there are five boys to every girl and the girls want the drug peddlers or musicians or any boy who has established himself as the hippie version of the letter man. The best the freshman can hope for is occasional group sex in a crash pad, a homosexual experience or a gang rape. While their parents are studying the Kama Sutra in a suburban bedroom in an effort to find the joys they imagine their children get spontaneously, the children are having sex, if at all, in the style their parents have forsaken as too square for the swinging sixties.

The hippies who left the suburbs in protest against the worship of money and material possessions found there is more talk about money on Haight Street than on Wall Street. Hippie bands fly first-class and buy extra seats for their instruments; Chester Helm of the Family Dog claims he earns a quarter of a million dollars a year; the owner of a hippie dance emporium has a corps of financial advisers; the poster makers are rich; the drug peddlers are rich; hippie bands are anxious to do singing commercials or play for the Opera Fol de Rol; Ken Kesey wanted desperately to sell the film made on his Intrepid Trips bus tour to General Electric for use in advertising.

Middle-class children, suddenly without money, become obsessed by it. There is resistance, but it is pitiful. "It's no good to have any money," a hippie boy said. "You get some money and you think of all the dope you could buy and sell and how much money you could get." The Diggers claim to despise money, but a leader of the group, which gives away food, clothing and furniture, finds it difficult to talk of anything else. "A cat comes up to me selling peace buttons. I say to him that he should give them away, be free, end the buyer-seller relationship; then we can be brothers." The cause of peace is insufficient; brotherhood must be established around the one theme that outshines drugs in the hippie world.

Having professed their disdain for middle-class values, the hippies indulge in them without guilt. It is the same talent for self-delusion they apply to other aspects of their lives: An obviously hostile young man is described by his girl friend in terms that would have astonished George Orwell's characters in "1984": "He's not hostile. He's got so much love in him that it comes out aggressively."

In the same vein, the leader of a hippie commune is called a "nonleader," and the "underground" newspapers sell hundreds of thousands, perhaps millions, of copies every month. The publisher of the first underground novel talks anxiously of the probability of having the unbound, mimeographed book reviewed in The San Francisco Chronicle. The people who blame the mass media for the failure of the movement continue to turn handsprings at the sight of a press card.

AT the height of the hippie movement, they were deluged with social services: a free medical clinic, free legal service, free stores, help for runaways, Jewish Welfare Organization social workers. Long lists of addresses, names and phone numbers to call in case of trouble were posted in the windows of Haight Street stores. White, middle-class children needed help and the white, middle-class community responded generously.

As the hippie world loses its lily-white complexion and black faces and Spanish accents become commonplace in the streets, the social services, perhaps coincidentally, are being withdrawn. The free medical clinic is closed; the legal organization is curtailing its services; the Diggers can't pay their rent and other organizations are phasing out.

The hippies' supporters plainly don't like the Negroes: "They are coming into the neighborhood to get white girls." The hippies themselves see the Negroes as intruders: "We had some grass, a lid [$5 worth]. And this spade comes up and grabs it. Then he pulls a switchblade. There were a couple of spades, big ones, but there were a hundred hippies. We could have got 1,000, 15,000. We could've creamed him. So he gave back the lid." Negroes are blamed for the increasing use of Methedrine: "They get some nice white chick, the kind your mother would want you to go out with, and they

BE-IN AND BE-OUT—Just last January, San Francisco hippies drew a crowd of 10,000 to a Human Be-In, addressed by Timothy Leary (above). This month, the same organizers, deciding they should change their image to that of "Free Men," staged a "Death of Hippie" funeral procession (right). It drew about a hundred die-hards.

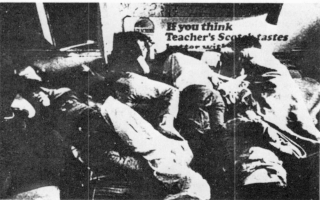

LIKE IT IS—A New York East Village Digger's pad, an apartment available to any wandering, lost hippie, at 11:30 of a morning.

shoot her full of speed. Then they gang her, 14, 15 of them, and she never knows what's happening." At the end of the Methedrine jag, when she crashes, she will know.

THE preponderance of hippies come from the middle class, because it is there even among adults that the illusion of the hippies' joy, free love, purity and drug excitement is strongest. A man grown weary of singing company songs at I.B.M. picnics, feeling guilty about the profits he has made on defense stocks, who hasn't really loved his wife for 10 years, must admire, envy and wish for a life of love and contemplation, a simple life leading to a beatific peace. He soothes his despair with the possibility that the hippies have found the answers to problems he does not dare to face. Unfamiliar with slum life, preferring illusions, he and his wife buy *art-nouveau* posters and smoke marijuana on Saturday night. The hippies. they say, have caused them to re-examine their own values, which they are more willing to suspect than those of the hippies.

Michael Stepanian, an attorney for HALO (Haight-Ashbury Legal Organization), says that when he calls the mother of a young girl from Connecticut who has been arrested for possession of marijuana, the mother invariably asks him: "Where did I go wrong?" In a time of race riots, the Vietnam war and the hydrogen bomb, it has not been difficult for the hippies to shake the confidence of the generation in power, the *malaise* generation. Of course, they raise valid questions; it is in their solutions that they fail.

Churchmen of several denominations have taken a deep interest in the hippies. A newly ordained priest, fresh from his first marijuana experience, said: "I want to work in the Haight-Ashbury; that's where it's at." The vice chancellor of the Archdiocese of San Francisco opened a conference of Catholic Charities by urging the delegates to visit the Haight-Ashbury to test their competency and their consciences. In an age of technology, during which organized religion has been losing its hold on the popula-

tion, particularly youth, the hippies offer new hope for the churches. Already attuned to mysticism, with a large percentage of close personal friends of God among them, claiming to have renounced worldly goods in favor of spiritual values, they have a kinship to the church which makes them attractive prospects for conversion. The nuns who walk down Haight Street tell them they are like the early Christians. However, the hippies have neither a Jesus of Nazareth nor a New Testament to sustain them. While persecution strengthened the bond among the early Christians, forcing them into close, secret groups, the hippies are faced with publicity.

"Men give more credit to things they understand not," wrote Montaigne, coming close to the true religion of the hippies, for they will believe in almost anything that fails the test of reason. The necromantic Bishop Pike is a hippie hero. Lenore Kandel, author of "The Love Book," is the leading witch in the Haight-Ashbury, where witchcraft is accepted with a seriousness unequaled since the Salem witch trials. Events are canceled because of curses or bad omens; astrology is the science of the movement, and stores advertise: "All your metaphysical needs here." The few serious students of Eastern religions abandoned the hippie life long ago, leaving their unlettered teeny-bopper brothers to rationalize drugtaking with sidewalk Sanskrit. Among the leftovers of the Eastern-religion aspect of the movement is a sign over a rack of psychedelic books:

## SHOPLIFTERS!
## Remember Your
## KARMA!

That sign and others like it in every store frequented by hippies are of little avail. Hippies steal — from stores, from tourists, from one another. The Diggers' Free Store has been looted at night of goods they would have given to the thieves during the day. A hippie who had been arrested on a narcotics charge complained that the police had left the door to his apartment unlocked when they took him to jail. A few hours later, released on bail, he returned

to the apartment to find it looted bare.

STEPHANIAN, the HALO attorney, says that a disproportionate number of all the arrests in San Francisco are made in the Haight-Ashbury district. He calls it police harassment and points out some of the ironies of the situation. Possession of narcotics, including that old rocking chair, marijuana, is a felony, but possession of Methedrine, by far the most destructive drug used by hippies, is only a misdemeanor. The majority of the arrests involve the very young, fresh from suburbia and making only a brief visit to the hippie life. They have no experience with city life or drug usage; consequently, they are often caught "holding," while the wily older hippies, peddlers and junkies rarely put themselves in danger.

The police harass the hippies and the hippies harass the police. The signs of the drug culture are everywhere in the movement. The underground papers, the art, even signs in the streets tell the police the hippies are using drugs. What choice do the police have? Two of the organizers of the Death of Hippie Funeral described the funeral this way, knowing they would be quoted:

"We stayed up all night before the funeral, drinking beer and smoking dope in the Psychedelic Shop. At about 2 in the morning, a taxi driver came in and he stayed up all night, too, smoking dope and laughing. It was a joyous night.

"The ceremony was at dawn. It was beautiful, first-class theater. Then a coffin appeared in the Panhandle [part of Golden Gate Park]. I don't know how. A guy from Kentucky played Blue Grass violin. He led the music while the funeral procession went around the police definition of the neighborhood. People put things in the casket, like clothes, beads, personal papers, marijuana. Then we burned the casket in the park and danced around the fire. Then the firemen came. Some people sat in the fire while the firemen were hosing it down."

The funeral coincided with the closing of the Psychedelic Shop, which had come to the

end of its lease, was $6,000 in debt, and was about to lose one of its co-owners to Napa State Hospital for 90 days of psychiatric observation at the request of the court. Its closing and the changing of the name to the Be Free Shop was announced with a poem:

### Psychedelic Shop
### Jan. 3, 1966–Oct. 6, 1967

*Once upon a time there was a Psychedelic Shop that tried to save the world and succeeded . . .*

A manifesto was published, entitled "Death of Hippy End/ Finished HIPPYEE Gone Good bye HEHPPEEEE DEATH DEATH HHIPPEE."

"Media created the hippie with your hungry consent," it began. "Be somebody. Careers are to be had for the enterprising hippie. The media cast nets, create bags for the identity-hungry to climb in. . . . NBC says you exist, ergo I am. Narcissism. Plebian vanity. . . . the FREE MAN vomits his images and laughs in the clouds because he is the great evader. . . . the boundaries are down. San Francisco is free now. The truth is out." It ended with the Declaration of Independence. Following the announcement of the Death of Hippie, the patrons of the I and Thou Coffee House completed a discussion of the subject by making signs and posting them on the windows and walls of the coffee house:

"LIFE TO THE DEATH & DYING."

"*Celebrate death/ mourn the living.*"

"*Thank you for telling us we can now be free.*"

"*A meaningless death in a meaningless life.*"

"NOW THAT YOU'VE FOUND ANOTHER KEY/ WHAT ARE YOU GOING TO PLAY?"

The effect of the state of the movement upon the pseudopsychedelic businesses in the neighborhood is documented by the history of one such store. "Before hippies got famous," said the owner, "we made $2 or $3 clear every day. It was enough for us to live on. That's all we wanted. This spring and summer we cleared $25 on weekdays and over $100 a day on weekends. Now it's down to $8 or $10 a day." The owner of a new store at the south limit of the Haight saw the Death of Hippie postings as "the handwriting on the wall" for his enterprise. Panicked, he put a sign in his window announcing an anti-Death of Hippie March to leave from his store on the closing day of the Death of Hippie Celebration, the day designated as "Silence Reigns." At the appointed time, five beardless boys appeared in front of the store.

THE concept of the Free Man, which was to replace the media's hippie label, is at best a murky one in the minds of its ex-hippie proponents. Philosophy is not a strong point with the high-school-dropout mentality of the movement; the unexamined life may be no life for man, but it appears to be satisfactory for love children. They express freedom with the fascist overtones of the true believer. To be free, according to the leaders of the Death of Hippie group, is to live the life of a hippie. Either one accepts the values of the Free Man movements and acts in accordance with them, or one is not free. But solipsism is not individualism. The Free Man is the complete follower, and nothing else will do, for the hippies are ruthless, utterly without empathy or compassion for anyone outside the movement.

Peter Berg, a nonleader of the Diggers, Death of Hippie, Free City, etc., defines freedom in part as "the end of the need to produce." And there the hippies are generally in agreement, for they are true consumers. In their utopian economy, the beggar takes the place of the owner of the means of production as the one who lives off the labor of the working class. After Eden, the choice is limited to being a producer or a parasite, and the hippies choose not to produce. Thus, the hippies become parasites on the flank of established society — albeit parasites with a certain sting—rather than an alternative to that society.

At one time the hippies hoped that their stores would all be cooperatives: "We thought we would export hippie arts and crafts to the straight world; that would sustain us." But their arts and crafts are controlled by a small group of young men on the make and there are no cooperative hippie stores.

"Prices in the Haight are very high," a hippie girl singer said. "In the Haight you pay double what you would pay anywhere else for incense." The stores are mostly boutiques catering to tourists and the hippies who get enough money from home to pause in their panhandling, as one girl did, and go into a boutique to buy a pair of $40 boots. An advertisement for flower children posters in The Oracle, a hippie newspaper dedicated to mysticism and incomprehensibility in an illegible format, contains a coupon urging the reader to "Fill out, cut out, chant an incantation, and send to: BEAUTIFUL POSTER THINGYS/ CAPITOL RECORDS DIST. CORP."

The hippies generally blame the mass media for commercialization, overcrowding and the other problems that made life in their communities intolerable; they will, in fact, agree to no other cause. An estranged hippie, who makes 8-mm. movies, said: "The movement is dead. It's being dissected. In order to be dissected a thing must be dead; we don't believe in vivisection in America."

Certainly the hippies are the most publicized meditative religious group in history. The publicity brought the tourists, and the tourists brought commercialization. Publicity also brought the record companies, dress manufacturers, social workers, researchers, teeny-boppers and a 70-year-old Hindu wise man who preaches from his storefront temple against the use of drugs. "It got too plastic," a retired hippie said. "The vibrations just aren't good any more. These new people are extremely selfish. They don't meditate." The manager of a rock 'n' roll band, who is of the mystic persuasion, said: "The hippie scene has moved to the country to get away from the center of infection. In the city there is too much compromise." He commutes daily to his San Francisco office from Marin County, whose per capita income is among the highest in the world.

THE love generation became the flower children, who have now taken up tribal relationships, in which the standard family unit is enlarged to a group of perhaps 10 or more. These tribes ordinarily live in one apartment, as in the case of a girl who supported herself and her tribe by baby-sitting. A month after the tribe moved in with her, she found that they had been using her telephone to make long-distance intertribal calls while she was out at her work. She threw them out. Now she has a new tribe living with her, but she has had her telephone disconnected. She is tenacious, but there is a limit to the tribal experiences she will put up with.

The shrinking of the movement began with the opening of school. The average age of the hippie, which dropped from 23 to 16 during the summer, is up again; social workers estimate that 90 per cent of the teen-age hippies have returned to school. The movement is seeking rejuvenation but its energy is gone, sapped by its own unreconcilable contradictions, by the vicious quality of hippie life, and by the commercial uses of its meager artistic production, which will be in evidence in Fifth Avenue and Union Square store windows and on Top-40 radio stations long after the movement that will replace the hippies has made a firm beginning in the underground.

Camus's statement, "I rebel, therefore, I am," is incapable of supporting life when the rebellion proves to be only a perversion of the values which set the world out of tune in the first place. The only clear thrust of the movement was its opposition to nuclear war, but hardly anyone is in favor of nuclear war; it is the circumstances of our lives that may drive us into the holocaust, and as the hippies come to realize that the movement has failed to redirect the inherent avarice and aggressiveness of its own members, let alone the entire world, they despair and abandon the movement.

The movement that was founded as an alternative to the "computerized, mechanized society" and chose electric musical instruments to play its leitmotiv has foundered in the very slough it created. Some hippies are moving to the country to live in garbage-heap communes, like the recently closed Morning Star in northern California, but the communes are only a prolonging of the death agonies of the movement. Most of the hippies are going back home or back to school; few of them ever intended to do anything else. "These were my wild years," said an ex-hippie college student. "I didn't want to spend them just sitting in a classroom. Now it's over. You have to get an education to get along in this world."

Although a formal census of the movement was never taken, there were reports that tens of thousands of young people had become hippies. It was an exciting vacation for at least that many American teen-agers, but the number of young people who intended permanently to drop out of society into a life of LSD, Methedrine and Eastern religion was never very large. Most of the hippies were "plastic," and they were the first to abandon the movement. Returning to "straight" society was easy for them. For the true believers a rapprochement with society is not easy. Transition is unacceptable to them, for faith mitigated is faith lost, and the movement had only faith and drugs to sustain it. There is nothing left now but the reluctance to admit failure, and that too is passing. All but a few have returned—or will return—to society, most of them with a better perspective for having been outlaws for a while. The others will remain somewhere outside, marked by venereal disease, life-shattering experiences, felony convictions, or with their minds jellied by LSD and Methedrine, the victims of a failed adventure in search of the perfect, ineffable groovy. ∎

### By DOTSON RADER

If you are a teenage runaway on the lam, or a 50-year-old executive finally gone bananas and about to drop out, then what you should probably read is Abbie Hoffman's "Steal This Book." It will tell you how to live for free and survive.

Hoffman has written a hip Boy Scout Handbook, a manual for survival in the counter culture. It tells you how to get the necessary stuff for free: food, clothes, housing, transportation, medical care, even money and dope. It tells you vital things, like what not to bring to a demonstration (contact lenses, ties, grass) and what to do if you are gassed, beaten up and arrested. It explains how to start an underground press, how to get in the newspapers, how to make stink bombs, procure false identification, cook Street Salad, Hog Farm Granola Breakfast, Weatherbeans and Yippie Yogurt; what towns are bad news for hitchhikers (Flagstaff, Ariz.); what boxcars to hop (ones with hydro-cushion suspension systems); how to employ the infamous "hopper-bopper method" to get a cheap ride on a Greyhound bus; and how to sell your hungry body to several universities at the same time. In the book you also learn that you can get

**Dotson Rader** is the author of "Government Inspected Meat" (a novel) and "I Ain't Marchin' Anymore." He is a contributing editor to Evergreen Review and editor of Defiance: A Radical Review.

## Steal This Book

*By Abbie Hoffman.*
*Co-conspirator: Izack Haber.*
*Accessories After the Fact:*
*Tom Forcade and Bert Cohen.*
*Illustrated. 308 pp. New York:*
*Pirate Editions. Distributed by*
*Grove Press. Paper, $1.95.*

your very own free elk or American buffalo from the Department of the Interior, and that you can acquire cheap guns and ammunition by starting a National Rifle Association Gun Club in your parents' basement. "Steal This Book" covers the turf from venereal disease and free movies—(did you know that you can have, just by writing a post card, a free copy of the movie, "More Fun With Parakeets"? Wow!)—to the newest techniques in the art of shoplifting, or "inventory shrinkage" as it is referred to in the trade. Do you want to drive the telephone company insane or give the president of Con Edison cardiac arrest? Do you want to unravel the credit bureaus' computer tape, and take the profitability out of pay toilets? Well, "Steal This Book" tells you how.

It also tells you something remarkable about Abbie Hoffman, something about the gentleness and affection for his people that lies hidden under his public rage. It reads as if Hoffman decided it was time to sit down and advise his children

on what to avoid and what was worth having in America. He says that if you want to be free, then America might kill you. You must know certain things if you are to survive. He warns of the baddies and meanies, the corrupt cops and lousy pushers and cheating landlords and shopkeepers and, more importantly, he warns about the crazy sad, bent kids who will lay awful trips and deadly vibes on you, who will do you irrevocable damage. So you must be prepared. You must be on your guard. "Steal This Book" is necessary to this age. It is a book of warning and practical knowledge. It should be read by the young, for it will help them to make it through life in hip America with their mind and body relatively intact.

Because "Steal This Book" tells you little more than the underground press has been reporting for years, because it hits hard against needle drugs and stupid violence, because it possesses its own peculiarly righteous morality, because it is not as subversive as many other books, nor as violent, say, as the speeches of Eldridge Cleaver or Senator Thurmond on the war, the attempt now being made to suppress it is all the more remarkable.

"Steal This Book" was rejected by 30 publishers. A senior editor at Random House, the first to reject the book, explained their action by saying, "How could we print a book that I wouldn't allow my 14-year-old child to read?" Other editors claimed more substantial reasons for rejection. Some stated they could not publish books that advocated illegal acts. By that logic books by Tom Paine, Karl Marx and others could not be published. Others were worried about possible Government reaction in the form of an I.R.S. inquiry. Still others took into account the probable response of booksellers plagued with rising "inventory shrinkage." Abbie Hoffman finally had to publish the book himself, through his own company, Pirate Editions (its logo shows a long-haired youth blowing up the Random House cottage). Grove Press agreed to distribute the book. Though it has sold 100,000 copies to date, the book has been subjected to various kinds of boycott since its publication April 15.

"Steal This Book" has yet to receive a single review—certainly an extraordinary reception, or rather lack of reception, for a work by a major national figure. Every "straight" newspaper in the country, with the exception of the San Francisco Chronicle, has refused to carry any advertising for the book. Gustin Reichback of the Law Commune, which represents Mr. Hoffman, stated that The New York Times Advertising Acceptability Department informed him that The Times does not take advertising for books advocating illegal acts. The reason given by FM radio stations WNEW and WCBS was that F.C.C. regulations prohibit their advertising the Hoffman book. Not one radio station in the United States has been willing to run advertising for "Steal This Book." In Canada it is even worse: the Government has banned it, released it, and banned it again.

This pattern of suppression is evident in the inability of Grove Press to convince regional distributors and booksellers to handle the book. Grove reports that over two-thirds of the stores that normally handle its trade list have refused to carry "Steal This Book." In the Boston area bookstores organized a boycott against it, and in New York the Doubleday bookstore chain, among others, has declined to stock the book.

The argument can be made that the publishing, distribution and advertising history of the Hoffman book gives credence to the radical notion of repressive tolerance in the United States. What meaning do First Amendment guarantees have if the work of even major figures cannot gain access to corporate publishing, advertising and distribution networks? As Hoffman remarks in his introduction, "To talk of freedom of the press, we must talk of the availability of the channels of communication that are designed to reach the entire population . . . wide-spread dissemination of information is the crux of the matter. To make the claim that the right to print your own book means freedom of the press is to completely misunderstand the nature of mass society. It is like making the claim that anyone with a pushcart can challenge Safeway supermarkets, or that any child can grow up to be president."

It is clear that without access to mass distribution networks, without the right to advertise, without reviews, freedom of speech and press becomes a vicious hoax. The right of freedom of press implies the right of fair and equal access to the machinery that disseminates ideas in a mass society. And that right has been denied, either through cowardice or design, to Abbie Hoffman.

Speaking as an American writer, I am frightened by the treatment accorded the Hoffman book by the publishing industry and the press. Everyone in publishing and distribution and in the press who has aided and abetted the restriction of Abbie Hoffman's freedom to be heard ought to be deeply ashamed. They are, as Lenin remarked in a different context, manufacturing the rope that will hang all of us. The irony is that those who refuse to publish or advertise or review or sell Hoffman's book in the name of legality are doing more damage to American freedom under law than Abbie Hoffman could do with all his books. A kind of fearsome censorship by tacit understanding within allied industries has been established. And everyone's freedom has been lessened because of it. ■

# BERKELEY STRIFE SET OFF BY LETTER

## Dean's Ruling in September Started Chain of Events

### By WALLACE TURNER
Special to The New York Times

BERKELEY, Calif., Dec. 5— The struggle between students and the administration at the University of California that boiled over this week began on Sept. 14 with a letter that took away some of the political privileges a few of the students had utilized.

A review of the conflict shows a series of steps leading straight to the events of this week that have thrown the largest state university in the West into a student strike and political turmoil that could have long term effects injurious to its enviable position in higher education.

That first step was a letter signed by Katherine A. Towle, the dean of students. It was a one-page letter and the last sentence urged "if you have any question, please do not hesitate to come to the office of the dean of students, 201 Sproul Hall."

Scores of girls went to the dean's office last Thursday, dragged there by the police who had turned them over to a matron who searched them before they were hauled away to jail. They had been arrested as sit-in demonstrators when hundreds of policemen were called by Gov. Edmund G. Brown to clear Sproul Hall after the Free Speech Movement took possession of it.

The Free Speech Movement was organized in the weeks after Dean Towle's letter brought on the conflict. Miss Towle, of course, did not write the letter to the president and chairman of student organizations without prior instruction. It has never been clear exactly who told her to write it, or precisely why it was written.

Clark Kerr, the president of the university, was out of the United States at the time, returning on Sept. 16. It has been assumed that the letter reflected the wishes of Edward W. Strong, chancellor of the Berkeley campus. No similar letters were sent on the other eight campuses.

But no comparable situation existed on the other campuses. At Berkeley a 25-foot-wide stripe of bricked-over earth was outside what appeared to be the entrance to the campus. Actually, it was the property of the university and as such was under control of the regents and the administration.

The University of California, unlike such Eastern institutions as Harvard, Yale and Princeton, is a state university subject for much of its operating revenues to appropriations from the California Legislature. This is a political aspect of the university's operations that has an unspoken but ever-present bearing on the decisions made in conflicts such as the one here.

The area in question had been used as a location for tables and posters and other activities of campus groups allied with off-campus political and civil rights group.

All of these were activities that the students were prohibited from carrying on elsewhere in the university. So the purpose of this 25 by 66 foot strip of ground was to be a safety valve. This is a fact widely recognized here these days, but it was not so well recognized on Sept. 14.

The students could make speeches on any subject in the "Hyde Park" area set aside for impromptu speeches. They could talk and discuss and belong to any groups they liked. They could feel safe from university interference with their off-campus activities, such as participation in civil rights demonstrations in San Francisco where many were arrested last spring at the Sheraton Palace Hotel.

At that time, President Kerr refused to discipline students arrested in the demonstration. He said in a controversial speech on the Davis campus that the university "assumes responsibility for the preservation of law and order upon its campuses," but he continued:

"It has recently been suggested that the university should also assume responsibility for the off-campus actions of individual students by expelling those who are arrested or convicted for illegal kinds of participation in civil rights demonstrations. I believe this proposal to be both impractical and improper."

From this position, President Kerr then felt that he had to hold that if the students were given freedom of political activity on campus, they would have to be held responsible by the university for illegal actions off-campus that were planned on campus. In short, if they misused the campus and abused their freedoms there, the university would have the duty of punishing them, President Kerr felt.

Thus, when Dean Towle's letter of Sept. 14 was circulated, it said in effect that students no longer would be permitted to use the 26-foot section of walkway as they had in the past.

This was a challenge to the most politically aware students on the campus and they moved to meet it. Protests were made, and rebuffed. The administration refused to move. By late September the protest was becoming well organized. There was a 12-hour sit-in demonstration in Sproul Hall on the night of Sept. 29. Eight students were suspended by Chancellor Strong for their participation in this.

Tables were set up at noon on Oct. 1 in the plaza in front of Sproul Hall, and organized violation of the no-politics rulings was continued to force more citations for violation of them. One nonstudent, Jack Weinberg, a local CORE representative, was arrested by the university police allegedly because he refused to identify himself, but was later released without charges.

## Alumni Stand

BERKELEY, Calif., Dec. 5 (UPI)—The University of California Alumni Association Council unanimously recommended tonight "firm disciplinary action, including expulsion and dismissal where warranted" against the student demonstrators

December 6, 196[

# The Berkeley Affair:
# Mr. Kerr vs. Mr. Savio & Co.

### By A. H. RASKIN

BERKELEY, Calif.

**W**HAT turned the University of California's world-renowned campus here into a snake pit of unrepressed animosities? As my helicopter rattled across the moon-dappled water of San Francisco Bay on its way toward this strangely riven academic center, it seemed to me two men were probably best equipped to supply the answer. In the process, they could go far toward explaining a simmering unrest on other campuses across the nation, and in every corner of our corporate society.

One man was Dr. Clark Kerr, 53, the quiet-spoken Quaker whose duties as president of the university make him Big Daddy to 72,000 students on nine California campuses. The other

A. H. RASKIN is assistant editor of the editorial page of The Times.

was Mario Savio, the charismatic 22-year-old undergraduate who had emerged as the archangel of student revolt at Berkeley.

My effort to get the answer from Savio got off to a rocky start. We had arranged to meet at the headquarters of the Graduate Coordinating Committee. This is a key unit in the Free Speech Movement (F.S.M.), the coalition of undergraduates, graduate students and teaching assistants that grew out of an ill-timed, worse-explained and now-rescinded administration order that barred all on-campus solicitation for political or civil-rights demonstrations mounted off the campus.

The committee office is a garret over the university's drama workshop, not far from the main gate to the huge, hillside campus. The visitor climbs a flight of wooden outside stairs and finds himself in a barren room that is dark despite the dazzling sunlight outside. The nearest thing to a real piece of furniture is a battered green sofa, with sags where the springs should be. A square table with a telephone fills one corner, and there are a half-dozen camp chairs. Under the table is a mound of picket signs. The mood is "Waiting for Lefty" done off-Broadway.

Savio, a slim six-footer with frizzy pale hair, peeled off the short, fleece-lined coat that has become a sort of personal trademark. His first words were a flat refusal to participate in any interview if I intended to focus on him as *the* communicator for the F.S.M. "Anything like that will just perpetuate a misrepresentation that the press has already done too much to build up," he said. "This is not a cult of one personality or of two personalities; it is a broadly based movement and I will not say anything unless it is made clear that the F.S.M. is not any single individual."

A way around that roadblock was ready at hand — a joint discussion with the six other members of the collective leadership who had accompanied Savio to the conference. It started with everybody sounding off against Sidney Hook's view in The Times Magazine (Jan. 3) that academic freedom was primarily for teachers and that the only imperative right for students was freedom to learn. Savio said they wanted equal space to reply; also they wanted to sue. I told them to go ahead if they thought they had a case. Finally, we got to what I wanted to talk about— namely, what they thought the issue at Berkeley had been and whether there was still any real issue left.

It was a somewhat formless encounter, a blend of a graduate seminar in political science and "Catch-22." People wandered out and others filled their chairs; getting in questions was harder than getting back answers. Yet, it was an engaging group—lucid in exposition, quick in rebuttal, manifesting no unease at differences of interpretation or emphasis within their own circle.

THE Berkeley mutineers did not seem political in the sense of those student rebels in the turbulent Thirties; they are too suspicious of all adult institutions to embrace wholeheartedly even those ideologies with a stake in smashing the system. An anarchist or I.W.W. strain seems as pronounced as any Marxist doctrine. "Theirs is a sort of political existentialism," says Paul Jacobs, a research associate at the university's Center for the Study of Law and Society, who is one of the F.S.M.'s applauders. "All the old labels are out; if there were any orthodox Communists here, they would be a moderating influence."

The proudly immoderate zealots of the F.S.M. pursue an activist creed —that only commitment can strip life of its emptiness, its absence of meaning in a great "knowledge factory" like Berkeley. That is the explanation for their conviction that the methods of civil disobedience, in violation of law, are as appropriate in the civilized atmosphere of the campus as they are in the primordial jungle of Mississippi. It was an imaginative strategy that led to an unimaginable chain of events.

Trouble began on Sept. 14, a week before the opening of classes, when the dean of students suddenly shut off the only area on campus where students had been free to collect funds and enlist adherents for off-campus political or social action. This island for activists was a 26-by-60-foot patch of bricked-over ground, called the Bancroft Strip, just outside the principal pedestrian entrance.

The decision to embargo the Strip, made in the climactic days of an election campaign that would settle both the Presidency and the fate of California's controversial fair housing law, forged a united front of protest extending from campus Goldwaterites to Maoist members of the Progressive Labor party.

With the memory of the mutiny thick in the gloomy garret, the collective leadership of the F.S.M. spent the next three hours telling me what they thought the rebellion was *really* about.

They are convinced that the abrupt decision to close the Bancroft Strip represented a university capitulation to right-wing forces angered by student picketing and sit-ins to compel the hiring of more Negroes in Bay area businesses. Specifically, they blame former Senator William F. Knowland, editor of The Oakland Tribune, whose paper was a special target. (Knowland says he didn't do it.)

The cutoff in political recruitment confirmed a conviction already held by some of the students that bankers, industrialists, publishers and other leaders of the Establishment in the Board of Regents were making a concentration camp out of the the "multiversity"—a term coined by Kerr in a series of lectures at Harvard nearly two years ago to describe the transformation of a modern university, like Cal, into a vast techno-educational complex.

This conviction was not diminished by the extreme freedom the university has long allowed students to express their own political views, however unorthodox, at "Hyde Park" areas inside the campus. Even during the ban on the use of campus property for organizing off-campus political action, students retained their liberty to invite Communists, Nazis or Black Muslims to address meetings at the university. They also could—and often did—agitate for the right to smoke marijuana, to be able to buy contraceptives at the University Bookstore or for other far-out objectives.

All this has been going on for years in an atmosphere

ATTRACTION—Folk singer Joan Baez entertains an F.S.M. rally.

particularly congenial to the flowering of undergraduate rebellion. The whole Bay area has a long Left Bank tradition of hospitality to radical movements and off-beat behavior. Czeslav Milosz, a Polish poet and defector, who served on the faculty, left convinced that Berkeley and Greenwich Village were "the only two places in America you can be free." The mild year-round climate also helps. "There is no place in the world where uncomfortable people can feel so comfortable," said a visiting British professor.

Taken aback by the vehement student reaction to the recruitment taboo, the Regents in November restored the right to mount political action—not only in the Bancroft Strip but in several areas where it had never been allowed before. However, the F.S.M. is still unhappy because the new ruling specifies that only "lawful" off-campus activities can be planned on campus.

The rebels argue that students should have the same right as other citizens to participate in the political and social affairs of the outside community. What is "unlawful" ought to be determined solely by civil and criminal courts, not by a university administration or faculty. The university's only area of proper regulation over political activity should be the establishment of minimal time-place-manner rules to guarantee that anything the students do on campus does not interfere with classes or the orderly conduct of university business. Such is the current focus of what is left of the "free speech" issue.

Remembering centuries of "town vs. gown" controversies all over the world, in which universities had always fought to keep their campuses from coming under police rule, I asked the F.S.M. leaders whether their insistence on leaving disciplinary authority to the municipal law-enforcement agencies might not destroy the whole concept of academic sanctuary and expose them to much harsher treatment.

Savio, a philosophy major who graduated at the top of his class from New York City's Martin Van Buren High School, had a blunt answer: "That is a specious argument. The campus is already crawling with cops of the most insidious kind from the 'Red

squad' and every other kind of undercover agency." Myra Jehlen, a comely, solemn Phi Beta Kappa from C.C.N.Y. and a Woodrow Wilson graduate scholar in English, added a postscript: "Immunity from police prosecution only applies to panty raids and fraternity guys. We're not interested in that."

She was the only coed in the group. Across the room was her husband, Carl Riskin, who had gone to Cambridge in England on a fellowship after graduating *magna cum laude* from Harvard and was now completing his Ph.D. thesis at Berkeley. He spoke seldom, but with force and precision.

Next to him sat Martin Roysher, a sophomore from Arcadia, Calif., whose casually correct clothes reflected the freshman year he spent at Princeton. He looked so young it was hard to believe he was out of high school, yet he, too, spoke crisply about everything from alienation to the importance of erasing any differentiation between the freedom of students and citizens to act upon their political beliefs.

Here, too, was Jack Weinberg, a former graduate student in math and now a civil-rights activist in CORE, who gained fame overnight as "the man in the police car" in the first of the mass upheavals last Oct. 1. Stephan Weissman, the red-bearded chairman of the Graduate Coordinating Committee, pulled a few picket signs from under the table and squatted on the floor. Robert Starobin, a Cornell B.A., who has been a teaching assistant in history at Berkeley for three years, is writing his Ph.D. dissertation on industrial slavery before the Civil War. Stocky and assertive, his talk bristled with complaints about the "power structure" and its determination to stifle civil-rights activity at Berkeley.

The one whose views evoked least challenge was the youth group's senior citizen, Hal Draper, a part-time librarian at the university who graduated from Brooklyn College in the Great Depression and is now fiftyish. A leader of the old American Student Union, he drifted through various wings of the Trotskyite movement and is currently an editor of New Politics, a journal intended to offer an outlet for all shades of Socialist thought. A Draper pamphlet called "The Mind of Clark Kerr" has become the F.S.M.'s bible in its fight

President Kerr: "The university is intertwined with all society."

against "the university factory." Dedicated to the students who immobilized the police car, the leaflet depicts Kerr as the preacher of docile submission to a technocratic juggernaut that will stamp out all individuality and all liberty.

The longer my conversation with the students went on, the clearer it became that the political battle was only a symptom of a larger revolt against the bigness and impersonality of the "multiversity" itself. If Clark Kerr is the high priest of the multiversity, social critic Paul Goodman is its Antichrist and thus beloved of the F.S.M. The opening theme of an F.S.M. pamphlet is a declaration by Goodman that in the United States today, "students—middle-class youth—are the major exploited class. . . . They have

no choice but to go to college." Rejecting their role as factory workers on an academic assembly line, the F.S.M. demands a humanized campus, a "loving community" based on comradeship and purpose.

"We must now begin the demand of the right to know; to know the realities of the present world - in - revolution, and to have an opportunity to think clearly in an extended manner about the world," says the F.S.M. credo. "It is ours to demand meaning; we must insist upon meaning!"

What is behind this manifesto? Does it betoken a desire to dismantle the University of California, or to establish a student soviet that would make all educational policy? The F.S.M. leaders disclaim such grandiose ideas.

"This is not a matter of rolling back the multiversity,"

Student Savio: "We committed the sin of being moral—and successful."

complished anything. Myra Jehlen answered first: "Of course, you never win finally. New problems will always arise. But there has been a great strengthening of democratic institutions on the campus. The kind of actions we've taken, the important function of students in society—these have been vindicated. Yes, we have won, though how much is not clear."

Savio was more succinct: "We committed the unpardonable sin of being moral and being successful."

THE setting was very different that evening when I visited Kerr at his home in El Cerrito, five miles from the campus. It is a glass-walled ranch house on a lofty bluff overlooking the Bay. Velvety lawns roll down to an old quarry in the canyon far below. There is a swimming pool, and flowers, shrubs and vines grow in junglelike profusion in a great glass-roofed patio.

But Kerr is not a man for rich living, even though his salary of $45,000 a year puts him $900 ahead of Governor Edmund Brown as the state's highest-paid official. He is frugal even of time. If Kerr gets to an airport and discovers the plane will be 15 minutes late, he is furious at the lost time. But if it will be an hour late, he is contented; he will sit quietly in a corner of the airport, begin writing memos, speeches, articles or even a chapter for a book.

Kerr works with the same intensity at home. Each afternoon a squad of eight secretaries at his office in University Hall pack a great sheaf of papers into a cardboard box. A driver returns them before noon the next day. Each carries a notation in green ink written in an incredibly pinched, yet distinct, hand—the marching orders by which the biggest of big universities is run.

The commander's invariable uniform is a navy blue suit and white shirt. His mind has extraordinary range and a rare capacity for turning discord into consensus. Kerr ranks among the country's half-dozen most effective peacemakers in the volatile realm of labor-management warfare—a skill that has prompted every President since Harry S. Truman to enlist his help. In the middle of the disturbances at Berkeley, President Johnson asked him to accept appointment as Secretary of Health, Education and Welfare. All Kerr will say

about that or any other post is that he still expects to be president of Cal on its centenary in 1968.

AMONG the many ironies of the Berkeley explosions is that Kerr now finds himself under savage attack from the left after more than a decade of demands for his ouster by right-wing critics. Leading the fight against a loyalty oath, he became so popular with the rest of the Berkeley faculty that in 1952, when the Regents decided to restore the goodwill they had lost in two bitter years, they named Kerr as chancellor. In 1959, a year after the Regents moved him up to president, Kerr again aroused right-wing ire by granting an honorary degree to Prof. Edward C. Tolman, who had been forced to resign for refusing to sign the oath. A year later he induced the Regents to name a new building in Tolman's honor.

When Berkeley students were arrested in 1960 for disrupting a hearing of the House Un-American Activities Committee in San Francisco, Kerr resisted demands to suspend or expel the demonstrators. He ignored similar conservative outcries last summer when undergraduates were arrested for a civil-rights sit-in at the Sheraton-Palace Hotel.

The liberalization of faculty and student rights during the Kerr administration earned for him and the Regents the American Association of University Professors' 1964 Alexander Meiklejohn award for conspicuous contributions to academic freedom. Less than six months later he was being denounced as an enemy of free expression by many on his own campus.

KERR was not consulted on the fateful order shutting the Bancroft Strip. He was in Tokyo on his way home from a seven-week economic mission to the Iron Curtain countries on the day it was issued.

"It was perfectly apparent," Kerr says, "that the decision was a mistake, both in the action itself and in the way it was done. There was no advance consultation with the students, the over-all university administration or anyone else. When a privilege had been extended as long as that had been, there should have been consultation — and especially against the background of an impending national election and intense student involvement in civil rights."

says Myra Jehlen. "But it is our view that this university does neglect its students. We have no contact with the community of scholars, except to see a professor across 500 feet of lecture hall. Teaching assistants have to serve as parents for the students."

Savio deplores the extent to which the university's professors and facilities are involved in research for the Government and giant corporations. "It is a distortion, and too bad, that the university does not stand apart from the society as it is. It would be good to return to an almost totally autonomous body of scholars and students. But what we have now is that the Pentagon, the oil and aircraft companies, the farm interests and their representatives in the Regents consider the university as a public utility, one of the re-

sources they can look on as part of their business."

And who should run things? Says Starobin: "Our idea is that the university is composed of faculty, students, books and ideas. In a literal sense, the administration is merely there to make sure the sidewalks are kept clean. It should be the servant of the faculty and the students. We want a redemocratizing of the university. Courses are clearly up to the faculty, but students should be able to convey their ideas. Dormitory regulations should be up to the students who live in the dorms. A bipartite or tripartite committee should have the final say in promulgating minimal rules on the time, place and manner of political activity."

There was much, much more before I asked whether they felt that the turmoil had ac-

(A Dostoevskian bit of background, still unknown to the students: Kerr foresaw in September, 1959, that the Strip would eventually be a source of trouble because there was no logical basis for exempting it from the no-politics rule that applied everywhere else on campus. He got the Regents to agree that it ought to be turned over to the city for use as a public plaza. But, for reasons still unexplained, the university's treasurer never carried out the instructions to deed over the Strip. If he had, the whole melancholy chain of events might never have begun.)

Kerr agrees with the F.S.M. thesis that students should have as much political freedom as anyone else in the community. The only difference is that he thinks they already have it. In his judgment, the rules governing political expression on campus, including the right to invite heretics of all political persuasions to speak at student meetings, give Berkeley undergraduates more freedom than bank clerks, factory workers or 99 per cent of the general citizenry.

He ridicules the notion that the university has been succumbing to the "power structure" in the dispute over civil-rights activity. "I had to fight some extremely tough battles against some very powerful legislators who felt we should kick out students who were arrested for sit-ins in the Bay area, but we never yielded an inch," Kerr says. "It just would not have been in character for us to say that the only place the students could fight for Negro rights was in Mississippi."

As for the Bancroft Strip, Kerr says that "whatever pressure preceded the order involved the loading of the galleries at the Republican convention with Berkeley students whooping it up for Scranton against Goldwater."

The F.S.M. indictment of the "multiversity" brings a special twinge to Kerr because every charge the insurgents now raise he foresaw with greater incisiveness as long ago as April, 1963, when he gave the Godkin lectures at Harvard.

Those talks described, with apparent fatalism but decided unenthusiasm, the evolution of a "mechanism held together by administrative rules and powered by money." Kerr predicted that undergraduates would feel so neglected and depersonal-

ized that the revolt they once engaged in against the faculty *in loco parentis* would turn into an even more destructive uprising against the faculty *in absentia*. Everything Kerr warned of then is embodied now in the F.S.M. lament that the student is being downgraded to the status of an I.B.M. punch card in a computerized multiversity.

Kerr concedes that the multiversity is a disturbing place for many students, but he disputes that it is devoid of meaning. "One of the advantages of a big city or a big university — as against a smaller and more monolithic closed community — is that people can find those things which may mean something to them," he says. "They are given a choice.

"It would be terribly stultifying to find yourself in a place which has a single meaning, and that meaning is the same for everyone. The only kind of society that has only a single meaning is an authoritarian one. It seems to me that is a place where you would really expect rebellion. Essentially, what the F.S.M. are saying is that they are rebelling against freedom of choice."

When I noted that the students objected not to too many meanings, but to the absence of any, Kerr replied:

"In fact, there is a lot of opportunity to participate, only it takes a little longer and requires more initiative to find it. Many tend to be overwhelmed by their opportunities; there are so many lectures to choose from, so many things to do, that they tend to become lost. They are torn too many ways and wind up condemning the whole structure."

The notion that the university, for all the magnitude of its Federal and industrial involvement (it is receiving $246 million this year for operating three giant atomic installations, plus $175 million in research grants and contracts), has become an arm of the Pentagon or big business also draws a rebuttal from Kerr. "The university," he says, "is intertwined with all society. And if it is overbalanced in any direction as compared with the surrounding society, it is in the fact that it is a source of dissent and social criticism. You could say it is a tool of the critics, and that is one of the things that make it so dynamic."

All this brought us back to the students' overriding complaint—the enormous size of

Berkeley, with 27,500 students on a single campus, and the obliteration of the individual's relationship to faculty and administration. Kerr's answer dwelt more on society's inescapable needs than confidence that alienation could be overcome.

"Every day makes it clearer that the university's invisible product, knowledge, is likely to be the most powerful single element in our culture," he says. "With so many young people pounding at our gates, we're up against a tremendous assignment. To take the position that we won't grow would be a terribly irresponsible thing."

**K**ERR is a philosopher-pragmatist of the technocratic society, probably the ablest and most creative in the educational field. His guiding principle is individual disengagement. He preaches the idea that each person can best protect his own happiness in a society of bigness by developing pluralistic attachments. "If you invest all of yourself in an institution," he says, "you become a slave. It becomes a prison, not an agency of liberation." This road to the independent spirit is just the opposite of that traveled by the F.S.M. and its leaders. Their goal is commitment, but there is a good deal of confusion about precisely what it is they are committed to.

And who is listening, now that the clear-cut issue created by the closing of the Bancroft Strip and the blackout of political recruiting has been resolved? The signs are that the overwhelming support for F.S.M. aims among students of all political hues and of no hues has evaporated along with the issue.

Moreover, there are strong indications of strain inside the F.S.M. steering committee, now a much more ingrown group than in the initial days of across-the-board coalition. Many would like to disband the movement. Hal Draper said frankly that it might go into "an inactive phase." Ed Rosenfeld, the F.S.M.'s press officer, says that one thought under consideration is to establish a cooperative coffeehouse, on a nonprofit basis, near the campus. "It would be a civilized gathering place in the best European manner," he says, "a suitable forum for debates and discussion."

**B**ACK at the heliport for the return flight, I tried to evaluate the Berkeley uprising

against the memories of my own days of rebellion as president of the C.C.N.Y. class of '31. It was a time when one worker in four was jobless and the misery of the Great Depression was beginning to grip the land. We had been ready to picket our own commencement in cap and gown, but we chickened out at the last minute for fear of losing our degrees.

These students, for all their talk of setting up an espresso joint as a monument to their mutiny, were a tougher, smarter breed, more ready to go for broke.

But what did they accomplish, besides effecting the cancellation of an order the university admits never should have been issued?

They have done one important thing that may prove of considerable help to Berkeley and all other big universities. They have cut through the multifarious concerns of an administration that must deal with every agency of government, including those in 50 countries abroad, and forced it to recognize that it is sitting on a volcano of neglected, seething students.

Kerr, who has always recognized the need for diversity in multiversity, already is hard at work on measures to improve the quality and the immediacy of instruction. He aims to break down the idea that research, not teaching, is the mission of the good professor. Both roles are vital, Kerr believes, and so does the man he has brought in as acting chancellor, Dean Martin Meyerson of the College of Environmental Design.

Last fall's earthquake also has shaken the administration and faculty into a heightened awareness of the need for teamwork to lessen the students' belief that no one cares whether they go or stay, that undergraduate needs are passed over in favor of lucrative research contracts, book-writing projects and traveling lectureships all over the world. Prof. Arthur M. Ross, the enterprising chairman of an emergency executive committee elected by the faculty in the blackest period last December, expresses confidence that a genuine educational overhaul is in prospect. Most of his colleagues agree.

What goes into the curriculum and who teaches what courses will be a matter for the faculty to determine, but both Kerr and Ross feel students can have a useful advisory role. A larger area of authority for students in disciplinary committees and in other forms of self-government also is in prospect. All these developments should help still the discord at Berkeley, but—much more important—they will help make it a better institution of learning.

**O**NE of the imponderables in trying to guess whether peace has really come to the campus is that some F.S.M. activists obviously have developed a vested interest in finding things to fight about. They seem to operate on the theory that, in a system they believe is basically corrupt, the worse things get, the easier it will be to generate mass resistance.

This is not a novel theory in radical movements, but it is not one that makes for stability. When the police dragged Savio and the 800 others out of Sproul Hall, he exulted, "This is wonderful — wonderful. We'll bring the university to our terms." When Paul Jacobs told an F.S.M. leader that he had advised Kerr to enter Sproul on the night of the sit-in and talk to the students (advice Kerr did not take), the insurgent asked sourly, "What side are you on?"

The reckless prodigality with which the F.S.M. uses the weapon of civil disobedience raises problems no university can deal with adequately. Mass discipline carries the danger of martyrdom and a spread of sympathetic disorders to other campuses.

Garrisoning the grounds with police runs so counter to the essential concept of the university as a redoubt of tolerance and reason that it is perhaps the worst solution of all. At Berkeley it brought the faculty into open alliance with the students against the administration. Yet, the alternative of giving students total immunity could engender a situation akin to that in the University of Caracas, where student revolutionaries use the campus as a fortress from which to sally forth to attack the general society.

"We fumbled, we floundered, and the worst thing is I still don't know how we should have handled it," Kerr acknowledges. "At any other university the administrators

wouldn't have known how to handle it any better."

Menacing as is this new disruptive device, one even graver danger sign outranks all others raised by the mess at Berkeley. That is the degree to which it evidences a sense of lost identity, a revulsion against bigness, that is affecting all of our society. On the campus it takes the form of antagonism against the multiversity. In the mass production unions this same feeling of impending obliteration recently spurred rank-and-file strikes against General Motors and Ford, and may erupt again in the basic steel industry this spring. The longshoremen, fearing the shiny face of automation, voted down contracts that gave them lifetime job security and a generous wage guarantee — principally because they felt the machine was grinding them and their jobs into nothingness.

A similar mood of irrationality, of vaporous but paralyzing apprehension, stalks all our institutions in a time of unmatched material prosperity and individual well-being. Young people, in particular, study the unemployment statistics and decide that society is in a conspiracy to provide security for the older generation at the expense of the youngsters outside waiting to get in. Education is the magic carpet over the hurdles that make the dropout the shutout in our society. But, even at this most distinguished of universities, bigness robs many students of individual dignity or purpose. This feeling helps explain the spread of drug addiction and senseless crime among many well-to-do youngsters. All are part of an alienation that turns even affluence and security into worthless prizes.

This may prove to be the nation's critical challenge, potentially more damaging than the international crises that monopolize so much of our concern and our budget. If Berkeley cannot imbue life with a sense of fulfillment and content, where will we find it? Kerr, the mediator-innovator, must become a gladiator—pioneering new paths in intergroup relations and giving new vitality to democratic standards that rest on knowledge.

# THE STUDENT LEFT: SPURRING REFORM

## New Activist Intelligentsia Is Rising on Campuses

### By FRED POWLEDGE

On a recent Saturday night, a group of University of Chicago students gathered at an apartment for a party. There was no liquor and no dancing and no talk about basketball, student politics or sex.

Instead, the young men, in sport coats and without ties, and the young women, in skirts and black stockings, sat on the floor and talked about such things as "community organization," "powerlessness" and "participatory democracy."

The host, Bob Ross, a 22-year-old graduate student in sociology who is the son of a factory worker, opened a window and found a cold bottle of beer on the fire escape. He offered it to a visitor and explained:

"I guess it seems pretty strange. I suppose some of us feel that we don't have time to drink or dance. We're too busy trying to change the world."

The young people in Chicago, and their counterparts in a dozen other college communities, are part of a new, small, loosely bound intelligentsia that calls itself the new student left and that wants to cause fundamental changes in society. Last week these young people, or people who feel the same as they, picketed in favor of: academic tenure for professors at St. John's College. Some of them participated in the recent New York school boycott.

They organized the Northern demonstrations and sit-ins that followed the civil rights uprising in Selma, Ala., and some of them went to Selma to help there.

They believe that the civil rights movement, the emergence of poverty as a national cause, and the possibility of nuclear extinction make fundamental change mandatory.

### Small Letters Preferred

They do not deny that they are a lot like the young radicals of the thirties in their aspirations. Some of them, who liken their movement to a "revolution," want to be called radicals.

Most of them, however, prefer to be called "organizers." Others reply that they are "democrats with a small 'd'" or "socialists with a small 's'". A few like to be called Marxists.

Most express contempt for any specific labels, and they don't mind being called cynics. Few have allowed themselves to develop a sense of humor about their work; they function on a crisis footing.

They are mindful that their numbers are tiny in comparison with the total in the nation's colleges. Now, as before, the great majority of their fellow students are primarily interested in marriage, a home, and a job.

### Forming Own Religion

Jeffrey Shero, a 23-year-old Texan, sat recently in the student union building at the University of Texas, drinking bitter institutional coffee and explaining his own particular cynicism in this way:

"This generation has witnessed hypocrisy as has no other generation. The churches aren't doing what they should be doing. There is lie after lie on television. The whole society is run and compounded on lies.

"People are manipulated. The kind of ethics that our parents preached are not practiced, because we now see how our parents really live.

"We are the first generation that grew up with the idea of annihilation. In a situation like this, you have to go out and form your own religion."

About 70 others were interviewed recently in New York, Chicago, San Francisco, Atlanta, Newark, Louisiana, and Austin, Tex.

### Skeptical of Communism

Although a few displayed a tendency to defend the Soviet Union as an example of the sort of society they want to create, the great majority of those questioned said they were as skeptical of Communism as they were of any other form of political control.

Their conversations indicated that they were neither directed nor inspired by Communism, as some of their critics have alleged. "You might say we're a-Communist," said one, "just as you might say we're amoral and a-almost everything else."

Although one of their goals is the elimination of the evils of a middle-class society, many of them come from middle-class, middle-income families.

They believe that the only way out of the nation's problems is through the creation of a new left. They reject many of the old leftist heroes, whom they describe as "sellouts"; they want to write their own philosophy, and they want to create an alliance between the millions of American whites

**ASSAYS YOUTH GROUPS:** Dr. Neil J. Smelser, assistant to the chancellor for political activity at the University of California. He believes that aims of student left will be achieved.

and Negroes who have no economic or political power.

Most of them express skepticism about their own chances of success, but they want to invest the rest of their lives in the cause.

One of them, Richard Rothstein, a 21-year-old worker in a district of Chicago that contains poor whites, Negroes, Mexicans and Puerto Ricans, was graduated from Harvard and was a Fulbright scholar at the London School of Economics. His father is a Federal civil servant.

### Working From Within

"We reject the idea that you can bring change through getting elected to the legislature and then handing down change from the top," he said. "Somehow, under that system, the poor still get treated poorly."

Mr. Rothstein is attempting to work from within to organize the residents of his adopted neighborhood into political groups.

It is this theory of "community organization" that is being practiced by almost all of these youth organizations now. The idea is to use the labor movement's techniques to organize deprived people around a central complaint.

### Jobs and Traffic Lights

The complaint may be poor housing, inferior schools, unequal job opportunities, capital punishment, the need for a traffic light at a busy corner, or the impersonality of a college administration.

There is little talk among the activists about racial integration. Some of them consider

the subject passé. They declare that integration will be almost as evil as segregation if it results in a complacent, middle-class interracial society.

"The civil rights movement has a built-in dead end," said one young man, "because when most of the basic civil rights issues are settled there still won't be enough jobs for everyone."

Said William Strickland, the executive director of the Northern Student Movement: "We have come to see that the attainment of full freedom transcends the secularity of 'civil rights.'

"Something more is needed: A movement which confronts the structural barriers to equality and enables people to assume the responsibility for their own lives."

### Bias at the Bottom

As a result most of the efforts at community action are based on grievances that arise from racial discrimination, but they are not aimed at eventual desegregation.

Some exponents of the community-action approach point out that young activists in the Southern movement, who originally worked almost exclusively in the fields of public accommodations or voter registration, are now talking more about other forms of organization.

Albany, Ga., was the scene of Selma-type demonstrations in the summer of 1962. Now a day-care center is being organized there.

In Newark, workers of the Students for a Democratic Society are trying to organize a Negro neighborhood that is faced with the probability of destruction through urban renewal.

Inside the college communities, some of the young people have found student freedom to be the issue around which a movement may be built.

On the campuses of a number of universities, the student leftists are planning demonstrations, marches, and political action around the issues of conscription, academic freedom, the war in South Vietnam, disarmament and poverty in general. They hope that an important side effect will be increased enrollments in the organizations they represent.

At present there is no reliable index of the strength of the student left. The hard core amounts to about 500 persons. However, thousands may rally around them from time to time in support of a given cause.

In the North, the movement is being run by a handful of organizations, along with a number of smaller or less important groups. The major groups are Students for a Democratic Society, the W.E.B. Du Bois Clubs of America, the Northern Student Movement and the Student Nonviolent Coordinating Committee.

### Port Huron Statement

Students for a Democratic Society was organized in June, 1962, at Port Huron, Mich., by "a band of young intellectuals who got most of their immediate inspiration from the sit-in movement," according to one of the founders, Tom Hayden, a 25-year-old Detroit native.

The Michigan meeting produced a 63-page paperback document called "The Port Huron Statement" that concluded as follows:

"We seek the establishment of a democracy of individual participation governed by two central aims: That the individual share in those social decisions determining the quality and direction of his life; that society be organized to encourage independence in men and provide the media for their common participation."

Students for a Democratic Society is affiliated with the League for Industrial Democracy Inc., a nonprofit educational institution founded in 1905 by Jack London, Upton Sinclair and Clarence Darrow.

It claims a national membership of 1,700 in 44 chapters, along with 50 staff members. It operates or cooperates with community action projects in Newark; Baltimore; Chester, Pa.; Cleveland; Chicago; Cairo, Ill.; San Francisco; Austin, Tex.; Hazard, Ky.; Boston, and New Brunswick, N. J.

### New York Headquarters

The group publishes an extensive list of essays, most of them written by its own members. The office is at 119 Fifth Avenue in New York. The president is Todd Gitlin.

The W. E. B. DuBois Clubs of America started in San Francisco about three years ago. The organization is named for the Negro leader who helped found the National Association for the Advancement of Colored People and who later turned to Communism.

Last June the clubs became a national organization. The preamble to its constitution states:

"It is our belief that this nation can best solve its problems in an atmosphere of peaceful coexistence, complete disarmament and true freedom for all peoples of the world, and that these solutions will be reached mainly through the united efforts of all democratic elements in our country, composed essentially of the working people allied in the unity of Negroes and other minorities with whites."

Last October, J. Edgar Hoover, the director of the Federal Bureau of Investigation, wrote that the DuBois Clubs had been spawned by the Communist Party, U.S.A., and that the clubs' ideology was one of "discord, hate and violence."

### Hoover Viewed as Threat

Many members reply that Mr. Hoover is part of the reactionary force that the Du-

Bois group believes is the greatest threat to American society.

One DuBois member on the West Coast, Bettina Aptheker, a 20-year-old University of California student, explained her philosophy this way:

"The basic thing is destroying or eliminating the corporate monopolies and nationalizing the control of the industries in the hands of the people.

"If this were done, a lot of other things would follow. There would be an elimination of the race thing, elimination of the preparations for war.

"That's the long-range thing. On a short-term basis, we should do whatever can be done within the present confines of the System—things like voter registration and political education.

"Being a member of the DuBois Club, I am also a Socialist, and I see the fight for further political freedom at Cal and the fight for civil rights in the rest of the country as part of the over-all fight to change the System. Any democratic movement to further the rights of the people is part of the democratic move toward Socialism."

### Daughter of Writer

Miss Aptheker, an American history major, is the daughter of Herbert Aptheker, a writer on Negro history and director of the Institute for Marxist Studies here. She calls herself a "Marxist Socialist."

She believes that "at present the Socialist world, even with all its problems, is moving closer than any other countries toward the sort of society I think should exist. In the Soviet Union, it has almost been achieved."

Robert Heisler, a 19-year-old sophomore at City College in New York, and the local coordinator for the club, shares the view of Miss Aptheker.

"The Soviet Union and the whole Socialist bloc are on the right track," he said. "They have broken loose from some of the basic problems that are at the heart of this country's social system.

"I don't mean that we're calling for a blueprint, a carbon copy of what they do. But I do believe that the Soviet Union and the Socialist bloc—including the new nations in Africa and Asia—are more on the way to getting this than is the United States at this point."

The DuBois Club claims a national membership of more than 1,000. Chapters are currently active in Madison, Wis.; New York City; Minneapolis; Chicago; Detroit; Los Angeles; Albuquerque; Berkeley; Oakland, Calif.; San Francisco; New Paltz, N. Y.; Philadelphia; New Jersey; Portland; Pittsburgh and Boston.

Phil Davis, the 25-year-old national president, is a hefty, bushy-haired young man who wears open-necked dress shirts and rough yellow boots, and who takes home $46.15 a week from his office in San Francisco. He calls himself a Socialist.

The Northern Student Movement was founded in 1961 as the Northern wing of the Southern-based Student Nonviolent Coordinating Committee.

The Northern group concentrates on tutorial programs and community organization in the Northern Negro ghettoes. It has field projects in Boston, Hartford, Detroit, Harlem and Philadelphia.

The Northern movement says it has 73 campus affiliates, 28 field secretaries, about 40 full-time volunteer workers and a constituency of about 2,000 students. The national office is at 514 West 126th Street, New York.

The Student Nonviolent Coordinating Committee, the inspiration for all the organizations of the new student left, was founded April 17, 1960. About 300 persons, almost all Negro youths heartened by the sit-ins that had started two and one-half months before in Greensboro, formed the Temporary Student Nonviolent Coordinating Committee. Their statement of purpose spoke almost exclusively of the virtues of nonviolence.

"By appealing to conscience and standing on the moral nature of human existence," it concluded, "nonviolence nurtures the atmosphere in which reconciliation and justice become actual possibilities."

The committee started out in a tiny office in Atlanta, upstairs from Dr. Martin Luther King Jr.'s headquarters. It had two employes. Now, more than a dozen campaigns later, it has 237 paid staffers. Twenty of them work in Northern Friends of S.N.C.C. offices and 25 in the Atlanta office. The others work in cities like McComb, Miss., and Selma, Ala.

The organization still retains its youthful, interracial composition, but its members have grown more cynical as the battle progresses. It now has 65 to 70 automobiles, more than 50 short-wave radio units, long-distance trunk lines and a ledger in which it can write its own airplane tickets.

Asked if the organization has adopted any defensive weapons, a member replied: "Yes. Our bodies."

On issues that involve the Southern campaign, S.N.C.C., or "Snick" as it is often called, and the Friends of S.N.C.C. can rally immediate Northern support. Most of the protests that issued from the North last week over the Selma crisis were organized by their people.

The organization is too involved in the highly realistic issues of Southern voting and the like to spend much time on academic freedom, conscription or ending in the war in Vietnam. Many Northern college students are active in its projects in the South in the summer time, community-organizing in the North during the academic year.

The Student Nonviolent Coordinating Committee has tended more and more toward political organization in recent months. Next summer's project, for example, will be centered on bringing pressure to bear **in Washington to provide equal representation in Congress for Southern Negroes.**

**Other organizations have formed as a result of its experiences in the South, and in some cases standard civil rights groups have altered their pro-**grams to accommodate those who believe in a new radicalism.

The Southern Student Organizing Committee was formed a year ago in Nashville to seek the involvement of Southern whites in the rights movement and is closely aligned with S.N.C.C. One of this group's first projects will be to seek the abolition of capital punishment in Tennessee.

Many members of the Congress of Racial Equality, a Northern group established in 1943 and devoted primarily to nonviolence, are working now on community organization. The group experienced a fundamental change last summer when some of its leaders declared that "demonstrations for demonstration's sake" were no longer a useful weapon.

### Sharing 'Powerlessness'

The members of the student left are hesitant about predicting the success or failure of their efforts. Most of them see the movement as one without end. The expression "not in my lifetime" occurs frequently in their conversations.

One man who has watched them feels confident that they will succeed in most of their aims. He is Dr. Neil J. Smelser, the 34-year-old editor of the American Sociological Review and the assistant to the Berkeley chancellor for student political activity. His job was created as a result of last fall's rebellions at the Berkeley campus.

"The students of the thirties considered themselves intellectuals," he said in an interview. **"They were Marxists. They were concerned with wealth, and their friends were the workers.**

**"The student intellectuals of this generation now find their** friends among the Negroes and Puerto Ricans and Mexicans. They share powerlessness with the minority groups. They're students and they have relatively little power and they're frustrated."

Dr. Smelser believes that "this movement will be as successful as the thirties' movement because it's as closely linked to the inevitable process of social change as the thirties' movement was."

### Foresees Moderation

Another faculty member at the University of California detects a note of sadness in the situation. Lewis S. Feuer, social scientist at Berkeley and a writer on the subject of student movements, said:

"The sad thing is that so many of these people have a sympathy for anything that's anti-American."

"The new student movements, by and large, differ from the older ones in that they believe in direct action," he said. "They don't lobby; they don't bother with legal procedures. They say 'By golly, we'll turn up with 500 people and compel the agreement to take place.'"

He believes that liberal student groups of a more moderate nature will come into existence to represent "the people who want to solve these problems through the traditional American democratic-liberal approach." But he adds:

"On the other hand, as long as there is an illness in America that makes some people look to others—Castro, Mao, or anyone else who comes along—this sort of thing will persist.

"Whatever makes in our society for any sort of emotional rejection of American character will cause this feeling, and this movement, to persist."

# F.B.I. Official Links Crime and the Advocates of 'Civil Disobedience'

Special to The New York Times

CHICAGO, Dec. 14 — C. D. DeLoach, associate director for crime records in the Federal Bureau of Investigation, today assailed "arrogant nonconformists" and characterized campus and street demonstrations as a disgrace.

Mr. DeLoach, who will assume the title of assistant to J. Edgar Hoover, director of the F.B.I., on Dec. 30, and who is Mr. Hoover's second in command, found a common denominator between criminals and extreme opponents of the Vietnam war and advocates of civil disobedience. It is that they believe they are above the law, he said.

Speaking to the annual convention of the American Farm Bureau Federation, Mr. DeLoach said defiance of the law was a "malignant disease" in a free society.

"Yet, throughout this great land of ours today, growing numbers of citizens — racketeers, Communists, narcotics peddlers, filth merchants and others of their ilk — hold themselves above the law," he said. "They represent a deadly cause —a cause which ironically is not only served but actually encouraged by expanding legions of its victims.

"Look, for example, at the 'celebrity status' which has often been accorded those mor-

Associated Press
**C. D. DeLoach**

ally and emotionally immature misfits who have cast a shadow of disgrace across the streets of many American communities and the campuses of some of our educational institutions."

Mr. DeLoach said that he referred to "the lawless demon-

strators, the draft card burners, the raucous exalters of the four-letter word." The latter was an apparent reference to the so-called "dirty speech movement" at the University of California, Berkeley, this year.

"I refer to the arrogant nonconformists, including some so-called educators, who have mounted the platform at public gatherings to urge 'civil disobedience' and defiance of authority," he said.

"And I refer also to those members of the self-proclaimed 'smart set' who consider it a sign of 'sophistication' to ridicule decency, patriotism, respectability and duty."

Mr. DeLoach said it was "inconceivable" that a member of the clergy would publicly commend draft-card burning as an act of loyalty to the United States "at an hour when Americans in uniform stand poised against the surging tide of Communist terror and aggression." He said that happened in New York last month, but did not name the clergyman.

"And it is equally inconceivable that anyone who enjoys the privileges and the blessings which this country conveys upon its citizens would advocate sending funds or supplies to the Communist forces in

Vietnam," Mr. DeLoach said. "Yet, this, too, has happened here in the United States."

Meanwhile, a sit-in at Holy Name Cathedral was continued by five persons protesting the alleged silencing of priests who have attempted to speak on Vietnam issues.

The protesters, who include students and Roman Catholic laymen, said they had been inspired by similar acts at Catholic colleges and churches across the nation, particularly by a partial fast conducted by students at the University of Notre Dame.

The vigil at the cathedral began Sunday night with two Loyola University students spending nine hours sitting in the cold on the steps. Six persons were permitted to spend last night inside the cathedral and five were there today with the intention of remaining all night.

Julian Sulgit, 22 years old, a senior philosophy major at Loyola, said the protest was over what he termed "oppressive attitudes within the church" in the alleged disciplining of the Rev. Daniel Berrigan of New York for criticizing American policy in Vietnam, and the alleged censuring of the Rev. William H. DuBay of Los Angeles, who spoke out on civil rights.

December 15, 1965

# Today's New Left, Amid Frustration and Factionalism, Turns Toward Radicalism and Direct Action

## The New Left Turns To Mood of Violence In Place of Protest

### By PAUL HOFMANN

"We are working to build a guerrilla force in an urban environment," said the national secretary of the left-wing Students for a Democratic Society, Gregory Calvert, one day recently.

"We are actively organizing sedition," he said.

Mr. Calvert, a 29-year-old former history teacher, spoke pleasantly about revolution in his dingy office on Chicago's Skid Row. The threat of violence in his words characterizes the

current radicalization of the New Left.

A maze of factions with a penchant for verbosity and a hankering for action, the New Left wants emphatically to be distinct from the old left—the socialist and Communist movements whose history goes back over generations.

**Ebullience and Frustration**

Just how distinct it has become was made clear during a three-week series of interviews with some 75 New Left activists and sympathizers from coast to coast. Most of them were younger than 30, and some sounded much more truculent than members of the Moscow-oriented Communist party, U. S. A.

The spirit of resistance

and direct action constitutes perhaps the major attitude in the New Left today. Other findings in this assessment of the New Left's mood are as follows:

¶An ebullience over the impact of opposition to the war in Vietnam, which emotionally involves some members of the middle class and leads them to New Left positions also on domestic issues.

¶A frustration resulting from the lack of New Left political power and the failures of "peace" candidates in national and local elections.

¶A virulent factionalism similar to the doctrinaire old left feuds, a factionalism that is being exploited by extremists.

¶A spreading tendency to link

up with leftist and "anti-imperialist" movements in Latin America, Europe and emerging nations.

¶The growth of a broadening "hippie" segment, mainly on the East and West Coasts, occasionally joining the New Left in demonstrations but also worrying it because drug users and beatniks tend to withdraw from society instead of attempting to reform or revolutionize it.

¶The drifting apart of young whites and Negroes, close allies in the civil rights battles in the South a few years ago, as black power extremism spreads in Northern ghettos.

**'Che Lives in Our Hearts'**

If there is one dominant hero of the New Left mood, perhaps he is Ernesto Che Guevara.

Mr. Calvert, the beardless, ruddy-faced national secretary of Students for a Democratic Society, said:

"Che's message is applicable to urban America as far as the psychology of guerrilla action goes. . . . Che sure lives in our hearts."

Che Guevara, the Argentine-born revolutionary who was an associate of Premier Fidel Castro of Cuba, disappeared more than two years ago and is rumored to be leading insurgents somewhere in the Andean fastnesses.

A long way from the South American sierras, a surprising number of young left-wing intellectuals were found to revere the Argentinian adventurer. Rebellious students who spoke with equal disdain about "Establishment liberals" and "Communist squares" professed the cult of the "pure" man of revolutionary action.

Posters of Che Guevara and of Malcolm X, the black nationalist slain here two years ago, are advertised for sale "at special bulk rates" in a San Francisco monthly, The Movement. The radical publication disaffiliated recently from the Student Nonviolent Coordinating Committee, the militant, Southern-oriented movement that used to be one of the pillars of the New Left but has lately veered toward black power goals and away from Students for a Democratic Society.

**'I'm No Pacifist'**

Che Guevara's bearded likeness was encountered on the walls of the littered offices of radical newspapers and left-wing groups. His name cropped up in talks in college cafeterias whenever the New Left's current infatuation with direct action was mentioned.

"I recognize that violence may be necessary, I'm no pacifist," said a vibrant young woman who has done much work for the New Left, Leni Zeiger. "I'm a white, middle-class girl, but I understand why Negroes, Puerto Ricans or Okies riot. I feel the same frustrations in myself, the same urge to violence."

Nevertheless, Miss Zeiger said during an interview at that citadel of the New Left, the University of California campus at Berkeley, "there are a lot of dilemmas about violence. . . ."

At the age of 21, Miss Zeiger considers herself "old New Left," because she believes more in community work and, possibly, political action than in urban guerrillas. She has been active in left-oriented projects in black and poor-white ghettos in Chicago and Cleveland and, while working for her B.A., is now on the staff of The Movement, doing research among poor Southerners and "hillbillies" in California.

Of the continual left-wing rifts, Miss Zeiger said:

"The trouble is that the politically minded people aren't very radical, and the radicals aren't very political."

Violence was a topic, too, in a talk with a University of Michigan economics teacher at Ann Arbor, Michael F. Zweig. He is a former president of the S.D.S. chapter there.

**Calls Violence Necessary**

"I think violence is necessary, and it frightens me," Mr. Zweig said. The 24-year-old graduate school teaching fellow, whose face is framed by a luxuriant blond beard, remarked:

"There isn't a great feeling of personal liberation in burning down a Cleveland store."

After another wave of urban riots like those of recent summers, Mr. Zweig suggested, local governments might decide to collaborate with left-inspired neighborhood groups, and poor people might even obtain guaranteed annual minimum earnings, a kind of negative income tax.

"If that's all we get," the teacher said "violence doesn't become so desirable."

He added: "I am very pessimistic about the prospects of change, even of meaningful reforms in this country. The quality of life [in America], that's what I am so pessimistic about."

Profound dissatisfaction with living in the contemporary United States was voiced by many other New Left backers. They saw the nation as oppressively dominated by an Establishment of political-corporate power structures that were hampering social and civil rights progress at home and tampering with the destinies of peoples abroad.

"Nicaragua and a lot of other countries should get together to resist the United States," said Gary Rothberger, a sociology student who succeeded Mr. Zweig as president of the Ann Arbor chapter of S.D.S.

Insurgency in Nicaragua and in other Latin-American countries is stirring news to the left wing on United States campuses. A California student, not yet 20, who looked like a younger Che Guevara, said he had spent last summer with Guatemalan guerrillas.

Ann Arbor is important on the New Left map because Students for a Democratic Society was born there some six years ago. The movement's first national convention in Port Huron, Mich., in June, 1962, produced a basic New Left manifesto.

This rejected "paranoic anti-Communism" while blaming the Soviet Union for suppressing opposition. It strongly attacked American capitalism, denounced the "hypocrisy of American ideals" and advocated a vaguely defined "participatory democracy."

Several S.D.S. members, asked for practical examples of "participatory democracy" in action, pointed to the Yugoslav

Peter E. Sutheim

**Gregory Calvert, national secretary of Students for a Democratic Society, aims at building guerrilla force.**

system of workers' councils' running nationalized business enterprises.

Amendments to the "Port Huron Statement" have made the S.D.S. program completely agnostic on Communism, opening the door to membership of Communists.

Since then, Students for a Democratic Society has gone through various phases. It aided the Student Nonviolent Coordinating Committee in the South, it went into the Northern ghettos to organize their inhabitants, and lately it has swung back onto the campuses.

Some of the ghetto efforts are still alive. Among them are the Newark Community Union Project—directed by Tom Hayden, a cofounder of S.D.S. and main author of the Port Huron manifesto— and Chicago's Jobs or Income Now (J.O.I.N.).

In the short but lively history of S.D.S., 1967 is the year of the "prairie guys," the national leaders who were elected at a convention in a Methodist camp at Clear Lake, Iowa, last September. Nick Egleson, president, Carl Davidson, vice president, Mr. Calvert and their friends are leading S.D.S., in Mr. Davidson's words, "from protest to resistance."

**Action Above Ideology**

Mr. Calvert described himself as a "post-Communist revolutionary," putting action above ideology. Dee Jacobsen, assistant national secretary and headquarters manager, said the North Vietnamese whom S.D.S. representatives had got in touch with "cannot understand why we don't take any direct action."

The three-room, $125-a-month national headquarters of Students for a Democratic Society is at 1608 West Madison Street, Chicago's Skid Row. It is close to the area of last summer's Negro rioting.

Despite the squalid setting, the headquarters looks more efficient than it did at its former location near the University of Chicago campus on the city's South Side.

Last year there was picturesque clutter; now there is drab orderliness. There are boxes for outgoing and incoming mail, staffers who answer telephones and an ancient safe with a combination lock.

"We are getting ready for the revolution." Mr. Jacobsen joked with a thin smile when a visitor remarked on the new look.

Mr. Jacobsen said he had abandoned psychiatric hospital work to become a full-time S.D.S. organizer because he felt "my life was getting unbearable."

Mr. Calvert and Mr. Jacobsen said S.D.S. had some 200 chapters, with 6,000 dues-paying members and at least 25,000 other supporters who participated in chapter activities.

These activities, the S.D.S. leaders said, are centered on assisting young men to evade military duty by "insubordination, legal and illegal emigration to Canada, going underground in America—everything."

Students for a Democratic Society is organizing "draft resistance unions" and has a "national draft resistance coordinator," Jeff Segal.

**A Change of Plan**

The resistance-fomenting new leadership has only contempt for electoral campaigns by "peace" candidates and is cool toward mere protest demonstrations. The leadership first decided not to participate in the Spring Mobilization antiwar demonstrations of last April 15, deeming them a futile exercise, but was overruled at a meeting of the movement's national council in Cambridge, Mass., early in April.

The national leaders still did not seem to think much of the mobilization, and they have hinted at possibly even sterner action than resistance to the draft.

"Some of our members undoubtedly will help" in ghetto riots this summer, Mr. Jacobsen said.

A former S.D.S. organizer, who asked that he not be named, ridiculed the present leadership's talk of urban guerrillas.

"Greg Calvert has read something about leftist terrorist commandos in Caracas," he said, "and he and his friends think they are Venezuelans. They are becoming a sect. Romantic and out of touch with reality."

He said infiltrators from the pro-Peking Progressive Labor party had gained control of at least one S.D.S. chapter in Chicago. He did not name it.

Other New Left moderates suggested that the verbal militancy in S.D.S. headquarters might mask an inferiority complex vis-à-vis Negro racists who had already made up their minds that violence was necessary to attain black power.

"Some of the black nationalists are stacking Molotov cocktails and studying how they can hold a few city blocks in an uprising, how to keep off the fire brigade and the police so that the National Guard must be called out," a white Ohio student said. "And they're right. We ought to help them where we can, but we oughtn't be hung up with leading or liberating the Negroes."

### In Praise of Black Power

Mr. Calvert conceded that S.D.S. had few Negro members. He said:

"Black power is absolutely necessary. When we have organized the white radicals we can link up with the Negro radicals."

This seemed to imply a lack of such a link at present.

In the view of Jack Newfield, assistant editor of The Village Voice, the Greenwich Village newspaper, and a former S.D.S. member, the radicalization of New Left movements results from a feeling of hopelessness.

"The situation is getting more oppressive," he said. "Look at Alabama, look at Georgia, look at the war in Vietnam."

At the Internal Security Division of the Department of Justice, an official said "it is obvious that these [New Left] groups are becoming more and more vociferous and threatening" in protesting against the war in Vietnam and calling for sedition. However, he said he was unable to comment on how serious a threat to law and order these groups were.

He said that "we are following closely the activities of some of these groups," keeping in mind that the First Amendment to the Constitution protects freedom of speech. He said violations of the Universal Military Training and Service Act and the Sedition Act were being investigated but declined to indicate whether prosecutions were on the increase.

Talks with police officers and community leaders in various cities found most in agreement that only a small hard core of leftist activists is determined to defy the law—maybe not more than a few hundred across the nation. The number of

young New Left militants who advocate violence is growing, it was found, but whether their increasingly radical talk will be translated into unlawful action is controversial.

A potential threat to public order from New Left radicals was seen in areas where racial disorders this summer are feared, including Cleveland, Chicago and, possibly New York.

Numerically, the New Left remains weak. The figure of 200,000 adherents nationwide that is often mentioned by sympathizers seems exaggerated.

### Staughton Lynd's View

In the New Left itself, the campus talk about direct action is only rarely frightening. It does not frighten Staughton Lynd, who at the age of 38 is often called an "elder statesman" of the New Left.

The guerrilla concept is "not descriptive" of the new radical trend, he said in an interview. He appeared to distinguish between active violence and civil disobedience, which he himself practiced at the end of 1965 when he defied the United States Government and visited Hanoi with Mr. Hayden, the S.D.S. cofounder, and Dr. Herbert Aptheker, the leading theoretician of the Communist Party, U.S.A.

Mr. Lynd, an associate professor of history at Yale University, who has been influenced by Quaker pacifism and Marxist doctrine, said he expected to receive a leave of absence from Yale and move to Chicago to teach at an S.D.S.-backed school for community organizers. Graduates of the school may lead draft resisters or defend the interests of the poor in housing and welfare, he said.

Mr. Lynd stressed that a "solid base of local organization" was more important to the New Left than going "too quickly" into national politics.

"I believe in local political candidates" of the New Left, he said.

A more sanguine assessment of the New Left's political possibilities was given by Paul Booth, who was S.D.S. national secretary before Mr. Calvert. Mr. Booth said in Chicago that the defeats of New Left and "peace" candidates in last year's primaries and Congressional elections "have given our people a better sense of how much work is to be done" to win political power.

### Third-Party Idea

Mr. Booth said the idea of setting up a third party on an antiwar and New Left platform deserved consideration.

He expressed hope that "maybe in three months" a vast alliance would rally behind the Rev. Dr. Martin Luther King Jr., the civil rights leader and Nobel Peace Prize winner, and Dr. Benjamin Spock, the pediatrician and antiwar leader, as

candidates for President and Vice President. Dr. King has said he does not intend to run.

Mr. Booth, a 23-year-old Swarthmore College graduate, is a board member of the National Conference for New Politics. ("Those left liberals!" Mr. Calvert sneered when the group was mentioned to him.)

The conference was established last year to help New Left and antiwar forces win political influence. Cochairmen are Julian Bond of the Georgia Legislature and Simon Casidy, a California Democrat. Dr. Spock was among the founders.

Another backer of Dr. King is Robert Scheer, the 31-year-old managing editor of Ramparts magazine. During a visit to New York he predicted broad popular support for the clergyman.

"I cannot think of any Negro minister attacking him," Mr. Scheer said. "Stokely Carmichael [chairman of the S.N.C.C.] embraced him publicly. The extremists will have to go along."

Mr. Scheer knows how to sound pretty extremist himself. In the Spring Mobilization rally in San Francisco he called President Johnson a "murderer" who was aiming at a "final solution" in Vietnam. The term "final solution" was used in official Nazi documents to describe the destruction of Jews ordered by Hitler.

The executive director of the Conference for New Politics, William F. Pepper, said in an interview at the group's New York headquarters, at 250 West 57th Street, that "we aren't a bunch of liberal do-gooders, we are revolutionary." ("Liberal" is a dirty word in the New Left.)

He said the conference aimed at affiliating with the hundreds of antiwar committees and left-oriented "single-issue and multi-issue" groups that had sprung up throughout the country.

Mr. Pepper said he once was a campaign coordinator for Senator Robert F. Kennedy in Westchester County but that in his present activity he was not "fronting for Senator Kennedy."

### A Meeting With Kennedy

Senator Kennedy has shown interest in the New Left and some time ago had a long talk with Mr. Lynd and Mr. Hayden at his home here. The meeting was arranged by Mr. Newfield, who is working on a biography of the Senator.

It was an aide of Dr. King, the Rev. James Bevel, who served as national director of the Spring Mobilization. The protest idea was originally conceived by pacifists around the Rev. A. J. Muste, who died last Feb. 11.

While Dr. King jolted the civil rights movement by saying that it was vitally connected with

the campaign against the war in Vietnam, leftists became prominent in the mobilization campaign. Some moderates withdrew.

The antiwar rally on April 15 in San Francisco's 62,000-seat Kezar Stadium, which was almost filled, was directed by a 21-year-old Trotskyite, Kipp Dawson. Outside the stadium, members of a Los Angeles-based pro-Peking group, wearing homemade uniforms with red-star insignia, sold copies of the "little red book" anthology of Chairman Mao Tse-tung's thoughts. The Maoists had denounced the April 15 demonstrations as a "revisionist Trotskyite betrayal," but did not pass up its possibilities for propaganda.

The W. E. B. DuBois Clubs, widely regarded as an unofficial youth arm of the Communist Party, U. S. A., played a subdued role in the antiwar drive or were missing altogether. Leftists of various shades wondered why.

An attempt to obtain an explanation at the Chicago national headquarters of the clubs was unsuccessful. The two-room office in the Great Lakes Building, 180 North Wacker Drive, was closed, and the telephone was disconnected.

### A Theory About the Clubs

Some DuBois Clubs have ceased their advertising of activities in local student publications. A Negro undergraduate had his own theory of why the clubs, which are named after a dead Negro Marxist scholar, seem dormant:

"The Communist Party desperately wants to look liberal and respectable. These DuBois cats, square as they are, are too swingin' for the party bureaucrats."

A former DuBois leader, Michael Myerson, is director of a newly formed Tri-Continental Information Center here that, according to a recent announcement, "has established contacts with anti-imperialist organizations and movements throughout the world." Among the sponsors are Communist party members such as Dr. Aptheker, S.D.S. backers and Dr. Spock.

Mr. Myerson, a 26-year-old University of California graduate, said the members of the center were offering their services and support as individuals and not as representatives of any organizations. The group has an office at 1133 Broadway and a two-man staff. It said it would issue a monthly bulletin and a series of pamphlets and would send fact-finding missions "to areas suffering from United States domination."

Students for a Democratic Society, too, is branching out internationally. A new Radical Education Project calls for creation of a network of "scholars, journalists, leftist youth leaders, government officials, guerrilla leaders, etc.," to gather international intelligence on insurgent movements and foreign policy developments.

The Young Socialist Alliance, an appendage of the Trotskyite Socialist Workers party, thoroughly committed its small but disciplined membership to the Spring Mobilization demonstration.

The Trotskyites' advocacy of all-embracing, "nonexclusive" antiwar alliances is met with deep distrust by many New Left adherents.

### 'Liars,' a Student Says

"The Trotskyites are liars and just want to take over the entire left," a Harvard University student said.

A visitor to the Spring Mobilization headquarters in San Francisco, a few days after the April 15 demonstrations, found the organizing committee's director there, the petite Miss Dawson, counting money contributions and arranging for the payment of bills.

It quickly developed during an interview that Miss Dawson's revolutionary idol is Che Guevara.

"The Cuban revolution is the most exciting thing that has happened in our time," said the Young Socialist Alliance activist, who was not yet born when Leon Trotsky was murdered in Mexico in 1940.

Trotsky, one of the chief organizers of the Russian October Revolution of 1917, advocated world revolution and establishment of uncompromising "pure" Communism. He was forced into exile by Stalin. Followers of Trotsky's doctrine of "permanent revolution" are influential in some Latin-American countries.

While the heirs of the old left thus identify with Che Guevara, his book "Guerrilla Warfare"—and not Mao's little red book—is becoming part of the young radicals' field kit.

Still on their required reading list is Albert Camus, the Algerian-born French author and moralist who groped for secular saintliness without God and would not cross the "tragic dividing line" from nonviolence to violence. But Camus seems to be losing ground on campuses to Major Guevara and to Frantz Fanon, the late psychiatrist from Martinique who glorified the Algerian war and wrote, in "The Wretched of the Earth," a passionate manifesto for global revolution.

"I'm just reading Fanon," remarked Miss Zeiger on the Berkeley campus. "I think I prefer Camus."

But then, she is old New Left.

# JOHNSON SUBMITS PLAN FOR VOTING BY 18-YEAR-OLDS

## Sends Congress Amendment to Assure Nation's Youth 'That They Are Trusted'

**By DAVID R. JONES**
Special to The New York Times

WASHINGTON, June 27—President Johnson proposed today a constitutional amendment that would lower the voting age to 18.

"Reason does not permit us to ignore any longer the reality that 18-year-old Americans are prepared—by education, by experience, by exposure to public affairs of their own land and all the world—to assume and exercise the privilege of voting," the President said in a message to Congress.

The President's proposal, which would be the 26th Amendment to the Constitution, would extend the franchise in national, state and local elections to more than 10 million citizens between the age of 18 and 21. Twenty-one is the voting age in 46 states now.

The amendment would not take effect unless passed by two-thirds of both houses of Congress and 38 of the 50 state legislatures. Most informed sources expressed doubt that the measure would pass during the current session of Congress, which is nearing an end.

### Prompt Action Sought

Joseph A. Califano Jr., a Presidential assistant, said at a White House news briefing that the amendment was proposed at this time in the hope that Congress would pass it this year so that the 47 state legislatures meeting in 1969 could consider the matter then.

Mr. Califano said the President had "a general purpose" to "enlarge the franchise and get people participating in the orderly political processes of Government."

This was an apparent reference to speculation that Mr. Johnson had decided to make the proposal now as a gesture to rebellious young students and as an effort to encourage them to channel their protests through traditional political channels.

### 'Commitment Is Honored'

Mr. Johnson seemed to allude to this in his message, urging Congress to approve the amendment as a signal "to our young people that they are respected, that they are trusted, that their commitment to America is honored and that the day is soon to come when they are to be participants, not spectators, in the adventure of self-government."

The nation's young people are asking an opportunity to give of their talent and energy, Mr. Johnson said, and that request must be answered. "For a nation without faith in its sons and daughters is a nation without faith in itself," he said.

The White House said Mr. Johnson's proposal was identical to a bill sponsored by the Senate Democratic leader, Mike Mansfield of Montana, the Senate Republican leader, Everett McKinley Dirksen of Illinois, and 36 other Senators.

Hearings on that measure were held in May by the Constitutional Amendments Subcommittee of the Senate Judiciary Committee. The President announced late last month that he would propose such an amendment.

The idea of lowering the voting age to 18 has been gaining popularity in Congress, where it has been a perennial loser. Both public and Congressional sentiment in favor of a lower voting age has tended to rise when the nation has sent its young men to war.

### Poll Finds 64% in Favor

Public support has climbed gradually, however, and a Gallup poll last month showed a record 64 per cent of the public approved the move.

Advocates generally argue that youths are better educated and more sophisticated now and should have the right to vote if they must bear arms. Lately, some have said lowering the voting age would help channel student protests in a more acceptable direction.

Those opposed generally contend it would violate states' rights. They dismiss the voteless-soldier argument on the ground that the vigor that makes a good fighting man does not necessarily make a wise voter. Lately, they have argued that lowering the age now would only reward unruly campus demonstrators.

The voting age is 21 in all but four of the 50 states, which at present under the Constitution are permitted to set their own age limits. Georgia has had a voting age of 18 since 1943, and Kentucky set the same age in 1955.

The voting age in Alaska is 19 and the age in Hawaii is 20. Several states have recently rejected efforts to lower the age.

## Hamlet Raskolnikov meets the dumb jock

# Out of Their League

By Dave Meggyesy.
Illustrated. 257 pp.
Berkeley, Calif.
The Ramparts Press. $6.95.

### By RICHARD ELMAN

At Syracuse University in the fifties, youth culture had not yet been designated with an imprimatur by the popes of alienation; the really large division in student sensibilities was between those who went to football games and those who didn't.

I did not.

On Saturday afternoons, hoping to seem sensitive—an intellectual—I sat drearily among books in the library seeking vicarious experience while my generation cheered raggedly, not too far away. But for the rest of the week I was even more aware that there were monsters inhabiting the campus in orange jackets who could diminish me with a glance, or a footstep. Having been raised to think of my physical self as a long extruded sleeve of waste, I rarely troubled myself to believe that mine was a perversion of nature every bit the equal of their physical assertiveness, but responded in the presence of so much gross, hard, professionally skilled flesh by mouthing a pip-squeak Marxian rhetoric.

Girls were always in danger of being turned on by these static pieces of violence. To turn their heads I played Hamlet Raskolnikov—pallid, trembling, inchoate, a crazy. It somehow seemed so much easier to make the leap from nice Jewish boy to literary assassin than to imagine any

Mr. Elman's new novel is "An Education in Blood."

empathy for these stolid engines of mayhem who were being subsidized to be my classmates. I laid them out with words like "dumb jock," and was always prepared to flinch.

Syracuse was just becoming big-time; Jimmy Brown was already on the scene, as was Jimmy Ringo. Dave Meggyesy, though he arrived a few years later, seems from this memoir to be very much the sort of brutal-honkey waif from Appalachia or Ohio whom Coach Schwartzwalder was expert at exploiting before the largely Jewish student body of this formerly Methodist institution, which now seemed to specialize in just about every aspect of Methodist hypocrisy. He was poor; he was used to hard treatment; he was eager to bruise or be bruised.

Or so it seemed to smug 6-foot-5-inch Jewish boys like myself from New York who may have thought they wanted to be great writers but could not bring themselves to imagine the consciousness of such a physical person. Was it possible that he and others like him knew we thought they were just "dumb jocks"? Meggyesy uses that word over and over again here to describe his own low self-esteem for having been an All American, a member of a championship team, a skilled professional for seven years. He quit at the height of his career, he tells us, as a protest against the dehumanization of athletes. (And he writes about that dehumanization at Syracuse and in the pros with honesty and insight.) He had fallen in love with an artist.

Later he was turned on to drugs and was led to join the Movement. The numerous injuries he suffered and inflicted, his exploitation, the slights he received, even his acts of physical cowardice are here—so vivid that I finally understood why my football-playing father had to label me a sissy whenever I shrank from pain. When Meggyesy describes his first contacts with "beatnik" stu-

dents at a place called the Orange (an off-campus bar and grill which, at totally dry Syracuse, was rumored to be the property of the university treasurer), I felt as if I was momentarily inside some time loop in which all my fearfulness toward fellows like him, mysteriously, had disappeared, and vice versa.

Not that I came to see him and know him in any fine detail; the work is fairly general and journalese, never sufficiently intense. But enough detail gets through so that one is able to feel that he and the author were, perhaps, once, one and the same possibilities. That Meggyesy was forced to opt for an armor plating of sinew and boney ligature, whereas I was raped into the pretense that I did not even have a body, but was pure mind, proves only that we were not worlds apart but driven so by an extremely vicious set of cultural preoccupations.

The bearded figure of the saint, contemplative, at Esalen Institute, which Meggyesy includes of himself in this book, intermingles camp and poignance. It seems almost like an affectation until one remembers that he has been prepared for sainthood by working at drudgeries of one sort or another since age 3, that his father was a bitter, impoverished brute, that he left home early and did not come back again, depending only on his physical prowess to get elsewhere—then it seems less affected than the bearded face with which I used to adorn my own books. One generation removed from this sort of poverty, my deprivations were entirely spiritual, as if the void left by the lack of love at home could somehow be filled with my father's boosterishly brutal enthusiasms for football, Syracuse and middle-class American WASP values.

I was a role playing rebel; Dave was a professional thug. I was told I was made of such fine stuff that my only thrill could come from being a spectator at those weekly acts of

violence on the gridiron that passed for sport. But at least a person like Dave was getting it off somehow. We middle-class momma's boys were supposed to internalize all our violence for the rest of our lives as successful professional men.

But now, like Meggyesy, I think I identify with a movement that speaks, albeit sentimentally, or ineptly, or brashly at times, in the name of human love. Isn't it just possible that we're both trying to overcome different aspects of the same profoundly-induced self-contempt?

I don't know Meggyesy. I wish I did. I have a feeling we could at least say hello to each other now and mean it. But, then, I have the feeling from reading his book that he was not the only "dumb jock" on the Hill who might have been worth getting to know. Maybe that's why he's so involved in seeking to undermine his métier through the Movement.

Reading "Out of Their League," I was aware again, as I had not been for quite some time, why we bother to read about others who seem so different from ourselves. It's the only way we have of knowing who we really are. I was moved by Meggyesy's efforts as a college freshman to enroll in regular academic courses against the wishes of his football coaches, who thought he would fail and be ruled ineligible for football. But it really all came home to me when he described a particular act of cowardice in high school when, at last down, with goal to go, Meggyesy got uptight about bucking through four men with his head down. I guess he was afraid they might break his neck. His team lost. His coach, a sort of spiritual father, refused to talk to him for nearly a week.

Who *was* Dave Meggyesy? Just another little "sissy," afraid, until recently, to admit how scared he really was. ∎

# Chicago Worried by Riot Potential in Convention Summer  as Racial Unrest in the Slums Increases

**By DONALD JANSON**
Special to The New York Times

CHICAGO, Feb. 5 — An already sizzling racial climate is worrying city officials pledged to maintain peace and tranquility during the Democartic National Convention here in August.

Developments and conditions contributing to the volatile atmosphere include the following:

¶For the sixth consecutive school day, seven Negro eighth-graders who have transferred to a less crowded neighboring white school were forced today to pass a gantlet of white adults whose taunts have included "Kill the niggers." The school is Mount Greenwood Elementary, on the Southwest Side.

¶Hearings forced by segregationists were started tonight after noisy and heated white opposition last month forced the Board of Education to reconsider a plan to bus slum pupils to distant white neighborhoods with classroom vacancies.

¶A South Side vocational high school in a Negro neighborhood was sealed off by the police today after 400 students joined in demonstrations protesting cancellation of a shop course and transfer of its teacher. They disrupted classes, rocked an automobile and surrounded a bus. A faculty member at the school, Dunbar Vocational, said they feared that a nearby housing development was accommodating mostly whites and that vocational courses were being replaced by academic courses to benefit white students planning to go to college.

¶Federal funds for job and other slum programs have been slashed. A Department of Labor report puts Negro unemployment here at three times the rate for whites. Edwin C. Berry, executive director of the Chicago Urban League, said in his annual report a week ago that the figure becomes "catastrophic" when underemployed Negroes are added.

¶Gains for the Negro poor in the last year have been "miniscule" here in education and housing, said Mr. Berry, an increasingly lonely voice of moderation among Chicago Negro leaders.

He stressed successful riot prevention efforts that gave Chicago its first relatively peaceful summer in three years last year. But he warned that this could not continue unless jobless Negro youths who rep-

resent the "social dynamite" of the city receive "first attention and ongoing attention."

His sober analysis has added to concern at City Hall for a cool summer and a safe Democratic convention. Mayor Richard J. Daley pledged law and order to get the convention. He has responded to threats of disruption with heated declarations that demonstrations going beyond peaceful picketing will be forcefully barred.

The Rev. Dr. Martin Luther King Jr., told a news conference in the Y.M.C.A. Hotel this afternoon that "the Democratic party should be demonstrated against" for its Vietnam policy and "failure to respond to economic problems in the urban areas that are causing riots." He said he would probably join the demonstrations if Congress did not act on his recommendations for economic programs for the poor.

Two kinds of trouble are brewing. One is massive, nationally coordinated demonstrations at the convention by antiwar and New Left groups such as the National Mobilization to End the War in Vietnam and the National Conference for New Politics.

Whether Negroes join in or demonstrate separately in line with the new emphasis on black power is yet to be decided. In any case, an even greater threat to peace is the riot potential fanned by anger over racial conditions.

None of the slum community organizations that now stress black political and economic power, such as the West Side Organization, advocate rioting. But their leaders openly write and talk of Chicago's violence potential. Membership in the militant slum organizations is small, but past riots have spread rapidly among the unorganized.

Many Negro leaders see peril in the combination of Negroes' heightened expectations and their lack of progress. These leaders include the Rev. C. T. Vivian, a former aide to Dr. King, and Chester Robinson, executive director of the West Side Organization.

## 'As Racist as Ever'

"Chicago is as racist and segregated as ever," Mr. Vivian commented in an interview. "Look at the bigoted reaction to the school busing plan. Look at the treatment of the seven little kids who transferred last week. A decade after Little Rock, we still have Little Rock in Chicago."

Mr. Vivian said most Chicago Negroes were convinced their "noneducation" was a deliberately planned strategy by the city's white power structure to make sure Negroes could not compete for jobs and power.

Anger and a desire for an "action now" type of self-expression among jobless Negro youths and young adults, Mr. Robinson said in an interview in his dingy storefront headquarters, make the crowded slums extremely volatile.

"Some people in Chicago want to see violence," he said. "This summer would be an ideal time for somebody who wanted to start a riot, with all the police tied up trying to control the students at the convention."

The National Mobilization to End the War in Vietnam has called a closed meeting in Chicago Feb. 24 and 25 to select a steering committee to plan demonstrations at the convention.

Rennie Davis, director of the Center for Radical Research here, said that "all the significant antiwar and black liberation groups" in the country were being invited. Mr. Davis recently visited North Vietnam at the invitation of the Hanoi government.

## Plan to Curb Protests

One of the demonstration planners, who asked not to be named, said efforts would probably be made to keep the large-scale protests "nondisruptive", until the Mississippi Freedom Democratic party delegation was rebuffed, as expected, in its quest for convention seats or President Johnson was nominated for re-election.

Either occurrence, he said, could set off civil disobedience by the demonstrators even if disruption was not planned in advance.

He envisioned blocking of foot and automobile traffic at the International Amphitheater and efforts to enter the hall to impede convention business. Side streets, alleys and the maze of stockyard pens and paths around the hall are under study, he said, as alternate routes for demonstrators in case the police block direct access.

Threats of disruption have been made by Dick Gregory, the comedian and civil rights activist, James Rollins, cochairman of the National Conference for New Politics, and a growing list of others.

The Chicago police called the threats "grossly exaggerated" but are making elaborate plans to cope with any contingency.

Capt. Thomas Frost, director of planning for the 12,000-man force, said riot control drills were now a part of police training.

### Police to Get Copters

For the tactical units established last year, he said, this includes training in use of rifles, shotguns and tear gas. He said supplies of the chemical Mace, a paralyzing gas, would be issued to all police officers soon.

He said the department would acquire three helicopters by summer, equipped with radios for communication with police cars and with loudspeakers for crowd control.

Policemen have already been assigned to serve as liaison officers with the Army, National Guard, Federal Bureau of Investigation, Secret Service and the state police, to coordinate riot-prevention efforts. The planning includes coordination of efforts to provide security for President Johnson.

Saul D. Alinsky, the "professional agitator" who returned to Chicago last week to seek negotiations with Mayor Daley on needs of the poor, said the Mayor seemed to be responding to legitimate protests with plans for repression. If so, he said, Chicago will explode.

Mr. Robinson said antiwar whites were showing a good deal more interest in convention demonstrations than Negroes were, but that blacks would be there, too.

Their demonstrations may be parallel but separate. The biracial peaceful marches and rallies organized by Dr. King and the 44-group Coordinating Council of Community Organizations here in recent years have lost favor with militant Negro leaders in Chicago.

Those efforts produced little gain for the poverty-stricken, who include a large proportion of Chicago's million Negroes.

Dr. King has not conducted a campaign here since 1966. A year ago he sent Hosea Williams and a Southern Christian Leadership Conference cadre for a voter registration drive to combat the Daley organization. It failed miserably.

The Coordinating Council of Community Organizations, which invited Dr. King here in 1965 for his first Northern drive "to end slums," has largely disintegrated. It has not met since Albert A. Raby, its convenor, left last September for graduate school.

Leadership in the slums has shifted to militant organizers of the poor for black-power, self-help programs. The principal surviving King program, Operation Breadbasket, under the Rev. Jesse Jackson, fits the new mold. It is successfully getting hundreds of jobs for slum Negroes by threatening economic boycott of slum businesses.

Whites, Mr. Robinson said, have no place in the reordered movement beyond offering money and resources.

"The hate and animosity in the ghettos is the worst I've seen in 33 years here," he said. "It is almost as if racist attitudes have been transferred from the white to the black community."

Mr. Vivian, the former King aide, said:

"We are in a great transition period for the whole civil rights movement. The accent now is on power instead of persuasion. The earlier period was worthwhile, however, because it produced in blacks a realization that white America is not due respect and a will to force change by themselves."

**Black Organizers Trained**

Mr. Vivian said the will was strong in Chicago. He has joined the staff of the new Chicago Action Training program, a school for black organizers.

"Students" in the three-month program, which ends March 31, include some of the principal slum organizers of tenant unions, welfare unions and neighborhood organizations. Whites are barred.

Black power goals of the Chicago slums, Mr. Robinson said, include ownership and operation of all businesses, to be forced by such measures as economic boycott. They also include "building an army" of Negro voters and activists as a political base for action on issues of self-interest.

"We want to break up the Daley machine," Mr. Robinson said.

In the meantime, he said, the mood in the slums is ideal for achieving a black coalition that "Chicago will have to deal with or face an alternative that will make Watts look like a picnic."

February 6, 1968

# Coalition Vows Peaceful Protest At Chicago National Convention

### By DONALD JANSON
#### Special to The New York Times

CHICAGO, March 25 — Spokesmen for a loose coalition of New Left and antiwar groups said today demonstrators at the Democratic national convention here in August would be peaceful rather than disruptive.

But they attacked Mayor Richard J. Daley, charging him with planning unconstitutional repression, and promised a legal challenge to insure their right to freedom of speech and assembly.

Spokesmen at a news conference at the Y.M.C.A. Hotel fresh from a planning meeting held over the weekend, were Rennie Davis of Chicago, director of the Center for Radical Research; David Dellinger of New York, editor of Liberation magazine, and Donald Duncan of San Francisco, military editor of Ramparts magazine.

"I don't think much would be gained by trying to storm the convention against all the tanks and other military equipment they would bring in," said Mr. Dellinger, a principal organizer of massive demonstrations in New York City last April 15 and at the Pentagon last Oct. 21.

Demonstrators may be aimed at induction centers rather than the convention, he said. He said they would take place simultaneously in other cities as well as Chicago.

Mr. Davis condemned the recent arming of all Chicago policemen with chemical Mace, a disabling spray. He said the "major disrupter" of the convention could be Mayor Daley for such "provocative actions."

The Mayor commented at a news conference that the rights of all citizens would be respected but that "no one, no matter who they are or who they represent, will be able to take over the convention hall or streets of Chicago."

The coalition initiated last weekend will be composed of such New Left student groups as students for a Democratic Society, such antiwar organizations as Women Strike for Peace, draft resistance groups and slum neighborhood organizations. Representatives will meet in June at an undisclosed site in the Midwest to plan the convention protest.

The aim stated today was "to use the Democratic convention as a national platform to heighten our impact and visibility and draw the movement together."

Demonstrations will seek to stimulate popular antiwar sentiment and build coalition membership.

Mr. Dellinger said the coalition would not try to impose peaceful demonstration tactics on other groups demonstrating at the convention.

Mr. Davis said Dick Gregory, Chicago entertainer and civil rights activist, conferred with Negro participants in the week-end meeting and an effort to effort to coordinate demonstrations at the convention.

Mr. Gregory has threatened such massive demonstrations that "the Government will be forced to bring the Army in" to protect the convention.

Mr. Davis said the coalition would also "work cooperatively" with the Youth International Party ("yippies"), which plans a massive "love-in" for Chicago parks during the convention.

"Yippie" elder statesmen include Allen Ginsburg, the poet, and Dr. Timothy Leary. "Yippie" observers attended the week-end planning conference of about 200 new left, antiwar, and black power leaders at a camp near Lindenhurst, Ill., 50 miles from here.

A conference resolution supporting the "yippie" convention project calls it "'a yippie festival seeking to contrast the celebration of life with the death-producing rituals of the politicians."

Mr. Dellinger said the coalition would support the candidacies of neither Senator Eugene J. McCarthy of Minnesota nor Senator Robert F. Kennedy of New York because their peace and domestic platforms did not go far enough.

The coalition, he said, wants immediate pull-out of American troops in Vietnam and self-determination for the Vietnamese people.

In the United States, he said, it wants a greater self-determination for slum residents rather than job and housing programs that would rely in part on private and business assistance as proposed by Senator Kennedy.

Mr. Dellinger said leaders of the coalition would confer tomorrow with the Rev. Dr. Martin Luther King Jr. to offer support for his "poor people's" demonstration in Washington next month.

March 26, 196

# Guard Is Called Up To Protect Chicago During Convention

### By DONALD JANSON
#### Special to The New York Times

CHICAGO, Aug. 20—Gov. Samuel H. Shapiro called up the National Guard today to keep order in the city during the Democratic National Convention.

At the request of Mayor Richard J. Daley, the Governor ordered 5,649 Illinois National Guardsmen to round-the-clock duty in Chicago beginning Friday to head off threats of "tumult, riot or mob disorder."

Meanwhile, an Army spokesman in Washington confirmed in a telephone interview that about 6,000 regular Army troops received rigorous riot-control training at Fort Hood, Tex., last week as a precautionary measure.

That exercise, he said, was called Operation Jackson Park, after the park in Chicago bivouacked last April when flown here from Fort Hood to help control Chicago's most recent riot.

Any deployment of Federal troops would await orders of President Johnson.

Three units of the National Guard will report for duty in Chicago at 8 A.M. Friday. Sixteen more will check into armories here 24 hours later.

The convention does not open till Monday, but anti-Administration dissidents who plan demonstrations are expected to arrive over the weekend. So are delegates to the convention. Pre-convention committee meetings are already under way.

### Fear of Riot Cited

In his Executive order calling up the guard, Governor Shapiro said in Springfield that "demonstrations by dissident organizations may result in tumult, riot or mob disorder, threatened by a body of men acting together by force."

He named no particular group, but said "it is deemed that a time of public danger and disorder exists."

Governor Shapiro said this assessment resulted from advice from Mayor Daley that the situation in Chicago next week might deteriorate "beyond the control of the civil authorities."

The convention thus became, before it even convened, the first national political convention in memory to require the protection of troops.

The presence of armed and uniformed guardsmen in the city will not be the only evidence of the tight security net enveloping the convention.

The Democrats will meet behind barbed wire at the International Amphitheatre in the Stockyards, not far from explosive South Side and West Side Negro slums.

A mile-long, chain-link fence, topped by strands of barbed wire, has been erected on the west side of the Amphitheatre for protection against invaders. It is joined to an existing fence on two other sides.

Halsted Street on the east side will be closed to nonconvention traffic, Deputy Police Chief John Hartnett said today. He said anyone entering the Amphitheatre area would be required to show credentials at a series of security checkpoints.

All doors on the Halsted Street side will be locked and guarded. Convention-goers will be funneled into the fenced-in Amphitheatre parking lot on the other side and enter the hall through heavily guarded doors there.

Chicago's entire 11,900-man police force will be on 12-hour shifts throughout the convention. Command posts inside and outside the Amphitheatre

have been established. Up to 2,000 uniformed and plainclothes men will be assigned to the area. They will be aided by contingents of Federal marshals, Secret Service men and Federal Bureau of Investigation agents.

It is expected that the Illinois Guardsmen, all riot-trained, will be on duty at armories in the city. However, several parks, including two near the Amphitheatre, have been reserved for bivouacs if needed. Several public schools have been designated for Guard command posts if riots occur.

### Firemen Assigned

Scores of firemen will be stationed, with fire-fighting equipment, in the Amphitheatre area. A pillared portico at the delegate entrance to the convention hall has been enclosed with bullet-proof materials for protection against sniper fire.

Even the manholes in the Amphitheatre area of Chicago have been sealed with tar to deny hiding places to anyone who would disrupt the convention.

So far the city has withheld parade and rally permits from anti-war and anti-Administration demonstrators who plan a march on the convention Aug. 28, the night they expect Vice President Humphrey to be nominated for the Presidency.

Rennie Davis and Thomas Hayden, coordinators of convention-week demonstrations for the National Mobilization Committee to End the War in Vietnam, charge the city has become an "armed camp" in a "garrison state."

The mobilization group's plans for picketing, marches and rallies by "tens of thousands" of peaceful demonstrators, they say, are being met with plans for violent repression that could lead to disorder.

The mobilization committee, which organized antiwar demonstrations in Washington and New York last year of 100,000 and 250,000 persons, released today an "open letter" to anti-Administration supporters of Senator Eugene J. McCarthy inviting them to "join our ranks."

Events listed in the invitation included "massive demonstrations at downtown hotels to greet arriving delegates" next Sunday and Monday, and, on Aug. 28, a "mass march on the

convention to protest ratification of the status quo."

Many McCarthy supporters are affiliated with the Coalition for an Open Convention, which lost a suit in Federal court here yesterday to force the city to permit the use of Soldier Field or Grant Park Sunday for a rally.

The anti-Humphrey organization announced this afternoon it had canceled the rally because of the "intractability" of Mayor Daley and the Democratic National Committee in refusing to respond to repeated requests for a site.

"We are quite sure that during the week of the convention there will be a seven-day moratorium on civil liberties in Chicago," said Martin Slate, rally coordinator. "We have told our people not to come to Chicago. Anyone who does come is taking a chance by walking into a police state."

Meanwhile, the mobilization committee and the Youth International Party (Yippies), began training marshals in Lincoln Park to provide self-policing for the line of march.

Both groups also began training in "self-defense" measures. Abbie Hoffman, New York Yippie leader, said those would include karate. He said the yippies and the mobilization groups would "pool" their self-defense efforts.

Police photographers recorded the strange exercises in the park. At one point plainclothes men seized two persons who were taking pictures, then released them when they produced Army intelligence credentials.

The Yippies, like the mobilization group, have sought without success for months to obtain from city officials permits for rallies and the use of parks for camping and sleeping next week.

Yesterday both groups took their plea to Federal District Court here, charging Mayor Daley and other city officials with conspiring to deny them the use of public facilities and the right to free speech and assembly.

No demonstrators will be allowed on a mile-long stretch of Halsted Street near the Amphitheatre, he said, the mobilization committee had planned to march there for a vigil outside the convention hall. Mr.

Davis has said repeatedly the demonstrations will be held whether or not permits are granted.

What concerns authorities more than antiwar or pro McCarthy demonstrators, however, is the possibility of rioting in the racially incendiary Negro ghettos.

Discontent with unemployment, housing conditions, the quality of schools and limited representation in the Daley administration has stirred unrest.

### Rumor of Plot Discounted

The unrest has tended to add credence to rumors, such as the rumor of a plot, reported in The Chicago Tribune today, to assassinate Vice President Humphrey and Senator McCarthy, the principal candidates for the Presidential nomination next week.

The plot, said to include the destruction by explosives of several police stations with the intent of producing chaos, was attributed to Negro extremists and members of a South Side street gang. The source was an unnamed prisoner in the county jail. Authorities said today no substance had yet been found for the report.

Mayor Daley officiated at the dedication today of the first of many modern, prefabricated houses to be erected in Negro neighborhoods in an attempt by the city to meet housing needs and allay tension.

In a speech, he urged Chicagoans to "build, not burn" and to "construct, not riot."

The Mayor announced at a luncheon that a factory would be established in the city next year with the objective of producing more than 2,000 similar homes annually.

He said the factory would be sponsored by construction trade unions, private industry and Government.

Delegates and others at the convention will be invited to inspect seven of the town houses.

The Mayor told a news conference he had requested the Guard call-up because "an ounce of prevention is worth a pound of cure."

He said he had acted on the advice of Police Superintendent James B. Conlisk "and other experts." The police superintendent has met regularly in recent days with Secret Service and F.B.I. agents in an effort to close every security gap.

## 7 Yippies Arrested With Pig 'Candidate' At Chicago Center

Special to The New York Times

CHICAGO, Aug. 23—Seven Yippies and the pig they are planning to run for President were arrested this morning.

Almost immediately, Abbie Hoffman, the backroom power behind the Youth International party, threatened to run a lion for President, but observers here believed the party would stick with its original nominee.

The arrests came as Yippies gathered for a nomination ceremony near the Picasso statue in the downtown Civic Center Plaza. Several of them carried signs reading "vote pig in '68" and "live high on the hog."

But, as the pig drew up in a battered station wagon, about 25 policemen swooped into the crowd.

Amid jeers, cheers, and cries of "pork power," the pig and seven supporters were quickly placed in a police van and driven off, while the police held back a crowd of about 250 spectators.

One Yippie was able to get off a fast nominating speech, shouting that the pig was an ideal candidate because he "was born in Montana, is 35 years old, studied law by candlelight for three years and walked five miles through the snow to school, plus the fact that he is affiliated with the Roman Catholic and Protestant churches, in addition to being a Jew."

The seven persons were charged with disorderly conduct, and one of them, Gayle Albin, of Chicago, the driver of the station wagon, was also charged with obstructing traffic. They were later released on $25 bail. Among those arrested were Jerry Rubin, the New York Yippie leader, and Phil Ochs, the folk singer and writer of topical protest songs.

## Hundreds of Protesters Block Traffic in Chicago

Special to The New York Times

CHICAGO, Monday, Aug. 26 — Hundreds of antiwar and anti-Humphrey demonstrators, driven out of a park on the shores of Lake Michigan here last night staged a series of hit-and-run protests today that blocked traffic and triggered angry shoving matches with heavily armed police.

One group of youths, numbering several hundred, congregated in a circle just outside Lincoln Park, which is on the edge of one of the city's plushest Near North Side neighborhoods, and confronted the police.

"Where's Dubcek?" some of the youths shouted, as the police, wearing plexiglass facemasks and carrying shotguns and tear gas guns attempted to disperse them. "Is this Czechosiovakia?"

Another group of several hundred moved from Lincoln Park to Michigan Avenue, one of the city's main streets, where the police threw up a line at the foot of a drawbridge across the Chicago River, halting traffic for blocks.

Several thousands of the youths had gathered in Lincoln Park earlier in the first show of strength by the young demonstrators who have been drawn here by the Democratic National Convention. The youths had been ordered out of the park at 11 P.M. because of the curfew.

Soon after the youngsters left the park, a large group congregated in the area of Clark Street and LaSalle Street, which is just southwest of Lincoln Park.

Some 400 policemen pursued the group into the maze of traffic circles, drives and islands that dot the area. Tempers flared as the police sought to disperse the crowd, which was almost entirely white.

At one point, a group of policemen charged into a mass of youngsters and about 20 were struck with nightsticks. The incident occurred after a bottle had arched out of the crowd and smashed on the ground near a policeman.

There were no immediate reports of arrests or serious injuries. Several persons, however, were reported to have suffered cuts and bruises during clashes with the police.

One of those who claimed to have been struck was Claude Lewis, a reporter for The Philadelphia Bulletin, who said he was struck by a policeman at the corner of Clark and LaSalle Streets. Mr. Lewis, a Negro, said he was wearing convention press credentials around his neck at the time.

Mr. Lewis said as he was making notes on the disturbances a policeman approached him and demanded: "Give me that notebook."

"He snatched the notebook out of my hand and started swinging away," Mr. Lewis said of the policeman. Mr. Lewis was treated for head lacerations at the Henrotin Hospital.

The incident on Michigan Avenue took place at about 12:30 A.M. when another group of the youngsters evicted from Lincoln Park streamed down Michigan Avenue toward a drawbridge that carries traffic across the Chicago River.

When the youths reached the foot of the bridge, they encountered a solid line of policemen, each brandishing a nightstick. The police lowered the gate of the drawbridge and an officer, using a bullhorn, ordered the youngsters to "move on out." The youths jeered, banged on the sides of police buses, but then retired. Traffic was delayed for about a half hour.

### Festival Is Conducted

The night of trouble in this tense convention city began when antidraft, antiwar, anti-Humphrey, New Left, hippie and Yippie youths collected in Lincoln Park to conduct their "Festival of Life."

There were isolated clashes between some of the youths and the police early last evening. At least eight persons were arrested at that time and at least one, identified as Stewart Albert of New York City, was struck by a policeman's club and injured.

But by midnight, an hour after the park was legally closed for the night, all but a handful of the young men and women appeared to have acceded to the pleas of their leaders to avoid a confrontation with the police and had left the park peacefully. Minutes later, however, the clashes erupted on the streets outside the park.

About 500 of the demonstrators, who began the afternoon at the camp site of the Youth International Party in Lincoln Park, marched two miles along the sidewalks through downtown Chicago to join other protesters in front of the Hilton.

As usual in such protests, there were widely divergent estimates on the number of protesters. Rennie Davis, a coordinator for the National Mobilization Committee to End the War in Vietnam, which is heading the demonstrations, estimated that 2,500 persons took part. Tom Hayden, another Mobilization committee coordinator, estimated between 1,500 and 2,500.

But newsmen on the streets around the three hotels generally agreed that there were between 900 and 1,000.

In an interview after the two-hour protest was over, Mr. Davis expressed satisfaction both with the turnout and the character of the demonstrations. "We proved that it was possible to hold peaceful demonstrations and marches in Chicago despite the provocative presence of thousands of armed police, National Guard and Federal troops," he said. "We did just what we set out to do."

Most of the demonstrators were young and white. Some of them wore McCarthy buttons in their lapels or McCarthy bumper stickers plastered across their backs. There were young girls with flowers woven in their long hair, college boys in sweatshirts and young radicals with Mao Tse-tung buttons.

And there were a few over 30 —a gray-haired man in a seersucker shirt with his two young sons grasping his hands; a grandmother in a white dress who sang softly over and over, "We Shall Overcome;" and a thin, intense man who carried a placard bearing Senator Robert F. Kennedy's picture topped by a small American flag.

# 300 Police Use Tear Gas to Breach Young Militants' Barricade in Chicago Park

## SHOUTING YOUTHS OPPOSE CURFEW

### Incident Follows March on Loop by Dissenters, Angry Over Leaders' Arrest

**By SYLVAN FOX**
Special to The New York Times

CHICAGO, Tuesday, Aug. 27 —The police unleashed a tear-gas barrage early this morning to breach a barricade that hard-line antiwar militants had erected in the heart of a downtown Chicago park.

At 12:20 A.M., after warning the young demonstrators that they must leave Lincoln Park, some 300 policemen, wearing plexiglass face shields, advanced on the protesters' makeshift baricade, firing tear gas as they moved forward.

The tear-gas shells hissed through the air and landed with dull thuds, unfolding a large brownish white cloud that forced the young demonstrators to retreat, gagging and gasping.

Some policemen, armed with shotguns, pursued clusters of youths out of the park and attempted to disperse them. Several youngsters were seen being clubbed and hauled away by the police.

At least 55 persons were arrested, the police reported, and at least 50 were injured, including one who was said to have been critically beaten about the head.

Almost 3,000 young men and women were in the park at the time of the tear-gas attack, which followed a tense hour-long confrontation between the police and the demonstrators. Most of the dissenters were massed behind a line of overturned picnic tables upon which three youths stood, holding Vietcong, black anarchist and peace flags.

**Police Cars Headed Off**

Minutes before the police began the assault a single police car flanked the barricade and approached the crowd from the rear. It was driven off by a hail of rocks and bottles, many of which slammed against the car.

"Kill the pigs!" some of the youngsters shouted, using a current New Left appellation for policemen.

"It was the most serious con-

Associated Press

**DEMONSTRATION IN CHICAGO:** Youths swarming over statue of Gen. John Logan, Civil War hero, in Grant Park yesterday. Flags, right, are of National Liberation Front.

frontation thus far in the tense situation that has developed here with the build-up of military and police force and the massing of demonstrators drawn here by the Democratic National Convention.

In the crowd, as the tear-gas shells flew, was Allen Ginsberg, the poet, who led about 300 Yippies in a gentle chanting of "om"—a mystic Indian chant of peace and relaxation.

The protesters' barricades had been erected by some 500 demonstrators who led the move to defy police orders to leave the park at 11 P.M., when the parks legally close. As the barricades went up, the police massed about a hundred yards from the crowd of Yippies, New Leftists and adherents of the National Mobilization Committee to End the War in Vietnam.

**Most Serious Encounter**

At about midnight, as the confrontation unfolded in the park, Thomas Hayden, a protest coordinator and one of the leaders of the New Left, was arrested for the second time in less than 12 hours. He had been arrested in Lincoln Park in the afternoon, but was released on bail.

Spokesmen for the mobilization committee said Mr. Hayden's second arrest occurred on a downtown street when policemen seized and hit him and a companion, Ronnie Davis, another committee leader. Mr. Davis was not arrested.

Mr. Hayden's first arrest touched off a march through the downtown Loop area by about 1,000 of his supporters.

The confrontation developed shortly before midnight when the youths, who had been driven out of the park last night, overturned picnic tables, put trash baskets between the upturned legs, filled the baskets with paper and wood and set them afire.

The result was a 20- or 30-yard-long flaming barricade behind which the 500 youngsters clustered, some waving Vietcong flags and some shouting, chanting and clapping their hands.

At 11:40 a police car began moving through the darkness, its loudspeaker announcing:

"This is a final warning. Please leave the park. The park is now closed. Anyone remaining in this park is in violation of the law. Everyone out of the park. This is a final notice."

The warning was met by a loud chanting of "Hell no, we won't go," by the youngsters.

As the police car moved through the park, its spotlight cut through the night to pick out the faces of youngsters standing defiantly behind the barricade or on top of it.

Across the no man's land that had been created by the two opposing forces, the youngsters shouted taunts at the policemen.

"Why don't you go home to your wife and kids," one youngster called. Another added, "While you still have them."

"Why don't we go up and clear them out," a policeman snapped.

The confrontation came after a day of high tension in which thousands of Yippies and other antiwar activists marched through the streets.

Medical volunteers working with the protesters reported that about a dozen demonstrators had been struck with Chemical Mace, an antiriot spray, and several others had been struck by policemen's clubs. The police department said it had no reports on the use of Chemical Mace.

About 2,00 young antiwar militants roamed the streets under the tense surveillance of the police during the early hours of the evening, as the Democratic National Convention got under way. None of the demonstrators attempted to go anywhere near the convention site, which is several miles from the downtown section of the city.

Another group of Yippies and protesters massed outside the Conrad Hilton Hotel, a focal point of convention activities, for a time. Later, this group moved to Lincoln Park. Smaller bands of youngsters wandered the streets late into the night.

At one point in the afternoon a march of protesters was halted by a solid line of policemen as the marchers attempted to move toward the Loop. The marchers then reversed their course and headed back to Lincoln Park and Old Town, which have been their principal bases.

Earlier in the day, some 1,000 of the protesters, angered over the arrest of two of their leaders, marched through the downtown Loop area, disrupting traffic and adding to the tension that besets this convention city.

August 27, 1968

## Microcosm of Nation

### Garrison Convention Is a Reflection Of Controversies Under Democrats

#### By ARTHUR KROCK

For the last eight years the Democratic party, its Congressional programs sustained by a Supreme Court majority appointed by Democratic Presidents, has been in executive and legislative charge of the state of the nation. The decision of the party authorities that its 1968 Presidential convention required protection by a military garrison to assure the orderly performance of its functions, and to safeguard the delegates and candidates from bodily harm, reflected in the microcosm of Chicago what the state of the nation actually is.

*News Analysis*

It is one of rising crime against persons and property; of violent disregard, in the racial conflict, of the laws by which the constitutional rights and liberties of the many are shielded from the violent infractions of the few; of assertions by the few of the right to obey only the laws of which they approve; of steadily mounting prices; of paralysis of the nation's economy and daily life when great labor unions chose to make this use of their excessive legalized immunities.

#### Bitter Division

The state of the nation also includes a bitter popular division over the executive decisions by which the American people have been committed to engage, in territory adjoining the boundaries of the two great Communist powers, in a major and militarily inconclusive war, on the representation that national security is vitally and directly involved in a Communist effort to take over the non-Communist section of a country thousands of sea miles distant from the western boundary of the United States in Hawaii.

It is true that the Republican candidate for President, Richard M. Nixon, endorses this concept of vital national interest, and apparently would press for military victory in the prolonged absence of a negotiated settlement.

But the reason the Chicago convention has been deemed to require the police and military protection the Miami Beach convention did not is that the official power to make war abroad and deal with social disturbances at home has for eight years been in the hands of a Democratic President-Commander in Chief whose chosen successor, if nominated and elected, endorses the fundamental uses of that power.

This made certain from the outset that the Democratic convention of 1968 would be embroiled in controversies that have grown out of these uses. Yet the first of these issues could not have been disposed of more tamely in the convention stockade—the retroactive abrogation of the unit rule.

There were reasons, of course, why the delegation from Texas, home state of the incumbent President, meekly accepted this overriding of the act of the Texas State Convention that approved the unit rule under the sanction of the Texas law.

#### Undercover Pact

The Administration (and Texas) candidate for President, Hubert H. Humphrey, would have been injured by militant Texas resistance to this trampling on precedent. And such resistance would have imperiled the obvious undercover pact by which shortly afterward the challenge to the credentials of the regular (Gov. John Connally) delegation was rejected.

But these prudent considerations so tamed the Texans that, when the name of Lyndon B. Johnson was first mentioned from the podium Monday night, and then repeated, not even a cheer arose from its ranks to break the indifferent silence of the convention.

That silence, and the docility with which the Texas delegation bowed to the shattering of the tenet of fair play that was inherent in changing the rules in the middle of the game, and nullifying the unit rule that the Texas convention had imposed with the full authority of state law, were practical political acceptances of the wisdom in these particular circumstances of Proverbs (16, 18): "Pride goeth before destruction."

However, as the turmoil broke out over the credentials dispute in Georgia and other Southern states, one preconvention expectation was fully sustained: that the Administration's assiduous courtship of the ethnic minorities, the Negroes especially, would run the risk of being broken off at the November polls if suspended or compromised by appeasing the South.

*August 28, 1968*

---

# HUMPHREY NOMINATED ON FIRST BALLOT; POLICE BATTLE DEMONSTRATORS IN STREETS

## VICTOR GETS 1,761

### Vote Taken Amid Boos For Chicago Police Tactics in Street

#### By TOM WICKER
Special to The New York Times

CHICAGO, Thursday Aug. 29 — While a pitched battle between the police and thousands of young antiwar demonstrators raged in the streets of Chicago, the Democratic National Convention nominated Hubert H. Humphrey for President last night, on a platform reflecting his and President Johnson's views on the war in Vietnam.

Mr. Humphrey, after a day of bandwagon shifts to his candidacy, and a night of turmoil in the convention hall, won nomination on the first ballot over challenges by Senator Eugene J. McCarthy of Minnesota and George S. McGovern of South Dakota.

The count at the end of the first ballot was:

| | |
|---|---|
| Humphrey | 1,761¾ |
| McCarthy | 601 |
| McGovern | 146½ |
| Phillips | 67½ |
| Others | 32¾ |

There was never a moment's suspense in the balloting, and throughout a turbulent evening, the delegates and spectators paid less attention to the proceedings than to television and radio reports of widespread violence in the streets of Chicago, and to stringent security measures within the International Amphitheatre.

Repeated denunciations of Mayor Richard J. Daley from convention speakers and repeated efforts to get an adjournment or recess were ignored by convention officials and Mr. Daley.

He sat through it all, usually grinning and always guarded by plainclothes security men, until just before the roll call. Then he left the hall. A few miles away, the young demonstrators were being clubbed, kicked and gassed by the Chicago police, who turned back a march on the convention hall.

### Watched From Hotels

Most of the violence took place across Michigan Avenue from the convention headquarters hotel, the Conrad Hilton, in full view of delegates' wives and other watching from its windows.

From the convention rostrum, Senator Abraham A. Ribicoff of Connecticut, denounced "Gestapo tactics in the streets of Chicago."

Julian Bond, the Negro insurgent leader from Georgia, in announcing his delegation's votes, spoke of "atrocities" in the city.

Wire services reported that Mr. Humphrey had chosen Senator Edmund S. Muskie of Maine for Vice President. Mr. Humphrey's staff denied that a decision had been made, although they would not rule out Mr. Muskie, 54 years old, a Roman Catholic of Polish extraction.

Even the roll-call of the states that nominated Mr. Humphrey could begin only over the protests of New Hampshire, Wisconsin and Mr. Conyers, all of whom moved for a recess or adjournment because of the surrounding violence and the pandemonium in the hall.

### Vote Begins Amid Boos

Representative Carl Albert of Oklahoma, the chairman, ignored all the motions and ordered the roll-call to begin amid a huge chorus of boos.

When Illinois's turn came to vote, the huge old amphitheater rocked with the sounds of boos and jeers, and the recording secretary had to ask for a restatement of its vote —112 votes for Mr. Humphrey.

Early in the evening, even Mr. Humphrey got a whiff of tear gas when it was wafted through his window at the Hilton, from the street fighting below.

Mr. McCarthy saw some of the violence from his window and called it "very bad." Later, it was reported at the convention hall, he visited a hospital where some of his young sup-

porters, wounded in the streets, were being treated.

At one point, the police broke into the McCarthy suite at the Hilton, searching for someone throwing objects out of the hotel windows.

Mr. McGovern described the fighting as a "blood bath" that "made me sick to my stomach." He said he had "seen nothing like it since the films of Nazi Germany."

### Pennsylvania Does It

Nevertheless, when Pennsylvania cast the votes that put Mr. Humphrey in nomination, the convention hall broke into a demonstration on his behalf that was loud and apparently happy. Mrs. Humphrey, watching from a box with her family, received congratulations with a gracious smile.

The day's events, moving swiftly toward Mr. Humphrey's nomination, began this morning with Edward M. Kennedy's disavowal of a draft movement in his behalf.

In an emotional afternoon debate, the delegates sealed the grip of Mr. Humphrey and Mr. Johnson on this convention by adopting a Vietnam plank drawn to the President's specifications.

They defeated by a comfortable margin a substitute proposal critical of much of the President's policy and supported by backers of Mr. McGovern, Mr. McCarthy and the "draft Ted" movement.

How united this would leave the party for the fall campaign remained to be seen. Mr. McCarthy has not yet pledged his support to the ticket, the platform fight left many antiwar Democrats disappointed and bitter, and there is a pervasive fear here, based on national polls, that Mr. Humphrey cannot win against Richard M. Nixon, the Republican nominee.

The delegations of New York and California, the two biggest states, voted largely against the Humphrey-Johnson forces on all issues here, including the platform plank and the Presidential nomination.

Humphrey sources said that the nomination of a Vice-Presidential candidate would probably not be made until Thursday night, although it had been planned for tonight. Mr. Humphrey conferred with advisers this afternoon and tonight on the choice of a running mate, and numerous names were bruited about among the delegates.

Two decisive breaks clinched the nomination, as well as the platform fight, for the Vice President. One was Mr. Ken-

nedy's Sherman-like refusal to be drafted; the other was the announcement by Mayor Daley that Illinois was casting all but six of its 118 votes for Mr. Humphrey.

Of almost equal importance was Gov. Richard J. Hughes's decision to drop his favorite-son's role; that let 61 of New Jersey's votes go to Mr. Humphrey.

By mid-day Lawrence F. O'Brien, a Humphrey manager, was claiming 1,654 delegates, without any help from the Illinois delegation then in caucus.

All the Southern states, except North Carolina, abandoned favorite-son candidacies, with most Southern votes lining K. Moore of North Carolina was expected to switch to the Vice President immediately after the first ballot.

The Southern shift to Mr. Humphrey which had been generally expected from the start of the campaign, caused Gov. Lester G. Maddox of Georgia to abandon the Presidential candidacy he had announced in the late days of the campaign. He withdrew before today's sessions.

Negro delegates here put forward a black candidate, the Rev. Channing Phillips, who had been the leader of the Kennedy slate of delegates from the District of Columbia.

Mayor Joseph L. Alioto of San Francisco was chosen to place Mr. Humphrey in nomination. Selected as seconders were former Gov. Terry Sanford of North Carolina and Mayor Carl Stokes of Cleveland.

Whether these selections had any Vice-Presidential significance could not be ascertained. Both Mr. Alioto, a Roman Catholic of Italian descent, and Mr. Sanford, a Southern progressive, have figured prominently in speculation here.

### Humphrey Backers Applaud

Mr. Alioto, avoiding mention of the Vietnam war, pounded out a thumping political speech that roused Mr. Humphrey's supporters to repeated roars of enthusiasm and the biggest and noisiest demonstration of the convention.

Citing the Vice President's 20 years of leadership in liberal causes, Mr. Alioto worked in the effective refrain "but he did it" after describing each of Mr. Humphrey's various achievements in terms of overcoming the impossible.

In fact, he said, in "a lifetime of courage," Mr. Hum-

phrey had become an expert practitioner of "the art of the impossible."

The Vice President, he said, is "a leader who can be impatient" at the slow pace of progress, and he cautioned those who were calling for "new options" that they were more likely to get them from a proved man of action than from mere talkers.

Mr. Ribicoff described Mr. McGovern as "a good man without guile" and a "whole man with peace in his soul," who could bring these qualities to a nation that needed them sorely.

"He brings out of the prairies of South Dakota a new wind," Mr. Ribicoff said, "a wind that will be able to lift the smog of uncertainty from this land of ours."

His voice rising in indignation, the Connecticut Senator then declared:

"With George McGovern as President, we would not have to have such Gestapo tactics in the streets of Chicago."

This set off a tremendous roar of approval and when it subsided briefly, Mr. Ribicoff added:

"With George McGovern, we would not have to have the national guard."

That renewed the applause but it also brought the Illinois delegates up in anger. Mayor Daley joined them in waving, catcalling and motioning for Mr. Ribicoff to sit down.

"How hard it is to accept the truth," Mr. Ribicoff replied —in a moment reminiscent of the booing of Governor Rockefeller of New York at the Republican National Convention of 1964.

Gov. Harold E. Hughes of Iowa, who was chosen to nominate Mr. McCarthy, said that "the people found Gene McCarthy for us. They found him; they follow him; he is more accurately the people's candidate than any other man in recent history."

The Governor, who seconded Lyndon B. Johnson at Atlantic City in 1964, called Mr. McCarthy "a leader who can arrest the polarization of our society—the alienation of the blacks from the whites, of the haves from the have-nots, and the old from the young."

The convention adjourned at 12:06 A.M., Chicago daylight time today. The final session is scheduled to convene at 7 o'clock tonight, Chicago daylight time (8 P.M. E.D.T.).

The session will choose its Vice-Presidential nominee and head acceptance speeches from him and Mr. Humphrey.

## Tribute to Kennedy Brings a Brief Moment of Unity

**By RUSSELL BAKER**
Special to The New York Times

CHICAGO, Aug. 29 — The Democrats paused tonight in perhaps the most violent convention in their history to honor their murdered President's murdered brother, Senator Robert F. Kennedy.

For 32 minutes they sat in the closest approximation to respectful silence they had managed all week, listening to the voice of the only surviving Kennedy brother, Edward, and then watching a memorial film entitled "Robert Kennedy Remembered."

When the partly dimmed convention hall lights came up at the movie's end, there were a few moist eyes visible in the audience, though not many.

Though open displays of grief were not so noticeable as they had been four years ago at Atlantic City when Robert Kennedy presided over a similar tribute to his brother, John, it seemed that the convention had been momentarily united in emotion for the first time all week.

### Battle Hymn Is Sung

Every delegate came to his feet in a standing ovation that lasted for five minutes before the chairman Representative Carl Albert of Oklahoma attempted to proceed with business.

It was the first occasion this week that had found the Democrats unanimous about anything, and even this momentary glimpse of harmony induced by the memory of death quickly deteriorated into another display of tension.

Those who wanted to continue the Kennedy demonstration—located principally in the New York and California delegations—answered Mr. Albert's plea for order by starting to sing "The Battle Hymn of the Republic."

Quickly, it was taken up all around the floor and through three sides of the four-sided gallery in a thunder of hand-clapping and foot-stamping that drowned out the chairman's gavelings.

The Texas and Illinois delegations, which all week had supplied the hard-core strength of the party's dominant old guard regulars, sat down, stopped applauding and affected a variety of expression ranging from bored to annoyed as the chorus of "Glory, glory, hallelujah" continued to roll through the hall.

On the floor and in the galleries, a few homemade signs spelled out such messages as "Bobby, We'll Remember You," and "Bobby, We'll seek Your Newer World."

After nearly 20 minutes, with the demonstration still unchecked, one of Mayor Richard J. Daley's men in the Illinois delegation stood up and gave a signal to the Daley claque in the hall's south gallery.

Almost instantly, the huge claque set up a howling chant of "We love Daley! We Love Daley! We love Daley."

The Mayor had passed them through the security guards earlier in the evening to assure himself a vocal defense against the booing he has been getting here the last few days and in their first test they proved powerful enough to shout the Kennedy demonstration into silence.

It was an end with a certain irony, for it was Mayor Daley's support that Robert Kennedy, in life, had considered essential to his quest for the Presidency.

At one point in his campaign he had once said, "Mayor Daley is the ball game." Tonight Mayor Daley was pitching for Hubert Humphrey.

The Kennedy tribute began with a brief speech by Senator Edward M. Kennedy relayed to the hall from the Senator's summer home at Hyannis Port, Mass.

At Atlantic City in 1964, Robert Kennedy had appeared in person to introduce the memorial film on the life of John F. Kennedy and had been received in tears and tumult.

Edward Kennedy's introduction tonight was couched in terms reminiscent of his funeral elegy to Robert in St. Patrick's Cathedral.

"If my brother's life, and death, had one meaning above all others," he said, "it was this: That we should not hate but love one another, that our strength should not be used to create the conditions of oppression that lead to violence, but the conditions of justice that lead to peace."

Those who had loved him, he said, "followed him, honored him, lived in his mild and magnificent eye, learned his great language, caught his clear accents, made his our pattern to live and die."

The film, shown on two screens high up in the gallery corners, was produced by Guggenheim Productions, Inc., of Washington, D. C.

Fred Dutton, a former aide to President Kennedy, said it had been commissioned by the Kennedy family for showing at this convention.

The film reflected the Kennedy taste for understatement. There was no broad attempt to produce tears, but instead an effort to evoke the sense of a life and the growth that had brought Robert Kennedy from young political technician to a man tormented in his final years by his sensitivity to the dark and poor underside of American life.

The delegates applauded three times as that familiar taut voice with the familiar sing-song rhythm articulated his vision of America in speeches that brought back familiar memories of his brief Presidential campaign.

The loudest applause perhaps was for his declaration that "This is a generous and compassionate country."

"That's what I want this country to stand for; not violence, not lawlessness, not disorder, but compassion and love and peace. That's what this country should stand for, and that's what I intend to do if I am elected President."

He was shot in the head at Los Angeles early on the morning of June 5 after winning the California Presidential primary that would have sent him to Chicago as a prime contender for the nomination. He died the next day.

---

# U.S. STUDY SCORES CHICAGO VIOLENCE AS 'A POLICE RIOT'

### Says Many Officers Replied to Taunts in August With Unrestrained Attacks

---

### PUNISHMENT ADVOCATED

---

### Panel's Staff Report Also Cites the Provocations of Some Demonstrators

**By MAX FRANKEL**
Special to The New York Times

WASHINGTON, Dec. 1—A graphic and comprehensive account of the violence in Chicago during the Democratic National Convention last August has been published, without evaluation, by the National Commission on the Causes and Prevention of Violence.

It concludes that many Chicago policemen responded to the misbehavior, obscene taunts and sometimes violent provocations of demonstrators with unrestrained and indiscriminate violence of their own.

It characterizes the attacks by policemen on peaceful demonstrators, innocent bystanders, newsmen, photographers and Chicago residents as often gratuitous, ferocious, malicious and mindless, and states that they amounted to "what can only be called a police riot."

### Asks Steps Against Police

Given the anxiety of the city, its leaders and its political guests and the "exceedingly provocative circumstances" that developed, the report says, the loss of control and discipline "can perhaps be understood, but not condoned."

If no action is taken against the offending policemen, it warns, there will follow only discouragement among the majority of the police who acted responsibly and a further strain between the police and the community, in Chicago and elsewhere.

These conclusions are for-

August 30, 1968

402

mally ascribed to one man—Daniel Walker, a prominent Chicago lawyer, a vice president and general counsel of Marcor, Inc., the parent concern of his old employer, Montgomery Ward & Co.; a former naval officer, and now president of the unofficial Chicago Crime Commission.

But his report is the work of a 212-member study team that took 1,410 eyewitness statements, reviewed 2,012 others provided by the Federal Bureau of Investigation and studied 180 hours of motion picture film, more than 12,000 still photographs and thousands of news accounts.

Operating under contract to the national violence commission, Mr. Walker built the study team with members of the F.B.I.-trained staff of the Chicago Crime Commission and with many lawyers and investigators lent to him by Chicago law firms and banks. They began work Sept. 27 and, "only by disregarding clock and families," he said, completed the report Nov. 18.

Entitled "Rights in Conflict" —in recognition of the rights of dissent and of public safety —the report contains a 233-page account of the violence in Chicago's parks and streets from Aug. 25 to 29 and of the events leading up to it; a 4,000-word summary statement supporting the call for disciplinary action against policemen, and 88 pages of photographs that provide their own chronology.

## Most Saw Report

Mr. Walker brought the study to Washington 10 days ago and it was rushed to most of the 13 commission members. Some, who were traveling, could not be reached, sources here said. But a "substantial majority" of the members were said to have authorized immediate publication, if only because the findings were bound to become known anyway.

Milton S. Eisenhower, former president of Johns Hopkins University and who is chairman of the commission, issued a brief comment attributing the prompt release to "the widespread interest." He said that the Walker report "carries neither the approval nor disapproval" of his group.

A commission statement said that the report would be studied along with testimony taken in recent months, similar studies of violence last summer in Cleveland and Miami, and many other documents being prepared by the staff and outside contributors.

## Epithets Transcribed

A striking feature of the Walker report is its liberal and literal transcription of the obscene epithets used by demonstrators and policemen alike to express their resentments and hostilities and, often, to provoke one another to violence. For many of the demonstrators, obscenity was said to have been the only weapon, and for many of the allegedly offending policemen it was the most vivid evidence of their rage.

The Government Printing Office refused to publish a document containing so much outrageous language. But Mr. Walker insisted, "with considerable reluctance," that it be retained as part of his record.

"Extremely obscene language was a contributing factor to the violence described in this report," he writes in a prefatory note, "and its frequency and intensity were such that to omit it would inevitably understate the effect it had."

His report suggests, however, that the violence of word and deed in Chicago was the product not only of momentary rage but also of the gradual conditioning of demonstrators and policemen. With some of the former determined to cause trouble and some of the latter determined to avenge it, only astute management could have averted an explosion, Mr. Walker implies.

Directly and by the weight of his presentation, he blames Mayor Richard J. Daley for his much-publicized criticism of police restraint in the riots in Chicago's black community last April. Though later modified, the Mayor's order to "shoot to kill arsonists and shoot to maim looters" undoubtedly had an effect, Mr. Walker writes.

## Negotiations Faulted

Implicitly, the report also criticizes the Chicago authorities, the Secret Service and others charged with public order for failing in negotiations with the demonstrators to authorize tolerable ways in which the demonstrators could register mass dissent peacefully, as the majority apparently wished to do.

Some rallies, marches and overnight bivouacs were eventually tolerated, but at least some of the violence, the report suggests, might have been averted through less literal enforcement of park curfews and other regulations.

Mr. Walker bemoans the general anxiety that built up in the weeks before the convention, inflaming passions and adding to the strain of an overworked police force. He says there was no machinery for distinguishing between real and imaginary threats of assassinations, sabotage of the city's water and

sewage systems and disruption of the Democratic convention.

The widespread characterizations of the crowds as hippies and yippies, anarchists and Communist sympathizers was "both wrong and dangerous," the report states, even as it records evidence that "many policemen looked upon the demonstrators in these ways." The "stereotyping" helps to explain emotional reactions of both the police and public, the study states.

Most of the demonstrators—including perhaps 5,000 from outside Chicago, and forming crowds that apparently never exceeded 10,000 — planned no disruption of the convention, no aggressive acts against the police and no assault against any person, institution or place of business, Mr. Walker reports. He also shows, however, that some demonstrators hoped for a violent "confrontation" and provocation of police violence and that others expected it to develop.

Corroborating many contemporary news accounts, the study reconstructs hundreds of incidents and clashes in which demonstrators alternately paraded their grievances and defied efforts to contain or disperse them. In their defiance, the demonstrators resorted to insulting the police but at times also to physical barricades, throwing rocks and other dangerous objects, attacks on police cars, burning trash cans and spreading foul-smelling chemicals.

## The Organizing Groups

The demonstrations from which the troublesome incidents developed were organized mainly by two loosely organized groups — the National Mobilization Committee to End the War in Vietnam, representing a variety of antiwar organizations, and the Youth International party (Yippies), bringing together hippies and other dissenters, dropouts and social critics strongly attracted to satirical and even absurd expressions of protest against American life.

But throughout the report, their offenses are set against testimony of indiscriminate police assaults, with billyclubs and gas and Mace, against crowds of protesters and even onlookers, against apparently stray and innocent citizens in the streets and even against seriously injured victims of the melees.

Many policemen are portrayed as eager to "bust the heads" of the demonstrators, to injure newsmen and to damage the equipment of photographers, and as so bent on the illegal use of force that they removed their identification numbers.

A few scenes of tender concern by a policeman for a young child or of heroic restraint by officers under rock attack relieve the narrative, but other small groups of policemen are said to have driven motorcycles into crowds, let the air out of private cars, illegally searched private quarters and insulted their occupants, and otherwise defied all training and discipline.

Mr. Walker believes that the clearing of Lincoln Park at curfew time on the first convention night, Monday, Aug 26, led directly to the violence symbolically and literally. By Wednesday, in the worst melee in Grant Park opposite the Conrad Hilton Hotel, he says "there is little doubt" that most of the violence came from the police.

An inspector-observer from the Los Angeles police who found the restraint of the police "beyond reason" for most of the week is quoted as follows on the Wednesday battle:

"There is no question but that many officers acted without restraint and exerted force beyond that necessary under the circumstances. The leadership at the point of conflict did little to prevent such conduct and the direct control of officers by first-line supervisors was virtually nonexistent."

The deputy superintendent of Chicago's police is reported to have pulled his men off demonstrators, shouting, "Stop, damn it, stop! For Christ's sake, stop it."

"It seemed to me," an observer is quoted as saying, "that only a saint could have swallowed the vile remarks to the officers. However, they went to extremes in clubbing the yippies. I saw them move into the park, swatting away with clubs at girls and boys lying in the grass."

## Attacks on Newsmen

Attacks on newsmen and photographers are treated in a special section of the report, with the conclusion that 49 were hit, Maced or arrested "apparently without reason," even though in 40 instances they were "clearly identifiable" by their credentials. The report also mentions "at least two occasions" on which camera crews staged violence and bogus injuries.

Some of the "worst" examples of police action were said by sources familiar with the study to have been omitted from the report at the request of the Department of Justice, which is placing the material before a Chicago grand jury.

In a statistical supplement, the study reports injuries to a total of 192 policemen, including 49 who were hospitalized. Flying objects caused 122 of the injuries, according to police records. Inadequate records were kept on demonstrators, but at least 101 were hospitalized and perhaps a thousand were treated elsewhere, nearly half for the effects of tear gas or Mace.

A total of 81 police vehicles were damaged, including 24 broken windshields. The police arrested 668 persons during convention week, the majority of those arrested being under 26 years old, male, residents of metropolitan Chicago and with no previous arrest records.

# Chicago 7 Cleared of Plot; 5 Guilty on Second Count

## Dellinger, Davis, Hayden, Hoffman and Rubin Are Convicted Individually

### By J. ANTHONY LUKAS
Special to The New York Times

CHICAGO, Feb. 18—All seven defendants in the Chicago conspiracy trial were acquitted today of plotting to incite a riot here during the 1968 Democratic National Convention, but five of them were convicted of seeking to promote a riot through individual acts.

The five men, David T. Dellinger, Rennie C. Davis, Thomas F. Hayden, Abbie Hoffman and Jerry C. Rubin, were found guilty of crossing state lines with intent to incite a riot and then giving inflammatory speeches for that purpose.

The two other defendants, John R. Froines and Lee Weiner, were acquitted on both the conspiracy and the individual counts.

After nearly 40 hours of deliberation, the jury returned its verdict at 12:20 P.M. in the brightly lit courtroom on the 23d floor of Chicago's Federal Building, where the four-and-a-half-month trial took place.

### Appeal Planned

William M. Kunstler, one of the defense attorneys, said later that the five convicted defendants would appeal. They face possible penalties of five years in prison, $10,000 fines or both.

It was an ambiguous end to the marathon trial, which has aroused passions on all sides.

Each side won something. For the defense, it was the Government's failure to persuade the jury that any conspiracy existed among demonstrators here during the convention. For the Government, it was the failure of five of the defendants to establish to the jury's satisfaction that their intent was innocent.

The defendants were apparently stunned, not so much by the verdict, but by the jury's capacity to produce it.

### Deadlock Expected

When the defendants were taken from their cells at Cook County Jail, where they had begun serving sentences for contempt of court, they believed they were to attend a hearing on the defense's motion to discharge the apparently deadlocked jury.

So they, their attorneys and most of the newsmen were astonished when Marshal Ronald Dombrowski announced to the hushed courtroom: "The jury has reached a verdict, Your Honor."

Before the jury was brought in, Richard G. Schultz, Assistant United States Attorney, asked Judge Julius J. Hoffman to exclude all spectators and the defendants' families from the courtroom to prevent the sort of disorders that often erupted during the trial's tensest moments.

Mr. Kunstler argued strenuously that at least the defendants' wives and girl friends should be allowed to remain.

"It would be the last crowning indignity of this trial," he said, "to make these men face this moment in a courtroom surrounded only by marshals and lawyers. At this moment, no man should be alone. I beg and implore you to reject the Government's motion."

But Judge Hoffman quickly approved the motion, and Federal marshals promptly moved towards four young women seated in the third row of the press section: Abbie Hoffman's wife, Anita; Mr. Rubin's girl friend, Nancy Kurshan; Mr. Weiner's girl friend, Sharon Avery; and Mr. Dellinger's 13-year-old daughter, Michelle.

As a marshal reached for Anita Hoffman, she stood and shouted at the defendants: "You will be avenged."

Then, as marshals propelled her down the aisle, she spun towards the judge and shouted: "We'll dance on your grave, Julie."

### 'I Love You'

"I love you," Michelle Dellinger called to her father as she was ejected.

Screams and shouts could be heard from the corridor outside as the women were pushed into elevators and ejected from the building.

A minute later, three marshals seized Mr. Froines's mother-in-law, who had been sitting quietly farther back, and half-dragged, half-lifted her from the courtroom.

Then, with only the defendants, the lawyers, about 40 carefully screened newsmen and about 20 marshals in the room, Judge Hoffman called in the jury.

After the 10 women and two men had taken their places in the jury box, where they sat for 20 weeks until last Saturday, Judge Hoffman asked whom they had selected as their foreman.

Edward F. Kratzke, a florid-faced cleaner for the Chicago Transit Authority, handed the written verdicts to Tony Bryce, the judge's clerk.

Then Mr. Bryce, a stooped, elderly man whose public duties during the trial have been to swear in witnesses and rap for silence, began to read the verdicts in a piping voice.

"We the jury," he read,

"find the defendant David T. Dellinger guilty as charged on Count No. 2 and not guilty on Count No. 1."

There was a small gasp around the defense table and, several defendants leaned over to whisper to the 54-year-old pacifist, who sat upright in his leather chair wearing the same brown tweed sports jacket he has worn during much of the trial.

Mr. Davis greeted his verdict with a tight-lipped grin. Mr. Hayden was expressionless under his tousled hair. Mr. Hoffman appeared despondent behind a two-day growth of beard, and Mr. Rubin, the normally ebullient Yippie, seemed on the verge of tears.

When Mr. Weiner's acquittal was announced the other defendants applauded and turned with broad grins toward the bearded sociology teacher, clapping him on the arm and tousling his hair.

"I'm happy for you, Lee," said Mr. Davis.

The last defendant, Mr. Froines, sank deep in his chair awaiting his verdict. When the acquittal was announced, he snapped upright, smiling and shaking his head incredulously.

A minute later, the husky, red-haired chemistry professor buried his head in his arms on the table, and his shoulders heaved with sobs.

When the verdicts had been read, Leonard I. Weinglass, the other defense attorney, asked that the jury be polled. Mr. Bryce asked the jurors if their votes had been correctly recorded, and one by one they said, "Yes, they were," or simply, "Yes."

Several of the jurors looked haggard and drawn from their long deliberations. Mrs. Jean Fritz, a housewife from Des Plaines, Ill., who was widely believed to be sympathetic to the defendants, seemed to have been weeping.

When the last of the jurors had affirmed the verdict, Judge Hoffman dismissed them, expressing his "deep appreciation" for their long labors. As they filed from the room. Mr.

Dellinger, Mr. Froines and Mr. Davis stood in a sign of respect. The other defendants remained sitting.

Judge Hoffman then announced that at 10 A.M. Friday he would determine the impact of admitted Government wiretapping on the case.

Before the trial began last September, the defense asked the judge to dismiss the Government's case because much of the evidence allegedly come from illegal wiretapping. But the judge said such a ruling would be required only if the trial produced convictions and said he would rule on the issue after a verdict. He is expected to reject the defense motion.

The judge set no date for sentencing, but presumably it will take place sometime next week.

Judge Hoffman rejected a defense motion for bond pending appeal.

"From the evidence in this case, from their conduct in this trial," he said, "I conclude that these are dangerous men to be at large."

Even if bond had been granted on today's convictions, the defendants would have had to go back to Cook County jail on contempt sentences imposed earlier. An appeal of the contempt convictions will be filed soon, and the defense is hopeful that the United States Court of Appeals for the Seventh Circuit will grant bail pending appeal on that offense.

At a news conference later, Thomas A. Foran, the United States Attorney, said, "the verdict proved that the jury system works."

He said this was true even if it turned out that the jurors had reached a compromise.

"I am satisfied because we got a verdict. If the verdict appears to be a compromise that's the way the system works. Everybody's feelings are in the verdict," he said.

Mr. Foran said he believed Judge Hoffman conducted the trial fairly, although he conceded that "Hoffman is a strict judge. He demands that attorneys stay within the rules of evidence."

Later, at a news conference, Mayor Richard J. Daley expressed satisfaction too. The Mayor, one of the first to contend there had been a conspiracy to cause riot in Chicago, said the verdict proved "that some people did come to our city to create a riot."

Before they went back to jail this afternoon, the defendants were permitted to meet with their lawyers for about an hour in the Federal Building.

At a news conference later, Paul Potter, one of the defense witnesses during the trial and a former president of Students for a Democratic Society, read a statement that he said had been written by the defendants.

It said: "This outrageous verdict results from the unholy combination of an unconstitutional law, a Daley prosecutor and a hostile authoritarian judge....

"Everyone who opposes the war against Vietnam—and everyone who advocates the liberation of black people—everyone with long hair and a free spirit—everyone who condemns the existence of poverty here and throughout the world—all have been found guilty by this verdict.

"This day will live in infamy. But the final jury is the people and their verdict is already beginning to come in. We await the final verdict of the people."

Terming the verdict "an outrage," Mr. Kunstler said it apparently had been a compromise between jurors determined to bring in a conviction and those holding out for acquittal.

"Some jurors believed in these defendants," he said, "but they were tired and worn out."

Mr. Kunstler said proof of such a compromise could serve as a ground for appeal. He said the defense planned to ask the appeals court for the right to interview jurors about how the verdict had been reached. Judge Hoffman forbade such contacts today.

Asked about the appeal the defense intends to file, Mr. Kunstler said: "There are so

many grounds it really staggers the imagination. The wiretaps, the mass of rulings on evidence where the judge ruled to admit the prosecution evidence and against the defense's."

Mr. Kunstler also emphasized that the five defendants had been convicted not for anything they did in Chicago but for what they said.

"It was all speeches. Speeches in Grant Park, speeches in Lincoln Park, speeches in churches around the country. All we have left is what the Government is most afraid of—speech."

The five so-called "substantive counts" on which the defendants were convicted refer to 13 speeches that the defendants gave between Aug. 1 and Aug. 28, 1968: Four by Mr. Davis, three by Mr. Hoffman, three by Mr. Rubin, two by Mr. Hayden and one by Mr. Dellinger. The speeches given before the convention, which took place Aug. 26 to Aug. 29, urged people to come to Chicago to participate in demonstrations. The speeches during the convention were generally made to groups in Grant or Lincoln Parks, urging them to action.

For example, a plainclothesman testified that on the evening of Aug. 26 in Grant Park he heard Mr. Davis yell over a bullhorn to a crowd around an equestrian statue: "Take the hill. Take the high ground. Don't let the pigs take the hill. If the police want a riot they can stay in the area. If they don't want a riot they can leave the area."

According to other testimony, Mr. Rubin told a crowd in Lincoln Park that same night: "The pigs started the violence, but tonight the people aren't going to give up the park. We have to fight them. They have guns and sticks so we have to arm ourselves with rocks, sticks and everything we can get."

On Aug. 28, according to testimony, Mr. Hayden told a crowd, "If blood is going to flow, let's make sure it flows all over this stinking city."

# DRAFT RESISTANCE AN OLD PROBLEM

## But Modern War Has Made It More Prominent

### By ALEXANDER BURNHAM

Although even in antiquity there were those who refused to bear arms, the conscientious objector to military service became most prominent in this century, when nations raised armies for wars on a global scale.

Conscription in the modern sense began with the French Revolution and was furthered by Napoleon. In this country both the Union and Confederate sides used the draft in the Civil War, but it was not until World War I that conscription became an acute problem to those who firmly objected to military service on the ground of conscience.

During World War II more than 70,000 men filed claims as conscientious objectors under the Selective Service Act of 1940. Of this number, 25,000 were assigned to noncombatant service and 12,000 to civilian work camps.

About 5,000 conscientious objectors were imprisoned during World War II; from 1948 to 1960, after the postwar Selective Service Act was passed, about 1,400 were imprisoned.

Under the 1940 act, members of recognized pacifist religions were allowed to substitute for military service either noncombatant military service, nonmilitary activity related to the war effort or activity considered socially valuable.

The 1948 act, amended in 1951, stated that conscientious-objector status could be achieved only if the applicant based his objection on religious belief and training that included a belief in a Supreme Being. The conscientious objector could then choose between noncombatant service or a public-service activity.

Mulford Q. Sibley and Philip E. Jacob, the authors of a study published in 1952 by the Cornell University Press, said it was not easy to define a conscientious objector. They stated, however, that the objector was "an individual whose scruples will not allow him to assist in the waging of war, and his refusal to assist inevitably leads to a clash between the conscientious claims that he supports and the demands of the state that professes to believe that it is fighting to protect social values and ideals."

### Dug Ditches During War

The resistance of the conscientious objectors was perhaps most widely publicized during World War II, when many engaged in a host of activities in substitution for active military service. They worked on soil conservation experiments, dug irrigation ditches and acted as guinea pigs for medical and scientific research.

One of the most famous objectors was the actor Lew Ayres, who starred in the antiwar film "All Quiet on the Western Front." Declining to bear arms, he enrolled instead at an Oregon camp operated by the Brethren and Mennonite churches. Later he entered the Army as a noncombatant, serving in the Medical Corps.

Asked how Private Ayres was doing, an officer replied: "I wish I had a whole battalion of men just like him."

Not all objectors win public sympathy, particularly those whose objections may be nonreligious. Such objectors have been criticized as self-centered, egotistic and ignorant of the world about them.

At one time the conscientious objector's scruples were considered for inclusion in the Federal Constitution. In 1789 James Madison proposed that the Bill of Rights provide that "no person religiously scrupulous of bearing arms shall be compelled to render military service in person."

However, the Congress decided not to include the exemption.

# General, in Farewell to Cadets, Stressed Ideals of West Point

### By ARNOLD H. LUBASCH

"Duty, Honor, Country."

The three-word motto of the United States Military Academy was the theme of a speech that General of the Army Douglas MacArthur delivered at West Point on May 12, 1962. The occasion was an award to the general, who observed then that it was the last time he would visit West Point.

On a brilliant spring morning, General MacArthur inspected the cadets in a full-dress brigade review on the parade ground, known as The Plain. He stood, in civilian dress, as future officers of the Army raised their ceremonial sabers to salute him.

Then, at a luncheon in Washington Hall, he accepted the fifth annual Sylvanus Thayer Award, presented by the Military Academy's Association of Graduates to a distinguished American whose service in the national interest exemplifies outstanding devotion to the West Point motto.

The ceremony was precise and perfunctory up to this point. But those in the audience who thought General MacArthur would make a routine acceptance speech were in for a surprise.

For 40 minutes, the hall resounded with the eloquence once so familiar to many Americans. The cadets listened respectfully at first, then attentively and even reverently to the words of General MacArthur.

The Sylvanus Thayer Award, named for the father of the Military Academy, was not being accepted as an award given to one personality, the general said. It was being accepted as a tribute to the American soldier, one of the world's noblest figures, who adhered to three words that provided courage when courage was most difficult and faith when faith seemed impossible.

"Duty, Honor, Country."

The bravery of the American soldier was proved to him on a hundred battlefields, he continued.

It is for others to engage in the discord of national and international controversies, the general told the cadets. Their mission, he said, is to win wars. The duty of the American soldier is to achieve victories, there is no substitute for victory, and the Long Gray Line of West Point has never failed the nation, General MacArthur continued.

If the cadets fail to keep faith with their motto, he said, thousands upon thousands of their predecessors will rise from beneath their white crosses to thunder those words that embrace the ideals they died to preserve.

"Duty, Honor, Country."

The companions of combat remained vividly clear to him around a thousand campfires, the general said. He could still hear the rumble of battle and the crash of guns, he said, and his memories were watered with tears.

When soon he crossed the final river, he pledged, his thoughts would be with the cadets at West Point. He called the cadets a beacon held high to the nation, and said his final thoughts would be of the Corps.

The shadows were lengthening for him, the general whispered. This was the twilight, the end of a long road, his last roll-call with the cadets, he said. He bade them farewell.

# U.S. INVESTIGATES ANTIDRAFT GROUPS

## Katzenbach Says Reds Are Involved in Youth Drive

**By AUSTIN C. WEHRWEIN**
Special to The New York Times

CHICAGO, Oct. 17 — Attorney General Nicholas deB. Katzenbach told a news conference here today that the Justice Department had started a national investigation of groups behind the antidraft movement.

Mr. Katzenbach, here for a speaking engagement, said: "There are some Communists involved in it." He also said, "We may very well have some prosecutions."

Mr. Katzenbach was questioned chiefly about the Students for a Democratic Society, a group of the "new left" that has headquarters here. But he said it was "one of many" that the Justice Department was investigating.

The society, which claims a membership of 300,000, mostly in colleges, has drafted a "strategy" for "the antiwar movement." Mr. Katzenbach said his department had a good deal of the literature it had passed out.

Speaking for the society, Paul Booth, a 22-year-old 1964 graduate of Swarthmore, who is the son of a University of Michigan professor, replied:

"The one basic thing is that we take a very principled civil liberties position. It sounds like a Red-baiting smear. The real issue is the war in Vietnam. This is a kind of a smokescreen. We are going right ahead. Our program is legal."

Mr. Booth, who was also interviewed before the Katzenbach news conference, denied that the society was the instigator of the demonstrations in many cities over the weekend. But he said that 50 of its campus chapters had staged demonstrations.

He said the society was "in communication" with the National Coordinating Committee to End the War in Vietnam, which has headquarters in Madison, Wis., and which did claim to be the instigator of the demonstrations. Mr. Booth declared that the society had put a "low priority" on demonstrations and denied it had anything to do with a mimeograph sheet passed out in Berkeley, Calif., called, "Brief Notes on the Ways and Means of 'Beating' and Defeating the Draft."

### Bribes Advocated

The Berkeley document advised, besides taking a conscientious objector's stand, such things as faking homosexuality, arriving at Selective Service examinations drunk or "high" on narcotics and bribing doctors for certificates of disability. Mr. Booth declared that the society was interested only in claims of conscientious objectors, which it wanted to encourage, and said he was a conscientious objector himself.

At the news conference, Mr. Katzenbach left the impression that the Justice Department did associate the society with the Berkeley "Beat the Draft" document. However, he did not elaborate on this point.

Mr. Katzenbach said he would hesitate to go so far as to call the demonstrations and related activities treason. He explained that there was a "large bite of constitutional protection," and added, "naturally, we are very careful to keep it [treason] confined within narrow limits, within overt acts."

### Notes Federal Statute

But he said that tearing up draft cards was recently made a Federal crime, and that urging or abetting draft evasion had long been a Federal crime, as had been sedition.

While he indicated that Chicago and California would be prime targets of the Federal investigation, he said that the investigation was still continuing.

Here in Chicago, Edward V. Hanrahan, the United States Attorney, has already set an investigation in motion with the aid of the Federal Bureau of Investigation, draft officials and the Chicago Police Department intelligence unit. But Mr. Katzenbach made clear that the Justice Department in Washington would decide whether any prosecutions would follow here or any place else in the country where investigations are going on.

Mr. Katzenbach was careful to avoid being drawn into specifics, saying that while he disagreed "strongly and violently" with the young antidraft demonstrators they had the right to express their views and opinions.

Asked about Communist influence, he said that in such groups "you are likely to find some Communists involved." Asked specifically about the society, he said that the identities of some Communists in the society and some Communists who claim association with it were known.

Asked if Communists were leaders in the society, he replied:

"By and large, no."

Mr. Katzenbach said he thought the danger was that the demonstrations might be **misunderstood abroad**, particularly in **Peking and Hanoi.** He said that "**an overwhelming majority of the American people stand with President Johnson's policy in Vietnam.**"

*October 18, 1965*

# POLICY IN VIETNAM SCORED IN RALLIES THROUGHOUT U.S.

## March to Base at Oakland Halted by Police — 38 Arrested in Michigan

## HUNDREDS GATHER HERE

## Youth Burns His Draft Card Outside Induction Center —Park Meeting Barred

**By DOUGLAS ROBINSON**

Demonstrations protesting the continuing United States involvement in the Vietnam War were conducted in cities across the country yesterday as part of a series of such rallies planned for the weekend.

The biggest of the demonstrations, a "peace march" that began at the University of California at Berkeley, was halted by the police before it reached its objective, the Oakland Army Base.

The demonstrators moved only three quarters of a mile on their projected seven-and-a-half-mile walk.

Three hundred Oakland police were mobilized to stop the marchers, whose number was estimated as high as 10,000. There were no disorders but a good deal of confusion. After they were halted, the demonstrators returned to Berkeley to hold a teach-in on a public square.

Thirty-eight persons, including six women, a professor of sociology and four other University of Michigan teachers, were arrested for conducting a demonstration at the Selective Service headquarters in Ann Arbor.

### Float Attacked

Earlier, a crowd of about 200 people there ripped apart a float depicting opposition to war. An American flag was torn from the float and stamped on.

There were several scuffles with counterpickets in Chicago. In Columbus, Ohio, four leaders of a planned rally were arrested by the police.

Here in New York, several hundred persons participated in a rally outside the Army Induction Center at 39 Whitehall Street. One youth burned his draft card while Federal agents looked on.

Meanwhile, a State Supreme Court justice declined to overrule a decision by Parks Commissioner Newbold Morris denying a permit for a protest rally in Central Park today.

The scores of demonstrations yesterday were a prelude to larger protests planned for 100 cities today and tomorrow.

The demonstrations have largely been organized by the National Coordinating Committee to End the War in Vietnam, with headquarters in Madison, Wis.

In Washington, the State Department said that the "noisy demonstrations" against United States policy reflected only an "infinitesimal fraction" of American public opinion.

One of the largest protests, a parade down Fifth Avenue from 94th Street to 68th Street, is due to start at 1 P.M. today. The sponsors said they expected 10,000 persons to participate.

In Chicago yesterday an angry spectator smashed the placard of a picket marching in front of Roosevelt University. A policeman intervened when the spectator attempted to punch the demonstrator.

The placard read: "I Only Followed Orders: Adolf Eichmann."

The spectator, who said he was Jewish, told the police that the sign offended him "because I lost three-quarters of my family over there." He was not arrested.

Later, some 400 young persons, apparently divided equally on the Vietnam question, gathered in a nearby park. The police kept the groups apart while the protesters made speeches and read poetry.

### Taylor Gives Warning

Also in Chicago, Gen. Maxwell D. Taylor warned that picketing against United States involvement in Vietnam might persuade Communist leaders that "there is a real division of strength in this country, and that may tempt them to prolong the war."

The former Ambassador to Saigon, who is now a special Presidential consultant, is on a speaking tour to explain United States policy on Vietnam. He told newsmen that North Vietnamese leaders "are on a sharp hook; they're looking for something to get them off, and they may think this is it."

Senator Wayne Morse, Democrat of Oregon, defended the demonstrators. Speaking in Washington, he predicted more demonstrations and said he was glad that there were some people "who will not be cowed into submission by the intolerant bigots who believe that because our country is on an illegal course of action, we must support its illegality."

In Columbus the four demonstration leaders were arrested as they walked along a street early yesterday morning. Two of the youths were stopped for questioning and all were taken into custody when they protested.

The four are scheduled to lead a demonstration outside the State Capitol.

At least 250 students and faculty members took part in a rally and march at Yale University. They were heckled by a group of undergraduates as they marched from the campus to a green in downtown New Haven.

The participants, who included a number of townspeople, carried signs reading "Fight Poverty, Not People" and "Heed the Pope's Message of Peace."

At the New York rally, a 22-year-old pacifist burned his draft card. The youth, David Miller of 175 Chrystie Street, said he was a volunteer worker for the relief program of the Catholic Worker movement, a pacifist religious organization.

After burning his card Mr. Miller told reporters that he hoped his action "will be a significant political act."

The draft card burning was the first in New York since recent passage of a law making such action a Federal crime.

Although several agents of the Federal Bureau of Investigation were in the throng outside the induction center, there was no move to arrest Mr. Miller. A city police official said the youth "can be picked up at any time."

### Speakers Jeered

At least 400 persons took part in the Whitehall Street rally. An equal number of spectators watched from across the street and several jeered the speakers with such epithets as "take a bath" and "join the war on poverty."

The rally was led by an amalgam of civil rights, peace, religious and political representatives.

Among the participating groups were the Students for Democratic Action, the Committee for Nonviolent Action, the Socialist Workers party, Youth Against War and Fascism, and the War Resisters League.

The speakers included Bob Parris, a civil rights worker and director of the 1964 voter registration project in Mississippi, and James Peck, editor of a newspaper published by the Congress of Racial Equality.

In the court action, State Supreme Court Justice Emilio Nuñez refused an appeal by the New York chapter of the American Civil Liberties Union to rule against Commissioner Morris's denial of a rally permit for Central Park.

In its appeal, the union contended that the commissioner's action was arbitrary and capricious in that plans for the rally were "beyond recall at this point."

Later in the day, Presiding Justice Charles D. Breitel of the Appellate Division rejected an appeal for an immediate hearing on Justice Nuñez's decision.

At City College, 600 students and faculty members staged a two-hour rally that was preceded by a four-hour "silent vigil" during which students carrying placards stood near the steps of the school library.

The students applauded a call to resist the draft and a demand that President Johnson recall American troops from Vietnam.

The rally was sponsored by the school chapter of the Independent Committee to End the War in Vietnam. Both the vigil and the rally were picketed by members of the campus Young Conservative Club.

At the Iowa State University campus in Ames, students supporting this country's policy gathered more than 250 signatures on petitions to Congress backing the Government. This occurred while a small group of anti-war pickets demonstrated in front of the headquarters of the Naval Reserve Officers Training Corps.

In Philadelphia, hundreds of students from colleges in that area massed at City Hall. About 10 persons backing United States policy picketed the rally.

The State Department's comments on the weekend demonstrations were issued by Robert J. McCloskey, a press officer.

"We are naturally aware of various noisy demonstrations that have taken place and are scheduled to take place," Mr. McCloskey said, "but I would like to point out that these groups constitute an infinitesimal fraction of the American people, the vast majority of whom have indicated their strong support of President Johnson's policies in Vietnam."

# Man, 22, Immolates Himself In Antiwar Protest at U.N.

### By THOMAS BUCKLEY

A 21-year-old former seminarian soaked himself with gasoline and then set himself aflame in front of the United Nations at dawn yesterday, as a protest against "war, all war."

Guards from the world organization and city patrolmen beat out the flames that enveloped him as he sat crosslegged on First Avenue and then rushed him to Bellevue Hospital.

He was drifting near death in the emergency ward last night, with second and third-degree burns covering 95 per cent of his body. The hospital staff said he had almost no chance of surviving.

The youth, Roger Allen LaPorte, was a member of the Catholic Worker movement, a charitable and pacifist organization with headquarters at 175 Chrystie Street on the Lower East Side. He lived in a tenement apartment leased by the organization at 58 Kenmare Street, a few blocks away.

Mr. LaPorte's self-immolation was the second in seven days attributable, at least in part, to continued United States' involvement in the war in Vietnam. Last Monday, Norman R. Morrison, a 32-year-old Quaker from Baltimore, burned himself to death in front of the Pentagon in Washington.

U Thant, the Secretary General of the United Nations, which has been seeking a solution to the Asian conflict, and Arthur Goldberg, the chief United States delegate to the world body, reacted with shock and horror to Mr. LaPorte's action.

Questioned at a city reception, Mr. Goldberg said that while the youth had undoubtedly been impelled by "the highest principles and motives," his action was "terribly unfortunate and terribly unnecessary."

"Perhaps there has been a failure on our part," he went on. "Perhaps we are not sufficiently communicating to the people of the world our dedication, our attachment and complete commitment to the idea that peace is the only way for mankind in the nuclear age."

A spokesman said that Mr. Thant was "deeply grieved over this human tragedy, whatever the motivation might be. U Thant regards human life as very sacred."

### Attended Union Sq. Protest

Friends of Mr. LaPorte said that he had been melancholy but not obviously emotionally disturbed since Saturday, when he attended the demonstration at Union Square at which five other youths burned their draft cards.

Robert Steed, a fellow member of the Catholic Workers, said that Mr. LaPorte had been unable to make up his mind to take part. However, he spoke little of politics and hardly mentioned Vietnam, Mr. Steed said.

On Monday night he helped to serve a simple meal to the members of the Catholic Worker's staff and several persons receiving assistance there, but after that his movements were unknown.

"He may have spent some time with a girl he knew," said Mr. Steed, "but I think he probably walked the streets all night coming to a decision."

Then, at about 5 A.M. the tall, slender blond youth, who looked nothing like the stereotype of the longhaired "Vietnik," or peace demonstrator, stepped onto the wide avenue in front of the Hammarskjold Memorial Library, at 42d Street.

He had a gallon can of gasoline, and now he stepped off the curb and knelt crosslegged on the asphalt in the posture of the Buddhist monks who set themselves on fire to protest the policies of the Diem regime in Vietnam.

Then he struck the light and blue and yellow flames enveloped his body.

### Guard Hears Scream

Henri Okai, a Ghanaian guard at the United Nations, saw the sudden flash and heard the seated figure scream. He called the Police and Fire Departments and then rushed to the burning man's side, trying to beat out the flames. He himself was sickened and treated for smoke inhalation.

A passing gasoline truck driver, who asked that his name not be used, call The New York Times a few minutes later, and in a shaking voice told what he had seen.

"Just as I stopped, three police cars screamed around the corner," he said. "The cops got out and beat with their hands. Then one of them got a fire extinguisher and squirted him with that. The flames weren't too high but they were coming from all over his body.

"While they were hitting at him, the guy sort of raised his head a little bit, then fell down onto the street. I couldn't look no more. I drove on.

"I only got a few blocks, though, when I stopped and called you. I don't know why I called a paper this time of

October 16, 1965

night. except that I had to tell someone."

The Times was open later than usual because of former President Eisenhower's sudden illness.

### Conscious in Ambulance

In the ambulancep that raced against the light traffic down to the Bellevue emergency room at 26th Street, the youth called repeatedly for water. He was conscious, the police said, and spoke coherently.

One of them asked why he had done it. They said he replied, "I'm a Catholic Worker. I'm against war, all wars. I did this as a religious action."

Why had he chosen the early morning hours?

"So no one could stop me," he said.

The police identified him from the contents of his wallet, including his draft card, which was undamaged. It put him in group 2-S, which is reserved for seminarians, but he was subject to reclassification.

At Bellevue, Dr. Jay Grosfeld, the 30-year-old chief resident physician of the New York University Medical School surgical service, had just arrived for his morning rounds. He was summoned to the emergency room to take charge of the fight to save the youth's life.

"He was conscious throughout." Dr. Grosfeld said, "and so badly burned that the nerve ends were destroyed and he was feeling almost no pain. He was in shock, however."

### Last Rites Administered

The Rev. Alexander Busuttil, a Carmelite who is one of the hospital's four Roman Catholic chaplains, gave the youth the last rites of the church.

"He made the most devout act of contrition I have ever

heard," the priest, who is a Maltese and has been in this country for only seven months, said. "His voice was strong and he meant every word."

Two hospital psychiatrists visited his cubicle, which was guarded from intruders by hospital and city policemen. They were quoted as saying that Mr. LaPorte, who was unable to speak because of tube that had been in his throat, had nodded when asked if he wanted to live.

In late afternoon, his parents, who are separated, arrived from Utica. They stayed with him briefly and then left without making any comment. Mr. La-Porte's older brother, Gary, first agreed to speak to reporters, then declined, saying, "Every one knows what happened. I don't want to make a soap opera out of it."

Mr. LaPorte was enrolled as a philosophy student at the Bronx branch of Hunter College. He formerly attended the Columbia University School of General Studies and worked as a Xerox operator in Butler Library on the campus.

He was born in Rome, N.Y., and was an honors graduate of Holy Ghost Academy in Tupper Lake, where he was a class officer and head of the debating society. The youth's original ambition was to be a Trappist monk and for a year, beginning in 1963, he attended the St. John Vianney Seminary in Barre, Vt. His friends said he never gave any reason for withdrawing.

### Members of Group Shocked

A spokesman for the Catholic Worker movement, James H. Forest, said that its members were "deeply shocked, perplexed and grieved by the immolation of Roger LaPorte."

"He never told us what he planned," Mr. Forest said. "If he had we would have discouraged him."

# Ordeal of the Pacifists

The action of the two American pacifists who have recently set themselves afire in protest against this country's involvement in the war in Vietnam has undoubtedly puzzled most of their fellow citizens. Except among the tiny minority that shares their pacifist convictions, there may be a tendency to dismiss their tragic deaths as the acts of emotionally unstable persons or even as the result of temporary insanity.

Although certain Asian peoples have a tradition of public suicide as a political gesture, suicide for political purposes is alien to the American temper. It also makes much less sense in a democracy such as the United States, where free political discussion is possible, than it does in autocratic nations where dissent is stifled, and extreme acts may seem the only way of making a point.

Yet the valor of a man who has unpopular convictions and is willing to kill himself for them commands a measure of respect. Unquestionably, the courage of an infantryman or a bomber pilot who volunteers for a dangerous mission and loses his life is the kind of courage that is readily understood and approved, as it should be. But it would be a mistake to demean or dismiss the self-abnegation of these pacifists.

As a practical political matter, it is unlikely that the suicides will have any effect on the conduct of the war or hasten the coming of peace. These men would have advanced their aims more effectively by staying alive and working for humanitarian causes. As a matter of logic, they have contradicted their own principles of non-violence by turning upon themselves the full fury of the violence they condemn.

Confused and misdirected though they have been, they may serve some useful purpose if their self-inflicted agony brings home—alongside the mounting casualty lists—the grisly cost of war. The violence of war feeds upon itself and begets demands for ever more intensifying violence, as the history of the Vietnam involvement makes clear. The prosecution of the war may be a hard practical necessity; it ought never to be an occasion for losing that self-control and that recognition of human kinship that distinguish men from animals.

To the Editor:

\* \* \* \* \*

As a 1959 graduate of Penn State with a commission as a second lieutenant in the Army, I, like many of my classmates, could have thought of numerous other ways to use my talents besides going into the service. And now as an active reservist working toward advanced degrees during summers, I would prefer to continue teaching my high school students as opposed to being called to active duty, just as many other officers and men in my unit would prefer to continue following their chosen civilian careers.

However, I am quite sure that it is the majority of us who would serve willingly if called upon and a minority who are willing to sacrifice their self-respect to "escape" the "horrors" of army life.

The idea of men who marry girls they do not love, father children they do not want, and pursue college degrees they do not need to evade the draft boards seems to be a cause for alarm. These men are no better than the misguided exhibitionists who burn their draft cards in public—always in public. In fact, one has to wonder whether this generation of W. W. II "babies" has experienced a genetic omission—lack of backbone.　JAMES T. COONAN
Binghamton, N.Y., Nov. 15, 1965

Associated Press Wirephoto

**AT INDUCTION CENTER IN HOUSTON:** Cassius Clay, having declined to be inducted into military service, is escorted out by Lieut. Col. J. Edwin McKee, commander.

# Clay Refuses Army Oath; Stripped of Boxing Crown

### By ROBERT LIPSYTE
Special to The New York Times

HOUSTON, April 28—Cassius Clay refused today, as expected, to take the one step forward that would have constituted induction into the armed forces. There was no immediate Government action.

Although Government authorities here foresaw several months of preliminary moves before Clay would be arrested and charged with a felony, boxing organizations instantly stripped the 25-year-old fighter of his world heavyweight championship.

"It will take at least 30 days for Clay to be indicted and it probably will be another year and a half before he could be sent to prison since there undoubtedly will be appeals through the courts," United States Attorney Morton Susman said.

#### Statement Is Issued

Clay, in a statement distributed a few minutes after the announcement of his refusal, said:

"I have searched my conscience and I find I cannot be true to my belief in my religion by accepting such a call."

He has maintained throughout recent unsuccessful civil litigation that he is entitled to draft exemption as an appointed minister of the Lost-Found Nation of Islam, the so-called Black Muslim sect.

Clay, who prefers his Muslim name of Muhammad Ali, anticipated the moves against his title in his statement, calling them a "continuation of the same artificially induced prejudice and discrimination" that had led to the defeat of his various suits and appeals in

Federal courts, including the Supreme Court.

Hayden C. Covington of New York, Clay's lawyer, said that further civil action to stay criminal proceedings would be initiated. If convicted of refusal to submit to induction, Clay is subject to a maximum sentence of five years imprisonment and a $10,000 fine.

Mr. Covington, who has defended many Jehovah's Witnesses in similar cases, has repeatedly told Clay during the last few days, "You'll be unhappy in the fiery furnace of criminal proceedings but you'll come out unsinged."

As a plaintiff in civil action, the Negro fighter has touched on such politically and socially explosive areas as alleged racial imbalance on local Texas draft boards, alleged discriminatory action by the Government in response to public pressure, and the rights of a minority religion to appoint clergymen.

#### Full-Time Occupation

As a prospective defendant in criminal proceedings, Clay is expected to attempt to establish that "preaching and teaching" the tenets of the Muslims is a full-time occupation and that boxing is the "avocation" that financially supports his unpaid ministerial duties.

Today, Clay reported to the Armed Forces Examining and Entrance Station on the third floor of the Federally drab United States Custom House a few minutes before 8 A.M., the ordered time. San Jacinto Street, in downtown Houston, was already crowded with television crews and newsmen when Clay stepped out of a taxi cab with Covington, Quinnan Hodges, the local associate counsel, and Chauncey Eskridge of Chicago, a lawyer for the Rev. Martin Luther King, as well as for Clay and others.

Half a dozen Negro men, apparently en route to work, applauded Clay and shouted: "He gets more publicity than Johnson." Clay was quickly taken upstairs and disappeared into the maw of the induction procedure for more than five hours.

Two information officers supplied a stream of printed and oral releases throughout the procedure, including a detailed schedule of examinations and records processing, as well as instant confirmation of Clay's acceptable blood test and the fact that he had obeyed Muslim dietary strictures by passing up the ham sandwich included in the inductees' box lunches.

Such information, however, did not forestall the instigation, by television crews, of a small demonstration outside the Custom House. During the morning, five white youngsters from the Friends World Institute, a nonaccredited school in Westbury, L. I., who had driven all night from a study project in

Oklahoma, and half a dozen local Negro youths, several wearing Black Power buttons, had appeared on the street.

### Groups Use Signs

Continuous and sometimes insulting interviewers eventually provoked both groups, separately, to appear with signs. The white group merely asked for the end of the Vietnam war and greater efforts for civil rights.

The Negroes eventually swelled into a group of about two dozen circling pickets carrying hastily scrawled, "Burn, Baby, Burn" signs and singing, "Nothing kills a nigger like too much love." A few of the pickets wore discarded bedsheets and table linen wound into African-type garments, but most were young women dragged into the little demonstration on their lunch hours.

There was a touch of sadness and gross exaggeration throughout the most widely observed noninduction in history. At breakfast this morning in the Hotel America, Clay had stared out a window into a dingy, cold morning and said: "Every time I fight it gets cold and rainy. Then dingy and cool, no sun in sight nowhere."

He had shrugged when Mr. Hodges had showed him an anonymously sent newspaper clipping in which a photograph of the local associate counsel had been marked "Houston's great nigger lawyer."

Sadly, too, 22-year-old John McCullough, a graduate of Sam Houston State College, said:

"It's his prerogative if he's sincere in his religion, but it's his duty as a citizen to go in. I'm a coward, too."

### 46 Called to Report

Then Mr. McCullough, who is white, went up the steps to be inducted. He was one of the 46 young men, including Clay, who were called to report on this day.

For Clay, the day ended at 1:10 P. M. Houston time, when Lieut. Col. J. Edwin McKee, commander of the station, announced that "Mr. Muhammed Ali has just refused to be inducted."

In a prepared statement, Colonel McKee said that notification of the refusal would be forwarded to the United States Attorney General's office, and the national and local Selective Service boards. This is the first administrative step toward possible arrest, and an injunction to stop it had been denied to Clay yesterday in the United States District Court here.

Clay was initially registered for the draft in Louisville, where he was born. He obtained a transfer to a Houston board because his ministerial duties had made this city his new official residence. He had spent most of his time until last summer in Chicago, where the Muslim headquarters are situated, in Miami, where he trained, or in the cities in which he was fighting.

After Colonel McKee's brief statement, Clay was brought into a pressroom and led into

range of 13 television cameras and several dozen microphones. He refused to speak as he handed out Xeroxed copies of his statement to selected newsmen, including representatives of the major networks, wire services and The New York Times.

The statement thanked those instrumental in his boxing career as well as those who have offered support and guidance, including Elijah Muhammad, the leader of the Muslims; Mohammed Oweida, Secretary General of the High Council for Islamic Affairs, and Floyd McKissick, president of the Congress of Racial Equality.

The statement, in part, declared:

"It is in the light of my consciousness as a Muslim minister and my own personal convictions that I take my stand in rejecting the call to be inducted in the armed services. I do so with the full realization of its implications and possible consequences. I have searched my conscience and I find I cannot be true to my belief in my religion by accepting such a call.

"My decision is a private and individual one and I realize that this is a most crucial decision. In taking it I am dependent solely upon Allah as the final judge of these actions brought about by my own conscience.

"I strongly object to the fact that so many newspapers have given the American public and the world the impression that I have only two alternatives in taking this stand: either I go to jail or go to the Army. There

is another alternative and that alternative is justice. If justice prevails, if my Constitutional rights are upheld, I will be forced to go neither to the Army nor jail. In the end I am confident that justice will come my way for the truth must eventually prevail. . .

"I am looking forward to immediately continuing my profession.

"As to the threat voiced by certain elements to 'strip' me of my title, this is merely a continuation of the same artificially induced prejudice and discrimination.

"Regardless of the difference in my outlook, I insist upon my right to pursue my livelihood in accordance with the same rights granted to other men and women who have disagreed with the policies of whatever Administration was in power at the time.

"I have the world heavyweight title not because it was 'given' to me, not because of my race or religion, but because I won it in the ring through my own boxing ability.

"Those who want to 'take' it and hold a series of auction-type bouts not only do me a disservice but actually disgrace themselves. I am certain that the sports fans and fair-minded people throughout America would never accept such a 'title-holder.'"

Clay returned to his hotel and went to sleep after the day's activities. He is expected to leave the city, possibly for Washington, in the morning.

April 29, 1967

# Punishment of Draft Foes Urged by Some in House

### Ignore First Amendment, They Say—Carmichael and Dr. King Scored

**By JOHN HERBERS**
Special to The New York Times

WASHINGTON, May 5 — Members of the House Armed Services Committee demanded today that the Justice Department disregard the First Amendment right of free speech and prosecute those who urged young men to defy the draft law.

"Let's forget the First Amendment," Representative F. Edward Hébert, Democrat of Louisiana, told Assistant Attorney General Fred M. Vinson Jr. in a loud voice during hearings on the draft.

"I know this [prosecution] would be rescinded by the Supreme Court," he said. "But at least the effort should be made. It would show the American people that the Justice Department and Congress were trying to clean up this rat-infested area."

Mr. Hébert was backed in his questioning by Representative L. Mendel Rivers, Democrat of South Carolina, the chairman, and Representative Alton Lennon, Democrat of North Carolina.

No one on the committee took issue with Mr. Hébert, but Mr. Vinson said:

"I am a firm believer in the First Amendment."

Mr. Hébert's statement was part of an outburst by committee members after Mr. Vinson told them that he saw no way

to amend the law or use it to prosecute those who advised others in a general way to evade the draft without coming into conflict with First Amendment rights, as interpreted by the Supreme Court.

The members specifically mentioned the Negro civil rights leaders, Stokely Carmichael of the Student Nonviolent Coordinating Committee and the Rev. Dr. Martin Luther King Jr.

The committee is conducting hearings on proposed revisions in the draft law. For the last two days, members have expressed less concern over the alleged inequities in drafting young men than in punishing those who either evaded the draft or urged others to.

Mr. Rivers set the tone for the exchanges yesterday when he told a representative of the Methodist Board of Christian Social Concerns, Everett R. Jones, who was testifying for voluntary service:

"There are only two ideologies in the world. One is represented by Jesus Christ and the other by the hammer and sickle. Which do you prefer?"

Mr. Jones did not answer.

When Mr. Jones said he thought the nation could suspend the draft and attract enough men for defense purposes by paying more money, Mr. Rivers said:

"I might recommend you to Secretary McNamara. You might be the man to lead us across the Jordan River."

Representative William H. Bates of Massachusetts, the ranking Republican, asked a conscientious objector, "You couldn't find it in your heart to help a wounded soldier?"

Representative Durwood G. Hall, Republican of Missouri, asked Raoul Kulberg, who was testifying for a Quaker group, the Washington Friends Joint Peace Committee:

"Are you now or have you ever been a member of the Communist party of the United States?"

Mr. Kulbert said he had not.

When Mr. Vinson appeared for questioning this morning, Mr. Rivers said the public was demanding that Congress take action against draft evaders. He said the Supreme Court was giving "these people license" to get out of military service.

### Punishment Prescribed

Popping a mint into his mouth and holding his gavel under his chin, Mr. Rivers said:

"There has been an 861 per cent increase in the mail since I became chairman of this committee. The committee is running days behind in answering it. I got down here this morning at 15 past five to sign the correspondence."

He implied that the mail was

**Representative F. Edward Hébert, Democrat of Louisiana, urged prosecution of counselors of draft evasion.**

from citizens demanding that the criminal provisions of the draft law be strengthened.

The New York Times

**Representative L. Mendel Rivers, Democrat of South Carolina, heads the panel.**

Mr. Vinson said that the Government had "a pretty good batting average" of convicting

draft law violators and that the problem had not increased appreciably in the last decade.

Mr. Rivers asked how many prosecutions there had been under the law, which contains a provision for punishment of up to five years in prison for aiding and abetting others to evade the draft.

He wanted to know why it had not been applied against those such as Mr. Carmichael, who had led students at Hampden Institute in chanting, "We ain't gonna go. Hell no."

Mr. Vinson replied that no one had been prosecuted under the provision and that the department could not prosecute Mr. Carmichael because of the First Amendment. He cited a decision going back to Oliver Wendell Holmes that utterances were protected by the First Amendment unless they constituted a "clear and present danger" to the country (Schenck v. United States, 1919).

"A great deal of the Constitution is intended to protect minorities and dissenters," Mr. Vinson said.

"We have been made aware of that in the past few years," Mr. Hébert replied. "How can the Carmichaels and the Kings stand before the American people and incite violation of the law while the Justice Department stands idly by?"

"No one," Mr. Vinson said, "has been prosecuted because the department felt no one has violated the law."

Could the law be amended to "get around the First Amendment?" Mr. Hébert asked.

"Any law that deals with utterances must be read in the light of the First Amendment," Mr. Vinson said.

It was then that Mr. Hébert said the First Amendment should be disregarded.

Mr. Lennon said he hoped "the American people will find out what type of Justice Department thinks it's all right for people to preach evading the draft."

"What can we do?" Mr. Hagan broke in.

"We can all applaud the 99 per cent of our citizens who vigorously support their country," Mr. Vinson replied.

The committee members wanted to know if any change could be made in the law that would speed draft evasion cases through the courts, reminding Mr. Vinson that some of their constituents were upset about the prospects of lengthy court action in the case of Cassius Clay, the heavyweight boxing champion, who refused to be inducted.

Mr. Vinson said that such cases had priority for trial, but he thought it would "not be good government" to give them preference on appeal.

"Would it hurt, would it hurt?" Mr. Rivers asked.

"What if every committee of Congress put such a provision in the law?" Mr. Vinson asked.

John R. Blandford, the committee's chief counsel said:

"This is the committee that controls the destiny of every youth in America."

At the end, Mr. Rivers said to Mr. Vinson with a smile, "I wish your father was Chief Justice."

The elder Vinson was Chief Justice from 1946 to 1953, when he died.

"I think we have a fine Chief Justice," Mr. Vinson replied.

May 6, 196

---

# Calley Pleads for Understanding

**By HOMER BIGART**

Special to The New York Times

FORT BENNING, Ga., March 30—Gasping for breath, First Lieut. William L. Calley Jr. made a final plea for understanding today as he faced the military jury that convicted him yesterday of the premeditated murder of at least 22 South Vietnamese civilians at Mylai.

The 5-foot 3-inch platoon leader, who has described himself in an interview as "just a finger, a fragment of a Frankenstein monster," said he never "wantonly" killed anyone. Shaken with sobs, he said the

Army never told him that his enemies were human.

The enemy was never described to him as anything but "Communism," he said.

"They [the Army] didn't give it a race, they didn't give it a sex, they didn't give it an age," said Lieutenant Calley, who had been accused by the Government prosecutor of slaying old men, women, children and babies.

After hearing Lieutenant Calley, the jury of six beribboned career officers retired to consider his punishment. Premeditated murder carries a mandatory penalty of death or life imprisonment.

The jury had not voted a sentence by 5 P.M. when the military judge closed the court, and it will resume deliberations tomorrow.

Too short to use the lectern, Lieutenant Calley spoke to the jury from behind a lowered microphone stand. His hands were jammed into his pockets. His chief counsel, George W. Latimer, stood nearby as if to catch him if he buckled. "I hope the boy won't cave in," Mr. Latimer told the court.

Lieutenant Calley, 27 years old, stood erect during his plea of 2 minutes 12 seconds. He wheezed noisily through the microphone and had to pause a number of times.

He said at the outset that he was not begging for his life. His voice quavering, he said:

"I don't really think it matters what type of individual I am. And I'm not going to stand here and plead for my life or my freedom."

### 'A Thousand More'

All he asked, he said, was that the court consider "a thousand more lives that are going to be lost in Southeast Asia" and the "thousands more" who would be maimed for life.

"I've never known a soldier nor did I ever myself," Lieutenant Calley said, "ever wantonly kill a human being in my entire life. If I have committed a crime, the only crime I've committed is in my judgment of values. Apparently I valued my troops' lives more than I did that of the enemy."

412

He said his troops were "massacred and mauled" by "an enemy I couldn't see, I couldn't feel, and I couldn't touch," an enemy, he said, that nobody in the military system had ever described as "anything other than Communism."

"They never let me believe [that Communism] was just a philosophy in a man's mind," he said. "That was my enemy out there."

Then, in a choked voice, he made his last statement:

"Yesterday, you stripped me of all my honor. Please, by your actions that you take here today don't strip future soldiers of their honor, I beg of you."

### Prosecution Replies

Capt. Aubrey M. Daniel 3d, the Army prosecutor, was quick to rebut Lieutenant Calley. Captain Daniel told the jurors:

"You did not strip him of his honor. What he did stripped him of his honor. It is not an honor — it has never been an honor — to kill unarmed men, women and children."

Captain Daniel did not specifically ask the jury to bring in a death penalty. "You know the facts," he said, "and I know you'll reach an appropriate sentence."

Not since April 13, 1961, has an American soldier been executed. On that day Pvt. John Bennett was hanged at Fort Leavenworth, Kan., for rape.

Before Lieutenant Calley spoke, his lawyers made pleas against the death sentence.

Flourishing a bunch of telegrams, Mr. Latimer told the jurors that the Calley case had "torn America apart." He declared:

"The flag may fly at full mast over military installations, but it will always be drawn at half mast over the homes of people whose sons may be going into military service. This case cuts very deep.

"When Lieutenant Calley went into the service of the United States Army he was not a killer, he was not an aggressive young man.

"It is one of the most unusual situations where a man was taught at Fort Benning, Ga., to kill, was not properly trained, when he comes back to Fort Benning, what's it for? To stand trial on a capital charge."

### 'That Oriental Area'

Mr. Latimer went on: "Lieutenant Calley, outside of an ordinary traffic violation, was a good boy and he remained that way until he got into that Oriental area over there in Vietnam.

"Maybe, shall we say, he used bad judgment, maybe he became too aggressive, went too far. But who trained him to kill, kill, kill?

"You don't have to have eyes of glass and hearts of stone. Somewhere along the line, there is some place where a few humanities ought to be worked into this case, where a maximum sentence isn't given, where it should not be."

Mr. Latimer asked that "some small consideration be given to a boy who did not necessarily want to go to Vietnam but was sent there, a boy who did not want to kill anybody but who thought he had to."

"I think there is a place for Lieutenant Calley to go on and make something of his life," Mr. Latimer said, "but he can't do it in the graveyard. Thank you all so much. I go away with a heavy heart for I see a life ruined."

The shooting of noncombatants was not unique, Mr. Latimer added. Many soldiers in Lieutenant Calley's company admitted shooting civilians indiscriminately at Mylai, but some had left the Army and charges against others have been dropped.

Of the whole company, said Mr. Latimer, only Lieutenant Calley and his commanding officer, Capt. Ernest L. Medina, would "go before the scales of justice and be measured whether they die or not."

March 31, 1971

## Medina:

# Another Of the Mylai Guiltless

It took the five officers on the military jury only 57 minutes to reach a verdict: not guilty on all counts. In the course of the month-long court-martial, the credibility of several Government witnesses had been damaged; others had changed their stories. Most of the charges, which had originally been for capital crimes, were successively reduced by the military judge to noncapital crimes and then, at the end, to mere misdemeanors. But even they didn't stick. Last Wednesday afternoon, Capt. Ernest L. Medina walked out of the courtroom at Fort McPherson, Ga., a free man.

With the acquittal of the 35-year-old former company commander of all charges of murder, assault on a prisoner during interrogation and responsibility for the murders of at least 100 Vietnamese civilians at the hamlet called Mylai (4) on March 16, 1968, the United States Army has closed the books on the prosecutions of those directly involved in the worst atrocity ever known to have been committed by American soldiers.

There is very little more to be done about the Mylai affair, officially at least. One court-martial remains, not for the crimes committed at Mylai but on charges of covering it all up after it happened. To that end, Col. Oran K. Henderson, Captain Medina's brigade commander, is now standing court-martial at Fort Meade, Md. Though he was in a helicopter over the scene during the assault, Colonel Henderson is not charged with any responsibility for the massacre itself, only with dereliction of duty by not investigating what happened there.

There were 105 American soldiers on the ground at Mylai (4) on that March morning. By their own testimony, the vast majority took part in the slaughter of unarmed and unresisting civilians there. By the time word of the incident had reached the American public 18 months later, and official Army investigations had begun, most of those men had been discharged and thus were beyond the reach of military courts—the only tribunals with jurisdiction over crimes committed by servicemen in Vietnam.

However, charges of murder, rape and other high crimes were lodged against a dozen officers and enlisted men still in the Army, with Captain Medina the highest-ranking officer indicted. Another dozen officers, from Captain Medina to Maj. Gen. (now Brig. Gen.) Samuel W. Koster, in 1969 commander of the Americal Division in Vietnam, were charged with covering up the massacre.

But only six men ever came to trial. Charges against all the others were dropped. And only one man was convicted: First Lieut. William L. Calley Jr., for the murder of an unknown number, but no fewer than 22 civilians. He was sentenced to life in prison, but a month ago his sentence was reduced to 20 years. It could be reduced still further as it is reviewed by military appellate courts and by President Nixon.

It seems certain that the acquittal of Captain Medina will raise again the cries that Calley was a scapegoat, a lonely and lowly lieutenant forced to shoulder by himself the blame for Mylai while all others involved — higher in rank and lower — have gone free. His conviction, many have said, came because the Army needed a fall guy and he was the most convenient one; not because of the desires of the Army, but despite them, as a result of the perseverance and determination of his prosecutor, Capt. Aubrey M. Daniel 3d.

It is apparent that the Army took the hardest road against Captain Medina. It could have prosecuted him for dereliction of duty, for neither reporting the massacre nor investigating it. Indeed, Captain Medina, both at his own court-martial and at Calley's, admitted that he was guilty of this offense. But that charge was dropped—the statute of limitations on it has now run out—and the decision was made to press the issue of command responsibility: that a commander must shoulder the blame for what his men do, even if he is unaware of their actions.

Command responsibility, of course, is basic to any army, for it is essential to the maintenance of discipline. The responsibility of commanders for the actions of their troops has been clearly spelled out both

413

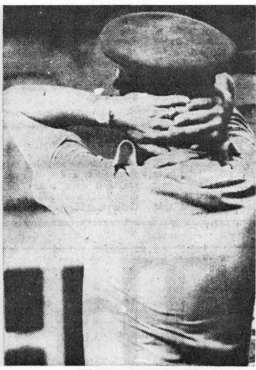

**Capt. Ernest Medina awaits the verdict. It was "not guilty."**

in army regulations and in the war crimes trials held after World War II—most notably that of Gen. Tamayuki Yamashita, who was hanged for the atrocities committed by his Japanese troops in the Philippines even though he was out of contact with them.

Captain Medina was a lot closer to the action at Mylai; though he claims to have been unaware of what was happening, he was on the fringes of the hamlet all during the two or three hours of the massacre.

But as many military-legal experts noted before the Medina court-martial began, to ask a jury of Army officers to convict a fellow officer of responsibility for the crimes of his troops, when some of those very same officers might find themselves in a similar situation at some future date, was probably expecting to much.

Judge Kenneth A. Howard, moreover, ruled, as the court-martial opened, that Captain Medina could not be convicted—despite the Yamashita rule—unless the Government could prove that the captain knew the slaughter was taking place and did nothing to stop it. Few witnesses supported this contention.

So now the official end is about to be written to the tragedy at Mylai. Though only one man, Calley, was convicted, the others involved have not escaped totally unscathed. Many, including Captain Medina, had looked forward to military service as their career. That future has now ended. Captain Medina and some others are leaving the service, or have already left it, and those who remain in uniform face official reprimand, dead-end assignments and even demotion.

—RICHARD HAMMER

# National Drive Seeks Amnesty For Deserters and Draft Evaders

### By BILL KOVACH
Special to The New York Times

BOSTON, Dec. 27 — A national debate is growing around the issue of amnesty for thousands of young men who have avoided or deserted from service in the Vietnam war.

Already, several political leaders, including Presidential contenders, have urged some form of amnesty, and at least three amnesty bills have been introduced in Congress by both liberal and conservative members.

The governing bodies of four major religious denominations have endorsed various amnesty proposals and the American Civil Liberties Union will open an office Jan. 1 to help coordinate organizations around the country now urging amnesty.

Although President Nixon has rejected any suggestions of action on amnesty, the Administration has acceded to a study of the problem.

Opponents of amnesty have not been so vocal as proponents, but there are many, including some antiwar activists, who reject the concept for various reasons, including the feeling that amnesty to deserters would be unfair to those who fought and died.

The issue has gained importance because of the large numbers of men involved. No war fought by the United States has generated the organized opposition Vietnam has. Influenced by education, the church antiwar organizations, personal convictions and political leaders who denounce the war, young men by the tens of thousands found means of escaping service.

In an effort to remove the threat of criminal prosecution and the possibility of wholesale imprisonment of those who refuse to serve in an unpopular war, the movement for amnesty is beginning its campaign.

Charles O. Porter, a former Representative from Oregon who opposed the war in the early nineteen-sixties, has formed Amnesty Now, a national organization whose sole purpose is to gain a general amnesty. As Mr. Porter sees the issue, these young men are the victims of the national debate over the war.

#### 'A Cruel Dilemma'

"Myself and other liberals like me unwittingly forced a cruel dilemma for these young men," Mr. Porter said from his law office in Eugene, Ore.

"We opposed the war and generated resistance. Idealistic young men caught in the middle of that debate had to make a decision, and some of them chose not to become involved in what has been considered an illegal and immoral war.

"We have felt for some time that amnesty is important, for it goes to the heart of the moral issue of this war. No man should be punished for refusal to participate in an immoral war."

Amnesty Now is preparing a draft of a bill for introduction in Congress that would offer amnesty to both draft resisters and deserters. It plans to develop an organization to lobby for the bill. Among the goals of the organization are to get amnesty planks in both national party platforms next summer, to obtain such commitments from Presidential and Congressional candidates and a petition campaign to support the bill.

Unlike bills currently in Congress—sponsored by Representative Edward I. Koch, Democrat of Manhattan, and Senator Robert Taft Jr., Republican of Ohio—the bill called for by Amnesty Now would require no "alternative service." Under both the Koch and Taft bills, draft evaders could avoid prosecution by volunteering for two or three years of alternative service in some Federal social program. Neither bill deals with deserters but leaves their disposition up to the military.

"I am totally opposed to alternate service," Mr. Porter said. "It is based on the need to punish, and to my mind these men have already paid a high price in exile or hiding."

Those who oppose any form of amnesty offer various arguments. One of the major ones is that to offer amnesty now could lead to the breakdown of the entire draft structure.

#### Change in Feeling

Another is that to grant amnesty to those who fled battle would be manifestly unfair to those who stayed and fought and died.

From their communities in exile, spokesmen for the thousands who will be affected by the final decision have entered the debate. One of these exiles, a draft resister now living in Toronto, Jack Colhoun, discussed the alternative service proposal in a published open letter to Representative Koch.

What Mr. Koch failed to comprehend, Mr. Colhoun wrote, "is that many of us would have been quick, willing and anxious to accept such a proposal five years ago. Indeed, many of us are exiles today precisely because such an alternative was denied to us in the past.

"We left the states because we did not want to become criminals of the heart and now feel that a Government which has the stain of Indo-China on its conscience has no business passing judgment on our 'crimes' and meting out punishment, no matter how seemingly tolerant and liberal it may be dressed up."

These young men denounced suggestions of amnesty for draft resisters and not for deserters as class legislation. Draft resisters, they point out, are largely college-educated middle-class young men who discussed the war and made a firm decision to avoid service. Deserters, on the other hand, tend to be less well-educated and less articulate men who are caught up by the draft and who turn against the military only after first-hand experience.

Participating in the developing pro-amnesty movement are a number of members of Congress and organizations such as the National Council of Catholic Bishops; the Presbyterian and Methodist churches and the Church of Christ; the Committee of Southern Churchmen; the Americans for Democratic Action; the National Student Association; the War Resisters League, and Clergy and Laymen Concerned.

Harry Schwarzschild, who will head the A.C.L.U. Amnesty Project office, which is to open next month in New York, is encouraged by the potential for commitment to the issue.

"We must overcome the divisions, hatred and bitterness built by this war," Mr. Schwarzschild said. "We must overcome the development for the first time in history of a group of American refugees made up of some of the most promising young men in our society."

The official reaction to these developments was summed up in the one-word answer President Nixon gave newsmen asking about the possibilities of amnesty on Nov. 12: "No."

Since that time Curtis W. Tarr, the Selective Service director, who earlier had told newsmen some sort of amnesty would have to be considered, now says: "It is the wrong time to talk about it as long as parents have sons in Southeast Asia. I just see a great potential for animosity."

The Department of Defense answers inquiries about amnesty with the statement that "There have not been nor are there any proposals under consideration for granting a general amnesty."

There are indications the Administration may have had second thoughts since President Nixon's rejection of the idea. The Sabre Foundation, a nonpartisan offshoot of the liberal Republican Ripon Society, is beginning a task force on amnesty to develop basic research information on the present situation, the proposals and the history of the question.

# PRESIDENT SAYS 'OPINION LEADERS' FAILED HIM ON WAR

## Holds Media, Business and University Critics Should Have Supported Mining

### By TAD SZULC
#### Special to The New York Times

WASHINGTON, Oct. 16— President Nixon attacked today "the so-called opinion leaders of this country" for not supporting him last May after he ordered the bombing of North Vietnam and the mining of its ports to deter the "specter of defeat."

Speaking extemporaneously and emotionally during a brief surprise appearance at a conference here of the National League of Families of American Prisoners and Missing in Southeast Asia, the President delivered a slashing indictment of critics of his Vietnam policies. He included critics in the news media, the universities and even the business community.

Pledging that the fate of the prisoners of war would not be left "to the goodwill of the enemy" and that draft evaders and deserters "will pay a price for their choice," Mr. Nixon addressed himself to key points in last Tuesday's Vietnam policy speech by his Democratic opponent, Senator George McGovern.

### McGovern's Promise

Senator McGovern promised that, if elected, he would send Sargent Shriver, his Vice-Presidential nominee, to Hanoi "to speed the arrangements" for the prisoners' return and would grant jailed and exiled draft evaders and deserters "the opportunity to come home."

Mr. Nixon, who received a standing ovation from the audience of about 1,000 persons at the Statler Hilton Hotel, told the conference in an eight-minute speech that his move last May 8 to interdict North Vietnamese supply lines was "the hardest decision I have made since becoming President of the United States."

He explained that as he was preparing for his Moscow meeting with Soviet leaders, "a massive Communist invasion took place in South Vietnam from North Vietnam."

### 'Had to Make a Choice'

"We were faced with the specter of defeat," the President said. "And I had to make a choice, a choice of accepting that defeat and going to Moscow hat in hand, or of acting to prevent it. I acted."

Mr. Nixon said that the decision was militarily "right" and that "those who predicted that it would lead to the dissolution of the summit and its failure proved to be wrong."

He then asserted that when a President makes "a hard decision, the so-called opinion leaders of this country can be counted upon to stand beside him, regardless of party."

He asked: "Who are the opinion leaders?

"Well, they are supposed to be the leaders of the media, the great editors and publishers and television commentators and the rest.

"They are supposed to be the presidents of our universities and the professors and the rest, those who have the educational background to understand the importance of great decisions and the necessity to stand by the President of the United States when he makes a terribly difficult, potentially unpopular decision. They are supposed to be some of our top businessmen who also have this kind of background.

"Let me tell you that when that decision was made, there was precious little support from any of the so-called opinion leaders of this country whom I have just described."

### Substitute for Kissinger

Henry A. Kissinger, Mr. Nixon's special assistant for national security affairs, had been scheduled to address the conference, but the President said that "I decided to substitute" for him to thank the prisoners' families for their support "and to urge you for your continued support."

He said the support he sought was not for "an election campaign" but for the "cause of an honorable peace."

Mr. Nixon said that "some very intensive negotiations have been under way" but that he would not comment on their status because "I would not want to raise false hopes" and because "any comments when negotiations are taking place could jeopardize their success."

Summing up the United States negotiating position, Mr. Nixon said that he would not agree "to any settlement which imposes a Communist government upon the people of South Vietnam," would "under no circumstances abandon our prisoners of war and our missing in action" and would "not betray our allies."

"We shall not stain the honor of the United States," he said:

Mr. Nixon said that when he used the word "abandon," he spoke "quite deliberately" to say that "we cannot leave their fate to the goodwill of the enemy."

Senator McGovern has said that he would send Mr. Shriver to Hanoi soon after halting the bombing of North Vietnam, would end all support for the South Vietnamese government and would arrange for the prisoners' return.

The Nixon Administration has maintained that the release of the prisoners must be "in parallel" with the withdrawal of United States troops from Vietnam and must not be left for subsequent disposition.

Although Senator McGovern did not use the word "amnesty" when he said last week that deserters and draft evaders should have the opportunity "to come home," the President said:

"I say that when thousands of Americans died for their choice and hundreds are now P.O.W.'s or missing in action for their choice, it would be the most immoral thing I could think of to give amnesty to draft dodgers and those who deserted."

"Your loved ones have and are paying a price for their choice, and those who deserted America will pay a price for their choice," the President said.

Mr. Nixon told the prisoners' families, "I know it has been a long, long vigil for you," but "you have never been away from my thoughts and you have never been away from my prayers, and there is nothing that I want more than to bring your loved ones home, and I will never let you down."

In a television interview on the Columbia Broadcasting System last Jan. 2, Mr. Nixon said: "I, for one, would be very liberal with regard to amnesty, but not while there are Americans in Vietnam fighting to serve their country and defend their country, and not while P.O.W.'s are held by North Vietnam."

The President said in January that amnesty would be considered after the end of the fighting and the release of the prisoners, "but it would have to be on a basis of their paying the price, of course, that anyone should pay for violating the law."

# A Famous Victory

## By Anthony Lewis

LOS ANGELES, Oct. 27 — In a strange election, this must have been the strangest moment: George McGovern about to leave Detroit for his day of campaigning, and suddenly the accompanying press hears that Henry Kissinger is talking on television about peace in Vietnam. Everyone piles out of the buses to watch in the cocktail lounge of a Howard Johnson's motel.

Watching, it was as if the real campaign were there in the White House briefing room—and Henry Kissinger the candidate. His account of the Vietnam negotiations was professionally masterful; it was also a skilled political performance. Here was a White House foreign affairs adviser promising "an act of healing" for domestic "anguish" over the war, and ending with a political peroration: "We believe that we can restore both peace and unity to America very soon."

But after all the suffering and heartache, domestic politics is unimportant compared to an end of this war—especially, for us, of America's role in it. As to that, the Kissinger statement and other events of the last few days have made a number of things clearer.

There is going to be a cease-fire: Kissinger's confidence about that is based solidly on the logic of the situation. President Nixon, having come this far, can hardly be seen to let peace slip away. Having at last engaged in a test of wills with his Saigon allies, he cannot afford to lose that contest.

Nguyen Van Thieu, for his part, prefers as always to have the United States go on bombing his own country and the other three states of Indochina until the last Communist is dead. But his leverage is limited. Four years ago he could deal from strength with President Johnson and candidate Humphrey because he had an alternative—Richard Nixon. This time he has no place else to go.

There was no comfort for Thieu in Kissinger's words. He said Saigon's views "deserve great respect." But he made clear that the South Vietnamese had not been informed during the crucial period of negotiation with Hanoi, and said coldly: "We will make our own decisions as to how long we believe a war should be continued."

As for Hanoi, its interest would also seem to lie in an early conclusion of the terms. It must have sought a timetable ending Oct. 31, as Kissinger disclosed, because it thought President Nixon was going to be re-elected and correctly believed that he would have the strongest motivation to put pressure on Saigon before Nov. 7. That is still the case.

The terms disclosed in Hanoi and Washington still leave fundamental questions completely up in the air: What will be the relationship between the Thieu Government and the new Council of National Reconciliation? How can the council conceivably operate under the proposed rule of unanimity? Who will really control the ground as attempts at a political settlement are made during the cease-fire? Who will control the police in South Vietnam?

Uncertainties of that kind were probably always going to be present in anything that passed for a negotiated settlement in Vietnam. Their existence now serves to emphasize the doubtful rationality—to put it mildly—of what the Nixon Administration has done over the last four years to obtain these particular terms.

It is true enough, as Kissinger said, that Hanoi has changed its position: It has agreed to separate military and political questions. But we have accepted a continued North Vietnamese presence in the south, and coalition of a sort. Will the substantive result for South Vietnam be meaningfully different from what might have happened if the United States in 1969 had simply announced its intention to end its part of the war in six months?

The cease-fire, with each side holding its territory in South Vietnam, could turn out to be the de facto political settlement if agreement on elections and administration proves impossible. Instead of having one coalition government of doubtful prospects, as the other side had always proposed, South Vietnam would then be a hodgepodge of territories governed by two authoritarian groups. From the viewpoint of the Vietnamese, would that be an improvement?

No one can say with assurance how the terms now proposed differ from what could have been obtained if President Nixon had moved boldly for peace in 1969. But any difference has been immensely outweighed by the cost of what the President has done in the four years—the cost to the people of Indochina and America.

Peace is more important than the particulars, and no one should niggle as it comes. But that has always been true. And the United States will not be at peace with itself until it recognizes the obsessive futility, the dishonor, of what it has done in the pursuit of particular terms in Vietnam.

A few years from now it is extremely unlikely that anyone except some scholars will be able to understand what it was that the United States gained by four more years of mass destruction. We shall look back at it all like the characters in Robert Southey's poem, "The Battle of Blenheim."

"But what good came of it at last?" Quoth Little Peterkin.
"Why that I cannot tell," said he; "But 'twas a famous victory."

# Ellsberg Yields, Is Indicted; Says He Gave Data to Press

## By ROBERT REINHOLD
### Special to The New York Times

BOSTON, June 28—Dr. Daniel Ellsberg declared today that he had given the Pentagon study of the Vietnam war to the press. Moments later he surrendered to the United States Attorney here for arraignment on charges of unauthorized possession of secret documents.

Later in the day a Federal grand jury in Los Angeles returned a two-count indictment accusing Dr. Ellsberg of the theft of Government property and the unauthorized possession of "documents and writings related to the national defense."

The 40-year-old scholar and former Defense Department official had been described as the source of the Pentagon documents that The New York Times drew upon for its Vietnam series, the publication of which began on June 13 and was stopped on June 15 by Federal Court order.

### Times Silent on Source

The Times refused again today to discuss the source of its documents.

After a one-hour hearing before United States Magistrate Peter W. Princi, Dr. Ellsberg was released on $50,000 bail. The Government had asked that bail be set at $100,000.

At almost exactly 10 o'clock this morning, as his lawyers promised Saturday, Dr. Ellsberg drove in a taxi to the Post Office Building, which houses the Federal courts.

Looking calm and confident and clutching his wife, Patricia, around the shoulders, he told the crushing throng of newsmen that in 1969 he gave the information contained in the documents to Senator J. W. Fulbright, chairman of the Senate Foreign Relations Committee.

"This spring, after two invasions and 9,000 more Americans deaths, I can only regret that at the same time I did not release them to the newspapers," he said. "I have now done so. I took this action solely at my own initiative.

"I did this clearly at my own jeopardy and I am prepared to answer to all the conse-quences of these decisions. That includes the personal consequences to me and my family, whatever these may be. Would not you go to prison to help end this war?"

In an interview later as he stood barefoot on the porch of his home in Cambridge, Dr. Ellsberg declined to discuss the details of how he gave the documents to the press. He would not confirm that The Times, the first newspaper to publish some of them, was the recipient of the 7,000-page study nor would he say whether he had a role in subsequent appearances of segments of it in other newspapers.

"I feel inhibited while there is litigation before the Supreme Court which turns in part on protection of sources," he said. "I don't want to say things that would make the case moot."

But, he added, "I was determined not to come forward without accepting responsibility."

### First Appearance in 10 Days

It was Dr. Ellsberg's first public appearance in the 10 days since his name was mentioned publicly as The Times's source of the study, of which he was one of 30 or 40 authors. A warrant for his arrest was issued in Los Angeles late Friday, but his lawyers advised him to await a regular business day to surrender. Over the weekend he eluded an intensive search by Federal Bureau of Investigation agents.

The warrant charges Dr. Ellsberg, a former Marine Corps officer, who is now a research associate at the Massachusetts Institute of Technology, with possession and failure to return the secret papers, under Title 18, Section 793E, of the United States Code. He is not accused of transmitting documents to anyone else.

After pressing through an almost impenetrable crowd of newsmen and cheering well-wishers, Dr. Ellsberg and his lawyers, Leonard B. Boudin and Charles R. Nesson, both professors at the Harvard Law School, entered the 11th-floor offices of the United States Attorney, Herbert F. Travers Jr.

There he was placed under arrest by F.B.I. agents and taken to the United States Marshal's office for photographs and fingerprinting. About 30 minutes later, with two Federal marshals holding his arms he was taken to a 12th-floor courtroom.

There Dr. Ellsberg sat alone behind a brass rail and listened intently, his chin propped on his hand, as his lawyers and the Assistant United States Attorney, Lawrence P. Cohen, presented arguments over bail.

### 'Severity of the Crime'

Mr. Cohen argued for $100,000 bail because of the "severity of the crime as measured by the punishment"—up to 10 years in prison and a $10,000 fine, or both—and because Dr. Ellsberg did not turn himself in immediately upon issuance of the warrant, eluding the F.B.I. over the weekend. "This suggests the defendant has the resources to remain in hiding and frustrate this court," Mr. Cohen said.

In response Mr. Boudin asked that his client be released in his own recognizance. Magistrate Princi expressed some doubt, saying that if the defendant was proved guilty of being insensitive to laws protecting secret documents, then "might he not be also insensitive to his obligation to appear if he found things were not going as he anticipated."

Mr. Boudin sought to establish Dr. Ellsberg's reliability by reading a long list of his accomplishments and former positions—as special assistant to the Assistant Secretary of Defense and as a special assistant to the United States Ambassador to Vietnam. The lawyer added that the defendant waited until today to surrender to avoid the "Roman holiday" atmosphere that sometimes surrounds major F.B.I. arrests.

The United States Attorney replied that it was a matter of public notice that Dr. Ellsberg "has been in concealment for two weeks."

"I'd like something concrete," the Magistrate said. "He is here this morning. Is there any reason to believe he would not be here next week?"

Eventually Dr. Ellsberg, a slim, intense-looking man, asked that he be allowed to "make myself responsible to appear." After several more minutes, he rose again and said, "I do ask that my responsibility for my appearance be accepted."

At this the Magistrate said: "I am going to take you at your word. I am going to put you on $50,000 bail without surety. You're going to walk out and be free." He then scheduled a hearing on July 15 for the removal of Dr. Ellsberg to Los Angeles, where the case will presumably be tried.

At the conclusion of the hearing Dr. Ellsberg and his wife, both smiling, descended to the street and held an impromptu news conference under the bright sun in the middle of Post Office Square, which was thronged with cheering supporters.

He urged everyone to read the documents and expressed the hope that the disclosures would help "free ourselves from this war."

Asked if he had any regrets, Dr. Ellsberg replied, "Certainly not" and added that he was very pleased with the way the newspapers had defended the First Amendment.

"As a matter of fact, it's been a long time since I had as much hope for the institutions of this country," he continued. "When I see how the press and the courts have responded to their responsibilities to defend these rights, I am very happy about that as an American citizen."

Earlier he said that "as a responsible American I could no longer cooperate in concealing this information."

After having consented somewhat reluctantly to the interview, he discussed his motives for publicizing the documents.

### Personal Responsibility

"I have wanted for about two years to try to raise the issue of personal responsibility and accountability of officials," he said, "not to punish but to make current officials conscious of their responsibility."

He took pains to dispute press reports that he was racked by guilt over his role in Vietnam, where he was connected with the pacification program.

"The simple fact is that I never felt tortured by guilt by anything I did in Vietnam," he asserted. "The kind of things I do blame myself for is not informing myself earlier than I did about the origins of the conflict."

He went on to say that his knowledge of the contents of the study was what drove him because it gave him a responsibility.

He maintained that not a single page of the documents he had disclosed "would do grave damage" to the country. He said he had not released documents that recounted direct negotiations between the Johnson Administration and foreign governments.

Dr. Ellsberg said he would expand on his comments tomorrow afternoon at a news conference at Faneuil Hall here.

June 29, 1971

# Ellsberg Trial Gave Insight on Intrusion of Executive Branch Into Judicial Process

## But Sudden End Leaves Vital Issues Unresolved

Special to The New York Times

LOS ANGELES, May 11—In an era of courtroom spectaculars, the Pentagon papers trial became one of the most spectacular of all.

This was so not only because of the issues that it raised but also because Daniel Ellsberg and Anthony J. Russo Jr., the defendants, did not contest the facts of the case: that Dr. Ellsberg removed the Pentagon papers from the Rand Corporation and that he and Mr. Russo copied them.

It started as a major test of the First Amendment to the Constitution, of the Government's authority to control information and of the public's access to that information.

And although the manner of the trial's conclusion left those constitutional issues largely unresolved, the denouement proved once again, in dramatic fashion, that finally truth is an army too many to turn back.

For in the last week of the trial, in a series of disclosures no novelist could invent, the Government admitted, chapter by chapter, the intrusion of the executive branch into the judicial process to a degree possibly unparalleled in American history.

### Break-In Disclosure

There was, for instance, on the 80th day of the trial, the disclosure that the office of Dr. Ellsberg's former psychiatrist had been broken into in an effort to obtain his "psychiatric profile," and that this had been done by a team of five persons led by E. Howard Hunt Jr. and G. Gordon Liddy, convicted Watergate conspirators who were operating then out of the White House.

This was quickly followed by other, even more stunning disclosures, all of them reluctantly offered. John D. Ehrlichman, President Nixon's former chief adviser for domestic affairs, said that acting on the President's orders he had directed an ex officio White House investigation into the public release of the Pentagon papers,

then into Dr. Ellsberg's background.

That investigation led to the break-in, and two of Mr. Ehrlichman's White House associates, Egil Krogh Jr. and David Young, were forced by the disclosure at this trial to quit Government service. Then Charles W. Colson, former special counsel to the President, admitted that he, too, knew about the break-in, but was told by Mr. Ehrlichman and John W. Dean 3d, the President's counsel, never to mention it because it had been done to protect national security.

Mr. Colson said that he had learned of the burglary and told no one, though he was assigned originally by the President to investigate the Watergate scandal. And it was revealed, at this trial, that Mr. Colson also ordered one of the burglars, Hunt, to forge State Department cables to directly implicate President Kennedy in the assassination of President Diem of South Vietnam.

Further, the trial showed that contrary to law, the Central Intelligence Agency does in fact operate clandestinely within the borders of the United States. Marine Corps Gen. Robert Cushman admitted that the burglary was committed on Sept. 3, 1971, with equipment and disguises supplied by the C.I.A., although the C.I.A. insisted it had not known a burglary had been planned.

At the time, General Cushman, now Commandant of the Corps and a member of the Joint Chiefs of Staff, was deputy director of the C.I.A.

### Disclosure by Judge

And in the midst of all these disclosures, the trial judge, William Matthew Byrne Jr., admitted in answer to a question put to him by Charles R. Nesson, a defense counsel, that twice last month he met with Mr. Ehrlichman to discuss the possibility of becoming director

of the Federal Bureau of Investigation.

Perhaps, too, the trial demonstrated that there exists even in government an inner dramatic tension similar to that of a finely written play. For former Attorney General John N. Mitchell, the man who ordered the prosecution of Dr. Ellsberg and Mr. Russo—the prosecution which led to many of the disclosures that embarrassed the Administration — has himself been indicted in an unrelated, campaign contribution case.

There was even a counterpoint to this: the promotion of two Government witnesses in this case. They were J. Fred Buzhardt, general counsel of the Defense Department, who was moved to the White House staff, and Army Gen. Alexander M. Haig Jr., another Government witness, who was made Chief of Staff of the White House staff.

The Pentagon papers are a 47-volume "top secret-sensitive" study of America's involvement in Southeast Asia. It was compiled by a special Vietnam History Task Force set up in the Defense Department by Robert McNamara, then Secretary of Defense, on June 17, 1967. The study was actually completed on Jan. 15, 1969, shortly before Clark Clifford left the office of Secretary of Defense.

The saga of the Pentagon papers actually started on the morning of Sept. 30, 1969, when Dr. Ellsberg telephoned his friend Mr. Russo and asked if he knew anyone with a Xerox machine. Mr. Russo said he did, and that evening Dr. Ellsberg removed portions of the Pentagon papers from the Rand Corporation in Santa Monica, where he was employed. Along with Mr. Russo and several others he started copying them. It took about eight sessions, lasting into November, to finish the job, Dr. Ellsberg testified.

It is now known that by

April, 1970, at the latest, and probably much earlier — even perhaps in October, 1969—the F.B.I. knew that Dr. Ellsberg was copying "top secret-sensitive" documents, but took no action against him.

In this trial he and Mr. Russo were originally accused of stealing and copying 18 volumes of the Pentagon papers, plus two other "top secret" documents — eight pages of a 1969 Joint Chiefs of Staff memorandum and a 1954 Geneva Accords memorandum. The judge later precluded the Geneva Accord memorandum from the trial.

The Pentagon papers were first disclosed to the public in The New York Times on June 13, 1971. On June 15, for the first time in American history, a newspaper of general publication, The Times, was restrained by prior court order from publishing articles—about the Pentagon papers.

In ordering The Times to halt publication of the material, United States District Judge Murray I. Gurfein said that any temporary harm done to the newspaper by his order was "far outweighed by the irreparable harm that could be done to the interests of the United States" if more articles and documents were published while the case was in progress.

The next day, June 16, 1971, the Justice Department asked Judge Gurfein to order The Times to turn over for the Government's inspection the secret Pentagon study from which its Vietnam series was drawn. But, Judge Gurfein later withheld action on the Government's demand. Instead, The Times gave the court and the Justice Department a list of descriptive headings for those portions of

the Pentagon archive in The Times's possession.

On June 18, The Washington Post in its late editions of that day began what it described as a series of articles based on "sections" of a Pentagon study

Front-page headlines from The New York Times in 1971 when publication of reports on the Pentagon papers was interrupted when John N. Mitchell, then Attorney General, opposed it. From top: June 13, June 15 and July 1.

"made available to The Washington Post" and the articles were distributed by The Washington Post-Los Angeles Times News service and decribed by The Associated Press and United Press International.

The next day Judge Gurfein refused to enjoin The New York Times from publishing more articles based on the secret Pentagon study, declaring that the press must be free to print sensitive matter even if it embarrassed the Government.

However, publication was blocked by Judge Irving R. Kaufman of the United States Court of Appeals. On June 23, the appeals court held that The Times could resume publication of its series but could not use any material that the Government contended was dangerous to national security. The Times

appealed to the Supreme Court the next day.

The restraint was lifted on June 30, 1971, by the Supreme Court, in a 6-to-3 ruling, but that ruling left important Constitutional questions unresolved, particularly the question of freedom of press under the First Amendment. It was left somewhat blurred by the fact that the case drew nine separate opinions from the Justices.

But the publication of the Pentagon papers in The Times set off another chain reaction. Dr. Ellsberg was arrested on June 25 on the eve of the oral arguments in the Supreme Court. He was charged with espionage. Later, in December, 1971, he was reindicted, and the charges against him then were greatly expanded.

Swarms of F.B.I. agents and Air Force investigators de-

scended on the Rand Corporation to interview employes and officials, and to find out what other "top secret" documents, if any, had been taken. A similar investigation shook up the Pentagon itself.

In the White House, President Nixon ordered the creation of his ex officio task force to investigate the leak, and nearly two years later Mr. Colson recalled that at the time there were many White House meetings about the disclosure —"kind of panic sessions," he called them.

### Second Jury Selected

The trial began on Jan. 3, 1973, with the start of selection of a second jury, the first having been dismissed because of a four-month delay over a previous wiretap argument.

The Government had charged the defendants with espionage,

theft and conspiracy covering a period between March 1, 1969, and Sept. 30, 1970—nine months to more than two years before the papers were first made public in The Times.

The broad constitutional issues involved were those of the First Amendment, for the Government was, in essence, charging Dr. Ellsberg with the theft of information, and with conspiring to deprive the Government not of materials—for the copied documents were returned—but of the information in those documents.

And, in a country where there was no Official Secrets Act, the Government was contending, for the first time, that the disclosure of information classified as "top secret" violated the espionage laws even though that information was not given to a foreign power.

Indeed, there is no law, only

Executive orders, pertaining to the disclosure of classified information. And so, legal authorities said, the Government was trying to make a jury create law where no Congressional statutes existed.

These legal authorities say that the way the trial ended—not by a jury verdict but because of legal technicalities—has left those constitutional issues unresolved.

The defense did try through the 89 days of the trial to litigate the war in Vietnam, and, for the most part, failed; it tried, too, to test the classification system, and, again, because of the judge's rulings, it failed.

But the American people were, through this trial, given a considerable insight into the intelligence-gathering methods of the United States.

There was weighty testimony, for instance, on how intelligence analysts do their work; and there was testimony about agents in the field, and about the wiretapping by intelligence agencies of even the heads of state.

The jury was told about the inner workings of secret diplomacy, about spy equipment in the sky, and even about infra red equipment that picked up the warmth of human beings at great distances and, therefore, was useful in detecting enemy troops in the field.

All this was developed to combat the Government's contention that disclosure of the papers could, in fact, have damaged the national security of the United States.

It was essential for the Government to prove this to convict the defendants on the espionage charges outstanding against them. But that issue was never resolved.

# President Says That 'Illegal' Ellsberg Break-In Need Never Have Been Disclosed

**By CHRISTOPHER LYDON**
Special to The New York Times

WASHINGTON, Aug. 22 — President Nixon said today that he had approved a preliminary decision to block disclosure of the break-in at the office of Dr. Daniel Ellsberg's former psychiatrist because the raid by White House "plumbers" had found a "dry hole," barren of evidence against the man charged with leaking the Pentagon papers.

After a 10-day reconsideration, the Justice Department reported the burglary late last April to the judge presiding at the trial of Dr. Ellsberg in Los Angeles. Two weeks later, the judge, William Matthew Byrne Jr., dismissed the charges against Dr. Ellsberg, citing the burglary among the "bizarre events" by which he said the Government had offended "a sense of justice" and destroyed its case.

Yet Mr. Nixon said today that even though the Ellsberg burglary was "illegal, unauthorized" and "completely deplorable," it need never have been disclosed to the judge or the defendants in the trial.

While condemning the Ellsberg raid, Mr. Nixon argued that a shortlived 1970 White House security plan that envisioned similar "illegal" burglaries and interception of mail did not exceed the "inherent power" of the Presidency in national security matters.

## Earlier Administrations

He added that during the six years of the Kennedy and Johnson Administrations that immediately preceded his own, "burglarizing of this type did take place" when it was authorized, on a very large scale. There was no talk of impeachment, he said, answering a news conference question whether approval of official burglaries violated his oath of office, "and it was quite well known."

To Nicholas deB. Katzenbach, however, who was Deputy Attorney General in the Kennedy Administration and Attorney General under President Johnson, President Nixon's charge was a surprise and a mystery.

"If official burglary did take place, I did not know about it," Mr. Katzenbach said in a telephone interview from his vacation home. "It's inconceivable to me it could have taken place without my knowledge. If such things did happen, the President should say who authorized them. I do not know what he is talking about."

President Nixon volunteered at his news conference that a higher level of wiretapping was officially reported in the Kennedy and Johnson Administrations than in the Eisenhower and Nixon Administrations.

Mr. Nixon referred obliquely to a Supreme Court decision last year that rejected the Administration's claim of an inherent authority to use electronic surveillance, without court authorization, in domestic security cases.

Then referring to the police burglaries outlined in the 1970 security plan, he said that the Supreme Court's opinion last year "indicates inherent power in the Presidency to protect the national security in cases like this."

### Robert Kennedy Cited

After mentioning "burglarizing of this type" between 1961 and 1966, he continued:

"I should also like to point out that when you ladies and gentlemen indicate your great interest in wiretaps, and I understand that the heights of the wiretaps was when Robert Kennedy was Attorney General in 1963. I don't criticize him, however. He had over 250 in 1963, and of course the average in the Eisenhower Administration and the Nixon Administration is about 110."

Mr. Nixon's comments on the administration of justice began in response to a question from Dan Rather, White House correspondent of the Columbia Broadcasting System, about Mr. Nixon's brief meeting with Judge Byrne last April when the Ellsberg trial was under way.

Mr. Rather asked whether the approach to Judge Byrne, in which a Presidential assistant asked the judge if he wanted to head the Federal Bureau of Investigation, constituted "a subtle attempt to bribe the judge" in the Ellsberg case.

Mr. Nixon bristled even before the question was posed, when Mr. Rather said that he was inquiring, "with due respect to your office."

"That would be unusual," Mr. Nixon interrupted.

"I'd like to think not," Mr. Rather replied.

In answering the question, Mr. Nixon said that he met with Judge Byrne "for perhaps one minute," on April 5, 1973, in San Clemente, and that John D. Ehrlichman, then his chief domestic assistant, had pointedly avoided mentioning the Ellsberg case in discussing the F.B.I. opening.

Mr. Nixon also put the burden on Judge Byrne for talking with the White House during the pendency of a case that involved other White House officials directly. Mr. Ehrlichman had asked the judge whether an unrelated discussion would "in any way compromise his handling of the Ellsberg case," the President said. "Judge Byrne made the decision that he would talk to Mr. Ehrlichman."

Mr. Nixon said today that Judge Byrne had told Mr. Ehrlichman "that he would be interested" in heading the F.B.I. — an account that differed from the one Judge Byrne gave last month.

In a written statement released on July 25, Judge Byrne said his "initial reaction," in his April 4 meeting with Mr. Ehrlichman, "was that I could not consider such a proposal at that time but would reflect upon the matter." In a brief second meeting on April 7, the judge said, he told Mr. Ehrlichman he was "rejecting consideration of any such proposal while the trial was in progress."

# Concerning Man's Basic Drive

SEXUAL BEHAVIOR IN THE HUMAN MALE. By Alfred S. Kinsey. 804 pp. New York: W. B. Saunders Co. $6.50.

By HOWARD A. RUSK

JUST as this was a difficult study to make, and a difficult book to write, so is it also a difficult book to review. Difficult, because of the magnitude of the subject—difficult, because it deals with man's basic drive to reproduce, a drive as strong as that for survival—difficult, because of our prejudices, taboos and preconceptions, preconceptions colored by personal experience which gives the individual the microscopic rather than the total concept. Now, after decades of hush-hush, comes a book that is sure to create an explosion and to be bitterly controversial.

The book is "Sexual Behavior in the Human Male," by 53-year-old Alfred S. Kinsey, Professor of Zoology at Indiana University. Although it is by far the most comprehensive study yet made of sex behavior, it has been preceded by hundreds of others. The author lists 500 titles in his bibliography. However, there are only nineteen articles on sex in that literature which have the "taxonomic" approach (measurement of the variation in a series of individuals that represent the species). The approach of this specific study is the taxonomic one of the trained scientist, and is based on over 12,000 personal interviews, each encompassing over 300 questions. It has required eight years to complete this first phase, "Sexual Behavior in the Human Male." The complete study, for which Dr. Kinsey plans to secure a hundred thousand interviews over a twenty-year period, will include sex behavior of the female, sex factors in marital adjustment, legal aspects, sex education and other problems.

Professor Kinsey began this study due to the frustrating experience of attempting to answer the sex queries of students when there were no adequate facts on which to base such answers. He is a brave man, for to publish this book took real courage, courage to fight taboos and prejudices, preconceptions based on ignorance and the confusion that comes from translating one's personal experience as universal practice.

That it took courage not only to publish this report, but to gather the data, is well evidenced by the fact that the author withstood violent opposition from medical groups and school boards, psychiatrists and sheriffs, scientific colleagues and politicians. In one city the president of the school board, a physician, dismissed a teacher because he had assisted in getting histories outside of the school, but in the same city. But for every individual or group that opposed the study, hundreds cooperated, ranging from Harvard and Columbia Universities to the Kansas State police and the Salvation Army's Home for Unwed Mothers. The auspices of the National Research Council, and the financial underwriting of the Rockefeller Foundation, bespeak the scientific solidarity of the project.

THE 12,000 subjects interviewed in the study by Professor Kinsey and his colleagues represented every level in our social strata—bootleggers and clergymen, professors and prostitutes, farmers and gamblers, ne'er-do-wells and social registerites. The final result—800 pages of text, with hundreds of charts and graphs analytically evaluated and statistically sound—is cold, dispassionate fact, starkly revealing our ignorance and prejudices.

These facts are presented with scientific objectivity, and without moralizing — but they provide the knowledge with which we can rebuild our concepts with tolerance and understanding. Here are a few of the significant findings:

Human sex patterns are established by three factors: physiological, psychological and social, the social being by far the most predominant. Using as a yardstick the educational level of eighth grade, high school and college, wide variations in sex concepts and behavior were found. "Most of the prejudices that develop in sexual activities are products of this conflict between the attitudes of different social levels."

We understand little of the range of human sex behavior. On the graph showing sexual frequency each individual differs only slightly from those next on the chart. This brings up the point of what is "normal" and "abnormal," and where such terms fit in a scientific study.

Dr. Kinsey points out that homosexual experience is much more common than previously thought. He indicates, however, that this is an extremely difficult problem to analyze "as very few individuals are all black or all white," and that one homosexual experience does not classify the individual as a homosexual. He decries the use of the noun, and finds that there is often a mixture of both homo and heterosexual experience.

To have or not to have premarital intercourse is a more important issue for a larger number of males than any other aspect of sex. Individuals in our American society rarely adopt totally new patterns of sex behavior after their middle teens. The peak of sex drive and ability comes in the late teens rather than in the late 20's or 30's as heretofore believed.

THE theory of "sex conservation" so commonly taught as reason for continence, is refuted. Boys who attain early puberty and begin sex activity earlier have the highest rate of sex activity and continue such activity to the older age level.

Comparing the sexual activities of older and younger generations evidences the stability of our sexual mores and does not justify the opinion harbored by some that there are constant changes in such mores.

The above are only a few of the revealing findings of the study.

Because we are all human, every individual is bound to interpret this study in terms of personal experience. For some it will be clarifying. Others it will confuse. Some will be alarmed, others will be shocked; a few will interpret the general findings as grounds for personal license. After the initial impact, when time permits sober reflection and analysis—the end results should be healthy. They should bring about a better understanding of some of our emotional problems, and the bases for some of our psychiatric concepts.

We can reorganize some of our attitudes and methods of sex education on the basis of need as dictated by experience rather than preconception, and we must surely re-examine the legal criteria by which we renounce and condemn individual sex behavior. Professor Kinsey states this well when he concludes:

To each individual, the significance of any particular type of sexual activity depends very largely upon his previous experience. Ultimately, certain activities may seem to him to be the only things that have value, that are right, that are socially acceptable; and all departures from his own particular pattern may seem to him to be enormous abnormalities. But the scientific data which are accumulating make it appear that if circumstances be propitious, most individuals might have become conditioned in any direction, even into activities which they now consider quite unacceptable. * * * There is an abundance of evidence that most human sexual activities would become comprehensible to most individuals, if they could know the background of each other's individual behavior.

L. Alan Gregg, in his concluding paragraph of the Preface to this study, has brilliantly summarized the many facets involved in this study as follows:

Certainly no aspect of human biology in our current civilization stands in more need of scientific knowledge and courageous humility than that of sex. The history of medicine proves that in so far as man seeks to know himself and face his whole nature, he has become free from bewildered fear, despondent shame, or arrant hypocrisy. As long as sex is dealt with in the current confusion of ignorance and sophistication, denial and indulgence, suppression and stimulation, punishment and exploitation, secrecy and display, it will be associated with a duplicity and indecency that lead neither to intellectual honesty nor human dignity.

These studies are sincere, objective and determined explorations of a field manifestly important to education, medicine, government and the integrity of human conduct generally. They have demanded from Dr. Kinsey and his colleagues very unusual tenacity of purpose, tolerance, analytical competence, social skills and real courage.

THE findings of Dr. Kinsey's report provide us with the material for sober thought, and a new basis for the personal understanding of our individual sex problems. It presents facts that indicate the necessity to review some of our legal and moral concepts. It gives new therapeutic tools to the psychiatrist and the practicing physician. It offers a yardstick that will give invaluable aid in the study of our complex social problems. It offers data that should promote tolerance and understanding and make us better "world citizens."

After recovery from the original impact due to the explosion of many of our preconceptions, this study should be most valuable if, in the words of Dr. Gregg, "the reader will match the authors with an equal and appropriate measure of cool attention, courageous judgment and scientific equanimity."

# Radio: Taboo Is Broken

## 'Live and Let Live' on WBAI Presents Homosexuals Discussing Problems

### By JACK GOULD

LAST night's discussion of homosexuality was handled with candor and tact on radio station WBAI, the frequency modulation outlet supported by the subscriptions of its listeners. The ninety-minute program was by far the most extensive consideration of the subject to be heard on American radio, and it succeeded, one would think, in encourag-ing a wider understanding of the homosexual's attitudes and problems.

•

The eight practicing homo-sexuals who participated in the taped roundtable covered such matters as their sexual drives, the patterns of their social and professional exist-ences and the prejudices they encounter in a heterosexual society.

Since the program, entitled "Live and Let Live," was in-tended to give the homosex-uals an opportunity to be heard without interruption, there was no challenge to their viewpoints. Perhaps on a sequel the subject could be explored with somewhat more penetrating questions. One area left hanging was the matter of a civilized legal ap-proach to homosexuality, par-ticularly in the distinction to be drawn between cases lim-ited to consenting adults and those involving minors.

But from the standpoint of broadcasting, the chief signi-ficance of the evening lay in the illustration of the value of the independent station's catering to a specialized fol-lowing. Such a station, know-ing the composition of its audience, can offer subject matter that, if addressed to coast-to-coast masses of all ages, might pose difficulties for a network.

•

Not ony WBAI but also many independent stations fi-nanced through advertising are playing a very consider-able role in wiping away old taboos in the arena of discus-sion. And in each instance the result has demonstrated that the contemporary public seems ready to accept almost any subject matter so long as it is presented thoughtfully

July 16, 1962

# DIVORCE LAWS AGAIN QUESTIONED

### By ROBERT E. TOMASSON

A cynic once wrote that for every marriage that ends in a divorce court, 100 couples would follow the same path if they knew the way.

Last year, 400,000 divorces were granted in the United States under the provisions of 50 state laws. No state Legisla-ture wants to contribute to the cynic's multiplier. Therefore, the lawmakers say, extreme caution is required in considering any change in the divorce laws. In-ertia, several bar associations have countered, is never an an-swer to the changing needs and attitudes of citizens.

Whether a state's approach to divorce involves caution or inertia, New York solidly fills the bill in both cases. Its di-vorce law, enacted in 1787 and essentially unchanged, is the only one that acknowledges a single ground for divorce—adultery.

### Potential Threat

The New York law was in the news last week as the result of a state Supreme Court decision invalidating a New York wo-man's Mexican divorce and or-dering her subsequent remar-riage of eight years annulled.

Justice Henry Clay Green-berg's ruling was viewed by lawyers as posing a potential threat to the estimated 250,000 Mexican divorce decrees held by New Yorkers.

Justice Greenberg's decision applies the state's legal force to only one case, Rosenstiel v. Ros-enstiel. A fellow justice sitting in the same court may in the future, as in the past, uphold

## Invalidation of a Mexican Decree May Lead to New Standards

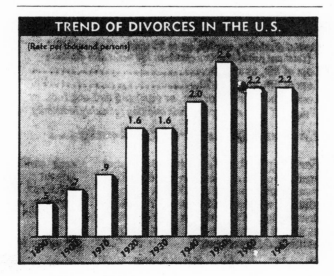

**TREND OF DIVORCES IN THE U.S.**

(Rate per thousand persons)

1.6  1.6  2.0  2.2  2.2

1890 1900 1910 1920 1930 1940 1950 1960 1962

similarly contested Mexican di-vorces. The decision does not invalidate all Mexican divorces in the state, nor does it consti-tute New York's legal attitude toward these divorces. Why, then, all the concern?

Initially, there are two basic considerations. First, one jus-tice has indicated what his views on the Mexican divorce issue are and what direction his fu-ture decisions on similar cases might take. Collaterally, the ruling provides other justices with a precedent—if they chose to accept it.

Second, Rosenstiel v. Rosen-stiel is expected to afford the Court of Appeals, the state's highest tribunal, an opportunity to rule for the first time on whether the New York courts are obligated, and to what ex-tent, to accept the validity of Mexican divorce decrees.

Any approach to New York's divorce law must stem from the virtually universal view held by judges, bar associations, law professors and lawyers that the law is archaic.

And these sources have said on many occasions that as a re-sult most divorces obtained by New Yorkers, whether here in the state, in other states or in Mexico, are based on collusive fraud.

Most New Yorkers seeking to end their marriages want to avoid the seamy aspects of a trial involving the sole issue of adultery. Only 7,235 divorces were issued in New York in 1960, compared with 49,276 in California, two states with about the same population.

### Mexico's Convenience

The appeal of Mexican di-vorces for New Yorkers is that under the divorce law of the state of Chihuahua, residency is established by "the respective certificate of the municipal reg-istrar."

The flight from New York to El Paso, Texas, takes four and one-half hours. The round-trip tourist fare is $234. For the New Yorker seeking a back door out of marriage, the ap-peal of El Paso is that it stands a few hundred yards from the courthouse in Ciudad Juarez in Chihuahua.

The walk over the Interna-tional Bridge into Mexico is not particularly scenic. But it is short. A perfunctory handshake with a waiting Mexican lawyer, several signatures on docu-ments, all in Spanish, a brief ap-pearance before a magistrate, have, as in the Rosenstiel case, constituted the elements of Mex-ican divorces for countless thou-sands of Americans, most of them New Yorkers.

### High Cost Cited

In 1960, 8,455 divorces were granted in Nevada. Although

considerable for a state that size, the number attests rather to the fact that, however desirable divorce decrees might be, few can afford the expense. The going price for obtaining a divorce in Nevada is conservatively estimated at $3,000, including residency and travel. In New York, it can be obtained for about $400.

Other states fall below Nevada's appeal because of longer residency requirements or because of more restrictive grounds. Nevada offers a choice of nine grounds including the favorite, mental cruelty.

Justice Greenberg's decision is significant because it involves a departure from what had come to be considered a settled matter. Although the Court of Appeals has not ruled on the validity of Mexican divorces, several Appellate Division and Surrogate court decisions have upheld Mexican divorces.

And tomorrow, if a couple applies for a marriage license in the New York Municipal Building and presents a certified Mexican decree, it will continue to be accepted as proof of the end of a previous marriage.

However, what concerns lawyers is that these divorces may soon go the way of Alabama divorces, often described by lawyers now as not worth the paper they are written on if seriously contested by a third, interested party.

The Alabama quickie divorce was created by that state's Legislature in 1945. Until then, Alabama required a year's residency for a plaintiff seeking a divorce. But under a brief amendment, the requirement was waived if the "court has jurisdiction of both parties."

### Invalidation

That phrase was interpreted by Alabama lawyers to mean that one day's residency would suffice as long as the plaintiff claimed "intent" to live in the state.

Two years ago, however, the Alabama Bar Association threatened to disbar any lawyer knowingly involved in the quickie divorces. And some judges there have since moved on their own motions to invalidate some divorces obtained by New Yorkers.

Each state's greatest right is its jurisdiction over its citizens. Does a New Yorker's brief visit to Mexico to obtain a divorce compromise that jurisdiction? The ultimate ruling of Rosenstiel v. Rosenstiel will determine the issue.

# Topless Suits Go on Sale This Week

### By BERNADINE MORRIS

THE first examples of Rudi Gernreich's topless bathing suit are expected in New York stores this week. The wool knit trunks with thin straps where the top conventionally would be will be available in black, brown, blue, red and orange, priced at about $24.

B. Altman & Co., Lord & Taylor, Henri Bendel, Splendiferous, 1312 Third Avenue (75th Street), and Parisette, 390 Fifth Avenue (36th Street), are the standard-bearers for the most radical development in swimsuit design since the bikini.

Some are carrying the banner reluctantly and hope that the theatrics caused by the introduction of the style two weeks ago by the West Coast designer will remain closet drama.

"We will not promote it or display it," said a representative of the store that placed the biggest order—21 pieces. "If a customer asks for it, we will take her into a fitting room and show it to her. Please don't quote me."

"Women will buy them to wear in their own pools or patios," said another store buyer, who also asked that her name not be used. "I hope some exhibitionist won't turn up with it at a public beach."

The stores' attitude is: "If they want it, we will have it for them," but they will not display or promote it.

"We have been first with other fashions before," said Ferris Megarity of Altman's.

The stores were pretty sure that some customers would want it, because they received inquiries—and orders—after a picture of the suit appeared in Look magazine.

Terry Ryan and Jerry Goldfarb, the operators of Splendiferous, said three customers told them about the existence of the suit before they themselves had seen it. One woman wanted to take it to Europe, another hopes to wear it on her terrace, and a third considers it a good conversation piece.

#### 150 Sold to Stores

One hundred fifty pieces have been sold to stores to date, Mr. Gernreich reported yesterday in his suite at the Gotham Hotel. He is here showing his sportswear line to retail buyers between visits from television crews immortalizing his new fashion development. He is somewhat upset that the swimsuit has detracted attention from the rest of his collection, which involves short skirts and long pants for fall, plus a tailored sheer shirt in lacquered chiffon that is meant to be worn with black satin pants and no underpinnings.

He said he was overwhelmed by the reaction to his swimsuit. "I never dreamed it would go beyond the fashion business into sociology," Mr. Gernreich explained.

Since his arrival at the Gotham a week ago, he has been deluged with press coverage, and now personal mail, some encouraging, but more of the vindictive variety.

On the positive side: "How delightful! A topless bathing suit. Where in Florida near Lakeland may my friends and I buy some?"

More typical: "I am a mother, aged 26, of three children, three, two and nine months. What are you doing to us?" or "How immoral can you get?"

The topless suit was first presented as a prediction for the future. While Mr. Gernreich was debating whether to put it into production, Hess Bros. in Allentown, Pa., placed the first order. It was followed by stores in other sections of the country, including the Dayton Company in Minneapolis, Joseph Magnin in San Francisco, the May Company in Denver, Neiman-Marcus in Dallas and Milgrims in Detroit.

Mr. Gernreich, who usually is considered America's most avant-garde designer, admitted that the pace of fashion change was even more rapid than he expected. He recalls that 10 years ago when he introduced the first leotard-like wool knit bathing suit in years, he was castigated for not including an inner bra. When he was 2 years old, he said, his parents were forced to take him off the beach at the Lido outside Venice because he was clad only in trunks, with no top. There has been some progress since then, he said.

As anyone with even a pinkie on fashion's pulse these day can tell you, you need a program, clothes-wise, to tell the boys from the girls. Trousers, once the Great Divide between the sexes, now scarcely offer a clue. If a trend noted at recent couturier showings in Paris, New York and London takes hold, the issue will be even further confused when women don man-tailored trouser suits designed for both town and country.

As for hair, the picture is even fuzzier. In England, teen-age boys and girls now sport hairdos exactly alike. And a hard-bitten group of British youths known as Mods not only flaunt long tresses, but also eye make-up, polka-dot blouses, shoulder-strap bags and 4-inch heels (beneath their skin-tight trousers). "When I wear the right gear I feel right," said a Mod recently queried by a London newspaper. "I know people are looking at me and I don't feel one of the crowd any more."

Extremist as all this may sound, it reflects a definite trend. Men's clothes are certainly getting lighter, brighter and, in sportswear at least, taking on more feminine hues. And by what may be the same token, women's apparel is becoming more masculine in cut and comfort. The ladies have also, of late, been raiding men's stores for their hats, jackets, shirts and bathrobes. (Abercrombie & Fitch reports a run on its Campobello hat, a white duck model of the headgear worn by the late Franklin D. Roosevelt at his summer home off the Maine coast.) And they may soon be stepping right into men's shoes. A designer of women's footwear has recently come up with a patent dancing pump that is the flat-heeled duplicate of a man's.

Predations such as these are heartily endorsed by Debbie Turbeville, Fashion Independent Editor of Harper's Bazaar, a publication that has been eying the His - is - Hers trend with approval. "There is a chic about women wearing men's clothes," says Miss Turbeville. "Some women, in fact, look more feminine in them. A really independent woman should be able to get her clothes anywhere. Why does it have to be a woman's shop?"

Miss T. is seconded by a man who has created clothes for both men and women, designer John Weitz. "American women have a complete talent for wearing men's clothes," he says. "And why not? Sports and the American way of life

LOOKALIKES—There was some similarity in men's and women's garb in savage epochs, but it was nothing to the sameness of today.

# Now His Is Hers

**One is hard put, these days, to determine which sex owns the pants. Where will the trend end?**

### By GRACE GLUECK

have dictated the necessity for clothes with male comfort. Lower heels, more pockets, blouses that fit under jackets. Take a woman who lives a busy suburban life. She gets up early, serves breakfast, gets the kids off to school, makes lunches, shops, picks her husband up at the station and when they go out at night and he gets looped, she has to drive him home. Can she do all that in a lace dress?"

Weitz cites a lady customer in Dallas who swears by his tailored silk evening ensembles. "Sometimes we go to parties 175 miles away," she says, "and yours are the only clothes I can wear to pilot my plane in comfort."

Fabric mills, figuring to work both sides of the street, have also had a hand in promoting lookalikeness in male-female dress.

"It's been happening more and more frequently that fabrics and color that are big in women's wear are picked up later by the men's-wear trade," said a stylist recently. "If suede is in for women one year, next year it's bound to be styled for men. So the mills have been playing it by ear."

As a result, "borderline" fabrics are burgeoning. Men's shirtings, for example—paisleys, foulards and regimental stripes — sell heavily to wo-

men's blouse manufacturers. Women's-weight cotton seersucker is appearing as a men's-wear fabric. Synthetic tricot, begun as a woman's fabric, has moved into men's shirts. Even women's suiting fabrics are invading the men's field. A small mill reports that a two-tone "hot" orange and beige stripe it's been producing as a woman's weave will appear in men's sports coats for next spring.

Now all this boundary-crossing is not exactly new, as may clearly be seen in the writings of Philip Stubbes, a dour 16th-century Puritan who felt quite firmly that Adam shouldn't try to be Eve (or vice versa). "Our apparel was given as a signe distinctive to discerne betwixt sexe and sexe," he wrote, "and, therefore, one to weare the apparell of another sexe is to participate with the same, and to adulterate the veritie of his own kinde." But if Stubbes thought things were bad in *his* day (he railed against the "wanton light colors" and "innumerable gewgawes" that men affected), what went on in the -18th century would undoubtedly have done him in.

By that time, male plumage had reached its effeminate peak. Suits were stiff with embroidery, men's hats were bedecked with gold lace, and

diamond buckles decorated their shoes. Both sexes wore cascades of lace and ran the gamut of fabric and color. Toward 1780, for example, a gentleman might be classily clad in a blue coat, a lilac waistcoat, black velvet breeches and yellow stockings. What's more, men carried muffs of fur or fabric, wore powdered wigs (in pre-Revolutionary France for a short period men and women were coiffed almost exactly alike) and, like the women, "made up" with rouge and beauty patches.

The rise of the common man, and his rebellion against courtly fripperies, helped put an end to all this finery, say style historians. So did the Industrial Revolution — which soiled fine clothes with the soot of commerce. And so, by 1850, men were doomed to the sartorial drabness from which they are only now emerging.

Oddly enough, it was just about then—100 years ago—that women began to win their trousers. But Mrs. Amelia Jenks Bloomer, the lady who first plumped for them in the eighteen-forties, could never have foreseen her spectacular success. The famed Bloomer costume that startled the world was really quite fetching—and certainly nothing to give men a moment's backlash. It consisted simply of a knee-length dress over snappy, Turkish-type harem pants gathered in at the ankle, a broad-brimmed hat and Congress gaiters. A few bold ladies wore it on lecture platforms to give punch to speeches advocating women's rights. But the Paris designers, particularly Worth, were as wily then as they are today. They were pushing the crinoline and within a decade after the Bloomer costume first appeared, women's clothes got fussier than ever.

The real emancipator in the field of women's dress was sport. Tennis and croquet could be played in skirts but more strenuous sports demanded less restrictive attire. In 1885, some divided dresses were shown at a Health Exhibition in London. One, a mountaineering get-up, boasted gaiters, knickerbockers, a skirt reaching to the knees and a short coat "like a gentleman's shooting jacket" with matching hat. But it was the bicycle that brought matters to a head. Its invention not only helped liberate young ladies from the onus of parental control, but absolutely forced a curtailment of the trailing skirts which had hitherto hobbled them. By the nineteen-twenties, short "flapper" skirts had exposed women's legs for almost the first time in history. With womanly modesty they hastened to encase them again—in trousers.

To a man, style authorities agree that the drift toward shared apparel cannot be lightly dismissed. Behind it is the steamroller of Female Emancipation. "There is a question as to whether this sex differentiation by clothing will continue in the world of the future, especially in view of the change which is now taking place in the power and position of women," wrote the

**BEES' KNEES**—There was a time when a man could tell that girls were girls. Twenty-three skiddoo!

late Lawrence Langner in his book, "The Importance of Wearing Clothes."

Should—can—the trend be contained? Neither, according to James Laver, a fashion philosopher who bears the heady title of Keeper of the Department of Paintings and Engraving, Illustration and Design at London's Victoria and Albert Museum. Along with other authorities, Laver believes that the trend toward similarity in dress reflects the end of the patriarchal system. "Emancipation of women must ultimately mean the emergence of a matriarchal society," he says. "In such an age, male and female costume will invariably come so close as to be nearly identical." (A Spanish cave painting, from the year 10,000 B.C., tends to bear him out. It shows a couple dressed in skins. The man wears what might correspond roughly to fur shorts, while the woman is hobbled by a long fur skirt that probably served to keep her close to the hearth.)

**PLUMAGE**—A proliferation of wigs and things in the 18th century made the sexes well-nigh the same.

What's more, Laver intimates, the British teen-agers may not really be so far out. "Innovation in clothes invariably starts with the young," he says, "and the grown-ups will in time catch up, not only because they copy the young, but because the young today are the grown-ups of a few years hence."

CAN women in men's clothes remain women? Anthropologist Ashley Montague says yes. "One is brought up—learns—to be either feminine or masculine," he says. "It's not really a question of what one wears."

The trend is not without its protestors—on a subconscious level, of course. The bushy beards men have been wearing lately, a psychiatrist has noted, may be a way of proclaiming their gender in a world they haven't made. As for women, a London newspaper recently suggested that they may have resorted to the topless bathing suit as a means of spelling out their sex.

Will clothes eventually become so homogenized that men and women will be wearing the same sort of comradely costumes; say, for example, the quilted jackets and trousers now favored by male and female alike in Communist China? Mr. Laver thinks not. "If women no longer need to marry men for their earning capacity or their social position," he says, "it is possible that men's clothes may reacquire an erotic principle that they have lost for the last 200 years. In that case, it may be that men will have all the fine clothes, and women will be reduced to wearing two kinds of clothing like the bees: dungarees and maternity gowns."

September 20, 1964

## Hoover Scores Trend In Hairdos and Clothes

WASHINGTON, Sept. 21 (UPI) — J. Edgar Hoover today deplored hairdos and clothing styles that he said sometimes made it difficult to tell the boys from the girls.

Mr. Hoover, deploring this and other current trends, in House testimony published today, said corrective steps should start in the family but that unfortunately they were not being taken.

The F.B.I. chief said most youths were sound, and the troublemakers were in the minority. He said he saw many cleancut youngsters on tours of the F.B.I. headquarters and encouraged them to apply for employment there after they graduated.

September 22, 1966

# Observer: The Bacchanalia Gap

### By RUSSELL BAKER

WASHINGTON, April 28— Malcolm Muggeridge, the English writer, reports that "America is drenched, if not submerged, in sex." Writing in The New Statesman, he describes a country that makes Sodom and Gomorrah sound by comparison like Philadelphia on a Sunday afternoon.

Sample: Sex "permeates every corner and cranny of life, from birth to grave. Dating begins at 9 years old and even earlier; tiny tots wear padded bras, paint their faces and howl like randy hyenas at the Beatles. Young lovers arm themselves with. . . ."

### A Familiar Ring

But let the curtain be decorously drawn, for Muggeridge's prose has scarcely begun to quiver at this point, and what follows will have a familiar ring to conscientious magazine readers. Scarcely a mail arrives without bringing a magazine or two containing one of these juicy reports on what is invariably called "The Sexual Revolution."

The message seldom varies: America is one enormous wild party. Look, Ma! We're decadent! Wringing your hands, lick your chops and read what a wonderfully immoral bunch we are!

It is the stock magazine piece of the 1960's. In the late 1950's they scolded us for too much cholesterol and flabby muscles. Now it's moral rot. Does this kind of thing really scare people?

### The 'Missing Out' Feeling

The answer is certainly "No." What it does do is make people feel that they are missing out on the scandalous life. Constant exposure to these shocked reports that America is a wild party may alarm the naive, but the sensible person will eventually start wondering why he never receives an invitation. Is he out of the mainstream? Is he un-American?

In his world, dating does not begin at 9 years old or earlier and, though there is some randy hyena-like howling at the Beatles, it is nothing more to him than a leering reminder that parental responsibility makes it impossible to drench or submerge himself in anything more erotic than a hot bath.

In the bath, with the Beatle-howling rising about him, he may read these reports of the

# The Pill and Morality

## By ANDREW HACKER

IT comes in a packet of 20, enclosed in a slim folder resembling a paper matchbook. There is a space on the inside flap for noting the starting date of the 20-day course and for checking off the day each one has been used.

What is being described is, of course, "the pill." There has been much talk about how its very existence is going to revolutionize, even subvert, moral standards in all parts of the civilized world. (Presumably in backward areas the pill merely controls population and does not become a moral issue.) To be sure, physicians understand that this form of contraception is not for everyone: There are women who experience side effects, some of them quite serious—hence the need for periodic checks to determine if the pill is being assimilated without any untoward consequences. While the pill can be had only on a physician's prescription, more and more women are nevertheless using it. And among these women are not a few who are unmarried.

THE question of whether college health clinics should give prescriptions for pills to unmarried female students is creating a stir on many campuses. This controversy, it should be remarked at the outset, has been highly overrated and certainly over-reported. The reason, quite simply, is that the clinics, far from giving out such prescriptions to all comers, have no intention of doing so now or in the near future.

A physician at one Ivy League college recently hit the headlines because he did write prescriptions for several coeds who were not only just about to be married but who brought notes attesting to this fact from their ministers. In other words, the college doctor in these cases was simply performing a service that physicians generally carry out for brides-to-be. Neither he nor any of the other university physicians I spoke with will write prescriptions for girls who do not have marriage firmly scheduled and announced.

"If we did," one clinic staff member said, "word would get around the dorms like wildfire and we'd be writing out prescriptions several times a day." There may be some truth to his view, for students are likely to take advantage of the free medical service they get while at college, but far

ANDREW HACKER teaches in the department of government at Cornell.

more critical for the university physician is the tacit approval that would be involved. "In giving the pills," this doctor went on, "we would be implicitly condoning the use they would subsequently make of them."

"We are not only adults but authority figures as well," a colleague added. "You'd be surprised how many undergraduates look to us for moral as well as medical help." This physician admitted that students may also bring their problems to professors, deans, and the sundry counselors and advisers on campus. "But I'm the only one who can turn theory into practice by actually signing a slip of paper they can take to the pharmacy."

The girls know they would get a firm but polite refusal. One junior said she wouldn't even think of approaching the college clinic for the pills. "They'd probably ask me for a note from my parents. That's silly. First, I wouldn't be telling my parents. And if I had told them then I wouldn't wait until I was at school to get them." The student is right in one respect at least. University physicians are terribly parent-conscious, to which must be added their sensitivity to alumni sentiment and public opinion. Whereas most professors have long given up regarding themselves as father-substitutes, the phrase in loco parentis is still uttered by most campus doctors. And they know that Daddy, if asked, would say, "No."

FOR years, college girls have been taking their sex-related concerns into the "town." Private practitioners, in fact, have a far greater awareness of the sexual activities of undergraduates than do the university physicians. And for good reason. Either the "town" doctor is the girl's family physician or, just as likely, a coed approaches him anonymously and on a one-visit basis. Far better to see a local gynecologist and to wait in a room filled with unknown townies than to sit among your classmates at the college clinic.

Local physicians are far more tolerant about the pills, and the cause of their leniency emerges early in any interview. They, unlike their university colleagues, have to deal with what happens when conception has not been prevented. "I see the tragic results all the time," one doctor remarked. "Don't think for a moment that all of my patients are married women. Unmarried girls are in my office along with the others every day. In a few cases I eventually deliver their babies. In other instances

---

wild party that is America and tell himself that life is passing him by. If he is over the age of 21, he knows better. He has been to too many parties. He knows what really goes on at them. They are all celery stuffed with cheese, women flushed with excitement about the P.T.A., cigar smoke and talk of insurance policies and politicians.

He has heard all his life about the wild parties. First in the fraternity house, then in the barracks. Men who claimed to have attended these wild parties inflamed his imagination. But when he went with these very men in search of bacchanalia, it always turned out to be beer and pretzels and, later, celery stuffed with cheese.

With age, he slowly accepted the drab truth: In the average city of three million people the number of wild parties held in the average year can be counted on the fingers of one hand. What is worse, these four or five wild parties are always attended by the same people—a handful of professional wild-party goers and 500 magazine writers who are gathering material for articles on sex-drenched America.

Every sensible adult knows that his chances of ever attending one of these parties are as remote as his chances of seeing a 9-year-old out on a date. The profound fact behind the big bull market for decadence reports is that there are millions of Americans, men and women, who know all too well that they will arrive at Social Security age without ever having experienced anything wilder than a wink from a widower or a convention night in Chicago.

These millions account for what the Muggeridges wrongly describe as "The Sexual Revolution." To fill out what they feel to be blank spots in their lives, they gobble the fantasies of the new novelists and sit through the ordeal of "La Dolce Vita" with its tantalizing view, for the decadence-starved, of what fun decadence can be.

## Sex Drenched and Bored

People who are genuinely sex-drenched and bored with the orgiastic excesses are unlikely to spend their time reading such stuff and watching imitations on the screen. Such people, as we know from the newspapers, prefer golf or sitting about in bar air trying to numb their central nervous systems.

The popular success of "The Sexual Revolution" article is its own argument against the Muggeridge case. Only the moral pay good money for sermons.

they disappear after I tell them I won't abort them."

Physicians know that illegitimacy is a reality and that a child who is born unwanted and out of wedlock may have a difficult time in this world. "If I refuse a girl's request for the pills," another local physician said, "then the consequence may be the creation of a life in the wrong place and at the wrong time." He went on: "It is not that I will feel personally responsible if she gets pregnant. It is that I have it in my power to prevent that eventually. If you had seen as much grief as I have, you wouldn't hesitate to exercise that power."

**W**HAT, then, about promiscuity? This is the specter inevitably raised by those who foresee a pill-inspired undermining of our traditional moral codes. Use of the pill obviously leaves behind the need for supplies and foreplanning that other methods entail. But more is involved here than simply convenience.

For a long time there has been a certain ritual, not without moral overtones, connected with birth control as practiced by unmarried people, college students or not. The young man is "prepared" on a date; the girl is not. If there is a seduction, he takes the initiative; she is "surprised." If she succumbs, he deals with the prevention of conception—which is proper, because she had no advance warning as to how the evening would turn out. Vital to this ritual is the supposition that the girl sets off on the date believing that it will be platonic; if it ends up otherwise she cannot be accused of having planned ahead for the sexual culmination. (Very few unmarried girls have owned their own birth-control devices.)

But now, for a girl to be "on pills" wipes out entirely the ritual of feminine unpreparedness. With the pill, one girl I talked with said, "you no longer have the ultimate excuse for saying 'No.'"

**W**ILL the pill sound the knell of traditional sexual standards? To answer that one requires the answer to the questions of how much (pre-pill) premarital sex has been going on, how much there is compared with other times, how many or how few girls get to the altar in a virginal state—and on these matters there have been all sorts of surveys, ranging from Kinsey's to those conducted periodically by campus humor magazines.

The consensus is that more girls, or at least more middle-class girls, than ever before are having sexual experience prior to marriage. Any hazarding of a then-vs.-now statistical

comparison would be guesswork, to say the least. It will have to suffice here to suggest that there is simply "more" now than there was 30 or 60 years ago.

Obstetricians, for example, agree that they are being confronted with a greater number of middle-class college girls who are pregnant and unmarried. "Even if only one in a hundred girls who has premarital sex ends up getting pregnant," a physician said, "I am getting a lot more of those ones in my office"—which means, of course, that there are many more hundreds who are not getting pregnant. Indeed, considering the availability of contraceptives of all sorts, it would seem that each illegitimate pregnancy today represents even more sex that does not end in pregnancy than was the case in the past.

**S**O far as attitudes are concerned, a survey I conducted among my freshmen students at Cornell is revealing. I asked all 200 of them, on a questionnaire, to indicate whether they thought the university clinic should be willing to prescribe the pills for undergraduate girls who request them. It is hardly necessary to say that a good majority of the boys thought this was a splendid idea. But what surprised me was that most of the girls also agreed with this proposal.

Considering that these are freshmen, just a few months removed from high school, it would appear that the new outlook is not simply a development of the college years but is actually being formulated at an earlier stage.

Closer analysis of the girls' replies showed that their religion or home background did not seem to make much difference. Coeds from small towns favored the easy availability of pills in equal proportion to those raised in the supposedly more sophisticated suburbs of large cities. While Jewish girls were slightly more permissive in attitude, a majority of their Protestant classmates also supported the pill prescriptions. (There were fewer than a dozen Catholic girls in the class, but even some of them took the relaxed view.)

Most striking of all was the fact that steady churchgoers were almost as strongly for the pills as were those who did not attend religious services or did so with only slight regularity. If there has been a loosening of standards with respect to premarital sex, it would seem that the producing forces are strong enough to obviate the traditional teachings of the churches. Indeed, there is reason to be-

lieve that nowadays churches and ministers cannot bring themselves to take a hell-and-damnation line on chastity, and by default are leaving young people to work out the decision for themselves.

Does all this, to raise the specter once again augur more promiscuity? I think not. For one thing, as a college physician pointed out, "Much of the pressing for more sexual freedom is in the nature of talk which might not to be followed by action." The endless discussions that are taking place on and off the campuses, admittedly more public than private in recent years, "serve as a safety valve which drains off some of the pressure to break with convention."

The freethinker and the free talker, in other words, are not necessarily free lovers. Indeed, one is now permitted to sow verbal wild oats and in that way satisfy the urge to startle one's elders and defy authority.

**T**O understand what is happening it is also necessary to appreciate the unwantonness of today's young people, to recognize their basic monogamy. They are pairing off, going steady, getting pinned, and entering into semiformal alliances at earlier and earlier ages. The age at which young Americans get married is also declining year by year, and this goes for middle-class college students as well as others in the population.

Thus, when a majority of girls state they would like to have the pills available, it does not mean that they are about to embark on a nymphomaniacal orgy. Quite the contrary, it suggests that they wish to catch themselves a husband and simply desire to have both a sexual relationship and contraceptive protection during the period of engagement.

If there is a good deal of premarital sex among college students, most of the activists are those who are in fact—if not by official announcement—engaged to be married. There is further reason to believe that most girls who have had sexual experience prior to marriage had only one partner, and he was the boy who is now their husband.

To be sure, there are engagements that are broken off or which do not last. Perhaps, for this reason, young couples should be criticized for not waiting until they are safely married. On the other hand, there are more than enough instances in which two people, after a serious and well-intentioned affair, discover that they were not in fact made for each other. Suppose they had "waited" and then come to this unhappy realization after a few months or years of marriage; it seems strange to assert that such an outcome would have been preferable on moral or prudential grounds

At all events, there is very little promiscuity on the part of college girls. Most, as has been said, are one-boy girls, and all but an insignificant handful are one-boy-at-a-time girls. Even if some do have more than a single premarital affair, how many of these does it take to make for "promiscuity?" Three? Four? Six? Considering that many girls go from 19 to 23 before being married, is intimacy with five men in five years a sign of easy virtue? The line between discretion and promiscuity becomes extremely difficult to draw. (And why, it should be asked further, is the term itself never applied to the conduct of unmarried men?)

THERE are, to be sure, girls who do not rush into marriage, and some of these see no reason why they should not have a sex life of their own during their early adult years. Girls have taken this view in every generation, and whether it is ill-advised is a perennial subject for debate. But in debates of this kind the chief participants are usually men, who see nothing untoward in the free standards that they set for themselves.

What does bear mentioning is that there are girls who are troubled by emotional problems that cause them to seek the semblance of affection wherever they can. Some come from broken homes and others wish, consciously or unconsciously, to hurt their parents. However, if moral strictures are in order, they should be directed at men who take advantage of girls in such an emotional condition. This kind of seduction is all too simple, and those men who achieve such success are hardly deserving of merit badges for their prowess.

If pills are wanted, then, it is primarily by girls who intend to use them sparingly and monogamously. That they may use them at all will obviously cause concern in many

quarters. However, we ought to face up to the fact that once a boy and girl enter into an engagement or begin considering the possibility of marriage, there is a good chance that they will go to bed together whether the pills are a' hand or not.

The fact is that an increasing proportion of young people, girls no less than boys, see nothing shameful or immoral about premarital sex. Anyone who wishes to proffer moral advice to this generation would do well first to apprise himself of the mood and temper that, quite independent of the adult world, are developing in the high schools and colleges of the nation.

THE "sexual revolution" has, of course, been going on for some time now. On a surface level the change is best reflected in what may be seen, read and heard in public. Throughout all of history it may be assumed that men and women thought about sex: they may have repressed such thoughts as soon as they arose, but people have always been people, and sex is no small part of any person's life. What is new is the public character of sex: the fact that respectable, not under-the-counter, agencies now deal with the subject for mass audiences.

Yet this, as has been said, is only the surface portion of the sexual revolution. What has emerged more importantly is a greater need for sex—that is to say, sex has assumed a more explicit role in people's lives because other things are missing. Some commentators have summed up this condition as the "crisis of identity": the problem, in our times, of knowing who we are and where we belong. This is a mass age and the individual is no longer sure that he or she counts in an identifiable way. There is more movement than ever before, from place to place, from class to class, with each step forcing adjustments in values and expectations.

What Americans, especially young Americans, are looking for is some kind of fixed relationship. The old ties of family, community, church and trade are no longer strong or satisfactory. Hence sex, as a meaningful liaison with another, becomes the route to

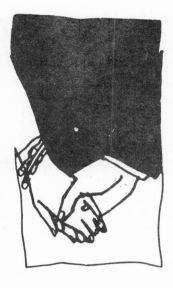

discovering and maintaining one's sense of self.

This is why there is the early rush into marriage, but it is also why there is a heightened tendency to sex before marriage. If Freud was influential a generation ago, today's intellectual rationale is to be found in existentialism. The best known exponents of this outlook are not so much philosophers, such as Sartre and Kierkegaard, but the film directors Antonioni and Fellini. The basic theme recurs throughout their films: how those in search of themselves try desperately to find the answer in sex. That this is not the solution need not imply that there is another way. There may be no solution at all.

It is worth noting, too, that the sexual revolution is revolutionary for only a portion of the population. There is no reason to believe that there was any less premarital or extramarital sex among men in the past than there is now. The rake, the unfaithful husband, the sower of wild oats have been with us, in fact and in fiction, as long as anyone can remember. Moreover, the lower or working classes have never really been subjected to what is essentially a middle-class sexual morality. All evidence is that both men and women in the lower strata have taken a free-and-easy attitude, if only because sex is one of the few enjoyments open to them in otherwise bleak lives.

The revolution, then, has primarily to do with women, and middle-class women in particular. They are the ones who have finally come to embrace ways of thinking and behaving that have long been customary for others. This change, as has been noted, has been precipitated by the search for identity, which probably hits the middle-class woman more deeply than others in society. The extent of the revolt among the younger members of this class may spring in large measure from their observing the apparent meaninglessness of the lives of their suburban mothers. They hope they can discover some genuine purpose for themselves in a new kind of personal—and sexual — relationship where both they and their partners will be equals.

THE pill, not necessarily this year or next, but certainly within the coming generation, is going to give rise to a clear-cut moral debate. Words of warning will be uttered, but with little ultimate effect. Moral standards become less absolute as the range of choices becomes wider. There can be no denying that the pill will tempt many to indulge momentary pleasures rather than exercise the self-restraint that has been the middle-class norm in matters of sex.

Whether national character will be weakened is a question that simply cannot be answered. What can be said is that a device like the pill does away with obsessive and irrational feelings about sex, and can serve to reduce the illegitimacy rate—which has been rising alarmingly in recent years.

Considering that most of today's young people are far more mature and responsible about sex than their elders like to think, there seems little danger that the pill by itself will be a corrupting force. On balance, it is needed, and should be welcomed. When it receives wide distribution, as it will, it will challenge our capacity to use yet another innovation with sophistication and responsibility. Just as we have adjusted our lives to the television set and the automobile, so—in 20 years' time— we shall take the pill for granted, and wonder how we ever lived without it.

November 21, 1965

# They Meet in Victorian Parlor to Demand 'True Equality'—NOW

**By LISA HAMMEL**

ALTHOUGH no one in the dim ruby and sapphire Victorian parlor actually got up and cried: "Women of the world, unite! You have nothing to lose but your chains," that was the prevailing sentiment yesterday morning at the crowded press conference held by the newly formed National Organization for Women.

NOW, which is the organization's urgent acronym, was formed three weeks ago in Washington to press for "true equality for all women in America . . . as part of the world-wide revolution of human rights now taking place."

The organization has been informally styled by several of its directors the "N.A.A.-C.P. of women's rights."

The board of directors asked President Johnson, in the text of a letter released yesterday, to give "top priority among legislative proposals for the next Congress to legislation which would give effective enforcement powers to the Equal Employment Opportunity Commission," which, the letter stated, "is hampered . . . by a reluctance among some of its male members to combat sex discrimination as vigorously as they seek to combat racial discrimination."

Separate letters were also sent to Acting Attorney General Ramsey Clark and the three current commissioners of the Equal Employment Opportunity Commission.

"As part of the Great Society program," the letter to the President read, "your administration is currently engaged in a massive effort to bring underprivileged groups — victims of discrimination because of poverty, race or lack of education — into the mainstream of American life. However, no comprehensive effort has yet been made to include women in your Great Society program for the underprivileged and excluded."

The press conference was held amid the dark Victorian curlicues and oriental carpeting in the apartment of the organization's president, Betty Friedan.

Mrs. Friedan, who became a household word when she gave "the problem that has no name" the name of "The Feminine Mystique" in a best-seller published three years ago, explained in her book to disgruntled housewives across the country that they had been sold a bill of goods by society.

Creative dishwashing and a life unremittingly devoted to the care and feeding of a husband and children is not the alpha and omega of a woman's existence, Mrs. Friedan maintained, nor is a woman likely to find complete fulfillment as an adult human being either among the diapers and soapsuds or in the boudoir.

"Our culture," Mrs. Friedan wrote, "does not permit women to accept or gratify their basic need to grow and fulfill their potentialities as human beings, a need which is not solely defined by their sexual role."

Mrs. Friedan said last week in an interview in her apartment that NOW had "just begun to think about methods" to implement its goals of enabling women to "enjoy the equality of opportunity and freedom of choice which is their right . . . in truly equal partnership with men."

Speaking in a gravelly alto from the depths of the large fur collar that trimmed her neat black suit, the ebullient author suggested that women today were "in relatively little position to influence or control major decisions."

"But," she added, leaning forward in the lilac velvet Victorian chair and punching the air as if it were something palpable, "what women do have is the vote.

"We will take strong steps in the next election," Mrs. Friedan continued, "to see that candidates who do not take seriously the question of equal rights for women are defeated."

The position paper issued by NOW at its formation on Oct. 29 stated that: "We will strive to ensure that no party, candidate, president, senator, governor, congressman, or any public official who betrays or ignores the principle of full equality between the sexes is elected or appointed to office" and that to this end the organization would "mobilize the votes of men and women who believe in our cause."

"Politics?" the Rev. Dean Lewis repeated yesterday in answer to a question. "What do you have for women in that field? Women's political auxiliaries. They are put aside in nice separate structures without policy-making powers."

### Reason for Joining

Mr. Lewis, a slender man with a neat pointed beard, is the secretary of the Office of Social Education and Evangelism of the United Presbyterian Church in the United States.

"Why did I join NOW?" he said. "It's like asking somebody why they joined the N.A.A.C.P. I'm interested in equal rights for anybody who desires them. The structure of both law and custom in our society deprives women of their rights."

Mr. Lewis is one of the 5 men on NOW's 28-member board of directors. The vice president of the organization is Richard Graham, director of the National Teacher Corps and a former Equal Employment Opportunity Commissioner.

NOW states in its position paper that it is concerned with discrimination where it exists against men as well as against women.

Mrs. Friedan explained that the organization believed that most alimony laws were discriminatory against men and that NOW intended to re-examine current laws.

The 500 members of NOW have been drawn from many fields, including education, labor, government, the social sciences, mass communications and religion. Two Roman Catholic nuns are members of the board of directors.

"There is religious discrimination in the church, but that is not my main reason for joining the organization," said Sister Mary Joel Read, chairman of the department of history at Alverno College, a Roman Catholic college for women in Milwaukee.

"This is not a feminist movement," the nun continued. "It is not a question of getting male privileges. In the past the possibility of realizing one's humanity was limited to an élite group at the top. Women are not equal in our society. This movement centers around the possibility of being human."

# Population Expert Terms Baby Boom Costly to Nation

A student of population patterns said yesterday that the postwar baby boom in the United States was "exacting a high price from the American people."

Dr. Philip Hauser, president-elect of the American Sociological Society, said the baby boom would do the following:

¶"Worsen the United States unemployment problem."

¶"Greatly increase the magnitude of juvenile delinquency."

¶"Exacerbate already dangerous race tensions."

¶"Inundate the secondary schools and colleges."

¶"Greatly increase traffic accidents and fatalities."

¶"Augment urban congestion."

¶"Further subvert the traditional American government system."

Dr. Hauser, who is professor of sociology and director of the Population Research and Training Center at the University of Chicago, spoke at the opening session of the two-day Eastern annual conference of the American Association of Advertising Agencies in the Plaza Hotel.

Looking ahead, he remarked:

"Even with the [currently] decreasing birth rate the United States will have added about 26 million people between 1960 and 1970 when the next census is taken; and we shall have added about 65 million between 1966 and 1985. Thus, between now and 1985, the United States will increase by about a population as large as that in the United Kingdom, Sweden and Norway."

## TV: Frank Exploration on 'Sex in Sixties' Program

### A.B.C. Documentary Reviews Morality

#### By JACK GOULD

PROBABLY the frankest review of sexual morality ever offered by television was presented last night on the American Broadcasting Company's "Stage '67." The Irving Gitlin production, "Sex in the Sixties," covered the more sensational manifestations of sexual expression and the serious aspects of where to-day's mores may be leading. The program itself in some ways was an example of the sexual revolution; in reporting on various methods of of contracption it was more specific than anything on evening TV before.

Mr. Gitlin's documentary opened with films of the bunnies of the world of Playboy magazine; topless waitresses, modern revealing fashions and the rise in nudity in nightclubs and burlesque houses. From there, it progressed to a discussion of sexual standards on the college campus, interviews with Dr. William H. Masters and Mrs. Virginia E. Johnson, authors of "Human Sexual Response," and a discussion of the growth of sex education in schools, partly a result of parental default.

"Sex in the Sixties" suffered from the common documentary handicap of trying to cover too much ground in too short a time, but the program will undoubtedly stand as a contribution to the national debate over the rise of premarital intercourse.

But where Mr. Gitlin totally failed to do an adequate job was in mentioning the role of advertisers on television in using sex in so many of their commercials. The omission is bound to raise eyebrows over whether A.B.C. and Mr. Gitlin were really committed to 100 per cent candor. It is on TV that many a child viewer probably gets his first sex education, and surely that is an essential part of the story of "Sex in the Sixties."

January 13, 1967

# The Class of 1942: What Happened to Those Girls in Saddle Shoes?

#### By MARYLIN BENDER

LIFE begins at 45 to 47. Or so it seems to one narrow segment of the female population, the Eastern college-educated woman.

The class of 1942 of the seven sister colleges, the women's Ivy League, has been returning to campuses for its 25th class reunion. But not before having itself polled, surveyed and analyzed.

As revealed in the questionnaires the alumnae answered, the average member of the class of 1942 has survived disgruntled housewifery and the conflict between home and career. Affluent, happily married (to a businessman or professional man), community-minded and churchgoing, she expects to charge off in new directions during the next 25 years. Many of them will seek further education and new careers.

Twenty-five years ago, they were the saddle shoe and baggy sweater girls who danced to the big-name bands and were graduated just in time to become war brides. Now they are mothers and grandmothers, graying or not (only 25 per cent of Vassar '42 admitted to dyeing its hair as against nearly one-third of Mount Holyoke '42), no more than five pounds heavier, but infinitely more energetic, they say, than they were at 20 to 22.

In theory they should feel passé. The merchants and the communications media have been assuring them that nearly half the population is under 25 and calling the turn. But the class of 1942 doesn't feel the least bit on the shelf. Half of the Barnard women who assembled yesterday to participate in a two-day lecture and discussion program entitled "New Approaches," said they viewed the future with equanimity, the other half with anticipation. Only a few were anxious, resigned or ambivalent.

"The Spread of My Life" was chosen as the theme for Smith College's 25-year reunion class last week. "The over-all sentiment seems to be that having had a good life for 25 years with my husband, family and community activities, and now that my children are grown, I'm going to start to spread out," said Mrs. Allen Howland of Warwick, R. I.

"We don't feel left out. We feel we have a whole new life ahead of us," said Mrs. Howland, wife of a chemical executive who served with the Navy in the Pacific for three years after their marriage. Mrs. Howland, who majored in music in college and taught it privately for several years, expects to study for a master's degree with an eye to teaching again. Her four children are in high school and college.

#### Living With a Label

The class of 1942 has been tagged with the "feminine mystique" label ever since Betty Friedan, Smith '42, wrote a best-selling book of the same name in 1963. It was based on a questionnaire she had circulated among her classmates at their 15th reunion. Mrs. Friedan, a trained psychologist as well as a housewife and mother, asserted that American women were trapped in domesticity. She urged them to find their identities in commitments outside the home.

Concurrently, colleges and universities were instituting experimental programs for women who wanted to resume professional development after a hiatus of marriage and child-rearing.

"The Feminine Mystique" dominated cocktail party conversation for several years and also put many women on the defensive about their previously esteemed roles as wives and mothers.

In answering the questionnaires, many of the class of 1942 referred to Mrs. Friedan, either negatively or positively, but the results show that the majority of them did not heed her advice immediately. Almost none of them find enchantment in housework, but they value being what one Vassar woman called "the mother-wife center, the cornerstone of family life."

Less than one-third of Vassar '42 has full or part time jobs. "I was surprised that more were not working," said Mrs. Seth C. Taft, of Cleveland, chairman of the 25th reunion, which takes place today and tomorrow in Poughkeepsie, N. Y. Mrs. Taft, chairman of the art history department of the Cleveland Institute of Art and a lawyer's wife, speculated that the reasons lay in suburban living patterns; "the great stress put on mothering as taught in the forties by the child study people"; and the fact that her classmates worked during World War II and may have appreciated homemaking more when they could get to it.

Their financial well-being (almost two-thirds reported family incomes between $20,-000 and $200,000 a year) and the rich and varied lives they are able to lead without working are responsible, too, Mrs. Taft suspects.

It also appears that a woman 25 years out of college is considerably more at peace than one 15 years removed from the ivy-covered halls. When Mrs. Friedan quizzed her classmates, they were "smack in the middle of the 3P period: Pablum, Playpen and P.T.A." as one Vassar woman put it.

#### Assailed by Doubts

"Surrounded by dirty dishes and diapers, with your husband on the rise and very busy, and not enough finances to do what you want to, you are in the middle of wondering why you ever went to college," Mrs. Howland recalled.

Nevertheless, by now, half of Smith '42 is taking postgraduate courses or intending to do so next year, so that they can establish or resume careers. Teaching, library service and social work are the most popular.

"Betty Friedan sent her questionnaire at a crucial time," said Mrs. Joseph Rotundo, of Schenectady, N. Y., who surveyed her Mount Holyoke classmates and discovered that 80 of the 186 who replied were working full-time but that others would join their ranks as their children left home.

431

"The 15th-year class is much more frustrated," she said. "It's natural that they would have bellyached, but would they have gone out and done anything about it? Now almost all have children old enough so that we don't feel we are deserting them."

Mrs. Rotundo, a widow, teaches English at the State University of New York at Albany. She is a candidate for a doctorate.

Barnard's class of 1942 feels its aspirations can be better satisfied in paid, rather than volunteer, work, said Mrs. Irwin Heimer who polled 138 co-alumnae and found 76 currently engaged in paid occupations, 40 of them interested in professional guidance. "Nobility has run its course," she added.

Mrs. Heimer, a physics major who was married to an Army Air Force pilot during her senior year (he is now a real estate manager), worked full and part time as a physicist until the third of her four children was born. Her 23-year-old daughter, a Barnard graduate, is married and teaching high school in Ohio. Her second daughter, a member of Barnard's graduating class, will attend Yale Medical School.

"I definitely have to get more education," Mrs. Heimer said. "My most serious thought is toward elementary school teaching because I can't work full time, with two children, 9 and 13, at home."

### Liberal Arts Backed

On the whole, the reunion-goers gave a resounding endorsement to the liberal arts education they received. Many of the Vassar women wondered, however, whether it had not fueled, rather than alleviated, the home-career conflict.

Some felt that they had been trained for important jobs they had never been able to fill and had suffered frustration and guilt as a consequence. "Vassar should help the girls to see realistically where and how they will spend the next 20 years," one suggested.

# Outside World Beckons Mothers

## By DEIRDRE CARMODY

Thirty million young mothers and millions of their own gray-haired mothers will awake tomorrow to the homage of their loving, or at least dutiful, families as the glow of Mother's Day spreads westward across the country.

The two generations of mothers have faced many of the same problems, as have generations of their mothers before them.

But now that women have been liberated from much old-fashioned drudgery by household aids, today's mother — particularly the educated urban mother—finds herself increasingly torn between her conflicting desires to spend that time rocking the cradle or ruling the world.

"There used to be a cultural myth about mothers," says Dr. Kitty La Perriere, a therapist with the Family Institute who has conducted research projects on young mothers. "It entitled you to be pampered. It entitled you to be more restricted."

Motherhood was once considered a full-time job and mothers were simply expected to be just that. There have, of course, always been mothers who worked for economic reasons. Pioneer women were as handy at wielding hatchets as at bathing babies and women in wartime took over their men's work inside and outside the some while their husbands were away. But this was work born of necessity.

The dilemma of today's educated middle-class mother arises from the realization of her potential in a world where women compete with men and by the nagging of a concerned conscience that tells her staying home and taking care of the children is not enough.

"We all try to be super-women; we try so hard not just to be good mothers but to add another string to our bow, which we've got to keep twanging" said one young mother of three children recently. "Becoming a great bovine mother of many children is a kind of cop-out. It's one way out of the identity crisis."

Though bringing up children is still a time-consuming job, young mothers are freer and more mobile than ever before. Long-haired girls stride the sidewalks carrying their babies, squaw-like, in slings on their backs. They drive around the countryside as carefree as teen-agers, their children perched beside them on special car seats.

Mrs. Sally Sarell, who lives in the 50's near the East River, can often be seen in local supermarkets or in the United Nations park, her blond hair flowing behind her and 1-year-old Chandra perched like a little blond papoose on her back.

"I feel free and liberated this way," Mrs. Sarell said. "It's just more fun than pushing a baby carriage."

### Casual Outlook

Instead of having to hire a babysitter or impose on grandmother, young mothers their children and a simple portable intercom system with them to dinner parties. The intercom system is quickly installed in the hostess's bedroom where the child is left to sleep, and in the living room where the mother can swing at the party and hear any sound from her child at the same time.

There is a general attitude of casualness among young mothers today. At a shopping area near the Henry Hudson Parkway in the Riverdale section of the Bronx, children doze in the sun in baby carriages and strollers while their mothers shop inside.

"Everyone leaves their babies outside," said Mrs. Alfred Hall, who lives in the neighborhood. "There seems to be some kind of honor system, because I haven't heard of any babies being stolen."

Another aspect of this casualness is that the system of priorities modern mothers have set up is different from that of earlier generations. There is less of a tendency to be a perfectionist housekeeper, an outlook that gives more time for other things.

"It took me a long time to realize that people don't care if there is a little dust around," said Mrs. Nan Socolow, mother of three children. "You have to learn about shortcuts," she said, stretching her legs out on the coffee table in her West End Avenue apartment. "Like this. I mean, putting your feet up and resting whenever you get a chance."

The college-educated mother, brought up in post-Depression years, tends to feel more imprisoned than other mothers, according to Dr. Benjamin Spock, the author and pediatrician.

### Yanked by the Leash

"These girls have been brought up with fantastic freedom," Dr. Spock said in a recent interview. "They're more likely to have more freedom than even men get.

Men almost never have that unencumbered feeling.

"Then after marriage, and maybe a career, the coming of the baby suddenly yanks her—you've seen a dog on a leash rush up and all of a sudden the collar grabs him—well, that's how it is for these young mothers."

Dr. Spock believes the worst period for a young mother is after the birth of her first child, when she thinks she should be "happy and proud and in a rosy whirl of mother love." As a result she does not dare complain openly about how imprisoned she suddenly feels.

"This is really a period of need that somehow our culture fails to acknowledge," said Dr. La Perriere, of the Family Institute. "The young mother says, 'What's happened? What's wrong with me?' But for a wife to admit that she's lonely, that she can't cope, is almost impossible. There used to be a folklore about it and these things were passed from mother to daughter, but not so much now."

There is a tendency today not to accept wholesale answers about anything but to work things our for oneself. This often causes loneliness for the young mother during the search, and excessive feelings of guilt when she does not live up to her own standards—standards that a more experienced mother could have told her are impossible to achieve.

Dr. Spock questions today's standards. He says that in America children are brought up to be happy, but that in other parts of the world children are brought up to serve their parents and their country.

"American parents say, 'We're bringing up the children for fulfillment,'" he said, "but of course we all know that you only find fulfillment in committing yourself to something. Here you have parents hovering over one or two children and saying 'Are you well-adjusted? Am I doing the right thing for you?'

"College-educated parents are afraid—afraid and guilty. They are afraid that if they are too firm in their leadership their children will become maladjusted, or worse still that their children will not like them."

Another difference between today's mother and yesterday's is that young couples tend to move more now.

"In another culture, when

Photographs for The New York Times by EDWARD HAUSNER

Young mothers like Mrs. Sally Sarell have no trouble getting about to stores and meetings with baby in a carrier

There is a look of casualness in young matrons nowadays

you lived near your people they took care of the baby," said Mrs. Frances L. Beatman, executive director of the Jewish Family Service. "Today you have cooperative relationships. People exchange babysitting, but you've got to do back for what you get. When your parents came in to take care of the grandchild, you didn't owe back in the same way.

"There is a loss. The child doesn't get the kind of giving that was given to it by the immediate family."

### Mothers Caught in Paradox

In many ways the young American mother is caught in a paradox: She is more liberated to pursue her own interests than her predecessors, but that very possibility of freedom only intensifies her dilemma. If she takes advantage of her freedom—either by part-time volunteer work or a full-time job outside the home—she feels guilty as a mother. If she devotes her entire time to her children, she feels she is betraying her education and her obligations to society.

"Accept your limitations, you've got to stop torturing yourself about what you can't do," one mother said philosophically. "You've got to keep the body fit, the mind fit and the soul fit, and you simply don't have time to do all three, so you've got to decide. Let the body go one year, let the soul go the next. It's the only way."

May 10, 1969

# Sex Education Battles Splitting Many Communities Across U.S.

## By DOUGLAS ROBINSON
Special to The New York Times

RACINE, Wis. — "The thing that hurt the most," said Richard B. Bliss, "was the letters from old friends that began, 'Dear Dick, I know you don't realize you're being used by the Communists, but . . .'"

Mr. Bliss is the science consultant to the Racine Unified School District 1 and the letters were only part of a campaign of harassment in a bitter fight over sex education in the public schools.

The battle in Racine was not unusual. In recent months, cities and towns across the nation have been torn by dissention over the issue. The battles have left a residue of suspicion, mistrust and hatred on streets where good neighbors once lived.

The dispute in Racine, a medium-size city on Lake Michigan, followed a pattern now familiar in many communities. Besides the letters, there were the telephone calls.

"'You're nothing but a dirty Communist traitor,' the anonymous callers would say, and the conversation went downhill from there," said Mr. Bliss, who considers himself a conservative.

The fight against a program about sex and family life in Racine was successful; the Board of Education voted to delay any action on the matter "until misinformation and misunderstanding are corrected."

In this area, too, Racine was not unusual, because such groups of the John Birch Society and the Christian Crusade have caused school officials and elected leaders to give way before the onslaught.

Congress and 19 state legislatures have before them measures to prohibit, control or curtail sex education in the public schools. Other legislatures have already acted.

"There are 10 states—Maine, New Hampshire, Vermont, Rhode Island, Alabama, Mississippi, Arkansas, Montana, North and South Dakota—that we haven't heard from yet," said Paul E. Putnam, assistant secretary for special studies of the Professional Rights and Responsibility Commission of the National Education Association. He said he assumed that those 10 "have no sex education programs planned or now functioning."

In the furor stirred up in many communities, more moderate criticism has been drowned out in the flurry of charges and counter-charges and in the wide distribution of literature that attempts to portray school officials as purveyors of filth and pornography.

### 'Lies and Distortions'

"I've never seen a more successful propaganda campaign," Mr. Bliss said in Racine. "They used lies and distortions to try to prove their contention that sex education is a Communist plot and that such a program would undermine the morals of their children."

"The extremists were really bothered by the use of the word 'sex,'" he continued. "They were convinced we were going to teach sexual intercourse. They had no understanding of such matters as hygiene, disease prevention, care of a child, family responsibility or mature values."

"It really made no difference to them," he added. "The venereal disease and divorce rates keep rising and these people refuse to understand. It's as if they were saying, 'There's an epidemic of polio, but we're not going to let you do anything about it.'"

"Now, even after the fight, former friends are distant with me," Mr. Bliss said. "I'm sure that if my standing in the conservative community here were not so solid, I'd have more enemies."

The issue of sex education in the schools has given the Birchers and their ideological counterparts a ready-made controversy that rivals disputes over religion in intensity.

Opponents of sex instruction in Minneapolis, for example, have been on the offensive for some time. They have yet to suffer a setback and there is no sex education course in the city's schools, despite a set of guidelines drawn by a group of educators three years ago.

Last week, Mrs. Elsie Zimmerman, the leader of those opposed to sex education courses in Minneapolis, said that a sex study program was "garbage."

### 'Master Plan' Cited

Her supporters, Mrs. Zimmerman warned, will use "every weapon," including court injunctions, to block sex education. There is, she said, a "master plan" for a "controlled, one-world society." Her followers, mostly women, applauded warmly when she added:

"We will no longer be old ladies in tennis shoes; we will be Paul Reveres in combat boots."

Two weeks ago, Gov. Ronald Reagan of California signed a measure that prohibits school districts from requiring students to attend sex education classes. The law allows parents to keep their children from such classes if they so choose.

In a related development today, the Anaheim Union School District in California's Orange County banned all sex education until there could be a complete evaluation of the courses that have been offered to the students.

There is no doubt that opposition to sex education comes from a small minority. A Gallup Poll showed that 71 per cent of all adult Americans want schools to offer such courses. By unofficial estimates, about two-thirds of the nation's school districts offer sex education in some form.

But this has been true for some time, according to Dr. Edward Mileff, consultant in health and safety education to the American Association for Health, Physical Education and Recreation.

"This demand for sex education is merely the formal outgrowth of courses that have been in the curriculum since the mid-30's," Dr. Mileff said. "In other years, it was usually presented under such euphemisms as senior problems, marriage and family or hygiene."

The new sex education courses, which are endorsed by a preponderance of educators, church groups and medical societies, go further than previous efforts in that they are designed to teach students about themselves as sexual human beings and inform them of the sexual responsibilities of adults. In short, children are taught that sexual feelings and attitudes are not forbidden mysteries, but facets of a normal life.

"Because moral judgments are bound to creep in to such courses," Dr. Mileff said, "we have worked out these courses with parental cooperation. We try never to go beyond the needs of individual communities."

Dr. Mileff said he was not worried by the opposition to formal sex education courses and professed surprise that there has not been more hostility.

Despite the criticism, he predicted that "the overwhelming problems emerging in our urban society will mandate a responsibility for sex education."

"The crisis nature of society will create such a program," he added.

### Attacks Began in '68

Mr. Putnam said opposition to sex education began late last summer, when the Christian Crusade, a right-wing organization based in Oklahoma and headed by the Rev. Billy James Hargis, published a book entitled "Blackboard Power— N.E.A. Threat to America" by Dr. Gordon V. Drake. The Christian Crusade also printed another attack by the same author, a pamphlet titled "Is the Schoolhouse the Proper Place to Teach Raw Sex?"

"The sudden attacks on sex education programs took the John Birch Society unawares," Mr. Putnam said in a speech this summer. "It took one of the most vocal organizations opposing Communists in our society six months to decide that sex education is a Communist plot."

In the January, 1969, issue of the John Birch Society Bulletin, however, Robert Welch wrote that what was needed was "organized, nationwide, intensive, angry and determined opposition to the now mushrooming program of so-called sex education in the public schools."

"Various stages of the program," he continued, "have already been imposed on some 5 to 10 per cent of the schools. Deep-laid plans have been carefully initiated to spread this subversive monstrosity over the whole American educational system, from kindergarten to high school."

"But a preponderant majority of the American people are not yet even aware of this filthy Communist plot . . ."

Birch people and other rightwing forces then sprang to the attack and MOTOREDE Committees, an ad hoc Birch group whose name was drawn from Movement to Restore Decency, were formed in several communities.

Birchers also heeded Mr. Welch's call to organize front groups to bring the message home. Thus, local groups with other names—usually acronyms such as MOMS, for Mothers Organized for Moral Stability, or POSE, for Parents Opposed to Sex Education — sprouted like mushrooms after a rain.

### 'The Innocents Defiled'

The society also put out a $30 film strip with sound entitled "The Innocents Defiled," in which the sex education program is depicted as a plot to confront American school children with pornography.

Birch members are particularly incensed over a slide film series entitled "How Babies Are Made," produced by Creative Scope. The rights to the series were purchased by Time-

Life, which also put out a book and a film strip.

"How Babies Are Made," aimed at elementary school children, frankly discusses reproduction and contains drawings of chickens and dogs mating as well as a male and female in bed with the woman lying in the man's arms. The scene of the man and woman has an aura of tenderness about it rather than sensuality.

The accompanying text for the pictures describes how sperm enters the female. Some schools and church groups use the film series, others do not.

Throughout the nation, literature that carried "horror" stories of what had happened in sex education classroom began to appear. After checking and cross-checking, all of the stories proved false but that the effects had already been felt in some communities.

For example, Mr. Bliss spent a good deal of money investigating allegations raised by rightwingers that boys and girls in a school near Racine had been instructed to go into a closet and feel one another as part of the sexual learning process. Officials and teachers in the school denied such activity.

### 'Illustrated' Lecture

The American Education Lobby, a right-wing group based in Washington, printed a number of horror stories. Among them was one telling of

a teacher in Lansing, Mich., who took off her clothes to illustrate a sex lecture. The local school board president declined to dismiss her, according to the story, saying that her activities were in the best interests of the students.

The story was checked out by Mr. Putnam at the N.E.A. He said that the incident occurred in a class for girls in home economics. The teacher was demonstrating various types of loose-fitting clothing and had changed costumes behind a screen.

"It's clear to anyone who reads the right-wing literature that they are opposed to public education by the state because they feel the state is a monolith vulnerable to Communist control," Mr. Putnam continued. "By seizing the emotional sex issue, they automatically get a larger audience for their views."

The organization that has borne the brunt of the assault is the Sex Information and Education Council of the United States (called SIECUS and pronounced Seek-us).

SIECUS, a tax-exempt, nonprofit voluntary health organization that consults with community leaders, educators, religious groups, colleges and medical schools about sex education programs only on request, is headed by Dr. Mary S. Calderone, an authority on sex education.

The Birch Society's film

strips and literature have described Dr. Calderone as the "Joan of Arc for sex education" and as a "sweet-faced, silvery-haired grandmother who shocks audiences by using four-letter words to make her point."

Although Dr. Calderone was not available to comment on the Birch attack, she has been quoted as saying that much of the material ascribed to her in right-wing publications was taken out of context.

The Birchers have also criticized Dr. Isadore Rubin, the editor of Sexology magazine and a former board member of SIECUS. Dr. Rubin is under attack because he once declined to answer Congressional investigators on possible Communist affiliations.

SIECUS has said its purpose is to "promote healthy, responsible relationships between male and female in all aspects of human behavior, not limited to the 'sex act.'"

"Education for sexuality," the organization continued, "does not attempt as its major goal to decrease venereal disease or out-of-wedlock pregnancies, but rather to help in producing more mature, responsible men and women and thus, eventually, parents who are strong and competent in their roles as spouse and parents."

"We feel that sex education is the prerogative of parents

and not the schools," replied Reed A. Benson, the director of public relations for the Birch Society and its Washington representative.

In a recent interview, Mr. Benson said that sex education was the work of "evil forces" who were "anxious to achieve the breakdown of morality in this country."

Mr. Benson identified these forces as Communists and said that sex education in the public schools was "one more means to break down and destroy the moral fiber of American youth."

In the cacophony of emotion over sex education, more moderate criticism has not been voiced.

"I know teachers I wouldn't want teaching math to my kids, let alone sex education," said a concerned parent in Racine.

It is this lack of more responsible questioning that has bothered such experts as Dr. Mileff, who believes that parental criticism will only make such programs stronger and better able to serve the particular needs of each community.

"Education doesn't supply the answer to living and dying, but sometimes it's the only answer," Dr. Mileff said, adding:

"No one claims that sex education programs will solve all the problems to this area of life. But how can you ignore sexuality? It's part of living."

September 14, 1969

# 80% Success Claimed for Sex Therapy

### By ROBERT REINHOLD
Special to The New York Times

BOSTON, April 25—Two experts on human sexuality who have developed an intensive two-week course of therapy for male impotence, female frigidity and other forms of sexual inadequacy say that their treatment has been effective in eight out of ten cases.

The new treatment consists of quickly educating a couple to break down their psychological fears while they perform carefully programed acts of sexual play and intercourse in private.

This differs from traditional lengthy psychotherapy mainly in that no attempt is made to correct the past emotional disturbances that some authorities believe cause disorders later.

The experts, Dr. William H. Masters and Virginia E. Johnson of the Reproductive Biology Research Foundation in St. Louis, say that their treatment proved successful for 80 per cent of the 790 persons treated over a period of 10 years.

The treatment is based in large part on a controversial 11-year scientific inquiry into the physiology of sex, the results of which were published four years ago as "Human Sexual Response." For that study, the authors observed hundreds of men and women as they engaged in coitus and masturbation.

The new study is generally thought to be the most comprehensive treatment of the subject to date, but some authorities dispute the conclu-

sions. It is being published tomorrow in Boston by Little, Brown & Co. under the title, "Human Sexual Inadequacy."

By "conservative guestimate," the authors said at a news conference, half of all American marriages are threatened by sexual dysfunction. The Kinsey Report found that sexual failure was a factor in three-fourths of all divorces in the United States.

The St. Louis team considers inadequacy more the product of a culture that has made sex dishonorable — "centuries of distorting the naturalness of sex function," as Mrs. Johnson put it—than of mental or physical illness.

Whether their techniques are valid is a matter of some debate among experts. "This is a real breakthrough," commented Dr. Wardell Pomeroy of New York, a psychologist who co-authored the Kinsey reports. "It

goes far beyond anything anybody's done before."

"Oversimplistic and naive," was the opinion of Dr. Natalie Shainess, a New York psychoanalyst who said that the method merely papered over symptoms without dealing with the complex psychosexual responses that underlie inadequacy and are likely to resurface.

Other experts said that many of the individual elements of the Masters and Johnson therapy were not new, but that the team had innovated by packaging them and developing an effective system.

Among the major conclusions of the work are these:

¶The outlook for treatment of almost all forms of sexual incompetence is very hopeful.

¶There is no such thing as an uninvolved partner. Both spouses must be treated, even if only one appears to have a problem.

435

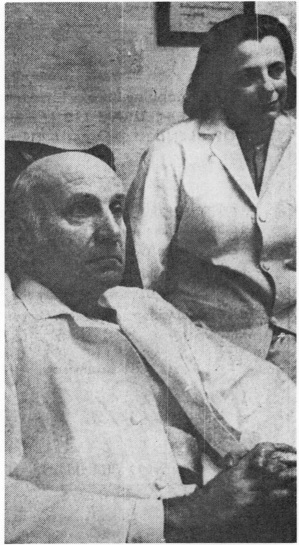

Dr. William H. Masters and Mrs. Virginia E. Johnson

The New York Times (by George Tames)

¶Treatment is best performed by a "dual sex therapy team." This consists of two therapists, one male and one female, each acting as a kind of "friend in court" for the spouse of the same sex.

Men and women over 50 can maintain active sex lives even into the 80's if they adjust their activities to the natural physiological changes of advancing age.

The largest single factor in sexual incompetence is a background in which the "thou shall nots" of religious orthodoxy were emphasized — at least in the group treated, which was not a cross section of society.

¶Much inadequacy is linked to fear of "performance," particularly now among women as they become more aware of their sexual responses. Therapy must restore the naturalness of the sex act.

## Written in Jargon

The book, couched in professional jargon, and complete with simple line drawings of suggested body positions for sex play and intercourse, is written for therapists, scientists and clergymen.

Nevertheless, the authors have no illusions about the potential public appeal of the work. "Human Sexual Response" is said to have sold more than 300,000 copies at $10 each. The new book, 450 pages long, is priced at $12.50 —high by most publishing standards.

"It's a hopeful book," said Mrs. Johnson, a 45-year-old psychologist. "If they [the public] insist on buying it, I'd like to think the hopeful nature of it will help." However, Dr. Masters, a 54-year-old gynecologist, warned that it should not be considered a "do-it-yourself kit."

To date, they have treated 510 married couples as well as 54 single men and three single women, for whom surrogate partners were provided. Among the patients were 89 physicians, including 43 psychiatrists, who had referred themselves for treatment. The ages ranged from 23 to 76 and they came mostly from the upper middle class.

Patients were accepted only on referral from some authority, such as a physician, psychologist, social worker or theologian. All had to agree to five years of followup to allow the therapists to test the permanence of the treatment.

The crux of the theory concept is the "dual sex" team, the theory is that a man can never really understand female sexual feelings and vice versa. One therapist is always a biologist and the other a behaviorist, such as a social psychologist.

After medical examinations and history taking, the couple meets with the team every day, seven days a week. At night, in the privacy of their room, they practice according to the instructions they get during the sessions. The couples are not observed in the laboratory during intercourse.

At the outset, there is a four-way roundtable discussion, with the therapists providing considerable direction, to re-establish communication and allow the couple to explore their personal interactions.

The couple is also educated in the facts of sexual response to dispel myths.

At the same time, they are directed to "pleasure" each other at night to stimulate gradual development of sexual pleasure. This involves the touching and fondling of each other.

The idea is to get the couple to think and feel sensuously without being obliged to reach climax or satisfy each other completely. With this rapport and confidence established, the treatment then progresses according to the specific problem.

Of the most prevalent forms of inadequacy, the best success has been achieved with premature ejaculation, a condition in which the man cannot control his orgasm long enough to satisfy his wife.

Somewhat smaller success was met in dealing with male impotence—the inability to maintain an erection. In dealing with this problem, the couple is told to engage in sex play, being careful to keep the man relaxed and undistracted.

For female frigidity, the couple are again helped to establish a nondemanding erotic climate. The husband is instructed in the means of stimulating his wife.

For the elderly the treatment is much the same, execept that special care is taken to dispel "one of the great fallacies of our culture," that sexual ability is impaired with age.

An attempt was made to follow up five years after treatment, the first time such a study has been made. This showed a very low percentage of reversal of success over the years.

Therapy is performed by Dr. Masters and Mrs. Johnson and two other teams at the foundation in St. Louis. The basic fee is $2,500, applied on a sliding scale depending on ability to pay. One-fourth of those treated paid only the cost to the foundation, $1,200, and another one-fourth paid nothing.

The foundation has completed, but not yet published, a study of homosexual response. It also expects to begin a postgraduate training program soon to teach the dual team technique to professional therapists.

The work is supported by fees for servicees, private citizens, and a number of small foundations, including the Playboy Foundation. A request for renewal of a grant from the National Institute of Health was turned down in 1962.

April 27, 1970

436

# The Price Men Pay For Supremacy

### By TODD GITLIN

SAN FRANCISCO—Feminists have pointed out how men benefit from male supremacy, in time, money, satisfaction, and above all, power; but far less attention has been paid to the price men pay for their power. Understandably so: women have been properly preoccupied with the price they pay. Meanwhile men, trapped in the same system, have been making token adjustments and wishing the whole subject would disappear. But it is long past time for men to reckon with the systematic damage done to their own lies, as well as women's, for most men are simultaneously accomplices and victims.

In the first place, women's oppression is intimately related to men's competitiveness and aggressiveness. A society whose cornerstone is aggressiveness, as a capitalist society must be, will inescapably keep women "in their place" and reserve for them the scorned higher virtues of warmth, sensitivity and tenderness which would only get in the way of men clawing their way to success. Women are converted into sexual objects to become rewards for competing men. Men compete for the attention of women, and compete for money and status for the "sake" of "their" women.

Thankfully, women are in revolt against their part of the vicious circle, but men continue to believe in the endless ladder of upward mobility, as if such Hobbesian individualism could result in anything but human wreckage for the many and hollow victory for a handful. In blissful unconsciousness, men acquire false selves, partly in order to justify their power and impress the captive female audience; the objectifiers become objectified.

Men suffer infinitely from the loss of the virtues bestowed upon women as rewards for their weakness; we fail to see how those virtues might be the strength of a civilization, when fused with work and potency, not divorced from them. A social system built on a pyramid of alienation is necessarily distortive of human need, imperialistic, violent, nasty, brutish, and, one hopes, short-lived.

Second, male domination suppresses love. Love is deformed, even eliminated, where there is no equality between the sexes. "Love Story" and similar entertainments fail to compensate for what we cannot discover in our lives; in fact the popularity of romantic fiction proves that the problem is not merely individual, but social. Men are only beginning to reap the whirlwind of centuries of domination. The consequences of lovelessness should be well known.

And third, along with race, sex is the primary division among the class of producers. Forced to sell themselves in the marketplace, men are compensated with castles in the shape of patriarchal homes. However little the little man, he knows he is bigger than the little woman. He comes home from factory or office, properly estranged or furious at his boss, and proceeds to mistreat his wife. Men's attention is diverted from their exploiters just as poor whites are tricked into blaming blacks for their troubles, just as overtaxed middle Americans displace their frustration onto "welfare bums."

Women in the labor force, along with minorities, also function as an "industrial reserve army" to drive down wages and obscure the common cause of the working class as a whole. Men, clutching their privileges vis-à-vis women, wail to recognize that the price of relative privilege is total alienation, endless insecurity (can the woman ever really be trusted?), and an inability to combine forces with women against the institutional titans of the entire society. Divided, we are contained and conquered.

Yet the male's fear is genuine: even given the most beneficent vision of future equality, in the short run men have their female cushions to lose. The psychic and pecuniary advantages of male power operate in the short run, in the household as well as in the factory and office. Male privileges are like those of a trusty in prison: real enough at the time, yet ultimately chimerical and counter-productive in light of the promise of general liberation.

Needless to say, women cannot be expected to delay their demands while waiting for men to discover that they too are victimized. Justice needs no higher purpose. But the painful revolutionary process may be accelerated and softened once men realize that their motives for change need not be restricted to fear, guilt and benevolence. The world women want to win, if their critique is taken to its logical extremity, is a world which would be easier for men to live in too.

*Todd Gitlin is a former S.D.S. organizer and co-author of "Uptown: Poor Whites in Chicago."*

# Homosexual Wins Fight to Take Bar Examination in Minnesota

Special to The New York Times

MINNEAPOLIS, Jan. 6—Jack Baker, an outspoken leader of the Gay Liberation Movement, has been ruled eligible for the Minnesota bar examination by examiners who found that he did not fraudulently obtain the license with which he entered into a homosexual marriage.

Mr. Baker was graduated from the University of Minnesota Law School in December, while serving his second term as student president.

After he applied for the bar examination the State Board of Law Examiners invited him to a hearing to answer questions about his 1971 application for a marriage license in Mankato, Minn.

At issue was a state law that requires candidates for the bar and for other professions, to be of "good moral character."

A question had been raised, not about Mr. Baker's avowed homosexuality, but about his responses in applying for the marriage license.

## High Court Appeal

In early 1970, Mr. Baker and James Michael McConnell, both now 30 years old applied for a license in Minneapolis but were refused. Supported by the Minnesota Civil Liberties Union, they carried an appeal to the United States Supreme Court, which dismissed the case last October "for want of a substantial Federal question."

During the appeal period, Mr. Baker and Mr. McConnell pursued other avenues toward union. On Aug. 3, 1971, Mr. McConnell legally adopted Mr. Baker in Minneapolis, with the goal of securing tax and inheritance advantages.

At that time, Mr. Baker legally assumed the name Pat Lynn McConnell, while continuing to use the name Baker in his daily affairs. Shortly after the adoption, Mr. Baker signed his new name to a marriage license application in Mankato, a college city 80 miles southwest of Minneapolis. On Aug. 16, 1971, Blue Earth County issued the license, and, on Sept. 3, Mr. Baker and Mr. McConnell were married in a private ceremony in Minneapolis by the Rev. Roger Lynn of the United Methodist Church.

Shortly after the ceremony John Corbey, the Blue Earth County Attorney, said that the license was defective and the marriage null and void because the address listed on the application "was not that of the bride." Minnesota law requires that marriage licenses be issued in the county of the bride's residence, and the address listed by Mr. Baker was that of a vacationing professor.

## Marriage Stays in Effect

Subsequently, the Hennepin County grand jury studied the legality of the marriage but found the question not worth pursuing. Thus the marriage remained in effect.

After the bar examiners studied the same issue last month, William J. Lloyd, the director of bar admissions in Minnesota, wrote to Mr. Baker, saying that the board "will make no objection to your application, which will be processed in due course."

Mr. Baker plans to take the bar examination in February. But, he said, "as far as I'm concerned, the last hurdle hasn't been met." If he passes the bar, he still must be sworn in by the Minnesota Supreme Court.

Next April, Mr. Baker and Mr. McConnell plan to test the same-sex marriage issue again by filing a joint income tax return.

# Some Accept Sex at Home for Young

**By ENID NEMY**

A changing concept of sexual morality, accepted as a matter of course by a number of teen-agers, is presenting an emotional problem in more and more homes.

What happens when the "liberated" young return for the weekend, with a friend of the opposite sex, and expect to share the same bedroom?

Some parents, a minority of no small proportions in a sampling of about 30 middle-class couples in and around New York, accept their childrens' sexual values with equanimity, if not enthusiasm. A smaller number wholeheartedly approve of what they call "the end of hypocrisy."

On the other hand, the situation has caused consternation in numerous households. It has frequently occasioned the first major rift between usually open-minded parents and their children, and it has widened an already existing difference in mores between conservative adults and their progeny.

It has led, too, to disagreement between husbands and wives. In some cases, liberal parents have realized, somewhat ruefully, that they are unwilling to accept emotionally what they are prepared to support intellectually.

The couples, drawn from various religious backgrounds, preferred to have their names withheld to spare their children any embarrassment. Many of them had younger children still at home, and, in those cases, almost invariably said that their stand against sexual freedom in the home was inflexible.

Almost all of the couples were resigned to, and not unduly concerned about, premarital sex away from home. The few who voiced objections conceded that, realistically, they were powerless to control it. Their concern, and the subject of discussion between themselves and with friends, was with upholding their particular standards in their own homes.

"I know my daughter has had affairs, and I can live with the idea as long as I'm not confronted with it," said one woman. "I may be acting like an ostrich, but that's the way it is. I'd rather have my head in the sand."

"There's a difference between acquiescing involuntarily to something you can't control, and giving it your blessing," said a father who described himself as "hung up on the Protestant-Puritan ethic." He "accepted unwillingly" his daughter's relationship with a fellow student, but drew the line at "complete surrender of parental authority."

An executive in the communications field was among the comparatively few parents who accepted his children's lifestyle without reservation.

"My whole attitude toward sex has changed enormously in recent years," he said. "I feel generally that the sexual ethics of young people now are better than those I had as a boy. It wasn't ethics then; it was hypocrisy."

The product of a traditional Jewish upbringing, he said that he and his wife, who is a Catholic, had discussed the question and decided that allowing their sons to share a room with girl friends was "the healthy way."

"It seemed a far more decent thing to do than say that they could sleep together away from home, but not at home. Sex is great. Why can't they enjoy it at home?"

But, like many broad-minded parents, he admitted the possibility of a somewhat different attitude if his children had been girls. And, he added, his wife's reservations might be even more marked. The reaction was not uncommon.

"I can understand some people not minding with sons—that's someone else's daughter being violated," said a lawyer active in human rights cases. "But you don't want the feeling that someone is doing that to your daughter."

"I'd be firmer with a daughter," said a business executive who has allowed his two teen-aged sons to share rooms with friends. "I don't know why, but the attitude is inbred. I don't like to think I have a double standard, but I guess it boils down to the fact that I do."

An aviation consultant and his wife, who did allow their 19-year-old daughter to share a room with her boy friend, have since regretted their decision.

"We allowed it, and heaven knows why," said the mother. "She came in with her friend and said he was staying for the weekend. We thought he'd stay in the guest room. When we came out in the morning, the guest room hadn't been used and that was that, but that night they shared her room again. We didn't say anything, and we had no discussion about it. We couldn't have been in our right senses."

The girl's father said he didn't like, want or approve of what happened but allowed it because, he said, "I didn't want to be a stupid reactionary father." However, if the occasion arose again, he would react differently.

"I'd knock at her door and say, 'Helen, I'm going to have to ask you to get that man out of your room.' What I would really be saying is that I don't care what you do as long as you don't do it in my house. I know it's narrow and unrealistic in the context of our times, but it's the way I feel, and it's purely a gut reaction."

A writer who has both a son and daughters said that he didn't even like to consider the idea that his daughters were having affairs.

"It would be different with my son," he said, conceding 'male chauvinism.' "But I still wouldn't let him share a room at home."

He recalled the first time one of his daughters brought home a boy with whom she said she was having an affair.

"He was supposed to sleep in the pool house, and, by sheer accident, the next morning I walked into a bedroom in the house and there they both were. I re-monstrated, and my daughter gave me that 'don't be old-fashioned . . . you know what is going on, so what's the difference?' argument. I said, 'We don't have a mixed dorm here and maybe I'm old-fashioned, but there it is.'"

His wife, a sophisticated career woman, indicated that she felt less strongly about premarital affairs.

"To them sex is a part of life, and I think it is a healthy thing," she said. "There's just no way for us to judge the way boys and girls feel about each other these days. We still judge them in terms of dates and popularity and things like that."

She had often turned her back, she said, "to the sneaky ways these things can be managed," but she would not permit "blatant shacking up" in her home.

"To me, it's a question of privacy," she said. "I'm still uncomfortable with friends of our own age, who have been living together for years and come to visit for the weekend. We put them together, but I still have that old-fashioned idea that nice people don't stay together if they are not married."

A middle-aged dentist admitted to permissiveness in dealing with his sons.

"It's difficult for me to say no to questions on which I think they are justified. When my son was 17, he came home with a girl and nothing was said. I just accepted it. I don't like sneaking around. I prefer to know what is going on."

But the practice of "carrying on" at home has been curtailed since the dentist's remarriage. His wife, who is in

---

"I feel generally that the sexual ethics of young people today are better than those I had as a boy. It wasn't ethics then; it was hypocrisy."

---

her early 30's, disagrees with her husband's attitude.

"I don't want my home a shack-up place," she said. "Of course, I admit the kids have been sleeping together, but what they do at college is another thing. They know you know but we play these games in life, and the sooner they learn the game, the better."

She believed, she said, the key word in any parent-child relationship was "respect."

"Before I was married, I was living with a guy," she said. "My mother knew I was, but I didn't think of asking her to share a room when I went home with him. I respected my mother and her house."

Respect for the home, and for their values, was a recurring theme among parents who disapproved of sexual freedom in the home.

"I believe strongly in being true to myself, and I think that kids' shacking up under my nose is ugly," said a mother who has not been told but is "sure" that her 16-year-old daughter has had an affair.

"What the hell belongs to you any more but your own home?" she asked rhetorically. "When you shut that door, it should be the way you want it."

Her attitude, she said, had nothing to do with morals.

"An affair should be a completely private thing between two people," she said. "If my daughter said 'Mommy, I need money for a weekend at a hotel' I'd probably give it to her. I wouldn't like one-night stands, but I've told her that I believe in trial before marriage."

Her husband, who is well known in the travel field, said he assumed "kids do a fair amount of sleeping around, and it's a situation you can't control unless you mount a 24-hour guard on them."

He said, however, that condoning sexual freedom in the home was "treating lightly a matter that should be handled with a heavier hand."

"The basic philosophy is, Are you going to function as a parent?" he said. "If you are going to be a buddy and pal, fine. All the rules are down. But I don't think kids need more buddies and pals. They need parents, and they have only two. It's much easier to let kids have their own way and win popularity contests, but parents are not in the business of winning popularity contests. They should be guiding."

# 2 Yankees Disclose Family Exchange

## Peterson and Kekich Give Details of Arrangement

### By MURRAY CHASS
Special to The New York Times

FORT LAUDERDALE, Fla., March 5—Fritz Peterson and Mike Kekich, the Yankees' starting left-handed pitchers, disclosed today details of an exchange of families.

The pitchers, who have been the two closest friends on the team for several years, said they and their wives began discussing last July the possibility of an exchange and that they put it into effect at the end of last season in October.

At this time, Peterson is living with Susanne Kekich and her two daughters, Kristen, 4 years old, and Reagan, 2, and they plan to be married as soon as they can divorce their spouses. That would be next October at the earliest, Peterson said.

### Kekich Is 'Dubious'

The other half of the relationship, though, hasn't worked out as well. Kekich lived with Marilyn (Chip) Peterson and her two sons, Gregg, 5, and Eric, 2, for two months last fall and then again briefly during the winter. They've also been together for the last 10 days here. Kekich said he hoped they could return to a good relationship, but "I'm dubious."

Both pitchers, in separate interviews after the Yankees disclosed the basic details, stressed that there was nothing sordid about the situation and it wasn't a matter of wife-swapping.

"It wasn't a wife swap," said Kekich, who married Susanne in 1965. "It was a life swap. We're not saying we're right and everyone else who thinks we're wrong are wrong. It's just the way we felt."

"It wasn't a sex thing," Peterson emphasized. "It was not a cheap swap."

Peterson and his wife, who were married in 1964, are legally separated. Peterson said he and Susanne Kekich planned to file divorces in New Jersey under what he said was that state's no-fault divorce law.

### Bitter Feelings

Both said they felt the situation wouldn't affect the Yankees as a team or themselves as pitchers. But it was obvious they had bitter feelings toward each other.

General Manager Lee MacPhail said he considered trading one of them after learning about the situation in January (Peterson said he told MacPhail he thought he should trade him), but he decided not to.

Manager Ralph Houk said he didn't think it could have any effect on the team.

"It doesn't bother me other than what effect it might have on their pitching," Houk said.

"Their personal lives are their own business. They live their own lives and they've got a lot of years to live. If you're not happy, you have to remember you only go through the world once. Why go through it unhappy?"

The other Yankee players know the situation now, but none evidently was aware of the plans of Peterson and Kekich during the last 2½ months of last season.

### Talk of Double Divorce

The two Yankees and their wives began discussing the possible exchange last July 15 on what the pitchers said was a high plane and amid "a tremendous amount of affection and compatibility." While remaining with their own families, they spent a lot of time together and individually —each player with the other's wife.

There was such harmony,

Associated Press

From left, on a sailing yacht last August, were Marilyn Peterson, Mike Kekich, Susanne Kekich and Fritz Peterson. They disclosed that they had exchanged families.

wanted Marilyn because "he wanted a wife with more education and zest." He himself, Peterson said, they even thought about having a double divorce and a double marriage and they discussed the possibility of dividing the children so that the older in each instance would go with the father and the younger with the mother.

Once the season was over, Kekich and Mrs. Peterson lived in the Petersons' rented home in Mahwah, N.J., and Peterson and Mrs. Kekich lived in the Kekiches' rented home in Franklin Lakes, N.J. Peterson said they even switched dogs.

"The only way I could justify giving up my daughters," said Kekich, 27, "was for a love far greater than I had ever known. By American standards, we both had good marriages; we had relative happiness with our families. But we were striving for something greater. Maybe that's too ideal. Now I feel hurt and the thing that hurts me most is I'm losing my children."

Peterson, 31, said Kekich

he said, wanted more freedom.

"Susanne is a perfect person for me," said Peterson, who hasn't signed his 1973 contract. "She's what I always wanted in a wife, a person and a mother. Before, we both felt dominated. Now we have free minds."

In relating the story, Kekich and Peterson disagreed on an interpretation of one aspect of the situation, a disagreement that has led to whatever ill feeling exists.

Kekich said the four had agreed that if any one of them at any time wanted to call the whole thing off and return to his or her original partner, they would do that. Peterson agreed that that was so until Dec. 14 but not afterward.

He explained that on Dec. 5, after the two pitchers had lived with each other's family for about two months they returned to their own families for what was to be a period of final decision. The Kekiches were in California, the Petersons in New Jersey. If they wanted to remain that way,

that's the way it would be. If they wanted to return to each other's wife, that also would be the path they would take.

On Dec. 14, Peterson said, after he called the Kekiches and said he wanted Susanne, she flew east to New Jersey and Marilyn flew to meet Mike in Portland, Ore. At that point, Peterson said, there was no turning back.

Kekich disagreed, contending Peterson had misled him into thinking Marilyn wanted to make the change at that time. Kekich said he and Marilyn both wanted to remain with their spouses for the time being.

"The morning Chip was going to leave," Peterson explained, "she asked me, 'How can you do this to me?' That was the first inkling I had that she had doubts. The night before she told me how much she wanted Mike."

Kekich said everything was fine until then. But he ex-

plained: "All of a sudden Marilyn and I were both left out in the cold and it changed our situation. It affected her because of her upbringing and her family. Her feelings put a great strain on me and a lot of friction was created between us. After a while I left Montana, where we were living, and went to New York.

"I would like it to work out with Marilyn and me, but I'm dubious. I've tried to stay with her throughout this whole thing, but love is funny. It can build fast, but it can wear on you, too."

Peterson said he had nothing to hide and nothing to be ashamed of but he had one regret.

"I never would have left my kids if I knew this was going to happen," he said. "I don't know what happened. I just have regrets for my kids. It's hard for me to think of them without a father and a family. If Mike and Marilyn don't get together, they'll be without a father. That eats me up. But I won't go back. I'll never go back."

March 6, 1973

# CHAPTER 5

# The Return to Normalcy

# Cybernetics, a New Science, Seeks the Common Elements in Human and Mechanical Brains

### By WILLIAM L. LAURENCE

The recent publication of Prof. Norbert Wiener's book, "Cybernetics," with the subtitle "Control and Communication in the Animal and the Machine" (John Wiley & Sons, Inc., New York), has brought to public attention the new science of cybernetics. Until now cybernetics has been known only to a small circle of the elite, among whom it had been regarded as something akin to a new revelation. Some of its more enthusiastic devotees in Dr. Wiener's inner circle believe that its further development will lead to a revolution in our understanding of the workings of the human mind and human behavior, both normal and abnormal, comparable to the revolutions in our understanding of the physical world brought about by the relativity and quantum theories.

Dr. Wiener, Professor of Mathematics at the Massachusetts Institute of Technology, has long been considered one of the world's ranking mathematicians. He is also an exceptional linguist, philosopher and literary scholar. While he is rightly the father of cybernetics, the new science is the outgrowth of extensive theoretical study and experimentation carried out by Professor Wiener in collaboration with outstanding scientists in other fields, including physiologists, psychologists, mathematicians and electrical engineers.

Cybernetics offers a new approach to the study of the human mind and behavior, based on a comparative study of the electrical circuits of the nervous system and those in the highly complex mechanical brains in the gigantic electronic calculating machines. It promises, in view of this relationship, to become of vital interest to psychologists, psychiatrists, physiologists, electrical and radio engineers, physicists, mathematicians, anthropologists, sociologists and philosophers. Indeed, it has already been used as the basis of a new philosophical approach to the relation of "ideological man to the scientifically known natural man" by the well-known Yale philosopher, Prof. F. S. C. Northrop. Professor Northrop uses cybernetics to correlate ideological and biological factors in social institutions.

### From the Greek

The word cybernetics is coined from the Greek word *kybernetes*, meaning steersman. Through its Latin corruption, *gubernator*, came the term governor, used for a long time to designate a certain type of control mechanism.

Cybernetics, Dr. Wiener states in The Scientific American, "combines under one heading the study of what in a human context is sometimes loosely described as thinking and in engineering is known as control and communication. In other words, cybernetics attempts to find the common elements in the functioning of auto-matic machines and of the human nervous system, and to develop a theory which will cover the entire field of control and communication in machines and in living organisms.

"It is well known," Dr. Wiener explains, "that between the most complex activities of the human brain and the operations of a simple adding machine there is a wide area where brain and machine overlap. In their more elaborate forms, modern computing machines are capable of memory, association, choice and many other brain functions. Indeed, the experts have gone so far in the elaboration of such machines that we can say the human brain behaves very much like the machines. The construction of more and more complex mechanisms actually is bringing us closer to an understanding of how the brain itself operates."

### Feed-Back System

The basic concept implied in the term cybernetics is that of a feed-back mechanism, represented by the steering mechanism of a ship, or the governor of a steam engine, or the common thermostat that maintains a house at a constant temperature. All these operate in response to information fed back to them; and since they tend to oppose what the system is already doing, they are known as negative feed-back systems.

Dr. Wiener's studies of feed-back systems began during the war, when he and Julian H. Bigelow were assigned the problem of working out a fire-control apparatus for anti-aircraft artillery which would be capable of tracking the curving course of a plane and predicting its future position. This job, which required collaboration between physiologist and mathematician, electronic engineer and physicist, led to startling observations. The outstanding one was that the voluntary activity of the nervous system operates on the negative feed-back principle in the same manner as the thermostat or other mechanical feed-back systems.

We do not will the motion of certain muscles, Dr. Wiener states. Indeed, we generally do not know which muscles are to be moved to accomplish a given task. We will a certain act, say, to pick up a cigarette. When we perform the act of picking it up, reports to the nervous system, conscious or unconscious, provide the information to the muscles so that they move just the right distance without overshooting or undershooting the mark.

This can be done only by a negative feed-back mechanism in our nervous system. As Professor Wiener puts it: "Once we have determined on picking up the cigarette, the motion of the arm and hand proceeds in such a way that we may say that the amount by which the cigarette is not yet picked up is decreased at each stage." The amount of the decrease at each stage is signaled to the muscles by a negative feed-back system in the nerve circuits so that we neither overshoot nor undershoot the mark.

### "Mechanism for Purpose"

This discovery that the voluntary nervous system, which includes our conscious activities and the operations of the brain, functions through a negative feed-back mechanism has already led Professor Northrop to the startling conclusions that neurophysiology, as interpreted by cybernetics, has found a "mechanism for purpose." Teleological (purposive) activity, he holds, is the correlate of negative feed-back systems by which signals from the goal can alter the behavior of a system after it has been initiated, the alterations making it possible for the system to reach the goal. This is the requirement, he tells us, for any mechanism to be goal-directed. A teleological system can be—and in the human nervous system it is—a mechanical system, in which the behavior of the system is controlled by a negative feed-back over the goal.

If this be so, then the ancient quarrel between the teleologists, who insisted on the freedom of the will, guided by purpose, and the determinists, who regard man as having neither freedom of choice nor purpose, may turn out to be a mere matter of semantics. Our actions are both mechanical and purposive. We have a goal but we reach it by mechanical means through the action of our negative feed-back mechanism.

The study of cybernetics, Dr. Wiener tells us, is likely to have fruitful applications in many fields, from the design of control mechanisms for artificial limbs to the almost complete mechanization of industry. But, he adds, "it encompasses much wider horizons. We are beginning to see that such important elements as the neurones—the units of the nervous complex of our bodies—do their work under much the same conditions as vacuum tubes."

### Intellectual Turning Point

The discovery that the human nervous system operates as a negative feed-back mechanism may well turn out to be one of the revolutionary discoveries of the age, marking an intellectual turning point in man's understanding of himself and of his universe. Professor Wiener assures us that a mechanical chess player could be constructed that "might very well be as good a player as the vast majority of the human race."

Since each mechanical brain provides the knowledge with which to build a better mechanical brain, it is conceivable that eventually we may build machines that will surpass the best human brains in thinking capacity; that may not only do all man's work for him but also solve such problems as the control of the atomic bomb and how to reconcile East and West. All that would be left for man to do would be to devise ways to stop the machine from destroying him.

December 19, 1948

# 'TOLL DIAL' PHONE LINKS TWO COASTS

## New Device Cuts Connection Time From 2 Minutes to 12 Seconds in Demonstration

### CITIES WILL BE NUMBERED

### Destination Picked by Machine That Is to Be Operated by Subscribers Later

Calling a person by telephone in San Francisco from New York, or vice versa, was reduced to a mere matter of dialing, and a few seconds, yesterday afternoon at the formal opening of the Bell System's "toll-dialing" circuits between the two cities.

The first call was placed by Mark Sullivan, president of the Pacific Telephone and Telegraph Company. He exchanged greetings with Dr. Oliver E. Buckley, president of the Bell Telephone Laboratories, and Keith S. McHugh, president of the New York Telephone Company, at the new "Looking Ahead with the Bell System" exhibit at 140 West Street.

When speaking with Mr. Sullivan over the circuit, Dr. Buckley predicted that technicians "soon will make it possible for toll operators to dial any telephone in the United States or Canada, and the machine will automatically select the best route to get it."

Mr. Sullivan's call was timed on a large recording clock. It took exactly twelve seconds from the moment the call was placed in San Francisco until the telephone extension rang at the Bell System exhibit here.

Ordinary New York-San Francisco calls require about two minutes, it was said. The exchange of greetings was reproduced over a battery of loudspeakers so visitors could both hear the call and watch the timing on the clock.

### Placing Cross-Country Call

A telephone subscriber in New York or San Francisco now may place a cross-country toll call merely by dialing 211 (long distance) and telling the special operator the desired number in either city. The operator then speeds the call on its way directly to the distant subscriber by "punching" out the number on a high-speed device resembling a small calculating machine.

For the time being a long distance operator will help to complete a call to a distant point, but eventually the telephone subscriber or user "will do it all on the phone dial in his home or office." For instance, when a New Yorker desires to call a business associate in St. Louis the former first will dial the number assigned to the city, then follow it, after a short interval, with the number of the person or concern.

In time every city or locality in the country is expected to have toll dialing in use. Long distance "city" numbers will be published in local telephone company books along with the numbers of phone subscribers. New York, for instance, has been assigned Code Area 212, Chicago 312 and San Francisco 415.

The exhibit downtown will be open to the public until Nov. 4. It traces the progress of the telephone from its earliest days to the present. Other displays include working models of television radio relays, coaxial cables, mechanized cost accounting and devices expected to be part of the country's telephone system of the future.

October 18, 1949

# ADJUSTMENT KEY TO SMOG SOLUTION

## Scientific Efforts Clash With Impatience of Populace in Suffering Los Angeles

### By GLADWIN HILL
#### Special to The New York Times.

LOS ANGELES, Sept. 26—This metropolis is experiencing a race between cold science and hot human tempers.

On the one hand, scores of slide-rule and test-tube manipulators are striving to solve the problems of smog. On the other is a populace of 5,000,000 periodically afflicted with a murky atmosphere that irritates eyes, nose and throat, blots out vistas of beauty and sometimes withers crops.

Less immediate, but no less definite, is the possibilty that continued smog can blight the city's development, jeopardize health and burgeon suddenly into a full-fledged disaster.

Scientists say the battle against smog is a chemically complex one that could be won quickly if motoring, factory operations and burning trash would cease. Otherwise, they say, it promises to take years of gradual suppression of air pollution sources.

### Ineffectual Wrangling

The citizen with streaming eyes and uneasy mind wants the battle won today. The question is to what extent his impatience will precipitate changes in the community's pattern of living.

At present, public dissatisfaction is still in the "let George do it" stage. People rail against air pollution caused by industry. But they have let their elected representatives wrangle ineffectually for months over the one step that would ameliorate smog quickly — substituting trash collection for the present system of backyard incineration.

Meanwhile, millions of dollars annually and the full-time effort of hundreds of persons are being directed at the problem on many fronts.

The Los Angeles metropolitan area covers several thousand square miles. Less than 500 square miles and only 2,000,000 of the area's 5,000,000 inhabitants are within the City of Los Angeles, subject to its police powers. The rest, along with many of the area's 15,000 industrial establishments, are in 100 outlying communities.

Hence, pollution-control efforts from a municipal base are meaningless. Fortunately, the metropolitan area coincides roughly with Los Angeles County. In 1948, the State Legislature authorized establishment of a County Air Pollution Control District, a governmental agency.

### Puts Out Criteria

The control district has a staff of 200, mostly engineers, chemists, physicists and field inspectors, and a current annual budget of $2,500,000. It has promulgated scientifically devised criteria of air pollution, based on optical and chemical measurements. Its standards have to be met by any fume-producing enterprise before it can get a permit to operate.

The authority's only legal weapon is the misdemeanor citation, which involves a maximum penalty of $500 fine or six months' imprisonment. These sanctions are considered less a punitive jailed—than an inducement for corrective measures. One nominal $12.50 fine is said to have proded a large factory into installing $75,000 worth of fume-suppression equipment.

Public pressure has forced a radical step-up in invoking the law. In the first seven years, there were only 1,200 citations. In the last six months, there have been 1,700.

Even after the anti-smog campaign began in 1948, Los Angeles' urge for growth was so strong that new industries were allowed to start operations and comply with air-pollution laws later. Public clamor seems to have ended this practice. Only thirty-two such permits are in effect.

The control district's regulatory activities are supplemented on the research front by the Air Pollution Foundation, a multi-million dollar non-profit civic organization. It is headed by Dr. Lauren Hitchcock, prominent consulting engineer, formerly of New York.

### $600,000 in Research Work

The foundation has $600,000 in research projects under way, scattered from here to Columbus, Chicago and Kansas City. The projects range from local atmospheric measurements so detailed they have to be correlated by "electric brain" punch-card machines to studies of how auto exhausts can be made less noxious.

The activities of these two organizations are being supplemented by teams of Federal and state engineers and scientists.

Under Federal air-pollution legislation enacted by the last Congress, Dr. Vernon Mackenzie, assistant chief of research and development for the United States Public Health Service, is here with an assistant making studies. A three-man state contingent is headed by Dr. Malcolm Merrill, State Health Director.

The control district and the foundation jointly establish standards for an "alert" system to warn the public of gathering pollution that might be dangerous, and to set in motion appropriate precautions.

445

The system hinges on complex chemical measurements. There are three "alert" stages. The first signifies the accumulation of an undue amount of smog; the second warns of a "preliminary health hazard," and the third of the presence of an actual hazard.

### First Stage Described

In the first stage, incineration is supposed to stop completely. In the second, secondary industrial and commercial activities producing fumes, including filling stations, are to stop. In the third, all but unavoidable fume-producing activities are to stop, including auto travel.

The alerts are sounded by radio. The system was put in effect July 29. Since then, there have been nine alerts. All were of the first degree, although officials said a recent ten-day smog had come close to producing a second-stage warning. Except for some reduction in home incineration, the "alerts" have had no perceptible effect on the populace's activities.

In addition to these ameliorative measures, a code of preventive measures was promulgated last week. It calls for daily announcements whether atmospheric conditions are conducive to a smog buildup. If they are, individuals and commercial enterprises are asked to minimize motoring, incineration and other fume-producing activities.

### Problems of Autos

It is hoped that such measures can keep the smog problem within bounds until scientists and engineers devise ways of maintaining relatively fume-free conditions.

Even with industrial air pollution eliminated, there would remain the problem of automobiles. Half of the 6,000,000 pounds of pollutant chemicals discharged into the air daily are attributed to car exhausts.

An extensive research program on alternative automobile fuels has just been reported as fruitless by the Air Pollution Foundation. Hopes are now pinned mainly on research in improved carburetion, in which the automobile industry is collaborating, and on developing effective muffler filters. But the perfection of these seems years away at best.

The first expert called in to appraise the problem nearly a decade ago was Dr. Louis McCabe, who cleaned up the air of St. Louis after years of community fumbling.

Dr. McCabe started the control districts here. He stressed that any community could have as clean air as it wanted, if it would make adjustments and sacrifices.

Los Angeles now is in the agonizing process of deciding where adjustments are to be made.

September 27, 1955

### Technological Booster

Neither scientific competence nor rich resources alone can assure a country a high living standard. A modern nation's real source of prosperity is its "technological potential" — the product of technical knowledge and business enterprise.

This is the view of Dr. B. D. Thomas, director of the Battelle Institute, technological research organization of Columbus, Ohio. He addressed a meeting here yesterday of the International Management Association, affiliate of the American Management Association.

The high value of this potential is the reason for the United States' high living standard, Dr. Thomas said. Its natural resources were helpful, he maintained, but not sufficient. The speaker noted that Switzerland, with limited natural resources, had the world's second-highest per capita income because of high technological competence and business enterprise.

Russia, he added, had high technological competence but low business enterprise, a combination producing low per capita income less than a fifth that of the United States.

May 25, 1957

# PRECISION URGED IN SCIENCE STUDY

### U.C.L.A. Dean Says Problem of Perfection Is the Same One Facing Society

### 'SLOPPY' WORK DECRIED

### Teachers Told Schools Can Make 'Magnificent' Gains in Controversial Time

**By ROBERT K. PLUMB**
Special to The New York Times.

DENVER, March 28—Problems that science teachers face in their classrooms are problems that run deep in American society, an educator suggested here today.

Dr. Howard E. Wilson, Dean of Education at the University of California in Los Angeles, addressed a session of the sixth national convention of the National Science Association. More than 1,500 science teachers and educational specialists have gathered for the four-day meeting.

A tradition of "sloppy craftsmanship" extends through American society, he asserted.

It extends from the garage mechanic, who does a sloppy job fixing a car, to the would-be English instructor who does not bother with proper punctuation and good grammar, Dr. Wilson reported.

"This is a problem as wide and deep as society itself," Dr. Wilson declared. "Our modes must change. We are living in an era when precision is becoming more essential to a successful career. We must learn to stimulate our students to achieve perfection or as near it as they can."

### Gains Seen Possible

According to Dr. Wilson, the present period of "controversy and creativity" about schools might well last until 1980. But out of it may come "magnificent" gains in education, he said.

The first of three periods of intense public interest in education occurred, he said, between 1830 and 1860 when the common school free to all was created; the second period came between 1893 and 1917 when the "muckrakers" got after education. That resulted in the modern comprehensive high school, he said. The third period, according to Dr. Wilson, has arrived.

Since World War II, the public has grown uncertain and uneasy with fears focused on the revolution that science has brought into every life, Dr. Wilson declared. Educators, he said, should see that their task is to make scientific education a central part of liberal education, to train citizens who understand what science is, rather than to train scientists themselves.

Following Dr. Wilson's address, science teachers at the meeting discussed how research in science teaching might be used to improve classroom instruction in elementary, secondary and college classes. Techniques might be evolved to increase the effectiveness of science teaching, it was suggested.

March 29, 1958

# Advertising: Love of Labor Lost

**By ROBERT ALDEN**

The mental picture of the daring, dashing, industrious American male may need some revision if a study by the Center for Research in Marketing, Inc., is valid.

More than 1,000 male respondents were given illustrations of six men in suitable dress. A jet pilot was illustrated wearing his flying suit complete with mask and helmet; a doctor in appropriate white garb examined an X-ray picture; a laborer held a welding torch; a business man, a brief case; a socialite in tails and wearing a top hat and cane casually lit a cigarette, a sportsman in sports shirt and

casual jacket leaned on his fishing pole.

Those shown the illustrations were then asked which of the men illustrated they would like to be.

The most popular choice by far was that of the sportsman. The business man and doctor tied for second place, the socialite came in third and the jet pilot finished fourth, but ahead of the laborer.

Further questioning disclosed that the sportsman won out because he represented a carefree life, a life of leisure, a life that represented no work. The illustration of the sportsman evoked images of vacations and retirement.

### Prestige Limited

The social prestige of being a doctor or a man in a gray flannel suit did not have the appeal that the researchers had expected. These categories represented work and they were not regarded as anywhere near as desirable as that of a sportsman who could go fishing whenever he wanted.

The experts also felt that the life of the socialite might prove very attractive to the men. They were wrong.

"That life is too fussy, too confining and demanding," was the general tenor of the comment of those interviewed.

As for the life of the jet pilot, which it was also felt would have wide appeal for the men, a serious drawback was encountered. "Too dangerous" was the general comment about this category of work.

As for the laborer, the category farthest down in the scale of preferences, here it appeared to be merely a matter of too much work. "Who wants to work?" asked one respondent, and his comment differed from many others only in that he was more outspoken.

### Conflict Is Found

William Capitman, president of the center, commented:

"Our results strongly indicate that men are in conflict with everyday working life with its pressures and uncertainties. There is a very great appeal to the idea of a carefree existence symbolized by the sportsman.

"Time to relax, freedom from constraint, the interest and excitement of sport are the goals men seek today. The status and material success open to professional and business men are valued, but not nearly so highly as what men perceive as the happiness and easy life of the sportsman."

However, a spokesman at the research center also gave another view:

"One interpretation of these findings is that in looking for a release from the responsibilities of modern life, men are returning to primal responsibilities, the pursuit of fish and game, for example.

"Men who no longer bring home the bacon but a pay check instead, are looking for more direct methods of asserting masculinity, without at the same time engaging themselves in the perilous and arduous tasks of, for example, fliers or welders."

But, no matter how the analytical house is built, it appears that that fellow who said: "Who wants to work?" came pretty close to hitting the nail on the head. ᐧ

*August 8, 1960*

# FAMILY IS CALLED VITAL TO INDUSTRY

## Business and Union Heads Say Man's Domestic Ills Affect the Economy

Twenty-four business leaders and the heads of organized labor in the United States have found family breakdowns to be a serious economic, as well as social, problem.

They said the worker who was having difficulties at home not only was less efficient, but also endangered his fellow workers.

Their views were set forth in a special fiftieth anniversary issue of Family Service Highlights, the publication of the Family Service Association of America. The issue was published last week.

"Family breakdown is a major human problem in America today," said Thomas J. Watson Jr., president of the International Business Machine Corporation, in his foreword to the special issue. He continued:

"I speak not only of families that are actually broken or on the verge of separation, divorce or desertion. More subtle is the effect of deteriorating family relationships, or the actual absence of healthy family life, on a substantial number of our population."

The great tragedy, he observed, is the effect on the human beings themselves. But, he said, the American economy also suffers.

"Business and industry, too, have a big stake in the community's efforts to maintain strong families," he said. "Most obvious is the fact that every employe is both a product of a family which shaped him and a member of one today which affects his everyday work for good or ill.

" * * * yesterday's family problems are today's community problems — delinquency, irresponsible parenthood, weak citizenship, mental illness, alcoholism, emotional distress and the inevitable costs of these and other problems to the voluntary contributor and to the taxpayer."

To bolster the contributors' conclusions, affiliated Family Service agencies presented brief case histories. A Southern agency told of an airline pilot with a troubled marriage who suffered stomach pains during critical moments of flying. Family counseling improved the relationship and relieved the pains in time, it reported.

### Connection Documented

This story, the national agency said in its introduction, dramatically documents the "connection between family problems and the many personnel problems that concern business and industry." It said the pilot's story showed that family difficulties could cause costly and dangerous human errors.

Recently, another airline pilot read a news report of a fatal plane crash in which no evidence of mechanical failure had been found. The report said the pilot had recently been divorced and lost custody of his children. Several days later the pilot who read the story phoned the local agency and asked for help with his family problems because "I know I have many lives in my hands."

Similar stories involving other industries were recounted by agencies.

George Meany, president of the American Federation of Labor and Congress of Industrial Organizations, stressed the value of counseling by family agencies.

### Many Unsolved Problems

Modern business and industry, said R. H. Collacott, director of public relations, Standard Oil Company, Ohio, have brought with them a host of unsolved social problems with which they must help to deal. He said social services had become as characteristic of this society as banking, legal and judicial services.

The greatest deficiency in these services today is in the shortage of them, he said. For its own good, the corporation should help to support and make these services available to its employes, he said.

The national agency said family services were facing a crisis. It said that only 10 per cent of family agencies had waiting lists in 1951 but that 45 per cent had lists in 1958. It was said that waiting lists were longer, too.

The special issue seeks to bring these facts closer to business and industry, said Frederick G. Storey, the association president.

*December 4, 1960*

## *Automation Report Sees Vast Job Loss*

Computers and automation threaten to create vast unemployment and social unrest, a planning consultant said in a report to be issued today.

Donald N. Michael, formerly of the Brookings Institution and now director of planning and programs for the Peace Research Institute in Washington, prepared the report for the Center for the Study of Democratic Institutions. The center was founded by the Fund for the Republic.

He said that while technology could replace human labor and even do much of the "thinking" for government and business leaders, cybernation might alter sharply the United States economic system.

Mr. Michael called his report "Cybernation: The Silent Conquest." The word is derived from cybernetics, pertaining to the processes of communication and control in men and machines.

He predicted that cybernation would eliminate entire job categories ranging from factory and farm workers to bank tellers and middle-management executives.

Mr. Michael saw no ready solutions for the resulting mass unemployment. But he found that Government would need to support part of the population through public works. The ultimate effects on society, he said, "certainly would not be conducive to maintaining the spirit of a capitalistic economy."

Mr. Michael maintained that cybernation's economic advantages make cybernation inevitable, in the Soviet Union as well as in this country.

As a result of smaller work forces, he said, cybernation would reduce management's human relations tasks, "whether these are coping with overlong coffee breaks, union negotiations, human errors or indifference."

Also, he said by handling routine administrative tasks, cybernation "frees management for attention to more basic duties."

On the other hand, he foresaw a severe displacement of blue-collar workers, especially in dock, factory and mine operations "where Negroes have hitherto found their steadiest employment."

He cited as outstanding examples of employment cutbacks the telephone and dry-cleaning industries, home maintenance and elevator operation. He said automation might eventually eliminate jobs now performed by bank tellers, statisticians, salesmen and retail clerks.

In sharp contrast, he said that professional people, such as teachers, doctors, scientists and engineers, would be "overworked." An unhealthy effect of cybernation, he added, may be the lack of jobs for "untrained adolescents," 26,000,000 of whom will be seeking work in this decade.

Mr. Michael was skeptical of proposed solutions, such as the retraining of workers and shortening of the work week to spread employment. Such efforts have not been successful, he said, and management "has not always been willing" to institute retraining programs.

As for shorter hours for the same pay, the report declared that "when the task is eliminated or new tasks are developed that need different talents, shorter shifts will clearly not solve the problem."

*January 29, 1962*

# Washington

## 'Major Domestic Challenge of the Sixties'

### By JAMES RESTON

WASHINGTON, Feb. 15—According to all well-informed and seasonally adjusted economists, machines are replacing everything in this country, except maybe pretty girls, and President Kennedy is worried about it.

He said at his press conference yesterday that we were going to have to find 25,000 new jobs every *week* for the next ten years to take care of these workers who are displaced by machines. He defined this as "the major domestic challenge of the Sixties" and this immediately produced two remarkable reactions.

First, his own Under Secretary of Labor, Willard Wirtz, said in Chicago that the machine-made unemployment problem was much worse than the President had indicated, and second, most of the press of the country paid very little attention to either of them.

### The Startling Statistics

Nobody questions the seriousness of the problem. Last year the major railroads of the country took in more money with 780,500 employes than they did in 1950 with 1,211,000 employes. In 1947, 655,000 United States workers produced 84,900,000 tons of steel; last year, about the same number, using new automatic machinery, produced nearly 100,000,000 tons—an increase of 17 per cent. Today the bituminous coal miners of America are producing as much coal as they did in 1949 with about one-third of the work force.

This is not merely a problem of electronic control devices replacing a man on a single machine. Machines are now beginning to replace other machines. The problem is that whole batteries of machines are now starting to regulate each other and operate whole factories and offices with predetermined automatic controls and very few workers.

Moreover, this is happening at a time when the population of the United States is increasing by over 3,000,000 a year—it has gone up by 28,000,000 since Eisenhower entered the White House in 1953—and when the lower-paid workers of Japan and Western Europe have mastered the techniques of automation and mass production.

The first fact about all this is that nobody knows what the facts are. If the President says that new machines and new workers mean that we have to find 25,000 new jobs every week and his Under Secretary of Labor says that the figure should be 35,000, it's not surprising that Walter Reuther and the National Association of Manufacturers disagree, or that Walter Heller, head of President Kennedy's Council of Economic Advisers, finds himself in a fight over the fact with Leon Keyserling, who was President Truman's economic adviser.

Therefore, the first thing is to do a more thorough job, even if it costs more money, of gathering reliable information about the effect of automation, rising population, exports, imports and all the rest, so that everybody can bicker amiably or even violently over some approximation of the facts.

### Those 'Bright' Newspapers

After that, it might be possible to get the newspapers and the radio stations to pay some attention to what the President called yesterday "the major domestic challenge of the Sixties—to maintain full employment at a time when automation is replacing men."

Yesterday the New York papers were wildly excited about Mrs. Kennedy's TV presentation of the Red Room in the White House, what's up in Vietnam and whatever happened to Ebbets Field and the Brooklyn Dodgers, but the bright boys had not a word to say about America and its problem of automation.

Nevertheless, serious questions remain, not all of them bright. What are the facts at this point when both automation and atomic energy are creating a new "automic" revolution in the world? What about the unskilled worker in America who will be displaced from his job or even the highly skilled worker who finds that his talent has been taken over by a machine? What about the small business man who lacks the capital to introduce automatic machinery into his plant and has to face competition of bigger firms whose capital resources enable them to build new automatic offices and factories? How can all this new power of automation and atomic energy be turned into a positive good instead of into a problem? And, probably more important than all, what will be the effect of all this new power and leisure on the American character?

In the introduction of the annual report of the Council of Economic Advisers to President Kennedy the point was made that economic goals were merely a means to human goals. The rest of the report, however, did not indicate how this was to be reached. There is, however, now agreement here in Washington that the main problems are to clarify what the facts are and get them discussed in the country so that this serious question can get the attention it deserves.

February 16, 1962

# Cape Canaveral

## Is the Moon Really Worth John Glenn?

### By JAMES RESTON

CAPE CANAVERAL, Fla., Feb 24—The examples placed before a nation are vital. What we constantly observe, we tend to copy. What we admire and reward, we perpetuate. This is why John Glenn himself is almost as important as his flight into outer space, for he dramatized before the eyes of the whole nation the noblest qualities of the human spirit.

Outside of the morality-play of our cowboy movies, where the hero always gets the girl and the villain always gets slugged behind the saloons, courage, modesty, quiet patriotism, love of family and religious faith are not exactly the predominant themes of our novels, plays, TV shows, movies or newspapers these days. Yet Glenn dramatized them all coast to coast and around the world.

This was no insensitive robot who landed here from the heavens yesterday morning, but a warm and thoughtful human being: natural, orderly, considerate and, at times, quietly amusing and even eloquent.

### All This and Annie Too

His departure from Cape Canaveral in a blaze of orange fire was a technical triumph, but his return was a human triumph. When he came back and saw his lovely wife, Annie, he put his head on her shoulder and cried. Thereafter nothing ruffled him, not the President, or the clamorous press, or the whirring cameras, or the eager shouting crowds.

This memorable performance, of course, may not stamp out juvenile delinquency overnight, but the models of the nation—not the uncovered cover girls of today but the larger models of human character—are probably more important than this age believes.

When Walter Bagehot, the English editor and scientist, made his famous study 100 years ago of why some nations progressed, he concluded that what a nation admired and despised was almost as important as its military power.

"Slighter causes than is commonly thought," he said, "may change a nation from the stationary to the progressive state of civilization, and from the stationary to the degrading."

It all depended, he insisted, on the model of character emulated or eliminated. If the enduring qualities of nobility, intelligence, perseverance and courage were uppermost, then he felt all was well.

For then, he asserted, "a new model in character is created for the nation; those characters which resemble it are encouraged and multiplied; those contrasted with it are persecuted and made fewer.

"In a generation or two, the look of the nation becomes quite different; the characteristic men who stand out are different; the men imitated are different; the result of the imitation is different. A lazy nation may be changed into an industrious, a rich into a poor, a religious into a profane, as if by magic, if any single cause, however slight, or any combination of causes, however subtle, is strong enough to change the favorite and detested types of character."

If this was true in the middle of the nineteenth century it has even more validity in this age of instantaneous communication. Only a few hundred people heard Lincoln's Gettysburg Address. New models and styles are now set by television every day, but most of them are models of cars and styles of dresses and hairdos.

What transcontinental television did for the nation on the Glenn story illustrates the wider application of the idea. It almost made up for what it does to us the rest of the time, but not quite.

### The Earth's Need

Meanwhile, the question remains: how many more John Glenns and Al Shepards are hiding in this country?

Outer space is a long way to go

to discover a new generation of leaders of men, but if we have to recruit them there, why not? Human weightlessness is almost our major problem in Washington and, since these astronauts know more about it than anybody else, maybe a couple of them should be transferred to the thin hot air of the capital.

After all, Glenn is 40 and even if he looks like the freshman football coach at Muskingum College he can't go off spinning around the earth without his Annie forever. Once Christopher Columbus had discovered America, Ferdinand and Isabella didn't insist that he go back every Tuesday.

Besides, is the moon worth John Glenn, when we need him so badly on earth?

February 25, 1962

# GLENN IS PRAISED BY LT. GOV. WILSON

## Colonel's Religious Attitudes Cited at Breakfast Here

Lieut. Gov. Malcolm Wilson praised Lieut. Col. John H. Glenn Jr. yesterday for having said "all the wrong things" according to prevailing attitudes toward religion and patriotism.

Mr. Wilson cited Colonel Glenn's statements that he believed in God and that it thrilled him to see children waving the American flag as examples of simple faith and patriotism now considered "old-fashioned."

Mr. Wilson spoke before 2,100 members and guests of the Holy Name Society of the Fire Department at the society's thirty's-eight annual communion breakfast at the Commodore Hotel.

Earlier, George P. David, chief of department of the Fire Bureau, said that because of the danger and hazards they faced, firemen had to have

strong religious faith. He referred to the average of 150 injuries a week to department personnel.

Mr. Wilson said Colonel Glenn's statements combined faith in God with love of country. He cited Saturday's Loyalty Day Parade and yesterday's mass and breakfast as an example of the same combination.

Mr. Wilson criticized those who favored "lukewarm" patriotism. He said, "If our country is not strong morally, it will not be strong in any other way."

He called on those present to exercise their personal responsibility for the morals of the nation and the world by fighting "so-called literature that befouls our newsstands" and "pictures and shows that cause revulsion to decent people."

The breakfast was held after a 9 A. M. mass in St. Patrick's Cathedral, celebrated by the Most Rev. Joseph F. Flannelly, Bishop of New York. Then the society paraded down Fifth Avenue.

The breakfast was the farewell appearance of Msgr. Leo G. Farley, the Department Chaplain. He has been named to the pastorate of St. Christopher's Church, Montrose, N. Y.

April 30, 1962

# 'Fail-Safe Syndrome'

## Blackout Recalls Fiction and Scientific Predictions of a Doomed Civilization

### By WALTER SULLIVAN

The British author E. M. Forster once drew a frightening picture of a civilization that surrendered to automation, then collapsed from the weight of its own complexity.

The consequences of Tuesday's electric blackout have given new meaning to this vision.

**News Analysis** — The breakdown in transport, the disruption of city life have called to mind recent warnings that our society may also collapse, some day, from its increasing complexity.

The breakdown of a far-flung, up-to-date and seemingly foolproof power system has also revived what some call "the fail-safe syndrome." This is the fear that, despite assurances to the contrary, a catastrophic war could be started by some "impossible" malfunction in the highly automated defense systems of the great powers.

In Forster's "The Machine Stops" everyone lives in his own underground cubicle, linked to others only by what would today be called television (the story was written before World War I). All human needs—light, food, even medical care—are provided by pushbutton control.

Civilization is thus one vast, global machine, driven by a "central power station" in France. If anything goes wrong—or if anyone gets out of line —the "Mending Apparatus"

takes care of it. Then, suddenly, the Mending Apparatus itself begins to fail. The power plant weakens. Lights dim. The artificial air becomes foul. Automatic beds the world over fail to function.

Finally there is darkness and frightful silence. Those born and raised under the Machine realize for the first time that it hummed. Then all perish.

### Hoyle vs. Malthus

Are we moving towards such a catastrophe? There are brilliant men who believe so. One of them is Fred Hoyle, a leading cosmologist, science fiction author and Plumian Professor of Astronomy and Experimental Philosophy at Cambridge University in England.

He has sounded his warning on a number of occasions, particularly in a lecture entitled "A Contradiction in the Argument of Malthus," given at the University of Hull. It was the English clergyman and economist Thomas R. Malthus who argued at the end of the 18th century that the population always increases faster than the food supply. He viewed starvation and war as the characteristic brakes on population growth.

Hoyle believes this is no longer the case. Technology is making it possible to provide for more and more people. As it does so, it becomes increasingly complex. Centralization and bigness make for greater pro-

duction efficiency, be it the generation of electric power or the processing of food.

But such societies become increasingly vulnerable to catastrophic disruption. When mankind was primarily rural, each family was largely independent and self-sufficient. Now we have already reached the stage where a disruption of the arteries of power, of food, or of fuel can be disastrous, as those planning Civil Defense are vividly aware.

### A New Society Predicted

Hoyle argues that our civilization will become so vulnerable that it will ultimately succumb to some such threat as a new disease, a nuclear war, or simply a general collapse like the one depicted by Forster.

Then, in his hypothesis, a new society will slowly evolve, populated by beings somewhat better equipped to deal with the problems of overpopulation and technology.

They, too, will ultimately fall, he says, to be replaced by an even more public-spirited and intelligent race of beings. This sawtooth pattern will continue, he theorizes, until a society finally emerges fully capable of long-term survival.

Harrison S. Brown, professor of geology at the California Institute of Technology, is less optimistic about the ability of successor societies to become technological. The easily accessible resources of this planet have been exhausted—the iron,

coal, copper, oil, etc. Hence he fears that those surviving a holocaust would be unable to build a new civilization such as our own.

### The Optimistic Side

The optimists, however, point out that the events of Tuesday night not only illustrated the weakness of our society but the marvelous ingenuity and adaptability of the human being. This, in fact, may prove to be the flaw in the argument of Hoyle. New Yorkers witnessed countless remarkable performances by their fellow citizens.

Young men, equipped by neighbors with white jackets made from bed sheets, wielded batons of rolled newspaper, directing traffic. Children, candles in hand, waited in apartment lobbies to lead those returning from work up the darkened stairways. The pushing, hurrying, competing of normal city life was laid aside as people worked to help one another.

This spirit of public service and cooperation in the face of common danger, so typical of wartime and other crises, may have roots in primeval fear instincts. Will mankind recognize the ultimate crisis in uncontrolled technological development? Or will profit-seeking, love of comfort and ultranationalism lead man down the road envisioned by Hoyle and Forster?

November 12, 1965

449

# Critic of Auto Industry's Safety Standards Says He Was Trailed and Harassed; Charges Called Absurd

**By WALTER RUGABER**
Special to The New York Times

DETROIT, March 5—A leading independent critic of the automobile industry has undergone an investigation of his affairs by private detectives.

The critic, Ralph Nader of Washington, has repeatedly charged that the car manufacturers are guilty of unsafe design. His attacks have helped generate a controversy over auto safety.

The investigators, working for unidentified clients, appear to have trailed Mr. Nader at different times in the last month and questioned a number of his friends.

In addition, Mr. Nader complained that he had received a series of harassing telephone calls and that women had sought to lure him into apparently compromising situations.

One of the men who conducted an inquiry said that while it was taking place, he found himself "tumbling over investigators all over the place."

## Report Is Supported

This report was supported by Vincent Gillen of New York, an attorney and detective, who said he had investigated Mr. Nader for an employment agency. Mr. Gillen said in a telephone interview:

"I've had reason to believe from what we saw and what we heard that other people were investigating Nader."

The detective said he had finished his inquiry.

Mr. Gillen called the employment agency he had worked for a "headhunter" but would not disclose its name. The detective maintains offices in Manhattan and Garden City.

Mr. Nader, the author of a scathing book entitled "Unsafe at Any Speed", has put the blame on industry for the inquiry. There have been no job discussions with anyone, he said.

Spokesmen for the major manufacturers in Detroit dismissed Mr. Nader's charge as ridiculous. Several indicated a belief that the investigation wouldn't be worth the trouble.

Mr. Nader said he believed the industry would order the investigation either to harass him or to impugn his standing before Congress and other opinion centers.

The critic, a 31-year-old bachelor who lives in northwest Washington, testified last month as a major witness before a Senate subcommittee investigating auto safety.

Mr. Nader lashed out at car design before the panel, headed by Senator Abraham A. Ribicoff, Democrat of Connecticut. Mr. Nader is expected to make another appearance before Congress when hearings begin on

President Johnson's measure to set nationwide safety standards for vehicles.

Many industry leaders deeply fear Federal standards because they believe Government regulation will lead to intolerable limitations on styling and performance.

Mr. Nader, an intense man, became interested in vehicle safety as a student and shows no signs of slacking off on what he considers a crusade.

## Attended Princeton

He was born in Winsted, Conn., where his father, a Lebanese immigrant, had established a restaurant and bakery. He attended Princeton University and the Harvard University Law School.

At Harvard, Mr. Nader was president of The Harvard Law Record and wrote a lengthy paper on unsafe auto design and its legal aspects.

For a short time after graduation, he worked as a research assistant to Harold J. Berman, a law professor at Harvard. He then spent six months in the Army.

Mr. Nader then traveled widely in Latin America, Europe and Africa, writing articles on a variety of subjects. He finally returned to Connecticut and started law practice.

Convinced of the national importance of safe design, Mr. Nader devoted more and more of his time to research on the subject and started getting in ouch with Government officials.

"Unsafe at Any Speed" was published last Nov. 30 by Grossman Publishers of New York. A spokesman there said about 20,000 copies had been sold.

Most of Mr. Nader's friends pictured him as a rather austere man who leads a Spartan life and spends most of his time working on various problems that interest him.

In late January, he said, he began receiving bothersome telephone calls at home despite his unlisted number. The callers were never obscene or abusive, he said.

"Mr. Nader?" a voice would inquire.

"Yes."

Then, suddenly, as if to a child:

"Cut it out now! Cut it out! You're going to cut me off I tell you! Cut it out!"

Then the connection would be broken. The other calls involved similar incidents. Mr. Nader believes they were made to harass him or to establish his whereabouts.

The telephone began to ring with increasing frequency, and on Feb. 9, the night before his testimony before Senator Ribicoff's committee, Mr. Nader said he received six calls.

They came as he was working on a statement to be read

the next morning. The calls continued until 4 A.M., he said, and as a result he overslept that morning.

On Feb. 11, the day following his appearance, Mr. Nader went to the National Broadcasting Company's television studios in the new Senate Office Building for an interview.

Two men followed him. They asked a guard for directions to the studio, described Mr. Nader and inquired whether he had gone in. The men waited outside the door.

Subsequent reports indicate they mistook a reporter for The Washington Post, Bryce Nelson, for Mr. Nader and began following him.

The mixup was discovered, but the Capital police came into the picture and an unidentified lieutenant ordered the two investigators to leave the building.

On Feb. 21, Mr. Nader flew to Philadelphia for another television interview and is positive he was shadowed, at least on the plane back.

He said he was late arriving at the plane but that men were in the waiting room though the craft was about ready to leave for Washington.

When he dashed for the ramp, Mr. Nader said, the two men followed him aboard. He said he managed to evade them at National Airport.

On the same day, Mr. Gillen conducted what appears to be the most extensive interview of Mr. Nader's acquaintances. The detective called on Frederick Hughes Condon.

Mr. Condon is assistant counsel and assistant secretary of the United Life and Accident Company of Concord, N. H. He was paralyzed in an auto crash, and Mr. Nader's book is dedicated to him.

Mr. Condon was reached at his home in East Andover, N. H., and said he had made notes and written a detailed memorandum of Mr. Gillen's visit.

The detective wore a sports coat and slacks and glasses with heavy, black frames, Mr. Condon said, and kept a tan attache case on his knees during the interview. The insurance company official said the investigator had asked about Mr. Nader's political beliefs and whether his ancestry had made him anti-Semitic.

Mr. Condon said Mr. Gillen had asked if there was any reason why Mr. Nader was not married. The insurance company official replied:

"Are you asking me if he is a homosexual?"

"Well, we have to inquire about these things," Mr. Gillen was quoted as having said. "I've seen him on TV and he certainly doesn't look like. . . . But we have to be sure."

Mr. Gillen confirmed in a tele-

phone interview that he had asked the questions and explained that an employer would want to know about such matters.

Despite such intimate questioning, Mr. Condon said he got the impression Mr. Gillen was most interested in a series of questions about Mr. Nader's driving record.

The insurance company official said the detective had asked three or four times whether Mr. Nader had a driver's license or whether he had ever seen Mr. Nader driving a car.

## An Important Job

The same question was raised on the same day in Lansing, Mich., by Frank Winchell, chief engineer for research and development at the Chevrolet Division of the General Motors Corporation.

Mr. Winchell, answering questions before a committee of the Michigan Senate, took a slap or two at Mr. Nader's biting criticism of General Motors in "Unsafe at Any Speed."

The engineer informed the Senators that Mr. Nader did not own an automobile and added that "I don't even know if he has a [driver's] license."

Mr. Condon, who said he had been told Mr. Nader was being considered for an important job assignment, said later he had been suspicious about the investigation.

Detectives interviewed more than half a dozen more friends of Mr. Nader. Some of these friends demanded complete identifications from the investigators, some did not.

Part of the inquiry appears to have been carried out by a detective agency in Boston. One person said he had been questioned by what he thought was a Washington-based agency.

Some of the interviews, such as one conducted with Mr. Berman at his office in Cambridge, were comparatively mild and involved only general questions about Mr. Nader's ability.

At a pharmacy on Feb. 20 and again in a supermarket on Feb. 23, Mr. Nader said he was approached by attractive young women in their 20's.

At the pharmacy Mr. Nader was leafing through an auto magazine when a woman apologized for being forward but asked if he would like to participate in a "foreign affairs discussion" at her apartment.

At the supermarket, where Mr. Nader said he was selecting a package of cookies, a young woman asked him for help in moving some heavy articles at her residence. Mr. Nader said that when he refused she did not ask anyone else for help although there were other men in the store.

Reliable sources within the auto industry report the existence at the major auto companies of an investigative apparatus for high-level security work.

Several big manufacturers are known to have a number of former agents of the Federal Bureau of Investigation in their employ, partly for counterespionage work on secret car designs.

### A Special Bureau

An informant at one company said it maintained a "special investigation bureau" that had contacts with police departments and private detective agencies.

The manufacturers that have such forces available also appear to use them for investigations into the backgrounds of executives they are considering for employment.

Mr. Nader has attacked other units of what he calls the nation's "traffic safety establishment" and one industry informant speculated that sources other than the manufacturers might have reason to be concerned about the young lawyer.

The establishment, as Mr. Nader defined it in his book, includes such groups as the American Association of Motor Vehicle Administrators and the National Safety Council.

The industry sources doubted a company would be responsible for the investigation of Mr. Nader, for several reasons. They all regarded its potential as limited. Also, one informant pointed out, "Think what a blunder it would be if a company was caught at it."

But the main point, in some instances expressed rather indignantly, was that the investigation of Mr. Nader appeared aimless and somewhat clumsily handled.

"You can bet that if one of us was doing it it would be a lot smoother," one source said. "If we were checking up on Nader he'd never know about it."

# G.M. Apologizes for Harassment of Critic

**By WALTER RUGABER**
Special to The New York Times

WASHINGTON, March 22 —The General Motors Corporation apologized today before a Congressional committee for investigating the private life of an outspoken advocate of safer cars.

James M. Roche, the company president, acknowledged that private detectives working for the concern had looked extensively into the personal affairs of Ralph Nader, Washington lawyer.

"I think there has been some harassment," Mr. Roche said.

He agreed with Senator Abraham A. Ribicoff, Democrat of Connecticut, that the General Motors inquiry was "most unworthy of American business."

Mr. Nader, author of a recently published book entitled "Unsafe at Any Speed," accepted Mr. Roche's apology. But he charged that the General Motors investigation had sought "to obtain lurid details and grist for invidious use."

The General Motors investigators questioned 50 to 60 of Mr. Nader's acquaintances and members of his family, today's testimony disclosed. The detective reports indicated the investigators asked about Mr. Nader's sex habits, political beliefs and attitudes toward Jews. The inquiry cost General Motors $6,700, an official testified.

Senator Ribicoff said he had read all the detective reports and that the investigators had failed to turn up anything detrimental to Mr. Nader.

"You and your family can be proud," Senator Ribicoff said. "They [the detectives] have put you through the mill and they haven't found a damn thing wrong with you."

Mr. Roche and Mr. Nader testified—both for the second time—before a Senate subcommittee that has conducted a year-long survey of traffic safety problems. Mr. Roche first appeared last summer. Mr. Nader was a witness last month and was under surveillance by the private detectives at the time.

In an opening statement at today's hearing, Senator Ribicoff said the "right to testify

freely without fear or intimidation is one of the cornerstones of a free and democratic society."

The Senator said it is "a crime to harass or intimidate a witness before a Congressional committee." Mr. Roche insisted that the General Motors investigation "was wholly unrelated to the proceedings of the subcommittee and Mr. Nader's connections with them."

With Mr. Roche at the witness table was Theodore C. Sorensen, former special counsel to President Kennedy and now a partner in the New York law firm of Paul Weiss, Rifkind, Wharton & Garrison.

Mr. Sorensen, holding a thin briefcase on his knees, sat silently throughout the appearance. The committee did not comment on his presence. He was hired yesterday as an adviser to Mr. Roche for his appearance.

The General Motors president said:

"This investigation was initiated, conducted and completed without my knowledge or consent, and without the knowledge or consent of any member of our governing committees. To say that I wish I had known about it earlier is an understatement, and I intend to make certain that we are informed of similar problems of this magnitude in the future."

Mr. Roche said he was "just as surprised and disturbed as all of you must have been" when he read on March 6 that Mr. Nader had been investigated.

"Two days later, in the process of ordering a formal statement denying our involvement, I discovered to my dismay that we were indeed involved."

General Motors then issued a statement, on March 9, admitting that it had ordered "a routine investigation . . . limited only to Mr. Nader's qualifications, background, expertise, and association" with attorneys suing General Motors.

That explanation provoked the sharpest questioning of the day. Senator Robert F. Kennedy, Democrat of New York, was particularly interested. He branded the statement "misleading and false."

### Inconsistency Conceded

Mr. Roche conceded that possibly the statement could have been "worded differently" and admitted it was "inconsistent" to the extent that it termed the investigation "routine."

Senator Kennedy brought the March 9 statement up again during the appearance of two General Motors lawyers, Aloysius F. Power, the general counsel, and Louis H. Bridenstine, the assistant general counsel.

Mr. Power got into an extended debate with Mr. Kennedy over whether the General

Motors statement was "correct." The company official finally admitted that "maybe we should have added the words, 'a routine investigation which developed into an intense investigation.'"

The Senator, in a quick series of verbal darts at Mr. Bridenstine, asked the lawyer if he "answered questions like this to Mr. Roche at General Motors."

"Now you remember that," Mr. Kennedy would say, or "you know what I'm talking about." Then the Senator called on the lawyers to be "completely candid . . . like Mr. Roche was."

### Jokes About President

The former Attorney General referred to the fact that the statement admitting the investigation was issued late at night. He said it reminded him of something his late brother had said about appointing him to the Cabinet.

"I'll open the door at 2 o'clock in the morning and say, 'It's my brother,'" Mr. Kennedy quoted the President as having said as a joke. The Senate Caucus Room, which was packed with spectators, laughed with the Senator.

Mr. Power explained to the committee that General Motors, the nation's largest industrial concern, was the defendant in 106 suits charging 1960 to 1963 Corvair automobiles with an unsafe rear suspension system.

Mr. Nader also had attacked the Corvair, Mr. Power said, and the investigation was undertaken to determine if the young critic had any connection with the suits.

General Motors ordered the investigation of Mr. Nader through a Washington lawyer, Richard G. Danner. Mr. Danner testified today that he in turn retained a New York private detective, Vincent Gillen, who is a former agent of the Federal Bureau of Investigation.

Mr. Gillen made frequent written reports as the investigation developed. Senator Ribicoff displayed a thick sheaf of them at the hearings.

### Shadowed in Capital

The investigation extended from mid-January to the end of February. Mr. Nader was shadowed by private detectives in Washington from Feb. 4 to Feb. 9. Mr. Gillen said the surveillance was discontinued "because it was not being very productive."

The detective reports were sent to Detroit periodically. Mr. Roche said there were "certain people on the legal staff [of General Motors] who were receiving these reports and knew the type of investigation that was being made."

Senator Ribicoff accused Mr.

March 6, 1966

Gillen of conducting a "smear" and Mr. Kennedy charged that the detective had carried out the investigation "as a lie."

"If you conduct an investigation in the open you don't get much information," Mr. Gillen asserted.

The personal questions asked by the detectives about Mr. Nader were held by General Motors to be part of the "pretext" of the investigation.

If investigators had asked questions solely about the Corvair design suits they would not have gotten very far, it was explained. So the detectives used the ruse that Mr. Nader was under consideration for a job.

Mr. Roche said the General Motors investigation "did not employ girls as sex lures, did not employ detectives giving false names, did not employ Allied Investigation, Inc. [a Washington detective agency], did not use recording devices during interviews, did not follow Mr. Nader in Iowa and Pennsylvania, did not have him under surveillance during the day [Feb. 10], he testified before this subcommittee, did not follow him in any private place, and did not constantly ring his telephone number late at night with false statements or anonymous warnings."

Mr. Nader had complained that he was approached by two young women in Washington, once in a supermarket and once in a drug store.

Both women invited him to their apartments, Mr. Nader reported, one to participate in a "foreign affairs discussion" and the other to help move some heavy furniture.

One of the people questioned by the investigators was Mr. Nader's stockbroker. He said he could not remember positively but that he thought the detective said he worked for Allied Investigation. Mr. Gillen disclosed today that part of the investigation was conducted by Arundel Investigative Agency of Saverna Park, Md.

A close friend of Mr. Nader's had said that when he was being interviewed Mr. Gillen held an attaché case on his lap. The detective said today that "it did not contain a recorder" but only "some paperwork."

"Surely," Mr. Nader told the Senators, "the questioning by private detectives of people who know and have worked with me as to my personal life in an attempt to obtain lurid details and grist for the invidious use and metastasis of slurs and slanders goes well beyond affront and becomes generalizable as an encroachment upon a more public interest."

Senator Ribicoff said he hoped today's hearing "will have a salutary effect on business ethics and the protection of the individual." He also asserted:

"There's too much snooping going on in this country."

March 23, 1966

# Society as a Learning Machine

## By JEROME B. WIESNER

E are living during one of history's most exciting periods — a dynamic time when man has almost limitless choices for good and for evil. We can make any kind of a world that man can agree upon, and if we don't learn to agree a bit better, man's days upon this planet may be numbered. I believe that this quarter century is likely to be the most decisive of any in man's long history for we are undergoing a test unlike any challenge man has ever faced before.

The dominant factor in the modern world is the mastery, albeit incomplete, that technology has given us over the physical world. There is growing suspicion, however, that the unanticipated side effects of new technology are causing more and more difficult problems that, in turn, require further expensive remedial actions. The population explosion, environmental pollution, and technology-induced unemployment are all examples of this problem. So too is the computer-created revolution in information processing that the world is now experiencing. In fact, the computer, with its promise of a million-fold increase in man's capacity to handle information, will undoubtedly have the most far-reaching consequences of any contemporary technical development. The potential for good in the computer, and the danger inherent in its misuse, exceed our ability to imagine.

Underlying all of this, I believe, is the fact that while most of us appreciate the individual creations of science for what they permit us to do, we do not really comprehend the fundamental change that the scientific revolution has brought about. We have actually entered a new era of evolutionary history, one in which rapid change is a dominant consequence. It will do no good to resent this, as many humanists do, or even to blindly fear the future as some others may. Our only hope is to understand the forces at work and to take advantage of the knowledge we find to guide the evolutionary process. Scientists and engineers, just as every other resident of this planet, are captives of the process that has been generated by the scientific revolution.

As man learns to apply his understanding of the physical world for practical purposes, he is substituting a goal-directed evolutionary process in his struggle against environmental hardships for the slow, but effective, biological evolution that produced modern man through mutation and natural selection. By intelligent intervention in the evolutionary process, man has greatly expanded the range of possibilities, but he has not changed the fundamental fact that it remains a trial-and-error process. This means that it is subject to the hazards of the evolutionary process, such as the danger of producing social dinosaurs unfit to live in the world that evolves.

A SOCIETY can be viewed as a giant learning machine, which, in principle, is not too unlike some of the more elaborate electrical systems that have been designed for recognizing patterns or solving mathematical problems. Trial and error are basic to technical and social change, but here the evolutionary process is not determined by chance as in the case of biological evolution. Man's intelligence intervenes and directs the process which remains, none the less, basically an experimental process. This view—which we at M.I.T. should call a cybernetic view of society since our late colleague, Norbert Wiener, did so much to introduce these concepts—points the way to interesting social science research and provides much common sense guidance in the planning of our affairs.

Any learning process requires feedback of information for a comparison of the accomplishment with goal. In a society there are always many goals. And on a few major goals there is general agreement — material well-being, individual identity, health, education and security.

SOME essential properties of a good learning system can be set forth. First, it should carry out experiments rapidly and, in general, this means many separate experiments going on simultaneously. Second, the response times of the communication channels should be rapid so that information about difficulties is transmitted quickly. Third, the error-detection system should be sufficiently sensitive to detect malfunction early in order to permit adjustments to be made quickly, before permanent harm is done.

In the economic sphere of a free economy, such as ours, when it is functioning properly, the profit motive encourages experimentation, and the feedback comes in the form of business success or failure. In those areas where individual initiative cannot respond to a problem—and more and more of these will arise as the population grows and the society becomes more complex—the feedback process performs less well. Many of the problems that worry us most are of this kind. There, research, education and effective communications are vital—research so that we have the knowledge available to make possible an early recognition of a potential problem; education so that the problem and possible solution can be agreed upon, and effective communications so that information can be transmitted with maximum speed and efficiency.

A poorly designed feedback system has a number of difficulties. If it is really bad, it can oscillate or hunt; that is, search violently around the correct position. The best way to correct this phenomenon is to build in a bit of prediction so that the behavior can be anticipated. The hunting can usually be stopped also by the brute-force method of just making the system do some work—by "loading" it. This slows it down and an adequate amount of loading will stop it from over-shooting. The only trouble is that it also becomes somewhat sluggish.

The economic system offers a very clear illustration of these phenomena. Not so many years ago our economic system hunted violently because of the lag betwen demand and the creation of capability to met it, resulting in periodic over-capacity. There is evidence that the widespread use of computers in industry has helped to keep supply and demand in balance and to regulate inventories and thereby has done much to dampen the oscillations that once plagued our economy. The heavy and progressive taxes instituted during World War II certainly have functioned as loading to further reduce oscillations.

**M**Y purpose is not to absolve either science or scientists as partial perpetrators of some of the ills of contemporary society. Nonetheless, the problems posed by scientific discovery will not disappear. The answer lies in gaining more understanding of the modern world based upon an integration of knowledge. Certain points stand out.

1. Our future is unfinished and unpredictable, and we must recognize that change will always be an integral part of our way of life. Only by accepting this aspect of our social evolution can we readily admit the need to modify or abandon plans, to change organizational and political structures, and to seek the best solution to a given problem.

2. One of our major areas of ignorance lies in the fields of human behavior and social organizations, and therefore we should encourage research in the behavioral and social sciences. The use of digital computers, both for processing the vast amounts of information inherent in many of these studies and for modeling the systems under investigation, offers the promise of a major breakthrough in research in social and behavioral sciences.

3. To find solutions to the problems of our environment, applied science, research and engineering—particularly of a systems engineering nature—are necessary. As the scale of human activities grows and becomes increasingly complex, the interaction between the individual parts becomes an even more important consideration. Here, too, one sees the need for more attention to the coupling between the various sectors of the society. The computer makes this feasible. First, because it is possible to gather and process the vast amount of information needed to understand what is going on. Second, the computer enables social scientists and economists to make models of many of the social problems that they want to study so that experiments completely impractical in the real world can be carried out on the models.

4. Human talents and abilities must be discovered and nurtured if coming generations are to continue to travel the road to effective participation in the world of the future, and our hope lies in better education for our youth. Here, too, the computer and other new information processing devices are certain to play an important role. For the teacher interested in improving educational methodology and for the computer expert seeking challenging and important problems, there is no more promising field.

Finally, our emphasis on material progress must be counterbalanced with greater attention to the nonmaterial goals of our society if we are to avoid being victims of our own good fortune.

**JEROME B. WIESNER,** Dean of Science at the Massachusetts Institute of Technology, served as science adviser to President John F. Kennedy. In his recent book, *Where Science and Politics Meet,* he examines the problems that governments face in meeting the challenge of modern technology.

# M'LUHAN'S VISION UNSETTLES P.E.N

### Canadian Urges Writers 'to Go to Control Tower'

**By HARRY GILROY**

Marshall McLuhan yesterday expounded at the International P.E.N. Congress on the alterations wrought in the writer's environment by the development of "electrical circuitry." The reaction of his audience of writers was generally both skeptical and scared.

Mr. McLuhan, the Canadian author and university professor, was the chairman of a panel discussion at the Loeb Student Center of New York University. It was the second day of sessions of the week-long P.E.N. (Poets, Playwrights, Essayists, Editors and Novelists) Congress.

Some of the 300 writers from around the world who heard Mr. McLuhan showed that they had read his book "Understanding Media: The Extension of Man." A program note pointed out that Mr. McLuhan argues in the book that "electrical technology has both narrowed the gap between thought and action and forced all humanity into immediate and intense social involvements."

Mr. McLuhan's remarks frisked over duplicating machines whereby "any reader can become a publisher," the computer with its "instantaneous retrieval system" and space capsules in which "the astronaut takes the planet with him in order to exist at all."

He likened the condition of the author in the electronic age to the astronaut in the space capsule.

Mr. McLuhan observed: "We are about to see an age where the environment itself is arranged as a teaching machine. The author is going to be engaged in programing the teaching machine."

There were some astonished murmurs as Mr. McLuhan developed this thought. Ivan Boldizsar, president of the Hungarian P.E.N. Center, said that he was "knocked out" by listening to Mr. McLuhan, just as he had been 30 years ago by the reading of Spengler's "The Decline of the West." He added, "I no longer feel knocked out by Spengler."

Mr. Boldizsar implied that after a while he would no longer feel knocked out by Mr. McLuhan's thoughts. The discussion circled around, but after a time it came back to Mr. Boldizsar, who said that Mr. McLuhan had sounded a note of doom for literature.

Mr. Boldizsar predicted that there would arise "a new type of writer, a craftsman in many fields, a renaissance type of writer. But such writers can

453

emerge only if writers resist the ideas of Mr. McLuhan, an obsessed man who is one of the nicest men I know."

Kathleen C. Nott, an English writer, said she too was haunted with a sense of doom in Mr. McLuhan's remarks. She said she was not sure whether the gathering was being told that there is not much future for writers or that "we must learn to love and live with the computer."

As the attack mounted on Mr. McLuhan, the author disclaimed any element of fatalism in his remarks. "To ignore the new devices is to put yourself in their fatalistic grip," he said. "Artists should go to the control tower not the ivory tower."

R. Buckmaster Fuller, the American engineer and author, supported Mr. McLuhan's thesis on the wide effects of new technology. "The dinosaur became extinct, he said, "because he carried everything with him—he had a one-ton tail to knock down a banana." Mr. Fuller added that each man in the United States now his in back of him about 30 tons of materials to extend his functions.

Unfortunately, he said, the new methods of communication are one-way and there is no way to answer back. "We must be coming to a point where we we will develop some two-way communications," Mr. Fuller said.

P. Tabori, the English writer, said that passive resistance was the course for the writer to follow when faced with the new machines. He spoke approvingly of a toy box that could be opened with pressure but all that happened when the lid was lifted was that a plastic hand came out and pulled the lid down again.

Haroldo de Campos, a poet from Brazil, said he agreed with Mr. McLuhan. He said that he and a group of friends had been writing concrete poetry since 1950. "The age of the literati is ended," he predicted.

Yves Gandon, a French novelist, said that after hearing Mr. McLuhan's remarks, "I was amazed, baffled and rather sickened." He hailed Mr. McLuhan as "a kind of mystic of the electrons," but indicated he was "scared" by the mysticism.

Books will not disappear, Mr. Gandon insisted. Television has not pushed out books in France, he said, noting that paperback sales there, as in the United States, had risen to great heights.

Tram Combs, an American poet from the Virgin Islands, said he disagreed with the statement of the Brazilian poet that men of letters were obsolete because of the new media. "Our problem is to see how we can best use the technological development" he said.

### Podhoretz Pokes Fun

Adolph Hoffmeister of Czechoslovakia conceded that people no longer dress for the opera but, instead, watch opera on television. And he agreed that the TV set had replaced the library in small apartments. But he insisted that even in a time of machines man has much need for art. Writers can still write he said "about love, the desire for money and human weaknesses."

Richman Lattimore, an American writer, observed "that a great deal of what is broadcast is what has been created by the writer in solitude."

Norman Podhoretz, the American critic and editor, said that he had been having trouble trying to get his electronic earphones to work during translations and he gibed that "Mr. McLuhan couldn't get his to work either." He also poked fun at Mr. McLuhan's "highly seductive" ideas.

Mr. McLuhan called on Pablo Neruda, the Chilean poet, to enter the discussions. In halting English Mr. Neruda said that "scientists have given us a Christmas Eve by opening the box of the universe." He said that there was a lack of union between science and literature.

Mr. Neruda said that he thought an airplane was beautiful when he first saw one in the sky when he was 10 years old, but that he had come to fear planes when he saw them drop bombs on Madrid. He added that he missed in the present time the feeling of warning against the dangers of mechanization that appeared in 19th-century humanist writing.

# Scientists Define Technology's Aims

Special to The New York Times

PASADENA, Calif. Oct. 28—Some of the nation's leading physical scientists and social scientists took time out this week to ponder the moral and social impact of their technological discoveries.

The scientists advanced some unorthodox proposals as to how to cope with fast-changing technologies.

Their observations were made at a special three-day convocation on Scientific Progress and Human Values marking the 75th anniversary of the California Institute of Technology. The meeting was attended by 124 delegates from universities and learned societies and by 1,500 students from Caltech and nearby institutions.

Speakers expressed disquiet about the applications of technology.

### New Direction Asked

Dr. Murray Gell-Mann, professor of theoretical physics at Caltech, said that society must give new direction to technology, diverting it from applications that yield higher productive efficiency and into areas that yielded greater human satisfaction. The "old drive" of science, he said, was to master, control and even destroy man's natural environment. The new drive, he continued, must be to create a richer and more satisfying life.

A symbol of this sort of change, he said, will occur when man no longer wants to channel resources into "building bigger, noisier aircraft" or when society decides to divert a new highway around a virgin forest rather than through it.

These sentiments were applauded by Carl Kaysen, director of the Institute for Advanced Study at Princeton, N. J., who emphasized that existing government institutions were no longer equal to the job of selecting and guiding the uses of technology.

"Technology is moving faster than our ability to assimilate it," said Dr. Simon Ramo, a prominent scientist and industrialist. Dr. Ramo urged the development of a new class of men called socio-technologists, who could "effectively link scientific developments with social betterment."

Science, he said, can provide many answers to improve the texture of human life, but scientists cannot persuade the public to utilize them. As an example, he observed that technology could provide a vastly more humane and efficient transportation system for sprawling Los Angeles, but only a new class of socio-technologists could persuade the public and the politicians to put that system into effect.

### 'Post-Industrial Society'

Dr. Daniel Bell, professor of sociology at Columbia University, said that these considerations were especially urgent in a "post-industrial" society such as the United States, where white collar workers involved in a service economy exceed the blue collar workers, who dominated the older manufacturing economy.

The sociologist argued that in this new post-industrial society the "scientific elite" functioned largely under the direction of the Government on projects the Government deemed important

This new "technical intelligentsia," he said, must "learn to question the politicians' often unanalyzed assumptions regarding efficiency," while the politician must become increasingly aware of the technical character of policy making.

Dr. Herbert J. Muller, professor of English and government at the University of Indiana, observed, "The popular American standards of material wealth and power or technological efficiency obviously won't do, since in these terms we are already by far the greatest society in history."

He continued: "The standard must be some civilized standard, involving moral, cultural, spiritual values, the kinds of achievements recognized in the broad agreement upon what were the great societies and the golden ages in the past. It requires value judgment."

In addition to debating the future applications of science, the convocation also heard some forecasts about the quality of human life from a panel of distinguished biologists.

Dr. James Bonner, professor of biology at Caltech, said that biologists were on the verge of finding a way to eliminate senility, thus facilitating a human life span of 200 years. Before long, he said, scientists will also be able to control reproduction, determine the most attractive life spans and, in general, direct the process of evolution.

Dr. Robert S. Morison, director of the Division of Biological Sciences at Cornell University, predicted that the family would suffer a great decline in prestige as society continued to grow more complex.

While the family is "a fine mechanism for transmitting conventional wisdom in a relatively static society," he said, "it is relatively poor at assimilating and transmitting new knowledge essential to survival in a rapidly moving world."

Dr. Morison said the growing awareness of the population problem and of human genetics would also "weaken the prestige of the family as the basic unit of human reproduction."

Finally, the biologist observed that "increasing knowledge in the plasticity of the human nervous system in early life will encourage further invasion of the home in the name of ensuring equality of opportunity."

Programs such as Operation Head Start, the Federal preschool training project for underprivileged children, represent a primitive example of this last trend, Dr. Morison said.

"It is idle," he said, "to talk of a society of equal opportunity as long as that society abandons its newcomers solely to their families for their most impressionable years."

# Man, The Mind-Making Animal

THE MYTH OF THE MACHINE. Technics and Human Development. By Lewis Mumford. Illustrated. 342 pp. New York: Harcourt, Brace & World. $8.95

### By EDMUND CARPENTER

WE know almost nothing about man's origins. Anthropologists don't always admit this to undergraduates, but among themselves, when they aren't trying to impress anyone, they acknowledge that we don't even know whether language dates from a million years ago, or half a million, or fifty thousand. There are lots of theories, but few facts — and the facts fit many theories.

It was once rather loosely believed that man was an alienated ape who, after becoming erect, commenced talking. This early walkie-talkie roamed several continents, producing pebble tools that remained nearly changeless for hundreds of thousands of years. Then, less than fifty thousand years ago, man burst forth with a plurality of tools and art.

Today it all seems far more complicated, largely as a result of new fossil discoveries, as well as the findings of ethnology and somatology. The long-standing ban on speculations on the origin of language, enacted because of lack of evidence, has been lifted, and intrepid scholars now venture back into this forbidden territory.

Lewis Mumford is by far the most audacious. In "The Myth of the Machine" he speculates on the full course of human development from the beginnings of ritual, language and social organization, down to Leonardo's inventions. There will be a sequel. History in the rough, full of gaps and irregularities, obviously disturbs Mumford. So he fills it in, insisting it "must have" happened this way. Perhaps it did. But reality often contradicts logic. He sees language emerging from a wordless but not soundless ritual, like Eliot's "The word within a word, unable to speak a word/Swaddled in darkness." This is plausible, but is it true?

Living evidence provides more interesting insights than speculations on the past. Alan Lomax, from the study of ethnic music, concluded that song is "danced speech." Bess Hawes found that the underlying principle in the songs of the Sea Islanders is the unheard beat — like an orchestra in which nobody plays the tune be-

MR. CARPENTER, an anthropologist who has worked in the Arctic, Borneo, Siberia and Micronesia, is the author of "Eskimo" and "Explorations in Communications."

cause everybody hears it. The underlying beat is a motor beat. The music is a dance executed while standing still.

Dreams, says Mumford, preceded speech. He believes they played a more important role in the lives of the ancients than in the lives of highly mechanized Western men. I wonder. On the face of it, dreams do appear very important in native life. Dream accounts are accorded great respect; there are rites of recitation and methods of interpretation. A day in an igloo begins, if no stranger is present, with dream recitals.

The point, however, of all this outward show is not that the inner dream life is so rich, but that private knowledge is feared. By making it public, weaving it into ritual, it becomes corporate. Dreaming itself, however, serves an even more indispensable psychic purpose than does dream-interpretation, and dreaming appears to be something that literate, mechanized man absolutely cannot do without. If subjects are carefully prevented from dreaming, then, no matter how much virtually dreamless sleep they get, they manifest emotional distress which increases as dream-loss continues.

Tribal Africans, however, are reported to require little sleep. It's only when they become 9-to-5 civil servants that they need eight hours a night. What they then need, of course, is dreaming, which means casting off the burden of isolating individualism and merging with cosmic powers. Natives achieve this experience of mystical participation in the cosmos through daily ritual, myth, dance and language. They go through the tribal dream wide awake. Detached, literate men, however, are dependent upon the dream proper as their only means of cosmic involvement.

I don't think it really helps to guess, as Mumford does, that dreams preceded language and were instrumental in its origin. The origin of language is largely unknowable, but language itself is everywhere available for study. Of course, what is closest at hand is often most difficult to see. Some of the California undergraduates I teach, especially the more intelligent ones, remind me, in their incapacity for formal speech, of Lancelot Andrewes's "The Word, and not to be able to speak a word." They either stand mute, with all the dumb pathos of inarticulate farm animals, or they stammer, their faces twisting, like aphasia victims. What's called illiteracy is not ignorance of meaning, but nonsensitivity to word arrangements.

Mumford is entitled to his speculations, but it turns out that these are really expectations. His entire account was written with a specific polemic purpose, which in fact has occupied him for years. His thesis is that man's relations with people (rituals) and particularly with himself (dreams) have always been more important than his invention of tools and his relations with machines. He feels we have overrated the part tools played in human development; that language, far more than tools, established human identity; and that man is pre-eminently a mind-making, self-mastering, self-designating animal.

Ethnology supplies unlimited evidence in support of this thesis. There is no such thing as a "primitive" language. People with only limited tools enjoy highly elaborate symbolic systems. Eskimo poems, Pygmy songs, Tsimshian carvings, are nowhere excelled, yet emerge from hunting cultures where machines are unknown.

Mumford finds much to admire in the tribal world. I'm with him there, of course. But other aspects, equally human, which are absolutely alien to everything he values, he either never sees or, in the case of the retribalized electronic world, he makes no effort to understand.

For 40 years he has criticized societies that mass-produce people and goods alike, and urged a return to joyful common toil, where no man is a stranger, afraid in a world he never made. If he has been naive, he has nonetheless been constructive. But in "The Myth of the Machine," he is dogmatic, petulant and out of date: "The present failure to use the words 'good' and 'bad,' 'higher' and 'lower,' in judging conduct, as if such differences were unreal, and such words nonsensical, has brought on a total demoralization of behavior." This is just an old man annoyed with his grandchildren.

To be out of date was once the mark of aristocracy and scholarship. Today no one can afford the luxury of being outmoded. Mumford's time-lag is brief but fatal: he fails to distinguish between the mechanical world of segmentation and sequence, and the electronic world of unity and simultaneity.

The Beats made this same error when they rejected all technology, including the electronic, which they mistook for machine. As soon as they recognized electricity as a means of human extension, they became Hip, and the Beatles walked on stage

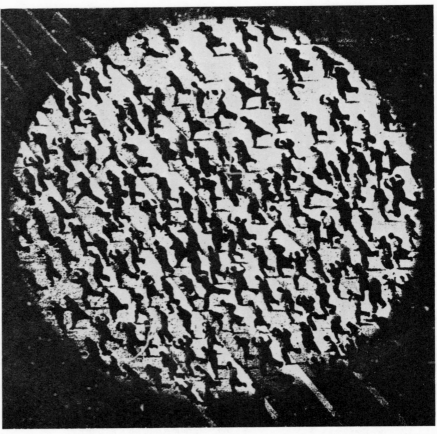

Detail from painting by Juan Genoves. Courtesy Marlborough-Gerson Gallery.

dragging their electronic muscles behind them. Electricity created Beautiful People and Flower Children in harmony with the cosmos.

One might expect that Mumford, who belongs to the Romantic school of organic sentimentality, would delight in this switch. But he neither recognizes nor likes what he sees. When he was young, Mumford did some hard thinking and came up with a mirage of a happy village community, so organic as to be almost medieval. He cannot bear to give it up. Nor will he give up his hostility toward the machine. He doesn't realize that electricity is not just another machine: it is antimachine. It makes machines obsolete. It's more organic than anything. It unites everyone.

A few weeks ago I attended an Eskimo conference held at El Siesta Motel located between a highway beanery and a drive-in on the outskirts of Winnipeg. A young Eskimo recited several poems, but instead of the traditional "Here I stand/Humble with outstretched arms . . . ," he began: "I drink, I smoke, I swear/I make love freely . . . ." He was the first Eskimo hippie I had met.

Recently a friend told me that when his plane was forced down in a remote part of the Arizona desert, a Navaho woman emerged from her *hogan* mud hut lugging the gasoline he needed. She knew all about credit cards. Like the rest of us, she had become a member of the biggest tribe ever.

Getting involved in the electronic world is probably easier for an Eskimo or Navaho than it is for mechanized man. The Eskimo simply switches tribes, but Western man must both accept an alien electronic world and give up a familiar mechanical one.

Mumford is at his best in describing the mechanical world, which began with writing, as an invisible architecture of the mind, and was then translated into a social structure, composed of rigid human parts, each a specialist in a great collective organization. This was the megamachine from which all mechanical machines derived. You can have mass production and mass achievement without machinery if you have enough labor. The Egyptians built the pyramids without machinery and the Romans mass-produced books by using teams of scribes. Where

fertile land produced large labor forces, all that was needed was organization to harness this for major production. Writing provided that organization. From it came "civilization," including the myth that the machine was absolutely irresistible and ultimately beneficent. In his love-hate affair with the machine, Mumford fails to see that just as the machine originated with literacy, so it disappears with literacy.

Anthropologists tend to dismiss armchair speculators as men who prefer not to live with the savages they love. I think this is unfair. Mumford just never penetrates the barrier of literacy. If he ever achieved an eyeball-to-eyeball confrontation with real tribesmen, whether in New Guinea or Haight-Ashbury, I think he would find them more vital than any hypothetical tribesmen.

We are all blind to the immediate, to the human reality. To understand the young and ourselves, we must understand both the mechanical world we have left and the electronic world we are entering. "Life can only be understood backward," observed Kierkegaard, "but it must be lived forward."

April 30, 1967

# Epitaph For An Age

### By JOSEPH WOOD KRUTCH

SOME years ago one of my acquaintances dropped in upon an aging professor of entomology at the University of Arizona. The old gentleman, who was at the moment pinning bugs in a museum case, looked up and exclaimed: "You know, I can never get over my astonishment that I get *paid* for doing this." In a way I share his feeling. For the most part I have been engaged in pursuits that only a small minority of our population would be willing to pay me for following, and yet society (perhaps just because it was too busy and too prosperous to pay attention to what was happening) has somehow maintained me in modest comfort while I made very little effort to please it.

I have been tormented by many anxieties, but most of them were needless. I have suffered no great tragedies, conspicuous failures or public disgraces. On the contrary, I have had and got much more of what I have wanted than most people have or get. Never having been insatiably ambitious or even normally aggressive, I am not wholly dissatisfied with my unspectacular achievements. I wanted to be a writer and I wanted even more to have an interesting life—in the sense that I myself would be usually interested in it. Both of these hopes have been fulfilled at least to the extent that I ever seriously hoped they would be.

From a purely selfish standpoint I have, therefore, no reason to complain about the world I live in. And yet, despite my feeling that my own existence has been, for me, a success, the world of my day has moved pretty steadily in directions that I find distressing.

Most men of my age feel, I suppose, that the world is going down the wrong road. I certainly do. It isn't that I am politically or economically a reactionary. On the contrary, I go along with most of the liberal and welfare legislation. But in another respect I find the world I live in increasingly alien. Those aspects of the physical world that make me happiest are certainly disappearing as a result of industrialization, exploding population and urban sprawl. To my mind, New York has become almost a horror; Arizona, vastly less attractive than it was 15 years ago. The latter's willingness, its eagerness even, to cloud once pure air with smog, to expand two cities in a most helter-skelter way, to be greedy for money at the expense of most other contributions to the good life, is typical of the country as a whole, and public figures, who once seemed to set themselves against all this, yield to political necessity and come out in favor of it.

To me it seems that most of my fellow citizens are crassly and cynically materialistic while most of the intellectual minority, which one might expect to oppose them, is nihilist—interested chiefly in destruction and violence, in nonart, nonmusic and nonpainting. Philosophy is bent on destroying itself as it becomes logical positivism on the one hand and verbal analysis on the other. The persons who appear most likely to shape the future are the scientists and technologists who tend to agree that all the culture of the past is irrelevant, and that the world should, and soon will, be a science-fiction writer's dream. Thus the physical, intellectual, esthetic and moral world in which I want to live seems to be disappearing.

The death wish is perhaps among the more dubious creations of psychoanalysis. Although some people do seem to seek self-destruction, the notion that it is an element in all men is harder to demonstrate. But a case could certainly be made out for the contention that modern man as a race has the death wish. Otherwise he would not be marching so resolutely toward literal extinction. But what impresses me most is not this wish for literal death in individuals or in society, but the desire for another sort of death that manifests itself so consistently in man's thoughts about himself. Can anyone deny that for at least a hundred years we have been prejudiced in favor of every theory, including economic determinism, mechanistic behaviorism and relativism, that reduces the stature of man until he ceases to be man at all in any sense that the humanists of an earlier generation would recognize?

I AM not unaware that I enjoy many conveniences and comforts unknown only a generation or two ago. I realize also that if it were not for recent advances in hygiene and medicine, I would probably be dead. And yet, although I consider this last fact a boon so far as I am concerned, I am not sure that it is such for mankind as a whole. The population increase is responsible for a number of the other developments I deplored in the preceding paragraphs, and a curious characteristic of our society is the antithetical attitudes of the two major sorts of intellectuals. Scientists and technicians tend to be optimistic and to predict a glorious future. The most esteemed and perhaps the most talented writers portray the present as ghastly and absurd and they can have little hope for the future since the source of their despair is not economical, political or technological but what they regard as the radical meaninglessness of the universe and, therefore, of human life.

Some will, no doubt, insist that this difference in mood means merely that science and technology represent the maturity that intellectuals of the other sort are unwilling or unable to understand or to face. But although I do not share the view of the universe held by so many contemporary intellectuals, I find it hard to believe that technology will be applied successfully to the solution of what seems to me the most serious of the threats to a better (or even a reasonably good) life for the future. I am ready to believe that smog, pollution, the horrors of war, and so forth *could* be controlled by technology just as the population explosion could be controlled by the means already at hand. But I see little indication that any of these things will be done since mankind as a whole, so bold in its attack upon the problems of achieving more speed, more power and more wealth, is very timid in its attack upon any of the other problems — partly, no doubt, because any such attack seems unfavorable to the increase of speed, of power, of wealth, or sometimes of all three. People demand high-speed automobiles no matter how dangerous, and economists tell us that our prosperity will collapse if we do not maintain sales by giving people what they want. Thoreau said "one world at a time," but we would spend billions on an attempt to go to the moon while being very careful

JOSEPH WOOD KRUTCH, the well-known essayist and former drama critic, now a resident of Arizona, has written extensively about nature and man's place in it. This article, reprinted from the summer number of The American Scholar, is the 50th in a series he began for that journal in 1955.

not to pay the price of pollution control—especially any price that includes outraging those most responsible for pollution. We have a crash program for getting to the moon, but there are always people of influence to urge slow-moving caution when it comes to regulating any of the forces that are destroying the healthfulness as well as the beauty of our country.

Tennysonian optimism — "O, yet we trust that somehow good/Will be the final goal of ill"—is very old-fashioned indeed in terms of what Tennyson was hoping for. But it is precisely what technologists say in their different way when faced with the threats they have created. Sometimes they go even so far as to be sure that "somehow good" will be the final goal of atomic fission, although, so far, it seems the greatest disaster of modern times. And it takes a faith at least as strong and as gratuitous as Tennyson's to believe that.

SECURITY depends not so much upon how much you have, as upon how much you can do without. And that is true for society as well as for the individual. Every technological advance is also a hostage to fortune. And the more we teach adjustment, group activity, getting along with the group, and so forth, the less any individual is prepared for the time, so likely to come in any man's life, when he cannot or will not call upon group support. Ultimate security for him depends upon the ability to stand alone or even just to be alone. Belonging is fine. But to belong to anything except oneself is again to give a hostage to fortune.

Many of those who do profess a faith in the somehow good would be willing to grant that the benefits of what they call progress are often not entirely unmixed, that we make one step backward for two steps forward as when, for example, automobiles pollute the air and good roads destroy the charm of the countryside. In other words, the Emersonian law of compensation works in reverse. For every gain there is a loss, and to me one of the most depressing aspects of this truth is the fact that a moral step forward seems so often to be accompanied by another step backward.

Most of us are shocked and almost incredulous when we read how common it was throughout most of history for armies to pillage and massacre whole populations as, for example, the Crusaders are said to have done when they captured Jerusalem. Quite a long time ago we stopped regarding things like that

as normal procedure. We don't put the inhabitants to the sword, anymore. Or rather we don't when we can see them face-to-face. But, of course, military necessity often compels us to do the same sort of job quite as effectively from a few thousand feet up, although the man who drops the bomb can't see his victims in the way a Crusader saw the woman or child through whose body he thrust his sword. This seems to me a wonderful example of committing one of the oldest sins in the newest kind of way, and I do not see how the most enthusiastic proponents of the theory that technological advance is an unmixed blessing can deny that only technology has permitted us to put a city to the sword without quite realizing what we are doing.

Not only technology but much of the so-called science of man seems to be leading us toward less and less interest in and less and less awareness of that inner life of which only the imaginative writer now seems to recognize the importance or even the existence. If the extremists are right and consciousness is a mere epiphenomenon, then we may gradually lose it and become, in fact, that man wound up like a watch which Thomas Henry Huxley said he was willing to become. Something like that may just possibly be what happened to the insects when they became so efficient that they no longer needed to think, even at the level of the lower organisms, and became, instead, efficient machines with, perhaps, no consciousness at all. Perhaps the obsession of the avant-garde with violence and unreason is a desperate effort to retain a hold upon something violent enough to prevent the lack of awareness.

THE fact that I have led a reasonably satisfactory private life in a world that I find increasingly unsatisfactory raises in an unexpected way the whole problem of free will or, in more concrete terms, the question of whether or not man is, as he tends increasingly to believe, controlled by forces outside himself. My own paradox—a satisfactory life in an increasingly unsatisfactory world —suggests to me a kind of answer.

I think that man is free to make those choices that can be made without reference to the way in which society is evolving, but that neither he nor, perhaps, collective humanity can resist the tendency of society to be molded by processes man cannot control.

When Emerson said that things are in the saddle and ride mankind, he

did not mean that we must let them do so. But that is exactly what the Marxists do mean when they talk about society as the product of evolving technology, and I think that there is a good deal of truth in the contention. A Thoreau can go to Walden Pond and (as he said) refuse to live in the bustling 19th century. But he could not have prevented the 19th century from bustling.

The paradox is somewhat like that of the unpredictable atom and the predictable behavior of any large aggregate of atoms. We can predict with a considerable degree of accuracy how many people will go to the seashore on a day when the temperature reaches a certain point, even

AT THE GRAND CANYON—The author photographed for an N.B.C. TV special, "Grand Canyon: A Journey With Joseph Wood Krutch."

how many will jump off a bridge. And although I am not, nor are you, compelled to do either, the statistics show that the group considered as a whole—like the group of atoms in a physical object—must obey the laws it does not formulate. That is why I believe that, although man's individual potentialities are much greater than commonly assumed today, he will probably not realize most of them, at least in any near future.

I THINK that I understand quite well what Natalie Barney wrote to Marguerite Yourcenar' in a letter of which a fragment was recently published. It translates something like this:

"I tell myself that you are lucky to have lived during an epoch when the idea of pleasure was still a civ-ilizing idea (which today it no longer is). I am especially pleased that you have escaped the grip of the intellectuals of this half century; that you have not been psychoanalyzed and that you are not an existentialist nor occupied with motiveless acts; that you have on the contrary continued to accept the evidence of your understanding, your senses, and your common sense." ■

*July 30, 1967*

# PICCARD DOUBTS MAN CAN SURVIVE

## Calls Technology 'Suicidal' and Pollution 'Tragic'

### By VAL ADAMS
Special to The New York Times

HOBOKEN, N.J., Nov. 14—Dr. Jacques Piccard, the oceanographer, said here today that he was "seriously doubtful" that man would still exist in the 21st century because of the dangers of technological progress and nuclear destruction.

"This technology we 'enjoy' today is litle else but a widespread suicidal pollution," Dr. Piccard said. "It is a blight affecting not only the air we breathe and the water we drink, but also the land we till and the outer space we hardly know."

"But most tragic of all, he added, "we now have the pollution of man in his body by insidious chemical products."

As for nuclear bombs, the scientist said he found it difficult to imagine that man could "play" with them forever without starting a war.

"The orientation of man's intelligence in this matter could not be worse," he said, "for unfortunately he is clever enough to build atomic weapons, but he is not clever enough not to use them."

### Others Less Pessimistic

Dr. Piccard spoke at a symposium on "Man in the 21st Century" sponsored by the Stevens Institute of Technology, which is holding a centennial convocation as it approaches its 100th anniversary in 1970.

Some of the other speakers also expressed concern about man's future, but offered more hope that problems could be overcome.

"Technology is working against man," said Dr. Piccard, "Man is working against nature and instead of natural selection, only technology remains."

Dr. Piccard asserted that the individual's interest was nearly always in conflict with the community's interest.

For example, he said, "When a physician keeps old people alive or when society establishes homes for the mentally ill, for the blind or similarly handicapped, they do not help humanity; they only help individuals, which is just the way to make mankind older and weaker."

### Adaptability Stressed

Dr. Albert Szent-Gyorgyi, director of the Institute for Muscle Research at the Marine Biological Laboratory, Woods Hole, Mass., and a Nobel prize winner, said that by the end of this century man "probably will have in hand all the essential factors of life."

"This new world demands an entirely new political, social and economic structure and thinking — new human relations," he said. "Our future, including our physical future, depends on the question how far we can adapt to the new conditions and keep alive in it."

During a morning symposium on "The Physical Man," Robert D. Lilley, president of New Jersey Bell Telephone Company, and the Very Rev. Malcolm Carron, president of the University of Detroit, said they believed man would overcome technological excesses and survive in the 21st century.

The Rev. Theodore M. Hesburgh, president of the University of Notre Dame, participated in an afternoon symposium on "The Philosophical Man." He called for a "unity of knowledge," which he said meant using all scientific and technological information to benefit all mankind, "not just for the people in the United States or th northern hemisphere."

*November 15, 1967*

# Make a Million? Not Interested, Youths Contend

### By VIRGINIA LEE WARREN

"I'D LIKE to be a millionaire, but I wouldn't want to spend my life getting there," said a 17-year-old Stuyvesant High School senior, Ira Myers, of Howard Beach, Queens.

"Most people who have a million have to spend their time trying to look after it and keep it," noted Charles Binder, 17, in his last year at Jamaica High School. The youth, who lives in Jamaica, Queens, added that after a certain point having more money loses its meaning.

"I don't want to be devoting my life till I'm 50 trying to make a lot of money," said Joel Lustig, 17, of Brooklyn, also a senior at Stuyvesant High. "If I don't have a million, I'll enjoy better whatever money I do have."

Are these typical American youths who are giving the great put-down to what has long been considered an American dream: becoming a millionaire?

### New York Attitudes Are Typical

According to a nationwide survey recently completed by the Youth Research Institute, the answer is yes. These New York boys could have been speaking pretty much for their counterparts in the rest of the country.

The percentage of today's high school seniors throughout the nation who see any point in bending all their energies toward amassing a million is only about 5 per cent, the survey, conducted by Lester Rand and based on 1,251 interviews, showed.

If the question had been, "Would you like to have a million dollars handed to you?" the result might have been different; what the boys made plain was that they did not want to concentrate on making the million. They believe, as the architect Mies van der Rohe said in another context, that "less is more."

Fourteen years ago, the Youth Research Institute conducted a similar poll and found that more than 14 per cent of those queried would be willing, even eager, to work toward a million.

While the present nationwide percentage of those indifferent to making a million is approximately 95 per cent, among the dozen 17-year old high school seniors queried here it turned out to be 100 per cent.

Economic and social backgrounds seem to have had almost nothing to do with their convictions. Although the 12 boys questioned go to two high schools with quite lofty scholastic standards—every student at Stuyvesant goes on to college and 80 per cent of those at Jamaica do—they represent a fairly wide spectrum.

### $40,000 a Year Would Be Fine

Richard Cantor of Rego Park, for instance, said that in his family there are a number of doctors and that he plans to study medicine. In terms of present monetary values, he thinks that $40,000 a year would be fine when he is in his late 30's or early 40's; that it would be enough to take care of the children he hopes to have, the two cars he wants and the house he wants in upstate New York, or, perhaps, Canada.

On the other hand, Clifford Barnes of Corona, who is in Jamaica High as part of the College Discovery Program, for disadvantaged youngsters, said rather shyly and after a good deal of thought, that he would be satisfied to make around $20,000.

Asked about cars, he decided that one car "would be nice." A degree in business administration is his goal; then he hopes to become an executive and to live not too far away from his present home. (All six boys at Stuyvesant, none of whom lives in Manhattan, hope to leave New York City.)

Clifford could have been speaking for all 12 when he said:

"The important thing is to get a job you can be interested in. I don't want to look forward to retirement; if you lose a job you lose a part of your life."

May 3, 1968

# Life Begins Anew With a 2d Career

### By DAMON STETSON

A California aeronautical engineer, fed up with the pressures and red tape of his big company, quits his job and goes back to the university to become a teacher. A Navy commander in his mid-40's retires from service and decides to become an Episcopal priest. A Staten Island teacher, described as tremendously competitive, leaves teaching to sell commercial real estate in Manhattan.

In today's affluent society, interlaced with critical social problems, such mid-course career changes appear to be increasingly common.

The patterns of mid-course career changes are too varied to be precisely defined, but the trend appears to be clear.

The current affluence, manpower shortages in many fields, changing technologies, earlier retirement, the availability of training and education — all are factors influencing men and women in all walks of life to reassess their futures and perhaps take a new tack in a more challenging and satisfying career.

"The two-career life, like the two-car garage, is beginning to become a part of the American scene," said Frank Coss, vice president in charge of research for Deutsch & Shea, specialists in manpower and personnel.

### Technology a Factor

Prof. Allan H. Stuart of the School of Continuing Education at New York University, cited the technological developments in such areas as computer programming and systems analysis as factors promoting change.

"It's amazing to see the parade of men between 35 and 50 who come in wanting to change jobs," he said. "Some of them feel obsolescent and want to be updated. Others have become financially stable, their kids are out of college and they're looking for a more exciting, more stimulating job for their later years."

Dr. Victor Fuchs of the National Bureau of Economic Research also observed in an interview that in a prosperous, full-employment economy, career change is more feasible and less of a risk than it used to be.

The reasons for these changes are diverse and complex. In some cases, men in their 40's become frustrated with dead-end jobs, realize that they will never become president of the company, editor of the newspaper or the top account executive. They decide to kick over the traces, get out of the "rat race" and try something they have always wanted to do.

## Women Active, Too

In addition, thousands of women are entering the marketplace to take new jobs as the demands of their families lessen — and to help put their children through college.

But for others the motive for a career change is more altruistic. Many, for example, have turned to jobs involving service to others—such as the Peace Corps or the International Executive Service Corps, which sends executives — both active and retired — to foreign countries to provide management skills for struggling businesses.

In 1964, William Dretzen was general manager of the Queensboro Motors Corporation, at that time the largest Volkswagen dealership in the United States, with annual sales of nearly $5-million.

"I was well rewarded," he said recently, "but somehow I felt it didn't matter in the bigger scheme of things. I felt that at some point everyone should put his life where his mouth is."

He recalled that both he and his wife were caught up in the "Kennedy mystique" and wanted to do something for their country and for people. Because of these strong feelings he gave up his job at the end of 1964 and joined the Peace Corps in March, 1965, at a fraction of his former salary.

Mr. Dretzen, his wife and three daughters went to the Cameroons in Western Africa. They returned to the United States last August. The executive, who is 42 years old, is now special assistant to Miss Josephine Nieves, regional director of the Office of Economic Opportunity.

"My wife and I feel strongly," he said, "that our Peace Corps experience was the most satisfying and at the same time the most frustrating experience we've ever had. It got us involved and we still are."

Some men motivated by a desire to be of greater service to a generation faced with critical social problems shift their career focus drastically but stay in the same occupational area.

John U. Monroe, former dean of Harvard College an-nounced in March, 1967, that he was resigning to devote full time to the education of struggling students at Miles College, a small Negro institution in Birmingham, Ala.

The 55-year-old educator emphasized at the time that he did not want anyone to think he was making a great sacrifice.

"I see it as a job of enormous reward," he said.

The position a man takes after he leaves college may provide a good income, but prove uninspiring and dull.

Frederick Byrne, 49, father of six children, was for years a successful salesman of men's and boy's underwear, but he never could get enthusiastic about his job. "I never really cared," he said. "It seems to me you ought to be imbued with a love for your product and the process of selling it. I wasn't."

Six years ago Mr. Byrne was elected a trustee of the public library in Mount Kisco, where he lives. He became interested in library operations and eventually decided he preferred library work to selling.

He had made enough money so he could take time out to spend a year at the Columbia University School of Library Services. He is now assistant librarian at Columbia's Graduate School of Business Administration.

## The Psysical Aspect

Men often tire of a job, find its physical demands excessively arduous, and look to new and potentially profitable fields.

Peter Karavitis, now 51, bought a vending-machine business in the Westchester area eight years ago. He has been working with 30 service clubs in the area and has placed candy machines in locations throughout Westchester and Dutchess counties. The clubs cooperating with him have received 20 per cent of the sales — amounting to more than $35,-000 a year.

Mr. Karavitis grew tired of the constant travel involved in the vending-machine business, but felt sure the many contacts he had made would be valuable in a new job. He is now in the process of selling his business and expects to go to work soon for a well-known stock brokerage house.

"I never thought that I would be able to do this," he said. "I've always been interested in stocks and I know I'm going to like the new job."

Dr. John E. Bourne, assistant dean of the School of General Studies at Columbia University, declared in an interview that half the career opportunities available today did not exist 20 years ago.

With such changing work and economic patterns, he said, many people become interested in new careers that appear more attractive, but that require further training or education.

"As a result of modern communications," he said, "people tend to dream a little more than they used to. And because of the general affluence, many are secure enough to get by for a year or two while they prepare for another career.

"These people are not escapist, they're venturesome and idealistic, a little dissatisfied but setting superior goals for themselves."

Dr. Bourne, who has been in charge of the New Careers Program at the School of General Studies, reels off a list of examples of career shifts to service occupations:

David Felix, a former financial writer and public-relations man who has completed courses at Columbia for a Ph. D. in history, is writing his dissertation, and is teaching history at Bronx Community College; A woman who had worked in radio and advertising who is now studying art and plans to teach; a trans-Atlantic airline pilot, now 31 years old, who took pre-medical courses at Columbia while still flying and is now in his second year of medical school.

Morton Feren, president of Marshall Leeman & Co., specializing in executive career advancement, said the least of the reasons for major job changes was money.

'It's frustration as much as anything," he said. "It's lack of opportunity for promotion, lack of recognition."

He cited a young Amherst graduate with an outstanding academic record who went into department-store work. By the time he was 33 he was merchandising manager for one of the city's largest stores, but as an ambitious individualist with many independent ideas he was not happy.

After consultations with Mr. Feren, he decided he would do better and be happier in his own enterprise. He is now running an importing business.

The early retirement age of police and firemen and men in the military services has been particularly conducive to a second career, made more secure of course, by a substantial pension.

Dominick DeLorenzo, 46, is a retired fire captain from Roslyn Heights, L.I. He had always had an interest in history and after retiring he entered Columbia's New Careers Program. He is now a full time student, working for his Ph.D. and planning a second career as a history teacher.

James J. Quinlivan, now 47, spent 21 years in the New York City Police Department, working mostly on traffic problems and safety enforcement. He retired last October.

He had no desire to vegetate in a rocker, so began immediately to look for a job. He answered an advertisement and got a position with the Long Island Rail Road as a clerk coordinating reports on personnel expenses and overtime charges.

"I don't make quite as much money as I did in the Police Department," he said. "but there are fewer tensions and I'm glad I made the switch."

Prof. Alan Gartner, of the New Careers Development Center at New York University, said that the poor and even the jobless are finding new lives as service agencies are established and old ones restructured.

He told of a mother who became a teacher-helper; a jobless young man who became an aide at a neighborhood service center, and a man who assisted in the Head Start program for pre-school children.

"The areas of greatest economic growth are clearly going to be in service areas," Professor Gartner said. "This means new types of jobs."

Van M. Evans, vice president of Deutsch & Shea, said that in today's generally wealthy society the risk has been taken out of most second career ventures.

"People use to worry about security," he said. "today they are open to adventure. They're looking for challenge and job satisfaction. They'll take risks and chances because they figure they can get another job tomorrow anyway."

# Advertising: How, and Why, to Retire at 47

**By PHILIP H. DOUGHERTY**

It came as quite a surprise when Neal O'Connor, the young chief executive of N. W. Ayer & Son, said he gave himself only about five more years in the job. He was going to have to move on to make way for the young tigers coming up, he said. And he said it at age 42.

Mr. O'Connor is of the opinion that any agency that wants to keep up the competitive pace of today's business world will need a boss that can "continually breathe contempory, innovative thinking into an agency."

"Any person in the top seat at, say, age 40," he said, "who intends to keep the reins until Social Security time will automatically eliminate much of the incentive for all of the talented people around him, for those who are coming up fast in the organization or for those who might otherwise be attracted to the company from the outside."

●

How's that for an interesting thought—kicking yourself out of a job before you're 50?

Well, anyhow, the idea, which came up during a casual conversation, seemed interesting enough to pass along for comment to some of the other new, young top executives in the business at such well-known shows as Ogilvy & Mather, Young & Rubicam and Grey.

At Grey last year, Richard S. Lessler became chairman at 43 and Edward H. Meyer, president at 40. Yesterday both seemed in general agreement with the Ayer president, but not necessarily with his timetable. Dick Lessler saw "the pressures of young talent in all business pushing upward," not just the ad game.

●

Ed Meyer, who said that "running an agency requires the health, vigor and flare of youth," thought that if agencies diversified into broader divisions, the talents of the older hands could be used, but if they stayed as they are, "working at the same frenetic pace," retirement age would probably end up in the mid-fifties.

And the agency business is not one particularly noted for early retirement. Ayer's Harry Batten, for example, died in harness at 69, and the late Stanley Resor of J. Walter Thompson didn't retire till he was 81. Thompson's mandatory retirement age of 60 goes into effect in 1971.

Even that comparatively low age must seem pretty far away to James R. Heekin, now only 41, who became president of Ogilvy & Mather at 39. He thought Mr. O'Connor's five-years-and-out plan "unnecessarily skeptical." The Ogilvy president agreed that there were more and more good people coming up. But, he said, today there are more places to use them as agencies become more decentralized.

Then he offered an interesting thought of his own, which for want of a better title we can call the Sardi's concept. Since, he said, most folks in the business agree that the most efficient agency to operate is billing $100-million, why not split up the bigger ones? That would mean in one town there'd be Thompson East, Thompson West and even North, South and South by Southeast.

When Stephen O. Frankfurt, the 36-year-old president of Y. & R.-U.S., was asked what he thought of Neal O'Connor's thoughts, his first comment was, "I'm too young to ask," but then he added, "I would have to disagree, you can't make a rule or a generalization. It depends on the guy."

As to the future of the early-retired ad executive, both the men at Grey mentioned public service and government service.

Mr. Lessler's own philosophical comment was, "people are now going to retire to something rather than away from something."

As for Mr. O'Connor, who sparked all this, he already has his plans made. "What I'd like to be," he said, "is the consultant who goes in and patches up agency-client relationships when they're in trouble."

Meanwhile, let's hope he doesn't get too much practice.

September 4, 1968

# Does Human Nature Change In a Technological Revolution?

**By KENNETH KENISTON**

SINCE the beginning of terrestrial history, man has been subject to nature. Last year ended with a feat that symbolizes the central revolution of our time: man's growing control over nature. Men have for the first time sped beyond the gravity of this earth, looked down upon our distant, spinning globe and asked in sudden mockery if this planet harbored life.

This escape from the pull of the earth symbolizes a revolution in human life and consciousness as profound as any before it. The Copernican revolution removed man from the center of the universe, and the Darwinian revolution deprived him of his unique position as not-an-animal. Today the technological revolution is depriving man of both the security and the constraint that came from subjugation to nature in its given visible forms.

## Old Reins Are Off

Man is learning to understand the inner processes of nature, to intervene in them and to use his understanding for his own purposes, both destructive and benign. Increasingly, the old reins are off, and the limits (if any) of the future remain to be defined.

But what of man himself? Do the constraints of human nature still apply? How will the change in man's relationship to nature change man? No one can answer these questions with assurance, for the future of humanity is not predestined but created by human folly and wisdom. Yet what is already happening to modern men can provide some insight into our human future.

If there is any one fact that today unites all men in the world, it is adaptation to revolutionary change in every aspect of life—in society, in values, in technology, in politics and even in the shape of the physical world. In the underdeveloped world, just as in the industrialized nations, change has encroached upon every stable pattern of life, on all tribal and traditional values, on the structure and functions of the family and on the relations between the generations.

## Rate of Change Rising

Furthermore, every index suggests that the rate of change will increase up to the as yet untested limits of human adaptability. Thus, man's relationship to his individual and collective past will increasingly be one of dislocation, of that peculiar mixture of freedom and loss that inevitably accompanies massive and relentless change.

As the relevance of the past decreases, the present—all that can be known and experienced in the here-and-now—will assume even greater importance. Similarly, the gap between the generations will grow, and each new generation will feel itself compelled to define anew what is meaningful, true, beautiful and relevant, instead of simply accepting the solutions of the past. Already today, the young cannot simply emulate the parental generation; tomorrow, they will feel even more obliged to criticize, analyze, and to reject, even as they attempt to re-create.

A second characteristic of modern man is the prolongation of psychological development. The burgeoning technology of the highly industrialized nations has enormously increased opportunities for education, has prolonged the postponement of adult responsiblities and has made possible an extraordinary continuation of emotional, intellectual and ethical growth for millions of children and adolescents.

In earlier eras, most men and women assumed adult responsibilities in childhood or at puberty.

## Prolonged Childhood

Today, in the advanced nations, mass education continues through the teens and

462

for many, into the twenties. The extension of education, the postponement of adulthood, opens new possibilities to millions of young men and women for the development of a degree of emotional maturity, ethical commitment and intellectual sophistication that was once open only to a tiny minority. And in the future, as education is extended and prolonged, a ever larger part of the world population will have what Santayana praised as the advantages of a "prolonged childhood."

This will have two consequences. First, youth, disengaged from the adult world and allowed to question and challenge, can be counted on to provide an increasingly vociferous commentary on existing societies, their institutions and their values. Youthful unrest will be a continuing feature of the future.

### Greater Complexity

Second, because of greater independence of thought, emotional maturity and ethical commitment, men and women will be more complex, more finely differentiated and psychologically integrated, more subtly attuned to their environments, more devel-

oped as people. Perhaps the greatest human accomplishment of the technological revolution will be the unfolding of human potentials heretofore suppressed.

Finally, in today's developed nations we see the emergence of new life styles and outlooks that can be summarized in the concept of technological man. Perhaps here the astronauts provide a portent of the future. Studies of the men who man the space capsules speak not of their valor, their dreams, or their ethical commitments, but of their "professionalism and feeling of craftsmanship," their concern "with the application of thought to problems solvable in terms of technical knowledge and professional experience," and their "respect for technical competence."

The ascendancy of technological man is of course bitterly resisted. The technological revolution creates technological man but it also creates two powerful reactions against the technological life style. On the one hand it creates, especially in youth, new humanist countercultures devoted to all that technological man minimizes: feeling, intensity of personal

relationships, fantasy, the exploration and expansion of consciousness, the radical reform of existing institutions, the furtherance of human as opposed to purely technical values.

### Three-Way Contest

On the other hand, technological change creates reactionary counterforces among those whose skills, life styles and values have been made obsolete. In the future, the struggle between these three orientations — technological, humanistic and reactionary — will inevitably continue. Technological man, like the technology he serves, is ethically neutral. The struggle for the social and political future will therefore be waged between those who seek to rehumanize technology and those who seek to return to a romanticized, pre-technological path.

Much of what will happen to men and women in the future is good—or if not good, than at least necessary. Yet it may not be good enough. The revolution over nature has already given men the capacity to destroy tenfold all of mankind, and that capacity will be vastly multiplied in the future. And many

of the likely future characteristics of men — openness, fluidity, adaptability, professional competence, technical skill and the absence of passion—are essentially soulless qualities. They can equally be applied to committing genocide, to feeding the starving, to conquering space or to waging thermonuclear war.

### Ethic Required

Such qualities are truly virtuous only if guided by an ethic that makes central the preservation and unfolding of human life and that defines "man" as any citizen of this spinning globe. So far, the technological revolution has neither activated nor extended such an ethic.

Indeed, I sometimes feel that we detect no life on any of the myriad planets of other suns in distant galaxies for just this reason. I sometimes fear that creatures on other planets, having achieved control of nature but lacking an overriding devotion to life, ended by using their control of nature to destroy their life.

In this regard, the future of man remains profoundly uncertain.

*Dr. Keniston is associate professor of psychology at the Yale University Medical School.*

January 6, 1969

# *Study Terms Technology a Boon to Individualism*

By WILLIAM K. STEVENS
Special to The New York Times

CAMBRIDGE, Mass.—Modern technology, far from crushing and dehumanizing the populace, has made Americans the most genuinely individual people in history, a Harvard-based corps of scholars is concluding after the first four years of a 10-year appraisal.

The group holds that technology has created a society of such complex diversity and richness that most Americans have a greater range of personal choice, wider experience and a more highly developed sense of self-worth than ever before.

"This is probably the first age in history in which such high proportions of people have felt like individuals,"

Dr. Emmanuel G. Mesthene, executive director of the Harvard University Program on Technology and Society, has written in the program's fourth annual report.

"No 18th-century factory worker, so far as we know, had the sense of individual worth that underlies the demands on society of the average resident of the black urban ghetto today," he said.

But there is another side of the story, too, as expressed by Prof. Edward Shils, a sociologist from the University of Chicago and England's Cambridge University, who is one of the program's researchers.

Professor Shils makes the point that the individual's new self-assurance has led him to make bolder and

more aggressive demands on governments at a time when the decline of authority and the sheer complexity of problems have made governments less self-confident than ever.

The result is an increased "probability of public disorder," according to Professor Shils, who cites this paradox:

"The social order which is made possible through the growth of individuality, and which I regard as one of the greatest accomplishments of our modern Western civilization, is simultaneously also endangered by the growth of the individuality which it has made possible."

Making sense of today's intricate society, and dealing effectively with its prob-

lems, may well require an expertise that most citizens don't have, Dr. Mesthene said in an interview a few days ago. He wrote in the annual report:

"If it turns out on more careful examination that direct participation [by the citizenry at large] is becoming less relevant to a society in which the connections between causes and effects are long and often hidden — which is an increasingly 'indirect' society, in other words—[then] elaboration of a new democratic ethos and of new democratic processes more adequate to the realities of modern society will emerge as perhaps the major intellectual and political challenge of our time." the 48-year-old Dr. Mesthene—

463

who started out as a college philosophy teacher and worked for 10 years as a "think-tank" economist for the Rand Corporation in Santa Monica, Calif. —heads what is said to be the nation's most comprehensive study of technology's impact on society.

His annual report, which contains the program's first summation of preliminary findings, is being distributed to 3,000 businessmen, professors, government officials and other interested individuals.

Under a $5-million grant from the International Business Machines Corporation, the program has awarded research stipends to more than 50 scholars at 11 universities, including Harvard, Columbia, Yale and the Massachusetts Institute of Technology.

In governing the nation, Dr. Mesthene said in the interview, it may well be essential to rely heavily on an emerging group of "technocrats": persons trained in the computer-based analysis techniques needed to sort out the complexities and subtleties of a rapidly evolving and highly interdependent society.

But he declared that making these "expert decision-makers" accountable to the citizenry posed a major problem. In his view, the rise of the expert analyst and decision-maker places a heavier burden of citizenship on the individual than before; that is, the ordinary citizen must learn more and work harder at his public role—almost as hard as he does at his private career—if he is to understand what the technocrats are doing.

### Individual Compromise

Each individual, he wrote in the annual report, must strike a balance "between his commitment to private goals and satisfactions and his desires and responsibilities as a public citizen.

"The citizens of ancient Athens seem to have been largely public beings in this sense, while certain segments of today's hippie population seem to pursue mainly private gratifications," he added.

Dr. Mesthene sees a rising tension between the expert technicians in government and those who want a direct voice in public policy but who are not equipped with the necessary science-based analytical skills. He acknowledged in the interview that this posed a crucial and continuing dilemma.

"If you go the full way of the technocratic élite you'll wind up with a technocracy. But if you go the way of those who want full participation you'll wind up with chaos.

"The question is how to take advantage of the knowledge necessary to run a big, complex society without giving up the values of participation. The answer we're looking for is a third way. We haven't found it yet."

The Program on Technology and Society operates from a three-story brick house tucked away on Kirkland Street just off Harvard Square. I.B.M. provided the money to install it there and finance its research, a company official said, in the hope of fostering an understanding of technology's impact so that its negative effects may be contained and its positive effects promoted.

In the year ahead the program's research will emphasize the effect of technology on the daily life of the individual and will continue its exploration of technology's impact on values. Before its work is finished in 1974, the program will have examined the interaction of technology with what its participants regard as the major phases of American life.

The impact of technology on society has become a subject of systematic scholarly inquiry largely since 1960, although there were earlier, scattered inquiries about narrow aspects of the matter. It is widely conceded that few solid conclusions of a general nature have emerged.

Technology, as defined by Dr. Mesthene in the annual report, is "the organization of knowledge for practical purposes." This includes tools in a general sense—not only machinery, but also contemporary tools of language, mathematics and analysis.

Dr. Mesthene described what he considered to be three fashionable, but distorted and "unhelpful,"-views of technology's role today.

One view sees technology as the villain of the age; an uncontrollable Frankenstein's monster that will ultimately reduce men to ciphers and ruin their environment.

A second sees technology as the engine of all progress, the solver of most of the nation's problems, the ultimate savior of America.

The third holds that technology as such is not worthy of special notice because it has been well recognized as a factor in social change at least since the Industrial Revolution and its unsettling effects are no greater now than then.

Each view contains a measure of truth, Dr. Mesthene concluded, but all are too uncritical and too one-sided to guide inquiry. Technology brings about both negative and positive effects inseparably intertwined, he argued, and those effects are profound.

The negative effects include diminished privacy, feelings of impotence in the face of "the machine," pressures to conform to the system, the crush of the cities, environmental pollution, and the social upheaval caused by automation.

On the other hand, Professor Shils is finding in his work for the program that the technological society has given the individual a greater range of choices than ever before in consumer behavior, picking a spouse, choosing an occupation, deciding where to live, and forming attachments to friends and groups.

The head of the faculty committee associated with the Mesthene program says that the complexity of society has resulted in an "increasing relegation of questions which used to be matters of political debate to professional cadres of technicians and experts which function almost independently of the democratic political process." The committee head is Dr. Harvey Brooks, dean of Engineering and Applied Physics at Harvard University.

Although the nature of the transformation wrought by technology is still unclear, wrote Donald A. Schon, president of the Organization for Social and Technical Innovation, it seems to be expressing itself in a series of basic shifts:

"From product to process, from component to system and to network, from static organizations (and technologies) to flexible ones, from stable organizations to temporary systems, to ways of knowing capable of handling greater informational complexity, from stable, substantive values to values for the process of change."

A hallmark of the current technological phase is the heightened importance and heavier flow of information, notes Prof. Alan F. Westin of Columbia University.

If information technology reaches the full potential claimed for it, he wrote, it could well lead to an era in which people and institutions rise and fall according to how adept they are at using the "information pools" of the "data-rich" society.

Prof. Karl W. Deutsch of Harvard sees the United States as moving from its present era of "half-technology," in which only some parts of the economy are dominated by the technology of the electronic age, to a coming age of "high technology" that will be distinguished by a much higher level of "intellectualization"—that is, a heavier, richer and more complex flow of information.

In an illustration offered by Dr. Mesthene, the mixed positive and negative aspects of technology can be seen in an aspect of the information revolution: mass communications, which has given "great benefit to education, journalism, commerce and sheer convenience."

"It has also been accompanied by an aggravation of social unrest, however," he went on, "and may help to explain the singular rebelliousness of a youth that can find out what the world is like from television before home and school have had the time to instill some ethical sense of what it could or should be like."

### 'Changes in Values'

Technology has a "direct impact on values by virtue of its capacity for creating new opportunities," Dr. Mesthene observed. "By making possible what was not possible before, it offers individuals and society new options to choose from."

The creation of new options in this way "can lead to changes in values in the same way that the appearance of new dishes on the heretofore standard menu of one's favorite restaurant can lead to changes in one's tastes and choices of food," he wrote.

Commenting on investigations by Dr. Harvey G. Cox, the Harvard divinity professor and author of "The Secular City," Dr. Mesthene wrote that technology was largely responsible for "the pluralism of belief systems that is characteristic of the modern world," and that religion must come to terms with this.

"The generation of knowledge and the use of technology are so much a part of the style and self-image of our own society that men begin to experience themselves, their power and their relationships to nature and history in terms of open possibility, hope, action and self-confidence," he continued.

"The symbolism of such traditional religious postures as subservience, fatefulness, destiny and suprarational faith begin then to seem irrelevant to our actual experience. They lose credibility, and their religious function is weakened."

As technology advances, Dr. Mesthene wrote, it usually changes the shape of society through a fairly well-defined sequence:

A given technological advance enables society to achieve some previously unattainable goal. If the new opportunity is to be taken advantage of, alterations in social organization are necessary.

As a consequence, the functioning of existing social structures is interfered with. And finally, goals served by the earlier social structure become somewhat neglected.

An example cited by Dr. Mesthene was medical care, in

which dramatic new lifesaving treatments and techniques force the medical profession to become more specialized and to concentrate its best efforts in a few major urban centers.

Consequently, the earlier system of general practitioners is weakened. Many persons are thereby deprived of the "medical general manager" and their everyday level of medical care suffers.

Studies by a group headed by Prof. Richard S. Rosenbloom of Harvard's Business School concluded that "existing institutions and traditional approaches are by and large incapable of coming to grips with the new problems of our cities," many of which are caused by technological change, and are "unable to realize the possibilities for resolving them that are also inherent in technology."

Dr. Mesthene offered several examples of this: failure to provice low-cost housing, increasing difficulty in controlling crime, intensified difficulties in education.

He mentioned a soon-to-be-published study by Prof. Anthony Oettinger of Harvard that says that computerized instruction — which is believed by some to make genuinely individualized learning possible for the first time—is likely to be stymied by the "institutional rigidity" of school systems.

"Human fallibility and political reality are still here to keep utopia at bay," Dr. Mesthene wrote, "and neither promises soon to yield to a quick technological fix."

He asserted that private corporations, organized for private profit, were not motivated or geared to deal with social problems, even the ones industry itself helps to create—environmental pollution, for instance.

These difficulties "are with us in large measure because it has not been anybody's explicit business to foresee and anticipate them," Dr. Mesthene wrote, and are a direct consequence of an unrestrained technological individualism much like the unrestrained economic individualism of pre-New Deal days.

The difficulties are traceable much less to "some mystical autonomy" presumed to lie in technology by such thinkers as Lewis Mumford, Jacques Ellul and Herbert Marcuse, Dr. Mesthene wrote, "and much more to the autonomy that our economic and political institutions grant to individual decision-making." He stated flatly:

"The negative effects of technology that we deplore are a measure of what this traditional freedom is beginning to cost us."

# Consumer Indignation

## Not Only Fly-by-Nights, but Big U.S. Companies Are Accused of Deception

### By PETER MILLONES

American business and many segments of government are being peppered these days with criticisms and questions from those who see themselves as defenders of the "consumer interest."

The consumer movement, infused with a growing number of restless youths, is now hoping to bring to public life what Prof. Richard Hofstadter said the Populists brought to it 80 years ago —"a capacity for effective political indignation."

*News Analysis*

That indignation is apparent almost daily as individuals or groups offer what they feel is evidence that corporations or their executives, often abetted by a silent government, are undermining the public interest.

Last week Robert M. Morgenthau, the United States Attorney here, said that "white-collar crime," like stock fraud and tax evasion, was becoming more prevalent—even though much was going undetected—and was encouraging crime by the poor.

#### Corporations Accused

More frequently the charges are that corporations, through deception or fraud, are inducing the public to buy products that are either overpriced or unsafe or poorly made, or all of these things.

The National Commission on Product Safety, for example, has pointed to, among other things, the widespread sale of children's toys that are dangerous because of certain chemical characteristics or because they are flammable, pressurized or radioactive.

Another example, only last week, was the request to the Interstate Commerce Commission by another Government agency that the license of Safeway Trails, Inc., an interstate bus company, be suspended for its alleged violation of one safety regulation more than 6,000 times in the last nine years.

(Why the I.C.C., which first accused the bus line of violations in 1960, had not acted despite allegedly repeated violations has added to the strong skepticism with which consumer advocates view the role of some regulatory agencies.)

#### Confusing Packaging Cited

In the area of deception, many consumers have long felt that manufacturers of goods sold in supermarkets have deliberately packaged products in a confusing array of ways, so as to defeat any reasonable efforts to compare prices. New York consumer officials are near endorsing a requirement that supermarkets clear up the confusion by more complete price labeling, a move that is said to be gathering support in other cities.

With these various abuses becoming more visible to the public, which is probably more alert now because inflation has forced consumers to watch their dollars more closely, there appears to be a growing willingness to see merit in Ralph Nader's argument:

"Consumers are being manipulated, defrauded and injured, not just by marginal businesses or fly-by-night hucksters but by the U.S. blue-chip business firms whose practices are unchecked by the older regulatory agencies."

#### New Doubts Raised

This view has startled the business community, which has long contended that abuses and dishonesty are the result of practices of only a few unscrupulous firms.

But Congressional and other hearings on drug hazards, auto safety, discriminatory credit practices, price-fixing and the disinclination of some businesses to sanction money-saving innovations have raised new doubts in many minds, consumer advocates believe.

What is perhaps most important now to the consumer movement is the indication that an increasing number of "sober types" are being attracted to Mr. Nader's views. This is not really surprising, since it is just as likely that the affluent, as well as the poor, will be victimized by unsafe household products and cars, and whose children will play with unsafe toys.

This indignation is also swelling among the young who are not a part of the student radical movement but who see the need for reforms in society. Thus Mr. Nader has attracted a large group of college youths, many of them law students, to help him investigate this summer various facets of American industry.

#### Moralistic Approach

These youths, and others, are bringing to the consumer movement a moralistic approach that does not consider it sufficient for a corporation to conduct its affairs legally if its ethics are open to question.

It is not an accident that much consumer legislation has been labeled "truth-in. . . ."

An additional reason the consumer movement appears to be swelling is that the movement has embraced efforts to fight air and water pollution and to protect natural resources. These are all areas in which industry has been on the defensive, even though many of its executives have been vigorous personal supporters of conservation.

In short, the movement appears to be attracting wider public attention as it espouses a philosophy along the lines stated by Bess Myerson Grant, the city's Commissioner of Consumer Affairs:

"We don't have to accept economic forces which we do not understand, which we did not create and which we cannot control. We need not surrender our social and physical environment to the vast corporate and political bureaucracies, which now too often stand beyond any meaningful public accountability."

## America: Learning to Relax

**By ANTHONY LEWIS**

LONDON, Nov. 9—A civilized Briton with much experience of the United States returned from an American lecture tour the other day struck by the tenacity of our dedication to the Protestant ethic — the notion that hard work is an aspect of Godliness. He found himself explaining to a Utah audience, he said, that the regular working day is a fairly recent invention and that life may offer alternatives.

Another British visitor, writing in the magazine New Society, regrets that America is so immune to decadence. He defines decadence in a non-pejorative way, a very English way, as a slightly weary sense of human limitations—not expecting much of oneself and charitable to others in their inadequacy or mere human difference.

### Intolerance and Hostility

No doubt we are less tolerant than the English of indolence and eccentricity. This must be one reason why the current youth phenomena arouse such violent reactions in middle America—the hatred and brutality explored in Dennis Hopper's film, "Easy Rider." And not only in the movie: Hopper has described the hostility met by the long-haired actors in the small towns where they did the filming.

The kids are getting something for nothing: that seems to be the objection. Money, pleasure, sex. We had to work for it. Why don't they?

### Signs of Change

But it is misleading to talk of these attitudes as if they were frozen. A little travel in the United States is enough to convince one otherwise. Things are changing.

Movies themselves are indicative. Middle-class, middle-aged people may be hostile to long hair and pot; they may complain at the lack of "good family pictures." But the lines are outside the theaters showing "Easy Rider" and "Alice's Restaurant." Along with the hostility there is clearly a certain amount of envy, sexual and otherwise.

Or take marijuana, that symbol of turning off, of rejecting the materialist society. Polls show an overwhelming majority of Americans still opposed to its use, but someone seeing the country after a long absence finds the change in attitudes toward marijuana amazing.

The Nixon Administration, after all, has proposed a reduction in the disproportionate criminal penalties—a step altogether unlikely even a few years ago. The Wall Street Journal has said that "marijuana use seems about as serious a crime as, say, public drunkenness." Time magazine has published a sympathetic essay on the problem.

Time is itself a symptom of change in middle-class America. In the old days the editors gave us their collective absolute truth about every subject they touched, sneering at those who differed. Now the certainties are gone; there is a tentative, insecure quality, as there is in American life.

It is not just the young, with their restless questioning. Something is moving deep under the conventional surface of politics and the economic struggle.

More Americans are growing skeptical of the Protestant ethic. They see that affluence is not enough, that it need not bring tranquility or fulfillment. They see that as it enlarges man's hopes, it may wither his surroundings.

### Utopia Needs Rules

And so they doubt the old values of work and ambition and progress, but they are not sure what to put in their place. The moral of "Alice's Restaurant" is that a Utopian communal life, without striving and without rules, does not bring peace or happiness either.

At the same time there are other Americans bitter because they have not reached the stage at which they can take affluence for granted. They are the black poor, turning in on themselves. And they are the white families worried about inflation and taxes, resentful of those who do not work.

### Disillusioned With System

What these elements have in common is a disillusionment with the way the American system is working. The viewpoints are totally different, but together they give an impression of social ferment that will sooner or later explode politically. The question is whether the result will be an angrier America or one more relaxed and charitable.

Michael B. Sadicario is a New York taxi-driver still under the magic age of 30. When another cab cut in front of him the other day, he did not shout.

"You take a driver like him," he said. "He's not relaxed. He's thinking about money. He's not going to listen to music all day. Another cab tries to take seventeen feet from him, and he goes crazy.

"I used to work in an office. I worked hard, but no one cared. Now I let my hair grow, and I wear dungarees. Last summer I went up to Woodstock."

*November 10, 1969*

---

## A Friedman doctrine—

# The Social Responsibility Of Business Is to Increase Its Profits

### By MILTON FRIEDMAN

**W**HEN I hear businessmen speak eloquently about the "social responsibilities of business in a free-enterprise system," I am reminded of the wonderful line about the Frenchman who discovered at the age of 70 that he had been speaking prose all his life. The businessmen believe that they are defending free enterprise when they declaim that business is not concerned "merely" with profit but also with promoting desirable "social" ends; that business has a "social conscience" and takes seriously its responsibilities for providing employment, eliminating discrimination, avoiding pollution and whatever else may be the catchwords of the contemporary crop of reformers. In fact they are—or would be if they or anyone else took them seriously—preaching pure and unadulterated socialism. Businessmen who talk this way are unwitting puppets of the intellectual forces that have been undermining the basis of a free society these past decades.

The discussions of the "social responsibilities of business" are notable for their analytical looseness and lack of rigor. What does it mean

---

**MILTON FRIEDMAN** is a professor of economics at the University of Chicago.

to say that "business" has responsibilities? Only people can have responsibilities. A corporation is an artificial person and in this sense may have artificial responsibilities, but "business" as a whole cannot be said to have responsibilities, even in this vague sense. The first step toward clarity in examining the doctrine of the social responsibility of business is to ask precisely what it implies for whom.

Presumably, the individuals who are to be responsible are businessmen, which means individual proprietors or corporate executives. Most of the discussion of social responsibility is directed at corporations, so in what follows I shall mostly neglect the individual proprietor and speak of corporate executives.

IN a free-enterprise, private-property system, a corporate executive is an employe of the owners of the business. He has direct responsibility to his employers. That responsibility is to conduct the business in accordance with their desires, which generally will be to make as much money as possible while conforming to the basic rules of the society, both those embodied in law and those embodied in ethical custom. Of course, in some cases his employers may have a different objective. A group of persons might establish a corporation for an eleemosynary purpose—for example, a hospital or a school. The manager of such a corporation will not have money profit as his objective but the rendering of certain services.

In either case, the key point is that, in his capacity as a corporate executive, the manager is the agent of the individuals who own the corporation or establish the eleemosynary institution, and his primary responsibility is to them.

Needless to say, this does not mean that it is easy to judge how well he is performing his task. But at least the criterion of performance is straightforward, and the persons among whom a voluntary contractual arrangement exists are clearly defined.

Of course, the corporate executive is also a person in his own right. As a person, he may have many other responsibilities that he recognizes or assumes voluntarily—to his family, his conscience, his feelings of charity, his church, his clubs, his city, his country. He may feel impelled by these responsibilities to devote part

of his income to causes he regards as worthy, to refuse to work for particular corporations, even to leave his job, for example, to join his country's armed forces. If we wish, we may refer to some of these responsibilities as "social responsibilities." But in these respects he is acting as a principal, not an agent; he is spending his own money or time or energy, not the money of his employers or the time or energy he has contracted to devote to their purposes. If these are "social responsibilities," they are the social responsibilities of individuals, not of business.

What does it mean to say that the corporate executive has a "social responsibility" in his capacity as businessman? If this statement is not pure rhetoric, it must mean that he is to act in some way that is not in the interest of his employers. For example, that he is to refrain from increasing the price of the product in order to contribute to the social objective of preventing inflation, even though a price increase would be in the best interests of the corporation. Or that he is to make expenditures on reducing pollution beyond the amount that is in the best interests of the corporation or that is required by law in order to contribute to the social objective of improving the environment. Or that, at the expense of corporate profits, he is to hire "hardcore" unemployed instead of better-qualified available workmen to contribute to the social objective of reducing poverty.

In each of these cases, the corporate executive would be spending someone else's money for a general social interest. Insofar as his actions in accord with his "social responsibility" reduce returns to stockholders, he is spending their money. Insofar as his actions raise the price to customers, he is spending the customers' money. Insofar as his actions lower the wages of some employes, he is spending their money.

The stockholders or the customers or the employes could separately spend their own money on the particular action if they wished to do so. The executive is exercising a distinct "social responsibility," rather than serving as an agent of the stockholders or the customers or the employes, only if he spends the money in a different way than they would have spent it.

But if he does this, he is in effect imposing taxes, on the one hand,

and deciding how the tax proceeds shall be spent, on the other.

This process raises political questions on two levels: principle and consequences. On the level of political principle, the imposition of taxes and the expenditure of tax proceeds are governmental functions. We have established elaborate constitutional, parliamentary and judicial provisions to control these functions, to assure that taxes are imposed so far as possible in accordance with the preferences and desires of the public—after all, "taxation without representation" was one of the battle cries of the American Revolution. We have a system of checks and balances to separate the legislative function of imposing taxes and enacting expenditures from the executive function of collecting taxes and administering expenditure programs and from the judicial function of mediating disputes and interpreting the law.

Here the businessman—self-selected or appointed directly or indirectly by stockholders—is to be simultaneously legislator, executive and jurist. He is to decide whom to tax by how much and for what purpose, and he is to spend the proceeds—all this guided only by general exhortations from on high to restrain inflation, improve the environment, fight poverty and so on and on.

The whole justification for permitting the corporate executive to be selected by the stockholders is that the executive is an agent serving the interests of his principal. This justification disappears when the corporate executive imposes taxes and spends the proceeds for "social" purposes. He becomes in effect a public employe, a civil servant, even though he remains in name an employe of a private enterprise. On grounds of political principle, it is intolerable that such civil servants—insofar as their actions in the name of social responsibility are real and not just window-dressing—should be selected as they are now. If they are to be civil servants, then they must be selected through a political process. If they are to impose taxes and make expenditures to foster "social" objectives, then political machinery must be set up to guide the assessment of taxes and to determine through a political process the objectives to be served.

This is the basic reason why the doctrine of "social responsibility" involves the acceptance of the socialist view that political mechanisms, not market mechanisms, are the appropriate way to determine the allocation of scarce resources to alternative uses.

ON the grounds of consequences, can the corporate executive in fact discharge his alleged "social responsibilities"? On the one hand, suppose he could get away with spending the stockholders' or customers' or employes' money. How is he to know how to spend it? He is told that he must contribute to fighting inflation. How is he to know what action of his will contribute to that end? He is presumably an expert in running his company—in producing a product or selling it or financing it. But nothing about his selection makes him an expert on inflation. Will his holding down the price of his product reduce inflationary pressure? Or, by leaving more spending power in the hands of his customers, simply divert it elsewhere? Or, by forcing him to produce less because of the lower price, will it simply contribute to shortages? Even if he could answer these questions, how much cost is he justified in imposing on his stockholders, customers and employes for this social purpose? What is his appropriate share and what is the appropriate share of others?

And, whether he wants to or not, can he get away with spending his stockholders', customers' or employes' money? Will not the stockholders fire him? (Either the present ones or those who take over when his actions in the name of social responsibility have reduced the corporation's profits and the price of its stock.) His customers and his employes can desert him for other producers and employers less scrupulous in exercising their social responsibilities.

This facet of "social responsibility" doctrine is brought into sharp relief when the doctrine is used to justify wage restraint by trade unions. The conflict of interest is naked and clear when union officials are asked to subordinate the interest of their members to some more general social purpose. If the union officials try to enforce wage restraint, the consequence is likely to be wildcat strikes, rank-and-file revolts and the emergence of strong competitors for their jobs. We thus have the ironic phenomenon that union leaders—at least in the U.S.—have objected to Government interference with the market far more

consistently and courageously than have business leaders.

The difficulty of exercising "social responsibility" illustrates, of course, the great virtue of private competitive enterprise—it forces people to be responsible for their own actions and makes it difficult for them to "exploit" other people for either selfish or unselfish purposes. They can do good—but only at their own expense.

Many a reader who has followed the argument this far may be tempted to remonstrate that it is all well and good to speak of government's having the responsibility to impose taxes and determine expenditures for such "social" purposes as controlling pollution or training the hard-core unemployed, but that the problems are too urgent to wait on the slow course of political processes, that the exercise of social responsibility by businessmen is a quicker and surer way to solve pressing current problems.

Aside from the question of fact—I share Adam Smith's skepticism about the benefits that can be expected from "those who affected to trade for the public good"—this argument must be rejected on grounds of principle. What it amounts to is an assertion that those who favor the taxes and expenditures in question have failed to persuade a majority of their fellow citizens to be of like mind and that they are seeking to attain by undemocratic procedures what they cannot attain by democratic procedures. In a free society, it is hard for "good" people to do "good," but that is a small price to pay for making it hard for "evil" people to do "evil," especially since one man's good is another's evil.

I HAVE, for simplicity, concentrated on the special case of the corporate executive, except only for the brief digression on trade unions. But precisely the same argument applies to the newer phenomenon of calling upon stockholders to require corporations to exercise social responsibility (the recent G.M. crusade, for example). In most of these cases, what is in effect involved is some stockholders trying to get other stockholders (or customers or employes) to contribute against their will to "social" causes favored by the activists. Insofar as they succeed, they are again imposing taxes and spending the proceeds.

The situation of the individual proprietor is somewhat different. If he

acts to reduce the returns of his enterprise in order to exercise his "social responsibility," he is spending his own money, not someone else's. If he wishes to spend his money on such purposes, that is his right, and I cannot see that there is any objection to his doing so. In the process, he, too, may impose costs on employes and customers. However, because he is far less likely than a large corporation or union to have monopolistic power, any such side effects will tend to be minor.

Of course, in practice the doctrine of social responsibility is frequently a cloak for actions that are justified on other grounds rather than a reason for those actions.

To illustrate, it may well be in the long-run interest of a corporation that is a major employer in a small community to devote resources to providing amenities to that community or to improving its government. That may make it easier to attract desirable employes, it may reduce the wage bill or lessen losses from pilferage and sabotage or have other worthwhile effects. Or it may be that, given the laws about the deductibility of corporate charitable contributions, the stockholders can contribute more to charities they favor by having the corporation make the gift than by doing it themselves, since they can in that way contribute an amount that would otherwise have been paid as corporate taxes.

In each of these—and many similar—cases, there is a strong temptation to rationalize these actions as an exercise of "social responsibility." In the present climate of opinion, with its widespread aversion to "capitalism," "profits," the "soulless corporation" and so on, this is one way for a corporation to generate goodwill as a by-product of expenditures that are entirely justified in its own self-interest.

It would be inconsistent of me to call on corporate executives to refrain from this hypocritical window-dressing because it harms the foundations of a free society. That would be to call on them to exercise a "social responsibility"! If our institutions, and the attitudes of the public make it in their self-interest to cloak their actions in this way, I cannot summon much indignation to denounce them. At the same time, I can express admiration for those individual proprietors or owners of closely held corporations or stockholders of more broadly held corporations who disdain such tactics as approaching fraud.

WHETHER blameworthy or not, the use of the cloak of social responsibility, and the nonsense spoken in its name by influential and prestigious businessmen, does clearly harm the foundations of a free society. I have been impressed time and again by the schizophrenic character of many businessmen. They are capable of being extremely far-sighted and clear-headed in matters that are internal to their businesses. They are incredibly short-sighted and muddle-headed in matters that are outside their businesses but affect the possible survival of business in general. This short-sightedness is strikingly exemplified in the calls from many businessmen for wage and price guidelines or controls or incomes policies. There is nothing that could do more in a brief period to destroy a market system and replace it by a centrally controlled system than effective governmental control of prices and wages.

The short-sightedness is also exemplified in speeches by businessmen on social responsibility. This may gain them kudos in the short run. But it helps to strengthen the already too prevalent view that the pursuit of profits is wicked and immoral and must be curbed and controlled by external forces. Once this view is adopted, the external forces that curb the market will not be the social conscience, however highly developed, of the pontificating executives; it will be the iron fist of Government bureaucrats. Here, as with price and wage controls, businessmen seem to me to reveal a suicidal impulse.

The political principle that underlies the market mechanism is unanimity. In an ideal free market resting on private property, no individual can coerce any other, all cooperation is voluntary, all parties to such cooperation benefit or they need not participate. There are no "social" values, no "social" responsibilities in any sense other than the shared values and responsibilities of individuals. Society is a collection of individuals and of the various groups they voluntarily form.

The political principle that underlies the political mechanism is conformity. The individual must serve a more general social interest— whether that be determined by a church or a dictator or a majority. The individual may have a vote and a say in what is to be done, but if he is overruled, he must conform. It is appropriate for some to require others to contribute to a general social purpose whether they wish to or not.

Unfortunately, unanimity is not always feasible. There are some respects in which conformity appears unavoidable, so I do not see how one can avoid the use of the political mechanism altogether.

But the doctrine of "social responsibility" taken seriously would extend the scope of the political mechanism to every human activity. It does not differ in philosophy from the most explicitly collectivist doctrine. It differs only by professing to believe that collectivist ends can be attained without collectivist means. That is why, in my book "Capitalism and Freedom," I have called it a "fundamentally subversive doctrine" in a free society, and have said that in such a society, "there is one and only one social responsibility of business—to use its resources and engage in activities designed to increase its profits so long as it stays within the rules of the game, which is to say, engages in open and free competition without deception or fraud." ■

September 13, 1970

# The Cultural Contradiction

**By DANIEL BELL**

The ultimate support for any social system is the acceptance by the population of a moral justification of authority. The older justifications of bourgeois society lay in the defense of private property. But the "new capitalism" of the twentieth century has lacked such moral grounding.

It is in this context that one can see the weakness of corporate capitalism in trying to deal with some of the major political dilemmas of the century. The issues here are not primarily economic but sociocultural. The traditionalist defends fundamentalist religion, censorship, stricter divorce, and anti-abortion laws; the modernist is for secular rationality, freer personal relations, tolerance of sexual deviance, and the like.

Now, the curious fact is that the "new capitalism" of abundance, which emerged in the 1920's, has never been able to define its view of these cultural-political issues. Given its split character, it could not do so. Its values derive from the traditionalist past, and its language is the archaism of the Protestant Ethic.

The fact that the corporate economy has no unified value system of its own, or still mouthed a flaccid version of Protestant virtues, meant that liberalism could go ideologically unchallenged.

But liberalism today is in trouble. Not only in politics, where its pragmatic style has been found wanting, but in an arena where it had joined in support of capitalism—in the economy. The economic philosophy of American liberalism had been rooted in the idea of growth.

The liberal answer to social problems such as poverty was that growth would provide the resources to raise the incomes of the poor. The thesis that growth was necessary to finance public services was the center of John Kenneth Galbraith's book "The Affluent Society."

And yet, paradoxically, it is the very idea of economic growth that is now coming under attack—and from liberals. Affluence is no longer seen as an answer. Growth is held responsible for the spoliation of the environment, the voracious use of natural resources, the crowding in the recreation areas, the densities in the city, and the like. One finds, startlingly, the idea of zero economic growth—or John Stuart Mill's idea of the "stationary state"— now proposed as a serious goal of government policy.

American society faces a number of crises. Yet these crises, I believe, are manageable (not solvable; what problems are?) if the political leadership is intelligent and determined. The resources are present (or will be, once the Vietnam war is ended) to relieve many of the obvious tensions and to finance the public needs of the society. The great need here is time, for the social changes which are required (a decent welfare and income maintenance system for the poor, the reorganization of the universities, the control of the environment) can only be handled within the space of a decade or more.

It is the demand for "instant solutions" which, in this respect, is the source of political trouble.

But the deeper and more lasting crisis is the cultural one. Changes in moral temper and culture—the fusion of imagination and life-styles (now so celebrated by Charles Reich of Yale)—are not amenable to "social engineering" or political control. They derive from the value and moral traditions of the society, and these cannot be "designed" by precept. The ultimate

sources are the religious conceptions which undergird a society; the proximate sources are the "reward systems" and "motivations" (and their legitimacy) which derive from the arena of work (the social structure).

American capitalism has lost its traditional legitimacy which was based on a moral system of reward, rooted in a Protestant sanctification of work. It has substituted a hedonism which promises a material ease and luxury, yet shies away from all the historic implications which a "voluptuary system"—and all its social permissiveness and libertinism—implies.

The characteristic style of an industrial society is based on the principles

of economics and economizing: on efficiency, least cost, maximization, optimization, and functional rationality. Yet it is at this point that it comes into sharpest conflict with the cultural trends of the day. The one emphasizes functional rationality, technocratic decision-making, and meritocratic rewards. The other, apocalyptic moods and antirational modes of behavior. It is this disjunction which is the historic crisis of Western society. This cultural contradiction, in the long run, is the deepest challenge to the society.

*Daniel Bell is Professor of Sociology at Harvard University and co-editor of The Public Interest.*

October 27, 1970

# A Man From Main Street

**By DOUGLAS E KNEELAND**

PONTIAC, Ill.—"My dad said this psychology to me," Frank Lehman said the other day, smiling from behind the counter of his men's store here, "that he'd rather have a peanut machine on the corner and have it belong to him than have the best job in America."

That is what Main Street was built on. That is the rock it clings to, whatever tides of change wash across the country.

For half a century, Main Street has stood as a symbol of self-satisfied provincialism and narrow boosterism. For half a century, since the days when the "war to end wars" was a proud and recent truth, that symbol has been accepted as the substance of small-town America, its merchants, housewives, doctors and philosophers.

Now Washington speaks more modestly of "a generation of peace"—if and when. Men have walked the moon and their footfalls have left marks on Main Street. Much has changed. But much has not.

Main Street's merchants are still often one with its philosophers.

Frank Lehman, for instance.

His allegiance to the Republican party, the Presbyterian Church, the Rotary Club, the Kiwanis Club, the Elks, the Moose, the Masons, the Chamber of Commerce and even Pontiac itself has not sufficed to keep Frank Lehman from asking himself

some disturbing questions about the times in which he lives—about the Vietnam war, ecological problems, the righteousness of denominational religion, the growing skepticism of the young.

But there are some verities. And for him, as for thousands of Frank Lehmans,

his father's words are among them.

Frank Lehman is 60 years old now, medium in height, somewhat thick through the waist, a little heavy in the jowls. And except for nine months at a business college in Kankakee ("I decided right then that I didn't care much for cities."), he has been on the square in Pontiac since he took a job at 13 as delivery boy for a department store.

●

For 47 years, he has been a part of Main Street. More

precisely, for most of that time, North Mill Street, on "the best side of the square."

Francis E. Lehman. That's the way it's written on the dashboard name plate of his 1964 Lincoln Continental. ("They'd have a hard time telling me that they ever built a better car than this Continental. But don't say that I ever said anything about the Cadillacs. The dealer's a customer of mine, too. I could get in a lot of trouble.")

But in Pontiac, it's mostly just "Frank."

Easing out the door of Lehman's Men's Store, he dropped a half-dozen first-name "good mornings" before he'd gone 20 feet along the sidewalk. Pausing, but not neglecting to smile and nod at the passers-by, he happily surveyed the busy square that surrounds the massive old brick courthouse adorned with white columns and pigeon-plagued towers.

"You see that new front on Penney's — that's in the last year," he said, squinting into the sun and pointing, "and that front on the furniture store — that's in the last year."

And on, around the square, cataloging, boosting, sometimes mildly apologizing before hastily prophesying a a future improvement. The words flowing in torrents as they always do when he talks of Pontiac. Excited, discovering again — as he had done almost every day of his life — the small wonders, the bright promise of his city of 9,000 enterprising mid-Americans.

Pontiac, 100 miles south-

west of Chicago on Interstate 55 and old Route 66, is a checkerboard of weathered frame houses and well-kept modern dwellings, split by the muddy meanderings of the Vermilion River, a springtime menace in these flatlands.

At the heart of a good farming area, the shopping center and seat of rural Livingston County, Pontiac has seen its once-thriving shoe industry dwindle to one small factory manufacturing heels.

But in the last few years a campaign to attract a more diversified set of employers, aided in part, of course, by Frank Lehman, has been successful. Now the city has more than a dozen small-to medium-sized plants, including Motorola and Interlake Steel, whose low, sprawling buildings on the edge of town are recent intruders among the corn fields.

A town of about 3,000 at the turn of the century, Pontiac has prospered, in its fashion, growing slowly and steadily. Houses worth $50,-000 to $85,000 grace the new subdivisions, some of them developed, of course, by Frank Lehman, around the nine-hole golf course.

But Pontiac's success has not been undiluted.

"I'm going to show you a bad thing here in town," Frank Lehman said, lighting another Pall Mall filter and maneuvering the Lincoln among the side street pot holes until he came to Winston Churchill College. The two-year institution, which has 127 students and occupies a former high school building, was started five years ago by the community.

470

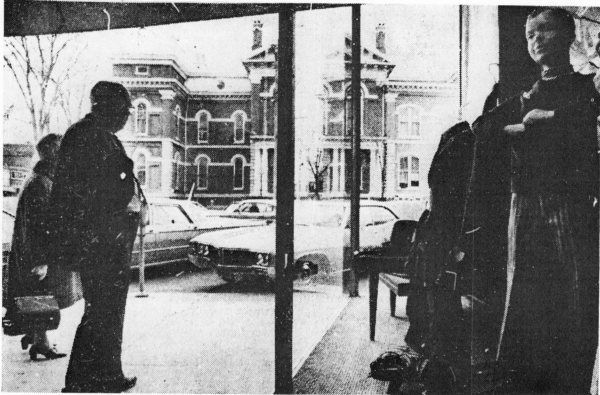

"Another fellow and I assumed the responsibility of raising $80,000 for the community college," he explained, "and we raised $147,000. I was on the board for a year, then I left. Later I went back on and helped raise another $60,000 for them."

●

Now the college, in financial difficulty again, must shut down at the end of this semester.

Frank Lehman may have gone to work as a delivery boy at 13, but it wasn't long before he was a salesman in the store's shoe department. Then, after his business school training at Kankakee, he set his sights higher.

"I went into this one clothing store to apply for a job," he recalled, "and this old German ran it. He said, 'if you came here looking for a job, it doesn't pay enough. If you came here to learn a business, it will be worth your while.'

"I asked him how long it would take. He said, 'Ten years.' He said, 'If you don't stay 10 years, the mistakes you make will be more than you can afford to pay.' And he was right.

"I worked for him eight and a half years. Then I worked three years for his competitor. He had a little more showmanship. I wanted to find out what he had."

Frank Lehman found out. And in 1939 he opened his own store on the square in a building bought by his father, a farmer turned realtor.

Some things have changed in 32 years at Lehman's Men's Store. The old maximum inventory of about $26,-000 has risen to $125,000. Overalls and work clothes are pretty much out, except for three low stacks of Levis stuck away behind a counter. Long underwear is almost a thing of the past, but a small supply is laid in for the traditionalists. White shirts have to be asked for, while the shelves are choked with vivid colors. Wide ties are the only ones displayed.

●

But Frank Lehman and his salesmen still work in their shirtsleeves and willingly model clothes for customers, especially the increasing majority of women who buy for their husbands. His three tailors still sew on lost buttons, mend rips and alter clothes for customers who have dieted or gained weight —all at no cost. And he still has a deal with some friends around town that they can return a suit if they don't get a compliment the first day they wear it.

Frank Lehman, in business, has lived by certain accepted truths:

"Every store has a person-

ality and we try to have a pleasing one.

"People want to see you in the store. They want you to know they've bought a suit there. I feel the same way when I go somewhere in town. I've instructed my salesmen to keep track of who buys a suit and tell me if I'm not there, so I can thank the fellow the next time I see him on the street.

"There's no reason in the world why we should let anyone go out of here with anything that doesn't look good on him.

"My dad told me when I went into business, 'You'll be doing a lot of business with farmers. Just as soon as you get some money ahead, you buy a farm.' So I did. I think I became more sympathetic toward them after I got involved."

The last of these truths also led to the passion of his later years, experimental farming. For seven or eight years now he has concentrated on organic farming on his 90 acres.

His farm trade has also led him into one of his few conflicts with his fellow merchants. Pontiac is one of the rare towns in the nation that has clung to Saturday night shopping hours and there has been talk of changing to Friday.

"I guess I've kind of stood in the way," Frank Lehman said modestly, although another man involved said

that last year the clothier somehow had singlehandedly managed to get a vote for the change reversed. "We get business from 40 miles around. I haven't got any way to get the word out to those farmers if we were going to close Saturday and that's the only day they have off. If they come in just once and I'm closed, that's it."

●

Business is still business on Main Street. But there are other truths.

"You've got a lot of memories that make life worth while, if you can kind of remember that other people need help, too," Frank Lehman mused as he shared a nightcap of ice cream and butterscotch sauce with his wife, Ferne, in the kitchen of their comfortable but unpretentious ranch house, which is on 30 acres overlooking the golf course. (He will take a drink or two, outside of business hours, but he doesn't keep liquor in his home.)

"You've got to be involved in life," he went on; "that's what makes it interesting— and it's good for business, too."

Frank Lehman has been involved.

For 16 years, until the Salk vaccine diminished the need, he ran the county polio fund drive. He has been active for 21 years on the board of St. James Hospital and not long ago headed a campaign that raised $222,-000 for a new wing. He used to serve on the county tuberculois board and is a member of the welfare board. He is a treasurer of the rural fire department, a past president of the Chamber of Commerce and a founder and past chairman of the board of the Bank of Pontiac.

Frank Lehman has done a lot. But that, too, is what it means to be on Main Street.

"Pontiac, like any small community," said John Verona, the young executive vice president of the Chamber of Commerce, "has taken people like Frank and worked them to death. The small businessman has made this community what it is— all of these Midwest communities. Every town has its leaders."

But Frank Lehman hasn't minded.

"I've thoroughly enjoyed life and everything I've done in this community," he said, relaxing on the long sofa in his living room as his son, John, 24, and his wife and infant daughter prepared to leave after an evening visit. "I only wish I was 20 now— everything is traveling at such a fast pace it's hard to keep up with it."

In Pontiac, he has kept up. But it's been almost a full-time job. Other than spending what time he can steal from his business and community affairs with his family or working on his farm or reading biographies (Lincoln is his favorite), recreation and socializing are not high on his list of priorities.

He's not a club man ("I haven't hardly been in the Elks Club for two years,"), although he's a joiner.

"I don't run in any social circles in particular," he explained. "I like to be able to be friends to all of them when you have to get something done. I'd rather spend my spare time working on community projects."

And over nearly half a century, Frank Lehman's love affair with Pontiac has not been severely tested. He has never taken a real vacation, never even exposed himself to the possible lures of New York or San Francisco or Florida or Arizona, let alone Europe or Asia.

"If I got in one of those places and I didn't know anybody," he explained earnestly, "I couln't operate like that.

"Besides, I'm not willing to come back and try to catch up with what's gone on while I'm gone. Every day is an interesting day to me and I don't want to miss anything.

"And, of course, we're close to Chicago and Peoria and places like that. It isn't as if we were off some place."

Frank Lehman is not way off some place. Frank Lehman is still on Main Street.

June 13, 1971

# City Increases Productivity by Piling Up the Work

By FRANCIS X. CLINES

Like a desk-top ant farm, one small nook of the city welfare bureaucracy has been fascinating Lindsay officials lately. It has become a classic case of how to finesse a 20-fold increase in work from a group of civil servants.

The project, involving the discarding of a huge collection of old Medicaid papers in 1,200 file cabinets, was assigned to a dozen clerks who viewed it, city officials said, as something less than a chance to celebrate the work ethic.

But a new time and efficiency expert—a "beakie" or a "shoo-fly" in Civil Service argot—looked in on the job and now has been credited with galvanizing the operation to legendary proportions.

The secret of the specialist, John A. Alexander, was as old as human pride. Instead of having the workers who were going through the old files discard obsolete dossiers into a common trash barrel, he had each one make his own pile of papers on the floor.

The result was a kind of growing bar graph of each individual's industriousness, according to administration officials. Since the work was carried out in a single large room, the man with a pile one-foot high was nagged toward matching his neighbor's four-foot-high pile without anyone having to say a word about laziness or culpability, Mr. Alexander said.

"We'd say something like, 'Gee, Larry, look at Suzy's pile—I wonder why it's so big!' and that was enough to do it," said Mr. Alexander, an assistant human resources administrator who was hired a year ago to direct management engineering.

The Lindsay administration currently is emphasizing the issuance of data-crammed productivity reports that contend city government has become more effective. Mr. Lindsay's sceptics are legion, of course, and the inch-thick "Quarterly Progress Report" issued Tuesday was quickly derided in one part of City Hall as deserving the subtitle "The Mayor's New Clothes."

Lindsay administration officials counter that there is more to the productivity campaign than dry statistics. And the file-culling at Medicaid was cited as a good example.

It received the status of a "classic" by being included in a breezy, informative memorandum entitled "Dictated Ramblings About Productivity," which was composed for top Lindsay officials by Andrew Kerr, the deputy budget director.

At the rate the project was initially begun last spring at Medicaid headquarters on West 34th Street, officials said, it would have taken months to complete, as the dozen clerks shuffled papers in the morgue-like fileroom, looking for telltale signs that a case was closed or out of date. Mr. Alexander's technicians discreetly measured the rate and found that an average of 150 files a day were being examined by each clerk.

Additional analysis and time studies determined that a "fair rate" of work would be the removal and scrutiny of 700 files an hour. Mr. Alexander turned to the technique of having each worker stack his own paperwork separately, a technique he said he had tried before in such positions as management engineer at the Allied Chemical Corporation.

Mr. Kerr's "Dictated Ramblings" described the result:

"Initially there were large discrepancies. Some workers had high stacks while others had low stacks. As time went on, the employes tried to keep their stacks equal in height. This became their unofficial standard."

The result of this delicate frenzy was an average for each worker of 400 files an hour—still short of the ideal but more than 20 times the old work pace.

The project was completed in six weeks, Mr. Alexander added, and the benefits included the elimination of overflowing files that had rendered the system virtually useless, the availability of empty cabinets for use in other offices and, Mr. Alexander hoped, some improvement in the over-all flow of Medicaid papers.

There was never any friction with union stewards or with individual sensibilities during the project, he said. The knack was to keep things impersonal.

"Right now, we're experimenting with the private-industry technique of measuring two groups of workers, and letting Group A know that they're behind Group B," he said. "We're not interested in singling out individuals."

While the debate about the productivity continues, Mr. Lindsay apparently feels convinced of its effectiveness—at least to the extent that he rewarded Mr. Kerr for his role in the program by naming him the new chief of the Housing Development Administration. The flaws and scandals charged to that superagency have been such lately that some of Mr. Kerr's well-wishers joke that his "Dictated Ramblings" could be reduced to mumblings.

October 20, 1972

# Where Do They Go From Here?

### By Richard Sennett and Jonathan Cobb

A Russian street-sweeper, an ardent believer in Communism, tells an interviewer he does not personally "matter as much as a party member"; German office workers are reported often to feel "humiliated" by their clothes; American construction workers tell a team of researchers they feel they have to give their sons cars in order to be respected as fathers. Without his possessions, every man walks with pride, preached the Abbé de Sieyès in 1790, but these workingmen and women of the modern world are not so sure. Just being a human being seems to them a state in which they are vulnerable. "I suppose I am not as dignified," the Russian remarks, "as people with more power and influence."

What these workers are saying is that the dignity of man is not believable as the Abbé de Sieyès preached it, even as they want to believe in themselves and have others respect them, even as they are outraged when others treat them like "part of the woodwork." Man alone, without making a demonstration of his worth, by just being, appears to them to be a vulnerable creature.

What the Enlightenment thinkers failed to create was an image of human dignity without a face. Once the character of a dignified man becomes in any way tangible, every man is saddled with the obligation to compare his own features to that ideal. To define what is dignified about mankind, rather than take it as an act of faith, sets up the machinery of individualism, for every man enters into the comparative process in order to be rewarded by feeling, and being treated as a special person with dignity.

Why is destroying concrete images of dignified living a matter of destroying classes? Tocqueville, after all, posed the prospect of an America without classes—an "equality of conditions"—yet one where people still remained restless unto death, forever seeking to find some manner of living in which they felt authentic, worthy of being respected, dignified.

America has not, however, become a society where an equality of conditions prevails, and the psychology of personal worth has come to have its uses in maintaining inequality and economic productivity along class lines. In addition to the old material incentives, the striving to become a developed, and therefore respectable person is an incentive that keeps men consuming and working hard. The goal now for most individuals is not to possess, to own, to wield power; instead, material things are aids to creating an inner self which is complex, variegated, not easily fathomed by others because only with such psychological armor can a person hope to establish some freedom within the terms of a class society.

Some social thinkers now believe it is foolish to talk of an end to social position through symbols of self-development, because in modern postindustrial society inner intellectual development becomes the direct basis for economic growth. Analysts like Alain Touraine and Daniel Bell claim that economic productivity now will expand only through the prestige system based on personal skills, with the professional intellectual occupying the highest status. In the process of each individual struggling for distinction against an ideal, the standard of excellence should change, Touraine says: competing individuals will thus create new forms of activity to display their talents, and these new activities will yield new goods and services.

This prediction of a postindustrial society ought to give pause. The injuries of class we have described will become worse, and a wider gap will open between those whom society accords respect and those who are not noticed. Further, the meaning of work for manual laborers will become less if a postindustrial system takes hold. Labor under these conditions becomes entirely a parade of ability; talent exists only as an exhibition, not as a commitment to a task.

If a postindustrial system is coming into being, if intellectual competition becomes a necessity for economic growth, there will very likely be an increase in men's feelings of anxiety about the actions which they are persuaded they must perform if they are someday to feel like their own masters. That is to say, to the extent that this linking of personal dignity and personal ability becomes more productive economically, class tension will become worse and worse, and the moral vices of the old capitalism will rise again on a new economic base.

*Richard Sennett, associate professor of sociology at New York University, and Jonathan Cobb of the Center for the Study of Public Policy, are co-authors of "The Hidden Injuries of Class."*

# Bobst Library's Benefactor, 88, Believes Dreams Breed Ideas

**By GEORGE GENT**

Elmer Holmes Bobst, whose gift of more than $11-million to New York University made possible the dedication of the school's new library yesterday — on his 88th birthday — has shaped his life and career around Victorian verities and the blueprinting of a lifetime's dreams.

Some years ago, looking back over an already long career, Mr. Bobst summed up the philosophy that had brought him riches, honors and the friendship of some of the great of the world.

"I have always believed most sincerely," he said then, "that first of all you have a dream. Then you blueprint and act on it. It's easy, but so few do it that there's little competition."

The rugged six-foot octogenarian reaffirmed that philosophy recently during an interview in his office at the Warner-Lambert headquarters at 7 East 60th Street, where he continues to play an active role in the company's affairs as its honorary chairman. The room is filled with testimonials for his many contributions to the American Cancer Society and other charities.

"I've never been a good sleeper," Mr. Bobst said. "My brain is too active to permit deep sleep. But I have always believed that dreams give birth to ideas, and ideas must be put into action. But they must be put into action quickly or they will die on the vine. Even after two or three weeks they will not be of much value because all of the enthusiasm with which they were born will have dried up."

The formula, while undoubtedly followed, is deceptively simple. From an impoverished childhood as the son of a Lutheran minister in the Pennsylvania Dutch town of Lititz, he rose to become one of the higher-paid men in America. Along the way, his dreams were frequently interrupted by such realities as inadequate education, early marriage and the vagaries of opportunity.

But, said Mr. Bobst, whose name is pronounced with a long "o" as in "go," the interruptions only forced him to change direction, never to lose a sense of purpose.

"When I undertake to do something," he said, "I put everything I have into it. I never let anything get me down. I get a great kick out of life and I have never watched the clock. I never allowed play to interfere with business, or business to interfere with play."

## Switched to Law

Hard work and home study, with books borrowed from local libraries ("I am paying off a lifelong debt to libraries," he says of his gift to N.Y.U.), helped him to qualify at the age of 20 as a licensed pharmacist in Pennsylvania.

"I had hoped to go on from there to work in a hospital pharmacy while studying medicine," he recalled. "But I became incensed over the corruption in Pennsylvania politics at the time and decided I would be a politician. I have always had a reformer's spirit. However, I realized that to be a good politician, I should be a lawyer."

Applying at a Philadelphia law office, he was told that because he lacked a college education he would have to take a preliminary state examination.

"I was emboldened by my success in qualifying as a pharmacist to undertake the study on my own," he said. "I borrowed about 75 books and, over a period of 10 months, devoted 1,000 hours to preparation for the examination. Those, I might add, were 1,000 hours lost to sleep, since I continued to work as a pharmacist. I passed the examination."

The grand design was to qualify as a lawyer and then to run successively for assistant district attorney of Philadelphia, Attorney General, Mayor and, finally, Governor. It collapsed with his marriage to his first wife, who died some years ago.

"I had to earn a living for two," he explained.

From then on his life was devoted to pharmaceuticals. He joined Hoffman-LaRoche in 1911 as a salesman, and by 1928 was its president. Retiring in 1944, the year he was named the fourth-highest salaried man in America, he was asked to assume the presidency of the declining Warner-Lambert company a year later, where he became known as the "Vitamin King" for his promotion of that commodity.

Mr. Bobst, who has two grandchildren and four great-grandchildren from his first marriage, remarried in 1961 Miss Mamdouha As-Sayyid, a social scientist with the Lebanese delegation to the United Nations, a woman 40 years his junior.

They share a 15-room apartment on Sutton Place, a large summer home in Spring Lake, N.J., and a Grecian villa in Palm Beach, Fla., where he fishes on a 53-foot boat named Dodo, after his wife's nickname, and swims and golfs several times a week.

## Views on Politics

Mr. Bobst, who is one of President Nixon's major financial backers and closest friends ("Our families used to have Thanksgiving and Christmas dinners together," he related, and the Nixon daughters call him "Uncle Elmer"), was asked if he ever regretted not entering politics. His brows knitted thoughtfully before he ventured an answer.

"I have mixed thoughts," he said at last. "I have found that, in politics, however clean a nominee may be, he will be forced to associate with people whom he ordinarily even disdains to look at. Politics seems to make everyone in the party a brother." Then, he interjected, "I don't refer to anyone in particular."

A religious man who says nightly prayers but is not a regular churchgoer ("Prayer is a great way to enhance your strength and I am convinced that belief in God is essential to happiness"), Mr. Bobst said that he might have been a successful lawyer or clergyman or almost any occupation that he set his mind to.

## $1.5-Billion in Sales

"I was born as an optimist," he explained. "I have a pleasing personality and I know how to smile. As time went on, I learned to develop the attributes of a salesman. Everyone who reaches out for success in this world, whatever his endeavor, must, I think, have to be something of a salesman."

Those attributes brought him more than the usual full measure of success. He rose to head two of the nation's largest pharmaceutical companies—Hoffman-LaRoche and Warner-Lambert, which this year, he said, will have net sales of $1.5-billion.

Firm advocate of purposeful endeavor, he recalled that he once gave President Nixon a poem containing the line, "He who aims too low will never hit the stars." "Don't you think that that is a beautiful line?" he asked. Mr. Bobst also had cast in bronze this motto: "I am not interested in doing the possible; I am only interested in doing the impossible."

"I have always believed in hard work," he said. "'By the sweat of thy brow thou shalt earn thy bread,' the Bible says. People today don't do enough of it. Everyone today is for a shorter week of work. That's the wrong direction. They are forgetting about productivity and the quality of work. Most people earn more than their efforts are worth."

# H.E.W. STUDY FINDS JOB DISCONTENT IS HURTING NATION

## Economic and Social Harm Linked to Dissatisfaction at All Worker Levels

### By PHILIP SHABECOFF
Special to The New York Times

WASHINGTON, Dec. 21 — A changing American work force is becoming pervasively dissatisfied with dull, unchallenging and repetitive jobs, and this discontent is sapping the economic and social strength of the nation, a Government report said today.

The massive study, entitled "Work in America," was issued by a study group of the Department of Health, Education and Welfare.

The report points to the increasingly familiar "blue collar blues" of bored, alienated assembly line workers. But it also tells of widespread "white collar woes" and serious job dissatisfaction or even despair at all occupational levels up to and including managers.

The discontent of trapped, dehumanized workers, the report says, is creating low productivity, increasing absenteeism, high worker turnover rates, wildcat strikes, industrial sabotage, poor quality products and a reluctance by workers to give themselves to their tasks.

### Health Decline Seen

Work-related problems are contributing to a decline in physical and mental health, decreased family stability and community cohesiveness, and less "balanced" political attitudes among workers, the report says.

Growing unhappiness with work is also producing increased drug abuse, alcohol addiction, aggression and delinquency in the work place and in the society at large, the report finds.

The H.E.W. study group suggests far-reaching, even radical, programs to reverse this process of job alienation and to replace "industrial efficiency" with "social efficiency." Among the recommendations are the following:

¶A basic "redesign of jobs" throughout business and industry to make work more challenging and rewarding by giving the worker more responsibility and autonomy in his tasks. A key to this program would be giving workers a share of company profits.

¶Massive worker retraining or "self-renewal" programs available to any worker who wants to enter them whether to acquire job mobility or to prepare for a second career. One such program would entail a sabbatical leave for all workers.

¶A governmental commitment not just to full employment, but to "total employment" — meaning that jobs would be provided not only to unemployed members of the work force but also to any American who wants a job, including youths, retired persons, housewives and others not now counted as part of the work force.

A number of findings and proposals contained in the report appeared to be in direct conflict with the policies and dogma of the Nixon Administration.

For example, its findings directly challenge President Nixon's repeated assertions that some Americans are abandoning the "work ethic" for the "welfare ethic."

The study group presents a mass of evidence indicating that satisfying work is a basic human need in that it establishes individual identity and self-respect and lends order to human life.

Work, the study says, is as meaningful to young people as to old, to poor people as to middle class, to black people as to white, to people on welfare as to people with jobs.

"It is illusory to believe that if people were given sufficient funds, most of them would stop work and become useless idlers," the report asserts. "People on welfare are as committed to the work ethic as middle-class people."

Elliot L. Richardson, the Secretary of Health, Education and Welfare, issued a somewhat cool statement along with the report today, stating that the report might be considered "controversial."

He also said that "its conclusions may not be fully supported by its data and it may in fact be off by quite a bit, but if it is anywhere near the truth, we had better start thinking about the implications." Mr. Richardson strongly suggested that he disagreed with portions of the study.

### Political Considerations

There are growing indications that the subject of worker discontent, and the report itself, are becoming political issues.

Senator Edward M. Kennedy, Democrat of Massachusetts, has announced that he will press for legislation to finance research and experimentation in the next session of Congress on problems of work.

Meanwhile, Labor Department officials have reportedly been criticizing and even ridiculing the report.

The report was ordered by H.E.W. and prepared independently under a contract with the nonprofit W. E. Upjohn Institute for Employment Research.

The study group was headed by Dr. James O'Toole, an anthropologist in the department, who was formerly director of field investigation for the President's Commission on Campus Unrest.

William R. Herman, a study group member and special assistant for policy analysis at H.E.W., said that there had never been a comparable study because awareness of the issue itself as well as the research techniques were relatively new.

Mr. Richardson named the study group, which consists of H.E.W. officials and outside experts, last Dec. 29. Although the study relies heavily on previous research, it draws together diverse facts of an issue that is only now rising to the surface of public consciousness: how work, both qualitatively and quantitatively, affects Americans and their society.

The unrest among blue collar workers has been receiving considerable attention recently, especially since young workers struck a General Motors plant in Lordstown, Ohio, last March because of an alleged speed-up of the assembly line.

The study points to "convincing evidence that some blue collar workers are carrying their work frustrations home and displacing them in an extremist social and political movements or in hostility to the Government."

It is also suggested that the growing ethnic phenomenon in industrial Northern cities is really an effort by blue collar workers, trapped in unsatisfying, low status jobs, to find esteem and identity elsewhere through association with ethnic "clans" or "tribes."

"The cause of blue collar blues is not bigotry, the demand for more money or a changing work ethic," the report says. The "blues" are said to stem from the fact that workers have rising expectations of status and mobility because of more education and income but cannot meet those expectations under the system.

The report says it is "striking" that the discontents of the assembly line are mirrored in white collar and managerial positions. "Much of the greatest work dissatisfactions in the country are among young, well-educated workers who were in low-paying, dull, routine and fractionated clerical positions," the report says.

There are also signs of growing discontent among middle managers who are losing influence, autonomy and authority in their impersonal corporate jobs, the report says.

According to the report, this management discontent is reflected in an increasing incidence of "mid-life crises" as well as a marked increase in the death rate of men between 35 and 40 years old.

The survey says that "more than any other group, it appears that young people have taken the lead in demanding better working conditions." But it also finds evidence that contradicts "the alleged revolt against work and the work ethic" among youth.

Young people, more affluent and better educated than in the past and brought up more freely than their parents, reject the authoritarianism of the work place, the study says.

This is a major threat that runs through the report. While Americans and their expectations are changing, the nature of work and the work place has remained largely static.

For example, little adjustment is found in business and industry to meet the needs and standards of minority groups in terms of dress, speech, education and other factors. "The most dissatisfied group of American workers is found among young black people in white collar jobs," it says.

### Work-Health Links

The study also says that "much of the work that women do outside their homes deflates their self-image." It notes, for example, that typist jobs are still thought of as women's work.

Older people, meanwhile, are thrust out of their jobs whether they want to retire or not, converting them to unproductive members of society with diminished self-worth, the report says.

Strong evidence of links between work quality and health are presented by the study.

A correlation was found between job satisfaction and longevity, while job dissatisfactions were found to be linked to heart diseases, ulcers, rheumatism and mental illness.

Workers often cope with work problems and discontents, the study says, by resorting to alcohol and drugs, to violence, to delinquency and to suicide.

The study concludes that the nation's health priorities are to a degree misdirected, with too much emphasis on medicine and not enough to preserving health through such measures as improving the quality of work.

The study also says that the nation's educational system is not meeting the needs of workers and that the job market is not responding to higher educational achievements of the work force.

The study group questions "conventional wisdom" that holds that high school dropouts face a bleak future. It suggests that many Americans are over-educated for the jobs they hold. It also finds little correlation between educational achievement and job performance.

### Majority Discontented

The study does not state precisely how many Americans are unhappy in their jobs. However, it summarizes the findings of polls asking questions such as "What type of work would you try to get into if you could start all over again?" The results suggest that a majority of Americans are discontent with their work.

After examining the economic, social and personal consequences of this wide job dissatisfaction, the study group asserts that "the main conclusion is that the very high personal and social costs of unsatisfying work should be avoided through the redesign of work."

The report contends: "Not only can work be redesigned to make it more satisfying, but significant increases in productivity can be obtained. In other words, workers can be healthier, happier in their work and better contributors to family and community life than they are now, without a loss of goods and services and without inflating prices."

The nature of the job redesign programs would vary from company to company, the study group says, but they would usually have two elements in common: the participation of workers in decision-making and profit-sharing.

Case histories of a number of companies that have tried job redesign programs, including the General Foods Corporation, the Motorola Company, Corning Glass and the Bankers Trust Company indicate that productivity gains almost always make up for higher costs.

At Banker's Trust, for example, dissatisfied workers were allowed to redesign their own jobs, the result of which was to eliminate the function of a checker, add interest to their work and save the company $260,000 a year.

At Corning, when women workers were allowed to conduct their own quality-control checks, rejects dropped from 23 per cent to 1 per cent and absenteeism from 8 per cent to 1 per cent.

And at Motorola, when workers were allowed to assemble entire receivers instead of components, more workers were required, but the extra cost was offset by higher productivity and lower inspection and repair costs.

Although unions have often opposed such job redesign and profit-sharing programs, evidence indicates that unions actually gain by these programs through increased loyalty from its members and a lower turnover.

For many workers, trapped in dead-end jobs or with failing careers, job redesign programs would not be enough to make work satisfying. To meet the needs of these workers, the report suggests massive retraining or "self-renewal" programs financed with Government help.

"Work in America" concludes with a quotation from Albert Camus: "Without work all life goes rotten. But when work is soul-less, life stifles and dies."

*December 22, 1972*

## Study Finds Incomes More Unequal

### By PHILIP SHABECOFF

Special to The New York Times

WASHINGTON, Dec. 26—A changing population and a changing industrial structure are producing a persistent trend toward inequality in the distribution of income among wage and salary earners in the United States, a study published by the Labor Department has found.

The trend is toward a concentration of an increasingly large share of average wage and salary income among people in jobs and professions that already bring higher pay, and it is likely to continue for some time, Peter Henle, author of the study, says.

The study, in the department's current Monthly Labor Review, departs from the widely accepted view that there has been little change in the distribution of income in America since World War II.

Most studies of income distribution examine family incomes, which include such nonearned incomes as welfare and Social Security payments. Family incomes also reflect the growing trend toward more than one wage earner per family.

The study by Mr. Henle, senior specialist on labor for the Library of Congress, examines only the money earnings, wages and salaries of male workers, so as to obtain a view of shifts in the distribution of payments for work performed.

### Male Workers Studied

In the period examined, 1958-1972, average earned income was steadily rising throughout the economy as a whole. But in the distribution of that income Mr. Henle found "a slight persistent trend toward inequality." This trend toward inequality was found between various occupations and industries and was also found within several occupations and industries.

For example, using unpublished data from the Bureau of the Census, Mr. Henle found that from 1958 to 1970 the share of aggregate wage and salary income earned by the lowest fifth of male workers declined to 4.60 per cent from 5.10. At the same time, the share of the highest fifth of male wage and salary earners rose to 40.55 per cent from 38.15.

This trend did not necessarily affect the very highest-paid and lowest-paid workers on the earned income scale, Mr. Henle said. For example, he noted that, while there had been a marked increase in the number of professionals earning $40,000 to $50,000 a year, there had been little change in the number of executives earning $200,000 or more.

### Denies 'Scheme Against Poor'

In a telephone interview, he stressed that the inequality in income distribution was not caused by any "nefarious scheme against poor people." Rather, the trend reflects a tendency in the economy to produce more higher-paying jobs without reducing the number of lower-paid workers, he said.

One reason has been a heavy flow of young people into the labor force as a result of the World War II baby boom, many of them poorly educated young men who took manual jobs at the bottom of the economic ladder, Mr. Henle said.

There has also been a shift in the structure of jobs. In some industries, including wholesale and retail trade, there has been a substantial increase in the use of part-time labor that has helped "tilt the earnings distribution toward inequality, he went on.

More important, there has been a shift toward employment among occupations and industries that pay higher earnings, including those involving high-technology and public sector jobs, Mr. Henle found. At the same time, the rate of compensation in these higher-paying industries has climbed more sharply than in the lower-paying sectors of the economy, he said.

For example, the number of Federal civil servants rose by 35 per cent in the 1958-70 period. In this same period, the number of employes in the upper pay echelons of the civil service more than tripled.

This kind of development is producing the growing inequality of earned income distribution, the study found.

The trend toward inequality in earnings, Mr. Henle concluded, is "perhaps almost inevitable in an advanced economy, as technological and organizational changes open the way for a higher proportion of

*December 27, 1972*

# To Tell The Truth

## By R. C. Gerstenberg

OAKLAND HILLS, Mich.—Ours is still a democratic republic. The people still have the power. Nothing moves —not on Capitol Hill and not here in Detroit—except by the will and vote of the American people. The individual American—whether we call him voter, or customer, or reader—is still the sovereign we must serve.

The future of our free enterprise economy is in his hands. If the American citizen is to shape that future to serve his own best interests, he must know more than he does about the laws of basic economics, about what makes a profitable business tick, and most important, why it is to his advantage to have business profitable.

The fact is that he knows too little about such vitally important matters. Few of our schools require studies in business or economics. Nor are many parents sufficiently well-informed on the subject of economics—or if they are, they don't seem to teach it at home. I do not have to tell you that the business section is not the most widely read part of newspapers and magazines.

Whatever the reason, the average American has only a hazy idea of what free enterprise means, much less how it works. One survey shows the typical American believes the average rate of after-tax profits for an American manufacturer is nearly seven times higher than it actually is—he thinks it is 28 per cent instead of only 4¼ per cent.

And in addition to that, other surveys suggest that the public's lack of understanding of business—as well as other institutions—has been worsening. In 1965, 70 per cent of the people thought business was doing a good job of achieving a proper balance between making a profit and providing a service. By 1971, however, this had been cut to less than half. Only 29 per cent thought business was doing a good job in balancing profits with service.

We would be wise to clear up some of the confusion that exists about profits—and also about productivity. Most Americans do not understand how essential both profits and productivity are to creating more jobs, for example.

If the average person in this country is confused about the tremendous importance of profits to his daily life, I sometimes think he is even more confused about the role of productivity. For example, another recent poll indicates that 70 per cent of the people believe stockholders are the chief beneficiaries of increased productivity. This supports a recent observation of Commerce Secretary Peter G. Peterson. According to him, many people today believe that "productivity is a 12-letter dirty word representing certain people getting exploited by others."

If what our public-opinion surveyors tell us is true, then the average American should be much better informed than he is on economic matters.

Great economic issues swirl around him. His judgment is critical, yet he has little or no economic knowledge or experience. Because he thinks profits are seven times higher than they are, because he is unaware of the direct linkage between profits and jobs and a prosperous society, he is often willing to accept regulation or legislation that would limit profits. He is a ready target for the propaganda of those who would break up what they call "big business," and subject the entire business community to progressively tighter governmental control and regulation. In my opinion, lack of understanding underlies much of the apathy which the public is showing toward efforts to eliminate or cripple the free-enterprise system.

Recent experience teaches us that the importance of public opinion should never be underestimated, that legislation follows opinion, and uninformed opinion can lead to bad legislation and to unreasonable controls and restraints by government. We in the auto industry have seen a great deal of this in recent years.

We cannot afford to let this continue. We cannot because the harsh lesson of history is that freedom lost in one sphere of human activity—in private enterprise, for example—inevitably leads to the loss of freedom in another.

Further, we depend on free enterprise to help fulfill the ambitious social agenda we, as a nation, have set for ourselves. We want to achieve even higher standards of education, health and welfare. We want to abolish poverty. We want to rebuild our cities. We want to restore and preserve the beauty of our land, our waters and our skies. We want to give every American—of whatever color, religion or background—an equal opportunity to become all he is capable of becoming.

It is urgently necessary—indeed an imperative of our times—that we improve the economic education of the American people.

The business community has a job to do. We know that. Individually and collectively, we must speak out more than we have. We must reach new audiences outside of the business community. We must enlist spokesmen whose support of free enterprise will not be dismissed as self-serving. And, most important, we must couple our words with actions. By our actions we must demonstrate that free enterprise is the most effective instrument that man has ever devised for both economic and social progress.

*R. C. Gerstenberg is chief executive officer of General Motors.*

# Work Ethic Or Idleness Envy?

### By Russell Baker

WASHINGTON, Feb. 7—"The work ethic" is one of those insidious shorthand terms—"women's liberation" is another—which seem to be useful for speeding conversation on to more vital essentials but aren't. What these terms usually do, instead, is sidetrack conversation into vacuity and noise.

Politicians just now are immoderate in lip service to "the work ethic," from which we may assume that "the work ethic," whatever it may be, is a first-magnitude vote-puller, right up there with "home" and "mother" among the treasured Americana all good-guy politicians will fight for until the last television floodlights go off.

We are presumed to reverence "the work ethic." And yet, after we have all agreed upon our devotion to it, how many of us would agree on what we were talking about?

The complicated idea for which "the work ethic" is shorthand has eroded down into a slogan, a shouted *viva!* from politicians certain that we, their conditioned audience, will return an automatic round of applause.

The term seems to be fairly new. A few years ago the cut-the-budget faction in Washington went through a period of talking about "the Puritan ethic," which would presumably have been honored by a cut in Federal outlays. "The Puritan ethic" never caught on. Who knows? Maybe because the stereotype Puritan, that blue-nosed child of repressed emotion, was all wrong for an age of Americans that had coined the battle cry, "Let it all hang out!"

In any case, "ethic" was a word that made all the right sounds on politicians' ears at a time when we were thought by the pols to be suckers for the calliope aspect of politics. They are still in love with "ethnics," probably because "ethnics" sound so much more sincere and sociological, you see, than "the Polish vote."

Whatever the explanation, "ethic" survived when "Puritan" failed, and when the public revulsion against welfare programs began to gather, there was good, sturdy, high-flown old "ethic," sounding like something high-minded we remembered from grave philosophy courses in college.

Sensitive, humane statesmen—as politicians quite naturally think of themselves—could scarcely go along with the more passionate welfare-haters' complaints that the recipients of the state's dole were "bums." The thought had to be agreed to—political reality can be very harsh at times—but the language was awkward. A solution was passionately required, and it turned out to be "the work ethic."

The trouble with welfare was that it violated "the work ethic." People on welfare were corrupted away from "the work ethic." And so on. As a piece of political shorthand for putting a tone of spiritual uplift into razor attacks on welfare, "the work ethic" has had the virtue of softening discourse at a time when some softening was much needed.

The phrase has become so popular, however, that we may be in danger of kidding ourselves into believing there is a "work ethic" that is vital to the nation. The fact, of course, is that the great argument for working hard, except among those who suffered repressed childhoods, has never been that hard work is good for you.

The reason for working hard was that the hard work might just possibly make you rich enough to enjoy a later life of leisure and easy days. In short, hard work had no ethical value; it was a means to an end, and the end was the option to not work at all.

Advancing national cynicism seems to have lessened the masses' faith in their chances of getting rich through hard work, although this is by no means demonstrable. What is demonstrable—we have just had an official report documenting it—is a spreading boredom of fatigue with the jobs that working Americans have.

There are many sociological theories about this. We needn't buy any of them to observe that the quality of much work being performed nowadays suggests that too many workers are not happy in their work. If Americans are so devoted to a "work ethic," how can they muster conscience to take pay for second-rate and sabotaged jobs?

It is surely not devotion to the spiritual value of toil which animates such persons to cheer politicians who demand more devotion to "the work ethic." It seems more likely that they are hooting at the jobless out of the malice of envy.

February 8, 1973

# Boulder, Colo., Shocked as Boy Hero Is Stripped of Title in Soapbox Derby Scandal

### By JAMES P. STERBA
Special to The New York Times

BOULDER, Colo., Aug. 24 —Not since some local dentists were accused of wholesaling marijuana has a local scandal set so many Boulderites afire. Corruption in politics is one thing, they say, but cheating at the Soapbox Derby is almost an affront to the flag.

From city fathers comes embarrassed silence.

From the District Attorney's office comes the specter of a "little Watergate."

From amateur investigators among the professors, scientists and researchers who largely inhabit this mountainside university town come clues and rumors and theories more.

Last Saturday, Jimmy Gronen, a local 14-year-old boy, was the hero of Boulder. He had won the 1973 All American Soapbox Derby in Akron, Ohio. On Monday he became the first winner in 36 years of Derby racing to be stripped of his title and a $7,500 college scholarship.

Derby officials announced that they had discovered in the car a sophisticated battery-powered magnetic system that illegally gave young Gronen a starting edge.

It worked like this: An electromagnet imbbeded in the racer's nose and powered by a battery concealed in its tail was activated by a button hidden in the head rest. The Gronen boy switched on the magnet by leaning his head back between special guides.

When the rectangular steel starting gate fell forward, beginning the race, it pulled the magnet and car forward quicker than gravity pulled the other racers' cars forward.

After that announcement, mystery piled atop scandal. Jimmy Gronen lived in the household of Robert Lange, a ski boot manufacturer until recently. Mr. Lange's son,

478

Robert Jr., won the Derby last year with an almost identical torpedo-shaped car.

No wrong-doing has been alleged in that race, but the car—which became Derby property—has been missing since it was shipped back to Boulder for promotional exhibits.

The Lange family, and Jimmy were also missing until last night when newsmen tracked them down in Oklahoma and Wisconsin.

Mr. Lange was found in Oklahoma City, where his daughter, Cornelia Wells Lange, 19, had entered her chestnut stallion in the International Arabian Horse Show. When approached by a reporter, he said, "I have nothing to say at this time. My lawyer is preparing a statement."

His lawyer, Ralph Hardin of Fort Collins, said today that he had talked briefly to Mr. Lange by telephone but would not prepare a statement until the two met Sunday or Monday upon Mr. Lange's return from Oklahoma City.

Derby officials in Akron and Boulder said that Mr. Lange had not been in touch with them since he left Akron last weekend.

The missing 1972 car was said to have been in the Lange house until Wednesday, when it was reportedly moved by a relative to an unknown place.

**Case Is Investigated**

Meanwhile, Mrs. Lange, her son, Robert Jr., and Jimmy Gronen — formally known as James H. Gronen —were reported to be staying at a lakeside lodge in Hayward, Wis.

Jimmy Gronen is a nephew of Mr. and Mrs. Lange's. He has been living with the Lange family since his father died of a heart attack two years ago.

County attorneys in Boulder and Akron were investigating the case for "possible

criminal violations." Stephan Gabalac, the prosecutor in Summit County, Ohio, told reporters, "I don't know if there has been any violation of criminal law, but I want to make sure this is an isolated event."

Soapbox derby rules prohibit the use of any other force but gravity to propel the racers down the 953.75-foot-long Akron course.

The rules also prohibit adults from helping contestants to build their racers.

Alex Hunter, the Boulder County District Attorney, said that a similar investigation had been opened here into possible violation of local derby rules. Boulder is one of several regional sites from which winners proceed to the national finals.

William Wise, another Boulder County Attorney, said today that his office was looking into the possibility that adults had helped to build the 1972 and 1973 winning car. Because the local winners received a $500 saving bond in 1972 and $100 in cash this year, plus trophies, there might be a po-

tential criminal fraud case, he said.

"It's like discovering that your Ivory Snow girl has made a blue movie," said Mr. Gabalac, the Akron prosecutor.

Mr. Wise said that the Boulder District Attorney's office had received telephone calls of complaint from several parents of local boys who had almost won the Boulder races.

One father called to say that his son, who finished near the front in 1972, begins to cry whenever he hears about the car that beat him and kept him out of the Akron final, Mr. Wise said. Another parent, he added, has said that he will file a civil suit.

The District Attorney's office here is investigating reports that both of the cars were engineered and partly assembled with expert adult advice at the Lange Company ski boot factory in nearby Broomfield, and that one or both of the cars were shipped before the races to the University of California, Los Angeles, for wind tunnel testing.

The investigators are also

looking into a report that the 1972 racer cost about $22,000 to build and test. Employes at the factory have been questioned by county investigators, a company spokesman said.

Derby rules state that no more than $40 can be spent on a car, excluding the four wheels that the Derby provides at a cost of $22.95, plus axles, paint and steering assembly. The rule of thumb limit for everything is about $75, although that is not mandatory.

Robert Lange Sr. manufactured plastic products in Dubuque, Iowa, until 1968, when he and two brothers started the Lange company ski boot factory in Broomfield and later established branch factories in Canada and Italy.

Last September the company was acquired by the Garcia Corporation in a stock trade. The three Lange brothers received three-year contracts as salaried employes. A company spokesman said today that their services were "terminated" earlier this summer, although they continue to receive salaries.

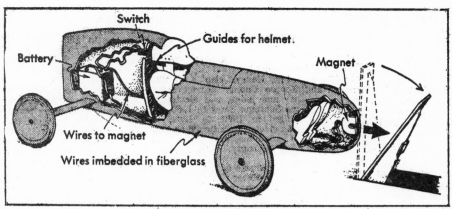

Chuck Ayres/The Akron Beacon Journal via United Press International

Jimmy's helmet fitted into guides to activate a switch for the battery. The battery activated an electromagnet in the nose, which rested against the steel starting plate at Derby Downs. When the plate dropped, the car was pulled by the force of the magnet. Apparatus was hidden under fiber glass. Drawing is based on X-ray photos.

# Washington: Roosevelt, Nixon and 'The Forgotten Man'

**By JAMES RESTON**

WASHINGTON, Sept. 7—The capital of the United States was very beautiful this weekend: clear, cool and serene. It has survived the heat of August and the political passions of Miami Beach and Chicago. It is the great prize, waiting to be captured, half way between a period that is dying and a period still unborn, the most feminine city in the world, the last great city full of trees and close to nature, and, like most women, it knows how to wait.

Washington has been dealing with the slippery ambiguities and imponderables of life for a long time. It knows the strengths and weaknesses of its suitors, and it has heard all their arguments for many years, and hears nothing very new from Nixon or Humphrey.

### Roosevelt Thesis

Roosevelt came to power here in 1932 appealing to "the forgotten man." Nixon is seeking the Presidency now by appealing to "the forgotten people." The technique is the same, but the facts are quite different, and this is the intriguing aspect of the 1968 Presidential election.

"The forgotten man" of the 1932 election was in terrible trouble, and his trouble was physical. He was out of work. He could not provide enough food and shelter for his family. The economic system had broken down. Roosevelt argued that the Federal Government had to rescue him, and on this hypothesis he not only won the election of 1932, but he kept the Democratic party in power for 28 out of the last 36 years.

Richard Nixon's argument for "the forgotten people" is quite different from Roosevelt's argument for "the forgotten man." The forgotten man of Roosevelt's day has made spectacular progress. He not only has a job a generation later, but he has property. He has benefited from the welfare state and the planned economy and has now moved out of the slums of the 'cities into the suburbs.

In fact, Roosevelt's "forgotten man," paradoxically, is now, a generation later, Nixon's "forgotten people." The vast army of the unemployed of Roosevelt's day—there were still nine million in 1937—are now employed. They have bought houses and now resent taxes, and are now indifferent and many of them even hostile, to the militant poor whites and blacks who are left behind.

### Nixon's Argument

Nixon's whole campaign now is directed to this "new class" of workers who have moved into the middle class as a result of the welfare state and planned economy policies the Republicans have held against Roosevelt for more than a generation. Nixon knows that there is still a "forgotten man" in the urban ghettos, black and white, but he also knows that there is a new and larger middle class, which resents the racial turmoil, the demonstrations in the cities and all the permissiveness of contemporary American life.

Nixon has been accused of appealing to racist bigots in the South, but this is not what he is really doing. He is basing his campaign on the workers who have benefited from Roosevelt's "New Deal," which his party opposed. He is saying that the workers of the middle class, liberated by Roosevelt, are now "the forgotten people," and this is his main hope of getting to the White House.

He is basing his campaign on the proposition that the blacks, the liberal intellectuals, and the liberal press are out of touch with the majority of the voters, and he may be right.

Humphrey and his aides are clearly worried about this Nixon strategy. They have lost their old allies in the universities and the press. They have the support of the labor union leaders but they are not sure of the support of the labor union voters. They have Mayor Daley of Chicago and George Meany of the AFL-CIO on their side, but not necessarily the workers or the poor who made up the Democratic labor vote of the past.

In short, the Democrats are in trouble. They are still appealing to "the forgotten man" as if this were 1932, but Nixon is appealing to "the forgotten people"—the new large middle-class workers and middle-class property owners who were the unemployed backers of Roosevelt at the beginning of the thirties.

### Political Switch

Washington is fascinated and astonished by this political switch.

It sees the Republicans benefiting from the welfare state and planned economy policies which Taft and Nixon opposed. It sees Humphrey accused of being a conservative warmonger, though it knows him over the years to be a liberal advocate of disarmament. So it waits and wonders.

It has seen all this before in other periods. It has heard all the predictions of disaster, now so common. It has been confronted by worse choices than Humphrey or Nixon for the Presidency; so it keeps going, cynical but hopeful, mainly through tradition.

September 8, 1968

# Agenda For the Nation

*Edited by Kermit Gordon.*
*620 pp. Washington:*
*The Brookings Institution. $6.95.*

**By EDWIN DALE**

In an important sense the Brookings Institution is part of the Establishment in the United States—just as much so as the Chase Manhattan Bank or Harvard University or Sullivan and Cromwell or the Secretary of the Treasury or General Motors or the Ford Foundation. And

*Mr. Dale is a member of The Times Washington bureau.*

there is a funny thing about the American Establishment: it's darn good.

The word itself is slightly foolish, but it has meaning. No radical need waste his time on this book, unless he might wish to be informed. Mr. Herbert Marcuse will be unimpressed. The trouble with the Establishment, in those people's terms, is that it believes in this society. The Establishment criticizes but never overturns—and that, incidentally, makes it different from an aristocracy, which does not even criticize.

Anyway, here is a sort of inner club of the American intellectual Establishment — 18 men (no women) producing essays on as many different matters, foreign and domestic, facing the nation as a new Administration takes office. Each essay is no more than the appraisal of one man, though there was a system for some critical review. It was not inevitable that Brookings would turn to Carl Kaysen on arms control or James Tobin on poverty or Edwin Reischauer on the Far East or Charles Schultze on the post-Vietnam budget, but they were, shall we say, natural choices. They were established.

With all that granted, come along, brethren, and see what the Establishment is feeling. Try Ralph Tyler on education, for example, or Anthony Downs on housing or Kenneth Clark on the city-*cum*-race matter. What emerges is a truly unhappy, almost despairing Establishment. The literary quality varies from the dreary in Tyler to the quasi-spritely in Tobin, but the impression is the same and overwhelming: our main domestic problems are very close to insoluble, quite apart from being agonizing and terrifying.

This was not the intention. Each of the authors, in good Establishment tradition, proposes solutions, and most even believe in them. Only a few are like Downs who comes right out and says that the just-established "national goal" of 26 million housing units in the next 10 years, including 6 million for low-income families, proclaimed by President Johnson and enacted by Congress, is an outright fraud (which it is because it cannot possibly be achieved). But where despair is not overt it is implicit.

Read 'em and weep: 20 per cent of our children are not getting educated at all, and Federal efforts to change the situation have failed. We have no idea, really, about what makes criminals or what to do about them (James Wilson). The only conceivable solution to the "pathology" of the black ghetto (the Establishment word used by Clark for stealing and dope and mugging and welfare and irresponsibility) is a truly integrated society, but that is further away than ever because white society has mixed up its decent, charitable instincts about poverty with the race question.

The present reviewer has no exalted view of mankind or mankind's history, and any careful reader of the newspapers can have learned much of what these men have to say. Still, given its origins, I can recall no more dispiriting book than this—which was not, of course, its purpose. The men who wrote these pieces are simply too good to be fools; most, particularly on the domestic side, have said how really bad the situation is. The mélange, and that is what it set out to be, is spoiling my breakfast. A million now on welfare in New York City — quadrupled in 10 years—is, one might say, explained here.

The foreign-affairs part is somehow more remote; perhaps all that is involved is whether we all blow up. Kermit Gordon, the brilliant head of Brookings, says in his foreword that "the initial menu of major policy issues," foreign and domestic, "ran to nearly 40 subjects" but that this had to be whittled down to 18. Lost in the grand shuffle, as Mr. Gordon is free to admit, was the small matter of world population, to name one item. Latin America got lost, too.

In any case, generalizations are not appropriate in the foreign-policy section (and they are perilous in the domestic). But these essays, too, contain a note of challenge, if not disillusion, about our earlier and simpler assumptions, whether about the Far East or foreign aid. There is great sophistication here, also, though variance in sharpness between, say, Francis Bator's subtle appreciation of our problems with Europe and Henry Kissinger's slightly Germanic vagueness on the matter of "central issues."

Foreign or domestic, there is no proper way to summarize or review this book. One could be a bit beastly and say that the eight essays in the foreign-policy section are not greatly more impressive than a good selection from the magazine Foreign Affairs, and that would be true. The same people wrote them. On the domestic side, every one of these authors has been prominently published somewhere, and there is, perhaps, nothing startling in their present papers, though some—Schultze on the limited amount of Federal money that will be available to be spent after Vietnam is the best example—are significantly updated.

What is startling from putting them all together is the discovery, or rather proof, of how troubled the American Establishment is. These are constructive men and just as much in the optimistic tradition as any other part of our leadership. But they are men without illusions—perhaps more so than at any time in our modern history. ■

January 26, 1969

# Nixon Plans to Enlist Citizens to Combat Social Ills

Special to The New York Times

WASHINGTON, April 30 — President Nixon announced today preliminary efforts to enlist citizen volunteers in the attack on social and economic ills.

He named Secretary of Housing and Urban Development George Romney, long an apostle of citizens' participation, to head a new Cabinet committee on voluntary action; instructed Mr. Romney to establish an Office of Voluntary Action in his department, and named Max M. Fisher, a Detroit businessman, to serve as a special Presidential consultant on voluntary action and, in effect, to oversee the program.

In what may turn out to be the most meaningful move, he also directed Mr. Romney to establish a clearing house for information on voluntary programs, where communities could seek advice on programs that have worked or failed in other communities.

## Questions Americans Ask

"At one time or another," the President observed in a statement, millions of Americans have asked themselves or others, 'What can I do? How can I help?' One of the chief aims of this new effort will be to make answers readily available.

"It is a remarkable and little-appreciated fact that for practically every one of the great social ills that plague us, solutions have been found somewhere—by citizen volunteers, who have devised programs that actually work in their own communities. In nearly every case, the experience can be helpful to those who are concerned with similar problems elsewhere."

These moves represent an effort by the President to fulfill a campaign pledge to mobilize the "voluntary sector" of American society. The President stressed that these steps represented "only a beginning," and Mr. Fisher, who appeared with Mr. Romney before newsmen at the White House this morning, cautioned against raising "false hopes" for the program and said that it would take "a great deal of time" to involve fully the voluntary energies of American citizens.

Both he and Mr. Romney said their plans were a bit vague at the moment. Mr. Romney said that thousands of student volunteers were now engaged in part-time teaching in slum schools in Michigan, and that similar programs might be tried elsewhere. Other officials suggested that volunteers could play a major role in the drive against hunger, serving as dietary counselors to poor families.

May 1, 1969

# Survey Finds College Students Are a 'New Breed'

Special to The New York Times

PRINCETON, N. J., May 25—A nationwide survey of college students conducted by the Gallup Poll has found that "students today are indeed a 'new breed.'"

The poll, known formally as the American Institute of Public Opinion, cited as representative of the new breed a Yale student who said:

"We are disenchanted with the ideologies of the adult population today, with their belief that a large Buick says something important about one's self. The urge of people for self aggrandizement repels us. Furthermore, we don't go along with the 'hard work mystique' —the notion that if one works hard he is therefore a good person."

Interviews were conducted for the poll with students across the nation—in private institutions such as Harvard University, in state-supported institutions such as Ohio State University and in denominational or church-related institutions such as Notre Dame University.

### Evidence of Differences

The institute said today that its findings provided ample evidence that today's students were different from earlier generations in these important aspects:

¶USE OF DRUGS. One student in every five (22 per cent) says he has tried marijuana. Less stigma seems to be attached to the use of marijuana now than a year ago; many students admit to taking marijuana as readily as they do to drinking beer. One student in 10 (10 per cent) says he has taken a barbiturate and four in 100 have tried LSD.

¶ATTITUDE TOWARD SEX. Two out of every three college students (66 per cent) think it is not wrong for men and women to have premarital sex relations, with 72 per cent of college males holding this view and 55 per cent of college women. A majority of students in both public and private colleges say sex before marriage is not wrong, but a majority of denominational college students holds the opposite view.

¶DRESS AND APPEARANCE. Many students consciously affect a slovenly appearance to drive home their anti-Establishment, nonconformist point of view. The interviewers found that beards, long sideburns and sloppy clothes were somewhat more prevalent in Eastern colleges and in private and public colleges than on denominational campuses. One student suggested that the longer the hair, the more radical the person's politics. However, another student said: "These things go in cycles. Five years from now, everyone will have his head shaved."

### Focus on Social Work

¶INTEREST IN SOCIAL WORK. Extracurricular social work used to be considered "square" in some college circles. Now, working among the poor and underprivileged is frequently a normal and expected part of one's college experience. A majority of all students (51 per cent) say they have done social work. The percentage is 58 per cent among women and 47 per cent among men. Among student demonstrator, 65 per cent say they have done social work, while among nondemonstrators the figure was 45 per cent.

¶GOALS IN LIFE. An uncertainty about the immediate future hangs over the campus today. The traditional goals of earning a great deal of money and making one's mark in the world have lost some of their charm. An extraordinarily high proportion of students today want to go into the "helping" professions, notably teaching. Asked what occupation they expected to be in at age 40, 29 per cent list teaching.

¶ATTITUDES TOWARD SOCIETY. Today's student has turned his anger at the Vietnam war on the closest representative of the Establishment —his own college. He has learned about demonstrations from the civil rights movement and about the effectiveness of "student power" from Senator Eugene J. McCarthy's campaign last year.

Seven in 10 college students think a "generation gap" exists, and the same proportion of older persons in the population holds the same view.

The biggest "gripe" of students about their parents is that they are "too set in their ways" (36 per cent). The biggest complaint of parents about young people is "undisciplined behavior" (30 per cent.)

May 26, 1969

# Topics: The Value Revolution

**By STEWART L. UDALL**

There is a deepening awareness that today's domestic turbulence is in reality a fundamental questioning of the value system of American society.

The protest of the blacks against the personal affronts and indignities of daily life is also a more general protest against the false and frequently inhuman values of our total social system. The widespread student antagonism toward the standards of "the establishment" represents an even broader disagreement with conventional values.

### Social Renewal

I believe this pervasive and pointed questioning of values may bring about a shift in those ideas and attitudes that ultimately shape the nation. In fact, we may already be engaged in the most vital sorting out of values since 1776.

Even our search for the roots of failure at the time of the Depression was more a questioning of the workability of the economic system than a radical search for the elements of thorough-going social renewal.

Our contemporary turmoil concerns human relationships: between the privileged and the impoverished, between black and white, between parents and children.

If we honestly believe, as I do, that the present young generation is not only the best educated, but also the most aware and idealistic in our history, we must be responsive to its causes and complaints. The anger of the young blacks against the built-in inequalities and hypocrisies of "the system" legitimately challenges the moral basis of the old order.

If a large proportion of the superior university graduates turn their backs on corporate careerism, if many of our most creative minds are turned off by conventional opportunities, we should question the incentives and concepts that make the system go. For there is no doubt that the desire to be merely affluent is yielding to the impulse to live in an environment that is life-giving and creative.

If most of our cities and countrysides are increasingly unclean and ugly we should begin to reconsider the policies that have made them a disordered mess. If technology is to continue its thrust, then it must be influenced by social considerations and aspirations—in short, technology must be civilized.

The thing that appalls the new generation the most, I believe, is the waste endemic in American life: the waste of young talent; the waste of the contributions the unmelted minorities could make if we gave them a chance; the waste of the beauty and bounty of a magnificent continent. The student protest against the Vietnam policy was and is a moralistic protest against waste.

### Excesses of War

With the benefit of hindsight we now realize it is a judgment wiser than Washington's —a judgment that the lives and wealth expended were excessive and misdirected, and thus demeaned us before mankind.

We will always need in this country all the idealism we can get, particularly from our youth, for the idealist is more sensitive to crucial moral issues, more attuned to the nonmaterialistic opportunities. Who indeed will pierce our old frauds and follies unless fresh minds question the habits and attitudes of the past?

The value revolution is upon us. It may transform our lives.

Those preoccupied with the selfish scramble for easy wealth, unmerited advantage and personal ease should become accustomed to the well-aimed arrows of those who have contempt for these aspects of American life.

The value doubters will continue to scorn our efforts to define the national well-being solely by Gross National Product, freight-car loadings, auto production, or the sufficiency of military preparedness. They want to assess (and they are entitled to raise the issue) what that product is, what the freight cars contain, what the rele-vance of individual wheels is to our mass transportation needs, how humanism fits into what can never again be a simple logistical measure of preparedness.

The time has come to recognize the worth of the value revolution and to encourage it toward constructive channels. It can have a profound and bene-ficial influence on our future if it causes us to renew our lives, revise our institutions, and reassess our directions and purposes.

*Stewart L. Udall served as Secretary of the Interior in the Kennedy and Johnson Administrations.*

June 7, 1969

# NIXON SELECTS AGNEW AS HIS RUNNING MATE AND WINS APPROVAL AFTER FIGHT ON FLOOR; PLEDGES END OF WAR, TOUGHNESS ON CRIME

## 'NEW LEADERSHIP'

## 'Long Dark Night' Over, Nominee Says, Pledging Action

Special to The New York Times

MIAMI BEACH, Aug. 8 — Richard M. Nixon called tonight for "new leadership" to restore the nation's prestige abroad and heal its wounds at home.

"The long dark night for America is about to end," the Republican Presidential nominee declared in his acceptance speech.

"The time has come for us to leave the valley of despair and climb the mountain so that we may see the glory of the dawn of a new day for America, a new dawn for peace and freedom to the world."

Mr. Nixon told the partisan audience of thousands and a nationwide television audience of millions that he would make the end of the war in Vietnam his first order of business.

Without offering specific solutions, Mr. Nixon suggested that only a new Administration "not tied to the mistakes and policies of the past" could bring a successful conclusion to the hostilities.

### 'Era of Negotiation'

Offering the hand of friendship to the nation's cold-war adversaries, he said that "after an era of confrontation, the time has come for an era of negotiation" with the leaders of Communist China and the Soviet Union.

On domestic issues, Mr. Nixon offered to solve the nation's internal difficulties by combining a firm approach to law and order with new remedies for the problems of poverty that would depend less on Government "billions" and more on activities of an enlarged private sector.

The speech was punctuated frequently by applause. The response was greatest after his appeals for law and order and his frequent references to what he portrayed as a decline in national prestige over the last eight years.

Early in his speech Mr. Nixon said that he had talked with Mrs. Dwight D. Eisenhower earlier in the day and that she had said that the best thing for the ailing former President would be a Republican victory in November.

"Let's win this one for Ike," Mr. Nixon urged, and the audience came to its feet cheering.

Mr. Nixon's running mate, Gov. Spiro T. Agnew of Maryland, in his acceptance speech, said his one objective if elected Vice President would be to "analyze problems without depending on the canned philosophy of either extreme liberalism or conservatism."

For the most part, Mr. Nixon's address amounted to a recitation of the basic themes that he offered to the voting public during the primary campaign.

In offering friendship to all peoples he said his policy in the world would be "open skies, open cities, open hearts, open minds."

He promised to restore what he said was dwindling national strength so that in the "era of negotiation" now beginning in the world, the United States would be able to negotiate from strength rather than weakness.

Regarding "law and order," Mr. Nixon declared:

"The first civil right of every American is to be free from domestic violence."

Such passages brought enthusiastic ovations from the delegates and spectators, particularly the Southern delegations, but Mr. Nixon said he was not using "law and order" as a catchphrase for "racism."

Rather, he said, he would try to provide an "equal chance" for black Americans through greater emphasis on private enterprise and self-help programs that would give them "a piece of the action."

### Warmly Applauded

The audience applauded warmly his calls for the abandonment of welfare and poverty programs "that have failed," and his promise that if elected he would use the "tax and credit policies to enlist the greatest engine of progress ever developed in the history of man —American private enterprise."

They applauded again when he promised to initiate a wide-ranging fight against "the merchants of crime and corruption in American society."

The loudest applause of all—except for the ovation that greeted him at the end—came at the conclusion of a passage that he first used in the New Hampshire primary and that has since drawn the warmest response of any single passage in any of his speeches.

It is, in effect, an appeal for the restoration of national prestige, an appeal similar to one that John F. Kennedy used to defeat him in 1960.

### On Vietnam War

Mr. Nixon said:

"When the strongest nation in the world can be tied down for years by a war in Vietnam with no end in sight; when the richest nation in the world cannot manage its own economy; when the nation with the greatest tradition of the rule of law is plagued by unprecedented lawlessness; when the President of the United States cannot

travel abroad or to any major city at home without fear of a hostile demonstration—then it is time for new leadership in America."

Yet, as he has throughout his efforts in the last year, Mr. Nixon summoned the nation to look not just at its problems but its promises as well.

He drew attention to what he called the "forgotten" majority of Americans—the "non-shouters, the non-demonstrators" who constitute "the real voice of America." And he declared that if properly mobilized by enthusiastic leadership they would respond.

"Just to be alive in America at this time is an experience unparalleled in history," he said. "Here is where the action is."

Mr. Nixon's delicate mixture of problem and promise has been characteristic of his approach to the issues this year.

Tonight, in pledging to use the promise of free enterprise to help solve the problem of black Americans, he declared that Negroes did not "want to be a colony in a nation."

### 'They Want the Pride'

"They want the pride, the self-respect and the dignity that can only come if they have

an equal chance to own their own homes, their own businesses, to be managers and executives as well as workers, to be a piece of the action in the exciting ventures of private enterprise," he said.

Mr. Nixon added some new imagery tonight as part of his appeal for a nation reconciled to itself and the world at large. He delivered a rolling, almost lyrical passage that described the two faces of "an American child."

The first face, he said, is the face of the poor: "He sleeps the sleep of childhood and dreams its dreams. Yet when he awakens, he awakens to a living nightmare of poverty, neglect, and despair."

The second face was the face of another child, who "hears the train go by at night," whose father "sacrificed everything so that his sons could go to college," who chose the "profession of politics" and who "tonight stands before you—nominated for the President of the United States."

Mr. Nixon then stated this wish to the convention:

"What I ask of you tonight is to help me make that [American] dream come true for millions to whom it's an impossible dream today."

Mr. Nixon's running mate, asserting that he stood on the rostrum with "a deep sense of the improbability of this moment," spoke of the challenges of the Vice-Presidency.

Governor Agnew said that he looked forward to participating in an Administration where he could assume some of the vital responsibilities of the cities.

"Changes must be made," he said, "and the Nixon administration will make those changes."

Mr. Agnew said the new Administration would look for new ideas to balance the relationship between Federal, state and local governments — a theme that Mr. Nixon also touched on in his speech.

The Federal Government must work harder and more creatively, the Vice-Presidential candidate said, to build independence and pride among Negroes.

And when it was all over, and both speeches had ended, and the vast convention hall was emptying, it seemed clear that both candidates had made the same appeal to basic, old-fashioned American values.

August 9, 1968

# PANEL FINDS NEED TO INSPIRE DEBATE ON NATION'S GOALS

## Study for Nixon Concludes Public, Not White House, Will Shape New Aims

By JAMES M. NAUGHTON
Special to The New York Times
WASHINGTON, July 18—A White House study on national goals has reached the conclusion that the White House cannot set goals for America.

A report of the National Goals Research Staff, released today by the White House, declares that the Government should instead provide the information the public needs to engage in debate about the sort of society it wants.

The first report of the goals staff, appointed last year by President Nixon, said that a national growth policy would "evolve in varying pieces through the nineteen-seventies; and it will probably never be completed because, by virtue of the dynamic nature of events, it will be open-ended."

At the same time, the report emphasized the importance of defining policy alternatives for the nation as it speeds toward the year 2000 in an era of inquiry, confrontation and technological achievement.

### Framework for Discussion

But few firm alternatives were specified in the 224-page document produced at the White House, nor were there many new facts. The report represented a conceptual framework for what President Nixon said last July should be "lively, widespread public discussion."

According to officials who took part in developing it, the

report deliberately skirted the volatile issues confronting the nation today and was tailored to coincide with the President's policies. It did, however, pose the following themes and invite challenge to them:

¶Contrary to earlier expectations, United States population growth will level off and the prediction of 100 million more Americans by the year 2000 will likely prove too high. Accordingly, the issue of population is one of distribution, not of concern over growth.

¶Schools must adapt to a period of widespread communication of ideas by shifting from efforts to give pupils information to an attempt to help them sift data and establish their own values.

¶The emerging emphasis on qualitative values in society must not lead to a rejection of quantitative values. Rising expectations cannot be met without continued economic growth.

¶Problems of today are a

result not of failures of American institutions but of their successes. By anticipating the consequences of government, business or social policies, the nation can avoid problems or be prepared to cope with them as they emerge.

### Garment Heads Staff

The report, entitled "Toward Balanced Growth: Quantity With Quality," was prepared by a staff directed by Leonard Garment, special consultant to the President, with the assistance of Daniel Patrick Moynihan, Counselor to the President, and Raymond A. Bauer, professor of business administration at the Harvard School of Business.

At a White House briefing before the report was released, Mr. Moynihan said that such a document could have been prepared by any of a number of private research institutions. "The purpose of doing it under the Great Seal," he explained, "is to make this kind of document available to the public for 95 cents."

The remark underscored Mr. Nixon's mandate to the study group not to set goals but, as the report stated it, to "inspire debate—and to help give that debate form, direction and meaning."

The report did not take up, however, the central issue of the debate today—whether efforts to achieve foreign policy objectives had been a factor in the nation's falling short of domestic goals. It avoided such controversies as those over racism, war, urban decay and minority dissent.

### Report Is Muted

Instead, the report discussed less heated issues, such as population growth, the environment, education and consumer activism, emphasizing that they did not represent a national agenda but were matters subject to analysis, tools to illustrate the concept of goal-setting.

Even in those areas, however, the report was muted, more often than not posing the issue less as a choice between polar alternatives than as a search for the proper "mixed approach."

The section on the history of the consumer movement was edited to delete all references to Ralph Nader, a leading consumer crusader and critic of the Government.

The report does mention Mrs. Virginia Knauer, Mr. Nixon's special assistant for consumer affairs. It cites her activities and notes the President's proposal for a "buyer's bill of rights."

One official who helped shape the document said that its frequent references to Mr. Nixon, his programs and his public statements were designed not to promote the Administration but to "convince the White House staff that the report was not at variance with the President's policies."

### The Swiftness of Events

The same official said that the staff agreed with the White House that, for two principal reasons, it should not set specific goals.

For one, as the report indicated, events change too swiftly for a table of priorities to have much permanence.

For another, unstated in the document, a list of goals would pose political problems for the Administration by setting up a yardstick against which to measure its success, restricting its options to make other decisions.

"It would be like giving the Democrats a campaign platform," the official said.

The report makes the point, nonetheless, that it is increasingly urgent for society to plan for its future and that the United States has the resources to do so.

Mr. Moynihan said that the

Government might set forth, on a regular basis, the trends, data and options as they develop so that priorities would not be established by an élite working in private.

Mr. Moynihan expressed hope that Congress would hold hearings on national goals and the Administration would conduct seminars on the subject for career bureaucrats.

The central ingredient of planning, the report said, will be the active participation of the American people. What needs to be done is not to formalize the process but to make it work better, it said.

Accordingly, the goals study made such points as the following:

### SCOPE OF DEBATE

For the first time, the virtues of economic growth are being questioned. The issue is normally put in terms of "quantity vs. quality." Yet the nation cannot have one without the other.

After a decade of increasing social concern and demands for citizen involvement, the nation now faces rising expectations and changing values.

Present projections are that the gross national product, the total value of the nation's economic output, will rise from $932-billion last year to $1.5-trillion in 1980. But this depends upon an expanding labor force and growth in productivity.

Even in the booming economy of recent history, the nation has learned that there is not always enough money to meet social needs. Thus, it must "set priorities more deliberately."

### POPULATION

Previous fears of a population explosion, with a 50 per

cent increase, or 100 million more people, in the next three decades, appear less valid, the report said.

The increase may be "considerably less" and the nation may reach the zero growth rate many demographers advocate. Mr. Moynihan said. "It doesn't really make as much difference to us at this point if we are

right or wrong as to get some discussion of it."

What is of concern is that if present trends continue to increase the population of metropolitan areas and decrease that of small towns and rural sections, the quality of life would deteriorate in both.

By 2000, there would be 70 per cent of the population in

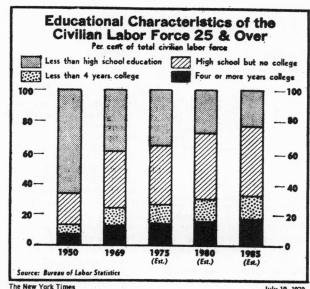

Source: Bureau of Labor Statistics

The New York Times                    July 19, 1970

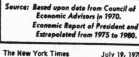

Source: Based upon data from Council of Economic Advisors in 1970.
Economic Report of President and Extrapolated from 1975 to 1980.

The New York Times          July 19, 1970

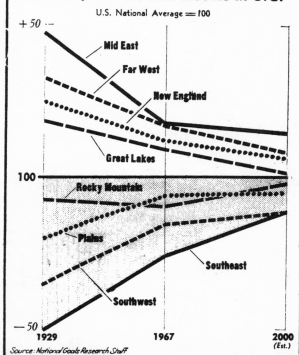

Source: National Goals Research Staff

The New York Times                    July 19, 1970

Chart shows the reduction, past and projected, in the gap between per-capita income levels in various U.S. regions.

12 metropolitan areas, more than half of it in three huge zones from Boston to Washington, Chicago to Pittsburgh and San Francisco to San Diego. The relative differences in percapita personal income among regions of the country would be aggravated more.

The alternative is to encourage internal migration, through programs and incentives that would generate growth in sparsely populated rural areas, foster expansion of existing small cities and towns or create new cities outside metropolitan regions.

### EDUCATION

The role of the school has been to transmit information and instill values. In a society of rapid change and common communication, children may get more information outside school and be buffeted by challenges to the established values.

Studies suggest that by 1980 some 4.7 million members of the labor force will still have less than a high school education. If even the graduates are not skilled at coping with society, demands for educational relevance may have increasing impact.

Knowledge for its own sake still has value to many. "By and large, it would seem that we must look for some appropriate mix rather than shift over to a complete doctrine of relevance."

### CONSUMERISM

American success at producing sophisticated products has, nonetheless, led to resentment that the range of products is so large, choice is difficult and untrained individuals cannot evaluate the products.

The key issue is how to protect the consumer and, at the same time, preserve an expanding economic environment.

### THE FUTURE

In the appendices to the report, there are predictions of such developments in the near future as three-dimensional television, portable telephones, ability to alter the weather, and chemical stimulation to aid in learning and retention of knowledge.

The report poses this challenge:

"Our nation in 1980 could be one in which cities are more clogged with immovable traffic, air is less breathable, streams polluted to the point where expensive processes will be necessary to get usable water, seashores deteriorating more rapidly, and our people suffering needlessly from having not developed the necessary institutional arrangements for achieving the promise of this decade of change.

"On the other hand, America in 1980 can be a nation which will have begun to restore its environment, to have more balanced distribution of regional economic development and population; a nation which has abolished hunger and many forms of social inequality and deprivation; and a nation which will have begun to develop the new social institutions and instruments necessary to turn the promises of this decade of change into reality.

"If we are to see the second of these possible futures realized in the America of 1980, we must begin now to define what we wish to have as our national goals, and to develop in both our public and private institutions the specific policies and programs which will move us toward those goals."

July 19, 1970

# Who Speaks for Ethnic America?

### By BARBARA MIKULSKI

The Ethnic American is forgotten and forlorn. He is infuriated at being used and abused by the media, government and business. Pejorative epithets such as "pigs" and "racists" or slick, patronizing labels like the "silent majority" or "hard hats" are graphic examples of the lack of respect, understanding and appreciation of him and his way of life.

The Ethnic Americans are 40 million working class Americans who live primarily in 58 major industrial cities like Baltimore and Chicago. Our roots are in Central and Southern Europe. We have been in this country for one, two or three generations. We have made a maximum contribution to the U.S.A., yet received minimal recognition.

The ethnics came to America from the turn of the century through the twenties, until we were restricted by prejudicial immigration quotas—65,000 Anglo-Saxons to 300 Greeks. We came looking for political freedom and economic opportunity. Many fled from countries where there had been political, religious and cultural oppression for 1,000 years.

It was this working class which built the Great Cities—constructed the skyscrapers, operated the railroads, worked on the docks, factories, steel mills and in the mines. Though our labor was in demand, we were not accepted. Our names, language, food and cultural customs were the subject of ridicule. We were discriminated against by banks, institutions of higher

*Patriotism—An interpretation by Edward Gorey*

learning and other organizations controlled by the Yankee Patricians. There were no protective mechanisms for safety, wages and tenure. We called ourselves Americans. We were called "wop," "polack" and "hunky."

For our own protection, we formed our own institutions and organizations and clung together in our new neighborhoods. We created communities like "Little Italy" and "Polish Hill." The ethnic parish church and the fraternal organizations like the Polish Womens' Alliance and the Sons of

Italy became the focal points of our culture.

These neighborhoods were genuine "urban villages." Warmth, charm and zesty communal spirit were their characteristics. People knew each other. This was true not only of relatives and friends but of the grocer, politician and priest. The people were proud, industrious and ambitious. All they wanted was a chance to "make it" in America.

Here we are in the 1970's, earning from $5,000 to $10,000 per year. We are "near poor" economically. No one listens to our problems. The President's staff responds to our problems by patronizingly patting us on the head and putting pictures of construction workers on postage stamps. The media stereotype us as gangsters or dumb clods in dirty sweat-shirts. The status of manual labor has been denigrated to the point where men are often embarrassed to say they are plumbers or tugboat operators. This robs men of the pride in their work and themselves.

The Ethnic American is losing ground economically. He is the victim of both inflation and anti-inflation measures. Though wages have increased by 20 per cent since the mid sixties, true purchasing power has remained the same. He is hurt by layoffs due to cutbacks in production and construction. Tight money policies strangle him with high interest rates for installment buying and mortgages. He is the man who at 40 is told by the factory bosses that he is too old to be promoted. The old job is often threatened by automation. At the same time, his expenses are at their peak. He is paying on his home and car, probably trying to put at least one child through college.

In pursuing his dream of home ownership, he finds that it becomes a millstone rather than a milestone in his life. Since FHA loans are primarily restricted to "new" housing, he cannot buy a house in the old neighborhood. He has no silk-stocking lawyers or fancy lobbyists getting him tax breaks.

He believes in the espoused norms of American manhood like "a son should take care of his mother" and "a father should give his children every opportunity." Yet he is torn between putting out $60 a month for his mother's arthritis medication or paying for his daughter's college tuition.

When the ethnic worker looks for some modest help, he is told that his income is too high. He's "too rich" to get help when his dad goes into a

nursing home. Colleges make practically no effort to provide scholarships to kids named Colstiani, Slukowski or Klima.

The one place where he felt the master of his fate and had status was in his own neighborhood. Now even that security is being threatened. He wants new schools for his children and recreation facilities for the entire family—not just the token wading pool for pre-schoolers or the occasional dance for teen-agers. He wants his street fixed and his garbage collected. He finds that the only things being planned for his area are housing projects, expressways and fertilizer factories. When he goes to City Hall to make his problems known, he is either put off, put down or put out.

Liberals scapegoat us as racists. Yet there was no racial prejudice in our hearts when we came. There were very few black people in Poland or Lithuania. The élitists who now smugly call us racists are the ones who taught us the meaning of the word: their bigotry extended to those of a different class or national origin.

Government is further polarizing people by the creation of myths that black needs are being met. Thus the ethnic worker is fooled into thinking that the blacks are getting everything.

Old prejudices and new fears are ignited. The two groups end up fighting each other for the same jobs and competing so that the new schools and recreation centers will be built in their respective communities. What results is angry confrontation for tokens, when there should be an alliance for a whole new Agenda for America. This Agenda would be created if black and white organized separately in their own communities for their own needs and came together to form an alliance based on mutual issues, interdependence and respect. This alliance would develop new strategies for community organization and political restructuring. From this, the new Agenda for America would be generated. It could include such items as "new towns in town," innovative concepts of work and creative structures for community control.

What is necessary is to get rid of the guilt of phony liberals, control by economic élitists and manipulation by selfish politicians. Then, let us get on with creating the democratic and pluralistic society that we say we are.

---

*Barbara Mikulski is a young Polish American and a member of a Baltimore community organization.*

---

## Market Place: The Attitude Of Personnel

### By ROBERT METZ

Perhaps you've heard a story like this. The irate customer brings his new car back to the dealer several times, complaining about a mysterious rattle. Bafflement turns to shock when it is discovered that a production line worker had deliberately welded the gas tank together with a pop bottle inside.

Such shenanigans don't shock Robert N. McMurry. He deplores this kind of thing as much as anyone, but he has come to expect it. As a personnel consultant and head of the McMurray Company in Chicago, he is a student of employes' go-to-hell attitudes.

Mr. McMurry is a Ph.D. in psychology and a prolific writer on business topics. His paper, "In Defense of the Protestant Ethic," has been submitted to The Harvard Business Review for possible publication.

Mr. McMurry says he believes the nation's value system has been drastically eroded with permissive attitudes replacing the Calvinist or Protestant ethic with Victorian overtones.

He blames life as portrayed on television where hedonism and self-indulgence are exalted along, on occasion, with crime, violence and sexuality.

Mr. McMurry says value systems are internalized and hard to change, except under conditions in which the worker's peers share the old values.

You'll find such people, by and large in rural or small city environments, in mid-America and in the South rather than on the West Coast (especially in California), and the East Coast between Norfolk and Boston.

He said people reared in areas of conflicting cultures are not likely to accept the Protestant ethic. They are likely to be somewhat confused and alienated in their values since they have been subjected to widely varying and conflicting ideologies.

Mr. McMurry is Protestant, but he stresses Protestant-type values as opposed to values strictly associated with Protestant denominations.

He believes that these values have contributed to the building of America into the colossus it is today. But he sees disaster if the old values are not restored.

Look at Russia, China and Japan, he says. Protestant-type values are in vogue there and these nations are beginning to prosper as a result. If we don't return to the old values, he says, we'll wind up emulating South American or Indian society with their "low standards of living" for all but a few.

Mr. McMurry's thrust is aimed at helping employers find employes with the old values and, where the values are weak or mixed with the new, he suggests ways to bring out the old.

He has a list of questions designed to turn up a prospective employe's values, including:

¶"What do you think about working Saturdays or Sundays?

¶"What do you think about working the second and third shifts?

¶"What do you think about 'sick-ins'?

¶"If you knew a fellow worker was stealing from the company, what would you do?

¶"What do you think of what is going on on the campuses?"

He has more sophisticated questions for executives, such as:

¶"What are your primary goals in life?

¶"What do you think of the 'Golden Handcuffs' some companies use to lock their executives into their jobs?

¶"What do you think about the legitimacy of the profit motive?"

Mr. McMurry thinks men with the wrong values should not be hired—or retained if already on the job.

To keep the man with the right stuff who is beginning to look fondly on the new freedom, Mr. McMurry suggests find a group of his peers who subscribe to a desired set of values—who believe in quality performance, etc. His peers will sense the fact that his values differ and will immediately apply pressure "(ostracization, ridicule or violence) to insure his conformity (this is a standard union tactic to 'convert' unbelievers.)"

Meanwhile, provide top executives who subscribe to the Protestant ethic who are of such competence and strength of character that they will be respected, trusted and emulated.

# The Cities: The 'Lower Class'

**By EDWARD C. BANFIELD**

The tangle of social pathologies that people mainly have in mind when they speak of "the urban crisis" arises principally from the presence in the inner districts of the central cities and of their larger, older suburbs of a small "lower class" the defining feature of which is its inability (or at any rate failure) to take account of the future and to control impulses.

The lower (as opposed to working) class person never sacrifices any present satisfaction for the sake of a larger future one. He lives from moment to moment.

This is to say, he does not discipline himself to acquire an occupational or other skill, to hold down a regular job, to maintain stable family ties, or to stay out of trouble with the law. His bodily needs (especially for sex) and his taste for "action" take precedence over everything else. The slum is his natural habitat. He does not care how dirty and dilapidated his housing is, and he does not notice or care about the deficiencies of public facilities like schools, parks, and libraries. Indeed, the very qualities that make the slum repellent to others make it attractive to him. He likes the feeling that something violent is about to happen and he likes the opportunities to buy or sell illicit commodities and to find concealment from the police.

For obvious reasons, "lower class" people are always unskilled and usually low income. However, the great majority of the unskilled and the low income — indeed, the great majority of slum dwellers — are not "lower class." It cannot be too strongly emphasized that being "lower class" is a matter of outlook and life style, not one of schooling, income, or social status.

Nor is it one of race. For historical reasons that are familiar to everyone the proportion of Negroes who are "lower class" is relatively large as compared to whites. This has little or nothing to do with race, however. Until a few decades ago the urban lower class was almost entirely white; every ethnic group, including the Anglo-Saxon Protestant one, contributed to it, and its outlook and style of life were strikingly similar to those of the present Negro lower class.

Now that relatively few whites are lower class, it is all too easy for whites (including, unfortunately, many teachers and many policemen) to make the mistake of assuming that a poorly dressed and poorly spoken Negro must be "lower class." This would be an unsafe assumption in dealing with whites but it is a highly implausible one in dealing with Negroes, many of whom have had little or no opportunity to acquire the outward marks of working or middle class culture. Because of their failure to look beyond externals, many whites classify as "Negro" behavior that they should classify as "lower class." Similarly, some of the behavior by whites that Negroes assume to be "racially prejudiced" is in fact "class prejudiced."

It is impossible to tell from Census or other existing data just how many lower class people there are in the cities. To make a count one would first have to decide where to draw the line between the lower and the not-lower classes, and of course any decision about this would have to be more or less arbitrary. Depending on where the line was drawn, it is likely that between 5 and 15 per cent of the population of the large central cities would be "lower class."

The size and importance of the problems that the "lower class" presents to the city are not at all well indicated by those figures, however. In St. Paul, Minnesota, a survey showed that 6 per cent of the city's families absorbed 77 per cent of its public assistance, 51 per cent of its public health services, and 56 per cent of its mental health and correction casework services. Studies in other cities have shown that a very small part of the population is responsible for most of the crimes of violence

So long as the city contains a sizeable "lower class" nothing basic can be done about its most serious problems. Good jobs may be offered to all, but some will remain chronically unemployed. Slums may be demolished, but if the housing that replaces them is occupied by the "lower class" it will shortly be turned into new slums. Welfare payments may be doubled or tripled and a negative income tax instituted, but some persons will continue to live in squalor and misery. New schools may be built, new curricula devised, and the teacher-pupil ratio cut in half, but if the children who attend these schools come from lower-class homes, the schools will be turned into blackboard jungles and those who graduate from them, or drop out of them, will in most cases be functionally illiterate. The streets may be filled with armies of policemen, but violent crime and civil disorder will decrease very little.

If, however, the "lower class" were to disappear — if, say, its members were overnight to acquire the attitudes, motivations, and habits of the working class—the most serious and intractable problems of the city would disappear with it.

If the problems of the city arise more from class cultural than from racial factors, not to recognize that fact may be a tragic error. Misplaced emphasis upon "white racism" is likely to make matters worse both by directing the attention of policy-makers away from matters that should be grappled with and by causing Negroes to see even more prejudice than actually exists.

---

*Edward C. Banfield is Professor of Government at Harvard University and author of "The Unheavenly City," from which this first of two articles is adapted.*

October 12, 1970

# Nixon's Nov. 3 Speech: Why He Took the Gamble Alone

**By ROBERT B. SEMPLE Jr.**

Special to The New York Times

WASHINGTON, Jan. 18 — President Nixon's State of the Union Message Thursday is eagerly awaited in Washington, but it is not likely to be as revealing or profoundly important—to him, to his staff, perhaps even to the country— as his speech to the nation on Vietnam last Nov. 3.

The Vietnam address has been largely passed over in the assessments of Mr. Nixon's first year in office, but his aides say that few episodes tell more about the President's style of operations and his instincts about the country, or about how he is likely to conduct himself at critical moments in the future.

They say that the Vietnam address represented his greatest gamble and greatest triumph of the year. In a substantive sense, he bought time and public patience for his Vietnam strategy with a direct appeal to the "silent majority" to trust him to withdraw American troops from Vietnam at a pace he would not disclose.

### A Deliberate Test

In psychological terms, he gave himself and his staff a welcome boost by putting his own capacity for leadership to what he considered to be a deliberate test.

Mr. Nixon's image in some quarters is said to be that of a man who is easily corseted by an overprotective staff, seeking a consensus, rationing his energie and avoiding major gambles. This may well be the prevailing Nixon style, but the Nov. 3 speech suggests that, on major occasions, he is likely to discard the entire apparatus in favor of his own instincts and judgments.

Against the advice of his chief foreign policy advisers, he offered a full justification for American intervention in the war; against the pleadings of his allies on Capitol Hill—notably Senator Hugh Scott of Pennsylvania, the minority leader — he proposed no further diplomatic initiatives.

According to his associates, Mr. Nixon relied little on his staff and almost entirely on his own perceptions of what the country would accept.

Rather than depend on his stable of six full-time speech writers, sources say, the President wrote the address almost entirely himself in the solitude of his Camp David retreat. The evidence suggests that his first thoughts about the speech survived a two-week personal drafting process with only minor changes.

"I must tell you in all candor," his chief foreign policy adviser, Henry A. Kissinger, told him during the drafting process, "that I have no way of knowing whether this speech has any chance of being listened to."

"What this speech will tell," the President reportedly replied, "is whether the American people can be led in the direction we have to go."

### Timing of the Decision

The decision to give the country an accounting of the Vietnam strategy was made during the President's August vacation in San Clemente, Calif., and was reaffirmed after he announced a second round of troop withdrawals in mid-September.

Mr. Nixon had told visitors all along that he wanted to key such an accounting of his war policy to the first anniversary of the bombing halt in early November. Lending urgency to the project was the fact that the negotiating package unveiled in the last full report to the people on May 14 had failed to energize the Paris peace talks and the related fact that, despite two separate troop withdrawals, public support for the Administration's position had rapidly eroded.

Accordingly, on Oct. 13, the White House press secretary, Ronald L. Ziegler, announced that the President would deliver a "major address" Nov. 3. Critics immediately charged that the announcement itself was timed to defuse the antiwar moratorium scheduled for Oct. 15, and that the speech was timed to achieve maximum impact in the scattered state and municipal elections on Nov. 4.

Mr. Nixon's associates insist otherwise. They contend that the President needed to announce the speech early, in the words of one high source, "to give Hanoi fair warning and a chance to turn around in Paris."

In addition, the President was said to have overridden the advice of his public relations specialists, who reasoned—correctly, as it turned out—that an early announcement would give critics three weeks in which to mount an attack and press for faster disengagement, and thus build expectations that the speech would contain precisely the sort of bold initiative that Mr. Nixon wished to avoid.

### Set of 'Talking Points'

Although he wrote the speech himself, Mr. Nixon turned for preliminary data to his policy-making machinery. Mr. Kissinger asked for memorandums from the Secretaries of State and Defense and from Ellsworth Bunker in Saigon and Henry Cabot Lodge in Paris. He also asked two members of his National Security Council staff to propose a set of "talking points" for the President.

The following Sunday, Oct. 19, Mr. Kissinger went to Cambridge, Mass., to solicit the advice of old friends in the Harvard community. What he heard apparently did not relieve his earlier nervousness about the speech. He reported that nearly all of his friends wanted the President to announce some concrete initiative, or, at the very least, disclose a definite timetable for withdrawal.

This was also the substance of much of the advice Mr. Nixon was repeatedly getting from his allies on Capitol Hill, in the press, and from the middle levels of the bureaucracy. But he remained convinced that the address would accomplish little at home or abroad, if he made yet another gesture of reconciliation. He felt that he should confine himself to the philosophical direction of American policy, according to his aides.

The President received little contrary pressure from his Cabinet, it is said, but on one point there was a fundamental disagreement. Most of the memorandums from the bureaucracy urged him to address himself to existing policies for disengagement and spend little time defending the original American commitment.

Even Mr. Kissinger, it is said, argued that the American presence in Vietnam created a logic of its own and that the President should give heaviest emphasis to what the Administration had done to turn a war it had not made into a peace with which both sides could live.

### Doing a Disservice

The President, however, reportedly argued that to dismiss the past would be a disservice to the mothers of 40,000 men who had died in conflict; and that to imply that America should never have entered the war in the first place would have involved criticizing the judgment of not only President Johnson but also Presidents Eisenhower and Kennedy, and might well have shaken public confidence in the institution of the Presidency itself.

Finally, he told friends, he himself had backed the original commitment, and to say that the war had been mishandled would, at this late stage, be mildly irrelevant.

According to White House sources, Mr. Nixon began making notes Oct. 21. The first jottings covered four pages of plain White House stationery and were dated "Oct. 21, 1 A.M." They began: "I speak on a problem that concerns every American. . . ." He used roughly the same phrase to begin the actual speech. Near the end, he jotted down two significant phrases:

"If you want defeat, let me know. If you want peace, now is the time to speak up."

This phraseology was later abandoned, in part because the President did not wish to issue so blatant an invitation to demonstrators of any kind, friendly or critical. But they suggest that, from the beginning, he intended to draw more boldly than ever before the line between the Administration and its critics.

His aides say that Mr. Nixon required extensive research material only on the middle portion of the speech, which set forth his efforts to achieve a negotiated settlement — including previously undisclosed private contacts—and a description of the parallel effort to transfer the bulk of the fighting to the Vietnamese.

Memorandums flew back and forth as the President tried to buttress his case with concrete detail. One, to Mr. Kissinger, reportedly requested the exact figures on enemy massacres in Hue; another requested a restatement of the three criteria on which, in his May 14 address, Mr. Nixon had said he would base further withdrawals.

### Trouble at the End

On Oct. 29, for the first time, the President read Mr. Kissinger an outline of what he had written, and the next day he gave three other close advisers—Attorney General John N. Mitchell, Secretary of State William P. Rogers and Secretary of Defense Melvin R. Laird —essentially the same presentation. He is said to have written a note to himself before the meeting and to have stressed it throughout his talk — "the burden is on them."

That afternoon, in his auxiliary office in the Executive Office Building, next door to the White House, Mr. Nixon read Mr. Kissinger the entire text, and the following day, the 31st, he read aloud the ending. Associates recall that he was having trouble with the ending, and had collected scraps of yellow paper covered with phrases he wanted to use but could find no place for.

"I don't want demonstrations," read one, "I want your quiet support."

That evening, after delivering an address on Latin-American policy, the President flew to Camp David. Arriving by helicopter the next day, Mr. Kissinger said, he discovered that the President had been up until 4 A.M., reworking the ending. It incorporated some of the thoughts from the first jottings of Oct. 21 and the scraps he had not found room for. From these emerged perhaps the decisive paragraph:

"And so tonight, to you, the great silent majority of Americans, I ask for your support."

Mr. Kissinger and the President reviewed the speech page by page on Saturday, Nov. 1. The President spent most of Sunday and Monday polishing it.

On Monday night, an hour before the President was to deliver the speech to the nation, copies were delivered to members of the press who had assembled for a briefing in the East Room of the White House. Fifteen minutes later, the Joint Chiefs of Staff—they were not consulted during the drafting process—received their copies.

Still nervous, Mr. Kissinger entered the East Room to brief the press. He says now that he fully expected to be overwhelmed with angry questions, because the speech contained none of the initiatives the press had forecast.

Mr. Nixon himself was not certain after the Vietnam speech whether he had accomplished anything. He called an aide, Patrick J. Buchanan, to ask: "How'd I do?" But on Nov. 4, telegrams of support began arriving in large numbers. The President said they came from the "silent majority," on whose existence he had risked the entire enterprise.

# The Rebirth of a Future: I

Tomi Ungerer

By CHARLES A. REICH

Day-to-day events leave us with a feeling of chaos; it seems as if we must be mere powerless spectators at the decline and fall of our country. But these same events are capable of being understood as part of a larger process of social change — a process that is fearsome and yet fundamentally hopeful. And we may be participants—we may regain the power to make our own future—if only we understand what is taking place.

In Spain, the American President rides in an open car with a military dictator who by using lawless force has repressed all meaningful social progress. In Vietnam, halfway around the world, young Americans are compelled to fight in support of another corrupt dictatorship. These are not separate events, they are symptoms of a larger pattern. Women's liberation, black militancy, the campaign against the S.S.T., Gay Liberation, the long hair of youth are not separate events either; they too are related. The many wars, the many revolutions, are one.

The agonies of the great industrial nations, and especially our own, are no mystery. They have been fully predicted and explained by many social thinkers. There is much room for argument among schools of thought, but the main outline is clear. Neither machines nor material progress is inher-

ently bad. But we have achieved our progress by a system which shortsightedly wastes man and nature by failing to protect them in the haste for gain. A rising crime rate, extremes of inequality, neglect of social needs, personal alienation and loss of meaning, disorder and war are all manifestations of the underlying process of corrosive exploitation.

This process has now reached a point where remedial action is desperately urgent. Knowing this, why are we unable to guide our progress along more rational lines? Why is our system so rigid that it ignores even the mild remedies proposed by its own Presidential Commissions? This brings us to a second element of our crisis, an element which also can be explained. American society has been amalgamated into a single monolith of power—the corporate state—which includes both the private and public structures. This monolith is not responsible to democratic or even executive control. The Corporate State is mindless and irrational. It rolls along with a momentum of its own, producing a society that is ever more at war with its own inhabitants. Again, there is plenty of room for different theories of the state, but the major pattern of unthinking and uncontrolled power must by now be accepted.

If our nation's immobility can be explained and understood, we must ask once more: why are we unable to refashion our system? All social systems are merely the creations of men; men make them and men can change them. But the power to act is limited by our consciousness. Today most Americans are not conscious of the realities of their society.

One segment of the American people remains at a level of consciousness that was formed when we were a land of small villages and individual opportunity; Consciousness I is unable to accept the reality of an interdependent society that requires collective responsibility. A second segment of the American people understands the realities of organization life but does not see that organizations and their policies are, by themselves, inhuman. Consciousness II supports the Corporate State and seeks happiness in its artificial rewards, mistakenly believing that such a state is necessary and rational in this industrial age.

These two forms of unreality, Consciousness I and II, render us powerless. We cannot act constructively so long as we are the prisoners of myth. Consciousness I exhausts its energy blaming scapegoats such as Communists, hippies, and liberals. Consciousness II offers solutions that would but strengthen existing structure. But the moment that our eyes are opened to the true causes of our self-destruction, there is hope.

What the times urgently demand, what our survival demands, is a new consciousness that will reassert rational control over the industrial system and the Corporate State, and transform them into a way of life that protects and advances human values. It is not necessary to destroy our machines or our material well-being; it is only necessary to guide them. Such a new consciousness must reject the old myths, must reject the mindless operation of the State, must reassert the reality of nature and of man's nature. Today, in this moment of most desperate need, that new consciousness is at last emerging—the spontaneous outgrowth of the fears and hopes of the new generation.

*Charles Reich is Professor of Law at Yale University. This article and one which follows tomorrow synthesize his views of the American condition as presented in "The Greening of America," to be published Friday.*

October 21, 1970

# The Eve of the Bluing of America

Jan Faust

## By PETER and BRIGITTE BERGER

A considerable number of American intellectuals have been on a kick of revolution talk for the last few years. It began in a left mood, with fantasies of political revolution colored red or black. The mood now appears to have shifted somewhat. The fantasies have shifted to cultural revolution, which, we are told, will color America green.

What the two varieties of revolution talk have in common is a sublime disregard for the requirements of technological society and for the realities of power and class in America. To be sure, drastic (if you like, "revolutionary") things are happening in this society, but the currently fashionable interpretations only serve to obfuscate them.

It is conceivable that technological society will collapse in America. In that case, as grass grows over the computers, we would revert to the ways of an underdeveloped country. Conceivable, yes; probable, no. The more likely assumption is that technological society will continue. If so, who will run it? We would venture, first, a negative answer: It will *not* be the people engaged in the currently celebrated cultural revolutions.

The "greening" revolution is not taking place in a sociological vacuum, but has a specific location in a society that is organized in social classes. There are enough data now to pinpoint this location. The cadres of the revolution are, in overwhelming proportions, the college-educated children of the upper middle class. Ethnically, they tend to be Wasps and Jews. Ideologically, they are in revolt against the values of this class—which is precisely the class that has been running the technological society so far. But the essentially bucolic rhetoric of this rebellion goes far beyond a radical (in

491

the leftist sense) rejection of American class society and its allegedly evil ways. The rhetoric intends a dropping out of technological society as such.

The matrix of this revolution has been the youth culture. What are the prospects for the children of the people of the emerging counterculture? We don't want to speculate in detail about the probable career of the son of a dropped-out sandal maker in Bella Vista—except for the suggestion that he is unlikely to make it to the upper-middle-class status of his grandfather. In sociological parlance, he is probably headed for downward social mobility.

The black revolution, for quite different reasons, is also headed for a counter or subculture, segregated from the opportunity system of technological society and subsidized through political patronage. The prospects here are for segregated social mobility. This may have its own cultural or ideological satisfactions. But upward mobility in a black ("community controlled") educational bureaucracy is unlikely to lead to positions of power and privilege in the enveloping technological society.

If the "greening" revolution will in fact continue to lure sizable numbers of upper-middle-class individuals out of "the system," and if the black revolution will succeed in arresting outward mobility among its adherents, a simple but decisively important development will take place: There will be new "room at the top." Who is most likely to take advantage of this sociological windfall? It will be the newly college-educated children of the white

lower middle and working classes (and possibly those nonwhites who will refuse to stay within the resegregated racial subcultures). In other words, precisely those classes that remain most untouched by what is considered to be the revolutionary tide in contemporary America face new prospects of upward social mobility.

A technological society, given a climate of reasonable tolerance, can afford sizable regiments of sandal makers and Swahili teachers. It must have quite different people, though, to occupy its command posts and to keep its engines running. These will have to be people retaining the essentials of the old Protestant ethic—discipline, achievement orientation and, last not least, a measure of freedom from gnawing self-doubt.

If such people are no longer available in one population reservoir, another reservoir will have to be tapped. There is no reason to think that "the system" will be unable to make the necessary accommodations. Should Yale become hopelessly "greened," Wall Street will get used to recruits from Fordham or Wichita State. Italians or Southern Baptists will have no trouble running the Rand Corporation. It is even possible that the White House may soon have its first Polish occupant (or, in a slightly different scenario, its first Greek).

There is one proviso—namely, that the children of these classes remain relatively unbitten by the "greening" bug. If they, too, should drop out, there would literally be no one left to mind the technological store. So far,

the evidence does not point in this direction.

Indeed, what evidence we have of the dynamics of class in a number of European countries would indicate that the American case is not all that unique. Both England and West Germany have undergone very similar changes in their class structures, with new reservoirs of lower-middle-class and working-class populations supplying the personnel requirements of a technological society no longer serviced by the old élites.

The aforementioned process is not new in history. It is what Vilfredo Pareto (that most neglected of classical sociologists) called the "circulation of élites." Even Marx, albeit in the most ironical manner, may be proved right in the end. It may, indeed, be the blue-collar masses that are, at last, coming into their own. "Power to the people!"—nothing less than that. The class struggle may be approaching a decisive new phase, with the children of the working class victorious—under the sign of the American flag. In that perspective, alas, the peace emblem represents the decline of the bourgeois enemy class, aptly symbolizing its defeat before a more robust adversary. This would not be the first time in history that the principals in the societal drama are unaware of the consequences of their actions.

"Revolutionary" America? Perhaps. We may be on the eve of its bluing.

---

*Peter Berger is professor of sociology at Rutgers University. Brigitte Berger is associate professor of sociology at Long Island University.*

February 15, 1971

# American Illusion

### By MICHAEL NOVAK

There are many reasons why a tragic sense of life does not come easy to Americans, and why a tragic sense of life is required if we are not to destroy ourselves. Until recently it was so easy not to believe evil of ourselves. Even when we saw the photographs used as evidence in the Calley trial, it was easy to be detached from them. They could not have connection to us.

To begin with, we were a new nation, born on a new continent, a people eager to forget past human history.

"I know America," President Nixon is fond of saying. "And the heart of

America is good." For three and a half centuries we have had to believe that about ourselves. That belief has been a necessary pillar of our sense of worth and meaning.

We had to believe that America would be hope. America would be beautiful. America would be "new." What would be newest about it would be the absence of tragedy, the advent of hope. Optimism became the one necessary foundation of the republic. Things must always be looking up.

We see now, after 350 years, that such ideological blinders prevented our ancestors—and ourselves—from recognizing the true history of our nation and its true relation to the rest of the world. Even when our children despair of us, it is not from despair. It is from too much hope. So powerful is the American illusion that our children are absorbed by it, and are full of rage not because their parents preached il-

lusion, but because their parents failed to live up to it.

The new world became hopelessly enmeshed in slavery and its deep psychic corruptions, which would entangle human relations as tragically as ever they had been in "the old world." In aggrandizement, greed, chicanery and exploitation, the men of the new world showed daily that the new history was all too like the old. Enormous advantages of a fresh beginning in a wealthy and beautiful land were all too quickly squandered.

The atom bomb was dropped on cities crowded with men of the yellow race. Torture, assassination, murder, and an unparalleled scorching of the land came to characterize, to an extent not yet explored, American tactics in a war full of dilemmas in Vietnam.

The artificiality of an economy based on advertising causes many men and women of sensitivity muted anguish in their daily work—was it this that in their youth they had in mind as "fulfillment"? Public duty and private escape divide the lives of many.

Had Americans a tragic sense, none of this would be surprising. What is more typical of the human story than such a denouement? Had we a tragic sense, we could perhaps admit military and political defeats, admit that "the heart of America" is not particularly good but ambivalent, admit that our public and private lives are shot through with falsehood and betrayal.

Nothing more common and ordinary than that. It is rather, the pretense of innate goodness that so bitterly divides Americans. Since each must think of himself or herself as good, it becomes necessary to project evil on the others.

Thus middle Americans blame "agitators" and "communists," radicals blame "pigs" and "fascists," black militants blame "honkies" and "imperialists," women's lib blames "men," liberals blame "ideologists."

The tragic sense of life suggests that the plague is not in others but in ourselves. It suggests that all things human, given enough time, go badly. And it does not find in such suggestions reason for shock, or crippling feelings of guilt, or dismay, or escape from action. On the contrary, the tragic sense of life differs from pathos precisely because it views humans as agents and actors, not as victims.

The tragic sense of life is a calm acceptance of despair, a firm determination to act well and unflinchingly, and forgiveness in advance for others and for oneself. No one escapes the burden of being fully human—even when each well knows himself to be incompletely human.

Tragedy arises precisely because we are called upon to act today with a wisdom, courage, honesty, and compassion we do not as yet possess. Had our people and our leaders a tragic sense of life, America would be less self-flagellant, more at peace with herself, and far less pretentious among others. Expecting less, we might quietly do more. Less righteous, we might be more honest with ourselves and with each other.

*Michael Novak teaches philosophy and religion at State University of New York, Old Westbury.*

# Beyond Freedom And Dignity

*By B. F. Skinner.
225 pp. New York:
Alfred A. Knopf. $6.95.*

## By RICHARD SENNETT

There are three B. F. Skinners. The first is Skinner the experimenter, the author of "The Behavior of Organisms," for more than 30 years an explorer of how far animals and men can be pushed to change engrained habits. This Skinner has created special environments within his laboratory: the famous "Skinner Box" is a device that enables a researcher to control totally the conditions in which a rat, rabbit or man acts; by carefully changing one element in the environment, from altering the temperature to rewarding only certain actions, the researcher hopes to see transformations in long-established patterns of behavior. The Skinner who invented these techniques belongs to an old school of psychology, founded by Pavlov, Thorndike and others at the end of the 19th century.

The second B. F. Skinner is bolder. His novel "Walden Two," published more than 20 years ago, is a utopian dream (or nightmare). The controlled environment that Skinner the experimenter creates in the laboratory, Skinner the utopian declares should be a model for planning the whole society. For example, violence is to be eliminated by scientifically changing a criminal's personality; laboratory experiments will determine what kind of carefully constructed exercises or tasks will induce him to change his behavior; the hope, as in "Animal Farm," is to create a citizenry who eventually can conceive only of actions that benefit everyone in society. In "Walden Two" Skinner dreams of a kind of scientifically induced altruism.

Like many utopian writers, Skinner Two hopes to show his model society

**Richard Sennett** is author of "Families Against the City" and "The Uses of Disorder" and teaches sociology at **New York University.**

is not a wild idea by demonstrating that everyday reality is already much as he describes it, but that people are unaware of what they are doing. Conditioning and reconditioning of behavior is going on all the time, Skinner says; recognize the reality that man is only as he is conditioned to behave, put away the unscientific ideas of a "mind" or a "soul" divorced from this conditioned behavior, and society can be organized more rationally.

This utopian program raises a terrible set of questions: Who makes decisions about what behavior will be praised and what behavior discouraged? Skinner says individuals have no free will, but isn't even the illusion of freedom from society's power necessary for human beings if they are going to fight society's injustices? Now, in a new book, "Beyond Freedom and Dignity," Skinner Three has appeared, a moral philosopher bent on answering, as the dust jacket puts it, "these and many other questions concerning so-called 'value-judgments.'"

The Skinner who appears in this book is different from the evangelistic author of "Walden Two." Where once he fantasized about a world controlled by social science, now he attacks the unscientific fantasies of others: the fantasy that people possess the right to freedom from society, or that mankind has an innate dignity which transcends the way society makes men behave. But this book is interesting chiefly because it shows us that Skinner the philosopher doesn't really believe in his own utopia, that he is at best a very troubled behaviorist.

The essays in "Beyond Freedom and Dignity" are bound together by a common enemy, an illusion of illusions that, by some quirk of environmental conditioning Skinner does not bother to explain, has haunted mankind for thousands of years; this falsehood is "autonomous man," a creature endowed with a "nature," an inner power to transcend the conditioning of society. Early in the book, Skinner makes a grand, not to say grandiose,

list of the fields this enemy idea has captured: autonomous man "is still an important figure in political science, law, religion, economics, anthropology, sociology, psychotherapy, philosophy, ethics, history, education, child care, linguistics,

493

architecture, city planning, and family life. These fields have their specialists, and every specialist has a theory, and in almost every theory the autonomy of the individual is unquestioned."

An amazing display of erudition (unfootnoted); in the field I know—sociology—the claim is simply untrue. But statements on this scale appear again and again in the book as Skinner tries to establish a peculiar tone: that he is a pioneer thinker proclaiming a hard and shocking truth to the multitudes who are too enslaved by the comfortable ideas of the past to listen fairly.

Had Skinner only listened to a modest piece of advice from Freud—we often love in private that which we condemn in others. The actual text of Skinner's new book reveals a man desperately in search of some way to preserve the old-fashioned virtues associated with 19th-century individualism in a world where self-reliance no longer makes sense.

This hidden agenda can first be detected in the way Skinner talks about controlling behavior. All his attention is centered on situations where one person is being controlled; he employs such phrases as "a person's behavior" or "operant conditioning of the subject." He seldom refers to different controls for different kinds of social groups. He hardly considers the variety of responses different people make to the same stimulus. Now of course it could be said that Skinner speaks of "the subject" as a general category; but then, anyone who really believes in the power of society to mold men knows that societies are so complex that they do not affect people "in general" in the same way.

This dissonance in Skinner's thinking becomes amplified when he tries to explain the ethical purpose of behavior conditioning. He tells us that the "technology of behavior" is of itself morally neutral; a saint or a devil could employ it equally well. Speaking, as it were, *ex machina*, he indicates a few purposes to which he personally would like to see the techniques put.

First, behavior control appears to him a way to get people hard at work again in an age where indolence is rife. "The species is prepared for short periods of leisure," he tells us, "but the result is very different when there is nothing to do for long periods of time." This is poor behaviorism; no genuine believer in the infinite malleability of human behavior should make statements about what "the species" is predisposed toward. But Skinner's beliefs have overtaken his theory; he personally believes in the virtue of hard work, and calls on what he condemns—an outmoded theory of innate human nature—to support a "value judgment" which his own value-free theory, as he says, is neither for nor against.

As a corollary to his belief in hard work, Skinner rails against the sexual and other sensual pleasures that he feels have become rampant today, and argues that such behavior needs to be redirected. "Sexual behavior . . . takes a prominent place in leisure . . . [as do] foods which continue to reinforce even when one is not hungry, drugs like alcohol, marijuana, or heroin, which happen to be reinforcing for irrelevant reasons, or massage" To equate heroin and massage takes a peculiar mind. The passage makes sense only if the writer feels all sensual pleasure leads to decadence. That, indeed, was the belief of the Victorian schoolmasters who admonished their young charges to be good and lose themselves in work.

Not surprisingly, Skinner also believes that the small group, the town, the village, the little neighborhood circle, is the scale at which behavior conditioning can operate morally. "A large fluid population cannot be brought under informal social or ethical control because social reinforcers like praise and blame are not exchangeable for personal reinforcers on which they are based. Why should anyone be affected by the praise or blame of someone he will never see again? Ethical control may survive in small groups, but the control of the population as a whole must be delegated to specialists—to police, priests, owners, teachers, therapists, and so on."

The character of this list is revealing. How in 1971 can a man equate industrial magnates with doctors of the soul? This is a child's view of society: there is no discrimination among controllers, everyone who has power is an "authority."

These beliefs should sound familiar. They are the articles of faith of Nixonian America, of the small-town businessman who feels life has degenerated, has gotten beyond his control, and who thinks things will get better when other people learn how to behave.

There has always been an incredible arrogance to Skinner's claim that his ideal society is supported by scientific evidence, but not until the appearance of philosopher Skinner in this book could the reasons for his emphasis on science be seen. As a moralist who believes in a way of life that is rapidly dying, Skinner has contrived the best possible defense for his "value judgments": science—modern, up-to-date, hard science — stands ready to support him. In the process Skinner, who has some harsh words for "pre-scientific" writers, misrepresents the character of modern scientific work.

*B. F. Skinner.*

Much of 20th-century physics has been built around Heisenberg's study of uncertainty in the behavior of matter; readers of James Watson's magnificent "The Double Helix" were able to observe how a fundamental problem in genetics was solved when the researchers began to imagine wild solutions rather than make precise deductions. While Heisenberg contemplated the unpredictable behavior of matter, Skinner insists that we must find unambiguous facts about human behavior; the difference is between wanting to explore the world as it is and wanting to possess knowledge. The possession of knowledge, of hard facts you can act on, is an echo of 19th-century positivistic science, just as Skinner's beliefs are an echo of that century's small-town society.

Skinner does a disservice to the social sciences as well, not only because his claims of hard truth confirm the stereotype many readers have that social scientists are dogmatic and naive, but also because Skinner acknowledges no peers. He says very little about allied work by Talcott Parsons, and very little about Karl Marx, who was, in fact, a thorough-going behaviorist; he too argued human beings were the creatures of their actions in society, that free will was a phantom, etc. Skinner never acknowledges him; for Skinner lacks a sense of perspective on himself.

In the end, Skinner's hidden agenda makes the reader doubt Skinner really believes that society intrudes into the deepest recesses of people's lives. Here, for example, is Skinner describing the plight of an alienated youth, translating into behaviorist terms the young man's feelings: "He has graduated from college and is going to work, let us say, or has been inducted into the armed services. ...He lacks assurance or feels insecure or is unsure of himself (his behavior is weak and inappropriate). . . . He is frustrated (extinction is accompanied by emotional responses); he feels uneasy or anxious (his behavior frequently has unavoidable aversive consequences which have emotional effects.)" But Professor, there's a war on! Why aren't you talking about the social cause of his behavi-

494

or? Why do you treat him as if he lives in a vacuum?

The unforgivable failing of this book is that it is incurious about the nature of society and has little to say about social life, though it proclaims a world of entirely socializable human beings. In the chapter on human dignity, we are told that dignity is simply a matter of "positive reinforcement," a matter of behaving so as to win praise. Were the rebels against Nazi Germany then undignified? Surely they suffered cataclysmic "negative reinforcement." The grandiose ideas in this book cannot handle historical events, which are, after all, how people actually have behaved. Indeed a conception of human dignity as simple-minded as Skinner's will never provide the insights that might stimulate a society to encourage more dignified behavior in its citizens.

This failure to do the intellectual work demanded by his own theory has made Skinner's behaviorism seem like a "monumental triviality" to Arthur Koestler and "intellectually bankrupt" to Peter Gay. (Characteristically Skinner has seen in these judgments of his ideas only personal "name calling.") I think these judgments are too harsh; behavior control has certain real uses in psychotherapy, and behaviorism in a form Skinner does not discuss is a ruling ideology in the Marxist countries of the world. It is Skinner who has weakened behaviorism by bending it to an inappropriate goal. Hoping to revive the morality of a less complicated age by invoking the certainties of an antiquated science, he appears to understand so little, indeed to care so little, about society itself that the reader comes totally to distrust him. ∎

October 24, 1971

# Welfare-Job Law Stirs Bitterness and Confusion

## By PAUL DELANEY
Special to The New York Times

WASHINGTON, Oct. 8 — Workfare, the controversial concept of a new law forcing welfare recipients to take jobs, has generated tremendous bitterness and confusion in the three months since the Federal measure took effect.

For the recipients, the law has meant additional frustration in dealing now with two bureaucracies—state employment services as well as state welfare agencies—rather than just the welfare offices as in the past.

And for officials of the agencies, judging from a survey of scores of state and city officials around the country, the new law has compounded a long-standing antagonism and led, in some cases, to open defiance of the law.

On one side are the welfare agencies, generally regarded as more sympathetic to the ways of the poor. And on the other are the employment services, historically better geared to serve highly motivated, middle class job seekers.

Shuttling between them, meanwhile, are the poor. When Leroy Begay, a 32-year-old Navajo, and his family arrived in Los Angeles not long ago, for example, they were penniless and without food and they went for help to the county welfare agency.

Under old welfare regulations, that agency would have determined whether the Begays were eligible for assistance and, if so, would have provided it straightway. But under workfare, the process is more complicated.

"First we went to the welfare office," Mr. Begay recalled. "They said they could not give us any help until we went to the employment office to sign up for work. I said we didn't have transportation to get down there, that it was a four-hour walk from our apartment. And I told them we didn't even have any food. But our counselor said there was nothing she could do."

Heretofore, workfare has been either voluntary or limited to experimental projects in such areas as New York and California. But the law that went into effect July 1 requires most able-bodied recipients of welfare under the Aid to Families with Dependent Children program to register for work and face a cutoff of benefits if they refuse a job.

So far the experimental workfare projects have provided jobs for a few recipients and forced greater numbers off welfare. Nixon Administration officials and other proponents believe that they have been successful.

Still, it is generally agreed among welfare officials and Federal manpower consultants as well as liberal members of Congress that the projects have failed in their over-all goals of substantially reducing welfare rolls and costs.

Just last week, the Senate killed further consideration of welfare reform programs that included various forms of workfare ranging from liberal work requirements to extremely stringent ones. The Senate voted instead to continue with experimental projects over the next five years.

The recent history of the controversial workfare concept winds through a thicket of politics, programs and projects. Since welfare rolls and costs have been steadily increasing, bringing about cutback has become a major political issue. Workfare is seen by its proponents as the answer to the problem.

Before enactment of the Federal law, experimental programs directed at up to 1.5 million of the nearly 11 million persons receiving welfare were under way.

### Failure is Charged

The most extensive was a Federal project called the Work Incentive Program (WIN). New York and California had the largest state programs, but several other states, such as New Jersey, Connecticut and Michigan, had some form of workfare, either as a state program, or as Federally funded experimental projects.

Most of the programs simply provide that recipients register for work or job training in order to get aid. Critics contend that most of these programs have been failures.

The work relief law of New York, for example, has been found to have minimal effectiveness in reducing welfare rolls and in putting welfare clients to work, according to reports made last May and last month.

Workfare became national law under what is called the "Talmadge Amendment" named for its sponsor, Senator Herman E. Talmadge, Democrat of Georgia.

Officials of many welfare agencies simply do not believe in the concept of workfare and do not feel it will work. Some not only predicted failure of the program but indicated that they would attempt to defy implementation of the Talmadge amendment.

On the other hand, many, but not all, employment service officials welcomed the changes, and some expressed delight in taking over welfare work projects, which was a kind of victory over welfare officials. The employment officials tended to be more optimistic than others that the situation would soon improve.

Both sides agreed that widespread and high unemployment and the historic failure of training programs would hamper the success of workfare.

"It just gives false hope and it is cruel," remarked Maurice A. Harmon, director of the Baltimore Department of Social Services.

"It takes a hard-crusted soul to build someone up for something phony like this," he said. "The jobs are just not there."

Many welfare recipients were found to be hopeful that they would be placed in jobs or in training programs that would lead to jobs. Several women interviewed at the state employment office on 8th Avenue North in Birmingham, Ala., were enthusiastic about work but pessimistic about training programs.

Welfare rights leaders were mixed in their reaction. They remained adamantly opposed to the principle of workfare, but they reflected the desire of recipients to get off welfare and into meaningful jobs.

### Delays Are Expected

Citing a lack of jobs, some welfare officials said that they would drag their feet in implementing the Talmadge amendment. Most believed that delays would occur anyway due to the normally slow process of setting up machinery and waiting for Federal guidelines to arrive.

The prototype for the national workfare program was the Work Incentive Program. In operation for five years, it provided that recipients participate in the work training program or face loss of benefits.

While Administration officials have insisted that the program has been successful, many critics, including Congressional committees, have concluded otherwise. For example, three evaluations of the California WIN program, all released earlier this year, found that the program had failed to provide meaningful training or permanent jobs.

WIN's success at placing its graduates in jobs has been about 20 per cent. But most of the jobs have lasted only a short time. Ninety-five per cent of the participants have been women.

Under the Talmadge amendment. the $455-million new WIN program would include $200-million for child care and other social services, $4-million for public service jobs and $46-million for staffing of the programs by state employment offices.

Further, employers could receive $1,000 for on-the-job training of each welfare recipient and a 20 per cent tax credit on the salary paid to a new worker. The employer must agree to train the prospective worker for six months and not discharge the worker without cause for two years.

### Exemptions From Program

Exempted under the Talmadge amendment is the bulk of the 11 million people on welfare under the Aid to Families with Dependent Children program. (These are children under 16 and those between 16 and 21 who are attending school and who make up more than half the program's rolls, the ill and those who care for them, mothers or other relatives caring for children under age 6 and recipients living too far from WIN projects).

The availability of jobs, most officials agreed, is a major problem. For example, William Bechtel, director of the Wisconsin Manpower Planning Council, said that there were only 300 jobs for the 19,000 registered recipients in the state.

An added hindrance is the reluctance so far of business to take advantage of the $1,000 tax credit for taking on recipients.

"First of all the economic situation is still bad," one employment service official in Birmingham, Ala., said. "But another thing, too, a lot of businessmen just don't like fooling around with the Federal Government. They don't like the red tape, the paper work and the Internal Revenue Service watching over them any more than is necessary."

# Nixon Vows to Back Individualist Values In a Second Term

### By ROBERT B. SEMPLE Jr.
Special to The New York Times

WASHINGTON, Oct. 21— President Nixon set forth today his vision of the moral values that animate the nation and pledged to champion those values in a second term.

In the third of a series of campaign radio addresses, he set aside what he called "current issues" to focus on his "philosophy of government" and to sketch in general terms "the principles which will guide me in making decisions over the next four years."

He did not mention his opponent, Senator George McGovern of South Dakota. But taken as a whole, his speech— the product of several weeks of work with William Safire, White House speechwriter, constituted an effort to draw a distinction between the values he holds and those he perceives to be held by Mr. McGovern and his followers.

Mr. Nixon's explicit message was that the majority of Americans still believe in individualism, the virtue of hard work, the rightness of receiving rewards for achievement and a sense of community and family.

His implicit message—reminiscent of some of the earlier speeches of Vice President Agnew—was that his opponents were élitist, "self-righteous" and scornful, that they had only contempt for basic values and were trying to make those who subscribed to them feel guilty.

The essential passages in the speech were as follows:

"To them," he said of his unnamed opponents, "the will of the people is the 'prejudice of the masses.' They deride anyone who wants to respond to that will of the people as 'pandering to the crowd.' A decent respect for the practice of majority rule is automatically denounced as 'political expediency.'

"I totally reject this philosophy.

"When a man sees more and more of the money he earns taken away by government taxation, and he objects to that, I don't think it is right to charge him with selfishness, with not caring about the poor and the dependent.

### Bigotry Charge Derided

"When a mother sees her child taken from a neighborhood school and transported miles away, and she objects to that, I don't think it is right to charge her with bigotry.

"When young people apply for jobs—in politics or in industry—and find the doors closed because they don't fit into some numerical quota, despite their ability, and they object—I don't think it is right to condemn those young people as insensitive or racist.

"Of course, some people oppose income redistribution and busing for the wrong reasons. But they are by no means the majority of Americans, who oppose them for the right reasons.

"It is time that good, decent people stop letting themselves be bulldozed by anybody who presumes to be the self-righteous moral judge of our society.

"There is no reason to feel guilty about wanting to enjoy what you get and get what you earn, about wanting your children in good schools close to home or about wanting to be judged fairly on your ability. Those are not values to be ashamed of; those are values to be proud of; those are values that I shall always stand up for when they come under attack."

### 'New American Majority'

Mr. Nixon identified himself with principles that he had found "deep in the American spirit" and portrayed himself as unusually sensitive to those principles. As evidence, he offered the positions and actions that he had taken on containing taxes, controlling inflation and on school busing and preserving the nation's national security.

"The new American majority," he said, "believes that each person should have more of the say in how he lives his own life, how he spends his paycheck, how he brings up his children.

"The new American majority believes in taking better care of those who truly cannot care for themselves, so that they can lead lives of dignity and self-respect.

"The new American majority believes in taking whatever action is needed to hold down the cost of living, so that everyone's standard of living can go up.

"The new American majority believes in a national defense second to none, so that America can help bring about a generation of peace.

### 'Values Deserve Respect'

"These are not the beliefs of selfish people. On the contrary, they are the beliefs of a generous and self-reliant people, a people of intellect and character, whose values deserve respect in every segment of our population."

In some passages, Mr. Nixon seemed almost to claim victory in advance, suggesting that Americans who shared his views represented a "new American majority" that would give him a second term in office.

The President said that he would take unpopular positions when necessary and would neither tailor his actions to the public opinion polls nor "follow the opinion of the majority down the line."

But, in what he perceived as a happy coincidence, he said that he had found that "what the new majority wants for America and what I want for this nation are basically the same."

Mr. Nixon's address was broadcast from his Camp David retreat in the Maryland mountains, where he is spending the weekend. He will deliver a Veterans Day radio address at 10:36 A.M. tomorrow over the Columbia Broadcasting System, the National Broadcasting Company and the Mutual Broadcasting System.

# Paul Goodman, Outsider Looking In

## By GEORGE LEVINE

Y the time Paul Goodman died at 60 last August, he had moved through what for most people would have been several careers: poet, novelist, urban planner, psychotherapist, social, literary and educational critic. As he noted many times himself, specialists in each of the fields he touched complained that he spread himself too thin. But almost everything he did was worth attending to, and his career has the coherence of a life lived both passionately and intelligently. He trained himself to live as an outsider looking in, and apparently he could not be seduced by the kinds of rewards his talents might have earned him—though his moving journal, "Five Years" (1966), makes clear how deeply he longed for an audience. But even after the success of "Growing Up Absurd" in 1960, when he began to seem a kind of guru for the young who were dropping out or turning left, he retained his power both to be engaged and to criticize. And in the years just before his death, he was describing himself as a "neolithic conservative," almost as if to ensure that he might remain outside all parties.

His last book, "Little Prayers and Finite Experience" (Harper & Row, $5.95), has the virtue of telling us a lot about him, though really not much more than his other books have revealed in passing. It is the kind of autobiography he was best equipped to write, requiring a personal voice talking to somebody, but being essentially about ideas; not the story of his life, not a summing up, but a rambling through his beliefs, obsessions, limitations, pains, sexual hungers, knowledge. It is an attempt

---

**George Levine** is chairman of the English department at Livingston College, Rutgers University.

to account for himself to an audience of students who wanted to know how he "went about" being. This may seem a little pretentious (though the point will be recognizable to anyone who has read "Growing Up Absurd"), but pretentiousness—except perhaps an occasionally excessive attempt to be direct, honest, concrete, earthy—was not Goodman's mode. He was right to assume that he had earned the right to talk about himself in this way, having lived a life of remarkable integrity, and having written a good deal without which we would be poorer.

Rather dubiously, the book is part of a series called "Religious Perspectives." Its inclusion is partly justified by the poems that make up half of it (the "Little Prayers"), full of invocations of "God," "Lord," "Father." But as Goodman himself says, these words have no meaning to him: they are part of an adopted convention. By and large, the convention doesn't work, and the "Finite Experience" of the prose section of the book (that is, every other page) is far more interesting and powerful, just as Goodman's nonfiction always seems more alive and touching than his novels and poems.

But it isn't hard to understand why he allowed this book to appear in an explicitly religious series. This isn't one of those fortuitous conclusions to a career in which a rationalist suddenly sees the light and turns to God. For a long time, Goodman had been identifying the crises of our time as religious. In earlier books he talked about the way modern society has deprived the young of the power to believe in anything outside themselves and, consequently, in themselves as well. They have no work that might enspirit them, no models (outside popular culture) to emulate, no communities to care about. In this sense, they have no faith. Goodman's own faith was his work as a writer. "Faith," he says, "is having a world-for-me. That my experience is given. That it will continue to be given. Next is not the brink of a precipice."

Thus in "Finite Experience" Goodman was doing the same job he had worked at for two decades. He had only one subject, he said in "Utopian Essays and Practical Proposals" (1962), "the human beings I know in their man-made scene." His work was to make life satisfying for human beings, largely by demonstrating that their social world is man-made and, therefore, man-changeable. The resources for change, he insisted, are in man himself.

Goodman's writing is touching because this faith in human possibility had always been manifest in its very texture. The writing is the faith because it is a kind of work—not the communication of a message, a means to an end, but a way of being in the world, an action. His prose has rarely been beautiful (it is striking how unbeautiful his fiction is), but the nonfiction has a life that grows from Goodman's almost physical sensitivity to the presence of his audience, and from an awareness of what he calls, in "Speaking and Language" (1971), the double life of words. Every speech must be ambiguous because it is almost impossible to tell "what of the meaning . . . comes from the experience and what meaning has been added" by the speaking. For various reasons, explained in his brilliant work in "Gestalt Therapy" (1951) — the only emotionally engaging textbook I know—Goodman always preferred to live with that duality. "If you want to make sense," he wrote in his dedication to "The Structure of Literature" (1954), "you had better take all important factors into account." And what could be more important than the self speaking and the self listening?

At its extreme, this view makes it difficult to distinguish rational argument from autobiography or dialogue. And it has evoked much criticism of Goodman from "experts." But who would prefer the value-free objectivity of the language of bureaucrats and social scientists, especially after hearing it in the dehumanized voice with which the Government denied its bombing of a hospital in North Vietnam?

Goodman's dislike of "objectivity" is the substance and the subject of most of his writing, and he picks it up again in the short section on gestalt therapy in this last book. "Perceiving," he quotes Aristotle as saying, "is the identity of the object and the activated sensory organ." Neurosis is the failure of creative adjustment between the perceiver and his environment. The contemporary apotheosis of objectivity is, therefore, neurotic because it alienates the self from its environment and diminishes our power to experience and grow. Perhaps Goodman would have had better luck in bringing about the changes he wanted had he pretended to the kind of objectivity that protects us from the implications of what we say and the reasons we say it. The importance of this way of seeing and feeling can be inferred from the terrible and all too accurate prediction he made in "Gestalt Therapy" over 20 years ago: that wars would become less and less passionate, more and more violent.

For me, the most satisfying aspect of Goodman's work is in precisely this power to connect the psychological with the social, to recognize the human in everything. His emphasis on the importance of "primary experience" leads him to his peculiar politics of communitarian anarchism. For him, politics was the activity of attempting to "remedy institutions that hinder experience from occurring." As he puts it here, "There is no politics but remedial politics; often the first remedy is to take 'Society' less seriously, and to notice what society one has." "Society" is not real. It's an abstraction that gets between us and the community we need in order, simply, to be. It keeps us from "noticing."

These attitudes allowed Goodman to anticipate the terrible malaise of the last decade and made him, for a while in the early sixties, a prophet to the young. Not trapped by abstractions, he could explain to us all what was happening and why, and he could creatively attack the various institutions that were trapped. For each institution he made "Utopian" proposals—that is, "practical" ones. He wanted us to ignore impractical obstacles erected by the institutions themselves and take each problem as it affects us directly. He regarded arguments that his proposals for radical change were impractical,

that we must compromise and face facts, as psychologically and sociologically neurotic.

In his brilliant and characteristically erratic "Utopian Essays and Practical Proposals" (1962), he argued that we have attempted to solve our problems by doing nothing more than more of the same —as the present frightening moment in our history seems to confirm. "If there's an increase of delinquency or addiction, our only recourse is more repressive legislation, although our experience and our theory prove that this does not work and creates worse problems. If there are urban problems of congestion, poor transportation, and slums, our recourse is to new and bigger technological wonders, although experience and theory prove that these create worse problems." By now this should be old hat, but it isn't. Clearly, whether or not Goodman's particular proposals are usable, his general proposal that we need a radical reconsideration of the way we go about solving problems is accurate.

He argued, long before reforming liberals were willing even to consider it, that the central practical problem of our society is how to handle bigness—how to avoid waste and fragmentation and dehumanization without centralization, which, by definition (we have discovered rather later than Goodman), increases these things even while it attempts to remedy them. Goodman would say, "our people suffer from a compulsion neurosis; they are warding off panic by repeating themselves."

This kind of criticism is misleadingly similar to that of the young who adopted Goodman as a spiritual leader. The desire to cut through red tape and abstractions, the deep moral urgency, the commitment to "primary experience," the insistence on radical rethinking — all seem the same. Both sides were misled by the similarities. Moreover, Goodman so passionately loved youth, energy and sexual vitality, and saw them as so essential to any real change, that he allowed himself to believe that the various political, communitarian, rebellious activities of the young in the sixties would lead to the kinds of reform he wanted. But in "New Reformation" (1969), he says, "In 1958 I called them 'my crazy young allies' and now I'm saying that when the chips are down, they're just like their fathers."

Yet "New Reformation" sounds like the same old Paul Goodman, as does "Little Prayers and Finite Experience." Some of the new difference might be accounted for by the disintegration of the youth movements toward hippiedom or the left that we are still watching (with exactly that sigh of relief that would have enraged Goodman); some by the dogmatic intolerance of those whose rejection of the "system" has hardened irrevocably. But one can see, with the clarity of hindsight, that Goodman's and youth's mutual disillusion was inevitably built into Goodman's way of being.

His career reminds me much of John Ruskin's, and like Ruskin he might be called a radical tory. Ruskin's astonishingly insightful critique of capitalist economics in "Unto This Last" was Utopian in precisely Goodman's way: it did not imply any alternative dogma or system except the primacy of human relations and of joy. Goodman's anarchism is in a way the ultimate laissez faire. It implies a deep faith in human powers of creative adjustment, a willingness to risk the dangers that come with the absence of system, and trust in other humans. In fact, among Goodman's Utopian proposals he includes the encouragement of conflict within communities: "Conflict," he says, "is not an obstacle to community, but a golden opportunity, *if the give-and-take continue, if contact can be maintained.*"

But this is hardly revolutionary. Marxists would argue that Goodman's anarchism implies that he too was trapped in the tradition of bourgeois individualism—the cause of the trouble, not the way out. "Practical" politicians would argue that you can't change the system by invoking individual responsibility and encouraging individual growth. Goodman wrote and acted as if you could. Wanting community, he worked at it by dealing with particular problems, but he couldn't believe that any institution—even one created by a revolution from the left—could improve the texture of individual life, of social and sexual intercourse, except by making itself go away. You can't be a revolutionary theorist and reject objectivity, abstractions and even theory itself. Marx, Lenin and Mao couldn't help him because Goodman wanted not more system but less. And so he has been attacked as a bourgeois reactionary by the young who expected something different.

In addition, like a good radical tory, Goodman had enormous respect for history, for language, for tradition, for science. In "Like a Conquered Province" (1967) he rejects the Ludditism of the fighters against technology. "Knowledge," he said, "must be pursued for its own sake, as part of the human adventure." His point has always been not that we should turn away from technological development, but that science and technology should be humanized. Scientists and engineers should engage themselves morally in their work and be responsible for it. Again, the attack turns out to be aimed not at the activities themselves but at the false idea of objectivity which has institutionalized and dehumanized them.

Another aspect of his radical toryism was manifest in "Growing Up Absurd," which contains (though most of us must have missed it the first time around) the last praise of patriotism I can remember from a serious writer. The problem, Goodman asserted over and over again, is that the young, seeing that none of the traditions around them seem worthy of respect, find it difficult to believe that there ever were or could be any.

Again, the last book Goodman published in his lifetime, "Speaking and Language," is a "Defence of Poetry." It is partly an attack on scientific linguistics, which Goodman thinks of as another example of false and deadly objectivity, but it is also an assertion of the values of the past, and of language intelligently, sensitively, carefully used. And it is thus, also, another implicit attack on the young, who, Goodman believed, in their disrespect for language and for the past, are as guilty of reifying abstractions as their parents, and hence as dangerous. Perhaps Goodman thought that with

sensible rebellion would come some sensible faith: some of the bitterness and anger of the last books reflects his awareness that it has not come.

But it would be wrong to think that Goodman's career ended with an old man's reaction from youth. He had lost none of his envy of, his love for the young—though the accidental death of his son must have helped lead to his disillusion. He attacked the young for the same reason he had supported them, because he cared for—even lusted after—them, and he knew, as he says in "New Reformation," that "they *are* the ball game."

Simple rejection was not his style. He never went in for polarities, and his writing is about sharing, about getting beyond dualisms of self and society, man and nature, I and Thou. We exist only insofar as we are in creative contact with the people and things around us. "You are what you eat," and what you see and feel and smell and touch.

As Goodman understood, accepting his way of thinking and being entailed danger; but risk is the price of growth—and of creative adjustment. Still, it is difficult not to play the role of the neurotic conformist in Goodman's scenario—the person who rejects his proposals because they just don't seem practical. In fact, I don't know what I think of many of his practical suggestions. Like many others —like Goodman himself, I think—I have been burned by trying out some of his ideas about education in my classrooms. But then I didn't fully understand, as many of his disciples still don't, that Goodman didn't believe that the classroom was a viable place for his sort of work. Because of its obvious failures, we now face a reaction to the idea of the open classroom which will allow us to relax into our old ways—again, probably, with a sigh of relief.

So Goodman, even in his death, remains an outsider. At one point, he quoted Ruskin as saying, "I show men their plain duty and they reply that my style is charming." That was Goodman's fate too. But unlike Ruskin, Goodman managed to stay sane, if also ineffectual. Maybe his Utopias are coming; probably not. But I confess to a quiet longing after them myself and to gratitude to Goodman for imagining them for me. He has taught me a lot about myself, about my world and about possibility. In "Five Years," in some few of his poems, in most of his essays, he has put me in touch with a man. I for one will miss him. ■

*Paul Goodman wrote more than 40 books. The following are in print today:*

"Adam and His Works: Collected Stories" (Random House-Vintage Books, paper, $2.45). "Empire City," novel (Macmillan, paper, $2.95). "Hawkweed: Poems" (Random, cloth, $5.95; Vintage, paper, $1.65). "Homespun of Oatmeal Gray," poems (Random, cloth, $5; Vintage, paper, $1.95). "Three Plays" (Random, $6.95).

"Five Years," journal (Vintage, $1.95). "Little Prayers and Finite Experience," poetry and autobiography (Harper & Row, $5.95).

"Compulsory Mis-education and The Community of Scholars" (Vintage, $1.95). "Growing Up Absurd" (Random, cloth, $6.95; Vintage, paper, $1.95). "Like a Conquered Province" (Random, $4.95). "New Reformation" (Random, cloth, $5.95; Vintage, paper, $1.95). "Speaking and Language" (Random, cloth, $6.95; Vintage, paper, $1.95). "The Structure of Literature" (University of Chicago-Phoenix Books, $2.45). "Utopian Essays and Practical Proposals" (Vintage, $1.95).

"Communitas," with Percival Goodman (Vintage, $1.95). "Gestalt Therapy," with F. S. Perls and Ralph Hefferline (Julian Press, $7.50). "Seeds of Liberation," editor (Braziller, $7.50).

# Four more years?
# Learning to live with Nixon

## By Garry Wills

"Four more years." Of what? Germaine Greer claims Arthur Miller gave her the answer in Miami: "If this man wins another term, the Supreme Court will be castrated, and The New York Times will be a single mimeographed page." Almost this Miller makes me a hardhat. He would no doubt have said the same kind of thing before the 1968 election; yet here is the same old Times, still very fat, like the rest of us. The apocalypse has better taste than to associate itself with American elections. Our party processes mash the candidates in toward the middle—a law best proved by those who try to defy it, like Senator McGovern. After denouncing the "regulars" in primaries and the convention, he was reduced to shameless capitulation by the end of his campaign; and even then he has been ineffectual. He started too far out from the perceived middle of things.

But, we are warned, electoral pressures no longer apply when a President is entering his final term. To re-elect Nixon is, in Sargent Shriver's lurid phrase, to "unleash" him. No longer controlled by the prospect of defeat at the polls, he can at last go bonkers for real. Another "unleashing" theory, which Daniel Patrick Moynihan applies to Nixon sycophantically, is that the President—quit of the task (and, for him, the temptation) of running for the office one more time—can look now to the history books. His deferred aspirations, held in abeyance during all those years of scrounging for votes, can at last be realized.

Both these approaches assume there is a "real" Nixon—an ogre barely restrained, or a closet egghead—kept under wraps for years because the sight of him would scare off voters. A third view exists: that there is no "real" Nixon, just a campaigner, trimming his sails and steering toward the next election date; and such a man will not know *what* to do when there is no campaign left for him. Each of these theories is based on a deeper assumption—that to go for re-election and to go for the history books are two different things. But a President who cannot carry the electorate with his program is going to be in trouble with the historians. The weavers of American mythology have been as nice as can be to Woodrow Wilson; but he failed, even though he was too ill to run for a third term (still legal in his day), when he could not get the people to "buy" his League of Nations. A President's public claim, and the source of his working power, is that he represents the

people. Whatever his aspirations to leadership, he can only be called a leader if people follow. And the test of having a following is, in our system, the vote. It does not matter that judgment is rendered vicariously in the case of a President who cannot run again. Most votes are retrospective sanctionings anyway; we know more about what has been done to us than what is being promised us. That is why we tend to vote the rascals out, to vote *against;* and no President wants to be the rascal, even at one remove.

So the pressure is never entirely off the President. He performs to win acceptance, not only election by election, but day by day. The idea of a free hand in the second term is most often used by Presidents to justify failures of performance during their first term—Kennedy got great mileage out of this. And when Lyndon Johnson tried to unleash himself as a peacemaker by declaring himself a lame duck, it did not do him much good, at home or abroad.

But the hopes or fears of an "unfettered" second term acquire special force in Nixon's case. He is widely believed to have "sold out" on his former convictions—his hawkishness, his crusading anti-Communism, his free-enterprise fundamentalism and opposition to guaranteed income—out of the desire for re-election. And now, with no further need to sell out, won't he revert?

That whole question has been badly posed. There is a sense in which Nixon "sold out" on taking office—most Presidents do. One of the self-balancing aspects of our system is that candidates not only try to "out-middle" each other, but also engage in compensatory blandishments toward those who have least reason to trust them. Thus the dovish side will peddle superhawkish wares—as Kennedy did, in his debates with Nixon, deploring the missile gap, the loss of Cuba, the lack of interventionist vigor in the Eisenhower years. By the end of this year's campaign, McGovern could rhetorically out-policeman Nixon at home and out-rabbi him abroad. That's part of the game. Indeed, McGovern's first backers have tried to assure each other that he was just foolin'. Once elected, he would "come home" to his friends on the Left. Forget the regrettable interim, said (e.g.) Gloria Steinem, and get him into the Oval Office; then he'll take good care of us. It is a variant of the "unleashing" theory.

But that's not the way it works, Ms. Steinem. All the sell-outable space is on the other side. The one group a President has least chance of pleasing is his primary constituency. Lyndon Johnson, trotted out to please the South in 1960, could not ever take a soft stand on civil rights. John F. Kennedy took the hardest position against aid to parochial schools of any recent President or candidate.

---

*Garry Wills, whose book "Bare Ruined Choirs: Doubt, Prophecy and Radical Religion" has just been published, is also the author of "Nixon Agonistes: The Crisis of the Self-Made Man."*

## It's likely to be four more years of roughly the same, "just the prosaic, unappealing task of getting along with ourselves."

Franklin Roosevelt was withering in his comments on the patrician class he came from. There is, thus, some reason to take the cynical view that a vote for your political enemy is the wisest course—he has no one to sell out to but you. Eugene Rostow, in his long New Yorker interviews, argued that Kennedy's tough stands were aimed more at domestic placation than foreign intimidation. Elected as a liberal Democrat, he was suspected of weakness toward "the Communist menace" and had to keep displaying his strength. The Left, in other words, gave a hostage to the Right by voting in its own man. By the dynamics of this process, a President McGovern would be automatically belligerent with regard to Israel's safety. Any weakening there would undercut a basic part of his support.

These pressures allow a President to achieve important things in the sell-outable territory. Only a Southerner like Lyndon Johnson could have passed the most extensive civil rights laws in our history. Only a Republican patriot of Ike's unquestionable standing could bring an end to McCarthyism (whose energies went far beyond its eponym). Humphrey, if elected in 1968, could not have gone to Peking or Moscow. Because a President has more room to maneuver near what seem to be his opponents, he is impelled to use that maneuverability; it allows him to achieve something, at least—an important consideration to any politician making a record. The effective President will be the one who moves into that open space on the other side. Roosevelt reversed his campaign promises to balance the budget and cut back on Hoover's spending, and did it with spectacular speed and efficiency. Ike would sell you out in a flash—something Richard Nixon learned over and over. In a way, Eisenhower kept people like Nixon and Dulles around to have somebody to sell out as occasion warranted.

Usually, of course the sellout is more apparent than real. Johnson, though a Southerner, had arrived at a sincere concern for black Americans by the time he became President. Eisenhower, though a General of the Army, sincerely detested the McCarthyites. And it is just on this question of sincerity that Nixon's critics have misgivings. If Nixon was sincere about anything, they feel, it was his early "hard-line" anti-Communism, a trait kept alive in his unyielding attitude toward the Vietnam war, despite any chumminess at Peking or Moscow. But his original connection with the Right was in large measure tactical. He was given the opportunity to achieve something in the Hiss case, and his subsequent reputation was used by Eisenhower to placate the Taft wing of the party while restraining its McCarthyites. He was programed to be Ike's concession to the Right — a role Agnew now plays. Nixon played the role well, in part from ambition, but also because he believes in such negotiatory balance over a broad spectrum. But all the time he was assigned to do the party's domestic dirty work, he yearned toward the larger opportunities of building a world order. The Dewey Establishment that put forward Eisenhower's candidacy thought in crude terms of "internationalists" (the good guys) being pestered by "isolationists" like Taft. Nixon was to drag isolationists into the world by tickling their anti-Communism. It was thought that the country would only indulge a foreign policy if it offered the chance of beating up on Commies somewhere along the line. The Establishment, both Democratic and Republican, put itself in the postwar position of inciting anti-Communist passions and then trying to check them—with strange results in a man like Acheson. Nixon's record of "toughness" has to be understood in this context.

But his hero from childhood was Woodrow Wilson. Nixon transcended his original constituency, and said so; but no one believed him. (The same thing may prove true, in time, of Agnew.) Men did not take Nixon seriously enough in his longstanding reverence for Wilson as the President of peace—a devotion bequeathed Nixon, he says, by his Quaker mother. Even as Vice President, he rescued Wilson's desk from White House-attic status, and made a cult of it. The same desk, now installed in the Oval Office, is the omphalos of American power—Nixon touched it reverentially, and told the nation he was working in Wilson's spirit, during a 1969 broadcast on Vietnam. He ordered Wilson's portrait hung in the Cabinet Room—the only Democratic icon on those walls. Wilson is Nixon's favorite superstition, a talisman of his own destiny as he perceived it all along.

This superstition is backed, as one would expect, by personal needs and deficiencies. Not a person of great charm, dispatched to personal confrontations where a mean response was desired, he liked the facelessness of large impersonal diplomacy, where statesmen rise above the pettier tricks of the politician. It has surprised some that he lets Henry Kissinger take so much credit for the face-to-face day-to-day negotiation of his very own grand alliance. People thus surprised forget (as he does not) what Nixon's face looks like in purely political terms. He has always had the brains to overcome his face; and now he has the chance to prove it. (McGovern aides, in their desperation, thought Nixon was salivating to rush out and lose votes by some ogre act in public—so little did they understand their foe.)

A far greater surprise than Nixon's "deference" to Kissinger is his conception of their relationship. The press has largely thought — with Kissinger's encouragement — of Kissinger as exercising academic restraint upon a naturally aggressive politician. Nixon, by contrast, welcomes Kissinger's nonideological "realism" of the Metternich school as a balance to his own — idealism. *Idealism?* Yes, yes, I know that Nixon plays ill the part of Oscar Wilde's hypocrite, merely pretending to vice but guilty, all the while, of virtue. Still, this has, in important ways, been the case with Nixon. Back in February of 1968, I asked him what the next President needed most of all. Others were saying, at the time, that a non-Johnsonian trustworthiness should be our highest priority. But Nixon thought something else was needed—which, by no accident, was what he had to offer: "a man who knows the world." Why this emphasis on worldwide expertise? Because, he said, the main task for America is "to forge a whole new set of alliances." The Peking and Moscow trips do not look so surprising against this background. Nixon was saying that kind of thing all during the spring of 1968, while Henry Kissinger was still busy running Nixon down in the cause of Nelson Rockefeler.

## August, Miami Beach

*Richard Nixon and Spiro Agnew wave to the delegates (and the cameras).*

Kissinger's role is suggested in other things Nixon said in 1968: "Wilson had the greatest vision of America's world role. But he wasn't practical enough. Take his 'open agreements openly arrived at.' That is not the way diplomacy is conducted. The Vietnamese war, for instance, will be settled at secret high-level negotiations." Secret, and high-level—calling, therefore, for a trusted intermediary. A President does not move obscurely. And "practical" — calling for a Metternichian, who will temper the grand vision with attention to detail, do the "tinkering," save a Wilsonian President from Wilsonian vagueness and mere vision. In a very revealing speech given last year by the President at the dedication of the Woodrow Wilson International Center for Scholars, Nixon said that Wilson "lit a spark that merged this nation with the cause of generosity and idealism . . . Woodrow Wilson helped make the world safe for idealism." But he knows that a Kissinger helps make idealism safe for the Presidency.

Nixon never conceived of the Vietnam war as an anti-Communist crusade. For one thing, he said in 1968 that it

could not be won at the military level. And by any sophisticated anti-Communist calculus, the war has proved a loss. It not only weakened the will to go on crusades, but also made the trips to Russia and China possible. Nixon has had something very different in mind during his efforts to disengage without admitting defeat. Even before his inauguration, he began saying that the greatest danger of Vietnam's aftermath would be "neoisolationism." That is what would make this country a pitiful giant, strong without the chance to use its strength. That would take away the game pieces Nixon means to play with on the big board. His perseverance in Vietnam has been, therefore, a *negotiatory* toughness—not at odds with overtures to Russia and China, but geared to them. What he calls, in the arms race area, the "bargaining chip" theory has much wider application in his scheme of things. If diplomacy is give and take, you have to have something to give. You soften only from toughness, trade only from possession. Even Wilson let himself be led into the war he "kept us out of" so that America could dispose of the peace, weighing the fate of conquered nations.

This explains how Nixon could take Kissinger into his Administration, at a time when Kissinger favored what he later mocked as "elegant bugout," and recruit him for the long haul in Indochina—meanwhile continuing to think of himself as the idealist and Kissinger as the tough guy!

Wilde was describing Nixon, after all—*guilty* of virtue. Nixon said, in that 1968 interview, "We are now in a position to give the world all the good things that Britain offered in her Empire without any of the disadvantages of 19th-century colonialism." That is the voice of America's devastating innocence—it might be Pyle speaking, the hero-villain of Graham Greene's "Quiet American," who went to Asia with "clean hands," to form a Third Force above the native darkness and the colonial "enlighteners." This attitude took us into Vietnam, and could take us into new conflicts under Nixon, who does feel the American burden on his shoulders and is determined to fight all "neoisolationist" attempts to shed it. He said in his dedication of the Wilson Center, "the greatest achievement of Woodrow Wilson was in opening the heart of America for the world to see."

Nixon, re-elected, would damn us with virtue if he could—but so would McGovern, whose national security white paper showed no difference from Nixon in principle. What he offered was more of the same, with (presumably) less maneuvering room. That, and instant peace in Vietnam—a peace Nixon seems at last to be accepting anyway, now that his initiatives in China and Russia have opened up other areas to negotiatory toughness (arms agreements, for instance, and the Middle East). He might well take us into a new war, especially if a confrontation with Russia shapes up in the Middle East; but if so, it will not be as part of an anti-Communist crusade, or out of a need to prove his manhood, or as a sign that he has gone bonkers. It will be for the same bright idealistic reasons that always take us to war. The country does not have much stomach for fighting at the moment, and even F.D.R. said, "I cannot go faster than the people will let me." Besides, Nixon would not have as much pressure to prove he is not an isolationist as McGovern would. But Nixon is *determined* to have a generation of peace, and it's just when we are most set on peace that we accept, as the price for it, war.

What of domestic policy? That interests Nixon less. It does not admit of the same impersonal long-term treaty arrangements (though things like the civil rights bills were essentially domestic treaties). One element in today's situation catches his attention, since it is kindred to alliance building—the realignment of the parties. If he wins the election Tuesday, as he no doubt will, the victory will be called a personal triumph for Nixon (how odd, for one supposed to be personally repugnant); he decided not to risk such victory by campaigning for candidates lower

on the ticket. But he conceives of this win as based on the New South strategy opened to Republicans by Barry Goldwater. As Goldwater, even in personal defeat, gave a new base to the party, shifting its center of gravity from the Eastern Establishment westward and south, Nixon can preserve that territory despite any partial setback for other Republican candidates. His own win will give him time and clout to stake out permanent ownership of the "Middle America" he has practically invented for electoral purposes. This meshes neatly with his "liberal" foreign policy, an area in which he can play the renegade to his first constituents; he can hug Communists at high-level meetings, so long as he cracks down on the kids and blacks at home. He can have Kissinger, at the price of Agnew—a cheap enough price to pay. He always knew he could "sell out" Leftward so long as he kept Agnew on the ticket. Announcing Spiro's reappointment before Miami took all the potential for even slight or symbolic trouble-making away from people like John Ashbrook. So, despite Moynihan's belief that the real angel-Nixon would emerge in a second term, we can expect little ardor for family assistance, and much chest-beating against welfare and busing. The mood of the nation is shifting that way, and McGovern might have been caught in the out-toughing trap. The chances are that Nixon will groom Agnew as his successor, since the Vice President starts with the all-important Southern and "heartland" base, and can move toward the middle with ease; he is not, any more than Nixon was, an extremist by conviction. The art is to disappoint your fans, without leaving them anywhere else to go; and Agnew should be as well positioned to do that as Nixon was before him.

On the economy, Nixon has

never been the purist his enemies made of him. He disagreed with Eisenhower's inflexible attitude on spending and controls. True, he is strong on the rhetoric—and even the philosophy—of the work ethic; but that is the domestic equivalent of negotiatory toughness. You've got to have chips to bargain with (arms in order to disarm)—in the same way, you must use controls to get freedom, spending to get incentive. One can manage the economy so long as one does not destroy initiative—which translates into giving to those who already have, and leaving the have-nots to fend for themselves. It's the American way, and Nixon doesn't want to change that. (McGovern couldn't change it, even if he wanted to—which he only marginally does. He is a very mild and meliorative sort of "populist.")

Four more years of roughly the same, then. Same dangers, deceptions, retreats; same large diplomatic ambitions abroad, and mean-spirited placation at home. The time may come for paying up some of our moral debts, foreign or domestic; but the debts are long-standing, and Nixon will inherit them by continuity of his policies, not violent breaks. We get the government we deserve, by sifting candidates down to those who are vaguely ingratiating over the broadest area. I could never vote for the man, myself—he combines the Wilsonian worst of liberalism with some very specific war crimes—but I can resign myself to him, as to most evils, without joining Arthur Miller in his thrill of anticipated Timesocide. Learning to live with Nixon is just the prosaic, unappealing task of getting along with ourselves. The four years will be added on, as if the election hadn't occurred. In many ways, it didn't. ∎

## AMERICANS' MOOD CALLED DOWNBEAT

### But Far From Helplessness, Upstate Seminar Told

The mood of the nation is downbeat, but far from one of helplessness, eight writers, educators and political polltakers agreed during a wide-ranging seminar called "President/Politics/People" held recently at the Institute on Man and Science in Rensselaerville, N. Y.

While the nation may appear indifferent to moral issues, the panelists agreed, it is not lacking moral fiber.

The program was directed and moderated by Lester Markel, former Sunday Editor of The New York Times.

The eight participants last weekend were Nasrollah Fatemi, director of the Institute of International Studies at Fairleigh Dickinson University; Betty Friedan, author of "The Feminine Mystique"; George Gallup, founder of the Gallup Poll; Sidney Hyman, historian at the University of Chicago; Paul Lazarsfeld, professor of social science at Columbia University; George Reedy, dean of the journalism college at Marquette University; Robert Semple Jr., White House correspondent of The New York Times, and Daniel Yankelovich, the polltaker.

#### Various Descriptions

They described the mood of the nation with words such as "lethargy," "resignation," "frustration," "impotence," "disillusionment," and "chaos."

"There's a tuning out of the old politics and nothing is coming in that tunes in to the needs of the people," Miss Friedan said.

Mr. Semple argued that the disillusionment was because "The speed of events has outrun man's ability to keep pace with them."

But there are bright spots in the blanket of despair, some of the panelists said. "Most people are not pessimistic about their personal situation," Mr. Yankelovich said, "but about what is happening in the country at large."

Dr. Gallup said he felt that "the mood has changed in the last six months from despair to watchful waiting; people are beginning to believe that things can change as a result of the agreements with Russia and China and the improving economic situation."

### Reedy Analyzes Mood

Mr. Reedy, a former press secretary in the administration of President Lyndon B. Johnson said he did not feel a lack of moral sense. "None of the present apparent lethargy," he said, "means that the peo-

ple are becoming moral monsters or losing their moral sense, but only a sort of feeling that they cannot do anything about it."

"Americans are not turning into monsters," Mr. Fatemi agreed. "There are certain pe-

riods when the people are disillusioned and uncertain. We are at one of those periods. This is not basically the fault of the people, but of the politicians."

The conference, attended by about 150 people, was part of

a series organized by Fairleigh Dickinson University to study problems in communications. Grants to support the programs were made by the university, the institute, The New York Times and The Record of Hackensack, N. J.

# President Pledges an End To 'Era of Permissiveness'

## In Pre-Election Interview, He Said Nation Passed Through 'Spiritual Crisis' — Calls Vietnam 'Only Part of Problem'

*Following is an account by Garnett D. Horner, White House correspondent of The Washington Star-News, of a pre-election interview he had with President Nixon. The interview took place last Sunday in San Clemente, Calif.*

#### Washington Star-News

WASHINGTON, Nov. 9— President Nixon, promising the American people the rigors of self-reliance instead of the soft life, says he hopes to use the second term to lead the nation out of a crisis of the spirit.

In an interview with The Star-News, the President vowed to work to end "the whole era of permissiveness" and to nurture "a new feeling of responsibility, a new feeling of self-discipline."

"We have passed through a very great spiritual crisis in this country," he said. He added that the Vietnam war was "blamed for it totally" by many but he said the war was really "only part of the problem and in many cases was only an excuse rather than a reason."

With a puritan fervor he has seldom shown in public, Mr. Nixon seemed to be closing the door on a time in which he felt the nation had been pampered and indulged, leaving its character weakened.

"The average American," he said, "is just like the child in the family. You give him some responsibility and he is going to amount to something. He is going to do something.

"If, on the other hand, you make him completely dependent and pamper him and cater to him too much, you are going

to make him soft, spoiled, and eventually a very weak individual."

In addition to setting the over-all tone for his next four years, the President dealt with a wide range of specific subjects. Some highlights:

¶Vietnam—He is "completely confident we are going to have a settlement" there. "You can bank on it."

¶Election—It was settled the day Senator George McGovern was nominated by the Democrats. Mr. McGovern's views "probably did not represent even a majority of Democrats."

¶Foreign Policy—The second round of arms limitations talks —SALT II—starting this month will be more important than SALT I. The Middle East "will have a very high priority." "Our policy toward Cuba will not change unless Premier Fidel Castro changes his attitude."

¶Domestic Policy — He will "shuck off" and "trim down" social programs set up in the 1960's that he considers massive failures largely because they just "threw money at the problems."

¶Taxes—"There will be no solution of problems that require a tax increase." He is convinced that the tax burden of Americans has reached "the

breaking point" and can go no higher.

¶The Courts—He intends to continue to appoint conservative judges. "The courts need men like Rehnquist and Burger and Blackmun and Powell."

¶His Aides — Some healthy "friction, competition" between Henry A. Kissinger and the State Department and John D. Ehrlichman and the domestic agencies is going to continue. "That is the way it is going to have to be with them or their successors."

He had just come through a campaign, the President recalled, in which he "didn't go out with a whole bag full of goodies."

#### Not All 'Goodies'

And he made it clear that there will be few social goodies in his second Administration.

He singled out the Federal payroll as a prime target for his attention in the new term. He said that some departments are "too fat, too bloated," and that civilian Defense Department employes "are getting in the way of each other."

His remedy: A thinning out all through the Government, including the White House.

Mr. Nixon noted suggestions that, no longer facing the problem of re-election, he might now be more free to advocate massive new social programs aimed at curing the nation's domestic ills.

"Nothing," he said, "could be further from the mark." He predicted, however, that the next four years would be an exciting period for Americans —on the international front because "we are going to continue to play a great role in the world" and domestically because of his determination to build a new national spirit.

He said that his general approach to the Presidency "is probably that of a Disraeli conservative — a strong foreign policy, strong adherence to basic values that the nation believes in and people believe in."

Repeatedly, during the conversation of nearly an hour last Sunday at his San Clemente office, the President indicated the conservative course — he called it basically centrist—he

was charting for the next four years:

¶ "This country has enough on its plate in the way of huge new spending programs, social programs, throwing dollars at problems . . . reform using money more effectively will be the mark of this Administration."

¶ "I honestly believe that Government in Washington is too big and is too expensive . . . we can do the job better with fewer people."

¶ "I am convinced that the total tax burden of the American people, Federal, state and local, has reached the breaking point. It can go no higher."

¶ "It is our responsibility to find a way to reform our Government institutions so that this new spirit of independence, self-reliance, pride that I sense in the American people can be nurtured."

The President said his position was not "over on the far right" but "basically . . . simply in the center" in standing for a strong national defense, for peace with honor in Vietnam, against busing for racial balance, against permissiveness, against amnesty for draft dodgers and deserters, against legalizing marijuana.

#### Central Position

President Nixon spoke with deep feeling about his desire to "exert that kind of leadership" required to make all Americans proud of their country.

"I think that the tragedy of the '60's," he said, "is that so many Americans, and particularly so many young Americans, lost faith in their country, in the American system, in their country's foreign policy."

"Many were influenced to believe that they should be ashamed of our country's foreign policy, and what we were doing in the world.

"Many Americans got the impression that this was an ugly country, racist, not compassionate, and part of the reason for this was the tendency of some to take every mole that we had and to make it look like a cancer."

# 1976 COMMISSION SCORED IN REPORT

## House Inquiry Says Panel Has Failed to Formulate Good Bicentennial Plan

Special to The New York Times

WASHINGTON, Dec. 29 — House investigators charged today that the American Revolution Bicentennial Commission was hampered by poor morale, lack of understanding of purpose and an unworkable structure and had failed to formulate a proper observance of the nation's 200th anniversary.

And, they concluded, the commission, as structured now, will not be able to provide the country with a proper commemoration by 1976.

The report was made by the staff of the House Judiciary Committee following a three-month investigation into charges of corruption and political impropriety by the Government-appointed commission.

The report, however, did not substantiate charges that the commission had manipulated the bicentennial for commercial purposes. The report also did not address itself to charges of political impropriety by some commission members.

Commission officials declined to comment on the findings of the committee staff.

Among private commission documents circulated here last August by an organization planning a counter-celebration was one written by Herbert G. Klein, the White House communications director. It urged that the commission consider hiring a well-known black educator who, Mr. Klein said, had "outlined a plan he believes would help blacks better understand and relate to the Republican party."

Among the Congressional staff findings were the following:

¶Six years after passage of the enabling legislation, the commission is still debating its role and still drafting resolutions designed to tell itself what it is supposed to be doing.

¶The 50-member decision-making body, meeting irregularly and at intervals of months, is not the best instrument for successfully running the administrative and operations aspects of the bicentennial celebration.

¶Commission and executive committee meeting suffer from a lack of attendance by a number of commission members.

¶There is evidence of lack of confidence in staff members by some commissioners and conversely a mistrust of the commission by some staff members.

¶The commission is guilty in many instances of abusing its hiring and personnel privileges, most often through the improper use of consultants and through inordinately high salaries paid to some staff members.

The report said that one case involved the hiring of a $10,-500-a-year business manager of a small community college as a $128-a-day consultant.

The report said that the man's civil service file indicated that he was not qualified for a high staff position. The consultant fee that he was paid is equivalent to the pay of a high-ranking staff job, the report said.

The report also charged that there were two major cases of financial mismanagement by the commission that appeared to involve violations of Federal law.

These, the report said, involved the expenditure of funds in excess of Congressional appropriation and about $26,000 of donated funds that were not deposited in the Federal Treasury.

The report was also critical of the commission for its "costly policy of conducting its meetings in various cities across the nation . . . necessitating large travel and per diem expenditures."

The report recommended that the commission be trimmed to 25 members from 50, and that all of them be appointed from private life by the President. In addition, all duties and responsibilities would be carried out by a nine-member board of directors selected by the President from the 25-member commission.

December 30, 1972

# Keep It Local

## By Elliot L. Richardson

It is my belief that never before in our national history has voluntarism and the voluntary ethic been so important to preserving what is best and most valuable in American society. At issue is our national response to the often necessary and seemingly inescapable growth of centralized government and the concomitant submergence of the individual, the community and the states to Washington-based authority.

At stake, I believe, is nothing less than the future of the individual— and of individual liberty—in the United States. The last forty years have seen us turning increasingly to central authority. And the trend continues to this day.

But as we increasingly turn to governmental authority and power to solve our problems, we must not lose sight of the costs to individual liberty involved. Orwell's "1984" and Huxley's "Brave New World"—fiction which has become all too real—projected political worlds in which government took control over the lives of the people it originally was to serve.

These portents of a world we don't want but may have begun to create serve to make it clear that we've reached a point in our history where either we submit to greater governmental authority over a lot of things whether we like it or not, or we begin to mold a different shape for our future.

It is an issue that is receiving a good deal of careful thought by this Administration in its comprehensive concept of "The New Federalism"—a blueprint for revitalizing government that outlines ways to make our institutions more responsive to individual needs. Beyond that, "The New Federalism" is a way of reversing the flow of power to Washington, to start it flowing back, in President Nixon's words, "to the states, to the communities, and most important, to the people."

The Administration is advancing this concept through revenue sharing and government reorganization—steps designed to give states, cities and citizens the power and authority they need to make decisions affecting their existence. State and local governments and private voluntary public service agencies must have the authority, the revenues, and the encouragement of the Federal Government in their task of delivering services to Americans in the communities where they live.

For the increasingly evident fact is that neither the President, nor the

Congress, nor a centralized bureaucracy, can keep neighborhood streets safe, clean up local pollution, meet local public health emergencies, unsnarl local traffic problems, or pick up local garbage. Such problems require local concern, local decisions and local action.

The answer to the drift of power toward the center must be a determination by citizens to wage an unending campaign to achieve local, personalized autonomy.

We estimate that to extend the present range of H.E.W. services equitably to all in need would cost a quarter of a trillion dollars—or the equivalent of the entire existing Federal budget. It would also require, according to our best estimates, the addition of twenty million trained personnel.

To the degree this nation can enlist volunteers for important, necessary tasks; to the degree we can tap the compassion, the concern and the commitment of our people as individuals—to that degree will we be able to deal simultaneously with shortages of manpower and money that cannot otherwise conceivably be overcome.

The concept, the ethic and the act of concern for the welfare of one's fellow-beings is, as we all know, a very deep part of the Hebraic tradition. It is a foundation-stone of the Judaeo-Christian ethic. It is also a particularly American quality.

---

*Elliot L. Richardson, the new Secretary of Defense, was formerly Secretary of H.E.W. This article is excerpted from a talk given in New York.*

# A Transcript of President Nixon's Second Inaugural Address to the Nation

*Following is the transcript of President Nixon's second inaugural address, as recorded yesterday by The New York Times:*

When we met here four years ago, America was bleak in spirit, depressed by the prospect of seemingly endless war abroad and of destructive conflict at home.

As we meet here today, we stand on the threshold of a new era of peace in the world.

The central question before us is: How shall we use that peace?

Let us resolve that this era we are about to enter will not be what other postwar periods have so often been; a time of retreat and isolation that leads to stagnation at home and invites new danger abroad.

Let us resolve that this will be what it can become: A time of great responsibilities greatly borne, in which we renew the spirit and the promise of America as we enter our third century as a nation.

## A New Pattern

This past year saw far-reaching results from our new policies for peace. By continuing to revitalize our traditional friendships, and by our missions to Peking and to Moscow, we were able to establish the base for a new and more durable pattern of relationships among the nations of the world.

Because of America's bold initiatives, 1972 will be long remembered as the year of the greatest progress since the end of World War II toward a lasting peace in the world.

The peace we seek in the world is not the flimsy peace which is merely an interlude between wars, but a peace which can endure for generations to come.

It is important that we understand both the necessity and the limitations of America's role in maintaining that peace.

Unless we in America work to preserve the peace, there will be no peace.

Unless we in America work to preserve freedom, there will be no freedom.

## New Policies Adopted

But let us clearly understand the new nature of America's role, as a result of these new policies we have adopted over the past four years.

We shall respect our treaty commitments.

We shall support vigorously the principle that no country has the right to impose its will or rule on another by force.

We shall continue, in this era of negotiation, to work for the limitation of nuclear arms, and to reduce the danger of confrontation between the great powers.

We shall do our share in defending peace and freedom in the world. But we shall expect others to do their share.

The time has passed when America will make every other nation's conflict our own, or make every other nation's future our responsibility, or presume to tell the people of other nations how to manage their own affairs.

## Rights of Nations

Just as we respect the right of each nation to determine its own future, we also recognize the responsibility of each nation to secure its own future.

Just as America's role is indispensable in preserving the world's peace, so is each nation's role indispensable in preserving its own peace.

Together with the rest of the world, let us resolve to move forward from the beginnings we have made. Let us continue to bring down the walls of hostility which have divided the world for too long, and to build in their place bridges of understanding—so that despite profound differences between systems of government, the people of the world can be friends.

Let us build a structure of peace in which the weak are as safe as the strong, in which each respects the right of the other to live by a different system, in which those who would influence others will we do so by the strength of their ideas and not by the force of their arms.

### The Noblest Endeavor

Let us accept that high responsibility not as a burden, but gladly—gladly because the chance to build such a peace is the noblest endeavor in which a nation could engage, and gladly also because only if we act greatly in meeting our responsibilities abroad will we remain a great nation, and only if we remain a great nation will we act greatly in meeting our challenges at home.

We have the chance today to do more than ever before to make life better in America—to ensure better education, better health, better housing, better transportation, a cleaner environment; to restore respect for law to make our communities more liveable and to ensure the God-given right of every American to full and equal opportunity.

Because the range of our needs is so great—because the reach of our opportunities is so great—let us be bold in our determination to meet those needs in new ways.

Just as building a structure of peace abroad has required turning away from old policies that have failed, so building a new era of progress at home requires turning away from old policies that have failed.

Abroad, the shift from old policies to new has not been a retreat from our responsibilities, but a better way to peace.

And at home, the shift from old policies to new will not be a retreat from our responsibilities, but a better way to progress.

Abroad and at home, the key to those new policies lies in the placing and the division of responsibility. We have lived too long with the consequences of attempting to gather all power and responsibility in Washington.

Abroad and at home, the time has come to turn away from the condescending policies of paternalism — of "Washington knows best."

A person can be expected to act responsibly only if he has responsibility. This is human nature. So let us encourage individuals at home and nations abroad to do more for themselves, to decide more for themselves. Let us locate more responsibility in more places. Let us measure what we will do for others by what they will do for themselves.

That is why I offer no promise of a purely governmental solution for every problem. We have lived too long with that false promise. In trusting too much in government, we have asked of it more than it can deliver. This leads only to inflated expectations, to reduced individual effort and to a disappointment and frustration that erode confidence both in what government can do and in what people can do.

Government must learn to take less from people so that people can do more for themselves.

### Building of Nation

Let us remember that America was built not by government, but by people—not by welfare, but by work—not by shirking responsibility, but by seeking responsibility.

In our own lives, let each of us ask not just what will government do for me, but what can I do for myself?

In the challenges we face together, let each of us ask not just how can government help, but how can I help?

Your national Government has a great and vital role to play. And I pledge to you that where this Government should act we will act boldly, and we will lead boldly. But just as important is the role that each and every one of us must play, as an individual and as a member of his own community.

From this day forward, let each of us make a solemn commitment in his own heart: To bear his responsibility to do his part, to live his ideals so that, together, we can see the dawn of a new age of progress for America, and together, as we celebrate our 200th anniversary as a nation, we can do so proud in the fulfillment of our promise to ourselves and to the world.

### Plea for Civility

As America's longest and most difficult war comes to an end, let us again learn to debate our differences with civility and decency. And let each of us reach out for that one precious quality government cannot provide: A new level of respect for the rights and feelings of one another and a new level of respect for the individual human dignity which is the cherished birthright of every American.

Above all else, the time has come for us to renew our faith in ourselves and in America.

In recent years, that faith has been challenged.

Our children have been taught to be ashamed of their country, ashamed of their parents, ashamed of America's record at home and its role in the world.

At every turn, we have been beset by those who find everything wrong with America and little that is right. But I am confident that this will not be the judgment of history on these remarkable times in which we are privileged to live.

America's record in this century has been unparalleled in the world's history for its responsibility, for its generosity, for its creativity and for its progress.

Let us be proud that our system has produced and provided more freedom and more abundance, more widely shared, than any other in the history of man.

Let us be proud that in each of the four wars in which we have been engaged in this century, including the one we are now bringing to an end, we have fought not for selfish advantage, but to help others resist aggression.

### Freedom and Abundance

Let us be proud that by our bold, new initiatives, and by our steadfastness for peace with honor, we have made a breakthrough toward creating in the world what the world has not known before—a structure of peace that can last, not merely for our time, but for generations to come.

We are embarking here today on an era that presents challenges as great as those of any nation, or any generation, has ever faced.

We shall answer to God, to history, and to our conscience for the way in which we use these years.

As I stand in this place so hallowed by history, I think of others who have stood here before me. I think of the dreams they had for America, and I think of how each recognized that he needed help far beyond himself in order to make those dreams come true.

Today I ask your prayers that in the years ahead I may have God's help in making decisions that are right for America, and I pray for your help so that together we may be worthy of our challenge.

Let us pledge together to make these next four years the best four years in America's history, so that on its 200th birthday America will be as young and as vital as when it began, and as bright a beacon of hope for all the world.

Let us go forward from here confident in hope, strong in our faith in one another, sustained by our faith in God who created us, and striving always to serve his purposes.

# 5 Charged With Burglary at Democratic Quarters

Special to The New York Times

WASHINGTON, June 17—Five men, said to have been carrying cameras, electronic surveillance equipment and burglary tools, were arrested shortly after 2 A.M. today after a floor-by-floor search that led to the executive quarters of the National Democratic Committee here. The suspects were charged with second-degree burglary.

None of the suspects disclosed any objectives for entering the committee headquarters or affiliations with any political organization in the United States.

The backgrounds of the suspects were hazy, but the following information was reported by the police here and sources in Miami, which was listed as the home of four of them.

Two of the men, born in Cuba, were said to have claimed past ties with the Central Intelligence Agency. A third was described as an adventurer who once tried to sell his services to an anti-Castro organization called Alpha 66.

The suspects were listed as:

Bernard L. Barker, alias Frank Carter, about 55 years old. According to Miami sources, he once worked in Cuba in the Buro de Investigaciones, the Cuban equivalent of the Federal Bureau of Investigation. Mr. Barker was said to have been a close associate of a leader of the Bay of Pigs invasion of Cuba.

Frank Angelo Fiorini, alias Edward Hamilton, about 48, who the police said had once been-arrested on a firearms charge. He was described by the Miami sources as an adventurer who had at one time transported arms to the Sierra Maestra when Fidel Castro was there fighting President Fulgencio Batista. Mr. Fiorini is also said to have been a close associate of Major Pedro Diaz Lanz, former Air Force chief under Fidel Castro, and to have been instrumental in spiriting Major Diaz Lanz out of Cuba. He is also said to have been involved later in buying arms for anti-Castro Cubans.

Eugenio L. Martinez, alias Gene Valdes, about 50, a native of Cuba who is also said to have fought against President Batista and to have been involved later in anti-Castro activities.

Raul Godoy, alias V. R. Gonzales, about 46, about whom Miami sources said they had no information.

James W. McCord, alias Edward Martin, about 54, of Rockville, Md., who said in court that he was a retired employe of the C.I.A.

The first four men were listed as Miamians.

The suspects were arraigned in District of Columbia Superior Court. Bond was placed at $50,000 for each of the Miami men and at $30,000 for the other.

A trial date was set for June 29 by Associate Judge James Belson.

Following is the sequence of events pieced together from reports by the police, a guard at the Democratic headquarters and from court testimony:

While making a hourly security check at about 12:05 A.M., Frank Wills, 24, the guard on duty noticed that three doors on the basement level were taped in such a way that the locks could not engage.

"I thought maybe it had been done by the building engineers or some other employes and I simply removed the tape and continued on my rounds." Mr. Wills said in an interview.

Mr. Wills said that he returned to the basement about 12:30 A.M. and this time found that all six doors there had been taped in the same manner. It was then, he said, that he summoned the police.

The police searched the sixth and eighth floors because they were burglarized about a month ago, according to Mr. Wills.

The eighth floor houses offices of the Federal Reserve Board, he said. The entire sixth floor is occupied by the Democratic committee.

Mr. Wills said that the exit door on the eighth floor was also taped and that the exit door on the sixth floor had been forced open.

He said that the police checked other offices on that floor and discovered five well-dressed men wearing gloves and carrying electronics surveillance equipment, cameras, burglary tools and walkie talkies.

"One officer told me that one man had more than $1,000 in $100 bills on him," Mr. Wills said.

## Agnew Says Public Is Tired of Hearing Corruption Charges

WASHINGTON, Oct. 29 (AP)—Vice President Agnew said today that "a calculated attempt to prove corruption on the part of the Administration . . . has fallen flat as a pancake in the eyes of the American people."

"The American people are tired of having all these insinuations made about the Nixon Administration," the Vice President said.

"We've seen it tried from every angle, and yet there is nothing but smoke. We haven't seen a bit of fire yet and I'm not sure there's going to be any fire."

Mr. Agnew was interviewed on the American Broadcasting Company program, "Issues and Answers."

The interview was the only thing on Mr. Agnew's schedule until Tuesday, when he will resume campaigning with trips to Michigan, Texas and California.

Asked about the Watergate burglary and bugging affair, Mr. Agnew said: "I still don't see a connection between the President of the United States and the Watergate case . . . What disturbs me greatly is the moral outrage of the same people who have in the past condoned this kind of conduct . . . I also feel that whether a person steals Larry O'Brien's secret papers or steals the Pentagon papers he should be punished. I didn't see any of these cries of moral indignation against the person-accused of stealing the Pentagon papers."

June 18, 1972

· October 30, 1972

# Watergate Trial Judge Indicates Political Aspects of Case Will Be Examined

**By WALTER RUGABER**
Special to The New York Times

WASHINGTON, Dec. 4—The judge in the Watergate case said today that "one of the crucial issues" in the forthcoming trial would be the motives behind the bugging of the offices of the Democratic National Committee last June.

The remark was made by Chief Judge John J. Sirica of the United States District Court here during a pretrial conference on the criminal proceedings against seven men charged with conspiring to spy on the party's Watergate headquarters.

The indictments confined themselves to certain aspects of the case, but the judge's statements today raised the possibility that the trial testimony may delve into more of the political questions raised by the case.

Two defendants in the trial, scheduled to begin on Jan. 8, are former White House aides. A third was the security adviser to President Nixon's campaign organization when he and four other men were arrested inside the Democratic offices.

"This jury's going to want to know the purpose [of the break-in and bugging]," Judge Sirica said. "What did these men go into the headquarters for? Was their sole purpose political espionage?"

"Were they paid?" the judge continued. "Were there financial gains? Who started this? Who hired them, if anyone hired them? A whole lot is going to come out in this case."

On several occasions, Judge Sirica questioned the principal Assistant United States Attorney, Earl J. Silbert, on whether the Government intended to offer evidence on the motives of the seven men.

"There'll be some evidence," Mr. Silbert said at one point.

"What do you mean, 'some evidence'?" the judge pressed. The prosecutor replied that the Government planned to present testimony that would allow the jury to draw various conclusions about the question.

Judge Sirica inquired specifically whether the prosecution would attempt to trace checks totaling $114,000 that passed through a Miami bank account controlled by Bernard L. Barker, one of the defendants.

It is generally conceded that the checks were intended as contributions to the president's re-election effort. Mr. Silbert indicated that the Government would try to show how the money had reached Mr. Barker.

Mr. Silbert informed the judge that the prosecution expected to offer as evidence between 150 and 200 exhibits. It will call between 50 and 60 witnesses, he said, and will summon 30 additional unless both sides stipulate they are unnecessary.

Today's session failed to resolve an issue raised by a defense effort to obtain a subpoena requiring The Los Angeles Times to produce tape-recordings of an interview with a key Government witness, Alfred C. Baldwin 3d.

Mr. Baldwin said in the interview that he had monitored the listening devices in the committee offices and that he had observed a number of pertinent developments in the case. The Los Angeles newspaper has said it will resist turning over the tapes.

William O. Bittman of Washington, the lawyer for E. Howard Hunt Jr., a former White House aide who is one of the defendants said the tapes were needed for the possible impeachment of Mr. Baldwin as a witness and for the possible development of leads useful to the defense.

Judge Sirica, suggesting that the defense request differs from other recent demands on the press because the source of the information is not in question, ordered memorandums on the issue from both sides next week.

He noted that if the subpoena was issued and if The Los Angeles Times refused to comply, representatives of the newspaper — its publisher and reporters were mentioned — could be jailed for contempt of court.

In addition to Mr. Barker and Mr. Hunt, the defendants in the case are G. Gordon Liddy, a former White House aide; James W. McCord, who was security coordinator for the Committee for the Re-election of the President; Frank A. Sturgis, Eugenio R. Martinez, and Virgilio R. Gonzalez.

December 5, 1972

# Watergate

# Mystery, Comedy, etc. —And Dirty Tricks

WASHINGTON—Scandal, like a lot of other things, never quite made it as an issue in the 1972 Presidential campaign. Last week, with the election two months past and the Inauguration at hand, there were some footnotes and some entirely new chapters in the scandal dossier.

● The Justice Department, on Thursday, charged the Finance Committee to Re-elect the President with eight criminal violations of the Campaign Spending Law. The committee spent $31,300 without reporting it as required, the Government said. The General Accounting Office had audited the committee's records last August and had reported a series of "apparent violations" involving about $350,000. The Justice Department said its charges last week stemmed "in part" from the G.A.O. report.

● It was alleged in court papers that President Nixon's personal lawyer, Herbert W. Kalmbach, had been a major solicitor of the dairy industry contributions to the Republican Party that came after the Administration reversed itself and raised milk price supports. According to a deposition in a law suit, Mr. Kalmbach first asked "quite unequivocally" for money and then tried to stop at least some of the gifts when industry officials made it plain they would make the donations public as required by law.

● Criminal Case No. 1827-72, the United States of America v. George Gordon Liddy, et al., came to trial on Monday in the United States District Court for the District of Columbia. Thus the first formal exploration of the Watergate affair got underway.

It had been by far the most malodorous item in the scandal bag, stemming as it did from the arrest on June 17 of five men—some of whom had links to the White House—inside the offices of the Democratic National Committee, and from the indictment on Sept. 15 of the five and two others.

The first five days of trial, like the six months of inquiry, speculation, and debate that preceded them, produced vast amounts of significant information, confusion, comedy, mystery, and pathos. The most important developments were these:

E. Howard Hunt Jr., author of 46 novels, onetime spy for the Central Intelligence Agency, and more recently a consultant to the White House, entered a plea of guilty to all charges of conspiracy, burglary, and eavesdropping that had been placed against

509

him. Hunt showed up in court looking bad. He had lost weight since his indictment, his face was very pale, his expression somber. Hunt's wife was killed last month in a plane crash, leaving him with three children at home between the ages of nine and 21. He is free on $100,000 bail, pending sentencing.

The publicity—as a C.I.A. agent he was anonymous for 20 years—seemed to bother Hunt more than it did any of his co-defendants, and he worked hard to avoid it. He was the most enigmatic of the defendants and perhaps because of that, the most interesting.

Bernard L. Barker of Miami, who served under Hunt in the planning of the Bay of Pigs fiasco, has said he would follow his old boss "to hell and back." By the end of the week there were reliable indications that he and three other defendants wanted to join Hunt in pleading guilty.

The legal situation was immensely complicated. The two other defendants, Liddy and James W. McCord Jr., both officials of the President's campaign organization at the time of the Watergate arrests, showed no signs of wanting to follow Hunt in changing their pleas. Since conspiracy is the major charge in the indictment and since Liddy and McCord are among the alleged participants, it appeared that as long as both or either of them stand trial the Government's case would have to be presented in full, regardless of the other guilty pleas.

The case was outlined in an opening statement to the jury by the principal Assistant United States Attorney Earl J. Silbert. The prosecutor sought to implicate no one except those charged, but he was scarcely shy in discussing the President's Campaign Committee. He said he would prove that the committee had paid Liddy $235,000 for an "intelligence operation" during last year's campaign. It was unclear, the prosecutor said, how most of this money—all of it was in cash—had been spent.

A previously unreported spy was also unveiled. A college student, Thomas James Gregory, testified that Hunt, who was alleged to have joined Liddy in recruiting for the intelligence effort, had hired him to get information from the campaign offices of Senators McGovern and Muskie.

—WALTER RUGABER

January 14, 1973

# *After 37 Days on TV, a Choice of Alternate Theories*

### By JAMES M. NAUGHTON
Special to The New York Times

WASHINGTON, Aug. 11 — The hearings have stopped but the question lingers on—was the President involved?

From the comic opera tapes holding open the locks at Watergate to the historic drama of a Congressional committee taking a President to court, the Senate's first-phase investigation of the 1972 campaign scandal has seemed immersed in incidents defying explanation and issues beyond resolution.

The 37 days of televised hearings that recessed on Tuesday established, beyond doubt, that there had been wiretapping of the Democratic National Committee offices at the Watergate and a subsequent effort to hide the extent of that conspiracy within the White House and the Committee for the Re-Election of the President.

At the same time, the Senate Select Committee on Presidential Campaign Activities was laying bare the White House. Former powers such as H. R. Haldeman and John D. Ehrlichman, only rarely glimpsed before, were questioned for days in public.

#### 'Enemies List' and I.T.T.

The committee was also displaying broad and often damaging glimpses of Administration life, such as the "enemies list," the aborted 1970 plan to spy on citizens and the 1971 effort to resolve the antitrust actions against the International Telephone and Telegraph Corporation.

Yet within the transcript of the Senate hearings on phase one of the inquiry there was no documented reply or irrefutable answer to the ultimate question of President Nixon's own role in Watergate.

The committee's lawyers went to the United States District Court on Thursday to seek White House tapes and documents that might—although the President said they would not provide the definitive evidence of innocence or involvement. The President went to Camp David to prepare his explanation of the matters raised in the hearings.

For the moment, perhaps for good, the seven Watergate Senators and their audience at large appeared to be faced with a choice between alternative theories whose outlines could be traced in the testimony taken since the hearings began on May 17.

The first plausible theory, based largely upon the circum-stantial evidence contained in the charges of John W. Dean 3d, the former White House legal counsel, was that Mr. Nixon had been committed personally to the Watergate cover-up.

The second, founded on the insistent denials by the President and the testimony of such key figures as Mr. Haldeman, Mr. Ehrlichman and former Attorney General John N. Mitchell, was that Mr. Nixon had been kept purposely unaware of the plot that had swirled about him until last March, when the cover-up began to crumble.

The Senators declared at the outset, and restated repeatedly, that they were not conducting a trial, that they had no defendants and that they sought not verdicts but facts. It remained true, nonetheless, that "with television, every citizen could sit in his living room and hear the evidence," as Samuel Dash, the chief counsel to the committee, said.

The New York Times
**Herbert W. Kalmbach, Mr. Nixon's former personal lawyer, said he was told his fund-raising efforts were not improper.**

During the three months that the evidence, the inferences and the witnesses' assumptions were sought and given, Mr. Nixon's ratings in the public opinion polls fell to the lowest point of his Presidency.

Simultaneously, Senator Sam J. Ervin Jr., Democrat of North Carolina, a constitutional crustacean who is chairman of the committee, became something of a folk figure and the idol of an Uncle Sam fan club.

#### Baker vs. Kennedy

The moralizing Republican vice chairman, Senator Howard H. Baker Jr. of Tennessee, had his own Presidential prospects charted in the polls—and finished, in one (Harris), ahead of Senator Edward M. Kennedy, Democrat of Massachusetts.

When he gaveled session one to a close on Tuesday, Senator Ervin, a former justice of the North Carolina Supreme Court, pronounced no judgment. Nor did Senator Baker, a former prosecutor, nor the other three Democratic and two Republican lawyers who make up the rest of the committee. They merely went home to rest before undertaking phase two, the inquiry into alleged political sabotage, and phase three, the examination of campaign finances, some time after Labor Day.

The record they left behind filled 7,573 pages, reached the height of the witness table and represented the question that the Senators left for the public to answer as individuals: What will reasonable men believe?

Barring release of the White House tapes of Mr. Nixon's conversations or a persuasive white paper from the White House, the options seemed to be these:

¶That, as Mr. Mitchell testified under oath, he and other senior associates of Mr. Nixon had placed the President's reelection last November ahead of disclosure to the President of the Watergate facts, confident that he would have "lowered the boom" on the offenders and thus have jeopardized his political standing.

¶That, as Mr. Dean testified under oath, the President was aware of the Watergate cover-up last Sept. 15, was engaged in discussions early this year about pledges of executive clemency and "silence money" for the seven Watergate burglars, and was undeterred by a warning from Mr. Dean on March 21 that the conspiracy was unraveling and Watergate was "a cancer growing on the Presidency."

Within the framework of each of the competitive rationales were central declarations by witnesses, and questions that reasonable men might ask in judging the value of the testimony.

Mr. Mitchell, who directed the President's campaign committee until he resigned two weeks after the June 17, 1972, Watergate burglary, testified that he had been so appalled at the White House "horror stories" involving defendants in the case that he and others — including Mr. Haldeman, then White House chief of staff, and Mr. Ehrlichman, then the President's domestic adviser—had made independent decisions to shield Mr. Nixon from the information.

Mr. Mitchell said that if the President had asked, "I would have laid out chapter .and verse of everything I knew," but that Mr. Nixon had not asked him.

Observers 'of the hearings wondered: Would a reasonable man believe that the President had not sought from the man who directed his campaign an explanation for a burglary involving campaign officials?

Mr. Haldeman and Mr. Ehrlichman each said that the President and they had been so preoccupied with diplomatic and domestic initiatives that they had been unaware of the cover-up until March, nine months after the Watergate break-in. They said that Mr. Dean, on the other hand, was a "self-starter" with time on his hands and sole White House responsibility for Watergate.

Would a reasonable man expect a second-echelon aide such as Mr. Dean, to be able to orchestrate a conspiracy — involving $450,000 of payments to Watergate defendants in campaign cash, perjured testimony by the deputy campaign director and intrigues among the President's personal attorney, former Attorney General and at least five others — without a clue reaching Mr. Dean's superiors or the President in nine months?

### Testimony About Money

Herbert W. Kalmbach, who had been Mr. Nixon's personal attorney, testified that he had been assured by Mr. Ehrlichman that there had been nothing improper in his efforts to help raise the money that went to the criminal defendants.

Mr. Ehrlichman and Mr. Haldeman declared that their understanding had been that the money had been used for bail, attorney fees and support for the defendants' families. It was, they said, no more unusual than the funds raised publicly for such figures as Dr. Daniel Ellsberg in the Pentagon Papers trial or the Berrigan brothers in the trial of the Harrisburg Seven.

Would a reasonable man argue that there was nothing untoward in the use of political funds in $100 bills, delivered according to the testimony of other witnesses in a series of covert "money drops" requiring keys taped beneath public telephones, boxes in airport luggage lockers or plain envelopes in motel lobbies?

By the same token, questions might be raised by reasonable individuals to test the validity of allegations made directly against the President by his dismissed legal counsel, Mr. Dean, or implicit in testimony of others who sat at the Senate committee's witness table.

Mr. Dean, in the most explosive testimony at the hearings, swore under oath that the President had congratulated him when the Federal grand jury indictments last Sept. 15 did not go beyond the seven original suspects in the Watergate burglary. He charged that Mr. Nixon had told him on March 13 that it would be "no problem" to raise $1-million in hush money and that he had promised clemency to E. Howard Hunt Jr., a convicted Watergate conspirator, threatening to talk.

Would a reasonable man expect the President to get involved in such discussions, knowing that his conversations were being tape-recorded and that his complicity could be documented' if the tapes ever got out?

Jeb Stuart Magruder, the deputy director of Mr. Nixon's 1972 campaign, and Mr. Dean told the Senators how Mr. Magruder had been coached on perjured testimony he gave to the Watergate grand jury. Mr. Magruder said it had been his "assumption'" that Mr. Dean reported to his White House superiors on the cover-up arrangements.

Would a reasonable man draw the most damaging conclusions from an "assumption" by a witness?

Former Attorney General Richard G. Kleindienst and Assistant Attorney General Henry E. Petersen, who directed the Justice Department's investigation of Watergate, recalled on Tuesday that Mr. Ehrlichman had inquired early this year about the likelihood of light sentences for Watergate defendents and the "technical" procedures for granting executive clemency.

Would a reasonable man necessarily believe that Mr. Ehrlichman had been acting on behalf of the President?

### Role of the F.B.I.

L. Patrick Gray 3d, the former acting director of the Federal Bureau of Investigation, testified on Monday that he had warned Mr. Nixon in a telephone conversation three weeks after the break-in that actions of White House aides could "mortally wound" the President. Mr. Gray said he was surprised that Mr. Nixon did not ask any questions — who, for instance, were the aides? — and merely told the F.B.I. chief to conduct a thorough investigation.

Would a reasonable man expect the President to do anything more than to instruct the successor to J. Edgar Hoover to proceed with the investigation?

Whatever reasonable men decided individually as they witnessed the unfolding of the dual themes, in the Watergate hearings, there was little doubt that the President would need to make a thorough accounting. Mr. Nixon was said to be considering the issuance of a white paper sometime next week, perhaps accompanied by a televised summary of its contents and followed by his first news conference in five months.

Moreover, the President's explanation may necessarily encompass far more than the roots and aftermath of the Watergate break-in.

While examining the campaign conspiracy, the Watergate committee turned up, and made public, a number of documents raising more general questions about the conduct of the Nixon White House.

The documents included the 1970 plan for a domestic surveillance program authorizing wiretaps and burglaries. Mr. Nixon has said that he rescinded the approval five days after granting it.

### Colson on I.T.T. Case

The Senate panel also produced a 1972 memorandum in which Charles W. Colson, a former special counsel to the President, expressed concern that a long list of other documents could implicate Mr. Nixon, Vice President Agnew and a number of other senior officials in the I.T.T. antitrust settlement if the documents ever came to light.

Mr. Ehrlichman told the Senators that the White House had not authorized the September, 1971, burglary at the office of a California psychiatrist treating Dr. Ellsberg. But he also said that it would have been within the President's inherent constitutional authority to order such a burglary if he thought it. was in the interest of national security.

The Watergate hearing record included, as well, testimony and documents related to a list of more than 200 political opponents of the President classed as "enemies" and about a secret White House intelligence unit whose alumni were among the Watergate burglars.

Mr. Nixon may feel compelled to offer assurance to reasonable men that an Administration involved in these other activities would not, all the same, resort to burglary and wiretapping to gain political intelligence.

# The Watergate Testimony So Far: Questions Remain on Eight Major Issues

*In 37 days of nationally televised hearings and 7,573 pages of testimony, the opening phase of the Senate's Watergate investigation produced a huge outpouring of evidence, assertion and insight.*

*Reduced to manageable proportions, the inquiry into last year's wiretapping at the Democratic National Committee offices and the subsequent cover-up turns on relatively few questions. But on most of them there are serious conflicts.*

*Witnesses hostile to the President—mainly John W. Dean 3d—have sought to show a pattern of words and actions implicating Mr. Nixon in the cover-up.*

*Loyalist witnesses such as H. R. Haldeman and John D. Ehrlichman have insisted on an innocent interpretation of the same words and actions, contending that the conspirators kept the truth completely hidden from the President.*

*Without additional evidence—the tape recordings of White House meetings withheld by Mr. Nixon, for example—any effort to resolve the conflicts must finally depend on ‹ ‹ perceptions of probability, of surrounding events, of men's characters.*

*What follows is ⌐ breakdown of the wiretapping and cover-up scandals into their main components and brief, compacted excerpts of what the most important witnesses had to say directly on each of the aspects selected.*

## To what extent, if any, was President Nixon aware of either the Watergate wiretapping or cover-up?

**DEAN.** "I cannot testify of any first-hand knowledge of that [the President's awareness in advance of the eavesdropping]. If Mr. Haldeman had advance knowledge or had received advance indications it would be my assumption that that had been passed along, but I do not know that for a fact."

**HALDEMAN.** "There doesn't seem to be much contention about what he knew [in advance of the Watergate arrests]. He knew [only] through the normal channels that the events had occurred. He expressed [afterward] just utter incomprehension as to how such a thing could have happened and why such a thing would have happened."

**NIXON.** "The burglary and bugging of the Democratic National Committee headquarters came as a complete surprise to me. I had no inkling that any such illegal activities had been planned by persons associated with my campaign; had I known I would not have permitted it." [May 22 statement].

**DEAN.** "The President told me [at a meeting on Sept. 15] I had done a good job, and he appreciated how difficult a task it had been; and the President was pleased that the case had stopped with Liddy. I left the meeting with the impression that the President was well aware of what had been going on regarding the success of keeping the White House out of the Watergate scandal."

**HALDEMAN.** "I recently reviewed the recording of that meeting. This was the day that the indictments had been brought down, and the President knew John Dean had been concentrating for a three-month period on the investigation for the White House. Naturally it was good news [that] there was not any involvement by anyone in the White House. This confirmed what Mr. Dean had been telling us. The President did commend Dean for his handling of the whole Watergate matter, which was a perfectly natural thing for him to do. I totally disagree with the conclusion that the President was aware of any type of cover-up, and certainly Mr. Dean did not advise him of it at the Sept. 15 meeting."

**DEAN.** "I told the President [on March 13] about the fact that there was no money to pay [the defendants] to meet their demands. I told him that it might be as high as a million dollars or more. He told me that that was no problem, and he also looked over at Haldeman and repeated the same statement."

**HALDEMAN.** "I seriously doubt that the conversation John Dean has described actually took place on March 13. A discussion of some of those matters actually occurred during a meeting on March 21. I did listen to the tape of the entire meeting. The President said, 'There is no problem in raising a million dollars; we can do that, but it would be wrong.'"

**NIXON.** "I did not know, until the time of my own investigation, of any effort to provide the Watergate defendants with funds." [May 22 statement].

**DEAN.** "The President then [March 13] referred to the fact that Hunt had been promised executive clemency. He said that he had discussed this matter with Ehrlichman and, contrary to instructions that Ehrlichman had given Colson not to talk to the President about it, that Colson had also discussed it with him later. [The President], in a nearly inaudible tone, said to me [on April 15] he was probably foolish to have discussed Hunt's clemency with Colson."

**HALDEMAN.** "There was no discussion while I was in the room [nor do I recall any discussion on the tape] on the question of clemency in the context of the President saying he had discussed this with Ehrlichman and with Colson. The only mention of clemency was Dean's report that Colson had discussed clemency with Hunt and the President's statement that he could not offer clemency and Dean's agreement."

**EHRLICHMAN.** "It was my strong feeling, that he [the President] ratified and adopted [in July, 1972] that this was a closed subject and we must never get near it, and that it would be the surest way of having the actions of these burglars imputed to the President for there to be any kind of entertainment [of clemency]. I mentioned [to Colson] that I did not think anybody ought to talk to the President about this subject—outsiders or staff people—that it is just a subject that should be closed as far as the President is concerned."

**NIXON.** "At no time did I authorize any offer of executive clemency for the Watergate defendants, nor did I know of any such offer."

**GRAY.** "I told the President [on July 6, 1972] that people on your staff are trying to mortally wound you by using the F.B.I. and the C.I.A. and by confusing the question of whether or not there is C.I.A. interest [in Watergate]." Mr. Gray was asked: "Do you think a reasonable and prudent man, on the basis of the warning that you gave him at that time, would have been alerted to the fact that his staff was engaged in something improper, unlawful, and illegal?" And he answered: "I do, because, frankly, I expected the President to ask me some questions. And when I heard nothing, you know, I began to feel that General Walters and I were alarmists, that we had a hold of nothing here."

**NIXON.** "On July 6, 1972, I telephoned the acting director of the F.B.I., L. Patrick Gray, [and] in the discussion Mr. Gray suggested that the matter of Watergate might lead higher. I told him to press ahead with his investigation."

## Who approved the eavesdropping conspiracy?

**MAGRUDER.** "Mr. Mitchell approved the project [at a meeting in Key Biscayne, Fla., on March 30, 1972] Mr. Mitchell simply signed off on it in the sense of saying, 'Okay, let's give him [Liddy] a quarter of a million dollars and see what he can come up with.'"

**MITCHELL.** "Well, it was very simple. [I said,] 'We don't need this; I am tired of hearing it; out; let's not discuss it any further'—this sort of a concept. In my opinion, it was just as clear as that. There could very well have been pressures [on Magruder] from collateral areas in which they decided that this was the thing to do. I can't speculate on who they might be."

# Figures Mentioned in the Text

Alfred C. Baldwin 3d, former F.B.I. agent hired by James W. McCord Jr. to monitor wiretap at the offices of the Democratic National Committee.

John J. Caulfield, former New York City policeman and investigator hired by John D. Ehrlichman.

Charles W. Colson, former Special Counsel to the President.

John W. Dean 3d, former Counsel to the President.

John D. Ehrlichman, former Assistant to the President for Domestic Affairs.

L. Patrick Gray 3d, former acting director of the Federal Bureau of Investigation whose nomination as director was withdrawn by the President.

H. R. Haldeman, former White House chief of staff.

Richard Helms, former head of the Central Intelligence Agency.

E. Howard Hunt Jr., former C.I.A. agent, former White House consultant and convicted Watergate spy.

Herbert W. Kalmbach, formerly the President's personal attorney and a major fund raiser in the 1972 campaign.

Frederick C. LaRue, former White House aide and deputy to John N. Mitchell at the Committee for the Re-Election of the President.

G. Gordon Liddy, one-time White House "plumber," later general counsel to the Committee for the Re-Election of the President, and leading Watergate spy.

Jeb Stuart Magruder, former deputy director of the Committee for the Re-Election of the President.

Robert C. Mardian, former Assistant Attorney General, employed at the Committee for the Re-Election of the President.

James W. McCord Jr., former C.I.A. employe, security co-ordinator for the Committee for the Re-Election of the President, convicted Watergate spy.

John N. Mitchell, former Attorney General, chief of President Nixon's re-election campaign until July 1, 1972.

Paul O'Brien, attorney for the Committee for the Re-Election of the President.

Herbert L. Porter, former scheduling director for the Committee for the Re-Election of the President.

Robert A. F. Reisner, an assistant to Jeb Stuart Magruder at the Committee for the Re-Election of the President.

Gordon C. Strachan, former political aide to H. R. Haldeman.

Anthony T. Ulasewicz, former New York City detective, aide to John J. Caulfield.

Vernon A. Walters, deputy head of the Central Intelligence Agency.

*From top to bottom: John D. Ehrlichman, H. R. Haldeman and John W. Dean 3d.*

**LARUE.** "Mr. Mitchell, to the best of my recollection, said something [at the March 30 meeting] to the effect that, 'Well, this is not something that will have to be decided at this meeting.'" Asked whether Mr. Mitchell had rejected the wiretapping program "out of hand," Mr. Larue said: "Not to my recollection, no, sir."

**REISNER.** "He [Magruder] appeared in my doorway [upon his return from Key Biscayne] and said, 'Call Liddy; tell him it is approved and that we need to get going in the next two weeks.'"

**DEAN.** In mid-February, 1973, eight months after the first wiretapping, Mr. Dean said, Mr. Magruder "told O'Brien that he had received his final authorization for Liddy's activities from Gordon Strachan and that Strachan had reported that Haldeman had cleared the matter with the President."

**STRACHAN.** "It is my opinion that that version of the facts was presented by Mr. Magruder to [force the White House into offering him an Administration job.]" At no time, Mr. Strachan said, did he give final authorization for the Liddy operation.

**DEAN.** "I had also received information from Magruder that he had been pressured by Colson and members of Colson's staff into authorizing the adoption of Liddy's plans on several occasions."

*Mr. Colson has not yet been summoned by the committee to testify, but he has said publicly on a number of occasions that he was unaware "Liddy's plans" involved any wiretapping or other illegal activity and that he simply wanted the Nixon organization to pursue legitimate intelligence goals.*

## Who received information from the wiretap?

**McCORD.** "He [Baldwin] was listening with headphones to the conversations that were being transmitted [in late May and early June, 1972] and would take down the substance of the conversations, the time, the date, and then ultimately would type up a summary of them and I would deliver them to Mr. Liddy."

**MAGRUDER.** "Approximately a week or a week and a half after the initial entry I received the first reports. I brought the materials into Mr. Mitchell in the 8:30 morning meeting I had each morning with him. He, as I recall, reviewed the documents and indicated, as I did, that there was really no substance to these documents, and he called Mr.

Liddy up to his office, and Mr. Mitchell indicated his dissatisfaction with the results of his work."

**MITCHELL.** That "happens to be a palpable, damnable lie. First of all, I had an 8:15 meeting every day over at the White House. Secondly, there was no meeting in any morning during that period when Mr. Magruder and I were alone. Thirdly, I have never seen or talked to Mr. Liddy from the fourth day of February, 1972, until the 15th day of June, 1972.".

**MAGRUDER.** "As I recall, because of the sensitive nature of these documents, I called Mr. Strachan and asked would he come over and look at them in my office rather than sending a copy to his office. As I recall, he did come over and look over the documents and indicate to me the lack of substance to the documents."

**STRACHAN.** "He [Magruder] did not show me the [wiretap reports]. His statement is couched with, 'As I recall, I called him up,' 'As I recall, he came over,' and 'As I recall, he read it.' Mr. Magruder told me that a sophisticated political intelligence gathering system had been approved [at Key Biscayne] and I repeated that to Mr. Haldeman. Unfortunately, he [Magruder] neither gave me nor did I ask for any further details about the subject."

HALDEMAN. "I had no knowledge of or involvement in the planning or execution of the break-in or bugging of the Democratic National Committee headquarters. To the best of my knowledge I did not see any material produced by the bugging of the Democratic headquarters. He [Strachan] confirmed that he had reread the contents [of political intelligence reports reaching the White House] many times and that they did not suggest any illegality or criminal activity."

## Who took part in destruction of possible evidence?

STRACHAN. "I said [to Haldeman immediately after the Watergate arrests on June 17] 'Well, sir, this is what can be imputed to you through me, your agent,' and I opened the political matters memorandum to the paragraph on intelligence, showed it to him [and] he told me, 'Well, make sure our files are clean.' I went down and shredded that document and others related."

HALDEMAN. "I have no recollection of giving Mr. Strachan instructions to destroy any materials, nor do I recall a later report from Strachan that he had done so or that the files were clean."

MAGRUDER. "Mr. Mitchell flew back [from California] that Monday [June 19, 1972] with Mr. Larue and Mr. Mardian. We met in his apartment with Mr. Dean. It was generally concluded that that file [containing the wiretap reports] should be immediately destroyed."

MITCHELL. "Not in my recollection was there any discussion of destruction of documents at that meeting."

LARUE. "I recall a discussion by Magruder of some sensitive files which he had, and that he was seeking advice about what to do about those files. As I remember, there was a response from Mr. Mitchell that it might be good if Mr. Magruder had a fire."

REISNER. "I think Mr. Magruder's secretary and I looked through his own files. I think other people on the committee did similar things, and virtually anything that concerned the opposition [was destroyed]."

GRAY. "Mr. Dean then [June 28, 1972] told me that these files contained copies of sensitive and classified papers of a political nature that Howard Hunt had been working on. I distinctly recall Mr. Dean saying that these files were 'political dynamite' and 'clearly should not see the light of day.' It is true that neither Mr. Ehrlichman [present during the transaction] nor Mr. Dean expressly instructed me to destroy the files. But there was, and is, no doubt

in my mind that destruction was intended. I burned them during Christmas week."

DEAN. "I remember well his [Ehrlichman's] instructions [prior to the June 28 turnover of the files to Mr. Gray.] He told me to shred the documents. I [later] suggested that they be given directly to Gray. At no time while I was present with Gray and Ehrlichman was he instructed by myself or Ehrlichman to destroy the documents."

EHRLICHMAN. "I don't think in my life that I have suggested to anybody that a document be shredded."

## Who was involved in paying the Watergate conspirators, and what was their purpose?

DEAN. "On the afternoon of June 28, in a meeting in Mr. Mitchell's office — and I believe that Mr. Larue and Mr. Mardian were also present — there was a discussion of the need for support money in exchange for the silence for the men in jail. Mitchell asked me to get the approval of Haldeman and Ehrlichman to use Mr. Herbert Kalmbach to raise the necessary money. They told me to proceed to contact Mr. Kalmbach."

KALMBACH. "My actions were prompted in the belief that such was proper and necessary to discharge what I assumed to be a moral obligation. I said [in a July meeting with Ehrlichman], 'It is just absolutely necessary, John, that you tell me, first, that John Dean has the authority to direct me in this assignment, that it is a proper assignment, and that I am to go forward on it.' He said, 'Herb, John Dean does have the authority, it is proper, and you are to go forward.' "

ULASEWICZ. "I said [in August], 'Well, Mr. Kalmbach, I will tell you something here is not kosher. He did agree with me that this was time to quit it."

LARUE. "After he [Kalmbach] got out, then I, in effect, became involved in it. My understanding of the payments of money is that this money was paid to satisfy commitments that had been made to them [the defendants]."

MITCHELL. "I became aware [of the payments] in the fall sometime. I was in New York [on June 28, when Mr. Dean said, payments had been discussed] and could not have been at such a meeting." Mr. Mitchell acknowledged that he had "acquiesced" in payments which, in the words of one questioner, "could have been pretty embarrassing, to say the least, if not illegal."

HALDEMAN. "I was told several times, starting in the summer of 1972, by John Dean and possibly also by John Mitchell, that there was a need by the [Nixon] committee for funds to take care of the legal fees and family support of the Watergate defendants. I had understood this was an important and proper obligation. I do not think I was called upon to condone or condemn."

EHRLICHMAN. "I was aware that there was a need for a defense fund. I do not know what [the] motives were." He denied that he had vouched for the propriety of the effort in his meeting with Mr. Kalmbach.

## Who was behind offers of executive clemency to the defendants?

DEAN. "He [Colson] said that he felt it was imperative that Hunt be given some assurances of executive clemency. Ehrlichman said he would have to speak with the President. On Jan. 4, I learned from Ehrlichman that he had given Colson an affirmative regarding clemency for Hunt."

EHRLICHMAN. "Clemency was obviously at the forefront of everybody's mind in this meeting as one of the things which was a potential danger, and I advised both people of a previous conversation that I had had with the President on that subject. The President wanted no one in the White House to get into this whole area of clemency with anybody involved in this case, and surely not make any assurances to anyone."

McCORD. "Political pressure from the White House was conveyed to me in January, 1973, by Jack Caulfield to remain silent [and] take executive clemency by going off to prison quietly. Caulfield stated that he was carrying the message of executive clemency to me 'from the very highest levels of the White House.' "

DEAN. "It was on Jan. 10 that I received calls from both O'Brien and Mitchell indicating that since Hunt had been given assurance of clemency Caulfield should give the same assurances to McCord."

MITCHELL. "That [Dean's testimony on Mitchell's role in the offer to McCord] is a complete fabrication because the negotiations with McCord started when I was entirely out of the way. I was down in Florida."

## What was the motive for involving the Central Intelligence Agency in the Watergate investigation?

HALDEMAN. "The President directed John Ehrlichman and me to meet with the director [Helms] and deputy director [Walters] of the C.I.A. on June 23. We did so and ascertained from them that there had not been any C.I.A. involvement. We discussed the White House concern [nonetheless] regarding possible disclosure of non-Watergate related covert C.I.A. operations or other nonrelated national security activities that had been undertaken previously by some of the Watergate participants, and we requested deputy director Walters to meet with director Gray of the F.B.I. to express these concerns. I did not, at this meeting or at any other time, ask the C.I.A. to participate in any Watergate cover-up."

EHRLICHMAN. "If the C.I.A. were involved in the Watergate then obviously that would be embarrassing, awkward, and difficult for the C.I.A. Mr. Helms and General Walters assured us that this was not the case. Then Mr. Haldeman said disclosure of C.I.A. operations disassociated from the Watergate would be awkward. It was there that we did not get the same kind of flat assurance, and so it was simply agreed that General Walters would make an early appointment with Pat Gray."

HELMS. "Mr. Haldeman said that there was a lot of flak about the Watergate burglary, that the opposition was capitalizing on it. Mr. Haldeman then said something to the effect that it has been decided that General Walters will go and talk to acting director Gray and indicate to him that these investigations might run into C.I.A. operations in Mexico and that it was desirable that this not happen."

WALTERS. "Mr. Haldeman said, 'It has been decided that General Walters will go to director Gray and tell him that the further pursuit of this investigation in Mexico could jeopardize some assets of the Central Intelligence Agency.' It was put in a directive form."

GRAY. "I believed, and General Walters believed, that people on his [the President's] staff were using the F.B.I. and the C.I.A. to confuse the question of whether or not there was C.I.A. interest in or noninterest in people that we wanted to interview, and it could very well have been activity on the part of over-zealous individuals over there [the White House] to protect the President."

*From top to bottom: John N. Mitchell, Jeb Stuart Magruder and James W. McCord Jr.*

### Who was involved in perjury during the first Watergate investigation?

MAGRUDER. "I personally felt that it was important to be sure that this story did not come out in its true form at that time. I want to make it clear that no one coerced me to do anything. I volunteered to work on the cover-up story. My primary contacts on the story were Mr. Dean and Mr. Mitchell."

PORTER. "He [Magruder] said, 'Would you corroborate a story that the money [paid to Liddy] was authorized for something a little bit more legitimate-sounding than dirty tricks?' I thought for a moment, and I said, 'Yes, I probably would do that.' It was a false statement."

DEAN. "I do not know when I first learned of Magruder's proposed testimony. I informed Haldeman and Ehrlichman of the story. We discussed it, and no one was sure it would hold up. We, of course, knew that it was a fabricated story."

HALDEMAN. "There was a reference to his [Dean's] feeling that Magruder had known about the Watergate planning and break-in ahead of it; in other words, that he was aware of what had gone on at Watergate. I don't believe there was any reference to Magruder committing perjury."

EHRLICHMAN. He said it was "not correct" that Mr. Dean had informed him of Mr. Magruder's perjury.

MITCHELL. "I became aware or had a belief [by the time Mr. Magruder testified to the grand jury] that it was a false story. To the best of my recollection I have never discussed it with them [Haldeman and Ehrlichman]."

# Old Story, New Words

## Nixon Merely Proclaimed Innocence, And Questions Remain Unanswered

### By JAMES RESTON

President Nixon left the Watergate crisis about where it was before he spoke. He rejected both the advice of those who urged him to mount a counteroffensive against the Senate investigating committee and those who urged him to confess error and seek reconciliation. In short, he redefined the conflict in different words, but he didn't remove it or even change it. His main theme was that he didn't know about the Watergate burglary or the cover-up, and that nobody except John W. Dean 3d had suggested that he did. So, he said, now that all these charges have been argued over television for weeks, let's all get on together to more important things.

**News Analysis**

This was not the appeal of a President who felt trapped or defeated. He looked drawn and a little sad, but his argument was that of a man who felt he was still very much in command. He seemed to be saying, "Now that I've explained it all to you, let's put our differences aside and get on to other things," but in fact he introduced not a single new fact and answered none of the major ambiguities or contradictions of the Ervin hearings. He merely proclaimed his innocence and appealed for trust.

The President spoke in a paradoxical situation. It was the first day of peace for America after nine years of the Indochina war. The dollar, twice devalued in the last year and a half, and badly battered in recent weeks on the world money markets, began to rally in the week before the President spoke, and the United States balance of international payments finally showed a surplus in the second quarter of 1973, just before he went on TV.

Still, mainly because of the Watergate scandals, the President's rating in the popularity polls dropped on the day before his speech to the lowest level of any President in the last 20 years—with only 31 per cent of those questioned in the Gallup Poll saying they thought he was doing a good job.

### Different Performance

His performance in this situation was quite different from his handling of previous personal crises. In his earlier explanations of the Watergate scandals, he talked about his personal responsibility for creating an atmosphere in which his staff had been too zealous.

This time, while repeating that he took responsibility for whatever was done in his name, he blamed the atmosphere of the sixties, the anti-war demonstrators and their supporters in the press, radio and television for establishing the notion that their higher ends justified illegal means.

Unfortunately, he suggested, some of his own people made the same mistake in the 1972 election, but they were merely following the mistaken lead of the dissidents. It was all wrong, he insisted, but it was somebody else's fault. Certainly not his.

### Second Theme

There was another unmistakable theme in the President's speech. This was that the Ervin Committee and the press, radio and television were going on and on reporting the Watergate affair, not because it was their duty to report the facts, but somehow, he suggested, because they were trying to exploit the crisis, maybe even glorying in the tragedy, not so interested in getting the facts as in getting the President.

This was stated rather carefully but unmistakably, and it is a critical point. For this suggestion, which ran through the speech — that Watergate was secondary and being used for unworthy reasons to keep the President from getting on with his larger primary and nobler objectives — is likely to be bitterly resented by the executive and legislative investigators who are only at the beginning of their inquiries.

### Raised the Questions

The odd thing about the President's speech is that in the beginning he raised the main questions, which he promised to answer, and then he didn't answer them. He said it was his constitutional responsibility to defend the "integrity" of the Presidency against "false charges" and then failed to define what was integrity and what was false.

"I also believe," he said, "that it is important to address the over-riding question of what we as a nation can learn from this [Watergate] experience, and what we should do now." But in the end he never defined the lessons of Watergate or answered the question of what we should do now.

The contrast between this Nixon speech and his first major speech—the "Checkers" speech of 1952—was also striking. In that other awkward situation, 21 years ago, when he was accused of having a political slush fund, he addressed himself to the moralities of the problem and not to the legalities.

"It isn't a question of whether it was legal or illegal," he said in September of 1952 when he was running with Dwight D. Eisenhower. "That isn't enough. The question is, was it morally wrong?"

Mr. Nixon did not deal with this question in personal terms last night. Nor did he leave the judgment of right and wrong and his own destiny to the people, as he did at the end of the Checkers speech.

### What He Said Before

He merely repeated what he had said before, what he had said in his legal brief denying the tapes to the courts, asserting his innocence and his rights to executive privilege and his power to deny evidence in his possession of possible criminal activity.

He avoided all the theatrical props this time: no pictures of his family or busts of President Lincoln behind him, but his presentation of his case, delayed for almost three months, after all the new charges in the Senate investigating committee, was not an answer to the questions and doubts folks had on their minds.

In fairness to the President, he said he wasn't going to answer the questions raised by the Senate hearings, and he kept his promise. It was hoped that after three months of silence, he would say something that would ease, if not remove, the doubts of the American people, but while he didn't make things any worse, he didn't' make them any better. He merely asked for trust, but he didn't offer any new evidence to change the political conflict or remove the public doubts.

August 16, 1973

# How About Some Honest Talk

### By James Reston

WASHINGTON, Aug. 25 — In every great crisis of violence or corruption in our national life, Americans tend either to turn away from it in cynicism or to attribute it to the moral decline of the nation as a whole. It's an old American habit: we either forget or bleed.

Still, at the beginning of a new school year, when even Washington is getting the first sweep of cool, clear autumnal air, one wonders whether we couldn't have a little more honest discussion in America about how all these strange things happened and what, if anything, they mean about our values and purposes.

After the murder of President Kennedy, and long before the Watergate burglary, the board of trustees of the Rockefeller Foundation met at Williamsburg, Va., to talk about precisely this question.

This foundation has spent hundreds of millions of dollars analyzing practical scientific problems, race problems, political and constitutional problems, cultural problems—but now its leaders were asking in William James' words how "to make an unusually stubborn attempt to think clearly" about values, morals and purposes. Could the thing be done?

They didn't know, but they got a few people together to talk about it— Dr. Hannah Arendt, Dr. Paul Freund, Irving Kristol, and Dr. Hans Morgenthau, and the new head of the Rockefeller Foundation, John H. Knowles, M.D., stated the fundamental question: What is the moral and ethical framework in which we are all living; of our work as a nation, as individuals, as institutions, in our relations with one another and with the world? We go on doing our jobs, but what's the meaning and purpose of all this energy?

This was the general question. And the specific question was why so many people felt isolated, pointless, and even helpless, and whether it was possible or useful to organize ways of talking, not only about legislation to deter violence and corruption, but about morals and values.

Everybody in this careful and illuminating Rockefeller Foundation discussion seemed to agree about the central issue: that we should be discussing all kinds of fundamental questions that are being ignored in the public dialogue today.

Paul Freund argued that it was important to discuss the questions of values and purposes, even if you couldn't resolve them, and also, that it was important that these questions should be discussed not only by the privileged or elitist university people but by the plain and ordinary people of the nation.

The tragedy is that such a sincere and careful analysis of our problems doesn't seem to lead anywhere. The people are left with the politicians and the reporters and the editorial writers and the thoughtful people at foundation meetings who do the best they can but in the end do not really answer the questions they raise.

The brilliant discussion by Arendt, Freund, Kristol and Morgenthau in the Rockefeller discussion defined the problem, but like the press and most of the rest of the people in Washington didn't help much in resolving it. Still, they were getting at something fundamental.

My own view is that, while the American people today don't believe in the old institutions, and are confused by this vague debate, they believe in the old values and yearn for some practical way to escape from the isolation and impotence that trouble their lives.

I also believe that there is a remnant in every institution in the nation, from the Congress or the churches to the universities or labor unions or Chambers of Commerce—that would welcome the chance to discuss the purposes of their work and lives, the "moral and ethical framework," if only somebody would give a lead on how to do it and define the questions for discussion.

Maybe this is where the foundations, like Rockefeller's, can help. The problem is not mainly to try to answer the questions of morals and values and purposes, but merely to get down on paper, as simply as possible, a definition or case study of the facts, questions and possible answers, with arguments for and against, so that thoughtful people can, if they wish, get together and talk coherently about the things that trouble them.

The way things are in the present crisis of Watergate, the people are dividing for and against the President, for and against the parties and the system and the press, but the causes of our present dilemmas are much more complex than that, and nobody brings the basic questions down to any practical form in which they can be debated.

"We would know how to build a good country," Robert Goheen told the Rockefeller Foundation trustees, "if we were confident what 'good' means. . . . We want to do the right thing but too often have trouble agreeing on what *right* means." The Rockefeller Foundation agreed and it is now searching for ways that these questions of values can be discussed effectively, not merely in foundations or by politicians or columnists, but by thoughtful people in their own communities and their own institutions.

August 26, 1973

# Suggested Reading

Aaron, Daniel. *Men of Good Hope: A Story of American Progressives.* New York: Oxford University Press, 1951. Paper edition: Oxford, 1961.

Allen, Frederic L. *Only Yesterday: An Informal History of the Nineteen Twenties.* New York: Harper & Bros., 1931. Paper edition: Harper & Row, 1972.

Brooks, John. *The Great Leap: The Past Twenty-Five Years in America.* New York: Harper & Row, 1966. Paper edition: Harper & Row.

Burlingame, Roger. *Engines of Democracy.* New York: Charles Scribner's, 1940.

Chafe, William F. *The American Woman: Her Changing Social, Economic and Political Roles, 1920-1970.* New York: Oxford University Press, 1972. Paper edition, Oxford, 1973.

Commager, Henry Steele. *The American Mind: An Interpretation of American Thought and Character Since the 1880's.* New Haven, Yale University Press, 1950. Paper edition, Yale, 1961.

Furnas, J. C. *The Americans: A Social History of the United States, 1587-1914.* New York: G. P. Putnam's Sons, 1969.

Galbraith, John K. *The Affluent Society.* 2nd ed. Boston, Houghton-Mifflin, 1969. Paper edition, revised: New American Library, 1970.

Hofstadter, Richard. *Anti-Intellectualism in American Life.* New York: Alfred A. Knopf, 1963. Paper edition: Random House.

Keniston, Kenneth. *The Uncommitted: Alienated Youth in American Society.* New York: Harcourt, Brace, Jovanovich, 1965.

Latham, Earl. *The Communist Controversy in Washington: From the New Deal to McCarthy.* Boston, Harvard University Press, 1966. Paper edition, Atheneum, 1969.

Lasch, Christopher. *The New Radicalism in America, 1889-1963: The Intellectual as a Social Type.* New York, Alfred A. Knopf, 1965. Paper edition: Random House.

Lerner, Max. *America as a Civilization.* New York: Simon and Schuster, 1957. Paper edition: Simon and Schuster, 1967.

Lynd, Robert S. and Helen M. *Middletown: A Study in American Culture.* New York: Harcourt, Brace, Jovanovich, 1929. Paper edition: Harcourt, Brace.

Nye, Russel B. *The Unembarrassed Muse: The Popular Arts in America.* New York: Dial Press, 1970. Paper edition: Dial.

Potter, David M. *People of Plenty: Economic Abundance and the American Character.* Chicago: University of Chicago Press, 1954. Paper edition: Chicago.

Powdermaker, Hortense. *Hollywood the Dream Factory.* Boston; Little, Brown, 1950. Paper edition: Little, Brown, 1972.

Riesman, David, *et al. The Lonely Crowd: A Study of the Changing American Character.* Rev. ed. New Haven: Yale University Press, 1969. Paper edition, abridged: Yale.

Rosenkrantz, Barbara Gutman and William A. Koelsch, editors, *American Habitat: A Historical Perspective.* New York: The Free Press, 1973.

Rourke, Constance. *American Humor: A Study of the National Character.* New York: Harcourt, Brace, 1931. Paper edition: Harcourt, Brace, Jovanovich. 1971.

Schneider, Herbert W. *A History of American Philosophy.* 2nd ed. New York: Columbia University Press, 1963. Paper edition. Columbia.

Smith, Henry Nash. *The Virgin Land.* Cambridge, Mass. Harvard University Press, 1950. Paper edition: Cambridge, Harvard, 1970.

Tocqueville, Alexis de. *Democracy in America.* (original publication, 1835) Phillips Bradley, trans. New York: Alfred A. Knopf, 1944. Paper edition: Random House.

Turner, Frederick Jackson. *The Frontier in American History.* New York: H. Holt & Co., 1920. Paper edition: Holt, Rinehart, and Winston.

Warner, Sam Bass, Jr. *The Urban Wilderness: A History of the American City.* New York: Harper & Row, 1972, Paper edition, 1973.

Westin, Alan F. *Privacy and Freedom.* New York, Atheneum, 1967.

Wills, Garry. *Nixon Agonistes: The Crisis of the Self-Made Man.* Boston: Houghton Mifflin, 1969. Paper edition: New American Library, 1971.

# Index